**2**

*Ani–Az*

# COMPTON'S ENCYCLOPEDIA & FACT-INDEX

*SUCCESS PUBLISHING GROUP, LTD.*
*Lombard, Illinois*

## 2002 COMPTON'S ENCYCLOPEDIA & FACT-INDEX

Published by *SUCCESS PUBLISHING GROUP, LTD.*

Library of Congress Catalog Card Number: 94-70149
International Standard Book Number: 0-944262-43-0

Printed in U.S.A.

*"To inspire ambition, to stimulate the imagination,*

*to provide the inquiring mind with accurate*

*information told in an interesting style,*

*and thus lead into broader fields of knowledge—*

*such is the purpose of this work."*

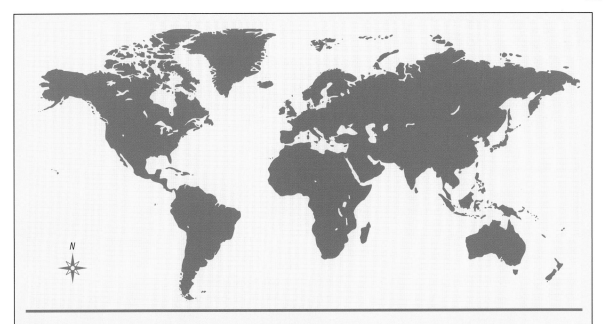

N

# HERE AND THERE IN VOLUME 2

*From the A-1 satellite to the zygote cell, thousands of subjects are gathered together in Compton's Encyclopedia and Fact-Index. Organized alphabetically, they are drawn from every field of knowledge. Readers who want to explore their favorite fields in this volume can use this subject-area outline. While it may serve as a study guide, a specialized learning experience, or simply a key for browsing, it is not a complete table of contents.*

(Top) Which large continent, claimed in part by seven countries, has never had any permanent human settlements? Page 476.

(Left) How does a serious art collector distinguish between antiques and antiquities? Page 493.

(Right) Which emperor, entombed here, gained the throne by imprisoning his ill father? Page 766.

Courtesy of the Victoria and Albert Museum, London; photograph, EB Inc.

Rapho—Photo Researchers

# EXPLORING VOLUME 2

Why does the tail of a comet always point away from the sun? Page 723.

How did prehistoric farmers develop arithmetic? Page 590.

Why is the sky blue? Page 750.

In how many different ways can animals communicate with one another? Page 448.

Where are the most automobiles produced? Page 866 chart.

How does a supermarket's automated checkout system work? Page 834.

What popular writer of science fiction also taught biochemistry? Page 709.

How did a barber become involved in the development of textile machinery? Pages 626–7.

Which architect called his houses "machines for living in"? Page 565.

When does a total eclipse take place? Page 720.

Which are the largest and the smallest of the apes? Page 499 illustrations.

What wood is often used in sports equipment? Page 671.

Why was the leader of the murderous *Hashshashin* nicknamed Old Man of the Mountains? Page 711.

Who was known as the "angelic doctor"? Page 520.

vi

B. Brander—Photo Researchers

Apricot Producers of California

*(Left) How long have aborigines inhabited Australia? Page 784.*

*(Top right) What widely grown fruit, a native of China, got its name from the Arabic and Greek words for "early ripening"? Page 512.*

Art Resource

*Which Buenos Aires barrio has become the home of Argentina's artist colony? Page 580.*

Which country has the largest army? Page 645.

Why does the "doodlebug" dig holes in the sand? Page 495.

What are ants' cows? Page 504.

Where was the secret ballot first used? Page 805.

What is the coldest temperature ever recorded on Earth? Page 473.

Why don't people sense the motion of Earth as it rotates? Page 718.

Why did W.H. Auden marry Erika Mann? Page 760.

What peninsula forms a bridge between Europe and Asia? Page 701.

What insects keep slaves? Page 471.

Why should an aquarium have plants as well as fishes? Page 516.

Why are all the young of an armadillo litter of the same sex? Page 628.

Who was the original "doubting Thomas"? Page 507.

What do leaf-cutting ants grow for food? Page 468.

Why was a citizen of the United States fined $100 in 1872 for trying to vote? Page 480.

How did dinosaurs become extinct? Page 460.

How was a "seaport" created in the inland state of Oklahoma? Page 626.

Where was the term Christian first used? Page 492.

Why did King Arthur and his knights gather at a round table? Page 654.

What are two major differences between a plant and an animal? Page 421.

What mineral can be woven into cloth? Page 671.

Department of Astronomy, University of Michigan   Flagstaff Chamber of Commerce

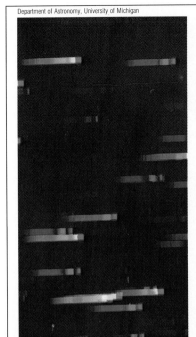

Photos Pack

*(Left) How does a spectrograph reveal a star's temperature and composition? Page 728.*

*(Top right) In what state is the extinct volcanic cone of Sunset Crater National Monument? Page 609.*

*(Bottom right) What is the significance of the pole that rises through a Japanese pagoda? Page 546.*

Why did human sacrifice play such an important part in the Aztec religion? Page 892.

What happened to most of the Parthenon sculptures? Page 742.

How fast can stock cars race? Page 874.

Why did the ancient astrologers study the motions of celestial bodies? Page 717.

On what continent did Judaism, Christianity, Islam, Hinduism, and Buddhism originate? Pages 683–4.

How do ants defend themselves? Page 471.

What was the first successful automobile in the United States? Page 857.

Where is the "queen of the East"? Page 492.

Why did the primitive Gilbert Islanders wear suits of coconut fiber? Page 629.

How is the larva of the ant lion beneficial to farmers? Page 495.

Why is the Atlantic the saltiest ocean? Page 744.

If the ice in the western part of Antarctica melted, how high would it raise the sea level throughout the world? Page 472.

When and where was Coca-Cola first sold? Page 743.

Where is the "Roof of the World"? Page 674.

What are the three orders (styles) of Greek architecture? Page 547 illustration.

Did Zebulon Pike climb the peak named for him? Page 626.

What is a driver's reaction time? Page 864.

What Greek philosopher classified the various branches of knowledge? Page 589.

Wm. Franklin McMahon

U.S. Navy Photo

*(Top) How can archaeologists learn about an ancient culture by studying the broken pieces of pottery and other artifacts they have unearthed? Page 534.*

*(Bottom) Name the state capital in which the United States Naval Academy has been located since 1845. Page 466.*

What is the vegetable lamb? Page 458.

What was the last important animal to be domesticated by humans? Page 456.

What are the 12 signs of the zodiac? Which planet or planets rules each sign? Page 716.

How do mammals differ from other vertebrates? Page 437.

How were the great temples and statues of Abu Simbel saved from submersion? Page 738.

Why was the original 'Birds of America' called the elephant folio? Page 762.

What has been one hope of scientists over the ages? Page 758.

Which group of Asian Americans operates more than half of the small family-owned grocery stores in New York City? Page 703.

How did the Great Depression advance archaeology? Page 536.

*The cheetah, or hunting leopard, is the fastest of the land animals over short distances. It has become an endangered species in Africa and is nearly extinct in Asia.*

# ANIMAL

All living things are divided into two main kingdoms—the animal and plant kingdoms—and two or three other kingdoms that include bacteria, blue-green algae, and one-celled creatures with definite nuclei. What is the difference between a horse, for example, and grass? A horse moves about in the pasture eating grass. It trots toward you when you offer it a lump of sugar and shows pleasure when you stroke its head. The grass, however, is rooted to one place. It does not respond behaviorally to people or to the horse in any way. (*See also* Plant.)

### Animals Move About and Sense Surroundings

Most animals move freely from place to place and can sense their surroundings; that is, they can taste, smell, hear, see, and touch. Certain simple animals, such as the corals and barnacles, spend most of their lives fastened to one spot, but they are able to swim freely when they are young. Even these rooted animals have parts that move in order to capture food. Plants, however, cannot shift about at their own will. They react to heat, light, chemicals, and touch, but their responses are involuntary and automatic, quite different from those of animals.

...........................................................................

*This article was critically reviewed and updated by J. Whitfield Gibbons, Senior Research Ecologist and Professor of Zoology, Savannah River Ecology Laboratory, University of Georgia.*

All living things are made up of cells of protoplasm. They may consist of a single cell, as does an amoeba, or billions of cells, as do trees and horses. The cell wall of a plant is composed of a woody material called cellulose. No true animal contains cellulose. Animal cells are bounded by a membrane composed chiefly of fat and protein.

Green plants make their own food. With the aid of the green substance called chlorophyll, they use the energy in sunlight to change carbon dioxide and water into carbohydrates and other food materials. No true animal contains chlorophyll.

Animals must eat, either directly or indirectly, the food manufactured by members of the plant kingdom. A horse cannot stand in the sun and wait for its body to make fat and proteins. It must move about the pasture in search of green grass. Even meat eaters—for example, lions—live on animals, such as zebras, which in turn subsist on plants.

### The Variety of Animal Life

More than a million different kinds of animals inhabit the Earth. The exact number is not known, for new kinds are continually being discovered. They live in the seas, from the surface down to the black depths where no ray of light penetrates. On mountaintops and in deserts, in mud and in hot pools some form of animal life may be found.

Ralph A. Reinhold—Animals Animals

*Foxes, bright and alert, are among the most intelligent of wild animals. They are famous for their cleverness in outwitting dogs, hunters, and other enemies.*

Animals are infinitely varied in form, size, and habits. The smallest animals are bits of protoplasm that can be seen only with a microscope. The largest, the blue whales, may be more than 100 feet (30 meters) long and weigh 300,000 pounds (136,000 kilograms).

Some of the most familiar animals, such as dogs, birds, frogs, and fish, have a backbone and a central nervous system. They are called vertebrates, meaning animals with backbones. Animals without backbones are called invertebrates and include arthropods, worms, mollusks, and many other groups. Most of the vertebrates and many invertebrates have a head where sense organs are concentrated and have legs, wings, or fins for locomotion. Vertebrates and many invertebrates, such as the arthropods and worms, have bilateral, or two-sided, symmetry. This means that they have two mirror-image sides (a right side and a left side), distinct upper and lower surfaces of the body, and a distinct front and rear.

Some invertebrates, such as jellyfish, sea anemones, and starfish, display radial symmetry, in which the parts of the body are arranged around a central axis, similar to a wheel. Animals with radial symmetry live in marine or freshwater aquatic environments. Some drift with the currents, unable to swim in any definite direction. Others become attached to a solid object by one end and float with the mouth end upright. Tentacles arranged in a circle around the mouth sweep in food particles and ward off enemies.

One-celled animals called protozoans live in fresh and salt water. Many are shapeless creatures and cannot swim toward their food. They move along by squeezing out a fingerlike projection from the body. This is called a pseudopod, from the Greek meaning "false foot." The pseudopod fastens to something solid, and the rest of the body flows into the fastened projection. The amoeba also moves in this manner. One-celled animals are very small. They are single blobs of liquid enclosed in a thin membrane and as such cannot attain a large size or a very definite shape.

## Animals with Outside Skeletons and Feet

Mollusks have soft bodies that are not divided into specialized sections such as head, thorax, and abdomen. Many mollusks are enclosed in hard, hinged shells. Snails have a single large, fleshy foot located on the stomach side.

The heads of the octopus and the squid are surrounded by a circle of eight or ten tentacles that act as arms and feet. Oysters, clams, mussels, and scallops all have a single ax-shaped foot which they burrow into sand.

Most mollusks do not move around efficiently. Oysters fasten themselves to something solid and settle down for life, letting food drift to them. Scallops may move in zigzag leaps by clapping their shells together.

## Joint-Legged Animals

Joint-legged animals, or arthropods, have bodies divided into segments that have specialized functions. These animals also have many jointed legs. Most arthropods are covered with a jointed skeleton made of a horny material. This outside skeleton is lighter than the shells of the mollusks. The legs and muscles and many organs of the arthropod are attached to the outside skeleton.

The arthropods include insects, lobsters, crabs, centipedes, millipedes, scorpions, and spiders. They can run, jump, swim, and crawl. Some live mostly on land, while others live mostly in water. Many of the insects have wings and can fly. Arthropods inhabit most of the Earth's environments, from the poles to the tropics, and are found in fresh and marine water and in terrestrial habitats.

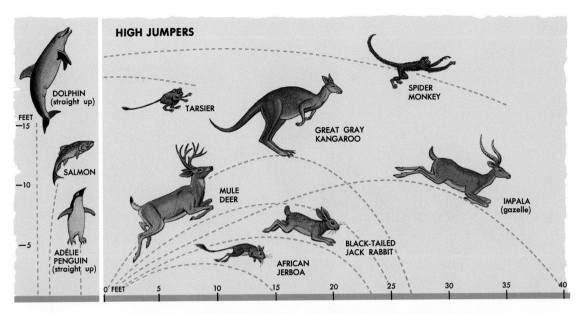

**HIGH JUMPERS**

DOLPHIN (straight up)

FEET
—15

—10

—5

SALMON

ADÉLIE PENGUIN (straight up)

TARSIER

GREAT GRAY KANGAROO

SPIDER MONKEY

MULE DEER

IMPALA (gazelle)

AFRICAN JERBOA

BLACK-TAILED JACK RABBIT

0 FEET    5    10    15    20    25    30    35    40

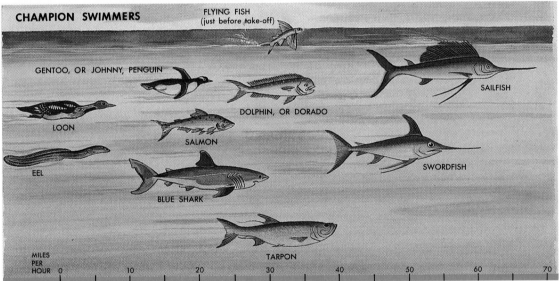

**CHAMPION SWIMMERS**

FLYING FISH (just before take-off)

GENTOO, OR JOHNNY, PENGUIN

SAILFISH

LOON

DOLPHIN, OR DORADO

SALMON

EEL

SWORDFISH

BLUE SHARK

TARPON

MILES PER HOUR    0    10    20    30    40    50    60    70

## How Backboned Animals Move

Vertebrates move through water and air and over the ground with great speed and skill. Birds, with their feathered wings, are the best fliers. Fish are the best swimmers. However, other vertebrates also can fly and swim. Bats fly on wings of membrane like skin. The flying squirrel glides on a broad membrane between its legs. The flying fish soars over the surface of the ocean by using its fins. Neither the fish nor the squirrel can soar great distances, however.

Some turtles swim with paddlelike front legs. Some water birds can swim underwater with their wings. The mudskipper and walking catfish are fishes that walk on mud by pulling themselves along on their front fins.

Frogs, kangaroos, various cats, and some fishes are superior jumpers. Salmon leap up waterfalls when they travel from the sea to their home streams to lay their eggs. Tarpon, swordfish, and sailfish make great leaps out of the water when pursuing their prey or trying to escape an enemy.

## Breathing

All animals must take in oxygen in order to change food into a form that the body can use. One-celled animals that live in water absorb oxygen directly through their membranes. The sponge is a very simple many-celled animal. The surface of a sponge is covered with millions of tiny pores. Water bearing dissolved oxygen and minute food particles flows through the pores and out of the opening at the top of the sponge.

## ANIMAL SPEED RECORDS

**Two-toed sloth, 0.5 mph; desert tortoise, 0.5 mph; roadrunner, 15 mph; African elephant, 24.5 mph; white-tailed deer, 30 mph; warthog, 30 mph; emu, 31 mph; giraffe, 32 mph; rhinoceros, 35 mph.**

Fish and tadpoles breathe by means of gills. Insects and caterpillars take air into the body through breathing pores called spiracles.

Mammals, birds, and reptiles obtain oxygen from the air. They take it into the lungs, and the oxygen passes through membranes in the lungs into particles called red blood cells. The bloodstream then carries the oxygen to all parts of the body. Amphibians have lungs, but they also have thin, moist skins that absorb oxygen directly. (*See also* Blood; Lungs; Respiratory System.)

### Reproduction

All animals reproduce their own kind. One of the most primitive forms of reproduction is by fission, in which the individual organism divides to produce a replica of itself. Some animals, such as sea squirts, reproduce by budding: lumps appear along a branchlike organ and develop into young sea squirts. Sea squirts, sponges, corals, and other creatures that bud often remain together and form large colonies. The hydra

**Different Ways of Breathing**

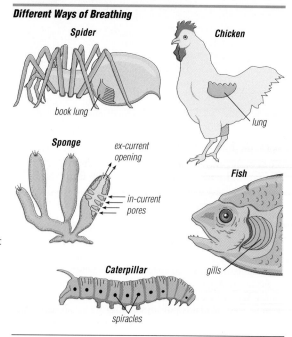

Spider — book lung

Chicken — lung

Sponge — ex-current opening; in-current pores

Fish — gills

Caterpillar — spiracles

*Greyhound, 36 mph; Mongolian wild ass, 40 mph; red fox, 45 mph; jackrabbit, 45 mph; ostrich, 50 mph;*
*Gobi gazelle, 60 mph; pronghorn antelope, 60 mph; cheetah, 70 mph.*

also reproduces by budding, but in time the young bud separates and goes off to live alone. (*See also* Reproductive System.)

Most animals reproduce by means of eggs from the female that are fertilized by sperm from the male. The eggs of some species are deposited in a nest or in some other manner before hatching. Most species of mammal and some species of reptile and fish bear their young alive, the fertilized eggs being retained within the body of the female.

The types of reproductive behavior among animals are almost as varied as the kinds of animals themselves. Some species, such as most insects and turtles, deposit their eggs and give them no further attention. In colonies of the social insects, such as ants and bees, a single female lays all of the eggs, and workers provide care and nourishment for the developing young in the nest. The females of some reptiles, such as the king cobra and the blue-tailed skink, and amphibians, such as the marble salamander, stay with their clutch of eggs until they hatch but provide no protection or nourishment for the young. Some fish guard their young after they are born. Crocodilians protect the eggs before hatching and the young for several months afterwards. Many birds provide not only protection but also nourishment for the developing young. Mammals, which feed their young with milk produced by the mother, provide care for their young much longer than do other classes of animals.

**Homes**

Many animals build temporary or permanent homes for themselves and their young. Birds occupy their nests only while they are incubating eggs and feeding the helpless nestlings. A few fish make temporary nests for their young.

No animal dwelling has excited more wonder and interest than the lodge built by the beaver. Almost as remarkable is the dome-shaped winter home of the muskrat. Underground burrows with sleeping rooms, food-storage rooms, connecting tunnels, and emergency exits are constructed by groundhogs, prairie dogs, European rabbits, gophers, kangaroo rats, and field mice. Chimpanzees and gorillas build temporary nests and sleeping platforms of sticks in trees. The living quarters made by the different kinds of ants

### Reproductive Facts of Common Mammals

| Animal | Age at which Female is Sexually Mature | Gestation Period, in Days | Average Number of Offspring per Litter | Average Weight of Offspring at Birth (Metric) |
|---|---|---|---|---|
| Armadillo | 1 year | 150 | 1–12 | 3 ounces (85 grams) |
| Bear, black | 4–5 years | 210–220 | 2–3 | 11 ounces (300 grams) |
| Bear, polar | 5 years | 240 | 1–4 | 20 ounces (600 grams) |
| Cat, domestic | 7–12 months | 65 | 1–8 | 3 ounces (100 grams) |
| Cattle | 18 months | 280–290 | 1 | 50 pounds (23 kilograms) |
| Chimpanzee | 7 years | 230 | 1 | 4 pounds (2 kilograms) |
| Dog | 10–24 months | 56–69 | 3–10 | 8 ounces (230 grams) |
| Donkey | 2–3 years | 365–380 | 1 | 50 pounds (23 kilograms) |
| Elephant, African | 14 years | 645 | 1 | 243 pounds (110 kilograms) |
| Elephant, Indian | 9–12 years | 645 | 1 | 220 pounds (100 kilograms) |
| Giraffe | 3½ years | 450 | 1 | 132 pounds (60 kilograms) |
| Guinea pig | 2–3 months | 68 | 1–13 | 4 ounces (100 grams) |
| Horse | 2–3 years | 337 | 1 | 50 pounds (23 kilograms) |
| Kangaroo | 20–36 months | 40–45* | 1 | 0.03 ounce (0.75 grams) |
| Lion | 3–4 years | 108 | 1–6 | 3 pounds (1.3 kilograms) |
| Mole | 10 months | 30 | 2–5 | 0.04 ounce (1 gram) |
| Mouse | 5–7 weeks | 20–21 | 3–12 | 0.04 ounce (1 gram) |
| Opossum | 275 days | 13* | 7–9 | 0.004 ounce (0.1 gram) |
| Rabbit | 80 days | 30–32 | 2–15 | 2 ounces (45 grams) |
| Whale, humpback | 6–12 years | 334–365 | 1 | 3,000 pounds (1,350 kilograms) |

*Marsupial. Figure does not include extended stay in maternal pouch.

Joe McDonald—Animals Animals

*Contrary to popular belief, the porcupine does not throw its quills in defense. However, some of its quills may become detached when the porcupine drives its powerful tail at its attacker.*

can be intricate and complex. Certain tropical bats cut palm fronds in such a way that they droop to form a leafy shelter from the hot sun and torrential rains.

### Defenses

All animals have some means of defending themselves against enemies. A cat can usually outrun a dog and climb the nearest tree. If cornered, it will scratch and bite.

Many animals rely on speed, camouflage, teeth, claws, and even intimidation to escape other animals. The variety of means of protection is extensive. Porcupines and hedgehogs roll into a ball and raise their sharp quills. The quills come off and stick into the nose or paw of an unwary dog or some other enemy.

Skunks spray a foul-smelling fluid from a gland when they are frightened. Deer, moose, and antelope fight with their antlers. An elephant's trunk is a powerful weapon. It can be used to pick up another animal and smash it to the ground.

Squids shoot out a cloud of inky material and escape under its cover. Torpedo fish and several other kinds of fish have built-in electric storage cells by which they can deliver a paralyzing shock. Some insects, snakes, and lizards protect themselves with their venom. Many amphibians produce poisonous skin secretions.

Many animals hide by means of protective coloration. A baby deer is almost invisible in the forest because its spotted coat looks like patches of sunlight in the brown leaves. Many fishes, birds, insects, lizards, and snakes use nature's camouflage to avoid being seen.

### Feeding Behavior

Many one-celled animals (the vorticella and collar flagellate, for example) live in water. These very tiny animals and their feeding habits can be studied only under a microscope. They feed on even tinier organisms in the water. The vorticella is attached by its stalk to some solid object. At the upper end is a mouth surrounded by tiny hairs called cilia. The hairs sweep food particles into the mouth by setting up a whirlpool action in the water. The food is enclosed in a bubble called a food vacuole, where it is digested.

The collar flagellate has a delicate, transparent collar. From the center of it grows a whiplike organ, the flagellum. The beating of the whip draws a current of water toward the cell. Food particles in the current pass through the wall of the cell into the food vacuoles.

The heliozoan, also called sun animal, moves about and captures food by means of pseudopodia. In this

**How Some Animals Capture Food**

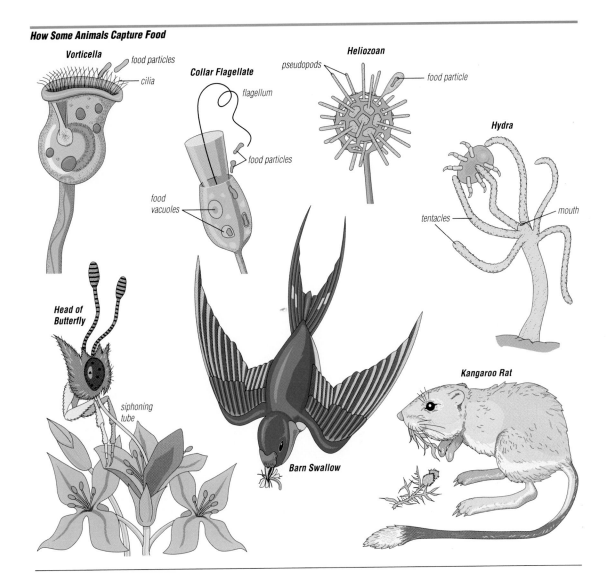

Vorticella — food particles, cilia

Collar Flagellate — flagellum, food particles, food vacuoles

Heliozoan — pseudopods, food particle

Hydra — tentacles, mouth

Head of Butterfly — siphoning tube

Barn Swallow

Kangaroo Rat

case the pseudopodia are stiff spines that radiate from the center of the cell. The spines wrap around the food and enclose it in a vacuole.

The hydra feeds most commonly on the larva of a kind of shellfish. It has a mouth surrounded with long tentacles. The tentacles sting and paralyze the prey and then shove it inside the mouth.

Butterflies and moths have tubelike mouth parts. With these they suck nectar from flowers. Grasshoppers and beetles have chewing, grasping, and tearing mouthparts.

Birds and bats catch insects in flight. Woodpeckers hammer into the bark of trees for grubs, other birds comb the leaves with their bills for small insects, and hawks swoop down on rodents and on other birds.

The kangaroo rat is a harmless little animal that lives in the deserts of the southwestern United States. It lives on dry thistle and cactus leaves, seeds, and small juicy tubers that grow abundantly in the desert 1 to 2 inches (2.5 to 5 centimeters) below the surface. It collects seeds in its cheek pouches and stores them in underground chambers. Gophers and chipmunks also collect food in their cheek pouches and store it in underground pantries for future use.

**Carnivores, Herbivores, Insectivores**

Animals that eat other animals are called carnivores. The shark is a fierce carnivore. It lives on smaller fish, such as mackerel. Many mammals are carnivores. They all have special kinds of teeth for tearing their food into chunks and chewing it (*see* Teeth and Gums). Most of them have claws for catching and holding their prey. Among the carnivores are cats, dogs, raccoons, weasels, bears, hyenas, and civet cats. Some fish subsist on plant and animal life known as plankton. The baleen whale is an enormous animal,

*How Other Animals Capture Food*

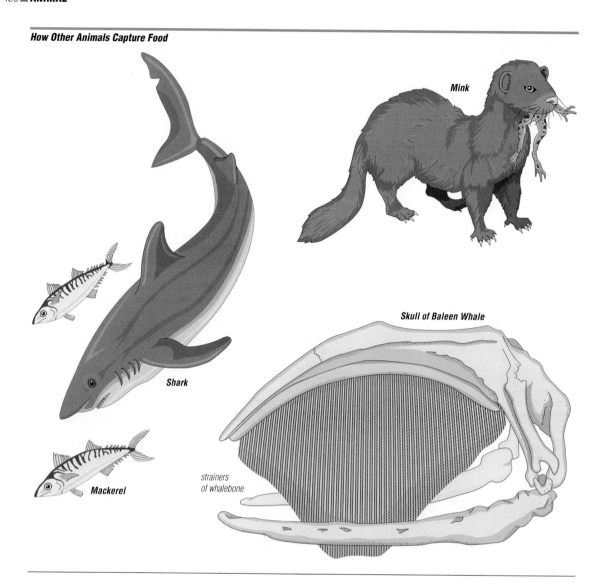

Mink

Shark

Mackerel

Skull of Baleen Whale

strainers
of whalebone

growing up to 100 feet long. It feeds upon shrimplike creatures only about 1 inch in length. When it finds a school of shrimp, it opens its mouth and gulps in several barrelfuls of water. Horny strainers that hang from the roof of its mouth catch the shrimp and drain out the water.

A large group of animals are plant eaters (herbivores). Many herbivores are prey of the carnivores. Insects are the dominant herbivores in most parts of the world, although they may be less conspicuous than plant-eating mammals and birds. Herbivorous mammals include horses, cattle, sheep, goats, rabbits, rodents, elephants, deer and antelope, and monkeys and apes.

A few mammals live on insects—moles, shrews, and hedgehogs, bats, armadillos, aardvarks, and anteaters. Many bird species are insect eaters, as are certain kinds of insects, such as ladybugs.

## How Animals Sense Their Surroundings

The ability of animals to sense and respond to their surroundings is one way in which they differ from plants. Higher animals have sense organs to perceive light, sound, touch, taste, and smell (*see* Senses).

Eyes are very important to most mammals. Animals that hunt and feed by night have very large eyes. Cats' eyes have pupils that can open wide in the dark and narrow down to slits in the sunlight. Insects have compound eyes, made up of tiny units that break up the image into many small pictures. They also have two or three simple eyes that probably detect motion. The eyesight of some fish is especially keen.

Ears are perhaps as important as eyes to some species. The fennec is a foxlike animal that lives in the Sahara and hunts by night. Its large ears help it detect its prey in the darkness of a hot, dry climate,

*How Animals Sense Their Surroundings*

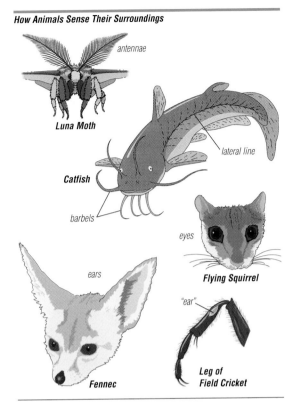

*antennae*

**Luna Moth**

*lateral line*

**Catfish**

*barbels*

*eyes*

**Flying Squirrel**

*ears*

*"ear"*

**Fennec**

**Leg of Field Cricket**

Miriam Austerman—Animals Animals

*Prairie dogs live in colonies that consist of well-defined territories, each one occupied and defended by a male, several females, and their offspring. Group grooming maintains social structure.*

where food may be very scarce. The cat is also a night prowler, and it too has large, erect ears. The hearing organs of the field cricket and katydid are located on their forelegs. The organ is a thin membrane that vibrates in response to sound waves.

Many animals have sense organs unlike those of the mammals. The antennae of the moths, butterflies, and other insects seem to correspond to the organs of taste, touch, smell, and hearing.

The barbels of the catfish and the whiskers of the flying squirrel and the cat are organs of touch. They are very useful for animals that explore in the dark. The lateral line of the fish is a rod of nerve cells running the length of the body. It probably helps the fish feel movements in the surrounding water.

The delicate forked tongue of the snake tastes the air. With it the snake can locate food and other snakes. The rattlesnake has sensory pits on the head through which it can detect a nearby warm-blooded animal. Even the simplest one-celled animals respond to touch. If a flatworm is touched, it may jerk away or curl up into a ball. It moves away from strong light or from water that is too hot or too cold.

In the warm, muddy rivers of Western Africa there are fish that send out small electric impulses and surround themselves with an electric field. Whenever another fish or other object approaches, the fish is made aware of it by the changes in the charged field. Thus a built-in electric system takes the place of eyesight in the dark waters and keeps the fish

informed of its surroundings. Bats emit high-pitched squeaks and use the reflected sound waves to avoid objects and locate prey while flying. Dolphins and whales send out ultrasonic signals and are able to detect objects by reflections of the sound.

**Migration and Hibernation**

When winter comes to northern or high-mountain regions, animals must find some way to keep warm. Many birds and some mammals seek a mild climate by moving south or to lower elevations. They are said to migrate. Other kinds of mammals (bears and woodchucks, for example) store up fat in their bodies in the fall by eating all they can. Then they curl up in a cave or some other protected place and sleep during the cold period—that is, they hibernate.

Most insects die in the wintertime. They leave well-protected eggs which hatch in the spring. Fishes, frogs, and aquatic arthropods and other water-dwelling animals may hibernate in mud or move to deeper water and become inactive.

**Living Together in Colonies**

Some animals live with others of their own kind. Ants, honeybees and bumblebees, and wasps are called social insects because they live together in highly organized societies.

Some birds live in large colonies. Penguins, anis, and eider ducks are examples. Weaver finches work together to build huge community dwellings.

South American monkeys travel through the jungles in family groups. They scatter while they are searching for food but stay within sight or hearing of one another. Toward evening they regroup and spend the night together. Baboons live in large bands. They

*How Long Animals Live*

| | mammals | | birds | | other vertebrates | | invertebrates |

*Maximum ages, in years, that certain animals may be expected to reach, based on reports of zoos and estimates of biologists.*
*(Data from S.S. Flower,"The Duration of Life in Animals," in 'Proceedings of the London Zoological Society'.)*

## Terms for Certain Animals and their Groups

| Animal | Male | Female | Young | Group |
|--------|------|--------|-------|-------|
| Bear | boar | sow | cub | sloth* |
| Beaver | . . . . | . . . . | pup, kitten | colony |
| Bee | drone | queen, worker | . . . . | hive, swarm (in flight) |
| Bison | bull | cow | calf | herd |
| Cat | tomcat | . . . . | kitten | litter, clowder* |
| Cattle | bull | cow | calf | drove, herd |
| Chicken | rooster | hen | chick | flock, brood (of chicks) |
| Crow | . . . . | . . . . | . . . . | murder* |
| Deer | buck, stag | doe | fawn | herd |
| Dog | dog | bitch | pup | litter, pack (wild), kennel |
| Donkey | jackass | jennet | colt | drove, herd |
| Duck | drake | duck | duckling | flock |
| Eagle | . . . . | . . . . | fledgling | aerie |
| Elephant | bull | cow | calf | herd |
| Fish | . . . . | . . . . | . . . . | school, shoal |
| Fox | reynard | vixen | kit, cub, pup | skulk |
| Goat | buck | doe | kid | herd, trip |
| Goose | gander | goose | gosling | flock, gaggle, skein (in flight) |
| Grouse, partridge, quail | cock | hen | chick | covey |
| Hog | boar | sow | shoat, farrow | drove, herd, litter (of young) |
| Horse | stallion, stud | mare, dam | foal, colt (male), filly (female) | stable, herd, string or field (of race horses) |
| Jay (bird) | . . . . | . . . . | . . . . | band |
| Kangaroo | buck, boomer | doe, flyer | joey | troop, herd |
| Lion | lion | lioness | cub | pride |
| Locust | . . . . | . . . . | . . . . | host |
| Ox | steer | cow | stot | drove, herd |
| Pheasant | cock | hen | chick | nye |
| Rabbit | buck | doe | kitten | colony, warren |
| Seal | bull | cow | pup | herd, rookery, harem |
| Sheep | buck, ram | ewe, dam | lamb | flock, hurtle* |
| Swallow, dove | . . . . | . . . . | . . . . | flight |
| Swan | cob | pen | cygnet | . . . . |
| Trout | . . . . | . . . . | . . . . | hover* |
| Turtle | . . . . | . . . . | . . . . | bale* |
| Walrus | bull | cow | cub | herd |
| Whale | bull | cow | calf | gam, herd |
| Wolf, coyote | . . . . | . . . . | . . . . | pack |
| Zebra | stallion | mare | colt | herd |

*Obsolete but still used in literature.

cooperate in getting food and post sentries to watch for danger when the group stops.

### Intelligence

Most animal activities that appear to indicate intelligence are simply instinctive. The most intelligent animals are the apes and monkeys. Dogs and elephants have been trained to serve humans in many ways. Horses, seals, porpoises, lions, and tigers are often taught to perform in circuses and aquariums. Talking birds, such as parrots, parakeets, and mynahs, learn to imitate sounds, but they do not have the capacity to think or to understand what they are saying.

### Relationship to Humans

Humans require the presence of other animals in a variety of ways. The domestication of animals has been important to the development of civilization (*see* Animals, Domesticated). By pollinating flowers, bees help in the cultivation of orchard fruits, alfalfa, clover, and many vegetables. The earthworm, by churning up the soil, improves the growth of plants.

Birds eat insect pests, weed seeds, and rodents. Certain bats eat so many mosquitoes and other insects that some communities erect shelters for them to encourage their help. Hyenas, vultures, and carrion beetles keep country regions clean by devouring dead animals.

Countless animal products are used by humans: pearls (from the oyster), shellac and lacquer (from the lac insect), glue, and fertilizers are only a few examples. Important drugs are produced from the blood and glands of animals. Serums and antivenins for snakebite are made from the blood of horses. Experiments performed on such animals as rats, mice, guinea pigs, and monkeys have been responsible for great advances in medical knowledge and the conquest of human disease.

Dangerous animals include the parasites in the human body and in domesticated animals that cause serious diseases. Fleas, lice, rats, and mosquitoes are also carriers of such serious conditions as malaria and encephalitis. Insect pests cause billions of dollars' worth of damage every year.

## How Animals Are Classified

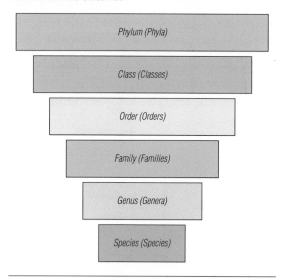

Phylum (Phyla)

Class (Classes)

Order (Orders)

Family (Families)

Genus (Genera)

Species (Species)

*The science dealing with the classification of animals is called taxonomy. The taxonomist creates from a varied array of organisms a hierarchy of groupings, or taxa (singular, taxon), that have an orderly relationship to each other. The basic unit is the species. Any animal that lacks a vertebral column, or backbone, in contrast to vertebrates (all of which possess some form of cartilaginous or bony internal skeleton) are called invertebrates. More than 90 percent of living animals are invertebrates. A few examples are shown at right. Apart from the absence of a vertebral column, invertebrates have little in common. Worldwide in distribution, they range in size from minute freshwater organisms to giant marine squids.*

## The Basic Forms of Animal Life and How They Differ

More than a million different kinds of animals inhabit the Earth. No one knows exactly how many kinds there are, for many new ones are discovered and named every year.

### Beginnings of Animal Life

The first organisms in the history of the Earth must have been one-celled bits of protoplasm floating in shallow seas and ponds. Here they remained for millions of years. They developed from one cell to many cells, becoming more and more complex. In time some animals moved into fresh water. Others began to live on land. In these surroundings they changed still more, until today there is a bewildering variety of forms.

The creatures that developed a backbone and an internal skeleton are called vertebrates. They include all the familiar animals—the mammals, reptiles, birds, fish, and amphibians. Animals without backbones are called invertebrates. They include insects, sponges, corals, jellyfish, clams, lobsters, and starfish.

## Animals Without Backbones

Fresh-Water Sponge

Sea Anemone

Sea Gooseberry

Dugesia (Planaria)

Whelk

Sea Urchin

Earthworm

Centipede

Fly

Crab Spider

Crawfish

---

**Animal Classification List**
*Higher Taxonomic Designations of All Major Groups of Animals**

| Scientific Classification | Popular Classification | Scientific Classification | Popular Classification |
|---|---|---|---|
| ***Kingdom Protista†*** | | | |
| Phylum Ciliata | ciliated protozoans | | |
| Phylum Cnidospora | cnidosporians | | |
| Phylum Mastigophora | flagellated protozoans | | |
| Phylum Sarcodina | pseudopodal protozoans | | |
| Phylum Sporozoa | sporulation protozoans | | |
| ***Kingdom Animalia*** | | | |
| Phylum Placozoa | trichoplax | Phylum Arthropoda | |
| Phylum Porifera | sponges |   Class Xiphosura | horseshoe crabs |
| | |   Class Arachnida | spiders, ticks, scorpions |
| Phylum Mesozoa | mesozoans |   Class Pycnogonida | sea spiders |
| Phylum Coelenterata | |   Class Crustacea | crabs, shrimp, lobsters, and other crustaceans |
|   Class Hydrozoa | hydras | | |
|   Class Scyphozoa | jellyfishes |   Class Chilopoda | centipedes |
|   Class Anthozoa | corals and sea anemones |   Class Diplopoda | millipedes |
| | |   Class Insecta | insects |
| Phylum Ctenophora | comb jellies | Phylum Chaetognatha | arrow worms |
| Phylum Platyhelminthes | | Phylum Echinodermata | |
|   Class Turbellaria | free-living flatworms |   Class Crinoidea | sea lilies |
|   Class Trematoda | flukes |   Class Asteroidea | starfish |
|   Class Cestoda | tapeworms |   Class Ophiuroidea | brittle stars |
| Phylum Acanthocephala | spiny-headed worms |   Class Echinoidea | sea urchins and sand dollars |
| Phylum Aschelminthes | | | |
|   Class Rotifera | rotifers |   Class Holothuroidea | sea cucumbers |
|   Class Nematoda | round worms | Phylum Hemichordata | acorn worms |
|   Class Nematomorpha | horsehair worms | Phylum Chordata | |
| Phylum Ectoprocta | bryozoans |   Subphylum Urochordata | tunicates |
| Phylum Brachiopoda | lamp shells |   Subphylum Cephalochordata | sea lancelets, amphioxus |
| Phylum Mollusca | |   Subphylum Vertebrata | |
|   Class Gastropoda | snails |     Class Agnatha | jawless fishes |
|   Class Scaphopoda | tusk shells |     Class Chondrichthyes | sharks and rays |
|   Class Pelecypoda | bivalves |     Class Osteichthyes | bony fishes |
|   Class Cephalopoda | squids and octopuses |     Class Amphibia | amphibians (frogs, toads, salamanders, and caecilians) |
| Phylum Pogonophora | beard worms | | |
| Phylum Annelida | |     Class Reptilia | reptiles (turtles, snakes, lizards, crocodilians, and tuataras) |
|   Class Polychaeta | marine segmented worms | | |
|   Class Oligochaeta | earthworms | | |
|   Class Hirudinea | leeches |     Class Aves | birds |
| Phylum Onychophora | peripatus |     Class Mammalia | mammals |
| | |       Subclass Prototheria | egg-laying mammals (duck-billed platypus and spiny anteater) |
| Phylum Tardigrada | water bears | | |
| Phylum Pentastomida | tongue worms | | |
| | |       Subclass Theria | marsupials and placental mammals |

*Both kingdoms of animals in this, one of several classification schemes, are given but some classes are not listed. In addition to those phyla listed, several primitive, poorly studied ones are also recognized: Gnathostomulida, Entoprocta, Priapulida, Phoronida, Sipunculida, Echiuroida. They have no common names.
†The Kingdom Protista also includes plant protists.

---

The vertebrates make up only about 5 percent of all animal species. Invertebrates compose the remaining 95 percent. There are some 4,000 species of mammals. Insects number about one million species.

## How Animals Are Classified

To study the many forms of animal life in a systematic way, scientists have divided the animal kingdom into groups. These groups are based upon the structure of the animal's body. The largest divisions are phyla (singular, phylum). The word phylum means "race" or "tribe." The phyla are groups of animals with fundamentally different body plans.

Each phylum is divided into classes, the classes into orders, and the orders into families. Families are subdivided into genera (singular, genus), and each genus is divided into species. All members of the same species are closely related. They are capable of interbreeding and producing fertile offspring. Animals of different species do not normally interbreed. Every animal has a scientific name, or binomial (having two names), consisting of the genus and species.

## How Classification Shows Relationships

Classification shows relationships between animals in an increasingly specific order, from remotely related members of the same phylum to closely related species within a genus. House cats (*Felis catus*) and bobcats (*Felis rufus*) belong to the same genus (*Felis*) and family (Felidae) but to different species.

Dogs and cats do not appear to be related. Both, however, have backbones and are meat-eating mammals. Hence they belong to phylum Chordata (having a spinal cord), class Mammalia (mammals), and order Carnivora (flesh eaters); because of differences between them, however, they belong to separate families (dog, Canidae; cat, Felidae).

Whales and sharks both appear to be kinds of fish. Both are strong, streamlined swimmers of the sea. However, the whale is a mammal. It has lungs and is warm-blooded, gives birth to live young, and nurses its offspring with milk. Whales therefore belong to the class Mammalia. The shark, on the other hand, is a primitive kind of fish with a skeleton of cartilage instead of bone. Sharks, whales, and true fishes all have a backbone. Thus, they are placed in the same phylum (Chordata) and subphylum (Vertebrata). Sharks and fishes, however, are also in different classes, the sharks being in the Chondrichthyes and the true fishes in the Osteichthyes.

Classification also suggests which kinds of animals may have descended from other types. All multicelled animals, for example, are supposed to be descendants of one-celled animals. This does not mean descent from one living kind of animal to another, however. All living animals are believed to have descended from common ancestors that were less specialized than they. These relationships may be shown on a treelike diagram called a phylogenetic tree. The word phylogenetic comes from two Greek words meaning "race history."

## Animals Without Backbones—Invertebrates

The simplest animal-like organisms consist of a single cell—a bit of protoplasm containing one nucleus. These organisms are called protozoans, which means "first animals" in Greek. These creatures are sometimes considered animals, but most classification schemes place them in a separate kingdom known as the Protista. Protozoans are very adaptable. They live in salt and fresh water, in moist earth, and as parasites in other animals.

Aside from the protozoans, all members of the kingdom Animalia have many cells and are referred to as metazoans. The simplest multicelled animals make up the phylum Porifera ("pore bearers"). The most familiar kinds are the sponges. They are called

**Zoogeographic Regions and Some Characteristic Animals**

red fox

red deer

Nearctic

opossum

pronghorn antelope

beaver

anteater

Neotropical

sloth

capuchin monkey

capybara

pore bearers because they are covered with millions of tiny holes. Water flows through the holes, and from the water the sponges take in oxygen and the tiny waterborne organisms that constitute their food and filter out wastes. Sponges have no mouth or digestive cavity, no nervous system, and no circulatory system. Several types of cells are present, but each generally functions as a unit without forming tissues, as in more complex metazoans. (Tissues are groups of similar cells bound together to perform a common function.)

## Pouchlike Animals

The next, less primitive structural pattern in invertebrates is a hollow gut. The representative phylum is Coelenterata, a term stemming from the Greek words *koilos* (hollow) and *enteron* (intestine). Among the coelenterates are the corals, hydras, jellyfishes, and sea anemones. The body is composed of two tissue

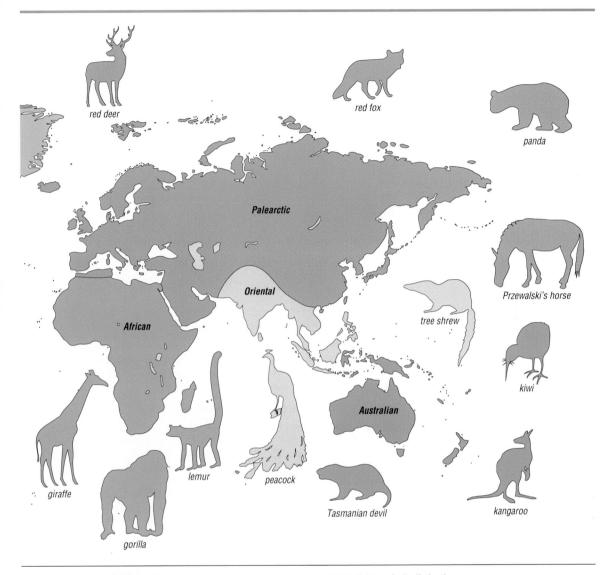

*Animal geographers divide the world into zoogeographic regions on the basis of the region's distinctive animal life. Each region more or less coincides with a major continental landmass, separated from other regions by oceans, mountain ranges, or deserts. Animals native to the Nearctic region include the red deer, red fox, pronghorn antelope, and beaver. (The red deer and red fox are also native to the Palearctic region.) Those native to the Neotropical region include the opossum, anteater, capybara, sloth, and capuchin monkey. Those native to the African region include the gorilla, giraffe, and lemur. Those native to the Australian region include the Tasmanian devil, kangaroo, and kiwi. Those native to the Oriental region include the peacock and tree shrew. Species distinctive to the Palearctic region are the panda and Przewalski's horse.*

layers. The inner layer, or endoderm, lines the central digestive cavity. The outer layer, or ectoderm, protects the animal externally.

The coelenterates have a mouthlike opening—the only opening into the gut—that takes in food and ejects waste material. Food-gathering organs such as tentacles and protective structures such as stinging cells surround the mouth. There is a primitive nervous system. (Coelenterates are also sometimes called cnidarians.)

### Bilateral Animals with Heads

All the animals described above are headless creatures—with shapes like a globe, a cylinder, a bowl, or a wheel. The latter are said to have spherical or radial symmetry; they have similar body parts arranged around a center or a central axis, respectively. Some drift around in ocean currents, unable to swim efficiently in any particular direction. Some of them in their adult stages—the corals and sponges, for

*Animals with Backbones*

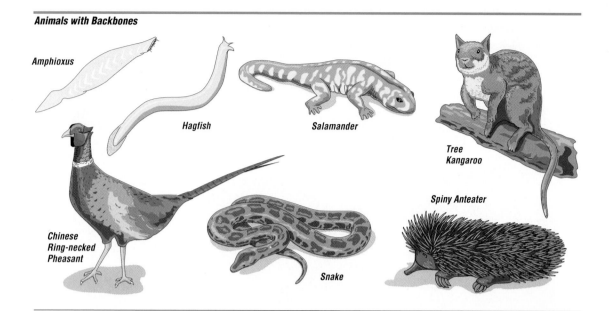

example—fasten themselves to fixed objects and do not move at all.

A flatworm called Dugesia, or planaria, is interesting because it shows two very important improvements in body structure. It belongs to the phylum Platyhelminthes (flatworms). It is the most primitive animal that has a definite head bearing sense organs. The mouth is on the underside of the triangular head. The body is differentiated into a front end and a rear end, a top and a bottom. It has bilateral symmetry: each half of the body is a mirror image of the other half. Most of the higher animals, including humans, are built on this pattern of body structure.

Platyhelminths are also the most primitive, living animals to have three cell layers. Between the ectoderm and the endoderm, which first appeared in the jellyfish and their relatives, is a middle layer: the mesoderm. Two-layered animals are small and fragile. The third layer gives solidity to the body and permits the animal to grow to a large size. Muscles and other complex organs develop from this layer.

### Segmented Worms

Segmented worms have a more developed digestive system than Dugesia, which takes in food and ejects waste material through the same opening in the head. Segmented worms have a digestive tube with two openings—a mouth and an anus through which wastes are expelled. The phylum Annelida (meaning ringed, or segmented) has a digestive system built on the same plan as the vertebrates. Earthworms and leeches are familiar annelids.

### The Soft-Bodied Animals

The phylum Mollusca (from the Latin word for "soft") includes the clam, oyster, chiton, snail, octopus, and squid. Mollusks have soft, fleshy bodies not divided

into segments. The main part of the body is enclosed in a fold of tissue called the mantle. They have bilateral symmetry. Many of them are covered by a shell. They have a solid, protective structure outside the body, called an exoskeleton.

### The Largest Group of Animals

The phylum Arthropoda ("jointed foot") has the largest number of species. In fact, about 90 percent of the million or more species living on the Earth today are arthropods. The insects total more than 800,000 species. Other arthropods include the centipedes and millipedes; the arachnids (spiders, scorpions, ticks, mites); and the crustaceans (barnacles, crabs, crayfish, lobsters, shrimp, water fleas). Obviously, the arthropod body plan has been highly successful. The members of this great phylum live on land, in fresh water, and in salt water. They can walk, fly, burrow, and swim. This is the only invertebrate group with jointed appendages (legs, feet, and antennae).

Arthropods, like mollusks, wear a supporting framework, or exoskeleton, on the outside of the body. Much more highly developed than the heavy, clumsy shell of the clams and snails, it is made of a substance called chitin. Rigid, waterproof plates of chitin are joined by thin, flexible membranes of chitin so that the animal can move freely and quickly. The muscles are attached to the inner surface of the armor. Many important structures are connected to the outer surface. For example, the wings, legs, jaws, and antennae of the insects are all made of chitin and are attached to the outer skeleton. The body is divided into sections, or segments.

### Spiny-Skinned Animals

One phylum with the characteristics of several others is the Echinodermata ("spiny-skinned"). All members of the group, which includes starfishes, sea urchins, holothurians (sea cucumbers), and crinoids (sea lilies), live in salt water—some in the shallow shoreline waters, others in the ocean depths. The young, called larvae, have bilateral symmetry, but the adults have radial symmetry, like the coelenterates. These are the most primitive creatures having an endoskeleton, or skeleton that is embedded in the flesh. It consists of a meshwork of plates that are made of calcium. The plates are joined by connective tissue and muscles. Spines project from these plates.

### Animals with Backbones

At the top of the animal kingdom is the phylum Chordata. This phylum consists of two groups of primitive chordates—the tunicates and the cephalochordates—and the main group of the vertebrates.

The major subdivisions, or classes, of the vertebrates are the fish, amphibians, reptiles, birds, and mammals. Members of this phylum possess the following structures at some period of their life, either as embryos or as adults:

**Notochord.** This is an internal supporting rod extending the length of the body. It is found in the embryos of all chordates, including human beings. Only the most primitive forms, such as the amphioxus, or lancelet, the lamprey, and the hagfish, retain it as adults. Remnants of the notochord are also present in sharks. In the higher chordates, such as amphibians, reptiles, birds, and mammals, the notochord is replaced during development of the embryo by a bony column of vertebrae, which gives the column and the animal flexibility.

**Nerve tube.** This lies in the midline of the body on the top (dorsal side) of the notochord. In the annelid worms and the arthropods the main nerve is solid and lies on the underside (ventral side). In most chordates the forward end of the nerve tube forms a brain; the remainder is the spinal cord.

**Pharyngeal gill slits or pouches.** The lower chordates, such as the fish, breathe through openings in the side of the neck in the region of the pharynx. The embryos of the higher chordates have these slits, but they disappear in the adult.

### Primitive Chordates

The amphioxus is characteristic of the most primitive chordates. This animal is a laterally compressed, semitransparent sea dweller about 4 inches (10 centimeters) long. Scientists believe that it may be one of the ancestors of the vertebrates. It has a notochord and a tubular nerve cord along the back. It has no well-developed brain, however, and only traces of eyes and ears. Pigment spots along the body are sensitive to light. The pharyngeal gill slits strain food from the water. The tunicates, or sea squirts, and acorn worms are other primitive chordates.

Lampreys and hagfishes are the most primitive of the true vertebrates. They have a notochord. The skeleton is composed of cartilage. They lack jaws and paired limbs.

### Mammals

Mammals differ from other vertebrates in that they have bodies that are covered with hair at some period of their lives. They are warm-blooded, meaning that their body temperature is largely unaffected by the temperature of the air or water in which they live. The females have milk glands to feed their young. Whales, as noted earlier in this article, dolphins, and porpoises are the most unusual-looking mammals because they resemble fishes. The most primitive mammals are the egg-laying platypus and the echidna, or spiny anteater. The marsupials, which incubate their unborn offspring in a pouch for a time, are also considered to be somewhat primitive. The remaining mammals transmit nourishment to their unborn young through a placenta and give birth to fully developed offspring.

**BIBLIOGRAPHY FOR ANIMAL**

**Books for Children**

**Alday, Gretchen.** Devoted Friends: Amazing True Stories About Animals Who Cared (Betterway, 1990).
**Aylesworth, T.G.** Animal Superstitions (McGraw, 1981).
**Gabb, Michael.** Creatures Great and Small (Lerner, 1980).
**Hirschi, Ron.** Who Lives In—the Forest? (Dodd, 1987).
**Hutchins, R.E.** Nature Invented It First (Dodd, 1980).
**Lauber, Patricia.** What's Hatching Out of That Egg? (Crown, 1979).
**Lopshire, Robert.** The Biggest, Smallest, Fastest, Tallest Things You've Ever Heard Of (Houghton, 1991).
**Lurie, Alison.** Fabulous Beasts (Farrar, 1981).
**McCauley, J.R.** Animals and Their Hiding Places (National Geographic, 1986).
**McGrath, Susan.** Saving Our Animal Friends (National Geographic, 1986).
**Patent, D.H.** Sizes and Shapes in Nature—What They Mean (Holiday House, 1979).
**Pope, Joyce.** Do Animals Dream? (Viking, 1986).
**Prince, J.H.** How Animals Move (Elsevier/Nelson, 1981).
**Pringle, L.P.** Feral: Tame Animals Gone Wild (Macmillan, 1983).
**Schulz, C.M.** Charlie Brown's Super Book of Questions and Answers About All Kinds of Animals (Random, 1976).
**Sundén, Ulla, ed.** Remarkable Animals (Guinness Books, 1987).
**Sussman, Susan and James, Robert.** Lies (People Believe) About Animals (Whitman, 1987).
**Windsor, Merrill.** Baby Farm Animals (National Geographic, 1984).

**Books for Young Adults**

**Adamson, Joy.** Born Free (Pantheon, 1987).
**Adamson, Joy.** Living Free (Harcourt, 1961).
**Argent, Kerry.** Animal Capers (Doubleday, 1990).
**Baker, M.L.** Whales, Dolphins, and Porpoises of the World (Doubleday, 1987).
**Burton, Maurice.** Cold-Blooded Animals (Facts on File, 1986).
**Burton, Maurice.** Warm-Blooded Animals (Facts on File, 1987).
**Burton, Maurice and Burton, Jane.** The Colorful World of Animals (Longmeadow, 1975).
**Gibbons, Whit.** Their Blood Runs Cold: Adventures with Reptiles and Amphibians (Univ. of Ala. Press, 1983).
**Herriot, James.** All Creatures Great and Small (St. Martin's, 1972).
**Herriot, James.** All Things Bright and Beautiful (St. Martin's, 1974).
**Herriot, James and others.** Animal Stories, Tame and Wild (Sterling, 1985).
**Kohl, Judith and Kohl, Herbert.** Pack, Band, and Colony: The World of Social Animals (Farrar, 1983).
**Milne, Lorus and Milne, Margery.** A Time to be Born (Sierra Club, 1982).
**National Geographic Book Service.** Wild Animals of North America, rev. ed. (National Geographic, 1987).
**Nowak, R.M. and Paradiso, J.L.** Walker's Mammals of the World (Johns Hopkins Univ. Press, 1983).

Patti Murray—Animals Animals

*Contact between baboons is necessary for their welfare. When baboons engage in grooming—a contact activity—they remove dirt and parasites from each other's hair. Grooming is a type of cooperative behavior.*

# ANIMAL BEHAVIOR

People have always been fascinated by the amazingly varied behavior of animals. Ancient humans observed the habits of animals, partly out of curiosity but primarily in order to hunt and to domesticate some animals. Most people today have a less practical interest in animal behavior. They simply enjoy the antics and activities of pets, of animals in zoos, and of wildlife.

But in modern times the study of animal behavior has also become a scientific specialty. The biologists and psychologists who study animal behavior try to find out why animals act in the specific ways they do and how their behavior helps them and their offspring survive. Some of them feel that the behavior of animals provides clues to the behavior of people.

A great deal of fanciful "animal lore" has arisen over the years in the mistaken belief that animals behave for the same reasons as people. The view that nonhuman things have human attributes is called anthropomorphism. An example of anthropomorphism is found in the following passage written in the 1st century AD by the Roman author Pliny the Elder:

*The largest land animal is the elephant. It is the nearest to man in intelligence; it understands the language of its country and obeys orders, remembers duties that it has been taught, is pleased by affection and by marks of honor, nay more it possesses virtues rare even for man, honesty, wisdom, justice, also respect for the stars and reverence for the sun and moon.*

Undeniably, the elephant can be taught to perform certain tasks, but no one today seriously believes that it reveres the sun and the moon.

Animal behavior can be studied in natural settings or in the laboratory. The study of animal behavior from the viewpoint of observing instinctive behavior in the animal's natural habitat is called ethology. An ethologist observes the ways in which animals solve their common problems—for example, eating, drinking, protecting themselves and their offspring from predators, reproducing, and grooming. A contrasting approach to behavioral studies is to observe animals in a laboratory setting. This area of study has concentrated mainly on learning processes, behavioral development, and the influence of behavior on an animal's internal workings—the action of nerve impulses and hormones, for example. Often, laboratory experiments are designed to test notions based on outdoor observation. Both approaches are important.

......................................................................................

*This article was contributed by Ethel Tobach, Curator, Department of Mammalogy, American Museum of Natural History, New York City.*

*Through the process of imprinting, Canadian geese formed a bond with a human being. Imprinting occurred when the newly hatched birds followed the first large object they encountered. If imprinted by a human "parent," the baby bird will follow the human even when a live adult bird of its own species is later present. This form of animal behavior is most often studied in birds, but it also occurs with other kinds of animals.*

Breck P. Kent—Animals Animals

## What Is Behavior?

Simply defined, animal behavior is anything an animal does—its feeding habits, its reproductive actions, the way it rears its young, and a host of other activities. Behavior is always an organized action. It is the whole animal's adjustment to changes inside its body or in its surroundings.

The group activities of animals are an important aspect of animal behavior. Bees, for example, communicate with each other about food, and birds may flock during migratory flights. Group activities are often adaptations to a new set of circumstances. Without adaptation, a species could not survive in an ever-changing environment.

Behavior can also be thought of as a response to a stimulus—some change in the body or in the environment. All animals, even those too small to be seen without a microscope, respond to stimuli.

## How an Animal Reacts to a Stimulus

A stimulus is a signal from the animal's body or its environment. It is a form of energy—light waves or sound vibrations, for example. All but the simplest animals receive a stimulus—light, sound, taste, touch, or smell—through special cells called receptors, located in many places on or in the body. For example, fish have hairlike organs over much of their body, sometimes even on the tail. These organs enable fish to feel changes in the water they swim through and thus to detect nearby food. Cats, who prowl the dark, rely on sensitive touch organs associated with their whiskers.

At the receptors the incoming energy is changed into nerve impulses. In complex animals these impulses may travel either to the brain or through reflex arcs to trigger the hormone or muscle actions of a response. (*See also* Brain; Nervous System; Reflexes.)

## Conditioning—A Way of Modifying Behavior

The behavior of many, perhaps all, animals can be modified by a kind of training called conditioning. Two types of conditioning have been studied— classical conditioning and operant conditioning. The first type was discovered by the Russian physiologist Ivan Pavlov; the second, by the American psychologist B.F. Skinner.

In classical conditioning, an animal can be made to respond to a stimulus in an unorthodox manner. For example, a sea anemone can be conditioned to open its mouth when its tentacles are touched—a response that it does not ordinarily make to this stimulus. When undergoing such conditioning, an animal is repeatedly offered two different stimuli in timed sequences. The first, called the neutral, or conditioned, stimulus, does not usually cause the animal to respond in the desired way; in the sea anemone experiment, touch is the neutral stimulus. The second stimulus, called the unconditioned stimulus, does cause the desired behavior. Squid juice is the unconditioned stimulus because it will cause the sea anemone to open its mouth. In classical conditioning, the neutral stimulus is followed by the unconditioned stimulus. The unconditioned stimulus may be given while the neutral stimulus is being delivered or afterward. The sea anemone was touched first, then given squid juice. After hundreds of such trials, it opened its mouth when touched even though no squid juice was offered.

In operant conditioning, an animal is given some type of reward or punishment whenever it behaves in a certain way—for example, whenever it pushes a lever, presses a bar, or moves from one place to another. The reward or punishment, called a reinforcement, follows the action. Food or water may be used as rewards; an electric shock, as a punishment. Rewarding the animal increases the probability that it will repeat the action; punishment decreases the probability. Operant conditioning has been used not only with laboratory animals but also in programmed instruction and teaching machines for people.

## Role of the Nervous System in Behavior

An important relationship exists between an animal's nervous system and its ability to respond to environmental changes. Animals with a fairly simple nervous system, such as ants, respond in a relatively fixed, or stereotyped, fashion as compared with animals that have a more highly developed and specialized nervous system, such as rats. A rat can link up, or

## AN EXPERIMENT IN ANIMAL BEHAVIOR

*Negative phototaxis—the movement of an organism away from light—can be demonstrated in a simple experiment. The experiment requires a blowfly larva, a sheet of black paper, and either two flashlights or a desk lamp with two bulbs that can be positioned and lighted independently. The larva may be obtained from sites where the blowfly breeds, such as garbage cans. The experiment should be performed away from the house in a garage or other enclosure.*

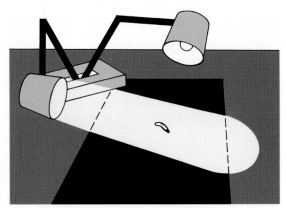

*Turn the second bulb on and the first bulb off. The larva will change course to avoid the light.*

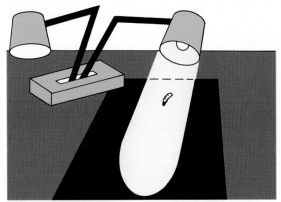

*Place the larva on the black paper and place the lamp bulbs at right angles to each other and at about a 30-degree angle to the paper. Since the blowfly larva generally avoids light by keeping its light-sensitive head end in its shadow, the larva will probably move away from the light.*

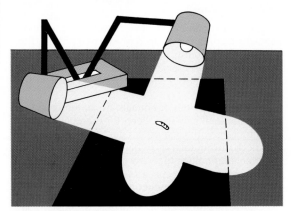

*Further phototactic responses of the larva can be observed by turning both bulbs on and by moving one bulb farther from the paper while both are on. In some instances, however, the larva will move toward the light or will not move at all. When the larva is close to pupation, it has a positive phototaxis and leaves its dark quarters to pupate in the light. When ready to pupate, it does not respond to light.*

integrate, different stimuli from the environment and can store and use the information from past experience to solve simple and complex problems far better than an ant can. However, the rat does not do as well as a higher mammal, such as a chimpanzee.

For example, a rat, an ant, and a chimpanzee can each learn a complicated pattern of responses to reach food. The rat is trained to run a maze—a number of pathways toward a goal, all but one of which end in blind alleys—to find food. Then the rat begins at the end of the maze and must learn to run the course backward in order to reach food placed at the starting point. The rat takes less trials to learn the maze backward than forward. An ant given the same training cannot benefit from its past experience. It must learn the backward path as though it were a new one. The chimpanzee shows the greatest learning ability of the three. When the chimpanzee solves a problem, such as discriminating between two geometric shapes, it can do so by generalizing from a "set to learn." That is, after it has learned that it can obtain food by making the correct choice between the two shapes, it easily makes the correct response on the next try. A rat requires a number of trials before it can associate "shape" with "food."

### The Evolution of Behavior

Behavioral scientists arrange living things according to the complexity of their behavior and the extent to which it can be modified. They have found that animals with more complex body and nervous systems have more complex and more modifiable behavior. In addition, however, the behavioral patterns that have

evolved among living things are particular ways of adapting to their environments—the places where they develop and reproduce. For example, though all animals feed, there are evident differences in the way they feed. Marine worms sift sand for edible organisms. An army ant stings a beetle and brings it back to the colony's bivouac, where it is dismembered by other members of the colony. A chimpanzee peels a banana before eating it.

It is possible to observe living animals and find out why they act as they do, but can anyone know how extinct animals behaved? There are fossil remains of extinct animals, but behavioral patterns cannot be left as fossils. Yet, equipped only with such fossil remains, scientists can get inklings about the behavior of extinct species. They achieve this by studying living species in the laboratory or in their natural habitats to determine their behavioral similarities and differences. Then they try to uncover the relationship between the structure of the body parts of these species and the particular function of each body part. Thus, if particular characteristics of the structure of a wing or a leg, for example, can be identified with a particular activity of a living animal, a scientist studying the evolution of behavior can make plausible guesses about the possible function of fossil bones. He can then develop notions about the possible behavior of extinct species that were ancestors of certain living animals.

For example, by studying the different groups of passerine, or perching, birds, researchers have identified the evolutionary relationships among them. One way is to use tail flick as a taxonomic character—a structural trait employed in analyzing the relationships among different species. Perching birds flick their tails in a particular way as they move through trees. By analysis of the extent of tail-feather spread during a tail flick and the direction and amount of tail movement, evolutionary relationships can be seen among such passerines as cardinals, buntings, weaverbirds, waxbills, and finches.

Evolutionary relationships among species may also be studied by analyzing different behavioral patterns. Among the most important behavioral patterns are orientation, social organization, and communication. All species exhibit each of these. However, within species considerable variation exists in the stimuli to which individuals respond, the age at which they respond, and the patterns of their response.

### Orienting Behavior

An animal orients by adjusting its posture and position in space. It does so in relation to the source of different forms of energy in its environment. These forms include light, heat, and chemicals in the air or water, pressure, electric current, air or water currents, gravity, radiation, and magnetic fields.

Orienting behavior may take the form of a tropism—an action in which the animal simply orients its body toward or away from the source of energy without changing location. Plants can also respond in this way. However, the orienting response may take the form of a taxis—a movement toward or away from the source of energy by swimming, flying, or locomotion. As a rule, only animals are capable of such responses. Still another type of orienting response is called a kinesis—an increase or decrease in an animal's activity, but in no particular direction.

Prefixes are usually added to the root words tropism, taxis, and kinesis to indicate the kind of energy to which the organism is responding. For example, geotropism is response to gravity; phototaxis, response to light. Prefixes may also indicate the type of response made. Thus klinokinesis refers to turning activities. In addition, the direction or intensity of a response may be described as positive, if directed toward a stimulus, or negative, if directed away from it.

Orientation makes it possible for an animal to feed, to exhibit social behavior, and to avoid obstacles and barriers. Some organisms, such as the bat, use sonar—reflected sound—to locate prey and to avoid obstacles. Some fish can navigate through tight crevices by detecting changes in their electric field. Electronic

*Penguins space themselves in a way that ensures a place for them and their young in a crowded rookery. The behavior through which an animal claims an area and defends it against others of its species is called territoriality.*

instruments enable researchers to detect and record the sound frequencies and electricity emitted by different species. (*See also* Bioengineering; Bionics.)

When foraging for food, the honeybee orients to the odor of flowers and the polarization of light. It also responds to cues from the sun's position off the horizon. This type of activity is called sun compass orientation. On returning to the hive the bee performs certain "dances"—a variety of motor patterns—that vary with the distance and direction of the food. These dances stimulate the other bees to travel the path of the returning bee. (*See also* Bee.)

Fish and birds also exhibit compass orientation when homing or migrating. However, scientists are not sure that animals navigate in the same way as man. When humans navigate, they use such instruments as the sextant to find the altitude of the sun and stars and a chronometer for timekeeping. It has not yet been demonstrated that homing and migrating animals can "shoot an azimuth" and "tell time." (*See also* Navigation.)

Some animals are known to return to the areas where they were born or spawned. The salmon, for example, upon reaching sexual maturity responds to the chemical characteristics of the stream in which it was spawned. The hormonal changes associated with sexual maturity are a cause of this new sensitivity. The stickleback moves from salty to brackish water to reproduce. Its behavior is related to endocrine gland responses to seasonal fluctuations in light. Similar

L. David Mech

Durward L. Allen

*Among social animals, dominance and submissiveness develop as a way of controlling breeding and territories. Two foxes engage in a mock battle for dominance (right). Among wolves, dominance denotes leadership as well. Alpha, or dominant, wolves usually lead the attack against prey (left). Even in an attack such as this, however, a healthy, fully grown moose will escape from the wolves.*

hormonal changes in birds lead to migration and reproduction. These cyclic changes in behavior due to hormonal regulation are considered evidence of a chronometer that might enable migrating or homing animals to correlate changes in visual cues during compass orientation with changes in internal rhythms and thus make navigation possible. (*See also* Biological Clock; Hormones.)

**Social Behavior**

All living things relate to other members of their species. In an amoeba, the relationship occurs only during the short time it takes the animal to split into two animals. In other species, such as the social insects, the relationship is so necessary that they cannot survive as individuals. This is true also of humans, who are dependent on others until they reach maturity. Social organization of some kind is common to all animals. However, the type of organization varies with the nervous system of the species. And in true social organization, animals of the same species react to each other.

Conspecifics, or animals of the same species, may at times be close to each other without exhibiting social behavior. For example, mollusk larvae may respond to changes in the intensity of light by swimming to the water surface. The resultant grouping, called an aggregation, stems from a common response to a physical aspect of the environment. But a response is truly social only when it is a response to visual, chemical, auditory, or other stimuli emanating from a conspecific. As a result of such stimuli, animals may approach each other to form a bond or to fight. Although dissimilar, both reactions are examples of social behavior.

The type of bond formed by conspecifics is a measure of their nervous and hormonal systems.

Organisms with relatively simple systems may respond to each other only as long as they give off attractive or offensive stimuli. For example, a worm will approach another worm during the reproductive state because certain chemicals are released. Once mating has occurred, they have nothing further to do with each other. A goby will remain near its eggs only as long as the hormonal state of the fish and the chemical and visual features of the eggs remain the same. Once the fry, or young, hatch, the fish responds to them as it would toward any small fish and tries to eat them. The goby does not recognize the fry as its own offspring.

Although orientation, changing hormonal levels, and other processes play a part, social bonding depends primarily on a mutual exchange of stimulation and food between animals. The give-and-take stimulation of a pair or a group is fundamental to the organization of social groups.

**The Army Ant Colony— An Example of a Social Group**

An army ant colony consists of many thousands of workers and a queen. The queen is capable of laying large batches of infertile eggs when she is fed sufficiently. These eggs hatch into workers, females incapable of sexual reproduction. However, at a certain stage of the queen's development she produces a brood of males and females capable of reproducing and starting new colonies.

The colony has a two-phase cycle of activity. The nomadic phase lasts about 18 days. By late afternoon or early evening, the larger workers cluster and leave the bivouac area where they spent the previous night. They move out over many yards in the area around the bivouac. As they crawl, they lay a chemical trail. Other ants in the colony travel over the trail, and as

Jeff Lepore—Photo Researchers

(Top) Eaton Burchell—OSF/Animals Animals; (bottom) Gregory G. Dimijian—Photo Researchers

*Birds fiercely protect their young and even their unborn offspring from harm. The killdeer protects its eggs by faking a broken wing to distract a predator's attention away from the eggs.*

*(Top) In an army ant colony a single queen is attended to by many thousands of workers, some of which climb on her back to assist her. (Bottom) As army ants travel to a new bivouac site, they lay a chemical trail for other ants to follow. The submajors carry the precious larvae under their bodies as they travel. A major, on the left, with large mandibles, protects the column as it moves along.*

the trail becomes more frequently traveled the concentration of chemical stimuli on it becomes stronger. The entire colony, queen and all, eventually move out from the bivouac along the trail. The ants range over large areas, preying on other insects and their young.

Army ants take in considerable food during the nomadic phase. The queen receives a good deal of it. She does not usually forage but is able to feed on the food brought back by medium-size workers. They return to the bivouac to lick the queen for the highly attractive chemicals she exudes. Chemicals that attract or repel conspecifics and heterospecifics (members of other species) are called pheromones. The exchanges of food and secretions between the queen and the workers produce a strong social bond that aids in keeping the colony together. The queen's increased food intake enables her to lay a batch of eggs. However, this affects her relationship with the workers. She becomes less stimulating to them, and their foraging, therefore, begins to decrease. Now the colony enters the other phase of its cycle—the statary phase. The number, frequency, distance, and area of foraging decreases considerably. The level of the entire colony's activity drops to a minimum.

After about 21 days the eggs hatch, and the larvae emerge. These squirming, active young are an intense source of stimulation to the workers. The workers are driven out of the bivouac and the nomadic phase starts again. They are now attracted by the pheromones of the larvae and the queen. When the workers return from foraging, they drop their food and feel and handle the larvae with their antennae and legs. As a result of this excitation, the number and frequency of raids again increase. The colony travels great distances, the larvae are fed, and the queen is overfed. At this point, the colony consists of the queen, workers, and larvae.

About 18 days after the eggs have hatched, the larvae enclose themselves in cocoons and become pupae. At about the same time, the queen lays her next batch of eggs. Now the colony consists of the queen, workers, pupae, and developing eggs. However, the pupae and the eggs offer little stimulation for the

workers, and the statary slowdown begins. But the queen continues to secrete pheromones that socially bind the colony. (*See also* Ant; Insect.)

## Dominance

In communities of certain animals the ruling, or dominant, animal is the largest, strongest, or most aggressive and thereby exerts the most influence on the other animals in the group. The dominant animal enjoys the greatest and most preferential access to members of the opposite sex and control of the best territory for feeding and breeding. Scientists have found that many groups of animals, most notably baboons, birds, foxes, lions, and crocodiles, establish dominance hierarchies. The best-known example is the pecking order of chickens. Flock members are arranged on the "rungs" of a social ladder, with each chicken superior to those below and subordinate to those above. The top animal has primary access to the necessities of life, such as the best food, mates, and living quarters. Submissive animals are left with less-desirable food, mates, and living quarters. Such animals may even be expected to groom dominant members and to help care for the offspring of more dominant animals, because subordinates are often prevented from having offspring of their own.

In other animal groups, dominance hierarchies are more complicated. Wolf packs, for example, are led by two dominants who have three subclasses of subordinates below them. Other animals have only one dominant leader with all other animals below him or her being exactly equal. Once an animal has established dominance, challenges to the order are rarely made from within the group, since animals are reluctant to fight other animals that are bigger, stronger, or more aggressive than they are themselves. Sometimes, however, animals from outside the group can successfully challenge and overthrow a longtime leader, but this is rare.

In more intelligent species, such as baboons, factors beyond mere size and strength determine the dominance hierarchy. Age seniority, hormonal condition, maternal lineage, and personality are sometimes factors that affect dominance in more intelligent animals. In baboon groups, furthermore, hierarchies are often elaborate. Adult males are dominant over less mature males and females; yet a fully mature female can be dominant over a less mature male. A dominant baboon displays its superiority with rapid "fencing" maneuvers, open-jaw displays, hitting, and other aggressive behavior.

### Close Bonds Among Animals

Animals with complex nervous systems, ranging from some fish to mammals, may form monogamous bonds. The mates of such species stay together for a breeding season or even for a lifetime. Their social ties are not restricted by the time-bound, immediate stimulation that simpler animals need. However, monogamous pairs must be able to identify their mates from other conspecifics. This requires the intricate action of an advanced nervous system.

Some birds and many mammals band in large groups, such as herds and families. These groups include adult males and females and offspring of different ages. The offspring in most mammalian groups remain with the group until they reach sexual maturity. The females frequently remain until the group splits up. Some socially bonded groups of mammals consist of an older male, a number of younger males, many females, and immature offspring. Among the howler monkeys, the younger males band together into a marginal bachelor group until each establishes himself as the older male in a new social group.

Not all mammals maintain elaborate group arrangements. Many live fairly solitary lives, coming together only for mating. Afterward, the female remains with the litter until the young become juveniles or are sexually mature. In some instances, the mating pair stay together until the young are born. Beavers behave in this way. Among other rodents, the male and the female separate immediately after mating.

### The Prairie Dog Coterie—A Complex Social Group

The prairie dog is a rodent that maintains an elaborate social organization. Bond formation among prairie dogs depends on the exchange of auditory, visual, and chemical stimuli. The coterie—the social unit of the prairie dog—is maintained in a network of burrows occupying a fairly restricted area.

Prairie dog pups are altricial at birth—that is, they are so undeveloped that they need adult aid for survival. When the pup is born, its mother is attracted to the helpless young organism. She licks the pup as it emerges from the birth canal, thus replenishing the salts she lost before and during birth. While licking the pup, she breaks the sac in which it developed as an embryo and thus stimulates its breathing response (*see*

*Wild animals usually run away when a person or any other possible enemy comes too close. However, an animal that cannot flee will attack when the enemy breaches its critical zone. Lion trainers rely on this behavior in circus acts. When a trainer steps into the caged lion's critical zone, it moves toward him. To stop the attack, the trainer steps back from the zone and the lion halts or turns around. Whips, guns, or other punitive devices used by the trainer are for show purposes only.*

Embryology). The pup, still wet from birth, is attracted to the warmth of the mother's body. Moments after birth, the mother and her offspring are exchanging highly attractive stimuli, quickly forming a social bond. As the pup nurses, it relieves the pressure in the mother's milk gland. Again, the exchange of stimulation strengthens the bond between the mother and her offspring, thus helping to ensure the infant's survival.

As the pup matures, other stimuli become attractive. When it is able to see and hear, the pup begins to recognize the relationship between stimuli that occur at the same time. Soon it leaves its burrow and encounters other adults that it stimulates. From birth, the prairie dog is constantly nuzzled and licked by its mother. When it emerges from its burrow, it is handled similarly by other prairie dogs.

These behavioral patterns maintain prairie dogs in a well-organized life space. There, the family unit reproduces, finds shelter, and feeds. Being grazers, prairie dogs check the growth of tall grasses that would prevent them from easily spotting predators. At the same time, their grazing habits encourage the dominance of fast-growing plants. Thus, the social organization of prairie dogs influences the ecological balances in their environment (*see* Ecology). Limited grazing space soon forces maturing prairie dogs to seek new areas. When they enter the burrows of another coterie their odor marks them as strangers, and they are rejected. Pairs of rebuffed animals band together to form new coteries.

### The Chimpanzee Family

The chimpanzee is one of the great apes. It lives in a family unit even more complex than that of the prairie dog. The chimpanzee family moves as a group through familiar feeding and resting areas. It has also evolved effective ways of defending itself against predators or from belligerent chimpanzees attempting to mate with the family's females.

When a chimpanzee has been attacked or has spotted a predator, it lets out an intense cry that raises the level of excitement of the other members of the family. They scream at the predator, throw rocks and other objects, and scamper off. As they flee, the females and the youngest chimpanzees are surrounded by the juveniles and the young males. The largest males guard the group. Thus, the action of a single chimpanzee serves as a signal that affects the behavior of the rest of the family.

### Animal Communication

Communication in the animal world takes many forms. These include chemical, visual, and audible signals. Attacked insects secrete a pheromone that so excites their conspecifics that they either attack or escape from the predator. Flocks of birds behave similarly, except that sounds rather than chemicals trigger the response. Vocalization also evokes social responses in the porpoise, an aquatic mammal. Porpoises communicate by means of whistles and other sounds. When a porpoise is born, females may be attracted by the mother's whistles. They swim to the baby and nuzzle it. The mother does not attack other females at this time. Possibly, this experience with many adult porpoises in the earliest days of infancy helps form the tight social bond of porpoises.

Reciprocal stimulation affects the behavior of any animal, whether briefly or for a long time. Each organism is the source of environmental changes that affect other organisms. For example, after an amoeba ingests a food particle, it excretes a metabolic by-product that changes the chemical characteristics of the environment. If another amoeba is nearby, it tends to approach the first, though it will not do so if the chemical concentration is too intense. A sexually mature male cricket stridulates—rubs its legs together and produces a sound—whether or not another cricket stimulates it. However, it is more likely to stridulate when it hears another cricket.

When one animal can prompt an anticipated response in another, it displays a more advanced type of communication. For example, in an experiment a chimpanzee was trained to obtain a banana by pulling

*A baby monkey seems contented with its mother (top). A baby monkey was "reared" by two "mothers"— one of wire, the other of wire and cloth (bottom). The baby would cling to the soft mother when resting or scared, even if nursed by the wire mother.*

Regional Primate Research Center, University of Wisconsin

on a rope attached to a weight. Then the experimenter increased the weight so that one chimpanzee could not raise it but two could. If the second chimpanzee had already been trained to pull the rope, the first was able to stimulate it to do so by gesture, vocalization, and shoving. The two would then pull together and get the banana. In this case, the consequence of the second chimpanzee's behavior was in some way anticipated by the first.

The directed activity of one animal toward another for the solution of a problem or the attainment of a planned goal is evident only in advanced species. Furthermore, man is the only species capable of transmitting ideas through a complex system of speech and writing.

The study of the evolution of language has given rise to a science called semiotics. This science attempts to understand the similarities and the differences among the many forms of communication.

### Heredity and Behavior

The evolutionary principle of selective adaptation holds that a species survives when it is able to adapt to environmental changes and when it is able to transmit to its offspring the genetic information that makes such adaptations possible. But how do genetic processes contribute to the development of behavioral

*Notions about animal behavior can be tested in laboratory experiments. A test box can be designed to deliver food, electric shocks, or other kinds of reinforcement. The consequent behavior of the animal is measured electronically and recorded on graph paper. A white rat is in the test box shown here.*

Elio Elisofon, *Life* © Time Inc.

patterns? Which behavioral patterns are hereditary? Which must be learned by each new generation?

In an effort to answer such questions, behavioral scientists have designed a number of experiments. In one type of experiment, closely related species with distinctly different behavior patterns are hybridized. For example, two species of parakeets that practically share a natural habitat but do not interbreed were crossed in the laboratory. The parakeets of one species ordinarily tuck nesting material under their tail feathers. The others carry it in their beaks. The hybrid female offspring made inadequate tucking motions with the nesting material, and the twigs fell out from their feathers. However, all the hybrids carried the nesting material successfully in their beaks. Scientists felt that since all the hybrids performed some part of the tucking behavior, it was probably the earlier form of behavior in the evolution of these species.

The relationship between heredity and behavior has fueled an old but continuing controversy in the behavioral sciences. Some scientists believe that genetic processes underlie every kind of behavior, while others think that the environment can modify genetically influenced behavior. In one type of experiment testing these views, animals with different genetic backgrounds are reared in the same environment. In another type, animals with the same genetic backgrounds are raised in different environments.

Cross-fostering is used to rear species with different genetic backgrounds in the same environment—that is, the young of one species are raised by a female of another species. In one cross-fostering study, a female great tit reared a baby chaffinch with her own babies. Great tits and chaffinches are closely related birds that feed in different ways. The great tit holds food under its feet; the chaffinch does not. A chaffinch hatched by a great tit did not use its feet during feeding, while its nestmates did. Its feeding behavior remained typical for its species, although it had no opportunity to observe other chaffinches.

However, when a great tit was reared in isolation, though it too demonstrated species-typical behavior by holding its food down, it did so very clumsily. Only after repeated tries did its performance improve. This experiment showed that experience may be important even in genetically determined behavioral patterns.

Manipulation of the physical environment was used to study the subspecies of deer mice. One subspecies lives in the forest, is a climbing animal, and has a longer tail and larger ears than the other, a prairie subspecies that lives in grassy fields. The two subspecies were reared in the same laboratory and then released in a room containing artificial grass and wooden posts with flat tops. Although neither subspecies had experienced its species-typical environment, the forest deer mice organized their life space around the "trees," and the prairie deer mice settled under the "grass." However, when prairie deer mice were bred in a laboratory for more than a dozen generations, they no longer showed a preference for the field. The environment eventually so altered the

Frank and John Craighead

*The behavior of large animals in their natural environments can be studied by means of telemetric devices. This grizzly bear was tranquilized and fitted with a radio transmitter (top left). When the drug wore off, the bear was released (top right). Radio signals from the bear's transmitter permitted its subsequent movements to be followed and plotted on a map (bottom left).*

genetic processes of these experimental animals as to change their species-typical behavior.

Bird-song patterns are species-specific and have, therefore, been regarded as genetically determined. Studies of the development of species-typical song patterns have helped to clarify the relative roles of heredity and experience in the development of such patterns. For example, if a meadowlark is exposed to another bird's song while it is learning to sing it will learn the other bird's song; however, if the meadowlark is exposed to the songs of other meadowlarks along with those of another species, it will learn only its own species-typical song. The bird instinctively chooses its species-typical song when it is in a situation in which there is a choice.

The response patterns of birds are so varied that the contributions made by genetic processes and by the auditory and other experiences of a bird during singing are hard to separate. It may be that in the course of its development a bird produces certain sounds that are a function of its peculiar body makeup. These sounds may be the fundamental vocalization of the bird's species. Additional experience by the bird with hearing and producing its own song, as well as hearing those of other birds in a social setting, may yield the "dialect," or song pattern, associated with the species. However, genes do not carry this pattern as such. Rather, they carry the code for the biochemical processes that develop certain body systems that, aided by experience, will affect the animal's behavior in its typical environment. (*See also* Animal; Biology; Genetics; Psychology.)

**BIBLIOGRAPHY FOR ANIMAL BEHAVIOR**

**Black, Hallie.** Animal Cooperation: A Look at Sociobiology (Morrow, 1981).
**Caras, Roger.** The Private Lives of Animals (McGraw, 1987).
**Fraser, A.F.** Farm Animal Behaviour, 2nd ed. (Saunders, 1983).
**Freedman, Russell and Morriss, J.E.** The Brains of Animals and Man (Holiday, 1972).
**Lydecker, Beatrice.** What the Animals Tell Me (Harper, 1982).
**McFarland, David, ed.** The Oxford Companion to Animal Behaviour (Oxford, 1981).
**National Geographic Society.** How Animals Behave (National Geographic, 1984).
**Pringle, L.P.** Animals at Play (Harcourt, 1985).
**Pringle, L.P.** The Secret World of Animals (National Geographic, 1986).
**Waller, E.J.** Why Animals Behave the Way They Do (Scribner, 1981).

**ANIMAL COMMUNICATION.** The act of giving out and receiving information is called communication. Anyone who has owned a dog or cat knows that animals can both give information and receive it. A dog's bark may be either a sign of warning or welcome; the meow of a cat may indicate hunger or loneliness. A pet owner can tell animals something by means of spoken or visual signs that the animal has learned to recognize. Some animals, particularly chimpanzees, have been taught to communicate with people through such devices as sign language and symbols.

The three primary purposes of animal communication are to make identification, give location, and influence behavior. The most important communications occur between members of the same species. A worker honey bee may find a source of food. To tell other bees in the hive in what direction and how far the food is, the honeybee initiates a specific dance pattern (*see* Bee). Ants leave an odor trail that the other ants can follow from the nest to a food source.

The actions that animals take to give information are called signals or displays. There are five types of signals or displays: sound or vibration, visual, chemical, touching, and electric. Often, the most effective way for an animal to give information is by a sound display. Sound spreads rapidly, and other animals in the vicinity can readily tell from what direction it comes. The most common sounds are vocalizations made by vertebrates (animals with segmented spinal columns), such as birds, reptiles, and mammals. A small bird may vocalize a sound of fear in the presence of a predator such as a hawk or a cat, thus warning other small birds in the area to flee. There are also nonvocal sounds. Some insects rub one body part against another, an act called stridulation. Beavers and gorillas, though they can vocalize, also use vibration sounds. To warn others of danger, beavers slap their tails on the water surface and gorillas beat their chests.

Visual communication can be conducted through the use of such badges as a patch of bright color or a set of horns. These badges give some indication of the communicator's identity, such as its species, sex, and age. Some species set aside a display arena or build a structure that is itself intended as a form of communication, such as the elaborate bowerlike nest of the bowerbird. Other visible signs include special dung heaps left by rabbits and the scars left on tree trunks by bears, both of which are used to mark territory. Such visual signals as the fluttering of a bird or the dance of a honeybee have the important advantage of pinpointing where the display originates. A major disadvantage is that such signals can be easily blocked from sight by, say, vegetation.

Many mammals, fishes, and insects secrete chemicals called pheromones to communicate with others of their species or to issue warnings. Some of these chemicals are distasteful or injurious to other animals. Many animals, for example moths, release pheromones into the air as sexual attractants. Ants secrete them to lay food trails or to warn the ant colony of danger. The disadvantage of pheromones is the rapid fading

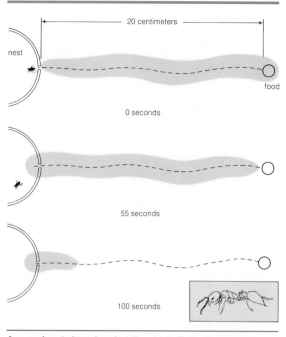

*An experiment shows how fast the odor trail of a fire ant worker disappears. The trail is made by the ant exuding a biological chemical called a pheromone.*

of the odor, making them an inadequate means of communication in situations that may change rapidly. Pheromone effectiveness is also considerably decreased in wind and rain.

Some species of animals, especially birds and mammals, use touching patterns to convey information. Birds and monkeys often engage in mutual grooming that seems to communicate acceptance. Wolves, dogs, and other canines have mock fights to establish and reestablish dominance and rank in a pack. A few species of fishes can emit electrical discharge patterns as part of a sensory system intended to gather information about surroundings and to fend off predators. Similarly, bats, dolphins, and porpoises have a sonar scanning system to enable them to perceive the environment without necessarily seeing it (*see* Bat; Dolphin and Porpoise).

Displays intended to convey or influence behavior are frequently more ambiguous or tentative in their nature than other kinds of signals. The snarling of a dog may indicate intention to attack or simply fear on the dog's part. A male spider, intending to mate with its partner, will strum on her web rather than face the danger of moving into the web too rapidly. Some animals, even of the same species, may signal the desire to escape or to attack.

**BIBLIOGRAPHY FOR ANIMAL COMMUNICATION**

**Goodenough, J.E.** Animal Communication (Carolina Biological, 1984).
**Lydecker, Beatrice.** What the Animals Tell Me (Harper, 1989).
**McDonnell, Janet.** Animal Communication (Child's World, 1989).

*A flock of geese prepares to land at the Tule Lake Refuge in California for feeding and resting on their way north. In the fall the geese fly south to central California.*

Robert C. Fields—Animals Animals

**ANIMAL MIGRATION.** Many people take trips periodically, often seasonally, in search of a fair climate, good food, and a change of scene in pleasant surroundings. Some animals are impelled to travel for similar reasons, and their trips, too, are often annual and linked to the seasons. These traveling animals are called migrants and their trips, migrations.

Most kinds of migrant animals make the round trip each year. Grazing animals, particularly the hoofed animals of Eastern Africa and the Arctic tundra, follow the seasonal changes in their supplies of green plants. Even fishes move about according to the season. Eels and many salmon make a round-trip only once in their life cycle. These animals return to the home waters where they were born to lay their eggs, and then they usually die.

Some animals make long journeys back and forth across land and ocean. Other migrations, however, take a vertical direction. During seasons of severe weather in mountainous regions, for instance, certain birds, insects, and mammals make regular trips down from the high altitudes where they breed into the foothills or plains below.

Many birds become gregarious during their travels, and even those that are fiercely individualistic at other times, such as birds of prey and those that hunt insects, often travel with a group of birds with similar habits. Large migrating flocks may be seen scattered along a broad airway hundreds of miles wide. Often the birds show remarkable grouping. The most characteristic migratory formation is the V shape of a flock of geese, ducks, pelicans, or cranes, the V pointed in the direction of the flight. Though birds usually follow specific, well-defined routes over long distances marked by rivers, valleys, coasts, forests, plains, deserts, and other geographic features they must cross, changes may be made because of wind and weather. The routes of some of the larger birds span oceans. Even small birds may cross as many as a thousand miles (1,600 kilometers) of water over the Gulf of Mexico, the Mediterranean Sea, and the North Sea.

In some cases the males migrate first. They fly ahead to select the nesting site in preparation for the arrival of the females. In other cases, males and females travel together and choose their mates along the way. Geese, which mate for life, travel as couples in large flocks. In the fall, female shorebirds often depart first, leaving the males to care for the young.

Birds fly faster during migration than during ordinary flying, but their speed depends upon the conditions through which they fly. Small songbirds may migrate at 20 miles (32 kilometers) per hour; starlings at 47 miles (76 kilometers) per hour; and ducks, swifts, and hawks at 59 miles (95 kilometers) per hour. Many birds are capable of speeds that would get them to their destination in a short time if they flew steadily. But most birds prefer leisurely journeys. After a flight of six or eight hours, they pause to feed and to rest for one or more days. The red-backed shrike covers about 600 miles (970 kilometers) in five days, but flies only two nights. It uses the other three nights for resting and the days for feeding.

Small land birds and shorebirds fly by night and feed by day. These nighttime migrants include water birds, cuckoos, flycatchers, thrushes, warblers, orioles, and buntings. Most of them fly until midnight or 1 A.M. and land soon after. Daytime travelers include most waterfowl, pelicans, storks, birds of prey, swifts, swallows, and finches.

Most birds fly at relatively low altitudes. Collisions between birds and airplanes seldom occur above 2,000 feet (610 meters), and many small birds fly at under 200 feet (61 meters). Skyscrapers and lighthouses

A COMPTON'S MAP

*The Pacific (far left) and the Central (left) flyways show the migration routes (arrows) followed by different kinds of birds from breeding grounds to winter homes. A flyway is a broader area (outlined in black) where many migration routes converge.*

are among the great dangers to migrants. Countless birds are killed by crashing into such structures. Many birds fly so low that their calls can be heard and identified. Some birds, however, fly much higher. Near Dehra Dun in northwestern India, geese have been seen at altitudes of about 30,000 feet (9,100 meters).

In true migration the birds always return to the same area. Most wading birds nest each summer in the tundra of the Arctic region and winter along the seacoasts from Western Europe to South Africa. Nomadic flights (flights without a fixed goal) may also occur, in response to irregular environmental conditions. After infrequent and unpredictable rains in the arid zones of Australia, for instance, ducks, parakeets, and seedeaters fly in suddenly, breed, and then move on.

Not all birds migrate. Migration is a response to ecological conditions, and birds that migrate do not differ much physically from those that do not migrate. For example, many kinds of birds are migratory in Northern and Eastern Europe, while comparable species in Western Europe are more sedentary. This is usually so in the case of goldfinches and tits.

Few terrestrial animals migrate, because walking is slow and requires a great deal of energy and time. Nevertheless, in regions where the climate and conditions fluctuate widely, vegetation is seasonal, and many hoofed animals must periodically seek fresh grazing lands. In the North American Arctic, for example, herds of caribou settle during the summer in the barrens. After the mating season, the animals begin to move irregularly southward and spend the winter wandering through the forests. Each herd seems to travel according to local conditions, without a definite pattern, apparently following good pasturage. Early spring finds the caribou again moving northward. Other North American mammals, such as elk, mule deer, and Dall sheep, migrate regularly in areas undisturbed by human habitation.

Large African mammals migrate with the wet and dry seasons. Many kinds of antelopes make seasonal

Anup & Manoj Shah—Animals Animals

*Wildebeests on the savannas near Mara, Kenya, cross a river during their migration. Herds of these animals move almost continuously, in search of fresh grasslands for grazing.*

movements over a large range. Zebras, wildebeests, and other plains animals travel more than 1,000 miles (1,600 kilometers) in their seasonal migrations in the Serengeti region of Tanzania. During the rains herds spread out. Then during the dry season they gather around watering holes. Elephants wander great distances in search of food and water. In Southern Africa hundreds of thousands of springbok once migrated according to the pattern of rainfall over their vast range. They moved in herds that were so dense that any animal encountered was either swept along with the herd or trampled. These huge migrations often resulted in enormous losses within the herd from starvation, drowning, or disease, which are natural methods of controlling overpopulation. Such movements, involving lesser numbers of animals, still occur in parts of Southern Africa.

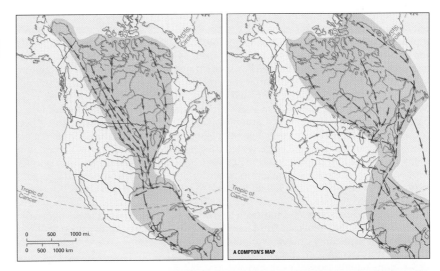

*The Mississippi flyway (right) is the most heavily traveled of the migratory routes for birds. In the north it spreads out across most of interior Canada. The Atlantic flyway (far right) has many west-east migration routes, in addition to the more normal north-south paths.*

A COMPTON'S MAP

Flying mammals, such as bats, show a greater tendency to migrate than do the terrestrial mammals. A few kinds of bats native to Europe and Asia travel to winter quarters in search of more habitable caves. These are short flights of 100 to 160 miles (160 to 260 kilometers) in response to seasonal conditions. Longer flights are made by other kinds of bats with stronger powers of flight. Red bats, large hoary bats, and silver-haired bats, which roost primarily in trees, make long flights from the northern part of their range in Canada to the southern United States. Individuals have been seen hundreds of miles out at sea. Apparently they are on their way to tropical islands; they are seen in Bermuda in the winter. Fruit bats, native to the tropical regions of the Old World, migrate regularly, following the seasons for fruit ripening.

Sea-dwelling mammals also migrate. Antarctic whales, including the humpback, a highly migratory kind, regularly winter in the tropics. Five distinct populations of Antarctic whales migrate separately, and individuals usually return to their zones of origin, though interchange may occur. Not all Antarctic whales travel; some stay at home. Whales south of the equator migrate northward during the winter (which begins in June in the Southern Hemisphere). They swim to areas rich in food, particularly the northwestern coast of Africa, the Gulf of Aden, and the Bay of Bengal. Northern whales have the same migratory habits. In the Atlantic Ocean, the humpback whales are found off Bermuda in the winter. As spring approaches, they leave for the waters around Greenland. The Pacific Ocean population of Northern whales winters in the Indian Ocean and in the seas bordering Indonesia. Dolphins and porpoises are migrants, but little is known about their travels. Harp seals range from the Arctic Ocean to the Pacific coast of southern California.

Many kinds of fishes travel regularly each year over great distances in migratory patterns that depend upon the currents, the climate, and topographical features. Eggs, larvae, and young fishes drift passively

Rick Frehsee

*Spiny lobsters migrate along the seabed every few weeks, in search of new places to feed. These animals forage for invertebrate prey at night, then return to their hiding places.*

with the current, but adults usually swim against the current toward their breeding grounds. For some kinds of fishes, these travels are part of the life cycle of the individual. The most famous examples are the salmon and the eels. Salmon from the Atlantic and Pacific oceans travel up the very same river in which they were born several years before to lay their eggs. Some may swim more than 1,850 miles (3,000 kilometers) to reach their freshwater spawning areas. Exhausted after their journey, some fish die after a single spawning. Others return to the sea and make the journey again, year after year.

Equally dramatic is the story of the eels of Western Europe and Eastern North America. Adult eels live in rivers that empty into the Atlantic Ocean. When it is time for them to breed, they swim thousands of miles to the deep of the Sargasso Sea, which lies south of Bermuda. There they lay their eggs, and soon after, they die. The young return to fresh water.

When conditions take a turn for the worse, most reptiles and amphibians are not capable of traveling far, so they lapse into a state of inactivity. This state makes it possible for them to stay in one place for an entire year. They may hibernate in the winter and estivate in the summer (*see* Hibernation). Their only migratory movements are made during the reproductive period. Frogs and toads migrate to the ponds, marshes, and lakes where they lived as tadpoles and lay their eggs there. Thousands travel to these sites from year to year. After the breeding season, they again spread out over their usual range. Sea turtles cover long distances to visit special sandy beaches where they lay their eggs, then disperse.

Certain insects, such as locusts, live but a single season. They move from the place where they hatched to lay their eggs and die elsewhere. These one-way trips are not migrations, but emigrations. Butterflies may travel as far as 80 miles (130 kilometers) in a day. The North American monarch butterfly has an extensive breeding range and has been known to migrate as far as 1,870 miles (3,010 kilometers). In the northern areas only one generation is born in a year, but in the southern range as many as five generations may be born. In summer the insects travel north to Hudson Bay. In autumn individuals of the last generation of the year migrate southward to Florida, Texas, and California. There they gather in sheltered sites, particularly on trees, clustering on trunks and large branches, and hibernate. In spring the survivors migrate back to the northern breeding areas. Some of these spring migrants are offspring of the overwintered insects.

Many little sea creatures drift with ocean currents. Plankton (tiny animal and plant organisms that float near the surface) also travel up and down in a daily rhythm. Numerous small or microscopic animals remain at great depths during the day and rise at dusk, concentrating in the upper layers of water during the night. Fishes and seabirds that feed on these organisms follow their rhythmic cycle.

Robber crabs and land crabs of tropical regions have adapted to life on dry land. But to lay their eggs, they journey to the sea so that their young can spend their early lives in salt water. After reproducing, they return inland, and their young follow at a later time.

### How Animals Navigate

Although they have no maps or compasses to guide them, many animals find their way over long distances. Animals use mountains, rivers, coasts, vegetation, and even climatic conditions such as prevailing winds to orient themselves. Even fishes use topographical clues to recognize their underwater range. Birds have been seen to hesitate and explore as they search for recognizable landmarks.

Birds can see ultraviolet light. They can also hear very low-frequency sound caused by wind blowing over ocean waves and mountains thousands of miles away. Many birds also possess a compass sense. They are able to fly in a particular, constant direction. Furthermore, they can tell in which direction to go in order to get home. They use the sun to get their bearings. Certain insects—bees, for example—do not even need to see the sun itself. They respond to the polarization of sunlight (which humans cannot detect) and orient themselves by the pattern it forms in a blue sky, even when the sun is behind the clouds.

Animals seem to have an internal clock and compensate for the movement of the sun. Many can orient themselves by gauging the angle of the sun above the horizon and the rhythm of daylight and darkness. (*See also* Biological Clock.)

Birds that fly at night use the patterns of the stars to find their way. It has been shown that birds can even orient themselves in a planetarium by the arrangement of night skies projected on the ceiling.

Fishes, too, use celestial bearings, though localization of the sun is much more difficult when its rays must pass through water. Sharks are known to be sensitive to electric fields, which probably aids them in navigating. Migrating salmon are also attracted by the particular odor of the waters of the stream where they passed their early lives. Still other researchers have concluded that genetics plays a significant role in the ability of offspring, such as that of salmon, to find their way back to their parents' mating grounds. The offspring seem to have inherited this homing ability from their parents.

Insects have an acute chemical sense and use it to navigate. The sense of smell is very important in the lives of many kinds of animals. But scented trails are probably helpful only for a limited time.

Many species of birds—such as pigeons, sparrows, and bobolinks—as well as some fish—such as yellow fin tuna—and honeybees, and even bacteria, have been known to migrate by orienting themselves to the Earth's magnetic fields. Researchers have found tiny crystals of a magnetic ore, magnetite, in the tissues of these animals that presumably help them navigate in this way. However, it is believed that birds in particular do not migrate by the polarity of the magnetic fields, but rather by detecting and then using the angle between the lines of the magnetic field and the horizontal plane of the Earth as guides.

### Explanations of Migration

Migration is part of the life cycle and depends upon the internal rhythm of the animal. Scientists have found that fats accumulate in the body tissues of certain migratory birds, and food consumption peaks at the start of the migratory season. These metabolic changes do not occur in the animals that do not migrate. The changes are triggered by hormones secreted by the pituitary gland, in the lower part of the brain. This gland also regulates the development of the sex glands, in which sex hormones are produced and reproductive cells are developed. Thus, the pituitary gland prepares the bird for both reproduction and migration. Before beginning its journey, the bird must be influenced by some ecological condition. Perhaps food becomes scarce, or the temperature drops suddenly.

What impels animals other than birds to migrate is not well understood. Mammals react to food shortages by moving to another region, and ecological conditions play an important part in the migrations of fishes and marine invertebrates as well.

**ANIMAL RIGHTS.** The Society for the Prevention of Cruelty to Animals was founded in England in 1824 to promote humane treatment of work animals, such as cattle and horses, and of household pets. Within a few decades similar organizations existed throughout Europe. An American society was founded in New York in 1866. Before long these organizations were protesting the use of animals in laboratory experiments and the use of vivisection for teaching. Until the mid-1970s the focus on humane treatment of animals continued these traditional emphases. After that period, animal rights activists enlarged their agendas considerably.

### Animal Experimentation

To increase medical, biological, or psychological knowledge, some scientists perform experiments using animals other than humans as their subjects. The effects of pollution, radiation, and many other stresses are determined by exposing animals to these conditions. It is estimated that 70 million animals are used in research every year in the United States alone.

Pharmaceutical and other industrial laboratories routinely use animals to screen drugs, cosmetics, and other substances before selling them for human use. Any new product or ingredient is usually tested on rats, mice, guinea pigs, dogs, or rabbits. The questionable substance may be applied to a small area of the animal's skin to determine primary irritation and sensitization (development of allergic responses after repeated applications). In the Draize test, developed in the 1940s, a substance is dropped into rabbits' eyes to determine eye damage and rate of recovery. Rabbits are used because their eyes produce no tears; thus blinking will not wash away an irritant. This test has been used by cosmetics firms to test the eye irritability of shampoos and other products.

A chemical may be fed to animals to determine toxicity, both acute (after one dose) and chronic (after repeated small doses over a period of time). One standard measurement for drugs and other chemicals is the Lethal Dose 50 ($LD_{50}$), the dose lethal to 50 percent of the test animals.

University, hospital, and public-health laboratories use animals to study both normal and disease processes. Cancer research, for example, requires a continuous supply of large numbers of animals, particularly mice. Vitamin requirements are usually determined by experiments using rats, chicks, dogs, and guinea pigs in which the increase in the animals' body weight is related to the amounts of vitamins in their diets.

Some schools require students to dissect cats, dogs, frogs, fetal pigs, and other animals. Such exercises are much more helpful than textbook illustrations in learning about body systems, but there are now computer programs that provide excellent simulation of these dissections for general classroom use.

The effects of various external influences on health are determined by studying animals that have been completely isolated to avoid contamination from

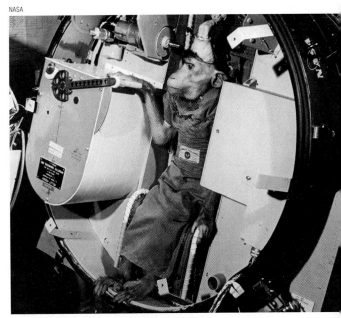

*A pig-tailed macacque in a test capsule reaches for a lever that triggers a food dispenser in an experiment.*

bacteria. Such studies may be continued over several generations of animals. The so-called germ-free animals are then compared with conventional animals.

The short life span of many animals as compared to humans is an advantage to experimenters since it allows them to observe several generations. Other requirements for a laboratory animal are that it be small, tame, hardy, and prolific. Rats are particularly well suited to laboratory study because they can breed at three to four months of age and produce up to seven litters in a year.

The greatest number of laboratory animals are specifically bred for laboratory use. In 1988 a strain of genetically engineered mice that was unusually susceptible to cancer was patented in the United States. Some animals are collected from the wild, particularly those that breed with difficulty in captivity, such as monkeys. In many countries, including the United States, stray dogs and cats are impounded and, if unclaimed, offered to laboratories.

Many animals resemble humans in elements of structure, physiology, and behavior, but because they also differ in some respects some scientists consider the results of animal studies of limited value and not necessarily applicable to humans. In the 1980s, however, researchers began to alter the systems of some animals in order to match them more closely to human systems. For example, in order to study AIDS (acquired immunodeficiency syndrome), researchers have transplanted parts of human immune systems into mice.

### Opposition to Experimentation

Publicity about commercial laboratory testing and pressure brought to bear by the noted animal rights activist Henry Spira led to the founding of the Center for Alternatives to Animal Testing in 1981 at Johns Hopkins University. The campaign against commercial testing was partially successful. In June 1989 two of the largest cosmetics firms in the United States, Avon and Revlon, announced that they would stop using animals in their laboratory testing. Avon had already dispensed with the Draize test.

Whether this singular success in commercial testing would lead to similar results in experimentation for medical purposes was far from certain. The great advances made in scientific and medical knowledge through experimentation made it unlikely that the scientific community would abandon the use of animals in the near future. Nevertheless, a significant body of legislation has been passed throughout the world to regulate, but not abolish, the use of laboratory animals. In 1989, for example, legislators of the European Communities recommended that the $LD_{50}$ test be dropped in favor of a more humane alternative known as the fixed-dose procedure.

The first organization founded to protest animal experimentation was the Society for the Protection of Animals Liable to Vivisection, started in England in 1875. (In 1897 its name was changed to the National Antivivisection Society.) By 1876 England's Parliament had passed the first national antivivisection law, the Cruelty to Animals Act. The law covered only vertebrate animals (mammals, birds, reptiles, fish, and amphibians), with more restrictive provisions on the use of donkeys, horses, mules, dogs, and cats. The law required all experimenters to have permits, and it established guidelines for the kinds of experiments and the way they were performed.

The American Antivivisection Society, founded in 1883, was the first such organization in the United States. The results it obtained, however, were far less impressive than those in England. The scientific community has strongly resisted most attempts to regulate the use of animals. Although bills were frequently introduced in Congress beginning in the 1890s, none passed. A few states abolished experimentation in public schools. Sending stray dogs and cats to laboratories was prohibited in some cities.

Not until 1966 was a national Animal Welfare Act passed by Congress. Most of its provisions dealt with animals in interstate transportation, because states are allowed to regulate such matters within their own borders. One of the act's purposes was "to insure that animals intended for use in research facilities or for exhibition purposes or for use as pets are provided humane care and treatment." This act and its subsequent amendments did not attempt to halt or curtail experimentation. A 1985 amendment, however, did call for seeking alternative methods of testing and asked that needless duplication of experiments cease.

By the second half of the 20th century most nations had animal welfare societies and anticruelty laws. In addition to national organizations there were several international societies: the World Federation for the Protection of Animals, the International Society for the Protection of Animals, and the International Fund for Animal Welfare.

## Animal Rights After 1975

Since 1975 advocates of humane treatment of animals have broadened their goals to oppose the use of animals for fur, leather, wool, and food. They have mounted protests against all forms of hunting and the trapping of animals in the wild. And they have joined environmentalists in urging protection of natural habitats from commercial or residential development. The occasion for these added emphases was the publication in 1975 of 'Animal Liberation: A New Ethics for Our Treatment of Animals' by Peter Singer, formerly a professor of philosophy at Oxford University in England. This book gave a new impetus to the animal rights movement.

The post-1975 animal rights activists are far more vocal than their predecessors, and the organizations to which they belong are generally more radical. Among the newer organizations are: People for the Ethical Treatment of Animals (PETA), the International Society for Animal Rights, Trans-Species Unlimited, the Fund for Animals, the Committee to Abolish Sport Hunting, the Scientists' Center for Animal Welfare, the Simian Society of America, United Action for Animals, Animal Rights International, and the Animal Liberation Front.

The tactics of the activists are designed to catch the attention of the public. Since the mid-1980s there have been frequent news reports about animal rights organizations picketing stores that sell furs, harassing hunters in the wild, or breaking into laboratories to free animals. Some of the more extreme organizations advocate the use of assault, armed terrorism, and death threats to make their point.

Aside from making isolated attacks on people who wear fur coats or trying to prevent hunters from killing animals, most of the organizations have directed their tactics at institutions. The results of the protests and other tactics have been mixed. Companies are reducing reliance on animal testing. Medical research has been somewhat curtailed by legal restrictions and the reluctance of younger workers to use animals in research. New tests have been developed to replace the use of animals. Some well-known designers have stopped using fur.

While the general public tends to agree that animals should be treated humanely, most people are unlikely to give up eating meat or wearing goods made from leather and wool. Giving up genuine fur has become less of a problem, since fibers used to make fake fur—such as the Japanese invention Kanecaron—can look almost identical to real fur.

Some of the strongest opposition to the animal rights movement has come from hunters and their organizations, such as the National Rifle Association. There were in 1991 about 16 million hunters in the United States, where about 165 million animals are killed annually. But animal rights activists have succeeded in marshaling public opinion to press for state restrictions on hunting in several parts of the nation.

Photos, Animals Animals, (left) Holt Studios, (right) E.R. Degginger

*A Filipino farmer (left) harrows a rice paddy behind a water buffalo. The water buffalo, a member of the ox family, was domesticated in Asia thousands of years ago. The camel (right) in Australia is a descendant of the dromedaries imported in the mid-19th century to be beasts of burden. Today there are thousands of wild camels living in the central Australian desert.*

**ANIMALS, DOMESTICATED.** The human race's progress on Earth has been due in part to the animals that people have been able to utilize throughout history. Such domesticated animals carry people and their burdens. They pull machinery and help cultivate fields. They provide food and clothing. As pets they may amuse or console their owners.

Domesticated animals are those that have been bred in captivity for many generations. While a single animal may be tamed, only a species of animals can be considered domesticated. In the course of time, by selective breeding, certain animals have changed greatly in appearance and behavior from their wild ancestors. There is a vast difference between the scrawny red jungle fowl of southern Asia and its descendant, the heavy-breasted, egg-laying farm chicken.

Not all domestic animals are tame at all times. An angry bull, a mother goose, or a mother sow with young pigs can be vicious. Some creatures confined in zoos breed in captivity. The lion is an example. These animals are not domesticated, however, for they remain wild and dangerous.

### How Animals Became Domesticated

Cattle, sheep, pigs, goats, and horses—the most important and widespread of the domestic animals—are all hoofed grass eaters and can be kept in herds. All of them were first mastered by the early peoples of southwestern Asia. It has been suggested that the grassy plains of that region began slowly eroding some 10,000 years ago. Humans were forced to share smaller and smaller oases of fertile land with wild animals. People gradually learned how to control the animals. Some animals were bred in captivity, and from them the domestic strains developed.

Another theory of how domestication came about points to the widespread human practice of making pets of captured young and crippled animals. Certain kinds of creatures became attached to their human masters. They followed the camps, and slowly humans built up herds. Several factors, rather than any one simple cause, must have led to domestication.

### When Domestication First Came About

There seems to be little doubt that the dog was the first animal domesticated by humans. Its bones are common in campsites of the late Neolithic that date back more than 10,000 years. At least five different kinds of dogs similar to the household pets of today have been identified from these remains. The beginnings of their domestication must therefore date many thousands of years earlier than that.

Possible wild ancestors of the domesticated dog are found on almost every continent. They include wolves and coyotes in North America, Europe, and Asia; jackals in Africa; and dingoes in Australia. One theory suggests that the wild dog "adopted" Paleolithic hunters of 100,000 years ago by scavenging on the edges of their camps for scraps of food. The hunters probably discovered that a litter of pups raised in camp became attached to their human companions and yet retained their hunting instincts. The pups joined in the hunt and shared in the feast. In some such way the hunting dog became the human race's first helper. (*See also* Dog; Human Origins.)

Beginning in about 8000 BC and continuing over a period of about 5,000 years, all the other animals important to humans today were domesticated. Remains of cattle, sheep, and pigs have been found among Mesopotamian ruins dating from some time before 3000 BC. At about the same time in the Indus River valley in India, people were raising buffalo, sheep, fowl, elephants, goats, and cattle. El Faiyûm, Egypt, an agricultural settlement of Neolithic people dating from about 3000 BC, kept cattle, pigs, and sheep or goats.

As suddenly as it began, the extent of human control over wild animals ceased to grow. Not one new species has been domesticated in the past 4,000 years, unless laboratory animals such as mice, rats, and monkeys can be considered domesticated.

Of the millions of species in the world, only a very few have been domesticated. The early peoples of Central and Southwestern Asia were the most successful in domesticating animals. They domesticated the cattle, sheep, pigs, goats, camels, horses, and donkeys that people use today. Indochina was the native habitat of the water buffalo, zebu, ox, chicken, and Asian elephant. The yak, domesticated in Tibet, still rarely leaves its high mountain home. Northern Europeans first domesticated the reindeer. Africa, with the greatest variety of animals in the world, domesticated only the cat, the ass, and the guinea fowl. South America has domesticated the llama, the alpaca, and the guinea pig. The highly civilized Inca of pre-Columbian Peru were the first to domesticate the llama and the alpaca. Only the turkey was domesticated in North and Central America.

### The Most Important Domesticated Animals

Cattle are among the most useful of all domestic animals. It has been said that modern civilization began when people first began milking cows and using oxen to plow their fields. Cattle have wild relatives in many parts of the world. They must have been domesticated in Asia first, however, for their bones have been found in settlements there earlier than anywhere else. Shorthorn cattle are supposed to have been introduced into Europe from Central Asia when the long-horned urus (now extinct) was still running wild. The urus and the Celtic ox were domesticated later than the Asian breeds of cattle.

Sheep have been so changed by breeding that their wild ancestors are hard to identify. Like the wild sheep, the domestic sheep of Egypt in 3000 BC had coats of coarse hair. The dense wool was gradually developed by selective breeding.

Pigs were derived from the wild boar, which can still be found in Europe, Asia, and Africa. In Egypt their flesh was not eaten. They were instead kept as scavengers. They loosened the soil by their rooting and so prepared it for planting. They were also used to trample down the seeds after sowing and to thresh the grain at harvesttime.

According to archaeological records, chickens were first domesticated in the cities of the Indus Valley in about 3000 BC. The donkey of Mediterranean lands is thought to be a descendant of the wild ass of Western Asia.

The horse was the last important animal to be domesticated. The only species of wild horse still living are Przhevalski's horse, very small numbers of which survive in the wild in western Mongolia, and the Riwoche horse, a few of which survive in northeastern Tibet. The tarpan, a wild horse of Europe and Northern Asia, became extinct in the mid-1800s. These two species were probably the ancestors of the modern horse breeds.

*In a mechanized age, domesticated animals still help people with their work. Cowboys on a ranch ride quarter horses, which are easy to maneuver and can run fast for short distances. These horses are also used for racing.*

A Semitic people who conquered the Mesopotamian region in about 2300 BC were mounted on horses. The ability of these people to domesticate horses may explain their success in war. The first sight of a person riding a horse must have struck terror into the hearts of people unaccustomed to such a sight. In addition, the myth of the centaur, half horse and half man, probably had its origin in just such an experience.

In North America before the arrival of the Europeans, the only domesticated animal among the Native Americans was the dog. After European settlers brought domesticated horses to the New World, the horse effected great changes for the peoples of the Plains (*see* Indians, American, or Native Americans).

### Other Attempts to Domesticate Animals

Humans have tried to domesticate many animals, but, as has been noted, they succeeded with very few. Dozens of kinds have been tamed and kept as pets or raised in menageries and zoos, but few have actually been domesticated. Many people keep unusual or exotic animals as pets, including boa constrictors, pythons, ocelots, tarantulas, and tropical birds. In the early 1990s the Vietnamese potbellied pig became a popular, though expensive, pet. This pig, in contrast to wild animals, can be readily domesticated. In some places, however, it is illegal to keep what are considered farm animals or animals that can be considered dangerous to the public.

Unsuccessful attempts at domestication have been made with the bison, related to cattle; with the zebra, related to the horse; and with the peccary, a cousin of the pig. The Egyptians kept herds of antelopes and gazelles in pastures. Why a few animals yielded to domestication while the majority refused to be mastered remains a mystery. (*See also* Ass; Camel; Cat; Cattle; Dog; Duck, Goose, and Swan; Horse; Pig; Poultry; and articles on other animals mentioned.)

The manticore, as depicted in a Latin bestiary (a collection of animal-based allegories), was a legendary creature with a human head, the body of a lion, and the tail of a dragon or scorpion. Thus it had qualities of both the griffin and the centaur.

The Granger Collection, New York

**ANIMALS, LEGENDARY.** People have always been interested in animals. Very early in the history of civilization hunters tracked down and domesticated the animals of their own surroundings. These remote peoples also listened eagerly to travelers from far places who told of strange beasts they had seen and even stranger ones they had only heard about.

Because early writers lacked scientific knowledge, they often confused fact with hearsay. Several books of travel and natural history that were dated from pre-Christian times and the Middle Ages were widely read, and their reports of fantastic animals were accepted. New versions, even more bizarre, were handed down. In the 1st century AD the Latin writer Pliny the Elder published a 37-volume 'Natural History', which was a massive compilation of 2,000 earlier works.

The most famous travel book of the Middle Ages was 'The Voyage and Travels of Sir John Mandeville, Knight', written in the mid-14th century. The mysterious writer's fanciful descriptions of monsters probably were derived from the writings of other noted authors.

In 1544 Sebastian Münster wrote the popular 'Cosmographia Universalis', which had vivid descriptions of dragons and basilisks. Even the great Swiss naturalist Conrad Gesner, in 'Historia Animalium' (1551–87), described the unicorn and winged dragons.

### Dragons, Centaurs, and Griffins

Of all the monsters in myth and folklore, the dragon is the most familiar and the most feared. Winged dragons with flame and smoke pouring from their nostrils dominate the legends of many countries. The various species whose parts were combined into the dragon's hybrid form differed from one land to another. (*See also* Dragon.)

The centaurs of Greek mythology were part human and part horse—wild creatures with a great fondness for wine and a reputation for carrying off helpless maidens. They may have originated in stories about the wild horsemen of prehistoric Asia. Never having seen men ride upon the backs of animals, people were filled with awe and terror of these mounted invaders.

The griffin had the head and wings of an eagle, the body of a lion, and the tail of a serpent or a lion. In legends of the Far East, India, and ancient Scythia, griffins were the guardians of mines and treasures. In Greek mythology they guarded treasures of gold and drew the chariot of the sun.

### Basilisk, Mermaids, Sea Serpents

The basilisk, or cockatrice, was a serpent so horrible that it killed with a glance. Pliny the Elder described it simply as a snake with a small golden crown. By

*A 12th-century Latin bestiary's version of the griffin showed it with the head and wings of an eagle, a body the size and shape of a lion, and a forked serpentlike tail.*

*The Lady and the Unicorn is one of the best-known medieval tapestries. Also called 'La Vue', it is from the late 15th century and is displayed at the Cluny Museum in Paris.*

the Middle Ages it had the head of a cock or sometimes a human head. It was born of a spherical egg, laid during the days of Sirius, the Dog Star, by a 7-year-old cock. The egg was then hatched by a serpent or toad. The sight of a basilisk was so dreadful that if the creature saw its own reflection in a mirror it supposedly died of fright. The only way to kill it, then, was to hold a mirror before it and avoid looking at it directly. The basilisk appears frequently in literature.

Mermaids lived in the sea. They had the body of a woman to the waist and the body and tail of a fish from the waist down. Irish legend says that mermaids were pagan women banished from Earth by St. Patrick. Sea serpents are still reported in the newspapers. Gesner's 'Historia Animalium' has a picture of a sea snake about 300 feet (90 meters) long wrapping its coils around a sailing vessel. The kraken of Scandinavian myth and the modern Loch Ness monster of Scotland have many similarities.

### The Vegetable Lamb

The vegetable lamb of Tartary, or Barometz, is a union of the plant and animal kingdoms. A picture of it appears in the Mandeville book, and Sir Thomas Browne described it in his 'Pseudodoxia Epidemica' (1646). Medieval travelers believed it came from a gourdlike fruit that grew on a tree.

It was believed that when the fruit ripened, it contained a little lamb. Garments could be woven from its fleece. Some accounts describe it as a plant whose shape resembles that of a lamb bearing a golden fleece. This as well as other accounts could be derived from fanciful descriptions of the cotton plant.

### The Unicorn

One of the most appealing legendary animals is the unicorn. It is a white horse, with the legs of an antelope, and a spirally grooved horn projecting forward from the center of its forehead. The horn is white at the base, black in the middle, and red at the tip.

The earliest reference to the unicorn is found in the writings of Ctesias. He was a Greek historian, at one time physician to the Persian king Artaxerxes II. Ctesias returned from Persia in about the year 400 BC and wrote a book on the marvels of the Far East. He told of a certain wild ass in India with a white body and a horn on the forehead. The dust filed from this horn, he said, was a protection against deadly drugs. His description was probably a mixture of reports of the Indian rhinoceros, an antelope of some sort, and the tales of travelers.

In early versions of the Old Testament, the Hebrew word *rĕ'ēm,* now translated as "wild ox," was translated "monocros," meaning "one horn." This became "unicorn" in English. By the Middle Ages this white animal had become a symbol of love and purity. It could be subdued only by a gentle maiden. The story of 'The Lady and the Unicorn' was a theme in the finest of medieval tapestries. In church art the unicorn is associated with the lamb and the dove. It also appears in heraldry.

The connection between the unicorn and the rhinoceros may be traced through the reputation of the powdered horn as a potent drug. Drinking beakers made of rhinoceros horn, common in medieval times, were decorated with the three colors described by Ctesias. As late as the 18th century, rhinoceros horn was used to detect poison in the food of royalty. In Arabian and other Eastern countries, the horn is still believed to have medicinal powers. (*See also* Pegasus; Sphinx.)

## Thunderbird, Phoenix, Roc

Early humans were very interested in birds and attributed magic and religious powers to them. The connection between birds and death that humans have imagined since prehistoric times still persists strongly in some modern folklore. There are also early hints of humans forming an association between birds and human reproduction. Somewhat later birds were regarded as weather changers and forecasters. Birds symbolized the mysterious powers that pervaded the wilderness in which humans hungered, hunted, and dreamed. Thus it is not surprising that many mythological creatures, such as thunderbird, phoenix, and roc, take the form of birds.

In the legends of native North Americans, the thunderbird is a powerful spirit in the form of a bird. Through the work of this bird, it is said, the Earth is watered and vegetation grows. Lightning is believed to flash from its beak, and the beating of its wings is thought to result in the rolling of thunder. It is often portrayed with an extra head on its abdomen. The majestic thunderbird is often accompanied by lesser bird spirits, frequently in the form of eagles or falcons. Evidence of similar figures has been found throughout Africa, Asia, and Europe.

In ancient Egypt and in classical antiquity, the phoenix was a fabulous bird associated with the worship of the sun. The phoenix was said to be as large as an eagle, with brilliant scarlet and gold plumage and a melodious cry. Only one phoenix existed at any one time, and it was very long-lived—no ancient writer gave it a life span of less than 500 years. As its death approached, the phoenix fashioned a nest of aromatic boughs and spices, set it on fire, and was consumed in the flames. From the pyre miraculously sprang a new phoenix, which, after embalming its predecessor's ashes in an egg of myrrh, flew with the ashes to the City of the Sun, in Egypt, where it deposited them on the altar in the temple of the Egyptian god of the sun. The phoenix was understandably thus associated with immortality and the allegory of resurrection and life after death. The phoenix was compared to undying Rome, and it appears on the coinage of the late Roman Empire as a symbol of the Eternal City.

In Arabic legends, the roc, or rukh, was a gigantic bird with two horns on its head and four humps on its back and was said to be able to carry off elephants and other large beasts for food. It is mentioned in the famous collection of Arabic tales, 'The Thousand and One Nights', and by the Venetian explorer Marco Polo, who referred to it in describing Madagascar and other islands off the coast of Eastern Africa. According to Marco Polo, Kublai Khan inquired in those parts about the roc and was brought what was claimed to be a roc's feather, which may really have been a palm frond. Sinbad the Sailor also told of seeing its egg, which was "50 paces in circumference." Thought of as a mortal enemy of serpents, the roc is associated with strength, purity, and life. (*See also* Folklore; Mythology; Pegasus; Sphinx.)

---

### *Some Famous Legendary Animals*

*Some legendary animals are not included below because they are covered in the main text of this article or in other articles in Compton's Encyclopedia (see Fact-Index).*

**Anubis.** Egyptian deity with the head of a jackal or dog and the body of a human. It leads souls of the dead to the underworld and helped Osiris at his final judgment. Anubis' particular concern is with the funeral cult and the care of the dead, and, Anubis is often considered the inventor of embalming.

**Apocalyptic beast.** A creature mentioned in the Book of Revelation in the Bible. It has two horns, speaks like a dragon, and bears the mystical number 666.

**Cerberus.** The three-headed watchdog of Greco-Roman mythology who guards the gates of Hades, the underworld. Cerberus was transported by Hercules into the world of the living.

**Harpy.** Greco-Roman mythological creature with the body of a bird and the head of a woman, often portrayed as very ugly and loathsome. It is sometimes associated with the wind, ghosts, and the underworld. Mentioned in the legend of Jason and the Argonauts and by the poets Virgil in the 'Aeneid' and Homer in the 'Odyssey.'

**Hydra.** In Greek legend, a gigantic monster with several heads (usually nine, though the number varies), the center one of which is immortal. It is said to haunt the marshes of Lerna near Argos. The destruction of the hydra was one of the 12 labors of Hercules. When one of the hydra's heads was cut off two grew in its place.

**Ki-rin.** The Japanese equivalent of the Pegasus. It lives in paradise and visits the Earth only at the birth of a wise philosopher.

**Kraken.** In Norwegian sea folklore, an enormous creature in the form of part octopus and part crab.

**Leviathan.** Biblical water monster, variously thought of as a whale or a gigantic crocodile. According to legend, it returns every year to be killed and thus represents the seasonal changes.

**Minotaur.** In Greek mythology, a bull-headed monster with the body of a man. It is known for eating human flesh. King Minos imprisoned the minotaur in his labyrinth in Crete.

**Nidhoggr.** Nordic serpent-monster representing the volcanic powers of the Earth. Since Nidhoggr also eats corpses, it symbolizes the decay of nature.

**Ryu.** A Japanese dragon able to live in the air, in water, and on land. It was considered one of the four sacred creatures of the Orient. Ryu symbolizes rain and storms.

**Satyr.** A wild creature of Greek legend whose bottom half is that of a beast, usually including a goat's tail, flanks, and hooves, and whose top half is that of a man. Satyrs are closely associated with the god Dionysus and known for their debauchery. The Italian version of the satyr is the faun. The female counterpart of the satyr is the nymph.

**Simurgh.** In Persian legend, a giant birdlike monster so old that it has seen the world destroyed three times over, and thus possesses the knowledge of all the ages.

**Siren.** In Greek legend, a creature half bird and half woman who lures sailors to their destruction by the sweetness of her song. Sirens are mentioned by Homer in the 'Odyssey' and in the legend of Jason and the Argonauts.

**Tatzlwurm.** A winged, fire-breathing dragon monster of Germanic legend.

**Wivern.** A winged, two-legged dragon with a barbed tail. The wivern often appears on heraldic shields and symbolizes guardianship.

**Yali.** In Indian legend, a creature with a lion's body and the trunk and tusks of an elephant.

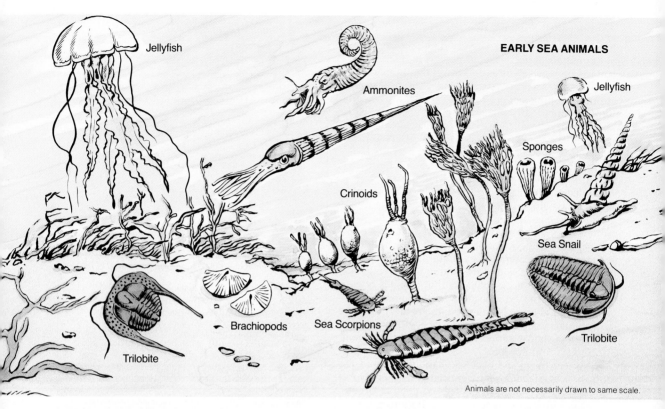

**EARLY SEA ANIMALS**

Jellyfish

Ammonites

Jellyfish

Sponges

Crinoids

Sea Snail

Brachiopods

Sea Scorpions

Trilobite

Trilobite

Animals are not necessarily drawn to same scale.

**ANIMALS, PREHISTORIC.** Because the era known as prehistoric covers the hundreds of millions of years before the first hominids, or humanlike creatures, existed, most prehistoric animals have never been seen by humans. Prehistoric animals evolved in two ways. Early, very simple kinds of animals gradually changed into new and more complex kinds; and the process of adaptation enabled some animals to survive in all parts of the Earth (*see* Adaptation).

While some prehistoric animals died out completely, becoming extinct, the descendants of others are still living on Earth. The best-known extinct animals are dinosaurs, huge animals that disappeared about 65 million years ago. Sponges, corals, starfish, snails, and clams—all familiar creatures today—can be traced back 500 million years or more. Spiders originated almost 400 million years ago. Insects and sharks also have long histories.

Dinosaurs dominated the Earth for more than 150 million years and then vanished. Scientists have many theories to explain this fact. Some say that when flowering plants appeared on Earth about 200 million years ago, they increased the amount of oxygen in the atmosphere, causing dinosaur breathing rates and heartbeats to increase to the extent that the creatures burned themselves out. Other theorists suggest that the dinosaurs were poisoned by plants they ate. Still others say that the huge animals began to die off after the Earth's continents, which had originally been a single landmass, broke apart, causing tremendous environmental changes, submerging huge areas, and

radically changing the climate. A more recent theory states that a giant meteor struck the Earth, exploded, and filled the atmosphere with debris for many years. This debris darkened the skies and blocked out the sunlight. The resulting lower temperatures on Earth caused the extinction of many animals.

Scientists have learned a great deal about prehistoric life by studying animal skeletons or shells. At times they have found bones and pieced them together. Often the remains were petrified (turned to a stony hardness) and discovered as fossils (*see* Fossils).

## EARLY SEA LIFE

The earliest fossils date from about 570 million years ago. In those days, shallow seas covered many places that have since become dry land. Jellyfish drifted about in the water; vase-shaped sponges grew on the bottom of the sea; small shellfish and worms crawled about under seaweed. Brachiopods—a large family of shell-covered animals with a kind of arm used to stir up the sandy bottom and to cause food to float near them—were common in ancient seas. Trilobites 6 to 7 inches (15 to 18 centimeters) long were the largest animals in those early seas. Some were oval and smooth while others had goggle eyes and spiny shells made up of several sections. These creatures had feathery legs and used jointed feelers to find food.

Echinoderms, or echinoids, named for the small plates that make up their outer coverings, are one of the most numerous animal groups to have lived in ancient seas. Starfish, sea urchins, and sea cucumbers survive today. The closely related crinoids, also a living species, are attached to the seafloor by stalks and resemble flowers somewhat; hence they are often called sea lilies. Two extinct kinds of echinoderms are cystoids, which had complex breathing organs, and blastoids, which resembled sea plants.

Also common were ammonites, some of which had ridged shells in the form of flat spirals. Others had cone-shaped hard coverings and bodies with long feelers that made them look like octopuses coming out of cones. Nautiloids, some species of which survive today as the nautilus of the South Pacific, were members of the ammonite family.

Fishes appeared about 450 million years ago, evolving perhaps from ancient soft-bodied organisms. Moving slowly along the sea bottom, they ate by straining food from water drawn through their gills. They did not look much like modern fishes: they had no jaws (and thus no mouth to open and close), no fins, and probably no head in the usual sense. Scientists imagine that their bodies were hose-shaped with simple digestive organs and a nerve cord running from front to back supported by a notochord, a kind of stiff supporting material. The notochord was extremely important because much later it was to evolve into a spine.

The first fish that resembled the present-day fishes was the ostracoderm, which lived about 400 million years ago. The creature had no jaws, a bony skull, and a thick shell-like armor on its back. A spinal cord ran from neck to tail, and it had two stumpy fins.

The numbers and species of fishes increased rapidly from the beginning of the Devonian period, some 395 million years ago. Fishes evolved jaws, which freed them to hunt food throughout the sea, and pairs of fins, which stabilized their bodies and made them faster swimmers. With mobility they lost their heavy back armor, growing scales as a replacement. Sharks appeared in Devonian times, with some species growing up to 50 feet (15 meters) long.

The lungfish is thought to represent a transitional stage between the fish (which lives entirely in the water) and the amphibian (which can survive on land or in water). Lungfish have real lungs, which means that they can rise to the water surface to breathe. They have pairs of fins at the fronts and backs of their bodies that they use like legs to crawl across the mud of river and lake bottoms. Although they live their entire lives in water, lungfish can survive long dry spells by slowing down their body functions (estivating) and by burrowing into the mud.

## THE FIRST LAND ANIMALS

At the beginning of the Devonian period, the Earth's surface changed as the continents drifted into new arrangements. Deep seas replaced shallow ones, and there was more dry land. Early forms of plants were algae, lichens, and probably mosses.

By that time, the structure and habitats of fishes were changing. Some forms, 2 to 3 feet (0.6 to 0.9 meter) long, also lived in pools on land. Called

crossopterygians, or lobe-fins, they had bony heads, sharp teeth, and simple lungs as well as gills. If the pools were fouled by decaying vegetation, these fish raised their heads to breathe air. If the pools dried up, the fish used their thick, short fins to crawl over strips of land that still contained small pools of water.

Amphibians, the descendants of certain crawling fishes, developed legs from fins and could move more easily. The first amphibians probably looked like salamanders, 3 to 4 feet (0.9 to 1.2 meters) in length, with sharp teeth and wide heads (see Amphibian).

During the next 50 million years, plants and animals changed greatly. About 280 million years ago, at the end of the Coal Age (Carboniferous, or Pennsylvanian, period), trees as much as 100 feet (30 meters) in height and 6 feet (1.8 meters) in diameter grew in swampy forests. Cockroaches grew 4 inches (10 centimeters) long, and dragonflies were enormous.

Labyrinthodonts also lived during the Coal Age. They were amphibians that may well have been the ancestors of all land vertebrates (animals with spines), including human beings. Some had body structures like those of reptiles. Many labyrinthodonts were as large as alligators, while some were as small as salamanders.

Reptiles represented the next step in animal development. On the evolutionary scale, they stand between the amphibians and the birds and mammals. Reptiles are vertebrates that breathe air and are covered with scales rather than hair or feathers. Cotylosaurs, extinct today, were probably the first reptiles, dating perhaps from about 300 million years ago. They were about $3\frac{1}{3}$ feet (1 meter) long with stumpy legs, short necks, and long tails.

Reptiles made the final break with life in the water. They lived entirely on land and thus could move to areas that lay far from seas and rivers. Reptiles also developed hard-shelled eggs that they could lay almost anywhere on the ground.

Insects began to evolve about 325 million years ago (see Insect). Fossils indicate that they developed from land-dwelling arthropods—invertebrate (spineless) creatures with shells and jointed legs. The earliest insects crawled but did not fly. Winged insects appeared about 300 million years ago.

### Dinosaurs and Other Reptiles

When prehistoric reptiles are mentioned, many people think of huge dinosaurs. But the first dinosaurs—called thecodonts—were no larger than turkeys. Living from about 230 million to 190 million years ago, thecodonts walked or ran upon their hind legs and used their long tails to balance their bodies. As millions of years went by, the descendants of these first dinosaurs grew larger and larger. Some of these dinosaurs began to walk on four legs while others remained on two; dinosaurs became some of the biggest animals that ever lived on land. (See also Dinosaur.)

The giant dinosaurs dwelt in deep swamps surrounded by forests about 150 million years ago. Apatosaurus (formerly called Brontosaurus) was an herbivore with a very small brain; it stood about 30 feet (9 meters) high and measured 90 feet (27 meters) from head to tail. *Apatosaurus* and smaller herbivorous (plant-eating) dinosaurs had massive bodies and legs, long necks, and even longer tails. When they were hungry, they pulled up water plants and swallowed them without chewing. When danger threatened, they waded into deep water. They could stand on the bottom of a body of water for hours with only their nostrils above the surface to breathe.

Dinosaurs lived all over the world except in the very coldest areas. There was a tremendous variety of species with a wide range of sizes and with scaly or heavily armored bodies. Some had ducklike bills full of sharp teeth. One type of dinosaur had two rows of bony plates on its back and long, bony spikes on its tail. Instead of running from danger, this creature swung its tail to and fro. The spikes delivered terrible blows against anything they struck.

The only animals that could harm the giant herbivorous dinosaurs were the carnivorous, or meat-eating, dinosaurs. These were savage creatures 30 to 50 feet (9 to 15 meters) long, with big heads and wide mouths set with daggerlike teeth. They stood on long, powerful hind legs, and their toes were armed with sharp, curved claws. They often attacked swamp-dwelling dinosaurs that had strayed too near the shore.

Advances in research techniques and many new excavations have resulted in the identification of more than 50 additional kinds of dinosaurs in recent years. Some scientists believe they have discovered the bones of two previously unknown, very large vegetarian dinosaurs—commonly called Supersaurus and Ultrasaurus. Supersaurus may have been 100 to 120 feet (30 to 37 meters) in length, and it is believed Ultrasaurus was even larger. Other discoveries have included very well-preserved baby dinosaur skeletons in nests.

Dinosaurs became extinct at the end of the Cretaceous period, about 65 million years ago. The mass extinction may have been caused by any number of events, as stated earlier, but a heavily favored theory is that a huge meteor struck the Earth, darkening the sky and blocking the sun with its debris. The subsequent cold temperatures may then have caused the extinctions on Earth. Paleontologists believe that a giant crater found in Mexico may be the site at which the meteor hit Earth.

Although dinosaurs were the most spectacular animals of their day, they were by no means alone on the Earth. Other reptiles walked the land, flew through the air, and swam in the water. There were birds, mammals, and some odd creatures that were halfway between the reptile and the mammal.

Mosasaurs, giant lizards that ranged from 16 to 33 feet (5 to 10 meters) in length, never left the sea. They had short paddles instead of legs and propelled themselves through the water by swinging their long tails from side to side. Icthyosaurs (meaning "fish-lizards"), smaller reptiles that lived entirely in the ocean, looked very much like sharks. Fossil evidence indicates that, like mammals, they gave birth to live young instead of laying eggs, as reptiles do.

Plesiosaurs were ocean-dwelling reptiles, most of which were about 15 feet (5 meters) long, though some later forms were as long as 43 feet (13 meters). Some species had very long necks and had flippers instead of legs.

Pterosaurs, flying reptiles, ranged from types the size of a sparrow to giant flesh-eating types with wingspans of up to 25 feet (8 meters). They had no feathers. To move through the air, they flapped large winglike webs of skin that stretched from their elongated front legs to their hind legs.

Theriodonts (meaning "mammal-toothed") were members of a reptile family that died out about 190 million years ago. They had skeletal features that suggest an evolutionary midpoint between the reptile and the mammal (see Reptiles).

**Birds and Mammals**

The great difference between the reptiles and the birds and mammals that followed them is warm blood. Reptiles are cold-blooded, which means that they must seek warmth for their bodies from an external source. Birds and mammals are warm-blooded; they can create their own body heat and have coverings of feathers or hair to conserve it.

Birds with teeth lived from about 150 million to 65 million years ago. These creatures might have evolved from flying reptiles, replacing their skin flaps with feathers. The earliest known bird, named archaeopteryx (meaning "ancient wing"), was about the size of a crow (see Birds, "The First True Bird").

Mammals represent an advance from birds because of their method of reproduction. Birds lay eggs that must be protected until they hatch. Mammals, the largest class of animals, develop their young within the mother's body (see Mammal).

Many of the early mammals were ancestors of familiar animals of today. Ancient horses had three toes and were not much larger than sheep. There were also little camels that had no humps and small rhinoceroses without horns. Mammoths and mastodons resembled elephants but were larger. The ground sloth was as large as an ox. Carnivorous mammals were common but not very large.

Several herbivorous creatures have no living relatives. Among these were the so-called "giant pigs", 5 to 6 feet (1.5 to 1.8 meters) in height. They had bony lumps on the sides of their heads and strong tusks, which they used for digging roots and for fighting. Even larger were plains-dwelling titanotheres. The biggest of these looked like a rhinoceros 8 feet (2.4 meters) high. On its nose it had two long, blunt horns of bone covered with hard skin.

It was during the Pleistocene epoch, or Great Ice Age, which began about 2 million years ago, that most of the recent animal extinctions took place. Since this epoch coincides with the appearance of humans on Earth, it is probable that some of the extinctions can be attributed to early humans.

*Animal tracks can tell an observer many things about the animal that made them. The distance between sets of prints helps to determine whether the animal was walking or running: the distance widens as an animal picks up speed. The number, length, shape, and position of the toes help a tracker distinguish between similar kinds of prints (see oppossum, skunk, and raccoon tracks on the following page). The amount of webbing between the toes also helps identify the animal. The gull (this page) uses its webbed feet as paddles; the spotted sandpiper (this page) swims only occasionally and so has only a small amount of webbing between its toes. Some animal tracks are accompanied by drag marks. The crow (this page) drags its tail as it walks and leaves a thin trail between its footprints, as does the muskrat (following page). The sidewinder rattlesnake (this page) throws first the front part of its body and then the back part sideways, leaving a trail of disconnected, parallel tracks with no drag marks between them. Noting the position of the hind-paw prints in relation to the forepaw prints is another way to distinguish between similar tracks. The hind feet of the woodchuck (following page) often land in the prints left by the front feet. As rabbits and squirrels hop (following page), their larger hind feet land in front of their forepaws, leaving a distinctive set of tracks.*

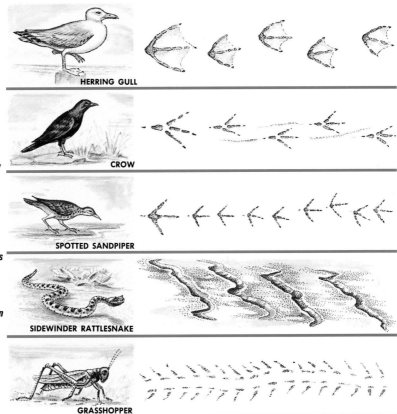

HERRING GULL

CROW

SPOTTED SANDPIPER

SIDEWINDER RATTLESNAKE

GRASSHOPPER

**ANIMAL TRACKS.** An observant outdoorsman can tell exactly what creatures have passed through an area from the impressions that they have left in the snow, soft earth, mud, or sand. Any person can make a walk outdoors more interesting by learning to "read" the tracks left by animals. Some people make a hobby of collecting plaster casts that they have made of various animal tracks. Some of the commonest animal tracks are shown on these pages. They include tracks of mammals, insects, snakes, and birds.

Snow can be a perfect medium for animal tracks. In winter the animals that do not hibernate are very active. Finding food is more difficult at this time, and they roam far and wide in search of something to eat. In all cases, fresher tracks show more detail, but experienced trackers prefer to wait a night and part of a day after a fresh snowfall before setting out so that both nocturnal and diurnal animals have had time to leave their prints.

In cities, squirrels and rabbits leave many tracks in the snow. In national parks and wilderness areas there may be the prints of large mammals such as deer, antelope, bobcats, mountain lions, bears, wolves, and coyotes to be found in the snow. In arctic regions visitors may see the tracks of polar bears.

The muddy bank of a stream or river or the edges of a lake may have a great variety of tracks left by animals that have come to the water to drink. On wet lakeshores and along the marshy shores of

ponds there may be tracks of gulls, sandpipers, and other birds that live around water. There may also be footprints of insects, crabs, turtles, and raccoons. A few feet from the sides of a sandy desert road may be the tracks of a jack rabbit, a kangaroo rat, or a kit fox. Sand dunes carry the impressions of snakes and insects as well as the tracks of bird and mammal travelers.

A knowledgeable tracker can tell many things from a set of animal tracks. The size of the prints gives a clue to the size of the animal, as does the distance between front and hind prints. The tracks of the front and back feet may occur in pairs or they may alternate, depending on the animal that made them. Some animals—beavers and porcupines, for example—walk with their toes pointed inward. The opossum's toes point slightly outward as it walks.

Tracks can reveal whether the animal was walking or running. For example, a walking deer places its hind foot directly in the print of the front foot on the same side. When a deer runs, however, its hind feet land in front of the forefoot prints. If it is running very fast, its toes may separate more than usual as its feet hit the ground.

The number of toes and the imprints left by toenails provide information about the kind of animal that made the tracks. Some animals with sharp claws, particularly members of the cat family, walk with their claws retracted, or pulled up away from the sole of the

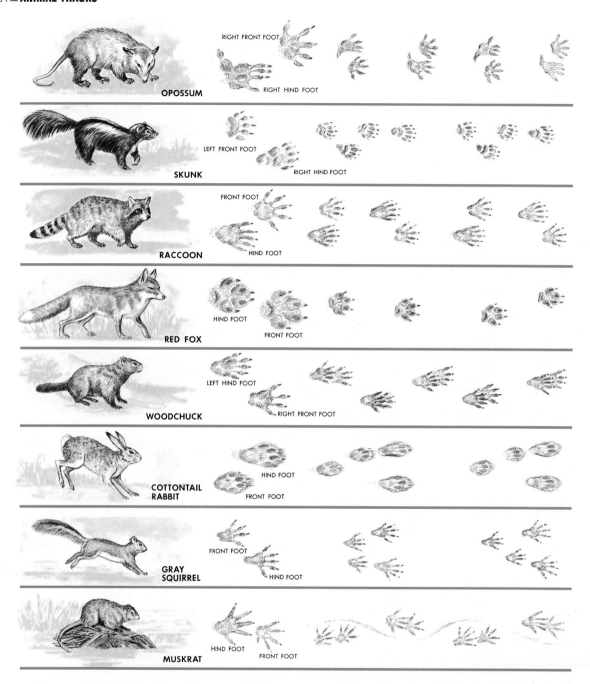

foot. Many tree climbers have long claws that leave deep imprints. Some animals, such as crows, muskrats, and weasels, drag their tails as they walk, leaving a thin trail between their footprints. The beaver's broad tail drags across the entire width of its footprints.

Sometimes tracks tell a dramatic story of flight and pursuit, of capture or escape. The animal may have crouched in waiting for some prey, leaving a depression in the snow, mud, or grass. A predator's tracks may suddenly bunch up and then stretch out at the point where the animal spotted its prey and took off in pursuit. Following the trail may reveal whether the animal caught its prey.

**BIBLIOGRAPHY FOR ANIMAL TRACKS**

**Branly, F.M.** Big Tracks, Little Tracks (Harper, 1960).
**DeLorme Publishing Company Staff.** Wildlife Signatures (1983).
**Guide to Animal Tracks** (Stackpole, 1976).
**Murie, O.J.** A Field Guide to Animal Tracks, 2nd ed. (Houghton, 1975).
**Stokes, L.Q. and D.W.** A Guide to Animal Tracking and Behavior (Little, 1986).

(*See also* bibliography for **Animal**.)

**ANIMISM.** A religious belief that everything on Earth is imbued with a powerful spirit, capable of helping or harming human needs, is called animism. This faith in a universally shared life force was involved in the earliest forms of worship. The concept has survived in many primitive societies, particularly among the tribes of sub-Saharan Africa, the aborigines of Australia, some islanders in the South Pacific, and North American Indians.

The word animism is derived from the Latin word *anima*, which means "breath of life," or "soul." Animists believe that all objects—animals, trees, rocks, rivers, plants, people—share the breath of life. According to their religious practices, all must live in harmony and be treated with equal respect.

In the world of the animist, communication with each spiritual being is vital. Prayers and offerings are given to assure the goodwill of the spirits. The Finno-Ugric peoples of Finland, Estonia, and Russia, for example, tie little bags of gifts around tree trunks to please the tree spirits so that the trees will thrive.

When an Ashanti in central Ghana chooses a tree for carving a mask or a drum, he does not simply chop it down. He explains to the spirit of the tree how its trunk will be used and asks permission for the sacrifice. If the tree has been transformed into a drum, the Ashanti musician speaks to the spirit of the instrument as he begins to play. Animists also believe that it is sinful to waste any element of a spirit that has sacrificed itself. North American Indians, for example, used every part of the buffalo they killed—for food, fuel, clothing, and shelter.

The English anthropologist Sir Edward Tylor coined the term animism in his book 'Primitive Culture' (1871). He defined it as the "belief in spirit beings." Most modern scholars have discredited Tylor's theory that primitive men could not distinguish whether things were dead or alive. The complex rituals, symbols, and myths that underlie animistic beliefs are no longer considered childish, primitive, or savage practices.

Tylor theorized that animism was low on a scale of religion that progressed to polytheism (belief in many gods) and then to monotheism (belief in one god). However, no evolutionary relationship between animism and later forms of religion has been demonstrated. In fact, animism may be practiced with, or even merged into, another religion, such as Christianity or Islam. For instance, a man setting off on a journey from his African village might stop at the local Christian church to pray for a safe and successful trip. In addition, he might kill a chicken and leave it in a special spot by the side of the road to placate the spirits of the roadway and to guarantee safe passage.

As a form of nature worship, animism has produced beautiful and varied art works. In religious rituals in Africa and the South Pacific, tribespeople dress up in masks and elaborate costumes to take on the spirit of a particular god. During the ceremony the spirit is believed to enter the human body and give advice through the person's mouth.

Beginning in the 1960s, a so-called neo-pagan religious movement has grown. This resurgence of animism is rooted in the increasing concern for ecology.

*Native Americans developed elaborate ceremonies in tribute to the spirits of the animals they hunted. Shown below is the 'Bull Dance of the Mandan Indians', an oil painting by George Catlin. Each of the six male societies of the Bambara of Africa has its own type of animist mask. The dance headdress at right is in the form of an antelope, representing the spirit of Tyiwara, the mythical being who introduced agriculture. In the Tyiwara ceremony, originally intended to assure fertile crops, farmers wear such masks as they imitate leaping antelopes.*

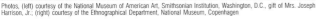

**ANKARA, Turkey.** The capital of Turkey and of Ankara *il* (province), Ankara lies at the northern edge of the central Anatolian Plateau, about 125 miles (200 kilometers) south of the Black Sea coast. It is an ancient city that, according to archaeologists, has been inhabited at least since the Stone Age.

Ankara is divided into old and new sections. The old city, which grew up on the slope around the citadel, is known as Ulus and contains Ankara's commercial center. Narrow, winding streets with wooden and mud-brick two-story houses are characteristic of the older residential areas high up the hill. The city's varied architecture is reflected in its Roman, Byzantine, and Ottoman remains. Yenisehir is the central district of the new city, which developed after Ankara was named the capital. It has broad avenues, hotels, theaters, restaurants, apartment buildings, government offices, and impressive foreign embassies.

The city has a variety of cultural and educational institutions, including the University of Ankara, founded in 1946, and the Middle East Technical University, established in 1956. Both the state theater and the Presidential Philharmonic Orchestra are based in Ankara. The National Library contains many periodicals, manuscripts, and other materials on microfilm. The main museums are the Archaeological Museum and the Ethnographical Museum.

Ankara is Turkey's second major industrial city after Istanbul. Its well-established factories produce wine, beer, flour, sugar, macaroni products, biscuits, milk, cement, terrazzo (mosaic flooring), construction materials, and tractors. Tourism and service industries have expanded rapidly. The communications industry includes well-developed radio and television broadcasting and the publication of more than 60 newspapers and some 200 magazines and journals.

This Muslim capital is an important trade crossroads and a major junction in Turkey's road network. The city is on the main east-west rail line across Anatolia; it has an international airport, and four military airports are located within the province.

Ankara survived under various rulers, including Alexander the Great, who conquered it in 334 BC, and the emperor Augustus, who incorporated it into the Roman Empire in 25 BC. As part of the Eastern Roman Empire (Byzantium), Ankara was repeatedly attacked by the Persians and the Arabs. Arab attacks continued into the 10th century, and by the 11th century the Turks threatened the city. Various rivals, including Mongol and Ottoman (Turkish) rulers, controlled Ankara until 1403. In that year the city was secured under Ottoman rule.

After World War I, Mustafa Kemal Atatürk, the Turkish nationalist leader, made Ankara the center of the resistance movement against both the government of the Ottoman sultan and invading Greek forces; he established his headquarters there in 1919. With the collapse of Ottoman rule, Turkey was declared a republic in 1923 and Ankara replaced Constantinople (now Istanbul) as its capital. (*See also* Turkey.) Population (1985 census), 2,235,000.

**ANNAPOLIS, Md.** The quaint capital of the state of Maryland is a port on the Severn River, about 2 miles (3.2 kilometers) from the river's entrance into Chesapeake Bay. It was called Providence by the Puritan exiles from Virginia who founded it in 1649. Later known as Anne Arundel Town, it was named Annapolis for Princess (later Queen) Anne of England after it became the colonial capital in 1694.

Annapolis has been the seat of the United States Naval Academy since 1845. It is also the site of St. Johns College, which was chartered in 1784. In 1965 the old area of Annapolis became a National Historic District. Among its historic buildings is the State House (1772–80), the oldest state capitol still in legislative use, where Congress ratified the Treaty of Paris ending the American Revolution.

Government offices are the major source of employment. Crab and oyster fishing, seafood processing, and boatbuilding are leading industries.

In colonial days Annapolis was a center of social and intellectual life. From November 1783 to June 1784 the United States Congress met in the tall-domed State House. In this city, on Dec. 23, 1783, George Washington resigned as commander in chief of the Continental Army. The Constitutional Convention of 1787 was requested by the Annapolis Convention held a year earlier. The city has a mayor-council form of government. (*See also* Maryland.) Population (1990 census), 33,187.

**ANN ARBOR, Mich.** The seat of Washtenaw County in southeastern Michigan, Ann Arbor is best known as the home of the University of Michigan. The city, located on the Huron River and founded in 1824, is named for the wives (both named Ann) of its two founders and for its natural groves, or arbors.

With the development of a hospital complex, along with the university's medical school, Ann Arbor has become a leading medical center. Private industrial research and development joined by the university's Institute of Science and Technology make Ann Arbor a major Midwest center for aeronautical, space, nuclear, chemical, and metallurgical research. Washtenaw Community College, founded in 1966, and Concordia (Lutheran) College, founded in 1963, are also located in Ann Arbor. Events of student interest dominate the life of the modern city. Ann Arbor produces such diverse items as ball bearings, scientific instruments, and precision machinery.

Ann Arbor was incorporated as a village in 1833 and as a city in 1851. It developed as an agricultural trading center after the arrival in 1839 of the Michigan Central Railroad, which connected it with Detroit, 38 miles (61 kilometers) to the east. The university, founded in Detroit in 1817, moved to Ann Arbor in 1837 and has played a major role in the town's growth. (*See also* Michigan.) Population (1990 census), 109,592.

**ANNE** (1665–1714). The last Stuart ruler of England was dull, obstinate Queen Anne. She was called Good Queen Anne, however, because she was goodhearted, conscientious, and deeply religious.

Anne was born in London on Feb. 6, 1665, the second daughter of James II by his first wife. When King James became a Catholic, Anne and her sister, Mary, remained Protestants. The Glorious Revolution of 1688 drove out James and put William III and Mary on the throne. In 1702 the crown passed to Anne.

For advice Queen Anne relied upon her close friend Sarah Jennings Churchill and Sarah's husband, who rose to be duke of Marlborough (see Marlborough). Under Marlborough's leadership in the War of the Spanish Succession, Britain and its allies put an end to the ambitions of Louis XIV of France. The Treaty of Utrecht (1713) gave England Gibraltar and important holdings in America, where the war was called Queen Anne's War (see Queen Anne's War). The Act of Union (1707) united the governments of England and Scotland.

Anne married Prince George of Denmark in 1683. She had 17 children, but none survived her. When she died, on Aug. 1, 1714, the crown passed to the nearest Protestant heir, the elector of Hanover, who became King George I (see George, Kings of England, Scotland, and Ireland).

**ANOREXIA NERVOSA.** The disorder anorexia nervosa, from the Latin words meaning "nervous loss of appetite," is characterized by a severe revulsion toward eating that results in extreme thinness and sometimes in death from self-inflicted starvation. The causes of anorexia nervosa are poorly understood, and its treatment is therefore difficult.

The usual victim is a girl between the ages of 14 and 17 years, though occasionally a male or an older woman may also develop a frantic preoccupation with body size. In most cases the illness begins with dieting to lose excess weight. The dieting turns into a refusal to take nourishment as anorexics relentlessly pursue an ideal of excessive thinness. They often follow strenuous exercise programs.

When the weight loss has continued for some weeks, the anorexic becomes malnourished, and imbalances in the body's chemistry begin to cause illness. Vitamins and minerals are depleted, and various glands are unable to function properly. Menstruation often stops, and physical development may slow. In some cases body weight may drop to half of normal. The anorexic usually claims to be eating adequately and refuses to acknowledge the emaciation that others can see. Death from starvation occurs in about 10 to 15 percent of anorexics despite the intervention of family and medical professionals.

The disorder often affects young women with what are called "perfectionist" personalities. This type of person is never satisfied that anything is done well enough. Many victims of the illness also have unusually heavy family responsibilities. Anorexia nervosa is viewed as a dangerous form of mental illness by most physicians, though a few are beginning to look for additional physical causes.

Treatment must begin with restoring nutrition. If starvation has reached a dangerous point, the anorexic is hospitalized and fed by stomach tube or through a vein. Because the illness is basically psychological, the help of a psychiatrist or other trained counselor is also necessary. When this condition begins in a girl who has just entered puberty, it is suspected that the illness is an unconscious desire to remain a child (see Adolescence). The patient needs to understand why she is starving herself and to recognize her value. Long-term psychotherapy, for both mental and physical recovery, is often necessary.

A related condition is bulimia, from the Greek *boulimia*, meaning "great hunger." It is characterized by gorging food, followed by forced vomiting, by fasting, or by laxative or amphetamine abuse. The distinguishing feature is regular gorging that leads to guilt and the compulsive desire to be rid of the hated food. Unlike the anorexic, the bulimic can usually function quite normally, though with difficulty, and rarely requires hospitalization. Recommended reading includes 'The Golden Cage' by Hilde Bruch (1978) and 'When Food's a Foe' by Nancy Kolodny (1987).

Ann Giudici Fettner

**ANSELM OF CANTERBURY** (1033?–1109). In the late Middle Ages the attempt to use philosophy to explain Christian faith was called scholasticism. The founder of scholasticism was St. Anselm, a philosopher, theologian, monk, and archbishop.

Anselm was born at Aosta, Italy, in about 1033. In his youth he resisted family pressure to enter politics and obtained a classical education instead. In 1057 he entered the Benedictine monastery at Bec, in northwestern France. In 1078 he became the abbot there. As Anselm's abilities and great learning became known, Bec became one of the leading schools of philosophy and theology.

While on inspection tours of monasteries in England, Anselm had been befriended by King William I. In 1093 William I's son and successor, William II Rufus, appointed Anselm archbishop of Canterbury. His term of office was an unhappy one, for he immediately became involved in one of the major conflicts of the time—the investiture controversy. At issue was whether a king had the right to invest a bishop with the symbols of his office. On this issue Anselm resisted both William II and his successor, Henry I. The matter was finally resolved in Anselm's favor by the Westminster Agreement of 1107. He lived only two more years, dying on April 21, 1109.

Anselm is remembered principally as one of the great theologians in the history of the Roman Catholic church. His main works—the 'Monologium' (Monologue), the 'Proslogium' (Addition), and the 'Cur Deus Homo?' (Why Did God Become Man?)—were outstanding attempts to use reason to explain belief. He was canonized a saint in 1163 and declared a doctor of the church in 1720.

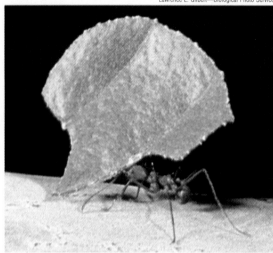

*The leaf-cutter ant* (Atta cephaloides) *is a serious pest that often strips the leaves from plants to provide nourishment for its fungus crop, which it eventually harvests and eats.*

**ANT.** Mankind is not alone in living in organized communities, working cooperatively and efficiently, creating a clear division of labor, waging war, and occasionally capturing slaves. The most common of the social insects, the ant, also exhibits these behaviors. Ants do not have the power of reason, however, by which humans err and experience freedom. They live in blind obedience to instinct, neither choosing nor willing to do anything.

Ants belong to the order Hymenoptera, which also includes bees and wasps. Ants constitute the family Formicidae, which has at least 8,000 species, and possibly as many as 14,000. Entomologists, scientists who study insects, have estimated that there are probably more ants than any other kind of insect. Ants have been in existence for at least 100 million years, and they probably evolved from wingless wasps.

Ants occur throughout the world. They have traveled from their original home, the tropics, to climates as varied as the polar regions, mountain ranges, and deserts. They make their nests in many materials, including soil, sand, wood, and leaves.

### Kinds of Ants

Although ants share many physical and social traits, there are many distinct varieties that differ in their habits and appearance. They are classified according to the shape of certain parts of their bodies and by specific behaviors.

**Myrmicines** are the most widespread subfamily. This is reflected in the word myrmecology, which means the scientific study of ants. There are more than 3,000 known species of myrmicines. Most have a stinger and a sound-producing organ.

**Formicines** are found throughout the world. There are at least 2,500 species. They possess poison glands, with which they spray or drip formic acid on their enemies to stun or kill them.

**Ponerines** are mainly tropical. The approximately 1,000 species are hunters, and they attack both ant and termite nests.

**Army ants,** also found in the tropics, are sometimes called driver ants or legionary ants. There are about 200 species. These wanderers do not build permanent nests; instead, they cling together on logs or in hollow trees. They travel in columns, sometimes at speeds of up to 65 feet (20 meters) per hour. Some of these columns have been said to contain up to 20 million ants. When a swarm of army ants marches through a human settlement, it can destroy all crops and any small animals in its path.

**Leaf-cutter ants** live in the tropics. These industrious ants carry cut-up flowers and leaves overhead like green umbrellas, which earns them the alternate name of parasol ants. They grow a fungus crop on decaying leaf pieces, carefully tending it like farmers and harvesting it for food.

**Bulldog ants** are meat-eating insects of Australia. There are about 100 species. They are among the largest ants, often reaching $\frac{4}{5}$ inch (20 millimeters) in length. They capture insects, which they feed to their young. The adults feed on plant juices.

**Amazon ants** are unable to gather food, build nests, or feed their young by themselves. They invade the nests of other species, killing the workers and bringing home the helpless young ants to raise as slaves and do the work of the amazon colony.

**Other varieties** of ants include carpenter ants, which live in wood; harvester ants, which store seeds, grass, and berries as food; weaver ants, which make nests from leaves and other materials held together by silk; and honey ants, which feed on a honeydew that is secreted by aphids.

### Physical Characteristics

Despite this great diversity in social behavior and habits, most ants have the same basic physical structure. They range in size from $\frac{8}{100}$ to 1 inch (2 to 25 millimeters). They are usually yellow, brown, red, or black. A few have a metallic luster.

Their bodies, like those of all insects, are divided into three sections: the head, the thorax, and the abdomen. The head is large, and the abdomen is slender and oval. The thorax, or midsection, is connected to the abdomen by a small "waist" section.

The mouth is an important working tool for most ants. It consists of two sets of jaws: the outer pair, used for carrying food and building materials for the nest, and the inner jaw, used for chewing.

Adult ants can swallow only liquids. In the back of the jaw is a storage pocket. Solid food goes first into this pocket, where a strong saliva breaks it down. The ant swallows the liquid part. The solids form into a ball that the ant spits out.

Different parts of ants vary according to the way a particular species lives. Harvester ants have short, heavy, crushing jaws for breaking seeds. The leaf-cutters have jaws with saw-toothed edges, so that they can shred leaves. The jaws of the amazon ant are

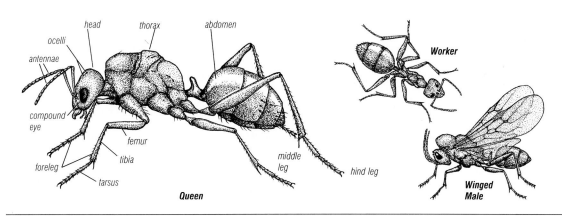

*The physical structure of the Argentine ant, like that of all ants, is typical of most insects. The body is divided into three sections—head, thorax, and abdomen. The legs are all attached to the thorax. In ants the "waist" section between the thorax and the abdomen is very small. The ocelli are simple eyes that are situated at the top of the head. The only winged ants are males and young queens. The workers are underdeveloped female ants.*

sickle-shaped, like a curved tool. They use these jaws to kill other insects efficiently.

Most ants have simple eyes, called ocelli, on top of the head, as well as a compound eye with many lenses on each side of the head. Nonetheless, their vision is probably poor. More useful than the eyes are the antennae, the two slender, pointed rods that wave constantly from the head as the ant moves about.

The senses of smell and touch are located in the antennae. With these rods, the ant recognizes its nest and the members of its colony. It can instantly detect an intruder from another colony by its smell. Ants also are able to communicate with one another by tapping with their antennae. Nursemaid ants clean the young with their antennae as well as with their tongues. Ants also clean themselves with a sort of comb called a strigil, which is located on the forelegs.

Males and queens are normally winged, although they only use these wings once—on their mating flight. All other ants lack wings.

Many ants have only simple stings, and instead of stinging their enemies they eject vapors of formic acid. Other ants, such as the bulldog ants and fire ants, have powerful stings at the tip of the abdomen.

Ants do not have lungs. They breathe instead through small holes called spiracles, which are located along the sides of the abdomen and the thorax.

## Life Cycle

The life cycle of the ant generally has four stages: egg, larva, pupa, and adult. Most ants live from 6 to 10 weeks, although certain queens may live for as long as 15 years, and some workers for up to 7 years.

The role, or caste, is the occupational group into which an individual ant is born. There are three major castes of ants: queens, workers, and soldiers. The queen is the mother and founder of the colony. She spends her life laying eggs. The workers are sterile

females, and do the jobs necessary to keep the colony in good working order. They care for the young, enlarge the nest, and gather food to feed the queen and the other members of the colony. The larger workers—the soldiers—defend the nest. They raid other colonies and often capture slaves.

At certain times of the year many species produce winged males and queens, which fly into the air, where they mate. The male deposits sperm in the queen's sperm sac. The winged males die soon after mating with the queens. They are not allowed to return to their original nests, so they starve or are eaten by other insects or by birds.

The queen digs a hole where she lays her eggs and waits until the first ants emerge. As she lays these eggs, she may or may not fertilize them with sperm from her sperm sac. Fertilized eggs result in females; unfertilized eggs produce males. The female eggs develop into fertile queens, sterile workers, or soldiers. Most of the ants in a colony are workers.

While the queen waits for her eggs to hatch, she is nourished by food stored in her body. The first eggs usually produce workers, which the queen feeds with other eggs. When the workers are able to bring in food from outside the nest, the queen devotes the rest of her life to laying eggs.

After the workers are born, soldiers, males, and winged females hatch. The larvae have no eyes or legs. Unlike adult ants, they can eat solid food, which the earliest workers obtain for them. The nurses lick the larvae constantly, in what looks like a show of affection. Actually, the nurse workers are greedily eating a sweet liquid that appears on the larvae.

After the larvae hatch out of the eggs, they shed their skin several times. Then most of them spin a silken cocoon about their bodies and rest inside while they change into adults. This protective covering is created from the ants' own saliva. In this form, when

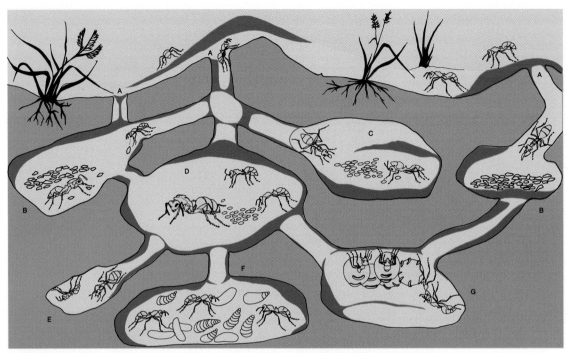

*An ant colony has several entrances (A), leading to a variety of subterranean chambers. Each chamber has a specific use. Some are for food storage (B). The queen has her own room (D). In another chamber workers tend unhatched eggs (C). A deeper room serves as a nursery for larvae and cocoons (F). In the replete gallery (G) are the worker ants whose expanded abdomens contain surplus food for the colony. In another room (E), worker ants are digging a new chamber.*

they look somewhat like ants but do not eat or move much, they are known as pupae.

When a pupa is ready to break out of its cocoon, the nurse ant bites a hole in the end of the silken wrapping and helps the weak little ant to free its legs and antennae. Then she washes and feeds it.

Many variations of this colonizing and rearing process occur. In one species, the queen is more than a thousand times larger than her workers. She is too large to feed her own young, so she must have workers to help her from the start. When she leaves her original nest on her mating flight, tiny workers go with her, clinging to her legs with their jaws.

### Behavior

The most distinguishing trait of ant behavior is sociability. Ants do not act individually; they behave according to the needs of the colony in roles dictated by the caste into which they are born. The major social unit is the colony, which forms a nest.

The nests of ants vary in structure and in material. Most of an ant's life is spent in its nest with from a few to more than a million other individuals. Some ants dig chambers and passages in the ground; others locate their nests under rocks, in trees, or in logs. The nests may be built of paper, twigs, sand, gravel, or other materials.

One colony can claim as its territory thousands of square yards. Some species pile large heaps of earth on top of their nests. These mounds can be more than 1

yard (0.9 meter) high and up to 4 yards (3.7 meters) in diameter. The nest is kept spotless. The ants remove all rubbish promptly. If an ant dies, a worker carries it from the nest to a spot that serves as both a cemetery and a garbage dump. If the queen dies, however, the workers continue to care for her as long as her body remains recognizable.

Ants like warmth and swarm out of their nests into the sunshine. But they can be frozen for long periods without harm. Packed in tight bunches, many spend the winter inside logs and stumps. Others lie under plant roots or in shallow nests in the ground.

Certain species deepen their nests below the frost line as winter approaches. There they crowd into their tunnels and chambers with their legs interlocked and sleep through the cold winter.

The social structure of the colony has led to several unusual living arrangements. Ants can be very hospitable. Some species live as guests with other ants or insects; some ants host other insects as guests. A few species live with parasites—insects or other small animals, such as mites, spiders, caterpillars, and beetles, that are fed and sheltered by the colony but that provide nothing in return.

The sociability of ants is especially evident in their feeding habits. The abdomen has two stomachs. The ant digests part of the food for its own use in the true stomach. The rest goes into a sac called the social stomach, or crop. This is a sort of storage tank for the use of the entire colony.

**How To Make An Ant Farm**

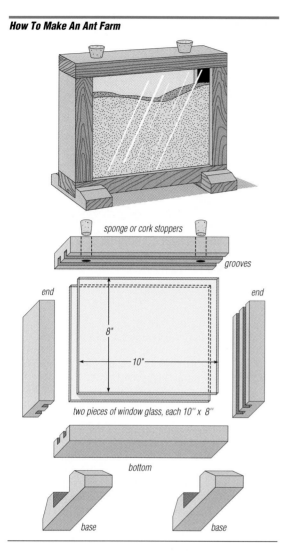

sponge or cork stoppers

grooves

end

end

8"

10"

*two pieces of window glass, each 10" x 8"*

bottom

base

base

*A simple ant farm can be made from two pieces of glass fitted into four sections of grooved wood and set on a wooden base. Fill the assembled farm two-thirds full with soil found near an anthill. A colony must contain a queen and should also have eggs, larvae, pupae, and parasites, along with the other ants. Ants should be fed bits of ground beef, dead insects, bread crumbs, and watered honey. The cork or sponge stoppers should be kept moist; ants must have moisture.*

When an ant is hungry, it strokes a worker with its antennae. The worker brings up a drop of liquid from her crop and passes it into the other's mouth. Thus the queen and other ants are fed by those whose job it is to find and bring back food.

Hospitality and cooperation are only one aspect of the ant's social character, however. It is also capable of warlike behavior. Ants are the only animals other than humans that carry on organized warfare, usually for the capture of slaves.

The dependence on slaves is clearly evident in the amazon ants. Because of physical limitations, they are inefficient workers. They use other species in their colony to care for their young, expand the nest, and do the other chores of the worker caste.

The ant's aggressive nature is also seen in robberies and quarrels over boundaries, which can lead to feuds lasting for years between different colonies of ants. Ants vary in their methods of defense. Some bite or spit out a disagreeable liquid. Others use their stings to shoot out formic acid. Still others run away when under attack, "play dead," or make sound signals to warn other members of their colonies.

In addition to being able to communicate, ants have an excellent sense of direction. They can find their way back to their nest by vision and smell. They orient themselves by the position of the sun and by the memory of landmarks such as trees. Some ants also leave scent trails to aid other ants.

**Relationship to Humans**

Although ants are generally considered an annoyance in houses, only a few species are capable of doing real damage to human property. Some species are actually quite helpful to humans.

Certain species help get rid of pests. Others, such as ground-dwellers, are useful to farmers. In the process of building their nests, they turn over the soil, which is good for crops.

**ANTANANARIVO, Madagascar.** Formerly called Tananarive, the high, inland city of Antananarivo is the capital of Madagascar, the world's fourth largest island. The country is located in the Indian Ocean nearly 200 miles (325 kilometers) off the southeastern coast of Africa.

The town was founded by Hova chiefs in the 17th century. It was captured in 1794 by Imerina kings, who had established a society in the island's central valley. They ruled until the end of the 19th century when the island became a French colony.

Antananarivo stands on a high hill. Avenues and flights of steps lead to a rocky ridge on which stands the Royal Estate, built by the Imerinas. Below are banks and administrative buildings, including the French Residency and the Anglican and Roman Catholic cathedrals. The city has research institutes, an observatory, the national library, and the University of Madagascar, founded in 1961.

Below this area is the commercial quarter. Industries include tobacco and food processing and the manufacture of leather goods and clothing. Antananarivo province, Madagascar's only landlocked province, is a region of hills, lakes, and hot springs. The province contains large rice fields, vegetable farms, orchards, and vineyards.

Antananarivo is a busy transportation center. The international airport at Ivato, 11 miles (17 kilometers) north of the city, is extensively used. A railway connects the capital with Tamatave, the island's chief port, and main roads from all directions converge at Antananarivo. (*See also* Madagascar.) Population (1980 estimate), 547,139.

*The sheer barrier face of the Ross Ice Shelf rises as high as 230 feet (70 meters) above the sea surface.*
*Mount Terror, approximately 2 miles (3.2 kilometers) high, rises in the background.*

**ANTARCTICA.** The icy continent around the South Pole is called Antarctica. This region, at the bottom of the world, is larger in area than the United States and Mexico combined. It is a cold and forbidding land that has no permanent human population and is almost devoid of animal or plant life. However, the oceans adjoining Antarctica teem with life.

Ice and stormy seas kept anyone from seeing Antarctica until about 1820. In 1950 more than half the continent still had not been seen. Now airplanes and tractors have taken people to most parts of Antarctica, and satellite photographs have revealed the rest. But Antarctica remains a frontier, and much is yet to be learned about it.

Almost no one goes to Antarctica except scientists and some adventurous tourists. The continent has natural resources that someday may be used, but the harsh environment of the continent makes them difficult to exploit. Nations interested in Antarctica have signed a treaty that reserves the region for science and other peaceful purposes.

### The Land

An ice sheet covers nearly all of Antarctica. At its thickest point the ice sheet is 15,670 feet (4,776 meters) deep—almost 3 miles (5 kilometers). It averages 7,000 to 8,000 feet (2,100 to 2,400 meters) thick, making Antarctica the continent with the highest mean elevation. This ice sheet contains 90 percent of the world's ice and 70 percent of the world's fresh water.

The Antarctic ice was formed from the snows of millions of years that fell on the land, layer on layer.

........................................................................

*This article was contributed by Guy G. Guthridge, Manager of the Polar Information Program at the National Science Foundation in Washington, D.C.*

The weight of new snow squeezes the old snow underneath until it turns to a substance called firn, then ice. As the ice piles up, it moves toward the coast like batter spreading on a pan. The moving ice forms into glaciers, rivers of ice that flow into the sea. Pieces of the floating glaciers break off from time to time, a process called calving. These icebergs float north until they reach warm water, break into pieces, and melt. Icebergs as large as 40 miles (64 kilometers) long and 30 miles (48 kilometers) wide have been sighted, but most are smaller. In some places the floating glaciers stay attached to the land and continue to grow until they become ice shelves. The Ross Ice Shelf alone is bigger than France and averages 1,000 feet (300 meters) thick.

The Transantarctic Mountains extend across the continent, dividing the ice sheet into two parts. The larger, eastern part rests on land that is mostly above sea level. It has been there at least 14 million years, and scientists do not think it is ever likely to melt. The smaller, western part is on land that is mostly below sea level. Scientists think that if the world were to warm a little, as it has in the past, the western part could melt—perhaps in as little as a one-hundred-year period. The melted ice would raise sea level throughout the world by about 20 feet (6 meters).

Other mountain ranges include the Prince Charles Mountains and smaller groups near the coasts. The Antarctic Peninsula has many mountains. The Ellsworth Mountains are Antarctica's highest, the Vinson Massif rising 16,066 feet (4,897 meters) above sea level. Mountains with only their peaks showing through the ice (called nunataks) are found in some areas. Several active volcanoes on the continent provide spectacular and scenic landforms at many places and are located near the Antarctic Peninsula and in the Transantarctic Mountains.

About 2 percent of Antarctica is ice-free. These unusual land areas, called oases, generally are near the coast and include the dry valleys of southern Victoria Land and the Bunger Oasis in Wilkes Land. High rims at the end of the valleys prevent entry of large glaciers. The warm local climate melts the ends of smaller glaciers extending into the valleys.

Surrounding Antarctica are the southern parts of the Pacific, the Atlantic, and the Indian oceans. The Antarctic Convergence, which encircles Antarctica roughly 1,000 miles (1,600 kilometers) off the coast, divides the cold southern water masses and the warmer northern waters. The Antarctic Circumpolar Current, the world's largest ocean current, moves eastward around the continent at an average speed of about half a knot (1 kilometer per hour). Sea ice up to 10 feet (3 meters) thick forms outward from the continent every winter, making a belt 300 to 1,000 miles (500 to 1,600 kilometers) wide. Even in summer the sea ice belt is 100 to 500 miles (160 to 800 kilometers) wide in most places.

Antarctica has three points that are called south poles. The best known is the geographic South Pole, at 90° S. latitude on the axis of the Earth's rotation. The geomagnetic south pole is at about 78° S. 110° E., in East Antarctica; it is the center of the Southern Hemisphere auroras. The magnetic south pole is the area toward which compasses point; it is just off the Adélie Coast at about 65° S. 140° E.

Antarctica does not have 24-hour periods broken into days and nights. At the South Pole the sun rises on about September 21 and moves in a circular path upward until December 21, when it reaches about 23.5° above the horizon. Then it circles downward until it sets on about March 22. This "day," or summer, is six months long. From March 22 until September 21 the South Pole is dark, and Antarctica has its long "night," or winter.

According to theory, some 200 million years ago Antarctica was joined to South America, Africa, India, and Australia in a single large continent called Gondwanaland. There was no ice sheet, and trees and large animals flourished. Today, only geological formations, coal beds, and fossils remain as clues to Antarctica's warm past.

## Climate

Antarctica is the coldest continent. The world's record low temperature of −128.6° F (−89.2° C) was recorded there. The mean annual temperature of the interior is −70° F (−57° C). The coast is warmer. Monthly mean temperatures at McMurdo Station range from −18° F (−28° C) in August to 27° F (−3° C) in January. Along the Antarctic Peninsula temperatures have been as high as 59° F (15° C).

Because it is such a large area of extreme cold, Antarctica plays an important role in global atmospheric circulation. In the tropics the sun warms the air, causing it to rise and move toward the poles. When these air masses arrive over Antarctica, they cool, become heavier, and fall from the high interior of

National Science Foundation

*Formed by moving ice, Mill Glacier is a river of ice that flows into the sea.*

the continent toward the sea, making some Antarctic coasts the windiest places in the world. Winds on the Adélie Coast in the winter of 1912 to 1913 averaged 40 miles (64 kilometers) per hour 64 percent of the time, and gusts of nearly 200 miles (320 kilometers) per hour have been recorded.

Antarctica's interior is one of the world's major cold deserts. Precipitation (if melted) averages only 1 to 2 inches (2.5 to 5 centimeters) a year.

## Plant and Animal Life

The severe climate has kept nearly all of Antarctica almost devoid of life. Nevertheless, botanists have found bacteria and yeast growing just 183 miles (295 kilometers) from the geographic South Pole. A lichen was found in a sunny canyon 266 miles (428 kilometers) from the pole, and a blue-green alga in a frozen pond 224 miles (360 kilometers) from the pole. Microbes related to lichens colonize in green and brown layers just beneath the surface of rocks facing the sun. Mosses and liverworts grow in some ice-free areas along the coast. Two species of flowering plants—a grass and an herb—grow on the peninsula.

The native land animals are limited to arthropods (such as insects), of which 76 species have been discovered. Nearly all of the species are found only in Antarctica. These springtails, midges, and mites live generally along the coast among plant colonies. The southernmost known animal, the mite, has been found 315 miles (507 kilometers) from the South Pole.

The immense numbers of birds and seals that live in Antarctica are, properly speaking, sea animals. They spend most of their time in or over the water, where they get their food. These animals come ashore only to establish rookeries and breed.

About 45 species of birds live south of the Antarctic Convergence. Two penguin species—the emperor and the Adélie—are distributed widely around the entire coastline. Gentoo and chinstrap penguins occupy Antarctic Peninsula coasts and some islands. Penguins,

*Lichens are common sights in the comparatively gentle environment of the peninsular region. Some species of lichens have even been found near the geographic South Pole.*

F. Erize—Bruce Coleman, Inc.

fine swimmers, catch their food—mostly krill (a shrimplike animal) and fishes—underwater.

Four species of seals breed almost exclusively in the Antarctic. They are the Weddell seal, which ranges as far south as the sea does and can dive as deep as 2,000 feet (600 meters) for nearly an hour; the crabeater seal, which spends most of its time around pack ice (sea ice); the leopard seal, which favors penguins as its food; and the Ross seal, rarely seen. Other Antarctic species include the fur seal and the huge elephant seal. Most populous is the crabeater, whose numbers are estimated at 50 to 75 million. Leopard and Weddell seals by comparison number only 250,000 to 500,000 each. The others exist in even smaller numbers.

Fishes peculiar to the Antarctic include the Antarctic cod and the icefish. These and other Antarctic fish have developed blood that enables them to live in seawater as cold as 28° F (−2° C).

The most important single member of the Antarctic marine food chain is the krill. This crustacean looks like a small shrimp and exists in huge numbers; one vast swarm stretching several miles in length was observed from ships, and some biologists think the total population may be 5 billion tons or more. Krill eat small marine plants (phytoplankton) and animals (zooplankton) and in turn are eaten in great numbers by squid, birds, seals, and whales.

*Emperor penguins, here at McMurdo Sound, can be found around the continent's entire coastline.*

Kevin Schafer—U.S. Navy/National Science Foundation

## Economic Development

Antarctica is so far from world markets, and its environment is so hostile, that little economic development has taken place. Also, little is known about the amounts of natural resources that exist there. But, if world shortages of food and energy products become severe enough, Antarctica may be more intensely explored. In anticipation of such a need, 15 nations have signed a convention for the conservation of living marine resources on the Antarctic continent.

The first people to make money by going to Antarctica were whalers and sealers, who first crossed the Antarctic Convergence in 1778. Seal hunters began catching Antarctic seals for their oil and fur in the early 1790s. Fur seals and then elephant seals were reduced almost to extinction by the mid-1800s, at which point the sealers finally stopped their Antarctic hunts. The populations of fur and elephant seals once again are growing.

In 1978 the nations interested in Antarctica agreed to prohibit the taking of fur, elephant, and Ross seals. This pact also limits the annual catch of crabeater, leopard, and Weddell seals. But no seal hunting has taken place in Antarctica since 1964.

Whaling began in Antarctic waters in the 19th century. The industry enlarged greatly in the early 1900s, when steamships, harpoon guns, and shore processing stations (notably at South Georgia) were introduced. During the 1912–13 season 10,760 whales were caught. After that time nearly all the whales caught in the world were caught in Antarctic waters. In 1931, a peak year, 40,199 whales were caught in the Antarctic, while only 1,124 were caught in the rest of the world. So many whales were caught that their numbers declined, just as had those of the seals. The industry declined after 1960. In the 1980–81 season fewer than 6,000 whales were caught in the Antarctic; all were minke whales, a relatively small-sized species also called the lesser rorqual.

Commercial fishing was begun by the Soviet Union in 1967. In 1971 a Soviet fleet of 40 trawlers and support ships in the southern ocean landed an estimated 300,000 tons—mostly cod, herring, and whiting. Today fleets of other nations, mainly Japan and Norway, also fish the waters.

Krill fishing began in the early 1970s, and by 1980 the Soviet Union and Japan were taking about 100,000 tons a year for use as a shrimp substitute and animal feed. Some scientists believe that huge amounts of krill could be harvested from the Antarctic, enough to double the worldwide catch of seafood. But much remains to be learned about the biology and population of krill to know how much damage would be done by huge harvests.

In 1982 the nations that were interested in Antarctica set up a scientific committee to study the Antarctic ecosystem and a commission to set catch limits. The nations wanted to protect the unique ecosystem and to avoid any activities that had already reduced the numbers of whales and seals in the area.

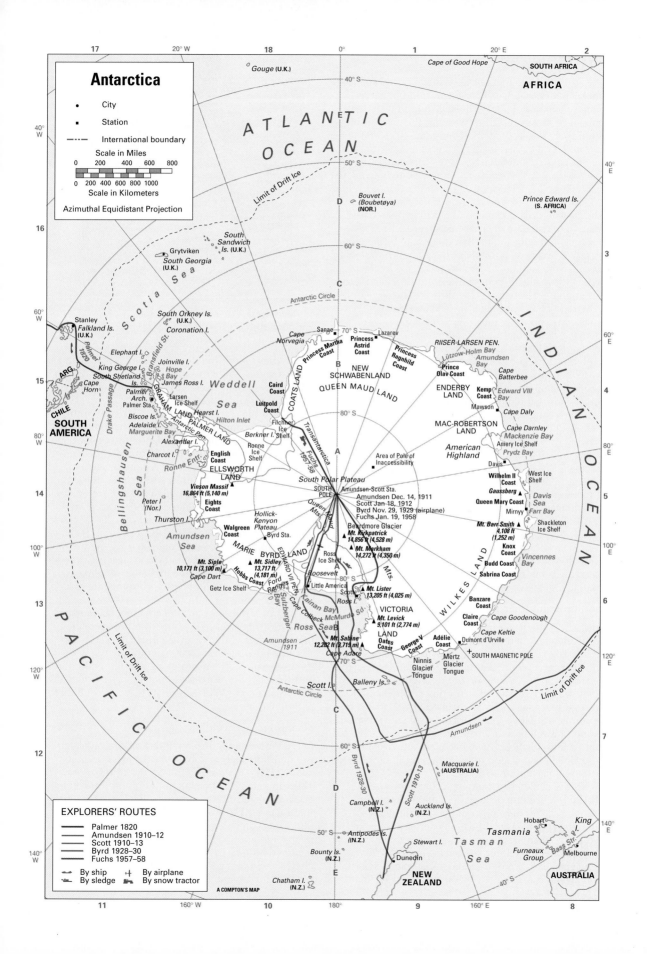

# Antarctica

- City
- Station
- International boundary

Scale in Miles
0 200 400 600 800 1000

Scale in Kilometers
0 200 400 600 800 1000

Azimuthal Equidistant Projection

**ATLANTIC OCEAN**

*Gouge (U.K.)*

*Cape of Good Hope*

**SOUTH AFRICA**

**AFRICA**

Limit of Drift Ice

*Bouvet I. (Boubetøya) (NOR.)*

*Prince Edward Is. (S. AFRICA)*

Antarctic Circle

*South Sandwich Is. (U.K.)*

Grytviken
*South Georgia (U.K.)*

**Scotia Sea**

Stanley
*Falkland Is. (U.K.)*

**ARG.**

*South Orkney Is. (U.K.)*
*Coronation I.*

*Elephant I.*
*King George I.*
*Joinville I.*
*Hope Bay*
*South Shetland Is.*
*James Ross I.*

**Bransfield St.**

*Cape Horn*
*Palmer Arch.*
*Palmer Sta.*
*Larsen Ice Shelf*
*Biscoe Is.*
*Adelaide I.*
*Marguerite Bay*
*Alexander I.*
*Charcot I.*

**GRAHAM LAND**
**PALMER LAND**
**Antarctic Pen.**

*Hearst I.*
*Hilton Inlet*

**Weddell Sea**

*Caird Coast*
*Luitpold Coast*
*Filchner Ice Shelf*
*Berkner I.*

**English Coast**
**ELLSWORTH LAND**
*Ronne Entr.*
*Ronne Ice Shelf*

**Drake Passage**

**CHILE**
**SOUTH AMERICA**

*Palmer 1820*

**Bellingshausen Sea**

*Peter I. (Nor.)*

*Thurston I.*

▲ *Vinson Massif 16,864 ft (5,140 m)*
**Eights Coast**

*Walgreen Coast*

**Amundsen Sea**

**MARIE BYRD LAND**
**EDWARD VII PEN.**

▲ *Mt. Siple 10,171 ft (3,100 m)*
*Cape Dart*

▲ *Mt. Sidley 13,717 ft (4,181 m)*
**Hobbs Coast**
*Ford Ranges*
*Getz Ice Shelf*

*Hollick-Kenyon Plateau*
■ *Byrd Sta.*

**COATS LAND**

*Cape Norvegia*

Sanae
70° S
Lazarev

*Princess Astrid Coast*
**Princess Martha Coast**

**NEW SCHWABENLAND**
**QUEEN MAUD LAND**

*Princess Ragnhild Coast*

**RIISER-LARSEN PEN.**
*Lützow-Holm Bay*
*Amundsen Bay*

*Prince Olav Coast*

**ENDERBY LAND**
*Kemp Coast*
■ Mawson

*Edward VIII Bay*
*Cape Batterbee*
*Cape Daly*

**MAC-ROBERTSON LAND**

*Cape Darnley*
*Mackenzie Bay*
*Amery Ice Shelf*
*Prydz Bay*

*American Highland*

■ Davis

**INDIAN OCEAN**

80° S

*South Polar Plateau*

Area of Pole of Inaccessibility

**SOUTH POLE**

Amundsen-Scott Sta.
Amundsen Dec. 14, 1911
Scott Jan 18, 1912
Byrd Nov. 29, 1929 (airplane)
Fuchs Jan. 19, 1958

*Fuchs 1957-58*
*Transantarctica*

*Queen Maud Mts.*

▲ *Mt. Kirkpatrick 14,856 ft (4,528 m)*
*Beardmore Glacier*
▲ *Mt. Markham 14,272 ft (4,350 m)*

*Ross Ice Shelf*

■ Roosevelt

■ *Little America*

*Kainan Bay*
*Cape Colbeck*
*Sulzberger Bay*

*Ross Sea*

*Cape McMurdo*
*Ross I.*
Scott
▲ *Mt. Lister 13,205 ft (4,025 m)*

**VICTORIA LAND**
▲ *Mt. Levick 9,101 ft (2,774 m)*

*Oates Coast*

**George V Coast**

▲ *Mt. Sabine 12,202 ft (3,719 m)*
*Cape Adare*
70° S

*Amundsen 1911*

**Wilhelm II Coast**
▲ *Gaussberg*
**Queen Mary Coast**
Mirny ■

**WILKES LAND**

▲ *Mt. Barr Smith 4,108 ft (1,252 m)*

*West Ice Shelf*
*Davis Sea*
*Farr Bay*
*Shackleton Ice Shelf*

*Knox Coast*
**Budd Coast**
*Vincennes Bay*
*Sabrina Coast*

*Banzare Coast*
*Claire Coast*
*Cape Goodenough*
*Cape Keltie*
*Dumont d'Urville*
+ **SOUTH MAGNETIC POLE**

**Adélie Coast**

*Ninnis Glacier Tongue*
*Mertz Glacier Tongue*

*Amundsen*

*Byrd 1928-30*
*Scott 1910-13*

*Macquarie I. (AUSTRALIA)*

**PACIFIC OCEAN**

Limit of Drift Ice

*Scott I.*
Antarctic Circle

*Balleny Is.*

Limit of Drift Ice

*Campbell I. (N.Z.)*
*Auckland Is. (N.Z.)*

*Antipodes Is. (N.Z.)*
*Bounty Is. (N.Z.)*
*Stewart I.*
Dunedin

*Chatham I. (N.Z.)*

**NEW ZEALAND**

*Tasmania*

Hobart

*King I.*

**Tasman Sea**

*Furneaux Group*
Melbourne
*Bass Str.*

**AUSTRALIA**

## EXPLORERS' ROUTES

- Palmer 1820
- Amundsen 1910–12
- Scott 1910–13
- Byrd 1928–30
- Fuchs 1957–58

By ship     By airplane
By sledge   By snow tractor

A COMPTON'S MAP

Petroleum and minerals have never been exploited in Antarctica. Minerals have been found in great variety but almost always in small amounts. Large mineral deposits probably exist, but the chances of finding them are small. Manganese nodules on the ocean floor, geothermal energy, coal, petroleum, and natural gas are potential resources that could perhaps be exploited in the future. Only two large mineral deposits have been found: iron ore in the Prince Charles Mountains and coal in the Transantarctic Mountains. But it would cost too much to get these materials to market to make them economically attractive.

Some authorities think that there may be large reserves of oil and natural gas in Antarctica, simply because the continental shelf is so large. However, very little exploration has been done, and even if they are found, extraction will be difficult. The edge of the Antarctic continental shelf is 1,000 to 3,000 feet (300 to 900 meters) deep, much deeper than the world average continental shelf depth of about 600 feet (200 meters), and Antarctica's huge icebergs would threaten drill rigs. Also, the environmental impact of spills would be greater in Antarctica than elsewhere because the low temperatures retard the growth of biological organisms that reduce crude oil to environmentally harmless components.

Some people have devised ingenious schemes for towing Antarctic icebergs north to warm, dry lands as a cheap source of fresh water. But many scientists and engineers believe that an iceberg, even if protected by the best possible means, would break and melt before it got to the place where it would be used.

Commercial tourist visits to Antarctica began in the 1950s. Between 1958 and 1980 an estimated 16,640 passengers on 80 ship cruises visited places along the Antarctic Peninsula and in the Ross Sea. Between 1977 and 1980 airliners from New Zealand and Australia carrying some 11,145 passengers made about 45 sightseeing flights over portions of the Antarctic continent.

### Political and International Relations

Because it has never had permanent human settlements, Antarctica has had an unusual political history. Seven nations have claimed pie-shaped sectors of territory centering on the South Pole. Three of the claimed sectors overlap on the Antarctic Peninsula. One sector is unclaimed. Most other nations do not recognize these claims. The United States policy, for example, is that the mere discovery of lands does not support a valid claim unless the discovery is followed by actual settlement. Also, like many other nations, the United States reserves all rights resulting from its explorations and discoveries.

This unsettled situation might have continued had it not been for a surge of scientific interest in Antarctica that developed in the middle 1950s. At that time scientists of 12 nations decided to make research in Antarctica the major portion of a large investigation, the International Geophysical Year. The 12 nations were Argentina, Australia, Belgium, Chile, France, Japan, New Zealand, Norway, South

Dave Thompson—U.S. Navy/National Science Foundation

*A geologist takes a sample of ice from the Ross Ice Shelf, the first step in determining the age of the ice in the area.*

Africa, the United Kingdom, the United States, and the Soviet Union. When this program was completed in 1958, these nations decided to continue their research programs in Antarctica.

Much of the research had been achieved through international cooperation, and the 12 nations carried their new, friendly ties from science into politics. They met in Washington, D.C., in 1959 to write the Antarctic Treaty. The treaty reserves the region for peaceful purposes, especially scientific research. It prohibits nuclear weapons and disposal of radioactive waste, and it does not allow military activities except to support science and other peaceful pursuits. The treaty does not recognize or dispute the territorial claims of any nation, but it also does not allow any new claims to be made. It allows members to inspect each others' installations, encourages the exchange of personnel, and requires each nation to report to the others on its plans and results.

The treaty does not include anything about sharing Antarctica's natural resources, but it does provide for meetings every other year to further its objectives. At these meetings the treaty nations have agreed on conservation plans and on responsible collection and sharing of resources. Other nations later joined the Antarctic Treaty, and by 1982 there were 26 that had signed it.

### Scientific Research

Every year about a dozen nations send scientists to Antarctica to do research. In the Antarctic summer about 2,500 people are in the region for this work. They operate research stations and camps; travel in airplanes, helicopters, and snowmobiles to the areas that they need to study; and operate ships for resupply and oceanic research. In winter fewer than 1,000 people remain to operate about 30 research stations scattered around the continent. The winter inhabitants are isolated for several months at a time because it is too cold for anyone to get to them, even in airplanes.

Biologists, geologists, oceanographers, physicists, astronomers, glaciologists, and meteorologists conduct experiments here that cannot be duplicated anywhere else. In the 1970s researchers began taking measurements of the protective ozone layer in the atmosphere over Antarctica. A seasonal hole (thinning) was reported over the region in 1985. By the 1990s the ozone depletion had reached alarming proportions and the effects had spread beyond Antarctica.

**Exploration and History**

The first expedition to come close to Antarctica took place from 1772 through 1775. The English navigator James Cook sailed around the continent and came within 100 miles (160 kilometers) of it. Land was seen in about 1820, when British and United States seal hunters and a Russian exploring expedition reached the Antarctic Peninsula. In the Antarctic summer of 1839–40 a United States Navy expedition headed by Charles Wilkes mapped 1,500 miles (2,400 kilometers) along the coast of East Antarctica. The next summer James Clark Ross of Great Britain sailed into the Ross Sea, traveling as far south as a ship can go. The first recorded landing on Antarctica was on Cape Adare in 1895, and the first group to spend a winter on the continent did so at Cape Adare during the period from March 1898 to March 1899.

The struggle inland and toward the geographic South Pole began with the first expedition by Robert F. Scott of Great Britain in 1901–04. But the first person to reach the pole was Roald Amundsen of Norway on Dec. 14, 1911. On another Antarctic expedition Scott arrived at the pole just a month later; he died on March 29, 1912, trying to return to the coast.

These early expeditions relied on sail power, dog power, and human power for their transportation. The mechanical age arrived on Nov. 26, 1928, when George Hubert Wilkins, leading an American expedition, made an airplane flight from Deception Island. On Nov. 29, 1929, Richard E. Byrd of the United States flew a three-motor Ford plane over the South Pole. Byrd also explored parts of Antarctica by air and on the surface in 1933–35 and 1939–41 and commanded the largest single expedition ever made to Antarctica—the United States Navy's Operation High Jump in 1946–47. Thirteen ships, many airplanes and helicopters, and thousands of men made surveys almost all the way around the continent. In 1990 a six-man international expedition led by an American named Will Steger completed a 221-day trek across Antarctica from west to east using dogsleds. At more than 3,700 miles (6,000 kilometers), it was the longest dogsled trek, as well as the first unmechanized passage through the South Pole. The team members were from the United States, the Soviet Union, France, China, Japan, and Great Britain.

The International Geophysical Year (IGY), 1957–58, was a major scientific effort that established 50 year-round stations, including one at the geographic South Pole and one at the south geomagnetic pole. In 1988 the IGY nations that had signed the Antarctic Treaty agreed on a convention to permit strictly controlled mining in Antarctica—probably by the end of the 20th century. There are no known mineral deposits of value, however, and the harsh climate does not encourage offshore oil exploration. Both the Antarctic Treaty and the new convention avoided the issue of sovereignty, claimed by seven nations over various parts of the region. (*See also* Polar Exploration.)

**BIBLIOGRAPHY FOR ANTARCTICA**

**Byrd, Richard.** Discovery (Columbia Univ. Press, 1991).
**Cook, Grahame, ed.** The Future of Antarctica (St. Martin's, 1991).
**Flaherty, Leo.** Roald Amundsen and the Quest for the South Pole (Chelsea House, 1992).
**Hackwell, W.J.** Desert of Ice (Scribner, 1991).
**May, John.** The Greenpeace Book of Antarctica: A New View of the Seventh Continent (Doubleday, 1989).
**Pringle, L.P.** Antarctica: Our Last Unspoiled Continent (Simon & Schuster, 1992).
**Steger, Will, and Bowermaster, Jon.** Crossing Antarctica (Knopf, 1992).
**Stewart, John.** Antarctica: An Encyclopedia, 2 vols. (McFarland, 1990).

**ANTEATER.** Members of the order of animals called Edentata (meaning "toothless"), anteaters are insect-eating animals of the family Myrmecophagidae. They live in tropical grasslands and forests from southern Mexico to northern Argentina and Paraguay. They are densely furred, long-tailed animals with long skulls. Their mouth openings are quite small, and their tongues are long and wormlike. Anteaters feed mainly on ants and termites. They use the long, sharp, curved claws on their forefeet to tear open the insects' nests. Then they insert their long, sticky tongues into the nests to get the insects out.

The largest of these animals is the giant anteater (*Myrmecophaga tridactyla*). It grows to about 4 feet (1.2 meters) in length and weighs about 55 pounds (25 kilograms). It lives on the ground and feeds during the day. The lesser anteater (genus *Tamandua*) and the two-toed, or silky, anteater (*Cyclopes didactylus*) live primarily in trees and feed during the night. Relatives of the anteater include the aardvark, the sloth, the armadillo, the numbat (or banded anteater), the pangolin (or scaly anteater), and the echidna (or spiny anteater). (*See also* Aardvark; Armadillo; Sloth.)

| The Continents Compared | | |
|---|---|---|
| **Region** | **Area** | |
| | **(sq mi)** | **(sq km)** |
| Africa | 11,667,000 | 30,218,000 |
| Antarctica | 5,500,000 | 14,245,000 |
| Asia | 17,236,000 | 44,642,000 |
| Europe | 4,056,000* | 10,505,000* |
| North America | 9,355,000 | 24,230,000 |
| Oceania | 3,284,000 | 8,506,000 |
| South America | 6,878,000 | 17,814,000 |
| World | 57,976,000 | 150,157,000† |

*Includes Russia.
†Details do not add to total given because of rounding.

**ANTELOPE.** The term "antelope" is zoologically somewhat imprecise. It refers to a variety of animals with similar characteristics but belonging to different families. The only true antelope is the North American antelope, also called the pronghorn or prongbuck. It belongs to the family Antilocapridae. The other antelopes belong to the family Bovidae, which also includes cattle, sheep, goats, and oxen. Of the Bovidae, there are about 50 kinds of animals considered antelopes, such as the gazelle, the impala, and the gnu. Most of these antelopes are native to Africa. Along with general similarities in appearance, all antelopes are browsing and grazing animals.

## Description

Antelopes of both families are noted for their beauty, grace, and speed in running. Most are distinguished by upswept, back-curving horns. Their coats of hair are usually golden, reddish tan, or grey, often with white beneath and on the face and rump. Some are strikingly marked. The bongo is red-orange with 12 thin white stripes down its side. The sable antelope is, as its name suggests, a rich, deep brown and black. The pronghorn is reddish brown with white underneath, two white bands on the throat, and a short, dark-brown mane. It can raise the hair on a round white patch on its rump to produce a vivid flash of white. It apparently does this as a signal to warn other animals of danger.

Antelopes have moderately developed brains and acute senses of smell and hearing. These, along with their unusual agility and speed, allow them to detect any lurking danger quickly and leap to safety.

Most antelopes are the size of goats and deer. The largest and tallest is the stately giant eland of Africa, a sturdily built animal standing about 69 inches (175 centimeters) tall at the shoulders and weighing about 1,764 pounds (800 kilograms). The smallest is the dainty royal, also of Africa, standing about 10 inches (25 centimeters) tall at the shoulders and weighing only about 6 pounds (2.7 kilograms). The pronghorn is medium-sized, with a shoulder height of about 35 inches (90 centimeters).

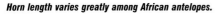

*Horn length varies greatly among African antelopes.*

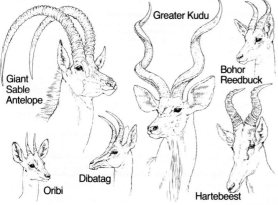

Giant Sable Antelope

Greater Kudu

Bohor Reedbuck

Oribi

Dibatag

Hartebeest

Drawing by R. Keane

Horns take many shapes and sizes among antelopes of the Bovidae family. The royal has spikes only one inch (2.5 centimeters) long; the giant sable antelope has imposing arcs, 63 inches (160 centimeters) long; the kudu has gracefully twisting spirals; the impala has long, elegant, lyre-shaped horns. None of the antelopes of the Bovidae family has branched horns, but the pronghorn has horns that branch from an erect stem into two prongs, the longer prong curving backwards and the shorter jutting forward. In some species, including the pronghorn, both the buck (male) and the doe (female) have horns. The four-horned antelope of India has two pairs of horns, one on its forehead and a larger pair on top of its head.

Antelope horns consist of a core of bone, an extension of the bone of the forehead, covered by a horny sheath. Antelopes of the Bovidae family never shed their horns, but the pronghorn sheds the horny sheath each year after the breeding season when a new sheath develops under the old one.

### Living Habits

Antelopes are herbivores—that is, they feed on grass and other plants. Since plants vary with the seasons, antelopes depend upon a succession of grasses, foliage, and other vegetation, and may eat a great variety. They have large, mobile tongues that they thrust forward to graze or browse. They are selective and often prefer similar parts of different plants rather than all of the same plant. Antelopes are ruminants (animals that chew the cud). They swallow their food and store it in the rumen, the first chamber of their stomachs; they later regurgitate it for chewing at leisure. Compared to carnivores (meat-eating animals), antelopes have larger stomachs and longer intestines because plants are somewhat more difficult to digest than meat.

The pronghorn can run 43 miles (70 kilometers) per hour and leap 20 feet (6 meters). Thomson's gazelle can run 50 miles (80 kilometers) per hour. The impala, noted for its great springing leaps, can jump to a height of $7\frac{9}{10}$ feet (2.4 meters) and cover 33 feet (10 meters) in a bound. The duiker is noted for quick, zigzag leaps and frenetic plunges into dense underbrush. In fast running, galloping, and bounding, antelopes raise their two front legs, one immediately after the other, then their two back legs, which give the animals their main propulsive thrust. In walking, they take a more stable position on diagonally opposite legs and move them in the order: left front, right rear; right front, left rear.

Antelopes are related to deer, camels, giraffes, and pigs, all of which belong to the order Artiodactyla, the even-toed ungulates (mammals that walk and run on their hoofs). Antelopes lost their "thumbs" and "big toes" at an early stage of evolution. They stand on the tips of their two center toes, which developed the large toenails that thickened and became hoofs (the so-called cloven, or split hoof, which is two toenails close together). The antelope's two outer toes became nonfunctional.

In this table, the heights of the antelopes are measured from the shoulder. The heights are averages and not extremes. This table represents a selection of some species, and is not intended to be inclusive.

**Habitat Key**

 Desert      Steppe

 Grassland      Scrub

 Savanna     Forest

**Pronghorn**
(*Antilocapra americana*)

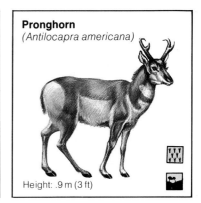

Height: .9 m (3 ft)

**Impala**
(*Aepyceros melampus*)

Height: .9 m (3 ft)

**South African Hartebeest**
(*Alcelaphus caama*)

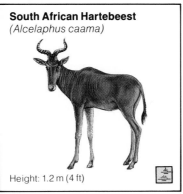

Height: 1.2 m (4 ft)

**Nilgai**
(*Boselaphus tragocamelus*)

Height: 1.5 m (5 ft)

**Blue Wildebeest**
(*Connochaetes taurinus*)

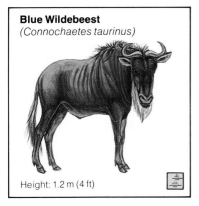

Height: 1.2 m (4 ft)

**Grant's Gazelle**
(*Gazella granti*)

Height: .9 m (3 ft)

**Waterbuck**
(*Kobus ellipsiprymnus*)

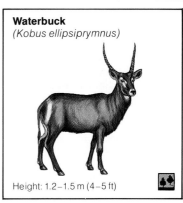

Height: 1.2–1.5 m (4–5 ft)

**Gemsbok**
(*Oryx gazella*)

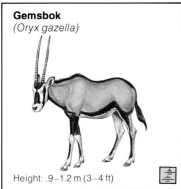

Height: .9–1.2 m (3–4 ft)

**Oribi**
(*Ourebia ourebi*)

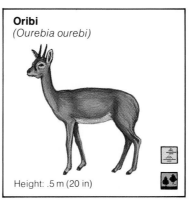

Height: .5 m (20 in)

**Greater Kudu**
(*Tragelaphus strepsiceros*)

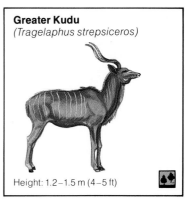

Height: 1.2–1.5 m (4–5 ft)

The antelope's great freedom of motion in running and leaping is partly due to an unusual anklebone. One of the bones between the leg and the foot, the astragalus, is pulley-shaped at both the upper and lower ends in Artiodactyls, in contrast to other mammals in which the bone is flat at the lower end and pulley-shaped only at the top.

### Native Habitats

Fossil records indicate that antelopes of the family Bovidae lived on the Eurasian continent and in Africa as long as 65 million years ago. Some still roam the central and southwest regions of Eurasia, but in the north temperate zones the winters are too severe to permit continued feeding on grasslands. The greatest number and variety of antelopes are now found in the grassy savannas, or plains, of Africa.

The American pronghorn once roamed the open plains and semi-deserts from Alberta, Canada, to northern Mexico. It lived alone or in small bands in summer and in large herds during the winter. Since the settlement of the Western United States, the number of pronghorns has been considerably reduced by hunting, while many of their grazing areas have been pushed back by civilization.

Antelopes make no permanent shelter, but roam about on a particular range where they make their home. In their grazing habits they follow a cyclic route that may cover more than 200 square miles (500 square kilometers) in a year. They generally travel in herds numbering several hundred antelopes. Some of them will travel with one herd in the summer and another during the winter. A few may seek solitude in marshes, along riverbanks, in dense tropical forests, on cliffs, and even in desert regions. These are usually old, infirm animals, bucks with no mates, or does about to give birth. A doe will eventually return to the herd once her young can follow her.

### Life Cycle

In the mating season male antelopes hold territories on which they attempt to detain a passing doe. They mark these territories as their own by rubbing their scent glands against plants and trees. Many species have scent glands in front of the eye, while others have them behind the horns, on the jaws, or on the tail, back, or feet. The American pronghorn and the African blackbuck, gazelle, and oribi are especially well endowed with such glands.

To defend his territory a buck will signal his intention to fight. Two males will lock horns and wrestle in a seemingly ritualized style that will not do either animal great harm. The African eland, however, has been known to fight to the death. Some antelopes gather harems of mates in the summer. Others have only one mate.

The gestation period, the time the doe carries her young before it is born, varies from four to eight months with the size of the species. In temperate climates birth takes place in spring or early summer. In tropical areas most births take place late in the rainy season or shortly afterward. Does normally have one young at each birth, but the pronghorn and the four-horned antelope frequently have twins. Newborn animals are well-developed and may weigh one tenth as much as the mother.

### Enemies

Tigers, lions, leopards, and other predators have a limited effect on a population of healthy and alert adult antelopes. It is the youngest and oldest that normally fall prey. While one animal in a herd may be killed, the others will escape.

Disease is also a marginal danger, although undernourished antelopes are susceptible to parasites. The African tse-tse fly carries disease-causing parasites, but the animals normally rid themselves of these pests by stamping their feet, twitching their skin, or shaking their heads and bodies.

The most dangerous threat to the existence of the antelope is the big-game hunter. Prime targets are the larger animals: eland, roan, greater kudu, waterbuck, nilgai (blue bull of India), mountain nyala, and bongo. Some species are almost extinct: the Arabian oryx, giant sable, blesbok, and bontebok. Others, formerly in danger of extinction, have been able to increase their numbers in preserves.

**ANTHONY, Susan B.** (1820–1906). For more than half a century Susan B. Anthony fought for women's right to vote. Many people made fun of her. Some insulted her. Nevertheless, she traveled from county to county in New York and other states making speeches and organizing clubs for women's rights. She pleaded her cause with every president from Abraham Lincoln to Theodore Roosevelt.

Susan B. Anthony was also active in the temperance movement and an ardent abolitionist. When blacks were given the right to vote by the 15th Amendment, she launched a campaign to extend the same right to women. In 1869 she helped to organize the National Woman Suffrage Association.

In 1890 this group joined the American Woman Suffrage Association to form the National American Woman Suffrage Association. She became the president of the new association in 1892 and held this office until she was 80 years old. In 1872 she voted in the presidential election to test her status as a citizen. For this act she was tried and fined $100, but she refused to pay the fine, declaring that "taxation without representation is tyranny."

At the time when Anthony began her work, women had few legal rights. Today, largely through her efforts and those of her associates, women have opportunities for higher education, the privilege of working at almost any occupation, the right to control their own property and children, the right to hold public office, and the right to vote. She lived to see many of these reforms put into effect. After she died in 1906, both major political parties endorsed women's suffrage. In 1920 the suffrage amendment to the Constitution was ratified.

**ANTHROPOLOGY.** The science that studies human cultures is called anthropology. It is a discipline that deals with the origins and development of human societies and the differences between them. The word anthropology is derived from two Greek words: *anthropos* meaning "man" or "human"; and *logos,* meaning "thought" or "reason." Anthropologists attempt, by investigating the whole range of human development and behavior, to achieve a total description of cultural and social phenomena.

### The Spheres of Anthropology

The science of anthropology is divided into two major disciplines, physical anthropology and cultural anthropology. Each of these is basically an independent science, although specialists in one field frequently consult and cooperate with scholars in the other. Physical anthropology is generally classified as a natural science, while cultural anthropology is considered a social science.

Physical anthropology is concerned with the biological aspects of human beings. In trying to learn about racial differences, human origins, and evolution, the physical anthropologist studies fossil remains and observes the behavior of other primates. Primates are an order of mammals that includes human beings as well as apes and monkeys.

Cultural anthropology deals primarily with the growth of human societies in the world. It is a study of group behavior, the origins of religion, social customs and conventions, technical developments, and family relationships. A major subfield of cultural anthropology is linguistics, the study of the history and structure of language. Linguistics is a valuable tool of the anthropologist because it enables him to observe a people's system of communication and to learn the ideas by which they view the world. It also enables

him to collect an oral history of the group being studied. Oral histories are constructed from a society's poems, songs, myths, proverbs, and folk tales.

Physical and cultural anthropology are connected by two other fields of study: archaeology and applied anthropology. In excavations, archaeologists find the remains of ancient buildings, tools, pottery, and other artifacts by which a past culture may be dated and described (*see* Archaeology).

Applied anthropology makes use of the research done by physical and cultural anthropologists in order to help governments and other institutions form and implement policies for specific population groups. It may, for instance, aid governments of underdeveloped countries in showing backward peoples how to cope with the complexities of 20th-century civilization. It may also be used by governments in the formulation of social, educational, and economic policies for ethnic minorities within their borders. The work of applied anthropology is often done by specialists in the fields of economics, sociology, history, and psychology.

Because anthropology is such a wide-ranging discipline, investigating as it does every facet of all human societies, it must draw upon research done in other disciplines to form its conclusions. Among these disciplines are history, geography, geology, biology, anatomy, genetics, economics, psychology, and sociology, along with the highly specialized tasks of linguistics and archaeology already mentioned.

### The Problem of Terminology

Different terms are used to describe the fields of anthropology in the United States and Europe. While in the United States the term anthropology is used to name the whole subject, in Europe the name ethnology is applied. (Ethnology is defined as the science that studies the many races of mankind—

*Linguist Francesca Merlin studies a little-known highland New Guinea language.*

Irven De Vore—Anthro Photo

their beginnings, characteristics, differences, and distribution.) What is called "cultural anthropology" in the United States is also termed "ethnology" in European countries. The term physical anthropology is used in both parts of the world.

The subareas of cultural anthropology in the United States are three: historical anthropology (or ethnology), prehistory (or prehistoric archaeology), and linguistics (or linguistic anthropology). In Europe the subareas are: ethnology (in the strictest sense as the historical description and comparison of races), prehistory (or prehistoric ethnology), and linguistics (or linguistic ethnology).

## PHYSICAL ANTHROPOLOGY

The science of physical anthropology has focused to a great extent on determining the place of human beings in nature, on comparing them with lower primates, and on interpreting the physical differences among the races. In pursuing its goals, physical anthropology has used the sciences of comparative anatomy, evolution, and genetics.

### Early Investigations

Modern physical anthropology began taking shape in the first half of the 19th century when there arose a great interest in studying the origins of mankind, the biological relationships between the races, and the changeability of man as an animal species. In working out their theories, anthropologists devised a framework called the "great chain of being." This was a model of nature that arranged all species in a hierarchical order, from the lowest to the highest. The point of this notion was to discover if there was steady progression from lower life forms up through the lower primates (apes and monkeys) to human beings. Since no continuous progression to human beings could at first be found, scientists theorized that there must be a "missing link" between the lower primates and man.

In order to classify and distinguish between the apes, monkeys, and races of man, the anthropologists have used comparative anatomy, measuring brain size, cranial capacity, arm and leg length, and height. They have also noted the color of skin and personality traits as clues for putting animals and races in their proper order.

The work of most 19th-century anthropologists was hampered by ignorance in a number of areas, including an ignorance that has since been dissipated by geology, astronomy, archaeology, and the biological sciences. The age of the Earth was unknown. Many

*An anthropologist working in the field demonstrates the preparation of groundnut milk in Karnataka, India. She has attracted a group of onlookers, some of whom seem to enjoy the operation as much as an entertainment as they do as a lesson. Anthropologists must often travel the world in order to do their work.*

Mimi Nichter—Anthro-Photo

Sara Hrdy—Anthro-Photo

*Daniel Hrdy, a physical anthropologist, weighs langurs as part of a general biological survey of a langur group that lives near Mount Abu in India.*

people, in accordance with the religious teachings of the time, believed it to be about 6,000 years old. Religious teaching also suggested that all species were created at one time, thus precluding any evolution from lower to higher forms. The first archaeological discoveries indicating the very ancient origins of mankind were not made until the middle of the 19th century, and then many anthropologists ignored or disputed them. The first major breakthrough for anthropologists came in the natural sciences when in 1859 Charles Darwin published his 'Origin of Species by Means of Natural Selection' (*see* Darwin, Charles).

**Evolution,** as first described by Darwin, was a crucial concept for anthropologists in reaching an understanding of the origins of man. The essential impact for the evolution of man was the idea of natural selection, although many decades passed before its implications were appreciated or employed. Darwin showed that nature selects those forms that are better adapted to a particular geographic zone and way of life. The notion of adaptation implied that organisms changed slowly over millions of years. It also disqualified any need for a "missing link," although this theory persisted well into the 20th century. The missing link had not been considered to be a product of evolutionary development but a creature placed between man and ape in the natural order of things (*see* Evolution).

## Modern Physical Anthropology

A major shift in the approach to physical anthropology occurred at the beginning of the 20th century with the discovery of genetic principles and of the ABO blood groups. Genetics was actually rediscovered. In 1865 an Austrian monk, Gregor J. Mendel, had formulated the first laws of heredity and laid the foundation of the science of genetics. His findings were almost entirely ignored at the time. In 1900 three other European botanists arrived at the same conclusions that Mendel had published 35 years earlier, and in researching the literature on the subject they found his work.

Genes are the units within sex cells such as the sperm and egg that transmit specific hereditary traits from one generation to the next. The study of inherited traits has become essential to anthropologists in seeking to understand human variations and differences between races. Genetics has modified the theory of progressive evolution somewhat, because it has been shown by experiment that there may be genetic reversals—that is, reversions back to traits and characteristics thought to be discarded in the hereditary process.

Early in the 20th century another Austrian, a physician named Karl Landsteiner, discovered the blood groups, or types, known as O, A, B, and AB. This led anthropologists to investigate blood differences among the races. They have noted that certain races and subraces have particular distributions of one or another blood type. This has enabled scientists to categorize the races and, since blood types are genetically determined, to trace early migration patterns.

**Dating** is crucial for physical anthropologists, as well as for geologists and archaeologists. It is a method that allows them to determine how old something is— whether it be a layer of rocks, a human-like fossil, or a collection of pottery.

There are two kinds of dating: relative and absolute. Relative dating shows the order in which events occurred but does not tell exactly when they occurred. Methods of absolute dating indicate with a fair degree of precision how old something is. Of the two types of dating, the determination of relative age relationships came into use first. Absolute dating depends upon technological advances that have been made in the 20th century.

Geologists and archaeologists have long used relative dating methods to determine the approximate age of the Earth and of fossils and artifacts. Geologists examine the many strata of the Earth's crust to determine the intervals of time from one layer of rock to another. Archaeologists also use the principle of layering to verify the sequence of human cultures. (For archaeological dating systems, *see* Archaeology, "Chronological Analysis.")

Another method of determining relative age is fluorine dating. It is based upon the principle that fossil bones absorb the element fluorine from the soil in which they are buried. The longer they are buried, the more fluorine the bones will contain. Determining the amount of fluorine is often not a practical means of relative dating because it requires many samples from an immediate area.

Absolute, or chronometric, dating attempts to pinpoint when a given rock, fossil, or other object reached its present condition. The basic method for determining absolute age is called radiometry—measuring the rate of radioactive decay of an element. This can be done with a high degree of accuracy, though no method is infallible without a great deal of corroborative testing.

One of the types of absolute dating that has been used by physical anthropologists is potassium-argon dating. It is a method of determining the time of origin of igneous rocks and sediments—and thereby the fossils found within them—by measuring the amount of decay of potassium-40, a radioactive isotope of the element potassium, into the stable isotope argon-40, one of the rare gases. The half-life of potassium-40, which is the time it will take one half of any quantity of it to decay into potassium, is 1,265,000,000 years. Potassium-argon dating has been used to measure the ages of a wide variety of objects up to 4,500,000,000 years old. The accuracy of potassium-argon dating declines, however, for dates more recent than about a million years ago. Such dating techniques applied to the remains and surroundings of ancient human beings have constantly pushed back the estimated age of mankind. By the end of the 20th century, the origins of humankind and its ancestors were believed to date back to at least 3 million years ago. This is based on the dating of a number of remarkable discoveries of fossil remains made in the Great Rift Valley of Africa. (For more information on the findings of physical anthropologists *see* Human Origins.)

## CULTURAL ANTHROPOLOGY

Cultural anthropologists are concerned with the origin and development of human societies in all their complexity. Cultural anthropology attempts to devise theories to explain the origin of aspects of various human cultures, each of which has unique features as well as characteristics in common with other societies.

Cultural anthropology has given rise to various schools of thought since the 19th century. Among them are evolutionism, historical particularism, diffusionism, functionalism, structuralism, and neo-evolutionism.

### Evolutionism

The theory of biological evolution was first formally presented by Charles Darwin in 'On the Origin of Species' in 1859. Darwin argued that man is an animal and has many of the same instincts and needs as do other social animals. Darwin stated that successful species adapted to changing environments, and that through a process he called natural selection only the most adaptable individuals or groups survive.

Nineteenth-century anthropologists applied these theories to their cultural studies. They believed that all societies develop in a universal sequence, and that all humans possess the same thought processes and basic mental structure. According to Lewis H. Morgan of the United States, the three basic stages that all societies pass through are savagery, barbarism, and civilization. Each of these stages, he believed, is characterized by specific technological developments.

A related 19th-century approach that applied the theory of evolution to society focused on different stages of religious thought. Edward Burnett Tylor, an English anthropologist, argued that these stages are animism, or a belief in the soul

*The United States–born Canadian anthropologist Richard B. Lee interviews !Kung San (Bushmen) in southern Africa's Kalahari Desert. He is aided by Bantu interpreters (wearing shirts).*

Irven De Vore—Anthro-Photo

(Right) © The Cleveland Museum of Natural History; (others) The Bettmann Archive

*Four leaders in the field of anthropology are (from left to right): Johann Friedrich Blumenbach (1752–1840), German founder of physical anthropology; Franz Boas (1858–1942), American founder of relativistic, culture-centered anthropology; Ruth Benedict (1887–1948), American cultural anthropologist; and Donald C. Johanson (born 1943), American physical anthropologist who has proposed a revision of early human evolution as a result of his work in Ethiopia and Tanzania.*

and in spirits; polytheism, or a belief in more than one god; and monotheism, or a belief in one god. Tylor also suggested that some groups could skip particular stages in their cultural development by learning from other cultures.

Another kind of cultural evolution was proposed by Karl Marx and Friedrich Engels. This theory defined a society by its method of producing goods and services and presented a developmental sequence that included necessary social conflict (*see* Marx).

Cultural evolutionists analyzed aspects of modern cultures that seemed to have survived from previous stages. They developed a number of points of view that are considered valuable contributions to anthropology. Among these are the concept of culture itself, the methods of comparing different cultures, and concepts for the study of social organizations.

Two major works in the field of anthropology, Sir James Frazer's 'Golden Bough' (1890) and Ernest Crawley's 'Mystic Rose' (1902), contained vast amounts of research on primitive and traditional societies and tended to reinforce the theories of evolutionists. Both were encyclopedic collections of customs, religious and magical practices, and much other curious data. Evolutionists saw evidence of a sequence of magical, religious, and scientific thought that seemed to be part of the development of every human society.

### Historical Particularism

By the beginning of the 20th century, anthropologists in Great Britain, Germany, and the United States were questioning the belief that all societies developed in much the same way. They suggested that each culture was unique because each had its separate geography, history, creativity, and degree of contact with its neighbors.

One of the first to reject evolutionism was a German-born American anthropologist, Franz Boas. Boas emphasized the importance of fieldwork and observation. Fieldwork involves seeking information about a particular group's behavior by gathering data and recording observable behaviors in that group's natural environment.

Boas believed that every aspect of a culture should be recorded and that the anthropologist studying a native culture should not only learn its language but should attempt to think like its people. Boas emphasized the importance of collecting information that described the individuals and their interrelationships in a particular culture. Such information was gathered through the recording of life histories and folklore, and then connecting these details with archaeological and historical data. Boas also believed that similarities among different cultures were the result of similar outside influences rather than to the similarity in thought processes or to any universal laws of development. He stressed the importance of analyzing a culture within its historical context.

Boas is known as the founder of the culture history school of anthropology, which dominated American cultural anthropology for much of the 20th century. Anthropologists who followed Boas' theories included Ruth Benedict, Alfred L. Kroeber, Margaret Mead, and Edward Sapir. (*See also* Boas; Mead.)

### Diffusionism

A group of Austro-German anthropologists, led by Fritz Graebner and Wilhelm Schmidt, rejected 19th-century evolutionism in favor of a belief that a few core cultures influenced all later societies. This diffusion, or spreading, of culture traits was believed to be the basic force in human development. By analyzing the cultural behaviors and aspects of a society, a diffusionist believed that he could determine from which core culture that society derived its civilization. Because the diffusionists called the original ancient civilizations "kulturkreise" (or "cultural clusters") they were also known as the kulturkreise school of anthropology.

A British group of diffusionists, led by Grafton Elliot Smith and William J. Perry, argued that only one civilization was responsible for all cultural development. They believed that the civilization fitting their theory was ancient Egypt and that ideas such as irrigation, kingship, and navigation were spread from the ancient civilization along the Nile throughout the world by voyagers who were seeking precious jewels. This theory was called the Manchester, or heliocentric (sun-centered) school of thought. The metaphor of the sun suggested that all cultures radiated from but a single source.

Although the diffusionist approach to anthropology was dominant in early 20th-century Europe, it was thought an inadequate point of view by later scholars. They claimed that it disregarded important geographical and psychological differences in culture.

### Functionalism

After World War I a school of thought developed that rejected historical approaches to the study of cultures. A leading proponent of this theory was Bronislaw Malinowski, a Polish-born British anthropologist. He believed that to understand a culture one must perceive its totality and the interrelationship of all its parts, much as if culture were a machine and the individual traits the cogs and gears that made it operate. Culture was to be interpreted at one point in time. The age of the elements composing it were of no importance. What mattered was the function the traits performed at any given time. Functionalism provided the field of anthropology with valuable contributions in the analysis of family, kinship roles, rites of passage, and political organization.

Closely related to functionalism was a theory proposed by the American anthropologist Ruth Benedict in the 1930s (see Benedict). She believed that each culture had, over the ages, given its members a unique orientation toward reality that determined how members saw and processed information from their environment. She believed it was necessary to study such mental or psychological conditioning to see how it functioned in a given society.

### Structuralism

Another influential 20th-century school of thought is structuralism, which is similar in many ways to functionalism. Its leading early proponents were the British anthropologist A.R. Radcliffe-Brown and Claude Lévi-Strauss, a Belgian-born French

ethnologist. They asserted that by taking all of the many aspects of a society into consideration one could arrive at a clear structural description, or model, of it— a model that the members of the society themselves are not fully aware of.

Radcliffe-Brown stated that all aspects of a society exist in order to maintain the social structure of the society. Lévi-Strauss was convinced that a culture, like a language, has a structure that can be similarly analyzed. The model that the anthropologist constructs is correct when it can account for all the observed data on a given society. One of the difficulties with structuralism is that it presumes a static condition and may find difficulty in taking historical changes into account.

### Neo-evolutionism

Since World War II there has been a revival of interest in evolutionism. The American anthropologist Julian Steward believed that similar stages of development are apparent in the cultural histories of various civilizations. His theory, termed "multilinear evolution" or "specific evolution," states that such similarities develop quite independently. A comparison of the sequences of change in sets of cultures should reveal regular patterns of change that are common to all of them.

Another American, Leslie White (1900–75), viewed culture as an inevitable natural process that develops from mankind's increasing ability to harness energy and use it effectively. The social and psychological makeup of a culture is therefore determined by its technology. From the work of Steward and White has come the term cultural ecology. This school of thought states that because a culture tends to reflect efficient use of the environment, similar environments will inevitably produce cultures that are similar.

### HISTORY

At least since the earliest times of the Greeks the study of mankind has been a major intellectual endeavor, a subject for speculation and for investigation. Philosophers, such as Plato and Aristotle, speculated on what it meant to be human and on what mankind's place was in nature and in the universe. Herodotus, on the other hand, was an investigator. In Western society he is considered the first historian and the first ethnologist.

In the 5th century BC he traveled over much of the known world, to Libya, Egypt, Syria, Mesopotamia, Asia Minor, Thrace, Macedonia, Scythia, and eastward into what is now southern Ukraine and Russia. The observations he made on his travels were published in his 'History'. Along with his narrative of the Persian Wars and other events involving the Greek city-states, he described the customs, social habits, religions, and political structures of many of the peoples he visited on his travels.

There were other ancient precursors of anthropology. In the 1st century BC the Roman philosopher Lucretius, in his 'On Nature', discoursed on the origin of religion, the arts, language, the division of labor, and the differences between the sexes. In AD 98 the Roman historian Tacitus wrote his 'Germania', an anthropological study of the Germanic tribes to the north of the Roman Empire.

In the Middle Ages the Christian religion dominated the thought of Europe. Mankind was not viewed as existing for itself. Mankind's status was that of crea-

tures of God whose ideal behavior reflected religious values. During the period called the Renaissance a change in attitude took place. Poets, painters, and scholars gained a renewed interest in the classical writings of Greece and Rome. They rediscovered the notion of studying mankind for its own sake.

It was during the 16th century that the term anthropology was coined and used by philosophy teachers in German universities. Anthropology was understood to be the systematic study of man as a physical and moral being. From the 16th to the beginning of the 19th century anthropology remained within the province of philosophy. Among the many writers who reflected upon the nature of man were the Frenchmen Michel de Montaigne, Jean Bodin, René Descartes, and Blaise Pascal; the Dutch philosopher Baruch Spinoza; the English philosophers John Locke and David Hume; and the German philosopher Immanuel Kant. (*See also* Bodin; Descartes; Hume; Kant; Locke; Montaigne; Pascal; Spinoza.)

With the work of the French naturalist Georges Buffon the divergence of anthropological studies from philosophy began to take place. He devoted two volumes of his 44-volume 'Histoire naturelle' (Natural History), published in the years 1749 to 1804, to man as a zoological species. Since that time anthropology has continued to diversify its approaches. Scholars have also maintained the necessity of using data from other sciences in their work.

Physical anthropology developed as a separate science under the influence of Johann F. Blumenbach in Germany. He was the first scholar to divide humanity into races. By the middle of the 19th century geologists and archaeologists had thrown a good deal of light on the age of the Earth and of human societies. For the first time, anthropologists saw the possibility of tracing mankind's origins into the very remote past.

---

## Some Major Anthropologists

*Some prominent persons are not included below because they are covered in the main text of this article or in other articles in Compton's Encyclopedia (see Fact-Index).*

**Blumenbach, Johann Friedrich** (1752–1840). The founder of physical anthropology. Born in Gotha, Germany, on May 11, 1752. Professor of medicine at Göttingen University. The first scholar to show the value of comparative anatomy in the study of man's history. Divided mankind into five families, or races. Died on Jan. 22, 1840.

**Johanson, Donald C.** (born 1943). A leading American anthropologist. Born in Chicago on June 28, 1943. Curator of physical anthropology at the Cleveland Museum of Natural History. In Ethiopia in 1970s, he found the oldest fossils showing man's bipedal stature and locomotion.

**Kroeber, Alfred Louis** (1876–1960). One of the major American anthropologists in the first half of the 20th century. Born in Hoboken, N.J., on June 11, 1876. Earned his doctorate under Franz Boas at Columbia University in 1901. Author of one of the first general texts in anthropology (1923). His field investigations centered on the Indians of California. Died in Paris on Oct. 5, 1960.

**Mauss, Marcel** (1872–1950). French anthropologist and sociologist. Born in Épinal on May 10, 1872. A nephew and student of pioneer sociologist Émile Durkheim. Professor of primitive religion at the École Pratique des Hautes Études in Paris. A major influence in the field of ethnographic studies. Died in Paris on Feb. 10, 1950.

**Morgan, Lewis Henry** (1818–81). American ethnologist and pioneer in the study of kinship systems. Born near Aurora, N.Y., on Nov. 21, 1818. His major work, 'Systems of Consanguinity and Affinity of the Human Family' (1871), inaugurated the scientific study of kinship. Died in Rochester, N.Y., on Dec. 17, 1881.

**Radcliffe-Brown, Alfred Reginald** (1881–1955). British social anthropologist. Born on Jan. 17, 1881, in Birmingham. Educated at Trinity College, Cambridge. Did fieldwork in the Andaman Islands and in Western Australia. Taught at University of Sydney, the University of Chicago, and Oxford University. His major contribution was in systematizing social structures of simple societies. Died in London on Oct. 24, 1955.

**Sapir, Edward** (1884–1939). American linguist and anthropologist. Born in Lauenburg, Pomerania (now in Poland), on Jan. 26, 1884. Educated at Columbia University, where he earned his doctorate under Franz Boas. Taught at the University of Chicago and at Yale University. His most significant contributions were in the study of American Indian languages. Died in New Haven, Conn., on Feb. 4, 1939.

**Tylor, Edward Burnett** (1832–1917). English anthropologist credited with originating the scientific study of culture. Born in London on Oct. 2, 1832. Investigation of primitive societies led him to develop the theory of an evolutionary, progressive relationship between preliterate and literate, technologically advanced cultures. His major work was 'Primitive Culture' (1871). Died in Wellington in Somerset, on Jan. 2, 1917.

---

**BIBLIOGRAPHY FOR ANTHROPOLOGY**

**Alland, Alexander, Jr.** To Be Human (Random, 1981).
**Benedict, Ruth.** An Anthropologist at Work (Greenwood, 1977).
**Benedict, Ruth.** Patterns of Culture (Houghton, 1989).
**Boas, Franz.** Race, Language and Culture (Univ. of Chicago Press, 1988).
**Campbell, Bernard.** Humankind Emerging, 4th ed. (Scott Foresman, 1985).
**Coon, C.S. and others.** Races: A Study of the Problem of Race Formation in Man (Greenwood, 1981).
**Coon, C.S.** The Story of Man, 2nd rev. ed. (Knopf, 1962).
**Fisher, M.P.** Recent Revolutions in Anthropology (Watts, 1986).
**Foster, G.M. and others.** Medical Anthropology (Random, 1978).
**Gregor, A.S.** Life Styles: An Introduction to Cultural Anthropology (Scribner, 1978).
**Haviland, William.** Cultural Anthropology, 5th ed. (Holt, 1987).
**Johanson, Donald and Maitland, Edey.** Lucy: The Beginnings of Humankind (Warner, 1982).
**Jolly, Clifford, ed.** Early Hominids of Africa (St. Martin, 1978).
**Malinowski, Bronislaw.** Scientific Theory of Culture (Univ. of N.C. Press, 1944).
**Mead, Margaret.** Coming of Age in Samoa, reprint (Morrow, 1971).
**National Geographic Society.** Primitive Worlds: People Lost in Time (National Geographic, 1973).
**Steward, J.H.** Theory of Culture Change (Univ. of Ill. Press, 1972).
**White, L.A.** The Concept of Cultural Systems: A Key to Understanding Tribes and Nations (Columbia Univ. Press, 1975).

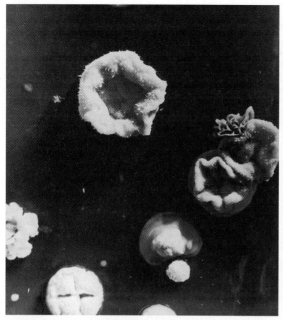 

*From such moldlike colonies (left) came the first broad-spectrum antibiotic. Dr. Benjamin M. Duggar (right) isolated the microorganism that produces chlortetracycline, or Aureomycin.*

**ANTIBIOTIC.** Certain medicinal substances have the power to destroy or check the growth of infectious organisms in the body. The organisms can be bacteria, viruses, fungi, or the minuscule animals called protozoa. A particular group of these agents is made up of drugs called antibiotics, from the Greek *anti* ("against") and *bios* ("life"). Some antibiotics are produced from living organisms such as bacteria, fungi, and molds. Others are wholly or in part synthetic—that is, produced artificially. Penicillin is perhaps the best known antibiotic. Its discovery and later development has enabled the medical profession to treat effectively many infectious diseases, including some that were once life-threatening.

### Antibiosis

The general relationship between an antibiotic and an infectious organism is one of antibiosis. This word refers to an association of two organisms in which one is harmed or killed by the other. The relationship between human beings and disease-causing germs is one of antibiosis. If a person is affected by germs, he is the injured organism; if the germ attack is repelled by the body's defenses, the germs are the injured organisms. When a person's defense system cannot control antibiosis in its own favor, antibiotics are used to tip the balance toward health.

### Homeostasis

The body's balance between health and illness is called homeostasis. This largely depends on the relationship of the body to the bacteria with which it lives. For example, bacteria are always present on human skin. When the skin is cut, the bacteria are able to get

inside the body and may cause infection. Usually the invading bacteria are destroyed by blood cells called phagocytes and by various actions of the immune system. When there are too many bacteria for the system to handle, or the infected person has a low resistance to infection, illness results and antibiotics are needed to help restore homeostasis.

### Action of Antibiotics

Antibiotics can be bacteriostatic (bacteria stopped from multiplying) or bactericidal (bacteria killed). To perform either of these functions, antibiotics must be brought into contact with the bacteria.

It is believed that antibiotics interfere with the surface of bacteria cells, causing a change in their ability to reproduce. Testing the action of an antibiotic in the laboratory shows how much exposure to the drug is necessary to halt reproduction or to kill the bacteria. Although a large amount of an antibiotic taken at one time might kill the bacteria causing an illness, such a dose usually would make the person suffer from illness caused by the drug. Therefore, antibiotics are given in a series of smaller amounts. This assures that the bacteria are either killed or reduced enough in numbers so that the body can repel them. When too little antibiotic is taken, bacteria can often develop methods to protect themselves against it. The next time the antibiotic is needed against these bacteria, it will not be effective.

### Administering Antibiotics

To work against infecting organisms, an antibiotic can be applied externally, such as to a cut on the skin's surface, or internally, reaching the bloodstream within the body. Antibiotics are made in several forms and given in different ways.

**Topical.** Topical application means "to a local area" such as on the skin, in the eyes, or on the mucous membrane. Antibiotics for topical use are available in the form of powders, ointments, or creams (*see* Antiseptic).

**Oral.** Tablets, liquids, and capsules are swallowed. The antibiotic is released in the small intestine to be absorbed into the bloodstream. Troches, or lozenges, are allowed to dissolve in the mouth, where the antibiotic is absorbed through the mucous membrane.

**Parenteral.** Applications outside the intestine are called parenteral. One form is an injection, which can be subcutaneous (under the skin), intramuscular (into a muscle), or intravenous (into a vein). Parenteral administration of an antibiotic is used when a physician requires a strong, quick concentration of the antibiotic in the bloodstream.

## Manufacture

**Natural.** At one time all antibiotics were made from living organisms. This process, known as biosynthesis, is still used in the manufacture of some antibiotics. It is actually the organisms that manufacture the antibiotic. The people involved merely provide favorable conditions for the organisms to do the work and then they collect the drug. For example, mold organisms are placed in a medium (a substance used for the growth of microorganisms) such as corn steep liquor to which milk sugar has been added. This forms a broth that is put into a tank, which is kept at a temperature of 25° C (77° F) and shaken for more than 100 hours. The mold organisms grow rapidly in this warm soup, producing penicillin as they do so. The penicillin is later extracted.

**Synthetic.** All penicillin types have an identical chemical nucleus called a ring. The chemical chain that is attached to the ring is different in each type. By changing the molecules of the chain, scientists devise drugs with potentially different effects on different organisms. Some of these drugs are useful in treating infections, some are not.

Pharmaceutical manufacturers now use computer-generated images of the rings and experiment with an endless variety of possible chains. Researchers have developed antibiotics with long half-lives (period of effectiveness), which allow taking the medication once in 24 hours instead of every few hours. The newer antibiotics are also more effective against a wider range of infections than were earlier drugs.

## Varieties

There are dozens of antibiotics. The following are in common use:

**Penicillins.** The various types of penicillins make up a large group of antibacterial antibiotics of which only those from benzyl penicillin are naturally produced from molds. Penicillin G and ampicillin are in this class. Another penicillin, called piperacillin, has been shown to be effective against 92 percent of infections without causing serious side effects. Penicillins are often given in combination with some of the following categories of drugs.

**Cephalosporins.** Similar to the penicillins, cephalosporins are often given when a sensitivity (allergic reaction) to the former is known or suspected in a patient. Cefotaxime sodium is a kind of cephalosporin that is very effective in combating deep infections such as those that occur in bones and those resulting from surgery.

**Aminoglycoside.** Aminoglycosides include streptomycin and neomycin. These drugs are used to treat tuberculosis, bubonic plague, and other infections. Because of potentially serious side effects, such as interference with hearing and their ability to make one sensitive to sunlight, these drugs are given with caution. (All antibiotics are given with care; caution implies more than usual possible negative consequences of drug administration.)

**Tetracyclines.** Tetracyclines are effective against pneumonia, typhus, and other bacteria-caused illness but can harm the function of the liver and kidneys. Tetracycline in a special gel base is used to treat many eye infections.

**Macrolides.** Macrolides are often used in patients who appear to be sensitive to penicillin. Erythromycin is the best known medicine in this group.

**Polypeptides.** The class of antibiotics called polypeptides is quite toxic (poisonous) and is used mostly on the surface of the skin (topically). Bacitracin is in this category.

## Sulfa Drugs

Sulfonamide was the first antimicrobial drug to be used. Sulfa drugs, which are made from chemicals, have largely the same effects as those of the later-developed penicillins. As sulfa drugs can have harmful effects on the kidneys—while being effective against kidney infections—they are always taken with large quantities of water to prevent the formation of drug crystals. Gantrisin is still among the most useful of these sulfa drugs.

## Other Antimicrobials

Other antimicrobials include furazolidone and tritethoprim. The first is used primarily in gastrointestinal infections; the latter, when combined with one of the sulfonamides, is effective in urinary and respiratory infections.

**Antifungal.** Antifungals combat illness caused by fungus such as candida. Fungus-caused infection requires long-term treatment. Drugs such as griseofulvin are often taken for six months. Most fungal infection occurs on the skin or the mucous membrane.

**Antiviral.** Very little is known about treating viral infections (the common cold is an example). A virus is thought to be the smallest infectious agent with the ability to replicate (reproduce) itself. Moreover, it seems able to mutate, or change, with great rapidity. The few drugs that are effective against viral infections interfere with the formation of new, normal cells

and are therefore used with extreme caution. Other microbial drugs have little effect on a virus and are given only to treat bacterial infections that accompany or result from the primary viral infection.

### Resistance and Side Effects

An antibiotic acts by limiting or stopping (and therefore killing) the growth of a specific microorganism. It probably accomplishes this by interfering with the wall of the bacteria cell at which it is targeted while at the same time having little effect on the body's normal cells.

When one is exposed continually to an antibiotic for an illness of long duration (such as rheumatic fever), the targeted bacteria may develop its own defense against the drug. An enzyme (*see* Enzymes) that can destroy the drug may be produced by the bacteria, or the cell wall can become resistant to being broken by the action of the antibiotic. When this happens, and it does most frequently in response to long or frequent treatment with penicillin or streptomycin, the patient is said to be "fast" against the drug. For example, one may be penicillin-fast, meaning penicillin is no longer able to help fight the infection and another type of antibiotic must be given.

Allergic reactions (*see* Allergy) to antibiotics are usually seen as rashes on the skin, but severe anemia

*Technicians (top) who work in producing antibiotics and testing them against disease organisms must wear germfree, protective garb. Some materials can only be handled with gloves attached to sealed boxes (bottom).*
Merck Sharp & Dohme

(too few red blood cells), stomach disorders, and deafness can occasionally result. It was once thought that allergic reactions to antibiotics—penicillin in particular—were frequent and permanent. Recent studies suggest, however, that many people outgrow their sensitivity or never were allergic. The large number of antibiotics that are now available offers a choice of treatment that can, in most instances, avoid allergy-causing drugs.

It is well to remember that all drugs can cause both wanted and unwanted effects on the body. The unwanted ones are called side effects, and these must be balanced against the effects desired in determining if a particular drug will do more harm than good. It is a fact that all drugs have the potential to be both beneficial and harmful.

### Choosing the Appropriate Drug

Physicians can generally determine the type of organism responsible for causing the most frequently seen infections and know which class of antibiotic will be the most effective in combating it. Sometimes the agent causing the illness is not known. In this event a culture from the infection is examined under a microscope to identify the invading organism. The results of the laboratory work permit the physician to prescribe the most effective antibiotic against the specific disease-causing bacteria.

### History and Future

The years between 1928 and 1940 were the most fruitful in the discovery and development of antimicrobial drugs. In 1928 Sir Alexander Fleming, a British bacteriologist, noticed that a mold growing in one of his laboratory cultures was able to destroy that culture's bacteria. Since the mold that produced the substance that killed the bacteria was a species of *Penicillium*, he named the germ-killing substance penicillin. The first use of an antibiotic, however, is not known, as folk medicine has used various molds to fight infections throughout history. In 1935 a German chemist, Gerhard Domagk, discovered the first sulfa drug, prontosil. In 1941 penicillin was used to treat serious infections. The results were dramatic because patients who received the drug made rapid and complete recoveries. Bacitracin, chlortetracycline, and streptomycin, naturally occurring antibiotics, were discovered by 1948. The penicillin ring was finally isolated in 1959 by British and United States scientists, and the way was open for the development of man-made, or engineered, antibiotics. The development of penicillin was the beginning of an era that has been called the golden age of chemotherapy. Since 1948, a large number of substances that inhibit or kill bacteria have been discovered.

Another use of antibiotics is as additives to the feed of animals. Chickens and beef cattle, for example, can be fed with these additives for better weight gains and to speed their growth.

Current work in antibiotics is largely in the area of viruses. Although some antivirals are available, most have toxic effects so severe that they can be used only in life-threatening diseases where the negative effects are the lesser danger. Preliminary studies, however, are reporting success in the development of safer antiviral drugs, and their use should be possible within the near future. (*See also* Drugs.)     Ann Giudici Fettner

---

### *Some Common Antibiotics and How They Are Used*

**Penicillins**
Otitis media (inflammation of the middle ear)
Cerebrospinal meningitis
Strep throat
Syphilis
Gonorrhea
Rheumatic fever
Prevention of bacterial endocarditis (infection of the lining of the heart)

**Cephalosporins**
Infections of the respiratory tract, skin and soft tissue, bone and joint, urinary tract, and bloodstream

**Streptomycin**
Tuberculosis
Tularemia (rabbit fever—acquired from infected animals)
Plague
Brucellosis (undulant fever—infection acquired from goats, cows, pigs)

**Neomycin**
Skin infections
Conjunctivitis (infection of the eye)

**Gentamicin**
Severe infections of bloodstream, urinary tract

**Tetracyclines**
Brucellosis
Chancroid (genital infection)
Trachoma (chronic eye disease found mainly in Asia and Africa)
Cholera
Rickettsial diseases (tick fever, relapsing fever)
Acne
Pelvic inflammatory disease
Syphilis

**Chloramphenicol**
Brain abscess
Meningitis
Typhoid

**Erythromycin**
Legionnaire's disease
Diphtheria
Whooping cough
Gonorrhea

**Lincomycin/Clindamycin**
Pulmonary, peritoneal, intraabdominal and pelvic infections

**Polymyxin**
Parenterally for life-threatening *Pseudomonas* infections; aerosolized for respiratory infection

**Rifampin**
Tuberculosis

**Nystatin**
Fungal infections (candidiasis)

Source: FDA Consumer

## ANTIETAM, BATTLE OF see CIVIL WAR, AMERICAN.

### ANTIGUA AND BARBUDA.
An island nation of the Lesser Antilles, Antigua and Barbuda lies at the southern end of the Leeward Islands. Located in the eastern Caribbean Sea, the independent state includes Redonda, an uninhabited rock. The total area of the three islands is about 171 square miles (443 square kilometers).

The main island of Antigua, unlike the other Leeward Islands, has no forests, mountains, or rivers and few springs. Prolonged droughts occur; rainfall averages only about 40 inches (100 centimeters) per year. The mean average temperature in this tropical climate is 81° F (27° C). Rainwater catchments and a desalinization plant supplement the water supply.

Barbuda, formerly known as Dulcina, lies 25 miles (40 kilometers) north of Antigua. A game reserve, it is a coral island, flat and well wooded. Although planned as a slave-breeding colony, it instead developed a unique system of communal landownership.

The major source of national income is tourism, which accounts for about 70 percent of the gross domestic product. Basic education is compulsory, and both teacher and technical training are offered at State Island College. The official language is English.

Antigua's major crop is sugarcane, though mangoes, melons, limes, eggplant, pumpkin, and sweet potatoes are also grown. Industries include manufacturing rum and assembling garments and appliances. The government operates a fish-processing corporation and a petroleum refinery.

In 1493 Christopher Columbus landed on Antigua, which was named after a church in Seville, Spain. The island was colonized in 1632 by English settlers, who grew tobacco there. Later in the century sugarcane proved to be a more profitable crop, and slaves were brought to the islands to work on the sugarcane estates. The slaves were emancipated in 1834. A fire in 1841, an earthquake in 1843, and a hurricane in 1847 were severe blows to the economy. The naval dockyard, closed in 1854, was reopened in 1961 as a historic monument and yachting center.

Until 1956 Antigua was administered by the British under the governor of the Leeward Islands. During the years 1958 to 1962, it was a member of the West Indies Federation. In 1967 it became an associated state in the Commonwealth. The neighboring Barbuda and Redonda were dependencies of Antigua. In November 1981 the three-island nation became independent as Antigua and Barbuda. Barbuda had been seeking separate independence. The capital and principal city is St. John's, on Antigua. The main settlement on Barbuda is Codrington. Population (1992 estimate), 64,000. (See also West Indies.)

**ANTIHISTAMINE.** The purpose of an antihistamine is to work against the effects of histamine, a chemical substance found in nearly all body tissues. Histamine is released in response to injury or invasion by foreign substances such as pollens (see Allergy). It is also the irritating agent in certain insect venoms. It appears to play a protective role in body chemistry, but its functions are not completely known. Histamines produce varied effects in the body, including widening of the blood vessels, constriction of the smooth muscles of the lungs, and stimulation of gastric secretion.

Some antihistamines are taken to relieve allergies such as hay fever and allergic skin problems. Other antihistamines are used to treat motion sickness and vomiting. Still others are used to control gastric secretion and to treat duodenal ulcers.

Antihistamines should be used carefully because some can cause such unwanted side effects as drowsiness, stomach upset, headaches, blurred vision, and dryness of the mouth. Driving a motor vehicle while under the influence of one of these drugs is dangerous because of these effects. Ann Giudici Fettner

## ANTIMATTER see MATTER.

## ANTIMONY see Fact-Index.

### ANTIOCH, Turkey.
Ancient Antioch was called the "queen of the East." The modern town, called Antakya, is a small trading center in the southern part of the country, about 20 miles (32 kilometers) from the Mediterranean Sea coast. The town has soap and olive oil factories, cotton textile mills, and other processing industries. The chief crops are wheat, cotton, grapes, rice, olives, vegetables, and fruit. Silk, shoes, and knives are also manufactured.

The old city was founded in about 300 BC by one of Alexander the Great's generals and became the capital of the Seleucid kings of Syria. It drew great wealth from the caravan trade to India and grew into a center of Greek culture. Just beyond its 70-foot (20-meter) walls lay the grove of Daphne, filled with magnificent temples that attracted pilgrims from many parts of the world. Antioch, even after it had passed under Roman rule, attracted the reforming spirit of the Apostles. Barnabas and Paul—and perhaps Peter—are said to have sown the seed that eventually converted half the population to Christianity. Here the name Christian was first used (Acts xi, 26). The most famous of the saints of the region was Simeon Stylites, who spent 30 years doing penance on top of a high pillar located near Antioch.

After suffering from many severe earthquakes, Antioch was sacked by the Persian king Chosroes I in AD 538 and never recovered its former glory. It was taken from the Seljuk Turks by the Crusaders after a nine months' siege in 1098, and for nearly two centuries it remained a Christian principality. Then it fell again to the Muslims, in 1268, after great fighting that caused much destruction and slaughter. This last blow destroyed ancient Antioch. Little remains of the old city except a few ruins of great aqueducts and parts of the walls. (*See also* Turkey.) Population (1985 census), 109,233.

**ANTIQUE.** United States customs law defines an antique as an object that is more than 100 years old. It is understood, however, that an object must be more than just old in order to be called an antique. Properly, an antique must also be distinguished by some degree of aesthetic or historic merit. An antique is usually both beautiful and decorative. It may also have additional interest and value because of its relationship to a historical period or to some well-known person. George Washington's teapot and dining room chairs, for example, are more valuable as antiques than are those that belonged to most other 18th-century Americans.

All decorative objects of great age are not automatically designated as antiques. In most cases the term is reserved for objects that survived from Western European cultures and from post-medieval times. Older things are usually termed antiquities, and they are often characterized by the name of the culture in which they originated, such as classical, Egyptian, pre-Columbian, Near Eastern, or Oriental. All of these objects are studied, collected, and bought and sold by specialists.

Antiques of all kinds are highly valued for their intrinsic beauty, craftsmanship, and quality of design. They may be made of rare materials such as gold or silver, but they may also be made of ordinary materials such as wood or paper. Most antiques are things that were originally used as household furnishings. These include furniture, silver, glass, ceramics, rugs, embroideries, and various kinds of metalware. In museums these objects represent the decorative arts. They are studied and exhibited in ways that are different from the ways in which the fine arts (paintings, prints, and sculpture, for example) are studied and presented.

Antiques are studied by cultural and social historians, who see them as direct clues to a people's way of life. Such scholars are less concerned with the beauty of a piece than with its typicality, craftsmanship, and role in the economic and social life of its owners. Washington's teapot and dining room chairs are studied as examples of 18th-century pottery and furniture-making. They are also studied for their roles in daily life at Washington's home, Mount Vernon. Such material culture studies have benefited private collectors greatly because the results have enhanced the associative or relic value of certain objects.

### Classification

Antiques are usually classified according to their countries of origin and the dates when they were

John Moss—Black Star

*An auctioneer recognizes a bid on an item displayed by an auction house employee. Antiques of all kinds and values are commonly sold at auction.*

made. The predominant classifications derive from styles that originated in London or Paris.

The names of the various periods into which antiques are classified may be derived from the reigning monarch of the time and place where they were made. A piece may be termed Charles II, Queen Anne, Georgian, Regency, or Victorian if it is English or Louis XIV, XV, or XVI, Napoleonic, or Empire if it is French. Unfortunately, it is not always as simple as that. Antiques, especially pieces of furniture, are sometimes called by the name of the leading craftsman or designer of their period—hence, the use of such names as Chippendale, Hepplewhite, Sheraton, or Phyfe. (*See also* Interior Design.)

### Collecting

There are many different kinds of antique collectors. Some enjoy furnishing their homes with beautiful old objects. Others confine their collecting to certain kinds of objects—for example, snuffboxes, candlesticks, dolls, or samplers. Most collectors define an area of interest and then seek to acquire objects of rarity and beauty within that area. Some are interested only in objects that come from a particular geographic area such as Virginia or French Canada. Others prefer things from a particular time period such as the English Regency or Puritan New England. Those who define their collections in terms of place and time are more likely to acquire objects of a wide variety of forms and materials.

### The Marketplace

Antiques are bought and sold in a variety of ways. Some are placed on consignment and sold at auctions. In the biggest auction houses, similar things are grouped together in sales for which catalogs are published. These sales receive international advertising and publicity. Bidding can be done in person, by agent, or by telephone.

At more modest auction sales, many kinds of goods are sold; furniture and rugs may be randomly mixed with dolls and firearms. House auctions or estate sales are those in which everything being sold has come from one family; sometimes lawnmowers and kitchen stoves are sold with fine antiques. Auctioneers cover their expenses and make a profit by charging the seller a percentage of the sale price. Some auctioneers charge the buyer an equal percentage, thereby doubling their profit.

Many antiques are sold by dealers—specialty merchants who buy objects from private owners, from auction houses, and from other dealers. Most antique dealers display their wares in their own shops.

The antique show is another popular way in which goods are sold. At a show many dealers rent small booths and display their wares for sale. Often a show is run for the benefit of a charity. Collectors like shows because they can see the wares of many dealers displayed together at one time and place.

### Documentation

An antique is valued for its form and beauty, the quality of workmanship evident in the way it is made, the rarity of the design, and the condition of the piece at the present time. Both the intellectual and financial value of a piece is considerably increased if specific information about its early history is known. If it is certain who made it, where and when it was made, who first owned it, or who first sold it, the piece is said to be documented. It can be studied as part of the culture in which it was originally made and used. If the history of all those who have owned a piece can be traced, this, too, increases its value.

### Varieties

**Clocks.** Clocks hold a special interest for many antique collectors. The many mechanical variations that affect the length of operation and the variety of striking devices and case designs have particular appeal. Since early clocks were handmade by individuals, the variations in the movements are almost infinite. Some collectors try to acquire as many different types as they can find or afford; others specialize in particular types. (*See also* Watch and Clock.)

**Ceramics.** Fine ceramics have been collected since ancient times, and Europeans have prized porcelains since Marco Polo first brought them from China. Ceramic collecting became a passion for those who could afford it. This area of antique collecting has often especially appealed to women. For example, Queen Mary, wife of Britain's George V, was an avid china collector.

Ceramic collections may be developed on the basis of the ware (porcelain, earthenware, stoneware, creamware, ironstone), the glaze (salt-glaze, lead-glaze), the ornamentation (transfer-printed, applied, gilded, hand-painted), the form (vase, jar, teapot, plate, soup tureen, garden seat), the maker, the country or region of origin, or the date when it was made. (*See also* Pottery and Porcelain.)

**Textiles.** Textiles are important vehicles of design concepts in any period; yet textiles are less eagerly sought as antiques than many other forms and materials. Printed cottons and silks are less collected than homespun pieces. The most prized are embroidered pictures and samplers, which can be framed and hung as pictures. (*See also* Textile.)

**Rugs.** Many different kinds of rugs are part of the story of antiques; yet it is the Oriental rug that has become the most highly prized. Here is an exception to the notion that antiques must be more than 100 years old and of Western European origin. Near Eastern rugs, called "Oriental" and usually made in the late 19th or early 20th century, exhibit handsome color and design. The study of the individual rug styles and of the peoples that made them is a complex parallel story. (*See also* Rug and Carpet.)

**Metalware.** Many kinds of metalwares are collected as antiques. Certainly the most valued is silver, but brass, pewter, iron, and some alloys are also collected. In each of these the collector seeks fine workmanship, good design, good condition, and some degree of documentation. (*See also* Metalworking.)

**Glass.** The forms of glass most commonly collected as antiques are those that were originally made as tableware, especially dishes, glasses, tumblers, decanters, bowls, and sweetmeat dishes. These may be handblown or molded in form and have cut, engraved, or applied decoration. Since glass is especially fragile, many early types are extremely rare. (*See also* Glass.)

**Folk Art.** Objects that are not directly related to the main currents of aesthetic design may be collected as folk art. Pieces are prized for their association with ordinary people and are said to be expressions of vernacular culture. Paintings, furniture, and various forms of carving are sometimes considered folk art as well. They are cherished for their bold use of color, strong form, and naive, often clever, concepts.

**Collectibles.** As rare and fine antiques have become harder and harder to find and the demand for them has grown, the field has expanded to include many kinds of things that would not formerly have been considered antiques. These pieces are not particularly rare, nor are they objects of great beauty. Often they are called "collectibles." Such things as baseball cards, beer cans, barbed wire, toys, and old bottles are part of this new aspect of the field. They are not antiques in the traditional sense, but they are bought and sold as if they were. (*See also* Hobby.)

Many kinds of things that are rare antiques today were fairly common in their own time. In fact, the things that were once the most common, such as white earthenware chamber pots, may be the most rare today. The qualities that make an object interesting to a scholar, a dealer, or a collector may vary, and this interest would probably have surprised the original maker or owner. The value of and interest in these objects become an interpretation of current times, part of the cultural story to be conveyed to future generations.

**ANTISEPTIC.** A chemical substance that slows or stops the growth of germs is called an antiseptic. The name comes from the Greek words *anti* ("against") and *sepsis* ("poison"). The many kinds of antiseptics can be divided into two categories—those that are used for internal conditions and those that are used to treat surfaces of skin and mucous membranes. Antibiotic is the term generally used to describe the internal use of these substances (*see* Antibiotic).

When the integrity of the skin is destroyed through a scratch or burn, various organisms often begin to grow in the wound. Viruses, bacteria, and fungi that may be present on healthy skin can multiply rapidly where the skin is broken. Unless this growth is prevented or stopped, serious infection can take place. The site of an injury also allows organisms to enter the body and cause illness.

To prevent such problems, antiseptics are applied to stop the infective growth until healing takes place. Antiseptics in weak solutions are also used on the mucous membranes. Boric acid is dropped in infected eyes, and silver nitrate is placed in the eyes of new-born babies to prevent the growth of any infection present at birth. Ulcers in the mouth and infection in the nose are treated with medicines containing antiseptics. Before surgery, all items and surfaces to be used are cleaned with antiseptics to prevent transfer of germs to the surgical wound. Different types of bacteria require different antiseptics. The most familiar ones are alcohol, Merthiolate, hexa-chlorophene, and peroxide. Antiseptics containing antibiotics and sulfa also work against a wide range of organisms. Antiseptics should not irritate the skin nor be toxic to the body when absorbed. Ann Giudici Fettner

**ANTITOXIN.** The waste products of certain bacteria are called exotoxins. These are poisons that can cause severe illness and death in people infected by bacteria such as those causing diphtheria and tetanus. To fight each exotoxin, the body produces a specific antitoxin. Antitoxins are proteins. They are made by special cells and circulate in the blood serum.

An antitoxin is created in a laboratory by injecting a healthy animal with a particular bacterium. The animal's body produces an antitoxin. A small quantity of blood is taken from the animal, and from the serum an antitoxin for human use is isolated. Antitoxins from horse serum are used to fight toxins associated with diphtheria, gas gangrene, botulism (food poisoning), and other disorders.

Because of allergic sensitivity to animal antitoxins (*see* Allergy), these substances are used with great care. A scratch test, in which a very small quantity of the antitoxin is injected into the skin, is tried first. If an allergic reaction (redness, swelling) results, the physician must find another way to combat the poison. Sometimes a patient is slowly given very small amounts of an antitoxin until the allergic reaction to the serum is no longer seen. Then the normal dose of antitoxin can be given.

When antitoxins produced from human blood can be used, allergic reactions seldom take place. These antitoxins are carried in the serum of the blood and are called gamma globulins. Gamma globulin is often given as a preventive against possible infection when a person has been exposed to a dangerous disease. Protection from the disease may be either long lasting or short lived. In the case of diphtheria, for example, being immunized by an antitoxin prevents reinfection. (So does having and surviving the disease.) In the case of certain other diseases, such as botulism, one can be reinfected any number of times. In these cases antitoxin treatment must be given each time there is exposure. Ann Giudici Fettner

**ANT LION.** The ant lion gets its name from the fact that its larva feeds chiefly on ants. The ant lion larva is often called a "doodlebug."

The adult ant lion is a winged insect. It prefers dry climates and in the United States it is found principally in the South and Southwest. A few species may be found in the Northern states.

The ant lion larva has powerful jaws with which it seizes its prey. It does not hunt the ants and other insects it feeds upon. Rather, it lies in wait for them in ingenious traps that it builds.

In making its trap the ant lion larva crawls backward, moving in small circles on the dry sand. As it moves it digs a small, round, funnel-like hole. This hole is about 1 to 2 inches (2½ to 5 centimeters) in diameter and about the same measurement in depth.

After the trap is completed, the ant lion hides in the hole. Only its jaws are exposed. When an ant, or some other small insect, approaches the trap, the doodlebug uses its large head to toss sand upward and out of the hole. The ant becomes confused and tumbles into the hole. The ant lion then seizes the insect in its powerful jaws.

After the doodlebug has eaten enough ants, it spins a cocoon around itself. In the cocoon the creature undergoes metamorphosis and emerges as a beautiful insect resembling a damsel fly. The adult fly has four long, slender, delicate wings.

The adult fly lays its eggs in the sand. The eggs produce the insect's larvae. The ant lion larva is considered beneficial because it destroys other insects, many of which harm crops.

*A marble bust of Mark Antony is in the Vatican Museum.*
Alinari—Art Resource

## ANTONY, Mark

ANTONY, Mark (83?–30 BC). Marcus Antonius (Mark Antony) was a brilliant Roman soldier, statesman, and orator. When he was past 40, he fell in love with the Egyptian queen Cleopatra. Because of his devotion to her he eventually destroyed his career and took his own life. He has always been more famous for this romance than for his part in ancient history.

Mark Antony belonged to an old aristocratic family of Rome. At the age of 25 he entered the army and served honorably in Palestine and Egypt. Soon after, he joined Julius Caesar in Gaul and became one of his lieutenants. Through Caesar's influence, Antony was appointed to various public offices. At the battle of Pharsalus Caesar made him head of a division. In 44 BC Caesar was assassinated. (*See also* Caesar.)

Following Caesar's murder, Antony persuaded the Romans to drive out the assassins. He then made himself dictator. Octavian, Caesar's adopted son, had similar ambitions (*see* Augustus). While Antony was away fighting the conspirator Brutus, Octavian won the Senate's support. The Senate sent an army against Antony, and he was captured at Mutina.

### Rule of the Triumvirate

Antony escaped and joined forces with Lepidus, one of Caesar's former soldiers. Together they marched on Rome. Octavian met them and the three came to terms. They formed a triumvirate and divided the Roman world among themselves. They continued to war against the conspirators and in 42 BC completely defeated the republican forces at Philippi. Antony went on to Tarsus, where he summoned Cleopatra to answer charges that she aided Caesar's enemies. Upon meeting her, however, he fell in love and followed her to Alexandria. (*See also* Cleopatra.)

News that his wife, Fulvia, and her brother, Antonius, were at war with Octavian brought Antony back to Rome. Fulvia's army was defeated, and she died soon afterward. The two triumvirs were reconciled when Antony married Octavian's sister. The Roman world was again divided. Antony took the eastern provinces. For several years he devoted himself to the service of the empire, but in 34 BC he returned to Cleopatra.

Antony gave large portions of the eastern empire to Cleopatra and their two sons. For this act the Roman Senate refused him support. In 32 BC, at the insistence of Octavian, the Senate deprived Antony of his power to rule. The following year the Roman army defeated him at Actium. Deserted by his followers, he fled to Egypt. On hearing a false report of Cleopatra's death, Antony committed suicide.

## ANTWERP, Belgium

ANTWERP, Belgium. While one of the largest seaports in Europe, Antwerp is also the largest Flemish-speaking city in Belgium. The city is located on the Scheldt River, 55 miles (89 kilometers) from the North Sea.

The various parts of Antwerp divide into historical sections: the old city, which lies within 16th-century walls; the 19th-century city, which stretches beyond the old section; and the post-World War II section of modern buildings. Many historic buildings survived the shellings of the two world wars. Dominating the port on the river is the fortresslike Steen, a medieval castle. Parts of it date back to the 10th century. The home and studio that the artist Peter Paul Rubens occupied from 1616 until his death in 1640 have been restored. His tomb is in the Church of St. James, which contains many works of art. The Flemish painters Van Dyck, Matsys, the Brueghels, the two Teniers, and Jordaens also lived and worked in Antwerp. The 16th-century printing house of Christophe Plantin is now a museum of typography.

Heavy pounding by German bombs destroyed much of Antwerp during World War II. The port has been rebuilt with new locks, docks, and railroad yards; an enlarged turning basin; and a new oil port. Railways, rivers, and canals connect Antwerp with other cities of the Low Countries, France, and Germany. The harbor and industrial areas are served by many import and export firms, banks, insurance companies, and road-transport businesses. Shipbuilding, sugar refining, brewing, distilling, and lacemaking are among the city's many industries. Automobiles, petrochemicals, and electronics are also manufactured. The city is a leading diamond-cutting center.

Founded in the 7th century, Antwerp at first was only a fortress and market village on a sluggish river. It became a seaport in the 12th century and soon had commerce enough to join the rich cities that formed the Hanseatic League. By 1560 Antwerp's prosperity was at its height. However, religious troubles with Spain brought war. The Spanish armies of Philip II massacred 7,000 citizens and burned 800 houses.

Napoleon recognized the city's strategic importance and rebuilt the harbor in the late 18th century. Since the second half of the 19th century, the seaport has grown continually except during wartime. The city was captured by the Germans in World War I. During World War II German troops occupied Antwerp. It was rapidly reconstructed after the war. (*See also* Belgium.) Population (1987 estimate), 479,700.

**ANZUS TREATY.** For protection against what was still perceived as a common danger in the Pacific after World War II, Australia, New Zealand, and the United States formed a mutual defense alliance. On Sept. 1, 1951, they signed the Tripartite Security Treaty—known as ANZUS, for the initials of the three nations.

The pact mainly provided for peaceful settlement of international disputes and maintenance of adequate defense capabilities. The three governments promised to defend one another if the security or territorial integrity of any member were threatened.

New Zealand's Labour party, which won the 1984 election, had campaigned on a pledge to refuse entry to ships carrying nuclear weapons—that is, United States Navy vessels. Party leaders called for withdrawal from ANZUS, and antinuclear legislation was proposed in 1985. In 1986 the United States officially suspended its treaty obligations to New Zealand. Its alliance with Australia and Australia's military ties to its neighbor were maintained, however.

**APARTHEID.** An Afrikaans word for "separateness," apartheid is the name that South Africa's white government applied to its policy of discrimination—racial, political, and economic—against the country's nonwhite majority. Since the 1960s apartheid, which affected white relations with all non-European groups, has often been referred to as "separate development."

Racial segregation, sanctioned by law, was widely practiced in South Africa before the National party won control of the government in 1948. The Nationalists passed new legislation to implement the policy.

The Group Areas Act of 1950 divided South Africans into three major groups—white, native (later Bantu or African), and Colored (those of mixed descent). The native and Colored groups were subdivided further on ethnic, linguistic, or cultural lines, and the act was also applied to the Asian section of the population. The government established residential and business areas for each race and strengthened existing "pass" laws by requiring passes, or permits, for living or trading outside a designated group area.

Under the Population Registration Act of 1950, identity cards that classified a registered person as white, Bantu, or Colored were issued. Other laws prohibited most interracial social contacts, authorized segregated public facilities, established separate educational standards, restricted each race to certain types of jobs, and denied nonwhite participation, even indirectly, in the national government.

The Bantu Authorities Act of 1951 reestablished tribal organizations, and the Promotion of Bantu Self-Government Act of 1959 created ten homelands for them. The Bantu Homelands Citizenship Act of 1970 made every black African, regardless of actual residence, a citizen of one of the homelands, thus excluding blacks from the South African body politic. Only four of the homelands were granted independence as republics, and the others, called Black States, had varying degrees of self-government. All remained dependent in some measure on South Africa.

Opposition to apartheid persisted, both within South Africa and from without. With some white support, black African groups—especially the African National Congress (ANC)—held demonstrations and strikes. South Africa was forced to withdraw from the Commonwealth in 1961 when other member countries would not accept its racial policies. Economic sanctions were imposed by the mid-1980s, and small reforms followed—most notably repeal of the pass laws.

A new government in 1989 relaxed so-called "petty" apartheid with the desegregation of some public facilities. The main symbol of change was the legalization of the ANC and the release from prison of its leader Nelson Mandela (*see* Mandela). In a landmark agreement with the government, the ANC suspended its armed struggle against white minority rule in exchange for the return of political prisoners. The ANC and the government entered into negotiations aimed at drafting a new constitution that would grant political rights to blacks. Limited school integration began in early 1991. By mid-year the last legal prop of apartheid, the 1950 act requiring the racial classification of all newborns, was repealed. (*See also* South Africa.)

**APENNINES.** The backbone of the Italian peninsula is the Apennine mountain system, a continuation of the Alpine system that extends into northern Italy. Some of the ancient Roman roads over its principal passes are still in use, and several railway lines now cross the mountains. The total length of the Apennines is about 870 miles (1,400 kilometers); their width ranges from 25 to 125 miles (40 to 200 kilometers).

In the northwest the Apennines form the background of the Italian Riviera. Then the range swings southeastward across the peninsula toward the Adriatic Sea, leaving only a narrow coastal plain. These central Apennines are the widest part of the chain and contain the highest mountains. The loftiest group is the Gran Sasso, which rises to 9,560 feet (2,914 meters) in Mount Corno. In the toe of the Italian boot the Apennines extend to the western coast. Near Naples is a volcanic region (*see* Vesuvius). The southern division, particularly the toe of Italy, has many earthquakes.

The Apennines form the watershed for peninsular Italy. In the north they furnish tributaries to the Po River. On the Adriatic side the streams are mountain torrents. To the west are larger rivers—the Arno, Tiber, and Volturno. The shorter streams flow only during the winter rainy season. Then their swift descent powers numerous hydroelectric plants.

The snow-white Carrara marble quarried in the northern Apennines was used by such famous sculptors as Michelangelo and Antonio Canova. Crops produced on the slopes include olives, citrus fruits, grapes, sugar beets, and potatoes. (*See also* Italy.)

**APES AND MONKEYS.** Both in behavior and in appearance apes and monkeys resemble human beings, which perhaps explains people's fascination with these animals. Because of their evolutionary relationship, apes, monkeys, and humans are placed in a single order, Primates, in the class Mammalia. Besides monkeys, apes, and humans, a variety of lower primates—unusual monkeylike animals such as lemurs, tarsiers, and lorises—belong to the order. A scientist who studies members of the order is called a primatologist.

## ANTHROPOID APES

The order Primates has ten families. The family Hominidae includes the four genera of true apes and humans. Apes are collectively referred to as hominids or anthropoids, meaning humanlike. The anthropoids existing today fall into the following classification scheme:

Order: Primates
Family: Hominidae
  Subfamily: Hylobatinae
    Genus: *Hylobates* (gibbons)
  Subfamily: Ponginae
    Genus: *Pongo* (orangutans)
    Genus: *Pan* (chimpanzees)
    Genus: *Gorilla* (gorillas)
  Subfamily: Homininae
    Genus: *Homo* (human beings)

The anthropoids have large, complex brains and no tails—features not shared with monkeys and lower primates. In appearance and behavior apes resemble humans in many ways. Apes can stand erect on occasion, and gibbons frequently walk upright, using their long arms for balance. Apes have opposable thumbs, which permit them to grasp and hold objects in their hands (they also have opposable toes, well suited for climbing). Like humans, apes have fingers and toes with flattened nails instead of claws. The anthropoids, in general, have keen vision and well-developed hearing but a poor sense of smell. Apes are native to the Old World tropics of Africa and Southeast Asia. They live in dense jungles and eat primarily leaves and fruit.

Although the life cycles of most kinds of apes have not been extensively studied, enough information is available to indicate several close similarities to the human cycle. Females undergo menstruation at monthly intervals and have gestation periods from seven months (in gibbons) to around nine months (in orangutans, chimpanzees, and gorillas). Normally, a single baby is born, although twins have been reported in most species. The baby is nursed by the mother for several months and may not learn to walk until it is 3 to 6 months old. Sexual maturity is reached after 8 to 12 years, depending upon species

..................................................................

*This article was contributed by J. Whitfield Gibbons, Senior Research Ecologist and Professor of Zoology, Savannah River Ecology Laboratory, University of Georgia.*

and conditions. Although the longevity of any of the species under natural conditions is uncertain, ages of 35 to 40 years have been reported for zoo animals.

### Gibbons

The gibbons (*Hylobates*) are represented by more than a half dozen different species in southern China, the Malay Peninsula, Java, Borneo, and Sumatra. They are the smallest and most agile of the apes. Of slight build and usually less than one meter (three feet) tall, they have exceptionally long arms, which they use to swing on limbs and vines, a great advantage for traveling in the dense upland forests where most species occur. They are a fascinating group for naturalists to study.

The Siamang gibbon (*Hylobates syndactylus*) is generally regarded as the most distinctive and impressive of the group. Siamangs are the largest gibbons. They have jet-black skin and hair, and a bright-red sac beneath the chin. In the jungle they rarely descend to the ground, being thoroughly at home in the upper canopy of trees where they swing, jump, and run among the highest limbs. The throat sacs are used to make low hooting sounds. Individuals join in a roaring chorus that occurs most frequently at dawn and dusk. These vocalizations and the enthusiastic treetop behavior of the Siamangs have attracted the attention of many naturalists.

### Orangutans

Orangutans, *Pongo pygmaeus,* are found in the lowland jungles on the islands of Borneo and Sumatra. They are large apes, standing up to 5 feet (1.5 meters) tall and weighing as much as 200 pounds (90 kilograms), with reddish-brown hair and facial features resembling those of an old man. They are the largest arboreal, or tree-dwelling, animals in the world. Although individuals often descend to the ground to feed, they usually spend the night in crude nests in trees. Orangutans have extremely long and powerful arms, which may span up to 8 feet (2.4 meters). Their legs are proportionately smaller and weaker. Of the three great apes, orangutans were discovered first, but even today many aspects of their life are poorly understood by scientists.

### Chimpanzees

Chimpanzees (*Pan troglodytes*) are the most familiar of the great apes because of their prevalence in zoos, their use in movies, and their extraordinary personalities. They are remarkable for their trainability. Some of them appear to understand and respond to human languages. They have the most extensive geographic range of any of the apes, occurring naturally in the jungles across all of equatorial Africa. In contrast to the common chimpanzee, which may stand taller than 5 feet (1.5 meters) and weigh over 175 pounds (80 kilograms), a pygmy form occurs in the southern Congo region. It is sometimes designated as a separate species. Chimpanzees are gregarious: they normally travel in family groups, and spend most of their time on the ground.

*Apes are native to the tropical forests of Africa and Asia. The gibbon (top left) is the smallest of the apes. The orangutan (top right) has long, well-developed arms for swinging from tree to tree. The chimpanzees (bottom left) are at home in trees or on the ground. The gorilla (bottom right) is the largest of the apes.*

### Gorillas

The largest and, paradoxically, the most gentle of the anthropoids are the gorillas (*Gorilla gorilla*), from tropical West Africa. These black-haired apes, which can attain a height of 5½ feet (1.7 meters), a weight of 600 pounds (270 kilograms), and an arm span of 9 feet (2.7 meters), were unknown until the mid-1800s. Despite their usually inoffensive behavior, both in the wild and in captivity, gorillas have been portrayed as vicious and aggressive villains in innumerable fictional tales, a completely unrealistic representation of their character.

Gorillas are currently recognized as a single species inhabiting three distinct regions of Africa. One population, known as the mountain gorilla, lives at elevations of 6,000–13,500 feet (1,800–4,000 meters) in the western part of the Democratic Republic of the Congo (formerly Zaire). The others are confined to the lowland forests from the west coast of equatorial

Africa to the rain forest of the Democratic Republic of the Congo.

Gorillas are strict herbivores (plant-eating animals) and lead a predominantly terrestrial life, except that smaller individuals often spend the night in tree nests similar to those constructed by orangutans. Family groups consist of a dominant male, two or more females, and various juveniles. Juveniles leave the family group as they near maturity. Despite interest in the ecology and particularly the humanlike behavior of gorillas, few studies have been conducted on the mountain gorilla in the wild.

### MONKEYS

Monkey is a term applied to the day-active, long-tailed primates. Although Old World and New World monkeys resemble one another, they have for so long evolved independently from one another that they are two distinct groups. Primatologists differ in their opinions about some classifications for the suborders, families, and subfamilies of monkeys, but all of

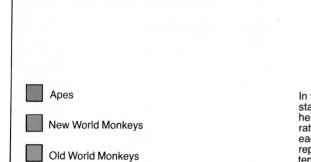 Apes

New World Monkeys

Old World Monkeys

In this table, the heights of the apes are measured while standing. The lengths of the monkeys are measured from head to rump, and tail measurements are given separately. Heights, lengths, and weights are averages for each male of the species and not extremes. This table represents a selection of some species and is not intended to be inclusive.

**Chimpanzee**
*(Pan troglodytes)*

Height: 1.25–1.5 m (4–5 ft)
No tail
Weight: 56–80 kg (123–176 lb)

**White-handed Gibbon**
*(Hylobates lar)*

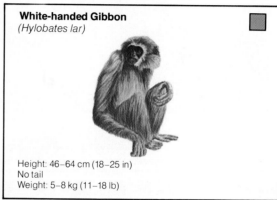

Height: 46–64 cm (18–25 in)
No tail
Weight: 5–8 kg (11–18 lb)

**Gorilla**
*(Gorilla gorilla)*

Height: 1.25–1.7 m (4–5½ ft)
No tail
Weight: 140–270 kg (309–600 lb)

**Orangutan**
*(Pongo pygmaeus)*

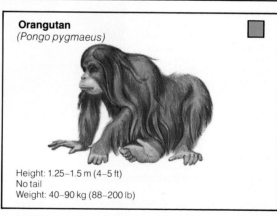

Height: 1.25–1.5 m (4–5 ft)
No tail
Weight: 40–90 kg (88–200 lb)

**Chacma Baboon**
*(Papio ursinus)*

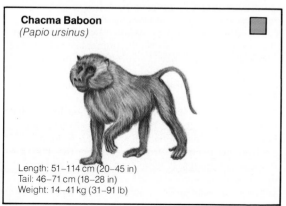

Length: 51–114 cm (20–45 in)
Tail: 46–71 cm (18–28 in)
Weight: 14–41 kg (31–91 lb)

**Diana Monkey**
*(Cercopithecus diana)*

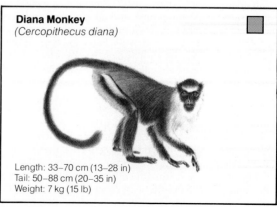

Length: 33–70 cm (13–28 in)
Tail: 50–88 cm (20–35 in)
Weight: 7 kg (15 lb)

**Mandrill**
*(Papio sphinx)*

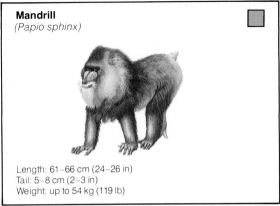

Length: 61–66 cm (24–26 in)
Tail: 5–8 cm (2–3 in)
Weight: up to 54 kg (119 lb)

**Proboscis Monkey**
*(Nasalis larvatus)*

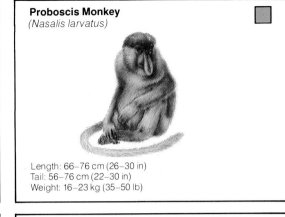

Length: 66–76 cm (26–30 in)
Tail: 56–76 cm (22–30 in)
Weight: 16–23 kg (35–50 lb)

**Rhesus Monkey**
*(Nacaca mulatta)*

Length: 54 cm (21 in)
Tail: 46 cm (18 in)
Weight: 10–13 kg (22–29 lb)

**Brown Howler Monkey**
*(Alouatta fusca)*

Length: 56–92 cm (22–36 in)
Tail: 59–92 cm (23–36 in)
Weight: 7–9 kg (15–20 lb)

**Capuchin Monkey**
*(Cebus capuchinus)*

Length: 31–38 cm (12–15 in)
Tail: 38–51 cm (15–20 in)
Weight: 1.65–4 kg (4–9 lb)

**Golden Lion Marmoset**
*(Leontideus rosalia)*

Length: 17–50 cm (7–20 in)
Tail: 23–39 cm (9–15 in)
Weight: 2.1–5.9 kg (5–13 lb)

**Spider Monkey**
*(Ateles belzebuth)*

Length: 38–64 cm (15–25 in)
Tail: 51–89 cm (20–35 in)
Weight: 7 kg (15 lb)

**Wooly Spider Monkey**
*(Brachyteles arachnoides)*

Length: 61 cm (24 in)
Tail: 67 cm (26 in)
Weight: 7–16 kg (15–35 lb)

the classification schemes recognize the distinction between the Old and New World species, and all separate monkeys from the lower primates and from the apes. Most authorities consider the Old World monkeys to be more closely related to the Hominidae than to the New World monkeys.

Monkeys are found throughout the tropics of Central and South America, Africa, and Asia. However, they are not native to North America, Europe, or Australia. A few species of monkeys, such as the rhesus monkey of northern China and the Japanese macaque, occupy temperate habitats. Most monkeys are forest inhabitants living in the trees, but some of the Old World species are open-country ground dwellers by nature.

Reproduction can occur at any time, but most species bear their young during periods of the year that are optimal for survival. Seasonal timing may be governed by annual wet-dry cycles. Monkeys have gestation periods ranging from almost five months to more than seven months. Most species have single young, though the marmosets and certain other monkeys ordinarily produce twins.

Like humans, monkeys are born with their eyes open. They stay with their mothers constantly and continue to nurse for several months following birth. They mature at three to four years in most species. Captive monkeys have been known to live for up to 45 years, but their life span in the wild is probably much shorter.

Monkeys have a varied diet, including fruit, leaves, flowers, insects, eggs, small reptiles, and even carrion; most species, however, are primarily herbivorous. Like the apes, most monkeys have thumbs and big

toes that are opposable. In addition, some species have a prehensile, or grasping, tail, like a fifth hand, which they use for clinging to branches. Color vision, acute hearing, and some form of vocalization are characteristic of monkeys.

The New World and Old World monkeys represent distinct evolutionary lines that differ in many respects and are confined, without exception, to their respective hemispheres.

**Old World Monkeys**

Old World monkeys belong to the family Cercopithecidae. They are generally larger than New World monkeys, and many live mostly on the ground. Their tails are not prehensile and may be very short. Their nostrils are close together and point downward.

**Baboons and mandrills.** These are predominantly African monkeys. They have doglike faces, are terrestrial, and walk on all fours. Baboons live primarily in open or rocky terrain, traveling in small bands. They are noisy, ferocious, and cunning. The young are boisterous and jolly; the old are boisterous and irritable. They occasionally make audacious raids on human settlements for food and have on occasion attacked people. Baboons are highly intelligent, and early Egyptians are believed to have actually trained the hamadryas baboon to serve food and perform other menial tasks.

The mandrills of West Africa are large-bodied, travel in small groups, and are noted for the bright colors on the rump and face of the males. The male mandrill's fearsome face is an extraordinary combination of a brilliant blue muzzle and bright crimson snout. The female is duller in color.

*The Old World mandrill (left) is one of the most colorful monkeys. The Indian macaque (center) is also called the bonnet monkey, for the thatch of hair on its head. In India the hanuman langur (right) is considered a sacred monkey.*

**Macaques.** These monkeys are primarily Asian. Many live mostly on the ground, and, unlike most monkeys, some can swim. Many are ill-tempered and aggressive. The rhesus monkeys, macaques of northern India and China, are used for medical research and have been exported by the thousands. They are hardy and have been successfully established in outdoor colonies in parts of the United States. The Barbary ape of northern Africa is also a macaque. A colony of these monkeys was established and has been maintained for many years on the Rock of Gibraltar by the British.

**Guenons.** These are common, medium-sized monkeys of Africa. All of them live mostly in trees, chattering from the treetops throughout the day. Guenons characteristically have long arms, legs, and tails; small, round heads; and whiskers and beards. Many have brightly colored coats and faces.

**Mangabeys.** These are large, slender-bodied monkeys of African forests. They are less aggressive than baboons or macaques. Mangabeys are unique among monkeys in being virtually mute, communicating by complex facial signals, which include fluttering eyelids. In species with white or light-colored eyelids the fluttering signals are visible even in the deep shade of an African jungle. Mangabeys form social groups that may include more than one family.

**Langurs and guerezas.** These are known as the leaf monkeys, because many subsist on a diet of leaves. Their stomachs consist of several compartments, like those of cows. The guerezas, or colobus, monkeys are ornately patterned tree dwellers of Africa. Many have been sought out and slaughtered for their fur. Langurs are long-limbed, long-tailed monkeys of Asia. Some are considered sacred by the Hindus of India and are allowed to roam the countryside at will. Some langurs live near the snow line in the Himalayas. One species of large langurs is suspected by some naturalists of being the legendary "abominable snowman." The legend presumably arose from the observation of partially melted, and thus enlarged, footprints in the snow, which appear to have been made by a much larger primate.

A final member of the leaf-monkey family that also deserves mention is the peculiar-looking proboscis monkey of Borneo with its long, banana-shaped nose.

*The saki (left), a New World monkey, has a head broader than it is long. The macaque (right), an Old World monkey, has a narrower and longer head and close nostrils that point down.*

Drawing by R. Keane

This strange animal swims for no other apparent reason than relaxation. The largest ones weigh more than 50 pounds (23 kilograms).

### New World Monkeys

The New World monkeys are placed in at least two and sometimes more families, depending upon the classification system. In contrast to the Old World monkeys, New World monkeys have widely separated nostrils that open to the sides. New World monkeys are tree dwellers and many have prehensile tails.

**Marmosets.** These are the smallest monkeys in the world. None gets larger than a small cat. An adult pygmy marmoset of the Amazon Basin can be cupped in a person's hand. They are restricted to the South American and Central American tropical forests. Marmosets do not have opposable thumbs but can grasp things with their long fingers. They make chirping sounds or birdlike trills. Some, such as the golden marmoset, are threatened with extinction because of continuing habitat destruction. These colorful and playful creatures are sometimes kept as pets.

**Howlers, spider monkeys, and capuchins.** The most commonly seen zoo monkeys are the capuchins, also known as the organ-grinder's monkey. The several species of capuchins live in social groups in tropical American jungles from Mexico to Argentina. The capuchins are popular because of their intelligence and hardiness in captivity. Howler monkeys, so called because they sit in treetops and howl, are the largest of the New World monkeys. They have powerful prehensile tails and occur in many colors including black, brown, and metallic gold. Spider monkeys are small and slender-bodied, with long tails.

**Other New World species.** Besides the major groups noted above, certain species warrant special mention. The owl or night monkey of South America is the only nocturnal monkey in the world, though many of the lower primates are night animals. The woolly spider monkey, an intermediate species between woolly and spider monkeys, is a rare species from Brazil. It has a thick coat of fur, no opposable thumb, and an extremely long prehensile tail. The so-called half-monkeys of South America include a number of unusual species whose ecology or behavior has been poorly studied. The uakaris have short tails, unlike any other New World monkeys.

### SURVIVAL OF APES AND MONKEYS

The fate of the apes and monkeys in their natural environment is uncertain. Anthropoid populations are diminishing in number and size as their habitats are destroyed by various human activities. Estimates indicate that only a few thousand orangutans are left and that the total number of gorillas may be as low as 5,000. The once extensive range of chimpanzees becomes smaller each year as their habitat is encroached upon. The extinction of the mountain gorilla will probably occur near the end of the 20th century if land-use practices, poaching, and human indifference continue unabated. The same fate will ultimately befall

Tierbilder Okapia, Frankfurt am Main

**The uakari, the only short-tailed New World monkey, lives in forest areas along the Amazon River in South America.**

most of the other species of apes within a few decades unless human attitudes toward the problem change.

Likewise, many species of monkeys are in imminent danger of extinction because of habitat loss. In the late 20th century large areas of rain forest in South America, Africa, and Asia have been destroyed. Commercial forestry programs in tropical habitats jeopardize the survival of entire species. International endangered-species laws place many monkeys and apes on lists of animals that cannot be brought live into many countries and whose skins cannot be sold. Such laws protect individual animals but do not prevent habitat destruction.

As a result of protection by the endangered species laws, some species of monkeys and apes are no longer sought commercially. Restrictions are placed even on the use of some species for zoo exhibits. However, most species in the world can still be captured legally and exported as pets or zoo animals. Monkey fur, particularly that of the African guerezas, is still marketed internationally, though legal restrictions have limited sales in some countries. Many monkeys (mainly rhesus monkeys) have been used extensively for psychological and medical research. However, waning natural populations and the laws in some Oriental countries have reduced the numbers of animals that can be exported for this purpose. Many rhesus monkeys are now reared in captivity for research needs.

**BIBLIOGRAPHY FOR APES AND MONKEYS**

**Fossey, Diane.** Gorillas in the Mist (Houghton, 1984).
**Goodall, Jane.** In the Shadow of Man, rev. ed. (Houghton, 1988).
**Goodall, Jane.** My Life with Chimpanzees (Simon & Schuster, 1988).
**Linden, Eugene.** Silent Partners: The Legacy of Ape Language Experiments (Ballantine, 1987).
**Wildlife Education, Ltd.** Apes (Wildlife Education, 1981).

**APHIDS.** On a stem or on the underside of a leaf sometimes a crowded colony of plant lice, or aphids, may be visible. They are parasites that have sharp sucking beaks and live on the sap of plants (*see* Parasite). There are many kinds. Most feed exclusively on a particular crop, weed, or tree.

The smallest aphids measure about $\frac{1}{20}$ of an inch (0.13 centimeter) in length and the largest about $\frac{1}{14}$ of an inch (0.64 centimeter). Most species are green, but some are pink, white, brown, or black. Those that migrate are born with wings. Most generations are made up of wingless females. During the feeding season these females, without mating, produce living young that are all females and that themselves produce several generations of young during the summer. In the fall a generation is born that includes both males and females. After mating, the females of this generation lay eggs that will hatch in the spring to start new colonies.

Aphids secrete from the alimentary canal a sweet watery liquid that is called honeydew. Ants relish this as food. Some species of ants care for whole herds of aphids (so-called "ants' cows"). The ants build mud shelters for them at the roots of plants and move them often to new pastures as the old ones wither. To induce the flow of honeydew the ants milk the "cows" by stroking them with the antennae. Most aphids, particularly the woolly aphids, spread a white, waxy secretion over themselves for protection.

Many aphids suck plant sap or inject poisonous saliva into plants, causing the plants' leaves to curl and sometimes drop off. Some aphids produce gall-like swellings on roots and bark. One of the most destructive aphids is the greenbug, which infests oats, wheat, and other small grains. Fields of corn are often destroyed by the corn-root aphis, which is dependent on the cornfield ant for survival.

Aphids reproduce so rapidly that if unchecked they can destroy entire fields of crops. Their numbers may be controlled by such natural enemies as ladybird beetles (ladybugs), aphid lions, and lacewings. Farmers frequently control the insects by spraying with pest-control agents (*see* Pest Control). Aphids belong to the order Homoptera and the family Aphididae.

*Rose aphids* **(Macrosiphum rosae)**

Anthony Bannister—EB Inc.

*The classic statue of Aphrodite is the world-famous Venus de Milo carved in about 150 BC, now at the Louvre in Paris.*

**APHRODITE.** Of all the goddesses of ancient mythology, none was more widely venerated than the goddess of love. The Greeks called her Aphrodite. The Romans worshiped her as Venus.

In Homer's 'Iliad' Aphrodite is said to be the daughter of Zeus and Dione, a Titan goddess. Other stories tell how she sprang, full-grown, from the foam of the sea near the island Cythera. (*Aphros* is Greek for "foam.") From there Zephyrus, the west wind, carried her gently on a shell to Cyprus, which was always regarded as her real home. There the Hours met her, clothed her, and brought her to the gods.

Every god—even Zeus himself—wanted this beautiful, golden goddess as his wife. Aphrodite was too proud and rejected them all. To punish her, Zeus gave her to Hephaestus (Vulcan in Roman mythology), the lame and ugly god of the forge. This good-natured craftsman built her a splendid palace on Cyprus. Aphrodite soon left him for Ares (Mars), the handsome god of war. One of their children was Eros (Cupid), the winged god of love.

Always eager to help lovers in distress, Aphrodite was equally quick to punish those who resisted the call of love. Cupid shot golden arrows into the hearts of those his mother wanted to unite in marriage. Aphrodite also had a magic girdle that made its wearer irresistible, and she sometimes loaned it to others. Under her influence Zeus more than once fell in love with mortal maidens. Afraid of being mocked someday by Aphrodite, Zeus decreed she should lose

her heart to Anchises, a shepherd of Troy. From this union was born Aeneas, the mythical ancestor of the Roman people (*see* Aeneas).

Aphrodite helped Paris of Troy win the beautiful Helen of Greece (*see* Trojan War). In the war that followed she proved to be a so-called "coward goddess." When Aeneas was wounded by Diomedes, she lifted him up in her soft arms and bore him from the field. Diomedes, advised by Athena that he could attack Aphrodite with safety, thrust at her with his spear and cut her hand. Aphrodite fled weeping to Mount Olympus to be healed and comforted.

Aphrodite was worshiped chiefly as the goddess of human love. She was also widely venerated as a nature goddess. Because she came from the sea, sailors prayed to her to calm the wind and the waves.

The poets of Greece and Rome never tired of singing the praises of the love goddess. Their sculptors carved countless figures of her. The most celebrated statue of Aphrodite in ancient times was that carved by Praxiteles at Cnidus, on the coast of Asia Minor. This has never been found by archaeologists. The most famous one that remains today is the beautiful 'Venus de Milo', now in the Louvre in Paris.

In the 'Iliad' Aphrodite is called the Cyprian or Cytherea. She is also referred to as Dionaea, after her mother, or even Dione. Other names for her are Aphrogenia, Anadyomene, and Astarte. It is often written Ashtoreth, particularly in Bible references to Philistine idols. The name may have been derived from that of the Assyrian goddess Ishtar.

**APOLLO.** Of the 12 great gods of Greece, the handsomest and best loved was Apollo. He was the god of light, youth, beauty, and prophecy. The priestess of the oracle at Delphi was his servant.

One of the earliest deeds of the young Apollo was the slaying of the deadly serpent Python. No man dared to approach the beast, which lived in the hills near Delphi. When the people asked Apollo to save them, he came down from Mount Olympus with his silver bow and a quiver of golden arrows. Apollo used one of the arrows to kill the serpent. In memory of this victory Apollo was believed to have started the Pythian games, which were held every four years in ancient Greece. The winners in feats of strength, in foot races, and in chariot races were crowned with wreaths of laurel leaves.

Apollo was also the god of song, music, and poetry. He charmed the gods with his playing at the banquets held in their palaces on Mount Olympus. It was said among the later Greeks that he invented both the flute and the lyre.

According to Greek mythology, Apollo was the son of Zeus and twin brother of Artemis (Diana). He was born on the island of Delos in the Aegean Sea. His mother was the goddess Leto (Latona). Later, through confusion with Helios, he came to be considered especially as the sun god. The Greeks connected him with agriculture and called him "protector of the grain," "sender of fertilizing dew," "preventer of

*The 'Apollo Belvedere' is a Roman copy of a Greek bronze.*

blight," "destroyer of locusts," and "destroyer of mice." They considered him the guardian of flocks and herds and a health-giving god. He was hailed as the "god of the silver bow" and in wartime as "the helper."

At Delphi in central Greece, near the foot of Mount Parnassus—sacred to Apollo and the Muses—was the famous oracle of Apollo. Here his priestess made known the future to all who consulted her. She gave guidance in matters of sickness, war and peace, and in the building of colonies. The tripod was dedicated especially to Apollo, and it was sacred to him as the god of prophecy. He was made one of the chief gods of Rome by an edict of the Emperor Augustus. The emperor regarded him as his patron deity and built a magnificent temple in his honor.

Apollo was represented by ancient sculptors as a beautiful youth with flowing hair tied in a knot above his forehead, crowned with a wreath of laurel and bearing his lyre or bow. The most famous statue of him is the 'Apollo Belvedere', which is a Roman copy of a Greek bronze original and is in the Vatican Museum in Rome.

**APOLLONIUS OF PERGA** (262?–190 bc). Admiring friends called him "The Great Geometer" for his numerous accomplishments in the field of geometry. Specifically, it was his theory of conic sections, elaborated in his major work, 'Conics', that earned Apollonius of Perga the plaudits of his contemporaries.

A solid cone can be cut into sections, producing several unusual forms. Apollonius examined these conic sections, noted their shapes, and introduced the terms ellipse, hyperbola, and parabola to describe them. He was the first to recognize that these three forms, along with the circle, are all part of any cone. His 'Conics', which brought order to a confused and ill-defined area of geometry, is considered one of the greatest scientific works of the ancient world. His theory of conic sections is still useful to engineers and mathematicians (for picture, *see* Geometry).

Born in Perga, an ancient Greek town that lies in present-day Turkey, Apollonius studied in Alexandria, Egypt, and later taught at the university there. He traveled to several libraries and universities to expand his understanding of mathematics. In his numerous books (most of which have been lost), Apollonius acknowledged those who had studied the field before him, summarized their work, and proceeded to make his own contribution. Only in the final volumes of 'Conics' did he break new ground. In addition to geometry, he studied the properties of light and the way curved mirrors reflect it.

**APOSTLE.** During his earthly ministry, Jesus Christ, the founder of the Christian religion, gathered many followers. These people were called disciples, or learners. Of the many disciples that Jesus had, there were 12 who formed an inner circle. After his death and resurrection, there were 11 disciples left, because Judas—who had betrayed Jesus—killed himself (*see* Jesus Christ).

To replace Judas, the other disciples chose a man named Matthias. He and the other 11 were sent out by Jesus as "apostles." The word is derived from a Greek term meaning "one sent forth." The other apostles were Simon (called Peter); Andrew, Simon's brother; James the Elder (son of Zebedee); John, James the Elder's brother; Philip; Bartholomew; Matthew (or Levi); Thomas; James the Younger; Judas (or Thaddeus, brother of James the Younger); and Simon Zelotes.

Except for meager accounts in the New Testament, the literature of the early Christian church is so fragmentary that there is no full or certain knowledge of the lives of the apostles. A mass of tradition has thus grown up around these men who by their teaching and martyrdom established Christianity. Typical of this tradition is the Apostles' Creed, a short three-part profession of faith ascribed to them, which began to be used in the Roman church in the 3rd century.

Peter, the fisherman whom Jesus had called to be "a fisher of men," was apparently the leader of the apostles. He witnessed most of the incidents in the life of Jesus recorded in the New Testament. With James the Elder and John, Peter formed an inner circle within the Twelve.

This favored group was present at such miracles as the raising of the daughter of Jairus and the Transfiguration. A widespread tradition holds that Peter went to Rome, where he was crucified in AD 64 (*see* Peter). Andrew, it is said, was crucified at Patras, Greece, on an X-shaped cross (hence the term "St. Andrew's cross"). What is believed to be part of

his cross is today enclosed in one of the four great piers supporting the dome of St. Peter's in Rome. John, "the beloved disciple," is represented throughout the Gospels as fiery but charming. After the Crucifixion he was associated with the other apostles in making converts in Jerusalem. After Peter, he was the most prominent of those who bore witness to the Resurrection. James the Elder was a steadfast worker in the early church and is said to have carried the Gospel as far west as Spain. The first martyr among the apostles, he was slain by order of Herod Agrippa I, king of Judea, in about AD 44 (Acts xii, 1–2).

Thomas was the original "doubting Thomas," so called because he would not believe in the Resurrection until he could see and touch the Master (John xx, 24–29). Tradition says that he went to India. Members of the ancient churches of southern India still call themselves "Christians of St. Thomas."

The New Testament tells little about the other seven apostles. According to one legend, however, Bartholomew was flayed and crucified while on a missionary trip to India. James the Younger is said to have been stoned to death when he persisted in his evangelistic work among the Jews.

The term apostle was later applied also to Paul because he was the equal of the Twelve in importance of office and in missionary zeal (see Paul). It was also bestowed on such apostolic assistants as Barnabas, Paul's traveling companion, and Luke, "the beloved physician," who is the traditional author of the Third Gospel and the Acts of the Apostles. Only two of the four Gospels bear the names of real apostles. The First Gospel is believed to have been written by Matthew, and the Fourth by John. Mark, who wrote the Second Gospel, assisted Paul and Barnabas in establishing the early churches in Asia Minor.

**APPALACHIAN HIGHLANDS.** Sweeping from Newfoundland to Alabama, the Appalachian Highlands dominate the landscape of the Eastern seaboard. Their peaks, ridges, hills, and valleys form a belt almost 2,000 miles (3,200 kilometers) long and up to 360 miles (580 kilometers) wide. These highlands have played an important role in the history and economic development of the United States. They formed a barrier that held the early settlers near the Atlantic coast until the colonies could develop the unity and strength to fight for independence and form a nation. When intrepid woodsmen found valleys and gaps through the ridges, a stream of pioneers moved on to settle the West.

Coal from the Appalachians was the foundation of the industrial development that made the adjacent manufacturing belt the most productive in the world. The uplands have also furnished iron, stone, oil, gas, and timber. Their tumbling streams have been harnessed to supply hydroelectric power.

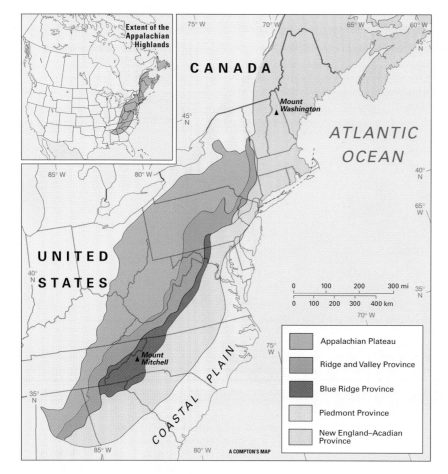

The forested mountains offer scenic beauty, with facilities for summer and winter sports. Trails and parkways serve hikers and motorists, and national and state parks preserve wilderness areas. (*See also* National Parks; Great Smoky Mountains.) The Appalachian Highlands may be grouped into five physiographic regions or provinces:

**1. The Piedmont Province** begins near New York City and extends to central Alabama. The word piedmont means "foot of the mountains." This province lies between the Coastal Plain and the eastern foot of the mountains. Most of the Piedmont is rolling farm and forested land, with scattered hills and ridges 1,200 to 1,800 feet (360 to 550 meters) in altitude.

**2. The Blue Ridge Province** is a chain of forested ridges that runs from Pennsylvania to Georgia. It is low in the north and lofty and much wider in the south. In the Great Smokies many peaks tower 6,000 feet (1,800 meters). Mount Mitchell (6,684 feet; 2,037 meters), in the Black Mountains of western North Carolina, is the highest point east of the Mississippi.

**3. The Ridge and Valley Province** lies west of the Blue Ridge. Its long, narrow valleys are separated by roughly parallel ridges. One small section in Pennsylvania contains nearly all the anthracite coal in the United States. The broad, fertile Great Valley begins in Alabama and continues northward through New York as the Hudson-Champlain Valley.

**4. The Appalachian Plateau** is the westernmost part of the highlands. Here narrow valleys wind between steep hills and level uplands. This province holds the world's greatest deposits of bituminous coal. The northern section of the plateau is known as the Catskill Mountains; the center, as the Allegheny Plateau; the south, as the Cumberland Plateau.

**5. The New England–Acadian Province** extends from Pennsylvania to Newfoundland. The Taconic, Green, and White mountains are its best-known ranges. Mount Washington (6,288 feet; 1,917 meters) is the highest peak in this forested area.

The provinces differ underground as well as on the surface. The Piedmont contains granite, very old crumpled formations, and tilted, broken strata. The Blue Ridge and the New England–Acadian provinces also contain granite and ancient crumpled rocks. The Ridge and Valley Province is underlain by beds of limestone, shale, and sandstone, bent in upward and downward folds. In the Appalachian Plateau, strata are gently tilted toward the northwest.

The geologic history of the Appalachians explains these differences. For ages the Blue Ridge and Piedmont were part of a very large island or group of islands known to geologists as Appalachia. Rocks in Appalachia were broken and changed, or metamorphosed. Molten material from the Earth's interior produced granite and other crystalline rocks.

Strata of the Ridge and Valley Province settled in shallow seas between Appalachia and the mainland. Some deposits of the Plateau also formed in the sea, but the coal deposits settled in swamps (see Coal).

A geologic revolution came in late Permian times, more than 200 million years ago. Appalachia sank slowly and pushed westward with such force that thick formations were squeezed into folds. Some folds broke and the rocks were pushed upward along inclined thrust faults, creating the first Appalachian Mountains. They were probably as high and steep as the modern Rocky Mountains, which were uplifted much later. The Plateau Province lay so far inland that its rocks were raised and tilted but not folded. Later, lavas erupted from volcanoes and fissures on the Piedmont, while sand and mud settled in valleys. Much of the land broke into narrow blocks that sank or tipped upward in long mountains.

Throughout Mesozoic and part of Cenozoic time, streams wore the mountains down to an almost level surface, or peneplain. Rivers in the plateau portion flowed to the interior. Those in the eastern sections found their way to the Atlantic Ocean.

During late Cenozoic times, the Appalachian region was repeatedly arched upward. Uplift gave speed to rivers. They eroded the land, dividing the peneplain into irregular hills and long ridges.

The streams of the Plateau Province traced an irregular network. The large rivers of other provinces remained in their courses. Since most of these led southeastward to the sea, the rivers often crossed the ridges and valleys. They carved channels, called water gaps. Their tributaries flowed between ridges of resistant rock, cutting narrow, parallel valleys.

Since final uplift and erosion took place late in the Cenozoic era, most of the Appalachian Mountains are less than 25 million years old. Only the highest peaks are remnants of the mountains formed long ago in the Permian period.

**APPLE.** Because of the apple's fine qualities, it is sometimes called the "king of fruits." The hardy apple flourishes over more parts of the Earth than any other fruit tree. Since the fruit keeps for months in cool storage, it was a dependable winter fruit supply before cold storage was developed.

The glossy red or greenish-yellow fruit is juicy and crisp, with a spicy aroma. It is delicious to eat raw or cooked. Apple juice and cider are popular drinks. Apples are also commercially canned, prepared as jelly or apple butter, and frozen as juice. The apple contains minerals and a fair amount of vitamins; the carbohydrates are readily digested fruit sugars. About one sixth is solid material and the rest water.

Although there are thousands of varieties of apples, relatively few are raised commercially. The most popular kinds include the Red Delicious, Baldwin,

*The apple tree belongs to the rose family, and its pink and white blossoms resemble those of the wild rose.*

Michigan Tourist Council

Cortland, Duchess, Early Harvest, Golden Delicious, Gravenstein, Grimes Golden, Jonathan, Maiden Blush, McIntosh, Northern Spy, Rambo, Rhode Island Greening, Rome Beauty, Spice Russet, Spitzenberg, Stayman, Winesap, Wealthy, Williams Red, Yellow Newton (Albemarle Pippin), and Yellow Transparent.

Early varieties ripen in July or August. The big harvest is in October. Firm fall apples may be stored at temperatures near their freezing point until the next summer's varieties appear on the market. Apples must be handled carefully to avoid bruising. Trees yield from 5 to 20 bushels each year.

An apple tree will grow from a planted seed, but the fruit will not be of the same variety as the parent apple. To grow trees of a selected variety, nurserymen cut a stem bud or a twig and graft it to a well-rooted little tree (see Fruitgrowing). The ground is cultivated and sometimes planted in a cover crop. As the trees grow they are pruned and sprayed. Extreme cold is harmful to the trees. They also require a dormant period in winter for rest.

The wild apple (Pyrus malus) of the family Rosaceae is the species from which most apples grow. Crab apple trees may belong to one of the trees native to North America, such as the Pyrus ioensis, or may have been developed from crosses of Asiatic species.

Charred remains of the fruit have been found in ruins of prehistoric lake dwellings. Stone Age men carved pictures of it. Apples are mentioned in the Bible. Greek mythology tells how the golden apple of discord led to the fall of Troy. In a Scandinavian myth the "apples of Iduna" brought youth to all who ate them (see Scandinavia).

Apples originated in southwest Asia, probably in the Caucasus between the Black and Caspian seas. The

**Red Delicious**     **Rhode Island Greening**     **Rome Beauty**     **Winesap**

**McIntosh**     **Jonathan**     **Grimes Golden**     **Stayman Winesap**

*The common apple has been paid tribute in a proverb ("An apple a day keeps the doctor away"), popular songs ('Don't Sit Under the Apple Tree'), and the Bible ("the apple of his eye").*

first apples were small, wild crab apples. The Romans probably introduced the apple into England. Colonists brought it to America, and pioneers carried seeds and sprouts across the continent.

Today apple orchards are found in the Old World from Scandinavia and Siberia to the mountains of Spain and India. The fruit grows throughout the temperate zones, both north and south of the tropics.

The United States is the world leader in apple production. In Europe, where much of the crop is used for cider and wine, the chief producers are France, Germany, Italy, Spain, and Turkey.

**APPLESEED, Johnny** (1774–1845). Pioneer children in the Middle West had apples to eat with their dull fare of hoecake and game, largely because of the efforts of the man they called Johnny Appleseed. The pioneers wove many tales about the strange, beloved hero of the frontier (*see* Folklore).

Johnny brought his first apple seeds to the Ohio wilderness early in the 19th century. He had gathered them at the cider mills of Pennsylvania. He cleared fertile spots along the streams and planted the seeds in these wild nurseries. He gave deerskin bags of seeds to families moving west in covered wagons.

All over Ohio and Indiana and into Illinois he tramped for 40 years, starting his nurseries and returning to tend them. If the settlers paid him money for the seedlings, he gave it to the poor, bought religious books, or fed broken-down horses. More often they paid him in cast-off clothing or cornmeal.

Although bears, wolves, and wildcats roamed the woods, he traveled without a gun. He walked barefoot through grass where rattlesnakes lurked. Indians hostile to other white men were his friends. They called him "great medicine man" because he scattered seeds of healing herbs. He tried to make peace between settlers and Indians; supposedly he saved Mansfield,

Ohio, from massacre by running through the night to alert troops 30 miles away. He lived to see thousands of acres of orchards planted in trees descended from his nursery stock.

Johnny Appleseed's real name was John Chapman. He was born in Leominster, Mass., in 1774 and died in Fort Wayne, Ind., in 1845.

**APPRENTICESHIP.** The learning of an art, craft, or trade under the tutelage of a master is called apprenticeship. There is normally some form of legal agreement that defines the relationship between teacher and student. Such matters as length of training period and service, financial remuneration, and living arrangements may be included in the agreement.

Before the Industrial Revolution and the modern era of mass production, most manufacturing was done on a fairly small scale in private shops or even in homes. People who made clothing, shoes, hats, jewelry, cooking implements, carts and wagons, glassware, and many other goods specialized in only their own craft. This was true also of the building trades and other occupations that required special skills.

It was not uncommon in preindustrial times for a craft or trade to remain in one family for generations. A craftsman's own sons were thus his chief apprentices. If he had no sons, he might find boys from his town who would be willing to learn his specific trade. Apprenticeship was almost always a family arrangement. If the apprentice was a neighbor rather than a son, he simply moved into the master's home for the duration of his training.

Although the number of workers trained in this way was always relatively small in proportion to a given population, apprenticeship did assure that trades and crafts would endure for generations. It also assured that the number of workers with a particular skill would be rather few in number. Hence the balance of supply and demand for a skill could be maintained at a constant level.

In the 20th century the number of workers trained as apprentices has been fairly small. Entrance into some trades, such as carpentry or masonry, is still closely regulated, and an unskilled worker must go through a period of apprenticeship before becoming a full member of the appropriate trade union. In other trades and crafts the necessary training is usually given in technical or vocational schools.

### Early History

The ancient societies of Egypt, Babylon, Assyria, Greece, and Rome all recognized the need for training in craft skills in order to have a sufficient supply of artisans to do the work. The laws of Hammurabi in Babylon required that artisans teach their skills to young men. In Greece and Rome the artisans and tradesmen were generally slaves. But as the Roman Empire began to break down in the 4th and 5th centuries, artisans organized themselves into groups called *collegia* in order to maintain standards and perhaps to limit membership.

In the Middle Ages the institution of apprenticeship first came into its own. European artisans and craftsmen organized themselves into guilds, or unions. These guilds regulated all aspects of a particular craft: production methods, quality control, prices, and guild membership. Leaders of the guilds were the master craftsmen. Limiting the number of apprentices was a means of assuring employment for themselves and adequate wages for the members of the guild (see Guild).

A master craftsman operated a shop in which apprentices, usually bound for a period of seven years, acted as his assistants. Apprenticeship became a kind of artificial family relationship; the apprentices even slept in the shop.

The apprentice "graduated" when he had finished the term of the agreement and completed a masterpiece, demonstrating his ability. There might then be an intermediate period when the young man did not yet have a business of his own but worked for another craftsman as a journeyman (from the French word *journée*, meaning "day's work" or "day's wages"). Eventually, when the worker went into business for himself, he became a master. This formal progression, from apprentice to journeyman to master, is still retained in some occupations.

Although this system was mainly suited to small-scale enterprises, it could be organized for large-scale projects such as the building of the great medieval cathedrals. Governments became involved with guilds when the latter abused their monopolies in particular crafts, keeping wages artificially high and causing shortages of competent workers.

With the coming of the Industrial Revolution in the 18th century, apprenticeship began to decline as an institution. Factory mass-production techniques eroded the personal relationship between master and assistant that apprenticeship demands. Labor was plentiful and cheap, and experience usually was gained on the job. Nevertheless, certain crafts maintained the tradition of apprenticeship and some professions, such as the legal profession in Britain, continued to rely on apprenticeship to provide practical training. In Britain articles of clerkship still bind a pupil to a solicitor or barrister until the young person is qualified to practice law independently.

Even though the Industrial Revolution opened the doors to unskilled labor, there was still a need for artisans and craftsmen. People were needed to build machines and to keep them running. The persistence of specialized tasks kept the institution of apprenticeship alive.

In colonial America apprenticeship was quite common: such famous Americans as Benjamin Franklin and Paul Revere learned their trades as apprentices. But America had fewer traditions and time-honored regulations than Europe, and many skilled workmen came as immigrants looking for a chance to make a living as free men. So the institution of apprenticeship never became so firmly established in the United States. During the 19th century many trades organized themselves into unions in order to protect their skills and maintain standards and wages.

In Europe, while the Industrial Revolution was changing the nature of work, there occurred during the 19th century a reaction in favor of the crafts and trades. Laws were introduced in such countries as France, Prussia, and England to protect the trade unions and strengthen the apprenticeship programs.

### Apprenticeship in the 20th Century

Today the prevalence of apprenticeship varies widely among nations. It remains a way of controlling, at a local level, growth in the number of workers in a particular occupation.

In Western countries, governments may promote apprenticeship, prescribe standards, and even offer employers and workers financial incentives. But in the end it is the employer, or the local union, that decides to take on an apprentice. In Communist and Socialist countries, manpower planning is a function of the state. Contractual apprenticeship, as a means of local economic control, has little or no place.

In continental Europe there is a long history of government involvement in apprenticeship training. There are frequently programs of payment to employers who institute training. Such programs are common in Germany, Austria, and Switzerland where approximately 5 percent of the working population are apprentices. In addition to the standard crafts and trades, entry-level jobs in offices, banks, insurance companies, travel and tourist services, hotels and restaurants, and the medical industry are often obtained through apprenticeship.

By contrast, in the English-speaking countries, apprenticeship is generally sponsored by craft unions and employers, and there is relatively little government involvement. The range of occupations in which apprenticeships are available is also much narrower than in other countries.

In Japan there is a personal relationship between employer and employees, a corporate version of the "artificial family" of the medieval guilds. A Japanese apprentice enters into his training agreement with the understanding that he will probably stay with the company for life. Thus he is trained not so much for a specific trade as for a particular company where a variety of skills may be required through a lifetime of employment with that company.

Aside from its immediate educational and vocational functions, apprenticeship has become an instrument of government social and economic policy in the United States and Britain. Apprenticeship programs are seen as an avenue for greater participation by minorities and women in the labor market.

The traditional form of master–learner relationship has survived from medieval times, but in the 20th century an entirely different concept of employee training has been developed by industries and corporations. "Corporate apprentice schools" were begun by major United States industries between 1905 and 1910 to fill a need for highly skilled workers required by new, sophisticated machinery.

The Italian "work schools" have refined this American practice. The Fiat and Alfa Romeo automobile corporations, as well as other very large businesses, provide the bulk of apprenticeship training in Italy. Such training programs obviously represent a broader interpretation of the term apprenticeship than has been traditional in European guilds or in American trade unions.

In the United States most recognized apprenticeship programs have two aspects. One part of training is on the job, under the eye of a skilled craftsman. Then there is classroom study in the theoretical aspects of the trade. There are in the United States apprenticeship programs for over 350 occupations in about 90 skilled trades.

In the field of printing, for example, craftsmen usually specialize in one type of operation, such as platemaking, presswork, or photography. Their training may be further confined to just one printing method: letterpress, lithography, or gravure. Apprenticeships in the printing trade usually last from four to six years. Besides training on the job, the program normally includes classroom or correspondence study. Applicants are required to be between 18 and 30 years old, to be physically fit, and to have good language and basic mathematical skills.

### Criticisms and Advantages

As a training method, apprenticeship has been criticized for a number of reasons. Many apprentices, especially in small- and medium-sized firms, are treated as workers rather than as learners and receive training only when it fits into production schedules. Classroom training is sometimes poorly coordinated with practical learning on the job.

Apprenticeship may lead to narrow job specialization in an era of rapidly changing technology requiring flexibility on the part of workers. A built-in weakness of apprenticeship is its dependence on economic or technological conditions that may change and eventually close off employment in a trade in which the would-be apprentice wishes to make a career.

On the other hand, apprenticeship can be a very attractive alternative to college for young people. The learner is paid, and apprenticeship programs are often a first step toward owning a business or gaining a management or labor leadership position.

Apprenticeship need not be confined to traditional trades and crafts, as the European experience has shown. With increasing worker participation in industrial management, skilled workers may begin taking responsibility for job training.

**APRICOT.** When the first warm days of spring relieve the winter chill, the buds of the apricot trees begin to stir. The little white or shell-pink blossoms begin to cover the bare twigs of the tree long before most other fruit trees have blossomed. Tiny leaves appear soon after the flowers.

The small green fruits grow very slowly until the stone is formed. Then they fill out rapidly and ripen in late June and in July. The name apricot is from Arabic and Greek words meaning "early ripening."

The apricot is closely related to the peach and plum. The fruit is less juicy. The bark is reddish and resembles peach tree bark. The leaves are almost

*The fruit of the apricot tree is similar to that of the peach tree, but it is somewhat smaller and less juicy.*

Apricot Producers of California

round, with a short point and heart-shaped base. The tree does not thrive as far north as the plum and peach because of its early blooming.

Each tree bears heavy clusters of golden fruit with a reddish blush. When fresh, the apricot has a mild, neutral taste. When canned or dried, its flavor sharpens into tartness. It is a good source of vitamin A.

There are three species of apricots. A native of China, the fruit was introduced into Europe in the time of Alexander the Great. It is widely grown in southern Europe and the Middle East. California, where it has been raised since mission days, Washington, and Utah produce nearly all the American crop.

Only a small share of the crop is used as fresh fruit. Formerly most of the crop was dried, but in recent years canners have taken the larger share. Apricots are also frozen and made into preserves, jam, nectar, and a liqueur. Both the dried and the canned fruit is exported. The seed kernel is a delicacy in tropical lands and is sold like the almond. The scientific name of the common apricot is *Prunus armeniaca*.

**APRIL** *see* CALENDAR; FESTIVALS AND HOLIDAYS.

**AQUACULTURE.** The growing of plants and animals on land for food and other products is agriculture. Raising animals and plants in the water is aquaculture. Practiced since ancient times in many parts of the world, aquaculture embraces such diverse activities as the Chinese tradition of growing carp in ponds, the harvesting and processing of seaweed in Iceland, and the artificial culture of pearls—a Japanese invention. Aquaculture can take place in water that is still or in running water, fresh or salt.

The practice of aquaculture has been growing rapidly. Experts have projected a fivefold increase in harvests during the final quarter of the 20th century. In the 1970s Asia accounted for approximately 85 percent of world production in the field.

Aquaculture is regarded as one possible solution to the world's food supply problems. The quantity of tillable land is limited and shrinking everywhere. But two thirds of the globe is covered with water; the supply of food animals and plants that may be grown there is almost limitless. In contrast to agriculture, which is practiced on the land's surface only, aquaculture is three-dimensional. Within the same vertical region several different crops can be grown at once—near the water surface, on the bottom, and in the area between. Multiple cropping of this kind, called polyculture, represents an efficient use of labor, materials, and energy. Aquaculture is less affected by climatic change—droughts, floods, and extremes of heat and cold—than is agriculture.

**Animal Aquaculture**

In animal aquaculture much effort has gone into controlling the breeding process. Some fish, such as trout, are easily bred in captivity. Eggs are squeezed from the female and fertilized. Once hatched, immature fish are raised in tanks or ponds. Carp and catfish, which do not breed easily in captivity, are caught in the wild while young and then raised to maturity by aquaculturists. In Indonesia, for example, when the rice paddies are idle during the time between harvest and planting, farmers may buy young carp and fatten them in the paddies. Mussels are raised in France by a process that involves hanging ropes over natural mussel beds in the ocean. The immature mussels, called spats, float after hatching and attach themselves to the ropes. The spat-covered ropes are next wound around large stakes in the sea. There the mussels mature. Similar methods are used to raise oysters in many parts of the world.

Aquaculturists keep their animals captive by such means as ponds, tanks, and underwater enclosures. In some areas fish are artificially bred, released into the wild, and then recaptured as adults. This is done in enclosed areas such as the Caspian Sea, where sturgeon are raised for their flesh and their eggs.

In some cases agriculture and aquaculture exist side by side, supporting one another. Rice farmers, for example, may flood their fields during the wet monsoon season. The incoming tidal water carries in fry, or fish young, and small crustaceans. These creatures become enclosed in the rice paddy, where they thrive on algae and rotting vegetable matter. After three months the farmers drain the paddies, netting the fattened animals. Next they bring in ducks to graze the paddies. The birds leave behind their droppings to fertilize the next rice crop.

Foods for the captive animals are chosen to yield maximum growth. In recent years the diets of many cultured fish have been supplemented with vitamins. (*See also* Fish Culture.)

**Plant Aquaculture**

Some water plants are as systematically cultivated as agricultural crops. Since the 17th century, for example, the Japanese have grown amanori (edible red algae) near estuaries, places where rivers meet the sea. Traditionally, farmers collected amanori spores by placing long pieces of split bamboo or tree branches in shallow, muddy river water. In two weeks spores settled onto the bamboo and developed into small plants. The bamboo was then moved toward the estuaries, where the amanori thrived on a nutritious mixture of fresh and salt water.

Amanori culture is tightly controlled and completely mechanized today. The spores collect on nets that hang in special hatching tanks. Farmers then truck the nets to bays along Japan's Pacific coast, where the amanori are mechanically tended until they are harvested.

The Chinese have also controlled and organized the culture of water plants such as kelp. Similar practices are developing in the Philippines, and interest is growing in many other parts of the world. An excellent book on aquaculture is 'Sea Farm', by Elizabeth Mann, published in 1980.

**AQUANAUT** *see* OCEAN.

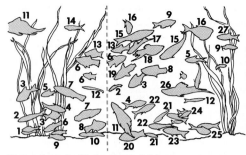

The most popular kinds of tropical fish were gathered in one tank to make this picture. The fish could not live together or in such numbers in a home aquarium. The key picture above and the list below identify them.

1. Golden Barb—southeastern Asia
2. Red-Fin Tetra—Brazil, Guyana, Suriname, and French Guiana
3. Sumatra Barb—Thailand and Malaysia
4. German Flag-Fish—Brazil
5. Red Rasbora—Malaysia and Sumatra
6. Red Platy—domestic variety
7. Black Mollie—southern United States
8. Black-Wag Platy—domestic variety
9. Zebra Danio—India
10. Guppy—Trinidad and Venezuela
11. Betta—Thailand
12. Pencil Fish—northern South America
13. Platy—Mexico, Guatemala, and British Honduras
14. Pearl Danio—Myanmar
15. Giant Danio—India and Sri Lanka
16. Hatchet Fish—Brazil
17. Black-Wag Swordtail—domestic variety
18. Swordtail Platy—domestic hybrid
19. Small-headed Characin—Brazil
20. Dwarf Cichlid—South America
21. Neon Tetra—Brazil and Peru
22. Oblique—Brazil
23. Red-nosed Tetra—Brazil
24. Glo-Lite Tetra—Guyana
25. Head-and-Tail-Light—Guyana and Brazil
26. Red Swordtail—domestic variety
27. Swordtail—Mexico, Guatemala, and British Honduras

**AQUARIUM.** The term aquarium may refer to a receptacle, such as a goldfish bowl or small tank, in which fishes and other aquatic organisms are kept, or it may refer to a building in which many different forms of aquatic life are put on display for the public or used in research. There are some open-air aquariums in places where the climate permits.

### THE PUBLIC AQUARIUM

A large aquarium may require a variety of specialists to maintain it: engineers, accountants, animal trainers, and biologists. Scientists on the staff of an aquarium make regular trips to many areas of the world to collect new specimens. They also exchange collections regularly with aquariums in other cities and countries.

There are two basic types of aquariums, which differ according to the water used and the kinds of fishes and other creatures kept in them. These are the marine, or seawater, aquarium and the freshwater aquarium. Ocean creatures are placed in seawater, while those from rivers and lakes require fresh water.

### Design and Maintenance

In a public aquarium huge exhibition tanks are often set into the walls. Thousands of fishes of many species swim in settings of rock, sand, or coral that imitate their natural habitats. Signs or charts indicate the popular and scientific names of the specimens, and where they originate.

Care must be taken in constructing containers for aquatic life, because many materials, such as certain plastics and adhesives, are poisonous to water-breathing animals. This is an even greater problem for marine animals since salt water can dissolve metals and produce substances that are toxic. Glass is considered the safest material. Other appropriate materials include polyethylene, polypropylene, Plexiglas, and fluorocarbon plastics. Effective adhesives

for sealing the tanks include epoxy resins, polyvinyl chloride, silicone rubber, and neoprene.

Large public aquariums are difficult to maintain because they must take into account the requirements of many different aquatic animals, including mammals, birds, reptiles, amphibians, and invertebrates, as well as fishes. These aquariums usually require a number of accessories such as filters, air pumps, lights, and heaters.

Filters are used to keep large aquariums clean. The most common types of filters are waterproof boxes through which the water circulates. They are packed with substances such as sand, gravel, fiberglass, and charcoal, which remove contaminants. Such filters can be placed inside or outside of the tank.

In a well-balanced aquarium, the plants and the surface of the water provide enough oxygen for the fishes and other animals. Often, however, the water must be aerated to get enough oxygen. Aeration is the process by which the water is stirred so that more oxygen is absorbed at the surface of the water.

Heaters are used by aquariums that house organisms that prefer higher than room temperatures. Electric heaters are often placed in an upper corner or on the bottom of the tank near the rear wall.

Natural lighting is too strong in summer, too weak in winter, and absent at night. The most effective method of lighting is by incandescent lamps above the front portion of the tanks. Fluorescent lights provide good illumination but may overlight the tank walls. Certain special bulbs emphasize natural colors and encourage the growth of aquatic plants.

Not all aquariums require special lighting, but all require good water quality. The water must be free of pollutants and must provide the right amount of oxygen. An aquarium must have water of the same temperature as the water from which the inhabitants were taken. Normally, five temperature levels of water

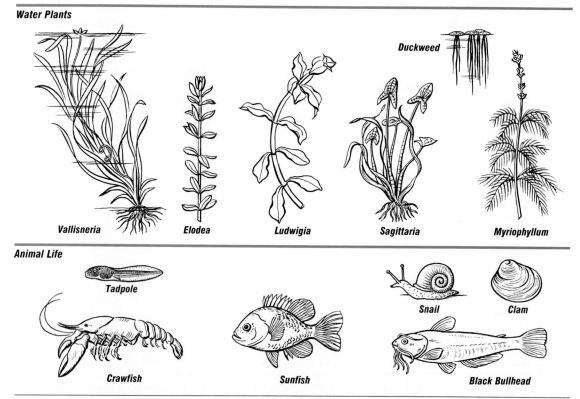

**Water Plants**

Duckweed

Vallisneria    Elodea    Ludwigia    Sagittaria    Myriophyllum

**Animal Life**

Tadpole

Snail    Clam

Crawfish    Sunfish    Black Bullhead

*Specific kinds of plants (top) are recommended for an aquarium because they give off plenty of oxygen. These plants also provide food and protection for various kinds of water life. Common freshwater fishes (bottom) thrive in an aquarium. Black bullhead and sunfish may be raised successfully. Snails, tadpoles, crawfish, and clams make interesting additions.*

are used, depending on the type of fishes and other animals in the aquarium: heated or chilled salt water and heated, chilled, or natural fresh water.

Aquariums located inland either must be provided with thousands of gallons of seawater or they must make their own blend of salt water by using artificial salts. This water is regularly cleaned, filtered, and allowed to settle so that it may be used for many years.

There are three basic types of aquarium water systems: open, closed, and semiclosed. In open systems, the water flows through the aquarium once and is then discarded. In a closed system, the water is renewed periodically and continuously recirculated. A semiclosed system differs from a closed system in that it is constantly connected to the water supply so the problem of dissolved wastes can be controlled by the regular addition of new water.

### Plants

Plants serve many purposes in an aquarium. In addition to providing beauty and authenticity, they help slow the growth of algae and provide food, hiding places, and spawning grounds for the animals that live with them.

The green plants remove carbon dioxide from the water and give off oxygen, while animal life uses

oxygen and exhales carbon dioxide. A proper ratio of oxygen and carbon dioxide creates an aquarium that is balanced with respect to these important gases. Another interrelationship is that fish droppings fertilize the plants and the fishes are able to eat the plants and organisms around them.

There are three types of aquatic plants: rooted plants, which require individual planting and have long roots; bunch plants, a type of rooted plant, which are obtained without roots and simply placed at the bottom of the tank; and floating plants, which are not planted in aquarium gravel or sand but live on the surface of the water.

Few plants will thrive in saltwater aquariums. These displays are decorated instead with rocks and corals. Some of the corals may look like plants.

### Care of Aquatic Animals

The collections in a public aquarium are often changed frequently. The various animals have different life spans. Some aquarium fishes may live 20 years, but their average span is about 18 months.

In order to prevent disease, the fishes and other animals are provided with suitable water, tankmates, and diet. New specimens are quarantined for two or three weeks before being placed with other fishes.

The inhabitants of aquariums survive best when supplied with the diet they were used to in their natural waters. Live foods often given to aquarium fishes include crustaceans, mosquito larvae, midge larvae, small worms, and fruit flies. Marine fishes can be fed fish roe, chopped mussels, lean fish, or shrimps. There are also several commercially prepared foods available to the professional and home aquarist.

## THE HOME AQUARIUM

Although goldfish are popular and easy to keep, the home aquarist often keeps many varieties of small tropical fishes. They are usually commercially collected or bred in such numbers that they may be bought at a relatively low price. The natural homes of many of these fishes include the Gulf of Mexico, the Caribbean Sea, the South Atlantic, the South Pacific, the Indian Ocean, and the swamps, streams, rivers, and lakes of Africa, Asia, South America, and Central America.

Among the most popular freshwater species of fishes are guppies (*Lebistes reticulatus*), swordtails (*Xiphophorus helleri*), and moonfish (*Platypoecilus maculatus*). These fishes bear living young. Among the most popular of the egg-laying species is the striped zebra danio (*Brachydanio rerio*). Another type, the "bubble-nest" builders, blow floating masses of bubbles into which the male places the eggs as fast as his mate lays them. The commonest of these are the paradise fish (*Macropodus opercularis*). But, they are so quarrelsome that they cannot be kept with other fishes.

Other fishes often kept in home aquariums include bettas (*Betta splendens*), which fight only among themselves, the dwarf gourami (*Colisa lalia*), which are extremely peaceful, and the brilliantly colored blue and red neon and cardinal tetras (*Hyphessobrycon innesi* and *Cheirodon axelrodi*).

Tropical fishes are generally easy to care for in a home aquarium, but one should make sure that the aquarium is not overstocked. The number of fishes that can safely be kept in any aquarium is based on a ratio of 1½ inches (3.8 centimeters) of fish length per square inch (6.5 square centimeters) of water surface. If filters and aeration are used, the ratio is 3 inches (7.6 centimeters) per square inch.

Tropical fishes require sufficient but controllable light, a water temperature of at least 70° F (21° C), and a variety of foods. Overfeeding is the most common cause of fishes dying. A good rule is to feed fishes only as much food as they totally consume in three to five minutes. Most fishes thrive best when fed only this limited amount from two to four times per day.

If the tank is covered with glass or a commercially manufactured full hood to prevent water evaporation, the water will rarely need to be completely changed. However, about 10 percent of the water should be removed and replaced with fresh water every week or two. Plants, filters, and heaters are helpful, even necessary in some cases.

To provide the most healthful habitat for fishes, chemicals help fight diseases and control water quality. Chemicals will also condition tap water

John G. Shedd Aquarium

*The coral reef exhibit at the John G. Shedd Aquarium is one of metropolitan Chicago's most popular points of interest.*

instantly for use in aquariums: they remove chlorine and fluorine, which would otherwise kill the fishes.

Many home aquarists add creatures other than fishes to their collection. The Japanese snail and the African paper-shell snail are examples. Snails are not, as was once thought, useful in helping keep an aquarium clean. Tadpoles, newts, and turtles, which may harm fishes, should be kept separate from them.

Saltwater home aquariums can house any of a number of beautiful tropical fishes, oysters, mussels, sea clams, shrimps, barnacles, and sea anemones. When the water from a saltwater aquarium evaporates, only fresh water should be used to replace it. If seawater were added, the salt left after continued evaporation would create a concentrated brine that would kill the animals. Saltwater home aquariums are not as popular as freshwater ones because they are more difficult and expensive to maintain.

## HISTORY

Aquariums have been kept for thousands of years. The Sumerians of Mesopotamia kept fishes in artificial ponds at least 4,500 years ago. Other early cultures that had aquariums include the Egyptians, Assyrians, Chinese, Japanese, and Romans.

These ancient aquariums served several purposes. They provided both entertainment and a place to breed fishes for market. The Chinese developed the practice of breeding ornamental fishes suitable for keeping in small containers. One result of their efforts was the goldfish, a type of carp.

Aquarium keeping did not become a well-established science until the relationship between oxygen, animals, and plants became known in the 1800s. The term aquarium first appeared in the works of Phillip Gosse (1810–88), a British scientist.

The first public aquarium was opened in 1853 in Regent's Park, London. It was followed by aquariums in Berlin, Naples, and Paris. By 1928 there were 45 public or commercial aquariums throughout the world. Growth then slowed because of the worldwide depression, and there were few new large aquariums built until after World War II.

Philip D. Gendreau—The Bettmann Archive

*The Pont du Gard aqueduct near Nîmes, France, was built by the Romans in 19 BC. It is composed of three tiers of semicircular arches and is about 160 feet high.*

**AQUEDUCT.** Most towns and cities arise on sites where water is plentiful, whether from lakes, rivers, or wells. As cities grow, the source of water is sometimes insufficient or even becomes too polluted for domestic use. Such cities must build artificial waterways, called aqueducts, to bring water from other sources. The distribution lines within the city are not normally classed as part of the aqueduct.

Aqueducts may be canals, open troughs, overland pipelines, or tunnels. The earliest aqueducts were dug through clay or cut out of solid rock. Ancient engineers used wood, stone, and primitive concrete. A few early aqueducts used siphons to carry water across valleys and over hills. For the most part, however, aqueducts had to follow gentle, downhill courses, sometimes taking paths around mountains, through hills, and atop long, bridgelike arcades. Pumps and pressurized construction allow modern aqueducts to carry water with little regard for the pull of gravity.

### Ancient Aqueducts

The earliest form of aqueduct was the *qanaat*. A *qanaat* is a tunnel that begins slightly below the water table in the foothills of a mountain or a range of hills. This tunnel leads away from the foothills, gradually downhill, to carry water to a village or city. *Qanaats* were used widely throughout the Middle East and Northern Africa (where they were known as *fogarras*). Their greatest development, however, was in Persia (now Iran). There *qanaats* are still in use and are constructed in much the same manner as they were in ancient times.

A famous early tunnel aqueduct was cut through solid rock in about 700 BC to carry water from the spring of Gihom to the Siloam reservoir in Jerusalem, a distance of about 1,750 feet (530 meters). In 691 BC, King Sennacherib of Assyria ordered construction of the aqueduct of Jerwan, which brought water from a tributary of the Greater Zab River to Nineveh, some 50 miles (80 kilometers) away. Another aqueduct, built on the Aegean island of Samos in about 530 BC, traveled through a hill by means of a tunnel about 3,300 feet (1,000 meters) long. Water flowed through clay pipes laid within the tunnel.

The most famous aqueduct builders of ancient times were the Romans. The word aqueduct comes from the Latin *aqua* ("water") and *ducere* ("to lead"). Roman engineers built the main portions of their aqueducts at ground level or underground where possible. The water fed through free-flowing conduits. When it was necessary for the Roman aqueducts to cross valleys or descend to plains, they were often carried on arched bridges, or arcades. Some bridges were built with two or three tiers of arches to gain the height needed to maintain an even flow. The bridges and arcades were more difficult to build and required more maintenance than the surface level or underground portions of the aqueducts.

Water for the city of Rome was supplied by 11 major aqueducts built over a period of more than 500 years. The first one, the Aqua Appia, was built in 312 BC and was 10 miles (16 kilometers) long. The last, the Aqua Alexandrina, was built in about AD 226. The longest was the 58-mile (93-kilometer) Aqua Marcia, built in 144 BC.

Roman engineers built aqueducts in numerous other parts of their empire, notably France, Spain, and Northern Africa. Remains of these aqueducts still exist.

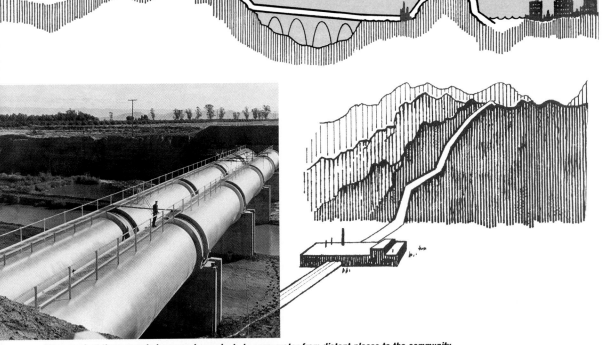

*Since ancient times people have used aqueducts to carry water from distant places to the community for use in homes or for irrigation. These man-made channels (top) may be one of several types or a combination of types. Tunnel aqueducts pass through mountains. Channels lined with planks, concrete, or brick cross valleys and open areas. In the United States, open aqueducts are often called flumes or sluiceways. Pipeline aqueducts carry a huge volume of water for long distances. Open aqueducts, such as the channel type (bottom left), are better suited to carrying small amounts for short distances. All aqueducts, at one time, had to be built to follow a gentle downhill slope so that the water flowed by the force of gravity. The modern pipeline aqueduct is not so restricted because the flow can be created by pressure from pumping stations (bottom right).*

A few of them, such as the one at Segovia, Spain, have remained in use. One of the most striking of the old Roman aqueducts is the Pont du Gard in southern France, which the Romans built to a height of 160 feet (49 meters) by stacking three bridges.

### Medieval Aqueducts

Roman aqueducts continued to be used even after the fall of the empire. Repairs were often inadequate, however, and most of the aqueducts gradually fell into disuse. A few were kept in operation through the Middle Ages. Some new aqueducts were built but none on the scale of the Roman ones.

Churchmen were often involved in aqueduct building in the Middle Ages. Aldric, the bishop of Le Mans from 832 to 856, constructed an aqueduct to bring water to two fountains. A monastery in Canterbury, England, built an aqueduct in about 1153 to supply its water.

Other waterworks were built by Cistercian abbeys in England, France, Germany, and Italy. In 1285 the convent of Chester, in England, laid a lead pipe 3 miles (5 kilometers) long to provide water.

A number of medieval aqueducts were built in African and Asian countries. One such aqueduct, an arched conduit, was constructed in the 9th century to carry water to Cairo, Egypt. In India an aqueduct

15 miles (24 kilometers) long was built in 1406, most of it cut through solid rock, connecting with the Tungbhadra Dam.

### Inca and Aztec Aqueducts

In pre-Columbian America, both the Incas and Aztecs channeled water to their cities and religious centers. The Incas built an elaborate system of aqueducts, some of cut stone, which wound through hills and valleys to bring water from the mountains. One of the Inca aqueducts leading from the highlands down to the sea was 360 miles (579 kilometers) long and 13 feet (4 meters) deep. Workers dug tunnels through mountains and cut channels into cliffs to complete the project. In seasons when too much mountain snow melted, the flood waters were carried to huge masonry reservoirs for storage.

### Modern Aqueducts

Aqueduct building has continued on into modern times, using more advanced engineering techniques. Improved materials, drills, and explosives were developed for tunneling. Horse-driven pumps, introduced in the late 1700s, were later replaced by mechanical pumps. One modern aqueduct, the Loch Katrine aqueduct of Glasgow, Scotland, completed in 1860, required 13 miles (21 kilometers) of tunneling over its total length of almost 26 miles (42 kilometers). One of the longest aqueducts, the Coolgardie Aqueduct in Western Australia extends 350 miles (563 kilometers) and was completed in 1903. The Apulian Aqueduct in Italy carries water 152 miles (245 kilometers) from the Apennines to Taranto.

In the United States the water supply system for New York City is among the most elaborate in the world. Most of the city's water comes from watersheds to the north. The water is stored there in reservoirs and natural lakes. The Croton, Catskill, and Delaware aqueducts deliver it to the city.

The Old Croton Aqueduct, completed in 1848, is 46 miles (74 kilometers) long. It was supplemented by the New Croton Aqueduct, 31 miles (50 kilometers) long, completed in 1893. The Catskill Aqueduct, 92 miles (148 kilometers) long, was completed in 1917. The Delaware System, 105 miles (169 kilometers) long, was completed in 1965.

Since the early 1900s the rapid growth in the population of California has required the building of an enormous aqueduct system to supply water. Probably the largest system ever constructed, it is still growing. The Metropolitan Water District of Southern California system alone has a total length of 672 miles (1,081 kilometers) and can deliver more than 1 billion gallons (3.8 billion liters) daily. The major part of this system is the Colorado River Aqueduct, completed in 1941. It brings water from Lake Havasu on the California-Arizona border to Los Angeles and other southern California communities. *James R. McDonald*

**AQUINAS, Thomas** (1225?–74). The Roman Catholic church regards St. Thomas Aquinas as its greatest theologian and philosopher. Pope John XXII canonized him in 1323, and Pius V declared him a doctor of the church in 1567. Leo XIII made him patron of Roman Catholic schools in 1880.

Thomas Aquinas, or Thomas of Aquino, was born in about 1225 in the castle of Roccasecca, near Naples. His father was the count of Aquino. The boy received his early education at the abbey of Monte Cassino before attending the University of Naples. While at the university Thomas came under the influence of the Dominicans, an order of mendicant preaching friars. In spite of the opposition of his family, he joined the order. His brothers captured him and imprisoned him at Roccasecca. After two years he escaped.

The Dominicans then sent Thomas to Cologne to study with Albertus Magnus, the most learned man of the time. In 1252 Thomas was in Paris composing his 'Commentaries on the Books of Sentences of Peter the Lombard'. He was later admitted as master of theology at the University of Paris.

In 1259 the pope called Thomas to Rome. He spent the rest of his life lecturing and preaching in the service of his order, chiefly in Italian cities and in Paris. He died on March 7, 1274, while traveling to a church council at Lyons.

A revival of learning had begun in Western Europe toward the end of the 11th century. By the 13th century many universities had been founded. They were linked to the church, and the chief subjects taught were theology and the liberal arts. The teachers were called Schoolmen or Scholastics. Thomas was recognized in his lifetime as the greatest of the Schoolmen and was known as the "angelic doctor."

The Schoolmen accepted Christian doctrines as beyond dispute, but they also studied the ancient Greek philosophers. Until the 13th century they relied on Plato as interpreted by St. Augustine of Hippo. Aristotle's treatises on logic were also admitted into the schools, but his other works, which were known in their Arabic translations, were forbidden because of their pantheistic tendencies. Albertus Magnus introduced Thomas to the works of Aristotle, which were beginning to be translated from the original Greek. Thomas set himself the task of harmonizing Aristotle's teachings with Christian doctrine. (*See also* Aristotle.)

Thomas held that there are two sources of knowledge: revelation (theology) and reason (philosophy). He held that revelation is a divine source of knowledge and that revealed truths must be believed even when they cannot be fully understood. His literary output was enormous. At times he dictated to several scribes on different subjects. His chief works are 'Summa Contra Gentiles' and 'Summa Theologiae', which form the classical systematization of Roman Catholic theology.

**AQUINO, Corazon** (born 1933). On Aug. 21, 1983, Benigno Aquino, a Philippine politician opposed to President Ferdinand Marcos, was assassinated as he got off an airplane in Manila. On Feb. 25, 1986, his widow, Corazon Aquino, became the first woman president of the Philippines. In so doing she ended the 20-year corrupt rule of Marcos (*see* Marcos).

Corazon Cojuangco was born on Jan. 25, 1933, in Manila. Her family was wealthy and politically active: her father and a brother were both congressmen. She attended school in Manila and in the United States in Philadelphia and New York City. She graduated from Mount St. Vincent College in New York in 1953. She met Benigno Aquino after her return to Manila.

After their marriage she helped him to pursue his political career. He hoped to be a presidential candidate in the 1973 election, but Marcos imposed martial law in 1972 and imprisoned Aquino and many other political opponents. After eight years Aquino was released and went into voluntary exile in the United States with Corazon and their five children.

After his death she became more active politically. When Marcos called an election for February 1986, she announced her candidacy. Although results of the election were disputed, Marcos was driven from the country on Feb. 25, 1986, and she assumed the presidency. She immediately released political prisoners and made overtures to Communist revolutionaries. In the 1992 presidential election Aquino supported retired general Fidel Ramos, her secretary of defense, who had supported her through seven coup attempts. Ramos won the presidency.

**ARABIA.** The "Island of the Arabs," *Jazirat al-Arab,* is located in southwestern Asia. Arabia, or the Arabian Peninsula, is the original homeland of the Arab population in the Middle East, of Arabic language and culture, and of the major world religion of Islam.

The central part of the Arabian Peninsula has never been conquered by a colonial power, though it has played a major role in the history of Islam and of the Muslim empires. Since 1932 the Kingdom of Saudi Arabia has predominated as the largest political unit of Arabia. Today the peninsula includes six other independent countries—Kuwait, Oman, Qatar, the United Arab Emirates, Yemen, and Bahrain. The peninsula also includes portions of Jordan, Iraq, and a Neutral Zone west of Kuwait that is shared by Iraq and Saudi Arabia. In addition to its economic importance because of its oil-producing nations, Arabia is also a strategically important part of the Middle East, as well as the religious focus of Muslims throughout the world.

Arabia lies in the belt of arid lands that stretch from the Sahara in northern Africa almost all the way across central Asia. It extends some 1,400 miles (2,250 kilometers) from Jordan and Iraq on the north to the Arabian Sea on the south. At its widest part, between the southern Red Sea and the Gulf of Oman, it measures about 1,250 miles (2,000 kilometers). The waters bounding it are the Gulf of Aqaba, the Red Sea, and the Bab el Mandeb on the west; the Gulf of Aden and the Arabian Sea on the south; and the Gulf of Oman, the Strait of Hormuz, and the Persian Gulf on the east. The peninsula's area is about 1¼ million square miles (3.4 million square kilometers). The population is 15,000,000.

Most of Arabia is a broad plateau that gradually slopes down from the Red Sea coastal mountains to the Persian Gulf. It is broken by hills and low mountains, notably the Jabal Tuwayq in central Saudi Arabia and the Jabal Akhdar in northern Oman. The highest point is a peak in Yemen that towers 12,336 feet (3,760 meters).

The vast stretches of desert in Arabia take many forms. The greatest part is steppe or desert-steppe. There the land receives enough seasonal rainfall to produce scattered patches of coarse grass and drought-resistant shrubs for grazing. In the An Nafud desert of northern Saudi Arabia, high parallel sand dunes roll like billows. Between the billows are troughs where pebbles, stones, and rocks are bared. Southward the sands of the Ad Dahna desert swirl in a crescent-like strip that ends in the Rub' al Khali (Empty Quarter), now the site of oil exploration.

### Climate, Vegetation, and Animal Life

The extensive arid portions of the peninsula are an extension of the Sahara's desert region. Rub' al Khali and An Nafud are the two largest areas of sand dunes. Little rain falls on the region, and there are no permanent rivers or lakes. Temperatures there reach 140° F (60° C) in the daytime, while at night they often drop to 30° to 40° F (−1° to 4° C). Along the coastal areas the humidity may reach 90 to 100 percent on

Standard Oil Co. (N.J.)

*Bedouins rest their camels at an oasis in Arabia. The numbers of these nomadic herdsmen have diminished.*

both the Red Sea and Persian Gulf shores in summer. Juniper trees grow in the mountainous regions of Asir Province in southwestern Saudi Arabia and Yemen. The mountainous regions of Oman also receive more adequate rainfall and consequently are used for agriculture.

The animals found in Arabia include the now-rare oryx, camels, hyenas, wolves, and jackals. The oryx with its two parallel horns is believed to have inspired the stories of the mythical unicorn. Other animals are similar to those found in Saharan Africa and the southwestern United States, including scorpions, snakes, spiders, lizards, hares, and rodents. Sheep, still kept by some tribes, are herded as far as Iraq and Syria for temporary spring grazing. The famous saluqi hound, a northern African desert dog, is used to hunt gazelles, while the prized Arabian stallions and falcons are owned by the ruling families. The bustard, a bird related to the cranes and hunted for food and sport, has virtually disappeared.

### The Economy

The most successful farmers are the Yemenis. On the terraced slopes leading to their hilltop villages they raise citrus fruits, grapes, figs, coffee, vegetables, and a variety of grains, including wheat, barley, and millet. The fertile Dhofar district, in southern Oman, produces livestock, coconut palms, and vegetables. Much of the cotton raised in Arabia is from Yemen. Apricots, peaches, pomegranates, and rice, which the Arabs were the first to bring to Europe, are raised in the oases of Saudi Arabia.

For centuries herding has been the chief means of livelihood of the pastoral nomads called Bedouins. On

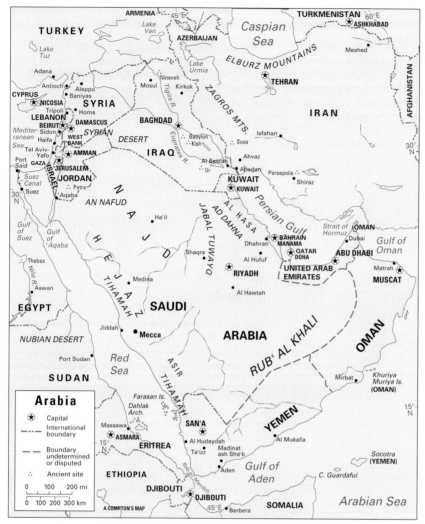

Arabia is the popular name for a large landmass in Southwest Asia called the Arabian Peninsula. A hot and arid land, it lies across the Red Sea from Africa on the west and is bounded by the Arabian Sea on the south and the Persian Gulf on the east. Until the late 1930s Arabia was a land of little commercial importance, noted chiefly as the birthplace of Islam, but petroleum discoveries in that period drew world attention to the peninsula. Arabia subsequently became a major source of world petroleum. Wealth from petroleum exports has enriched most of the Arabian countries and brought many social benefits to their peoples.

the desert-steppe they find pasturage for their camels, sheep, goats, donkeys, and horses. Wool, hides, and ghee (clarified butter), the chief products, are sold to oasis settlements. (*See also* Nomads.)

Petroleum was discovered along the Persian Gulf coast in the early 1930s. Most of the oil fields were developed by United States, British, Dutch, and Japanese interests. Among them are the Abqaiq, Berri, Safaniya, and Ghawar fields in Saudi Arabia, the Burgan field in Kuwait, and the Dukhan field in Qatar. Refineries are located at Ras Tanura in Saudi Arabia, at Mina al Ahmadi in Kuwait, and on Bahrain. An oil pipeline, completed in 1981, links the Red Sea to the Persian Gulf.

The royalties paid by foreign oil companies have greatly increased the revenues of some Arabian governments. Some states have used this huge income to benefit the people; in Kuwait, for example, oil profits have been used for new schools, hospitals and other medical facilities, sanitation systems, and electric power stations. Others are using it to modernize irrigation and

to improve means of communication and transportation. The United Arab Emirates, Kuwait, Bahrain, Qatar, Oman, and Saudia Arabia formed the Gulf Cooperation Council in 1981 to plan for the defense of the area. To diversify the economy the oil-producing states along the Persian Gulf established petrochemical plants and related industries.

The countries of Arabia benefit from the latest health facilities, though the personnel that operate them are largely Western. Generally there is a lack of local personnel qualified to deal with the new technology that has been introduced into these nations.

## The People

The pattern of life in the Arabian Peninsula has changed drastically in the past decades. In the 1950s a series of droughts forced many nomadic and semi-nomadic groups to dispose of their herds and move to the urbanareas. Many governments established programs to settle these people, providing them with plots of land, wells, and seeds to enable them to start farms. Also, the need for education and health care for their children made it necessary for families to move to places that provided schools and other facilities. The oil wealth enabled many to acquire houses, automobiles, and other conveniences of modern-day life previously unavailable to them. For these reasons little is left of the old nomadic life, though tribal affiliations, the importance of the family, and other customs still remain. Traditional female roles are also undergoing change, and education for women is available through university levels.

One of the three major world religions, Islam is practiced by an estimated 750 million people, called Muslims (*see* Islam). Among them are most of the inhabitants of the Arabian Peninsula. Until 1948, when Israel was established, there was a significant number of Jews in Yemen. Various forms of religious practices involving several gods preceded Islam, particularly among the nomads. With the advent of Islam these people were incorporated into a religious state led by Muhammad, considered the last of the prophets by Muslims throughout the world (*see* Muhammad).

Historically the Arabs have maintained a rich oral tradition that was based on the recitation of poetry and stories of tribal valor. The poet, a strong political influence in the community, was both revered and feared. Arabic, a Semitic language rich in vocabulary, easily lends itself to rhyming, and couplets arranged in a form called the *qasidah* are part of Arabia's early literary heritage. The art form calligraphy was used to decorate tombs and the pages of the Koran—the holy book of Islam. The carved wooden latticework seen in the window screens of 19th-century homes in Jiddah, Saudi Arabia, attests to the expertise of Arab carpenters. (*See also* Islamic Literature; Koran.)

## History

Arabia was the original home of a number of Semitic tribes who after years of wandering settled in the Fertile Crescent to the north of the peninsula. There they developed some of the earliest civilizations. The southwestern part of Arabia also contained advanced kingdoms. The Minaean flourished in about 1200 BC. Other notable kingdoms were Himyarite and Sabean, or Sheba, whose queen is reputed to have visited Solomon. (*See also* Babylonia and Assyria; Mesopotamia; Phoenicians; Solomon.)

The Arabs were famous traders. In ancient times caravans brought frankincense and myrrh from the Hadhramaut Valley in southern Arabia to Egypt and the eastern Mediterranean lands. Later, as trade with the Orient expanded, they carried spices from the East Indies, silks from China, and ivory from India. Long before Europeans explored the African continent, Arabs had colonized Ethiopia, sailed down the east coast, and traded in the interior.

Islam—literally "submission" (to the will of Allah)—was brought by Muhammad to the tribes of the Arabian Peninsula in the 7th century. It refocused tribal loyalties to a monotheistic (single god) religious state that extended its territory from Afghanistan westward across North Africa into Spain and part of France by 732. The area of the Fertile Crescent, including Syria and Mesopotamia, housed the capitals of the Umayyad and 'Abbasid caliphates in the 8th and 9th centuries. After having been ruled in the Middle Ages by the Fatimid and Mameluk dynasties, in 1517 the Hejaz, or western littoral of Arabia, was incorporated into the Ottoman Empire. During the Ottoman period the Hejaz was granted special subsidies, and the sultan (Ottoman ruler) appointed a representative, the grand sharif of Mecca, to oversee the hajj (the pilgrimage to Mecca made by Muslims) and administer the province. (*See also* Caliphate.)

In the 18th and 19th centuries various rival leaders outside the Hejaz fought to assert their control of the peninsula. Most powerful were the emirs (princes) of the House of Saud and the emirs of the House of Rashid in Ha'il in north-central Arabia. The Ottoman viceroy in Egypt, Muhammad 'Ali Pasha, sent forces to regain control from the Wahhabis in the early 19th century. Great Britain, concerned over its route to India, established treaties with the sheikhs along the eastern coast of Arabia to protect the Arabian Sea from raiding pirates. In the early 20th century the Ottoman Empire declined to a point where various sheikhs and emirs made new attempts to exert control in Arabia. (*See also* Ottoman Empire.)

At the beginning of World War I the Wahhabis, under Ibn Saud, gained control of the province of Al Hasa in eastern Arabia and Najd. In the Hejaz Sharif Husayn of Mecca aligned himself with the British against the Ottomans to establish an independent Arab kingdom. His rival to the south, the Idrisi of Asir, also made treaties with the British. In Yemen the Ottoman sultan was forced to recognize the virtual independence of its imam (ruler).

During the war Sharif Husayn, with British aid and joined by the tribes of Transjordan, led a successful revolt against the Ottomans. Ibn Saud overthrew the Rashids and drove the sharif from the Hejaz in 1924 and proclaimed himself ruler of the kingdom of Saudi Arabia in 1932. With the acquisition of Asir in 1934 he became undisputed leader. The League of Arab States was formed in 1945. Its apparent failure to achieve unity led to the formation of regional common markets, such as the Arab Cooperation Council in 1989. The accord was signed by Iraq, Jordan, Yemen, and Egypt. (*See also* Arabs; Ibn Saud.)

Sheila A. Scoville

**BIBLIOGRAPHY FOR ARABIA**

**Katakura, Motoko.** Bedouin Village: A Study of a Saudi Arabian People in Transition (International Scholastics, 1977).
**Netton, I.R., ed.** Arabia and the Gulf (B & N Imports, 1986).
**Philby, J.B.** Arabian Highlands (Da Capo, 1976).
**Raban, Jonathan.** Arabia: Journey Through the Labyrinth (Simon & Schuster, 1980).
**Stark, Freya.** The Southern Gates of Arabia (JP Tarcher, 1983).
**Time-Life.** Arabian Peninsula (Silver, 1985).
**Trench, Richard.** Arabian Travellers: The European Discovery of Arabia (Salem, 1986).
**Winder, R.B.** Saudi Arabia in the Nineteenth Century (Octagon, 1980).

*Morgiana, with dagger in hand, entertains Ali Baba and his son. The picture is by Walter Crane, an English artist and illustrator of children's books, for an 1873 edition of 'Arabian Nights'.*

**'ARABIAN NIGHTS'.** The colorful tales called the 'Arabian Nights' have come down through the centuries. Nobody knows who told them first or where, though they existed as early as the 10th century. Of Middle East origin, the tales have given to the world such interesting heroes or rogues as Sinbad the Sailor, Ali Baba and the story of the 40 thieves, and Aladdin and his magic lamp.

The legendary heroine of the tales of the 'Thousand and One Nights' is a girl named Scheherazade. It was said of Scheherazade that she was "learned, prudent, and witty." She was the elder of the two daughters of the grand vizier (chief councilor of state) of a kingdom that lay somewhere between Arabia and China. The younger daughter was named Dunyazad. The ruler of the kingdom was Sultan Shahriyar.

### The Sultan's Revenge

Shahriyar loved his first wife dearly, but the sultana betrayed him. His brother, the ruler of a neighboring kingdom, had had the same experience. Shahriyar, crushed and angry, ordered the grand vizier to put the sultana to death. Then the sultan decided to revenge himself on all women. He issued a decree stating that he would take a new wife each night and have her executed the next morning.

For three years the sultan's cruel order was carried out. The kingdom was in danger of losing all its eligible young women. Many parents with young daughters fled the land.

At last, Scheherazade conceived a plan to put an end to the daily executions. She asked her father to present her to Shahriyar as his next bride. The grand vizier was horrified, but finally he yielded. Scheherazade, accompanied by her sister, Dunyazad, was taken to the sultan.

### Scheherazade Begins the First Tale

Shahriyar was pleased with Scheherazade's beauty and wit. He warned the grand vizier, however, that she would not be spared the fate of his previous wives. After the marriage Scheherazade wept because she had to leave her sister. She begged the sultan to permit Dunyazad to sleep in the bridal chamber. Shahriyar was surprised but granted her request.

Just before daybreak, as Scheherazade had previously planned, Dunyazad begged her sister to tell once more one of the delightful stories for which she was famous. The sultan became interested and agreed to listen. So began the first of the tales called the 'Arabian Nights'.

Scheherazade's plan was to tell her story up to its most interesting point and then stop, leaving Shahriyar in suspense. To hear the end of the tale, he decided to let Scheherazade live for another night. Her supply of stories was so large that her scheme worked for a thousand and one nights.

During this time Scheherazade bore the sultan three sons. He became convinced of her wisdom and wifely devotion. In the end he revoked his barbaric decree, and they continued to live happily together.

### The Origin of the Tales

Where the 'Arabian Nights' originated is not known. The tale of Scheherazade is pure fiction. It merely serves to bind the stories together. An ancient Persian book was named 'A Thousand and One Nights'. Scheherazade and her Bluebeard husband, Shahriyar, were in it. The framework of this Persian collection, however, differs somewhat from that of the versions that are known today.

The fairy tales in the more modern collections probably had a Persian origin. The beast tales undoubtedly came from India. The anecdotes and the stories with morals are distinctly Arabic. There are also tales that must have come from China and Japan.

During the later part of the 8th century the stories were introduced into the court of Harun al-Raschid, the caliph of Baghdad. Harun al-Raschid was a scholar, a poet, and a patron of literature. He loved stories. The storytellers of his court flattered the caliph by making him the hero of many of their tales. Harun al-Raschid liked to disguise himself and roam among his subjects in the streets of Baghdad. It is in this role that he usually appears in the 'Arabian Nights'.

### The Tales Are Carried to Other Lands

Most modern versions of the 'Arabian Nights' have an Arabian background. The manners and customs of the myriad characters are those of medieval Muslim people. Scholars have found no original collection of the stories that can be called authoritative. For hundreds of years the tales were kept alive by word of mouth. Only in the framework and their division into nights was there any constant pattern. In about 1400, Egyptian scholars recorded the stories. Fragments of these collections were carried into other countries.

One of these collections, coming by way of Syria, fell into the hands of the French orientalist Antoine Galland. In 1704 he brought the 'Arabian Nights' tales to Europe. Galland's colorful and romantic collection was eagerly accepted. Galland was a talented storyteller, and he both told and wrote the stories, but his translation was never completed. The last volumes of his collection were made up of stories that are said to have been told to him in France by an Arab named Hanna. These include the well-known tales of 'Ali Baba and the Forty Thieves' and 'Aladdin'.

In Egypt, meanwhile, scholars had continued to collect the 'Arabian Nights' tales. In the beginning of the 19th century an unknown editor gathered a large number of them into manuscript form. All subsequent editions of the 'Arabian Nights' are based upon this Egyptian collection and later translations of it. These include the three famous English editions of Edward William Lane, John Payne, and Sir Richard Francis Burton (see Burton, Richard).

Lane's edition of the 'Arabian Nights' in three volumes was published in 1838 to 1840. It was the first of these three English translations made directly from the Arabic text. More literal in translation, though possibly less scholarly, is the translation in nine volumes by John Payne, a lawyer who devoted his later life to literature. The volumes in the Payne edition were published in 1882 to 1884.

Burton entered military service in India in 1842. He became one of the best-informed students of Asian life and languages of his time. The original and uncensored Burton translation was published in 16 volumes in 1885 to 1888. It is especially useful for its footnotes describing Muslim customs.

Many artists have illustrated various editions of the 'Arabian Nights'. Among the most successful were Vera Bock, Edmund Dulac, Walter Crane, Eric Pape, Maxfield Parrish, Willy Pogany, Arthur Rackham, and Lynd Ward.

The shortened, well-illustrated editions of the 'Arabian Nights' arranged for reading by young people are the best known. These collections vary somewhat in content, but almost all include the stories of 'Sinbad the Sailor', 'The Young King of the Black Isles', 'The Three Sisters', 'The Enchanted Horse', and 'Prince Ahmed and Periebanou'. Versions of the 'Arabian Nights' have appeared in virtually all the European languages, Hebrew, Yiddish, Chinese, Japanese, Malaysian, and Swahili.

Some well-known children's editions are 'Arabian Nights: Tales of Wonder and Magnificence', edited by Padraic Colum and illustrated by Lynd Ward (Macmillan, 1964); 'Arabian Nights: Their Best-Known Tales', edited by Kate Douglas Wiggin and Nora Archibald Smith and illustrated by Maxfield Parrish

(Macmillan Child Group, 1993); and 'Arabian Nights', edited by Andrew Lang and illustrated by Vera Bock (Watts, 1967). A paperback edition, 'Arabian Nights Entertainments', was edited by Lang with illustrations by H.J. Ford (Dover, 1969).

**ARABIAN SEA.** Located between the Indian and Arabian peninsulas in the northwestern section of the Indian Ocean, the Arabian Sea forms part of the major trade route between India and the countries of Europe. It is also bounded on the north by Pakistan and Iran, and on the west by the Horn of Africa. The principal waterway draining into the Arabian Sea is the Indus River (see Indus River). The total area of the sea is about 1,491,000 square miles (3,862,000 square kilometers).

There are no islands in the middle of the Arabian Sea, where depths generally exceed 9,800 feet (3,000 meters), though there are coastal islands. The mean depth is 8,970 feet (2,734 meters). Deep water reaches close to the bordering lands except in the northeast, off Pakistan and India. The sea's deepest known point, at Wheatley Deep, is more than 19,000 feet (5,800 meters).

Minimum surface temperatures of about 75° to 77° F (24° to 25° C) occur in the central Arabian Sea in January and February. Temperatures higher than 82° F (28° C) occur both in June and in November. The rainy season occurs when the southwest monsoon winds blow from April to November.

High levels of phosphates and other inorganic nutrients that support a rich fish life have been recorded in the western part of the sea. Fishes living at or near the sea's surface but far from the land borders include tuna, sardines, billfish, wahoo, sharks, lancet fish, and moonfish. Mass mortality of fishes is a periodic phenomenon in the Arabian Sea. For example, in an area of approximately 77,000 square miles (200,000 square kilometers) about 20 million tons of fishes were believed to have died in 1957. This occurrence was attributed to the unusual presence of certain unfavorable surface water conditions that caused the fishes to die from lack of oxygen.

From about the 8th or 9th century onward, Arabian and Persian mariners learned to navigate by using the surface currents generated by the summer and winter monsoon winds. Between the 9th and 15th centuries various navigators compiled instructions for sailing between southern Arabian, East African, and Red Sea ports, as well as ports in India, Malaysia, and China. Some of these works, called in Persian *rahmangs* (book of routes), contain useful information on navigating by the stars and on winds, currents, soundings, descriptions of coasts, approaches, and islands of the Arabian Sea.

## ARABS.

The term Arab is of uncertain origin and meaning. The word probably means "those who speak clearly"; so, in its most general application, it refers to those who speak Arabic as their native language. The term did not come into general usage until the 7th century, when all the peoples of the Arabian Peninsula were united by the religion of Islam (*see* Islam). For the first time, all the peoples of the region, who had led separate tribal existences for centuries, found a common identity in religion, law, and language. They have maintained that unity ever since. (*See also* Arabia.)

Today the word Arab refers not only to the people of the Arabian Peninsula, but also to large segments of the population of the Middle East and North Africa, as well as minorities on the east coast of Africa, in the Americas, and in Chad, Iran, and elsewhere. In fact, most of the world's more than 100 million Arabs live in Saudi Arabia, Jordan, Qatar, Kuwait, Oman, the United Arab Emirates, Bahrain, Yemen, Iraq, Egypt, Syria, Israel, Lebanon, Libya, Algeria, Morocco, The Sudan, Tunisia, and Turkey.

All Arabs consider the Arabian Peninsula their ancestral home. It is where their language originated, and it is the locale of their most sacred religious shrine, at the Grand Mosque in the city of Mecca.

Long before the founding of Islam, Arabia was inhabited by tribes, some of whom lived in settled communities, while others were nomadic or seminomadic herders. These tribes traced their ancestry back many centuries to one of two branches of Arabs. One branch, called true Arabs, traced its descent from an ancient patriarch named Qahtan.

The other branch of Arabs was considered to be descended from Ishmael, a son of the Hebrew patriarch Abraham. These people are called arabized Arabs, because it was believed that they came from Abraham's original home in Mesopotamia, now called Iraq (*see* Abraham).

### Arab Society

The family is the basic unit of Arab society, and Arabs tend to be known by the family to which they belong. Family life, like all of Arab society, is dominated by men. Women are considered to be the property of their fathers or husbands. Most marriages are monogamous—one husband and one wife—but in Saudi Arabia and some African countries a man may legally have as many as four wives. Marriages are usually arranged by parents for their children.

Beyond the family, Arabs distinguish among themselves on the basis of descent, tribal affiliation, and social status. A tribe is a collection of families headed by a sheikh, or sheik, who has the obligation of protecting the tribe's weak and poor. When disputes arise within or between tribes, the matter is put before an arbiter who is familiar with tribal customs.

The members of wandering tribes are called nomads, or Bedouins (*see* Nomads). These tribes make up about one fifth of the Arab population in the Middle East and North Africa. They live on the coarse grasslands and deserts that make up much of the

P. Keen—F.A.O.

*A camel herder getting water for his animals at the "Well of the Ticks" in Algeria is typical of the Bedouins who live in the Middle East and North Africa.*

terrain in that part of the world. They use camels for transportation and herd camels, sheep, and goats.

Most Arabs, although descended from nomadic tribes, are farmers or city dwellers. Those who live in towns and cities engage in businesses and commerce. Many work for the petroleum industry, which has become a major factor in the economy.

The most powerful force in the Arab world is Islam. This religion shapes all social attitudes and customs and the operation of the system of justice. Islam is a conservative, tradition-oriented religion, based on strict interpretation of its holy book, the Koran. In recent decades, perhaps because of the prosperity brought by the petroleum industry, there has been some unofficial relaxation of traditional observances in matters of dress, food, and law. This has occurred mostly in the larger cities.

In the smaller towns and desert areas, social attitudes remain traditional. Women wear a dark robe and a veil or shawl to cover the face. Men may wear a long robe (*jallabiyah*) and a felt cap covered by a hat of cloth wound around the head and kept in place by a cord. Some men wear ample trousers, with a long shirt outside that may fall below the knees.

Law in the Arab world is believed to rest on divine revelation given to Muhammad, the founder of Islam. Because revelation came to an end with the death of Muhammad in 632, the law is regarded as virtually unchangeable. For devout Muslims everything in life is related to religion. Therefore the law includes all human action within its scope. Because life in the Arab world is strictly regulated, the law can seem unbending to Westerners. Harsh penalties existed for criminals in the Middle East many centuries before the Koran sanctioned them.

**Past and Present**

The history of the Arab peoples since the founding of Islam may be divided into two major periods: that of the caliphate from 632 to 1924 and the era of modern Arab nationalism since 1924. The word caliph is derived from an Arabic word meaning "successor." The caliphs were the successors of Muhammad. It was intended that Muslims would always live under a Muslim who ruled from the city of Medina, but this principle did not endure.

From 632 to 732 the Arab tribes united to conquer the Middle East, North Africa, and Spain. Although frequently torn by internal power struggles, this phase of the caliphate lasted until the Arab-controlled territories, except for Spain, were conquered by the Ottoman Turks early in the 16th century. The Ottoman Empire was dismantled after World War I, and the caliphate was abolished by the new Turkish government in 1924. (*See also* Caliphate; Ottoman Empire.)

Arab nationalism began to grow early in the 20th century, largely inspired by European ideas of nationhood. The essence of Arab nationalism was defined in 1938 as "all who are Arab in their language, culture, and loyalty." Because of the Arabs' common adherence to Islam, this nationalism ideally transcends national boundaries. But Arab states have frequently been at odds with one another.

To consolidate Arab unity, the Arab League was founded in 1945. The members are Algeria, Bahrain, Djibouti, Iraq, Jordan, Kuwait, Lebanon, Libya, Mauritania, Morocco, Oman, Qatar, Saudi Arabia, Somalia, Sudan, Syria, Tunisia, the United Arab Emirates, Yemen, and the Palestine Liberation Organization. Egypt, one of the founding members, was suspended in 1979 for signing a treaty with Israel but was officially readmitted in 1989. The aims of the league were to strengthen and coordinate political, military, economic, cultural, and social programs. After 1948 the unity of the league coalesced around opposition to Israel (*see* Israel). Various forces tended to disrupt unity and render the league almost powerless. The Iraqi invasion of Kuwait in 1990 and the subsequent international conflict caused a deep rift as members took different sides in the war (*see* Persian Gulf War).

Algeria, Libya, Mauritania, Morocco, and Tunisia established a common market, known as the Arab Maghreb Union, on Feb. 17, 1989, to boost trade among North African countries by allowing free movement across borders. Another regional common market, the Arab Cooperation Council, was created by Egypt, Iraq, Jordan, and North Yemen, also in 1989.

**ARACHNID** *see* **SCORPION; SPIDER; TICK AND MITE.**

**ARAFAT, Yasir** (born 1929). The controversial leader of the Palestinian people in their attempt to achieve statehood was Yasir Arafat. In 1969 he became the chairman of the Palestine Liberation Organization (PLO), an alliance of many Palestinian organizations that exists as a government-in-exile in the Arab world of the Middle East.

Arafat was born in Jerusalem on Feb. 17, 1929. He attended Cairo University in Egypt, where he became president of the Union of Palestinian Students. In 1948, when the state of Israel was established, an estimated 726,000 Palestinians were displaced. Arafat devoted his life to gaining a permanent homeland for his people. He studied guerrilla tactics and joined the Egyptian army. In 1959 he helped organize al-Fatah, the largest of the Palestinian guerrilla units. This group took control of the PLO in 1969. Under Arafat's leadership, the PLO received official recognition from many nations. He addressed the United Nations General Assembly in 1974.

After the 1967 Arab-Israeli War, Arafat moved the PLO to Jordan. In 1970 the Jordanian army expelled the PLO in a bloody civil war. From Lebanon the PLO continued its attacks against Israeli targets until 1982, when an Israeli invasion forced the PLO to disperse to various Arab nations. On Nov. 15, 1988, the PLO under Arafat declared Palestine an independent state. On Dec. 14, 1988, Arafat affirmed "the right of all parties concerned in the Middle East conflict to exist in peace and security, including the state of Palestine, Israel, and their neighbors." In September 1993, after months of secret negotiations, Arafat signed a mutual recognition pact between the PLO and Israel. A few days later, Arafat's representative signed a peace accord with Israel. (*See also* Israel; Palestine; Palestine Liberation Organization.)

**ARAL SEA.** Once the fourth largest lake in the world, the Aral Sea is also called Lake Aral. Its two main tributaries are the Amu Darya and the Syr Darya. It lies more than 200 miles (320 kilometers) east of the Caspian Sea. It is bordered by Kazakhstan on the north and Uzbekistan on the south. To the southeast spreads the great desert Kyzyl-Kum.

Drought and overuse of its tributary waters for irrigation purposes caused the Aral Sea to lose more than half of its volume, shrinking to an area of 15,800 square miles (41,000 square kilometers) by the late 1980s. This shrinkage caused the salt concentrations of the water to rise drastically, killing off the once-abundant supplies of freshwater fishes and making the water undrinkable. In 1988 the Soviet government announced a 20-year program to increase the flow of water into the lake.

© Marc Riboud—Magnum

The summit of Mount Ararat, at the eastern border of Turkey, is nearly always shrouded in clouds.

**ARARAT, MOUNT.** An isolated mountain of volcanic origin, Mount Ararat is located in the extreme eastern part of Turkey. It overlooks the point at which the frontiers of Turkey, Iran, and Armenia intersect. The Ararat Massif, the entire mountain mass, extends for about 25 miles (40 kilometers).

Ararat, traditionally known as the landing place for Noah's Ark at the end of the flood, is a sacred place to the Armenian people. There is a Persian legend that refers to Ararat as the cradle of the human race. The name Ararat, as it appears in the Bible, is the Hebrew equivalent of Urartu, the name of an Assyrian-Babylonian kingdom that flourished between the Aras and the Upper Tigris rivers from the 9th to the 7th century BC.

Ararat consists of two extinct volcanoes, their summits about 7 miles (11 kilometers) apart. Great Ararat, which rises 16,853 feet (5,137 meters) above sea level, is Turkey's highest peak. Little Ararat rises in a smooth, steep, nearly perfect cone to an altitude of 12,877 feet (3,925 meters).

Great Ararat is always snowcapped. It was first climbed in modern times in September 1829 by Johann Jacob von Parrot, a German. Twentieth-century attempts by international expeditions to locate Noah's Ark were unsuccessful. A village, monastery, and chapel—the last settlements on the mountain—were destroyed by an earthquake and avalanche in 1840.

**ARBITRATION.** One method of settling disputes between individuals, groups, or nations is by arbitration. The two parties simply choose some disinterested and qualified person or persons to judge the matter and agree in advance to accept the decision. The decision is called an award, to distinguish it from a court judgment.

Arbitration has been practiced in America since colonial times. It was one of the English customs the colonists brought with them, along with the common law. George Washington in his will directed that if any disputes should arise they should be decided by three "impartial and intelligent" men, "two to be chosen by the disputants, each having the choice of one, and the third by those two."

The chief use of arbitration today is in settling disputes between business firms. If the matter is highly technical, an arbitrator can be chosen who is better qualified to give a decision than jurymen or a judge. Arbitration also avoids the delays and expense of lawsuits. Most trade associations and chambers of commerce write into their membership forms a "future disputes" clause. The members thus agree in advance to arbitrate disputes that may thereafter arise between them.

In colonial times good faith and public opinion were counted on to make arbitration awards effective. In 1920, New York was the first state to pass a law making commercial arbitration agreements enforceable in the courts. Today practically all states as well as the federal government have such laws.

The American Arbitration Association was set up in 1926 to advance commercial arbitration. In 1937 unions became eligible for membership. It is a non–profit-making organization, supported by its members. Its panels of arbitrators include hundreds of lawyers, accountants, bankers, and other specialists, in addition to business and labor representatives.

Both employers and unions are usually unwilling to allow an outsider to decide wages and conditions of work. Arbitration is therefore seldom used to settle the terms of a new or revised union contract. During the life of a contract, however, many disputes arise concerning its interpretation. These are usually decided by arbitration. Some industries and some large companies have a permanent arbitrator. Others appoint an arbitrator as each case arises. The method of choosing an arbitrator or arbitration board is usually provided for in the union contract.

Although labor and management prefer to make their own contract decisions, they frequently accept outside help in the form of mediation or conciliation. Unlike arbitrators, mediators and conciliators have no power to make an award.

In actual practice there is little difference between mediation and conciliation. Strictly speaking, a mediator is a go-between. When negotiations break down, he talks to both parties separately and carries messages back and forth. If he can bring them together, he may then act as conciliator. A conciliator serves as chairman and may offer advice.

The United States Conciliation Service was established as a bureau of the Department of Labor in 1913. This was replaced in 1947 by the Federal Mediation and Conciliation Service, an independent agency set up by the Labor-Management Relations Act (Taft-Hartley Act).

### International Arbitration

During the Middle Ages kings and princes frequently called on the pope to act as mediator. Then national states arose, and arbitration was abandoned for several centuries.

The United States and Great Britain revived international arbitration with Jay's Treaty (1794). This provided that several disputes that existed between the two nations should be settled by arbitration commissions. The United States and Great Britain in 1872 also arbitrated the celebrated *Alabama* claims case. The Bering Sea controversy was arbitrated in 1893, and the Alaska Boundary dispute in 1903. Latin American states have frequently submitted boundary disputes for settlement by arbitration. (*See also* 'Alabama' Claims; Alaska Boundary Dispute; Bering Sea; Jay, John.)

In 1899 the Permanent Court of Arbitration—known as the Hague Court—was established at The Hague, in The Netherlands (*see* Hague Peace Conferences). Instead of judges sitting continuously, this court simply provided a list of qualified jurists and an administrative office. Each of the member nations named not more than four persons for the list. The parties to a dispute then each chose two arbitrators from the list, and these four chose an umpire.

The Permanent Court of International Justice was established in 1920 by the League of Nations. After World War II it was succeeded by the United Nations International Court of Justice (the World Court). Like its League of Nations predecessor, the World Court is a court of justice rather than a court of arbitration. (*See also* United Nations; Peace Movements.)

International arbitration is likely to be successful only when neither party feels very strongly about the dispute. It is hard to find an arbitrator who is really impartial. If one nation thinks the decision is unfair, it may refuse to accept it and even go to war to force a decision in its favor.

**ARBOR DAY** *see* table in Fact-Index.

**ARBORETUM** *see* **BOTANICAL GARDEN AND ARBORETUM.**

**ARBORVITAE.** The Latin term *arbor vitae* means "tree of life." This evergreen tree was probably so named because of the supposed healing properties of its aromatic leaves. It is native to North America, Japan, and East Asia.

In North America there are two species. American arborvitae (*Thuja occidentalis*), also called white cedar, grows throughout southern Canada, the north-central and northeastern United States, and the Appalachian Mountains. It forms dense forests in wet and marshy regions. It grows 40 to 60 feet (12 to 18 meters) tall and 2 to 3 feet (0.6 to 0.9 meter) in diameter. It is used as an ornamental tree or shrub.

The giant arborvitae (*T. plicata*), or Western red cedar, is found in the Rocky Mountains and on the western coast of North America from Alaska to California. It may reach 150 to 200 feet (46 to 61 meters) in height and 4 to 8 feet (1.2 to 2.4 meters) in diameter. The wood is used for shingles, siding, and posts.

The arborvitae has tiny scalelike and awl-shaped leaves packed closely on the flat branches. It belongs to the cypress family, Cupressaceae.

**ARCADIA.** In Greece, on the central plateau of the Peloponnesus, the ancient district of Arcadia was isolated from the coast, surrounded on all sides by high mountains. The plateau is also subdivided by smaller ranges. The Arcadians lived simple lives, untouched by the progress that marked the rest of Greece. The name Arcadia thus came to be a symbol of ideal simplicity, rural beauty, and contentment. It was represented as a kind of paradise in Greek and Roman poetry and Renaissance romances.

What is now the Greek department of Arkadhía roughly corresponds to the ancient district. It covers an area of 1,706 square miles (4,419 square kilometers) and extends to the Gulf of Argolis. It has a coastline of about 40 miles (64 kilometers). The region has a few vineyards but no olive trees. There are patches of oak forest, but the eastern areas are drier.

**ARCHAEOLOGY.** The field of study called archaeology combines the excitement of treasure hunting with the investigative labor of detective work. Archaeology is the scientific study of the material remains of mankind's past. Its discoveries are the principal source of knowledge about prehistoric cultures.

The materials of archaeological study are both the things made by people and the things used by them. All the things fashioned by people—including settlements, buildings, tools, weapons, objects of ornament, and pure art—are called artifacts. Nonartifactual materials—things that were used but not made or fashioned—include the unworked bones of the animals that were eaten, the traces of the plants that were either grown or collected for food, and the charcoal from ancient hearths.

*An archaeological excavation reveals many levels that contain records of the nearly 11,000 years of human occupation of Jericho, one of the earliest continuous settlements in the world.*

University of London

The word archaeology is derived from two Greek terms—*archaios,* meaning "ancient," and *logia,* meaning "science" or "study of." Thus archaeology originally meant the study of ancient things. By the beginning of the 20th century, however, archaeological study had expanded to include the reconstruction of the arts, technology, societies, religions, and economies of past cultures.

Since the mid-20th century there has been another shift in the emphasis of archaeological study: from finding out how cultures change to trying to understand why they change. Some modern archaeologists are trying to establish archaeology as a true science from which generalizations or laws can be made about the causes of cultural change.

## Branches and Training

There are two main branches of archaeology: classical, or historical, archaeology and anthropological, or prehistoric, archaeology. The education and training of an archaeologist are divided along these two lines, though the general sequence of each is similar. Usually a student of archaeology obtains a Bachelor of Arts degree and then pursues a doctorate in a chosen field of archaeology. In addition to classwork, the graduate student must complete work in the field and in the laboratory. The student often uses this work to support a thesis—an original dissertation outlining and supporting the solution of some specific archaeological problem of the student's choosing. Once students have earned their Ph.D. degrees, they are ready to look for a job in archaeology. Archaeologists are employed in museums, colleges and universities, government agencies, and private research foundations.

**Classical archaeology** explores the records and artifacts of ancient civilizations. Classical archaeologists are particularly interested in the early cultures of the Mediterranean and the Near East—especially Greece, Rome, Persia (now Iran), Egypt, and Mesopotamia (now part of Iraq)—and also in the civilizations of ancient China, of the Indus River valley in modern Pakistan, and of Southeast Asia (*see* Ancient Civilization). The field of classical archaeology has become prominent in many countries interested in preserving their national heritage.

Naturally the curriculum for classical archaeology includes the basic principles and methods of archaeology. However, it also emphasizes historical studies—including art history and the study of classical civilizations—as well as philology (the study of literature and linguistics), ceramics, architecture, mineralogy, and other subjects.

**Anthropological archaeology** focuses on prehistory—the time before written records were kept. The curriculum emphasizes such studies as physical and cultural anthropology and linguistics as well as

. . . . . . . . . . . . . . . . . . . . . . . . . . . . . . . . . . . . . . . . . . . . . . . .

*This article was contributed by Richard Stockton MacNeish, Director, Andover Foundation for Archaeological Research, former Director, Robert S. Peabody Foundation for Archaeology, and winner of the Lucy Wharton Drexel Medal for Archaeological Research.*

archaeology itself. The anthropological archaeologist is involved in interdisciplinary studies—with particular emphasis on the way such fields as paleontology, human evolution, geomorphology, geology, and aerial photography relate to archaeology and how their principles and methods can be used by the archaeologist.

## HOW ARCHAEOLOGISTS WORK

The great majority of archaeological work involves collecting, analyzing, and synthesizing data. The process of collecting data is divided into two parts: reconnaissance—locating and recording a site and studying the geography of the area—and excavating, or actually digging at the site. Once materials are collected, they are analyzed to determine the time period and the civilization from which they came and to reconstruct the people's way of life. Then the information obtained from this analysis is synthesized, or collected in reports that provide histories, sometimes called cultural-historical integrations.

Most archaeological research ends here. Some archaeologists, however, may go on to analyze the histories themselves in order to produce hypotheses, or educated guesses, about why particular cultural changes took place. Then they test those hypotheses against archaeological data to see whether that data supports their hypotheses. If it does, the archaeologists believe they have arrived at a law or generalization that explains the development of the human race and why certain changes took place thousands or even millions of years ago.

## The Archaeological Team

The size of an archaeological team depends on the financial resources available. Teams range from a solitary digger to the kind of militarylike organization that Mortimer Wheeler directed at Mohenjo-daro in Pakistan. A team as large and well-funded as the latter may have three branches: administrative, laboratory, and excavational. Under the administrative director or chief are the quartermaster corps, accountants, secretaries, and mechanical and nonskilled staff that keep the whole organization going. The laboratory chief supervises artists, draftsmen, scientific analyzers, repairers, and specimen numberers, as well as computer staff. The excavational, or digging, branch includes various crew chiefs and their assistants, recorders, photographers, artists, and the diggers themselves, who are often students. The diggers may work at a variety of jobs or they may specialize in certain jobs such as troweling, screening, or removing dirt or refuse.

## Preliminary Fieldwork

The first stage of collecting archaeological data—the discovery and recording of sites and their superficial examination—is called preliminary fieldwork. Many sites have been found by pure luck. The famous 20,000-year-old wall paintings in Lascaux, France, for example, were discovered by boys who climbed into a

Jay W. Sharp—D. Donne Bryant Stock

*Before beginning the main excavation, archaeologists near El Paso, Tex., dig a checkerboard pattern of test holes to determine which area may yield the most useful artifacts.*

hole to find their missing dog. Some sites have been uncovered in the course of preparation for construction projects or as the result of bombing. Today, however, most sites are located by careful and well-planned survey programs.

**Reconnaissance techniques.** The exact methods of finding archaeological sites vary, primarily because there are so many different types of sites. Some sites—such as mounds, temples, forts, roads, and ancient cities—may be easily visible on the surface of the ground. Such sites may be located by simple exploration: by an individual or group going over the ground on foot, in a jeep or car, or on a horse, mule, or camel. This kind of survey can be comprehensive—that is, the entire area may be covered—or it can involve the technique of sampling. In sampling, a limited number of strategic spots in the region are checked for signs of an underlying archaeological site. Sampling was not widely used in the United States until passage of the Archaeological Resources Protection Act of 1979. This act, designed to protect the archaeological heritage of an area, has encouraged archaeological sampling of areas in which archaeological remains might exist that are in danger of being destroyed by construction or by the growth of cities.

To find sites that have no surface traces, archaeologists may use aerial photographs taken from balloons, airplanes, or satellites by cameras with remote sensors, infrared film, or other devices. The archaeologist checks these photographs for clues such as variations in soil color, ground contour, or crop density that may indicate the existence of a site.

Archaeologists may simply probe the ground with sound to check for variations in reflection of sound that would indicate the presence of structures or hollows in the ground. A probe, or periscope, may be inserted into the ground to locate walls and ditches. The archaeologist Carlo Lerici used such a probe, called a Nistri periscope, to locate and photograph Etruscan tombs in Italy in 1957.

Other modern devices use electricity and magnetism to locate buried structures. Electron or proton magnetometers or even mine detectors may be used to force currents through the earth and record any unusual features, such as a large, solid object, that lie beneath the soil. Similar magnetometers are dragged through the water to locate sunken ships or structures. The 20th-century archaeologist George Bass and the explorer Jacques Cousteau both had considerable success using this technique.

**Reconnaissance records.** All survey programs must be properly recorded and the sites designated—that is, given some sort of name or number. The simplest ways of designating a site are to name it after its discoverer, after the owner of the property on which it was found, or after its location. Another simple method is to give the site a serial number: site 1 for first site found, for example, or Fo$^v$1 to mean the first (1) village ($^v$) in Fulton County (Fo). More complex systems of identification may involve grid coordinates such as latitude and longitude, township and range, or geographic blocks.

Although there is no universally accepted system for recording the discovery of a site, most survey records include the site's designation, its exact location, the date it was found, the discoverer, the size of the site, and some sort of description of the site itself and what was found there. Of particular interest are structures such as mounds, temples, and houses and artifacts such as pieces of pottery and stone tools.

## Excavation

Perhaps the most important idea for an archaeologist to keep in mind during excavation is that any archaeological digging is, in fact, destroying a nonrenewable resource. Careful excavation and scrupulous record keeping and specimen preservation are therefore critical.

**Preparation.** The first step in excavation is to make a record of the site before it is dug or changed in any way. This preliminary record often involves making a contour map and taking photographs of the site. To make such maps and photographs meaningful, some mechanism must be set up to measure locations on the site. Vertical measurements—depths and heights—are often taken with respect to an agreed-upon base point, called the datum point, and are recorded as so many centimeters below or above the datum. The site may also be divided into horizontal units so that the provenience, or original location, of artifacts may be exactly recorded. Often the site is gridded, or staked out into squares. Then a system is devised for designating the location of each unit or square.

Before major digging actually begins, some sort of test is generally performed to determine the best part of the site in which to carry out the main part of the excavation. (Large sites are usually not dug out entirely.) One way to do this is to dig test holes called sondages. These may be spaced throughout the site at random, or they may be dug in certain strategic locations or in a checkerboard pattern. Crosswise, parallel, or crisscross trenches may be dug through the site instead.

**Digging.** Although the stereotypical tool of archaeology is the spade, the archaeologist's real tool is actually the trowel, which is used to scrape, slice, or clean away soil. Other tools of the trade include spoons,

(Left) Donald Miller—D. Donne Bryant Stock; (right) Institute of Nautical Archaeology

*An archaeologist uses a pick and screwdriver (left) to remove soil from the teeth of a human skeleton found in Chiapas, Mexico, and dating from about 500 BC. Archaeologists search each square of a gridded underwater site in Turkey (right) for artifacts from an 11th-century shipwreck.*

picks, paintbrushes, and dissecting needles.

There are a wide range of excavational techniques, and the method that an archaeologist uses depends very much on the type of the archaeological site. Usually the dirt is removed by stripping off horizontal layers to expose the artifacts and other materials. The layers may either be of an arbitrary thickness or they may correspond to natural strata, or layers of sedi- mentary rock or earth. Sometimes excavation is done vertically by slicing down through the different strata. Sometimes a combination of both techniques is used. The excavator must scrupulously record and preserve all archaeological materials as they are uncovered.

**Record keeping.** Archaeologists use various methods for recording data from a dig. Traditionally, they have made field notes and kept diaries describing what was being done and what was found. These records were generally accompanied by maps and drawings to show both the horizontal units dug from the site, called floor plots, and the vertical units, called cross sections, and indicating the artifacts and other materials found in them. Photographs or films might also accompany these records. Other methods for recording specific data include square-description forms, diary forms, soil forms, pollen forms, and similar kinds of recording aids. In the mid- to late 20th century, archaeological recording has increasingly been done using computers, digitizing cameras, and various other advanced devices.

**Preservation.** As with most other steps in the excavation process, the methods used for preserving archaeological specimens depend on the nature of the site. A less delicate specimen may be placed in a bag with a label and number. In some cases artifacts are coated with preservative chemicals. The advances in technology and chemistry made since the 1950s have enabled archaeologists to perform remarkable feats of preservation that would probably have been impossible a few decades ago.

### Interpreting Archaeological Finds

Ideally, analysis of the materials found on a site begins in the field laboratories while excavation is still in progress. Often, however, reconnaissance and excavation are completed in a relatively brief period of time, and the records and preserved remains are taken back to a museum, university, or laboratory for more analysis. This analysis has many aspects, which include describing and classifying objects by form and use, determining the materials from which they were made, dating the objects, and placing them in environmental and cultural contexts. These aspects may be grouped into two broad categories: chronological analysis and contextual analysis.

**Chronological analysis** of archaeological materials—identifying their time periods and sequence in time—is often done first. Archaeologists use two general kinds of dating methods: relative dating, or establishing when the various materials found at a site were made or used in relation to each other, and absolute dating, or assigning a fairly precise, chronometric date to a find.

The oldest method of establishing relative dates is by analyzing stratigraphy—the arrangement of strata in a site. This technique is based on the assumption that the oldest archaeological remains occur in the deepest strata of the excavation, the next oldest in the next deepest strata, and so on. By following this assumption, archaeologists can place the materials collected from the various strata into a rough chronological sequence.

If archaeologists digging in an undated site find a distinctive type of pottery for which the date is known, they may conclude that the other materials found in the site along with the pottery bear the same date as the pottery. This is an example of a relative-dating technique called cross dating.

Similarly, archaeologists may assign a date to an artifact based on the geologic region or strata with which the artifact is associated. For example, archaeologists may conclude that hand axes found in the high terrace of the Thames River in England are older than arrow points and pottery found in the lower terrace because they know that the high terrace was formed earlier than the low one. The association of artifacts with animal or fossil remains can also be used for relative dating. For example, it is known that superbison became extinct in the Great Plains of what is now the United States and were replaced by modern bison. Thus if archaeologists discover one site in which Folsom fluted points (the distinctive tips of a kind of prehistoric man-made weapon) are found imbedded in superbison remains, and they discover a second site in which a different kind of points, called Bajada points,

Tom McHugh—Photo Researchers

*The Hudson-Meng site in the United States reveals a layer of bison bones and the weapons used to kill the animals.*

are sticking in the remains of modern bison, they may conclude that Folsom points were made before Bajada points. This kind of relative dating may also be done using plant remains, particularly plant pollen, which is often preserved in archaeological strata.

If archaeologists know how certain types of artifacts—styles of pottery or burial objects, for example—evolved over time, they may be able to arrange groups of these artifacts in chronological order simply by comparing them. This method is called seriation.

Archaeologists can judge the relative dates of bones by analyzing their fluorine content, since the amount of fluorine in buried bones increases over time. In the 1840s Dr. Montroville Dickeson proved that a human pelvis found in Natchez, Miss., dated from the same time as mammoth bones found with it because both had accumulated the same proportions of fluorine.

There are many other methods of relative dating. None of them is as accurate as the absolute-dating methods, however, because the assumptions on which many relative-dating techniques are based can be misleading. Nevertheless, sometimes relative dating is the only method available to the archaeologist.

In absolute, or chronometric, dating, a definite age—in numbers of years before the present—is assigned to an archaeological specimen. When applied correctly, the methods of absolute dating can yield highly accurate dates. The remains found by classical archaeologists—coins or written records, for example—may have dates already written on them, but this is not always the case. It is never the case for anthropological archaeologists, who study prehistoric materials.

One system of absolute dating, called varve dating, was developed in the early 20th century by Gerard de Geer, a Swedish geologist. He noted that the mud and clay deposited by glaciers into nearby lakes sank to the lake bottom at different rates throughout the year, forming distinct layers, called varves, on the lake

bottom. Because each year's layer was different, the researchers were able to establish dates for artifacts or sites associated with a specific varve.

A similar absolute-dating method—dendrochronology, or the dating of trees by counting their annual growth rings—was first developed for archaeological purposes in the early 1900s by the American astronomer Andrew Ellicott Douglass. If an ancient structure has wooden parts, archaeologists can compare the number and widths of the growth rings in those parts with sequences from other samples to find out when that structure was built. Other techniques yield absolute dates based on the thickness of the patina, or residue, that forms over time on certain stone artifacts.

Advances in the physical sciences during the 20th century greatly improved absolute-dating methods. One of the best-known and most valuable techniques is radiocarbon dating (also called radioactive carbon dating, carbon dating, and carbon-14 dating). All living things contain small amounts of carbon-14, a radioactive form of carbon. After death, this carbon-14 changes, or decays, into a more stable form of carbon. Archaeologists can determine the age of once-living things such as bones, wood, and ash by measuring the amount of carbon-14 remaining in the specimen (*see* Radiocarbon Dating).

Radiocarbon dating cannot be used to make accurate age measurements of very old materials—materials more than about 70,000 to 100,000 years old. For such objects, archaeologists can use similar techniques involving other chemical elements. Potassium-argon dating, for example, can be used to date rocks millions of years old. A related dating method called fission-track dating can be used on certain stone samples of almost unlimited age. Another modern dating method, thermoluminescence dating, can be used to find out when ancient pieces of pottery or other fired-clay objects were made.

**Contextual analysis.** Determining the chronology of an artifact is only half of the archaeologist's task; the other half is reconstructing the ancient culture from which the artifact came. This process is called contextual analysis.

The lowest, or most basic, level of contextual analysis consists of analyzing a culture's systems of subsistence and technology—that is, the ways in which ancient people adapted to their environment. The next level involves reconstructing their social structures and settlement patterns. Finally, archaeologists try to reconstruct a culture's ethos, or guiding beliefs.

Each of these levels requires different analytical methods. Archaeologists may start reconstructing an ancient subsistence system by determining what the people ate. They may do this through coprology, the examination of fossilized feces, or by analyzing human bones for the presence of certain forms of carbon and nitrogen. The study of the plant remains found in a dig can also provide clues to a people's diet.

By studying ancient tools—such as arrow tips, butcher knives, and grinding stones—archaeologists can find

*An archaeologist sorts pottery shards excavated from the site of an ancient palace in Yugoslavia onto labeled cards.*

out how people obtained and prepared their foods. Archaeologists may also be able to determine how ancient people made and used their tools. Studying the work of a modern flint knapper, for instance, may show an archaeologist how ancient people made flint tools. (In archaeology, this type of reasoning or interpretation is called ethnographic analogy.)

When archaeologists attempt to reconstruct ancient social structures, they often use data gathered by ethnographers, social anthropologists, and historians. The excavated materials themselves may also provide hints of ancient social organization. Specialized artifacts that are found concentrated in certain areas may indicate that the ancient culture had full-time craft specialists, and different types of burial arrangements may indicate that social classes existed.

Reconstructing the highest level of a culture, including its values, ethos, or religion, is the most difficult type of contextual analysis. Such items as statues or paintings of figures that appear to be supernatural, buildings that may have been temples, and evidence of religious ceremonies can all be used to help reconstruct ancient systems of beliefs.

The goal of chronological and contextual analysis is to write and publish records of ancient history. Excavated materials have value only if the information gained from them is disseminated through books, magazines, and other publications. Such publications not only keep track of how techniques have changed but also record great archaeological discoveries.

## HISTORY

Like any history, the development of archaeology may be divided into stages. To some degree these periods reflect changing interests and objectives as well as changing techniques in archaeology. The stages are also marked by great finds and famous names.

### Before 1860

The interests and objectives of the first archaeologists are the most difficult to define. Perhaps they acted more out of curiosity than for any well-defined, scholarly goal. In the Old World, a landmark event in early archaeology was the removal of ancient Greek sculptures, now known as the Elgin Marbles, from their site in Athens, Greece, to England from 1803 to 1812. This acquisition, which was arranged by the English diplomat and art collector Thomas Bruce, 7th earl of Elgin, aroused violent controversy, and Bruce was widely denounced as a vandal.

By 1812 a national museum of archaeology had already been established in Denmark. By 1818 its curator, Christian J. Thomsen, had developed the three-part chronological system that divides human prehistory in Europe into the Stone, Bronze, and Iron ages. Thomsen was assisted by Jens Worsaae, whose subsequent discovery of ancient human remains established the Paleolithic as a period of prehistory.

In 1837 the French archaeologist Jacques Boucher de Crèvecoeur de Perthes discovered Stone Age tools and other remains in France. He was the first to draw scientific attention to evidence that mankind had lived on Earth much earlier than had been previously thought. The English archaeologist Austen Henry Layard was responsible for two milestones in early archaeology. During the 1840s he excavated Calah, the capital of Assyria under King Ashurnasirpal II, and Nineveh, the oldest and most populous city of the ancient Assyrian Empire and its capital for hundreds of years. At both sites Layard discovered the remains of palaces, including the palace of the Assyrian King Sennacherib, and a large number of significant artworks. Perhaps most important, however, was his discovery of many cuneiform tablets from the state archives, from which much about Assyrian and Babylonian culture and history was learned. Other archaeological milestones were the translation of the Rosetta stone by French scholar Jean-François Champollion and Henry Rawlinson's translation of the cuneiform inscriptions on the Bisitun rock. These translations provided the key to deciphering the writings of ancient Egypt and Mesopotamia, respectively.

In the New World the Father of American Archaeology, Thomas Jefferson, excavated burial mounds in Virginia in the early 1790s to determine if the mound builders were Native Americans. Other early American research included the mapping of Mayan ruins by the American archaeologists John Lloyd Stephens and Frederick Catherwood.

### 1861–1901

With the rise of Darwinism and the theory of evolution, archaeology underwent a momentous change (*see* Darwin, Charles). During the second half of the 19th century the idea of the Paleolithic evolved—a period in the Stone Age that represented a stage, or level, of human development characterized by the use of rudimentary chipped-stone tools. The French archaeologist Gabriel de Mortillet refined the concept by subdividing the Paleolithic into six subperiods.

Archaeological evidence of human physical evolution included specimens of such human ancestors as Java man (discovered in 1891–92) and Neanderthal man (1856). In 1879 magnificent Paleolithic wall paintings were discovered in the Altamira caverns in Spain. (*See also* Evolution.)

Inspired by these Old World finds, American anthropologists Frederic Putnam, William John McGee, and others began a search for evidence of Paleolithic man in the New World. A more immediate concern of most American archaeologists, however, was determining who built the mysterious ancient mounds in the Midwest United States. Archaeologists who studied the mounds included Clarence Moore, Warren Moorehead, Stephen Peet, and Charles Willoughby.

In the Mediterranean other archaeologists excavated classical sites. In the early 1870s the German archaeologist Heinrich Schliemann began exploring the ruins of ancient Troy (*see* Schliemann). The British archaeologist and Egyptologist Flinders Petrie conducted numerous valuable excavations in Egypt beginning in the 1880s, including explorations of the Great Pyramid at Giza and the Temple of Tanis.

Beginning in the late 1890s the British archaeologist Arthur Evans excavated the ruins of the ancient city of Knossos in Crete and uncovered evidence of a sophisticated Bronze Age civilization, which he named Minoan. Art treasures from historic and prehistoric archaeological sites flowed into the museums of Europe and the United States.

## 1901–32

In the New World in the early 20th century, the field of anthropology came to be dominated by the theories of the German-born anthropologist Franz Boas. His view that different human groups developed in different ways not because of genetic differences but because of differences in their environmental, cultural, and historical circumstances changed the theories and practices of his colleagues not only in anthropology but also in other fields, including archaeology. (*See also* Boas.)

Under the direction of anthropologist Fay-Cooper Cole, the University of Chicago established its now-famous school for archaeological fieldwork and University of Chicago teams excavated mounds and sites in Fulton County, Illinois. Frank Roberts' discovery of Folsom fluted points alongside extinct bison bones in Folsom, N.M., firmly established that humans had been living in the Americas for as long as 10,000 years.

In Europe studies of the Paleolithic progressed as more human fossil remains were uncovered. Danish and British archaeologists established the existence of Mesolithic culture, and the Australian-born British archaeologist Vere Gordon Childe began his famous studies of Neolithic cultures in the region of the Danube River.

For European classical archaeology this was the era of the great expeditions. The British archaeologist Leonard Woolley conducted his famous excavation of the ancient Sumerian city of Ur in present-day Iraq and

David L. Brill © National Geographic Society

*A mass spectrometer counts the atoms of radioactive argon in a sample. The results of potassium-argon dating tests can be used to determine the age of the sample.*

made many valuable archaeological finds; the French archaeologist Jean-Vincent Scheil headed an expedition to the site of Susa in present-day Iran and uncovered, among other objects, the Code of Hammurabi—the most complete existing collection of Babylonian laws; and the British archaeologist Howard Carter found a magnificent treasure in the unlooted tomb of King Tutankhamen in Egypt.

Archaeologists also studied remains of the high cultures of the New World—the Aztecs, Maya, and Incas. George Vaillant undertook excavations of ancient sites and cities in the Valley of Mexico; Sylvanus Morley started work on Mayan sites in the Yucatán Peninsula; and Max Uhle and other archaeologists explored the great sites of Peru.

## 1932–62

It is ironic that in the United States the Great Depression did more to advance archaeology than did any other single event. As part of his program to employ American citizens, President Franklin D. Roosevelt established the Work Projects Administration and set up a government-sponsored archaeological program to rescue archaeological sites that would be covered by water in the Tennessee Valley Authority project.

In South America the basic chronologies of ancient cultures were established by Wendell Bennett, Junius Bird, and J.C. Tello in Peru; by Irvin Rouse in the Caribbean; and by J.M. Cruxent in Venezuela. In Mexico and Central America, Alfred Vincent Kidder continued Sylvanus Morley's investigation of Mayan sites on the Yucatán Peninsula and in Honduras and Guatemala. George Vaillant, Paul Tolstoy, and others continued reconstructing chronologies in the Valley of Mexico. In Palenque, Mexico, Alberto Ruz opened the tomb in the Mayan Temple of Inscriptions. Richard MacNeish and Paul Mangelsdorf began their long search for the origins of corn agriculture, the basis of subsistence of Meso-American cultures.

World War II followed close on the heels of the Great Depression, and in the Old World achievements in prehistoric archaeology declined considerably. The British archaeologists Graham Clark and Vere Gordon Childe dominated the field of Mesolithic and Neolithic studies. Paleolithic studies flourished worldwide with the work of François Bordes and Hal Movius in Europe; Mary and Louis Leakey in Africa; Davidson Black in China; and Robert Braidwood and Dorothy Garrod in the Middle East.

Developments in classical archaeology continued, though also on a reduced scale. Among the most notable events were Kathleen Kenyon's excavation of Jericho to its Stone Age foundations, the discovery of the Dead Sea Scrolls, and the deciphering of Mycenaean script by Michael Ventris. Underwater archaeology began during this period, and various technological improvements—satellite photography, radiocarbon dating, the use of computers and metal detectors to locate sites and to record data—aided archaeological efforts.

One of the most pressing challenges for modern archaeology is preventing the loss of data, and so of knowledge, that results from the destruction of archaeological sites. With the cooperation of governmental authorities, archaeologists hope to find a way of stopping such destruction and of preserving the traces of humankind's ancient history.

## Recent Trends and Discoveries

In the second half of the 20th century there has been an emphasis on theory in archaeology—particularly dealing with the question of why cultures change. Other trends in modern archaeology include an increasing reliance on computers and other technological advances and a tendency toward well-planned interdisciplinary programs designed to answer specific archaeological questions.

Archaeology in the United States has been greatly affected by passage of the Archaeological Resources Protection Act and by the Environmental Protection Agency's establishment of cultural resource management programs. These measures require that, before any government-sponsored project begins, archaeologists search the area affected for any possible archaeological sites that might be destroyed. If such sites are found, the government requires that they be excavated or protected to preserve any data.

The period has already produced some sensational finds. These include the discovery in Ethiopia of a 3-million-year-old skeleton called Lucy, regarded by many as intermediate between ape and human; the discovery of the tomb of Philip II of Macedon, father of Alexander the Great, in northern Greece; and the discovery in northern Guatemala of Nakbe, the earliest-known Mayan center.

Major finds in the late 1980s included the unearthing in Oklahoma of stone tools that might be evidence of the earliest groups of humans to inhabit North Amer-

ica; the discovery in Iraq of the world's oldest statue, an 11,000-year-old stone in the shape of a human; and the discovery in London of the remains of Shakespeare's Globe Theatre. A virtually intact body of a man from the late Stone Age was discovered in the Austrian Alps in 1991. The body was so well preserved it still had its skin, internal organs, and fingernails, as well as its clothes, shoes, and weapons. Dubbed the Iceman from the Similaun, the body is believed to be at least 5,000 years old.

In February 1996 a team of United Nations–sponsored archaeologists announced that they had discovered the ancient birth chamber of Prince Siddhartha Gautama, the founder of Buddhism, beneath the Mayadevi temple in southwestern Nepal. The site, which was located in Lumbini, more than 200 miles (350 kilometers) southwest of the Nepalese capital, Kathmandu, appeared to settle an international debate over whether Buddha was born in India or Nepal.

A team of American and Russian archaeologists made some interesting discoveries when they excavated the tombs of the 6th century BC Sauromatian and Sarmation nomadic tribes, along the westernmost border of Kazakhstan. Most surprising was the discovery that the women had been buried along with swords, daggers, bows, and arrows, leading many of the archaeologists to the preliminary conclusion that at least some of the female members of the tribes served as warriors. Some observers suggested that the women warriors bore some relation to the mythical Amazons, powerful female warriors of whom the Greek historian Herodotus had written.

For more than two and a half centuries, the final resting place of one of history's most notorious sea vessels remained a mystery. In 1718 *Queen Anne's Revenge*, which had been the fleet flagship of the infamous pirate Edward Teach, known popularly as Blackbeard, escaped from the sinking vessel along with his crew. Legend has it that they were able to save the vast treasures they had accumulated during two years of plundering ships and towns along the Eastern seaboard. The location of the ship had remained undetermined for more than 270 years, mostly because of the clutter of other ships at the bottom of the ocean in the area where it was believed to have sunk. A team of marine archaeologists, however, consulted a rare book from 1719 that chronicled the story of the sinking of Blackbeard's notorious ship and provided an exact description of the location where the ship went down. They also used a sophisticated device designed to detect the large amounts of metal in the ship's numerous cannons.

In November 1996, after a decade-long process of research and underwater searching, the team of marine archaeologists finally located the hull of a ship that seemed consistent with known information concerning the design of the *Queen Anne's Revenge*. It was only after a team of divers salvaged several artifacts from the hull, including the bell of the ship, that they were able to conclude that the ship in question was most likely Blackbeard's legendary vessel. The bell had been inscribed with the date 1709, the year that construction was believed to have been completed on the ship.

## Milestones in Archaeology

**1. 30,000–13,000 BC.** Paintings of animals made in caves by Stone Age artists. Altamira Cave (Spain) found, 1879; Lascaux Cave (France), found 1940; Cosquer Cave (France), found 1991.

**2. 25,000–10,000 BC.** Asian hunters, ancestors of American Indians, crossed Bering Strait to North America over land bridge now under the sea.

**3. 9000–8000 BC.** Flint embedded in bison bone and other artifacts, evidence of humans in southwest United States by 9,000 BC, found near Folsom, N.M., 1926.

**4. 9000 BC.** Jericho, one of the world's oldest cities. Human skulls 7,000 years old found by Kathleen Kenyon, 1952.

**5. 4500–2500 BC.** Swiss lake villages occupied. Drought lowered Lake Zürich and revealed pilings on which buildings stood, 1853–54.

**6. 3000–2050 BC.** Ur of the Chaldeans; occupied before 3000 BC by Sumerians in what is now Iraq. Sir Leonard Woolley found remarkable royal graves, 1922.

**7. 2686–2345 BC.** Pyramids of Giza, near Cairo, erected. Sir William M.F. Petrie began scientific study, 1880.

**8. 3100–1550 BC.** Stonehenge, Salisbury Plain, England; Stone Age circle of stones forms what is thought to be a temple.

**9. 1750 BC.** Babylonian king Hammurabi's code of 282 laws on slab of stone, brought to Susa in 1200 BC, found, 1901.

**10. 1600–1400 BC.** Height of Minoan culture, at Knossos, Crete. Sir Arthur Evans uncovered palace of King Minos; began excavations, 1900.

**11. 1450 BC.** Mycenaeans wrote in Linear Script B on clay tablets. Michael Ventris deciphered it, 1952; found it to be archaic Greek.

**12. 1361–52 BC.** King Tutankhamen ruled Egypt. Howard Carter found Tut's tomb, 1922; among treasures was a golden mask covering the king's mummy.

**13. 1200 BC.** Fall of Troy. Heinrich Schliemann began excavating, 1870. He and his successors found at least nine cities.

**14. 1000–474 BC.** Etruscan civilization at its peak. Wall paintings and jewels in tombs show advanced culture.

**15. 705–681 BC.** Sennacherib built up Nineveh, which in 720 BC became capital of Assyria, already 1,000 years old. Sir Austen Henry Layard began excavating, 1845.

**16. 500–400 BC.** Athens' golden age. Lord Elgin removed many sculptures, later called Elgin marbles, and took them to London, 1801.

**17. 196 BC.** Rosetta stone records decree of Egyptian priesthood. Found, 1799. Hieroglyphics deciphered by Jean François Champollion, 1822.

**18. 100 BC.** First of Dead Sea Scrolls, religious manuscripts written between 100 BC and AD 68, found, 1947.

**19. AD 692.** Temple of Inscriptions, Palenque, Mexico, built by Mayan Indians over tomb of ruler Pacal. Opened by Alberto Ruz, 1949.

**20. AD 650–670.** Burial of Saxon ship and treasure at Sutton Hoo, near coast of Suffolk, England, discovered, 1938; restored by British Museum.

*1. Lascaux cave paintings*

*6. Headdress, cemetery of Ur*

*2. Asian hunters*

*7. Pyramids of Giza*

*3. Folsom point*

*8. Stonehenge, England*

*4. Jericho artifacts*

*9. Code of Hammurabi*

*5. Swiss lake village*

*10. Cretan wall painting*

*11. Mycenaean mask and script*

*16. Parthenon, Athens*

*12. Mask of King Tut*

*17. The Rosetta Stone*

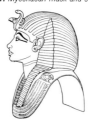

*13. Jewel from Troy*

*18. Dead Sea scrolls*

*14. Etruscan wall painting*

*19. Palenque temple*

*15. Nineveh relief*

*20. Treasure of Sutton Hoo*

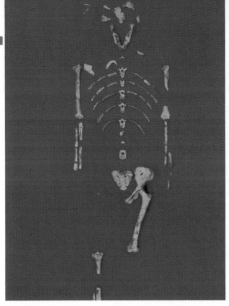

*The skeleton of "Lucy" (Australopithecus afarensis) (left), a 3-million-year-old find that may be intermediate between apes and humans, has been almost half reconstructed from recovered bones and bone fragments. To be sure that they did not miss any small bones or other materials, archaeologists at the Lucy site in Ethiopia (right) spread gravel from the site on long cloths and sifted through it handful by handful.*

(Left) Cleveland Museum of Natural History; (right) David L. Brill © National Geographic Society

**Deep-sea Roman treasure found.** A team of marine archaeologists led by Robert Ballard, an internationally renowned scientist who made headlines when he located the remains of the oceanliner *Titanic* in 1986, announced in 1997 yet another extraordinary discovery made in the depths of one of the world's most well-traveled bodies of water, the Mediterranean Sea. Using a sophisticated nuclear submarine on loan from the United States Navy, the marine archaeologists located five ships in the depths of the Mediterranean that had sunk over a period of 2,000 years. Three of the wrecks were relatively modern, but the other two were believed to have originated in the classical world, when the imperial powers of Rome and Carthage dominated the region and its shipping routes. Both ships contained numerous objects that indicated they were trading ships. Because the ships were found so far out in the middle of the sea, the discovery was praised as one that would redefine modern perceptions of trade in the ancient world. Previous to the 1997 discovery and an earlier 1989 discovery of Ballard's, historians had believed that trade between ancient overseas empires was largely confined to coastal routes along the Mediterranean.

**Ancient ruins discovered in Cambodian jungle.** A team of archaeologists studying the ancient Khmer civilization of Cambodia announced in 1998 that they had discovered a series of previously unknown Khmer temples and a man-made mound in the jungle of northwestern Cambodia. The newly discovered temples predate by as much as 300 years the nearby temple of Angkor Wat—a well known and magnificent Hindu temple constructed by the Khmer people in the middle of the 12th century.

The newfound archaeological structures were first detected during a space shuttle mission conducted by the National Aeronautics and Space Administration (NASA) in 1994. In December 1996, NASA, working in coordination with archaeologist and Khmer civilization expert Elizabeth Moore of the University of London, surveyed the densely vegetated region using advanced microwave radar imaging. The radar images produced enough evidence to suggest that some sort of man-made structure existed deep beneath the thick foliage. In December of 1997 Moore led a team of archaeologists through the Cambodian jungle—regions controlled by guerrilla armies—eventually discovering the remains of six additional temples in the area near Angkor Wat, as well as a man-made mound that was built as early as the 6th century BC.

The discovery of the new temples profoundly changed archaeological conceptions of the Khmer civilization and the ancient Khmer city of Angkor, because it indicated that the region was probably regularly inhabited for much of the 1,000 years preceding the construction of Angkor Wat.

(*See also* Aegean Civilization; Ancient Civilization; Anthropology; Babylonia and Assyria; Earth, "The Earth Through Time"; Egypt, Ancient; Indus Valley Civilization; Maya; Mesopotamia.)

**FURTHER RESOURCES FOR ARCHAEOLOGY**

**Bertman, Stephen.** Doorways Through Time (JP Tarcher, 1991).
**Fagan, B.M.** Quest for the Past: Great Discoveries in Archaeology (Waveland, 1988).
**Gallant, R.A.** Lost Cities (Watts, 1985).
**Hodder, Ian.** Reading the Past (Cambridge Univ. Press, 1991).
**Joukowsky, Martha.** A Complete Manual of Field Archaeology (Prentice, 1980).
**Lampton, C.F.** Undersea Archaeology (Watts, 1988).
**Stuart, G.E.** Your Career in Archaeology (Society for American Archaeology, 1986).
**Thomas, D.H.** Archaeology, rev. ed. (Holt, 1989).

(*See also* Further Resources for Ancient Civilization; Anthropology; Human Origins.)

**ARCHANGEL** *see* **ANGEL AND DEMON.**

**ARCHERY.** The sport of archery—shooting arrows from bows at targets—has its roots in prehistoric times. Arrows were used by ancient peoples to battle their opponents and to hunt wild game. In some societies, people still use bows and arrows as weapons.

No one knows exactly when the first bows and arrows were used. Researchers have found evidence of of archery that leads many of them to believe that it originated in more than one place. Other evidence has been found that shows the use of bows and arrows by peoples in every part of the world except Australia. The earliest bows and arrows were probably used for hunting rather than warfare. They were very important to primitive hunters, who used them to kill game that could not be outrun.

Archaeologists have found indications that people used hunting bows as long as 50,000 years ago in what is now Tunisia. Those early bows probably were wood branches or saplings cut into a "D" shape. To make the bowstring, primitive archers cut a long thong, or strip, from the hide of an animal. For arrows, they used straight sticks sharpened at one end. At the other end, they cut a notch so the arrow and bowstring fitted together snugly.

Other evidence of prehistoric archery has come from cave drawings in Spain, France, and North Africa. These drawings, which date back thousands of years, show bows and arrows being used for hunting and warfare. Archery was also a sport in ancient Egypt, China, and India. The ancient Egyptians were famous for their skill with the bow. However, the most advanced bows of ancient times came from the Far East. Craftsmen there glued wood, bone, and animal tendons together to make extremely accurate and powerful bows.

As the bow became a better weapon, it gained new importance in warfare. Military leaders began to use massed bowmen, who shot hundreds of arrows toward the enemy at the same time. The use of archery in warfare reached its peak in the Middle Ages with the English longbow. English bowmen used this effective weapon against the French during the

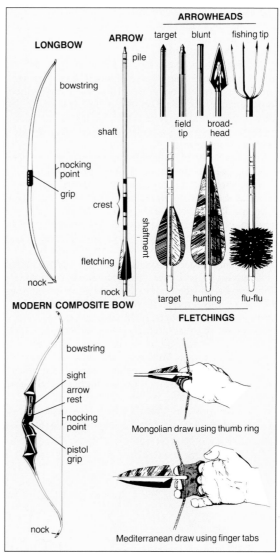

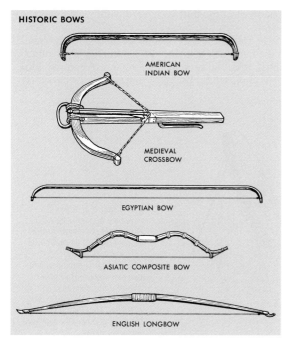

Hundred Years' War, and their skill helped England become a world power.

The bow began to have less importance in war after the invention of firearms. In 1595 the British army replaced the longbow with the gun. Through the years, archery in Europe, whether competitive or for hunting, became entirely a sport.

The North American Indians, like other ancient peoples, used the bow and arrow for hunting and warfare. After the English and other Europeans settled in North America, the Indians rather rapidly adopted firearms, and archery was left to develop as a recreational activity.

### Types of Bows and Arrows

A bow consists of two parts—the bow itself and the bowstring. The bow is made of a long, narrow strip of flexible material that snaps back to its original shape after being bent. The design of bows comes from both the English longbow and ancient Asian bows. Modern bows may be made of wood, aluminum, or fiberglass. Woods used for bows include hickory, yew, lemon, orange, and osage orange.

There are three major kinds of bow designs. Self bows consist of a single piece of wood. Backed bows are made of two layers of wood that have been glued or laminated together. Composite bows are made of wood and other materials bonded together; the modern composite bow consists of laminated wood with a fiberglass surface.

Just below the middle of the modern composite bow is a grip that fits the hand. At the bottom of the grip, a small shelf called the arrow rest holds the arrow in place as it is drawn and released. Each end of the bow has a nock, or notch, for the string. The bowstring is looped at both ends, and the loops fit into the nocks and hold the string in place. The string is shorter than the bow, and so it becomes taut and puts the bow under great tension. As the bow is bent and released, this tension snaps the bowstring forward, propelling the arrow with tremendous force. Most wooden bows have bowstrings made of linen fibers. Modern bows use strings of a synthetic fiber, such as Dacron.

Bows are classified according to bow weight, which is the force needed to pull the bowstring back the length of the arrow. The higher the bow weight, measured in pounds, the greater the force that must be used to pull the string. Bows of higher weight also make the arrow travel farther and faster. Most men's bows measure about 6 feet (1.8 meters) long and have a bow weight of 37 pounds (17 kilograms). Women's

bows average 5½ feet (1.7 meters) in length and 30 pounds (14 kilograms) in bow weight.

Like bows, arrows may be made of wood, aluminum, or fiberglass. An arrow has four main parts: the pile, or tip, of which there are various kinds for different purposes; the shaft; the nock, or notch, at the end of the shaft for the bowstring; and the fletching, or feathers (also called vanes), near the end of the shaft. The fletching, which may be actual goose or turkey feathers or, especially in target arrows, may be made of plastic, make an arrow spin in flight. The spinning motion steadies the arrow and keeps it flying straight. Most arrows measure between 25 and 28 inches (63 and 70 centimeters) long.

### The Sport of Archery

Archers should place their feet comfortably apart and point them at right angles to the shooting direction. A right-handed person holds the bow grip with the left hand. The archer fits the arrow into the bowstring, rests it on the left side of the bow, and raises the bow to a vertical position. The bowstring is usually drawn back with the middle three fingers of the right hand, keeping the arrow between the first and second fingers. The head is turned to face the target. The right elbow stays high, on a line with the arrow, which is drawn back smoothly in one motion. At full draw, the string touches the archer's chin. When releasing the arrow, the archer lets it roll off, rather than snap off, the fingertips. The shooter remains still until the arrow reaches the target.

Target archery is the most popular form of archery in the United States and Europe. Archers shoot from various distances at circular, straw-filled targets called butts. These targets are 6 inches (15 centimeters) thick and measure 48 inches (122 centimeters) in diameter. The front of the butt is covered with oilcloth or canvas painted with five concentric circles. The innermost circle, called the bull's-eye, is painted gold and has a diameter of 9¾ inches (24 centimeters). The other rings, from the center outward, are colored red, blue, black, and white. Each is 4⅘ inches (12 centimeters)

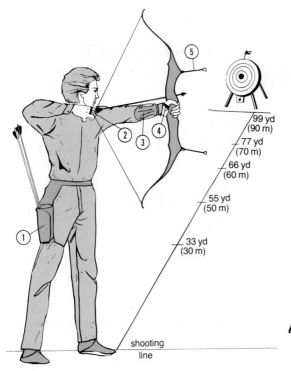

99 yd (90 m)
77 yd (70 m)
66 yd (60 m)
55 yd (50 m)
33 yd (30 m)

shooting line

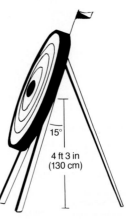

15°

4 ft 3 in (130 cm)

*This target archer has equipped himself with a quiver (1) to hold his arrows and with finger tabs (2), an arm guard (3), and a hand protector (4). His bow is equipped with two stabilizers (5) to offset a lateral force exerted on the bow when the arrow is released. The distances on the field and the target height are international standards.*

wide. Starting with the bull's-eye, the circles have point values of 9, 7, 5, 3, and 1. The outermost area of the butt, known as the apron, is painted green and has no point value. The butt stands on an easel, with the center of the bull's-eye 48 inches above the ground. In international competition the butt has ten rings and is centered 51 inches (130 centimeters) above the ground.

In modern competition, archers shoot in one or more rounds. A round consists of a certain number of arrows that are shot at a target from a specified distance. Different rounds are used in various competitions. In the United States national tournament men shoot 36 arrows from 99 yards (90 meters), and women shoot 36 arrows from 77 yards (70 meters).

Other types of sport archery include field shooting, clout shooting, and flight shooting. In field shooting, archers shoot at figures of animals painted on backdrops. Scoring rings are marked over the animals. In clout shooting, the contestants try to shoot arrows high into the air so they fall on a target marked on the ground. In flight shooting, archers try only for distance and are not concerned with accuracy.

The first formal competition was held in England in 1673, and England's first modern national archery tournament took place in 1844. The National Archery Association of the United States was founded in 1879 and held its first competition that year. The Fédération Internationale de Tir à l'Arc (FITA), which is the international governing body for archery, was established in 1931. The first world archery championship took place in Poland in 1931. Target archery was an event of the Olympic Games in 1900, 1904, 1908, and 1920. It was then dropped from the Olympics but was reinstated in 1972. (*See also* Arrowhead.)

**ARCHIMEDES** (287–212 BC). The first scientist to recognize and use the power of the lever was Archimedes. This gifted Greek mathematician and inventor once said, "Give me a place to stand and rest my lever on, and I can move the Earth." He also invented the compound pulley and Archimedes' screw. Archimedes was a brilliant mathematician who helped develop the science of geometry. He discovered the relation

*In Archimedes' screw, water or any other liquid is carried up the tube by the turning blade.*

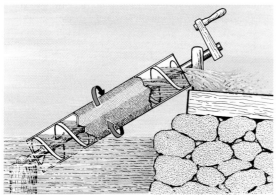

between the surface area and volume of a sphere and those of its circumscribing cylinder. (*See also* Geometry; Mechanics.)

A legend says that Archimedes discovered the principle of displacement while stepping into a full bath. He realized that the water that ran over equaled in volume the submerged part of his body. Through further experiments, he deduced the principle of buoyancy, which is called Archimedes' principle. According to this principle a body immersed in a fluid loses as much in weight as the weight of an equal volume of the fluid. (*See also* Hydraulics.)

Another legend describes how Archimedes uncovered a fraud against King Hieron II of Syracuse using his principle of buoyancy. The king suspected that a solid gold crown he ordered was partly made of silver. Archimedes first took two equal weights of gold and silver and compared their weights when immersed in water. Next he compared the weights of the crown and a pure silver crown of identical dimensions when each was immersed in water. The difference between these two comparisons revealed that the crown was not solid gold.

Archimedes was born in Syracuse, Sicily. He lived there most of his life. When the Romans attacked Syracuse, Archimedes invented weapons to defend the city. He is said to have suggested a method of employing mirrors to set enemy ships afire. After a two-year siege the Romans finally entered the city, and Archimedes was killed in the battle that followed.

*According to legend, Archimedes invented a large solar mirror to set fire to Roman ships attacking Syracuse, Sicily.*

Culver Pictures

**ARCHITECTURE.** By the simplest definition, architecture is the design of buildings, executed by architects. However, it is more. It is the expression of thought in building. It is not simply construction, the piling of stones or the spanning of spaces with steel girders. It is the intelligent creation of forms and spaces that in themselves express an idea.

Construction becomes intelligent and thus architectural when it is efficient and immediately appears so. If it is the simplest and most advanced type of structure, solving the task set for it, and conceivable in its age, construction will have the quality of perfect appropriateness and will also be the expression of the mechanical knowledge of a culture. It becomes intelligent also when it is made to emphasize its simplicity and to express its system of support so that both can be immediately understood.

Construction, however, only became a basic factor in architectural thought during the Roman era at the time of the birth of Christ. Before then architecture had been almost exclusively symbolic in form and decoration. The symbols that were materialized in the Egyptian pyramid, Sumerian ziggurat, Hindu stupa, and Japanese pagoda were the most powerful expression of each culture's religious beliefs. They were designed according to the most complex and all-embracing symbolic systems; their shape, decoration, dimensions, and orientation to the sun were the result of the most profound meditation. But they enclosed little or no internal space. They were works of architecture but not of construction.

When intelligent, permanent construction enclosing space replaced the symbolic architecture of primitive cultures, a new type of architectural art appeared. It

Photos, facing page: (top left, top right, middle left) Alinari/Art Resource; (top center) Anderson/Art Resource; (middle) Art Resource; (middle right) Louis Goldman—Rapho/Photo Researchers; (bottom center) Bildarchiv Foto Marburg; (bottom left) GEKS; (bottom right) from 'The New Churches of Europe' by G.E. Kidder Smith. This page: (top left) Michelle Stone—Art Resource; (top center left, top right, middle left) Alinari/Art Resource; (top center right) Todd Webb—Photo Researchers; (middle) F.B. Grunzweig—Photo Researchers; (middle right) Yan—Rapho/Photo Researchers; (bottom left) GEKS; (bottom center) French Cultural Services/Photo Researchers; (bottom right) from 'A Pictorial History of Architecture in America' by G.E. Kidder Smith.

became possible for a whole city to become a work of architecture with each contributing element—places of worship, government institutions, markets, houses—enclosed in an appropriate structure and decorated to express its individual character.

The cities of Rome, Ravenna, Constantinople, and Isfahan became possible with their colorful domes, cavernous markets, and decorated palaces. Their interior spaces also became symbolic in their shape and decoration as seen in the Islamic mosque and in Byzantine and Gothic churches.

With the Renaissance in Europe around 1400, there came a new sort of architecture in which mass

*This article was contributed by David Van Zanten, Ph.D., former Associate Professor of Art History, Northwestern University, and the late Ann Van Zanten, Ph.D., Curator of the Architectural Collection, Chicago Historical Society.*

and interior space were manipulated to produce aesthetically pleasing pictures like those in paintings and sculptures. The elaborate symbolism of primitive and medieval art disappeared. In its place was a purely human-centered handling of form and space to produce visual delight.

The demystification of architecture during the Renaissance prepared the way for modern design. In the 19th century the picturesque, the design of both buildings and their landscape surroundings as if they were pictures, evolved.

But the simultaneous evolution of society, science, and industry collided with this view of architecture, suggesting the very different idea that building could be an important instrument of social betterment if made healthy and efficient. Thus it has come about that next to the theater-set architecture of New York City's Fifth Avenue there is that of the hospital-like housing projects, which has left many architects with the difficult choice between working as decorative artists or as social planners.

### Symbolism

Mankind first used indestructible materials to erect large structures not to live in but to worship their gods. From the beginning of settled habitation about 10,000 BC to the rise of the Roman Empire, houses were built of the flimsiest materials and were not expected to outlast the lives of their inhabitants. A few early civilizations—especially the Assyrians, Persians, and Minoans—erected monumental palaces, but these were the residences of priest-kings. Architecture originated in the religious impulse and thus was originally symbolic.

The earliest permanent constructions consist of huge stones, roughly shaped, arranged in lines or circles. The one at Stonehenge in England is the best known

of these complexes. The stones were set up by several successive peoples inhabiting the region between 3000 and 1600 BC. They are grouped in four concentric circles, two of which are formed by paired uprights bearing huge capstones.

Because they are arranged to align with the sun at the summer and winter solstices, it is generally assumed that the complex served as a monumental calendar in which rites were performed on significant days of the year. Similar circles of stones were set up elsewhere in England, at Avebury most particularly, and in France at Carnac. Clusters of stones spanned by roof slabs, called dolmens, and single stones that stood on end, called menhirs, were also erected in large numbers, especially in Europe.

**Egypt.** The Egyptian pyramids were far more sophisticated and larger in size but similar symbolically: sacred stones. The fertile Nile Valley permitted civilization to develop there around 3000 BC ruled by god-kings, the pharaohs. The necessity of carrying out extensive irrigation projects meant that the Egyptians were organized to build on a large scale. Furthermore, the high limestone cliffs hemming in the valley provided an inexhaustible supply of fine building stone.

Royal tombs were built along the edges of cliffs, at first as low rectangular mastabas, then as tall four-sided pyramids. The earliest of the pyramids was that of the pharaoh Zoser erected at Saqqara about 2700–2600 BC. Three huge pyramids built at Giza, near Cairo, about 2500 BC were the culmination of the series (*see* Pyramids). The largest of these, the great pyramid of the pharaoh Cheops, measured 756 feet (230 meters) on a side at its base and was 481 feet (147 meters) high. In spite of its huge size, however, it enclosed no space other than a narrow passage leading to a small tomb chamber in its center. It was constructed of

*The ziggurat of the moon god Nanna at Ur in Mesopotamia was built in about 2100 BC. The three 100-step staircases in the northeastern façade converge in a gateway between the first and second terraces. A single flight then leads to the top terrace and to the door of the god's shrine.*

*The Horyu-ji temple at Nara in Japan was built in 722. Beside the towering pagoda in the courtyard is the image hall, or kondo.*

Robert Harding Associates

limestone blocks weighing between 3 and 15 tons that were simply piled on top of each other.

The Egyptians worshiped the sun as their chief god, often represented by a symbolic pyramidal stone, or *ben-ben*. The Egyptian hieroglyph for the sun was a triangle divided into three zones horizontally—red, white, and yellow. It would seem to represent the sun (the top, or yellow zone) spreading its rays upon the Earth (the bottom, or red zone). The pyramids at Giza were once faced in a smooth coating of white marble with a band of pink at the base and a pyramidal block of pure gold at the top.

It has been concluded that the pyramids themselves were huge *ben-ben*s, symbols of the sun and its rays reaching down to Earth. When the pharaoh died he was said to ascend the sun's rays to join his father, the sun-god. Thus the pyramid would also seem to have been the symbolic staircase up which its occupant, the pharaoh, would climb to reach heaven. What breathtaking symbols these must have been lined up on the west rim of the Nile Valley!

To the east of Egypt another civilization appeared about 3000 BC, that of the Sumerians in the river valley of the Tigris and Euphrates called Mesopotamia, or the "land between the rivers." This too was a highly organized culture capable of carrying out large irrigation and construction projects. But it differed from Egypt in two respects: it had no stone with which to build, only river clay, so that its architecture is entirely in brick; and it had no single divine ruler but was divided into a number of independent city-states and worshiped unseen gods.

**Sumeria.** The Sumerian temple was a small brick house that the god was supposed to visit periodically. It was ornamented so as to recall the reed houses built by the earliest Sumerians in the valley. This house, however, was set on a brick platform, which became larger and taller as time progressed until the platform at Ur (built around 2100 BC) was 150 by 200 feet (45 by 60 meters) and 75 feet (23 meters) high. These Mesopotamian temple platforms are called ziggurats, a word derived from the Assyrian *ziqquratu*, meaning "high." They were symbols in themselves; the ziggurat at Ur was planted with trees to make it represent a mountain. There the god visited Earth, and the priests climbed to its top to worship.

The ziggurat continued as the essential temple form of Mesopotamia during the later Assyrian and Babylonian eras. In these later times it became taller and more towerlike, perhaps with a spiral path leading up to the temple at the top. The Greek historian Herodotus wrote that the main temple of Babylon, the famous Tower of Babel, was such a tower divided into seven diminishing stages, each a different color: white, black, purple, blue, orange, silver, and gold.

**India.** A third civilization emerged about 300 BC east of Mesopotamia, beyond the Iranian plateau, in the Indus River valley of India. From it evolved the Hindu culture of India that produced another characteristic temple form, the stupa. The earliest example surviving in its entirety is that at Sanchi, erected during the 1st century BC. More is known about the symbolism of the stupa because the Hindu religion has survived to the present day, while the religions of the ancient Egyptians and the Sumerians have not.

The Hindu stupa again symbolized a sacred mountain. It was an ovoid mass of stone blocks that became increasingly tall as time progressed. Here, however, the deity was placed deep inside a small, unlit womb chamber at its core, directly under the structure's highest peak. During ceremonies a statue of the god placed there was believed to be inhabited by the deity. These statues had originally been placed in rock-cut caves deep in the faces of cliffs, and it was only after many centuries that the Hindu place of worship emerged from the Earth and became a freestanding construction symbolizing the mountain in which it had formerly been excavated.

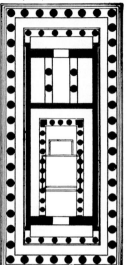

*The Parthenon on the Acropolis in Athens, Greece (left), was built from 447 to 438 BC by the architects Ictinus and Callicrates for the statesman Pericles. A floor plan (right) reveals something of the inner detail of this, one of the most famous of all structures.*

As in the case of the pyramid and the ziggurat, there is very little space inside a stupa. But its exterior was richly carved in decorative patterns derived from the wooden construction of palaces and covered with masses of statues and reliefs depicting religious scenes. These statues were placed to mark the hieratic system of the Hindu universe so that around the tiny womb chamber and its sacred image there spread a series of secondary blocks, courtyards, and avenues. At Angkor Wat, erected in Cambodia in the 12th century AD, these grew to huge size and complexity (*see* Angkor Wat).

**Japan.** Angkor Wat was a Buddhist rather than a Hindu shrine. In the early centuries of the Christian Era, Buddhism spread eastward from India across China, becoming established in Japan by AD 600. There the Indian stupa reappeared in the similar but greatly transformed pagoda. The earliest and most perfect surviving example of the pagoda is that in the monastery of Horyuji, which was erected in 607. Built in 711, the pagoda is in wood, the primary material of construction in Japan. Its basic form is that of a house, repeated five times vertically. The spreading roof of each tier displays the characteristic construction in posts and lintels joined by elaborate brackets perfected in the houses and palaces of China and Japan. There is little internal space. A relic of the Buddha is set in the stone base of the tall pole that rises the entire height of the pagoda, emerging at the peak as a finial. Located around the base of the pole are four statues that face the four cardinal points.

Buddhism in Japan also emphasized other, newer architectural forms, most particularly the image hall. At Horyuji this is called the golden hall and is set beside the pagoda in the monastic courtyard to share its ritual emphasis. The golden hall encloses a large space, like a palace hall, but is occupied principally by cult statues and painted screens. Religious ceremonies took place chiefly out-of-doors in the courtyard. The wooden palace construction of the pagoda is repeated in the golden hall and in all the monastic buildings, producing a lighter and more habitable environment than the stone masses of Sanchi and Angkor Wat.

**Greece.** The greatest of the early religious types is the Greek temple, which evolved during the thousand years before the birth of Jesus. Until the age of Alexander the Great, the Greeks erected permanent stone buildings almost exclusively for religious monuments, like the Egyptians, Sumerians, and Hindus. Their temples were not large enclosures of space but statue chambers containing a god's sacred image. These chambers were accessible only to priests. Yet the Greek temple has always been seen as fundamentally distinct from and superior to most other early religious types, partly because of the simplicity of its form, partly because of the exquisite refinement of the best examples (especially the Parthenon on the Acropolis in Athens), and partly because it is seen to reflect the emergence in Greece of a rational, philosophical approach to art that replaced earlier belief systems. (*See also* Acropolis.)

There are two types of Greek temple: the Ionic, evolved in Ionia on the eastern shore of the Aegean Sea, and the Doric, evolved on the western shore. The two systems are called orders because their parts and proportions are ordered and coordinated. Their forms must originally have had symbolic meaning. Both show the same basic plan: a central windowless statue chamber, the cella; a porch, usually with two columns in front; and a ring of columns, the peristyle, around the four sides. The cella and porch seem to have been the original elements of the temple. They reproduce the primitive Greek house so that the god is symbolically depicted as living like a chief. The temple is usually set on a natural hill, or acropolis, but has no artificial platform beyond a three-step foundation, or stylobate. The peristyle was a later addition, apparently borrowed from the Egyptians, evidently to enlarge and ornament the symbolic god-house inside. A low, sloping roof tops the building with gables, called pediments, on the short sides.

The Ionic and Doric temples differ in their details. The Doric temple is simple in plan, the Ionic larger with a double peristyle. The columns differ: the Doric has a dish-shaped top, or capital, and no base, while the Ionic has paired volutes at its capital and carved rings at its base. The lintels, or entablatures, spanning the columns are also distinct, the Doric having a row of projecting blocks, or triglyphs, between sculpted metopes. The Ionic elements are smaller and taller, the Doric forms shorter and broader.

What is remarkable and unique about the Greek temple is the conscious adjustment of these orders by Greek architects for purely aesthetic effect. For the first time in history, architects, not priests, directed these building projects. Many of their names are known, and several wrote books about their aesthetic experiments. A book that has survived to the present is 'De Architectura' (On Architecture) by the Roman architect Marcus Vitruvius Pollio, who was active at the time of the birth of Christ. It is an authoritative source of information on much of Greek architectural theory and practice.

Greek designers sought perfect orderliness in their rendition of the temple form. They adjusted the number of columns across the ends in relation to those down the sides. They aligned all the accents along the elevations so that each unit defined by one column (in the Doric order) was divided in the entablature into two triglyphs and metopes, four mutules under the cornice, four water spouts along the roof edge, and eight roof tiles. The most perfect example of this, the Parthenon in Athens, was built in 447–438 BC by the architects Ictinus and Callicrates for the political leader Pericles.

Within this strictly ordered framework, the Greek architect worked to endow every part with interest and life in the carving of its surface. The spiral of the Ionic volute, the curve of the Doric capital, the depth and breadth of the flutes were varied endlessly for effect. The translucence and fine grain of the marble used in the most important buildings were an important help in making these refinements perceptible. Most amazing was the application of this work of adjustment to the temple as a whole, particularly in the case of the Parthenon. Here the stylobate and entablature are very slightly curved so that they rise in the center of each side, while the columns are made to lean slightly inward—the angle increasing as they approach the corners—and the distance between the shafts varied. Nor are the column shafts themselves straight but bulge slightly toward their middles in entasis. Thus the whole building was treated with the subtlety and delicacy of the marble sculptures that filled its metopes and pediment. Callicrates and Ictinus' attitude toward religious architecture ceased to be that of the superstitious priest-architect held subject to unvaryingly precise (and often hypnotically elaborate) repetition of prescribed forms and became instead that of the artist rationalist—adjusting, refining, and simplifying forms to make them quietly effective and satisfying to the eye.

In the 5th century BC, the age of Pericles, Greece was still an assortment of independent city-states, many of them democracies. In 338 BC Philip II of Macedon forced them all together into a single empire. Between 334 and 323 his son, Alexander the Great, conquered Egypt, Mesopotamia, Iran, and parts of India, transforming the whole into the most powerful state in the civilized world. Greek architecture suddenly became that of this rich, powerful Hellenic empire and was forced to break out of the fixed, small-scale vocabulary of forms that had been satisfactory for the Periclean temple. The orders were retained and a new one added, the Corinthian, a variation of the Ionic with realistic leaves of the acanthus plant on its capital.

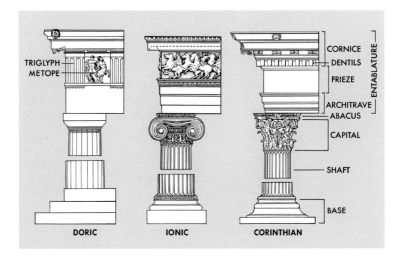

*Greek architecture developed two distinct orders, or styles—the Doric and the Ionic—and later a variant of the Ionic, the Corinthian. Although each order has characteristic differences in each of its parts, it is the capital that is most distinctive.*

Alinari/Art Resource

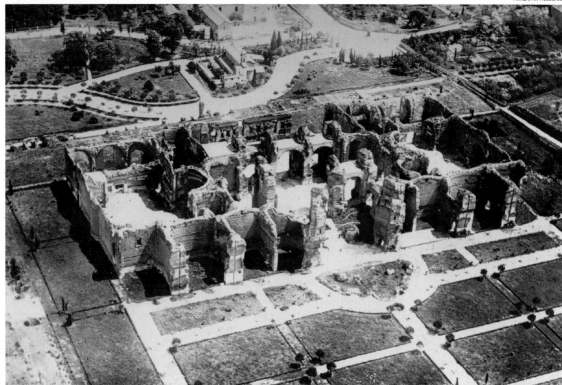

*The Baths of Caracalla in Rome were completed in AD 217 by Alexander Severus. There were three large vaulted bath chambers and a central great hall, with courts and auxiliary rooms, surrounded by a garden for exercise and games. It is the only great Roman bath to survive in large part.*

Construction was still in stone blocks—preferably marble—following the system of the column-post and entablature-lintel. But now this simple system was extended and multiplied to make monumental cities with colonnaded avenues and squares, palaces and public meeting halls, libraries and tombs. A series of great Hellenistic metropolises grew up, Alexandria in Egypt in particular (today completely buried underneath the modern city). At the royal city of Pergamum, which was built during the 3rd and 2nd centuries BC, one can see even today a series of colonnaded plazas stepping up a concave hillside, a single huge composition of architectural forms that are expressive of Hellenistic wealth and political power.

This was no longer an architecture of detail and refinement but one of massive (if simple) construction and political show. The vocabulary of the Periclean temple was no longer appropriate, and the Roman Empire that succeeded the Hellenistic adopted another, revolutionary solution.

## Space

**Pagan Rome.** The Roman Empire, founded by Augustus Caesar in 27 BC and lasting in Western Europe for 500 years, reorganized world politics and economics. Almost the entirety of the civilized world became a single centralized state. In place of Greek democracy, piety, and independence came Roman

authoritarianism and practicality. Vast prosperity resulted. Europe and the Mediterranean bloomed with trading cities ten times the size of their predecessors with public amenities previously unheard of: basilicas (law courts), theaters, circuses, public baths. And these were now large permanent masonry buildings as were the habitations, tall apartment houses covering whole city blocks, or *insulae*.

This architectural revolution brought about by the Romans required two innovations: the invention of a new building method—concrete vaulting—and the organization of labor and capital on a large scale so that huge projects could be executed quickly after the plans of a single master architect.

Roman concrete was a fluid mixture of lime and small stones poured into the hollow centers of walls faced with brick or stone and over curved wooden molds, or forms, to span spaces as vaults. The Mediterranean is an active volcanic region, and a spongy, light, tightly adhering stone called pozzolana was used to produce a concrete that was both light and extremely strong.

The Romans had developed pozzolana concrete about 100 BC but at first used it only for terrace walls and foundations, as, for example, at the Temple of Fortuna Primigenia at Palestrina, erected about 80 BC. It apparently was the notorious emperor Nero who first used the material on a grand scale to rebuild a region of the city of Rome around his palace, the expansive Domus Aurea (Golden House), after the great fire of AD 64 (which he is erroneously said to have set). Here broad streets, regular blocks of masonry apartment houses, and continuous colonnaded porticoes were erected according to a single plan and partially at state expense. The Domus Aurea itself was a labyrinth of concrete vaulted rooms, many in complex geometric forms. An extensive garden with a lake and forest spread around it.

The architect Severus seems to have been in charge of this great project. Emperors and emperors' architects succeeding Nero and Severus continued and expanded their work of rebuilding and regularizing Rome. Vespasian (emperor AD 63–79) began the Colosseum. Domitian (81–96) rebuilt the Palatine Hill as a huge palace of vaulted concrete designed by his architect Rabirius. Trajan (97–117) erected the expansive forum that bears his name (designed by his architect Apollodorus) and a huge public bath. Hadrian (117–138)—proud to serve as his own architect—built the Pantheon as well as a villa the size of a small city for himself at Tivoli. Later Caracalla (211–217) and Diocletian (284–305) erected two mammoth baths that bear their names, and Maxentius (306–312) built a huge vaulted basilica, now called the Basilica of Constantine.

The Baths of Caracalla have long been accepted as a summation of Roman culture and engineering. It is a vast building, 360 by 702 feet (110 by 214 meters), set in 50 acres (20 hectares) of gardens. It was one of a dozen establishments of similar size in ancient Rome devoted to recreation and bathing. There were a 60- by 120-foot (18- by 36-meter) swimming pool, hot and cold baths (each not much smaller than the pool), gymnasia, a library, and game rooms. These rooms were of various geometric shapes. The walls were thick, with recesses, corridors, and staircases cut into them. The building was entirely constructed of concrete with barrel, groined, and domical vaults spanning as far as 60 feet (18 meters) in many places. Inside, all the walls were covered with thin slabs of colored marble or with painted stucco. The decorative forms of this coating, strangely enough, were derived from Greek architecture as though the Romans could build but could not ornament. Therefore, what is Roman about the Baths of Caracalla and the other great constructions of the Romans is merely the skeleton.

The rebuilding of Rome set a pattern copied all over the empire. Nearby, the ruins of Ostia, Rome's port (principally constructed in the 2nd and 3rd centuries AD), reflect that model. Farther away it reappears at Trier in northwestern Germany, at Autun in central France, at Antioch in Syria, and at Timgad and Leptis Magna in North Africa. When political disintegration and barbarian invasions disrupted the western part of the Roman Empire in the 4th century AD, new cities were founded and built in concrete during short construction campaigns: Ravenna, the capital of the Western Empire from 492–539, and Constantinople in Turkey, where the seat of the empire was moved by Constantine in 330 and which continued thereafter to be the capital of the Eastern, or Byzantine, Empire.

**Christian Rome.** One important thing had changed by the time of the founding of Ravenna and Constantinople; after 313 this was the Christian Roman Empire. The principal challenge to the imperial architects was now the construction of churches. These churches were large vaulted enclosures of interior space, unlike the temples of the Greeks and the pagan Romans that were mere statue-chambers set in open precincts. The earliest imperial churches in Rome, like the first church of St. Peter's erected by Constantine from 333, were vast barns with wooden roofs supported on lines of columns. They resembled basilicas, which had carried on the Hellenistic style of columnar architecture. Roman concrete vaulted construction was used in certain cases, for example, in the tomb church in Rome of Constantine's daughter, Santa Costanza, of about 350. In the church of San Vitale in Ravenna, erected in 526–547, this was expanded to the scale of a middle-sized church. Here a domed octagon 60 feet (18 meters) across is surrounded by a corridor, or aisle, and balcony 30 feet (9 meters) deep. On each side a semicircular projection from the central space pushes outward to blend these spaces together.

**Byzantine Empire.** An impressive series of domical churches was built about the same time as San Vitale, especially in the Eastern Roman Empire at Constantinople. Here in 532–537 the emperor Justinian had his architects Anthemius of Tralles and Isidorus of Miletus build Hagia Sophia. A low dome 107 feet (33 meters) in diameter is supported on four triangular vaults, or pendentives, so that two half-domes of the same dimension can open at either side. The central space measures 107 by 220 feet (33 by 67 meters). A deep aisle and balcony surround this, opening into it through arcades and blending with it across semicircular recesses. Externally the building is brought to a rectangle that is 220 by 320 feet (67 by 98 meters) on a side, terracing upward by stages to the dominant central dome.

The symbolic religious buildings of Egypt, Mesopotamia, India, Japan, and Greece stood apart from the surrounding cities and stated a religious belief in every detail. The Byzantine church, however, was buried in the new masonry city, another domical block like the baths and basilicas nearby. But symbolic expression found a new and powerful medium in the illusionistic decoration of the vast interior church spaces. The interiors of the Baths of Caracalla had been decorated with fragments of Greek architecture, and the walls of Nero's Domus Aurea had been painted in fantastic stage architecture and landscapes. Now the interior of the Byzantine church was covered with glass mosaic pieces. These depicted Biblical scenes and images of saints set against a continuous gold background. The mosaics at Hagia Sophia have been plastered over, but an impression of the original effect survives in the smaller, later churches at Daphni and Hosios Loukas and, especially, San Marco in Venice, begun in 1063. Here the walls of the space are

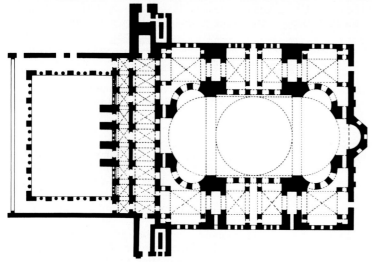

*The Hagia Sophia (top left) in Constantinople (now Istanbul, Turkey) was built in 532 to 537 by Anthemius of Tralles and Isidorus of Miletus for the emperor Justinian I. The minarets and wall buttresses date from the Turkish conquest in 1453. An interior view (top right) and floor plan (bottom left) provide added detail.*

Photos, (top left) GEKS; (top right) Hirmer Fotoarchiv, Munich; (bottom left) D. Talbot-Rice, 'The Byzantines' (1962), Praeger Publishers, Inc., and Thames and Hudson Ltd.

made to disappear in a glow of mystical light, and the worshiper seems to be carried up into the court of Heaven with Christ and all the saints.

**Islam.** Roman concrete vaulted construction was paralleled and indeed preceded by brick vaulted techniques evolved in Mesopotamia during the thousand years before the birth of Christ. This tradition created a sophisticated type of palace design, seen, for example, in that at Ctesiphon, near Baghdad, built in AD 550. It was passed on to the Islamic dynasties after the foundation of that aggressive religion in 622. Islam, like Christianity, required large covered interior spaces. Also like Christianity, it first created such spaces by the erection of broad wooden roofed enclosures divided by lines of columns, as are seen in the Mosque of Cordoba, Spain, built between 786 and 987. Vaulting was restricted to palaces. In the 12th century, however, masonry vaulting was used in Persia to span the wide spaces of the "Friday" Mosque at Isfahan. Here four deep tunnel vaults open from each side of a courtyard with a dome extending the vault on the side facing toward Mecca. This became the model of the great Egyptian and Iranian mosques of the 16th and 17th centuries. It is seen expanded in scale and ornamented in glowing blue ceramic tile in the Royal Mosque (Masjid-i-Shah) at Isfahan. With their conquest of Constantinople in 1453, the Ottomans developed a type of mosque that combined the Persian type, especially its tile decoration, and the single domical space of the Byzantine church. The celebrated architect Sinan built a series of mosques in the 16th century that displayed a structural resourcefulness and decorative refinement equal to that of his European contemporaries of the High Renaissance. The Islamic tradition closed impressively with the Taj Mahal, erected in Agra, India, in 1630–48, during Muslim rule. It is a domical tomb monument covered in carved marble (*see* Taj Mahal).

**Romanesque.** For seven centuries, from 300 to 1000, Europe was a shambles of crude wooden houses and churches. This was in sharp contrast to the continuation of Roman building techniques in the Byzantine and Islamic empires in the East. There had been only one short break in these Dark Ages: the reign of Charlemagne (768–814) was marked by the erection of his palace and palace chapel (792–805) at Aachen (now in Germany), which is a copy of San Vitale in Ravenna. Shortly after 1000, however, a miraculous transformation occurred. Large masonry churches were simultaneously begun all over Europe. The 11th-century monk Raoul Glaber wrote that it was as if the continent was putting on "a white mantle of churches." This was religious architecture built by anonymous architects according to symbolic prescriptions.

A new period of architecture commenced, called Romanesque today because it was the reproduction of Roman vaulted style. The methods of construction were the same, although often very crudely carried out, but great originality was shown in interior spatial planning and in exterior massing and decoration. A new type of church evolved that is excellently represented in St. Sernin at Toulouse, built from about 1080 to 1120. The plan is cross-shaped instead of centralized as at Hagia Sophia. The longest of its four arms extends westward and is the nave. It is crossed by shorter transepts and is balanced by a short chevet, or head, where the altar is set in front of a semicircular end-wall roofed with a half dome. Each arm has an aisle on either side below a high balcony, or triforium. These arms are vaulted with simple half-cylindrical barrel vaults and are narrow so that the intersection, or crossing, is less important for the tiny dome inside than for the tall tower built in tiers above it on the exterior. In the chevet the aisles are carried around the curved end as an ambulatory from which open individual semicircular chapels.

Romanesque churches of this type are in France and northern Spain and Italy and have been called pilgrimage churches because they stand along the route of pilgrimage roads leading to San Juan Campostella. Relics were displayed for veneration in the chapels around the chevet, and sleeping space for pilgrims was provided in the triforium.

Other similar Romanesque church types developed all over Europe. Along the Rhine River large churches were built with narrow, vaulted naves, no transepts, and groups of tall towers at both ends. In northern France the Norman Romanesque evolved with skillful vaulting and pairs of tall towers at the west facades. This style was carried to England by William the Conqueror after 1066 and produced the Anglo-Norman Romanesque of Durham and Ely cathedrals.

The Romanesque's most striking manifestation was probably in Italy, among the ruins of the ancient Roman Empire and near the continuing Byzantine culture. Here trading cities were experiencing new prosperity. The Venetians, beginning in 1063, built San Marco with five domes, an elaborate imitation of Byzantine architecture. In Pisa, beginning in 1053, a complex of structures was built—a cathedral, bell tower, baptistery, and monumental cemetery—of sparkling colored marbles covered with carved decoration, in part Roman, in part fantastic and barbarian.

**Gothic.** The prosperity and the building campaigns of the Romanesque period were slight, however, in comparison to the vast development of economic and building power of the Gothic period, which began in the late 12th century. In France, between 1140 and 1200, a new and more efficient type of masonry vaulted construction was invented. The Roman vault was a consistent mass of concrete that had been poured over a heavy wooden mold and left to harden. The new Gothic vault consisted of a network of separate stone arches, or ribs, spanning the space, between which were laid a thin webbing of small stones. This kind of vault was lighter and its thrusts were more clearly defined, since they passed down the ribs. This meant that the walls of the building supporting the vaults could be made thinner and opened with

*The church of San Marco in Venice was begun in 1063 and consecrated in 1085. The mosaics in the interior date from about 1100 to the middle of the 15th century.*

G.R. Richardson—Taurus Photos

*The Royal Mosque (Masjid-i-Shah) in Isfahan, Iran, was built in 1612 to 1638 by Ustad (Master) Abul Qasim for Shah Abbas I. It is noted for its tile mosaics.*

large windows. Furthermore, beginning in 1194 with the construction of Chartres cathedral, the weight of these vaults was supported on flying buttresses, light structures of stone piers and arches standing outside the mass of the building itself.

The plan of a Gothic church resembled that of the Romanesque but was more unified because the arms were shorter, the spaces broader, and the walls between the parts made thinner or entirely removed. Gothic interior spaces, however, did not look at all the same. The efficient vaulting system enabled these spaces to be much taller and to be entirely surrounded with windows that were filled with stained glass depicting Biblical scenes and saints. These figures, in deep red and blue colors, seemed to float above the worshiper like the figures depicted in Byzantine mosaics, but they glowed as daylight beamed through. To hold these great expanses of glass in place, thin stone ribs of tracery in decorative forms were built across the windows.

Externally the Gothic church was more complex and expressive than the Romanesque. Tall towers with tiers of openings and slender stone spires marked at least the facade and crossing, and usually were intended at the transept ends as well. Along the sides flying buttresses stood out from the wall and bore pinnacles and tracery as well as carved figures and fantastic rainspouts called gargoyles. At the doors at the end of the nave, and sometimes also at those at the ends of the transepts, were elaborate symbolic sculptural compositions of Biblical scenes and saints. Above would sometimes be a huge round stained-glass rose window. The Gothic style was used not only in the construction of churches but, like the Roman vaulted style, was a building technique and permitted a whole city-full of masonry vaulted forms to be created.

Although Europe was as prosperous as it had been under the Romans, it was disturbed by continual wars between the separate city-states. Thus the finest achievements of the Gothic builders were the mighty rings of city walls, like those at Carcassonne in France, or castles, like Harlech Castle in England. Inside these were expansive rib-vaulted rooms and chapels. In the free-trading cities of France, the Netherlands, and northern Germany, there arose large town halls, like the Cloth Hall (about 1250–1300) at Ypres (now in Belgium). There were also palaces such as that at Nuremberg, with its wooden beamed ceiling. Rich merchants built expensive houses with traceried windows and carved fireplaces, as Jacques Coeur did in Bourges, France, in 1443–51.

### Art

About 1400 a great change took place in society and culture in Italy. As it evolved it came to be called the Renaissance, the "rebirth," because of the rediscovery of ancient Roman literature and art in the period. This was, however, only one of its aspects, and many would say only a minor one. First of all, it was the moment of the discovery of individuality, of people able to think and act for themselves. The medieval worker had been an anonymous toiler for the glory of God. On the medieval facade of the church of St. Hubert in Troyes, one reads *non nobis, Domine, non nobis, sed nomini tuo da gloriam*—"Not to us, O Lord, not to us, but to your name be glory." But one reads across the front of the Renaissance church of San Francesco in Rimini simply the name of the ruler who built it, Sigismondo Malatesta, and the date. The building came to be called Tempio Malatestiano, the Temple of Malatesta.

The Renaissance individual, freed from medieval superstition, cynically experimented in politics (as can be seen in Machiavelli's book 'Il Principe' [The Prince] of 1513), explored new areas of science and nature (as did Galileo), conceived a new philosophy—Neoplatonism—that combined Christian and ancient thought, reintroduced realism into painting and sculpture, and created a new style in architecture. The Renaissance architect was a new and different sort. In place of the medieval craftsman-architect, there were now men skilled in all artistic media, men who understood theory as well as practice and who pretended to personal worth and even genius. Among the leading architects of the period were two sculptors—Filippo Brunelleschi and Michelangelo—and three painters—Leonardo da Vinci, Raphael, and Giulio Romano. Leonardo was a scientist, Michelangelo a philosopher and poet. Leon Battista Alberti and Andrea Palladio wrote treatises on architecture. To these men architecture was not a mechanical art pursued by traditional craft rules but a liberal art controlled by abstract intellectual speculation.

**Alberti.** The new state of architecture can be seen most clearly in the person of Alberti. Medieval architects had risen from the anonymity of stonemasons, but Alberti was a gentleman and sportsman who

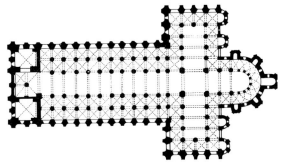

*The church of St. Sernin at Toulouse, France, was built from about 1080 to 1120. An example of Romanesque architecture, it has semicircular chapels around the chevet at the east end (top left) and heavy Roman vaults in the nave (top right).*

practiced painting and music and who applied his general theorizing to architecture. In 1452 he wrote 'De re aedificatoria' (Ten Books on Architecture), which was the first theoretical essay on building. Here he sought to rewrite the ancient Roman architectural book 'De architectura' (On Architecture) by Vitruvius to clarify and Christianize it as his philosopher friends in Florence were then rewriting and Christianizing the philosophy of Plato. Alberti conceived of architecture in terms of simple geometric volumes and numerical proportions, combining Plato's belief that beauty lies in numbers and Vitruvius' assertions that the orders were fixed in proportion. Alberti described an ideal city with all its streets laid out geometrically, centering on a cylindrical domed church set on a high base, with its windows placed far up the walls so that only the sky could be seen from inside. The church's decoration was to be very simple and its ornament to be faithfully copied from ancient Roman buildings. (*See also* Alberti.)

**Brunelleschi.** Alberti's vision was a startlingly new one and a difficult one to realize. Alberti's young friend Filippo Brunelleschi had made the first attempt in his design for the church of San Lorenzo in Florence, begun in 1421. The plan is not centralized, but the dark stained glass and tall proportions of the Gothic style have been replaced by light, open regular spaces in the proportion of one to two. Greek columns and entablatures in dark gray stone define the spaces and measure the white stucco walls. Alberti had not yet written 'De re aedificatoria' in 1421, but he was working on a treatise on perspective in painting, which was dedicated to Brunelleschi, and San Lorenzo seems to reflect Alberti's interest in the precise definition of space. (*See also* Brunelleschi.)

Alberti himself, beginning about the time of Brunelleschi's death in 1446, designed a number of buildings. Some were only exteriors added to existing structures, like the Tempio Malatestiano or the Rucellai Palace in Florence. He made the church facade in the form of a three-part Roman triumphal arch, intending that the tombs of Sigismondo Malatesta and his wife should be set on each side of the entrance opening. Alberti decorated the palace facade with a grid of Roman pilasters, setting up a proportional system followed also in the windows and doors. Two churches he later built in their entirety, those of San Andrea and San Sebastiano, were given pediments and pilasters surmounting broad flights of stairs like ancient Roman temples.

**Bramante.** Alberti moved from Florence to Rome about 1450. The power and the wealth of the pope at

*The main part of the cathedral at Chartres, France, was begun in 1194 and finished less than 30 years later, giving the representative Gothic structure a rare unity.*

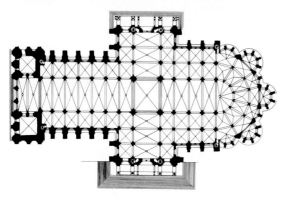

Rome were increasing, and about this time the center of the Renaissance moved there. The years from 1503 to 1513 marked the glorious papacy of Julius II. He brought Michelangelo and Raphael to work for him in Rome, and in 1506 he commenced the huge project of rebuilding St. Peter's. The man he employed to replace the venerable but dilapidated basilica (built by the emperor Constantine) was Donato Bramante. He was about 60 when he went to Rome from Milan, and he is supposed to have been trained as a painter by Piero della Francesco and Andrea Mantegna. While working as an architect in Milan, he would have known Leonardo, who was there at the time working out a series of geometric solutions for an ideal centralized church on Alberti's lines. From 1506 until his death in 1514, Bramante worked to design and begin construction of the first full expression of the new Renaissance church.

Only the four central piers and the four arches linking them to support the central dome were completed before Bramante died, and he seems to have still been changing his design. It was a composition of spaces defined by piers, vaults, and domes like the great Roman ruins nearby. It was principally, if not completely, centralized with a huge central dome at the meeting of four vaulted arms. This form was repeated in the cross-shaped, domed spaces set in the corners. From the exterior it would have made a unified composition of simple geometric forms, building step by step to a hemispheric dome supported on a ring of Roman columns. (*See also* Bramante.)

**Michelangelo.** Delay and confusion followed Julius' and Bramante's deaths within a year of each other, but in 1546 work was recommenced by a worthy successor, Michelangelo. He was 70 but had been executing architectural projects in Florence since the 1520s. His Medici Chapel in the church of San Lorenzo of 1520–34 and his Laurentian Library of 1523–59 were extraordinary for the expressive distortions of their details. Michelangelo extended these to his new design for St. Peter's. He simplified Bramante's composition, strengthened the proportions, and designed details as huge and powerful as the construction itself. He made the exterior wall to ripple in response to the intricate

Bildarchiv Foto Marburg

*The church of San Lorenzo in Florence was designed by Filippo Brunelleschi. Built in about 1421 to 1460, it typifies the Renaissance style. All of the ornament is Classical, with Corinthian columns and pilasters, but the plan is based on the earlier basilica in proportions of one to two.*

interior spaces as though they were pushing against an elastic membrane. He made its thickness palpable with deeply cut windows and niches and then held it together with a row of massive pilasters. (*See also* Michelangelo.)

**Giulio Romano.** Bramante had realized Alberti's Neoplatonic ideal. Michelangelo's architecture shows an elaboration and expressiveness that might seem excessive and that has been called Mannerist. The painter Raphael lived to 1520, and, in his last works as well as in architectural designs done at the end of his life, he displayed similar Mannerist tendencies. In the hands of Raphael's student Giulio Romano, Mannerism received its most dramatic expression. In the Palazzo del Te in Mantua (erected and decorated from 1524 to 1535), Giulio Romano made the most adventurous distortions: keystones that seem to be falling from arches and painted ceilings that appear to be collapsing.

**Palladio.** While Mannerism dominated Rome and central Italy, the rich island city of Venice and its region experienced in the work of Andrea Palladio the extension and final perfection of the balanced Neoplatonic architecture of Alberti and Bramante. Palladio had begun as a stonemason, but beginning about 1535 he was educated as a scholar by the literary reformer Giangiorgio Trissino. He later became a close friend of other scholars, most particularly the editor

of Vitruvius, Daniele Barbaro, and in 1555 Palladio became a founding member of the Accademia Olympica in Vicenza. In 1570 Palladio published his highly respected treatise, 'I Quattro Libri dell'architettura' (Four Books on Architecture). His work is remarkable for applying geometry and proportion as well as simplicity and correctness of precedent to all genres of architecture. He coordinated the proportions of every room in designs such as that for the Villa Rotonda near Vicenza of 1550. He also tried to apply the simple forms of the Roman temple—the evenly spaced rows of columns and the pediment—to both villas and churches, developing a uniquely satisfying type of church facade in San Giorgio Magno and Il Redentore in Venice. His buildings, especially as illustrated and described in his book, were to become the principal models of imitation as the Renaissance spread outward from Italy around 1600.

### Organization

About 1600 European culture was again revolutionized. In northern Europe the Renaissance had become the Protestant Reformation. In Italy, beginning with the foundation of the Jesuit Order in 1539 and the Council of Trent of 1545–63, the Roman Catholic church began the Counter-Reformation, a campaign to strengthen itself in reaction. There resulted a more purely Catholic and emotional style, the baroque.

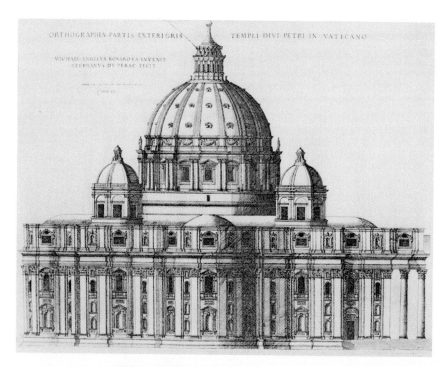

*St. Peter's Basilica in Rome was redesigned by Michelangelo after 1546 (engraving by Dupérac of south elevation, top), simplifying the 1505 plan (bottom) by Donato Bramante.*

Photos, (top) courtesy of the Metropolitan Museum of Art, New York, Harris Brisbane Dick Fund, 1941; (bottom) from 'Art Through the Ages' by Helen Gardner, fifth edition, edited by Horst de la Croix and Richard G. Tansey, © 1970 by Harcourt Brace Jovanovich, Inc. and reproduced with permission.

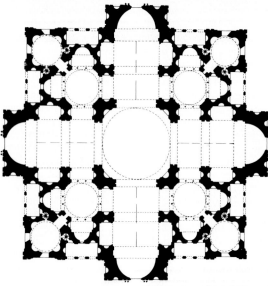

Italy, however, was becoming less and less the center of European civilization. The discovery of America brought great wealth to Spain in the 16th century; the expansion of trade made Holland and Britain major powers in the centuries following; and political centralization made France under Louis XIV the most influential state on the Continent. In these northern states religious architecture was overshadowed by political building—palaces and government institutions. The profession of architecture evolved in response. The architect had become a gentleman during the Renaissance. Now he became a government official, a bureaucrat, a part of the centralized administration of building. The greatest architects of the age—Jules Hardouin-Mansart, Sir Christopher Wren, Jacques-Germain Soufflot, Balthasar Neumann—were heads of corps of designers and builders who were assembled to carry out national construction projects of all sorts. These were educated men, but they were not (with the exception of Wren) philosophers or (with the exception of Bernini) practitioners of many arts.

**Italy.** The first great architect of this period was the Italian Giovanni Lorenzo Bernini. He was the last Renaissance architect in the sense that he was equally able in sculpture, painting, and building. But already there was a difference; instead of being a free-thinking Humanist like Alberti or Leonardo, Bernini was a faithful Catholic and a lay member of the Jesuit Order. This was reflected in his works, which were stage sets for the dramatization of Catholic ritual. (*See also* Bernini.)

A nave, at the clergy's insistence, had been added to the front of Michelangelo's St. Peter's by Carlo Maderna in 1607–15. In 1656 Bernini began a plaza in front of it defined by dramatic curving and angled colonnades. Connecting this to the papal apartments, he erected the Scala Regia of 1663–69, made dramatic by concealed light sources and a progressive diminishing of width as it rises. His little church of San Andrea al Quirinale of 1658–78 was his most perfect work. It is no longer round, like Alberti and Bramante's ideal, but expressively oval. A concealed light source illuminates a vision of religious figures in stucco over the altar that seems to float in the real space of the building. What in the 16th century had been cerebral and static became, in the 17th century, actual and dynamic.

*The Villa Rotonda near Vicenza, Italy, was designed by Andrea Palladio in 1550. It has Classical porticoes on each of its four sides.*
Alinari/Art Resource

Bernini had a brilliant assistant, Francesco Borromini, who in the 1630s emerged as his competitor in architecture. If Bernini's designs appear dramatic, Borromini's seem bizarre. His largest work, the chapel of San Ivo della Sapienza in the Collegio Romano of 1642–60 displays a distorted triangular space internally and a stepped dome that culminates in a spiral on the exterior. His intentions were evidently symbolic. The plan shows the triangular emblem of divine wisdom, and the spiral evokes the pillar of truth. The whole building has thus been made to become the Domus Sapientiae, the "House of Wisdom," expressive of its location in a college and its dedication to a saint of learning. (*See also* Borromini.)

At the end of the 17th century, Bernini's use of dramatic lighting and Borromini's free spatial geometry were combined by Guarino Guarini in a series of churches in Turin. Here space opens mysteriously behind space, and webs of dome ribs seem to float in front of bursts of divine light, producing the highest expression of the Italian baroque.

**Spain.** The Spanish Empire in the 16th and 17th centuries enjoyed great prosperity as well as close proximity and political interrelationship with Italy. In 1563–84 there arose the first great non-Italian work of the High Renaissance, Philip II's Escorial. It was simultaneously a monastery, mausoleum, fortress, and palace—a symbol of royal piety and power that became characteristic of the age. The principal architect, Juan de Herrera, worked closely with the king. The result, built in black granite, has the clarity of Bramante and the massiveness of Michelangelo and achieves the king's desire that it have "simplicity of form, severity in the whole, nobility without arrogance, majesty without ostentation."

**France.** France equaled Spain in power and finally, during the reign of Louis XIV (1643–1715), outshone its rival. The Renaissance had arrived early there also, during the reign of Francis I (1494–1547) in his palace at Fontainebleau. He had imported Italian artists, including Leonardo (who died at Amboise in 1519), but the architectural results during the 16th century were largely decorative and fantastic. In 1615, however, an equivalent to the Escorial began to rise in Paris in the Luxembourg Palace designed by Solomon de Brosse for the regent Marie de Medicis. This was followed by the châteaux and churches of François Mansart, especially his Val de Grace of 1645–67, and by the whole town and château of the Cardinal Richelieu commenced to a single design by Jacques Lemercier in 1631.

It was Louis XIV, upon his accession to power in 1661, who carried the combined expression of central power and state church to a new plane. He started by projecting the completion of his city palace, the Louvre, and in 1664 invited Bernini to Paris to execute it. But what had started as an admission of Italian supremacy ended as an assertion of French independence when Bernini returned to Rome after a few months' stay, and his baroque project was superseded by a simpler, more correct one by Claude Perrault, executed from 1667 to 1670.

Paris, however, was becoming too small a canvas for Louis XIV's architectural display of royal authority. His superintendent of finances, Nicolas Fouquet, had employed in 1657–61 the architect Louis Le Vau, the painter Charles Le Brun, and the landscape gardener André Le Nôtre to coordinate their three arts to produce his château at Vaux-le-Vicomte. Louis was deeply impressed. He had Fouquet's finances investigated,

The chapel of San Ivo della Sapienza at the University of Rome (top) was built by Francesco Borromini in 1642 to 1660. A view inside (bottom) reveals some of the rich interior detail.

The church is at the center of El Escorial, a palace-monastery built for Philip II by Juan de Herrera in 1563 to 1584 near Madrid in Spain.

He rose to be first royal architect and then, in 1699, superintendent des bâtiments. He designed Louis XIV's last and largest projects in a style that finally began to show baroque complexity and richness—the château at Marly (begun 1679), the Dome of the Invalides (1679–91, intended as Louis's mausoleum), and the Place Vendôme (begun 1698). Significantly, Hardouin-Mansart was one of the first architects to be accused by his contemporaries of not producing his own designs but of using the talents of skillful assistants.

**Holy Roman Empire.** To the east of France lay the Holy Roman Empire with its capital at Vienna. Beginning in 1690, Johann Bernhard Fischer von Erlach worked there, starting the baroque Karlskirche in 1716. The most extraordinary work in the German sphere was produced in the early 18th century in the bishopric of Würzburg, where Balthasar Neumann, trained locally as a military engineer, served as state architect. He designed the magnificent bishop's Residenz (palace), with ceiling frescoes by Giovanni Battista Tiepolo, as well as the pilgrimage church of Vierzehnheiligen (1741–71, near Lichtenfels in Bavaria). In the latter building the spatial geometry of Borromini is combined with a richness of decoration and an openness of structure that make the whole space a religious apparition.

**England.** France's real competitor for domination of northern Europe, however, was the developing

took over his team of artists, and in 1668 set them to work producing an even grander ensemble for him at Versailles. Here huge expanses of formal gardens on one side and three monumental avenues on the other culminate in a vast palace designed in the severe style of the Louvre and the Escorial (*see* Versailles).

Versailles was built slowly in parts. Upon Le Vau's death in 1670, Jules Hardouin-Mansart took over, designing the famous Galérie des Glaces (begun 1678).

Aerofilms, Ltd., London

*The palace at Versailles, in France, was built chiefly by Louis Le Vau and Jules Hardouin-Mansart for Louis XIV during the last half of the 17th century. Hardouin-Mansart more than trebled the size of the original from 1678 to 1708.*

maritime nation of England. The Renaissance had arrived especially late there. After an almost abortive introduction of Palladianism by Inigo Jones in the early 17th century, the development was suspended until Sir Christopher Wren's appointment as surveyor of the king's works in 1669. He was the last scholar-architect, having pursued mathematics and astronomy before becoming involved in building. He became one of the most brilliant and prolific architect-bureaucrats of the age. Before his death in 1723 he had designed 52 London churches (after the 1666 fire), carried through the construction of St. Paul's Cathedral from foundation to cupola-top between 1673 and 1710, extended several palaces, and built two huge military hospitals at Chelsea and Greenwich. (*See also* Wren, Christopher; London, England.)

He is chiefly remembered for St. Paul's. It is French in its severity but original in its Gothic plan (insisted upon by the cathedral chapter) and ingenious in its vaulting and dome. From Wren's office emerged Nicholas Hawksmoor who, together with the gentleman-architect Sir John Vanbrugh, erected a series of huge ducal palaces in the early 18th century, notably Blenheim Palace near Oxford (begun 1705).

France continued in the 18th century to be the center of northern European culture and architecture, producing Ange-Jacques Gabriel's Place de la Concorde (begun 1757) and Jacques-Germain Soufflot's

Pantheon (1755–92). The latter structure was built originally as the church of Ste-Geneviève, and all of its complication of colonnades, domes, and windows restates the original Renaissance theme of the centralized, vaulted space that is decorated with sober ancient Roman ornamentation.

**Neoclassicism**

Soufflot's Pantheon was not only the culmination of the baroque tradition but also the first hint of the future course of architecture. It shows a growing awareness of the possibility of achieving pictorial effects. The building uses an ingenious hidden system of Gothic buttresses, which make possible the high windows that bring light streaming through the layers of columns and arches, which, in turn, support the roof vaults. The interior of the Pantheon is dramatized in much the same way as the contemporary Italian engraver Giovanni Battista Piranesi dramatized his views of ancient Roman monuments and buildings.

Piranesi's engravings influenced many architects in France and England and helped to begin a movement toward what has been called Romantic Classicism, or Neoclassicism. Classical forms began to be put together for dramatic and expressive effect rather than purely to create orderly compositions. With the writings of the theorist Marc-Antoine Laugier in France, architecture began to be seen as originating in natural

*The church of Vierzehnheiligen (top) in Bavaria was built in 1741 to 1771 by Balthasar Neumann. The Pantheon (bottom left and right) in Paris was built as the church of Ste-Geneviève in 1755 to 1792 by Jacques-Germain Soufflot.*

rather than human form, and architects began to try to recreate the effect of landscape in their works. This point of view paralleled the thinking of philosophers like Jean-Jacques Rousseau, who saw nature as the source of mankind's fundamental character. About the time of the French Revolution, the architect Étienne-Louis Boullée worked on projects for buildings that were intended to evoke natural phenomena such as the four seasons through their forms and character.

Many of Boullée's projects also reflected a popular philosophical concept, that of the sublime, which was put forward by the Englishman Edmund Burke in 1756 in his 'Philosophical Inquiry into Our Ideas of the Sublime and Beautiful in Art'. Burke tried to categorize the natural effects that combined to make something sublime; that is, those that are impressive beyond the normal range of experience. An offshoot of his theory was the development of the concept of the picturesque, which was based on a painter's interpretation of nature. The picturesque caught the imagination of architects, particularly in England, where the ancient form of the Roman villa was now freely adapted to suburban and country houses with features such as asymmetrical towers. A system of purposely irregular landscaping, whose best known practitioner was Humphrey Repton, was developed to complement these houses.

**Picturesque and Gothic Revival.** The picturesque soon came to include exotic forms from the Near East and the Orient, as well as from Gothic architecture, by then a form of building that had survived only in rural areas. As early as 1750, the writer Horace Walpole had put Gothic decorations on his villa, Strawberry Hill, just outside London. But the fashion for the medieval historical novel, introduced by Sir Walter

Scott, combined with enthusiasm for the picturesque, made the Gothic an alternative style of building by the early 1800s.

Early efforts at reviving the Gothic style tended to be superficial, involving the application of pointed arches, battlements, and finials to fundamentally classical buildings. The first architect to study Gothic forms and structure carefully with the aim of accurately reproducing them was the Englishman Augustus Welby Northmore Pugin, who worked in the 1830s and '40s. Pugin, a convert to Roman Catholicism, linked the revival of Gothic architecture to the revival of religion in society. He espoused the Gothic as a morally correct form of building.

Pugin's ideas were adopted and further developed by the art critic John Ruskin, who contrasted the structural honesty of Gothic architecture with the manipulations and concealments of structure practiced by Renaissance architects. Ruskin's writings, notably 'The Seven Lamps of Architecture' (1849) and 'The Stones of Venice' (1853) in which he defended truthfulness of structure and richness of ornament in natural forms, were enormously influential. Their effect was reinforced by that of the Anglican ecclesiological movement, which inspired Gothic-revival churches in England and America.

These ranged from the extraordinarily expressive and richly decorated church of All Saints, Margaret Street, in London of 1849–59, by William Butterfield, to the modest wood and stone churches designed for rural United States sites by Richard Upjohn in the 1840s and '50s. The idea of structural honesty was also extended to secular buildings, resulting in the United States in the simple country villas designed by Andrew Jackson Downing and his followers and

A.F. Kersting

*The church of All Saints, Margaret Street (top), in London was built in 1849 to 1859 by William Butterfield. Strawberry Hill (bottom) at Twickenham outside London was acquired by Horace Walpole in 1747 and made into a showplace villa.*

A.F. Kersting

*The unusual apartment house Casa Milá in Barcelona, Spain, was built in 1905 to 1910 by Antonio Gaudí.*
Archivo Mas, Barcelona

culminating in the great houses of the shingle-style movement of the 1870s and '80s and the buildings of Henry Hobson Richardson.

Structural honesty became structural rationalism in the works and writings of the French architect Eugène-Emmanuel Viollet-le-Duc. The most conscientious 19th-century student of Gothic structural techniques, Viollet-le-Duc wrote in favor of the creation of a modern architecture that would use modern materials like iron and glass as rationally as Gothic architecture had used stone. Viollet-le-Duc's writings were widely read in Europe and the United States well into the early 20th century, and they influenced architects as diverse as the Spaniard Antonio Gaudí and the Belgian Victor Horta (both designers in the naturalistic Art Nouveau style) and the American Frank Lloyd Wright, who espoused the organic use of materials.

**New Forms.** At the same time that the revival of Gothic architecture and the development of new forms based on Gothic structure were taking place, Classicism was continuing to develop in European and American architecture. The monumental Romantic Classicism that appeared about the time of the French Revolution, and its parallel—though more modest—in the new American republic, gradually gave way to more experimental forms.

When Thomas Jefferson designed the University of Virginia at Charlottesville in 1817–26, he used Classical forms to evoke the spirit of ancient republics and to teach proper taste to the students. The German architect and painter Karl Friedrich Schinkel put a vast row of columns across the front of his Altes Museum in Berlin (1824–28) in order to produce the sense of grandeur appropriate to a major public building. But even in the work of Schinkel, the Classical style was beginning to be abstracted into a system of post-and-lintel construction that organized space into regular bays.

By the 1830s architects were beginning to question whether the repetition of ancient forms had any meaning for modern society with its new industries, institutions, and standards of living. When Henri Labrouste designed the Bibliothèque Ste-Geneviève in Paris in 1838–51, he used the more practical and less imposing arched forms of the Renaissance in a building whose composition and decoration were dictated by its interior organization and purpose rather than by historical model. As the century progressed, architects turned to using the forms of the Classical tradition in more decorative and pictorial ways. In France, Charles Garnier's Paris Opéra of 1861–75 reflected the opulence of contemporary society in its

*The Bibliothèque Ste-Geneviève in Paris was built in 1838 to 1851. Henri Labrouste designed the building with shape and form to serve the needs of a library.*

Bildarchiv Foto Marburg

*The Paris Opéra (interior, top; exterior, bottom) was built in 1861 to 1875 by Charles Garnier and became the showpiece of the reign of Napoleon III.*

Photos, Photo Researchers: (top) Goursat—Rapho, (bottom) Pierre Berger.

baroque forms and rich decorations. It also served as a set piece in the new system of grand boulevards laid out by Baron Georges Eugène Haussmann with the encouragement of the emperor Napoleon III. In the United States the Renaissance and baroque became favored styles for the houses of wealthy businessmen and for the buildings where they worked and the public institutions they endowed. The firm of McKim, Mead, and White was the best known and most successful architectural servant of the merchant classes, designing such varied works in New York City alone as the Villard houses of 1885 (now part of the Helmsley Palace Hotel), Columbia University of 1893, the University Club of 1900, and Pennsylvania Station of 1906–10.

### Technology

A dramatic growth in the influence of technology on architecture occurred in the 19th century. With the Industrial Revolution architecture developed a relationship with manufacturing. Industry created a need for new types of buildings, and at the same time new building materials and techniques were being made available by industry. Huge spaces, unobstructed by bulky vertical supports, were needed for factories and mills. The goods they produced were stored in warehouses and shipped from docks and train sheds. When they reached their destinations, they were sold in shops joined by great covered passages or, later in the 19th century, vast department stores. These new buildings were made possible by the development of new technology: first, cast and wrought iron in the late 18th century, and, after the Bessemer process was invented in 1856, steel. Iron and steel are lighter than stone and stronger than wood and can be made quickly into structural elements at a factory and shipped to a construction site.

**Skyscraper.** It soon became clear that the technology of industrial buildings could be turned to other uses, the most important of which was building more efficiently in the cities where growing population pushed up land values until it became desirable to put tall buildings on small lots. In the booming cities of the United States in the late 19th century, the skyscraper gradually came into being. Little by little, iron and steel supporting elements were added to stone and brick buildings, until in 1885 William LeBaron Jenney designed the Home Insurance Company Building in Chicago, Ill. It was the first building in which the exterior walls were entirely supported on a steel frame. By the 1890s United States cities were dotted with tall office buildings. Architects like Louis Sullivan of Chicago tried to emphasize the simplicity and rugged strength of the steel frame in their works but also strove to make them artistic by shaping them or decorating their surfaces. Sullivan, though claiming originality, drew from the geometric and naturalistic

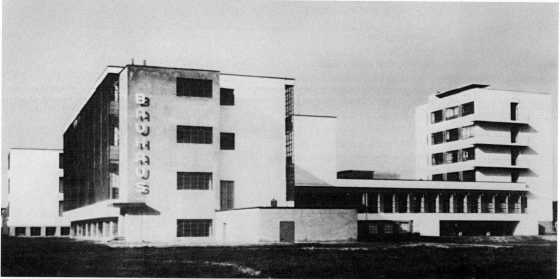

*The Robie house (top) in Chicago was built in 1909 by Frank Lloyd Wright. The Bauhaus school building (center) was built in 1925 to 1926 in Dessau, Germany, by Walter Gropius. The chapel of Notre-Dame-du-Haut (bottom) in Ronchamp, France, was built in 1950 to 1955 by Le Corbusier.*

Photos, (top) Hedrich-Blessing; (center) Bauhaus-Archiv, Berlin; (bottom) Marilyn Silverstone—Magnum ornament of the past, like the Moorish and Gothic, in tall office buildings such as the Wainwright Building in St. Louis of 1890–91.

Other architects turned to Classical and medieval forms. The blend of steel construction and stylistic revival produced some of the great United States skyscrapers of the early 20th century such as Cass Gilbert's Woolworth Building of 1911–13 in New York City and Raymond Hood and John Mead Howells' Tribune Tower of 1922–25 in Chicago.

**Wright.** American technical and stylistic innovations of the period were quickly recognized in Europe. Not only the skyscrapers but also the houses of Chicago architect Frank Lloyd Wright were widely written about and admired (*see* Wright, Frank Lloyd). The abstract, floating planes of the exterior of a building like the Robie house of 1909 in Chicago were seen by Europeans as an escape from historical forms. After the crisis of World War I and the political changes of that period, architects in France, Germany, and Russia started looking for ways to create a new architecture that did not use past styles.

**International Style.** The architecture that developed during this period came to be called the International Style because it spread throughout Europe and the United States. It was not really a style in the traditional sense of the word, with features like Doric columns or pointed arches, but was rather an attitude toward design. The buildings that were grouped together under this name tended to be nonsymmetrical in form, with flowing interior spaces, flat roofs, and large areas of glass in plain, undecorated walls. They were intended to represent an abstract, machined simplicity of built form and a modern clarity of thought and action in the lives of those who designed and used them.

The architects of these buildings also tried to extend their modernist ideals to every area of design through the medium of craft and manufacturing. Thus a group of German architects and artists formed the Deutscher Werkbund in 1907 to promote craft education and production through groups modeled on medieval guilds. The Werkbund sponsored an exhibition in Cologne in 1914 in which exhibition pavilions were assigned to architects representing a range of philosophies. This was the first time that modern buildings were put "on display" as a group of works of art.

**Bauhaus.** The Deutscher Werkbund gave way to a school of design and was refounded as the Bauhaus. Directed by architect Walter Gropius and, after 1926, housed in a building designed by him at Dessau, Germany, the Bauhaus produced designs for furniture and household goods that are still used today and laid the groundwork for the creation of a modern aesthetic that dominated the next 50 years. Extensive postwar building in Germany also provided opportunities to try new building techniques and modernist forms. Many housing developments were built in the 1920s in major German cities, including the Weissenhof Siedlung near Stuttgart, where 17 architects from Germany and other European countries were

invited in 1927 to contribute designs for houses and apartment buildings.

**Le Corbusier.** Modernist architecture developed in two main directions between the late 1910s and the 1960s. These were led by the work of two individuals: Charles-Édouard Jeanneret-Gris (known as Le Corbusier), who was a Swiss working in France, and Ludwig Mies van der Rohe, a German working first in Germany and then in the United States.

Le Corbusier created architecture of asymmetrical volumes enclosed by smooth white walls raised off the ground by slender, cylindrical columns, the best known example of which is the Villa Savoye of 1929 at Poissy, near Paris. He called his houses "machines for living in," emphasizing their organization around modern domestic life rather than a formal ideal. As Le Corbusier's career developed, his buildings became more complex in form, using curves and irregularly shaped solid elements, as in his distinctive chapel of Notre-Dame-du-Haut (1950–55) at Ronchamp, France. These late works inspired an entire generation of architects who worked in roughly finished forms of poured concrete. Le Corbusier was also important

*The Wainwright Building in St. Louis was built in 1890 to 1891 by Louis Sullivan. It is an early steel-framed skyscraper faced in red stone, brick, and terra-cotta with strong vertical lines and recessed horizontals.*

© 1982 Sadin-Schnair Photography

## Some Distinguished Architects

*Some prominent persons are not included below because they are covered in the main text of this article or in other articles in Compton's Encyclopedia (see Fact-Index).*

**Aleijadinho** (Antônio Francisco Lisboa) (1738?–1814). Brazilian architect and sculptor known for rococo statuary and religious articles. Designed, built, and decorated church in Ouro Prêto and sanctuary in Congonhas do Campo. He helped shape the decorative baroque movement of 18th-century Brazil.

**Bulfinch, Charles** (1763–1844). Dominant American architect in the Federal period. His numerous buildings in the Boston area include the Massachusetts State House. He successfully supervised completion of the United States Capitol (1817–30).

**Burnham, Daniel** (1846–1912). American city planner and architect, in partnership with John Wellborn Root. He is known for his comprehensive scheme for Chicago. His commercial buildings include the Rookery (1886) and Reliance (1894), both in Chicago, and Flatiron (1902) in New York City.

**Churriguera, José Benito de** (1665–1725), **Joaquín** (1674–1724), and **Alberto** (1676–1750). Leading Spanish architects of their time who created works that featured fantastically complicated ornamentation.

**Erickson, Arthur C.** (born 1924). Canadian architect whose original and varied work includes buildings at Simon Fraser University, in British Columbia (1963) and the University of Lethbridge, in Alberta (1971). He also designed the prize-winning Canadian pavilion at the Expo 70 fair in Osaka, Japan. He is known for his use of detailing and neutral colors.

**Fathy, Hassan** (1900–89). Egyptian architect devoted to housing in developing nations. He planned the village of New Gourna, Egypt (1945–48), and is noted for blending ancient design methods with modern organizational skills.

**Fischer von Erlach, Johann Bernhard** (1656–1723). First and chief architect of the Austrian imperial baroque. He is known for his Karlskirche (begun 1716) and library in the Hofburg (imperial palace, begun 1723), both in Vienna.

**Foster, Norman** (born 1935). English architect who first gained notice as a partner in the Team 4 group. His minimalist approach is seen in the Sainsbury Centre for the Visual Arts at the University of East Anglia.

**Gabriel, Ange-Jacques** (1698–1782). First architect to Louis XV of France. His masterpiece is the Petit Trianon (1762–68) at Versailles. His work shows the influence of Mansart, Michelangelo, and Bernini.

**Gehry, Frank** (born 1929). Canadian-born American architect whose flair for art and sculpture is seen in the warehouse and offices of the Mid-Atlantic Toyota Distributorship in Glen Burnie, Md. (1978). He designed the Hollywood Bowl Shell, phase I, Los Angeles, Calif. (1976), and the American Center in Paris (1994).

**Gibbs, James** (1682–1754). Scottish-born English architect and disciple of Christopher Wren in such structures as the Radcliffe Library, Oxford (1737–49), and church of St. Martin-in-the-Fields, London (1721–26). His 'Book of Architecture' (1728) quickly became a classic.

**Giulio Romano** (1499?–1546). Roman artist and architect who assisted Raphael on Vatican frescoes. The Palazzo del Té at Mantua is an example of his mannerist style, which combined a classical precedent with detailed romantic freedom.

**Graves, Michael** (born 1934). Influential American postmodernist whose trademark themes include the liberal use of cubism, color, and texture. He is known for his concern with a structure's relationship to its physical and historical setting. Among his works are the Claghorn House, Princeton, N.J. (1974), and the House in Aspen (Colo.) project (1978).

**Greene, Charles S.** (1868–1957) and **Henry M.** (1870–1954). American architects known for their California houses in the Western stick style characterized by the use of wooden elements.

**Hardouin-Mansart, Jules** (1646–1708). French architect who was a disciple of his great-uncle, François Mansart. He is known for his Grand Trianon (1687) at Versailles and work on the church of Les Invalides (completed 1691) in Paris.

**Hawksmoor, Nicholas** (1661–1736). With John Vanbrugh he created the English baroque style. His six dramatic London churches, which include St. George-in-the-East and St. Anne, display bold stonework and original tower designs.

**Hoban, James** (1762?–1831). Irish-born American architect who designed the White House in Washington, D.C. (1793–1801). He also designed the new, enlarged White House (1815–29) after the first was destroyed by the British in 1814.

**Holabird, William** (1854–1923) and **Roche, Martin** (1855–1927). Partners whose commercial buildings exemplify the Chicago school and are landmarks in the development of the skyscraper. Among their most noted works are the Champlain (1894), the Cable building (1899), and the Mandel Brothers Annex (1900, 1905), all in Chicago. Their 333 North Michigan building marked the introduction of the Art Deco style to Chicago.

**Horta, Victor** (1861–1947). Belgian architect of the art nouveau style who in his houses, hotels, and stores built between 1893 and 1903 created a new curvilinear style that broke with 19th-century traditions.

**Hunt, Richard Morris** (1827–95). First American student at the École des Beaux-Arts in Paris. He began the beaux-arts movement in the United States.

**Isozaki, Arata** (born 1931). Prolific Japanese architect recognized for his innovative use of space. His major works include the Saga Branch of the Fukuoka Mutual Bank, Saga City (1973), and the Yano House, Kawasaki (1975).

**Jahn, Helmut** (born 1940). German-born postmodern rationalist. His attention to function is key in such works as Kemper Arena, Kansas City, Mo. (1974), and the Agricultural Engineering Building, University of Illinois, Champaign (1984).

**Jenney, William Le Baron** (1832–1907). American engineer and architect whose Home Insurance Building in Chicago (1884–85) was the first with an interior frame supporting an exterior shell. He trained Louis Sullivan, William Holabird, Martin Roche, and Daniel Burnham.

**Johnson, Philip** (born 1906). Coauthor of 'The International Style' (1932) and American leader in movement by that name. He served as director of the department of architecture at the Museum of Modern Art in New York City and designed the museum's sculpture garden (1953) and two additions (1950, 1964). His transparent Glass House in New Canaan, Conn. (1949) was based on projects by Ludwig Mies van der Rohe. He later championed postmodernism.

**Kahn, Louis** (1901–74). Estonian-born American architect known for his government buildings in Dhaka, Bangladesh, and the Kimbell Art Museum in Fort Worth, Tex. He is recognized as an influential modern designer and poetic writer on architecture.

**Latrobe, Benjamin** (1764–1820). English-born American neoclassic architect who contributed to the design of the United States Capitol and was one of the first champions of the Greek revival style in the United States.

**L'Enfant, Pierre-Charles** (1754–1825). French-born architect and engineer who planned the city of Washington, D.C. (1791–92). He fought in the American Revolution serving as captain of engineers. Commissioned by President George Washington to prepare plans for the federal capital, he was dismissed before his plans were carried out.

**Loos, Adolf** (1870–1933). Leader of Vienna's avant-garde in the 1920s whose best-known structure is Steiner House (1910). His influential essay "Ornament and Crime" argued for a modern style freed from nonessential ornamentation.

**Lutyens, Sir Edwin L.** (1869–1944). Revered as England's premier architect of the early 20th century, his design of country homes was influenced by the Renaissance style. He is known for his plan for the city of New Delhi, India, which included the Viceroy's house, staff residences, and stables (1912–30).

**McKim, Charles Follen** (1847–1909); **Mead, William Rutherford** (1846–1928); and **White, Stanford** (1853–1906). Largest and best-known American architectural firm of its time, which established neoclassicism as a prevailing style.

**Mackintosh, Charles Rennie** (1868–1928). Scottish art nouveau designer and architect whose School of Art, Glasgow (1898–99), was a pioneer work of modern architecture. As a craftsman he stressed that all details, including those of the furniture, are integral to a building's overall appearance. Hill House, Helensburgh (1902–06) is hailed as his best domestic project.

**Meier, Richard** (born 1934). American modernist influenced by Le Corbusier, he believed architecture should contrast with natural surroundings. He designed the Atheneum visitors' center, New Harmony, Ind. (1979) and the High Museum of Art, Atlanta, Ga. (1983); and was chosen in 1984 to construct the J. Paul Getty Center in Los Angeles, Calif.

**Mendelsohn, Erich** (1887–1953). German-born British-American architect known for pioneering work in steel and concrete as in his Einstein Tower, Potsdam (1921).

**Mills, Robert** (1781–1855). Leading American figure in the Greek revival who designed the United States Treasury building (1836) and Washington Monument (completed 1884), both in Washington, D.C.

**Nash, John** (1752–1835). British architect noted for grand visual effects as in Regent's Park, a London residential development with facades in an amalgam of classical styles.

**Neumann, Balthasar** (1687–1753). Bohemian architect of the late baroque in Austria and Germany known for his bishop's residence in Würzburg (1724–44). His small churches of the early 1740s are each centered on a large, low dome.

**Neutra, Richard** (1892–1970). Austrian-born American architect known for luxurious private homes that blend with natural settings in the Los Angeles, Calif., area. His use of large areas of glass stressed a relationship between interior and exterior space.

**Niemeyer, Oscar** (born 1907). Brazilian architect influenced by Le Corbusier. He is known for his designs for government buildings in Brazil's capital, Brasília (1962–67). Many of his works are marked by dramatic geometric images.

**Pei, I.M.** (born 1917). Chinese-American architect known for design simplicity in large-scale corporate and governmental projects. His many works include the National Center for Atmospheric Research, Boulder, Colo. (1967); the east wing of the National Gallery of Art, Washington, D.C. (1978); and Mount Sinai Medical Center Complex, New York, N.Y. (1988).

**Renwick, James** (1818–95). American Gothic revival architect best known for St. Patrick's Cathedral in New York City (1859–79).

**Rogers, Richard** (born 1933). Italian-born English "Hi-Tech" architect known for his design of Centre Beaubourg, Paris (1977) and Lloyd's of London Headquarters (1979).

**Root, John Wellborn** (1850–91). American architect who, with Daniel Burnham, practiced the Chicago school of commercial architecture. Their Chicago office buildings include the Montauk Building (1882), the Rookery (1884–86), and the Monadnock Building (1889–91).

**Rossi, Aldo** (born 1931). Italian rationalist architect, magazine editor, and architectural historian. He collaborated with others on such projects as the Peugot Building, Buenos Aires, Argentina (1961); Sandicci City Hall, Italy (1968); and the plans for the city of Florence, Italy (1981).

**Rudolph, Paul** (1918–97). Prominent American architect, and student of Walter Gropius, whose buildings are notable for creative and unpredictable designs that appeal strongly to the senses. From 1958 to 1965 he was chairman of the department of architecture, Yale University, where his building—School of Art and Architecture (1958–63)—is characterized by a complex massing of interlocking forms and a variety of surface textures.

**Scarpa, Carlo** (1906–78). Italian architect heavily influenced by the Venetian tradition and Frank Lloyd Wright. Designed or restored many museum interiors including the Correr Museum, Venice (1953, 1960) and the Castelvecchio Museum, Verona (1964).

**Sinan** (1489?–1588). Possibly born in Greece, great Turkish architect under Süleyman "the Magnificent." He was responsible for more than 300 mosques, palaces, and public-works projects. He was the founder and most influential representative of classical Ottoman architecture.

**Skidmore, Louis** (1897–1962); **Owings, Nathaniel** (1903–84); and **Merrill, John O.** (1896–1975). Formed architectural firm that after World War II became the leading American designer of skyscrapers and other large commercial buildings. Among the firm's many corporate projects are PepsiCo Inc., World Headquarters, New York, N.Y. (1960); Sears Tower, Chicago, Ill. (1974); and Citicorp Plaza, Los Angeles, Calif. (1985).

**Soane, John** (1753–1837). English professor of architecture at the Royal Academy who designed the Bank of England (1799–1800). He is noted as one of the most original exponents of neoclassicism.

**Soleri, Paolo** (born 1919). Italian-born American architect who proposed the idea of *arcologies* (from the words *ar*chitecture and ec*ology*), urban settlements of three-dimensional complexes. In 1970 he began work on the community of Arcosanti near Cordes Junction, Ariz., which would provide housing and other needs to 5,000 people.

**Soufflot, Jacques-Germain** (1713–80). Major figure in the early development of neoclassicism in France. His most important building is the Panthéon in Paris (1757–90) He introduced to France the horseshoe-shaped theater in Lyons (1753–56), one of the first modern theaters in the country.

**Stirling, James** (born 1926). Scottish-born English architect noted for his concern with the humanization of an environment. Some examples are the Engineering Department, University of Leicester (1959–63) and Runcorn New Town Housing, Cheshire (1967–76).

**Stone, Edward Durell** (1902–78). American architect whose work ranged from the international style to eclecticism. Examples include the United States Embassy, New Delhi, India (1954) and the John F. Kennedy Center for the Performing Arts, Washington, D.C. (1971).

**Tange, Kenzo** (born 1913). Japanese architect and urban planner who combined traditional Japanese structural ideas with Western methods, especially those of Le Corbusier. Examples of this influence include his Hiroshima Peace Center (1949–55) and Kurashiki City Hall, Okayama (1958–60). His National Gymnasium for the Tokyo Olympics (1961–64) is considered the peak of 20th-century Japanese architecture.

**Upjohn, Richard** (1802–78). English-born American leader in the Gothic revival as exemplified in Trinity Church in New York City (1839–46). An advocate of professionalism for architects, he was founder and first president of the American Institute of Architects.

**Vanbrugh, John** (1664–1726). Prominent figure in the English baroque movement who collaborated with Nicholas Hawksmoor on Castle Howard (begun 1700) and Blenheim Palace (begun 1705). He was knighted in 1714.

**Van de Velde, Henri** (1863–1957). Belgian architect and designer who was one of the leaders of the art nouveau movement. In numerous writings he set his goal at raising the status of architects to that of fine artists. He designed the Saxon School of Arts and Crafts, Weimar, Germany (1906) and the Werkbund Exhibition Theater, Cologne (1914).

**Venturi, Robert** (born 1925). American architect and author of 'Complexity and Contradiction in Architecture', considered one of the most important books on the subject. He is known for the Walker and Dunlop Office Building, Transportation Square, Washington, D.C. (1968) and Franklin Court, Philadelphia, Pa. (1976).

**Viollet-le-Duc, Eugène-Emmanuel** (1814–79). Architect and champion of the neo-Gothic movement in France. He was chosen to restore many medieval buildings, including the cathedral of Notre Dame in Paris (restoration begun 1845) and the cathedral of Clermont-Ferrand (1864).

**Wagner, Otto** (1841–1918). Founder of modern Austrian architecture. As a professor at the Austrian Academy of Fine Arts, he argued that architecture had not kept pace with social change. His most important works are iron structures for Vienna's urban railway system (1894–1901).

**Walter, Thomas Ustick** (1804–87). American architect associated with the Greek revival style in Washington, D.C., and Philadelphia, Pa. Designed the United States Capitol's House and Senate wings and cast-iron dome (1851–65).

## *Architectural Terms*

**acropolis.** Elevated group of buildings that serves as a civic symbol.

**aisle.** Space alongside a church nave, usually separated by columns. Also a passageway between rows of seats in a public building.

**ambulatory.** Passageway around the apse of a church; also a covered walk of a cloister.

**apse.** Semicircular or semipolygonal space at one end of a church, occupied by the altar.

**arcade.** Arches in series with columns, roof, and other structural parts closed or open on one side.

**arch.** Curved or pointed construction that spans an opening.

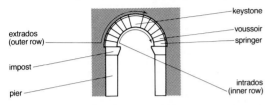

**atrium.** Forecourt of an early Christian basilica with colonnades on all four sides and often a fountain in the center.

**baptistery.** Part of a church or separate building used for baptism.

**basilica.** Oblong building consisting of a nave with clerestory, lower side aisles, and apse, often with a narthex and atrium, and sometimes with a transept.

**bay.** Area of a building between adjacent piers or columns. Also a protruding structure with windows.

**buttress.** Masonry structure projecting beyond a wall or free of a wall that receives lateral pressure from construction within a building such as vaulting.

**cella.** Sanctuary that contains statue of a god in a classical temple.

**chancel.** Sanctuary and choir of a church.

**chevet.** Apse, ambulatory, and radiating chapels of a church.

**choir.** Space between the sanctuary and the nave of a church.

**clerestory.** Upper section of nave wall pierced with windows; located above the triforium and above the roof of the aisle.

**cloister.** Covered walkway around a courtyard that usually connects a church with other buildings of a monastery.

**coffering.** Ceiling with deep recesses, often ornamented.

**colonnade.** Series of columns set at regular intervals that usually supports the base of a roof.

**corbel.** Masonry projection or series of stepped projections that support overhanging construction.

**cornice.** Projection at the top of a wall finished by a blocking course.

**crossing.** Place where the transepts cross the nave and chancel of a church.

**crypt.** Lower story of a church, below or partly below ground level, that often contains chapels and tombs.

**curtain wall.** Nonbearing exterior wall that is not supported by the skeleton frame.

**dome.** Hemispherical roof structure that spans an area.

**dormer.** Small windowed structure that projects from a sloped roof.

**façade.** Exterior side of a building that can be seen at one view, especially the front.

**finial.** Ornament at the top of a spire or steeple.

**fluting.** Concave channels cut on the shafts of columns.

**fresco.** Decoration in color on plaster. True fresco is painted while the plaster is wet.

**gable.** Triangular end of a pitched roof building between the level of the eaves and the ridge of the roof.

**gable roof.** Roof consisting of two sloping sides like an inverted trough.

**gargoyle.** Waterspout that projects from a roof gutter, often carved grotesquely.

**groin.** Line of intersection of two (arched) vaults.

**half timber.** Building framed with heavy timbers and the spaces between filled with plaster or stucco.

**hip roof.** Roof that rises with equal angles from all four sides.

**iconostasis.** In an Eastern rite church, screen of icons (flat pictorial representations) that separates the chancel from the laity.

**isometric drawing.** Three-dimensional projection with lines parallel to the edges drawn in true length.

**lintel.** Beam across the top of an opening such as a doorway.

**mansard roof.** Roof with four sloping sides, each slope broken into two pitches.

**mastaba.** Egyptian freestanding tomb of rectangular shape with inclined sides and a shaft leading to underground chambers.

**mosaic.** Design formed by small pieces of glass, stone, or tile, usually set in cement (*see* Mosaic).

**narthex.** Enclosed porch or vestibule at the entrance of a church.

**nave.** Central part of a church from the narthex to the choir.

**pagoda.** Multistoried tower, usually with projecting roofs at each story that curve upward, often topped with a stupa.

**pediment.** Low triangular, ornamental area over doors, windows, or the fronts of buildings.

**pendentive.** Curved wall surface that forms a transition between a dome or drum and its supporting masonry.

**peristyle.** Colonnade around the outside of a building, an enclosed room, or a court.

**pilaster.** Rectangular, columnlike projection from a pier or wall.

**pyramid.** Funerary structure with a square base and four sloping triangular sides that meet at the apex (*see* Pyramids).

**post-and-lintel construction.** System of construction with vertical columns (posts) and horizontal beams (lintels) that carry the load over an opening.

**quoin.** Stone or brick used to reinforce corners of masonry walls.

**rib.** Curved structural member that supports a curved shape.

**rose window.** Circular window with tracery radiating from its center.

**rotunda.** Circular room under a dome.

**sanctuary.** Area around the altar of a church; sacred shrine of a god.

**spandrel.** Irregular triangular space between the outside curve of an arch and the rectangular frame enclosing it. Also space between the upper frame of a window and the lower frame of a window above it.

**stupa.** Buddhist hemispherical mound that enshrines a relic or commemorates a sacred site.

**tracery.** Decorative openwork of stone or wood, as in the upper part of a Gothic window.

**transept.** Armlike extensions of a church between the nave and the choir, forming the shape of a cross.

**triforium.** Shallow, usually open passages above the arches of the nave and choir and below the clerestory.

**vault.** Arched masonry structure that forms a ceiling or roof.

barrel vault · cross, or groined, vault

**volute.** Spiral scroll-shaped ornament that forms the chief feature of the Ionic capital.

**ziggurat.** Mesopotamian temple tower of pyramidal shape, built in successive stages with outside staircases and topped by a shrine.

Photo Media, Ltd.

*The Seagram Building in New York City was completed in 1958 by Ludwig Mies van der Rohe and Philip Johnson. Its bronzed skeleton and amber-colored windows make it a distinctive landmark on the Manhattan skyline.*

for his lifelong interest in urban planning—giving a new form to the city. As early as 1922 he proposed a contemporary city for 3 million inhabitants with low residential blocks separated by large areas of park. This idea has since been adapted many times for housing projects. (*See also* Le Corbusier.)

**Mies van der Rohe.** Ludwig Mies van der Rohe designed mainly steel-and-glass structures in simple geometric forms, developing a vocabulary of steel detailing that was almost the equivalent of the ancient orders. As early as 1919 Mies was making projects for steel-and-glass towers, though he did not have the chance to build any until his Lake Shore Drive apartments of 1948–51 in Chicago. His early buildings, all done in Europe, were mostly houses and were highly abstract compositions of vertical and horizontal planes that shaped, but did not completely enclose, spaces.

When Mies came to the United States in 1938, he started a new and influential architectural career for himself. His buildings for the Illinois Institute of Technology in Chicago, where he taught architecture from 1938 to 1958, and his high-rise office and apartment buildings set the pace for new commercial and institutional architecture in the United States. American business embraced his sleek, modern-looking style to the extent that most of the tall office buildings constructed since the 1950s in the United States were based on Mies's use of the steel-and-glass curtain wall. His Seagram Building of 1958 in New York City—which he designed in collaboration with distinguished United States architect Philip Johnson—was recognized as a masterpiece of American corporate architecture. (*See also* Mies van der Rohe, Ludwig.)

**Postmodernism.** In the 1960s some modification of the prevailing attitudes toward design of the previous 50 years began to take place. There was a revival of interest in traditional forms and historical styles. The United States architect Louis Kahn reacted to the abstraction in the works of Le Corbusier and Mies by using regular geometric compositions and materials such as brick, stone, and wood that made reference to the spirit of some of the architecture from the past, especially Egyptian, Greek, and Roman. Other architects rejected International Style modernism in more literal ways, using past forms like Classical columns or drawing on the architecture of modern popular culture, the highway, and the suburb for inspiration. This artistic experimentation has run parallel to the explosion of construction for purely practical purposes. (*See also* Kahn, Louis I.) (For table of world structures, *see* Building Construction in Fact-Index.)

**BIBLIOGRAPHY FOR ARCHITECTURE**

**Adams, Henry.** Mont-Saint-Michel and Chartres (Penguin, 1986).
**Brown, David.** The Random House Book of How Things Were Built (Random Books Young Reader, 1992).
**Curl, J.S.** Classical Architecture (Van Nostrand Rheinhold, 1993).
**Hiller, C.E.** Caves to Cathedrals: Architecture of the World's Great Religions (Little, 1974).
**Huntington, L.P.** Americans at Home (Coward, 1981).
**Huxtable, A.L.** Inventing Reality: Architectural Themes and Variations (New Press, 1993).
**Kostof, Spiro.** America by Design (Oxford Univ. Press, 1987).
**Lampugnani, V.M.** Encyclopedia of 20th-Century Architecture, rev. ed. (Abrams, 1986).
**Lang, Jon.** Urban Design: The American Experience (Van Nostrand Rheinhold, 1994).
**McAlester, Virginia, and McAlester, Lee.** A Field Guide to American Houses (Knopf, 1984).
**Macaulay, David.** City: A Story of Roman Planning and Construction (Houghton, 1983).
**MacGregor, Anne, and MacGregor, Scott.** Skyscrapers (Lothrop, 1981).
**Perrella, Stephen.** Aspects of Modern Architecture (St. Martin's, 1991).
**Pierson, W.H., Jr.** American Buildings and Their Architects (Oxford Univ. Press, 1986).
**Platt, Richard.** Incredible Cross Sections (Knopf Books Young Reader, 1992).
**Pressman, Andy.** Architecture 101 (Wiley, 1993).
**Roth, L.M.** Understanding Architecture (HarperCollins, 1993).
**Stelle, James, ed.** Architecture for a Changing World (St. Martin's, 1993).
**Trachtenberg, Marvin, and Hyman, Isabelle.** Architecture (Prentice, 1986).
**Wright, F.L.** American Architecture (Horizon, 1955).
**Yarwood, Doreen.** The Architecture of Europe (Trafalgar, 1993).
**Yarwood, Doreen.** A Chronology of Western Architecture (Facts on File, 1987).

(*See also* bibliographies for **Housing; Shelter.**)

Joe Rychetnik—Photo Researchers

**An Arctic polar bear has roamed miles offshore on pack ice of the Chukchi Sea, an arm of the Arctic Ocean.**

**ARCTIC OCEAN.** By far the smallest of the world's oceans, with an area of 5,440,000 square miles (14,090,000 square kilometers), the Arctic Ocean covers the northern polar region of the Earth. The North Pole is located approximately at its center.

Russia, Canada, Greenland, Iceland, Norway, and the United States (Alaska) border on the Arctic Ocean. There are islands around the ocean's outer edges but none in its central region.

In the center of the Arctic Ocean is an immense area of floating pack ice several hundred miles in diameter. The pack ice moves slowly in a clockwise direction, making a complete revolution around the top of the world every ten years. It consists of countless gigantic islands of ice that crash and grind together as they move. There are many small areas of open water. People and animals regularly travel across the pack ice, but they do so in constant peril from the ice itself and from the region's brutally cold climate.

The pack ice restricts the amount of sunlight that can penetrate to the waters beneath it. This reduces the occurrence of photosynthesis, which is fundamental to plant growth. As a result, few of the microscopic plants called phytoplankton grow beneath the ice cap. Since phytoplankton, directly or indirectly, provide the food for all oceanic life, the number of fishes is also limited. Overall, the Arctic Ocean has less than 10 percent as much marine life as the other oceans. It is a kind of frigid, watery desert.

At the ocean's borders, however, where its waters mix with those of the Atlantic and Pacific, animals thrive. Fishes and birds are numerous. Mammals common to the area include seals, walruses, and the most famous Arctic animal of all—the polar bear.

The major circulation of water into and out of the Arctic Ocean takes place through a single deep channel between Greenland and the Norwegian islands of Svalbord. Only 2 percent of this water leaves the ocean as ice—pieces broken loose from the pack—but this tiny amount creates great problems. The channel is one major source of icebergs in the North Atlantic. Although their movements are constantly monitored by satellites and radar, these huge floating masses of ice have destroyed innumerable ships.

Despite the inroads of modern civilization, many of the native peoples of the Arctic regions still follow their traditional ways of life as reindeer herders (primarily in Eurasia) or hunters. Some Inuit, or Eskimo, live near the edge of the pack ice and spend most of their lives hunting and fishing (*see* Inuit).

Early European explorers tried to find a Northwest Passage—a sea route through the Arctic Ocean from Europe to the Orient. Modern explorers have conducted climatic and other scientific research (*see* Polar Exploration).

The discovery of oil, gas, and other minerals in the lands bordering the Arctic Ocean and beneath its floor greatly increased economic activity there after the 1960s. Russia, which has the longest coast on the Arctic Ocean, estimates that 70 percent of its untapped oil resources are located under its northern continental shelf.

Canada, which also has a long Arctic coast, can give only rough estimates of the oil, gas, coal, and other mineral resources in its northernmost territories, but they are thought to be substantial. After finding huge oil reserves on the Arctic coast of Alaska, the United States constructed a pipeline across that state from Prudhoe Bay in the north to the ice-free port of Valdez in the south. The Arctic Ocean floor may someday be mined as well. There are indications that valuable metals may be present.

The increased economic activity in the Arctic Ocean area has caused considerable environmental concern. Habitats and living patterns of wildlife and sea life have been disturbed. The potential dangers from oil spills and other forms of pollution are immense. The Arctic ecosystem is fragile, with comparatively few species; therefore any disruption has far-reaching effects. Because of the harsh Arctic cold, many areas that border the pack ice are open for shipping and construction of drilling platforms for only a few weeks each year. When this "summer" season is over, the ocean freezes and becomes impassable. This raises the danger that an oil leak might continue for months before it could be stopped and the spill cleaned up. Also, in the frigid Arctic climate, the rate at which crude petroleum and other pollutants decompose into environmentally harmless components is extremely slow. The effects of such pollution on wildlife and sea life could be catastrophic.

So far the Arctic Ocean has survived increased human activity. Scientists are seeking ways to exploit its abundant resources without damaging the fragile environment. (*See also* Arctic Regions.)

James Balog—Black Star

*When it is summer in the Northern Hemisphere, the Arctic is the land of the midnight sun. Daylight lasts 24 hours during the summer, but the sun does not rise at all during the long, frigid winters.*

# ARCTIC REGIONS

A vital zone between North America's and Russia's northernmost frontiers consists of the Arctic regions. Once only explorers, traders, and Inuit, or Eskimo, hunters were interested in the vast, icy area at the "top" of the world. Today, because of its strategic location and its value to scientists, the Arctic is the scene of much activity.

The Arctic is studded with air bases, constant reminders that the shortest air routes between the United States and Russia are over the area. Only a narrow channel separates Little Diomede Island, of the United States, from Big Diomede Island (Ostrov Ratmanova), which is Russian territory. The long-range missile and the nuclear-powered submarine have made distances between the two countries seem even shorter. Year-round scientific research stations are maintained to study weather, climate, and mineral resources of the Arctic.

The Arctic is sometimes defined as the area that lies within the Arctic Circle. The Arctic Circle is a parallel of latitude (66° 30′ N. latitude), 1,650 miles (2,660 kilometers) from the North Pole, the northern end of the Earth's axis. Actually, the Arctic Circle does not enclose all the Arctic regions. The true Arctic is the area in which the mean temperature for the warmest month is less than 50° F. The coldest region, the "polar segment," is where the mean temperature of the warmest month is below freezing.

The subarctic region is the area that has a mean temperature above 50° F (10° C) for more than three but less than four months a year. The boundary of the Arctic is sometimes said to be the line beyond which no trees grow. This is based on the theory that tree life cannot exist unless there is at least one month a year with a temperature of 50° F.

## Arctic Ocean and Arctic Land

The greater part of the 8,000,000 square miles (21,-000,000 square kilometers) within the Arctic Circle is occupied by the Arctic Ocean (5,440,200 square miles, or 14,090,050 square kilometers). Around the pole, the ocean is about 13,800 feet deep (4,200 meters). Islands dot the southern two thirds of the ocean. Then comes a rim of land provided by the northern continents.

The most important islands north of America are Baffin, Victoria, and Ellesmere, belonging to Canada. Svalbard, a Norwegian group, and Franz Josef Land and Novaya Zemlya, belonging to Russia, are the largest islands north of Europe.

North of Asia, near Siberia, lie Severnaya Zemlya and the New Siberian Islands. Other islands in the Arctic regions are Wrangel, Prince Patrick, Devon, and Banks islands, and the Parry Islands. Alaska and northern Canada form the Arctic lands of North America. Farther east is the world's largest island, Greenland. It is part of the Danish kingdom. At Dundas, Greenland, the United States has a large air base.

In Northern Europe, the Laplands of Norway, Sweden, Finland, and western Russia jut into the Arctic. Eastward stretches the Russian territory of Siberia. (*See also* Alaska; Canada; Siberia.)

## The Greatest Cold Is Not at the Pole

The most extreme winter cold and summer heat in the Arctic are not at the pole because the Arctic Ocean prevents extremes. The water absorbs heat during the summer and gives it out in the winter.

Greater extremes occur near the Arctic Circle because the land there is less effective than water in storing heat. Alaska has had a winter temperature

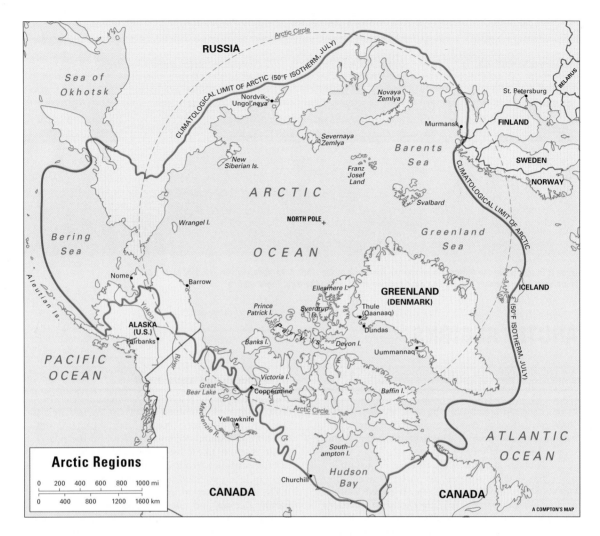

Arctic Regions

A COMPTON'S MAP

of −80° F (−62° C). In summer the temperature has reached 100° F (38° C). The coldest weather in the Arctic regions occurs near Verkhoyansk in Siberia. The January temperature there can reach −90° F (−68° C). The Arctic is warmer than Antarctica (see Antarctica).

Within the Arctic Circle winter cold is bearable because there is little wind (see Wind). Blizzards and gales occur only when the air is flowing strongly outward across the Arctic Circle or where a break in the land level disturbs the circulation. The winter air is very dry. Most of the moisture in the region is frozen. Snowfall totals less than in Chicago or New York City.

### The Cause of Arctic Climate

The Arctic climate is determined by the amount of heat and light received from the sun. The slant of the Earth in relation to the sun prevents the sun's rays from reaching the Arctic regions for part of each year. The North Pole has no direct sunlight for six months. In summer the Arctic has long hours of sunlight. The sun's rays strike at a great slant, however, and do not give as much heat as they do farther south (see Earth).

More than half the Arctic Ocean is covered with a layer of ice all the time. Much of it stays in place as a jumbled mass called pack ice.

### Animal and Plant Life

Many animals live in the Arctic wilderness. Although not as numerous as in other oceans, countless microscopic plants called diatoms live in the polar sea. They furnish food for shrimps and other crustaceans. These, in turn, are eaten by fishes. Both the crustaceans and the fishes are eaten by seals, walruses, and the few whales that still live in the sea.

Much of the land in the Arctic region is covered with a treeless grassy carpet called tundra. In summer flowers and grasses spring up in some places.

Caribou, reindeer, and musk oxen eat the tundra. In winter they paw away the snow to get moss and lichens. Polar bears, wolves, and foxes prey on these larger animals and the sea animals. Smaller meat eaters live mainly on sea life.

During the long cold season fox, ermine, muskrat, beaver, marten, mink, and other animals grow thick,

Photos, (left) Glenn Knudsen—Tony Stone Worldwide; (right) Kurt Scholz—SUPERSTOCK

*Many human societies flourish in the Arctic. A Lapp in Kautokeino, Norway (left), uses a reindeer as a pack animal. These animals also provide milk. Thousands of miles east, the Russian town of Provideniya (right) on the Bering Sea has a tannery and facilities to produce dairy products.*

rich furs. In the lengthy days of summer many species of migrating land birds, such as the redpoll, snowbird, pipit, and rock ptarmigan, fatten on the swarming insects. Seabirds eat the abundant fish. The snowy owl and the raven often winter here.

### People of the Arctic

The Arctic plains have only a sparse and scattered native population. These people manage to live comfortably, however, by making use of everything the bleak surroundings afford.

The Inuit who dwell in Arctic America and Greenland depend upon hunting and fishing (*see* Inuit). They have no fruits or vegetables. They make clothing and tents of animal skins. Snug igloos are built of snow and ice for temporary shelter on winter hunting trips. For more permanent homes the Inuit use sod, stones, and driftwood.

The Lapps of Northern Europe rove about the tundra with their grazing herds of reindeer. These animals supply milk, meat, and skins for clothing and tents (*see* Lapland). Reindeer-herding tribes also live in Siberia. Other Mongoloid people of the Asian Arctic hunt and fish in summer and trap fur-bearing animals in winter.

### Growing Importance of the Region

Many attempts to explore the Arctic ended in tragedy. Growing appreciation of the region's importance, however, has stimulated experiments in Arctic living. The Soviets began setting up weather stations on Arctic islands in the 1930s. In 1944 scientists from the United States and Canada founded the Arctic Institute of North America for polar research.

World War II brought weather stations to Arctic America and Greenland. In 1958 the submarine *Nautilus*, sailing beneath the icecap, made the first

undersea crossing of the North Pole (*see* Polar Exploration).

### A Radar Picket Fence

Along the extreme north rim of North America stretches the Distant Early Warning (DEW) line, built in the 1950s. This series of radar outposts would signal the alarm should enemy planes attack via the polar route. Stations of the Ballistic Missile Early Warning System (BMEWS) were added in the early 1960s in Greenland and Alaska (*see* Greenland). South of the DEW line is the Mid-Canada line. Roughly along the United States–Canada border is the Pinetree System. All these warning systems are connected with the combined North American Air Defense Command (NORAD) headquarters at Ent Air Force Base in Colorado.

Along the western flank of the United States Arctic defenses is a web of air, land, and sea bases. The bases are kept constantly in touch by a communications system called White Alice. The system speaks across hundreds of miles in Alaska with signals that are deflected from the troposphere, a layer of air up to 7 miles (11 kilometers) above the Earth's surface.

### The Permafrost

In much of the Arctic, earth, ice, and rock are frozen solid permanently. The solid mass is called permafrost. It is covered with a layer of ice and snow which melts in summer. In winter the Earth's crust in the Arctic is a solid frozen mass as deep as 1,000 feet (300 meters) in some places. In summer, however, the surface thaws to a depth of 2 to 6 feet (0.6 to 2 meters). The surface then becomes swampy. The water cannot drain off or be absorbed because the earth beneath is frozen.

Great care must be taken that buildings erected in the Arctic do not thaw the permafrost layer and sink.

Arktika, *the flagship of the Soviet Atomic Icebreakers' Fleet, plows through the ice fields of the Kara Sea on its maiden voyage in June 1975. The* Arktika *was equipped with the world's most powerful power installation, which made it possible for the vessel to break through the heavy ice of high latitudes.*
TASS from Sovfoto

The top cover of earth was removed in building the runways at the United States Thule Air Base near Dundas (formerly called Thule, which is now the name of a town to the north). A rock pad was then laid down in layers to form a base over the permafrost. This was covered with further layers of compacted materials and then paved with asphalt. Buildings at the air base were made to sink slowly.

**Scientific Arctic Investigation**

During the International Geophysical Year (IGY), from July 1957 to December 1959, scientists studied weather and ice in the Arctic. Teams stationed on floes, or ice islands, found that their chief problem was summer thawing. Giant cracks appeared in one island, and the campsite broke away from the main part of the floe. Men and equipment had to be airlifted to another island.

Four such drifting ice stations (two Soviet, two American) were set up in the Arctic during the IGY. Driven by wind and current, they traveled as far as 4,000 miles (6,400 kilometers). Soundings made daily from one of the American stations revealed the existence of an unsuspected submerged mountain ridge.

Another floe team took the first photographs of the ocean bottom in the central polar region. This team collected samples of sediment and measured ocean depths, the Earth's magnetic field, temperatures, and ice movements. Studies made on McCall Glacier during the IGY indicate that glaciers swell rather than shrink as the weather becomes warmer.

The United States Navy's nuclear-powered submarines *Sargo* and *Sea Dragon* reached the North Pole in 1960. An ice island 12 feet (4 meters) high was found about 150 miles (240 kilometers) north of Point Barrow, Alaska, in May 1961. It probably was part of a glacier that broke off and drifted away. As the island melted, glacial debris was exposed. This floe became the United States Navy's Arctic Research Laboratory Ice Station II (ARLIS II). Weather and oceanographic studies were carried on there.

The United States Army Corps of Engineers has studied the properties of ice and problems of construc-

tion and living in the Arctic in two subsurface camps on the Greenland ice cap. At Camp Century, 138 miles (222 kilometers) from Thule Air Base, engineers built tunnels and insulated buildings beneath the snow for their activities. The tunnels are deep trenches cut with a rotary snowplow. As the plow moved downward, the cuts were widened. The narrow top was roofed over. At Camp Tuto, occupied in January 1962, tunnels were constructed through solid ice.

In addition to an extensive scientific research program, Canada is encouraging a widespread search for significant mineral deposits in its Far North. It holds 28 percent of the Earth's Arctic land surface. Only Russia has more—40 percent. Mineral riches have been under development in the Canadian subarctic. In the late 1960s huge reserves of natural gas were found on Melville and other Canadian Arctic islands, and in 1970 oil was discovered near the mouth of the Mackenzie River. Oil and gas were found in the shallow waters of the Beaufort Sea. Extensive reserves of oil were discovered at Prudhoe Bay on Alaska's North Slope in 1968. Construction of an 800-mile (1,290-kilometer) crude-oil pipeline from Prudhoe Bay to the ice-free port of Valdez was completed in 1977.

The Arctic lands of Russia are known to contain rich reserves of minerals, including cobalt, nickel, coal, and iron. The gold and diamond mines of eastern Siberia place Russia high among world producers of these minerals. Natural gas and oil have been found in several places. The first nuclear power station in the Arctic was opened by the Soviet Union on the Kola Peninsula in 1974. In 1977 the Soviet nuclear icebreaker *Arktika* became the first ship to break its way through to the North Pole.

The discovery phase of Arctic exploration is over; there is no longer any possibility of finding new lands. Photo surveys have provided accurate maps, and improved aircraft and base facilities are making the once formidable region increasingly accessible. The emphasis now is on studying the area's geology and ecology. The bed of the Arctic Ocean has also been the subject of increasingly intensive studies. (*See also* Polar Exploration.)

Donald B. MacMillan

© Lisl Steiner—Photo Researchers

# ARGENTINA

*Gauchos in traditional dress round up cattle on the Argentine pampas. The gaucho is a popular figure in the country's arts and literature.*

Within Latin America the nation of Argentina is second in area only to Brazil and fourth in population only to Brazil, Mexico, and Colombia. This large land covers more than 1 million square miles (2.7 million square kilometers), in the southern part of South America east of the Andes Mountains. It extends from the Tropic of Capricorn south to the tip of the continent—within about 700 miles (1,100 kilometers) of Antarctica. Argentina claims a portion of that continent as well as the Falkland Islands (Islas Malvinas) and several other islands of the South Atlantic Ocean. The country is bounded by Chile on the west and south, Bolivia and Paraguay on the north, and Brazil, Uruguay, and the Atlantic Ocean on the east.

The official language of Argentina is Spanish, and more than 90 percent of the population is Roman Catholic. The country was settled from the 16th through the 18th centuries by colonists from Spain and other parts of South America. Emmigrants from many European countries, including Italy and Germany, settled in the central plains and south during the 19th century. Agriculture, based on grain and livestock, became the dominant factor in the Argentine economy and accounts for most of its exports. Industry in general has not kept pace with the country's population growth. A United States-style constitution was adopted in 1853, but military government and political instability have been the norm.

## The Land

The Argentine landscape slopes downward from the Andes Mountains in the west to the Atlantic coast in the east. The western border with Chile follows the crest of the Andes, where heights of peaks range from more than 20,000 feet (6,000 meters) in the north to less than 5,000 feet (1,500 meters) in Tierra del Fuego at the southern tip of the continent. One of these peaks, Aconcagua (22,831 feet; 6,959 meters) is South America's highest mountain. The highest part of the Andean area lies in Argentina's Northwest region, which tapers from a width of nearly 350 miles (560 kilometers) in the north to about 200 miles (320 kilometers) in the south. In the northern Andes is a dry altiplano, or high plain, surrounded by mountains. A string of artesian oases lies along the eastern foothills.

Eastward from the northern Andes lies an arid plateau called the Gran Chaco. It is a region of scrub woodland mixed with grassy savannas. Farther to the east, between the Paraná and Uruguay rivers, is the region called Mesopotamia. It has extensive subtropical pine forests and fertile plains on which are grown rice, oranges, and flax. Gran Chaco and Mesopotamia together form the Northeast region of the Argentine Republic.

The next region to the south is the Pampa, a low, flat plain interrupted only by low hills or sierras. Over millions of years the Pampa has been covered by a fertile wind-borne soil known as loess, and by waterborne alluvium eroded from the Andes. The pampas, or plains, are the homeland of the famous Argentine gaucho, or cowboy.

South of the Colorado River is Patagonia, the largest region of Argentina. It extends from the Pampa to Tierra del Fuego and was named in 1520 by the Portuguese explorer Ferdinand Magellan, while sailing for Spain, on his trip around the world. The landscape is dominated by the Andes in the west and plateaus that stretch eastward to the Atlantic, forming cliffs along much of the shoreline. The climate is dry and windy.

Sizable rivers flow across Argentina. The Northeast is drained by the Paraguay and Paraná rivers, which originate in the Central Plateau of Brazil. The Upper Paraná is the site of the famous Iguazú (Iguaçu) Falls,

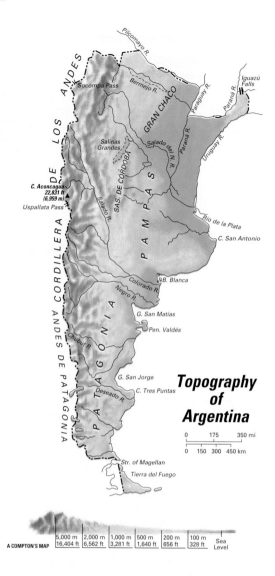

**Topography
of
Argentina**

| 0 | 175 | 350 mi |
| 0 | 150 300 | 450 km |

| 5,000 m | 2,000 m | 1,000 m | 500 m | 200 m | 100 m | Sea |
| 16,404 ft | 6,562 ft | 3,281 ft | 1,640 ft | 656 ft | 328 ft | Level |

A COMPTON'S MAP

Ocean, seasonal temperature extremes are moderated. Only in the Northwest do continental extremes similar to those in North America occasionally occur.

Argentina's very great north–south distance covering 33 degrees of latitude also influences the climate of the country. In the Northwest, for example, only the Andean peaks that rise above 20,000 feet (6,000 meters) high are covered by snow, whereas at the southern tip of the nation the snow line is below 1,500 feet (500 meters). Glaciers can be found in mountain lake valleys, such as that of Lago Argentino, as far to the north as 50° S. latitude.

Moist mid-latitude winds rise from the Pacific Ocean to bring rain and snow to the higher slopes of the Andes. Winter snow cover has made the area near San Carlos de Bariloche a world famous ski resort known as the Argentine Switzerland. As the prevailing westerly winds descend the eastern slopes of the Andes, they become warmer and increase their capacity to absorb moisture. Consequently, few clouds form and precipitation is minimal throughout the western plateau of Argentina. Locally these drying winds are called the zondas.

In addition to the presence of the zondas a cold offshore ocean current in the Atlantic contributes to the dryness of the climate. Moist air over the Atlantic cools over the frigid waters of the current and loses its moisture as fog or rain before it can move inland.

The two conditions described combine to keep most of Patagonia dry. There, precipitation of less than 10 inches (250 millimeters) falls per year. More than two thirds of Argentina does not receive soil moisture sufficient for nonirrigated agriculture. As is typical of such regions occasional short-lived heavy rains produce flash floods. At other times dust storms cover extensive areas. In central north Argentina the precipitation is not sufficient to sustain the flow of rivers, especially during the warm summers when evaporation is highest. Many end in salt lakes, like the Mar Chiquita, or in large saltwater swamps. Storms moving in the westerly wind belt across Patagonia occasionally become diverted to the northeast and may bring frost and even light snow to Buenos Aires. Such storms are usually accompanied by strong south winds and are called pamperos. They occur several times a century and cause crop damage in the Gran Chaco and Misiones.

In the extreme south of Patagonia precipitation once again increases because the Andes are lower. There the climate is cool and moist throughout the year and much of the land is forested. In Ushuaia, Argentina's southernmost city, winter snows are sometimes heavy, and, because of the high latitude of nearly 55° S., the sun in June and July barely rises above the mountainous horizon even at noon.

Another notable weather condition is caused by an Atlantic storm called the *sudestada* that passes over northeastern Argentina. This storm produces heavy rains that cause the sudden flooding of rivers.

The Pampa can be divided into two climatic zones, the coastal humid pampa, or *pampa húmeda*, and the

where the river plunges over the plateau edge. Also in the Northeast is the Uruguay River, which forms Argentina's border with both Uruguay and Brazil. These three north-south flowing rivers and their Andean tributaries, such as the Pilcomayo, the Bermejo, and the Salado, empty into the so-called Río de la Plata, an estuary between Argentina and Uruguay. The most important rivers of central and southern Argentina are the Colorado, Negro, Chubut, Deseado, Chico, and Santa Cruz. They all originate high in the Andes.

### Climate, Soil, and Vegetation

The climate of Argentina is marked by seasonal change characteristic of the temperate middle latitudes. In Argentina, because it is in the Southern Hemisphere, the seasons are reversed from those in North America, winter occurring during June, July, and August and summer extending from January through March. Because most of Argentina is close to the Atlantic dry pampa, or *pampa seca*. The *pampa húmeda* receives abundant precipitation and is Argentina's major grain and livestock region. In the *pampa seca*, precipitation is less abundant and crops grown there must be irrigated.

The soils of Argentina's two main agricultural zones, the Pampa and the Northeast, differ greatly. In the Pampa sufficient moisture and grass cover have combined with sedimentary and windblown material to form brown-black phaeozems, which have considerable organic matter at the surface, and deep, fertile prairie soil sometimes called chernozem. In certain areas alfalfa roots penetrate 15 feet (4.5 meters) into this soft, easily crumbled soil.

In northeastern Argentina deep red soils that are derived from basaltic (volcanic) rocks of the Paraná plateau extend over most of Misiones Province. These red soils are unlike many similar-looking ones that are found elsewhere in the tropics and the subtropics in that they are only slightly acidic, possess some plant nutrients, and are well-drained. Consequently, such crops as citrus fruits, sugarcane, and maté can be grown well in them, especially when fertilizers are used.

Relatively intensive settlement in the most habitable parts of Argentina has decimated the formerly abundant animal life. The two most notable remaining forms are members of the wildcat family in Misiones Province, and the rhea, the American three-toed ostrichlike bird of the pampas. Some ranches feature rides for children on the backs of rheas.

### The People

The first people to live in what is now Argentina were American Indians. The most important groups belonged to the Guaraní tribes in the Northeast. They were farming Indians among whom the Roman Catholic Society of Jesus (Jesuits) during the colonial era established Utopia-like missions (Misiones Province). A group of nomadic Indians lived on the pampas. When they obtained horses from Spanish invaders, they became highly successful military opponents of the Europeans and were not finally conquered until the 20th century. Scattered tribes inhabited the Andean zone from north to south. Most of the native peoples died in warfare and from diseases following the Spanish invasion, which began in 1516. Today only 3 percent of the people of Argentina are Indians and mestizos (mixed). The rest of the people are of European descent.

Modern Argentina is inhabited by many people of European descent and by a few American Indians. Although various estimates have been made for the Indian population before the Spanish conquest, a conservative number might be 300,000 for the present national area. After the various phases of discovery,

The scenery around shimmering Lake Moreno in the Andean foothills of Río Negro province is similar to that of the Swiss Alps. Nearby is Nahuel Huapí National Park and the town of San Carlos de Bariloche, a world famous ski resort.

Chip & Rosa Maria Peterson

*Iguazú Falls on the Argentina–Brazil border is one of South America's scenic wonders. The horseshoe-shaped falls are four times the width of Niagara Falls in North America.*

exploration, and settlement, the Indian population had been drastically cut. About 40,000 live in Argentina today, primarily in remote Andean valleys and in the Gran Chaco. However, their physical features are sometimes apparent in many gauchos—the Pampa cowboys descended from Spanish fathers and Indian mothers and who are, therefore, mestizos.

It should be noted that African slaves were never important in Argentina because neither mining nor plantation agriculture played a significant role in the colonial economy. Consequently, as European settlers arrived, a white population soon became dominant. By the time Argentina achieved its independence in 1824, the vast majority of the populace had been born in South America.

After independence was gained, political chaos prevented unification of the country. However, the idea of planned pioneer settlement for the purpose of inhabiting the country's vast empty spaces was carried forward from time to time. In 1856, for example, Swiss and German settlers were invited to found new colonies in the provinces of Buenos Aires and Santa Fe. Other small European groups went to Misiones Territory far to the northeast on the Brazilian border. Then a great wave of foreign immigration began in the early 1880s and lasted for a decade. At that time Italians along with some Spaniards arrived to open the pampas. This marked the beginning of change in the Argentine economy, as European demand for wool, tallow, mutton, and hides increased rapidly until the end of the century. Domestic sheep flocks replaced wild cattle on the plains, and cattle breeding from new European stock began.

Another immigration wave occurred from 1904 to 1913. Prosperity brought about the construction of a railroad network, which began to stretch across the pampas, and the blossoming of the city of Buenos Aires with its international port. Everything was paid for by the productivity of agriculture on the rich soils of the immediate hinterland. By the time World War I began 30 percent of the Argentine population was foreign-born.

Another period of immigration between the two world wars marked the onset of the modern development of Misiones Territory by many groups from Europe, especially Germans. A more recent immigration between 1947 and 1955 brought tens of thousands of Italians and Spaniards to the country. Thereafter, immigration from Europe ceased because of the improved economic conditions there. Moreover, the Argentine economy began to falter seriously at the same time.

Though immigration from Europe stopped in recent years, Argentina at this time began to attract migrants from other South American countries. This resulted in such oddities as the largest population of urban Paraguayans not being in Asunción, Paraguay, but in Buenos Aires. In northwestern Argentina Bolivians cross the border in sizable and growing numbers, and a small but steady migration from Chile has influenced the population in Patagonia since the early 1900s.

In addition to immigration there is also a seasonal movement of foreign labor into various parts of Argentina. This is due largely to the lack of mechanization for harvesting crops in much of the nation. For instance, thousands of Paraguayans cross the border to work during the maté harvests in Misiones between December and March. Others come from Bolivia and Chile to help with grape picking in Cuyo and Mendoza from April to July and following that for the sugarcane, cotton, and tobacco harvests in the northern sections of Argentina.

In the early 1900s the Argentine population structure reflected a growing rural element with the majority of the people less than 20 years of age. In more recent years, especially in the cities, the 30- to 50-year-olds have emerged as the dominant group. These data reflect the composition of the capital city of Buenos Aires, in which more than 12 million people live—more than one third of the country's population. By the early 1990s there were 17 other cities in the country of more than 100,000, reflecting a trend that shows the nonurban population of Argentina steadily declining. (*See also* Buenos Aires.)

*Ushuaia, the capital and port of Argentina's Tierra del Fuego national territory, is the southernmost city in the world.*

### The Economy

Argentina has traditionally been one of the more prosperous Latin American countries. Unlike many of its neighbors, the country has developed a strong manufacturing industry and has become less dependent on agriculture. Today the country is largely self-sufficient in consumer goods. However, the Argentine economy in the late 20th century, like that of many countries, suffered from severe inflation. This condition was complicated by an unstable government and continuing domestic and international political problems. By the mid-1990s, however, economic reforms implemented by the government of President Carlos Saúl Menem succeeded in bringing inflation under 5 percent.

**Agriculture and livestock.** Argentina is one of the world's chief exporters of food and other agricultural products. Wheat, the chief crop, occupies about one seventh of the nation's cropland and is raised mainly in the Pampa. Corn (maize) covers less land, but the crop yields are high. Flax, grown for linseed oil, and rye, barley, and oats, used mainly for livestock feed, are also important. Sunflower seeds are a major source of the nation's cooking oil.

Cotton is raised in the Chaco for use in the nation's textile factories. Near Tucumán, in the Northwest, stretch Argentina's principal sugarcane fields. Vineyards and fruit orchards thrive farther south around Mendoza and San Juan.

The country has vast pasturelands. The first cattle, horses, and sheep were introduced by the early Spanish settlers. The cattle were stringy animals used chiefly for hides and jerked beef. After the 1880s fields were fenced and high-grade breeds were introduced. The construction of railways by foreign, mainly English, investors made it possible to ship stock and crops to markets and ports. Refrigerating plants and refrigerator ships permitted the meat to be exported.

Today Argentina is a world leader in the raising of livestock. Animal products such as fresh and canned meat, wool, and hides rank high among the country's exports.

**Mining and lumbering.** Argentina does not have adequate mineral resources. The leading minerals produced are petroleum, lead, and zinc. From the Northwest come tungsten, beryllium, and manganese. The country has little iron ore or other ores necessary to modern industry. It is poorly supplied with coal, especially high-grade coking coal for steel manufacture. Natural gas is piped to more than a million homes and factories, but more is needed.

Lumbering is limited mostly to the quebracho forests of the Gran Chaco and the pine and broadleaf forests of northern Mesopotamia and, especially, Misiones Province. One variety of quebracho is cut for telephone poles, railway ties, and fence posts. Another is a source of tannin, used in making leather.

**Manufacturing.** Argentina is one of the leading manufacturing countries of Latin America. For a number of years it has been following a trend of breaking away from dependence on food processing and consumer goods and placing greater emphasis on heavy industry. A large integrated iron-and-steel plant, for example, has been constructed at San Nicolás. The petrochemical, plastics, synthetic rubber and fiber, and motor vehicle industries are all developing.

Food processing, however, is the leading industry. Meat-packing, flour milling, sugar refining, and vegetable and fruit canning are principal activities. The processing of linseed oil and the production of wine, beer, and soft drinks are also extensive. Other manufactures include textiles, metal goods (excluding machinery), chemicals, drugs, vehicles and machinery, wood and lumber, clay, glass, and stone products. The publishing business is also significant.

In recent decades the Argentine government has played a strong role in the development of industry. It has assisted with the production of aircraft at Córdoba, steel at San Nicolás, and petroleum-based industry at Comodoro Rivadavia.

**Trade.** More than 90 percent of Argentina's exports are made up of crops, especially wheat, and livestock products. Countries that usually buy extensively from Argentina include the United States, Russia and other Eastern European countries, The Netherlands, Brazil, Germany, China, and Italy.

Chip & Rosa María Peterson

*A dazzling nighttime light display rims the central obelisk of the Plaza de la República in Buenos Aires. More than one third of the Argentine people live in the Buenos Aires metropolitan area, which is one of the largest urban centers in the Western Hemisphere.*

The largest quantity of imports comes from the United States. Germany, the United Kingdom, Venezuela, and Brazil are other major suppliers. The chief imports are iron and steel products, fuels, chemicals, nonferrous metal products, lumber, and paper.

**Transportation and communication.** Argentina's airlines, railways, and bus and ship lines constitute the most extensive transportation system in Latin America. The rail network is the most complete on the continent, fanning out from Buenos Aires in all directions. Rail lines are government owned. Roads are extensive and link all parts of the nation with the capital. Telephone and telegraph networks are mainly government owned.

### Architecture and the Arts

In colonial times Argentina's culture was mainly adopted from Spain. Churches and public buildings in such cities as Córdoba and Salta reflect Spanish architectural styles. Development of a national culture based on Argentine life came about in the 19th century. Foremost among artists was Prilidiano Pueyrredón, who is noted for his paintings of the Pampa region and of gaucho life.

Melancholy songs sung to the accompaniment of a guitar formed the basis of Argentine folk music. This music figured prominently in the rise of Argentina's major contribution to popular music, the tango. In 19th-century literature the gaucho's decline is mourned in the popular gaucho poem 'Martín Fierro' by José Hernández. (*See also* Latin American Literature.)

French, Spanish, and Italian influences have been strong in art, music, and literature. Argentina has about 100 art museums, many with schools. Numerous painters and sculptors reside in the picturesque La Boca district on the waterfront of Buenos Aires. The large Italian population helps account for the strong support of grand opera. There are symphony orchestras in many of the country's cities. The Teatro Colón in Buenos Aires is one of the world's largest performing arts centers and attracts many famous artists during its regular June to August season. It is also the headquarters of the national ballet and national symphony.

### Education

Argentina has one of the highest literacy rates in South America. Public schools were built by government subsidies, especially under the leadership of President Domingo F. Sarmiento from 1868 to 1874. Primary education is compulsory and free, but further training is expensive. Vocational schools offer commercial, agricultural, and industrial instruction.

The first university in the country was established at Córdoba in 1613. Other national universities were founded in Buenos Aires (1821), La Plata (1884), San Miguel de Tucumán (1914), Santa Fe (1919), Mendoza (1939), Bahía Blanca (1956), Corrientes (1957), and Santa Rosa (1959).

### The Government

The constitution of Argentina was adopted in 1853 and has been amended several times. It established Argentina as a federal republic with separate executive, legislative, and judicial branches. The constitution calls for an executive branch to be headed by a president, who is elected directly by the people for a term of

*A vineyard thrives in an area south of Mendoza, the largest city of the Cuyo region in west-central Argentina. With the use of extensive irrigation the region has developed a flourishing fruit-growing agriculture. The crops are exported to eastern markets.*

Chip and Rosa Maria Peterson

four years and who may serve only two terms. The president and the vice-president must both be Roman Catholics and at least 30 years old. The president also serves as commander in chief of the armed forces.

According to the constitution the legislature—the Argentine National Congress—is to consist of two houses, the Senate and the Chamber of Deputies. The Senate is to be composed of three members from each of Argentina's 22 provinces, the Federal District, and the National Territory of Tierra del Fuego. Provincial senators must be 30 years of age and are elected by their local legislatures for six-year terms. Members of the Chamber of Deputies must be at least 25 years old and are elected directly by the people for four-year terms. The number of deputies is based on population. Voting is compulsory for all citizens between the ages of 18 and 70 with exceptions based on such conditions as health and distance from a polling place. Some people have also been deprived of the right to vote for legal reasons.

The judiciary consists of a Supreme Court and a series of lower courts. The five justices of the Supreme Court are appointed for life by the president with the consent of the Senate. Federal court jurisdiction includes those cases that involve the constitution and laws and treaties of the nation.

In 1976 the elected civilian government was deposed by the armed forces, an event that has often occurred in Argentine history. A military junta then took control of Argentina under a revised constitution that called for the president to be a retired army officer in addition to the other requirements. All activity by political parties was suspended by the regime established by the junta. With the return to civilian rule in 1983, the constitution of 1853 was restored.

In international affairs Argentina is a member of the United Nations, the World Bank, and the General Agreement on Tariff and Trade. To participate in regional matters it belongs to the Organization of American States.

## History

The level of Indian civilization before the arrival of the Europeans in the early 16th century did not approach that of the Aztecs, Mayas, and Incas farther north. Some of the Indians in what is now Argentina were nomadic hunters, while others grew crops.

*Shepherds tend their sheep flocks on a ranch in bleak, windswept Patagonia, the major sheep-raising region of Argentina. The continual growth of sheep production in Patagonia has helped Argentina to become one of the major wool-producing countries of the world.*

© Carl Frank—Photo Researchers

*Sides of beef hang in a long row in a refrigerated warehouse in Buenos Aires. Much of Argentina's beef is exported.*

Initial attempts by the Spaniards, the first Europeans to arrive, in 1516, in Argentina, to found settlements on the south bank of the Río de la Plata as well as on the Paraná River failed because of Indian attacks. The original colony of Buenos Aires, which was founded in 1536 by Pedro de Mendoza, was abandoned four years later, and a new settlement was established in safer territory far upstream at Asunción. The Spaniards first succeeded at Asunción because the more sedentary Guaraní Indians living there were friendlier than the nomadic types farther south. Finally, working downstream from Asunción, the Spaniards founded Santa Fe in 1573. They resettled Buenos Aires in 1580, and this time it became a permanent settlement.

The Spaniards hoped to establish an inland trade route leading from Buenos Aires to the silver mines located at Potosí, Bolivia. Transport of silver and supplies over this route never succeeded because of flooding during the wet season and low water in the Pilcomayo River region of the Gran Chaco during the dry season. As a result of their interest in the silver trade and also because of hostile Indians to the south the Spaniards did not settle the fertile pampas until the 19th century.

Before the Spaniards tried to open the northwest trade route to Bolivia, other conquistadores had crossed the Andes in Chile and Peru and founded a line of cities stretching from north to south along the east side of the mountains. Their purpose was to supply the Bolivian mining region with food and mules for transport and to secure the region for trade. The latter was important to Buenos Aires, which

received supplies from Spain via Panama, the Pacific Ocean, and Chile rather than directly across the Atlantic. The whole La Plata region was a subdivision of the viceroyalty of Peru and did not carry on direct trade with Spain until after 1776, when it was made a separate viceroyalty.

Because of this enforced isolation the inhabitants of what is now Argentina had to develop their own production. For example, escaped horses that roamed wild on the pampas were periodically hunted for their hides and tallow and were also used in the transport of cargo and for riding. There quickly arose a gaucho tradition much like the cowboy tradition once found in the western United States. Indians who captured wild horses became formidable enemies who were not conquered easily. They were the basic reason that forts had to be built near Buenos Aires and that horses were obtained from hunting expeditions rather than raised by breeding ranches, or estancias. These horse ranches were not even developed until after the Indian threat had ended.

As local agriculture and industry grew in the La Plata region, surplus products such as hides, vicuña (a small llama-like animal) wool, and silver were used to trade for smuggled European goods. The long Pacific trade route with Spain was time-consuming and expensive, and so Spanish settlers bargained with the Portuguese who sold merchandise in Colonia, a town they had built on the left bank of the Río de la Plata opposite Buenos Aires. However, after the creation of the Río de la Plata viceroyalty in 1776 Buenos Aires traded directly with Spain. Hides and meat preserved by salting were shipped to Spain and became the most important trade items. The interior Andean towns declined in importance after the center of trade became focused on the Atlantic coast.

In 1806 British troops occupied Buenos Aires. Deserted by the Spanish viceroy, the people (*porteños*) ousted the British by themselves. After Napoleon I conquered Spain, colonial resistance to Spanish rule spread in Latin America. The *porteños* set up a revolutionary government on May 25, 1810. The formal independence of the new United Provinces of the Río de la Plata was declared on July 9, 1816. Several years of fighting followed before the Spanish royalists were finally defeated. The hero of the war was Gen. José de San Martín (*see* San Martín). Rival parties sought control of the new government. The resulting chaos permitted Juan Manuel de Rosas to seize power in 1829. He maintained a cruel and repressive dictatorship until it was overthrown in 1852. In 1853 Argentina became a federal republic.

During the next several decades the nation's economy expanded. As Indian tribes were defeated on the pampas, tracts of their land were given away by the government. In 1880 Gen. Julio Roca, hero of the Indian wars, became president. Other presidents of that era were Bartolomé Mitre (1862–68) and Domingo Faustino Sarmiento (1868–74), who fostered educational reforms (*see* Sarmiento). Roque Sáenz Peña (1910–14) established the secret ballot and allowed

© Frank Nowikowski

*Calle Florida (Florida Street), a pedestrianized street in Buenos Aires is a major shopping venue.*

adult males to vote. Hipólito Irigoyen (1916–22 and 1928–30) instituted advanced labor laws.

Argentina remained neutral during World War I. The postwar economic depression and growing corruption in government led in 1930 to a military coup, after which Gen. José Félix Uriburu was installed as president. A gradual return to democratic government in the 1930s was countered by a strong dictatorial trend. Argentina remained neutral in World War II until 1945, when it finally declared war on Germany.

Colonel Juan Perón emerged after the war as Argentina's new strongman. Promising a better living for the urban workers, Perón was elected president in 1946. He repressed demands for democratic government, but, aided by his popular actress-wife, Eva, was reelected by an overwhelming majority in 1951. He was determined to make Argentina industrially self-sufficient. Supported by constitutional reforms adopted in 1949, he nationalized railways, utilities, and other foreign-owned properties. Perón's downfall came when students, bankers, industrialists, and other groups turned against him. In 1952 the death of his wife, who had her own political following, also weakened his support. In September 1955 the armed forces rebelled, and Perón fled the country. After Perón's ouster, the country suffered from high unemployment, high inflation, and a series of military dictatorships.

Political unrest brought Perón back to leadership for a short time. He died in 1974, and he was succeeded by his third wife, María Estela (Isabel) Martínez de Perón, the first woman head of state in South America. In 1976 she was forced by the military to resign because she was unable to curb the extreme inflation rate. The military took over, and Gen. Jorge Rafaél Videla assumed the presidency. During the so-called dirty war that followed, thousands of leftists and other political opponents were killed or imprisoned or simply disappeared. The Argentine government, maintaining that it was fighting a civil war, was subject to much criticism at home and abroad for civil rights violations. (*See also* Perón.)

In 1982 a military conflict took place between Argentina and Great Britain over control of the Falkland Islands, known in Argentina as the Islas Malvinas. Although the islands lie about 300 miles (480 kilometers) off the east coast of Argentina, they have been controlled by Britain since 1833. Argentina also claimed the Falklands, and in 1982 Argentine troops invaded East Falkland. A British naval force counterattacked soon after the Argentine occupation, and the British quickly regained control over the islands. (*See also* Falkland Islands.)

The defeat caused Lieut. Gen. Leopoldo Galtieri to resign as president of Argentina; his successor, Maj. Gen. Reynaldo Bignone, promised a return to civilian rule. In October 1983 a lawyer, Raúl Alfonsín of the centrist Radical Civic Union, was elected president. His victory ended the military regime and the domination the Peronist party had held since the 1940s. In 1987 and 1988 there were uprisings by military officers who opposed Alfonsín's government. In 1989 the country faced its worst energy crisis in 40 years and continued to be plagued by severe inflation. In May 1989 Carlos Saúl Menem of the Peronist party was elected president. Alfonsín resigned at the end of June, and Menem was inaugurated on July 8, five months ahead of schedule, so he could tackle the huge economic problems of the country. Menem reversed five decades of state control of the economy by planning a free-market economy, with lower tariffs based on wage-price pacts between labor, business, and government, and by declaring that all major state-owned industries would be privatized by 1993. He also sought to quell the military's discontent by pardoning those involved in the dirty war of the 1970s, a move for which he was strongly criticized. Menem was reelected to a second term in May 1995.

By the mid-1990s, widespread poverty gripped a large portion of the nation's 33 million inhabitants. During the years of Menem's presidency, hundreds of thousands of workers lost their jobs during the privatization of nationalized industries. From mid-1996 until mid-1997, the unemployment rate across Argentina exceeded 17 percent. In 1997 citizens unhappy with the government's continuing policies of economic austerity staged mass demonstrations and riots in major cities and towns across the country. The mass outpouring of anger threatened to bring down Menem's government. (*See also* South America.)

Robert C. Eidt

**FURTHER RESOURCES FOR ARGENTINA**

**Crawley, Eduardo.** A House Divided: Argentina 1880–1980 (St. Martin, 1984).

**Hintz, Martin.** Argentina (Children's, 1985).

**Lye, Keith.** Take a Trip to Argentina (Watts, 1986).

**Waisman, C.H.** Reversal of Development in Argentina (Princeton Univ. Press, 1987).

# Argentina Fact Summary

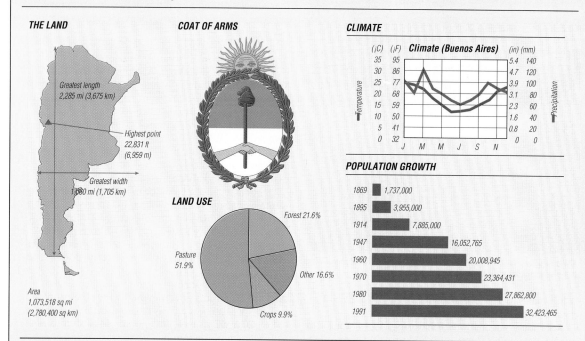

**THE LAND**

Greatest length
2,285 mi (3,675 km)

Highest point
22,831 ft
(6,959 m)

Greatest width
1,060 mi (1,705 km)

Area
1,073,518 sq mi
(2,780,400 sq km)

**COAT OF ARMS**

**CLIMATE**

Climate (Buenos Aires)

**LAND USE**

Forest 21.6%

Pasture
51.9%

Other 16.6%

Crops 9.9%

**POPULATION GROWTH**

| 1869 | 1,737,000 |
| 1895 | 3,955,000 |
| 1914 | 7,885,000 |
| 1947 | 16,052,765 |
| 1960 | 20,008,945 |
| 1970 | 23,364,431 |
| 1980 | 27,862,800 |
| 1991 | 32,423,465 |

**Official Name.** Argentine Republic.
**Capital.** Buenos Aires.
**Argentina.** From Latin *Argentum,* meaning "silver."
**Coat of Arms.** Adopted 1813. Cap is symbol of liberty; hands clasping each other symbolize brotherhood and unity.
**Flag.** Three horizontal stripes: blue, white, and blue (*see* Flags of the World).
**Anthem.** 'Oíd, mortales, el grito sagrado Libertad!' (Hear mortals, the sacred cry of Liberty!)

## NATURAL FEATURES

**Mountain Range.** Andes.
**Highest Peaks.** Aconcagua, 22,831 feet (6,959 meters); Bonete, 22,546 feet (6,872 meters); Mercedario, 22,211 feet (6,770 meters).
**Largest Lake.** Mar Chiquita.
**Major Rivers.** Bermejo, Carcarañá, Paraguay, Paraná, Pilcomayo, Río de la Plata, Salado, Uruguay.
**Natural Regions.** Pampa: vast fertile plain covering about one quarter of the country. Northeast: including the warm, moist plains of the Chaco and an area between the Paraná and Uruguay rivers called Mesopotamia. Northwest: Andean highlands, including Cuyo and Pampean Sierras. Patagonia: semiarid plateau.
**Climate.** Mostly temperate; great variations because of latitudinal extension and varying altitudes. Extreme heat in Chaco region; mild climate in central Pampa; mild to cold in southern Patagonia. Seasons the reverse of those in Northern Hemisphere.

## PEOPLE

**Population** (1996 estimate). 34,995,000; 32.6 persons per square mile (12.6 persons per square kilometer); 86.9 percent urban, 13.1 percent rural (1991 estimate).
**Major Religion.** Roman Catholicism (official).
**Major Language.** Spanish (official).
**Literacy.** 96.2 percent.
**Major Cities** (1991 estimate).
Buenos Aires (city, 2,960,976; metropolitan area, 9,621,345). Capital of Argentina; chief port; industrial, commercial, railroad, and cultural center. Córdoba (1,179,067). Processing and commercial center; auto manufacturing; resort; railway and highway hub.
**Leading Universities.** National Universities at Bahía Blanca,

Córdoba, Corrientes, La Plata, Mendoza, Santa Fe, Santa Rosa, San Miguel de Tucumán; University of Buenos Aires.

## GOVERNMENT

**Form of Government.** Federal republic.
**Chief of State and Head of Government.** President.
**Legislature.** National Congress.
**Voting Qualifications.** Compulsory over 18 years of age except for clergymen, army personnel, and those deprived for legal reasons.
**Political Divisions.** 23 provinces: Buenos Aires, Catamarca, Chaco, Chubut, Córdoba, Corrientes, Entre Ríos, Formosa, Jujuy, La Pampa, La Rioja, Mendoza, Misiones, Neuquén, Río Negro, Salta, San Juan, San Luis, Santa Cruz, Santa Fe, Santiago del Estero, Tierra del Fuego, Tucumán. 1 federal district: Districto Federal.

## ECONOMY

**Chief Agricultural Products.** *Crops*—sugarcane, soybeans, corn (maize), sunflower seeds, grapes, potatoes, sorghum, tomatoes. *Livestock*—cattle, sheep.
**Chief Mined Products.** Siver, gold, coal, crude petroleum, petroleum products, natural gas.
**Chief Manufactured Products.** Cement, wheat flour, vegetable oil, sugar, paper, soda, wine, beer.
**Monetary Unit.** 1 peso = 100 centavos.

## PLACES OF INTEREST

**Aconcagua.** Peak in Andes Mountains; highest peak in the Western Hemisphere.
**Christ of the Andes.** Statue in Uspallata Pass commemorating boundary settlement between Chile and Argentina; dedicated in 1904.
**Iguazú (Iguaçu) National Park.** Includes Iguazú Falls, 269 feet (82 meters) high, more than 2 miles (3 kilometers) wide.
**Nahuel Huapí National Park.** In the Andes; lakes, glaciers, waterfalls, rapids, forests, resorts, skiing, and cable cars.
**Santiago del Estero.** Oldest city on Argentine soil; founded 1553; parks; colonial buildings; convent and Church of Santo Domingo dating from 1590; warm springs at nearby Río Hondo.
**Tierra del Fuego.** Isolated island group forming the southern tip of South America.

# Argentina

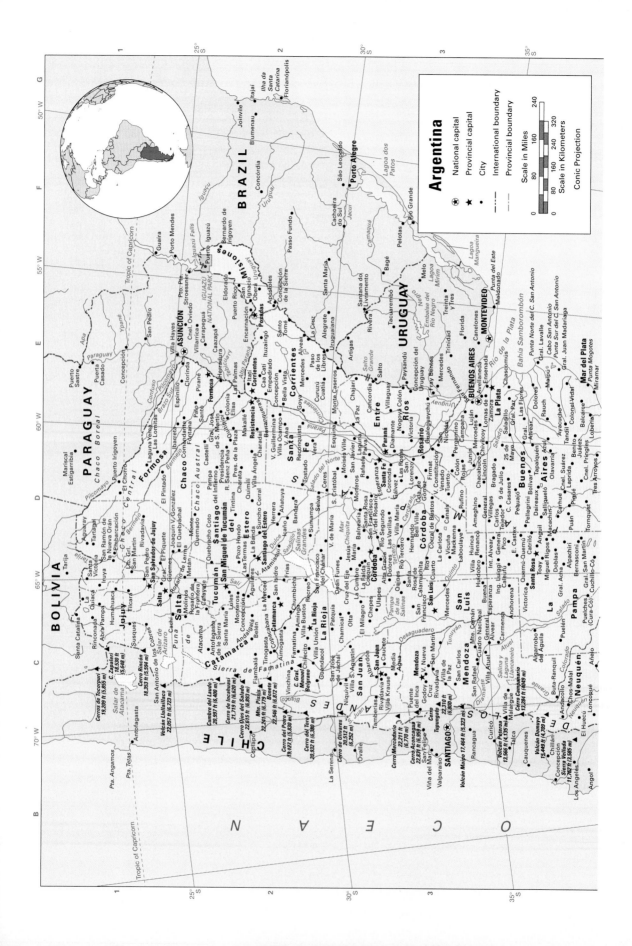

## Argentina

- ⊛ National capital
- ★ Provincial capital
- • City
- –·–·– International boundary
- –··–··– Provincial boundary

Scale in Miles
0   80   160   240

Scale in Kilometers
0   80  160  240  320

Conic Projection

**BOLIVIA**

**PARAGUAY**

**BRAZIL**

**CHILE**

**URUGUAY**

**ANDES**

**OCEAN**

**BUENOS AIRES**

**SANTIAGO**

**ASUNCIÓN**

**MONTEVIDEO**

Tropic of Capricorn

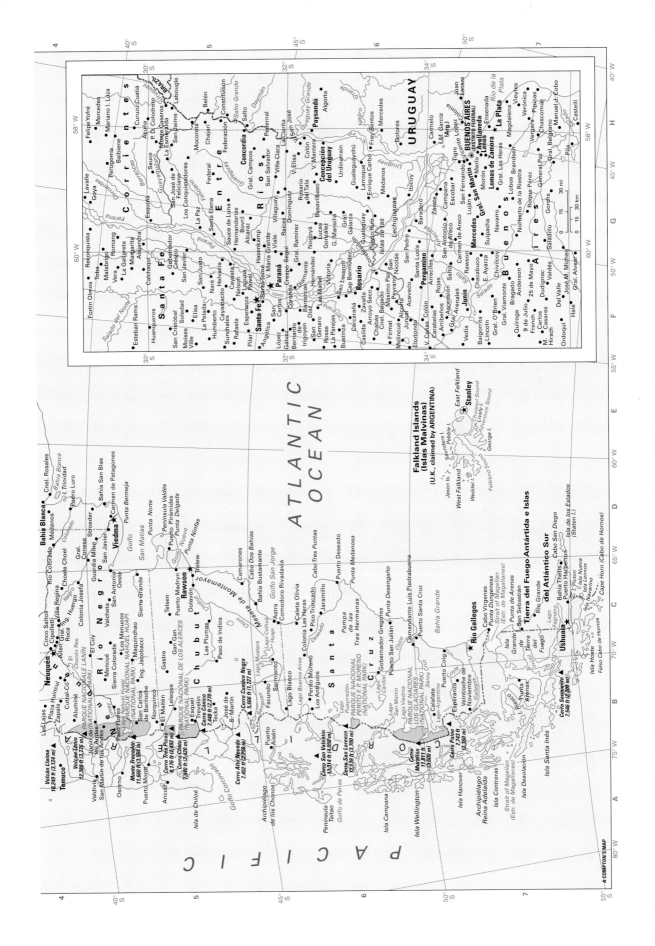

**ARGON** *see* Fact-Index.

**ARIOSTO, Ludovico** (1474–1533). One of the masterpieces of Italian Renaissance literature is the romantic-comic epic poem, 'Orlando furioso', written by Ludovico Ariosto. Its author was a man who would have gladly devoted his whole life to poetry and drama, but the needs of his family forced him into the role of soldier-statesman.

Born in Reggio Emilia, Italy, on Sept. 8, 1474, Ariosto grew up in the city of Ferrara. He studied law in the years 1489 to 1494, then devoted himself to literature for several years. The death of his father in 1500 left him the sole support of his nine younger brothers and sisters.

For most of the next 25 years Ariosto was in the service of the House of Este, the ruling family of Ferrara. Much of his time was spent on military or diplomatic missions. Only in 1525 was he able to return to Ferrara and settle down to a quiet life of writing. Ariosto died on July 6, 1533, at Ferrara.

'Orlando furioso' was written and reworked from 1503 to 1533. Based on the exploits of the legendary French hero Roland, it was first published in 1516. An expanded version came in 1532. The book was a sequel to the 'Orlando innamorato' of Matteo Boiardo, a less popular poetical work of the 15th century. Ariosto's book, on the other hand, enjoyed great popularity throughout Europe and influenced Renaissance literature.

*A woodcut of Ariosto was made from a drawing by Venetian artist Titian for the third edition of 'Orlando furioso'.*

Reproduced by courtesy of the British Library; photograph, J.R. Freeman & Co. Ltd.

*A bust of Aristophanes is a Roman copy of a Greek original.*
Cliche Musees Nationaux, Paris

**ARISTOPHANES** (448?–385? BC). Eleven of the plays of the great ancient Greek writer of comedy Aristophanes survive almost in their entirety. His plays have stood the test of time, having been frequently produced on the 20th-century stage and for radio.

Little is known of Aristophanes' life. Most of what has been pieced together is based on references in his own plays. Although it is known that he was born about 450 BC and was an Athenian citizen, his place of birth is uncertain. His first play was produced in Athens in about 427 BC.

Most of his work is about the social, literary, and philosophical life of Athens. Many of his themes, however, relate to the folly of war, especially the Peloponnesian War (431–404 BC) between the city-states of Athens and Sparta.

Aristophanes is thought to have written 40 plays in all, an average of one per year during his dramatic career. His success is attributed to his witty dialogue, comical though sometimes spiteful satire, brilliant imitations, clever and absurd scenes and situations, and charming songs. Criticism has centered on the loose construction of plots and the feeble development of characters.

The 11 works of Aristophanes that survive are: 'The Acharnians', 'The Knights', 'The Clouds', 'The Wasps', 'The Peace', 'The Birds', 'Lysistrata', 'The Thesmophoriazusae', 'The Frogs', 'Women in Parliament', and 'The Plutus'.

Shortly after producing 'The Plutus' in 388 BC, Aristophanes died. His son, Araros, staged two more of his plays in about 387 BC. (*See also* Drama.)

**ARISTOTLE** (384–322 BC). One of the greatest thinkers of all time was Aristotle, an ancient Greek philosopher. His work in the natural and social sciences greatly influenced virtually every area of modern thinking.

Aristotle was born in 384 BC in Stagira, on the northwest coast of the Aegean Sea. His father was a friend and the physician of the king of Macedonia, and the lad spent most of his boyhood at the court (*see* Macedonia). At 17, he went to Athens to study.

Alinari/Art Resource

*A Roman copy of a Greek statue of Aristotle stands in the Galleria Spada in Rome.*

He enrolled at the famous Academy directed by the philosopher Plato (*see* Plato).

Aristotle threw himself wholeheartedly into Plato's pursuit of truth and goodness. Plato was soon calling him the "mind of the school." Aristotle stayed at the Academy for 20 years, leaving only when his beloved master died in 347 BC. In later years he renounced some of Plato's theories and went far beyond him in breadth of knowledge.

Aristotle became a teacher in a school on the coast of Asia Minor. He spent two years studying marine biology on Lesbos. In 342 BC, Philip II invited Aristotle to return to the Macedonian court and teach his 13-year-old son Alexander. This was the boy who was to become conqueror of the world (*see* Alexander the Great). No one knows how much influence the philosopher had on the headstrong youth. After Alexander became king, at 20, he gave his teacher a large sum of money to set up a school in Athens.

### The Peripatetic School

In Athens Aristotle taught brilliantly at his school in the Lyceum. He collected the first great library and established a museum. In the mornings he strolled in the Lyceum gardens, discussing problems with his advanced students.

Because he walked about while teaching, Athenians called his school the Peripatetic (which means "to walk about") school. He led his pupils in research in every existing field of knowledge. They dissected animals and studied the habits of insects. The science of observation was new to the Greeks. Hampered by lack of instruments, they were not always correct in their conclusions.

One of Aristotle's most important contributions was defining and classifying the various branches of knowledge. He sorted them into physics, metaphysics, psychology, rhetoric, poetics, and logic, and thus laid the foundation of most of the sciences of today.

Anti-Macedonian feeling broke out in Athens in 323 BC. The Athenians accused Aristotle of impiety. He chose to flee, so that the Athenians might not "twice sin against philosophy" (by killing him as they had Socrates). He fled to Chalcis on the island of Euboea. There he died the next year.

### Aristotle's Works

After his death, Aristotle's writings were scattered or lost. In the early Middle Ages the only works of his known in Western Europe were parts of his writings on logic. They became the basis of one of the three subjects of the medieval trivium—logic, grammar, and rhetoric. Early in the 13th century other books reached the West. Some came from Constantinople; others were brought by the Arabs to Spain. Medieval scholars translated them into Latin.

The best known of Aristotle's writings that have been preserved are 'Organon' (treatises on logic); 'Rhetoric'; 'Poetics'; 'History of Animals'; 'Metaphysics'; 'De Anima' (on psychology); 'Nicomachean Ethics'; 'Politics'; and 'Constitution of Athens'.

**ARITHMETIC.** The foundation of all other branches of mathematics is arithmetic, the science of calculating with numbers. Without the ability to use numbers, it would not be possible to measure distance or tell time. People would not be able to figure out how many gallons per mile they get with an automobile; they would not be able to judge how tall they are or how high a building is; they could not buy something in a store and figure out if they got the correct change in return. All of the simple operations done with numbers would be virtually impossible without arithmetic: it is one of the most useful of all sciences. (*See also* Mathematics.)

Arithmetic is also one of the most fundamental sciences. It includes six basic operations for calculating with numbers: addition, subtraction, multiplication, division, involution (raising to powers), and evolution (finding roots).

These operations are used in all other branches of mathematics; without arithmetic, geometry, algebra, and calculus would not be possible. This article is not a course in arithmetic; rather, it focuses on the operations of arithmetic.

### The Beginnings of Arithmetic

**One-to-one Correspondence.** The term arithmetic comes from *arithmos,* the Greek word for number; but people began doing arithmetic long before the Greeks invented the word, even before anyone invented numbers. Historians believe that as early as 10,000 years ago, when prehistoric people started farming, they began to use arithmetic. They needed to know such things as how many sheep they owned, or how many rows of grain they planted, or how long it would be before harvest season arrived.

According to historians, prehistoric farmers devised an ingenious method for keeping track of things; they used a process of matching that mathematicians call one-to-one correspondence. A shepherd, for example, could keep track of his flock by dropping a pebble into a pile or by cutting a notch in a twig for every sheep that went to pasture in the morning. He could make sure that all his sheep returned home by matching them, one by one, to the pebbles in his pile or the notches on his twig.

This process of matching pebbles or notches with objects was the first step in the development of arithmetic. In fact, two of the words that people use to describe doing arithmetic, calculating and tallying, come from the Latin words for pebble (*calculus*) and notch (*taleus*). One-to-one correspondence is still the most basic arithmetic process, and it is so simple that even very young children use it. Before they learn to count, children can often put the right number of forks on the dinner table by laying out "one for mama, one for daddy, one for brother, one for sister, and one for me."

**Counting.** It is just a short step from one-to-one correspondence to counting, which is the process of matching objects with the names of numbers. Counting is the second simplest arithmetic process. The earliest mathematicians, thousands of years ago, probably learned to count in much the same way as little children do today—with their fingers. When a young child wants to show how many people are in his family, he might hold up a finger for each family member. The child begins to count by reciting a specific number name for each consecutive finger he holds up: "one, two, three, four."

It is not just coincidence that the Latin word for finger is *digitus* and that the ten numerals used in writing numbers (0, 1, 2, 3, 4, 5, 6, 7, 8, and 9) are often called digits. The names that people invented for numbers came directly from counting. Most modern languages, including English, have base ten number systems—that is, they have separate number names only for the first ten numbers, corresponding to the ten fingers used for counting. Beyond ten the cycle of number names begins all over again. For example, in English the word eleven comes from the Old English word *endleofan*, which means "one left over." Twelve is from the word *twelf*, meaning "two left over." Thirteen is clearly a version of "three and ten," and twenty comes from the Old English word *twentizh*, which means "two tens."

The numbers that are used for counting—one, two, three, four, and so on—make up a special class of numbers and are referred to as a class by several different terms. They are called counting numbers, whole numbers, or positive integers (from the Latin word *integer*, meaning "whole"). People use these

numbers to count whole things, such as one whole apple, two whole days, or three whole words. They are also referred to as natural numbers because they were the first kinds of numbers that occurred to people, and for a long time they were the only numbers that anyone used.

All the laws of arithmetic are based upon these counting, or whole, numbers. When people learn to add, subtract, multiply, divide, raise to powers, and extract roots, they are learning to calculate with whole numbers. Other kinds of numbers, such as fractions, negative integers, and zero were not introduced until much later, when it was realized that new kinds of numbers were needed to make all the operations of arithmetic possible.

### Arithmetic Operations

Arithmetic evolved as a tool to help people solve practical problems involving numbers or quantities. Because they had to solve several different kinds of number problems, people had to develop several different kinds of number operations. In arithmetic, the word operation refers to a method of combining two numbers to get a third. Addition, for example, can solve the problem of how many cows a farmer will have altogether if he buys ten more. Subtraction can solve the problem of how many potatoes a family will have left for tomorrow if it eats six for dinner today. By using multiplication, a woodsman can tell how many trees he will be able to cut in a day if he can cut two in an hour. And division can tell a mother how to split up a basket of 12 apples so that each of her six children gets an equal number.

When arithmetic is used to solve such practical problems, it is called practical, or applied, arithmetic. Early in the history of arithmetic, however, mathematicians discovered that they could deal with numbers that are unrelated to objects. Arithmetic can be used to solve abstract problems, such as $14 + 25 = 39$. By studying abstract problems, or pure arithmetic, mathematicians have isolated certain rules that govern the operations of arithmetic. The following sections will outline the different operations that make up arithmetic and will explain how they developed, how they are used, how they work, and what the laws are that govern them.

**Addition.** The process of combining two or more numbers to find the quantity represented by them altogether is called addition. Because addition is so closely related to counting, it was probably the first arithmetic operation that man discovered. Imagine a farmer, thousands of years ago, who found a stray herd of goats. If he combined the stray goats with his own animals, he would probably want to know how many goats he had in all.

One way he could find the number was by counting. If he started out with four goats and found five more, he could count each goat and learn that he had nine altogether. If the farmer counted four and five together often enough, he would soon learn that they always equal nine. He would no longer need to count. He could simply add four and five and know instantly what the answer would be.

At that point the farmer would have learned an addition fact. In school, children who are learning to add often memorize 81 of these addition facts:

$$1 + 1 = 2, 1 + 2 = 3, 1 + 3 = 4,$$
all the way to $9 + 9 = 18.$

But no one can memorize the answer to every possible addition problem; some are too complex. For example, it would not be easy to know automatically the total of 87 and 45, and it would take too long to count that number of objects. In ancient times there was no easy way to compute addition problems in writing. Even though people began writing numbers as early as 5,000 years ago, ancient systems of written numbers were too cumbersome to use for calculating. Adding 87 and 45 in Roman numerals would mean adding LXXXVII and XLV. Even in Roman times only special scribes could perform this feat. Roman and Greek numeration systems used letters to represent numbers. The letters were useful for recording but they were not useful for adding.

Many ancient peoples used a simple mechanical calculating device called an abacus (*see* Abacus). This ancestor of the modern adding machine was probably invented by the Babylonians, but it was used in almost all ancient societies from China in the East to Rome in the West.

On an abacus, each vertical column has room for many pebbles. The pebbles in the column farthest to the right represent units, or ones. Those in the next column stand for tens, then hundreds, and so on.

Adding 87 and 45 on an abacus is easy. First the pebbles presenting 87 are placed in the proper columns. (This number is called the augend, which means "supposed to be increased.") Then the pebbles representing 45 are added to them. (The number to be added is called the addend.) The combined total, or the sum, usually needs abbreviating, which is done by regrouping. Ten pebbles in any column can be replaced by one pebble in the column to its left. The replacement is called a carry.

In approximately AD 700, the Hindus of India invented a numeral system that made adding with written numbers as easy as adding on an abacus. The Arabs soon adopted this number system, and in 1202 the discovery reached Europe by way of an Italian mathematician, Leonardo Fibonacci. The new system, called Arabic numerals, simplified written addition and other calculations so dramatically that none better has been found and it is still in use.

Why are Arabic numerals so easy to use? The answer is that they are modeled on the abacus. Like the abacus, the Arabic numeral system is a decimal system; that is, it groups numbers by tens. The Hindus originally invented nine different symbols, corresponding to the nine pebbles used in each column of the abacus. These symbols changed shape over the years, but when printing was invented in the

15th century, the symbols became standardized: 1, 2, 3, 4, 5, 6, 7, 8, 9.

The Arabic number system can use these nine symbols to represent very large numbers because the system is positional: a numeral's position determines its value. In the Arabic system, as on an abacus, a nine in the ones column means nine, but a nine in the tens column means ninety, and in the hundreds column it means nine hundred.

Eventually the Hindus had to invent a new symbol to stand for an empty column on the abacus. The concept of zero and symbol 0 are taken for granted today; but until the Hindus invented it around AD 700, no number system had found an easy way to distinguish between 17, 107, and 1,070. The invention of zero revolutionized arithmetic.

When people add, they use Arabic numerals to represent the quantities they want to combine. By adding the numerals together in much the same way that pebbles are added together on the abacus, people get the same answer as if they had actually counted objects one by one.

In the course of adding with numbers, mathematicians discovered two fundamental laws about addition. First, the order in which numbers are added never affects the sum:

$$3 + 6 = 9 \text{ and } 6 + 3 = 9;$$
$$7 + 3 + 6 = 16 \text{ and } 6 + 7 + 3 = 16.$$

Mathematicians have called this property the commutative law of addition because the numbers can commute, or change places, but not change their total value. To show that the law is true for all addition problems, mathematicians illustrate it with letters rather than numbers:

$$a + b = b + a$$

The other fundamental property of addition that mathematicians discovered is this: when someone is adding more than two numbers, it makes no difference in what order the numbers are added. $1 + 2 + 3$ can be added together in several different orders and still give the same sum. To show which numbers should be combined first, mathematicians enclose them in parentheses:

$$\text{So, } 1 + (2 + 3) = 1 + 5 = 6$$
$$\text{and } (1 + 2) + 3 = 3 + 3 = 6.$$

Mathematicians refer to this property as the associative law of addition, indicating that the numbers can associate in different orders. They illustrate the law:

$$(a + b) + c = a + (b + c)$$

Those who have been doing arithmetic for a long time may wonder why these laws are worth noting. It seems obvious that $1 + 2 = 2 + 1$ and that $(1 + 2) + 3 = 1 + (2 + 3)$. But not every process of addition is commutative and associative. In chemistry, for instance, the order in which chemicals are added often makes a great deal of difference to the result. If sulfuric acid is added to water (water + sulfuric acid), the result will be dilute sulfuric acid. If water is added to the acid (sulfuric acid + water), the result can be an explosion. Only in arithmetic is addition always commutative and associative.

These laws are also worth considering because they help explain why the commonly used methods of addition work. For example, they help explain how numbers can be switched to simplify addition: 20 + 6 + 90 can be switched by the commutative law to 20 + 90 + 6. By the associative law, 20 + 90 can be combined first, so (20 + 90) + 6 = 110 + 6 = 116.

The laws also help explain how the column addition method works. When 41 + 15 + 72 are added together, the addition looks like this:

$$\begin{array}{r} 41 \\ 15 \\ 72 \\ \hline 128 \end{array}$$

As the numbers are added, what actually happens is that all the ones are grouped together and added first; then all the tens are grouped and added. In other words 41 + 15 + 72 is broken down to (40 + 1) + (10 + 5) + (70 + 2). The numbers are regrouped by the associative law:

$$(40 + 10 + 70) + (1 + 5 + 2) = 120 + 8 = 128$$

**Subtraction.** Although many people choose to think of subtraction as a separate and distinct arithmetic process, it is not. Subtraction is just the reverse of addition.

Primitive people probably needed subtraction to solve basic problems as much as they needed addition. If a prehistoric father picked an armful of 14 apples to feed his family of 10 and he dropped four apples, he would want to know how many he had left to feed his family. Or if he had collected only four apples, he might want to know how many more he would need to feed everyone at home.

Subtraction answers both kinds of questions. When a number of things are taken away, subtraction answers how many things are left. And if two quantities are being compared, subtraction answers how many more are needed to make them equal or what the difference is between the two.

Like addition, subtraction can be done by counting. The apple picker could hold up four fingers and then count the remaining fingers on his hand to see how many more he needed to reach ten. Once he learned that 10 − 4 always equals 6, he would have learned a subtraction fact. If he memorized 81 of these subtraction facts, he would be prepared with answers for most of his daily subtraction problems. But when people began to face more complicated subtraction problems, they required some subtraction procedure

that would be more practical than either counting or memorizing.

In ancient times, most complicated subtraction was probably done on an abacus. If an abacus has pebbles representing 7,438, it is easy to subtract 5,236 by taking away five pebbles from the thousands column, two from the hundreds, three from the tens and six from the ones.

Subtracting in the Arabic numeral system follows much the same process as abacus subtraction. The problem 7,214 minus 5,236 can be written

7000 and 200 and 10 and 4
minus 5000 and 200 and 30 and 6

Because six cannot be subtracted from four, or thirty from ten, numbers have to be borrowed; the top numbers have to be regrouped and rewritten. After the regrouping, the problem would look like this:

$$\begin{array}{l} 6000 \text{ and } 1100 \text{ and } 100 \text{ and } 14 \\ \underline{\text{minus } 5000 \text{ and } \quad 200 \text{ and } \quad 30 \text{ and } \quad 6} \\ 1000 \text{ and } \quad 900 \text{ and } \quad 70 \text{ and } \quad 8 \text{ or } 1{,}978. \end{array}$$

The process of borrowing and regrouping helped solve some sticky subtraction complications. Other complications were more difficult to solve. How, for example, can five be subtracted from four? Some ancient mathematicians declared it could not be done, since 4 − 5 would be less than nothing. It was not until the 16th century that the Italian mathematician Girolamo Cardano first began to use numbers less than zero. Cardano put to use what his predecessor Leonardo Fibonacci had recognized three centuries earlier: there can be an amount smaller than zero—for example, a debt. If someone had six dollars and paid it toward a nine-dollar debt, he would still owe three dollars. In subtraction that problem could be written 6 − 9 = −3. Because subtraction is indicated by a minus sign (−), numbers less than zero are marked with that sign also.

Early mathematicians recognized the usefulness of numbers less than zero but were not happy about having to use them. They gave these numbers the unflattering name negatives from the Latin word meaning "to deny." Two more-appropriate terms for negative numbers are additive inverse and opposite. As these names suggest, all negative numbers require an equal and opposite amount to be added to them to give zero. A debt of five dollars requires payment of five dollars before the account is cleared. An air temperature of −5 degrees requires the air to get five degrees warmer before the temperature reaches zero. In other words −5 + 5 = 0 just as 5 − 5 = 0. This view of negative numbers suggests another way to understand subtraction. Subtracting any number is the same as adding its opposite:

$$a − b = a + (− b)$$

**Multiplication.** When people learned to add, they had developed a timesaving device. Addition is just a shortcut method of counting, but even addition can be time-consuming, especially when the same number must be added repeatedly. Situations requiring repeated addition must have arisen often, even in ancient times. If a shepherd wanted to trade 16 of his sheep for a supply of wheat, and if each sheep was worth 29 bushels of wheat, the shepherd would have to add sixteen 29s to calculate his price. Ancient mathematicians developed multiplication to simplify repeated addition problems.

One of the earliest multiplication techniques was called doubling or duplation. The shepherd who had to add sixteen 29s probably began by adding 29 + 29 to get 58; but he may have recognized that eight 58s would give the same sum as sixteen 29s. Probably much encouraged, he added again: 58 + 58 = 116. Could the eight 58s be replaced by four 116s? Yes, and the four 116s could be replaced by two 232s, which gave the sum 464. The whole problem could be done by four doublings instead of 16 additions—quite a time-saver.

The multiplication technique used today is faster than doubling. It is a mechanical method of manipulating numbers which can be used to calculate the sum of large numbers but only requires two digits to be multiplied at a time. In order to multiply quickly it is necessary only to memorize all the possible multiplications of two digits, from $1 \times 1 = 1$ to $9 \times 9 = 81$. These are called multiplication facts or the multiplication table. The sign "$\times$" is read "times" and the problem $9 \times 9$ actually means nine added nine times. The answer to this multiplication problem, 81, is called the product. One additional multiplication fact must also be remembered: any number multiplied by zero equals zero. This fact makes sense because $3 \times 0$ actually means 0 added three times, a process that would result in zero.

Arithmetic textbooks teach the multiplication technique thoroughly. Many people, however, have lost touch with the principle behind multiplication— why the technique works. The problem $29 \times 26$ can serve to illustrate the principle. Worked out by the standard multiplication method, the problem will look like this:

$$
\begin{array}{r}
26 \\
\times\ 29 \\
\hline
234 \\
52\phantom{0} \\
\hline
754
\end{array}
$$

It is easier to see what is actually happening if the two numbers to be multiplied (called multiplicands) are broken down into their positional components:

$$
\begin{array}{r}
20 \text{ and } 6 \\
\times\ \underline{20 \text{ and } 9}
\end{array}
$$

Each of the components on the top line is multiplied by each of the components on the bottom line; after this is done all the answers (called partial products) are added up.

$$
\begin{array}{r}
20 \text{ and } 6 \\
\times\ 20 \text{ and } 9 \\
\hline
54 \\
180 \\
120 \\
400 \\
\hline
754
\end{array}
$$

This method of multiplication works because multiplication is distributive. In other words, when the sums of numbers are multiplied, all the multiplications are distributed evenly. Each of the addends of one sum is multiplied by each of the addends of the other sum. To illustrate, $5 \times 5$, which equals 25, can be broken down into the product of two sums, $(2 + 3) \times (4 + 1)$. According to the distributive law, the sums are multiplied in the following way:

$$
\begin{array}{c}
(2 + 3) \times (4 + 1) = \\
(2 \times 4) + (2 \times 1) + (3 \times 4) + (3 \times 1) = \\
8 + 2 + 12 + 3 = 25
\end{array}
$$

Mathematicians illustrate the distributive law

$$a(b + c) = (ab) + (ac)$$

Because multiplication is a shortened form of addition, it has two other fundamental properties that it shares with addition. Multiplication is both commutative and associative. According to the commutative law of multiplication, $ab = ba$, the order in which numbers are multiplied never affects their product: $4 \times 5 = 20$ and $5 \times 4 = 20$. According to the associative law, $ab(c) = a(bc)$, when someone is multiplying more than two numbers, it makes no difference in what order the numbers are multiplied:

$$
\begin{array}{c}
8(2 \times 9) = 8 \times 18 = 144 \\
\text{and } (8 \times 2) \times 9 = 16 \times 9 = 144
\end{array}
$$

**Division.** While multiplication combines numbers to obtain sums, division separates numbers into equal parts. Division is the opposite of multiplication— multiplication is a shortened method of adding, and division is a shortened method of subtracting.

One of the difficulties in learning division is understanding that it is really a process that works backward. Rather than learning division facts, one must learn to apply multiplication facts in reverse. The problem "What is $18 \div 3$?" is the same as asking: "What number times 3 equals 18?" According to the multiplication table the answer is 6.

Some examples can illustrate exactly how division is related to both multiplication and subtraction. Division can solve the problem of how to split 12 apples into three equal groups. This problem calls for a kind of backward multiplication: $3 \times ?$ apples = 12 apples. The answer that you get, according to the multiplication table, is 4.

Division can also solve another kind of problem: if the milk filling a 12-quart container has to be transferred to three-quart containers, how many three-quart containers will be filled? This problem may be worked out literally with cans. The milk from the 12-quart container can be poured to fill one three-quart can, then a second three-quart can, then a third can, and a fourth can. This problem in effect calls for a kind of repeated subtraction—subtracting three quarts of milk four times.

Both problems pose the question "How many times does 3 go into 12?" and both problems are written $12 \div 3 = 4$ (12 divided by 3 equals 4). The number to the left of the division sign, 12, is called the dividend; the number to the right, 3, is called the divisor; and the answer to the problem, 4, is called the quotient, derived from the Latin word meaning "how many times."

The division method commonly used to solve complicated problems is called long division, and it is a mechanical process of unmultiplying. As this example illustrates, long division repeats a cycle of guess-multiply-subtract until the problem is solved.

$$
\begin{array}{r}
21487 \\
12\overline{)257844} \\
24 \\
\hline
17 \\
12 \\
\hline
58 \\
48 \\
\hline
104 \\
96 \\
\hline
84 \\
84 \\
\hline
0
\end{array}
$$

Solving this problem requires (1) guessing "what number times 12 equals 25?"; (2) multiplying the answer, 2, by 12; and (3) subtracting that answer, 24, from 25. The next digit is dropped down, and the cycle repeats until the entire problem is unmultiplied and the last subtraction yields zero.

Most division problems do not end so neatly in a zero. What happens, for instance, when 175 is divided by 2? There is no exact whole number that can be multiplied by 2 to give 175. The closest is 87: 2 times 87 is 174 and 1 is left over. It would be extremely impractical for mathematicians to avoid this type of problem because it does not come out evenly. It is often necessary to divide such numbers.

If a father insists upon dividing his 175 acres of land equally between his two children, he would give each of them 87 acres and a half of the remaining acre. To deal with division problems that do not yield whole numbers, mathematicians have developed a kind of number to represent a part of a whole unit: the fraction.

People have been using fractions since ancient times. The Rhind papyrus, an Egyptian mathematical document written about 1700 BC, makes use of fractions

in which the numerator (the top number) is one: ¼, ½, etc. It is easy to see why fractions were discovered at almost the same time as whole numbers. People began using whole numbers as soon as they found it necessary to count, and they used whole numbers to count separate and individual objects.

Numbers were needed not only for counting but also for measuring. People had to measure land area and distance, food, and time. Land and food and time do not always exist in evenly measurable amounts. A farmer may own only a part of an acre of land. An activity may last for some amount of time less than an hour. Early in history, people needed numbers smaller than whole numbers.

At first only the simplest fractions were used. People tried to avoid more complex fractions whenever possible by subdividing their units of measurement into smaller units. An hour, for instance, is divided into 60 subunits called minutes. A foot is divided into 12 subunits called inches. A circle is divided into 360 subunits called degrees.

The reason that 12, 60, and 360 appear so often as numbers of subunits is that each of these numbers has several factors—that is, several numbers can be divided into them evenly without leaving fractions. Twelve, for instance, can be divided evenly by 1, 2, 3, 4, 6, and 12.

There are many occasions when units must be divided into parts. If two acres of land must be divided into three equal portions, each portion will be smaller than one acre. The size of each portion is represented by the fraction ⅔, which is read as "two thirds," or "two over three," or "two divided by three." A fraction is actually a compact division problem, and any division problem can be represented as a fraction. The father who needed to divide his 175 acres between his 2 children would divide 175 by 2 and give each of them ¹⁷⁵⁄₂ acres or 87½ acres.

Calculating with fractions was originally more complicated than calculating with integers because fractions did not fit neatly into the positional notation system. By the 17th century, however, people began to use a positional method for representing portions of whole numbers—decimal fractions.

Any fraction written as a division (¾, ¹¹⁄₁₂, ²⁹⁄₇₂, etc.) can be converted to a decimal fraction by dividing the numerator by the denominator. In order to convert ¾ into a decimal fraction, three is divided by four, and a decimal point is used to separate any integers from the fraction:

$$
\begin{array}{r}
.75 \\
4\overline{)3.00} \\
28 \\
\hline
20 \\
20 \\
\hline
0
\end{array}
$$

The major advantage in using the decimal system is that decimal fractions can be added, subtracted, multiplied, and divided exactly as whole numbers can.

**Involution.** The process of simplifying arithmetic calculations continues beyond the process of multiplication. When multiplication is viewed as a shortened form of arithmetic, it seems like a great advance. But even figuring out the product of a simple multiplication problem like $15 \times 15 \times 15$ requires a significant amount of work:

$$
\begin{array}{r}
15 \\
\times 15 \\
\hline
75 \\
15 \\
\hline
225
\end{array}
\qquad
\begin{array}{r}
225 \\
\times \ 15 \\
\hline
1125 \\
225 \\
\hline
3375
\end{array}
$$

Repeated multiplications often arise in arithmetic. To calculate the volume of a cube with a three-foot edge, for example, the length of the edge must be multiplied three times: $3 \times 3 \times 3 = 27$ cubic feet. René Descartes, the father of modern mathematics, adopted a shorthand notation. He used a new type of symbol called an exponent. In exponential notation $8 \times 8$ is written as $8^2$. The small number above the line, the exponent, indicates the number of times the base number, 8, is to be multiplied, or used as a factor. The process of repeating the multiplication of a number is called involution, or raising that number to a certain power. So $14 \times 14 \times 14 \times 14 \times 14$ is written $14^5$ and is called 14 to the fifth power.

Exponential numbers are useful to arithmetic in an important way: they provide an easy method to calculate with very large numbers. Scientists and mathematicians have adopted the practice of expressing very large numbers in exponential form—especially as powers of 10. The number representing the speed of light—30,000,000,000 centimeters per second—is written by scientists as $3 \times 10^{10}$. Suppose the scientist wanted to find out how far light had traveled in 100,000,000 seconds. Standard multiplication techniques would result in a huge number. But the scientist can multiply with the exponential numbers. The rule for multiplying with exponents is: To multiply two powers with the same base, add the exponents and use their sum as the exponent of the common base. The scientist's problem would look like this:

$$3 \times 10^{10} \times 10^8 = 3 \times 10^{18}$$

Dividing exponential numbers calls for subtracting the exponents: $3^4 \div 3^2 = 3^2$. Working through this problem will illustrate this rule:

$$3^4 \div 3^2 = \frac{3 \times 3 \times 3 \times 3}{3 \times 3} = \frac{81}{9} = 9 = 3^2$$

Exponents can be used to represent extremely small numbers and fractions. Use the rule for dividing exponents: $3^2 \div 3^3 = 3^{-1}$. If these numbers are represented in the standard Arabic numeral form the problem would read $9 \div 27$ or $\frac{9}{27}$ or $\frac{1}{3}$. So $3^{-1}$ actually equals $\frac{1}{3}$. The negative exponent signals that the exponential number is a fraction.

**Evolution.** Every arithmetic operation has its reverse. The reverse of addition is subtraction. The reverse of multiplication is division. And the reverse of involution is called evolution. Since involution is a process of repeated multiplication, it stands to reason that evolution is a process of repeated division. This process of repeated division leads to finding the foundation, called the root, of a number. If the number 64 is divided by 4 three times, the answer will be 1:

$$
\begin{aligned}
1: 64 \div 4 &= 16 \\
16 \div 4 &= 4 \\
4 \div 4 &= 1
\end{aligned}
$$

Four is the third root of 64 and is written as

$$\sqrt[3]{64}$$

People are not called upon to work out roots very often, and the method is too complicated to use unnecessarily. Fortunately mathematicians have developed an alternative notation that simplifies calculating with roots. They represent roots as fractional exponents. The square root (or second root) of 16 can be written as either

$$\sqrt{16} \qquad 16^{\frac{1}{2}}$$

In both cases the number equals 4.

Fractional exponents, like regular fractions, can be converted to decimal form:

$$16^{\frac{1}{2}} = 16^{.5}$$

Once these equivalences were worked out, it became possible to express all the real numbers in a similar exponential form.

In the early 17th century, a Scottish mathematician, John Napier, and a British mathematician, Henry Briggs, developed a system that put the properties of exponents to their most practical use and greatly simplified arithmetic. They invented a system of logarithms. A logarithm is an exponent. Napier discovered that if every possible number could be expressed as a power of a common base, then all problems of multiplication and division could be reduced to problems of adding and subtracting exponents. Briggs suggested that this common base be ten. He created a table that recorded the log (or power of ten) for every number. The log for 100 is 2, which stands for $10^2$. Numbers that are not natural powers of 10 are represented in the table by decimal logs. The log of 1,074 equals 3.0311 because $1,074 = 10^{3.0311}$.

Since the advent of electronic computers and pocket calculators, complicated arithmetic operations are accomplished much more easily. Raising to powers, figuring roots, and calculating logs can be done in a matter of seconds with a calculator. But it is still necessary to know what the operations of arithmetic are to be able to use them correctly for the many purposes which they serve.
Kenneth Rose

Rene Pauli—SuperStock

*The Grand Canyon of the Colorado River in northern Arizona is one of the world's great scenic wonders. Much of its overwhelming beauty is the result of erosion by water and wind.*

# ARIZONA

The Grand Canyon State is a combination of the changeless past and the volatile present. On lonely mesa tops high above the plains are Native American villages where ancient rituals are still observed, their origins lost in the mists of time. The modern-day counterparts of tribal medicine men, Lowell Observatory scientists, use the most advanced techniques to map the contours of the moon's surface.

Out on the mountain-rimmed Arizona desert the beautiful mission of San Xavier del Bac, white-walled and serene, recalls the days when Spanish priests converted the Native American Indians to Christianity. There has been an active mission church of the Papago on the site ever since Father Eusebio Kino founded the mission in 1700. Earlier missionaries arrived in the companies of swashbuckling 16th-century conquistadores. The first European visitors, however, were members of the ill-fated Narváez expedition, which was shipwrecked in the Gulf of Mexico in 1528. The ship's treasurer, Álvar Núñez Cabeza de Vaca, and three other survivors years later roamed the Southwest after escaping from hostile Native American Indian captors.

Another of the four survivors of the shipwreck was a slave called Estéban, or Estevanico (little Stephen),

. . . . . . . . . . . . . . . . . . . . . . . . . . . . . . . . . . . . . . . . . . . . . . . .

*This article was critically reviewed and updated by Neil M. Shpritz, Program Director of Research and Information Services, Arizona Department of Commerce.*

who is honored in black history as one of the earliest American pioneers. In 1539 he led a small search party from Mexico to locate the Seven Cities of Cibola that Cabeza de Vaca had claimed to have found. Although this search ended with the explorer's murder by Zuni Indians, he had paved the way for a Franciscan friar, Marcos de Niza, to claim the region for Spain.

After the Spaniards came professional big-game hunters, Mormon settlers, Confederate veterans, gold seekers, cattle and sheep ranchers, and the gunslingers who made Tombstone, Bisbee, and other mining towns notorious. Annual festivals re-create the past— Flagstaff's Annual Navajo Marketplace; Prescott's Frontier Days Rodeo; All-Indian Days and Pow Wow in Scottsdale; Gold Rush Days in Wickenburg; and Native American religious observances like the Hopi Snake Dance.

Arizona's population growth in the last half of the 20th century has been tremendous, especially in its major urban centers. Between 1950 and 1960 its population increased more than 74 percent. In the next decade the increase was 36 percent—still larger than any state except Nevada. In the 1970s the increase in residents was more than 53 percent. According to the 1990 census, it was one of the five Southwestern states that continued to attract more Americans in search of a better environment. Arizona's population continues to grow; in the 1990s it increased by 40 percent, second only to Nevada.

## State Symbols

**FLAG.** Arizona's distinctive flag was adopted in 1917. The central copper star symbolizes the importance of minerals in the state's economy. The lower half of the flag is a blue field, and the upper half consists of 13 alternate red and yellow rays, suggesting the setting sun over the desert. The colors of the rays signify the period of Spanish dominion over Arizona; it has been said that their number represents either the 13 original United States or the 13 counties that made up Arizona in 1911, when the flag was designed. The battleship *Arizona*, later sunk at Pearl Harbor in 1941, received one of the first copies made.

**SEAL.** The Arizona state constitution of 1911 described the state seal that replaced earlier territorial seals. In the background is a mountain range with the sun rising behind it, a dam, and a reservoir. In the middle distance and foreground are a miner with pick and shovel, standing by a quartz mill; irrigated fields and orchards; and grazing cattle. The motto "Ditat Deus" (God Enriches) is placed above the scene.

**AMPHIBIAN.** Arizona Treefrog.

**FISH.** Arizona Trout.

**GEMSTONE.** Turquoise.

**NECKWEAR.** Bolo Tie.

**TREE:** Palo Verde

**FLOWER:** Blossom of the Saguaro Cactus

**BIRD:** Cactus Wren

## Facts About Arizona

A COMPTON'S MAP

**Nickname.** Grand Canyon State.

**Motto.** Ditat Deus (God Enriches).

**Song.** 'Arizona March Song', words by Margaret Rowe Clifford and music by Maurice Blumenthal.

**Entered the Union.** Feb. 14, 1912, as the 48th state.

**Capital.** Phoenix.

**Population** (2000 census). 5,130,632—rank, 20th state. Persons per square mile, 45.1 (persons per square kilometer, 17.4)—rank, 36th state.

**Extent.** Area, 114,006 square miles (295,276 square kilometers), including 364 square miles (943 square kilometers) of water surface (6th state in size).

**Elevation.** Highest, Humphreys Peak, 12,633 feet (3,851 meters), near Flagstaff; lowest, Colorado River at southwest corner of state, 100 feet (30 meters), average, 4,100 feet (1,250 meters).

**Geographic Center.** 55 miles (89 kilometers) southeast of Prescott.

**Temperature.** Extremes—lowest –41° F (–41° C), Hawley Lake, Jan. 7, 1971; highest 127° F (53° C), Parker, July 7, 1905. Averages at Flagstaff—January, 27.3° F (–2.6° C); July, 65.5° F (18.6° C); annual, 45.6° F (7.6° C). Averages at Phoenix—January, 52.1° F (11.2° C); July, 90.7° F (32.6° C); annual, 70.7° F (21.5° C). Averages at Yuma—January, 53.4° F (11.9° C); July, 91.0° F (32.8° C); annual, 71.8° F (22.1° C).

**Precipitation.** At Flagstaff—annual average, 18.31 inches (465 millimeters). At Phoenix—annual average, 7.64 inches (194 millimeters). At Yuma—annual average, 3.27 inches (83 millimeters).

**Land Use.** Crops, 2%; pasture, 56%; forest, 22%; other, 20%.

*(See also* ARIZONA FACT SUMMARY.)

*Arizona's Capitol, known as the State House, is in Phoenix. The central section was completed in 1900. A figure symbolizing Liberty and Peace crowns the dome.*
SuperStock

Mark Keller—Four By Five

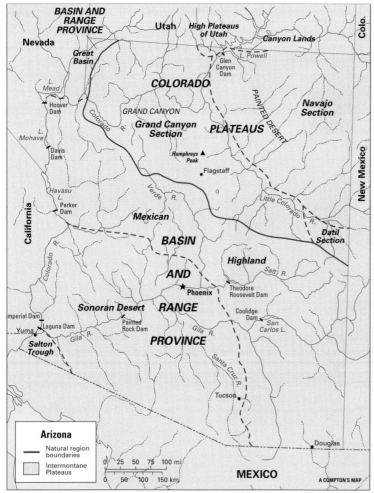

*Saguaro National Monument east of Tucson covers more than 63,000 acres, set aside in 1933 to preserve the saguaro cactus. Many of these unusual plants are more than 100 years old.*

Miners and farmers, war veterans and senior citizens have swelled the number of settlers and visitors. Although Arizona's economy has developed rapidly, employment opportunities and housing construction have not always kept pace with the influx. Irresponsible land-promotion schemes also caused concern. Yet the newcomers continue to pour in, seeking jobs, recreation, or retirement.

The state's name may come from the Pima Indian word *Arizuma* or from the Papago words *aleh-zon* or *ari-sonac*, or *ali-shonak*, all translated as "little spring" or "place of the little spring." The Spanish first used the name for a mining camp by the Planchas de Plata mine. When settlers petitioned for the Arizona district to become a territory, other place-name suggestions were Gadsonia and Pimeria. Arizona's nickname is the Grand Canyon State, after the spectacular gorge in the northern part of the state. Other nicknames have been the Copper State, the Apache State, the Aztec State, the Italy of America (for its mountains), and the Baby State and the Valentine State because it was the last state in the Union when it was admitted on Feb. 14, 1912.

## Survey of the Grand Canyon State

Located in the arid Southwest, Arizona is bounded on the north by Utah, on the east by New Mexico, and on the south by the Mexican state of Sonora. On the west the Colorado River flows for almost the entire length of the state. The river separates Arizona from California and part of Nevada.

The Grand Canyon State is almost square. From north to south its greatest length is 395 miles (636 kilometers), and its greatest width is 343 miles (552 kilometers). Its total area is 114,006 square miles (295,276 square kilometers), including 364 square miles (943 square kilometers) of water surface. Arizona is the nation's sixth largest state in area.

## Natural Regions

The surface of Arizona rises from a low point of approximately 100 feet (30 meters) above sea level, in the southwestern corner of the state to a high point of more than 12,000 feet (3,600 meters) in the northern part. Northern and northeastern Arizona are on the Colorado Plateau, which extends into Utah, Colorado, and New Mexico. Southern and southwestern Arizona are in the Basin and Range Province. Almost the entire state is drained by the Colorado River and its chief tributaries—the Little Colorado, the Bill Williams, and the Gila. After entering Mexico, the Colorado drains into the Gulf of California (*see* Colorado River).

**The Colorado Plateaus** region is gashed and scarred by deep canyons and gullies that snow-fed streams have been carving for millions of years. It is studded with mountain ranges, lofty peaks, and great flat-topped sandstone mesas. The Grand Canyon, Oak Creek Canyon, the Painted Desert, and the Petrified Forest are all in this region. Here too, near Flagstaff, is Humphreys Peak—the highest point in the state at 12,633 feet (3,851 meters).

**The Basin and Range Province** is made up of mountains and plains. The province's mountain, or range, section is formed by an irregular belt of mountains that crosses the state from southeast to northwest. This section, 70 to 150 miles (110 to 240 kilometers) wide, contains many extinct volcanoes. The mountaintops rise 4,000 to 6,000 feet (1,200 to 1,800 meters) above the valley floors. On the south the mountains drop sharply to a series of low ridges and terraced mesas. From the edge of this belt the land slopes gently toward the province's plains, or basin, section. Here the vast irrigated desert plains are broken by valleys, detached mountain ranges, and solitary peaks.

### Climate

Arizona has a widely varied climate. In the southwest part of the state, summer daytime temperatures above 100° F (38° C) are frequent. The extremely dry air, however, allows the heat to radiate rapidly so that the nights are usually cool. At higher elevations in the east-central part, winter temperatures as low as –37° F (–38° C) have been recorded. The growing season in the northeast is less than three months. In the lower areas of the southwest there are sometimes no killing frosts for two or three years at a time. On the irrigated desert truck crops and citrus fruits are grown throughout the year. Arizona receives very little rain because the high Pacific coast mountains block moisture-laden clouds from the ocean. Most of the rain clouds that reach the state are blown up from the Gulf of Mexico. Average annual precipitation (rain and snow) ranges from about 3 inches (8 centimeters) at Yuma in the southwest, to 18 inches (46 centimeters) at Flagstaff in the central part of the state.

Despite the scanty rainfall, the state has an interesting and varied plant and animal life. Most characteristic is the desert vegetation—the cactus, mesquite, agave, yucca, creosote bush, and sagebrush. More than a hundred varieties of cactus are found in Arizona, ranging from the little prickly pears to the giant saguaro cactus—20 to 50 feet (6 to 15 meters) high. Coyotes, mountain lions, deer, antelope, and wildcats are found in the north. The desert is the home of such creatures as scorpions and the venomous Gila monsters, whose bite is fatal to small animals. There

Tom Algire—SuperStock

*The White House at the base of a cliff in Canyon de Chelly National Monument is the best preserved of the 138 ruins of Native American Indian dwellings. This Pueblo Indian ruin dates from the 11th century.*

are also rattlesnakes and other reptiles, as well as many kinds of birds.

### Natural Resources

About 45 percent of the land in Arizona is owned by the federal government. The United States Department of the Interior works with the Arizona Department of Land and the Department of Game and Fish on many reclamation and conservation projects.

Much of the state's wealth lies in its mineral deposits. Rich copper veins make Arizona the principal copper-producing state as well as one of the great copper-producing areas of the world. Arizona also ranks among the leading states in the production of gemstones, construction sand and gravel, and silver. Most of the uranium mined in the United States comes from the Colorado Plateau region, but the amount mined has been greatly reduced since the end of the Cold War era.

In northern Arizona is the largest ponderosa pine forest in the United States. The state's chief commercial trees are yellow pine, fir, and spruce. Most timbered areas are set aside as forest reserves.

A fine climate, magnificent scenery, open spaces for recreation, and the Native American cultural influence make tourism a major industry. One of the state's most profitable enterprises is the dude ranch—a vacation resort that offers horseback riding and other activities typical of working Western ranches to its guests, who are usually dudes (city people).

**Irrigation.** Arizona is sometimes thought of as a desert, but irrigation has changed much of the fruitless desert into rich farmland with highly productive citrus, cotton, and truck farms. There are Native American

*Glen Canyon Dam is one of the world's highest dams. Its reservoir, Lake Powell, has a capacity of more than 9 billion gallons. Glen Canyon National Recreation Area occupies nearly 1.3 million acres in northern Arizona and southern Utah.*

Werner Wolf—Black Star

Indian pueblos on the mesas and cattle towns on the plains. Mining communities cling to mountain ledges in the highlands.

Grasses of many varieties grow throughout the state, especially in the north. These furnish excellent grazing for cattle and sheep. Some grasses seem to be almost independent of rainfall and flourish except in times of long droughts. Only about 2 percent of the total land area of the state is harvested cropland, of which nearly 75 percent depends upon irrigation. With adequate water the fertile soil in the river valleys and desert plains produces huge crop yields.

Since rain is sparse, a long chain of dams and reservoirs has been built to store precious water. It is brought into the fertile valleys through irrigation canals and ditches. Theodore Roosevelt Dam, completed in 1911, is the largest of seven multipurpose dams on the Salt and Verde rivers. These dams store water for nearly 238,000 acres (615,000 hectares) in the Salt River valley. Painted Rock and Coolidge dams are on the Gila River.

Arizona shares with California the waters of the Colorado River. These waters are diverted at Imperial and Laguna dams into the delta lowlands around Yuma and the Gila Valley east of the city. Parker, Davis, and Hoover dams are farther up the Colorado. Hoover Dam, one of the largest water and power projects ever undertaken, and Glen Canyon Dam— both on Arizona's northern borders—are among the highest dams in the United States. (*See also* Colorado River; Dam; Imperial Valley.)

### People of Arizona

The first Europeans to reach what is now Arizona were Spanish explorers and missionaries. Later a few trappers visited the region. Among the many Native American tribes they encountered were the Hopi, Papago, and Pima. The warlike Apache were not found there until after the middle of the 16th century.

The first wave of new settlement took place during the early 1800s. Most of the newcomers were from the southern and eastern United States. During this period many Mexicans also moved into the region. Arizona boomed after gold and silver were discovered in the 1850s. Mormons from Utah formed the first group of pioneers to settle on Arizona farmlands. With the completion of the first transcontinental railroads in the 1880s, still more people were brought into the area.

Today about 13 percent of the people in Arizona are foreign born. Mexicans make up more than half the total foreign population. African Americans make up 23.1 percent of the population, and 5 percent are Native Americans.

The majority of Arizona's Native American Indian population live on 21 reservations. The Navajo have the largest tribe and reservation, located in the northeastern section of the state and extending into New Mexico and Utah. Other large reservations include Fort Apache, San Carlos, Tohono O'odham, and Hopi.

Several thousand Native Americans live off the reservations. Scattered over the state are the ruined cliff dwellings and pueblos of ancient Indian communities. (*See also* Indians, American.)

### Cities

Phoenix, the state capital and largest city, is a shipping point for truck crops, cotton, fruits, and beef and an important industrial city (*see* Phoenix). The second largest city, Tucson is a manufacturing and resort center in the cotton and mining area (*see* Tucson).

Of the next seven cities in size, all of them are in the Maricopa County area surrounding Phoenix. They are Mesa, Tempe, Glendale, Scottsdale, Chandler, Peoria, and Gilbert. Sun City is a fast-growing retirement community and the largest of its kind in the nation. Also in the area is Yuma, a shipping port for large quantities of farm products. The northern city of Flagstaff is an educational and cultural center.

Comstock

(Top) Christopher R. Harris—Stock South; (bottom) Steve Northup—Black Star

*Phoenix is the capital and largest city of Arizona. It was founded in 1867 and became capital in 1889. Its climate has made it one of America's chief tourist attractions.*

## Manufacturing

At one time Arizona's economy was said to be based on the "Five Cs"—copper, climate, cotton, cattle, and citrus. During and after World War II, however, manufacturing became increasingly important. Today Arizona plants produce copper, processed foods, transportation equipment, communications equipment, semiconductors, and electric and electronic equipment. Arizona has been successful in attracting high technology industries, which have a total economic impact of more than $3.3 billion per year. More than half of all manufacturing employment is in this sector.

One of Arizona's major industries is the smelting and refining of metals. Copper production is the most important branch of this industry. The Copper Mountain district at Morenci in Greenlee County is the leading copper-mining area in the state. Other large copper-producing districts are the Miami in Gila County, the Bisbee area in Cochise County, and Ajo in Pima County. Copper production, while still a billion-dollar industry, fell during the late 1990s due to low market values.

## Agriculture

Although Arizona is known for a relatively dry climate, the river valleys and desert lands where irrigation is used are suitable for farming and ranching. More than a million acres are under irrigation. With a year-round growing climate and relatively low cost of water, agriculture adds $6.3 billion to the state economy. The average farm size—some 4,300 acres (1,740 hectares)—is the largest in the nation, but much of the area is grazing land for cattle.

Arizona is a leading state in the production of cotton and ranks high in lettuce and orange output. Truck crops, cattle, hay, dairy products, and wheat are also important in the state's economy. Wine producers have enjoyed success with a number of varietal grapes.

*Open-pit copper mining (top) is one of the major industries in Arizona. The state leads the nation in copper production. The largest mine in the state is at Morenci. A water desalination plant (bottom) is in operation in Yuma. The arid Southwest has long suffered from inadequate and uncertain water supplies. Removing minerals from seawater should alleviate this problem.*

## Transportation

Until the close of the 19th century, when Arizona's mining and agriculture became significant, people were mainly interested in finding easy ways to get to California. Tales of wealth to be found in the Golden West, told by wagon drivers who had crossed the region, brought in many of the first settlers. The wagon and stagecoach routes used by the Arizona pioneers evolved into the network over which the modern state highway system was developed.

When Arizona began to be settled, the Colorado and some of the other rivers were used for transportation. During the American Civil War the Confederates of Texas almost stopped land transportation in the state by taking over important overland express lines. Arizona was cut off from the rest of the country until new stage lines—and later railroads—spanned the

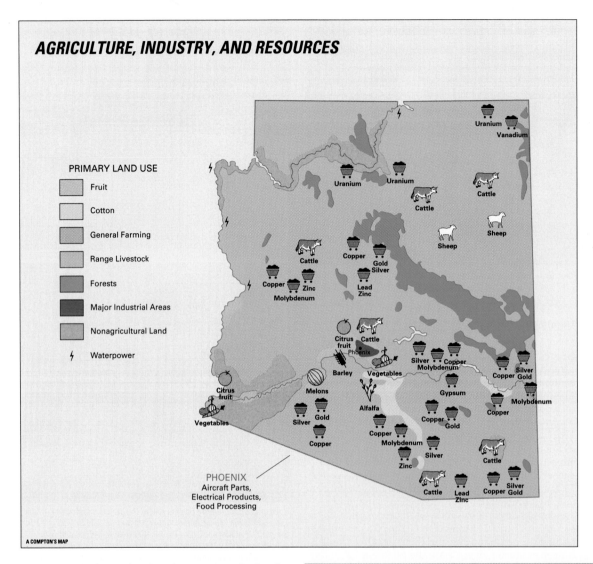

## AGRICULTURE, INDUSTRY, AND RESOURCES

PRIMARY LAND USE

- Fruit
- Cotton
- General Farming
- Range Livestock
- Forests
- Major Industrial Areas
- Nonagricultural Land
- ⚡ Waterpower

Uranium
Vanadium
Uranium
Uranium
Cattle
Cattle
Sheep
Sheep
Cattle
Copper
Gold
Silver
Copper
Zinc
Molybdenum
Lead
Zinc
Citrus fruit
Cattle
Phoenix
Silver Copper
Molybdenum
Copper
Silver
Gold
Barley
Vegetables
Gypsum
Citrus fruit
Melons
Alfalfa
Copper
Molybdenum
Vegetables
Silver
Gold
Copper
Gold
Copper
Copper
Molybdenum
Silver
Cattle
Zinc
Cattle
Lead
Zinc
Copper
Silver
Gold

PHOENIX
Aircraft Parts,
Electrical Products,
Food Processing

A COMPTON'S MAP

continent. The first railroad in the state was the Southern Pacific, which crossed the Colorado River to Yuma in 1878 and reached Tucson in 1880. With the coming of the railroads, the waterways and stage routes became obsolete. Arizona's highway and rail network link key cities in the Southwest, northern Mexico, California, Texas, and Colorado. In 2000 some 7.3 million motor carriers were processed through Arizona's 27 ports of entry. The state has more than 200 airfields including Phoenix Sky Harbor International Airport, one of the fastest growing commercial airports in the world.

### Recreation

Southern Arizona's mild winters and northern Arizona's cool summers draw millions of vacationers and $12.5 billion to the state each year. Arizona has more national parks and monuments than any other state (*see* National Parks). Tourists also visit the state's golf and tennis resorts, Native American Indian villages, natural scenic splendors, dude ranches, and

Courtesy of the Arizona Office of Tourism

*Cotton covers the ground near Coolidge after the harvest is finished. Good soil and a long growing season enable Arizona farmers to grow a variety of warm-weather crops.*

*The University of Arizona (top left), situated in Tucson, opened in 1885. The clock tower is part of its Student Union Memorial Building. Kitt Peak National Observatory (top right), located on the Papago Indian Reservation 50 miles west of Tucson, was established in 1958. It is the site of the world's largest collection of ground-based telescopes as well as the world's largest solar telescope. Lake Powell (bottom), with is remarkable rock formations, was formed by water impounded behind Glen Canyon Dam in the Colorado River.*
(Top left) James Blank—Tony Stone Worldwide; (top right) Scott Berner—Gartman Agency; (bottom) William Waldron—Stock South

desert and mountain playgrounds. In professional sports are basketball's Phoenix Suns, football's Arizona (formerly St. Louis) Cardinals, and baseball's Arizona Diamondbacks.

Many people settle in Arizona because of health concerns. The dry climate alleviates certain chronic diseases. Retirement communities are also growing in number. Almost everything is air-conditioned, from shopping malls to racetrack grandstands.

### Education

The first schools in Arizona were founded by Jesuit missionaries from Mexico. The first public school opened at Tucson in 1871. From 1869 to 1877 Governor A.P.K. Safford worked to establish a system of public education in the territory. In 1879 the territorial legislature created the office of state superintendent of public instruction. Actual organization of the public school system began in 1883.

Arizona has three state universities—the University of Arizona, at Tucson; Arizona State University, at Tempe; and Northern Arizona University, at Flagstaff. Arizona has more than a dozen private colleges, and the Maricopa Community Colleges form the largest community college system in the nation.

At Taliesin West, near Phoenix, students experiment with new architectural ideas. The center was founded by Frank Lloyd Wright (*see* Wright, Frank Lloyd). Near Glendale is the American Graduate School of International Management, which grants degrees in its highly specialized course of study.

Lowell Observatory, near Flagstaff, was established in 1894. From here, the planet Pluto was discovered in 1930. Atop Kitt Peak, near Tucson, is one of the world's largest solar telescopes. A revolutionary multiple mirror telescope was introduced at the University of Arizona's Smithsonian Astrophysical Observatory in 1978. The ground-breaking telescope was recently

The old courthouse in Tucson still stands (top) as a reminder of the days of frontier justice. The Heard Museum (bottom) in Phoenix has exhibits of Native American artifacts from prehistoric times to the present. The Goldwater Kachina doll collection is also housed in the museum.
Courtesy of (bottom) the City of Phoenix; (left) Don & Pat Valenti—Tony Stone Worldwide

converted to a single 21.5 foot (6.5 meter) mirror. ( *See also* Telescope.)

### Government and Politics

Arizona's territorial government was organized in 1863. The first capital was Fort Whipple. Phoenix was made the territorial capital in 1889 and the state capital in 1912. Arizona became a state in 1912, the year after its constitution was adopted.

The chief executive officer is the governor. The legislature consists of the Senate and the House of Representatives. The Supreme Court heads the judiciary. The state constitution guarantees maximum citizen participation via initiatives, referenda on legislature, and the right to recall elected officials.

While the majority of the territorial governors were Republican, at first the state governors were more likely to be Democratic. Raul H. Castro was Arizona's first Mexican American governor (1975–77). The first woman to govern the state was Rose Mofford (1988–91), who had been named acting governor after Evan Mecham (1987–88) was removed from office for campaign violations—only the seventh governor nationwide to be impeached. (Mecham failed in his 1990 bid for the Republican nomination to succeed Mofford.) That nomination and the election went to Republican J. Fife Symington III who went on to win a second term in 1994. However in 1997, Symington became the second governor in nine years to lose his seat. Two days after being convicted on seven counts of fraud, he resigned the office. Jane Dee Hull took office after Symington's resignation. In 1998 she became Arizona's first elected female governor.

Arizona voted Democratic in presidential elections from 1932 to 1948 and 1996. Before and since then it supported the Republican nominees, including Barry M. Goldwater of Phoenix, who was defeated by President Lyndon Johnson in 1964. Once branded an extremist, Goldwater was considered the symbol of high-minded Republican conservatism by the time he retired from the United States Senate in 1987. Carl T. Hayden, whom he replaced in 1969, at 91 had been the

THE HEARD MUSEUM
ANTHROPOLOGY · PRIMITIVE ART

oldest member of Congress and served a record 56 continuous years—since Arizona became a state. In 1990 Arizona's senators, Republican John McCain and Democrat Dennis DeConcini, were both among the so-called Keating Five, under investigation for using their influence improperly in a savings and loan scandal. McCain made an unsuccessful bid for the 2000 Republican presidential nomination.

### HISTORY

In 1848, as a result of the Mexican War, the United States gained both New Mexico and the part of Arizona that lies north of the Gila River. In 1853 the remaining part, south of the Gila, was obtained from Mexico by the Gadsden Purchase. In 1863 Arizona was made a territory. Its boundaries have remained unchanged since it became a state in 1912.

### Exploration and Settlement

One of the first Europeans to explore the territory now included in Arizona was the Franciscan priest, Marcos de Niza. A former slave called Estéban, who reportedly had explored the region earlier, led the way northward from Mexico in 1539. After learning that the black man had been murdered by Indians during his search for their legendary golden cities,

**Meteor Crater, near Winslow, is 560 feet (170 meters) deep and 4,150 feet (1,260 meters) from rim to rim. The best-preserved such crater in the world, the site is now used for astronaut training.**
Pete Winkel—Stock South

605

the priest simply claimed the land for Spain and returned to Mexico.

Other missionaries seeking converts and armor-clad Spanish conquistadores seeking riches and adventure followed. In 1540 Friar Marcos acted as guide for the expedition of Francisco Coronado. The reports of fabulous wealth stored in the Zuñi Indians' stone villages (the Seven Cities of Cibola) continued to spark explorers from Mexico to press on in spite of hostile tribes and other difficulties. Coronado spent many months in the quest, but no gold was ever found. (*See also* Coronado, Francisco.)

For almost 300 years the Spaniards continued their efforts to explore and colonize the country. They brought cattle, horses, sheep, and new farming methods to the Indians. In 1692 Father Eusebio Kino established the first of many missions, among them Tumacacori and San Xavier del Bac, which still stand (*see* Kino, Eusebio). Settlement remained slow. The first important city to rise was Tucson, established as a presidio (fort with soldiers) in 1776. (*See also* Spanish Missions table in Fact-Index.)

While under Spanish and Mexican rule, Arizona was considered a part of New Mexico. The Treaty of Guadalupe-Hidalgo at the close of the Mexican War gave the region to the United States (*see* Mexican War). The territorial government was organized formally on Dec. 29, 1863, at Navajo Springs.

**From Territory to Modern State**

The Apache Wars lasted from 1871 until 1876. They began with the Camp Grant Massacre of April 30, 1871, in which white settlers from Tucson killed about 100 Native American Indian women and children. The wars lasted until Geronimo surrendered to Gen. George Crook in 1886 (*see* Geronimo). These wars did not prevent early economic growth. Between 1870 and 1891 the number of grazing cattle increased from 5,000 to more than 1.5 million.

Miners found their way to Arizona to exploit its mineral wealth. Gold was discovered along the Gila River in 1857 and mining flourished there until the early 1860s. Silver, which proved more profitable, was discovered at the site of Tombstone in 1877. The silver boom ended in 1886, when the mines flooded. In the long run, copper was the most abundant mineral, and it became the basis of a large industry that prospered until the 1980s. The extraction of copper is expensive, so it was necessary for outside companies and investment to come to Arizona to open the mines and build the processing and shipping facilities. The first mine was opened at Ajo in 1854, but the richest lode was found at Bisbee in 1877.

While the mining and cattle industries were thriving, Arizonans sought statehood. In 1910 Congress passed the act authorizing the territory to draft constitution. President William H. Taft vetoed the first constitution because it contained a "recall of judges" clause. Once this clause was removed, Taft signed the constitution. Arizona became the 48th state on Feb. 14, 1912. The controversial clause was later restored.

Farming, cattle, and mining were the basis of the state's prosperity until World War II. The clean, dry air proved beneficial for people with respiratory problems. As war loomed in 1940 the federal government opened military bases, especially for training pilots. After the war many servicemen returned with their families to go to school or to work in the various industries. By the 1980s Arizona had become one of the leading high-technology states.

As the nation prospered, more people began moving to the Southwest from the older, and often colder, states. Arizona became one of the fastest growing states. (*See also* United States, "Western Basins and Plateaus"; individual entries in Fact-Index on Arizona persons, places, products, and events.)

**FURTHER RESOURCES FOR ARIZONA**

**Cheek, L.W.** Arizona, 2nd ed. (Fodor's, 1993).
**Fradin, Dennis.** Arizona: In Words and Pictures (Childrens, 1980).
**Heinrichs, Ann.** America the Beautiful: Arizona (Childrens, 1991).
**Marsh, Carole.** Arizona Timeline (Gallopade, 1992).
**Miller, Tom, ed.** Arizona: The Land and the People (Univ. of Ariz. Press, 1986).
**Powell, L.C.** Arizona: A History (Univ. of N.M. Press, 1990).
**Trimble, Marshall.** Arizona: A Panoramic History of a Frontier State (Doubleday, 1977).
**Varney, Philip.** Arizona's Ghost Towns and Mining Camps (Arizona Hiway, 1994).
**Wagoner, J.J.** Arizona's Heritage (Gibbs Smith, 1983).
**Writers' Program.** The WPA Guide to 1930s Arizona (Univ. of Ariz. Press, 1989).

## *Notable Events in Arizona History*

**1200.** Oraibi, oldest Indian community in what is now continental United States, is founded.

**1528.** Cabeza de Vaca, shipwrecked off Gulf of Mexico coast, wanders to Arizona and Mexico.

**1539.** Estéban, black companion of De Vaca, guides Friar Marcos de Niza to Zuñi villages in Arizona; Friar Marcos claims region for Spain.

**1540.** Coronado, guided by Friar Marcos, reaches Zuni River; detachment under García López de Cárdenas discovers Grand Canyon.

**1582.** Antonio de Espejo finds silver near Prescott.

**1680.** Hopi Indians rise against Spanish priests.

**1692.** Father Eusebio Kino begins missionary work among Pima Indians; founds Guevavi Mission; Tumacacori Mission founded in 1696; Mission San Xavier del Bac, in 1700.

**1751.** Pima and Papago revolt. Spanish build presidio (fort) at Tubac in 1752; garrison moved to Tucson in 1776.

**1771.** Father Francisco Garcés begins missionary work.

**1781.** Yuma kill Garcés; Spanish retaliate in 1782.

**1821.** Mexico wins its independence from Spain.

**1824.** Mexico creates New Mexico Territory, including Arizona. American traders enter region.

**1846.** Col. Stephen W. Kearny leads Army in Mexican War; takes Santa Fe; crosses Arizona to San Diego. Mormon Battalion captures Tucson.

**1848.** Mexico cedes Arizona region north of Gila River to United States. New Mexico Territory, including Arizona, established by United States in 1850.

**1853.** Lieut. A.W. Whipple makes railroad survey. Gadsden Purchase gives southern Arizona to United States.

**1854.** First copper mine in area opened at Ajo.

**1861.** Arizona declared Confederate territory.

**1862.** California Volunteers take Tucson for Union; only Civil War skirmish in Arizona is at Picacho.

**1863.** Congress creates Arizona Territory; capital, Fort Whipple; governor, John N. Goodwin.

**1864.** Capital moved to Prescott; to Tucson in 1867; to Prescott in 1877; to Phoenix in 1889.

**1869.** John Wesley Powell explores Grand Canyon.

**1878.** Southern Pacific Railroad reaches Yuma; extended to Tucson in 1880.

**1885.** University of Arizona chartered at Tucson.

**1886.** Chief Geronimo surrenders.

**1900.** Present State Capitol built; wings added in 1960.

**1911.** Theodore Roosevelt Dam completed.

**1912.** Arizona becomes 48th state, February 14; capital, Phoenix; governor, George W.P. Hunt.

**1919.** Grand Canyon National Park established.

**1930.** Coolidge Dam dedicated.

**1936.** Hoover (Boulder) Dam completed.

**1938.** Parker and Imperial dams built.

**1939.** Bartlett Dam completed.

**1949.** Davis Dam built.

**1959.** Glen Canyon Bridge dedicated.

**1960.** Kitt Peak National Observatory dedicated.

**1963.** Glen Canyon Dam completed.

**1966.** In Miranda *vs.* Arizona case, Supreme Court curbs police interrogation by ruling an arrested suspect must be informed of rights to remain silent and have counsel during questioning.

**1971.** Historic London Bridge reconstructed in Lake Havasu City.

**1974.** Raul H. Castro, state's first Mexican American governor, elected.

**1988.** Voters narrowly approve proposition to make English the official language of state government.

'Coronado's March', from an 1898 illustration by Frederic Remington, shows the Spanish explorer and his associates searching in vain for the Seven Cities of Gold in what is now Arizona.

The Granger Collection

## Some Notable People of Arizona

*The people listed below are associated with Arizona, though some of them may not have been born there. Some prominent people are not included below because they are covered in other articles in Compton's Encyclopedia (see Fact-Index).*

**Castro, Raul H.** (born 1916). Public official. Born on June 2, 1916, in Cananea, Sonora, Mexico. He moved with his family to Arizona when he was 10 years old. After graduating from the University of Arizona in 1949, he practiced law and served as a judge. He was the United States ambassador to El Salvador for four years and ambassador to Bolivia for one year. He was elected governor of Arizona in 1974, becoming the first Mexican American to hold a chief executive office in Arizona. He resigned in 1977 to become the United States ambassador to Argentina.

**Goldwater, Barry** (1909–98). Public official. Born on Jan. 1, 1909, in Phoenix, Ariz. He became president of the family department store, Goldwater's, Inc., in 1937. After serving with the Army Air Force in World War II, he was elected to the United States Senate in 1952. In 1960 he published 'The Conscience of a Conservative', and in 1962, 'Why Not Victory?' He left the Senate to run for president in 1964. He lost that race but was reelected to the Senate in 1968. He retired in 1987.

**Hayden, Carl** (1877–1972). Political leader. Born on Oct. 2, 1877, in Hayden's Ferry (now Tempe), Ariz. When Arizona became a state in 1912, he was elected to the United States House of Representatives and served 15 years. In 1927 he became a senator from Arizona and served until 1969, setting a record for the most time served in the Senate.

**Jacobs, Helen Hull** (1908–97). Tennis player. Born on Aug. 8, 1908, in Globe, Ariz. She shared a rivalry with Helen Wills Moody Roark that dominated women's tennis between 1928 and 1938. Jacobs won the United States women's singles crown four times (1932–35) and won one Wimbledon singles title (1936). In 1933 she was awarded the AP Athlete of the Year award, becoming the first woman tennis player to win the award. She was ranked among the top ten in women's tennis for 12 years and was ranked first in 1927 and 1932–35. She was inducted into the International Hall of Fame in 1962.

**Kay, Ulysses** (1917–95). Composer. Born on Jan. 7, 1917, in Tucson, Ariz. In the 1940s he composed a ballet, 'Dance Calinda'; choral compositions; orchestral compositions, including 'A Short Overture' and 'Portrait Suite'; and the score for the motion picture 'The Quiet One'. In 1958 he was chosen as one of the composers to participate in a cultural exchange mission to the Soviet Union. Other works include an opera, 'The Boor' (1955), and 'Essay on Death' (1964), a tribute to John F. Kennedy.

**Poston, Charles D.** (1825–1902). Explorer and author. Born on April 20, 1825, in Hardin County, Ky. In 1856 he went to what is now Arizona to open mining and irrigation properties. After the Territory of Arizona was created, he became the first delegate to the United States Congress from Arizona, in 1864. He was often called the Father of Arizona. His writings include 'Europe in the Summer-Time' (1868).

**Ronstadt, Linda** (born 1946). Country-rock singer. Born on July 15, 1946, in Tucson, Ariz. She helped form a group called the Stone Poneys in the mid-1960s. In 1968 she went solo and made her big break in 1974 with her album *Heart Like a Wheel*, which included the songs 'You're No Good' and 'When Will I Be Loved'. Other albums include *Simple Dreams* (1977), *Mad Love* (1980), and *Cry Like A Rainstorm, Howl Like the Wind* (1990). She has sold more than 50 million records and has won 10 Grammy Awards

**Udall, Morris** (1922–98). Public official and lawyer. Born on June 15, 1922, in St. Johns, Ariz. In 1949 he graduated from the University of Arizona and began practicing law. He was the county attorney for Pima County in 1953 and 1954. In 1961 he was elected to the United States Congress to fill the vacancy left by his brother, Stewart Udall. He was reelected for every subsequent term through 1990 and retired in mid-1991.

**Linda Ronstadt** — Steve Schapiro—Sygma

**Barry Goldwater** — Dan Ford Connolly—Gamma-Liaison

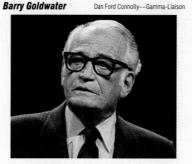

**Ulysses Kay** — G.D. Hackett—Pictorial Parade

**Helen Hull Jacobs** — AP/Wide World

**Charles D. Poston** — Culver Pictures

# Arizona Fact Summary

## POPULATION TRENDS

Rank Among States

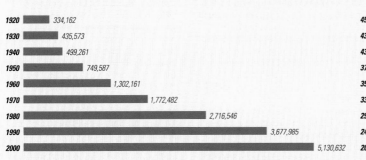

| Year | Population | Rank |
|------|-----------|------|
| 1920 | 334,162 | 45 |
| 1930 | 435,573 | 43 |
| 1940 | 499,261 | 43 |
| 1950 | 749,587 | 37 |
| 1960 | 1,302,161 | 35 |
| 1970 | 1,772,482 | 33 |
| 1980 | 2,716,546 | 29 |
| 1990 | 3,677,985 | 24 |
| 2000 | 5,130,632 | 20 |

## THE LAND

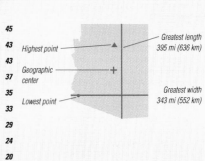

Highest point

Greatest length
395 mi (636 km)

Geographic center

Greatest width
343 mi (552 km)

Lowest point

## LARGEST CITIES (2000 census)

**Phoenix** (1,321,045). State capital; resort city in irrigated Salt River valley; electronics; museums; South Mountain Park nearby (*see* Phoenix).

**Tucson** (486,699). Winter resort; cotton, livestock; University of Arizona; Arizona Historical Society Museum; mountain park and Arizona-Sonora Desert Museum nearby (*see* Tucson).

**Mesa** (396,375). Resort-residential city; fruit, ancient Indian irrigation ditches; Mormon Temple.

**Glendale** (218,812). Irrigated area; vegetables, fruit; American Graduate School of International Management nearby.

**Scottsdale** (202,705). Resort-residential city; art galleries and craft shops.

**Chandler** (176,581). Winter resort in Salt River Valley; Gila River Indian Reservation nearby.

**Tempe** (158,625). Trade center for agricultural and stock-raising region; Arizona State University.

## VITAL STATISTICS 1998 (per 1,000 population)

**Birthrate.** 17.0 (1999)
**Death Rate.** 8.2
**Marriage Rate.** 8.1
**Divorce Rate.** 5.5

## GOVERNMENT

**Capital.** Phoenix (became territorial capital, 1889; state capital, 1912).

**Statehood.** Became 48th state in the Union on Feb. 14, 1912.

**Constitution.** Adopted 1911; amendment may be passed by majority vote of legislature; ratified by majority voting on it in an election.

**Representation in U.S. Congress.** Senate—2. House of Representatives—6. Electoral votes—10.

**Legislature.** Senators—30; term, 2 years. Representatives—60; term, 2 years.

**Executive Officers.** Governor—term, 4 years; may succeed self. Other officials—secretary of state, treasurer, and attorney general; all elected; terms, 4 years.

**Judiciary.** Justices and judges are all elected. Supreme Court—5 justices; elected at large; term, 6 years. Court of Appeals—18 judges; term, 6 years. Superior courts—101 judges; term, 4 years.

**County.** 15 counties.

## MAJOR PRODUCTS

**Agricultural.** Cotton and cottonseed, hay, vegetables and melons, citrus fruit, dairy products, lettuce, wheat.

**Manufactured.** Electric and electronic equipment, transportation equipment, semiconductors, communications equipment, nonferrous metal products.

**Mined.** Copper, molybdenum, cement, gold, silver, gypsum, manganese, zinc, uranium, coal, vanadium.

## EDUCATION AND CULTURE

**Universities and Colleges.** Arizona State University, Tempe; Northern Arizona University, Flagstaff; University of Arizona, Tucson.

**Libraries.** Arizona State University Library, Tempe; Northern Arizona University Library, Flagstaff; University of Arizona Library, Tucson.

**Notable Museums.** Amerind Foundation Museum, Dragoon; Museum of Northern Arizona and Arizona Historical Society Pioneer Museum, Flagstaff; Heard Museum and Phoenix Art Museum, Phoenix; Arizona State Museum at the University of Arizona, Tucson; Tuzigoot National Monument, Clarkdale.

## EMPLOYMENT Percentage by Industry

*Total Number of Persons Employed: 2,502,000.*

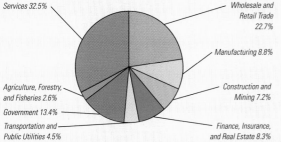

Services 32.5%

Wholesale and Retail Trade 22.7%

Manufacturing 8.8%

Construction and Mining 7.2%

Agriculture, Forestry, and Fisheries 2.6%

Government 13.4%

Transportation and Public Utilities 4.5%

Finance, Insurance, and Real Estate 8.3%

## GROSS STATE PRODUCT Percentage by Industry

*Total GSP: $143,683,000,000. Per Capita Income: $25,578.*

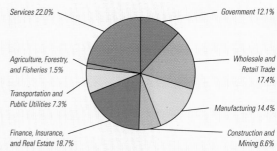

Services 22.0%

Government 12.1%

Agriculture, Forestry, and Fisheries 1.5%

Wholesale and Retail Trade 17.4%

Transportation and Public Utilities 7.3%

Manufacturing 14.4%

Finance, Insurance, and Real Estate 18.7%

Construction and Mining 6.6%

## PLACES OF INTEREST

**Apache Trail.** Between Apache Junction and Globe; scenic mountain drive.

**Bisbee.** Open-pit copper mines; Queen Mine; Lavender Pit.

**Boyce Thompson Arboretum.** Near Superior; collection of more than 10,000 plant varieties.

**Buckskin Mountain State Park.** Near Parker; water sports.

**Coolidge Dam.** Multiple-dome dam on Gila River forms San Carlos Lake.

**Coronado National Memorial.** Near Bisbee, where Spanish explorer Coronado entered what is now United States in 1540.

**Glen Canyon National Recreation Area.** In Arizona and Utah; one of the highest arch dams in United States forms Lake Powell.

**Grand Canyon National Park.** Colorado River canyon, 277 miles (446 kilometers) long, average of 10 miles (16 kilometers) wide; includes Toroweap Point and Vulcan's Throne.

**Hopi Villages.** In middle of Hopi Indian Reservation; Snake Dances.

**Jerome State Historic Park.** At Jerome; old mining town; museum.

**Kitt Peak National Observatory.** Near Tucson; solar telescope.

**Lake Havasu State Park.** Behind Parker Dam on Colorado River; camping; water sports.

**Lake Mead National Recreation Area.** In Arizona and Nevada; Hoover Dam.

**Meteor Crater.** Near Winslow; 4,000 feet (1,200 meters) wide, 600 feet (180 meters) deep.

**Mission San Xavier del Bac.** Near Tucson; founded in 1700.

**National Monuments.** Canyon de Chelly; Casa Grande Ruins; Chiricahua; Montezuma Castle; Navajo; Organ Pipe Cactus; Pipe Spring; Saguaro; Sunset Crater; Tonto; Tumacacori; Tuzigoot; Walnut Canyon; Wupatki.

**Oak Creek Canyon.** Between Sedona and Flagstaff; colorful, deep chasm.

**Painted Desert.** Large area in northeastern part of state; brightly colored mesas and desert pavement.

**Painted Rocks State Historic Park.** Near Gila Bend; prehistoric rock painting.

**Petrified Forest National Park.** Near Holbrook; petrified prehistoric trees.

**Picacho Peak State Park.** Near Picacho; scenic area; landmark visible in any direction for 40 miles (64 kilometers).

**Prescott.** Resort; Territorial Governor's Mansion, built in 1864; Smoki Museum, Indian relics.

**Theodore Roosevelt Dam.** Major dam of Salt River irrigation project.

**Tombstone Courthouse State Historic Park.** In Tombstone; old mining town restored; museum.

**Tubac Presidio State Historic Park.** At Tubac; ruins of old mission.

**Yuma Territorial Prison State Historic Park.** At Yuma; remains of prison opened in 1876; museum.

*All Fact Summary data are based on current government reports.*

# Arizona

### COUNTIES

Apache, 69,423 ... D 2
Cochise, 117,755 ... C 4
Coconino, 116,320 ... B 2
Gila, 51,335 ... C 3
Graham, 33,489 ... C 3
Greenlee, 8,547 ... D 3
La Paz, 19,715 ... A 3
Maricopa, 3,072,149 ... B 3
Mohave, 155,032 ... A 2
Navajo, 97,470 ... C 2
Pima, 843,746 ... B 3
Pinal, 179,727 ... C 3
Santa Cruz, 38,381 ... C 4
Yavapai, 167,517 ... B 2
Yuma, 160,026 ... A 3

### CITIES AND TOWNS

Aguila ... B 3
Ajo, 3,705 ... B 3
Alpine ... D 3
Arlington ... B 3
Ash Fork ... B 2
Avondale, 35,883 ... B 3
Bagdad, 1,578 ... B 2
Bapchule ... C 3
Bellemont ... C 2
Benson, 4,711 ... C 4
Bisbee, 6,090 ... D 4
Bouse ... B 3
Bowie ... D 3
Buckeye, 6,537 ... B 3
Bullhead City–Riviera, 33,769 ... A 2
Bylas ... C 3
Camp Verde 9,451 ... C 2
Casa Grande, 25,224 ... B 3
Cave Creek, 3,728 ... B 3
Central Heights–Midland City, 2,694 ... C 3
Chambers ... D 2
Chandler, 176,581 ... C 3
Chinle, 5,366 ... D 1
Chino Valley, 7,835 ... B 2
Chloride ... A 2
Clarkdale, 3,422 ... B 2
Clay Springs ... C 2
Claypool, 1,794 ... C 3
Clifton, 2,596 ... D 3
Colorado Riv. Ind. Res. ... A 3
Concho ... D 2
Congress ... B 2
Coolidge, 7,786 ... C 3
Cornfields ... D 2
Cornville, 3,335 ... B 2
Cottonwood, 9,179 ... C 2
Davis Dam ... A 2
Douglas, 14,312 ... D 4
Duncan, 812 ... D 3
Eagar, 4,033 ... D 2
El Mirage, 7,609 ... B 3
Elfrida ... D 4
Eloy, 10,375 ... C 3
Flagstaff, 52,894 ... C 2
Florence, 17,054 ... C 3
Fort Apache ... C 3
Fort Apache Ind. Res. ... C 2
Fort Defiance, 4,061 ... D 2
Fort McDowell Ind. Res. ... C 3
Fort Thomas ... D 3
Fredonia, 1,036 ... B 1
Ganado, 1,505 ... D 2
Gila Bend, 1,980 ... B 3
Gila Bend Ind. Res. ... B 3
Gila River Ind. Res. ... B 3
Gilbert, 109,697 ... C 3
Glendale, 218,812 ... B 3
Globe, 7,486 ... C 3
Grand Canyon, 1,460 ... B 1
Green Valley, 17,283 ... C 4
Gu Achi ... B 3
Happy Jack ... C 2
Hayden, 892 ... C 3
Heber-Overgaard, 2,722 ... C 2
Holbrook, 4,917 ... C 2
Hopi Ind. Res. ... C 1
Hotevilla, 767 ... C 2
Houck, 1,087 ... D 2
Huachuca City, 1,751 ... C 4
Hualapai Ind. Res. ... B 2
Humboldt ... B 2
Joseph City ... C 2
Kaibab Ind. Res. ... B 1
Kayenta, 4,922 ... C 1
Keams Canyon, 260 ... C 2
Kearny, 2,249 ... C 3
Kingman, 20,069 ... B 2
Klagetoh ... D 2
Klondyke ... C 3
Lake Havasu City, 41,938 ... A 2
Lakeside ... C 2
Littlefield ... B 1
Lupton ... D 2
Mammoth, 1,762 ... C 3
Marana, 13,556 ... C 3
Maricopa Ind. Res. ... B 3
Maverick ... D 3
Mayer, 1,408 ... B 2
McNary, 349 ... D 2
Mesa, 396,375 ... C 3
Miami, 1,936 ... C 3
Morenci, 1,879 ... D 3
Naco, 833 ... D 4
Navajo Ind. Res. ... C–D 1
Nelson ... B 2
Nogales, 20,878 ... C 4
North Rim ... C 1
Oracle, 3,563 ... C 3
Oraibi ... C 2
Page, 6,809 ... C 1
Papago Ind. Res. ... B 3
Parker, 3,140 ... A 2
Patagonia, 881 ... C 4
Payson, 13,620 ... C 2
Peach Springs, 600 ... B 2
Peoria, 108,364 ... B 3
Phoenix (cap.), 1,321,045 ... B 3
Phoenix—Meza (met. area), 3,251,876 . B 3
Picacho ... C 3
Pima, 1,989 ... D 3
Pinetop-Lakeside, 3,582 ... C 2
Plantsite ... D 3
Polacca ... C 2
Prescott, 33,938 ... B 2
Quartzsite, 3,354 ... A 3
Queen Creek, 4,316 ... C 3
Quijotoa ... B 3
Roll ... A 3
Sacaton, 1,584 ... C 3
Safford, 9,232 ... D 3
Sahuarita, 3,242 ... C 4
St. David, 1,744 ... C 4
St. Johns, 3,269 ... D 2
St. Michaels, 1,295 ... D 2
Salome, 1,690 ... B 3
San Carlos, 3,716 ... C 3
San Carlos Ind. Res. ... C 3
Sanders ... D 2
San Manuel, 4,375 ... C 3
San Xavier Ind. Res. ... C 4
Scottsdale, 202,705 ... C 3
Sedona, 10,192 ... C 2
Seligman, 456 ... B 2
Sells, 2,799 ... C 4
Show Low, 7,695 ... D 2
Shungopavy (Shongopovi), 632 ... C 2
Sierra Vista, 37,775 ... C 4
Silver Bell ... C 3
Skull Valley ... B 2
Snowflake, 4,460 ... C 2
Solomon ... D 3
Somerton, 7,266 ... A 3
South Tucson, 5,490 ... C 3
Springerville, 1,972 ... D 2
Sun City, 38,309 ... B 3
Superior, 3,254 ... C 3
Tacna, 555 ... B 3
Tanque Verde, 16,195 ... C 3
Taylor, 3,176 ... C 2
Tempe, 158,625 ... B 3
Thatcher, 4,022 ... D 3
Tolleson, 4,974 ... B 3
Tombstone, 1,504 ... C 4
Tonopah ... B 3
Topawa ... C 4
Topock ... A 2
Tubac, 949 ... C 4
Tuba City, 8,225 ... C 1
Tucson, 486,699 ... C 3
Tucson (met. area), 843,746 ... C 3
Wellton, 1,829 ... A 3
Wenden, 556 ... B 3
West Yuma ... A 3
Whiteriver, 5,220 ... C 3
Wickenburg, 5,082 ... B 3
Willcox, 3,733 ... D 3
Williams, 2,842 ... B 2
Window Rock, 3,059 ... D 2
Winkelman, 443 ... C 3
Winslow, 9,520 ... C 2
Wittmann ... B 3
Yarnell, 645 ... B 2
Young ... C 2
Yuma, 77,515 ... A 3
Yuma Proving Ground ... A 3

### OTHER FEATURES

Agua Fria (riv.) ... B 3
Alamo (lake) ... D 2
Black (mesa) ... C 1
Black (mts.) ... A 2
Canyon de Chelly Nat'l Mon. ... D 1
Casa Grande Nat'l Mon. ... C 3
Chinle Wash (stream) ... C 1
Chino (valley) ... B 2
Chiricahua Nat'l Mon. ... D 4
Colorado (plat.) ... B 1
Colorado (riv.) ... A 3
Coolidge (dam) ... C 3
Coronado Nat'l Mem. ... C 4
Davis (dam) ... A 2
Fort Bowie Nat'l Hist. Site ... D 3
Gila (riv.) ... B 3
Gila Bend (mts.) ... B 3
Glen Canyon (dam) ... C 1
Graham (mt.) ... D 3
Grand Canyon Nat'l Park ... B 1
Havasu (lake) ... A 2
Hoover (dam) ... A 1
Hualapai (peak) ... B 2
Hubbell Trading Post Nat'l Hist. Site ... D 2
Humphreys (peak) ... C 2
Imperial (res.) ... A 3
Kaibab (plat.) ... B 1
L. Mead Nat'l Rec. Area ... A 1
Little Colorado (riv.) ... C 1
Mazatzal (peak) ... C 2
Mead (lake) ... A 1
Meteor Crater ... C 2
Mogollon (plat.) ... C 2
Mogollon Rim (cliff) ... C 2
Mohave (lake) ... A 2
Montezuma Castle Nat'l Mon. ... C 2
Navajo Nat'l Mon. ... C 1
Organ Pipe Cactus Nat'l Mon. ... B 3
Painted (desert) ... C 1
Painted Desert Section (park) ... C 2
Painted Rock (dam) ... B 3
Parker (dam) ... A 2
Pastora (peak) ... D 1
Petrified Forest Nat'l Park ... D 2
Pictograph Rocks ... B 3
Pipe Spring Nat'l Mon. ... B 1
Powell (lake) ... C 1
Saguaro Nat'l Mon. ... C 3
Salt (riv.) ... C 3
San Carlos (lake) ... C 3
San Pedro (riv.) ... C 3
Santa Cruz (riv.) ... C 3
Sulphur Spring (valley) ... D 4
Sunset Crater Nat'l Mon. ... C 2
Theodore Roosevelt (dam) ... C 3
Theodore Roosevelt (lake) ... C 3
Tonto Nat'l Mon. ... C 3
Tumacacori Nat'l Mon. ... C 2
Tuzigoot Nat'l Mon. ... C 2
Verde (riv.) ... C 2
Virgin (riv.) ... A 1
Walnut Canyon Nat'l Mon. ... C 2
Wupatki Nat'l Mon. ... C 2

2000 census information is unavailable for cities listed without population figures.

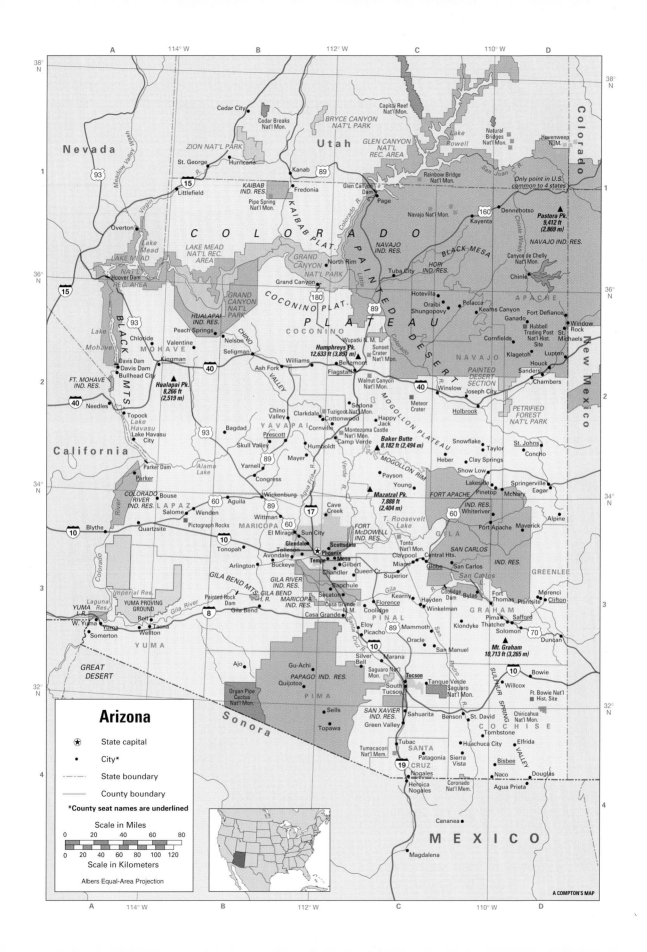

Tom Coker—SuperStock

**Farmland, such as this acreage near Fayetteville, provides a rustic picture of the recent history of Arkansas. Since the 1960s agriculture has given way to industry as the mainstay of the economy.**

# ARKANSAS

In pioneer days Arkansas was known as the Bear State. Then the Native Americans who first farmed and hunted the land were driven westward, and the sloths (packs) of brown bears began to disappear too—along with the once-abundant bison, panthers, and wolves. Now numerous bears again roam the forested hills of Arkansas and leave their tracks in the mountain snow. Wildlife is plentiful, and Arkansas claims to lead the states in fishable lakes and streams. Scenic attractions—the Ozark Mountains, hot mineral springs, limestone caverns, and the only diamond mine open to the public in North America—have made the state a family vacationland.

Arkansas has two national forests—Ouachita and Ozark. The original Ouachita tract has been greatly expanded since its boundaries were defined in 1907. Quick-growing shortleaf pine predominates in the area of the former Arkansas National Forest. The somewhat smaller Ozark National Forest, which was created in 1908 in northwest Arkansas, has pine and hardwood. The forests of Arkansas have made lumber and wood products and pulpwood and paper some of the state's leading industries. More vital are the farms of the Mississippi Floodplain and the Gulf Coastal Plain.

. . . . . . . . . . . . . . . . . . . . . . . . . . . . . . . . . . . . . . . .

*This article was critically reviewed and updated by the staff of the Arkansas Department of Economic Developement.*

A mild climate, long growing season, fertile soil, and ample rainfall helped make Arkansas a place where most people were close to the land in the past. Its small homesteads and large plantations created a major agricultural region soon after it became a state in 1836. But the modernization of farming methods has gradually released laborers from the soil. Now the number of Arkansas workers in manufacturing surpasses the national average, and that industry accounts for one third of the state's gross product.

In a roundabout way Arkansas was named for a Siouan-speaking people who left their allied tribes to journey south on the Mississippi River. They were known as the *Ugakhpa,* or *Quapaw,* meaning "those going downstream or with the current." The state General Assembly officially subtitled Arkansas the Wonder State in 1923 to reflect its wealth of resources. Thirty years later the state legislature adopted the nickname Land of Opportunity "because of the future outlook for the development of business, industry, and agriculture." In 1989 the official nickname was changed to The Natural State to reflect the state's natural beauty and vast resources. In addition to the nickname Bear State, during the frontier era Arkansas was known as the Bowie State due to the heavy use of bowie knives for hunting there. Other nicknames were the Toothpick State (an allusion to the knives), the Hot Water State (for its hot springs), and the Guinea Pig

## State Symbols

A COMPTON'S MAP

**FLAG.** In 1913 the Arkansas state legislature approved a flag design that had been chosen from among 65 others by a state commission. The flag consists of a red field with a large white diamond bordered with blue in the center, signifying that Arkansas is the only state in which diamonds are found. The blue border bears 25 stars to symbolize the state's order of admission to the Union. The name of the state is in the middle of the diamond and is surrounded by four stars, one above and three below the name. The three stars below represent France, Spain, and the United States, the three nations that have ruled Arkansas. The fourth star was added by law in 1923 to commemorate the state's association with the Confederacy.

**SEAL.** On Arkansas' state seal, adopted in its present form in 1907, can be found symbols utilized by other states. At the bottom of the seal is an eagle holding in its beak a scroll that says "Regnat Populus" (The People Rule), the state motto. In front of the eagle is a shield like that of Pennsylvania's, divided into three parts. The figure of Liberty, as on North Carolina's seal, holds a pole and liberty cap. An angel on the left is inscribed "Mercy," while a sword on the right reads "Justice."

**GEM.** Diamond.

**INSECT.** Honeybee.

**MAMMAL.** White-tail Deer.

**MINERAL.** Quartz Crystal.

**ROCK.** Bauxite.

**TREE:** Pine

**FLOWER:** Apple Blossom

**BIRD:** Mockingbird

## Facts About Arkansas

**Nickname.** The Natural State.

**Motto.** Regnat Populus (The People Rule).

**Song.** 'Arkansas', words and music by Eva Ware Barnett.

**Entered the Union.** June 15, 1836, as the 25th state.

**Capital.** Little Rock.

**Population** (2000 census). 2,673,400—rank, 33rd state. Persons per square mile, 51.3 (persons per square kilometer, 19.8)—rank, 34th state.

**Extent.** Area, 53,182 square miles (137,742 square kilometers), including 1,107 square miles (2,867 square kilometers) of water surface (27th state in size).

**Elevation.** Highest, Mount Magazine, 2,753 feet (839 meters), southeast of Paris; lowest, Ouachita River at south boundary, 55 feet (17 meters); average, 650 feet (198 meters).

**Geographic Center.** 12 miles (19 kilometers) northwest of Little Rock.

**Temperature.** Extremes—lowest, –29° F (–34° C), Pond, Feb. 13, 1905; highest, 120° F (49° C), Ozark, Aug. 10, 1936. Averages at Little Rock—January, 41.8° F (5.4° C); July, 81.9° F (27.7° C); annual, 62.4° F (16.9° C). Averages at Texarkana—January, 41.9° F (5.5° C); July, 80.8° F (27.1° C); annual, 61.5° F (16.4° C).

**Precipitation.** At Little Rock—annual average, 49.49 inches (1,257 millimeters). At Texarkana—annual average, 48.24 inches (1,225 millimeters).

**Land Use.** Crops, 30%; pasture, 6%; forest, 55%; other, 9%.

*(See also ARKANSAS FACT SUMMARY.)*

**The present State Capitol, completed in 1915, was the third government center to be built in Little Rock, which also served as a territorial capital before Arkansas became a state.**
Carlos Elmer—SuperStock

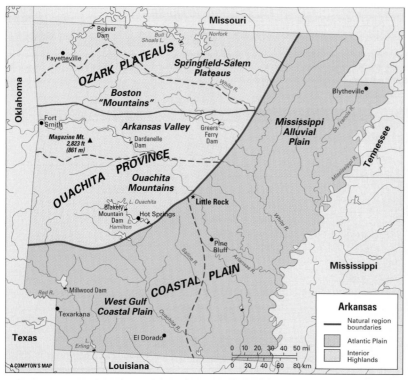

*The Goat Trail is a narrow path high on a sheer cliff overlooking the Buffalo National River. The river runs through Buffalo River State Park, which covers 1,735 acres. The park and river together offer fishing, swimming, and other recreation.*

Courtesy of the Arkansas Department of Parks & Tourism; photo, A.C. Haralson

State (for its willingness to be used as a proving ground for government experiments in agriculture during the 1930s).

## Survey of the Natural State

Arkansas lies in the south-central part of the United States. It is bounded on the north by Missouri, on the west by Oklahoma, on the southwest by Texas, and on the south by Louisiana. On the east the Mississippi River separates it from Mississippi and Tennessee.

The state's greatest length, from east to west, is 275 miles (443 kilometers). Its greatest width, from north to south, is 245 miles (394 kilometers). The total area of Arkansas is 53,182 square miles (137,742 square kilometers). This includes 1,107 square miles (2,867 square kilometers) of inland water surface.

## Natural Regions

Arkansas is divided into two contrasting geographic divisions by a line running from Randolph County, in the northeast, to Sevier County, in the southwest. North and west of this line are the interior highlands containing three distinct natural regions. To the south and east are two different types of plains.

The highest point in the state is Mount Magazine with an elevation of 2,753 feet (839 meters) above sea level. The tallest mountain from the Mississippi River to the Rockies, it is in the Ouachita Mountains, southeast of Paris, the seat of Logan County. The lowest point in the state is about 55 feet (17 meters), located in the southeast where the Ouachita River crosses the Arkansas-Louisiana line.

**The Ozark Plateaus** rise in the northwestern part of Arkansas. Their tree-covered highlands extend north into Missouri and west into Oklahoma (*see* Ozark Mountains). The Boston Mountains in the south of the region overlook the Arkansas Valley. These mountains are the most rugged part of the Ozarks.

**The Arkansas Valley** is a trough between the Ozark Plateaus and the Ouachita Province. It was formed by the Arkansas River (*see* Arkansas River). The average width of the valley is about 40 miles (60 kilometers). Near Little Rock it merges with the eastern plains.

**The Ouachita Province.** The Ouachita Mountains rise in narrow east-west ridges south of the Arkansas Valley. This rugged range of the Ozark Plateaus extend from the Oklahoma border eastward to near Little Rock. These highlands are covered with pine trees.

**The Mississippi Alluvial Plain** extends inland from the river to cover all the eastern part of the state. It is a fertile, flat land that is broken only by narrow Crowley's Ridge. Rising about 200 feet (60 meters) above the surrounding delta, this series of small hills runs from Clay County south into Phillips County.

**The West Gulf Coastal Plain** covers the southwestern corner of the state. It is slightly higher than the Mississippi Alluvial Plain and is heavily forested. This plain extends south to the Gulf of Mexico.

All the rivers of Arkansas flow to the south and east and are part of the Mississippi system. The Arkansas River divides the state almost in half. Between the Arkansas and the Mississippi in the north are the White and St. Francis rivers. South of the Arkansas are the Red, the Ouachita, and the Saline.

## Climate

Throughout the state the climate is generally mild. The southeast lowlands have a near-tropical climate with long, hot summers and short winters. The northwest highlands are cooler in both summer and winter.

Each year Arkansas receives enough precipitation to grow all types of crops. Polk County has about 54 inches (137 centimeters) of rainfall; the region east of Fort Smith, 44 inches (112 centimeters). The growing season varies from 240 days a year in Pulaski County to 180 days in the northwest.

## Natural Resources

Most of the natural wealth of Arkansas lies in its fertile cropland. Underground are a variety of minerals, with fuels supplying the bulk of the income. Almost half of the state is forested. The chief commercial coniferous trees are loblolly and shortleaf pine, with a mixture of various hardwood species, in the southwest, shortleaf pine and hardwoods in the Ozarks and Ouachitas, and bottomland hardwoods in the east.

The Mississippi River, with an outlet to the Gulf of Mexico, and other navigable waterways provide a low-cost means of transportation. There are more than 500,000 acres (202,000 hectares) of lakes and more than 9,700 miles (15,600 kilometers) of fishable streams in Arkansas. The United States Corps of Engineers has constructed 16 dams, all of which are multipurpose structures.

Water resources in the state are administered by the Soil and Water Conservation Commission. Wildlife is protected by a game and fish commission. A forestry commission and the Department of Parks and Tourism supervise much of the state-owned land.

## People of Arkansas

The early European explorers found the Arkansas region inhabited by several tribes of Native Americans. The Caddo lived in the southwest, the Osage in the north, and the Quapaw, or Arkansas, near the mouth of the Arkansas River. In 1817 Fort Smith was established to keep peace among the groups. Two tribes from east of the Mississippi, the Choctaw and Cherokee, were granted land in the Arkansas region during the early 1800s. By 1840, however, all the major groups of Indians had been forced to leave the state.

In 1820 Arkansas had fewer than 15,000 people. During the next 20 years a land boom increased the population to more than 97,000. The first white settlers came to start small farms. As cotton became important, thousands of settlers from nearby Southern states moved into the area. Many brought their slaves along and established large plantations in the lowlands. As a result Arkansas became a proslavery state.

Arkansas's population growth began to slow down toward the end of the 1800s. Much of this was due to the lack of immigration from abroad. The African American population now makes up more than 15 percent of the total. African Americans predominate in the counties of the Mississippi Delta area.

*Little Rock, the capital and largest city of Arkansas, sits on the Arkansas River at the foothills of the Ouachita Mountains in the central part of the state.*

## Cities

Little Rock, near the center of the state, is the capital and the only city with a population of more than 180,000. It is a transportation, industrial, and commercial center. Across the Arkansas River is North Little Rock, part of the same metropolitan area and the third largest city in the state. (*See also* Little Rock.)

Fort Smith, the second city in size, is the business center of western Arkansas. It stands on the south bank of the Arkansas River at the Oklahoma–Arkansas border. Pine Bluff is also on the Arkansas. It is a lumbering center downstream from Little Rock.

The Fayetteville-Springdale-Rogers metropolitan area in the northwest is one of the fastest growing areas in the country. Hot Springs, the state's chief tourist attraction, is a noted health resort in the west-central part of the state. The principal city in southern Arkansas is El Dorado, the so-called "oil capital" of the state.

## Manufacturing and Services

Manufacturing represents 18.3 percent of statewide employment. The food processing industry is the largest manufacturing employer in the state. Benton and Washington counties are the chief canning areas.

The state's forest resources provide the basis for two other leading industries—lumbering and the manufacture of pulp, paperboard, and paper. Other important manufactures are electrical machinery, transportation equipment and supplies, fabricated metal products, and chemicals and allied products.

# AGRICULTURE, INDUSTRY, AND RESOURCES

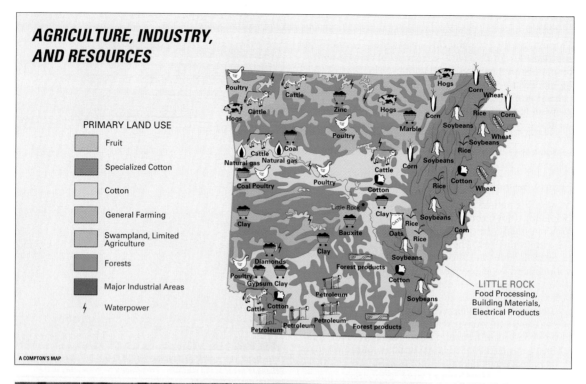

PRIMARY LAND USE

Fruit

Specialized Cotton

Cotton

General Farming

Swampland, Limited Agriculture

Forests

Major Industrial Areas

⚡ Waterpower

LITTLE ROCK
Food Processing,
Building Materials,
Electrical Products

A COMPTON'S MAP

*A poultry farmer in central Arkansas adjusts the feeding and watering system in his chicken barn. The state has become a leading poultry producer since 1960.*
Courtesy of the Arkansas Department of Parks & Tourism

Arkansas's service sector is another fast-growing industry, particularly business services.

## Agriculture

More broilers (chickens for broiling) are produced in Arkansas than in any other state. They are raised principally in the mountainous and hilly areas in the western part of the state. In 1998 the processing of broilers was valued at around 2.14 billion dollars. Arkansas is also a leader in egg and turkey production.

Before the American Civil War Arkansas had many great plantations of a thousand or more acres each. Almost all of these were later broken up into smaller farms. Today the state has fewer than 50,000 farms, with an average size of 318 acres (129 hectares). Only a small percentage of Arkansas workers are engaged in agriculture, and very few people now live in rural areas.

Arkansas is the top producer of rice among the states and accounts for almost half of the nation's rice crop. Soybeans and cotton are also major crops.

*Rice is harvested on a farm in Arkansas. Rice was first planted in the state in 1904 and has since become one of its most valuable agricultural products.*
Photri

Courtesy of the Arkansas Industrial Development Commission; photo, Mark Morgan
*A bromine extraction plant operates in Union County. Bromine use ranges from medicines to photographic film. Industrialization is a major factor in Arkansas's economic development.*

Aquaculture is also important, and Arkansas is a top producer of catfish. Rice, cotton, soybeans, and wheat are found principally in the delta region of eastern Arkansas. The western uplands are the chief source of hay, truck crops, and fruits. Many beef cattle ranches and dairy farms are located there. Corn is grown in most Arkansas counties.

## Mining and Fishing

The most valuable mineral in Arkansas is petroleum, produced chiefly from fields along the mid-southern border. Arkansas is also the leading domestic producer of bromine. Stone, sand and gravel, and natural gas are also significant minerals. Coal is mined chiefly in the west-central part of the state. Near Murfreesboro diamonds have been found in the rock where they were formed. The only other diamonds discovered in the United States have been in glacial drift.

The annual yield of fish caught in the Mississippi River and its tributaries is worth about a half million dollars. Buffalofish rank high in importance. Other valuable commercial catches include catfish, carp, drum, and gar. Arkansas is also well known for the fine sport fishing that is afforded by its many lakes and streams.

## Transportation

Arkansas's many rivers provided the first means of transportation through the state. Barge traffic is still important, particularly on the Mississippi (*see* Mississippi River). On land, Indian trails gradually gave way to wagon roads. A military road was completed in 1828 between Little Rock and Memphis. In 1858 the Southern Overland Mail (Butterfield) stage line was opened through Fort Smith. The State Highway Commission, created in 1913, now manages about 16,100 miles (25,900 kilometers) of state highways.

Railroad construction began in the 1850s but was halted by the American Civil War. The first line to be completed connected Little Rock with Memphis in 1871. Today the state is served by four major railroads and several leading airlines.

## Recreation

The state's chief tourist attractions are its natural scenic beauty and its clean air, well-stocked streams and lakes, rivers, and mountains. The state maintains 51 state parks that range from mountaintop hideaways, such as Queen Wilhelmina State Park, to Crater of Diamonds State Park, the world's only diamond site open to the public.

The largest single attraction in Arkansas is Hot Springs National Park, which offers outdoor recreation

*A high waterfall is one of many natural attractions in Petit Jean State Park, located on the mountain of the same name. The park was established in 1923 with about 3,000 acres.*

*Resort hotels and bathhouses attract visitors to Hot Springs, where the mineral waters are believed to be therapeutic.*

and luxury hotels throughout the year. Another popular resort is Eureka Springs, which is known for its arts community and Victorian architecture.

### Education

During the 1820s missionaries taught both Native American and white children at Dwight Mission in Pope County. A so-called "system of common schools" was established by the state legislature in 1843. The 1868 constitution provided the basis of the modern public education system.

The largest institution of higher learning is the University of Arkansas, at Fayetteville, with campuses at Little Rock, Monticello, and Pine Bluff. The University of Arkansas law schools are located at Fayetteville and Little Rock. The University of Arkansas for Medical Sciences is at Little Rock. There are several other state-supported universities.

### Government and Politics

Arkansas Post was the first territorial capital. In 1821 the new seat of government was moved to Little Rock. This city became the state capital when Arkansas was admitted to the Union in 1836. The state is governed under a constitution adopted in 1874.

The chief executive officer is the governor. Lawmaking is in the hands of the General Assembly, made up of a Senate and a House of Representatives. The Supreme Court heads the judiciary.

The state's most controversial governor was Orval E. Faubus, who served a record six terms (1955–67). He used the National Guard to turn away nine African American students who were trying to desegregate a Little Rock high school in 1957; the next year he closed the public high schools to delay integration. Faubus' successor, Winthrop Rockefeller, was the first post-Reconstruction Republican governor of Arkansas (*see* Rockefeller Family). Another Republican succeeded Democrat William Clinton after his first term (1979–81), but Clinton was consistently reelected thereafter and served as governor until 1993, when he became president of the United States.

Faubus was the unsuccessful National States' Rights party presidential candidate in 1960. In 1968, Alabama's George Wallace of the American Independent party was the first non-Democratic candidate for president to carry Arkansas. In the next election Richard M. Nixon became the first Republican candidate for president to win the state since 1876. Except for the 1976 election, which was won by Democrat Jimmy Carter, and Clinton's election in 1992 and 1996, the state continued to support Republican presidential nominees. Arkansan Hattie Wyatt Caraway became, in 1932, the first woman elected to the United States Senate.

### HISTORY

The Louisiana Purchase of 1803 gave Arkansas its eastern boundary, the Mississippi River. The southern and northern boundaries were fixed when the Arkansas Territory, which became separate, was carved out of the Missouri Territory in 1819. The western boundary was established by an 1825 treaty with the Choctaw Indians and an 1828 treaty with the Cherokee

Courtesy of the Arkansas Department of Parks & Tourism

Courtesy of the Arkansas Department of Parks & Tourism; photo, A.C. Haralson

*"Old Main" has been the administration building of the University of Arkansas, at Fayetteville, for about a century. The structure also serves as a museum of ethnology and natural history.*

*The Stuttgart Agricultural Museum offers exhibits of farming equipment used in the development of the agricultural industry, as well as displays of swamp, prairie, and woodland wildlife.*

Indians, who agreed to leave the territory. The present southwestern boundary was determined in 1874.

The first European to explore the Arkansas region was the Spaniard Hernando de Soto in 1541–42. Two Frenchmen, Marquette and Jolliet, descended the Mississippi as far as the mouth of the Arkansas River in 1673. Another Frenchman, Henri de Tonti, built the first permanent settlement in the present state in 1686. It was Arkansas Post, near the mouth of the Arkansas. (*See also* De Soto; Jolliet; Marquette.)

France ceded the region to Spain in 1762, received it back in 1800, and then sold it to the United States in 1803 (*see* Louisiana Purchase). The future state was part of the Louisiana Territory until 1812, when it was included in the Missouri Territory. Made a separate territory in 1819, Arkansas was admitted to the Union in 1836 as the 25th state—the third state west of the Mississippi, after Louisiana and Missouri. Beginning in 1849 Fort Smith and Van Buren served as outfitting points for wagon trains bound for California.

## Statehood and Secession

Settled largely by slaveholders, Arkansas seceded from the Union when the Civil War broke out in 1861. The most important battle fought in the state was the battle of Pea Ridge (Elkhorn Tavern) in 1862. Both Arkansas Post and Little Rock were captured by federal troops in 1863. (*See also* Civil War, American .)

Arkansas was readmitted to the Union in 1868 after it adopted a constitution that gave the vote to blacks and withheld it from former Confederate soldiers. Hostilities broke out in the Brooks-Baxter War of 1874: the supporters of Elisha Baxter fought the rival backers of Joseph Brooks after a disputed election for the governorship. President Ulysses S. Grant finally declared Baxter to be the lawful governor.

## The Modern State

The present development of Arkansas's natural resources began in 1887 when John C. Banner

discovered bauxite ore near Little Rock. The first natural-gas well in the state was drilled near Fort Smith in 1901. A short-lived search for quick wealth was started in 1906 when John Huddleston found diamonds near Murfreesboro. A new source of wealth was the El Dorado oil field, discovered in 1921.

Lumber production reached a peak in 1909. Most of the land cleared of timber in the Mississippi Delta was turned into fertile fields for cotton. Rice became an increasingly important crop during the 1900s. More recently soybeans have also made great gains.

Between 1940 and 1960 Arkansas's population declined. During the 1950s the state lost about 12,000 residents a year as they looked for work elsewhere. The population increased about 8 percent in the 1960s and 18 percent in the 1970s after a remarkable economic upturn in the state. This economic growth was partly the result of the completion in 1971 of the McClellan-Kerr Arkansas River Navigation System. The project controls the river's regular flooding and provides a navigable waterway for year-round shipment of the region's products. The Arkansas Industrial Development Commission, established in 1955, also helped bring in new manufacturing plants and create new jobs. Arkansas also became a popular tourism and retirement destination.(*See also* United States, "The South"; individual entries in Fact-Index on Arkansas persons, places, products, and events .)

### FURTHER RESOURCES FOR ARKANSAS

**Ashmore, H.S.** Arkansas: A History (Norton, 1984).
**Branscum, Robbie.** Johnny May (Avon, 1976).
**Carpenter, Allan.** Arkansas, rev. ed. (Childrens, 1978).
**Fradin, Dennis.** Arkansas: In Words and Pictures (Childrens, 1980).
**Heinrichs, Ann.** America the Beautiful: Arkansas (Childrens, 1989).
**Tucker, D.M.** Arkansas: A People and Their Reputation (Memphis St. Univ. Press, 1985).
**Writers' Program.** The WPA Guide to 1930s Arkansas (Univ. Press of Kan., 1987).

## Notable Events in Arkansas History

**1541–42.** De Soto explores Arkansas region.

**1673.** Marquette and Jolliet descend Mississippi River to mouth of the Arkansas.

**1682.** La Salle claims Mississippi Valley for France.

**1686.** Henri de Tonti builds Arkansas Post, first permanent settlement in lower Mississippi Valley.

**1717.** John Law takes possession of "Louisiana" territory in "Mississippi Bubble" plan; company collapses in 1721.

**1762.** Arkansas included in area ceded by France to Spain; Spain secretly returns it in 1800.

**1769.** Spain takes possession of Arkansas region, renaming Arkansas Post Fort Charles III.

**1800.** Cotton first grown commercially.

**1803.** Louisiana Purchase makes region part of United States.

**1804.** Ouachita River explored; United States Army takes over Arkansas Post; Louisiana Territory created; includes Arkansas.

**1808.** Osage Indians clash with Cherokee.

**1812.** Arkansas included in new Missouri Territory.

**1817.** Cherokee granted land in western Arkansas.

**1818.** Quapaw cede large area to United States.

**1819.** Congress creates Arkansas Territory; capital, Arkansas Post; governor, James Miller.

**1820.** Homesteaders flock into territory. Choctaw granted land in western Arkansas. *Comet,* first steamboat on Arkansas River, reaches Arkansas Post; *Eagle* arrives at Little Rock in 1822. Little Rock chosen capital; legislature moved in 1821.

**1825.** Choctaw cede land to United States.

**1828.** Cherokee agree to leave territory.

**1836.** Arkansas becomes 25th state, June 15; capital, Little Rock; governor, James S. Conway.

**1849.** Fort Smith, established in 1817, becomes outfitting point for California gold seekers.

**1861.** State troops seize Federal arsenal at Little Rock and Fort Smith. Arkansas secedes from Union.

**1862.** Battle of Pea Ridge (Elkhorn Tavern) is first Civil War battle fought in Arkansas; site dedicated as national military park in 1963.

**1863.** Federals capture Arkansas Post and Little Rock; Washington becomes Confederate state capital.

**1864.** Unionists frame new state constitution.

**1867.** Arkansas put under military rule.

**1868.** Arkansas readmitted to Union.

**1871.** University of Arkansas chartered at Fayetteville.

**1874.** Joseph Brooks ejects Gov. Elisha Baxter from office, beginning Brooks-Baxter War. President Ulysses S. Grant declares Baxter the lawful governor. Present state constitution adopted.

**1887.** Deposits of bauxite discovered near Little Rock.

**1906.** Diamond deposit discovered near Murfreesboro.

**1915.** Present State Capitol completed.

**1927.** Mississippi River floods about one fifth of state.

**1934.** Sharecroppers organize Southern Tenant Farmers' Union.

**1957.** Resistance to school desegregation receives nationwide attention; integration of Little Rock's high schools begins in 1959.

**1964.** Gov. Orval E. Faubus wins unprecedented sixth term.

**1966.** Winthrop Rockefeller becomes first Republican governor since Reconstruction period.

**1971.** McClellan-Kerr Arkansas River Navigation System dedicated; Arkansas and Verdigris rivers in Arkansas and Oklahoma now navigable to Mississippi River.

**1988.** United States government reveals that Pine Bluff Arsenal is producing chemical weapons.

**1992.** Gov. Bill Clinton elected 42nd president of the United States; reelected in 1996.

*The painting 'Discovery of the Mississippi River by Hernando de Soto in 1541', by William H. Powell, shows the Spanish explorer and his party viewing the great river for the first time on May 21, 1541, across from what is now Arkansas.*

The Granger Collection

# Some Notable People of Arkansas

*The people listed below are associated with Arkansas, though some of them may not have been born there. Some prominent people are not included below because they are covered in other articles in* Compton's Encyclopedia *(see Fact-Index).*

**Anthony, Katharine S.** (1877–1965). Writer. Born on Nov. 27, 1877, in Roseville, Ark. She was a biographer whose works, including 'Catherine the Great' (1925), and 'Louisa May Alcott' (1938), focused on the lives of famous women. Her later books included 'Dolly Madison, Her Life and Times' (1949) and 'Susan B. Anthony, Her Personal History and Her Era' (1954).

**Campbell, Glen** (born 1936). Singer. Born on April 22, 1936, in Delight, Ark. He gained recognition in 1967 with his singles 'Gentle on My Mind' and 'By the Time I Get to Phoenix'. In 1975 he released the hit single 'Rhinestone Cowboy', and in 1977 he had another hit with 'Southern Nights'. His albums include *Wichita Lineman* (1968), *That Christmas Feeling* (1968), and *Somethin' 'Bout You Baby I Like* (1980).

**Caraway, Hattie W.** (1878–1950). Political leader. Born on Feb. 1, 1878, near Bakerville, Tenn. She and her husband, Thaddeus Caraway, moved to Arkansas, where he became involved in politics. When he died during his second term as United States senator from Arkansas, Hattie was appointed to his seat. She became the first woman ever elected to the Senate when she won a special election for the rest of the term, and she served for 13 years.

**Dean, Dizzy** (1911–74). Baseball player. Born Jay Hanna Dean on Jan. 16, 1911, in Lucas, Ark. He was nicknamed Dizzy because of his eccentric behavior, including playing practical jokes. He played with the St. Louis Cardinals for a total of eight years beginning in 1930. He and his brother Paul pitched the Cardinals to a world championship in 1934. He was elected to the National Baseball Hall of Fame in 1953.

**Fulbright, J. William** (1905–95). Educator and public official. Born on April 9, 1905, in Sumner, Mo. He joined the faculty at the University of Arkansas law school in 1936 and served as president of the university from 1939 to 1941. In 1942 he was elected to the United States House of Representatives and two years later was sent to the Senate. In 1946 he sponsored the Fulbright Act for funding an educational foreign exchange program.

**Johnson, John H.** (born 1918). Publisher. Born on Jan. 19, 1918, in Arkansas City, Ark. He moved with his mother to Chicago in 1933 and was hired by Supreme Liberty Life Insurance Company three years later. One of his duties there was to gather news concerning African Americans to put in the company newspaper. In 1945 he founded *Ebony* magazine, which became an immediate success. In 1950 the Johnson Publishing Company began publishing *Tan*, and in 1951 it introduced *Jet*. He received the Spingarn Medal in 1966.

**Pike, Albert** (1809–91). Lawyer and soldier. Born on Dec. 29, 1809, in Boston, Mass. He moved to Arkansas and became a teacher in 1833. He was hired by the *Arkansas Advocate* and later became sole owner of the paper. He sold the paper in 1837 and began to practice law. He was a brigadier general in the American Civil War but was released from duty in 1862. He had meanwhile become a Freemason and was elected Sovereign Grand Commander of the Supreme Grand Council in 1859. He was in that position for 32 years during which time he rewrote the rituals of the Freemason order and produced many poems.

**Rose, Uriah** (1834–1913). Jurist. Born on March 5, 1834, in Bradfordsville, Ky. He graduated with a law degree from Transylvania University in 1853 and moved to Arkansas to form a law partnership. He served as president of the Arkansas Bar Association and of the American Bar Association. In 1907 he was appointed as a delegate to the Second Peace Conference at The Hague in The Netherlands. His works include 'The Constitution of the State of Arkansas' (1891) and 'Addresses of Uriah M. Rose' (1914).

**Glen Campbell**    Larry Dale Gordon—Sygma

**John H. Johnson**    Jonathan Kirn—Gamma-Liaison

**Dizzy Dean**    AP/Wide World

**Albert Pike**    The Bettmann Archive

**Hattie W. Caraway**    UPI/Bettmann

# Arkansas Fact Summary

## POPULATION TRENDS

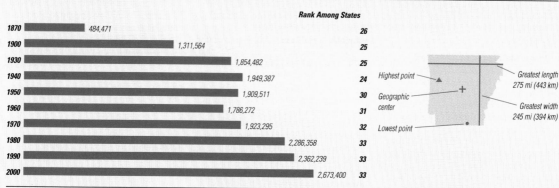

| Year | Population | Rank Among States |
|---|---|---|
| 1870 | 484,471 | 26 |
| 1900 | 1,311,564 | 25 |
| 1930 | 1,854,482 | 25 |
| 1940 | 1,949,387 | 24 |
| 1950 | 1,909,511 | 30 |
| 1960 | 1,786,272 | 31 |
| 1970 | 1,923,295 | 32 |
| 1980 | 2,286,358 | 33 |
| 1990 | 2,362,239 | 33 |
| 2000 | 2,673,400 | 33 |

## THE LAND

Highest point

Geographic center

Lowest point

Greatest length 275 mi (443 km)

Greatest width 245 mi (394 km)

## LARGEST CITIES (2000 census)

**Little Rock** (183,133). State capital; industrial, financial, trade, and transportation center; Old State House; Arkansas Territorial Restoration (see Little Rock).

**Fort Smith** (80,268). Chief industrial city; livestock market; Fort Chaffee.

**North Little Rock** (60,433). Opposite Little Rock on Arkansas River; industrial center; railroad shops.

**Fayetteville** (58,047). Poultry; fruit growing; University of Arkansas.

**Jonesboro** (55,515). Farm area; cotton, rice, soybeans; Arkansas State University.

**Pine Bluff** (55,085). Cotton market; lumber and wood products; stockyards.

**Springdale** (45,798). City in agricultural region; part of Fayetteville metropolitan area.

**Hot Springs** (35,750). Health resort; national park; Lakes Catherine, Hamilton, and Ouachita nearby.

**Jacksonville** (29,916). Industrial city near Little Rock; Little Rock Air Force Base nearby.

**West Memphis** (27,666). Industrial city on Mississippi River; trade center; agriculture.

## VITAL STATISTICS 1998 (per 1,000 population)

**Birthrate.** 14.4 (1999)
**Death Rate.** 6.1
**Marriage Rate.** 15.1
**Divorce Rate.** 10.8

## GOVERNMENT

**Capital.** Little Rock (became territorial capital, 1820; state capital, 1836).

**Statehood.** Became 25th state in the Union on June 15, 1836.

**Constitution.** Adopted 1874; amendment may be passed by majority vote in each house; ratified by majority voting on it in an election.

**Representation in U.S. Congress.** Senate—2. House of Representatives—4. Electoral votes—6.

**General Assembly.** Senators—35; term, 4 years. Representatives—100; term, 2 years.

**Executive Officers.** Governor—term, 4 years; may succeed self. Other officials—lieutenant governor, attorney general, secretary of state, treasurer, auditor, and land commissioner; all elected; terms, 4 years.

**Judiciary.** All justices and judges elected. Supreme Court—7 justices; term, 8 years. Court of Civil Appeals—12 judges; term, 8 years. Chancery, Probate, and Circuit Courts—115 judges; term, 6 years.

**County.** 75 counties.

## MAJOR PRODUCTS

**Agricultural.** Soybeans, rice, cotton and cottonseed, hay, cattle, poultry, eggs, and catfish.

**Manufactured.** Processed foods, electric and electronic equipment, paper, construction, lumber.

**Mined.** Crude petroleum, natural gas, bromine, stone, bauxite, diamonds.

## EDUCATION AND CULTURE

**Universities and Colleges.** Arkansas State University, Jonesboro; University of Arkansas, Fayetteville; University of Arkansas, Little Rock; University of Central Arkansas, Conway.

**Libraries.** Central Arkansas Library, Little Rock; Craighead County and Jonesboro Public Library, Jonesboro; University of Arkansas Libraries, Fayetteville; Mississippi County Library System, Blytheville; North Arkansas Regional Library, Harrison; Ozarks Regional Library, Fayetteville; Pine Bluff and Jefferson County Library System, Pine Bluff.

**Notable Museums.** Museum of Automobiles, Morrilton; Historic Arkansas Museum, Museum of Science and History, Old Statehouse Museum, Little Rock; Old Fort Museum, Fort Smith; Delta Cultural Center, Helena; University of Arkansas Museum, Fayetteville; Shiloh Museum, Springdale; Arkansas Museum of Natural Resources, Smackover.

## EMPLOYMENT Percentage by Industry*

*Total Number of Persons Employed: 1,431,000.*

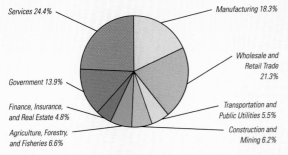

Services 24.4%
Manufacturing 18.3%
Wholesale and Retail Trade 21.3%
Government 13.9%
Finance, Insurance, and Real Estate 4.8%
Agriculture, Forestry, and Fisheries 6.6%
Transportation and Public Utilities 5.5%
Construction and Mining 6.2%

## GROSS STATE PRODUCT Percentage by Industry

*Total GSP: $64,773,000,000. Per Capita Income: $22,257.*

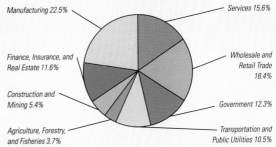

Manufacturing 22.5%
Services 15.6%
Finance, Insurance, and Real Estate 11.6%
Wholesale and Retail Trade 18.4%
Construction and Mining 5.4%
Government 12.3%
Agriculture, Forestry, and Fisheries 3.7%
Transportation and Public Utilities 10.5%

## PLACES OF INTEREST

**Arkansas Post National Memorial.** Near Gillett; site of first permanent European settlement in lower Mississippi Valley.

**Bauxite.** Bauxite (aluminum ore) mines.

**Bella Vista.** Resort in Ozarks near Bentonville; Wonderland, mountain cave; Big Springs.

**Blanchard Springs Caverns.** Near Mountain View; crystalline formations; underground river.

**Confederate State Capitol.** In Washington; State Capitol during American Civil War (1863–65); built in 1833.

**Eureka Springs.** Picturesque health resort on slopes of Ozarks; more than 60 springs in city; antique and craft center.

**Fort Smith National Historic Site.** At Fort Smith; United States military post (1817–71).

**Great Hurricane Cavern.** Near Western Grove; rock formations.

**Hampson Museum.** Near Wilson; artifacts of the prehistoric Indian Mound Builders.

**Herman Davis Museum.** In Manila; honors World War I hero Pvt. Herman Davis.

**Hot Springs National Park.** Adjoins Hot Springs in Ouachita Mountains; 47 mineral hot springs with therapeutic value; bathhouses.

**Jacksonport.** Early settlement on White River; old courthouse converted to museum.

**Magazine Mountain.** Near Paris; state's highest point; in Ozark National Forest.

**Magnet Cove.** Near Malvern; crater of extinct volcano; magnetic ore and other minerals.

**Mammoth Spring.** In Mammoth Spring; one of world's largest springs; 200-million-gallon (760-million-liter) outflow daily.

**Murfreesboro.** Only diamond mine in United States.

**Narrows Dam.** Impounds Lake Greeson on Little Missouri River for power and flood control.

**Norfork Dam.** Forms Norfork Lake on North Fork of White River; fishing.

**Old Davidsonville State Park.** Near Pocahontas; historic community; camping, fishing, picnicking.

**Pea Ridge National Military Park.** Near Rogers; scene of Civil War battle (1862).

**Prairie Grove Battlefield.** At Prairie Grove; scene of Civil War battle (1862); relics of battle scattered about park.

**State Parks.** Total of 39, including Bull Shoals, Crowley's Ridge, Daisy, Devil's Den, Lake Catherine, Lake Charles, Lake Chicot, Lake Dardanelle, Lake Ouachita, Mount Nebo, Petit Jean, Queen Wilhelmina, Withrow Springs.

**Stuttgart.** Rice center of state; rice fields and mills; fishing; annual national duck-calling contest.

**White Oak Lake.** Near Camden; camping; water sports.

**Wolf House.** In Norfork; oldest building in Arkansas—constructed in 1809.

*All Fact Summary data are based on current government reports. Details may not total 100% due to rounding.*

# Arkansas

### COUNTIES

Arkansas, 20,749 D 3
Ashley, 24,209 D 4
Baxter, 38,386 C 1
Benton, 153,406 A 1
Boone, 33,948 B 1
Bradley, 12,600 C 4
Calhoun, 5,744 C 4
Carroll, 25,357 B 1
Chicot, 14,117 D 4
Clark, 23,546 B 3
Clay, 17,609 E 1
Cleburne, 24,046 C 2
Cleveland, 8,571 C 4
Columbia, 25,603 B 4
Conway, 20,336 C 2
Craighead, 82,148 E 2
Crawford, 53,247 A 2
Crittenden, 50,866 E 2
Cross, 19,526 E 2
Dallas, 9,210 C 3
Desha, 15,341 D 4
Drew, 18,723 D 4
Faulkner, 86,014 C 2
Franklin, 17,771 B 2
Fulton, 11,642 D 1
Garland, 88,068 B 3
Grant, 16,464 C 3
Greene, 37,331 E 1
Hempstead, 23,587 B 4
Hot Spring, 30,353 B 3
Howard, 14,300 A 3
Independence, 34,233 D 2
Izard, 13,249 D 1
Jackson, 18,418 D 2
Jefferson, 84,278 C 3
Johnson, 22,781 B 2
Lafayette, 8,559 B 4
Lawrence, 17,774 D 2
Lee, 12,580 E 3
Lincoln, 14,492 D 3
Little River, 13,628 A 4
Logan, 22,486 B 2
Lonoke, 52,828 D 3
Madison, 14,243 B 2
Marion, 16,140 C 1
Miller, 40,443 B 4
Mississippi, 51,979 E 2
Monroe, 10,254 D 3
Montgomery, 9,245 B 3
Nevada, 9,955 B 4
Newton, 8,608 B 2
Ouachita, 28,790 C 4
Perry, 10,209 B 3
Phillips, 26,445 E 3
Pike, 11,303 B 3
Poinsett, 25,614 E 2
Polk, 20,229 A 3
Pope, 54,469 B 2
Prairie, 9,539 D 3
Pulaski, 361,474 C 3
Randolph, 18,195 D 1
St. Francis, 29,329 E 2
Saline, 83,529 C 3
Scott, 10,996 B 3
Searcy, 8,261 C 2
Sebastian, 115,071 A 2
Sevier, 15,757 A 3
Sharp, 17,119 D 1
Stone, 11,499 C 2
Union, 45,629 C 4
Van Buren, 16,192 C 2
Washington, 157,715 A 2
White, 67,165 D 2
Woodruff, 8,741 D 2
Yell, 21,139 B 3

### CITIES AND TOWNS

Alma, 4,160 A 2
Altheimer, 1,192 D 3
Amity, 762 B 3
Arkadelphia, 10,912 B 3
Arkansas City, 589 D 4
Armorel F 2
Ashdown, 4,781 A 4
Ash Flat, 977 D 1
Atkins, 2,878 C 2
Aubrey, 221 E 3
Augusta, 2,665 D 2
Bald Knob, 3,210 D 2
Barling, 4,176 A 2
Batesville, 9,445 D 2
Bauxite, 432 C 3
Bay, 1,800 E 2
Bearden, 1,125 C 4
Beebe, 4,930 D 2
Beirne B 4
Benton, 21,906 C 3
Bentonville, 19,730 A 1
Berryville, 4,433 B 1
Black Rock, 717 D 1
Blytheville, 18,272 F 2
Booneville, 4,117 A 2
Bradford, 800 D 2
Bradley, 563 B 4
Brinkley, 3,940 D 3
Bryant, 9,764 C 3
Cabot, 15,261 C 3
Calico Rock, 991 C 1
Calion, 516 C 4
Camden, 13,154 C 4
Cammack Village, 831 C 3
Caraway, 1,349 E 2
Carlisle, 2,304 D 3
Carthage, 442 C 3
Cave City, 1,946 D 2
Charleston, 2,965 B 2
Clarendon, 1,960 D 3
Clarksville, 7,719 B 2
Clinton, 2,283 C 2
Coal Hill, 1,001 B 2
Conway, 43,167 C 2
Corning, 3,679 E 1
Cotter, 921 C 1
Cotton Plant, 960 D 2
Crawfordsville, 514 E 2
Crossett, 6,097 D 4
Curtis B 3
Damascus, 306 C 2
Danville, 2,392 B 2
Dardanelle, 4,228 B 2
De Queen, 5,765 A 3
De Valls Bluff, 783 D 3
De Witt, 3,552 B 3
Deer B 2
Dermott, 3,292 D 4
Des Arc, 1,933 D 3
Dierks, 1,230 A 3
Doddridge B 4
Dover, 1,329 B 2
Dumas, 5,238 D 4
Earle, 3,036 E 2
El Dorado, 21,530 C 4
Elaine, 865 E 3
England, 2,972 D 3
Ethel D 3
Eudora, 2,819 D 4
Eureka Springs, 2,278 B 1
Evening Shade, 465 D 1
Fayetteville, 58,047 A 1
Fayetteville-Springdale (met. area), 311,121
Fordyce, 4,799 C 4
Foreman, 1,125 A 4
Forrest City, 14,774 E 2
Fort Smith, 80,268 A 2
Fort Smith (met. area), 207,290
Gentry, 2,165 A 1
Gillett, 819 D 3
Glenwood, 1,751 B 3
Gould, 1,305 D 4
Grady, 523 D 3
Gravette, 1,810 A 1
Green Forest, 2,717 B 1
Greenwood, 7,112 A 2
Gregory D 2
Gurdon, 2,276 B 4
Hamburg, 3,039 D 4
Hampton, 1,579 C 4
Hardy, 578 D 1
Harrisburg, 2,192 E 2
Harrison, 12,152 B 1
Hartford, 772 A 2
Hazen, 1,637 D 3
Heber Springs, 6,432 C 2
Helena, 6,323 E 3
Hensley, 150 C 3
Holly Grove, 722 D 3
Hope, 10,616 B 4
Horatio, 997 A 4
Hot Springs, 35,750 B 3
Hoxie, 2,817 D 1
Hughes, 1,867 E 3
Humphrey, 806 D 3
Huntington, 688 A 2
Huntsville, 1,931 B 1
Huttig, 731 C 4
Jacksonville, 29,916 C 3
Jasper, 498 B 1
Jenny Lind A 2
Joiner, 540 E 2
Jones Mill C 3
Jonesboro, 55,515 E 2
Judsonia, 1,982 D 2
Junction City, 721 C 4
Keiser, 808 E 2
Kensett, 1,791 D 2
LaGrange, 122 E 3
Lake City, 1,956 E 2
Lake View, 531 E 3
Lake Village, 2,823 D 4
Lamar, 1,415 B 2
Laneburg B 4
Leachville, 1,981 E 2
Lepanto, 2,133 E 2
Leslie, 482 C 2
Lewisville, 1,285 B 4
Lexa, 331 E 3
Lincoln, 1,752 A 2
Little Rock (cap.), 183,133 C 3
Little Rock A.F.B. C 3
Little Rock–North Little Rock (met. area), 583,845
Lockesburg, 711 A 4
Lonoke, 4,287 D 3
Luxora, 1,317 F 2
Madison, 987 E 2
Magazine, 915 B 2
Magnolia, 10,858 B 4
Malvern, 9,021 C 3
Mammoth Spring, 1,147 D 1
Mandeville B 4
Manila, 3,055 E 2
Mansfield, 1,097 A 2
Marianna, 5,181 E 3
Marion, 8,901 E 2
Marked Tree, 2,800 E 2
Marmaduke, 1,158 E 1
Marshall, 1,313 C 2
Marvell, 1,395 D 3
McCrory, 1,850 D 2
McGehee, 4,570 D 4
McNeil, 662 B 4
Melbourne, 1,673 D 1
Mena, 5,637 A 3
Mineral Springs, 1,264 B 4
Monette, 1,179 E 2
Monticello, 9,146 D 4
Morrilton, 6,550 C 2
Mount Ida, 981 B 3
Mountain Home, 11,012 C 1
Mountain Pine, 772 B 3
Mountain View, 2,876 C 2
Mountainburg, 682 A 2
Mulberry, 1,627 A 2
Murfreesboro, 1,764 B 3
Nashville, 4,878 B 4
Newark, 1,219 D 2
Newport, 7,811 D 2
North Little Rock, 60,433 C 3
North Little Rock–Little Rock (met. area), 583,845
Ola, 1,204 B 2
Osceola, 8,875 E 2
Ozark, 3,525 B 2
Palestine, 741 E 3
Paragould, 22,017 E 1
Paris, 3,707 B 2
Parkin, 1,602 E 2
Perryville, 1,458 C 2
Piggott, 3,894 E 1
Pine Bluff, 55,085 C 3
Pine Bluff (met. area), 84,278
Pine Bluff Arsenal C 3
Plainview, 755 B 3
Pleasant Plains, 267 D 2
Plumerville, 854 C 2
Pocahontas, 6,518 D 1
Portland, 552 D 4
Powhatan, 50 D 1
Prairie Grove, 2,540 A 2
Prescott, 3,686 B 4
Proctor E 2
Rector, 2,017 E 1
Rison, 1,271 C 4
Rogers, 38,829 A 1
Roland C 3
Russellville, 23,682 B 2
St. Paul, 163 B 2
Salem, 1,591 D 1
Searcy, 18,928 D 2
Sheridan, 3,872 C 3
Sherwood, 21,511 C 3
Siloam Springs, 10,843 A 1
Smackover, 2,005 C 4
Sparkman, 586 C 4
Springdale, 45,798 A 1
Springdale-Fayetteville (met. area), 311,121
Stamps, 2,131 B 4
Star City, 2,471 D 4
Stephens, 1,152 B 4
Strong, 651 C 4
Stuttgart, 9,745 D 3
Summers A 2
Swifton, 871 D 2
Taylor, 566 B 4
Texarkana, 26,448 B 4
Texarkana (met. area), 129,749
Thornton, 517 C 4
Trumann, 6,889 E 2
Tuckerman, 1,757 D 2
Turrell, 957 E 2
Tyronza, 918 E 2
Urbana C 4
Van Buren, 18,986 A 2
Waldo, 1,594 B 4
Waldron, 3,508 A 3
Walnut Ridge, 4,925 E 1
Warren, 6,442 C 4
Weiner, 760 E 2
West Helena, 8,689 E 3
West Memphis, 27,666 E 2
Wickes, 675 A 3
Wilmar, 571 D 4
Wilmot, 786 D 4
Wilson, 939 E 2
Woodson, 445 C 3
Wynne, 8,615 E 2
Yellville, 1,312 C 1

### OTHER FEATURES

Arkansas (riv.) D 3
Arkansas Post Nat'l Mem. D 3
Bayou Bartholomew (riv.) H 6
Beaver (lake) D 2
Black (riv.) D 2
Blue (mt.) A 3
Boston (mts.) A 2
Buffalo Nat'l Riv. B 1
Bull Shoals (lake) C 1
Dardanelle (lake) B 2
De Gray (lake) B 3
Erling (lake) B 4
Fort Chaffee B 3
Fort Smith Nat'l Hist. Site B 3
Greers Ferry (lake) C 2
Greeson (lake) B 3
Hot Springs Nat'l Park B 3
Magazine (mt.) B 2
Millwood (lake) A 4
Mississippi (riv.) D 4
Norfolk (lake) C 1
Ouachita (lake) B 3
Ouachita (mts.) A 3
Ouachita (riv.) C 3
Ozark (plat.) A 1
Pea Ridge Nat'l Mil. Park A 1
Red (riv.) A 4
St. Francis (riv.) E 2
Saline (riv.) C 3
Table Rock (lake) B 1
White (riv.) D 3

2000 census population is unavailable for cities listed without population figures.

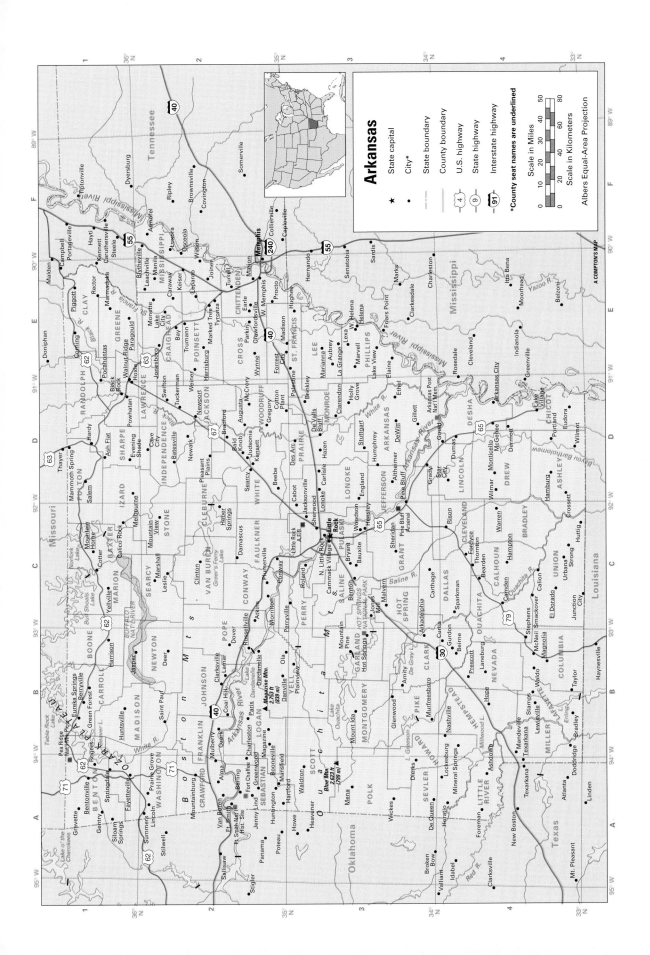

# Arkansas

★ State capital
• City*

- - - State boundary
——— County boundary
⑷ U.S. highway
⑼ State highway
91 Interstate highway

*County seat names are underlined

Scale in Miles
0  10  20  30  40  50

Scale in Kilometers
0  20  40  60  80

Albers Equal-Area Projection

A COMPTON'S MAP

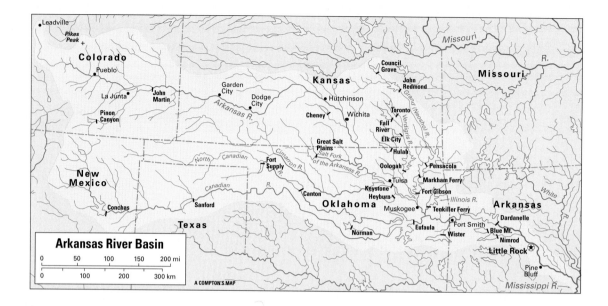

**Arkansas River Basin**

```
0    50    100   150   200 mi
0    100       200      300 km
```
A COMPTON'S MAP

# ARKANSAS RIVER

**ARKANSAS RIVER.** "Pikes Peak or bust!" That was the slogan of thousands of fortune seekers who came to the Colorado region of the United States when gold was discovered there in 1858. In 1806 Zebulon M. Pike, a United States Army officer, had explored the upper part of the Arkansas River. On a side trip he unsuccessfully tried to climb the mountain named for him, Pikes Peak. He then continued to explore the headwaters of the Arkansas.

The Arkansas River rises on the east slope of the Rocky Mountains near Leadville, Colo. It flows generally southeast through Kansas, Oklahoma, and Arkansas. It enters the Mississippi River in Desha County, Ark., about 275 miles (443 kilometers) upstream from New Orleans. The Arkansas is the largest tributary of the Mississippi-Missouri river system. It is 1,450 miles (2,335 kilometers) long. It drains about 160,500 square miles (415,700 square kilometers) in the south-central United States.

Between Canon City and Parkdale, Colo., the Arkansas flows through the Royal Gorge. This scenic canyon is about 10 miles (16 kilometers) long and 1,000 feet (300 meters) deep. As the Arkansas enters southwestern Kansas it flows through a dry plains region once known as desert. Today this irrigated region produces much wheat.

The Grand (Neosho) River joins the Arkansas in Oklahoma. Other tributaries entering the river in northeastern Oklahoma include the Salt Fork, Cimarron, Verdigris, Illinois, and Canadian. Tulsa, an important Oklahoma oil city, is on the Arkansas near the Cimarron fork.

Entering western Arkansas, the river flows between the Boston Mountains on the north and the Ouachita Mountains on the south. The four largest cities in Arkansas are all located on the Arkansas River. These are Little Rock, Fort Smith, North Little Rock, and Pine Bluff. Near its mouth the Arkansas is connected with

the White River by a short cutoff formed as a result of backwater from the Mississippi River.

About 750,000 acres (303,500 hectares) are under irrigation in Kansas and Colorado. Here grain, sugar beets, and fruit are grown. Stock raising is also important in the river valley. Wheat and cotton are grown in Oklahoma, and cotton and rice are cultivated near the mouth of the river. Some local cargo is shipped on the Arkansas and its tributaries.

The Arkansas River's volume of water varies greatly, and serious floods have occurred. To guard against these, levees have been built along much of its lower course. An inland waterway extends on parts of the Arkansas and Verdigris rivers from the Mississippi to Catoosa, Okla. The navigation channel, 436 miles (702 kilometers) long, was completed in 1971, thus creating the first "seaport" in Oklahoma. The many dams used in the construction of the waterway not only aid navigation but also produce hydroelectric power.

**ARKWRIGHT, Richard** (1732–92). The father of the modern industrial factory system was Richard Arkwright. A self-educated man, he invented many machines for mass-producing yarn and was responsible for establishing cotton-cloth manufacture as the leading industry in northern England.

Richard Arkwright was born Dec. 23, 1732, in Preston, England, a seaport town. He was the youngest of 13 children of a poor laboring man. Apprenticed to a barber in Bolton, Arkwright married in 1755. After the death of his first wife, Patience Holt, by whom he had a son, he married Margaret Biggins in 1761. Margaret had a small income, which enabled Arkwright to expand his barbering business. He acquired a secret method for dyeing hair and traveled about the country purchasing human hair for use in the manufacture of wigs. His travels brought him into contact with people who were concerned with weaving and spinning. When the fashion for wearing wigs declined, he looked to mechanical inventions in the field of textiles to make his fortune.

By 1767 a machine for carding cotton had been introduced into England, and James Hargreaves had invented the spinning jenny. These machines called for considerable hand labor, however, and Hargreaves' jenny produced inferior yarn. With the help of a clockmaker, Arkwright constructed a spinning machine that produced a stronger yarn. He then built his first spinning mill.

Arkwright's horse-driven spinning mill at Preston was the first of his many mills. By 1775 he had developed mills in which the whole process of yarn manufacture was carried on by one machine. His system of division of factory labor is still used today. He was also the first to use James Watt's steam engine to power textile machinery, though he used it only to pump water to the millrace of a waterwheel. From the combined use of the steam engine and the machinery, the power loom eventually was developed.

Arkwright's patents were attacked and declared void in 1785, largely as a result of testimony by the clockmaker. His machinery was widely copied by other manufacturers. Arkwright was knighted by George III in 1786. For several years he was able to fix the price of cotton yarn in England, and he was able to leave a large fortune at his death, in Cromford, on Aug. 3, 1792.

**ARMADA, SPANISH.** Beginning on July 21, 1588, a great fleet of ships from Spain engaged English forces in combat in English waters. This was the Invincible Armada, sent by Philip II, king of Spain. The Armada was made up of 130 ships, not more than 50 of them real men-of-war. They carried 30,493 men, of whom 18,973 were soldiers.

Philip II had many reasons for attacking England. In part, his was a religious war against heretics. Mary Stuart, queen of Scotland and the Catholic hope for succession to the throne of England, had been executed. With her died the chance of defeating the Protestant Reformation. Pope Sixtus V urged Philip to the holy war, promising him financial aid.

Another reason for Philip's wrath was that English pirates, chartered by Queen Elizabeth I, had challenged Spain's dominions. English privateers captured Spanish ships carrying treasure from the New World and from Africa. This booty made up a large part of England's Royal Treasury. A climax was reached when Francis Drake sailed around the world, trading at will in Spanish territory, and was knighted by Elizabeth I on his return.

The original Spanish plan of attack was made by the foremost Spanish seaman of his time, Don Álvaro de Bazan, marquis of Santa Cruz. The plan, which called for an invading force of 556 ships and 94,222 men-at-arms, was spoiled by Drake's raids. Drake entered the harbor of Cádiz with 23 English vessels in April 1587 and destroyed or captured 38 of the Spanish ships that were to make up the Armada. He took still more ships at Cascaes Bay and off Cape St. Vincent, and Philip had to change his strategy.

The new Spanish plan of attack called for fewer ships and men. The land invasion was to be commanded by Alessandro Farnese, duke of Parma, an experienced soldier and head of Philip's occupation army in the Netherlands. Santa Cruz opposed this selection, but his resistance ended with his death in January 1588. The Armada was then placed under the command of Don Alonso Pérez de Guzmán, duke of Medina Sidonia, an inexperienced warrior.

The Armada sailed from Lisbon on May 20, 1588. After putting in at Coruña for repairs, it was sighted in the English Channel on July 19. The English fleet that met it had 197 ships; many were small coastal vessels, so the total tonnage of the two forces was about equal.

The battle was decided by the superior speed and maneuverability of the long, low English ships and by their long-range firepower. The Spanish were accustomed to the Mediterranean style of fighting, which called for ramming and boarding. The English raked the Spaniards with broadsides at long range. In the first engagement, near Eddystone, a Spanish flagship was destroyed and other vessels of the Armada were severely damaged. Other battles were fought off St. Alban's head on July 23 and off the Isle of Wight on July 25. The Armada retreated to Calais. Medina Sidonia sent a message requesting Parma's help. Blockaded, Parma was unable to aid him.

At midnight on July 28 eight fire ships drifted into the harbor of Calais and burst into flames. The Spaniards panicked, cut their anchor cables, and drifted near Gravelines. Attacked again, the Armada fled north, intending to sail around Ireland's west coast and return to Spain. Buffeted by gales, many ships sank or ran aground. In all, 63 Armada ships were lost. Only four had been sunk in battle.

**ARMADILLO.** Native to Central and South America, the armadillo is a piglike creature with bony armor. Jointed plates, which cover the back and sides of the animal, look like the armor worn by medieval knights. They protect the armadillo from attacks by enemies and from thorns and cactus. When danger threatens, some species are able to roll up into tight round balls, with nothing showing but the thick, hard plates on their backs.

The armadillo is a timid creature with very poor eyesight. It depends almost entirely upon its senses of hearing and smell for guidance. It has short legs, but when alarmed it can run with considerable speed. The animal's digging claws enable it to bury itself in an incredibly short time. It makes its burrow in the dry soil of arid regions. By swallowing air to make itself buoyant in water, the armadillo can be a good swimmer. It feeds at night, largely on insects, worms, roots, fruits, and sometimes carrion. Its flesh is occasionally eaten as a delicacy.

Armadillos belong to a group of toothless or nearly toothless animals. They are usually brownish black, marked with yellow above and yellowish white underneath. The female normally bears two to 12 young at a time. They come from a single egg, or ovum, and are all the same sex. The three-, six-, and nine-banded armadillos—belonging to *Tolypeutes, Euphractus,* and *Dasypus* genera, respectively—are named for the number of movable bands in their armor. Species may range in length from about 6 inches (15 centimeters) to 5 feet (1.5 meters).

**ARMENIA.** One of the world's oldest centers of civilization and once the smallest republic of the Soviet Union, Armenia is an independent republic in the Caucasus Mountains.

Armenia covers an area of 11,500 square miles (29,800 square kilometers). It is situated in the southern part of the Caucasus, the region between the Black Sea and the Caspian Sea (*see* Caucasus). Armenia borders on Azerbaijan, Georgia, Turkey, and Iran. Yerevan, near the Turkish border, is the capital and chief city, with a population of about 1.2 million (*see* Yerevan).

The land is a lofty plateau, crossed by mountain ridges and cut by valleys. The highest peak is Mount Aragats, an extinct volcano 13,418 feet (4,090 meters) high. The climate is cool in the highlands and warm in the lowlands.

About 90 percent of the people are ethnic Armenians. The remainder of the population is made up primarily of Azerbaijanis and Russians, with a small number of Kurds, Ukrainians, and other groups. The Armenians belong mainly to the Armenian Apostolic church or the Armenian Catholic church.

The chief agricultural and industrial region is the Araks River valley. Irrigated fields produce wine grapes—the most important crop—figs, olives, pomegranates, cotton, and fruits. In higher altitudes grains, sugar beets, tobacco, potatoes, and hay are grown and cattle, sheep, and goats are pastured. Mineral resources include metal ores.

The development of hydroelectric power transformed ancient Yerevan into a major industrial city. Its chief products are chemicals, clothing, precision instruments, and machinery. Other Armenian industries include food processing and textiles.

**History.** In ancient times Armenia was conquered by Assyria and by Persia, but it continued to be governed by native kings. Following conquest by Alexander the Great, it was ruled by a Greek dynasty.

In AD 300 the Armenian king Tiridates III was converted to Christianity. He at once made Christianity the state religion and took steps to stamp out the old Persian religion, Zoroastrianism. In the 5th century a separate Christian church was established. In 653 Armenia fell to the Arabs, who were spreading their new Islamic religion. Persia took Armenia again in

1502, but the Turks soon wrested most of it from them and brought it into the Ottoman Empire. Both the Persians and the Turks oppressed their Christian subjects. The Armenians began to leave their homeland and scattered over Asia and Africa.

In 1828 Russia took from Persia the region later known as Russian Armenia. In 1878, at the Congress of Berlin that followed the Russo-Turkish War, Russia gained part of Turkish Armenia. Kurds, who had been resettled on Armenian land, massacred thousands of Armenians in 1894, 1895, 1896, and 1909. During World War I the Turkish government systematically began to annihilate the Armenians. Many fled and immigrated to Russia, Syria, Egypt, the Balkans, Western Europe, and the United States.

The Treaty of Sèvres (1920) between Turkey and the victorious Allies recognized the independence of Armenian territories in both the Soviet Union and Turkey. In December 1920, however, the Soviets sent troops to Yerevan and set up a Soviet government over Russian Armenia. In 1922 Russian Armenia became part of the Transcaucasian Soviet Federated Socialist Republic. In 1936 the Armenian Soviet Socialist Republic was made a separate constituent republic of the Soviet Union.

Since 1988 violent ethnic riots and armed demonstrations have been common between Armenians and Azerbaijanis. The unrest followed a vote in 1988 by the Nagorno-Karabakh Autonomous Oblast, which is mostly populated by ethnic Armenians but is part of Azerbaijan, to secede and be united with Armenia. Soviet troops were sent to restore order in the disputed region and in Yerevan. Azerbaijanis blockaded Armenia's rail lines to the region, and fighting continued to break out along the border even though the Supreme Soviet voted to return control of the region to Azerbaijan.

A massive earthquake, measuring 6.9 on the Richter scale, devastated a widespread area near the Turkish border on Dec. 7, 1988. About 25,000 people were killed and more than 500,000 left homeless. The cities of Spitak, Kirovakan, and Leninakan were partially or totally destroyed.

Armenia was one of six republics that boycotted a referendum on March 17, 1991, on continuing the union. Armenia, Georgia, Moldavia, Latvia, Lithuania, and Estonia declared their intention to secede from the Soviet Union, and refused in May to sign a union treaty that would fundamentally change the structure and formal name of the Soviet Union. The union treaty collapsed after the August 1991 attempted coup to oust Soviet leader Mikhail Gorbachev. Armenia declared its sovereignty and its independence in late August, and proclaimed its independence again in September. On Dec. 21, 1991, with ten other former Soviet republics, Armenia joined the Commonwealth of Independent States, which was to be an alliance of fully independent states (*see* Independent States, Commonwealth of). (*See also* Azerbaijan; Union of Soviet Socialist Republics.)

In 1999 there was an attempted coup d'état in which Prime Minister Vazgen Sarkisian and several other officials were killed inside the parliament in Yerevan. The rebel-gunman surrendered the next day. Population (1995 estimate), 3,548,000.

**ARMOR.** As long as men have fought with one another they have doubtless used armor of some kind to protect themselves. Stone-Age men cushioned their bodies against the blows of clubs with layers of furry hides. The primitive Gilbert Islanders used war clubs armed with shark's teeth. The suits of coconut fiber they wore as armor were designed to snag these clubs. Quilted or padded coats have been worn as armor.

The Egyptians wore coats made of layers of woven flax, a light and practical defense. Primitive quilted armor was often reinforced with small plates of hard material, such as bone, horn, horse hoofs, leather, or metal. Such scale armor originated in Asia. Iron scale armor was used by the ancient Persians and Assyrians. Mail, which is formed of interlinked rings of metal, was also worn at least as early as Assyrian times.

The Greeks wore a helmet, a corselet consisting of breastplate and back plate, and greaves, or armor for the shins. These defenses were made of sheet bronze and were fashioned to fit the mold of body and limbs. Another type of corselet was made of scales secured to a leather or quilted foundation. The Greek soldier did not protect his abdomen and thighs because he wanted to keep his movements free. The great round shield of bronze or wood remained his principal defense.

The Roman legionnaire wore armor that was suited for long marches and active movement. His corselet and shoulder defenses were formed of bands of iron. The bands were joined by leather straps so that the whole was flexible and comfortable. Because most of

*A magnificent suit of etched plate armor is detailed in this portrait of Maurice of Saxony, painted by Lucas Cranach the Younger in 1578. The helmet, bottom left, enveloped the head.*

this iron armor has rusted away, knowledge of armor of the Roman Empire is based mainly upon the reliefs carved on Trajan's Column in Rome (AD 114). Here in great wealth of detail appear Roman officers, legionnaires, and the barbarians they fought against. The pictures of barbarians on Trajan's Column show that scale armor and mail were in frequent use.

*In 1480, the valet of Maximilian I rode a completely armored horse (left). Relief from Trajan's Column (right) shows Roman legionnaires, bottom, and barbarians, top, in armor of the period. Scale armor was much used by ancient Oriental warriors.*

*The Japanese suit of armor (left), worn in about 1800, had thousands of small overlapping plates that were held together by laces. The 18th–19th century Indian "coat of a thousand nails" (right) was reinforced with steel plates.*

## Mail and Plate Armor

After the collapse of the Roman Empire, new styles of arms and armor were developed. In the time of Charlemagne, early in the 9th century, the soldiers wore jackets covered with scales of leather or iron. Another early type of medieval armor was composed of iron mail, so closely interlinked that it was proof against dagger, sword, and arrow.

In the 8th century, mail appeared in the equipment of the Norsemen, who were acquainted with objects of Oriental origin. In Europe mail remained the standard defense for more than 400 years, known as the period of mail. With only minor variations it remained the chief protection of knights until late in the 13th century.

Already, however, the use of maces, military flails, and war axes had discouraged the use of yielding materials. By the middle of the 13th century weapons had improved so greatly that one piece of plate armor after another was being added. The first reinforcing plates appeared on the knee, for this was a vulnerable spot to the mounted knight. The knee defenses were extended downward in the form of shin guards, and so the evolution of the complete suit of plate began.

By 1400 suits composed entirely of plate armor were in general use for mounted knights. Such suits weighed about 60 pounds (27 kilograms), practically twice as much as a complete suit of mail. The plate armor was more comfortable, however, as it was supported by the wearer's body at all points. An armored knight on an armored horse could readily trample down foot soldiers. As the weapons of foot soldiers further improved, the knight increased the weight of his armor and lost some of his mobility.

For centuries the typical European infantryman wore a quilted jacket reinforced with pieces of metal, bone, or leather. Armored jackets were used by archers, musketeers, and pikemen during the time that plate armor was worn by their superiors. Such jackets were less costly and far more comfortable than plate armor as they allowed more ease of movement. This type of armor remained in general use long enough to be imported into the New World. Among the items sent from London, England, to Jamestown, Va., in 1622 were brigandines (armored jackets), jacks (coats) of mail, and shirts of mail.

The struggle for superiority between armor and missiles never ceased. Armorers tested the armor against the powerful crossbow bolts and bullets to prove it, and this meant making the plates heavier and heavier if they were to continue to be effective. In the 17th century, reinforced armor became unbearable to wear while marching long distances in quick time, and it was discarded piece by piece. Leather, a favorite material for defensive purposes, reappeared in the 17th century. The soldier's buff coat and heavy boots of that period were then of practically the same defensive value as the ancient armor of furry hides. After this era armor was unused for more than two centuries.

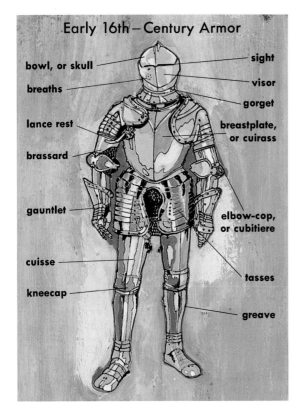

Early 16th – Century Armor

bowl, or skull
breaths
lance rest
brassard
gauntlet
cuisse
kneecap

sight
visor
gorget
breastplate, or cuirass
elbow-cop, or cubitiere
tasses
greave

## Types of Modern Armor

Ancient and medieval armor has been important in the 20th century because it is of practical value in designing modern armor. In both world wars, the steel helmet was as much a standard part of the fighting soldier's equipment as the rifle. These helmets were machine pressed from sheet steel, many of them on punch presses designed for automobile parts. In World War I body armor was experimented with as a means of defense against machine gun fire, and in World War II flak suits were worn by the air forces.

During the Korean War, United States forces were protected by light and flexible body armor that was made of fiberglass, nylon, and heat-treated aluminum. The field vest, weighing only eight pounds (four kilograms), was effective against grenade fragments from an explosion a few feet away.

Bulletproof jackets ordinarily have a lining of overlapping steel disks. The protective devices are either contained in pockets within a synthetic-fiber vest or snapped into a plastic framework. Metal is being replaced by synthetic materials like fiberglass, which make the garment less cumbersome and more bullet resistant.                    Stephen V. Grancsay

**ARMOR PLATE.** Most ships, land vehicles, and airplanes that are used in warfare have thick metal sheets to protect them from enemy fire. These sheets are called armor plate. Some of the earliest forms of armor plate were used in making shields, which warriors carried into battle. Many early shields were made of bronze and later ones of iron. Armor plate is also used on commercial vehicles, especially those used for transporting money and other valuables.

### Ship Armor

A few armored ships were made by Scandinavian shipbuilders in the 11th century. Iron plates protected the ships from ramming, but the weight of the armor slowed the vessels too much to be of great value. During the 19th century, improvements in cannons encouraged the use of armor to protect warships. Early in the American Civil War, the armored ships *Monitor* and *Merrimack* demonstrated its value.

Early armor plate consisted of wrought iron backed by wood. In the 1880s, after more powerful, rifled cannons came into use, compound armor plates of steel backed with iron were used to provide better protection. During the next 20 years, shipbuilders devised new methods of tempering steel plate and developed new alloys, such as nickel steel and nickel-chromium steel. The goal was armor plate that combined softness, so that it would not crack, and toughness, so that it could not be punctured.

As armor-piercing cannons improved, ships were built with increasingly heavier armor plate. Many of the largest ships had armor 18 to 24 inches (46 to 61 centimeters) thick along the hull's waterline.

### Tank Armor

Tanks are the most heavily armored land vehicles. The first tanks, developed by the British during World War I, were armored for protection against machine-gun fire. With the creation of antitank weapons, tank armor was improved and strengthened. However, in tanks, even more than in ships, weight limitations hampered the design of armor plate. Stronger, lighter alloys did not provide enough protection. Therefore, manufacturers designed armored tanks with sloping sides so that shells would be more likely to strike at an angle and then glance off. During World War I, the armor of most tanks measured from ⅜ to ¾ inches (9.5 to 19 millimeters) thick. Tanks from World War II had armor ranging from 2 to 6 inches (5 to 15 centimeters) thick.

Most tank armor is made of heat-treated steel alloys. Other metals used include aluminum, magnesium, and titanium. Nonmetallic materials used as tank armor include plastic laminates, nylon fabrics, and concrete and other stone products. Armor similar to tank armor, but much thinner, protects armored cars and other land vehicles.

### Aircraft Armor

During World War II aircraft armor was used in the bodies of fighter planes and other low-flying aircraft. It was also built into the pilot's seat to protect him from enemy fire from below and behind. To keep planes as light as possible, manufacturers used armor plate made of thin sheets of a steel or aluminum alloy. (*See also* Armor.)                    James R. McDonald

**ARMSTRONG, Edwin H.** (1890–1954). The static-free circuits that make all radio and television broadcasting possible were invented by Edwin H. Armstrong, an American engineer. When he was only 21, he devised the regenerative, or feedback, circuit that not only brought in signals loud enough to be heard across a room but also generated wireless waves.

Edwin Howard Armstrong was born in New York City on Dec. 18, 1890. As a child he was interested in mechanical contraptions. At age 14, having decided to become an inventor, he built a maze of wireless apparatus in the family attic. He attended the Columbia University School of Engineering.

During World War I, while serving in the United States Army Signal Corps, Armstrong invented the superheterodyne circuit. This is a highly selective means of receiving, converting, and greatly amplifying very weak, high-frequency electromagnetic waves. It is the basis for almost all radio, radar, and television reception. In 1933 Armstrong secured the circuit patents that were the basis of the frequency modulation (FM) system. He died in New York City on Jan. 31, 1954. (*See also* Radio.)

**ARMSTRONG, Louis** (1900–71). The prolific trumpeter who became a world ambassador for jazz, Louis Armstrong learned to blow on a bugle in reform school when he was 13. His intuitive genius for improvisation changed the course of jazz, but after the 1940s mugging dominated his performances and he had his greatest success as a pop singer.

Louis Daniel Armstrong—popularly known as Satchmo and Pops—was born on July 4, 1900, in New Orleans, the birthplace of American jazz. His father, Willie, was a day laborer in a turpentine plant, and his mother, Mayann (Mary Ann), worked chiefly as a domestic. His grandparents had been slaves. Dippermouth (his original nickname) picked up small change by singing and dancing with other street urchins in the notorious Storyville district.

After Louis celebrated New Year's Eve by firing a .38 pistol that belonged to one of his "stepfathers," he was sent to the Colored Waifs' Home for Boys in 1913. There he tried several instruments until he found his voice in the cornet, and, though self-taught, he became the leader of the school band.

Armstrong was 18 when he replaced his idol, King Oliver, in Kid Ory's Brownskin Band. A mellophonist taught him how to read music when he joined a Mississippi riverboat band. In 1922 he went to Chicago to play second cornet with Oliver's Creole Jazz Band. His time with Fletcher Henderson's big band in New York City in 1924 expanded his music beyond the traditional New Orleans style. Soon he switched to the trumpet on theater dates because of its brighter sound and flashier look.

The first band built in the image of one personality was the one Armstrong organized in Chicago in 1925. With his phenomenal tone, instrumental range, stamina, and stunning gift for melodic variations, he was able to turn jazz from ensemble music to a solo

art. His Hot Five and Hot Seven recordings were jazz landmarks. He introduced scat on 'Heebie Jeebies', supposedly because he dropped the sheet music. The voice was first used as an instrument on 'Skid-Dat-De-Dat', also the first tune built completely on breaks. With 'Cornet Chop Suey' he had created the stop-time solo break. Another Armstrong innovation was high-register playing in jazz, and his sandpaper voice influenced more conventional jazz singing.

Armstrong's contagious humor and flamboyant style made him an ideal goodwill ambassador for American music. In 1933, during his first European tour, he dedicated a hot trumpet break to King George VI with "This one's for you, Rex!" As his non-jazz audience grew, he appeared frequently on television and made more than 35 film shorts or movies, including 'High Society' and 'Hello Dolly!'.

Satchmo classics include 'West End Blues', 'Weather Bird', 'Tight Like This', 'Hotter than That', and 'S.O.L. Blues'. Among his best-selling records were 'Mack the Knife' and 'C'est si bon'.

The musician had four wives—Daisy Parker, a prostitute (1918); Lil(lian) Hardin, a jazz pianist who gave him some formal musical education (1924); Alpha Smith (1938); and Lucille Wilson, a showgirl (1942). He died July 6, 1971, in New York City.

**ARMSTRONG, Neil** (born 1930). The first man to set foot on the moon was United States astronaut Neil Armstrong. As he stepped onto the moon's dusty surface, he spoke the now famous words, "That's one small step for [a] man, one giant leap for mankind."

Born in Wapakoneta, Ohio, on Aug. 5, 1930, Neil Alden Armstrong knew early in life that he wanted an aviation career. On his 16th birthday he became a licensed pilot; a year later, in 1947, he was a naval air cadet. After studying aeronautical engineering and serving in the Korean War, in 1955 he became a civilian research pilot for the National Advisory Committee for Aeronautics, later known as the National Aeronautics and Space Administration (NASA).

Armstrong joined NASA's space program in 1962. On March 16, 1966, as command pilot of the Gemini 8 spacecraft, he and David R. Scott docked with an unmanned Agena rocket, thus completing the first manual space-docking maneuver.

On July 16, 1969, Armstrong, along with Edwin E. Aldrin, Jr., and Michael Collins, blasted off on the Apollo 11 mission to land men on the moon. On July 20, the "Eagle" lunar landing module, with Armstrong and Aldrin aboard, separated from the command module and, guided manually by Armstrong, touched down. During their 21 hours and 37 minutes on the moon, they collected soil and rock samples, took photographs, and deployed scientific instruments, while millions watched on television. The voyage back to Earth began on July 21, and the trio splashed down in the Pacific on July 24.

Armstrong resigned from NASA in 1971 to become professor of aeronautical engineering at the University of Cincinnati, Ohio. (*See also* Moon; Space Travel.)

Wally McNamee—Woodfin Camp

**ARMY.** An army is an organized, land-based military fighting unit. From the ancient world to modern times, the organization and composition of armies has varied considerably.

The earliest armies consisted of warriors in horse-drawn chariots; of infantry—armed foot soldiers; and of cavalry—armed soldiers on horseback. These units were sometimes accompanied by engineers who operated siege weapons and by supply trains to feed and outfit the fighters.

With the introduction of cannon in the 15th century, artillery units were added to the combat sections of armies. In the 19th and 20th centuries, as a result of great advances in technology, other units were added: signal troops, engineer corps for building bridges and entrenchments, medical units, administrative troops, mechanized units to replace cavalry, transportation and communication units, and explosives and munitions experts. The number of such backup or support units has tended to increase as warfare has become more sophisticated.

Recruitment for armies takes different forms. Soldiers may be volunteers, conscripts, or mercenaries. Volunteers fight willingly, usually for a cause or a country. Conscripts are drafted by their country to serve in its armed forces (*see* Conscription). Mercenaries serve for pay. They are not necessarily citizens of the country they fight for.

The command structure of armies has undergone considerable change in the course of centuries. The earliest armies followed a single leader, either a tribal chief or a king. As nations grew in size and armies became larger, it was necessary to divide command among officers, of whom generals were the highest rank. Officers, some of whom were professional soldiers, normally came from the wealthiest class in a society. They alone had the money to pay soldiers, buy weapons, and supply horses for war.

In the 20th century, with the spread of both demo-cratic and socialist types of government, permanent officer classes based on wealth or heredity have tended to disappear. Except in states that have military dictatorships, the army is kept under the control of elected civilian officials. Officers are promoted from within the ranks or are trained at military schools (*see* Military Education).

Command structures of modern armies vary somewhat. The officer ranking system discussed here is based on that of the United States Army as it has developed since World War II.

All army personnel are ranked according to level, from the lowest level—privates—to the highest level—generals. Above privates there are three levels of officers: noncommissioned officers, warrant officers, and commissioned officers. The difference between noncommissioned officers and commissioned officers is one of training and also of authority. Commissioned officers are graduates of military academies or of officer training schools.

Noncommissioned officers include corporals and sergeants. There are several ranks of sergeants including staff sergeant, master sergeant, and command sergeant major. The duties of these officers vary considerably, depending on the complexity of the makeup of an army. Some are in combat command positions, others in backup units such as maintenance, transportation, or communications. Noncommissioned officers are promoted from within the body of enlisted personnel.

Warrant officers are neither commissioned nor noncommissioned officers, but in rank they are between the two. In the modern army warrant officers are highly trained technical experts who usually operate in one area of specialization throughout their whole military career. Most helicopter pilots, for instance, are warrant officers. They may also operate in an advisory or administrative position, but they do not command troops. Although they remain warrant officers, their pay schedules may rise to that of some commissioned officers.

The levels of commissioned officers are as follows:

1. Line officers, also called company grade officers or junior officers, include second lieutenants, lieutenants, and captains. The highest rank, the captain, is usually in command of a company, a unit of 160 soldiers in the United States Army. A lieutenant commands a platoon, a unit of 38 soldiers. He is assisted by a second lieutenant.

2. Field grade officers, also called senior officers, are majors, lieutenant colonels, and colonels. Colonels command brigades, units of 3,800 soldiers. Lieutenant colonels command battalions, units of 817 soldiers. They are assisted by majors.

3. General officers are the highest ranking officers in an army. They are brigadier general, major general, lieutenant general, and general. Some European armies have as the highest rank the field marshal. The United States has conferred the unique title of general of the armies on a few generals of notable achievement such as John J. Pershing, George C. Marshall, Dwight D. Eisenhower, Douglas MacArthur, Omar Bradley, and Henry H. Arnold. This title is the equivalent of the European field marshal. In terms of rank, major generals are in charge of divisions (18,700 soldiers); lieutenant generals command an army corps (two or more divisions); and generals command a field army (100,000 or more soldiers). The army units named here are based on the modern United States Army and do not coincide exactly with those of other major armies of the world.

In most modern armies the distinction is made between line officers and staff officers. Line officers are those in charge of the purely combatant section of an army. Staff officers are general officers who assist the commander of a military force. The United States, for instance, has a Department of the Army responsible to the president as commander-in-chief. The staff officers plan and coordinate the activities of an army in both peace and war.

The first such officer staff was the General Staff established in Prussia in 1806 by Gen. Gerhard von Scharnhorst. With the unification of Germany in 1871 it became the German General Staff, a highly effective model for all other command systems. By the start of World War I all major armies of the world had command staffs.

Since World War II the staffs of the separate military branches—army, navy, and air force—have been combined into a joint staff arrangement. The United States has a Joint Chiefs of Staff responsible to the secretary of defense and to the president. Other major military powers such as Great Britain, France, and Israel have similar military command structures.

## HISTORY OF ARMIES

### The Ancient World

The first historical evidence of army organization comes from the Middle Eastern Sumerian empire in Babylonia. Figurines from the 4th millennium BC show foot soldiers in copper helmets and heavy cloaks carrying short spears. The Sumerians used wooden chariots; but, with four solid wooden wheels, these were probably too slow to ride into battle.

The army of the Babylonians (2nd millennium BC) included both lifetime soldiers drawn from the highest social class and citizens from the merchant class. The lifetime soldiers received grants of land for their service. They could pass the land on to their sons only if the sons, too, became soldiers. The conscripts may have been rewarded for their service with special trading or fishing privileges.

The Egyptians of the New Kingdom (1560–1085 BC) built up their army in two ways: by recruiting citizens and by enlisting foreign troops. Some of the foreign troops were slaves from conquered lands. In this way Egypt shifted to her subject nations the burden of supplying fighting men. Other foreign fighters were mercenaries paid in land or plunder. The resulting settlements of Nubian, Libyan, and Greek mercenaries in Egypt became so powerful that it was difficult for later pharaohs, or kings, to rule them. From about 945 to 730 BC Egypt was ruled by descendants of Libyan settlers.

The army of Egypt's New Kingdom was divided into infantry and chariot forces. Each light, two-wheeled chariot carried a driver and an archer. Foot soldiers fought with copper or bronze axes, daggers, scimitars, and bows and arrows. In 1320 BC the standing army consisted of two divisions of 2,000 men each. Each division had eight companies of 250 archers and spearmen. Each company had five platoons of 50 men. These soldiers wore helmets and either leather breastplates covered with metal scales or cloth tunics covered with crocodile skin.

Egypt's army was probably strongest under the warlike Pharaoh Ramses II (reigned 1304–1237 BC), who commanded four Egyptian infantry divisions, bands of Nubian archers, and many other mercenaries—a total of 20,000 men.

Four centuries later an Assyrian king, Shalmaneser II, boasted that he could raise an army of 120,000 men. The core of the Assyrian army was the king's bodyguard, a group of highly trained professional soldiers. Every Assyrian landowner could also be drafted. Assyrian sculptures show the king riding out to battle in a chariot surrounded by the Royal Guard. The richest men could afford to have chariots, horses, and attendants. Chariots probably led the attack. The riders had to fire arrows while driving at a gallop.

The Assyrians had the first known cavalry, a force of men on horseback. These men wore coats of iron scales and leather breeches. They either thrust at the enemy with nine-foot spears or shot arrows. Most Assyrian soldiers fought on foot. The foot soldiers were divided into heavily armed troops with pointed helmets, coats of mail (linked metal armor), and metal or wicker shields, and lightly armed troops with helmets and wicker shields. Slingers hurled stones at the enemy with slingshots. Other groups carried six-foot spears and straight swords made of bronze or iron. The favorite weapon of the Assyrians seems to have been the bow and arrow. Baggage animals and

herds of animals to feed the army followed behind the soldiers. (*See also* Babylonia and Assyria.)

While Assyria was a unified empire, Greece was made up of independent city-states, each with its own army. At first the armies were small and made up of free men. Slaves were not used as soldiers because defending the city was considered an honor. All men served as border guards from age 18 to 20. During this time, they learned how to use shield, spear, and sword and to fight in a formation called a phalanx.

A phalanx consisted of eight or more lines of infantry, one behind the other, drawn up across a battlefield. The men stood shoulder to shoulder, and each successive line followed the one in front of it closely. An individual soldier was called a hoplite, from the Greek word for heavy infantry. The lines moved forward at the same time, making a charge a heavy shock to the enemy. As men in the front line fell, those in the next line moved forward to replace them in combat. Fighting in this manner did not require much training, but Greek soldiers in Athens and most city-states did not remain in the army very long. After age 20 they fought only when called upon. Each soldier supported himself and bought his own weapons and supplies. Command of the army did not belong to a king or to one powerful general. Instead, a group of men often commanded together. At the battle of Marathon, in 490 BC, Athens had 11 generals who voted on strategy. Every day a different one of the 11 took charge (*see* Marathon).

In Sparta, the most militaristic Greek city-state, all free male citizens were full-time soldiers. They began training at age seven. At 20, each man joined a company made up of 15 men. Each member of the group had to help pay for the food. The men in the company ate, trained and fought together. Even if they had families, the soldiers lived with their company in a military camp until age 30. Because the soldiers did no other kind of work, the state gave each

*A relief sculpture now in the British Museum depicts an Assyrian battle scene. Foot soldiers and charioteers using swords and bows and arrows are on the attack.*

one some land and slaves to support himself and his family. The Spartans had two kings, one of whom led the army. (*See also* Sparta.)

As the Greek city-states expanded, they had to modify the way they fought. The phalanx was not very flexible. Once it started moving, it was hard to change its direction. An opponent with cavalry or lighter troops could outflank the phalanx and attack it on the sides. To protect their flanks, the Greeks hired professional skirmishers or peltasts. The peltasts carried small round shields, swords, and javelins. They did not fight in formation but moved forward and back with the flow of battle. Gradually the Greek armies became paid professional forces.

Philip II of Macedon did a major army reorganization and created one of the most effective land-based fighting units in history. He changed the structure of the phalanx by making it 16 lines deep instead of eight. A single division of hoplites numbered 4,096— 16 lines of 256 soldiers each. Preceding the hoplites into battle were four lines of 256 *psiloi*, light infantry. Behind the phalanx division were eight lines of 256 peltasts, also light infantry. Cavalry units covered the flanks. Including cavalry, a full division consisted of 8,192 men. Attached to the army were a medical corps and a corps of engineers. This army was inherited by Philip's son, Alexander the Great, and used to conquer a great portion of the Mediterranean world (*see* Alexander the Great).

In the western Mediterranean, somewhat removed from the activities of Greece and Macedon, two other military powers emerged: Carthage and Rome. Both began as city-states and both enlarged themselves into empires. Carthage in North Africa and Rome on the Italian peninsula were close enough to come into conflict over the control of the Mediterranean and adjacent lands. Between 264 and 146 BC they fought three wars that resulted in final victory for Rome.

The army of Carthage, based on the early Greek phalanx, was comprised of mercenaries, yet it had

*The battle formation developed by Macedonian king Philip II and his son, Alexander the Great, improved the phalanx.*

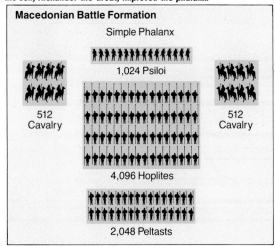

**Macedonian Battle Formation**

Simple Phalanx

1,024 Psiloi

512 Cavalry

512 Cavalry

4,096 Hoplites

2,048 Peltasts

the distinction of nearly annihilating the Roman army during the Second Punic War in 218 to 201 BC. The great Carthaginian general Hannibal was, like Napoleon 2,000 years later, a master strategist who had the ability to select the most favorable terrain for a battle (*see* Hannibal). His successful tactic at the battle of Cannae in 216 BC was to allow his light infantry to fall back before the Roman advance. The Carthaginian cavalry then moved out to the flanks to surround the numerically superior Roman army.

This victory was not followed up for several reasons: Hannibal's lack of naval support, his very long supply lines, and inadequate recruitment policies to obtain more mercenaries. The war ended eventually in a Roman victory. In the Third Punic War from 149 to 146 BC Rome destroyed the city of Carthage and annexed the region as a Roman province.

The history of Rome is basically the history of its highly successful armies. Between the 2nd century BC and the 1st century AD Rome expanded from a city-state to an empire controlling the whole Mediterranean basin. This achievement was the work of its legions (*see* Roman Empire).

The earliest Roman army formation was the phalanx, the formation used by the Greeks, Macedonians, and Carthaginians. For the Romans the phalanx proved to be too unwieldy a unit to fight on hilly and broken ground and they soon began to change the nature of their battle formations. The result was the legion. Unlike the phalanx, the legion was not a static form; it varied greatly over the centuries.

The term legion did not originally mean any specific type of military formation. Its origin probably denoted those who were chosen for military service during the annual public assembly of citizens. As it developed, the legion became a unit of from 4,000 to 6,000 heavy infantry supported by cavalry and light infantry. The term infantry simply means soldiers who fight on foot; the terms light and heavy refer to the kinds and weight of their weapons.

The advantage the legion had over the phalanx was flexibility and mobility. The legion did not have to move in a solid block of men as did the phalanx. The legion was divided into maniples, groups of 120 men, which were able to fight in a much more open and versatile battle array; they marched in lines instead of solid formation.

On the march soldiers carried weapons, armor, cooking gear, and tools. Each day the army would stop and build a camp surrounded by a wall of logs and a deep ditch. With the army went a train of baggage animals, armorers, supply staff, engineers, and secretaries.

From the earliest days of the Republic until the end of the 2nd century BC the armies of Rome were made up of citizens called up for duty each year. Every male citizen between the ages of 17 and 46 was liable for duty. In times of extreme emergency all male citizens could be called up, even the young and the aged. Each class of citizens had to furnish a specific number of companies made up of 100 men. These units

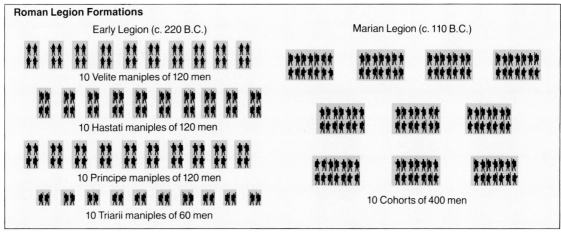

**Roman Legion Formations**

Early Legion (c. 220 B.C.)

10 Velite maniples of 120 men

10 Hastati maniples of 120 men

10 Principe maniples of 120 men

10 Triarii maniples of 60 men

Marian Legion (c. 110 B.C.)

10 Cohorts of 400 men

*The small fighting units of the Romans were more flexible in battle than was the Greek phalanx.*

were called centuries, or hundreds, and they were commanded by officers called centurions. Even after the units of one hundred were abandoned, the term centurion persisted as an officer designation.

Shortly before the end of the 2nd century BC a number of changes were made in the Roman army system that were to change the very nature of Rome itself. Reliance on an annual call-up of citizens meant that Rome never had a permanent army. This practice was abandoned. The citizen army was replaced by a standing army made up of landless city dwellers and newly created citizens from outlying provinces. The allegiance of these new legions was to their commander rather than to the Roman state. The commander was expected to pay his soldiers in money or land supplied by the state.

The leader in this reform of Rome's military system was the general Gaius Marius. He reformed the legion, substituting for the maniple a 600-man unit that was called the cohort. The soldiers swore an oath to him, binding them to service for a period of ten years. This transformation from a temporary citizen army to a professional one made better training possible. It also meant that each Roman commander had his own private army, with legions that were faithful to him for their term of service.

This new army system paved the way for the destruction of the Roman Republic and the establishing of the empire. Army commanders not only went abroad making new conquests and fighting barbarians, but also vied with each other for political control of the Republic. During the 1st century BC, Roman legions often fought each other under the leadership of such generals as Pompey, Julius Caesar, Mark Antony, and Octavian.

In the end, it was Octavian, later called Augustus Caesar, who defeated all his opponents and instituted imperial rule at Rome. Once in power, he revised the army system by cutting the number of legions from 60 to 28, requiring 20 years of service from the soldiers, and setting up a military treasury to pay the armies in the field and in retirement.

Under the empire the main task of the legions was not conquest, but defense. The extensive borders of the empire in Europe, the Middle East, and Africa had to be continually held against domestic insurrection and foreign invasion. Most of the legions were deployed at the outposts of the empire. More and more, the army's manpower was derived from conquered barbarians rather than Roman citizens.

In the 3rd and 4th centuries AD the army was again reorganized, first by the emperor Diocletian, and later by Constantine. The number of men in a legion was cut from 4,500 to 2,000 in order to gain mobility in fighting border wars. Total manpower was raised to 500,000, and discipline was strengthened. Constantine reorganized the legions into border guards and organized a mobile field army for a reserve force.

During the 5th and 6th centuries the western portion of the Roman Empire was overrun by invading barbarians. The center of power shifted to the Eastern, or Byzantine, Empire, with its capital at Constantinople. The Byzantine Empire was able to defend itself with a small, professional army consisting of barbarian mercenaries and landless peasants who volunteered as lifetime soldiers.

In the 7th century the Byzantine Empire reformed the army. It recruited citizens. These men were granted tracts of land to support their families. Over the years, the military families became powerful factions within the empire. The empire also brought the army under government control: the empire was divided into districts, and the viceroy of each district was made head of both the government and the army in his territory.

The emperor assumed the exclusive right to grant any military appointments. Prior to this time each general could reward his own men with promotions, money, and plunder.

The Byzantine army combined infantry and cavalry. Heavy cavalry, called cataphracts, wore iron helmets, shirts of metal scales called hauberks, and iron shoes. Their chief weapon was the bow and arrow, but they also fought with lance and broadsword. They carried no shields because both hands had to be free to shoot arrows. The Byzantine forces had the best medical service that was available in their time. Bearers carried the wounded out of battle to physicians behind the lines. (*See also* Byzantine Empire.)

Little noticed at the time, but of great consequence for the makeup of armies, were some inventions that had originated in Persia and other eastern areas during the time of the Roman Republic. The stirrup, saddle, and horseshoe were devised. Also a new breed of large warhorse was developed. It became possible to mount a cavalryman wearing heavy armor and carrying heavier weapons. These innovations changed the nature of warfare in Europe until after the Middle Ages. Heavy cavalry came to dominate armies to such an extent that the use of foot soldiers became at times negligible.

**The Middle Ages**

The first fighters to make extensive use of the new horse power were the barbarians who invaded and eventually overran the Roman Empire in the West: the Goths, Huns, Vandals, and others. The end of this portion of the empire in the 4th and 5th centuries inaugurated the 1,000-year period called the Middle Ages. During this era, from approximately 476 to 1500, armies were almost continually on the march somewhere. Muslims, Mongols, and European states vied with each other for the control of territory, for trade routes, and for wealth and power. They also sought to spread their respective religions.

The two most effective cavalry forces of the Middle Ages belonged to the Muslims and the Mongols. The Muslims, fanatic followers of the religion of Islam, set out in the 7th and 8th centuries to conquer the world for their faith. They launched jihad, or holy war, against all unbelievers. All able-bodied men were obliged to serve in their armies.

The main Muslim force was the cavalry. The men wore helmets and mail and fought with swords, javelins, bows, daggers, and scimitars. The scimitar is a curved sword made of strong steel. Another vital weapon was the six-foot, pointed lance.

Only after encountering European armies did the Muslims realize that a strong infantry force such as the phalanx or legion was useful in war. For their foot soldiers they hired mercenaries, reserving the privilege of membership in the cavalry for Muslims.

Within 100 years after the death of Muhammad, their founder, in 632, Muslim armies had conquered the whole Middle East, all of North Africa, and Spain. The threat that they posed to Europe was finally turned back in 732 at the battle of Tours in France. They were defeated there by Charles Martel and his Frankish army.

One of the best-trained and most disciplined armies the world has ever seen was that of the Mongols who swept across Asia and into Europe in the 13th century. Led by Genghis Khan, this army was virtually all cavalry, and the quality of their horsemanship was unmatched by any other army.

A Mongol force usually numbered 30,000 men in three *toumans,* or groups of 10,000. Each touman was divided into ten regiments of 1,000 men; each regiment into ten squadrons of 100; and each squadron into ten troops of ten men each. Under leaders like Genghis Khan and his general, Subotai, entire columns could travel great distances separately and reach the same battleground in time to fight.

Part of the Mongols' success was owing to the hardiness of the troops. They needed no supply train. The men could travel ten days while eating only a dried milk paste and drinking blood taken from each man's extra horse. The Mongols fought in a battle line five men deep. The first two lines, with helmets, leather breastplates, and small shields, attacked with

*A parade of ancient Roman cavalry is part of a relief sculpture on the column of Antoninus Pius in Rome.*
By courtesy of the Vatican Museums

*The Mongols do battle with the Turks. Perhaps the best horsemen of the Middle Ages, the Mongols had highly successful armies.*

lances and sabers. They used iron hooks to pull their opponents off their horses. The three back lines threw javelins and shot arrows; they wore no armor. Mongol commanders directed their men with black and white signal flags. Mongol armies conquered a vast empire stretching from China across Russia to the Middle East and Hungary.

At the same period in Western Europe, fighting was the business of mounted knights in armor. For most of the Middle Ages there were no standing armies in Europe. Military service was linked to owning land. Only big landowners could afford horses, armor, and weapons for themselves and their supporters, called men-at-arms. Small landowners became vassals (servants or tenants) of the more powerful. A vassal swore to fight and work for his lord in return for protection. The wealthiest men attracted many vassals and became more and more powerful. Even the wealthiest lords were vassals to a king, but it was difficult for a king to rule these powerful men (*see* Feudalism).

A fully armed medieval knight wore a cylindrical helmet and a suit of mail. He carried a shield and fought with sword and lance. His horse had to be large enough to bear the weight of the armor and the shock of a lance thrust. Many young noblemen practiced horsemanship and the use of weapons from their youth (*see* Armor).

Foot soldiers played no significant role during the Middle Ages. For one thing, they could not wear armor as heavy as that of mounted men, and so did not stand much chance against a charge by knights. Nor was much time spent drilling knights and foot soldiers in fighting together. In battle, foot soldiers were often trampled by the knights on their own side.

Vassals swore to fight for their lords 40 days every year. If a campaign lasted longer, many vassals simply went home. Medieval armies were cumbersome and poorly organized. Command was fragmented because vassals were loyal to their own lord first.

With the rise of strong kings and the development of new weapons like the longbow (a wooden bow from five to six feet long), the medieval army was gradually replaced by more disciplined forces. Kings allowed their vassals to contribute money instead of providing men. A king could then use the money to hire armies of mercenaries. In some states the native populations played no role in military campaigns.

As the Middle Ages were drawing to a close in the 14th and 15th centuries, the supremacy of the foot soldier began to reassert itself. This development was in part the result of improved weaponry that enabled infantry units to defeat cavalry.

In England infantrymen used the longbow, which could shoot a yard-long arrow with great accuracy up to 200 yards. Trained English archers could fire six arrows a minute that could pierce a knight's armor. With the longbow an English army of 11,000 defeated a French army of 60,000 at Crécy, France, in 1346. The longbows drove back the slower-firing French crossbowmen, then shot down the knights' horses. Once the horses fell, it was a simple matter for the English to stab or club the clumsy armored knights. Once the enemy line was broken, the English cavalry charged. (*See also* Hundred Years' War.)

More important even than the longbow in the revival of infantry warfare was the renewed use of the Greek phalanx in modified forms. It was the Swiss who rediscovered the phalanx. Unable, as a citizen army, to afford horses and armor, they contrived, through constant drill and good discipline, to learn how to maneuver and coordinate a mass of men in such a way as to defeat cavalry. The weapon that made this tactic feasible was the 19-foot pike carried by the first four ranks of the phalanx. While the pikemen speared charging horses, the troops behind them ran forward to attack the unhorsed knights.

The Swiss used three phalanxes, one behind the other. This prevented an enemy from outflanking the front lines. It also allowed the front phalanx to fall back into the one behind it for added strength. If surrounded, the Swiss formed a hedgehog, a hollow square with pikes pointing out on every side.

Innovations in weaponry during the late Middle Ages were to change the nature of warfare permanently. Firearms appeared in the late 14th century, and cannon were introduced in the 15th century. These weapons gradually made the pike, crossbow, longbow, and sword obsolete. They also promoted the infantry over the cavalry as a fighting force. Horses made better targets than men, and once the horseman was dismounted he had no advantage over the infantryman. (*See also* Artillery; Firearms.)

Between 1300 and 1648 the feudal system of Europe declined. The many social transformations that occurred significantly altered the makeup of armies (*see*

*At the battle of Crécy, during the Hundred Years' War, the heavily armored French soldiers, left, were no match for the English archers with their lighter weapons.*

Feudalism, "Decline of Feudalism"). The breakdown of the vassal-master relationships forced kings, nobles, and city-state leaders to find other ways of raising armies. England turned to the citizen-soldier concept, while on the Continent the use of mercenaries became the standard method.

In England the practice of hiring foreign mercenaries was stopped by the Magna Carta of 1215. This document, limiting the powers of the monarchy, was imposed on King John by the nobles (*see* Magna Carta). The feudal system of calling up vassals proved unsatisfactory, for it often resulted in an untrained, undisciplined assemblage whose main thought was to get military service over with and go back to family and work. The outcome was that paid military service became the right and duty of all Englishmen. To fill out the army, specific numbers of men were drafted from each county for service in wartime.

On the Continent the decline of feudalism led to the hiring of mercenaries by kings and nobles alike. Even the city-states found it to their advantage to hire armies to fight their wars for them. The advantage of mercenaries over vassals was great: mercenaries were professional soldiers who devoted their whole lives to combat. This, in turn, led to war becoming a more professional and calculated affair on the part of kings and princes.

Groups of professional mercenaries banded together in what were called "free companies" to hire themselves out as units. The two most outstanding types of free companies were the condottieri (contractors) of Italy and the Swiss mercenaries. The condottieri were men who contracted for the services of units of mercenaries, then hired out units to princes for their wars. From the 13th through the 15th centuries, the condottieri and their troops monopolized warfare on the Italian peninsula. Their chief advantage was their professionalism; their main disadvantage was their lack of loyalty to a cause. Since they fought for money, they were frequently willing to change sides for higher pay.

The Swiss provided the best mercenary units in Europe. Their use of the phalanx and pikemen made them the champion fighters on the Continent. Every ruler in Europe wanted Swiss mercenaries in his army. These Swiss Guards, as they were also called, saw action in many wars from the 15th through the 19th centuries. In the 20th century the only remaining vestige of the Guards is the personal bodyguard of the pope in Vatican City. This Vatican Swiss Guard has been in existence since 1505.

In Germany, men called *landsknechts,* who were mercenaries, imitated the Swiss phalanx. After a time they became capable fighters.

Spain was the one state of Europe that did not use free-company fighters. The Spanish armies, among the most powerful of the early modern period, consisted largely of mercenaries from Germany, The Netherlands, and Italy. These mercenaries were led by well-trained Spanish officers who infused them with a spirit of loyalty to Spain and its monarchs.

### Development of Standing Armies

The end of the Middle Ages is generally dated about 1500, but militarily it did not end until the time of the Thirty Years' War, fought from 1618 to 1648. By this time several strong nation-states had developed in Europe, among them France, Sweden, Spain, and the Holy Roman Empire consisting of the German states, Austria, and northern Italy. These monarchies had the manpower for large armies and the money to support them. The emergence of the national standing army comprised of citizen soldiers spelled the gradual decline in the wholesale use of mercenaries and free companies, although the tradition of the mercenary has persisted on a limited scale into the 20th century.

Gustavus II Adolphus (1594–1632), king of Sweden, has been called the father of modern warfare. It was he who forged the first national standing army, one that was to be a model for other states for 150 years. All Swedish males over 15 years of age were drafted for military service. The forces he raised by conscription were augmented by mercenaries.

Gustavus organized the army into companies of 150 men. There were four companies in a battalion and three battalions in a brigade. To fight a battle, he arranged his infantry into regiments, each containing as many as ten companies, with the cavalry in front. The cavalry led the charge, while the infantry came forward behind them, stopping to fire and reload. The front row of the infantry fired from a kneeling position, while the next two fired standing. Prior to starting a battle, the artillery bombarded the enemy. This coordination of artillery, cavalry, and infantry was an innovation devised by Gustavus and soon adopted by other European armies.

To increase the mobility of his armies, Gustavus made improvements in weaponry. His soldiers used lighter muskets that could be loaded faster than previous models. Early muskets took two men to load and fire. The newer muskets were shorter and lighter. The powder charge was measured ahead of time and packed with the ball in a paper cartridge. The soldier had simply to bite off the end of the cartridge and ram the shot down the muzzle. Gustavus made similar improvements in his artillery. Heavy cannons were replaced with lighter ones that one horse could pull. Cannon shot was measured ahead of time. Supplies of powder, cannon balls, and musket shot were stored in depots all over the country so that the army did not have to carry excessive loads of ammunition.

During the Thirty Years' War, Gustavus taxed conquered districts to pay his soldiers. His armies were supplied with uniforms, weapons, food, and housing. His enemies, the armies of the Holy Roman Empire, had to find their own food and shelter in the lands they marched through; hence they lived by plunder and made enemies of local populations.

The first military leader to imitate the work of Gustavus Adolphus was Oliver Cromwell, during the English Civil War in the middle of the 17th century. His army was patterned after the Swedish army, and his only major innovation was the introduction of basic training for his troops (see Cromwell, Oliver).

After Gustavus Adolphus the next outstanding military genius of Europe was Frederick the Great, king of Prussia. He came to the throne in 1740 and ruled for 46 years. The first 23 years of his reign were spent in making Prussia a great military power and in fighting two major wars: the War of the Austrian Succession, from 1740 to 1745, and the Seven Years' War, from 1756 to 1763. Both of these wars were against Austria. Frederick's goal was the annexation of Silesia, a Polish province that had come under Austrian control in the 16th century. Frederick's greatest military strengths lay in enforcing strong discipline and in devising tactics. Frederick's father, Frederick William I, had raised the strength of the Prussian army to 80,000. Frederick increased this number to 140,000, then to 180,000. All young men of the lower classes could be drafted. Sons of the middle classes did not have to serve. Officers came from the class of nobles and wealthy land owners known as Junkers. (See also Frederick the Great; Seven Years' War.)

The Prussian army consisted of infantry, cavalry, and artillery. The foot soldiers carried muskets with bayonets. By constant drilling they learned to load and fire their muskets five times a minute, while other armies could only do so twice a minute. This did not give the soldiers much time to aim, but careful aim did not matter, since the muskets were not accurate at more than 50 yards. Targets were not individual soldiers, but the mass of the enemy line.

The Prussian army formed a line three men deep. The line advanced until it was about 100 yards from the enemy. The soldiers delivered a succession of volleys, then paced forward, reloading as they moved. When they came close to the enemy line, they charged with their bayonets.

On the flanks of the infantry rode the heavy cavalry in close formation. Its charges were carefully coordinated with the advance of the infantry to take advantage of any weakness in the enemy lines.

In his drill formations Frederick inaugurated the tactic of wheeling his line to change direction, thus enabling it to face an attack from a different direction. He also adopted the practice of arranging his line in echelon formation. This meant that a line would not be straight as it advanced, but each soldier, beginning with the second in line, would be at least one step behind the next. It would give the appearance of a diagonal line marching across a battlefield. The advan-

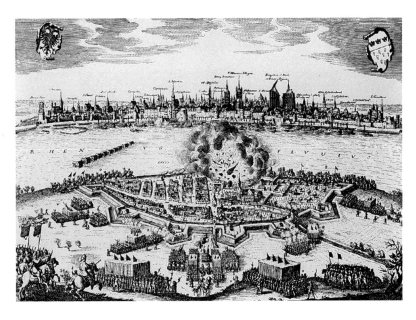

*The Swedish armies (in formation in the foreground) bombard the city of Cologne, Germany, in 1632 during the Thirty Years' War.*

*The second line of infantry fires over the heads of the first line in a battle scene of the Seven Years' War in Germany.*
Historical Pictures Service, Chicago

tage of the echelon formation was that it exposed only one flank of his army.

The methods that Frederick the Great instituted in Prussia were adopted by the armies of Europe and the United States. His drill formations and tactics were used by most armies up through World War I. Modern mechanized warfare with airpower, tanks, and missiles has made them much less useful.

### The French Revolution and Napoleon

What happened in France between the Revolution of 1789 and the defeat of Napoleon at Waterloo in 1815 was of far greater political than military significance. The Revolution began in 1789 as a class war. Within a few years the monarchy had been destroyed and class distinctions had been erased. Each person became a citizen of the reconstructed nation. (*See also* French Revolution.)

The import of what had happened in France was not lost upon the other monarchies of Europe. They saw this social upheaval as a threat to their very existence. The French were in part responsible because they wanted to spread their revolution to the rest of Europe. In response, Prussia and Austria formed a coalition to defeat the revolution and restore the monarchy.

With the monarchy gone, the immediate reaction of the French was to identify defense of the revolution with defense of the nation. For the first time in history, all the loyalties and aspirations of a people were bound up with the fate of their country. Modern patriotism was born: a nation would go to arms to defend itself. A new relationship had been forged between a state and its army, a relationship that has played a vital role in most nations of the 19th and 20th centuries.

France's call to arms in 1793 brought forth more than one million men, the first army of such size in modern times. The revolutionary government decreed that every citizen—young or old, man or woman—was to work for victory against the Austrian-Prussian coalition by making ammunition, providing and moving supplies, and nursing the wounded. War was no longer left to the professionals; the day of the citizen soldier had arrived. To raise its armies, the French used conscription, a practice that soon was to spread to the rest of Europe (*see* Conscription).

Napoleon was the general who welded the French armies into a combat force that defeated the other armies of Europe for 20 years, from 1795 to 1815. His division contained infantry, artillery, and cavalry. He assembled two or three divisions into a corps to make larger units for battle.

Napoleon had two main strategies: he sought out terrain most favorable to his armies to fight on, and he used artillery and masses of men to breach the enemy's weakest point and disrupt its battle plans. His methods were normally direct and simple: use a fast-moving army to breach the enemy lines, then outmaneuver and outflank them. Napoleon was finally defeated at Waterloo, Belgium, because the armies of the Prussians and the English had learned to use some of his own tactics and employed them against him. (*See also* Napoleon I; Waterloo.)

### The 19th Century

In the history of armies, the 19th century covers the period from Napoleon's defeat at Waterloo in July 1915 to the start of World War I in August 1914. The two features that stand out in this period are the great strides in technology and invention and the major organizational changes made in armies.

The Industrial Revolution of the 18th and 19th centuries brought with it improvements in manufacturing such as the assembly line and interchangeable parts (*see* Industrial Revolution). This meant that weapons would be made more rapidly and they could be standardized. The use of steel instead of cast iron or bronze meant that rifles, revolvers, and cannon were of better quality and more durable.

In addition to weaponry, there were a number of other inventions and new processes that had an impact on the way armies fought. The canning and refrigerating of food made feeding armies easier. The invention of the steamship, railroad, telegraph, telephone, light bulb, automobile, airplane, and tank changed warfare markedly between 1815 and the end of World War I by improving transportation, communication, and combat effectiveness.

In terms of organization, few changes were made in European armies and none in the United States Army in the first half of the 19th century. The unification of Germany under Otto von Bismarck in the 1860s made a complete change in the military situation, however. In the next few decades Europe became an armed camp. Every nation of any size instituted conscription and greatly increased the size of its army. Large reserve forces were also built up. Germany, for instance, increased the size of its army from 400,000 to 850,000 and kept a reserve of more than 4 million in the period immediately before World War I. France, Austria, and Russia followed a similar course. The exception was Britain, essentially a naval power until the World War made conscription necessary.

While the nations of Europe were arming themselves and reorganizing their land forces, the greatest conflict of the century was fought across the Atlantic. The American Civil War (also called the War Between the States in the South), fought from 1861 to 1865, has been called the first modern war. It was a gigantic struggle in which more than 617,000 died and at least 375,000 were wounded. The theater of war was 1,500 miles wide from east to west, and 800 miles from north to south. It was the first war in which railroads, telegraph, ironclad ships, torpedoes, and modern breech-loading rifles were used. It was a war in which the industrial might of one side, the North, was able to wear down and defeat a largely agricultural economy, the South. (*See also* Civil War, American.)

The number of soldiers who fought in the war was huge. There were about 2,375,000 in the Union armies of the North and 900,000 in the Southern Confederacy over the course of the war. Most of these men were volunteers, along with a few thousand professional soldiers from the regular army. The commanders on both sides were officers trained at the military academy of West Point. Infantry regiments numbered 1,000 men, and cavalry units were about the same size. Artillery batteries were small in size at the start of the war—usually about six guns—but by the end of the war they had been organized into brigades of five batteries to increase concentration of fire power at key points on the large fronts in most battles.

Two aspects of Civil War battles are notable because they were to become standard procedures in World War I: entrenchment and advance. For the first time in warfare the construction of hasty field fortifications and trenches before battle became customary. When a battle began, the cavalry and infantry of both sides charged forward.

The infantry, as the war dragged on, adopted the tactic of advance by rush: half the men would fire at the enemy while standing still, and the other half ran ahead. Then that half would stop and fire while the others in turn rushed the enemy. Cavalry soldiers of the North usually dismounted to fight, while those of the South remained on horseback.

The size and complexity of the Civil War made it necessary for both the Union and the Confederacy to increase the size of their staff systems. Neither side had a staff like the general staffs of the nations of Europe. In the course of the war there were advances in military engineering because of the need for building bridges, fortifications, and entrenchments.

Other wars were fought between 1815 and 1914: the Crimean War (1854–56), the Franco-Prussian War (1870), the Boer War (1899–1902), the Russo-Japanese War (1904–5), and the Balkan Wars (1912–13). None was of the magnitude of the American Civil War. Yet the military establishments of Europe and Japan were not disposed to learn much from the Americans. The Europeans and the Japanese considered the American Civil War to be a conflict between amateur armies and therefore tended to ignore its tactics. (*See also* Balkan Wars; Boer War; Crimean War; Franco-Prussian War; Russo-Japanese War.)

### World Wars of the 20th Century

The failure of the Europeans to learn from the American Civil War led them to fight the same kind of war in World War I as they always had fought. The armies of Europe, and finally, of the United States, fought for four years, only to end in a stalemate. Nothing was settled despite massive loss of life.

Some of the tactics used were much the same as those used in the American Civil War: principally, the building of fortifications and digging of trenches before charging the enemy with rifle fire, and the falling back to the trenches if no gain was made.

The armies of World War I were the largest put into the field up to that time. The Germans were able to mobilize 2 million men in two days, and within five days about 1 million soldiers were on the march toward France. Austria mobilized 500,000 men, while France started out with 1,600,000; Russia called up an army of 1,400,000; Great Britain, with the only all-volunteer army in Europe, had only 120,000 at the start of the war.

By 1917 the British Army had increased tenfold; the French land forces had been enlarged to 2,600,000; and in 1918 the American Army in France numbered 1,200,000. It was the addition of troops from the United States that made it possible to defeat German forces numbering about 2.5 million.

Army organization for all the belligerents remained the same as it had been throughout the 19th century. They all had similar infantry and cavalry divisions, artillery brigades, engineering companies, supply units, and medical units.

The advances in technology that had been made since the American Civil War were not sufficient to tip the balance either way. Both sides made use of airplanes, tanks, radio, machine guns, and other inventions. The newness of these technologies meant that they had to be adapted to wartime use on a trial-and-error basis. Many inventions were developed for commercial use, such as the telephone, radio, and internal-combustion engine, and were only gradually adapted for use in warfare. It was not until World War II that full advantage was taken of the technologies of mechanized warfare. (*See also* World War I.)

The interwar period, from 1918 to 1939, was marked by a feeling of revulsion to all war on the part of most of the belligerents. The armies of the Allies—France, Britain, and the United States—were all drastically reduced in size. Only Germany differed in these matters. Convinced that their country had been betrayed by its politicians in World War I, the Germans continued to prepare secretly for another conflict. Russia, allied with France against Germany, had been knocked out of the conflict by the Revolution of 1917 and a hastily arranged treaty with the new Communist government.

The gravest mistake made by the former Allies between 1919 and 1939 was the failure of the military to keep up with industrial development and new technologies. The one change that was made was the addition of air force auxiliaries to the several armies (*see* Air Force).

While Germany was secretly modifying its industries for rapid changeover to wartime production, the other nations were convinced a war could not occur again. When war did come in 1939, the Allies had to make very rapid changes in their industrial capacity to meet the German challenge. They also were forced to use conscription.

Civil war in Spain from 1936 to 1939 provided a small-scale dress rehearsal for World War II. Volunteers from other countries went to Spain to fight. Soldiers on leave from Germany and Italy went to fight on the side of Francisco Franco (*see* Franco). Americans, Canadians, Englishmen, and others went to fight for the Spanish republic. Italy and Germany, both dictatorships and both preparing for war, had a chance to try out their new airplanes and tanks as well as other weapons. Tanks were used for frontal attack and airplanes for the strafing of infantry and for bombing missions. (*See also* Spanish Civil War.)

During the early decades of the 20th century a great military power emerged in the Far East. Japan had for some decades been mobilizing all of its industrial and human resources to increase the strength of its armed forces. By 1941, when Japan entered World War II, it had built up an army of about 55 infantry divisions and 35 tank regiments. Its army air force had about 1,600 combat planes.

*The front line of Confederate general P.G.T. Beauregard engages Northern forces at Petersburg, Va.*

World War II, fought from 1939 to 1945, had several characteristics that distinguished it from World War I: the coordination of all services—armies, air forces, and navies—in one common effort; the use of amphibious (combined land–sea operations) warfare; the coordination of tanks and airplanes in initial attacks (a tactic the Germans called blitzkrieg, meaning "lightning warfare"); and the use of radio communications among areas, both in the air and on the ground. It was the first fully mechanized war. The cavalry, which had been part of armies for hundreds of years, was finally obsolete. The term cavalry, however, continued to be used to describe mechanized units.

More combatants were mobilized for World War II than at any previous time. For the major belligerents the total number of fighting men in all services was: Australia, 1,000,000; Canada, 1,041,080; China, 17,250,-521; Germany, 20,000,000; Great Britain, 5,896,000; Italy, 3,100,000; Japan, 9,700,000; the Soviet Union (army only), 12,000,000; the United States, 11,000,000; and Yugoslavia, 3,741,000.

The organization of armies changed very little from the prewar period. Divisions numbered from 11,000 to 15,000 men, depending on national policy. Airborne divisions numbered from 6,000 to 10,000. The major change was in the number of backup and support troops such as engineers, signal troops, supply troops, mechanics, communications experts, and medical personnel. For the first time, women served in uniform in fairly large numbers. They did administrative and communications work and performed many other support functions.

The command structures of the armies remained as they had been before the war, but there were two innovations in the scope of command. For the first time, joint and combined commands were used. Joint commands meant placing all of the armed services of a nation—army, navy, and air force—under a single command in a theater of operations. Combined command involved two or more nations. For example, Gen. Dwight D. Eisenhower of the United States was supreme commander of all Allied forces operating in Europe. (*See also* World War II.)

### Armies in the Nuclear Age

World War II was brought to an end by the dropping of atom bombs on two Japanese cities in the summer of 1945. With the dawn of the atomic, or nuclear, age, military personnel and civilians alike at first believed that the nature of warfare had been changed forever. This did not prove to be the case. All the major nations of the world maintain standing armies, and conventional weapons—albeit highly sophisticated—are still used. Many more or less conventional wars have been fought since 1945, including conflicts in Vietnam, Korea, and the Middle East. (*See also* Iraq; Israel; Korean War; Persian Gulf War; Vietnam War.)

One major factor armies have had to deal with since World War II is guerrilla warfare. The term guerrilla means "little war"; it is a type of warfare characterized by fighting limited actions, often on terrain difficult for a regular army to dominate. Guerrillas use hit-and-run tactics, sabotage, terrorism, and propaganda. They are highly mobile, use unorthodox methods, obtain weapons from any available source, and normally live off the country without regular supply lines. Most of the wars and revolutions since 1945 have involved guerrilla warfare: particularly notable were the Cuban Revolution of 1959, the Vietnam War (1965–75), and the Afghanistan war (1979–89).

### THE ARMY OF THE SOVIET UNION

With 5,081,000 members in the late 1980s, the Soviet Union's Army was second only to China's in size. This huge force was deployed within all the major regions of the Soviet Union itself, as well as in the satellite nations of Eastern Europe.

The Red Army was founded in January 1918, shortly after the Russian Revolution. Conscription was introduced, and by 1936 the Army numbered more than 1.5 million. Between 1936 and 1939 tens of thousands of Army officers were executed in Stalin's political purges. Following this disaster the Army was reorganized by Marshall K.E. Voroshilov and proved itself a worthy instrument in the defeat of Germany in World War II.

Following the war more reorganization was undertaken, and the name Red Army was replaced by Soviet Army. Command was placed under the Ministry of Defense headed by a civilian official. The Ministry was responsible to the Presidium of the Supreme Soviet, which was the governing body of the Soviet Union. Each branch of the armed services had its own military commander-in-chief. With the fall of Communism and the collapse of the Soviet Union in 1991, the newly formed Commonwealth of Independent States and the individual republics began negotiations to determine who would gain control of the armed forces.

### THE UNITED STATES ARMY

As the commander in chief of the armed forces, the president of the United States maintains civilian control over the Army. The Department of the Army is a branch of the Cabinet-level Department of Defense, which is headed by a civilian secretary who is appointed by the president. The secretary of the Army, also a civilian appointed by the president, is under the authority of the secretary of defense and of the president.

Civilian control of the Army is also maintained by the United States Congress through its reviews of Army programs and its appropriations. Each house of Congress has an Armed Services Committee.

The top military officer of the Army is the Army chief of staff, a four- or five-star general appointed by the president. Along with the heads of the Air Force, and Navy, the Army chief of staff is a member of the Joint Chiefs of Staff, who serve as the principal military advisers to the secretary of defense and to the president. The Army chief of staff is assisted by an inspector general and an auditor general and by a policy committee on the Army Reserve forces.

The Army General Staff consists of a comptroller and of offices of operations and plans; personnel; logistics; research, development, and acquisition; intelligence; and automation and communications. Special Staff agencies include the offices of the adjutant general, chief of engineers, surgeon general, chief of chaplains, and judge advocate general. The chiefs of the Army Reserve forces and of the National Guard Bureau are also members of the Special Staff.

### Organization

**The active United States Army,** which is made up of the officers and the enlisted men and women who are on active duty, is one of the three parts of the total Army. The other two are the Army Reserve and the Army National Guard.

**The Army Reserve** is made up of civilians, many of whom also hold full-time jobs. The Army Reserve is divided into three categories: the Ready Reserve, forces available for immediate mobilization; the Standby Reserve, forces available in times of national emergency; and the Retired Reserve.

Although the Army Reserve has several designated combat units, most of its units provide the Active Army with combat support during national emergencies. The Army Reserve also assumes important training responsibilities in times of crisis.

**The Army National Guard** is the oldest military force in the United States. It traces its origins to the trained bands in the Massachusetts Bay Colony that date from 1636. There are Army National Guard units in all 50 states, the District of Columbia, Puerto Rico, and the United States Virgin Islands. Most Army National Guard members are assigned to combat units.

The Army National Guard is both a federal and a state military force. The governors of the states command the Army National Guard during peacetime.

Units of the Army National Guard often assist state or local officials in dealing with natural disasters and civil disorders. On the order of the president, the Army National Guard can be called to federal duty and its units made part of the Active Army.

The Army's responsibilities are divided among 15 major commands:

**The United States Army Forces Command** supervises Active Army and Army Reserve troops in the continental United States. Headquartered at Fort McPherson, Ga., the command divides the continental United States into four Army areas. These are the First Army, which is headquartered at Fort George G. Meade, Md.; the Second Army at Fort Gillem, Ga.; the Fifth Army, at Fort Sam Houston, Tex.; and the Sixth Army, at San Francisco, Calif. The Army Forces Command is also in charge of the training of units of the Army National Guard. Other responsibilities include the development of plans for mobilization.

**The United States Army Training and Doctrine Command** directs combat training programs for forces of both the Active Army and the Army Reserve. It is headquartered at Fort Monroe, Va.

**The United States Army Materiel Command** is in charge of the equipment used by the Army. Its responsibilities include development, procurement, storage, delivery, and maintenance. It is headquartered at Alexandria, Va.

**The United States Army Information Systems Command** is responsible for the Army's worldwide communications system, including air traffic control facilities. It is headquartered at Fort Huachuca, Ariz.

**The United States Army Health Services Command** provides health services for Army personnel and supervises medical training and education. It is headquartered at Fort Sam Houston, Tex.

**The United States Army Intelligence and Security Command** performs intelligence and security functions above the corps level. It is headquartered at Arlington Hall Station, Va.

**The Military Traffic Management Command** controls the movement of freight, personal property, and passengers for the Department of Defense. Another duty is the administration of highways for national defense. It is headquartered at Washington, D.C.

**The United States Army Military District of Washington,** which supports the activities of the Army and of the Department of Defense, is primarily responsible for protecting the nation's capital. Other duties include arranging state funerals and supervising military participation in ceremonies for foreign dignitaries. It is headquartered at Washington, D.C.

**The United States Army Criminal Investigation Command** is responsible for all criminal investigations that are conducted by the Army, including those overseas. It operates a criminal intelligence element. It is headquartered at Falls Church, Va.

**The United States Army Corps of Engineers** is responsible for both military engineering projects and civil works programs. It is headquartered at Washington, D.C.

In addition to these commands in the United States, there are five Army components of Unified Commands overseas. The United States Army Europe is part of the **United States European Command.** The Eighth United States Army is part of **United States Forces Korea.** The United States Army Japan is part of the **United States Forces Japan.** The United States Army Western Command is part of the **United States Pacific Command.** There is also a **United States Army Special Operations Command.**

### Arms and Divisions

The branches of the Army fall into three broad categories: combat arms, combat support arms, and combat service support arms. Combinations of these arms function as teams.

**Combat arms** are the branches that are directly involved in fighting. They include the infantry, armor, air defense artillery, field artillery, and aviation.

**The infantry** engages the enemy by using firepower and maneuvers. Although infantrymen may be transported by any means, they normally fight on foot. The infantry is the basic fighting force, but it functions as a part of a team that includes other arms.

**Armor** conducts mounted mobile, land, and air cavalry warfare. Most armor units are organized around a nucleus of tanks.

**Air defense artillery** destroys enemy aircraft and missiles. It is also capable of attacking ground targets with guns, missiles, and automatic weapons.

**Field artillery** also destroys enemy targets and is the primary support for infantry and armor. Its weapons include both cannon and missiles.

**Aviation** primarily works with field troops. A group of aircraft assigned to a field unit is under the control of the commander of the unit.

**Combat support arms** are branches of the Army including the Corps of Engineers, The Signal Corps, the Military Police Corps, the Chemical Corps, and Military Intelligence.

—The Corps of Engineers has combat units that are responsible for construction and demolition.

—The Signal Corps installs, operates, and maintains communications and electronic equipment.

—The Military Police Corps performs such duties as supervising prisoners of war, preventing crime, and providing security.

—The Chemical Corps assists combat units principally through activities such as chemical reconnaissance and decontamination.

—Military Intelligence units provide background information on the enemy and on the weather and terrain. They also monitor enemy communications and interrogate prisoners of war.

**Combat service support arms** are branches of the Army that perform logistics and administrative functions that support the combat arms. There are 17 branches of combat service support arms: Adjutant General's Corps; Corps of Engineers; Chemical Corps; Finance Corps; Ordnance Corps; Quartermaster Corps; Military Police Corps; Signal Corps; Judge

Advocate General's Corps; Transportation Corps; Chaplains; and the six branches of the Army Medical Department—Army Medical Specialist Corps, Army Nurse Corps, Dental Corps, Medical Corps, Medical Service Corps, and Veterinary Corps.

## The Division

The division is the smallest force that includes all of the combat arms and support arms of the Army. The standard elements of a division are a headquarters and headquarters company; an aviation battalion; an air defense artillery battalion; an engineer battalion; a combat electronic warfare and intelligence battalion; an armored cavalry squadron; a signal battalion; a chemical company; a military police company; a division field artillery headquarters with attached field artillery firing battalions; a support command that provides medical, transportation, supply, field maintenance, and administrative services; and three or more combat brigades.

Several divisions make up a corps. Two or more corps comprise a field army. Two or more field armies make up a group. The Army has 24 divisions, which include 16 Active Army divisions and 8 Army National Guard divisions.

**The infantry division** uses the foot soldier as its basic component. It is the oldest type of division and continues to be the core of the Army.

**The armored division** uses the tank as its principal weapon (see Tank). This type of division developed after World War I.

**The airborne division** uses Air Force and Army aircraft to drop troops by parachute behind enemy lines or in remote places (see Parachute). After they land, paratroopers fight as infantrymen.

**The mechanized infantry division** relies on several types of combat vehicles. This type of division was first organized in the mid-1960s.

**The airmobile division** uses helicopters for transport and for fire support (see Helicopter). This type of division was also developed during the mid-1960s.

## Special Forces

The Special Forces of the Army are trained to infiltrate deep behind an enemy's lines and to carry on guerrilla warfare. Because of the hazards of this type of fighting the Special Forces is made up entirely of volunteers. Special Forces candidates first complete basic and advanced training and the basic airborne course. They are then assigned to the Special Forces Training Group, located at Fort Bragg, N.C. Upon completion of training they become members of 12-man detachments, the basic Special Forces unit.

A Special Forces detachment is made up of two officers and ten noncommissioned officers. Each of the noncommissioned officers is proficient in one of the five basic Special Forces skills. Two are skilled in the use of all types of weapons. Another two are communications experts. A third pair, trained in medicine, are capable of performing limited surgery and of treating illnesses and diseases common to a particular region.

A fourth pair are demolitions specialists. The fifth pair are senior noncommissioned officers trained in operations and intelligence.

All members of a Special Forces detachment also have training in the areas outside their specialties. Many are proficient in a foreign language or receive language training after assignment.

## Rapid Deployment Force

The Rapid Deployment Joint Task Force consists of Army, Navy, Marine, and Air Force elements. It was developed as a strategic force capable of mobilizing quickly anywhere in the world.

The Army element of the force consists of 110,000 troops specifically trained to fight a conventional or nuclear war in any climate and terrain. The principal components of the Army element are an airborne division, an air assault division, a mechanized division, and a cavalry brigade.

## History of the United States Army

After the American Revolution the Continental Congress declared its belief that a standing army was contrary to democratic principles, and it disbanded the veteran forces. It soon found, however, that regular troops were needed to protect the frontier forts and lands against Indians and other enemies of settlers. When the government was organized under the Constitution, there was a force of about 1,000 officers and enlisted men.

The country entered the War of 1812 with only about 7,000 trained soldiers (see War of 1812). After the war Congress authorized a regular force of 10,000. At the outbreak of war with Mexico in 1846 the Regular Army consisted of only about 8,000. This small force, augmented by volunteers, won the Mexican War (see Mexican War). Congress then authorized strengthening the Army to 18,000 men. This force furnished the framework for the Northern armies of the Civil War.

After the Civil War Congress set the size of the Regular Army at 45,000 men but later reduced it to 25,000. Most of these men saw constant service in the Indian wars in the West (see Indians, American). The Army was primarily an Indian-fighting force when war erupted with Spain in 1898, but Spain's weakness and the success of the Navy soon ended the conflict (see Spanish-American War). After the war the United States had to garrison overseas possessions, necessitating an increase in Army strength to 100,000 men.

The National Defense Act of 1916 created the framework of the Army that fought in World War I. The act increased the strength of the Regular Army to 287,846 men and provided for a reserve corps of officers and enlisted men. It also authorized the president to call the state National Guard units into federal service. Most of the American forces in World War I, however, were raised by means of the Selective Service Act of 1917. Of the 3,700,000 men under arms at the end of the war, 2,800,000 had been drafted into the service.

In the years of peace that followed, lack of Congressional appropriations cut the Army's strength to 12,000 officers and 118,000 enlisted men. In 1939 President Franklin D. Roosevelt's proclamation of a "limited emergency" included an order to increase the size of the Regular Army and the National Guard. The first National Guards and Reserves were called into federal service in 1940.

Swift expansion of the Army resulted from the Selective Training and Service Act of 1940. The United States entered World War II with a force of 1,600,000 men. By 1945 the Army had 8,300,000 men. Two thirds of them were drafted through Selective Service. With this force the Army organized 89 combat divisions. These consisted of 66 infantry, 16 armored, five airborne, one dismounted cavalry, and one mountain division.

After V-J Day (victory over Japan in August 1945) the Army demobilized rapidly. By 1947 the number of men on active duty had fallen below the authorized peacetime strength of 670,000. National Guard and Organized Reserve enlistments, however, were greater than ever. The Selective Service Act of 1948 established a peacetime draft. In 1947 the Army Air Force was separated from the Army. It became the United States Air Force, coequal with the Army and the Navy. In addition, control of some operations was withdrawn from the individual services and placed under the Joint Chiefs of Staff.

At the outbreak of the Korean War in 1950 the draft was extended to 1959. (It was extended for additional four-year periods in 1959, in 1963, and in 1967, and was extended for a two-year period in 1971.) During the Korean War the Army expanded to more than 20 combat divisions.

The Reserve Forces Act of 1955 initiated compulsory reserve training. It enabled men from 17 to 18½ years of age to enlist in the Ready or the Standby Reserve. In 1963 the reorganization of National Guard and Organized Reserve divisions under the ROAD plan was completed. The period of service for reservists was cut from eight to six years. Further restructuring of the Army Reserve and Army National Guard was ordered in 1965.

Beginning in the mid-1950s, United States Army personnel served in South Vietnam in an advisory capacity. After United States bases were attacked by the Viet Cong in 1965, the Army played an active part in the Vietnam War. By 1968 seven Army divisions, plus other units, were fighting in Vietnam. Army manpower totaled about 1,470,000. After the war manpower was about 830,000.

During the 1960s many people criticized Selective Service. Some critics opposed United States military involvement in Vietnam. Many argued, however, that the system itself was unfair since, through its exemptions, it allowed certain groups—for example, college students—to escape military service. To correct such inequities, Congress instituted a draft lottery in 1969.

In January 1973, six months before the Selective Service Act expired, the draft was ended, and the Army began using all-volunteer forces. The Army, and the other armed services, attracted disproportionate numbers of blacks and of poor, undereducated volunteers. In addition, low pay scales caused reenlistment rates to drop. Registration, without conscription, was resumed in 1980. In the early 1990s the United States Army had a strength of 731,700, with reserves of almost the same number in the Army National Guard and the Army Reserves combined. Units of the Army were deployed in the continental United States, Alaska, Hawaii, Europe, Asia, and Latin America.

During the Persian Gulf War in early 1991 the Allied coalition against Iraq reached a strength of more than 700,000 troops, including 539,000 American personnel. After a massive Allied air war lasting several weeks the Allies sent in large numbers of ground troops to destroy Iraqi fortifications, weapons stockpiles, and tanks. Within four days the Allies had destroyed most of Iraq's elite Republican Guard and President Bush had declared a cease-fire. After the war, proposals were made by Congress to cut the total armed forces by some 22 percent over the next five years.

**BIBLIOGRAPHY FOR ARMY**

**Binder, L.J.** Front and Center: Heroes, War Stories, and Army Life (Pergamon, 1991).
**Collins, R.F.** Qualifying for Admission to the Service Academies: A Student's Guide (Rosen, 1987).
**Depuy, R.E., and Depuy, T.N.** The Encyclopedia of Military History, 2nd rev. ed. (Harper, 1986).
**Keegan, John.** The Face of Battle (Penguin, 1983).
**Keegan, John, and Holmes, Richard.** Soldiers: A History of Men in Battle (Viking, 1986).
**Knötel, Richard.** Uniforms of the World (Scribner, 1980).
**Lampton, Christopher.** Star Wars (Watts, 1987).
**Morris, J.P.** History of the U.S. Army (S & S Trade, 1987).
**Nalty, B.C.** Strength for the Fight: A History of Black Americans in the Military (Free Press, 1986).
**O'Neill, Richard, ed.** An Illustrated Guide to the Modern U.S. Army (Arco, 1984).
**Salzman, Mariann, and O'Reilly, Ann.** War and Peace in the Persian Gulf: What Teenagers Want to Know (Peterson's High School Series, 1991).
**Slappey, M.M.** Exploring Military Service for Women (Rosen, 1986).

**ARMYWORM** *see* **BUTTERFLY AND MOTH.**

**ARNOLD, Benedict** (1741–1801). The name Benedict Arnold has become a synonym for a traitor to one's country. In the first years of the American Revolution, however, Arnold was a brilliant and dashing general, highly respected for his service to the patriot cause (*see* Revolution, American).

Benedict Arnold was born on Jan. 14, 1741, in Norwich, Conn. His father, Benedict, was a well-to-do landowner. His mother was Hannah King Waterman Arnold. While a boy, young Arnold twice ran away to join the colonial troops fighting in the French and Indian War. When he was 21 he settled in New Haven. In time he became a prosperous merchant and a captain in the Connecticut militia. He married Margaret Mansfield in 1767. They had three sons.

Arnold played a gallant part in the American Revolution and became a major general in 1777. His wife had died in 1775. Early in 1779 he married Margaret Shippen, by whom he had four sons and one daughter. Arnold lived lavishly and soon found himself badly pressed for money.

He then began his treasonable activities. Most historians agree that Arnold did so for money, though he may also have resented lack of further promotion. Whatever his motive, he regularly sent vital military information to the British and was well paid for it. His wife helped him, often acting as messenger. In 1780 Arnold obtained command of West Point and at once conspired to turn over the garrison to the British. He met Maj. John André, a British spy, and made final plans. André was captured, however, and his papers indicated Arnold's treason.

Arnold heard of the capture and fled to the British headquarters in New York City. He was given a command and about £6,300. He served with the British for the rest of the war, leading troops on raids in Virginia and Connecticut. After the war he lived with his family in England. He failed to obtain a regular commission in the British army and failed also in several business ventures, including land speculation in Canada. He died in London on June 14, 1801.

**ARNOLD, Matthew** (1822–88). One of the most noted 19th-century English poets and critics was an inspector of schools. For more than 30 years Matthew Arnold visited English schools and compiled lengthy reports and recommendations. He also found time to write poems marked by profound sincerity and essays that probed deeply into basic problems.

Matthew Arnold was born on Dec. 24, 1822, in Laleham, England. He was the eldest of nine children. His father, Dr. Thomas Arnold, was a famous educator. Matthew went to school at Winchester and Rugby and spent summers with his family in the Lake District. He entered Balliol College, Oxford, when he was 18. After graduation in 1845 he won a fellowship to Oriel College, Oxford.

In 1851 Arnold secured his school inspectorship and married Frances Wightman. His poetry and criticism early won recognition, and from 1857 to 1867 he also served as professor of poetry at Oxford. He died in Liverpool on April 15, 1888.

Among Arnold's volumes of essays are 'Culture and Anarchy' (1869) and 'Literature and Dogma' (1873). His poems include 'The Scholar-Gypsy' and 'Sohrab and Rustum'. (See also English Literature.)

**ARROWHEAD.** Prehistoric man used bows and arrows in hunting. American Indians also used these weapons in hunting, as well as in waging war.

There were different kinds of arrows, depending upon their use and where they were made. Because they were handmade, no two were identical.

Arrowheads varied in design. Early Indians used flint or animal bone. Arrowheads were also made of shell, horn, metal, antlers, and precious stones.

The heads of hunting arrows were oval so they could be withdrawn easily. War arrowheads, however, were barbed to prevent easy withdrawal. (See also Indians, American; Archery.)

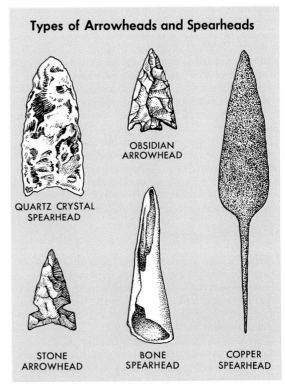

### Types of Arrowheads and Spearheads

QUARTZ CRYSTAL SPEARHEAD

OBSIDIAN ARROWHEAD

STONE ARROWHEAD

BONE SPEARHEAD

COPPER SPEARHEAD

**ARSENIC.** The semimetallic element arsenic is a dangerous poison. It has served mankind well, however, as a killer of germs and insect pests.

Doctors use chemical derivatives of arsenic to treat certain tropical diseases. The arsenic preparation known as "606," Salvarsan, or arsphenamine is historically important as the first drug to kill the germs of syphilis (see Ehrlich). Among the compounds of arsenic that have been used to fight insect pests is Paris green (a complex compound of arsenic with copper, hydrogen, and oxygen). Manufacturers produce arsenical drugs, insecticides, and similar preparations from "white arsenic," or arsenious oxide. White arsenic also takes the color out of glass.

A small percentage of arsenic in alloys makes them more brittle and lowers their melting point. Arsenic in molten lead delays hardening and makes possible the production of perfectly spherical lead shot. Arsenic in lead-base bearing alloys improves their durability, especially at high temperatures. In copper alloys arsenic increases the resistance to corrosion.

Arsenic is on the border line between metals and nonmetals (see Chemistry). Its chemical symbol is

---

**Properties of Arsenic**

| | | | |
|---|---|---|---|
| Symbol . . . . . . . . . . . . . . As | Density at 32° F . . . . . . . . 5.73 |
| Atomic Number . . . . . . . . . 33 | Boiling Point . . . . . . . 1,139° F. |
| Atomic Weight . . . . . 74.9216 | Melting Point (under pressure) |
| Group in Periodic Table . . . V A | . . . . . . . . . . . . . . . . 1,497.2° F. |

As. It occurs in nature chiefly in combination with other minerals. Among the common compounds are arsenopyrite, or mispickel (FeSAs); leucopyrite (FeAs); realgar ($As_2S_2$); and orpiment, or king's yellow ($As_2S_3$). Arsenic compounds usually appear in metal-bearing ores. Most of the world's supply of white arsenic is recovered as a by-product of the smelting of lead and copper ores. Sublimation of mispickel or leucopyrite in the absence of air is a common method of obtaining metallic arsenic.

Arsenic is crystalline and very brittle. When cut it is silver gray in color, but it turns yellow and then black on exposure to air. When burned, arsenic emits a vapor that smells like garlic. The element is insoluble in water, acids, and alcohol. It reacts readily with oxygen, the halogens, and sulfur. (*See also* Poison.)

**ARTESIAN WELL** *see* **WATER.**

**ARTHRITIS.** The term arthritis refers to more than 100 diseases that affect the skeletal system and muscles. These diseases make up the leading cause of physical disability in much of the world. In the United States alone, as many as 31 million persons suffer from some form of arthritis.

There are four common forms of arthritis. Osteoarthritis, or wear and tear on joints, mainly occurs as part of the aging process. Rheumatoid arthritis (RA) mostly affects women of all ages and is a serious, often crippling, form of the disease. Ankylosing spondylitis (AS) occurs in young men 15 to 40 years of age and can result in a "frozen" spine. A form of arthritis can follow injury, resulting in conditions such as tennis elbow and lower back pain.

The tendency to contract some of these diseases appears to run in families. Genetic markers, detectable variations in the genes, are often found in the white blood cells of those with RA and AS. Yet many people with these markers or in families in which there is arthritis never get the disease. It is not known what triggers arthritis, but viruses, bacteria, and stress are all suspected of playing a part.

In some forms of arthritis, such as RA, the immune system, which normally protects against such outside invaders as bacteria and viruses, begins to attack the body (*see* Immune System). Many parts of the body are affected by inflammation of tissue. This is the main cause of damage, mostly to the joints. Inflammation in the joints causes heat and swelling. The lining of the joints, or synovium, may be eaten away. In severe cases, if medication is not effective in stopping inflammation, the affected joints can be destroyed.

There is no cure for arthritis. It sometimes goes into remission, which means that the symptoms disappear for a period of time—from a day to a lifetime. Many different kinds of drugs are used to induce remission and to fight the inflammation that causes the damage. The most common medicine is aspirin taken in large doses. Taken this way, it is an anti-inflammatory as well as a painkiller. Drugs compounded from steroid hormones, such as cortisone, are also used. The

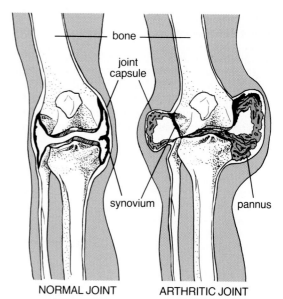

bone

joint capsule

synovium

pannus

NORMAL JOINT ARTHRITIC JOINT

*A normal joint has a healthy synovium lining a joint capsule that keeps the joint lubricated and the bones in proper position. With arthritis comes deterioration of the synovium and formation of useless pannus.*

precious metal gold is often used in a solution that is given by injection. Immunosuppressive drugs that discourage the body's attacks on itself are used in severe cases. All of the drugs for arthritis can produce dangerous side effects. Because what helps one person may not help another, different drug treatments often must be tried until the right one is found. Other treatments for arthritis include heat, cold, and physical therapy to ease pain and to keep the joints movable.

When joints have been badly damaged or are so painful that they are useless, surgical replacement of the affected joints with artificial joints can be performed. Most joints can be replaced by long-wearing plastic or stainless steel substitutes. Successful joint replacement, particularly in the hips, has allowed many people to return to more normal lives.

Because the causes of most forms of arthritis are not yet known and there is no cure for this painful, often disabling, and chronic disease—which means most people have arthritis for life—many unproven and quack remedies are sold to victims. Nearly 1 billion dollars is spent each year in the United States on useless, sometimes dangerous, items advertised as cures or remedies.

Medical researchers are looking at the immune system to discover how and why the body turns against itself when afflicted with arthritis. They are also looking for drugs that can permanently stop the inflammation of arthritis and prevent joint damage. Although the causes of most forms of arthritis are not known and there is no known cure for the disease, early diagnosis and proper medical treatment can often prevent its disabling effects.　Ann Giudici Fettner

**ARTHROPOD** *see* **CRUSTACEAN; INSECT; SPIDER.**

Gramstorff Brothers

*21st President of the United States
(1829–86; president 1881–85)*

# CHESTER A. ARTHUR

On the evening of Sept. 19, 1881, Vice-President Arthur was in his home at 123 Lexington Avenue, New York City. Through the open windows he could hear newsboys shouting, "President Garfield is dying!" About midnight he received a telegram from the members of Garfield's Cabinet informing him of the president's death and advising him to take the oath of office without delay. Arthur took the oath with firm resolution, but his heart was heavy. He knew that millions of Americans regarded him as unfit for the presidency of the United States.

## A Baptist Minister's Son

Chester Alan Arthur was born in the village of Fairfield, Vt., Oct. 5, 1829. His father, William Arthur, had immigrated to America from northern Ireland when he was 18 and had become a Baptist minister. His mother, Malvina Stone Arthur, was born in New Hampshire. The Arthurs had four daughters when Chester was born. When the family was complete, Chester had a brother and another sister.

Elder Arthur, an eloquent preacher, was restless, and moved constantly from one town to another. In 1839 he settled down at Union Village (now Greenwich), in eastern New York. Chester attended the academy there and was remembered by his teacher as being "frank and open in manners and genial."

Five years later Elder Arthur moved to Schenectady. There Chester was admitted to Union College as a sophomore when he was only 15, because his father had taught him Latin and Greek. His father, however, could give him no financial help; so the next year Chester began to teach during the long winter vacations. After graduation at 18, near the top of his class, he continued to teach while studying law.

## He Defends Civil Rights

Elder Arthur was an abolitionist, and his son shared his views on slavery. In the minister's congregation was a congressman, Erastus D. Culver, who also had strong antislavery principles. Culver moved his law office to Brooklyn and agreed to take young Arthur into his firm to train him. The tall, handsome young man entered Culver's office in March 1853. The next year he was admitted to the bar and taken into partnership.

Chester Arthur arrived in time to assist Culver in the famous Lemmon slave case. In 1852 Jonathan Lemmon and his wife had brought eight slaves from Virginia to New York by boat. They intended to stop over only until the next boat left for Texas. The court decided that slaves passing through New York became free.

Meanwhile Arthur was fighting another civil rights case. A black woman, Lizzie Jennings, had been forced off a Brooklyn streetcar by the conductor and some of the passengers. Arthur won $500 damages for her and, more important, obtained a court decision that blacks should be allowed the same accommodations on street railways as white passengers.

## He Marries and Enters Politics

In 1856 Arthur went into partnership with another young lawyer in a modest office in the Wall Street district. To build up a practice, he needed to enlarge his circle of acquaintances; so he joined clubs and entered politics. He soon numbered among his friends prominent literary people as well as politicians. He could talk equally well on literature, politics, or fishing—his only sport.

In 1859 Arthur married Ellen Lewis Herndon of Fredericksburg, Va., who was living in New York City with her mother. Her father, Capt. William Lewis Herndon of the United States Navy, an explorer of the Amazon, had heroically gone down with his ship in the Caribbean after saving many lives. Ellen had a winning manner, and she and her mother belonged to a prominent social group.

## Time Line of Presidents, Events, and Periods

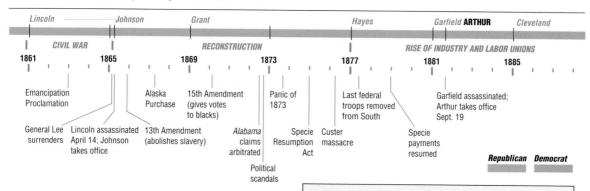

Lincoln  Johnson  Grant  Hayes  Garfield **ARTHUR**  Cleveland

CIVIL WAR  RECONSTRUCTION  RISE OF INDUSTRY AND LABOR UNIONS

1861  1865  1869  1873  1877  1881  1885

Emancipation Proclamation

General Lee surrenders

Lincoln assassinated April 14; Johnson takes office

Alaska Purchase

13th Amendment (abolishes slavery)

15th Amendment (gives votes to blacks)

*Alabama* claims arbitrated

Political scandals

Panic of 1873

Specie Resumption Act

Custer massacre

Last federal troops removed from South

Specie payments resumed

Garfield assassinated; Arthur takes office Sept. 19

Republican  Democrat

The Granger Collection

*An engraving shows Vice-President Arthur taking the oath of office to become president in New York City on Sept. 20, 1881.*

---

**ARTHUR'S ADMINISTRATION 1881–85**

American Red Cross established (1882)
Chinese Exclusion Act (1882)
Immigration act bars paupers, criminals, and insane from United States (1882)
First steel cruisers authorized to modernize United States Navy (1882)
Star Routes postal fraud cases prosecuted (1882)
Pendleton Civil Service Act (1883)
Tariff Act (1883)
Civil government established in Alaska (1884)

---

Arthur played an important part in the organization of the new Republican party in the state of New York, but he was never interested in holding political office. His activities soon brought him to the attention of the governor, Edwin D. Morgan.

On April 13, 1861, the day after Fort Sumter was fired on, Morgan asked Arthur to take over the duties of quartermaster general in New York City. The post involved supplying barracks, food, uniforms, and equipment for the thousands of troops who passed through the city. Arthur quickly built up an efficient organization and forced contractors to meet specifications. He could not be bribed to accept inferior materials. A friend quoted Arthur as saying, "If I had misappropriated five cents, and on walking downtown saw two men talking on the street together, I would imagine they were talking of my dishonesty."

Morgan was succeeded by a Democratic governor, and Arthur turned over his organization to a Democratic successor on Jan. 1, 1863. He left the office poorer than he was when he went in; but he soon acquired a considerable fortune in private practice.

Arthur's first son, born in 1860, died before he was three years old. Another son, born in 1864, was given his father's name but was called Alan. A daughter,

born in 1871, was named for her mother, Ellen Herndon Arthur.

### Collector of the Port of New York

Arthur's political activities brought him into close association with Senator Roscoe Conkling, the Republican boss of New York State. In 1868 Arthur worked with Conkling to promote Grant's election. President Grant rewarded Arthur by appointing him, in 1871, collector of the port of New York. The *New York Times*, reporting the appointment, said of Arthur: "His name very seldom rises to the surface of metropolitan life, and yet, moving like a mighty undercurrent, this man during the last ten years has done more to mold the course of the Republican party in this state than any other man in the country." The secret of his success, said the *Times*, was his executive ability and his knowledge of men.

The New York Custom House, on Wall Street, collected about two thirds of the nation's tariff revenue and employed about a thousand people. It was the usual practice for the collector to give appointments to people who had worked for the party and to accept from them "voluntary contributions" to campaign funds. Arthur was scrupulously honest but he was a practical politician, not a reformer. He did not remove good men to make way for others, but when an appointment was to be made he looked for a qualified political friend to do the work. Like Conkling and many other men in government, he believed that the spoils system ("to the victor belong the spoils") was necessary to maintain a political organization.

## Major World Events During Arthur's Administration

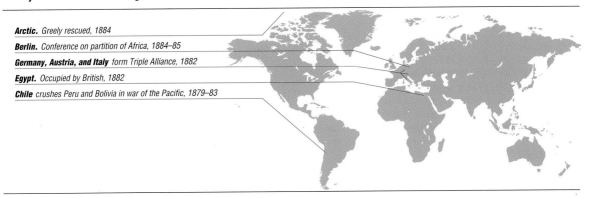

**Arctic.** *Greely rescued, 1884*

**Berlin.** *Conference on partition of Africa, 1884–85*

**Germany, Austria, and Italy** *form Triple Alliance, 1882*

**Egypt.** *Occupied by British, 1882*

**Chile** *crushes Peru and Bolivia in war of the Pacific, 1879–83*

Civil-service reform was in full swing when Hayes succeeded Grant in 1877. Hayes decided to organize the New York Custom House on a strictly business basis (*see* Hayes). In 1878 he replaced both Arthur and his associate, Alonzo B. Cornell, with men of his own choice. Conkling's machine, however, managed to retain its political power in the state, and Arthur remained dominant in New York City.

Arthur's wife died on Jan. 11, 1880, and was buried beside her son and Arthur's parents in a rural cemetery near Albany. With his wife and his parents gone and his Custom House administration discredited, Arthur was desolate.

### Vice-Presidency

The Republican party was seriously divided in 1880. Conkling, as leader of the Stalwart Republicans, tried to nominate Grant for a third term in 1880. The "half-breed" Republicans wanted Senator James G. Blaine. The deadlock in the convention lasted until the 36th ballot, when James A. Garfield was unexpectedly nominated. To make sure of the Stalwarts' aid in the election, the convention nominated Arthur for vice-president. The Republicans won the election and Arthur took the Senate chair; but he did not lose his interest in New York politics.

After the election, the split in the party widened. Garfield appointed Blaine, Conkling's bitter enemy, as secretary of state and refused to allow Conkling to name the secretary of the treasury, who would control the Custom House. Finally, Garfield proposed to appoint William H. Robertson, the outstanding "half-breed" Republican of New York State, to the Custom House.

Conkling feared Robertson would use Custom House patronage to build up his own machine. Arthur shared his apprehension. As a protest, Conkling resigned from the Senate and took with him the junior senator from New York, Thomas C. Platt. Arthur went with them to Albany to work for their reelection.

Garfield was shot on July 2, 1881, by a crazed office seeker who boasted that he was a Stalwart Republican (*see* Garfield). During the weeks when Garfield lingered between life and death, popular indignation against the Stalwarts ran high. "Arthur for president!" Hayes wrote in his diary, "Conkling the power behind the throne, superior to the throne!" Arthur remained in seclusion until Garfield's death made him president.

### Refurnishing the White House

Arthur was wealthy and used to modern conveniences. He refused to move into the White House until a real bath was installed, walls refinished, and worn furniture and carpets replaced. He gave his personal attention to the new fittings and had 24 wagonloads of discarded relics removed and sold at auction. Then he moved in with his French chef and black valet. One of his sisters, Mary Arthur McElroy, acted as hostess for him and cared for his 12-year-old daughter Nelly. Arthur's son Alan was at Princeton during this time.

After a period of mourning for Garfield, Arthur began to entertain on a lavish scale. He enjoyed balls and receptions and had an epicure's taste for food and drink. After two or three hours at the dinner table he would still urge his friends to stay because he disliked to bring a pleasant evening to a close. Then he would work late into the night. This type of life caused him to gain weight and lose energy. In 1883 he went on a fishing trip to Florida to regain his health. He contracted a fever on this trip and never fully recovered from the effects of the illness.

### Presidency

Arthur's simple and sincere inaugural address helped to reassure the people. In his first message to Congress he surprised everyone by coming out strongly for civil-service reform. In 1883 he signed the country's first civil-service law, the Pendleton Act. This act set up a civil-service commission to conduct open competitive examinations for about 14,000 officeholders. Succeeding presidents extended the merit system (*see* Civil Service).

Before Garfield's death, frauds in the so-called Star Routes had come to light. The Star Routes were those in the Far West where mail was still carried by horseback or stagecoach. Large sums had been drawn from the post office for services that were never rendered. Arthur tried earnestly but unsuccessfully to bring the guilty to justice.

Arthur is called the Father of the American Navy because he took a personal interest in modernizing and expanding it. The Navy had declined steadily after the American Civil War. In 1882 Congress appropriated money for the nation's first all-steel vessels. The so-called "white squadron," which was completed in Cleveland's administration, formed the nucleus of the modern United States Navy.

Few governments in history had ever complained of too much money in the treasury. Throughout the 1880s, however, each year the United States government had a large surplus over ordinary expenditures. At this time government funds were stored in vaults rather than in banks. With each increase in the treasury surplus, more money was taken out of circulation, which resulted in a deflation of prices. Moreover this was happening in a period of rapid economic expansion. The most pressing problem of the administration therefore was how to return money to circulation. The flood of money was caused largely by the high tariffs that had been imposed by the government during the Civil War. Arthur wanted to attack the surplus by lowering tariffs. He set up a commission, which recommended a reduction in duties. Manufacturers who prospered under the high tariffs, however, had powerful lobbies in Washington. The so-called "Mongrel" tariff of 1883, which Congress passed, stamped the Republicans as favoring a high protective tariff. The Democrats at this time began to demand a lower tariff—"for revenue only."

In Arthur's administration the first acts to restrict immigration were passed. The Chinese Exclusion Act of 1882 restricted the immigration of Chinese laborers for a ten-year period. In the same year paupers, criminals, convicts, and the insane were barred from the United States. (*See also* Migration of People.)

Arthur's popularity grew with each year of his presidency. He had struggled to hold together the bitterly divided Republican party, and he hoped to receive approval from the nominating convention of 1884. The convention, however, did not seriously consider him. Senator Blaine was nominated but lost the election to Grover Cleveland, the first Democratic president to be elected since 1856. Despondent, Arthur returned to his New York home and tried to resume his law practice, but he lacked the energy for it. He died on Nov. 18, 1886. (For Arthur's Cabinet and Supreme Court appointments, *see* Fact-Index.)

### BIBLIOGRAPHY FOR CHESTER A. ARTHUR

**Doenecke, J.D.** The Presidencies of James A. Garfield and Chester A. Arthur (Regents Press of Kansas, 1981).
**Kane, J.N.** Facts About the Presidents: A Compilation of Biographical and Historical Information, 5th ed. (Wilson, 1990).
**Poole, S.D.** Chester A. Arthur: The President Who Reformed (M. Bloomfield, 1977).
**Reeves, T.C.** Gentleman Boss: The Life of Chester Alan Arthur (Knopf, 1975).
**Simon, Charnan.** Chester A. Arthur: 21st President of the United States (Childrens, 1989).

*A part of a French wool tapestry pictures King Arthur. The tapestry is attributed to Nicolas Bataille in the 14th century.*

Courtesy of the Metropolitan Museum of Art, New York, The Cloisters Collection, Munsey Fund, 1932

**ARTHURIAN LEGEND.** The virtues of knighthood were more completely embodied in King Arthur, the legendary prince of the ancient Britons, than in any other figure in literature. According to legend, Arthur was the son of King Uther Pendragon. Immediately after his birth, Arthur was given into the keeping of Merlin, the magician. Merlin took him to Sir Hector, who brought the child up as his own son. After Uther's death Arthur proved his right to the throne by pulling out a sword that had been fixed in a great stone and which no one else had been able to move. This was the first of Arthur's two magic swords, both called Excalibur. The other was given to him by the Lady of the Lake. According to the story, her arm appeared above the surface of the lake with the sword in hand. When Arthur took it, her arm disappeared.

King Arthur married Guinevere and held his court at Camelot, which is also sometimes identified as Caerleon, on the River Usk in England, near the Welsh border. Around him he gathered many strong and brave knights. They all sat as equals about a great round table, and thus they ultimately came to be known as the Order of the Round Table. King Arthur extended his conquests far and wide. Then dissension appeared, and his traitorous nephew, Mordred, rose in rebellion. In a great battle Mordred was defeated and slain, but Arthur himself was mortally wounded. His body was mysteriously carried to the Island of Avalon to be healed. He was expected to return at some future time and resume his rule.

Is there any truth in these stories of King Arthur? The answer is best given in the words of one of the old writers: they are "not all a lie nor all true, not all fable nor all known. . . ." Some scholars believe that there was a historical Arthur, who lived in Britain in the 5th or 6th century and gained fame as a leader of the Christian Celts in the wars against the heathen Saxon invaders. He was defeated and killed in battle. His people fled to the mountains of Wales and to Brittany in France. There they told stories of Arthur's valor and goodness—stories that became more glorified in the telling until he was elevated to a wise and powerful king.

Other old stories then attached themselves to the name of Arthur—myths of ancient Celtic gods and tales of magic and the supernatural. Later, because Arthur had been a Christian fighting against the heathen, the knights and poets of chivalry fancied him a knight like themselves, even though he had lived long before the age of chivalry. Stories of other knights, such as those of Tristram and of Gawain, were drawn into the Arthurian cycle. Sir Lancelot was considered the most chivalrous of the legendary knights and his son, Sir Galahad, the noblest. Some of the romances involved Lancelot with Guinevere. A religious element was added with the legend of the quest for the Holy Grail, the cup that had been used by Jesus Christ at the Last Supper and which only the pure in heart and deed might behold (see Holy Grail). Thus the Arthurian stories are a combination of history, myth, romance, fairy tale, and religious parable.

One of the earliest chronicles that mentions Arthur is the 'Historia Britonum' (History of the Britons). It is supposed to have been written by a Welsh monk named Nennius, about two centuries after the hero's death. In the 12th century another Welshman, Geoffrey of Monmouth, first gave literary form to the Arthurian stories in his 'Historia Regum Britanniae' (History of the Kings of Britain). In this chronicle Geoffrey fused together history and legend with his creative imagination. Geoffrey, like Nennius, wrote his stories in Latin, which was then the learned and literary language of all Europe.

The stories were carried throughout the continent. The English historian Edward Gibbon said of them: "Every nation embraced and adorned the popular romance of Arthur and his knights of the Round Table; . . . and the voluminous tales of Sir Lancelot and Sir Tristram were devoutly studied by the princes and nobles, who disregarded the genuine heroes and heroines of antiquity."

In the 15th century Sir Thomas Malory translated many of these romances. They appeared as 'Morte d'Arthur' (Death of Arthur), one of the first books to be printed in England. Malory's work is the chief source of the Arthurian legend. T.H. White's 'The Once and Future King' became the basis for the musical 'Camelot' (1960) and the animated film 'The Sword in the Stone' (1963).

**BIBLIOGRAPHY FOR ARTHURIAN LEGEND**

**Bulla, C.R.** The Sword in the Tree (Harper, 1988).
**Lang, Andrew, ed.** King Arthur: Tales of the Round Table (Schocken, 1987).
**Pyle, Howard.** The Story of King Arthur and His Knights (Macmillan, 1984).
**Stewart, Mary.** Arthurian Saga, 4 vols. (Fawcett, 1985).
**Sutcliff, Rosemary.** The Sword and the Circle (Dutton, 1981).
**Twain, Mark.** A Connecticut Yankee in King Arthur's Court (Morrow, 1988).
**White, T.H.** The Book of Merlyn (Univ. of Tex. Press, 1988).
**White, T.H.** The Once and Future King (Berkley, 1983).
**Winder, Blanche, ed.** Stories of King Arthur (Airmont, n.d.).

**ARTICLES OF CONFEDERATION.** The first constitution of the United States was known as the Articles of Confederation. The Articles were written in 1776–77, after independence from Great Britain had been declared and while the American Revolution was in progress. As a constitution, the Articles had a short life. The document was not fully ratified by the states until March 1, 1781, and it remained in effect only until March 4, 1789—the date on which the present Constitution went into effect. Under the Articles, Congress was the sole organ of government.

When the United States declared its independence in July 1776, the only institution acting as a central government was the Continental Congress (see Continental Congress). The states were operating under old colonial charters. Previously, the British Parliament had been the closest thing the colonies had to a national government. Thus, at the same time the united colonies were fighting to assure their independence, they were faced with the need to improvise a permanent national government and to formulate state constitutions.

**The First State Constitutions**

To accomplish this, the states between 1777 and 1780 adopted written constitutions, or fundamental laws. The first of these were drawn up by the legislatures, but many believed that a constitution should not be made by the same method as that used in making ordinary laws. In Massachusetts, a constitution was rejected because it was prepared by the legislature. Then the state called a special convention, the sole purpose of which was to frame a constitution. This set the fundamental law apart from acts of the legislature. Other states also followed this plan, which has become the typical American method.

In 1776 Americans were inclined to mistrust all government. Their troubles with England made them believe that officials who had much power would become unjust. To prevent this, seven states put into their new constitutions what were known as bills of rights (see Bill of Rights). These listed many things that the government could not do. Among other things, it could not take a citizen's property without compensation, keep a citizen in prison without just cause, or deny a citizen the right of jury trial.

The government was further limited by dividing its powers among the legislature, the executive, and the courts, so that each might act as a check on the others. If one department alone had all the power, it might use it unwisely or unfairly.

The patriot leaders remembered how the governors sent from England had generally acted contrary to the wishes of the people. For the most part, the new constitutions provided that the governor could not veto laws or dismiss the legislature, and they restricted his power to appoint local officers.

Democratic as they were in principle, the first state constitutions did not give all citizens equal political rights. In most states less than half the men could vote, since there were fairly high property qualifications for voting and holding office and sometimes religious qualifications as well. Women were denied the right to vote, and slaves received no rights. The people of the seaboard obtained more delegates in the national legislature than did the poorer settlers of the interior. Yet the new governments were far more democratic than those immediately preceding. The governor was now elected by the legislature or the voters. More people could vote. The states also did away with primogeniture—bestowing a landed estate on the oldest male heir by inheritance, leaving none to the other children.

The new constitutions were so well made that they lasted in many cases more than 40 years. They set in writing the rights for which English subjects had been fighting for centuries. They also preserved the institutions to which the Americans had grown accustomed: representation of the people, legislatures of two houses, town and county governments, and courts open to all.

### Need for a Federal Government

At the same time, a plan for national government was being produced by members of the Second Continental Congress. On June 7, 1776 (nearly a month before the Declaration of Independence was signed), delegate Richard Henry Lee of Virginia proposed that the Congress appoint a committee to draw up a plan of national government. The committee was composed of one delegate from each state. On July 12 it presented for approval a plan of union put together by John Dickinson of Pennsylvania (see Dickinson, John).

Strong differences of opinion among the 13 states about a variety of issues kept debate on the document going for more than a year before the new constitution, or Articles of Confederation, was actually submitted to the states for approval. In addition, debate was delayed when the Congress was forced by events of the war to move its headquarters from Philadelphia to York, Pa., in 1777.

The first aim of the Articles was to give Congress the powers required for winning the war. But the citizens of the states knew that in time of peace they would have to continue working together. They would have to defend their frontiers and protect their trading vessels. They needed a common postal service and diplomatic agents abroad. So the Articles created a perpetual union—not merely an alliance for war—and declared that the name of the nation should be The United States of America.

### Powers Granted to Congress

The main problem in drafting the Articles was that of dividing the powers of government between the states and Congress. England had formerly supplied the navy, the postal service, and the diplomatic agencies for America. It had also taken charge of the wars in which the colonies had participated. The patriots realized the value of having a single government do these things. Accordingly, the Articles gave Congress the power to raise and maintain an army and a navy, to make war and peace, to negotiate treaties, to fix standards of coinage and of weights and measures, and to provide a postal service.

On the other hand the patriot leaders had objected to England's claim that Parliament could tax the colonies, regulate their trade, restrain them from issuing paper money, interfere in their local concerns, and take charge of relations with the Indians. Therefore the Articles did not allow Congress any control over the domestic affairs of the states. Nor could it levy taxes; it could only ask the states for funds. Congress could make commercial treaties and also superintend Indian affairs so far as its acts did not conflict with state laws.

Each of the 13 states was to have only one vote in Congress, though it might send from two to seven delegates, and nine of the 13 votes were required before Congress could act. The enforcement of all laws and the administration of justice were left to the states. The Articles could be changed only by unanimous vote of the Confederation. Any power not specifically granted to Congress was reserved to the states.

### Advantages and Weaknesses of Union

The Articles were adopted by Congress on Nov. 15, 1777, and submitted to the states for ratification. The smaller states, especially Maryland, objected to the claims of Virginia, Massachusetts, the Carolinas, Georgia, New York, and Connecticut to the lands west of the Appalachians. Maryland felt that if these states had all the western land they claimed, they might become overwhelmingly powerful. Only when the states with western land claims agreed to turn over these lands to Congress for the use of all the states would Maryland ratify the Articles. It finally signed them on March 1, 1781.

Thus the Articles, which had been laid before the states in 1777 and which were intended to help win the war, did not come into effect until a few months before the close of the war. The new Congress had only to keep the armies in the field until the war was won. It provided four executive offices to superintend foreign affairs, finance, war, and marine. Through the efforts of the able superintendent of finance, Robert Morris, money was borrowed from Holland and France, and further sums were obtained from the states. Congress also negotiated the peace treaty that secured independence and granted the new country the land west to the Mississippi River.

Congress worked out important policies with reference to the western lands ceded by the states. An Ordinance of 1785 provided for dividing these lands into townships of 36 square miles and allowed the sale of 640-acre tracts at about a dollar an acre. Many settlers were able to buy farms of their own. The Ordinance of 1787, also known as the Northwest Ordinance, opened the territory to settlement and outlined the representative government later used for all the continental territories. It promised that the region should eventually be divided into new states that would enter the Union on an equal footing with the original 13.

After the war the states refused to pay taxes requested by Congress; hence the general government could not pay the public debt or even the interest on it. The Navy was inadequate to protect foreign commerce. Now that the states were out of the British Empire, they were not allowed to trade freely with England and its West Indies colonies. The settlers in the West needed an outlet for their produce down the Mississippi. Spain, however, held the mouth of the river and refused to allow them to ship their products from New Orleans. Congress found that it could not get commercial favors from either England or Spain. Since the states had the final say in commercial regulations, a treaty of Congress had little force and the European countries preferred to deal separately with the states.

After the American Revolution a period of hard times set in. The price of farm products was very low, and the farmers bought manufactured goods on credit. Then they found great difficulty in paying their debts. They soon asked their legislatures to issue paper money that creditors would have to accept. Massachusetts experienced a violent struggle between the debtor farmers and their creditors known as Shays's Rebellion (see Shays's Rebellion). Congress, however, could not prevent the states from issuing cheap paper money or act to put down a civil war.

The first Union allowed people to move freely throughout the country. The Congress, however, could not enforce a law or collect a tax. It had no power to control foreign trade, or to restrain the states from trade wars among themselves. And there was neither an executive to carry out the acts of Congress nor a federal court to interpret and enforce the laws. The Union under the Articles, however, carried the United States through a critical period and paved the way for the "more perfect union" of the Constitution. (See also United States Constitution.)

**ARTIFICIAL INTELLIGENCE (AI).** In 1637 the French philosopher-mathematician René Descartes predicted that it would never be possible to make a machine that thinks as humans do. In 1950, the British mathematician and computer pioneer Alan Turing declared that one day there would be a machine that could duplicate human intelligence in every way and prove it by passing a specialized test. In this test, a computer and a human hidden from view would be asked random identical questions. If the computer were successful, the questioner would be unable to distinguish the machine from the person by the answers.

Inspired by Turing's theory, the first conference on AI convened at Dartmouth College in New Hampshire in 1956. Soon afterwards an AI laboratory was started at Massachusetts Institute of Technology by John McCarthy and Marvin Minsky, two of the nation's leading AI proponents. McCarthy also invented the AI computer language, Lisp; but by the early 1990s AI itself had not been achieved. However, logic programs called expert systems allow computers to "make decisions" by interpreting data and selecting from among alternatives. Technicians can run programs used in complex medical diagnosis, language translation, mineral exploration, and even computer design.

Machinery can outperform humans physically. So, too, can computers outperform mental functions in limited areas—notably in the speed of mathematical calculations. For example, the fastest computers developed are able to perform roughly 10 billion calculations per second. But making more powerful computers will probably not be the way to create a machine capable of passing the Turing test. Computer programs operate according to set procedures, or logic steps, called algorithms. In addition, most computers do serial processing: operations of recognition and computation are performed one at a time. The brain works in a manner called parallel processing, performing operations simultaneously (see Brain, "How the Brain Works"). To achieve simulated parallel processing, some supercomputers have been made with multiple processors to follow several algorithms at the same time (see Computer).

Critics of this approach insist that solving a computation does not indicate understanding, something a person who solved a problem would have. Human reasoning is not based solely on rules of logic. It involves perception, awareness, emotional preferences, values, evaluating experience, the ability to generalize and weigh options, and more. Some proponents of AI have, therefore, suggested that computers should be patterned after the human brain, which essentially consists of a network of nerve cells.

By the early 1990s, the closest approximation to AI was a special silicon chip built to behave like a human brain cell. It was modeled after the internal workings of neurons in the human cerebral cortex. Unlike the conventional silicon chip, which works in digital mode, the new silicon chip works in analog mode, much the way a human brain cell works.

**ARTIFICIAL LIMBS** see PROSTHETIC DEVICE.

**ARTIFICIAL SWEETENER** see SWEETENER, ARTIFICIAL.

**ARTIGAS, José Gervasio** (1764–1850). Although his country did not become independent from Spain until after he was forced into exile, José Gervasio Artigas is regarded as the father of Uruguayan independence.

Born on June 19, 1764, in Montevideo, Artigas was a gaucho, or cowboy, in his youth. He joined the army in 1797 and after 1810 helped Argentina in its war for independence. In 1814 he was forced into a civil war to keep Argentina from absorbing Uruguay, which was at that time little more than a huge cattle range between Brazil and Argentina. He became a champion of federalism and for a short time ruled most of Uruguay and some of Argentina.

In 1816 his forces were defeated. He continued a resistance movement for three years, but an invasion of Portuguese forces from Brazil drove him into exile in 1820. Uruguayan independence was achieved in 1828. Artigas died in Paraguay on Sept. 23, 1850.

**ARTILLERY.** Military weapons that shoot large projectiles are known as artillery. This class of weapons includes not only the many types of cannons, but also rockets and guided missiles. Traditionally, the difference between artillery and small arms has been that soldiers cannot carry the larger weapons. According to an older tradition, artillery fires projectiles larger than .60 caliber (15 millimeters or 0.6⅗ inch in diameter), and small arms shoot projectiles of no more than .60 caliber. However, some modern rockets and guided missiles are much larger than .60 caliber, and yet soldiers carry them and launch them from the shoulder. (*See also* Ammunition.)

### Ancient Artillery

Ancient types of artillery, such as the catapult, ballista, and petrary, hurled large stones and spears and arrows. The Assyrians apparently developed the earliest forms of catapults during the 13th century BC. Ancient military leaders used artillery only to defend cities or lay siege to them. In the 300s BC, Philip of Macedonia and his son, Alexander the Great, developed smaller, portable catapults and ballistae. These weapons could be transported into battle and used much as field artillery is used now. Philip and Alexander often carried additional equipment for the catapults, using timber from nearby trees to build the main structure of the weapons.

Alexander used catapults and ballistae to lay siege to cities, much as others had done before. However, he also protected his troops with the weapons when the men climbed mountainous terrain and crossed rivers in the presence of enemy forces.

Some ancient Greek warships carried catapults and ballistae. The Greeks used these weapons to fire broadsides of spears and stones in battle against enemy ships to clear their decks of soldiers before boarding the vessels.

Roman legions used catapults and ballistae not only as siege weapons and field artillery, but also to bombard enemy troops before a battle. After the Romans, military commanders relied on catapults almost exclusively to besiege cities and rarely took them into the field.

Catapults and ballistae both operated by means of one of three principles—torsion, tension, or counterweight. Torsion is a force created by twisting heavy cords, most of them made of rope, hair, or animal tendons. One end of a long arm of timber between the cords was pulled back and then released to shoot a spear or stone as it spun forward. Tension was used by mounting a large bow on a base, arming it with a spear, and drawing the string back with a winding device called a windlass. Soldiers fired the spear with a trigger mechanism. Counterweight was used in the petrary, a weapon of the Middle Ages. This device had a lengthy timber hinged toward one end to which a heavy weight was attached. The other end of the timber had a spoon-shaped device or a sling that held a large stone. The stone, when fired, was flung up and forward by the heavy weight on the opposite end.

Through the centuries, until the introduction of gunpowder, armies used such devices of many sizes. The largest of these machines hurled projectiles that weighed up to 60 pounds (27 kilograms) as far as 400 to 500 yards (365 to 460 meters).

*Ancient artillery was powered by torsion, as in the catapult; by tension, as in the ballista; or by a counterweight, as in the petrary.*

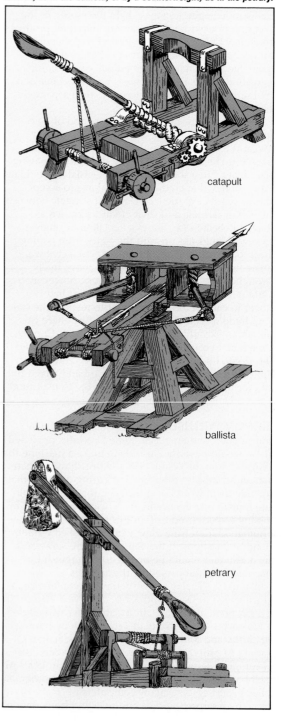

catapult

ballista

petrary

*Types of modern artillery include the recoilless rifle, which can be jeep-mounted (top), and the field artillery cannon, such as the 155-millimeter howitzer (bottom) that can be towed or airlifted into the field.*

(Top) U.S. Army; (bottom) Condec Corporation

## Artillery of the Middle Ages

Fragmentary records show that gunpowder was known in Europe during the mid-13th century. The invention of firearms came about 100 years later.

Early cannon had little value in battle because they were so crude and clumsy. Made of wrought iron, usually rods welded together, these cannon lacked the strength to shoot balls made of iron or lead, and so soldiers fired stone balls.

The 14th and 15th centuries brought the development of larger and larger cannon, which came to be called bombards. Armies used them in sieges to smash the walls of cities and castles. The Russians made the largest bombard, called the Tsar Cannon, which weighed almost 40 tons (36,360 kilograms) and had a bore diameter of 36 inches (91 centimeters). Such cannon, though too cumbersome except for use against large cities, made castle walls and other fortifications obsolete by the end of the 15th century.

The invention of smaller cannon provided artillery that could be pulled into the field of battle. The French introduced horse-drawn gun carriages in the 1590s, and these, plus lighter cannon built of bronze, made mobile artillery a reality. The French also developed the trunnion, an axle-like device near the middle of the cannon tube, which simplified the task of mounting the cannon. In addition, trunnions provided more secure mounting of the cannon on its carriage, and enabled the weapon to be raised or lowered with greater ease for aiming.

At first, cannon were much more effective than small firearms, and all the European armies adopted artillery. This rush to arm with artillery led to the development of hundreds of varieties of cannon. Cannonmakers experimented with new lengths, bore diameters, and barrel thicknesses in a continuing search for better artillery.

By the middle of the 16th century, Spain brought some order to the wide variety of cannon. King Charles I decreed that only seven types of artillery would be made for his army, with their projectiles weighing from 3 to 34 pounds (1 to 15 kilograms). Other nations soon standardized their artillery, and all artillery came to be grouped into three classes: culverins, cannon, and pedreros and mortars. Culverins were long, thick-walled artillery designed to shoot accurately at long range. Cannon were somewhat shorter, lighter pieces that had greater mobility than culverins but less accuracy and shorter range. Pedreros and mortars were short, thin-walled pieces that fired heavy projectiles a short distance.

During the first half of the 17th century, King Gustavus Adolphus of Sweden developed lighter, more mobile artillery that could keep up with his cavalry. Using three standard weapons, which fired projectiles weighing 24, 12, and 3 pounds (11, 5, and 1 kilograms), Gustavus' artillery supported both cavalry and infantry. However, his light cannon could not fire continually for very long, because they became overheated. Other armies did not adopt the Swedish artillery innovations until further improvements in artillery design had been made during the 18th century.

From the 16th century until the mid-19th century, improvements in cannon came gradually. Cast iron, bronze, and brass cannon changed little, even though machining and casting techniques improved. The improvement of gunpowder increased the certainty of igniting powder charges and of controlling them. The types and sizes of artillery became further standardized. Cannon manufacturers combined powder and shot into one cartridge that could be rammed down the muzzle faster. However, the most far-reaching improvements came in the lightness and mobility of artillery pieces and in the efficiency of their carriages and mountings.

New types of ammunition, including grapeshot and canister, came into common use, in addition to solid iron cannon balls. These new projectiles consisted of cases of small metal balls that were loaded into cannon as a single unit. Improvements in fuzes and the appearance of shrapnel made explosive shells important elements of artillery by the 19th century.

## Early Modern Artillery

The 19th century brought greater advances in cannon than ever before, primarily because of a considerable amount of progress in engineering and the basic sciences. Munitions companies perfected rifled cannon, which have spiral grooves on the inside of the barrel. These grooves cause the projectile to spin, stabilizing its flight and providing greater accuracy and longer range. Further improvements resulted from the introduction of bullet-shaped projectiles, which replaced spherical ones.

The invention of smokeless powder provided greater propellant force and did not foul cannon barrels as much as black powder did. Further improvements in metallurgy enabled manufacturers to build larger cannons that could withstand heavier propulsion forces and achieve longer ranges. The most important improvement may have been the introduction of the all-steel cannon in 1851 by Alfred Krupp, a German munitions manufacturer.

Two other advances played important parts in the development of modern cannon. The first successful system of breech loading for cannon permitted faster loading. The introduction of the recoil system, in which only the barrel recoils after the cannon has been fired and then automatically returns to its original position, allowed much more rapid and accurate fire. Earlier cannons bucked greatly when fired, and after each shot the gunners had to move these heavy weapons back into their original position and aim again before refiring.

With these advancements the era of rapid-firing artillery had arrived. Using brass cartridge cases that held a unit, or round, of ammunition—projectile, powder, and primer—small and medium-sized artillery could fire up to 20 times per minute. The empty shell casings were ejected automatically when the gun recoiled.

Some new forms of artillery were developed and used during World War I and World War II. For example, the shell of a new kind of mortar could simply be dropped into the breech of the vertical weapon. When the shell reached the bottom of the mortar tube, a fixed firing pin triggered its propulsive charge, hurling the shell high into the air, where it fell toward its target.

Another new artillery weapon, the recoilless rifle, has small openings located in the rear of the cannon. These openings let small amounts of the exploding gases escape. The escaping gases provide just enough force to balance the recoil effect of the shell as it leaves the barrel, so that little or no recoil actually occurs. Recoilless rifles can be mounted on small vehicles or on tripods, making these weapons more mobile than ordinary artillery.

With the development of improved ammunition, such as the armor-piercing shell and the proximity fuze, artillery played broader roles in combat. During both world wars, armies used artillery as major weapons against tanks, airplanes, fortifications, and massed troop formations.

## Rockets and Guided Missiles

The role of conventional artillery has been supplemented by new artillery weapons, including rockets and guided missiles. Rockets date back to ancient times and were used extensively through the 19th century. They then fell into disuse until World War II, when armies fired rockets from antitank weapons called bazookas. Numbers of larger rockets were used much like massed cannon against troop formations. (*See also* Guided Missile; Rocket.)

Germany developed crude forms of guided missiles, the V-1 and V-2 rockets, during World War II. They had internal guidance systems that controlled their flight. Following the war, guided missiles underwent rapid development and began to play a major role in armed warfare. Guided missiles are classified as surface-to-surface, surface-to-air, air-to-surface, or air-to-air, depending on their use.

Some small guided missiles are controlled by signals sent over thin wires that extend from the missiles as they streak toward their target. Most of these wire-guided missiles are short-range weapons. Other missiles are guided by radio.

Some types of sophisticated guided missiles have built-in radar and electronic equipment that enable them to find their target without external control. Others fly toward sources of heat, such as the jet engines of aircraft.

James R. McDonald

*The Pantheon in Rome, Italy (top left), is a 2nd-century architectural masterpiece that combines beauty with use. 'The Discus Thrower' (top right)—seen here is a Roman copy of the Greek original by Myron—attains a goal of sculpture in depicting the human form. Rembrandt's 'The Slaughtered Ox' (bottom left), painted in 1665, is an exceptional example of representational art. The musical motion picture 'Hello, Dolly!' (bottom right) featured Barbra Streisand in the lead role. A musical combines drama, music, and dance into one art form.*

# THE ARTS

Paintings and power shovels, sonatas and submarines, dramas and dynamos—they all have one thing in common. They are fashioned by people. They are artificial, in contrast to everything that is natural—plants, animals, minerals. The average 20th-century person would distinguish paintings, sonatas, and dramas as forms of art, while viewing power shovels, submarines, and dynamos as products of technology. This distinction, however, is a modern one that dates from an 18th-century point of view.

In earlier times the word art referred to any useful skill. Shoemaking, metalworking, medicine, agriculture, and even warfare were all once classified as arts. They were equated with what are today called the fine arts—painting, sculpture, music, architecture,

literature, dance, and related fields. In that broader sense art has been defined as a skill in making or doing, based on true and adequate reasoning.

The earlier and more comprehensive understanding of art can be seen in the Latin and Greek words that were used to describe it. The Latin word *ars* (plural, *artes*) was applied to any skill or knowledge that was needed to produce something. From it the English word art is derived, as is artificial, which means something produced by a human being. The Greek word is even more revealing. It is *technē*, the source for the term technology, which most people would never confuse with art.

The more general meaning of art survives in some modern expressions. The liberal arts, for instance, refer to the seven courses of university study that were offered during the Middle Ages: grammar, rhetoric, logic, arithmetic, geometry, music, and astronomy. The student who finished these courses received a bachelor of arts degree.

The liberal arts originated in ancient Greek and Roman attitudes toward different types of skill. The Greek philosophers, primarily Plato and Aristotle, did not separate the fine arts from the so-called useful arts, as is done today. They distinguished between the liberal arts and the servile arts, and fine arts were classified among the labors of the lower classes in ancient Greece and Rome.

---

### FACT FINDER FOR THE ARTS

The subject of art is a broad one. Readers will obtain additional information in the articles listed here. (*See also* related references in the Fact-Index.)

| | |
|---|---|
| Acting | Jewelry and Gems |
| Advertising | Knitting |
| Antique | Lace |
| Architecture | Literature |
| Ballet | Lithography |
| Basketry | Magic |
| Batik | Mask |
| Bead and Beadwork | Metalworking |
| Book and Bookmaking | Mime and Pantomime |
| Braiding | Mosaic |
| Calligraphy | Motion Pictures |
| Cartoons | Museum and Gallery |
| Counterfeiting and Forgery | Music |
| Dance | Musical Comedy |
| Decorative Arts | Needlework |
| Design | Opera |
| Directing | Operetta |
| Doll | Painting |
| Drama | Performing Arts |
| Drawing | Photography |
| Embossing | Poetry |
| Enamel | Pop Culture |
| Fashion | Pottery and Porcelain |
| Finger Painting | Puppet |
| Folk Art | Quilt |
| Folk Dance | Realism |
| Folklore | Renaissance |
| Folk Music | Romanticism |
| Furniture | Rug and Carpet |
| Glass | Sculpture |
| Glassware | Spinning and Weaving |
| Graphic Arts | Stained Glass |
| Greek and Roman Art | Tapestry |
| Hairdressing | Tattoo |
| Handicrafts | Textile |
| Heraldry | Theater |
| Holography | Ventriloquism |
| Industrial Design | Vocal Music |
| Interior Design | Wagon and Carriage |
| Jazz | Writing, Creative |

(*See also* fact finders for LITERATURE; MUSIC; PAINTING; PERFORMING ARTS.)

---

The word liberal comes from the Latin *liberalis,* meaning "suitable for a freeman." Studies that were taken up by free citizens were thus regarded as the liberal arts. They were arts that required superior mental ability—logic or astronomy, for example. Such arts were in contrast to skills that were basically labor.

*Servilis,* the Latin word for slavish or servile, was used to describe the handiwork that was often done by slaves, or at least by members of the lower classes. The servile arts involved such skills as metalworking, painting, sculpture, or shoemaking. The products of these arts provided material comforts and conveniences, but such arts were not themselves considered beautiful or noble.

### Aesthetics and Beauty

The concept of *beaux-arts,* a term that was coined in France during the 18th century, is expressed in English as fine arts. But the French word *beau* (plural, *beaux*) is usually translated as meaning "beautiful." This usage is the decisive clue to the separation of the fine arts from the useful arts and technology in the 1700s. The arts of the beautiful were separated from the arts of the useful because of the belief that the fine arts had a special quality: they served to give pleasure to an audience. The type of pleasure was called aesthetic, and it referred to the satisfaction given to the individual or group solely from perceiving—seeing or hearing—a work of art. The work could be a painting, a performance of music or drama, a well-designed building, or a piece of literature. The satisfaction could come from a perceived beauty, truth, or goodness; but since the mid-18th century the emphasis has been on beauty.

**Aesthetics** is the study, or science, of the beautiful. The word is derived from the Greek *aisthētikos,* meaning "of sense perception." The term aesthetics was coined by a German philosopher, Alexander Gottlieb Baumgarten in a two-volume work on the subject. Written in Latin and titled 'Aesthetica Acroamatica', it was published from 1750 to 1758. This unfinished work, which established aesthetics as a branch of philosophy, influenced some noted German philosophers—particularly Immanuel Kant. Kant retained Baumgarten's use of the term to apply to the entire field of sensory knowledge, and his interpretation was adapted by the German writers Johann Wolfgang von Goethe and Friedrich Schiller to present their own studies of the subject. It was Kant's 'Critique of Aesthetic Judgment'—the first part of his 'Critique of Judgment' (1790)—that proved to be the pivotal work on the subject, not Baumgarten's earlier work.

For Baumgarten, aesthetics had two emphases. First, it was a study of the theory of beauty; second, it was a theory of art. These two emphases, when drawn together in one science, served to distinguish the fine arts from the other activities of humankind.

The recognition of these arts as something distinctive and designed for pleasure really began during the Renaissance (primarily the 15th and 16th centuries in

Europe). For the first time artists of great skill gained individual reputations and their works were eagerly sought. After a 1,000-year period (from about AD 400 to 1400) during which the church dominated European culture, the arts were taken up by wealthy aristocrats and newly rich merchants and bankers. They competed with one another in the possession of beautiful things—homes, gardens, collections of paintings and sculpture, fine books, and theatrical performances.

The arts of decoration and design also gained a prestige they never had enjoyed earlier. Architects, landscape artists, painters, and sculptors gained a new prominence and, often, great financial rewards. Monarchs, nobles, and the growing middle class became patrons of the arts: they hired composers, dramatists, and other artists to create works for them. By the time Baumgarten published his 'Aesthetica Acroamatica' the fine arts had taken hold of the imagination of Europe. His new terminology served to enhance their reputation, while Kant and his successors provided the intellectual framework for understanding them.

Since the late 18th century aesthetics has become a fairly large and diversified field of study. Like the other sciences, it has moved out from the umbrella of philosophy and become a discipline of its own. It attempts to classify the arts—to understand, for example, what such diverse things as ballet and sculpture have in common that allows them to be categorized together as fine arts. The study of aesthetics also tries to describe the forms and styles of the various arts. It devises theories of art history in an attempt to trace patterns of development and change, along with analysis of outside influences on artists and their styles.

**Beauty**—unlike aesthetics, which was not used as a term until after the 1750s—has been a matter of thoughtful discussion and disagreement for many centuries. The Greek philosopher Plato could, in fact, be considered the true originator of aesthetics because he spoke a great deal about the nature of beauty in several of his dialogues. For Plato, true beauty was an ideal beyond human perception; like truth and goodness, it was eternal. Beauty that was visible could not be absolutely beautiful, he believed, because it was subject to change, growth, and decay. Beauty such as this was, in his judgment, merely a reenactment, or imitation of real beauty.

For all that Plato said about beauty, his writings never give a precise definition of it. The Greek artists and artisans knew how they wanted to present beauty in such masterpieces as the Parthenon in Athens and the statue of Helios in Rhodes. They demanded proportion and harmony, in accordance with their principle of moderation: nothing too much or too little. But examples do not create definitions. During the late Middle Ages, St. Thomas Aquinas tried to define beauty as "something pleasant to behold." In imitation of the Greeks, he noted that "beauty consists in due proportion, for the senses delight in things duly proportioned."

Bildarchiv Foto Marburg—Art Resource

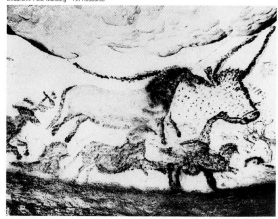

*The cave paintings at Lascaux, France, may date from as early as 15,000 BC, but the passing of millennia has not diminished their vivid realism or artistic merit.*

As a definition the words of Aquinas are unsuccessful. That is one of the two chief problems with beauty—the inability to give a clear and concise definition that everyone can understand and agree upon. The second problem is equally vexing: are there real standards of beauty, or is it only a matter of what the audience thinks? The familiar statement, "Beauty is in the eye of the beholder," is the most common way of saying that what is beautiful depends on the viewer. In other words, one person's beauty may be another's ugliness. The opposite opinion holds that beauty can be separated from ugliness, just as truth can be separated from falsehood and good from evil.

### Art, Technology, and Progress

At one time, as noted above, the same meaning was given to art that was applied to techniques. The blanket description that each involves the skill to make or do something is no longer true or accepted, however.

Technology is now generally thought of as applied science. The old terminology still has some validity in the role that skill plays and also in the transformation of matter. The skills of the artist, the craftsman, and the technologist all generally involve changes in the natural world. A block of marble is shaped into a statue by a sculptor. Silicon, metal, and plastic are shaped into a microchip by a technician using a machine. Otherwise art and technology have diverged completely. The goal of artists is to give permanence to the present, to speak to their age by creating works that will endure for all time. The goal of technicians is to press on to the future and to new discoveries.

Technology suggests permanent change and improvement. Once a new technique is discovered and adopted, society does not attempt to revert to the former technique. The automobile displaced the horse and buggy; the electric light replaced kerosene lamps; sound movies replaced silent films; and word processors are rapidly making typewriters obsolete.

This forward march of technology is called progress. In the fine arts such progress does not exist. The skill

*Art in the 17th century was concerned primarily with representing nature. 'Quince, Cabbage, Melon, and Cucumber' (top left) was painted by Spaniard Juan Sánchez Cotán. A marble portrait of Pietro Mellini (top right) by Benedetto da Majano was a product of the Italian Renaissance. The Chinese woodcut 'Bird and Blossom' (bottom) was done by Hu Cheng-yen in 1633.*

of the artist rests upon knowledge and experience, just as the skill of the technician does. But the creative processes involved seem to be different. Today, for example, one can admire the design of a Roman chariot, but few people would ever want to depend on it as a regular means of transportation. By contrast, it is still possible to walk into the Vatican's Sistine Chapel and be astounded by the magnificence of Michelangelo's frescoes. These paintings have an excellence that will never become outmoded.

A work of art, whether it be a painting by Titian or a concerto by Mozart, is not a stepping-stone to something else that will someday be considered better. It is not like the vacuum tube, which served its purpose well enough until the transistor was invented. Each artwork stands on its own—distinctive

for all time. Even poor imitations cannot damage the goodness and integrity of the original.

All the paintings and pieces of sculpture that have been done since Michelangelo and Leonardo da Vinci are different from the works of those two masters. But the more recent work can in no sense be viewed as an improvement in the same sense that the steamship is an improvement on the sailing ship. Painting of the 20th century, no matter how good it is, cannot be considered an improvement over the prehistoric cave paintings discovered near Lascaux, France; it can only be considered different.

In the late 20th century art and technology have been united by the computer. It is possible to create musical compositions on a computer. It is also common to design three-dimensional models of commercial products or to sketch out blueprints. Computers are used by sculptors, filmmakers, architects, printmakers, and other workers in the visual arts. It is even possible to create finished works of fine art on a computer screen. But the distinction between technology and art persists. Computers make the execution of some kinds of art more challenging and interesting; they do not, however, make art better.

## Useful Arts

Once the fine arts had been exalted by aesthetics into a class by themselves, the word art, when used alone, was normally understood to signify fine art. Otherwise it was modified by various adjectives when referring to other skills. Today, for instance, it is common to hear the terms decorative arts, commercial arts, industrial arts, or graphic arts. Sometimes the word art is omitted altogether, and terms such as applied sciences, technologies, or industries are used instead.

The term useful arts may be used to describe what does not specifically belong to the fine arts. The term is not at all precise, of course. It is obvious that a piano concerto is meant to be heard and enjoyed, without its having any other purpose. The same cannot be said for a well-designed building. While architecture is one of the fine arts, its products have uses other than aesthetic. The principal functions of buildings are as homes and workplaces.

Use and beauty also tend to overlap in other arts whose primary goal is to make useful objects. Furniture, jewelry, china, or carpets made by skilled craftsmen are intended to be beautiful as well as useful. Home-made trunks and quilts and other folk art crafted in rural areas have simple but attractive designs. The patterns created for wall coverings, draperies, and carpets also belong to the general category of decorative arts.

Mass-production industries spend much effort and money to make automobiles, boats, television sets, computers, and home appliances appealing to the eye as well as functional. Commercial art used in advertising usually tries to attract customers to its product or service.

### Classifications of the Arts

The arts have been classified as liberal or servile, fine or useful, as noted above. They can also be classified by the sense to which they appeal or by the number of skills needed to create the final product.

**Sensory appeal.** Arts are usually classified by their appeal to the senses of sight or hearing. Because painting, sculpture, and architecture depend for their aesthetic appreciation on eyesight, they are all visual arts, but a sculpture might also involve the sense of touch. Some useful arts, such as furniture making,

also appeal to the touch. Music is an auditory art, related as it is to the hearing. Literature can be both visual and auditory. When an individual reads a novel, the words are conveyed through visual impressions. Talking books provide an auditory experience of the same art. If cooking is included among the useful arts, its appeal is to both taste and smell.

**Single or composite arts.** Painting, sculpture, music, and literature are single arts. Each is independent of the others in that representative works can be enjoyed alone—one painting, one statue, one symphony, or one poem. Architecture, opera, drama, and dance are composite arts. They depend for their success on a variety of talents.

The great religious structures of medieval and Renaissance Europe were the results of collaboration among architects, stonemasons, glassmakers, sculptors, painters, and mosaicists, to name a few. An opera brings together a dramatic plot, music that is both played and sung, well-designed scenery and costumes, acting, and perhaps dance. A motion picture brings together writers, actors, directors, musicians, costume and set designers, camera operators, and a great variety of other technicians. Ballet combines dance, music, plot, costumes, and scenery.

*Art as expression emerged in the late 19th century. Claude Monet's 'Impression—Sunrise' (top) of 1872 prompted a critic to call the new art movement impressionism. It measures 45 by 55 centimeters. 'The Palace at 4 a.m.' (bottom left) is a surrealist construction in wood, glass, wire, and string by Alberto Giacometti from 1932–33. It is 64 centimeters high, 72 centimeters wide, and 40 centimeters deep. Expressionist painter Franz Kline's 1952 work, 'Painting No. 7' (bottom right), is an oil on canvas measuring 146 by 208 centimeters.*

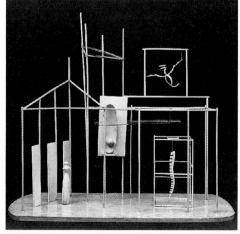

The development of architecture as a composite art was probably a normal division of labor. No one individual who designed a large building would ever have been expected to have expertise in all phases of its construction. As the designer, the architect probably worked as the foreman and coordinator of the project. The specialists who worked under the architect belonged to their own guilds, just as many artisans belong to unions today.

## Imitation and Expression in the Arts

In the fourth chapter of his 'Poetics' Aristotle says, "Imitation is natural to man from childhood, one of his advantages over the lower animals being this, that he is the most imitative creature in the world, and learns at first by imitation. And it is also natural for all to delight in works of imitation." By "works of imitation," Aristotle meant works of art. This included products of human skill that are now regarded as technological. Other terms he could have used for imitation are "representation" and "depiction."

Throughout the whole history of art, from the ancient world until the early 20th century, it was taken for granted that art imitated nature. The 16th-century English poet Thomas Overbury said simply, "Nature is God's. Art is man's instrument." About 300 years later the English critic John Ruskin noted, "Art does not represent things falsely, but truly as they appear

'Ministry of the Virgin', a panel painting from the Amiens School in 1437, is Gothic in style and measures 38½ by 23 inches. Gothic art combined elements of realism with abstraction.

Giraudon—Art Resource

to mankind." "Art is the child of nature," wrote the American poet Henry Wadsworth Longfellow in his "Kéramos and Other Poems."

Imitation was considered an aspect of the useful arts as well as what are now called the fine arts. The shoe imitates the foot and the glove the hand. The most enduring theme of the sculptor has been a representation of the human body. A great deal of Far Eastern painting depicts nature. Plato, in his "Sophist" dialogue, remarked that the painter is able to imitate anything in the world, and it is true that a painter's choice of subjects is virtually unlimited—landscapes, buildings, people, animals, scenes of battle, and still lifes of bowls of fruit or flowers. Literature can imitate the drama of all humankind or the individual life. Poetry, in the classical sense, has attempted to imitate truth itself. Music imitates the human passions. Music can also be descriptive in its presentation of sounds that remind a listener of an event—the roar of cannons as Napoleon invaded Russia in Tchaikovsky's '1812 Overture', the rolling waves in Claude Debussy's 'La Mer' (The Sea), and the insect noises in Rimski-Korsakov's 'Flight of the Bumble Bee'.

Imitation, in this sense, does not mean duplication. A real house is three-dimensional, but a painting of the house, though only two-dimensional, could still be a realistic representation. Sculpture, which is three-dimensional, makes a closer approximation of reality, but it lacks the life of what it depicts.

A divorce of art from nature (or at least a partial separation) occurred in the 20th century. The period through the 1960s witnessed such movements in art as cubism, Dadaism, nonobjectivism, abstract expressionism, surrealism, pop art, and minimalism.

The denial that art has to be imitative is at the heart of a statement by Pablo Picasso. When asked whether he painted what he saw, he replied: "I paint what I know is there." To paint what one sees is a description of art as imitation. Picasso's rather cryptic statement clouds the issue of imitation and puts the origin of artistic creation entirely within the artist. The artist's goal is self-expression, not necessarily imitation of any feature of the outer world. Both the inspiration and the subject matter derive from within. Or the artist may be trying to distill the essence of what is seen, to create an abstraction of its qualities.

The movement away from art as imitation, or representation, probably started in France with the work of the impressionists in the 19th century. The word impressionist is itself suggestive. The artist is not just painting a representation, because the artwork is giving a personal impression of what is seen. The artist is not trying to be a photographic realist.

The late 19th and early 20th centuries, therefore, created a sharp break with all past understandings of art. A painting or a piece of sculpture no longer had to refer to something familiar. It could instead consist only of abstract lines, shapes, and colors. Such art can be said to express the inner life, imagination, or emotions of the artist. Or it may be art that refers to nothing at all—just pure abstraction for its own sake.

The art-as-expression theory has generally replaced the art-as-imitation belief. Critics have contended, for instance, that all representational art is to some degree abstract. While some features of its subject are emphasized, others are ignored or downplayed. The Gothic art of the Middle Ages was abstract to some degree in that it did not pretend to depict literal reality. It was intent on portraying religious symbolism, but the abstractions were not so removed from normal experience that they were not easily recognizable by the viewers. Abstract portraits of saints and depictions of events in the life of Jesus Christ had become familiar to viewers by long association.

The performing arts in particular, have the quality of expression. A piece of music can express happiness or sorrow. George Gershwin's 'Ol' Man River' has an air of sadness and fatalism about it. The marches of John Philip Sousa bring to mind the arts of warfare, while some of George M. Cohan's music seems to proclaim patriotism. Paintings can express a large array of emotions, while works of literature can encompass the whole range of human activities. Tragic drama, according to Aristotle, was intended to arouse fear and pity in the viewer, thus affording an emotional release.

### Principles of Form

Metro-Goldwyn-Mayer, the motion-picture studio, has long used the Latin motto *Ars gratia artis* (Art for art's sake). The statement is basically meaningless since it is quite doubtful that anything can exist for its own sake, with no other purpose or goal. Art is at least meant to be enjoyed. But there is a school of art theory that contends the visual arts serve no ends other than their own. The enjoyment of each painting or piece of sculpture is based solely on the visible forms—colors, lines, and shapes, which are sufficient to satisfy the aesthetic tastes of the audience.

This theory of art is on firmer ground when dealing with principles of form. The ancient Greeks had their own principles—harmony, proportion, no excess, no deficiency. Aristotle laid down principles of form for dramatic literature in the 'Poetics'. His first principle was unity: a play must have a beginning, middle, and end; everything in the drama must belong and have a purpose. He also demanded diversity: an artist could paint a canvas one solid color, which would have unity, but it would be completely uninteresting. So too Aristotle demanded with drama. It needs diversity and complexity to make it appealing to an audience, but all the complexity must be drawn together at the end so nothing is left unresolved.

Close to the issue of diversity is a multiplicity of themes. Longer works of fiction often have one dominant story line and several minor themes. This is true, for instance, of Leo Tolstoi's 'War and Peace'. The main themes are Napoleon's invasion of Russia in 1812 and the love stories of Natasha, with Andre and Pierre. But there are numerous underlying plots and themes that occupy the novel's dozens of characters.

Even paintings can have two thematic levels. Some of the religious works of Hieronymus Bosch,

Bildarchiv Foto Marburg—Art Resource

*'The Garden of Earthly Delights', painted by Hieronymus Bosch in about 1500, consists of three panels. The center one, part of which is shown, measures 86¹/₂ by 76³/₄ inches.*

the Dutch painter, are quite complex. His 'Garden of Earthly Delights' has one major theme, but it is composed of isolated scenes with themes of their own. Longer pieces of music, especially symphonies, are multithematic; and epic poems weave together several stories within a major theme. Homer's 'Iliad', the greatest of the epics, is a classic example.

Some works of art—notably drama, novels, long poems, and music—should display development as they progress from beginning to end. There should be no parts that are interchangeable or capable of being shifted from one place to another. Nor should there be breaks that leave the audience wondering what is missing. The process of development should demonstrate balance. Each segment of a work of art needs adequate time—the overture to an opera, for example, cannot be longer than the opera. In a drama the action should be distributed throughout the acts. In a painting, objects in the background must appear smaller than those in the foreground, unless the work is completely abstract.

### Style in the Arts

The term style is most easily understood as a way of doing art. When two authors have a different way of writing, each is said to have a personal style. The style of Herman Melville was his own, quite different from that of Mark Twain, for instance. If a writer attracts followers who try to imitate the author's particular way of writing, they help perpetuate a style. Imitators of James Joyce, for example, use his stream-of-consciousness effects, and their writings are called Joycean.

*Changes in technology bring about changes in style. The flying buttresses on the south side of Chartres Cathedral (right) supported the walls and made large windows and lofty interiors possible. The advent of steel-frame construction permitted the building of modern skyscrapers. The Home Insurance Company Building (left), an early skyscraper, was designed by William Le Baron Jenney in Chicago in 1884–85.*

(Left) Chicago Architectural Photographing Company; (right) Bildarchiv Foto Marburg—Art Resource

Ancient Greek temples, medieval Romanesque churches, and 20th-century skyscrapers have different characteristics. What is peculiar to each one is its style. A movement in painting, such as impressionism, can be called a style. A school of painting, such as the Hudson River School in the early 19th century, suggests a specific style. There are, in fact, so many ways to describe style that the word has become almost impossible to define.

Many styles of popular music have emerged in the 20th century. One of the most dominant is rock, which itself represents a merging of earlier styles. Within rock several substyles developed. Elvis Presley, who appeared in the mid-1950s, was followed by the Beatles in the early 1960s. At the same time the Rolling Stones began playing a cruder form of rock. The Stones led the way to the punk rock of the Sex Pistols. By 1990 the music of Elvis Presley and his inspiration, Chuck Berry, was called classic rock, in contrast to the later, more extreme or violent styles.

The word style itself is from the Latin *stilus,* which originally referred to a stake and later was used for a sharpened writing instrument. The word has come into English as stylus, to denote such a pen. Because of its association with the written word, *stilus* also absorbed a colloquial meaning that referred to a skillful use of words in either writing or speaking. For many centuries other kinds of art were discussed in terms of their manner, characteristics, or similar qualities. The term style was limited to literature and rhetoric.

Not until about 1600 in Italy was style applied to different types of music. Its use for the visual arts came shortly after 1700. Today it is the most common word used to describe distinctive characteristics of individual artists, periods of art, national arts, regional types, and other variations in the arts. Thus the terms Romanesque, Byzantine, Gothic, realistic, postimpressionist, cubist, baroque, rococo, classical, neoclassic, mannerist, pointillistic, surrealistic, minimalist, and similar adjectives can be understood as indicating styles.

In the visual arts especially styles emerge and develop in different ways and for different reasons. A style in architecture, for example, may originate from an attempt to solve structural problems. When the Gothic cathedral first appeared in France in about 1140, those who designed it found a way to support the weights of the walls and ceilings by using external buttresses. As a result greater expanses of the thinner wall were available for windows, something that could not easily be accomplished earlier.

Once the structural solutions of Gothic architecture became generally accepted, new cathedrals were built throughout northern France. The new way of building quickly became a style that was consciously imitated throughout Europe. As a consequence, Gothic substyles developed. England's York Minster (Cathedral of St. Peter), Germany's Cologne cathedral, and Italy's Milan cathedral are all recognizably Gothic. But they also differ from each other in striking ways.

The 20th-century skyscraper was also the product of new technology and imagination. The Sears Tower, in Chicago, and the World Trade Center and the Empire State Building, in New York City, were made possible by steel-beam construction. The introduction of the elevator had made tall buildings feasible, but traditional masonry construction still limited the height of downtown buildings. This problem was solved by William Le Baron Jenney, the engineer who designed the Home Insurance Company building (1884–85) in Chicago. The forerunner of the modern skyscraper, it had a skeleton of cast-iron columns, covered with masonry, and wrought-iron beams. It is probably no coincidence that the most famous tall structure of the time was the Eiffel Tower in Paris, an entirely steel-beam construction (*see* Eiffel Tower).

Sometimes stylistic changes are little more than a matter of decoration. The three best-known kinds of classical Greek columns were Doric, Ionic, and Corinthian. All three types served essentially the same purposes, and from a distance they looked pretty much alike. A closer view showed their stylistic differences, particularly in decoration. Whereas the top of a Doric column was fairly plain, there were a snaillike carving on the Ionic and acanthus leaves atop the Corinthian.

All arts are influenced by the times in which they flourish. They are subject to an era's limitations or abundance—especially the quality and availability of materials for the visual arts. Great works of sculpture by Leonardo da Vinci, Michelangelo, and other artists benefited from nearby Italian marble quarries. Architecture has always been subject to the technical knowledge of its various periods. What is expressed and the way it is expressed are also grounded in specific epochs. Great events usually spawn a good deal of art. The French Revolution and the career of Napoleon were powerful influences on all the arts of France in both style and content.

The political and economic ideas of a time may have a vivid impact on literature. The Industrial Revolution and its aftermath inspired many writers during the 19th century. Charles Dickens could never have written 'Hard Times' except against the background of a newly industrialized society. Mass poverty and the brutalization of workers in the late 19th and early 20th centuries were among the factors that inspired the styles called realism and naturalism. Émile Zola in France and Theodore Dreiser in the United States were notable realists in fiction.

No really good style is ever out of style. The funeral and temple arts of the Egyptians and Mesopotamians became obsolete even in the ancient world. But later styles that developed in Western society have endured. The classical architecture of Greece and Rome reappeared during the Renaissance and again under 19th-century Romanticism. Some modern structures still use classical or neoclassic lines. Gothic has never gone out of style for houses of worship, though most modern Gothic is entirely inauthentic as a way of building. (The problems that the style was designed to solve can now be dealt with in other ways.) The same is true of Byzantine architecture, a product of ancient and medieval Constantinople (now Istanbul).

The Renaissance styles of the late Middle Ages have a broader appeal and are still used in a wider assortment of buildings—museums, educational institutions, and government buildings, to name a few. The mosque, which was developed as a house of worship in Islam, has persisted for centuries, though there are striking regional and national varieties of the style. In traditional societies, such as exist in India, styles may persist almost unchanged for centuries.

### The Artist's Training

Artists and their works belong, first and foremost, to specific places and times. Through their works artists interpret their societies to their own generation. At the same time, they distill the essence of their time and place for later generations. An illustration by Norman Rockwell perfectly captures the quality of life in rural, small-town America in the first half of the 20th century. The great rose window of the cathedral at Chartres vividly depicts the objects of belief for 12th-century Christians. Eero Saarinen's Trans World Airlines terminal at John F. Kennedy International Airport in New York City symbolizes the technology and adventure of flight.

As artists are products of their time, they absorb the prevailing ideas, beliefs, and techniques of their generation. They are also individuals with special talents, who in most cases have devoted significant portions of their lives to training and to sharpening their skills.

Today it is possible to study the arts in a college or university. There are also specialized schools of architecture, music, design, and other arts. These educational institutions are a fairly modern development, mostly from the mid-19th century. From ancient times through the 16th century, artists were trained by other artists in their workshops or studios. Becoming an artist required an extended apprenticeship (see Apprenticeship). The neophyte artist became an apprentice as a young teenager and did the most menial tasks around the studio before being trained in the more difficult tasks of an art or craft. The normal period of service was seven years.

By the 17th century the budding artist was considered more a pupil than an apprentice; the training of student artists by masters lasted well into the 19th century. By the 17th century, however, the early academies had begun to flourish as training centers. In Italy the Accademia di San Luca was founded in Rome in 1593. In France the Royal Academy of Painting and Sculpture, which was patterned after it, was founded in Paris in 1648. England's Royal Academy of Arts was started in London in 1768.

*Old styles do not disappear. The 190 S. LaSalle Building in Chicago, designed by John Burgee and Phillip Johnson in the 1980s, has elements of Gothic and Renaissance decoration.*

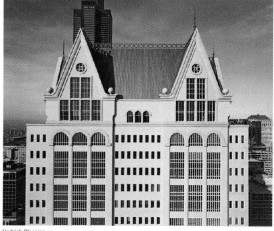

Hedrich Blessing

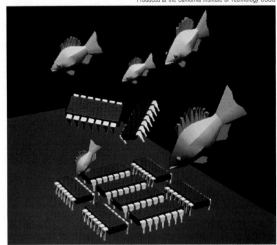

*The computer graphic 'Fish and Chips' (1985) by Vibeke Sorensen is an example of what an artist can do with technologies that have been developed since the early 1970s.*

These academies became a vital force in the instruction of young artists, and they exerted a powerful influence on the development of the arts generally. Because the academies limited their enrollments, they created artistic elites within their countries. They also set standards of taste for whole societies. By their insistence on correct technique, the schools tended to standardize art and reward conformity.

Reactions against the monopoly of the academies arose in the 19th century. In London the government-sponsored School of Design opened in 1837. In 1852 the Victoria and Albert Museum was founded, and at the same time a number of other art schools were set up by the government. The combination of museum and art school took hold in other countries as well. A basic part of the artist's training was painting imitations of the old masters in museums. In Paris the French Institute (now the National Superior School of Fine Arts) was set up in 1795 to supervise the arts and displaced the Royal Academy of Painting and Sculpture as a training institution.

In England, under the leadership of William Morris, schools were established to teach both fine arts and applied arts. This merger of fine and applied arts was furthered by the Bauhaus (house of building), a school of design founded in Weimar, Germany, in 1919 by Walter Gropius. With its outstanding faculty of architects, painters, and other artists, the Bauhaus completely transformed art education. Through its influence, schools of art that embraced its methods and ideals were incorporated into colleges and universities, especially in the United States.

Schools for music training began with the founding of a conservatory in Paris in 1795. Other conservatories were started in European and American cities in the next few decades. Some of these eventually became associated with universities. The first modern school for dance, the Royal Academy of Dance, was founded in France by King Louis XIV in 1661. With this and

other French schools, Paris became the leading training center for ballet. Training for the theater was, until the 20th century, similar to an apprenticeship system. Young actors worked in theaters to learn their craft from experienced performers. Today there are two main types of drama school. Some, like the Actors Studio in New York City and the Royal Academy of Dramatic Art in London, teach only acting. Others, such as the Yale School of Drama, are workshops associated with universities and colleges.

**BIBLIOGRAPHY FOR THE ARTS**

**Barasch, Moshe.** Theories of Art: From Plato to Winckelmann (N.Y. Univ. Press, 1985).
**Caplin, L.E., ed.** The Business of Art (Prentice, 1982).
**Curtiss, Deborah.** Introduction to Visual Literacy (Prentice, 1987).
**De La Croix, Horst and Tansey, R.G.** Gardner's Art Through the Ages, 8th ed. (Harcourt, 1986).
**Dissanyake, Ellen.** What Is Art For? (Univ. of Wash. Press, 1988).
**Goodman, Cynthia.** Digital Visions: Computers and Art (Abrams, 1987).
**Hartley, Marsden.** On Art (Horizon, 1981).
**Kurtz, B.D.** Visual Imagination: An Introduction to Art (Prentice, 1987).
**Langer, S.K.** Reflections on Art (Ayer, 1979).
**McConnell, R.B., ed.** Art, Science, and Human Progress (Universe, 1983).
**Roskill, Mark.** What is Art History? 2nd ed. (Univ. of Mass. Press, 1989).
**Scruton, Roger.** The Aesthetic Understanding (Routledge, 1984).
**Taylor, J.C.** Learning to Look: A Handbook for the Visual Arts, 2nd ed. (Univ. of Chicago Press, 1981).
**Wolfe, Tom.** The Painted Word (Farrar, Strauss, 1975).

*Norman Rockwell's 'Freedom From Want' was one in a series of Four Freedoms works that perfectly capture the spirit of early 20th-century small-town life in the United States.*

**ARUBA.** A self-governing island of The Netherlands, Aruba is approximately 50 miles (80 kilometers) west of Curaçao and 15 miles (24 kilometers) north of Venezuela. The island is mostly flat and covers an area of about 75 square miles (194 square kilometers).

Tourism benefits from Aruba's deepwater harbors for cruise ships, its international airport, long stretches of white sandy beaches, and a favorable climate. The Lago Oil refining complex was the main source of employment until it closed in 1985. Two plants produce low-sulfur fuel oil, and a petrochemical plant produces ammonia.

More than half the people are of Indian ancestry; the rest are European or other immigrants. The official language is Dutch, but the native language used in daily life is Papiamento, a mixture of Portuguese, Dutch, Spanish, and African origin.

Aruba's earliest inhabitants were Arawak Indians. Aruba was claimed by Spain in 1499. The Dutch West India Company garrisoned the island in 1634, and it has remained under Dutch control, except for 13 years of intermittent British rule in the early 1800s.

On Jan. 1, 1986, Aruba seceded from the Netherlands Antilles. All local affairs are handled by an island government. The Netherlands, however, still controls the island's defense and foreign affairs. Aruba is expected to gain complete independence in 1996. (*See also* West Indies.) Population (1991 estimate), 66,000.

**ASBESTOS.** A natural mineral fiber that is either mined or quarried, asbestos can be spun, woven, or felted, almost like cotton and wool. It has been valued since ancient times for its resistance to fire. It is composed of strands that are flexible and very strong.

Airborne asbestos fibers have been shown to cause cancer. Some manufacturers of asbestos products have been sued by people who have been exposed in some way to these fibers and later gotten cancer. Asbestos can also cause a lung disorder known as asbestosis.

Only the longest asbestos fibers, called spinning fibers, are made into threads and yarns. From them are woven tough fabrics for making brake-band linings, clutch facings, gaskets, wicks, fireproof theater curtains, fire fighters' suits, gloves, and conveyor belts for hot materials. The shorter, or nonspinning, fibers are used for molded brake linings, acid filters, soundproofing materials, and paints. They are combined with magnesia for heat-insulating materials and are made into paper for covering pipes and wires.

The brittle, smooth-surfaced asbestos fibers are usually blended with a rough-surfaced fiber, such as cotton, which may constitute 10 to 25 percent of the blend. At the mill the fibers are freed from rock by hand sledges or by machines that crush, dry, recrush, and screen the rock. The fibers are then separated from the surrounding material and graded.

In a natural state, asbestos fibers are tightly packed in veins and pockets of rocks. The chief commercial variety is chrysotile. It has crystalline fibers composed of magnesium, silicon, hydrogen, and oxygen. Other useful varieties are amosite, which is exceptionally long-fibered, and crocidolite (blue asbestos), which is valued for its strength. The world's largest producers of asbestos are Russia and Canada. (*See also* Fibers, Natural.)

**ASH.** Among the finest forest and timber trees in North America are the ashes. About 65 species are found throughout the Northern Hemisphere. The most abundant and economically useful is the white ash (*Fraxinus americana*). Its tough, elastic, straight-grained wood can be used for baseball bats, skis, oars, tennis rackets, tool handles, and ladders.

This graceful tree grows in deep, well-drained soil in moist locations. It may reach 120 feet (37 meters) in height. The compound leaves may be 12 inches (30 centimeters) or more in length, with five to nine leaflets, each a few inches long. Reddish-purple flower clusters bloom in the early spring.

The flowering ash (*F. ornus*) of Southern Europe produces creamy white, fragrant flowers, has leaves with usually seven leaflets, and reaches about 60 feet (18 meters) in height. *F. cuspidata,* from southwestern North America, has similar flowers, seven leaflets, and reaches 20 feet (6 meters) in height. Among the taller ashes are *F. floribunda,* from the Himalayas, and the European ash.

Mexican ash (*F. uhdei*), a broad-crowned tree widely planted along Mexico City streets, is evergreen except in dry or freezing seasons. It reaches 50 feet (15 meters) in height and has leaves with five to nine leaflets. The velvet ash (*F. velutina*), also a mild-climate tree, has three to five narrow leaflets. The so-called mountain ash is not a true ash (*see* Mountain Ash). The ashes belong to the olive family, Oleaceae.

**ASHKHABAD, Turkmenistan.** Located in an oasis near the Kara-Kum Desert is the city of Ashkhabad, capital of the Central Asian republic of Turkmenistan. From 1924 to 1991 it was the capital of the Turkmen Soviet Socialist Republic.

Situated near the foot of the Kopet-Dag Range Ashkhabad is an administrative, industrial, transportation, and cultural center. The city is renowned for its carpet-weaving industry, as well as glassworks, cotton mills, and metalworking shops. There are several institutions of higher education, including the Turkmen Academy of Sciences, founded in 1951, which is home to the world-renowned Institute of Deserts. Other attractions include an opera house, theaters, and several museums.

Ashkhabad was founded in 1881 as a Russian military fort and took the name of a nearby Turkmen settlement. Because of its position on the caravan routes and on the Transcaspian Railway, its population numbered more than 45,000 by 1911. After the Russian Revolution the city was renamed Poltoratsk, for a local revolutionary; in 1927 it reverted to its original name. An earthquake virtually destroyed the city in October 1948. A chronic water shortage was alleviated considerably when the Kara-Kum Canal reached the city in 1962. Population (1991 estimate), 412,200.

Pictor/Uniphoto

*Framed by bamboo plants, the sun rises over the Li River near the town of Yangshuo in Guangxi Province. The sharp hill formations in southern China are unique to Asia.*

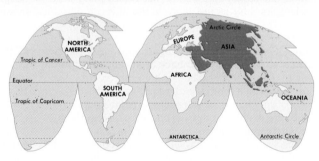

# ASIA

A land of extremes and contrasts, Asia is the largest and the most populous continent. It has the highest mountains and most of the longest rivers, highest plateaus, and largest deserts and plains of all the continents. Asia is also home to some of the world's oldest cultures. It has some of the poorest as well as some of the richest nations in the world. It contains a major share of the world's largest cities, yet most of Asia's people are rural dwellers. Because of its size, age, population, and rich resources Asia has long been of great interest to the rest of the world. During much of Asia's history, outsiders, principally Europeans, have tried to exploit and control it and its

*This article was written by Jack F. Williams, Professor of Geography, Michigan State University, and author of numerous publications on China and other Asian subjects.*

## PREVIEW

*The article Asia is divided into the following sections:*

people. In the 20th century, however, Asia has been the scene of great change. Many of the undeveloped countries of the region are taking various approaches to modernizing their economies and societies, some under Communism. Progress has often been slow because of physical and cultural barriers, but there have been some notable advances and the efforts to upgrade living standards continue.

## Two Definitions of Asia: Classical and Modern

Asia is actually just one part of the Eurasian landmass, the largest body of land on Earth. Through time, a division of Eurasia into two parts, Europe and Asia, became generally accepted. The dividing line started with the Ural Mountains in Russia and then continued south to the Caspian Sea, turning west to follow the boundary between today's Iran and Turkey and Georgia, Armenia, and Azerbaijan. Turkey thus was the westernmost part of Asia. Asia then, in the classical sense, extends east as far as the Pacific Ocean, north to the Arctic Ocean, and south to the Indian Ocean and the islands of Southeast Asia. Europeans called Asia the Orient, meaning "east," and the Western world was referred to as the Occident, meaning "west." These old terms are seldom used anymore.

Some geographers prefer to define Asia in a narrower sense. This smaller Asia is based on the region's more recent political, cultural, and economic changes. Thus, modern Asia would exclude two subregions, Russian Asia (Siberia) and Southwest Asia. Remaining in the modern version of Asia are three subregions: South Asia, Southeast Asia, and East Asia. Although this article on Asia uses the classical, larger definition of the continent, some recognition is given to the modern interpretation of Asia.

## THE NATURAL ENVIRONMENT

### Land and Population

Even the modern, smaller definition of Asia would make it the largest and most populous of the continents. Classical Asia is even larger. Its area of more than 17 million square miles (44 million square kilometers) accounts for almost one third of the Earth's land surface, or an area greater than the two Americas or Europe and Africa combined. From a population perspective, Asia leads the world even more. There are about 2.6 billion people in Asia, 60 percent of the world total. Most of those people, some 2.2 billion, are concentrated within the modern limitations of Asia (South, Southeast, and East), which is one reason for trying to confine the study of Asia.

Regardless, the share of the world's people living in Asia is increasing steadily. By the year 2000, Asia's share should reach about 3.8 billion or about 61 percent of the world total. This fact alone demonstrates the importance of Asia. Asia's population density thus is high, about 151 persons per square mile (58 per square kilometer), compared to around 40 per square mile (15 per square kilometer) in North America. Moreover, Asia's population is unevenly distributed,

so that in some of the most populous countries of the continent, the densities are far higher. In Japan, for example, the density is about 850 per square mile (330 per square kilometer).

### Seas and Islands

One of the major characteristics of Asia is that most of the population is crowded onto a broad fringe extending to the ocean; an area that is relatively fertile, level, and well-watered. This can be pictured as an arc extending through the three subregions of East, Southeast, and South Asia. The association with the sea is strong. Three oceans border Asia, the Arctic, Pacific, and Indian, but the latter two are by far the most important to the people of Asia. Within the areas where these oceans touch the continent are many of the world's largest and most important islands and archipelagoes.

On its eastern side Asia is strung with island arcs that enclose many seas. In the northeast, Asia comes closest to North America, where the Alaskan mainland lies only 53 miles (85 kilometers) from Siberia. The Aleutian Island chain encloses the Bering Sea. The Kamchatka Peninsula and the Kuril Islands fence off the Sea of Okhotsk in Siberia. Sakhalin Island and the main islands of Japan bend in another arc toward the Korean Peninsula to set off the Sea of Japan. The Ryukyu Islands arc southward to the island of Taiwan, enclosing the Yellow Sea and East China Sea. From Taiwan south, the Philippine archipelago picks up the pattern, blending into the island of Borneo to delimit the South China Sea. Much of Southeast Asia is a complex mix of islands and seas.

This distinctive pattern of island arcs is the result of the so-called Ring of Fire that largely encloses the Pacific Ocean. In this area the land is geologically young and still developing. The islands along the ring are thus rugged, and volcanoes and earthquakes are common in this region.

In South Asia, the pattern of seas and islands is not so striking, and the region is dominated by the mass of the Indian Ocean fronting directly on the mainland. The largest island, Sri Lanka (formerly Ceylon) lies off the tip of the Indian subcontinent. The Bay of Bengal directly to the east is separated from the Andaman Sea by the Andaman and Nicobar islands that trail southward toward Sumatra. To the west of India there is a sprinkling of mostly coral atolls in the Laccadive Islands and Maldives, running south out of the Arabian Sea. Southwest Asia is distinctly shaped by the peninsulas of Arabia and Turkey and the seas that surround them, particularly the Black Sea, Mediterranean Sea, Red Sea, and Persian Gulf.

### Continent of Extremes

Asia's great expanse from the equatorial tropics to the arctic (6,000 miles; 9,650 kilometers) and from the Pacific Ocean to the Mediterranean Sea (5,900 miles; 9,500 kilometers) results in a continent of extreme contrasts. Asia contains virtually every kind of natural landscape. Roughly half the continent consists of

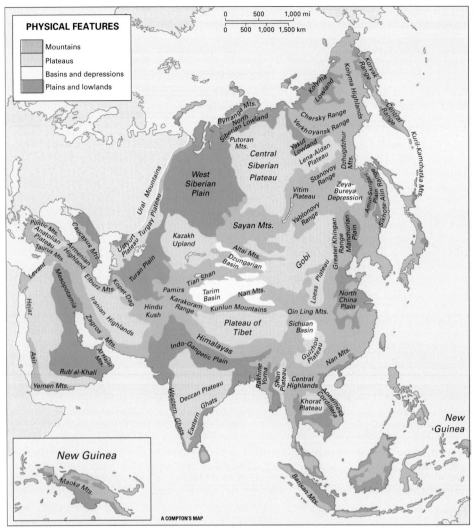

*Physiographic regions of Asia*

highlands, and about 8 percent is more than 10,000 feet (3,000 meters) above sea level. Asia's average elevation exceeds that of all the other continents except Antarctica.

**Mountainous Center**

Dominating the Asian landscape is the huge Tibetan-Qinghai Highlands, which occupy much of western China. This plateau is the highest and largest in the world. According to some geologists it was created by movements of the Earth's crust between India and Tibet that forced the plateau upward. Geologists say it is still rising. (*See also* Earth.)

In the western part of this plateau are the Pamir Mountains, called the Roof of the World, where China, Tajikistan, Pakistan, and Afghanistan meet. From this mountain knot, lofty ranges spread outward in many directions. The Hindu Kush runs southwest through Afghanistan. To the northeast extends the Tian Shan.

The Karakoram runs southeast and merges into the Himalayas, the highest mountain range in the world. Mount Everest, the tallest peak (29,023 feet; 8,846 meters), is located there, as are the other eight highest peaks of the world. The Himalayas are a favorite challenge for mountain climbers.

The largest area of highlands in Asia thus is connected with the Tibetan plateau. Most of western and northern China, as well as all of Mongolia and much of southern Siberia, is dominated by mountains and plateaus.

To the north is the great plain of Siberia that rims the Arctic Ocean and stretches west, with few physical barriers, to European Russia. The Caspian Sea and the Ural Mountains mark the traditional western limit of Asia. South, southwest, and east of the highland core of Asia, the landscape is a mix of lower mountain ranges, hills, plains, and valleys, which blends into the island arcs of the east and southeast.

Harrison Forman

*The lofty snow-covered peaks of the Hindu Kush range rise up beyond the Bololo Canyon, north of Kabul. Asia's landscape includes the highest and most rugged mountains in the world.*

## Great Rivers and Their Basins

The drainage pattern of Asia is also dominated by the central highland core. With the exception of Southwest Asia, all the great rivers of Asia flow out of this central highland region. Eight of the twenty longest rivers in the world are found in Asia. Those that flow to the Arctic through Siberia include the Ob, Yenisey, and Lena. The valleys they form are largely uninhabited because of the harsh climate.

The rivers that flow to the east and south, however, have been home to millions of people since the beginning of history. Their valleys have the combination of warmth and moisture that was favorable to early civilizations. These rivers include the eastward flowing Amur (or Heilongjiang), the Huang He, the Yangtze, and the Hsi, all in China. Southeast Asia has the great rivers of the Mekong, Chao Phraya, Salween, and Irrawaddy. In South Asia are located the Ganges-Brahmaputra and Indus rivers. Southwest Asia is arid and has few major rivers. The most important are the Tigris and Euphrates, which flow out of the highlands of Turkey.

Not all of Asia's rivers reach the sea. From the Caspian Sea eastward through parts of the central mountain core of western China is a region of interior drainage. Here rivers flow from the mountains across arid lands and disappear into salty lakes or swamps. This is a rugged land and is among the least populated parts of Asia.

## Extremes of Climate

Asia has every type of climate found in the world. The major factors that influence Asia's climate pattern are its huge land area, its location between the tropics and the arctic, and its great range in elevations from sea level to high plateaus and mountains. The dominant climatic pattern over most of the inhabited part of Asia is the monsoon, the seasonal shift in wind patterns between winter and summer. Most of Asia's people live in what is sometimes called "monsoon Asia." This includes the subregions of East, Southeast, and South Asia. During winter, cold, dry air moves southward out of the Mongolian Plateau, giving northern Asia little precipitation in winter. In summer the pattern reverses, with warm, moist air moving northward from the tropics. Rainfall is heaviest at this time, especially in the coastal band of the three subregions. By the time the air masses reach farther north, most of the moisture is gone. Precipitation is therefore heaviest in southern and eastern Asia where most of the people live.

To the north, in Siberia, the climate is cold and dry. The extreme northern fringe, as well as much of the Tibetan-Qinghai Plateau, has a tundra climate, sometimes also called a cold desert because the land is dry like a desert but with cold temperatures. Most of the remainder of Siberia has a subarctic climate. In this area stands a vast evergreen forest known as the taiga. There, some of the world's coldest temperatures have been recorded.

Steppe and desert climates dominate the regions just south of the subarctic; they affect most of north and west China, Russia, and virtually all of Southwest Asia and western South Asia. These are regions of low precipitation and hot summers. Because of the dryness and lack of sources of fresh water, large parts of the steppe and desert regions are uninhabited.

Parts of northern China, plus North and South Korea and part of Japan, have a continental warm summer climate. Winters are fairly cold, but summers warm and humid, and thus the land is well-suited for agriculture and human settlement. To the south a large humid subtropical climate zone prevails. It stretches from southern Japan through all of southern China and parts of northern Southeast Asia and South Asia. Because of the mild climate of this region, it is one of the most densely populated parts of Asia

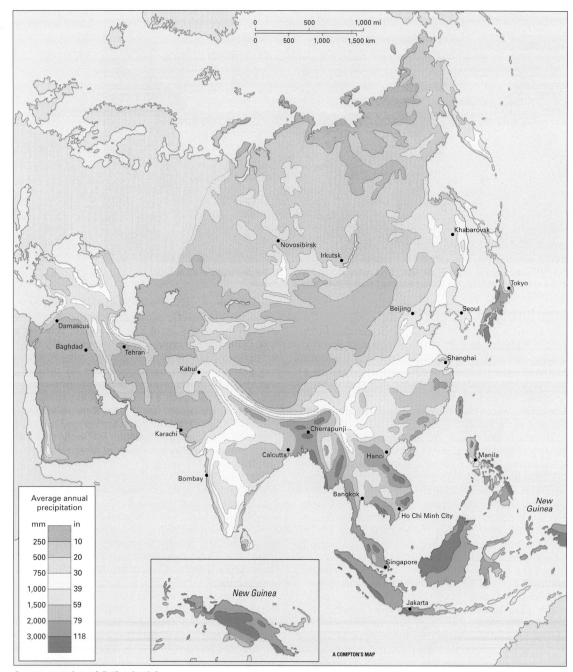

*Average annual precipitation for Asia*

and the world. Nearly 1 billion people live in this hospitable climate zone of Asia.

Farther south are the tropical humid climate zones of South and Southeast Asia. They have high year-round temperatures and heavy precipitation, which have given rise to some of the world's densest tropical rain forests. On the mainland, where the winter monsoon effect is felt, precipitation is concentrated in summer and there is a winter dry season, producing a savanna

climate. Particularly in a high population density region such as India, the timely arrival of the summer monsoon is critical to millions of people who depend on the rains for agriculture.

**Plant and Animal Life**

The distribution of Asia's natural vegetation and wildlife is directly related to the continent's climate patterns. Thus, the types of plant and animal life are

*Evergreen taiga forest extends across much of Siberia, where some of the world's coldest temperatures have been recorded.*

strong policies for protecting wildlife, and uncontrolled hunting has often been allowed. Nevertheless, some unique animal species that are found only in parts of Asia still survive, including the yak, giant panda, Siberian tiger, Bactrian camel, Bengal tiger, Indian leopard, Indian elephant, Indian rhinoceros, Malay tapir, gibbon, and orangutan.

### Asia's Geographic Regions

The five major regions, or realms, into which classical Asia is divided are distinguished primarily by culture, history, political development, and, to some extent, natural environment. The five regions, as stated earlier, are: Russian Asia, Southwest Asia, South Asia, Southeast Asia, and East Asia.

**Russian Asia.** Russian Asia (largely Siberia) accounts for about three fourths of the territory of the former Soviet Union. It includes Kazakhstan, Kyrgyzstan, Tajikistan, Turkmenistan, and Uzbekistan. This region was controlled by Imperial Russia during the 17th to 19th centuries. A vast, largely barren land, it has always resisted human settlement because of severe cold in the north and dryness in the south. Only a small proportion of Russia's people live there today despite the area's size. The population is denser in a narrow band running east and west along the southern border of the region, just north of Iran, Afghanistan, Pakistan, Mongolia, China, and North Korea. This is the route of the Trans-Siberian Railroad.

Russian Asia extends all the way to the Bering Strait, which separates it from North America. The principal economic activities in Russian Asia are mining of the region's rich mineral wealth, particularly coal and oil, and logging in the taiga, the world's largest forest. Heavy industrial activities include petroleum and gas refining, chemical and metal production, machine building, and construction. The harsh climate and vast area hamper greater development.

**Southwest Asia.** Like Russian Asia, Southwest Asia is a subregion that is not regarded as part of the modern concept of Asia. The area extends from Asian Turkey and Iran in the north, south through Iraq, Syria, Lebanon, Israel, Jordan, and Saudi Arabia and the other states of the Arabian Peninsula. This

as various as the climate. Wherever humans have been present in large numbers for a long time, such as India and China, the need for land for agriculture and settlement has meant the destruction of wildlife and natural vegetation. In Southeast Asia the once extensive tropical rain forest is rapidly disappearing because of logging operations, population growth, and agricultural expansion. China has barely 12 percent of its land under natural forest cover, the lowest proportion of any major country in the world. Only in Siberia, where the population is small, has the natural landscape survived relatively unchanged. To a lesser extent that is also true in the steppes and deserts.

Asia was once the range for countless species of wildlife, including some found only in Asia. Now many species have been drastically reduced in numbers, some close to the point of extinction. The governments of most nations in Asia have not had

*Horses graze on the steppe grass in the southern region of the Gobi, a cold desert that straddles the China-Mongolia border. The Altai Mountains loom up to encompass the desert's western reaches.*

*Dense tropical vegetation covers the Cameron Highlands in Malaysia, a nation of Southeast Asia. Tropical forest is prevalent in this region, though it is being reduced by population expansion.*
Mort Beebe—Photo Researchers

is a region dominated by a dry climate, and thus the total population has never been large. Of the more than 134 million people in the region, Iran and Turkey account for more than half. Culturally, the region is the easternmost extension of the Middle East–North Africa realm, that area dominated by the Arabic-Islamic culture. Although Southwest Asia has had long historical associations with the rest of Asia to the east, its main economic and political ties have been to the West, with North Africa and Europe.

Southwest Asia was the site of some of the earliest civilizations. This was in the Fertile Crescent, starting in the Tigris-Euphrates valleys in present-day Iraq and curving down through the valley of the Jordan River and the Dead Sea in present-day Jordan and Israel. Although economically limited by the arid climate, Southwest Asia has been fortunate during the 20th century because of the vast oil deposits found there, especially around the Persian Gulf. The wealth earned from oil exports has economically transformed much of the region and made some of the nations among the richest in the world. Oil has made Southwest Asia a region of vital importance to the world's industrial countries. In the 20th century Southwest Asia has been the focus of numerous world crises, both because of cultural conflicts and the attempts of industrial nations to influence and control the oil-rich region.

**South Asia.** South Asia is sometimes referred to as the Indian subcontinent. It consists of modern India, plus the smaller nations of Pakistan and Afghanistan to the west, Bangladesh to the east, Nepal and Bhutan to the north, and the island nations of Sri Lanka and the Maldives to the south. The northern boundary of South Asia is the great Himalayan mountain chain, which forms the southern border of Tibet, a part of China. South Asia is about half the size of the United States and has a great range of natural features and climates. Nepal and Bhutan are landlocked mountain states with limited agricultural potential. The same is true of Afghanistan, though it has a much larger territory.

Afghanistan's strategic location near Russian Asia has made it a crossroads and the target of numerous invasions including one by the Soviet Union in 1979.

Most of western South Asia, including parts of Pakistan and western India, is extremely arid. Irrigation, mainly from the Indus River, has long been vital to agriculture there. In the east, Bangladesh shares the valleys of the Ganges and Brahmaputra with India. This is the heartland of South Asia, with the most humid climate and best conditions for agriculture. More than half of South Asia's 1 billion people live in these valleys. South of the Ganges Valley the land slopes to the Indian plateau and the climate is subtropical to tropical. With the development of irrigation and hydroelectric projects, the region has made industrial progress.

All of South Asia was controlled by the British, as part of their worldwide colonial empire, until independence was granted in the late 1940s. The British left a legacy of many economic improvements, including an extensive railway system, and a strong political and cultural imprint on the traditional societies of the region. However, the great diversity of peoples, languages, and religions in South Asia, combined with overpopulation and extensive poverty, left the region with many problems of national development.

Since independence, there have been many improvements characterized by growth of industry, mechanization of agriculture, urbanization, and an increase in literacy. The South Asian nations are still poor, but they are developing.

**Southeast Asia.** Southeast Asia consists of two main parts: mainland and insular (largely the island area). The mainland is composed of parallel mountain ranges and river valleys that run south and southeast out of the Tibetan plateau and surrounding highlands. Thus, the mainland nations of Myanmar (formerly Burma), Thailand, Laos, Cambodia (Kampuchea), and Vietnam consist of river valley cores in which most of the people live. These cores are surrounded by less populous highlands. In Myanmar the core is the Irrawaddy Valley. In Thailand it is the Chao Phraya. In Laos, Cambodia, and southern Vietnam, the cores center along the Mekong River. In northern Vietnam the core is in the Red River valley. Insular Southeast Asia consists of the Malay peninsula and the many islands that make up the nations of Malaysia,

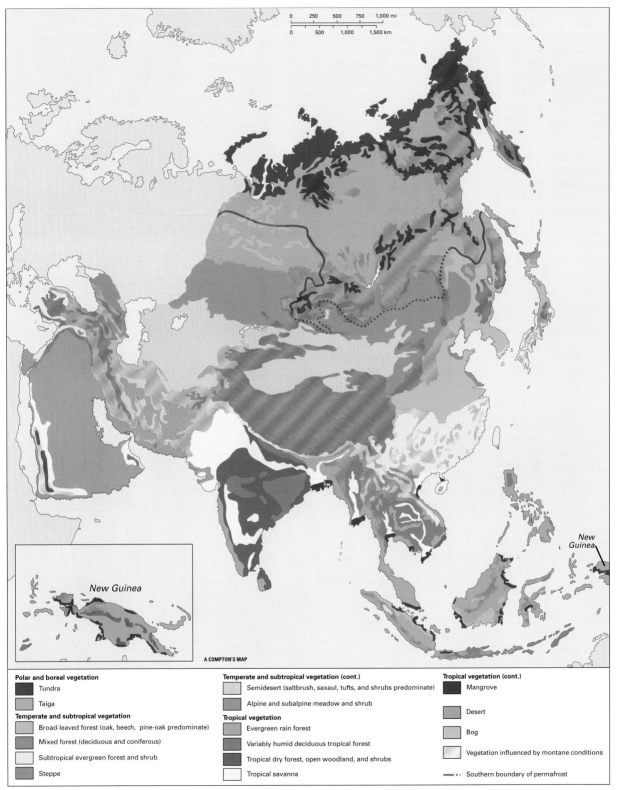

**Vegetation zones of Asia**

**Polar and boreal vegetation**
- Tundra
- Taiga

**Temperate and subtropical vegetation**
- Broad-leaved forest (oak, beech, pine-oak predominate)
- Mixed forest (deciduous and coniferous)
- Subtropical evergreen forest and shrub
- Steppe

**Temperate and subtropical vegetation (cont.)**
- Semidesert (saltbrush, saxaul, tufts, and shrubs predominate)
- Alpine and subalpine meadow and shrub

**Tropical vegetation**
- Evergreen rain forest
- Variably humid deciduous tropical forest
- Tropical dry forest, open woodland, and shrubs
- Tropical savanna

**Tropical vegetation (cont.)**
- Mangrove
- Desert
- Bog
- Vegetation influenced by montane conditions
- Southern boundary of permafrost

A COMPTON'S MAP

New Guinea

Singapore, Indonesia, Brunei, and the Philippines. Indonesia alone has about 13,000 islands. People on these islands live largely along coastal plains and short river valleys that flow out of the mountainous interiors of the islands. Most of the islands are mountainous, and many are of volcanic origin. The most famous and important of the islands is Java in Indonesia.

Southeast Asia's population of about 440 million is much smaller than that of South or East Asia, but the land area of Southeast Asia is also smaller. The population is unevenly distributed, and population densities in parts of the region range among the world's highest. Indonesia alone has more than 181 million people, more than half of them on the island of Java. All of Southeast Asia was under colonial rule or influence until after World War II. Independent civilizations, such as the Khmer and Thai, flourished in the region long before the colonial rule of the British, French, Dutch, Spanish, and Portuguese was imposed starting in the 16th and 17th centuries. Since independence these countries have struggled to develop their natural resources and industries. For example, Singapore and Jakarta have become modern industrial centers. Indonesia is a major petroleum producer, and Malaysia is a major tin producer. Throughout the region new techniques are being used to increase production of rice and other grain crops. Plantation crops such as rubber, bananas, coconuts, sugarcane, tea, palm oil, and spices are also important.

The Indochina conflict that raged from World War II until the mid-1970s hampered progress in the states of Indochina, of which Vietnam has become perhaps the most powerful. Turmoil has continued in the region, especially in Cambodia, further complicating economic growth.

**East Asia.** East Asia consists of the nations of Japan, North and South Korea, China, Taiwan, and Mongolia, and the colonies of Macao and Hong Kong. An old term for the region is the Far East, dating from earlier history when the area was "far" from Europe and "east" of Europe in terms of traveling time and direction. It lies mostly within the Temperate Zone, and thus the climatic patterns and natural environment are similar in many ways to those of Europe and southern North America.

China, with its huge size and population, dominates East Asia physically. The remaining much smaller states are located along the eastern side of the region, which includes the peninsula of Korea, divided today into the two nations of North Korea and South Korea. The island nation of Japan is also there. In the southeast is the island of Taiwan (formerly Formosa), where the Republic of China government rules in exile as a legacy of the Chinese Revolution. The government of the People's Republic of China also claims control of Taiwan. Hong Kong, on China's southeast coast, is still administered as a British colony. There is also the tiny Portuguese colony of Macao just across the bay from Hong Kong. Both Portugal and Britain agreed in the 1980s to transfer control over these colonies to China in the 1990s. Culturally, the Republic of Mongolia

*A Kyrgyz horseman hunts with a royal eagle in a valley of Central Asia.*

*A Jordanian Bedouin in flowing robes with his grandson in a jogging suit reflect changing traditions in the Middle East.*

AP/Wide World

AP/Wide World

*A gardener works amid blooming plants on the Royal Summer Palace grounds at Paro, a high Himalayan valley in Bhutan. The kingdom's valleys resemble those of the Swiss Alps.*

is also part of East Asia. However, Mongolia was politically tied to the Soviet Union for much of the 20th century and plays no significant role in current East Asian affairs.

East Asia is the most populous region in the world, with about 1.4 billion people, or more than one fourth of the world total. More than 1 billion of those people are in China alone. Most of these people are concentrated in the eastern fringe of the region, where there are extensive lowlands and the most favorable climate. In this area population densities are among the highest in the world.

China was the first great civilization in East Asia and strongly influenced the cultural development of the other peoples in the region. For this reason, East Asia is also sometimes referred to as the Sinic (meaning "Chinese") culture realm. During the 19th and early 20th centuries, China was gravely weakened by internal political and economic problems, which were aggravated by Western and Japanese colonial efforts to exploit the country. The Chinese Revolution, which started in 1911, resulted finally in the Communists seizing power in 1949. Since then China has struggled to overcome its problems of overpopulation and

*Vietnamese children play near construction work in a village of Cai Lay, a district of Vietnam in the Mekong Delta region. Most of the Vietnamese people live in the lowlands of the Mekong Delta and Valley while other peoples of the country mostly occupy the hill regions.*

Marilyn Silverstone—Magnum

Sven Gillsater—Tiofoto Bildbyra

*Some of the world's largest cities are in Asia. (Top) Barges jam a canal in downtown Singapore, a densely populated city-state and one of the world's busiest ports. (Bottom) Small shops line the narrow streets of Hong Kong, one of the few colonies left in Asia.*

lack of technology in order to develop as a modern industrial nation. Progress has been gradual but slow. Although much smaller in size and population, Japan is the economic giant of the region and one of the most powerful industrial nations in the world. South Korea, Taiwan, and Hong Kong are rapidly industrializing, following the Japanese model.

## PEOPLES AND CULTURES

The racial pattern of Asia is extremely complex. The three main racial groups are found there: Caucasoid, Mongoloid, and Negroid. The Caucasoid dominates in South and Southwest Asia, and the Mongoloid in East and Southeast Asia, as well as in Siberia. The Negroid peoples, much fewer in numbers, are found mainly in South Asia. The Aryo-Dravidians of India are also sometimes regarded as a separate main racial group. Among these racial families are many variations, commonly based on language and culture differences. On the one hand, there has been considerable mixing of the races. On the other hand, many groups have been isolated because of physical barriers, such as mountains, deserts, and seas. This isolation has influenced the development of special ethnic characteristics among certain groups.

### Languages

The language patterns of Asia reflect the great diversity of peoples. Ural-Altaic languages are predominant in Siberia. In East Asia and parts of Southeast Asia various Sino-Tibetan languages are spoken. Korean and Japanese are unique variations derived from both the

Tom Putnam

Adapted from Norton S. Ginsburg (ed.),*Aldine University Atlas* (1970), Aldine Publishing Co., Chicago; copyright © 1970 by George Philip & Son Ltd., London; with permission from the author and Aldine-Atherton, Inc.

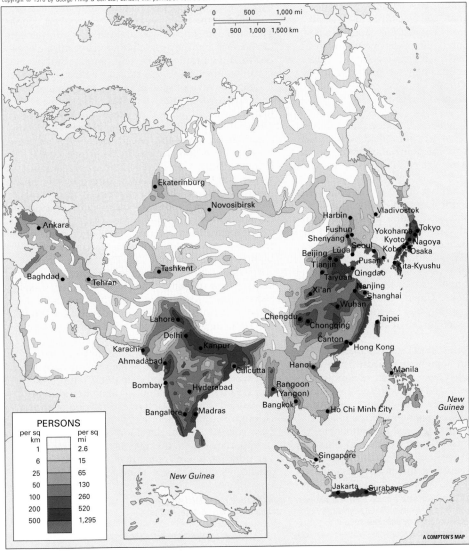

*Population density of Asia*

Ural-Altaic and Sino-Tibetan groups. The peoples of insular Southeast Asia speak various Malay languages. In South Asia the Dravidian and Indo-Aryan are the main language families. In Southwest Asia, Arabic and Irano-Armenian languages are the most common. These are the broadest patterns. Actually, the language situation in Asia is far more complex, because there are often dozens of variations in each language family. South and Southeast Asia are especially complex in their language patterns. Indeed, the great variety of spoken and written languages is often one of the main obstacles to developing a sense of national unity in the countries of these regions. In some places, inhabitants share a common written language but are unable to understand the spoken dialects of their neighbors.

To overcome problems of communication, most Asian countries have adopted a national or official language. Often this is the language spoken by a large segment of the population. Hindi spoken in India and Bahasa Indonesia (Javanese) in Indonesia are examples. In China the spoken dialect of the Beijing region of northern China has been the national language for decades. As a result of past colonialism, European languages, especially English and French, are widely used in Asia. Throughout Asia most schoolchildren study English for at least a few years. Most educated people in Asia know more than one language. English remains the unofficial national language of India and a number of other former British colonies. Dutch, Spanish, and French may also still be heard in other former colonies.

## Religions

Asia was the birthplace for most of the great world religions, including Christianity, Judaism, Islam, Hinduism, and Buddhism. The first three emerged out of the ancient Middle East (Southwest Asia). These three faiths share the belief that there is but one God. There are other similarities, but there are also some fundamental differences among the three. Such differences have often been among the causes that led to bloody conflict between followers of the faiths, beginning with the Crusades of the Middle Ages and most recently in the Israeli-Arab struggle. Fierce internal struggles have also taken place between factions within each religion. Of these three religions Islam has become the most widespread on the Asian continent. Muslims are the dominating group in the countries of Southwest Asia and in parts of South and Southeast Asia.

Hinduism and Buddhism developed in South Asia. The latter was carried to East and Southeast Asia where it is still significant. Buddhism, however, is no longer a major religion in South Asia itself. Sikhism, a combination of Islamic and Hindu elements, also grew out of South Asia. Confucianism emerged in China more than 2,000 years ago. Not a true religion, Confucianism is more of a social-ethical system, and it profoundly influenced China's development. Many elements of Confucianism still play important roles in Chinese society, even under Communism, which discourages religion.

Other religions confined to East Asia include Taoism in China and Shintoism in Japan. These are also not considered true religions. In Southeast Asia, Buddhism dominated the mainland area and Islam spread through most of the insular area. As a result of Spanish colonialism, many of the peoples of the Philippines were converted to Catholicism. That country has one of the only dominant Christian populations in all of Asia today, though there are notable Christian minorities in many Asian countries.

Christian missionaries worked throughout much of Asia during the colonial era, trying to convert people. Their religious impact was slight in terms of numbers of converts, but they sometimes made contributions to health and education, especially among rural people. Christian missionaries are still active throughout Asia.

Religious divisions, often related to language and cultural differences, have been the source of many social and political problems. For example, the partition of British India after World War II was mainly the result of the inability of the Muslims (believers in Islam) and Hindus to live peaceably together. Thus, a Muslim Pakistan was created in two sections on the subcontinent, leaving a mostly Hindu India in between. The two nations have frequently feuded since. In Southeast Asia, religious and cultural differences between Muslim Malays and nonreligious Chinese have been a source of tension in some of the countries there. In Iran, after the overthrow of the shah in 1979, a militantly orthodox Shi'ah Muslim government attempted to suppress other religious faiths. Islamic militancy has marked much of Asia's history and has continued in the 20th century.

As the nations of Asia have modernized, the hold of traditional religions has weakened. This is particularly true in East Asia. During the era of Mao Zedong in China, from 1949 to 1976, for example, religion was officially discouraged. Some religious freedom, however, has been restored. In non-Communist East Asia social and technological modernization has tended to weaken the role of religion in society. Through Southeast, South, and Southwest Asia, where there is less economic development, religion still plays an important role in the daily life of millions of people.

In addition, there are many other Asians who practice various forms of animism. These are tribal

*Young Tai pupils (left) of Southeast Asia receive their lessons from a monk outside a Buddhist temple. Most Tai youth serve some time as monks. Hindu pilgrims in India travel long distances to bathe in the Ganges River (right), whose waters they consider sacred.*

S.E. Hedin—Ostman Agency

Paul Popper Ltd.

*A carved jade beast represents sculpture from the Six Dynasties of China in the 4th and 5th centuries AD. Most jade carving comes from China, where the art form originated.*

*A leafy design decorates a ceramic dish by the 20th-century Japanese artist Hamada Shoji. The potter's art has a particularly rich tradition among East Asian cultures.*

*Buddhist art and architecture are reflected in the shimmering Shwe Dagon pagoda, built in Rangoon (Yangon), Myanmar, in the 15th century.*

*Winged creatures sit amid flowering stems and birds in paradise in a detail from a Persian silk hunting carpet made in Kashan, Iran (then Persia), in the 16th century. Carpet making reached its highest artistic level in Asian countries such as Iran and Pakistan.*

religious beliefs concerned with spiritual beings that can help or harm the believer. Animistic peoples are generally isolated and have little contact with others.

## Arts and Literature

The richness of Asia's cultures is reflected in its arts and literature. China, for example, developed one of the world's most distinctive cultures over a period of some 3,000 years. The Chinese developed unique forms of art, such as painting, ceramics, and bronzeware, as well as architecture, literature, and music. These profoundly influenced the cultures of Korea and Japan. The Indian civilization of South Asia also developed distinctive art forms, different from those of East Asia and in many ways related to the arts of the Middle East. Islamic art and architecture have also had a major influence on world culture. The art, architecture, and literature of Asia have long been highly appreciated by Westerners.

## Education and Health

In the more developed countries, especially Japan, there are high standards for education and health care. Most of the developing nations of Asia face major problems in improving education and health care for their large populations. Overpopulation remains the chief obstacle to improving the lives of the people. This is not only because of the large populations within each nation. It is also because such a large proportion of the population is young. In China,

*A young Indian woman listens intently in a nursing class. Many Asian countries are emphasizing health care education.*

WHO

for example, more than 60 percent of the people are under 30 years old. In most of the region it is not uncommon for 40 to 50 percent of the population to be under 21. Subsequently there is an enormous demand for education, and the demand for health care and various other social services is growing continually.

Most Asian countries, however, do not have economies strong enough to provide adequate services. Young people often receive only a primary school education. Many get no education at all and remain illiterate. A lucky few go on to high school, and even fewer to college. The labor forces thus tend to be poorly trained. Combined with low incomes and poor nutrition, this means that millions of Asians have shortened life-spans and suffer from chronic illnesses, untreated diseases, and reduced energy levels. Population control is generally recognized as a major requirement in solving these health and education problems in Asia's poorer countries.

## THE ECONOMY

Great poverty contrasted with great wealth characterizes Asia's economies. Parts of Asia, such as Japan, Singapore, and some of the Middle East oil-rich nations, have standards of living equal to that of most Western countries. Other parts of Asia, such as Indonesia, Myanmar, Indochina, and Bangladesh, have much lower standards of living. Many of the people live in poverty. Within many of the countries of Asia, there are great gaps in income levels, with a relatively small and wealthy elite living beside large masses of people who struggle to survive. Many factors account for this inequality; probably one of the most important is that Asia's people still depend largely on agriculture for their living; so a middle class has not been able to develop through industrial growth. What limited industrialization there is in most Asian countries tends to be concentrated in a few large cities. The wealth produced by such urban-centered industry tends not to spread evenly throughout the countries. Asia's traditional societies, reluctant to change customs, also foster inequality.

The situation caused by these conditions is that of dual economies. In many of the smaller countries this means there is a small, relatively modern industrialized economy concentrated in the largest city, which is often the national capital. A small proportion of the people live there, but their average income tends to be higher than that of the majority of the people living in rural areas, where most of the people work in agriculture. There is little industry, and income levels are low. Society changes slowly in these areas. Because of this gap between rural areas and the large cities, millions of rural people have been moving from the countryside to the cities to seek a better life. This migration burdens the large cities with too many people, who often cannot find jobs, adequate housing, and other social services. The rural areas also suffer because most of the migrants are young men. This trend is one of the major problems facing Asian nations that are still largely agricultural.

## Agriculture

Most of Asia's peoples are farmers who struggle just to produce enough food to survive. Throughout the continent, the average person consumes only about 2,000 calories a day, which is just barely enough for minimum nutrition. Moreover, those calories tend to be high in starches and low in protein. Meat is a luxury for most Asians, eaten only on special occasions. The diet tends to consist mostly of rice or other grains, plus small amounts of vegetables and fruits, and protein from nonanimal sources, such as beans. In many countries fish is another source of protein.

**Subsistence farming.** The type of agriculture practiced by most farmers is called subsistence farming. The whole family works hard in farming; there are few if any farm machines, and little surplus is produced for market. Farms tend to be small, an average of no more than two to three acres (about one hectare). Farming thus tends to be intensive; that is, the farmer must get a small land area to produce the highest possible yields. Fortunately, much of Asia lies in the tropics and warmer climates, so that

double-cropping, or growing two crops each year, is possible. Rice is preferred in the warmer, wetter places; wheat and other dry grains are grown in the cooler and drier areas. The farmers often raise a little poultry or livestock as well, usually for the market.

In hilly and mountainous areas farmers practice slash and burn cultivation, which is the crudest form of subsistence agriculture. This kind of agriculture consists of cutting down the forest cover, then burning it. Seed is then planted in the ground among the tree stumps; nothing more is done to help the plants grow until harvesttime. Yields are low, and after a few harvests the farmer must abandon the land and move on to a new forest area, where he starts the process again.

**Commercial agriculture.** Commercial agriculture, in the form of plantations and small holdings, is also widespread in Asia, especially in the countries of Southeast and South Asia. European colonial rulers began this type of agriculture. The Europeans first acquired control over huge estates of land all over Asia and then planted them with a single crop, such as rubber, sugarcane, coffee, tea, or bananas. Labor

*Agriculture is still the basis of most Asian economies. A Philippine farmer (top) uses animal power to pull a plow through his rice paddy. Fishermen on Eastern Lake in Wuhan, China (bottom), use nets to pull their catch into small boats. Fish is a major source of protein in many Asian countries.*

(Top) Ted Spiegel-Black Star;
(bottom) Herbert Lanks—SUPERSTOCK

was supplied by local peasants who worked for small wages. Most of the profits were returned to Europe.

Plantation farming has declined greatly since the early 1950s, because most of the nations in which it was practiced regained independence. A few countries, such as Malaysia and Sri Lanka, have encouraged plantation farming in order to increase exports. Some countries have encouraged local farmers to produce commercial export crops on their small holdings. Most commercial production now comes from small holdings, and these crops provide a major source of export income for a number of Asian countries.

**Nomadic herding.** In the drier parts of Asia, especially Southwest Asia, most rural people make a living by raising livestock. Many are nomads who move with their herds of animals over large territories, constantly seeking good supplies of grass and water. The people live simply and carry their tents and belongings with them. Such animals as goats, sheep, camels, and yaks, raised by these herders, are able to withstand dry climates (*see* Nomads).

**Collectivized agriculture.** In the Communist nations of Asia, particularly China and the Soviet Union before its dissolution, agriculture has been collectivized. Governments ordered the farmers to pool their land and other resources with their neighbors to make large farms. In China these are called communes. The farmers work the land together and share the income produced. The government's goal is to produce more than was possible on the traditional small subsistence farms of the past. With more-efficient farming, surpluses would be produced to help feed the huge Chinese population. The commune system, however, did not meet expectations. In the era after Chairman Mao Zedong's death in 1976, the government determined that the commune system might not be providing enough incentives for farmers.

To encourage farmers to produce more, China experimented with changes in the commune system.

For example, in some areas families are given free use (but not ownership) of a plot of land. They can grow what they want on the land, as long as they turn over a fixed quota to the commune after the harvest (*see* China).

**Fisheries.** Much of the Asian population has traditionally relied upon fishing as an occupation and fishes as a source of protein in the diet. Most of the fishing is traditional and is done in small boats that stay close to shore. Japan and Russia have Asia's largest and most highly developed oceangoing fishing industries. They send large, modern fleets throughout the world in search of sea products, including whales. Aquaculture, or sea farming, is also common in Asia. This consists of raising shellfishes and other seafood, such as oysters, clams, shrimp, and seaweed, in offshore shallow waters. Freshwater fishes are also raised in ponds or caught in rivers in inland areas. This practice is widespread in warm, humid areas. (*See also* Aquaculture; Fish Culture.)

**Forestry.** Timber for construction, firewood, and many other uses is widely harvested in Asia. In wetter, warmer areas, especially in the Southeast, bamboo plays a vital role in some traditional societies because of its many uses. The young bamboo shoots are even an important source of food. Commercial logging is most developed in Southeast Asia, where large areas are still covered with tropical and subtropical forests. Teak and mahogany are two notable wood products of this area. However, the demand for forest products for local use and for export has resulted in abuse of the forest cover. One of the main threats to the forest is that the people must use wood as cooking fuel. In parts of South Asia, such as India and Nepal, for example, the forest cover is rapidly disappearing for this reason. Soil erosion and other problems commonly result from this stripping of the forests. Increased conservation programs are sought, but they are difficult to implement where people depend on forest products for survival.

*Goats graze on sparse grasses alongside an oil pipeline at Masjed Soleyman in Iran. Oil discoveries have transformed the economies of many countries in arid Southwest Asia.*

Fred J. Maroon—Photo Researchers

## Minerals and Power

Asia contains some of the richest mineral deposits in the world. The mining industry, however, is still poorly developed in many areas, and both total output and per capita output are low. The extent of mineral resources is still not fully known, and discoveries made since the early 1950s have improved projections for the future. Other natural resources that would serve as the basis for industrial growth, such as waterpower, are also plentiful.

## Energy Resources

The development of cheap energy for industrial growth is essential to the improvement of most Asian economies. Asia's energy resources are among the world's largest, but still only partially tapped. China, for example, contains the world's third largest coal deposits. Large coalfields are found in Siberia as well. India and Southeast Asia also have notable deposits.

The richest oil reserves in the world are in Asia, mainly in Southwest Asia around the Persian Gulf. Most of the world's oil is produced there. But China and Russia have also become major petroleum producers, and Indonesia is the largest producer in Southeast Asia. Much of Russia's oil comes from Siberia. Oil exploration is being carried out all along the perimeter of Asia, from the waters off Korea and China south to Indonesia and west to the Persian Gulf. Oil exports have become important sources of income for an increased number of Asian nations. China and Malaysia now enjoy wealth from petroleum, and prospects for further finds are promising. Russia is the continent's chief producer of natural gas.

Asia has the greatest waterpower potential of all the continents, but only a tiny fraction of this power has been developed. China has enormous quantities of undeveloped waterpower, especially along the Yangtze River (see Yangtze River). With so many of the world's major rivers located in Asia, it is under-standable that the continent has such great potential power. However, the obstacles to development of this resource are many, including the cold climate in Siberia and the lack of capital in other areas. Dams for tapping waterpower are extremely expensive to build. A number of nations have been involved for decades trying to develop the waterpower of the Mekong River in Southeast Asia. Unfortunately, the Indochina conflict delayed that cooperative effort. Although hydroelectric power is continuing to grow, thermal power is generally a more widely used source for producing electricity.

Another growing power source in Asia is nuclear energy. Nuclear power plants are operating in a number of Asian countries, but especially Japan, which is probably the largest producer and user of power in Asia. India, Pakistan, South Korea, and Russia are other places served by nuclear power, and many more plants are planned.

**Metals and Other Minerals for Industry.** Among the mined metallic minerals useful to industry, iron ore is one of the most important because it is the basis of steelmaking. India and China are the largest iron ore producers in Asia. Accordingly, those two countries have the largest iron and steel industries in Asia, using their abundant coal supplies as fuel. Other iron ore deposits are located in North Korea, Malaysia, and Siberia. Bauxite, for aluminum production, is found in large amounts in India and Indonesia. Copper is mined in the Philippines and in other parts of Southeast Asia. Much of the world's tin comes from the tin belt that stretches from South China through Thailand and the Malay Peninsula to Indonesia. There are deposits of most of the other metallic minerals in Asia as well. Nonmetallic minerals are also abundant, but unevenly distributed, as are the metals. Sulfur, one of the most important, is produced in Japan, Korea, and China, as well as parts of Southwest Asia and Siberia. North and South Korea and China produce a large share of the world's graphite.

*Workers at a huge steel foundry in Songnim, North Korea, stoke furnaces to a white heat. Heavy industry in North Korea and other East Asian countries has developed more rapidly than in most Asian regions.*

Jean Mohr, Geneva

Most of Asia's nations are not major consumers of minerals, because of their low levels of industrial development. One of the primary exceptions is Japan, which largely lacks the most important minerals but is highly industrialized. Japan must buy minerals from other parts of Asia and the rest of the world. Japan is one of the largest world importers of mineral products. European powers started mining industries in many of the former colonial states of Asia. Foreign investment in mining is still common throughout the region, especially in oil prospecting and drilling.

## Manufacturing

Asia has some of the most highly industrialized countries in the world, like Japan, and some of the least, such as Bangladesh, Laos, Nepal, and Afghanistan. Between these extremes are found all levels of industrial development, from countries just beginning to develop modern manufacturing to those that have already made some marked progress. The latter are sometimes referred to as the NICs (newly industrialized countries). Three of the most successful NICs—Hong Kong, Taiwan, and South Korea—are in East Asia and one—Singapore—is in Southeast Asia. Malaysia has also achieved considerable progress. Overall, East Asia ranks as the most heavily industrialized of the five subregions of Asia, followed

*A supervisor and a worker discuss production in the spinning mill of a textile works at Ulaanbaatar, Mongolia.*

UPI/Bettmann

in order by Russian Asia, Southeast Asia, Southwest Asia, and lastly South Asia.

Throughout Asia there is a strong movement to change traditional agrarian societies into modern industrial societies. Various economic plans have been used to accomplish industrialization in socialist and nonsocialist countries. Some countries have used features of both socialist and nonsocialist programs.

In Communist lands—notably China, North Korea, Vietnam, most of the rest of Indochina, and the Soviet Union before its dissolution—largely socialist programs of industrial development have been followed. Generally in this approach there is no private ownership of industry. Everything is owned by the state, and workers are employed by the state. The system is highly centralized, with decisions made by the central government. Orders are then sent out to the various regions and factories to produce specific products in specific quantities. The emphasis tends to be on heavy industry rather than consumer goods or light industry, though this trend has shifted somewhat. These countries have made progress in manufacturing, especially China. One of the main problems in socialized industry is the difficulty of balancing supply and demand. It is difficult to avoid frequent critical shifts in shortages of some goods and surpluses of others. This, of course, is a problem to some degree in any industrialized society. Some economists also feel that the lack of an incentive system, like those in capitalist countries, also affects production. Some socialist countries have begun to introduce incentive systems as a result. Since the late 1970s, for instance, China has experimented with economic reforms. It is decentralizing management and using wage bonuses to encourage production. China is also stressing production of consumer goods to meet the needs of its huge population. Some small private enterprise is also being permitted. Since 1991 Russia and the other former Soviet republics have been in transition between socialism and capitalism.

Various forms of the free enterprise, or capitalist, system are being used to develop manufacturing in much of Asia. Private ownership of businesses and factories is encouraged. Governments primarily are involved in regulating and planning and sometimes investment in expensive manufacturing, such as iron and steel or transportation.

Some of the manufacturing developed since the early 1950s followed that first established by the former colonial rulers. In India, for example, the British established the still important modern textile industry. The Japanese began much of the industrialization in Taiwan, South Korea, and northeastern China (Manchuria) when they ruled those territories. For the most part, however, colonial rulers in Asia were interested in extracting the mineral resources and agricultural products of Asia. Manufactured products were mostly imported from the colonial mother countries. Today the former colonial countries are developing industries that will turn out products for their own needs and, perhaps, for export.

By the 1980s Japan was by far the most successful Asian country in industrialization. It was also the first Asian nation to industrialize, starting in the late 19th century. By World War I Japan was already a highly developed nation. However, its greatest growth as an industrial power has been since World War II. Japan has been so successful that it now has the second largest industrial production in the world, even greater than that of much larger Russia, and it is rapidly gaining on the United States. Japan is one of the leading world producers of many important manufactured products, such as automobiles and electronics. Unlike most other Asian countries it is a major exporter of manufactured goods.

China has the potential to become a great industrial power, if it can solve its vast problems of overpopulation and develop more-productive economic policies. In the late 1980s its value added to the economy by manufacturing was at the level of Canada. Perhaps the greatest potential for industrial development is in some of the oil-rich nations of the Middle East. Many of them, such as Saudi Arabia, are using their vast earnings from oil exports to undertake industrialization programs. However, money alone is not enough. These countries are critically short of skilled labor, managers, and technology. Environmental limitations, such as the shortage of fresh water, and political problems have also hampered their progress. India has made considerable progress in industrialization, but is also beset with severe problems of overpopulation and political and social instability. Indeed, these problems afflict many nations of Asia.

**Transportation and Communications**

Efficient networks of transportation and communications are a key requirement for industrial development. Goods, people, and ideas must move quickly and efficiently. The pattern throughout Asia is still uneven and closely parallels the level of industrial development. Thus, at one extreme there is Japan, with its highly sophisticated railway, superhighway, and airline systems plus the latest in telecommunications, equal to the best found in the Western world. At the other extreme there are parts of Asia that are still virtually as isolated and cut off from the modern world as they were centuries ago. In most Asian countries most people spend their entire lives without ever traveling more than a few miles from their village or farm. Their extremely limited knowledge of the outside world is learned primarily from word of mouth or occasional radio broadcasts. Extensive transportation and broadcast facilities are being developed throughout the Asian continent as a means of improving this condition.

Asia's vast space and enormous physical barriers have hindered progress in transportation. Traditionally travel and trade have moved largely around the edges of the continent rather than inland. Until the 19th century, caravans on land routes, supplemented by oceangoing vessels, were the chief means of

*The spacious Haj terminal at the King Abdul Aziz International Airport in Jiddah, Saudi Arabia, is a major depot for thousands of Muslim pilgrims who visit the city each year.*

Corning Incorporated

transportation. After the mid-19th century oceangoing vessels continued to be important and rail transport significantly improved overland travel.

Road and rail systems continue to improve, but slowly. One of the more notable advances was the completion in 1915 of the Trans-Siberian Railroad in Russian Asia. A massive highway network begun in the 1960s was designed to link Istanbul, Turkey, with Singapore in Southeast Asia. China joined the system in 1989. The development of air transport in the 20th century has played a key role, especially in such landlocked countries as Afghanistan, Nepal, and Laos. In some of the less advanced countries, however, animal transport remains the main method for moving goods from farm to market.

Inland waterways provide transportation routes in some countries and are especially important in South, Southeast, and East Asia. Bangladesh, the Indochinese countries, and China all have well-developed inland water transport systems.

**INTERNATIONAL RELATIONS**

Since ancient times, Asia has had contact with the rest of the world. This began with caravans carrying the silks, spices, and other exotic products of Asia westward to Europe. This trade benefited Asian economies, and it also brought knowledge about Asia to Europe. Unfortunately, that knowledge led eventually to the colonial takeover of much of Asia by the 19th century. Colonialism is now virtually gone, but the economic and political linkages established by colonialism remain strong. Since World War II Eastern and Western powers have competed to be the dominant influence in Asia.

Many of Asia's trade links are with former colonial rulers, because those tend to be industrialized nations that still need the mineral resources and agricultural products of Asia. Although most Asian nations are trying to industrialize, the industry that has developed produces goods primarily for the domestic market, not for export. Thus, in order to buy abroad what they need, Asian nations must still rely upon exports of their traditional primary products.

Since the 1950s important trade relations have developed between Japan and the rest of Asia, and between the United States and Asia. Those two nations account for the major share of exports and imports in most of Asia's world trade. They are also the major source of foreign-investment capital that has flowed into Asia. In 1967 the Association of Southeast Asian Nations (ASEAN) was formed by Indonesia, Malaysia, the Philippines, Singapore, and Thailand. Brunei joined in 1984. In 1991 ASEAN signed an agreeement to start a regional common market within the next 15 years. The policies of the Organization of Petroleum Exporting Countries (OPEC) created a series of energy crises that seriously affected economic development in the region during the 1970s.

The political ties of the past have also been maintained in many parts of Asia. One important development since World War II was the expansion of United States political and military influence in Asia. This influence resulted from the defeat of Japan in World War II and the emergence of the United States as a chief world military power. With the outbreak of the Cold War in the late 1940s, followed by the Communist victory in China and the Korean War, the United States assumed a policy of combating Communist influence in Asia. The growing dependence of the Western world, especially the United States, on petroleum supplies from the Middle East has made that area highly valued, especially since the world energy shortages that developed in the 1970s.

After its failure in the mid-1970s to prevent Communist control of Indochina, the United States changed the emphasis of its role in Asia. One of the most significant developments has been the dramatic change in relations with China that ended in United States recognition of the Beijing government in 1979. Because of its difficulties in relations with the Soviet Union and a desire to modernize more rapidly, China became a major economic and political partner with the United States. Not wanting to jeopardize that relationship with the United States, China agreed to a summit with the Soviet Union in 1989 as the first step in normalizing relations, which had been suspended in 1960. In 1989 Vietnam announced the final withdrawal of troops from Cambodia that had been deployed there since 1979. Some 160 nations were represented in a gathering of world unity at the funeral of Japanese Emperor Hirohito in Tokyo in 1989.

**HISTORY**

Humans have lived in Asia since prehistoric times, when they roamed large stretches of the continent in quest of food and shelter. As they began to organize together into societies, three of the earliest civilizations for which there are historic records emerged in parts of Asia. These were the ancient cultures of Mesopotamia in the Tigris-Euphrates River valley, beginning in about 10,000 BC; the early cultures in the Indus River valley, beginning in about 3500 BC; and the early Chinese civilization in the Huang He valley, beginning in about 2000 BC.

Asia's long history can be divided into three major periods. The first and longest period was from earliest times until around AD 1500, when the Europeans began to arrive. During this long period, many empires and kingdoms rose and fell, and distinctive cultures evolved in certain regions. Those cultures came to dominate Asia in spite of periodic political upheavals and wars through the centuries.

The development of those cultures provides a basis for dividing Asia into three subregions. In East Asia the Chinese civilization emerged first, and from it the Korean and Japanese cultures evolved. China is renowned for the splendor and extraordinary continuity of its civilization. In South Asia the Indian civilization, with its complex mix of Hindu, Muslim, and other influences, came to dominate. In Southwest Asia, the Arabic-Muslim culture spread widely beginning in the 7th century AD.

Japan National Tourist Organization

*Trains on Japan's Shinkansen high-speed railway can travel at speeds of up to 160 miles (260 kilometers) per hour.*

These three cultures achieved high levels of development within the traditional agricultural economies on which they depended. As already noted, there were brilliant achievements in art, architecture, language and literature, as well as early science and technology. Many of the devices that Europeans later came to depend on originated in Asia, such as gunpowder, paper, the wheel, and the compass.

While European civilization was slow developing during the Middle Ages, Asia's great civilizations flowered in unmatched brilliance and prosperity. When Marco Polo traveled to China in the 13th century, he marveled at the magnificence of China's great civilization, already 3,000 years old. Less famous Europeans were to echo him later.

### European Contact and Conquest

The second major phase of Asian history was the period of European contact and conquest, starting around 1500 and continuing into the mid-20th century. Some historians contend that this period is still not over. The European interest in Asia was partly just curiosity and awe, but it became mainly a desire to exploit the wealth of Asia. To do this, the Europeans had to conquer and colonize much of Asia. This process mainly took place in the 19th and early 20th centuries. By World War I, most of Asia was under European control. Asian traditional societies proved to be no match for the militarily and technologically superior Europeans.

The three or four centuries of European contact and control had both good and bad consequences for Asia. European contributions included new ideas and techniques for agriculture, industry, trade and commerce, health and education, political administration, and warfare. A few Asian cultures were able to adapt these new ideas without being physically taken over by the Europeans. Most notable was Japan. Although most of the Asian cultures were not able to do this, even under physical occupation by European rulers large

parts of Asia gained as they were forcibly introduced to the modern world and provided with benefits, such as railroads or control of diseases, that proved helpful after independence.

European colonialism also brought problems. It drained away much of the wealth of Asia, exporting it to the mother countries in Europe. The Europeans also divided up Asia in such a way that post-independence political boundaries were often poorly located in relation to natural divisions of peoples, cultures, and physical regions. There were also social and political problems that resulted from the introduction of alien minorities into colonial states. The French culture in Indochina and the Spanish culture in the Philippines, for instance, clashed with existing cultures in these places. Many of these aspects of European rule still cause problems for Asian nations.

### Independence and Struggle

The third phase of Asian history began after the end of World War II. Within the next 30 years, between 1945 and 1975, colonialism ended and virtually all the countries of Asia had become independent. In some cases independence came peacefully; but in others there were prolonged and bloody conflicts. By the 1990s only two small relics of the colonial era remained—Hong Kong and Macao—and these were scheduled to revert to China's control by the year 2000.

Independence came to the Indian subcontinent in 1947. As far as Great Britain was concerned, the separation was peaceful at the time, but the former colony had struggled for decades to end British rule. As independence approached, the strife continued within the subcontinent between Muslims and Hindus. This was resolved by partitioning India into two separate countries, India and Pakistan, which received independence simultaneously. The two new countries watched each other warily. India and Pakistan fought a short war over disputed territory in 1965. A more serious conflict in 1971 resulted in the loss to Pakistan of its eastern territory, which subsequently became Bangladesh. After that, tension remained as Muslims sought to gain control of more land along the India-Pakistan border, but no more wars took place. Most of the subcontinent's violence after 1980 was in the south, in Sri Lanka's civil war.

A major upheaval and power shift in Asia came with the establishment of the People's Republic of China in 1949 (*see* China). This was a result of decades of civil war between the Communists, based in the north, and the Nationalist government of Chiang Kai-shek, based in Nanking. The Communist victory had enormous political influence on the entire region—indeed, on the entire world. It seemed, at the time, to indicate that Communism was the wave of the future. The new rulers in Beijing encouraged revolution everywhere, especially in Third World countries. And they were eager to help neighbors fighting to end colonialism. One such neighbor was just to the south, in Indochina.

After World War II France had tried to regain its colonies in Southeast Asia following their occupation by Japan. By the early 1950s the French found themselves bogged down in a guerrilla war. After a humiliating defeat at the battle of Dienbienphu in 1954, the French forces withdrew. The worst was not over for Indochina, however. Soon the United States was involved, determined to contain the expansion of Communism in that part of the world. The determination of the Americans was met with an even greater resistance on the part of the North Vietnamese and their allies in South Vietnam—leading to a long and very destructive war that ended with Communist victory in 1975 and more than a decade of great suffering for the people of Indochina. (*See also* Indochina; Vietnam War.)

Meanwhile, another serious conflict had occurred to the north. In June 1950, North Korea, urged by the Soviet Union and cheered on by the Chinese Communists, invaded South Korea. The United States responded immediately, and a United Nations coalition force was sent to fight the North Koreans. The massive intervention of China nearly turned the tide, but in the end a truce was arranged in 1953. An uneasy peace endured, and in the 1990s North and South Korea were working toward reunification. By then North Korea had become isolated. The Soviet Union was rapidly disintegrating, and China was conducting business with the United States, Japan, and even South Korea. (*See also* Korean War.)

Southwest Asia is usually called the Middle East. It had been in turmoil since the end of World War I. The Arab countries had traditional disagreements. With the creation of the State of Israel, however, the Arabs united to oppose the new state. An Arab-Israeli conflict began in 1948 and continued through four more wars. In the 1967 war Israel acquired much new territory, including the West Bank (formerly part of Jordan), the Gaza Strip, and Syria's Golan Heights. Israel kept these lands as occupied territory and built settlements on them. This land policy, plus the diffi- cult relations with the Palestinians, kept Arab-Israeli tensions high. Only after the success of the United States and its allies against Iraq in 1991 were peace talks arranged between Israel and its Arab neighbors.

Another struggle developed in Afghanistan, which was invaded by Soviet troops in 1979 to support a Soviet-sponsored government. The Soviets withdrew in defeat by 1990, and the puppet government was overthrown by Afghan guerrillas in April 1992.

A war between Iran and Iraq from 1980 to 1988 threatened the precarious stability of the Persian Gulf region and claimed more than 1 million lives in both countries. After Iran became an Islamic republic early in 1979, Muslim fundamentalism seemed to pose a threat to all the Arab states. By 1990 Iran found itself isolated because of its fanaticism and was seeking more normal relations with other countries. In August 1990 Iraq invaded Kuwait. This resulted in massive retaliation against Iraq and its defeat by a coalition of forces led by the United States. These conflicts have severely complicated the efforts of Middle Eastern countries to deal with serious problems of overpopulation, lack of industrial development, and ancient cultural attachments, which hinder progress in education and health. (*See also* Afghanistan; Iran; Iraq; Israel; Palestine; Persian Gulf War.)

The breakup of the Soviet Union in 1991 was one of the most significant events in modern history. It added several independent countries to the map of Asia, and it ended the Cold War. But it also portended serious problems of economic reconstruction to societies that had lived under Communist domination for about 70 years. (*See also* Soviet Union, "The Revolution of 1991".)

**The New Prosperity**

While regional conflicts and civil wars were tearing some societies apart, other nations were working economic miracles. The foremost and earliest success was in Japan, which had to rebuild itself after the devastation of World War II. By the late 1970s Japan had become the economic giant of the Far East, carving out market shares for its products in all parts of the world. By the 1980s Japan's success was being emulated by the "Four Little Tigers" of Asia: Taiwan, South Korea, Hong Kong, and Singapore. These dynamic economies were soon challenging Japan's leadership in manufacturing and finance.

By 1990 even larger areas were undergoing significant economic development. Among these were Indonesia and Malaysia. Both of these multi-island nations are very populous, and development was un- even. The most surprising change took place in South China. In June 1989, when the democracy movement was brutally put down, outsiders felt China was disowning reform. The contrary was true. Guangdong Province, just north of Hong Kong, had become one of the fastest growing economies in the world by 1992. Its prosperity was broadly based, a striking contrast to the failed enterprises run by the state. It was a contrast as well to the Communist ideology preached by the government, but there was no doubt that the reforms in Guangdong were accomplished with the government's consent.

**BIBLIOGRAPHY FOR ASIA**

**Chapman, William.** Inventing Japan (Prentice, 1991).
**Fairbank, John K.** China: A New History (Belknap, 1992).
**Horsley, W., and Buckley, R.** Nippon: New Superpower (BBC Books, 1990).
**Mansfield, Peter.** A History of the Middle East (Viking, 1991).
**Naipaul, V.S.** An Area of Darkness (Viking-Penguin, 1992).
**Rees, David.** A Short History of Modern Korea (Hippocrene, 1988).
**Salisbury, H.E.** The New Emperors: China in the Era of Mao and Deng (Little, Brown, 1992).
**Stewart, Gail B.** India (Crestwood House, 1992).
**Tweddell, C.E.** Introduction to the Peoples and Cultures of Asia (Prentice, 1985).
**Ulam, Adam B.** The Communists: The Story of Power and Lost Illusions 1948–1991 (Scribner's, 1992).
**Vogel, Ezra F.** The Four Little Dragons (Harvard, 1991).
**Williams, L.E.** Southeast Asia: A History (Oxford, 1987).
**Winchester, Simon.** Pacific Rising (Prentice, 1991).

## Political Units of Asia

| Political Unit | Status | Area (sq mi) | Area (sq km) | Population (2000 est.) | Capital |
|---|---|---|---|---|---|
| Afghanistan | Transitional Regime | 251,773 | 652,090 | 25,889,000 | Kabul |
| Bahrain | Monarchy (Emirate) | 260 | 668 | 691,000 | Manama |
| Bangladesh | Republic | 55,598 | 143,998 | 129,194,000 | Dhaka |
| Bhutan | Constitutional Monarchy | 17,800 | 46,000 | 667,000 | Thimphu |
| Brunei | Monarchy (Sultanate) | 2,226 | 5,765 | 336,000 | Bandar Seri Begawan |
| Cambodia | Constitutional Monarchy | 69,898 | 181,035 | 12,371,000 | Phnom Penh |
| China | People's Republic | 3,692,000 | 9,561,000 | 1,265,207,000 | Beijing |
| Cyprus | Republic | 3,572 | 9,251 | 865,000 | Nicosia |
| Hong Kong | Administrative Region (China) | 405 | 1,050 | 6,782,000 | Victoria |
| India | Federal Republic | 1,269,419 | 3,287,782 | 1,014,004,000 | New Delhi |
| Indonesia | Republic | 741,101 | 1,919,443 | 209,342,000 | Jakarta |
| Iran | Islamic Republic | 636,000 | 1,648,000 | 62,704,000 | Tehran |
| Iraq | Republic | 168,928 | 437,522 | 22,676,000 | Baghdad |
| Israel | Republic | 8,000 | 20,700 | 6,107,000 | Jerusalem |
| Japan | Constitutional Monarchy | 145,842 | 377,728 | 126,920,000 | Tokyo |
| Jordan | Constitutional Monarchy | 34,343 | 88,947 | 4,982,000 | Amman |
| Kazakhstan | Republic | 1,049,200 | 2,717,300 | 14,913,000 | Astana |
| Korea, North | People's Republic | 47,077 | 121,929 | 21,688,000 | Pyongyang |
| Korea, South | Republic | 38,211 | 98,966 | 47,275,000 | Seoul |
| Kuwait | Constitutional Monarchy | 6,880 | 17,818 | 1,984,000 | Kuwait City |
| Kyrgyzstan | Republic | 76,600 | 198,500 | 4,895,000 | Bishkek |
| Laos | People's Republic | 91,429 | 236,800 | 5,497,000 | Vientiane |
| Lebanon | Republic | 3,950 | 10,230 | 3,578,000 | Beirut |
| Macao (Macau) | Administrative Region (China) | 6 | 16 | 440,000 | Macao |
| Malaysia | Federal Constitutional Monarchy | 127,316 | 329,747 | 23,260,000 | Kuala Lumpur |
| Maldives | Republic | 115 | 298 | 285,000 | Male |
| Mongolia | Republic | 604,800 | 1,566,500 | 2,399,000 | Ulaanbaatar |
| Myanmar (Burma) | Military Regime | 261,228 | 676,577 | 41,735,000 | Rangoon (Yangon) |
| Nepal | Constitutional Monarchy | 56,136 | 145,391 | 24,702,000 | Kathmandu |
| Oman | Monarchy (Sultanate) | 120,000 | 310,000 | 2,416,000 | Muscat |
| Pakistan | Military Regime | 307,374 | 796,095 | 141,553,775 | Islamabad |
| Philippines | Republic | 115,800 | 300,000 | 76,320,000 | Quezon City/Manila |
| Qatar | Monarchy (Emirate) | 4,400 | 11,400 | 599,000 | Doha |
| Saudi Arabia | Monarchy | 864,900 | 2,240,000 | 22,024,000 | Riyadh |
| Singapore | Republic | 239 | 618 | 3,278,000 | Singapore |
| Sri Lanka | Republic | 25,332 | 65,610 | 19,246,000 | Colombo, Sri Jaya-wardenapura-Kotte |
| Syria | Republic | 71,498 | 185,179 | 16,306,000 | Damascus |
| Taiwan | Republic | 13,900 | 36,000 | 22,186,000 | Taipei |
| Tajikistan | Republic | 55,300 | 143,100 | 6,312,000 | Dushanbe |
| Thailand | Constitutional Monarchy | 198,456 | 513,998 | 62,423,000 | Bangkok |
| Turkey | Republic | 301,380 | 780,570 | 65,667,000 | Ankara |
| Turkmenistan | Republic | 188,500 | 488,200 | 4,885,000 | Ashkhabad (Ashgabat) |
| United Arab Emirates | Federation of Seven Emirates | 30,000 | 77,700 | 3,022,000 | Abu Dhabi |
| Uzbekistan | Republic | 172,700 | 447,300 | 24,756,000 | Tashkent |
| Vietnam | Socialist Republic | 127,207 | 329,465 | 78,774,000 | Hanoi |
| Yemen | Republic | 207,270 | 536,830 | 17,479,000 | San'a |

## The Continents Compared

| Region | Area (sq mi) | Area (sq km) | Population | GNP per Capita (U.S. $) | Literacy (%) (Male) | (Female) | Life Expectancy (Male) | (Female) |
|---|---|---|---|---|---|---|---|---|
| Africa | 11,667,000 | 30,218,000 | 669,752,000 | 650 | 56.4 | 36.8 | 53.1 | 56.4 |
| Antarctica | 5,500,000 | 14,245,000 | — | — | — | — | — | — |
| Asia | 17,236,000 | 44,642,000 | 3,335,672,000 | 1,780 | 77.6* | 58.8* | 63.3 | 66.0 |
| Europe | 4,056,000 | 10,505,000 | 727,997,000 | 11,100* | 96.7* | 98.0* | 69.3 | 77.0 |
| North America | 9,355,000 | 24,230,000 | 442,115,000 | 12,380 | 91.3 | 89.5 | 68.5 | 74.8 |
| Oceania | 3,284,000 | 8,506,000 | 27,641,000 | 12,730 | 94.2 | 91.3 | 69.8 | 75.4 |
| South America | 6,878,000 | 17,814,000 | 308,770,000 | 2,450 | 87.1 | 84.6 | 64.4 | 69.9 |
| World | 57,976,000 | 150,157,000† | 5,511,947,000 | 4,100 | 80.8 | 67.9 | 63.4 | 67.5 |

*Includes data for all 15 republics of the former Soviet Union.
†Details do not add to total given because of rounding.

# Asia Fact Summary

## NATURAL FEATURES

**Mountain Ranges.** Himalayas, Karakorum, Hindu Kush, Elburz, Caucasus, Pamirs, Taurus, Kunlun, Tian Shan, Altai, Urals.

**Highest Peaks.** Everest (29,023 feet; 8,846 meters); K2 (28,238 feet; 8,607 meters); Kanchenjunga (28,208 feet; 8,598 meters); Lhotse I (27,923 feet; 8,511 meters); Makalu (27,824 feet; 8,481 meters).

**Largest Lakes.** Aral Sea (15,800 square miles; 41,000 square kilometers); Baikal (12,160 square miles; 31,494 square kilometers); Balkhash (7,300 square miles; 18,900 square kilometers); Caspian Sea (143,000 square miles; 370,000 square kilometers); Dead Sea (394 square miles; 1,020 square kilometers).

**Major Rivers.** Amu Darya, Amur, Brahmaputra, Chao Phraya, Euphrates, Ganges, Huang He (Yellow), Indus, Irrawaddy, Irtysh, Jhelum, Jordan, Lena, Mekong, Ob', Salween, Shinano, Tigris, Yalu, Yamuna (Jumna), Yangtze, Yenisey.

**Climate.** Regions—equatorial, tropical monsoon, warm temperate, cold temperate, hot desert, midlatitude desert, steppe, Mediterranean, and tundra.

Total annual precipitation and average annual temperature at selected stations:

| Station | Precipitation | | Temperature | |
|---------|-----|------|-----|-----|
| | *in* | *mm* | °F | °C |
| Amman | 11 | 279 | 64 | 18 |
| Dhaka | 80 | 2,032 | 79 | 26 |
| Irkutsk | 18 | 457 | 30 | −1 |
| Istanbul | 26 | 660 | 55 | 13 |
| Jakarta | 67 | 1,702 | 81 | 27 |
| Manila | 82 | 2,083 | 81 | 27 |
| Ulaanbaatar | 8 | 203 | 27 | −3 |

Extremes in temperature and precipitation:

Al Jizah, Saudi Arabia, and Perim Island and Kamaran, Yemen, highest annual average temperature, 86° F (30° C). Oymyakon, Russia, lowest annual average temperature, 2.7° F (−16.3° C). Cherrapunji, India, highest annual average precipitation, 450 inches (11,430 millimeters). Masira Island, Oman, lowest annual average precipitation, 0.6 inch (15 millimeters).

## PEOPLE

**Population** (1993 estimate). 3,335,672,000.

**Density.** 193.5 persons per square mile (74.7 persons per square kilometer).

**Vital Statistics** (per 1,000 population). Birthrate, 27; death rate, 9.25; annual growth rate, 1.8 percent.

**Main Language Groups.** Chinese (1,105,150,000); Hindi (347,610,000); Bengali (180,230,000); Japanese (123,360,000); Punjabi (89,210,000); Javanese (74,210,000); Korean (66,600,000).

**Principal Religions.** Hinduism (721,113,000); Islam (668,298,000); Buddhism (746,512,000); Christianity (300,383,000); minorities of Shintoism, Taoism, and Zoroastrianism.

**Literacy.** 65.5 percent.

**Largest Cities (population of city proper).** Seoul, South Korea (10,612,577); Bombay, India (9,925,891); Jakarta, Indonesia (8,259,266); Tokyo, Japan (8,129,377); Shanghai, China (7,496,509); Delhi, India (7,206,704); Istanbul, Turkey (6,620,241); Beijing, China (5,769,607); Hong Kong (5,609,951); Karachi, Pakistan (5,208,132).

**Agricultural and Food Products.** *Crops*—bamboo, bananas, cassava, coconuts, coffee, corn (maize), cotton, hemp, jute, mangoes, millet, palm nuts and oil, peanuts (groundnuts), pineapples, rice, rubber, sesame seed, sorghum, soybeans, spices, sugarcane, tea, tobacco, wheat. *Livestock and fish*—buffalo, camels, cattle, donkeys, fish, goats, pigs, poultry, sheep, yaks.

**Manufactured Products.** Aluminum, automobiles, cement and building materials, chemicals and petrochemicals, electronic equipment, fertilizers, iron and steel, machinery, pharmaceuticals, plastics, processed food, pulp and paper, refined petroleum, textiles, transportation equipment, wood products.

**Mined Products.** Bauxite, chromite, coal, copper, crude petroleum, gold, graphite, iron ore, lead, manganese, mercury, molybdenum, natural gas, nickel, platinum, sulfur, tin, tungsten, uranium, zinc.

**Total Foreign Trade.** $1,923,950,000,000; imports, 44.5 percent; exports, 55.5 percent.

## THE LAND

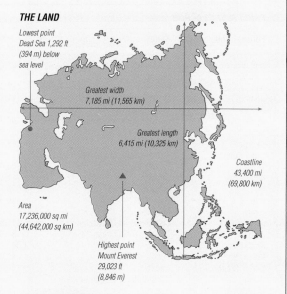

Lowest point
Dead Sea 1,292 ft
(394 m) below
sea level

Greatest width
7,185 mi (11,565 km)

Greatest length
6,415 mi (10,325 km)

Coastline
43,400 mi
(69,800 km)

Area
17,236,000 sq mi
(44,642,000 sq km)

Highest point
Mount Everest
29,023 ft
(8,846 m)

## POPULATION TRENDS

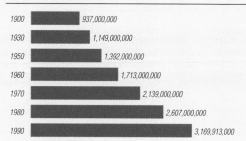

| 1900 | 937,000,000 |
| 1930 | 1,149,000,000 |
| 1950 | 1,392,000,000 |
| 1960 | 1,713,000,000 |
| 1970 | 2,139,000,000 |
| 1980 | 2,607,000,000 |
| 1990 | 3,169,913,000 |

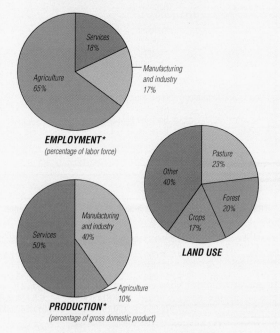

Services 18%

Manufacturing and industry 17%

Agriculture 65%

**EMPLOYMENT***
(percentage of labor force)

Pasture 23%

Other 40%

Forest 20%

Crops 17%

**LAND USE**

Services 50%

Manufacturing and industry 40%

Agriculture 10%

**PRODUCTION***
(percentage of gross domestic product)

*Excludes countries of former Soviet Union.

# Asia

Abadan, Iran — F 6
Abakan, Russia — L 4
Abha, Saudi Arabia — F 8
Abu Dhabi (cap.), U.A.E. — G 7
Adana, Turkey — E 6
Aden (gulf) — F 8
Aden, Yemen — F 8
Afghanistan — H 6
Agra, India — J 7
Ahmadabad, India — J 7
Ahvaz, Iran — F 6
Ajmer, India — J 7
Akita, Japan — P 6
Aksu, China — K 5
Aktyubinsk, Kazakhstan — G 4
Al Hudaydah, Yemen — F 8
Al Huful, Saudi Arabia — F 7
Al Jawf, Saudi Arabia — F 7
Al Mukalla, Yemen — F 8
Al Wajh, Saudi Arabia — E 7
Aldan, Russia — O 4
Aldan (riv.), Russia — P 3
Aleksandrovsk-Sakhalinsky, Russia — R 4
Aleppo, Syria — E 6
Allahabad, India — K 7
Alma-Ata (cap.), Kazakhstan — J 5
Altai (mts.) — K 5
Altun Shan (range), China — K 6
Amami (isls.), Japan — P 7
Ambon, Indonesia — O10
Amman (cap.), Jordan — E 6
Amritsar, India — J 6
Amu Darya (riv.) — H 5
Amur (riv.) — P 5
An Najaf, Iraq — F 6
Anadyr', Russia — U 3
Anadyr' (gulf), Russia — V 3
Anadyr' (riv.), Russia — U 3
Andaman (sea) — L 8
Andaman (isls.), India — L 8
Andizhan, Kyrgyzstan — J 5
Angara (riv.), Russia — L 4
Angarsk, Russia — M 4
Ankara (cap.), Turkey — E 5
Anshan, China — O 5
Antalya, Turkey — D 6
Anzhero-Sudzhensk, Russia — K 4
Aomori, Japan — R 5
Aqaba (gulf) — E 7
Arabian (sea) — H 8
Arak, Iran — G 6
Aral (sea) — G 5
Aral'sk, Kazakhstan — H 5
Ararat (mt.), Turkey — F 6
Aras (riv.) — F 6
Arctic (ocean) — C 1
Ardabil, Iran — F 6
Argun (riv.) — N 4
Asahikawa, Japan — P 5
Ashkhabad (cap.), Turkmenistan — G 6
At Ta'if, Saudi Arabia — F 7
Ayaguz, Kazakhstan — K 5
Ayan, Russia — P 4
Babol, Iran — G 6
Babuyan (isls.), Philippines — O 8
Bacolod, Philippines — O 8
Baghdad (cap.), Iraq — F 6
Baghlan, Afghanistan — H 6
Baguio, Philippines — N 8
Bahawalpur, Pakistan — J 7
Bahrain — G 7
Bali (isl.), Indonesia — N10
Balikpapan, Indonesia — N10
Balkhash, Kazakhstan — J 5
Balkhash (lake), Kazakhstan — J 5
Bam, Iran — G 7
Banda (sea), Indonesia — O10
Banda Aceh, Indonesia — L 9
Bandar 'Abbas, Iran — G 7
Bandar Seri Begawan (cap.), Brunei — N 9
Bandung, Indonesia — M10
Bangalore, India — J 8
Bangka (isl.), Indonesia — M10
Bangkok (cap.), Thailand — M 8
Bangladesh — L 7
Banjarmasin, Indonesia — N10
Baoji, China — M 6
Baotou, China — M 5
Bareilly, India — K 7
Barnaul, Russia — K 4
Baroda, India — J 7
Basra, Iraq — F 6
Bassein, Myanmar — L 8
Batan (isls.), Philippines — O 7
Batang, China — L 6
Batdambang, Cambodia — M 8
Baykal (lake), Russia — N 4
Beijing (cap.), China — N 5
Beirut (cap.), Lebanon — E 6
Belogorsk, Russia — O 4
Bengal (bay) — K 8
Benxi, China — O 5
Bering (sea) — V 4
Bering (str.) — W 3
Bhavnagar, India — J 7
Bhopal, India — J 7
Bhutan — L 7

Bikaner, India — J 7
Billiton (isl.), Indonesia — M10
Birjand, Iran — G 6
Birobidzhan, Russia — O 5
Bishkek (cap.), Kyrgyzstan — J 5
Biysk, Russia — K 4
Black (sea) — E 5
Blagoveshchensk, Russia — O 4
Bodaybo, Russia — N 4
Bogor, Indonesia — M10
Bol'shevik (isl.), Russia — N 2
Bol'shoy Lyakhov (isl.), Russia — R 2
Bombay, India — J 8
Bone (gulf), Indonesia — O10
Bonin (isls.), Japan — R 7
Borneo (isl.) — N 9
Brahmaputra (riv.) — L 7
Bratsk, Russia — M 4
British Indian Ocean Territory — J 10
Brunei — N 9
Bukhara, Uzbekistan — D 5
Bursa, Turkey — D 5
Buru (isl.), Indonesia — O10
Bushire, Iran — G 7
Butuan, Philippines — O 9
Butung (isl.), Indonesia — O10
Cabanatuan, Philippines — O 8
Calcutta, India — K 7
Cambay (gulf), India — J 7
Cambodia — M 8
Can Tho, Vietnam — M 9
Canton (Guangzhou), China — N 7
Caspian (sea) — G 5
Cebu, Philippines — O 8
Celebes (isl.), Indonesia — N10
Celebes (sea) — O 9
Ceram (isl.), Indonesia — P10
Chagos (arch.), Br. Ind. Ocean Terr. — J 10
Chang Jiang (Yangtze) (riv.), China — N 6
Changchun, China — N 7
Changde, China — N 7
Changsha, China — N 7
Changzhi, China — N 6
Chardzhou, Turkmenistan — G 6
Chefoo, China — O 6
Cheju (isl.), S. Korea — O 6
Chelyabinsk, Russia — H 4
Chelyuskin (cape), Russia — M 2
Chengdu, China — M 6
Cheremkhovo, Russia — M 4
Cherskiy, Russia — T 3
Cherskiy (range), Russia — R 3
Chiang Mai, Thailand — L 8
Chimkent, Kazakhstan — H 5
China — L 6
Chita, Russia — N 4
Chittagong, Bangladesh — L 7
Chokurdakh, Russia — R 2
Chongjin, N. Korea — P 5
Chongqing, China — M 7
Choybalsan, Mongolia — N 5
Christmas (isl.), Australia — M11
Chukchi (sea) — W 3
Chukchi (pen.), Russia — V 3
Cirebon, Indonesia — M10
Cocos (isls.), Australia — L 11
Coimbatore, India — J 8
Colombo (cap.), Sri Lanka — J 9
Communism (mt.), Tajikistan — J 5
Comorin (cape), India — J 9
Cuttack, India — K 7
Cyprus — E 6
Da Nang, Vietnam — M 8
Dahana (desert), Saudi Arabia — F 7
Daito (isls.), Japan — P 7
Damascus (cap.), Syria — E 6
Damavand (mt.), Iran — G 6
Dandong, China — O 5
Davao, Philippines — O 9
Delhi, India — J 7
Dezful, Iran — F 6
Dhahran, Saudi Arabia — F 7
Dhaka (cap.), Bangladesh — L 7
Diego Garcia (isl.), Br. Ind. Ocean Ter. — J 10
Dili, Indonesia — O10
Diyarbakir, Turkey — F 6
Doha (cap.), Qatar — G 7
Dondra head (cape), Sri Lanka — K 9
Dongting (lake), China — N 7
Dudinka, Russia — K 3
Dushanbe (cap.), Tajikistan — J 5
Dzhambul, Kazakhstan — J 5
Dzhezkazgan, Kazakhstan — H 5
Dzhugdzhur (range), Russia — P 4
East China (sea) — O 6
East Siberian (sea), Russia — T 2
Ekaterinburg, Russia — H 4
Engaño (cape), Phillipines — O 8
Erenhot, China — N 5
Ergun Zuogi, China — O 4
Erzurum, Turkey — E 5
Eskişehir, Turkey — D 6
Etorofu (isl.), Japan — S 5
Euphrates (riv.) — F 6
Everest (mt.) — K 7
Faisalabad, Pakistan — J 6

Farah (riv.) — H 6
Fergana, Uzbekistan — J 6
Feyzabad, Afghanistan — H 6
Flores (isl.), Indonesia — O10
Flores (sea), Indonesia — N10
Formosa (str.) — N 7
Fukuoka, Japan — O 6
Fushun, China — O 5
Fuxin, China — O 5
Fuzhou, China — N 7
Galle, Sri Lanka — J 9
Ganges (riv.) — K 7
Garyarsa, China — K 6
Gauhati, India — L 7
Gaziantep, Turkey — E 6
Gejiu, China — M 7
George Town, Malaysia — M 9
Gobi (desert) — M 5
Godavari (riv.), India — J 8
Golmud, China — L 6
Gorgan, Iran — G 6
Grand (canal), China — N 6
Great Wall (ruins), China — N 5
Greater Khingan (range), China — O 5
Guangzhou (Canton), China — N 7
Guilin, China — N 7
Guiyang, China — M 7
Guntur, India — K 8
Gur'yev, Kazakhstan — G 5
Gwalior, India — J 7
Gyda (pen.), Russia — J 2
Hadd, Ras al (cape), Oman — H 7
Hadhramaut (reg.), Yemen — F 8
Hadiboh, Yemen — G 8
Haikou, China — N 8
Hail, Saudi Arabia — F 7
Hainan (isl.), China — N 8
Haiphong, Vietnam — M 7
Hakodate, Japan — R 5
Halmahera (isl.), Indonesia — O 9
Hamadan, Iran — F 6
Hamamatsu, Japan — P 6
Hami, China — L 5
Han (riv.), China — N 6
Handan, China — N 6
Hangzhou, China — N 6
Hanoi (cap.), Vietnam — M 7
Harbin, China — O 5
Hefei, China — N 6
Hegang, China — O 5
Helmand (riv.), Afghanistan — H 6
Hengyang, China — N 7
Henzada, Myanmar — L 8
Herat, Afghanistan — H 6
Himalaya (mts.) — L 7
Hindu Kush (mts.) — J 6
Hiroshima, Japan — P 6
Ho Chi Minh City, Vietnam — M 8
Hohhot, China — N 5
Hokkaido (isl.), Japan — R 5
Homs, Syria — E 6
Hong Kong — N 7
Honshu (isl.), Japan — P 6
Hotan, China — K 6
Hovd, Mongolia — L 5
Howrah, India — K 7
Huainan, China — N 6
Huang He (riv.), China — N 6
Hue, Vietnam — M 8
Hungnam, N. Korea — O 6
Hyderabad, India — J 8
Hyderabad, Pakistan — H 7
Igarka, Russia — K 3
Ili (riv.), Kazakhstan — J 5
Iloilo, Philippines — O 8
Imphal, India — L 7
Inchon, S. Korea — O 6
India — J 7
Indian (ocean) — H10
Indigirka (riv.), Russia — R 3
Indonesia — M10
Indore, India — J 7
Indus (riv.) — H 7
Inner Mongolia (reg.), China — N 5
Ipoh, Malaysia — M 9
Iran — G 7
Iraq — F 6
Irbil, Iraq — F 6
Irkutsk, Russia — M 4
Irrawaddy (riv.), Myanmar — L 7
Irtysh (riv.) — J 4
Isfahan, Iran — G 6
Ishim (riv.), Kazakhstan — H 4
Islamabad (cap.), Pakistan — J 6
Israel — E 6
Issyk-Kul (lake), Kyrgyzstan — J 5
Izmir, Turkey — D 6
Iwaki, Japan — R 6
Izmit, Turkey — D 5
Jabalpur, India — K 7
Jaffna, Sri Lanka — K 9
Jaipur, India — J 7
Jakarta (cap.), Indonesia — M10
Jambi, Indonesia — M10
Jammu, India — J 6
Jamnagar, India — H 7
Jamshedpur, India — K 7

Japan — R 6
Japan (sea) — P 6
Jask, Iran — G 7
Java (isl.), Indonesia — M10
Java (sea), Indonesia — M10
Jerusalem (cap.), Israel — E 6
Jialing (riv.), China — M 6
Jiddah, Saudi Arabia — E 7
Jilin, China — O 5
Jinan, China — N 6
Jinzhou, China — N 5
Jixi, China — P 5
Jodhpur, India — J 7
Johore Baharu, Malaysia — M 9
Jordan — E 6
K2 (mt.) — J 6
Kabul (cap.), Afghanistan — H 6
Kagoshima, Japan — O 6
Kaifeng, China — N 6
Kakinada, India — K 8
Kalat, Pakistan — H 7
Kamchatka (pen.), Russia — S 4
Kampong Cham, Cambodia — M 8
Kanazawa, Japan — P 6
Kandy, Sri Lanka — K 9
Kanpur, India — K 7
Kansk, Russia — L 4
Kaohsiung, Taiwan — N 7
Kara (sea), Russia — H 2
Karachi, Pakistan — H 7
Karaganda, Kazakhstan — J 5
Karaginskiy (isl.), Russia — T 4
Karakorum (ruins), Mongolia — M 5
Karamay, China — K 5
Karbala, Iraq — F 6
Kashgar, China — J 6
Kathmandu (cap.), Nepal — K 7
Kayan (riv.), Indonesia — N 9
Kayseri, Turkey — E 6
Kazakhstan — H 5
Kemerovo, Russia — K 4
Kerman, Iran — G 6
Kermanshah, Iran — F 6
Kerulen (riv.) — N 5
Khabarovsk, Russia — P 5
Khanka (lake) — P 5
Khanty-Mansiysk, Russia — J 3
Khatanga, Russia — M 2
Khyber (pass) — J 6
Kirkuk, Iraq — F 6
Kistna (riv.), India — J 8
Kitakyushu, Japan — P 6
Kobe, Japan — P 6
Kokchetav, Kazakhstan — H 4
Koko Nor (lake), China — L 6
Kolhapur, India — J 8
Kolpashevo, Russia — K 4
Kolyma (range), Russia — S 3
Kolyma (riv.), Russia — S 3
Komandorskiye (isl.), Russia — T 4
Komsomolets (isl.), Russia — M 1
Komsomol'sk, Russia — P 4
Konya, Turkey — E 6
Korf, Russia — T 3
Koryak (range), Russia — U 3
Kota, India — J 7
Kota Baharu, Malaysia — M 9
Kota Kinabalu, Malaysia — N 9
Kotuy (riv.), Russia — M 2
Kozhikode, India — J 8
Krasnovodsk, Turkmenistan — G 5
Krasnoyarsk, Russia — L 4
Kuala Lumpur (cap.), Malaysia — M 9
Kuching, Malaysia — N 9
Kumamoto, Japan — P 6
Kunashiri (isl.), Japan — R 5
Kunlun (range), China — K 6
Kunming, China — M 7
Kupang, Indonesia — O11
Kurgan, Russia — H 4
Kuria Muria (isls.), Oman — G 8
Kuril (isls.), Russia — R 5
Kurnool, India — J 8
Kushiro, Japan — R 5
Kustanay, Kazakhstan — H 4
Kutch, Rann of (salt marsh) — H 7
Kuwait — F 7
Kuwait (cap.), Kuwait — F 7
Kwangju, S. Korea — O 6
Kyakhta, Russia — M 4
Kyoto, Japan — P 6
Kyrgyzstan — J 5
Kyushu (isl.), Japan — P 6
Kyzyl (riv.), Russia — L 4
Kyzyl-Orda, Kazakhstan — H 5
La Pérouse (str.) — R 5
Laccadive (isls.), India — H 8
Lahore, Pakistan — J 6
Lanzhou, China — M 6
Lao Cai, Vietnam — M 7
Laoag, Philippines — N 8
Laos — M 8
Laptev (sea), Russia — O 2
Latakia, Syria — E 6
Lebanon — E 6
Lena (riv.), Russia — O 3

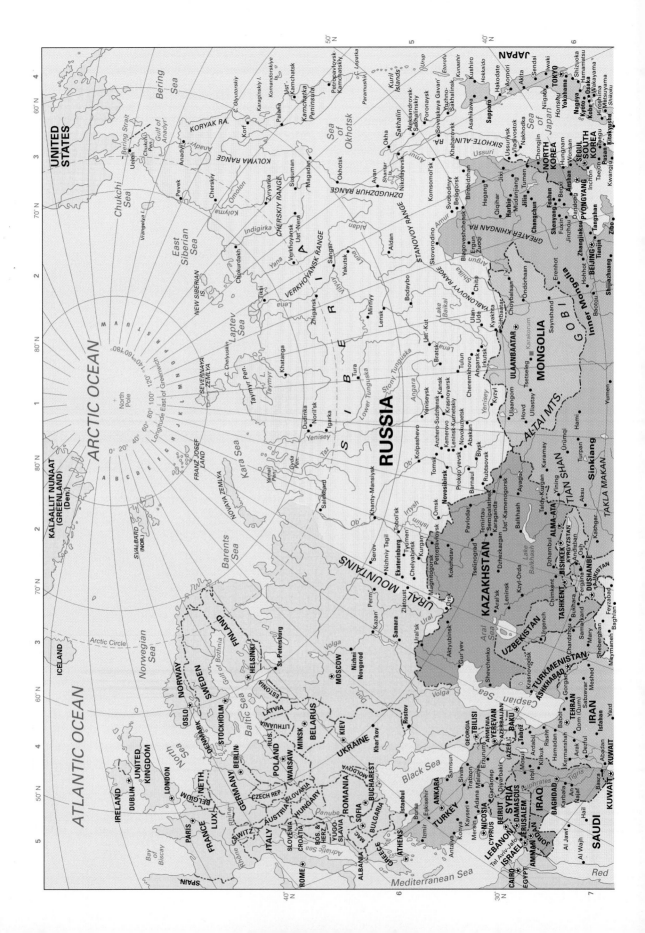

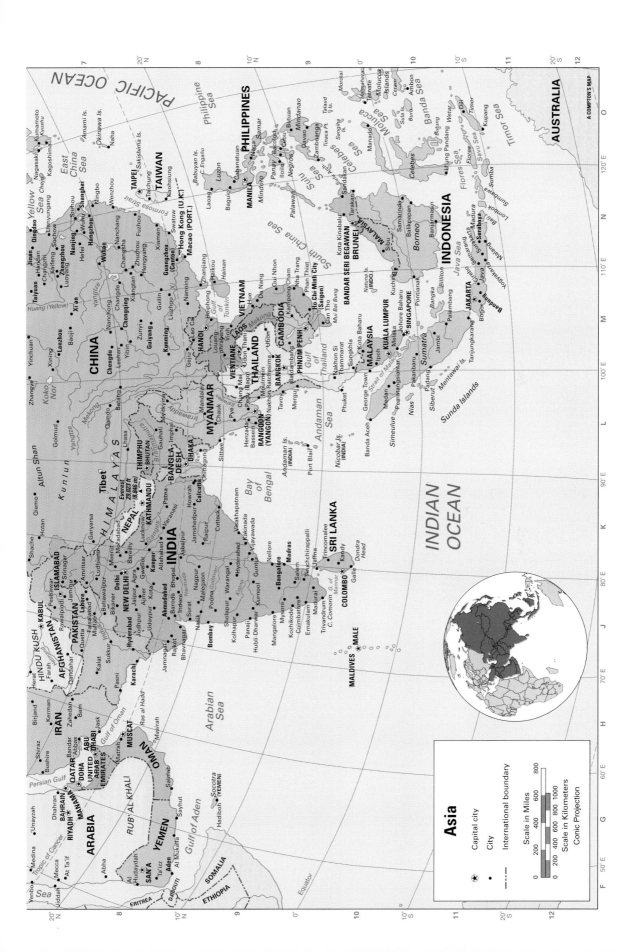

# Asia

⊛ Capital city

• City

-·-·- International boundary

Scale in Miles

0  200  400  600  800  1000

Scale in Kilometers

0  200  400  600  800  1000

Conic Projection

A COMPTON'S MAP

PACIFIC OCEAN

Philippine Sea

PHILIPPINES

TAIWAN

TAIPEI ⊛

MANILA ⊛

East China Sea

Yellow Sea

CHINA

Celebes Sea

Sulu Sea

South China Sea

BRUNEI

BANDAR SERI BEGAWAN ⊛

MALAYSIA

Borneo

INDONESIA

Molucca Sea

Banda Sea

Timor Sea

AUSTRALIA

Java Sea

Flores Sea

Sumatra

KUALA LUMPUR ⊛

SINGAPORE ⊛

JAKARTA ⊛

VIETNAM

HANOI ⊛

LAOS

VIENTIANE ⊛

THAILAND

BANGKOK ⊛

CAMBODIA

PHNOM PENH ⊛

Ho Chi Minh City (Saigon)

Gulf of Thailand

Gulf of Tonkin

MYANMAR

MANDALAY

RANGOON (YANGON) ⊛

BANGLA-DESH

DHAKA ⊛

BHUTAN

THIMPHU ⊛

NEPAL

KATHMANDU ⊛

Everest 29,023 ft (8,846 m)

HIMALAYAS

Tibet

Kunlun

Altun Shan

Koko Nor

HINDU KUSH

KABUL ⊛

AFGHANISTAN

PAKISTAN

ISLAMABAD ⊛

NEW DELHI ⊛

INDIA

Calcutta

Bombay

Bay of Bengal

Andaman Sea

Andaman Is. (INDIA)

Nicobar Is. (INDIA)

SRI LANKA

COLOMBO ⊛

MALDIVES

MALE ⊛

INDIAN OCEAN

IRAN

QATAR

DOHA ⊛

BAHRAIN

MANAMA ⊛

UNITED ARAB EMIRATES

ABU DHABI ⊛

OMAN

MUSCAT ⊛

RUB' AL-KHALI

ARABIA

RIYADH ⊛

YEMEN

SAN'A ⊛

Persian Gulf

Arabian Sea

Gulf of Oman

Gulf of Aden

Red Sea

SOMALIA

ETHIOPIA

ERITREA

DJIBOUTI

Tropic of Cancer

Equator

## Asia—Continued

Leninsk, Kazakhstan H 5
Leninsk-Kuznetskiy, Russia K 4
Lensk, Russia N 3
Leshan, China M 6
Leyte (isl.), Philippines O 8
Lhasa, China L 7
Lianyunggang, China N 6
Liao (riv.), China O 5
Liuzhuo, China M 7
Lombok (isl.), Indonesia N10
Lop Nor (lake), China L 5
Lopatka (cape), Russia S 4
Louangphrabang, Laos M 7
Lower Tunguska (riv.), Russia L 3
Lucknow, India K 7
Lüda, China O 6
Ludhiana, India J 6
Luoyang, China O 6
Luzon (isl.), Philippines O 8
Macao N 7
Madras, India K 8
Madura (isl.), Indonesia N10
Madurai, India J 9
Magadan, Russia R 4
Magnitogorsk, Russia H 4
Makassar (str.), Indonesia N10
Malacca (str.) M 9
Malang, Indonesia N10
Malatya, Turkey E 6
Malaya (state), Malaysia M 9
Malaysia M 9
Maldives J 9
Male (cap.), Maldives J 9
Malegaon, India J 7
Manado, Indonesia O 9
Mandalay, Myanmar L 7
Mangalore, India J 8
Manila (cap.), Philippines N 8
Mannar (gulf) J 9
Martaban (gulf), Myanmar L 8
Mary, Turkmenistan H 6
Masirah (isl.), Oman G 7
Matrah, Oman G 7
Matsuyama, Japan P 6
Maya (riv.), Russia P 4
Mecca, Saudi Arabia F 7
Medan, Indonesia L 9
Medina, Saudi Arabia F 7
Meerut, India J 7
Mekong (riv.) M 8
Melaka, Malaysia M 9
Mentawai (isls.), Indonesia L 10
Mergui, Myanmar L 8
Mersin, Turkey E 6
Meshed, Iran G 6
Meymaneh, Afghanistan H 6
Mindanao (isl.), Philippines O 9
Mindoro (isl.), Philippines N 8
Mirnyy, Russia N 3
Molucca (isls.), Indonesia O 10
Molucca (sea), Indonesia O 10
Mongolia M 5
Moradabad, India J 7
Morotai (isl.), Indonesia O 9
Mosul, Iraq F 6
Moulmein, Myanmar L 8
Mudanjiang, China O 5
Mui Bai Bung (pt.), Vietnam M 9
Multan, Pakistan J 6
Muscat (cap.), Oman G 7
Myanmar (Burma) L 7
Myitkyina, Myanmar L 7
Mysore, India J 8
Naga, Philippines O 8
Nagasaki, Japan O 6
Nagoya, Japan P 6
Nagpur, India J 7
Naha, Japan O 7
Nakhodka, Russia P 5
Nakhon Ratchasima, Thailand M 8
Nakhon Si Thammarat, Thailand M 9
Nanchang, China N 7
Nanchong, China M 6
Nanjing, China N 6
Nanning, China M 7
Narmada (riv.), India J 7
Nasik, India J 8
Natuna (isls.), Indonesia M 9
Nefud (desert), Saudi Arabia F 7
Negros (isl.), Philippines O 9
Nellore, India K 8
Nen (riv.), China O 5
Nepal K 7
Neutral Zone F 7
New Delhi, India J 7
New Guinea (isl.) P 10
New Siberian (isls.), Russia R 2
Nha Trang, Vietnam M 8
Nias (isl.), Indonesia L 9
Nicobar (isls.), India L 9
Nicosia (cap.), Cyprus E 6
Niigata, Japan P 6
Nikolayevsk, Russia P 4
Ningbo, China O 7
Nizhniy Tagil, Russia H 4
Noril'sk, Russia L 3
North Korea O 5
Novokuznetsk, Russia K 4
Novosibirsk, Russia J 4
Nukus, Uzbekistan H 5
Ob' (gulf), Russia J 3
Ob' (riv.), Russia H 3
October Revolution (isl.), Russia K 2
Okha, Russia R 4
Okhotsk, Russia R 4
Okhotsk (sea), Russia R 4
Okinawa (isls.), Japan O 7
Olenëk (riv.), Russia N 3
Olyutorskiy (cape), Russia U 4
Oman G 8
Oman (gulf) G 7
Omolon (riv.), Russia S 3
Omsk, Russia J 4
Öndörhaan, Mongolia N 5
Osaka, Japan P 6
Osh, Kyrgyzstan J 5
Pacific (ocean) T 5
Padang, Indonesia L 10
Pakanbaru, Indonesia M 9
Pakistan H 7
Palana, Russia S 4
Palawan (isl.), Philippines N 8
Palembang, Indonesia M10
Pamir (plat.) J 6
Panaji, India J 8
Panay (isl.), Philippines O 8
Paramushir (isl.), Russia S 5
Parece Vela (isl.), Russia P 7
Pasni, Pakistan H 7
Patna, India K 7
Pavlodar, Kazakhstan J 4
Pegu, Myanmar L 8
Pematangsiantar, Indonesia L 9
Persian (gulf) G 7
Peshawar, Pakistan H 6
Petropavlovsk, Kazakhstan J 4
Petropavlovsk-Kamchatskiy, Russia T 4
Pevek, Russia U 3
Phan Thiet, Vietnam M 8
Philippine (sea) O 8
Philippines O 8
Phnom Penh (cap.), Cambodia M 8
Phuket, Thailand L 9
Pontianak, Indonesia N10
Poona, India J 8
Poronaysk, Russia R 5
Port Blair, India L 8
Poyang (lake), China N 7
Prokop'yevsk, Russia K 4
Pusan, S. Korea O 6
Pye, Myanmar L 8
Pyongyang (cap.), N. Korea O 6
Qaidam Pendi, China L 6
Qamdo, China L 6
Qandahar, Afghanistan H 6
Qatar G 7
Qazvin, Iran F 6
Qiema, China K 6
Qilian Shan (range), China L 6
Qingdao, China O 6
Qiqihar, China O 5
Qom (Qum), Iran G 6
Quetta, Pakistan H 6
Qui Nhon, Vietnam M 8
Qum (Qom), Iran G 6
Raipur, India K 7
Rajkot, India H 7
Rangoon (Yangon) (cap.), Myanmar L 8
Rasht, Iran G 6
Rawalpindi, Pakistan J 6
Red (river) M 7
Red (sea) E 7
Riyadh (cap.), Saudi Arabia F 7
Rub 'al Khali (desert), Saudi Arabia G 7
Rubtsovsk, Russia K 4
Russia L 3
Ryuku (isls.), Japan O 7
Sabah (state), Malaysia N 9
Sabzevar, Iran G 6
Saigon (Ho Chi Minh City), Vietnam M 8
Sakhalin (isl.), Russia R 4
Sakishima (isls.), Japan O 7
Salalah, Oman G 8
Salekhard, Russia H 3
Salem, India J 8
Salween (riv.) L 8
Samar (isls.), Philippines O 8
Samarinda, Indonesia N10
Samarkand, Uzbekistan H 6
Samsun, Turkey E 5
San'a (cap.), Yemen F 8
Sandakan, Malaysia N 9
Sangar, Russia O 3
Sangihe (isls.), Indonesia O 9
Sapporo, Japan P 5
Sarawak (state), Malaysia N 9
Saudi Arabia F 7
Savu (sea), Indonesia O10
Sayhut, Yemen G 8
Saynshand, Mongolia M 5
Selenga (riv.) M 5
Semarang, Indonesia N10
Semipalatinsk, Kazakhstan K 4
Sendai, Japan R 6
Seoul (cap.), S. Korea O 6
Serov, Russia H 4
Severnaya Zemlya (isls.), Russia M 1
Shache, China J 6
Shanghai, China O 6
Shantar (isls.), Russia P 4
Shaqra, Saudi Arabia F 7
Sheberghan, Afghanistan H 6
Shelekhov (gulf), Russia S 3
Shenyang, China O 5
Shevchenko, Kazakhstan G 5
Shijiazhuang, China N 6
Shikoku (isl.), Japan P 6
Shilka (riv.), Russia N 4
Shiraz, Iran G 7
Shizuoka, Japan P 6
Sholapur, India J 8
Siberia (reg.), Russia M 4
Siberut (isl.), Indonesia L 10
Sibu, Malaysia N 9
Sikhote-Alin (range), Russia P 5
Simeulue (isl.), Indonesia L 9
Singapore M 9
Sinkiang (aut. reg.), China K 5
Sittwe, Myanmar L 7
Sivas, Turkey E 5
Skovorodino, Russia O 4
Socotra (isl.), Yemen G 8
Songhua Jiang (riv.), China P 5
Sorong, Indonesia P10
South China (sea) N 8
South Korea O 6
Sovetskaya Gavan', Russia R 5
Sretensk, Russia N 4
Sri Jayawardenapura-Kotte (cap.), Sri Lanka K 9
Sri Lanka K 9
Srinagar, India J 6
Stanovoy (range), Russia O 4
Stony Tunguska (riv.), Russia L 3
Suchow, China N 6
Sühbaatar, Mongolia M 5
Sula (isls.), Indonesia O10
Sulu (arch.), Philippines O 9
Sulu (sea), Philippines N 9
Sumatra (isl.), Indonesia L 9
Sumba (isl.), Indonesia N11
Sumbawa (isl.), Indonesia N11
Sunda (isls.), Indonesia L10
Sunda (str.), Indonesia M10
Surabaya, Indonesia N10
Surakarta, Indonesia N10
Surat, India J 7
Susuman, Russia R 3
Sutlej (riv.) J 6
Suzhou, China O 6
Svobodnyy, Russia O 4
Swatow, China N 7
Syr Darya (riv.), Kazakhstan H 5
Syria E 6
Tabriz, Iran F 6
Taegu, S. Korea O 6
Taejon, S. Korea O 6
Taichung, Taiwan O 7
Taipei (cap.), Taiwan O 7
Taiwan N 7
Taiwan (isl.) N 7
Taiyuan, China N 6
Ta'izz, Yemen F 8
Tajikistan H 6
Takla Makan (desert), China K 6
Talaud (isls.), Indonesia O 9
Taldy-Kurgan, Kazakhstan J 5
Tangshan, China N 5
Tanimbar (isls.), Indonesia P10
Tanjungkarang, Indonesia M10
Tarakan, Indonesia N 9
Tarim (riv.), China K 5
Tashkent (cap.), Uzbekistan H 5
Tatar (str.), Russia R 5
Tavoy, Myanmar L 8
Taymyr (lake), Russia L 2
Taymyr (pen.), Russia L 2
Taz (riv.), Russia K 3
Tehran (cap.), Iran G 6
Tel Aviv-Yafo, Israel E 6
Telanaipura, Indonesia M10
Temirtau, Kazakhstan J 4
Ternate, Indonesia O 9
Thailand M 8
Thailand (gulf) M 9
Thimphu (cap.), Bhutan L 7
Tianjin, China N 6
Tian Shan (range) K 5
Tibet (reg.), China K 6
Tigris (riv.) F 6
Tiksi, Russia P 2
Timor (sea) O11
Timor (isl.), Indonesia O10
Tinaca (pt.), Philippines O 9
Tiruchchirappali, India J 8
Tobol (riv.) H 4
Tobol'sk, Russia J 4
Tokyo (cap.), Japan R 6
Tomini (gulf), Indonesia O10
Tomsk, Russia K 4
Tonkin (gulf) M 8
Trabzon, Turkey E 5
Trincomalee, Sri Lanka K 9
Trivandrum, India J 9
Tselinograd, Kazakhstan J 4
Tsetserleg, Mongolia L 5
Tulun, Russia M 4
Tumen, China O 5
Tura, Russia M 3
Turkey E 6
Turkmenistan G 6
Turpan, China L 5
Tyumen, Russia H 4
Ubon, Thailand M 8
Udaypur, India J 7
Udon Thani, Thailand M 8
Uelen, Russia V 3
Ujung Pandang, Indonesia N10
Ulaanbaatar (cap.), Mongolia L 5
Ulaangom, Mongolia L 5
Ulan-Ude, Russia M 4
Uliastay, Mongolia L 5
'Unayzah, Saudi Arabia F 7
United Arab Emirates G 7
Ural (mts.), Russia G 4
Ural (riv.) G 5
Ural'sk, Kazakhstan G 4
Urgench, Turkmenistan G 5
Urmia (lake), Iran F 6
Ürümqi, China K 5
Urup (isl.), Russia S 5
Ussuri (riv.) P 5
Ussuriysk, Russia P 5
Ust'-Kamchatsk, Russia T 4
Ust'-Kamenogorsk, Kazakhstan J 5
Ust'-Kut, Russia M 4
Ust'-Nera, Russia R 3
Ust'-Urt (plat.), Kazakhstan G 5
Uvs Nuur (lake), Mongolia L 4
Uzbekistan H 5
Van (lake), Turkey F 6
Varanasi, India K 7
Verkhoyansk, Russia P 3
Verkhoyansk (range), Russia O 3
Vientiane (cap.), Laos M 8
Vietnam M 8
Vijayawada, India K 8
Vilyuy (riv.), Russia N 3
Vinh, Vietnam M 8
Visakhapatnam, India K 8
Vitim (riv.), Russia N 4
Vladivostok, Russia P 5
Vrangelya (isl.), Russia U 2
Wakayama, Japan P 6
Warangal, India J 8
Wenzhou, China N 7
Wetar (isl.), Indonesia O10
Wonsan, N. Korea O 6
Wuhan, China N 6
Wuhu, China N 6
Wuxi, China O 6
Xi (riv.), China N 7
Xiamen, China N 7
Xi'an, China M 6
Xiangtan, China N 7
Xigazê, China K 7
Xining, China M 6
Yablonovyy (range), Russia N 4
Yakutsk, Russia O 3
Yalong (riv.), China M 7
Yalu (riv.) O 5
Yamal (pen.), Russia H 2
Yana (riv.), Russia P 3
Yangtze (Chang Jiang) (riv.), China N 6
Yarkand (riv.), China K 6
Yazd, Iran G 6
Yelizavety (cape), Russia R 4
Yellow (sea) O 6
Yemen F 8
Yenbo, Saudi Arabia E 7
Yenisey (riv.), Russia K 3
Yeniseysk, Russia L 4
Yibin, China M 7
Yinchuan, China M 6
Yining, China K 5
Yogyakarta, Indonesia M10
Yokohama, Japan R 6
Yuan (riv.), China M 7
Yumen, China L 6
Yuzhno-Sakhalinsk, Russia R 5
Zahedan, Iran G 7
Zamboanga, Philippines N 9
Zaysan (lake), Kazakhstan K 5
Zhangjiakou, China N 5
Zhangye, China M 6
Zhanjiang, China N 7
Zhengzhou, China N 6
Zhigansk, Russia N 3
Zhuzhou, China N 7
Zibo, China N 6
Zlatoust, Russia G 4
Zunyi, China M 7
Zyryanka, Russia S 3

**ASIA MINOR.** One of the great crossroads of ancient civilization is a broad peninsula that lies between the Black and Mediterranean seas. Called Asia Minor (Lesser Asia) by the Romans, the land is the Asian part of modern Turkey. It lies across the Aegean Sea to the east of Greece and is usually known by its Greek name Anatolia.

Asia Minor juts westward from Asia to within half a mile (800 meters) of Europe at the divided city of Istanbul, where a suspension bridge over the strait of Bosporus links the two continents. Asia Minor is also bordered by the Sea of Marmara on the northwest. The area of the peninsula is about 292,000 square miles (756,000 square kilometers).

The interior is a high arid plateau, about 3,000 feet (900 meters) in elevation, flanked to the north and south by rugged mountain ranges. Within the plateau a number of ranges enclose broad, flat valleys, where several salty lakes have formed.

A Mediterranean-type climate of hot, dry summers and mild, moist winters prevails in the coastal areas. The dry central plateau has hot summers and cold winters. During all seasons high winds are common; moist Mediterranean winds bring rain to the coastal regions in the winter. There is little summer rainfall.

In about 2000 BC Asia Minor was in the hands of the Hittites, who migrated from the area east of the Black Sea. Their civilization rivaled that of the Egyptians and Babylonians. In the 12th century BC their empire fell to the Assyrians. Small seaboard states grew up, only to fall to the Greeks, who colonized the entire coast in about the 8th century BC. According to legend, they first laid siege to the city-state of Troy during the Trojan War. (*See also* Aegean Civilization; Greece, Ancient; Hittites.)

In 560 BC Croesus mounted the throne of Lydia in Asia Minor and soon brought all the Greek colonies under his rule. Croesus was overthrown by Cyrus the Great of Persia. Two hundred years later Alexander the Great again spread Greek rule over the peninsula. (*See also* Alexander the Great; Croesus; Persia.)

After its conquest by Rome in the 2nd century BC, Asia Minor enjoyed centuries of peace. During the Middle Ages, as a part of the Byzantine Empire, it became a center of Christianity and the guardian of Greek and Roman culture. One of the chief medieval trade routes passed through the region. As the power of the empire declined, Arabs and Mongols invaded. In the 15th century the Ottoman Turks conquered the peninsula and made Istanbul (then known as Constantinople) the capital. The Ottoman Empire lasted until 1922. The next year Asia Minor became the larger part of the Turkish republic under Kemal Atatürk. He had set up a government at Ankara, which became the new capital of Turkey. (*See also* Ankara; Atatürk; Byzantine Empire; Istanbul; Ottoman Empire. For physical map, *see* Turkey.)

Alex Webb—Magnum

*An Asian American student studying in a Harvard University library typifies the determination of his generation to succeed.*

# ASIAN AMERICANS

Success story of the 80s has been the catchphrase used in the media to describe certain groups of Asian Americans—especially the American-born children of emigrants from China, Japan, and Korea. While the media focus was usually on the outstanding success in school or business of these Asian Americans, their remarkable achievements were often matched by young Asian immigrants for whom English was a second language. Part of the success story has been the old-world ethics of their parents, who often left their Asian homes without any material possessions and who had to work hard to achieve their goals.

Beyond their common struggles for success in an alien world, the various Asian American ethnic groups should not be lumped together as if they were homogeneous. Their cultures are distinct, and each of these ethnic groups came to the United States under widely varying circumstances.

*This article was contributed by Bill Hosokawa, former Associate Editor and Editor of the Editorial Page,* Denver Post, *and author of books on Japanese American history and numerous magazine articles on Asian Americans.*

*The many Asian American populations of the United States brighten their communities and homes with traditions from their homelands. Japanese in native costumes (top left) participate in the Festival of American Folk Life, sponsored by the Smithsonian Institution each year in Washington, D.C. Children's Day (top right) is sponsored by the Korean Baptist Church in Los Angeles. Two Buddhist monks (bottom left) of the Khmer community in New York City perform a ceremony in a private home. Chinese New Year (bottom right) is celebrated annually in Boston's Chinatown.*

Asian Americans vary as much as Norwegians differ from Spaniards or the English from the French and Italians, though all are Europeans. The term is broad enough to include people from all of what was Soviet Central Asia (including Russia east of the Ural Mountains, Kazakhstan, Kyrgyzstan, Tajikistan, Turkmenistan, and Uzbekistan), as well as citizens of the Indian subcontinent (including India, Afghanistan, Pakistan, and Bangladesh), Thailand, China, Japan, Korea, Indochina, the Philippines, Indonesia, and some Pacific islands (mainly the Hawaiian islands, Samoa, and Guam).

The real success story of Asian Americans is epitomized in their overall pursuit of excellence. The median family income of Asian Americans exceeds that of the general population by several thousand dollars. (An exception is emigrants from Southeast Asia, refugees from the Vietnam War who only began coming to America after the war ended in 1975.)

Asian American children of high school age generally outscore other students on the Scholastic Aptitude Test (SAT), and their overall grades are higher. They make up a disproportionately large segment of student bodies in the most prominent colleges and universities. There were complaints that discriminatory quotas were being applied against these students, however, as a higher percentage of high school graduates sought entrance to the top schools.

Japanese Americans in college today are the second and third generations of their families born in the United States. Chinese Americans in college today

range from individuals whose families have lived in the United States for five generations to the children of educated urban Chinese newcomers. These individuals are American by birth, outlook, training, and philosophy, and are influenced only peripherally by ancestral traditions. This is not wholly true of the offspring of recent arrivals in the United States. Many are strongly influenced by the ancient legacy of their parents, whose traditions emphasize family solidarity, discipline, hard work, and schooling.

A traditional emphasis on hard work and the willingness to undertake the most menial jobs to get ahead are perhaps the most obvious characteristics of the more recent immigrants. It is often the case that all adult family members work, while the children go to school. Asian American immigrants usually move into the economy through small business enterprises—for example, newsstands, grocery stores, motels, and restaurants. In New York City, for instance, Korean Americans operate more than half of the small family-owned grocery stores.

Those Asian Americans whose families have been living in the United States for several generations resent being singled out and stereotyped as part of a superminority. They feel that their achievements are only comparable to what other immigrant groups have done in the past. They are also aware that they have often had to work harder to overcome the hurdles of racism and ethnic discrimination. Even after six generations American citizens of Asian descent are still identified as Asian Americans, and they believe that they are not fully accepted as Americans. (Americans of European descent are usually referred to as Americans after a single generation, while Americans with an African background have only recently chosen to be called African Americans.)

## Historical Background

There were more than 7 million Asian Americans in the United States in 1990. This represented a sharp increase from the 891,000 who were accounted for in 1960. The statistics published by the Bureau of the Census for 1980 gave a total of 3,726,440 Asians, including Pacific islanders, which represented 1.6 percent of the population.

Emigration from Europe began in the 17th century but from Asia not until the 19th. The total emigration from the Far East consistently remained below the number of European arrivals, with one exception. There was substantial immigration to Hawaii, which was not a state until 1959—mainly to work on the sugar and pineapple plantations. Hawaii thus became a stepping-stone for many Asians to the American mainland. Today, Hawaii is the only state whose population has its roots mainly in Asia. Apart from this exception, the total Asian immigration to the United States never approached the nearly 33 million people who arrived from European nations between 1820 and 1929. One reason for the smaller number of Asians was the discriminatory legislation passed by the United States Congress and several of the states.

According to the Naturalization Act of 1790, only free, white immigrants could gain citizenship through naturalization procedures. Although the provisions of this law were set aside in 1870 in favor of African Americans who were former slaves and their descendants, Asians were still excluded. Several Western states also passed discriminatory legislation against Chinese, Japanese, and other Asian immigrants, which severely limited their rights. The phrase aliens ineligible to citizenship was used in what were called antialien land laws to deny Asians the right to own property. These laws, passed in the early 1900s, had the effect of dooming Asian immigrant farmers to lives as farm laborers, sharecroppers, or tenant farmers.

The Immigration Act of 1924, which became known as the Asian Exclusion Act and the National Origins Act, prohibited the entry into the United States for permanent residence of all persons whose national origin sprang from nations within what was called the Asia Pacific Triangle. These countries included Japan, China, the Philippines, Laos, Siam (Thailand), Cambodia, Singapore (then a British colony), Korea, Vietnam, Indonesia, Burma (Myanmar), India, Ceylon (Sri Lanka), and Malaysia. The act halted the immigration of all Asians and was deeply resented by the affected countries because it maintained that their people were undesirable because of race. The 1924 law was modified during World War II, after some embarrassment to the United States, to provide immigration quotas for China and the Philippines,

which were allies of the United States against Japan.

Under vigorous lobbying by the Japanese American Citizens League, Congress passed the Immigration and Nationality Act of 1952 (also known as the McCarran-Walter Act), which eliminated race as a consideration in both immigration and naturalization. This was a significant piece of legislation in that it recognized Asians other than Chinese and Filipinos as being worthy of immigrating to the United States. It established only minimal quotas for them, however.

The Immigration Act of 1965 permitted residents of the Asia Pacific Triangle to enter the United States as quota immigrants, which resulted in heavy emigrations from Korea, Taiwan, Hong Kong, and Indochina. From Southeast Asia came about 130,000 refugees after the Vietnam War ended in 1975, and five years later the number increased to more than 560,000.

Further legislation after the war had created an immigration system that aided family reunification and created preferences for immigrants with good educational backgrounds. The Refugee Act of 1980 brought some order to admission of emigrants coming from Southeast Asia's war zone.

More than half of the Asian Americans were living on the West coast by the late 1980s. California, with 35 percent, had the largest Asian population. (*See also* Migration of People.)

## Chinese Americans

The first Chinese immigrant arrived in 1820, according to United States government records. Fewer than 1,000 arrived during the next 27 years. The discovery of gold in California in 1848 drew the first significant number of Chinese. They came to do menial work for the growing population of gold seekers. By 1852 there were about 25,000 Chinese in California. By 1880 the total had climbed to 105,465, and most lived in the Far West.

### Asian Population in the United States, 1990

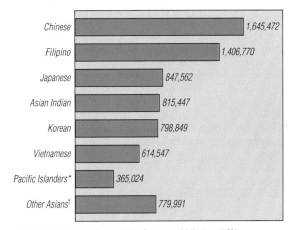

| | |
|---|---|
| Chinese | 1,645,472 |
| Filipino | 1,406,770 |
| Japanese | 847,562 |
| Asian Indian | 815,447 |
| Korean | 798,849 |
| Vietnamese | 614,547 |
| Pacific Islanders* | 365,024 |
| Other Asians† | 779,991 |

*Includes Hawaiian, 211,014; Samoan, 62,964; Guamanian, 49,345; others, 41,701.
†Includes Laotian, 149,014; Cambodian, 147,411; Thai, 91,275; Hmong, 90,082; Pakistani, 81,371; Indonesian, 29,252. The total Asian population (1990 census) is 7,273,662.
Source: Bureau of the Census, U.S. Dept. of Commerce

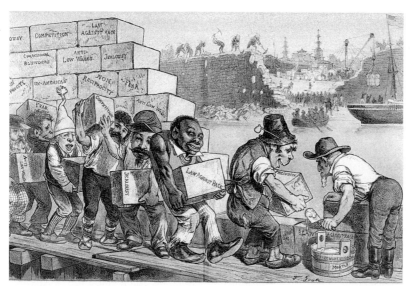

Anti-immigrant sentiment and legislation were held up to ridicule in a 19th-century cartoon. Ethnic figures representing non-Asian groups are depicted building a wall to keep out Asians, as China itself becomes more open to foreign trade. The original caption reads, "The Anti-Chinese Wall: the American wall goes up as the Chinese original goes down."
Library of Congress

Many thousands more of the Chinese who came to America returned home after a few years.

Nearly all of the early Chinese immigrants were young, poorly educated males from Guangdong (Kwangtung) Province. They came from a war-torn country where job opportunities were few. Many of them planned to work in the United States only until they could return home with a modest nest egg.

When the Chinese first arrived in California, they were regarded as welcome additions to a very small work force. Later, when anti-Chinese agitation was at its height, it was also for economic reasons that they were persecuted. The Chinese performed every type of menial job that was available. They worked in the gold mines, the lumber industry, the fisheries and canneries, and as migrant farm laborers. Some of them opened laundries, and within a few decades there were Chinese laundries in many American cities. The laundry business was a service for which there was a demand and one that required no capital or skills to start. The early immigrants, however, should be remembered for their heroic efforts in the building of the transcontinental railroad. The Central Pacific Railroad employed about 15,000 Chinese.

By the time the transcontinental railroad was completed in 1869, the population of the Far West—especially in California—had increased dramatically. The overwhelmingly white labor force, made up largely of first-generation European immigrants, soon found itself in competition with thousands of unemployed Chinese rail workers. Only a year earlier (on July 28, 1868) Congress had ratified the Burlingame Treaty—a document that allowed the free and unlimited migration of Chinese but excluded them from naturalization. Even before the treaty became law, however, anti-Chinese feeling was being stirred up throughout the West. American citizens regarded the immigrants as serious competition for jobs.

Two other factors prompted an upsurge in anti-Chinese sentiment. The first was the increase in Chinese immigration after 1869. The second was the depression that started in 1873. Adding fuel to an already dangerous situation was the use of Chinese workers as strikebreakers in different parts of the United States and the attempts to replace the freed black slaves with Chinese laborers on Southern plantations. Throughout the West organizations were formed to stop emigration from the Far East. In some cities there were anti-Chinese riots. In San Francisco, an Irish immigrant named Denis Kearney started a movement to fight the "Oriental menace."

The demands for an end to Chinese immigration became a major issue in West coast politics. Finally Congress passed the Chinese Exclusion Act of 1882. It effectively ended the immigration of Chinese laborers. Afterwards the number of Chinese in the United States gradually decreased as many of the immigrants returned home or went to more hospitable places. Very few Chinese women had come to the United States to join the young Chinese men. Since Asians were forbidden by law to marry whites, there was little opportunity to have families and there were few children to replace the aging Chinese population. The Geary Act of 1892 extended the 1882 exclusion policy. And in 1924 the National Origins Act drastically restricted immigration to the United States from all of Asia. By this time the total number of Chinese in the United States had dropped to fewer than 62,000.

The end of this discrimination against Asians began during World War II. With China as a wartime ally in fighting Japan, the 1882 exclusion act became a national embarrassment. In 1943 Congress repealed the law and granted naturalization rights to foreign-born Chinese.

**Chinatowns.** The Chinese normally settled in communities of their peers, as did most other immigrant groups. They created small Chinatowns in which they opened their own stores and restaurants, built temples, and formed societies. The most useful of the early associations were the Chinese Six Companies—family or clan organizations that helped immigrants to get established. These associations also governed affairs within the Chinese communities, particularly in San Francisco's large Chinatown. The Chinese Six Companies also served American employers as employment bureaus to hire workers.

Somewhat better known beyond the Chinatowns were their tongs. These started out as benevolent protective associations, much like the Chinese Six Companies, but they were rooted in secret Chinese societies in Asia. In California the tongs developed into criminal gangs, each of which staked out its own territory. Feuds between these gangs, popularly called tong wars by outside observers, began during the 1850s and lasted until the 1920s. Some Chinatowns experienced a renewal of urban gang problems in the 1980s. This situation was related less to tongs than to the disillusionment felt by young unemployed immigrants toward the lack of economic opportunity.

**Japanese Americans**

In 1868 the first group of Japanese laborers arrived in Hawaii. A year later the first Japanese settlement on the American mainland was founded: the Wakamatsu Tea and Silk Colony in Gold Hill, Calif. The colony failed as an enterprise within two years. Thereafter there was a small, but steady, immigration of male Japanese, mostly students, to the United States. Significant numbers of workers did not begin arriving until after 1890, when the Chinese Exclusion Act had been in effect for eight years. By that year there were only 2,039 Japanese in the United States according to the census. In the next decade about 22,000 arrived, followed by 58,000 in the decade from 1901 through 1910 (compared to nearly 9 million European immigrants in the same period).

Like the Chinese, the Japanese were welcomed as laborers when they first arrived. They lived in small colonies of their own, especially in San Francisco and in Los Angeles after the San Francisco earthquake. The Japanese also worked in similar industries—the lumber camps, railroads, fisheries and small factories—and in agriculture as farmers or migrant workers. Some started small businesses. Unlike the Chinese, many planned to remain in the United States in spite of the denial of naturalization privileges.

To establish families, many Japanese men sent for picture brides, wives chosen through the exchange of photographs. The picture marriage might be contracted after a man had asked parents, relatives, or friends to act as go-betweens, and the groom was not necessarily present for the ceremony. Usually the immigrant hoped to return to Japan someday, but, when families were formed and roots were established, returning to Japan became difficult.

Hardly had the Japanese established themselves on the West coast when an anti-Japanese movement began. As with the opposition to the Chinese, it was led by California labor leaders, newspapers, and politicians. The Asiatic Exclusion League was founded in San Francisco in 1905. A year later the city's Japanese schoolchildren were segregated from white students by the school board. Protests from Japan, countered by pressures from California, led President Theodore Roosevelt to make a "Gentlemen's Agreement" with Japan in 1907. Under its terms, the government of Japan stopped issuing passports to laborers. Enforcement of the agreement by both nations effectively slowed Japanese immigration; some 70,000 Japanese returned home in the decade that ended in 1920.

The end of immigration in 1924 did not stop discrimination in California and other Western states. To stem the prosperity of the hardworking Japanese, the California legislature passed the first in a series of alien land laws in 1913. The law did not mention the Japanese by name, but it provided that aliens ineligible for citizenship could not own land and limited leases to three years. Other states followed suit, and California soon closed legal loopholes. In 1922 the United States Supreme Court affirmed the ban against naturalization of Japanese immigrants.

Hostility from the majority population forced the Japanese to live in social isolation. They formed their own organizations and built their own churches and Buddhist temples. They also started their own protective associations, such as the Jikei-Kai that was organized after the San Francisco earthquake of 1906 to provide charity for its victims. By 1939, when about half of the Japanese population was American born, the second generation (called nisei) founded the Japanese American Citizens League. Its goals were to combat racism and to promote Americanism.

**Pearl Harbor.** "Yesterday, December 7, 1941—a date which will live in infamy—the United States of America was suddenly and deliberately attacked by naval and air forces of the Empire of Japan." With these words, President Franklin D. Roosevelt opened his speech requesting a declaration of war against Japan. The attack on Pearl Harbor proved disastrous for Americans of Japanese descent. Anti-Japanese sentiment, which had been dormant, quickly surfaced, encouraged by political opportunists and the press. It spread throughout the United States but was especially rampant on the West coast, where it was feared that the Japanese navy might launch attack. Japanese American residents were all viewed as potential traitors.

By law, the foreign-born Japanese were denied citizenship, just as the Chinese were. But their American-born children were United States citizens. The two groups of Japanese Americans were classified in Army terminology as aliens and nonaliens, but all were treated as enemy aliens. On Feb. 19, 1942, President Roosevelt signed Executive Order 9066, designating military strategic areas on the West coast. On March 18 an order was issued for the relocation of all individuals of Japanese ancestry from the strategic areas. The Japanese naturally lost their jobs, along with their legal and constitutional rights.

Up to 120,000 Japanese Americans were transported to ten concentration camps, called relocation centers.

Only 2,000 Japanese voluntarily moved to other parts of the country. Widespread hostility discouraged Japanese Americans from venturing into unfamiliar areas. Strangely, the larger Japanese population of about 150,000 on the Hawaiian Islands was not interned, though theoretically it posed a more serious threat to the United States war effort. The relocation provided an opportunity for non-Japanese on the West coast to despoil the evacuees of their land, homes, and businesses.

After World War II the United States confronted a new enemy—the Soviet Union. Japan became an American ally after the war. And the devastation caused by the atomic attacks on Hiroshima and Nagasaki in August 1945 helped to dispose public opinion in favor of the Japanese Americans. This sentiment was intensified by the outstanding feats of Japanese American fighting units—notably the famed 442nd Regimental Combat Unit—during World War II. (The 442nd Regimental Combat Unit consisted of second-generation Japanese Americans, and it became the most decorated army unit of its size and length of service in American history.) Altogether, about 33,000 Japanese Americans served in the war, including some 6,000 linguists who translated captured documents and intercepted messages, interrogated prisoners, and otherwise provided valuable intelligence.

Although Japanese American internees were allowed to leave the camps on an individual basis, the disgraceful episode was not brought to a close legally until 1989. In 1988 Congress passed a bill apologizing for the internment and offering cash payments of 20,000 tax-free dollars to each victim still living (about 60,000 at the time). The bill acknowledged that an injustice had been committed "without adequate security reasons and without any acts of espionage or sabotage." Its sponsors were four Japanese Americans: Representatives Norman Y. Mineta and Robert T. Matsui of California and Senators Daniel K. Inouye and Spark M. Matsunaga of Hawaii. Because Congress failed to appropriate the necessary funds, a second bill had to be passed in 1989 to guarantee the reparations.

## Korean Americans

The focus of Korean immigration from 1900 to 1946 was Hawaii. The first 100 Koreans arrived on the islands in 1903 to work on the sugar plantations. Soon the Hawaiian Sugar Planters' Association was arranging for recruitment of Korean workers.

The reasons for emigration from Korea were more internal than external. The country, from the time of the Sino-Japanese War of 1894–95, was in almost constant turmoil. This war was followed by the Russo-Japanese War and a few years later by the Japanese takeover of Korea itself. About 8,000 Koreans had gone to Hawaii before Japan stopped the emigration in 1905. Japan took this action to keep Koreans from competing with Japanese immigrants to the islands and to the West coast of the United States.

After 1905 only limited numbers of Koreans came to the United States. These were mostly students, a few political refugees, and some picture brides for Korean men. The political refugees formed organizations to promote Korean independence. One of the leading activists was Syngman Rhee, who became president of South Korea in 1948 (see Rhee).

Even more than the Japanese, the Koreans wanted to remain in their new home—especially since they did not wish to return to a homeland dominated by Japan. The earlier Korean immigrants had been mostly peasants. Later arrivals included many intellectuals. A sizable number were Christians, and their churches became the chief communal organizations.

Because there were so few Koreans in the United States prior to World War II, there was less agitation against them. They were, however, subjected to the San Francisco school segregation rule of 1906, along with the Japanese. And they were not allowed to become naturalized citizens. Arrivals from Korea ceased after the 1924 immigration act was passed.

After World War II, Korea was divided in two. North Korea became a Communist ally of the Soviet Union, while South Korea was allied with the United States. There was no emigration from South Korea, with the exception of a few isolated cases, until 1952. There was no emigration from North Korea because the North Koreans had dropped an iron curtain across the peninsula following the division. After the Korean War (1950–53), North Korea became a closed society.

Before the passage of the Immigration Act of 1965, the South Koreans who immigrated to the United States were mainly of three types: brides of American servicemen, college students, and children born to Korean women and American servicemen. Many of

**As second-generation Japanese Americans of the highly decorated 442nd Regimental Combat Unit (right) fought in Italy in 1943, many of their families and friends were confined to Manzanar detention camp (left) in California and in similar camps throughout the western United States.**
Library of Congress; photo by Ansel Adams; AP/Wide World

these Amerasian children were orphans who were brought to the United States to be adopted.

By 1970 there were a few more than 70,000 Koreans in the United States. As provisions of the 1965 immigration law began to take effect, this number grew dramatically. By 1990 there were more than 798,000 Koreans. A large number of the new immigrants were urban professionals, including physicians. In general, the later immigrants came from a broader spectrum of the population than earlier Koreans.

### Asian Indian Americans

There were approximately 815,000 Asian Indians and their descendants in the United States in 1990. More than 354,000 emigrants from India arrived in the two and a half decades from 1961 to 1986. Most members of this group were well educated, and there were many professionals among them. They tended, therefore, to be city dwellers and formed residential and business communities in major urban centers. Mass emigration from the Indian subcontinent became possible only with the passage of the 1965 act. Prior to that date, East Indians were generally excluded by provisions of the 1924 immigration law, along with other Asians. The small Indian population in the United States prior to 1960 consisted mostly of college and university students, in addition to descendants of Asian Indians who had arrived earlier.

The first significant emigration from India occurred in the years 1901–10. Most of the arrivals went to the West coast, either directly from India or from the Canadian province of British Columbia. The number of arrivals was not large: 271 were admitted in 1906; 1,072 in 1907; and 1,710 in 1908. In 1909 the federal government began a policy of restricting admissions, largely as a result of political and social pressures from West coast residents. Many Indians were turned back because of health problems, while others were denied entry because it was feared they would be forced to live off public charity.

When the East Indians began arriving in numbers, it was as a result of active recruitment by West coast industrialists who wanted a continuous supply of cheap labor. Many of the Indians were put to work at menial jobs in lumber camps or on railroads. A sizable number ended up as migrant farm workers in the San Joaquin and Imperial valleys in California.

### Filipino Americans

The United States acquired the Philippine Islands from Spain in 1898 during the Spanish-American War and established an American colony there. The islands were not granted their independence until 1946. During that period there was some Filipino immigration to the mainland of the United States, but the number of arrivals was never large. Most emigrants from the islands went to Hawaii. They were actively recruited by agents of the Hawaiian Sugar Planters' Association. From 1909 to 1931 about 113,000 Filipinos went to Hawaii. When hard times struck the

E. Hartmann—Magnum

*A Korean-owned neighborhood grocery store is one of hundreds of immigrant-owned markets in New York City.*

agriculture industry there, many Filipinos returned home, while nearly 20,000 of them went to the West coast. Some of these Filipinos worked most of the year on California farms but spent the summers working in Alaska salmon canneries.

In 1934 Congress passed the Tydings-McDuffie act, which provided for the eventual independence of the Philippines. This legislation limited the emigration from the islands to only 50 each year. This quota was raised to 100 in 1946, and the immigrants were allowed to apply for citizenship. Since the passage of the 1965 immigration law, the Philippines has become one of the major sources of American immigration.

### Indo-Chinese War Refugees

Since the Vietnam War ended in 1975 approximately 150,000 Vietnamese refugees have begun their lives in the United States in Westminster, Calif., a community south of Los Angeles in Orange County. This area became the American capital of the Vietnamese immigrant population. The region had a Little Saigon, a Vietnamese chamber of commerce, and about 2,000 Vietnamese-owned businesses.

Similarly, ethnic communities of Laotians and Cambodians sprang up in such states as Texas, Louisiana, Illinois, Washington, Oregon, Virginia, Minnesota, Florida, and Pennsylvania. California had the largest concentration of all Indo-Chinese groups, except for the Indo-Chinese Hmong, formerly a mountain-dwelling people of Vietnam and Laos, whose largest community was in Minnesota. Each group had its own language and culture and preferred to live isolated from the others.

(Left) Herman J. Kokojan—Black Star; (right) © Dick Swanson, 1989

*Many Indo-Chinese immigrants who arrived after 1975 were less educated than their predecessors, and so they worked in trades they had practiced at home. Some Vietnamese went to the Gulf coast of Texas, where they competed with native-born Americans in the fishing industry (left). A Hmong girl (right) works at quilt making, a common folk art, in Lancaster County, Pa.*

The refugee problem in Southeast Asia had been escalating ever since large-scale bombing attacks were launched on North Vietnam in the mid-1960s. By the end of the conflict thousands were homeless and thousands more sought refuge from the victorious Communists. Many of the Vietnamese (among whom were large numbers of ethnic Chinese) were evacuated by American military forces. As repression and genocide followed the Communist takeover, still more refugees fled. Among them were vast numbers of boat people, who used any sea vessel at their disposal to escape Indochina. Many were first sheltered in refugee camps throughout Southeast Asia before reaching the United States.

While these immigrants were allowed into the United States under various refugee laws, the government sought the help of volunteer agencies to find American sponsors and to arrange for jobs and housing. The immigrants were then sent to various parts of the country to begin new lives. The government's purpose in this program was to scatter them and thus prevent the growth of ethnic colonies such as the one that developed in Westminster. The plan failed quickly. Not long after their original settlement the refugee families, driven by loneliness, began to relocate to ethnic communities. Thus the present settlement of the Indo-Chinese refugees developed from this second migration.

These resettled immigrants found life difficult. While most of the first Indo-Chinese refugees had been well-educated city dwellers, the later arrivals came from rural backgrounds and had limited, if any, schooling. (The Hmong, for example, were subsistence peasants without a written language.) They did not speak English, and their few skills were useless in an urban, industrialized society. Many suffered from

## Some Successful Asian Americans

*Some prominent persons are not included below because they are covered in other articles in Compton's Encyclopedia (see Fact-Index).*

**Chandrasekhar, Subrahmanyan** (1910–95). Indian American physicist, born in Lahore (now in Pakistan). To United States in 1936 and joined University of Chicago faculty. "Pure theorist of modern astronomy," received 1983 Nobel prize.

**Chung, Connie** (born 1946). Chinese American broadcast journalist, born Constance Yu-Hwa Chung in Washington, D.C. On CBS newscasts in 1970s, NBC anchor in 1980s. Anchored various newsmagazine shows in the 1980s and 1990s.

**Chung, Dae Hyun** (born 1934) Korean American geophysicist, born in Jeongup. To United States in 1956. With Lawrence Livermore National Laboratory from 1974.

**Howe, James Wong** (1899–1976). Chinese American cinematographer, born Wong Tung Jim in Canton. Noted for realistic effects and innovative techniques, was nominated 16 times for Academy award (won twice).

**Khorana, Har Gobind** (born 1922). Indian American chemist and educator, born in Raipur. With Rockefeller Institute from 1958, Massachusetts Institute of Technology from 1970. After winning Nobel prize (1968), developed first artificial gene.

**Lee, Bruce** (1940–73). Chinese American martial artist, born in San Francisco, Calif. Child actor in Hong Kong. Appeared in martial arts films in Chinese (made in Hong Kong) and English ('Enter the Dragon'). Created martial arts philosophy, jeet kune do.

**Masaoka, Mike M.** (born 1915). Japanese American civil-rights activist in the Japanese American Citizens League. He is credited with persuading the United States Congress to grant Asians equal immigration and naturalization rights.

**Mehta, Zubin** (born 1936). Indian American conductor, born in Bombay. To United States 1961. Musical director of Montreal Symphony and Los Angeles, Israel, and New York Philharmonic orchestras.

**Onizuka, Ellison** (1946–86). Japanese American aerospace engineer, born in Kealakekua, Hawaii. Became astronaut candidate 1978. Assigned to film Halley's comet with handheld camera on fatal space shuttle *Challenger* mission.

**Ono, Yoko** (born 1933). Japanese American artist, born in Tokyo. To United States 1951. After murder of third husband, ex-Beatle John Lennon, continued their mission of promoting world peace.

**Tandon, Sirjang Lal** (born 1941). Indian American computer engineer. To United States to attend Howard University 1960–62. Head of Tandon Corporation.

**Wang, An** (1920–90). Chinese American inventor of computer memory core, born in Shanghai. To United States 1945. In 1951 founded Wang Laboratories, pioneer in office computers.

physical and psychological traumas that they had experienced before fleeing Indochina. Desperate for money and humiliated by their oppressed situation, a few turned to criminal activities, but most worked hard to become less dependent upon public aid. Members of large families usually helped one another with living expenses and education costs.

---

**FURTHER RESOURCES FOR ASIAN AMERICANS**

**Armor, John, and Wright, Peter.** Manzanar (Times Books, 1988).

**Brownstone, D.M.** The Chinese-American Heritage (Facts on File, 1988).

**Chan, A.B.** Gold Mountain: The Chinese in the New World (Left Bank, 1983).

**Chandrasekhar, Sripati, ed.** From India to America (Population Review Books, 1982).

**Chen, Jack.** The Chinese of America (Harper, 1990).

**Daniels, Roger.** Asian America: Chinese and Japanese in the United States Since 1850 (Univ. of Wash. Press, 1990).

**Hosokawa, Bill.** Nisei (Morrow, 1969).

**Irons, Peter.** Justice at War: The Inside Story of the Japanese American Internment (Oxford, 1983).

**Kim, Hyung-Chan.** Dictionary of Asian American History (Greenwood, 1986).

**Kitano, H.H., and Daniels, Roger.** Asian Americans: The Emerging Minority (Prentice, 1988).

**Lehrer, Brian.** The Korean Americans (Chelsea House, 1988).

**Mangiafico, Luciano.** Contemporary American Immigrants (Praeger, 1988).

**Rutledge, Paul.** The Vietnamese in America (Lerner, 1987).

**ASIMOV, Isaac** (1920–92). The author of more than 400 books on a broad range of subjects, Isaac Asimov called himself a "born explainer." His streamlined versions of science facts are as popular as his science fiction, and his works include history and mysteries.

Asimov was born in Petrovichi, Russia, on Jan. 2, 1920. His family moved to the United States when he was 3. When he was about 9, he began reading the science fiction magazines stocked in his parents' candy store in Brooklyn, N.Y. In 1938, while he was still a teenager, he sold his first short story, "Marooned Off Vesta," to *Amazing Stories*.

After postgraduate work at Columbia University, Asimov began teaching biochemistry at Boston University in 1949. The next year his first books—the futuristic satire 'Pebble in the Sky' and the thriller 'I, Robot'—were published. As the pace and scope of his writing increased, he moved to New York City for a free-lance career but retained his academic title.

Decades ahead of their time, Asimov's 'The Intelligent Man's Guide to Science' (1960) and 'Today and Tomorrow and . . .' (1973) are still popular with researchers. With his wife, Janet, he wrote a series of children's books about a mixed-up robot named Norby. Two volumes of autobiography—'In Memory Yet Green' and 'In Joy Still Felt'—cover the years 1920 to 1954 and 1954 to 1978.

The more than 30 subjects in Asimov's 'How Did We Find Out' series range from numbers (1973) to photosynthesis and microwaves (both 1989). Other subjects in the young people's series are dinosaurs, germs, volcanoes, DNA, and the brain. In 1989 he also published the novel 'Nemesis'; *SciQuest* selections, 'The

Tyrannosaurus Prescription and 100 Other Essays'; and 'Asimov on Science', a collection of *Fantasy and Science Fiction* columns written over a 30-year period. He died in New York City on Apr. 6, 1992.

**ASOKA.** (died 232 BC?) The Maurya Empire in India lasted from 321 to 185 BC. Its most outstanding ruler was Asoka, a man known more for his contributions to Buddhism than for his role as a monarch.

The dates of Asoka's birth and death are uncertain. He is believed to have been emperor from about 274 to about 232 BC. He governed most of the Indian subcontinent. Early in his reign he conquered the Kalinga territory in a bloody war on the east coast of India (the modern state of Orissa). The sufferings inflicted on the defeated people led him to renounce warfare and to devote himself to the welfare of his subjects.

Asoka became a Buddhist and made every effort to live according to the precepts of this religion. He was no narrow fanatic, however. He insisted on tolerance toward all sects within his realm. At the time Buddhism was a religion of diverse schools and sects that Asoka attempted to meld into a uniform point of view. He built monasteries, encouraged the study of Buddhist scriptures, and had statements of his beliefs inscribed on pillars for all to read. To spread Buddhism he sent missionaries to other lands. His son, Mahinda, led a delegation to Ceylon (now Sri Lanka) and is considered responsible for its conversion to Buddhism. After Asoka's death the Maurya Empire began to disintegrate, and his religious work was discontinued. (*See also* Buddhism; Maurya Empire.)

**ASPEN** *see* **POPLAR.**

**ASPHALT.** A strong, versatile binding material almost immune to weather and decay, asphalt adapts itself to a variety of uses. It cements crushed stone and gravel into firm, tough surfaces for roads, streets, and airport runways. It lends its preservative, waterproof qualities to roofing, paints, and rustproof coatings for metal pipes.

Asphalt is a heavy, brown-to-black mineral substance, one of several mixtures of hydrocarbons called bitumens. Asphalt is obtained either from natural deposits (native asphalt or brea) or as a by-product of the petroleum industry (petroleum asphalt).

Some petroleums—such as those in California and Mexico—have an asphalt base. When such petroleum is heated, the lighter oils in it, such as gasoline and kerosine, are driven off, leaving the heavy, sticky asphalt. Native asphalt is probably also a residue of petroleum, left when the lighter oils evaporated or seeped into rock fissures. It is more solid than petroleum asphalt and is sometimes brittle. When heated and fluxed with petroleum oils, it softens and becomes sticky. Petroleum asphalt does not require fluxing. (*See also* Petroleum, "Refining Petroleum.")

Native asphalt occurs widely. In some places the deposits appear on the surface of the Earth and are so large they are called lakes. Pitch Lake on the island of Trinidad occupies about 115 acres (47 hectares) and at the center has a depth of about 135 feet (40 meters). Bermudez Pitch Lake, in Venezuela, covers about 1,000 acres (400 hectares) but is shallow, averaging only 5 feet (1.5 meters) in depth. Lake asphalt is semisolid and is dug out in chunks. It is identical in its properties to impure petroleum asphalt.

Another form of native asphalt, called vein asphalt or asphaltic coal, is mined from rock crevices. Jet black, brittle, and lustrous, it is the purest of all asphalts. The vein asphalt of New Brunswick is called albertite. Other types of vein asphalt are uintaite (known also as Gilsonite), wurtzilite, and grahamite. Porous rock, such as sandstone and limestone, that has become impregnated with asphalt is called rock asphalt or bituminous rock. Vein asphalt is used to make heat-resistant enamels.

One of the principal uses of asphalt is for highway surfacing. The paving mixture is a dull black, flourlike material, usually a combination of asphalt, sand, and powdered limestone. After being heated it is dumped out steaming hot onto a concrete roadbed, raked by hand, and then smoothed by a steamroller (see Roads and Streets). On cement highways asphalt is used for expansion joints and patches. Because of its resiliency, it is also used as a surfacing for airport runways, tennis courts, playgrounds, and floors in buildings. Road oils, which are light forms of petroleum asphalt, are used to settle dust, to bind gravel, and to help prevent disintegration of roadways.

Much asphalt goes into the manufacture of asphalt shingles and roll roofing, which consist usually of felt or asbestos saturated with asphalt. Asphalt is used also to waterproof tunnels, bridges, dams, and reservoirs and to soundproof walls and ceilings.

Thousands of years ago the people of Mesopotamia used asphalt to build temples, irrigation systems, and highways. The ancient Egyptians impregnated the wrappings of mummies with this preservative. In ancient India it served as a reservoir sealant.

**ASS.** Obstinate and slow, the ass, or donkey (much like its relative, the mule), is a symbol of stubborn stupidity; but it is fairly intelligent in its deliberate way. It was the first member of the horse family (Equidae) to be domesticated.

The ass was brought to the New World by the Spanish colonists and is known in Mexico and the southwestern United States by its Spanish name, *burro*. The burro is smaller than some of its Old World relatives, standing only 40 to 50 inches (1.0 to 1.3 meters) high at the withers and weighing about 500 pounds (230 kilograms). Its shaggy coat is brownish, except for a white nose and belly and a black stripe over the withers. Its ears are long, its scrubby mane is stiff and erect, and its tail is smooth, ending in a tuft.

Stock raisers in the United States have developed a mammoth ass, 4 ½ to 6 feet (1.4 to 1.8 meters) tall and weighing up to 1,200 pounds (540 kilograms), to breed with horses. The male ass, called a jack or jackass, is

Galen Rowell—Mountain Light

*Herds of fleet-footed wild Tibetan asses called kiangs roam the high rugged plateaus of Tibet and the Gobi Desert in Mongolia.*

mated with a mare to produce the sturdy mule for farm work; and the she-ass, or jennet, is mated with a stallion to produce the hinny. These hybrids are not fertile: they cannot reproduce.

The stolid domestic ass is probably a descendant of the fleet-footed wild asses of Ethiopia, which the Egyptians caught and tamed more than 4,500 years ago. Wild asses still roam northeastern Africa from Somalia to Ethiopia. In the highlands and deserts of Central Asia, Iran, and northwestern India are found wild asses called onagers. The kiang roams the high plateaus of Tibet. The scientific name of the ass is *Equus asinus;* of the onager, *E. hemionus onager;* of the kiang, *E. kiang.* (See also Horse.)

**ASSAD, Hafez al-** (1930–2000). Throughout his three-decade dictatorship of Syria, Hafez Assad remained unyielding in his relationships with other countries. While Egypt, Israel, and the Palestinians all made strides along the path to peace in the Middle East, Syria and Assad only crawled forward. Known as the Lion of Damascus, Assad was a survivor in the most volatile of regions, even if it was—at times—only as a result of brutal means.

Assad was born in Qardaha, a mountain farming village in the province of Latakia, in 1930. He was a member of Syria's smallest ethnic group, the Alawite, a Muslim group which follows both Christian and Islamic teachings. As a youth, he became president of the Union of Syrian Students. Soon after, he joined the Ba'ath party. He became a pilot, and when the Ba'ath party came to power in 1963, was made commander-in-chief of the air force. Soon he became Defense Minister. While Defense Minister, Assad lost the Golan Heights to Israel, after Israel invaded in 1967. In 1970 Assad seized the leadership of Syria from then-President Atassi in a coup. The next year he held official elections and was elected President. When Syria and Egypt retaliated against Israel in 1973, Israel again defeated Syria. In 1976 Syria interceded in the Lebanese civil war and never withdrew its forces. As Anwar Sadat of Egypt began peace talks with Israel in 1977, Syria broke off relations with Egypt, its former ally. Soon thereafter Syria officially allied itself with the Soviet Union. Though Syria has been on the United States terrorism list since the list began in 1979 and is a known backer of Hezbollah, it also fought on the side of the United Nations in the Persian Gulf War.

Even with his own people, Assad was often brutal. In 1982 in the town of Hama, during the rebellion of a group of Sunni fundamentalists—Sunni being the Syrian Muslim majority—in which the rebels murdered some local leaders, Assad had his army attack the town. Approximately 10,000 are believed to have died.

Assad had two sons. His son Basil, whom Assad was grooming to take over Syria after his death, himself died in a car accident in 1994. Assad then began grooming his son Bashar, a Western-educated opthalmologist, for that position. Hafez Assad died in June of 2000. His son Bashar took over the country after his death. (*See also* Assad, Bashar; Hezbollah; Syria.)

**ASSASSINATION.** One of the most conspicuous facts of public life in the 20th century has been the killing, usually for political reasons, of public figures. Such murders are called assassinations. Since 1900 many world leaders have been the victims of assassins. After 1970 ordinary citizens and military personnel also became targets of assassins. American citizens were especially singled out by terrorist organizations in the Middle East and other Third World areas.

Such killings have taken place in all parts of the world and in every period of history. Ancient Greeks and Romans sometimes practiced tyrannicide, the killing of a dictator or tyrant in order to bring in another leader. The slaying of Julius Caesar on March 15, in 44 BC, was considered by its perpetrators to be an act of patriotism to save the Roman republic from a would-be king. This murder took place only four years after Caesar's great rival, Pompey, was assassinated in Egypt. (*See also* Caesar; Pompey the Great.)

The adoption of assassination as a political weapon derives from the Islamic world of the 11th century. A secret order of Muslims was founded in Persia in about 1090 by a man named Hasan-e Sabbah. After gaining control of a mountain fortress near the Caspian Sea, Hasan founded a sect to fight his political enemies by means of murder. Hasan and his followers were known as Nizaris and belonged to the Isma'ili branch of Islam. For two centuries this secret organization terrorized the Middle East.

Hasan, who gained the nickname Old Man of the Mountains from his fortress hideaway, is said to have given his followers a vision-inducing drug called hashish, made from Indian hemp. The visions of Islamic paradise brought on by the drug persuaded his disciples they would have a glorious afterlife if they followed Hasan's orders and killed his enemies. The killers were called *Hashshashin*, the plural of a word meaning "one who smokes hashish." This name was eventually corrupted into its present form, Assassins.

The Assassins were a threat to the stability of the Middle East until 1256, when the Mongol khan Hülagü stormed their fortresses and massacred 12,000 of them. A branch of their organization in Syria was destroyed by the Egyptian sultan Baybars I a few years later. From that time on, the sect of Assassins became little more than another Muslim faction, with no political influence. Followers of the sect are still to be found in Central Asia. (*See also* Islam.)

Political leaders and other well-known personalities have continued to be victims of public murderers. Henry IV of France was killed on May 14, 1610, by a fanatic named François Ravaillac. In 1793 Jean-Paul Marat, the radical French revolutionary politician, was knifed in his bath by Charlotte Corday. On Dec. 8, 1980, former Beatle John Lennon was shot to death outside his home in New York City by Mark David Chapman, a former mental patient. (*See also* Beatles; Henry, Kings of France; Marat.)

Since 1900, assassination has remained a terrifyingly frequent defect of civilization. The reasons for such killings are various. But apart from purely irrational behavior on the part of the killer, there are three basic motives: personal vengeance, propaganda purposes, or the hope of political revolution.

**Personal vengeance.** Assassination in which a political figure is killed for the private reasons of the murderer is usually based on the murderer's determination to carry out an act of personal or social revenge for real or imagined wrongs. The killing of American presidents has often fallen into the vengeance category. The murder of President James Garfield in 1881 is considered a typical example of vengeance assassination. Garfield was shot on July 2, 1881, by Charles Guiteau, a disgruntled office seeker. Guiteau was convinced he had been wrongly denied the political rewards that were due him. (*See also* Garfield.)

The assassination of President Abraham Lincoln on April 14, 1865, is a less clear example of vengeance. It has traditionally been assumed that John Wilkes Booth was attempting to avenge the South's defeat in the American Civil War. But some historians have suggested that Booth was perhaps part of a conspiracy that may even have involved members of Lincoln's Cabinet. (*See also* Lincoln, Abraham.)

Similar uncertainty surrounds the killing of President John F. Kennedy in Dallas, Tex., on Nov. 22, 1963. The general assumption is that Lee Harvey Oswald was a lone gunman who acted from undisclosed personal motives. There have been, however, frequent allegations that Oswald was part of a conspiracy that has yet to be uncovered (*see* Kennedy, John F.).

Some privately motivated assassinations have been prompted by idealism. The victim was chosen because the murderer believed the death of that person would benefit humankind or a particular cause. Probably the most notable incident involving such idealism was the failed attempt on the life of Adolf Hitler in the summer of 1944 (*see* Hitler, Adolf).

**Propaganda purposes.** Another type of assassination is often called "propaganda by the deed," an attention-getting device designed to gain publicity for some particular point of view. The 19th-century anarchists were perhaps the most prominent advocates of such crimes prior to the last half of the 20th century. The anarchists argued that violence and assassination were moral responses to immoral institutions and governments. In the years between 1881 and 1914, several heads of state were killed by anarchists: Alexander II of Russia (1881), President Sadi Carnot of France (1894), Premier Antonio Cánovas del Castillo of Spain (1897), Empress Elizabeth of Austria-Hungary (1898), King Umberto of Italy (1900), President William McKinley of the United States (1901), and Premier José Canalejas of Spain (1912). (*See also* Anarchism.)

Probably the most significant assassination of the 20th century for propaganda purposes, with the most devastating outcome, was that of Archduke Francis Ferdinand of Austria-Hungary. He and his wife were killed by Gavrilo Princip, a Serbian nationalist, on June 28, 1914, in Sarajevo, Bosnia. The furor aroused in Europe by this assassination fed the already explosive international tensions that erupted into World War I five weeks later. (*See also* World War I.)

The second half of the 20th century has known its share of propaganda assassinations. One of the most notorious killings was that of former Italian Premier Aldo Moro. Moro was kidnapped on March 16, 1978, by members of the Red Brigades, an Italian terrorist group responsible for many kidnappings, bombings, and killings. His body was found in a parked car in Rome nearly two months later.

**Political revolution.** Political killing has as its goal a change in leadership or form of government. Such assassinations often occur during a military coup. On April 12, 1980, the president of Liberia, William R. Tolbert, was executed by members of the Liberian army, and a new government was installed. On Oct. 26, 1979, the president of South Korea, Park Chung Hee, was killed by one of his associates, but there was no change in the form of government. The killing of Czar Nicholas II and his family in 1918 was meant to guarantee the abolition of the monarchy in Russia.

The Hindu nationalist who killed Mahatma Gandhi in 1948 probably intended to alter the course of India's domestic policies. Assassinations for political reasons have not always brought about the change desired.

### The 20th-Century Record

In addition to the previously mentioned assassinations that have taken place since 1900, there were more than 150 attempts on the lives of national leaders between 1918 and 1968. Of these, nearly 70 attempts were successful. Chief executives in the United States, Portugal, Japan, Ireland, Brazil, Iran, and Germany were among those slain.

Some 25 individuals who were politically connected but were not government officials were also murdered during this period. Among them were Pancho Villa of Mexico (1923), Leon Trotsky of the Soviet Union (1940), and the American civil rights leader Martin Luther King, Jr. (1968).

---

## Some Notable Assassinations Since 1900

*Some notable 20th-century assassinations are not included below because they are covered in the main text of this article or in other articles in Compton's Encyclopedia (see Fact-Index).*

**Abdullah ibn-Hussein.** King of Jordan. On July 20, 1951, in Jerusalem, by a young Palestinian Arab.

**Aquino, Benigno S.** Philippine political opposition leader. On Aug. 21, 1983, in Manila, allegedly by Rolando Galman, an ex-convict.

**Cermak, Anton J.** Mayor of Chicago. On Feb. 15, 1933, in Miami, Fla., by Giuseppe Zangara. It is believed that President-elect Franklin D. Roosevelt was the intended victim.

**Dollfuss, Engelbert.** Chancellor of Austria. On July 25, 1934, by a group of Nazis raiding the chancellery.

**Evers, Medgar.** American civil rights leader. On June 12, 1963, in Jackson, Miss., by Byron De La Beckwith.

**Faisal.** King of Saudi Arabia. On March 25, 1975, by his nephew, Prince Faisal ibn Musad, in Riyadh.

**Gandhi, Indira.** Prime minister of India. On Oct. 31, 1984, in New Delhi, by two Sikh bodyguards.

**Gandhi, Mahatma.** Indian nationalist and spiritual leader. On Jan. 30, 1948, in Delhi, by Hindu extremist Nathuram Godse.

**Gandhi, Rajiv.** Former prime minister of India. On May 21, 1991, near Madras, allegedly by a Tamil woman with explosives strapped to her waist.

**Gemayel, Bashir.** Newly elected president of Lebanon. On Sept. 14, 1982, in Beirut, by unknown assailants.

**Kennedy, John F.** President of the United States. On Nov. 22, 1963, in Dallas, Tex., presumably by Lee Harvey Oswald.

**Kennedy, Robert F.** United States senator and presidential candidate. On June 5, 1968, in Los Angeles, Calif., by Sirhan Sirhan, a Jordanian-born Arab immigrant.

**King, Martin Luther, Jr.** American civil rights leader. On April 4, 1968, by James Earl Ray in Memphis, Tenn.

**Long, Huey P.** United States senator. On Sept. 8, 1935, in Baton Rouge, La., by Dr. Carl Austin Weiss.

**Lumumba, Patrice.** Former premier of the Congo (now Zaire). On Jan. 17, 1961, in Katanga Province, probably by followers of President Joseph Kasavubu.

**McKinley, William.** President of the United States. On Sept. 6, 1901, in Buffalo, N.Y., by Leon Czolgosz, an anarchist.

**Malcolm X.** American civil rights leader. On Feb. 21, 1965, by black nationalists in New York City.

**Moawad, René.** Newly elected president of Lebanon. On Nov. 22, 1989, in Beirut, by unknown assailants.

**Mountbatten, Louis.** Member of the British royal family. On Aug. 27, 1979, by members of the Provisional Irish Republican Army, on a fishing boat off the coast of Ireland.

**Ngo Dinh Diem.** President of South Vietnam. On Nov. 2, 1963, in Saigon, during a military coup.

**Palme, Olof.** Prime Minister of Sweden. On Feb. 28, 1986, by an unknown assailant in Stockholm.

**Rasputin.** Politically powerful Russian monk. On Dec. 31, 1916, by a group of noblemen.

**Sadat, Anwar el-.** President of Egypt. On Oct. 6, 1981, by Muslim fundamentalists in Cairo.

**Somoza Debayle, Anastasio.** Former president of Nicaragua. On Sept. 17, 1980, in Asunción, Paraguay, in an ambush.

**Somoza García, Anastasio.** President of Nicaragua. On Sept. 21, 1956, in the Panama Canal Zone, by Rigoberto López Pérez.

**Trujillo Molina, Rafael.** Dictator of the Dominican Republic. On May 30, 1961, near Ciudad Trujillo (Santo Domingo), by an unknown assailant.

Assassinations and assassination attempts persist. A number of present-day terrorist organizations have used kidnapping and murder as political and economic weapons. Among the better known of these organizations are the so-called Baader-Meinhof gang in Germany, the Red Brigades in Italy, the Provisional Irish Republican Army in Northern Ireland, the Palestine Liberation Organization in the Middle East, and Basque organizations in Spain.

Assassinations by drug traffickers increased dramatically in the 1980s, especially in Colombia. Colombian drug leaders targeted judges, court workers, and journalists in efforts to show their stronghold on the nation. Senator Luis Carlos Galán, a presidential candidate, was killed on Aug. 18, 1989, near Bogotá. On the same day, Colombian President Virgilio Barco Vargas announced a crackdown and reinstated a treaty that allowed drug dealers to be extradited to the United States. In turn, members of the powerful Medellín drug cartel pledged an "all-out war," while a group known as the Extraditables threatened to kill ten judges for every Colombian extradited.

**ASSAYING.** In chemical analysis the process of determining proportions of metal, particularly precious metal, in ores and metallurgical products is called assaying. The most important technique, still used today, grew largely out of the experiments of the ancient alchemists and goldsmiths, who tried to find or create such precious metals as gold and silver by experimenting with base metals and minerals. (Base metals include lead, bismuth, tin, antimony, and copper.)

Precious metals often occur as particles dispersed throughout an ore, so that a large sample of the ore must be used for the assay. Such large samples—typically containing gold, silver, and lead—can be most economically assayed by the fire method.

In the fire method a representative sample is taken and melted with other chemicals to produce a button—usually mostly lead, containing the precious metal—and slag, which is discarded. In a step called cupellation, the button is melted in an atmosphere that oxidizes impurities, including lead and other metals, and leaves a gold-and-silver-alloy bead.

The bead is weighed to determine the total of gold and silver. The bead is then treated with hot dilute nitric acid to dissolve out the silver. The remnant of gold is weighed and that weight is subtracted from the weight of the gold-silver bead to find the weight of the silver.

If platinum, palladium, or rhodium are present, they dissolve in the molten lead and are collected in the same manner as gold and silver. If iridium is present, it forms a black deposit that clings to the bead. Osmium and ruthenium, on the other hand, are largely lost during cupellation; if their presence is suspected, chemical methods instead of fire analysis are used. ( *See also* Chemical Analysis.)

**ASTAIRE, Fred** (1899–1987). Top hat, white tie, and tails, with a formal cane, epitomized the elegance of Fred Astaire's dancing style, but in his routines he used many other props—a mop, a hat rack, dumbbells, golf clubs, firecrackers, even funhouse mirrors. He danced on the tops of bottle-stacked bars and pianos, over furniture and, in a memorable 'Royal Wedding' number, up the walls and across the ceiling.

Fred Austerlitz was born on May 10, 1899, in Omaha, Neb. His Austrian immigrant father, Frederic E. Austerlitz, was a traveling beer salesman. When Fred was 4, he began taking lessons at the ballet school where his sister, Adele, was studying. After learning tap in New York City, the youngsters began touring as vaudeville hoofers in 1906. Their mother was their tutor, manager, and promoter.

The brother-sister act's first Broadway success was 'Over the Top' in 1917, by which time they had changed their name to Astaire. The Astaires teamed in many hit shows until Adele's retirement in 1932. The next year Fred began a movie career that lasted half a century. He developed a debonair flair for comedy and an appealing delivery of pop songs, while his choreography became increasingly inventive and fluid.

After Joan Crawford in 'Dancing Lady', Astaire had more than a dozen dancing partners, including Rita Hayworth, Judy Garland, Eleanor Powell, Cyd Charisse, Leslie Caron, Ann Miller, and Audrey Hepburn. His most popular partner was Ginger Rogers; from 'Flying Down to Rio' (1933) to 'The Barkleys of Broadway' (1949), they danced together in ten movies. Their sophisticated style, the grace and technical excellence, and the integration of plot and music in their films revolutionized the musical comedy.

In 1949 Astaire received a special Academy award for his unique artistry and his contributions to the musical genre. Between Astaire's last musical films—'Silk Stockings' (1957) and 'Finian's Rainbow' (1968)—he experimented with dance on television. 'An Evening with Fred Astaire' (1958) won a record nine Emmy awards. Television specials in 1959 and 1960 garnered more awards. In motion pictures he began concentrating on straight roles, both dramatic and comedic. He was nominated for an Academy award for his work as a con artist in 'The Towering Inferno' (1974).

Astaire married Phyllis Livingston Potter, a socialite, in July 1933; she died in 1954. The couple had two children. Horse racing preoccupied Astaire for many years, and he married a 35-year-old jockey, Robyn Smith, in June 1980. His autobiography, 'Steps in Time', was published in 1959. He died in Los Angeles on June 22, 1987.

**ASTATINE** *see* Fact-Index.

**ASTEROID.** Through a telescope one may sometimes see a point of light that looks like a star but is seen to move against the background of stars. It may be a planet or it may be an asteroid—a minor planet.

The discovery of these tiny planets dates from Jan. 1, 1801, when the Italian astronomer Giuseppi Piazzi found the first one and named it Ceres. At least 3,000 asteroids have been cataloged, and more are discovered each year. The largest asteroid, Ceres, is about 578 miles

(930 kilometers) in diameter. Next in size are Pallas, about 343 miles (552 kilometers); and Vesta, about 324 miles (521 kilometers).

Asteroids, like planets, revolve around the sun. Most of them have orbits that lie between the orbits of Mars and Jupiter. A few, however, approach the sun more closely. Asteroids whose orbits cross that of the Earth are called Apollo asteroids. Because these asteroids cross the Earth's orbit, there is the possibility of a collision between them and Earth. In 1937 the asteroid Hermes passed within 465,000 miles (748,300 kilometers) of Earth.

Many scientists believe that some asteroids have actually impacted on Earth. One hypothesis put forth to explain the mass extinction of the dinosaurs on Earth some 65 million years ago is that a large asteroid slammed into the Earth, causing a massive disturbance in global climate and humidity. Evidence for this scenario lies in Chicxulub, a region located at the tip of the Yucatan Peninsula in Mexico. A crater at Chicxulub, buried under slightly more than a half-mile (1 kilometer) of Cenozoic sediment, contains deposits of iridium, an element that is rare on Earth, but found in large quantities in asteroids and meteorites. The presence of iridium in a crater is considered to be evidence of an asteroid or meteorite impact.

The Chicxulub asteroid, measuring approximately 6 to 12 miles (10 to 20 kilometers) in diameter, has been theorized to have crashed into Earth with a force equivalent to $10^8$ megatons of explosives. An impact of that magnitude would have caused, at minimum, a global dust cloud that could have blocked sunlight for several years. This would have drastically affected global temperature and humidity, ultimately resulting in the mass extinctions that occurred at that time.

Theories of asteroid impacts are not limited to terrestrial events. Suspicions of a past oceanic asteroid impact began to grow in the 1980s after scientists discovered iridium in cores taken from the floor of the Bellingshausen Sea north of Antarctica during expeditions in the 1960s. In 1997 scientists revealed evidence for, and the consequences of, an asteroid that landed in the southern Atlantic Ocean during the Pliocene epoch, approximately 2 million years ago. The asteroid—named Eltanin—crashed into the deep ocean basin approximately 930 miles (1,500 kilometers) southwest of Chile in South America. Although it failed to leave an impact crater, researchers determined that its size, along with the force of the impact, was sufficient to cause huge tsunamis, or tidal waves, to sweep over portions of South America and Antarctica. The researchers estimated that Eltanin's size ranged from 0.6 to 2.5 miles (1 to 4 kilometers) in diameter, a small asteroid when compared to the Chicxulub asteroid. However, Eltanin's size was significant enough to cause disturbances in sediments as far as 310 miles (500 kilometers) away from the suspected impact site and may have removed the overlying sediments from the surrounding seamounts altogether. In addition to far-ranging disruption in sedimentary layers, disturbances were present in sedimentary layers at a depth formed 45 million years earlier. Although there is no evidence of a mass extinction around the time of Eltanin's splash landing, the researchers believe that, due to Eltanin's size, its impact affected aquatic and terrestrial life. An asteroid 2.5 miles (4 kilometers) in diameter would cause the sweeping of large water waves, or megatsunamis, over the coasts and some inland regions of South America and Antarctica, and the deposition of large amounts of water and salts in the upper atmosphere. This scenario is supported by the presence of coastal marine sediments in South America containing a jumble of marine and terrestrial mammal skeletons dating back to aproximately 2 million years ago. Additionally, the fossilized remains of diatoms have been identified in sediments well above sea level along the eastern coast of Antarctica. While researchers lacked an irrefutable proof of asteroid impact at the site—an intact asteroid or an impact crater—they were confident that additional evidence would be found to support their hypothesis of a large asteroid crashing into the deep ocean basin 2 million years ago. They suspected that their strongest line of evidence would perhaps lie in the frozen reaches of the Transantarctic Mountains.

The first spacecraft to encounter and photograph an asteroid was the space probe Galileo, which flew very near to the asteroid Gaspra in 1991. Until then scientists had only been able to study asteroids through ground-based telescopes. (*See also* Astronomy; Solar System.) (For tables of asteroids, *see* Asteroid in the Fact-Index.)

**ASTHMA** *see* **ALLERGY.**

**ASTOR FAMILY.** A renowned Anglo-American family that made a fortune in New York City real estate was founded by John Jacob Astor (1763–1848). The forefather of the Astor family was a butcher's son and was born near Heidelberg, Germany, on July 17, 1763. He emigrated to America in 1783 and by 1786 was established in the fur business. He devoted many years to organizing the fur trade from the Great Lakes to the Pacific Ocean and from there to China and Japan, exchanging fur for tea at great profit. His American Fur Company was the first American business monopoly.

Astor was also investing in the New York City real estate that became the foundation of the family fortune. When he died on March 29, 1848, he was the wealthiest person in the United States. He bequeathed 400 thousand dollars of his estimated 20 million dollars to found a public library, which was eventually consolidated with others as the New York Public Library in 1895.

John Jacob Astor's son, William Backhouse Astor (1792–1875), was born in New York City on Sept. 19, 1792. He more than doubled the family fortune by building hundreds of stores and dwellings in New York City. Accused of being a slumlord, he tried to renovate some of the older Astor tenements. He died on Nov. 24, 1875, leaving the bulk of his estate to his two sons.

John Jacob Astor III (1822–90) was born in New York City on June 10, 1822. Inheritances from his father and his grandfather made him the largest private owner of real estate in the city. His brother, William Astor (1830–92), became interested in land development in Florida and increased the family holdings through the yacht-building business.

William Waldorf Astor (1848–1919) was the son of John Jacob Astor III, from whom he inherited 100 million dollars. William was born in New York City on March 31, 1848. From 1882 to 1885 he was the United States minister to Italy. In 1890 he moved to England, becoming a naturalized citizen in 1899, and in 1917 was made First Viscount Astor. After moving to England, he razed his Fifth Avenue home and built the Waldorf Hotel. (In 1897 John Jacob Astor IV built the Astoria Hotel next door, and the two hotels were run as one until 1929, when they made way for the Empire State Building; a new Waldorf-Astoria Hotel was erected on Park Avenue in 1931.) William Waldorf Astor died on Oct. 18, 1919.

His elder son, Waldorf Astor (1879–1952), was born in New York City on May 19, 1879. He was educated at the University of Oxford in England and was a member of Parliament from 1910 to 1919. After World War I he took control of the London Sunday newspaper, *The Observer* (founded in 1791 and formerly owned by his father), which he ran until 1945. Waldorf Astor also held various positions in the British government. He died on Sept. 30, 1952.

In 1906 Waldorf Astor had married an American, Nancy Witcher Langhorne (1879–1964). She was born on May 19, 1879, in Danville, Va. In 1919, after her husband retired from Parliament when he succeeded to the viscountcy, she became the first woman member of the British House of Commons. The witty and energetic Lady Astor served there until 1945. Her chief interests were women's rights, improved public education, and temperance, but she was more famous abroad as the hostess of a salon at Cliveden, their country home. She died on May 2, 1964, at Grimsthorpe Castle, Lincolnshire.

The younger son of the First Viscount Astor, John Jacob Astor (1886–1971) was born in New York City on May 20, 1886, and was also educated at Oxford. He served as an aide to the viceroy of India (1911–14) and with the British Army in World War I. He was chief owner (1922–66) of *The Times* newspaper (London) and a member of Parliament (1922–45). He died on July 19, 1971, in Cannes, France, where he had lived since 1962.

Gavin Astor (1918–84), his son, was born on June 1, 1918, at Hever Castle, the family home in Kent, England. He assumed directorship of *The Times* in 1952 and became chairman of the Times Publishing Company (1959–66).

In the United States branch of the family, John Jacob Astor IV (1864–1912), another great-grandson of the founder, was born in Rhinebeck, N.Y., on July 13, 1864. After graduating from Harvard University in 1888, he continued the real estate tradition of the family. He was on board the *Titanic* when the ship sank on April 15, 1912, and was among the 1,513 persons who died in the disaster.

His son, William Vincent Astor (1891–1959), was born on Nov. 15, 1891, in New York City. After attending Harvard, he served in the United States Navy in both world wars. Under his direction the family real estate holdings underwent significant change. Major portions of Astor property in the heart of New York City were sold, including the site for the Empire State Building. William Vincent Astor died in New York City on Feb. 3, 1959. He willed most of his fortune to the Vincent Astor Foundation.

**ASTRAKHAN', Russia.** On the north shore of the Caspian Sea is Europe's only desert, a region with less than 6 inches (15 centimeters) of rainfall a year. The only large city in the desert is Astrakhan', at the head of the Volga River delta, about 60 miles (100 kilometers) from the sea. The city, situated on several islands between two branches of the river, is a major fishing port.

Spires and onion domes etch the skyline of Astrakhan'. On the tallest hill stands the city's chief landmark, the Kreml', a fortress built in 1580. This looks out over the fine arts conservatory, technical schools, and public gardens, and beyond to sprawling suburbs with wooden houses and crooked streets. The people are chiefly Russians, Kazakhs, and Tatars.

Astrakhan' owed its rise to its location on the Volga, the greatest river in Russia, and on the caravan and water routes. The chief industry is processing and canning fish products, especially caviar, obtained from sturgeon from the Caspian Sea. Other industries include metalworking, woodworking, and the manufacture of chemicals.

The city was formerly capital of the Astrakhan' Khanate and the province of Astrakhan', a political division of the old Russian Empire. Until 1991 it served as capital of Astrakhan' Oblast, an administrative division of the former Russian Soviet Federated Socialist Republic. Population (1989 estimate), 509,000.

**ASTROLOGY.** The study of heavenly bodies to learn what influence they may have on human life is called astrology. From the dawn of civilization, humans have looked with wonder and awe at the heavens, seeking to understand the nature of the sun, moon, planets, and stars. With the limited means available to them, ancient Mesopotamians, Egyptians, and Greeks studied the regular movements they saw in the sky. The calculations they made laid the foundation for the science of astronomy (see Astronomy). A pseudoscience, astrology also originated in speculations about how the heavens influenced life on Earth (see Pseudosciences). In ancient times, and for many centuries afterward, no distinction was made between astrology and astronomy.

Although many people—especially astronomers and other scientists—believe astrology is nothing more than a kind of superstition, it has had a popular following in the past century. Many Wall Street brokers hired specialized astrologers in the 1980s. The most publicized acknowledgment of astrological influence occurred after an assassination attempt on United States President Ronald Reagan on March 30, 1981. For the

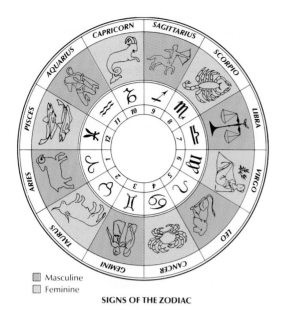

Masculine
Feminine

**SIGNS OF THE ZODIAC**

next seven years his wife, Nancy, consulted a California astrologer about the most favorable times and dates for major events in the president's life—the takeoff and landing of Air Force One, State of the Union addresses, surgery, the signing of treaties, presidential debates, even press conferences.

Astrological advice and forecasts appear in many daily newspapers and are sold in vending machines. Numerous magazines and books are published on the subject every year. Most of the advice that is given appears in a form called a horoscope—originally an elaborate chart drawn up to indicate what influences the heavenly bodies would have on the life of an individual born at a particular time. The shorter capsules of advice that appear in print for a wider audience are more generalized horoscopes, drawn according to the 12 birth signs.

An individual's astrological horoscope—that is, the natal, or birth, chart—is determined by the position of all the planets at the exact moment of birth. Astrologers divide the year into 12 equal sections, called the zodiac, which originally corresponded to 12 constellations lying in a great belt around the heavens (see Constellation). This scheme was based on the notion that the sun passes through the 12 constellations of the zodiac during the course of a year. Each constellation was regarded as the house of a particular planet, though some planets ruled more than one constellation. Each planet was believed to have either a strong or a weak influence on a person's life, depending on its position in the heavens. Each of the 12 signs of the zodiac was also believed to have a relation to parts of the human body and to the four classical Greek elements—earth, air, fire, and water. Greek astrologers associated feminine or masculine traits with each birth sign.

The divisions of the zodiac are called signs because ancient astrologers assigned descriptive names, mostly of animals, to various constellations and devised abstract symbols to fit these names. The position of the sun in one of these 12 constellations at the moment of birth determines an individual's sun sign. A person born just at the time of change from one sun sign to the next is said to be on the cusp, sharing qualities of both signs. The word cusp originally meant "point," so the astrological cusp is the point of exit from, or entry to, a given sign.

In addition to the signs, all horoscopes are also divided into 12 houses. A house denotes some human characteristic or aspect of experience such as romance, home, family, travel, death, employment, health, and thought. All the houses are related to the signs, but the signs represent planetary influences, while the houses deal with earthly life.

The astrology practiced today is based on a system of beliefs derived from the early Greeks. A major error in their astrological sophistication was the assumption that all the planets and the sun rotate around the Earth. It was not until the work of Copernicus and Galileo in the 16th and 17th centuries that the sun was discovered to be the center of the solar system. (See also Copernicus; Galileo; Solar System.)

Early astrologers had different opinions on the relationship of planetary influences to the will of God. Some said that astrology foretells what will and must happen, without the possibility of events being changed either by humans or by God. (Christianity and Islam both take issue with astrologers because of this theory.) Less rigid astrologers claimed that astrology only predicts possible influences. One school of early Christian astrologers believed that astrology reveals what God has already planned.

In most cultures where astrology has long been practiced—among them Egyptian, Greek, Indian, and Chinese—the animistic religious systems claim all nature to be alive and to possess almost human qualities (see Animism). In these traditions, astrology is simply another form of divination, of telling the future by consulting the will of natural forces.

"What's your sign?" was a cliché of the 1970s. For instant character analysis, distinct personality traits have been identified with each of the signs (gregarious Aquarius, nit-picking Virgo). Many people still like to check their daily horoscope for the general outlook of their sign. Others have their own personal horoscopes drawn up for more specific information that might help them make wiser decisions.

With the help of computers, astrologers can make the complex mathematical computations for a horoscope in five or ten minutes. Such computations used to take hours or even days. Many professional astrologers use computers in this way to save their time and energy for the art of interpreting the data.

No one has been able to prove the scientific accuracy of astrological predictions. Results vary with the individual astrologer's interpretive skill—a skill that is part intuition and part training. Attempts to measure and define such skill have been inconclusive.

**ASTRONAUTICS** *see* **AEROSPACE INDUSTRY; SPACE TRAVEL.**

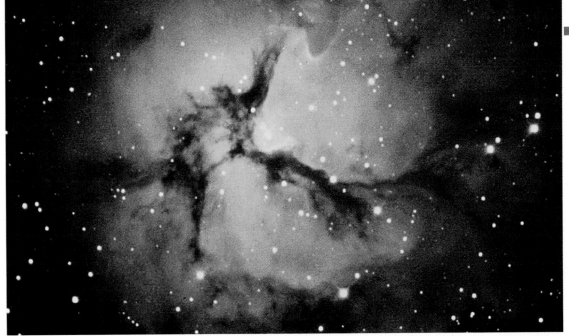

U.S. Naval Observatory

*The Trifid nebula is a cloud of glowing gas and dark streaks of dust. It is in the constellation Sagittarius.*

# ASTRONOMY

Since the beginnings of humankind people have gazed at the heavens. Before the dawn of history someone noticed that certain celestial bodies moved in orderly and predictable paths, and astronomy—an ancient science—was born. Yet some of science's newest discoveries have been made in this same field. From simple observations of the motions of the sun and the stars as they pass across the sky, to advanced theories of the exotic states of matter in collapsed stars, astronomy has spanned the ages.

For centuries astronomers concentrated on learning about the motions of heavenly bodies. They saw the sun rise in the east, cross the sky, and set in the west. After the sun had set, they saw tiny points of light appear as the sky was growing dark.

Most of these lights seemed to stay in the same place in relation to one another, as if they were all fastened to a huge black globe surrounding Earth. These lights were called stars. Other lights, however, seemed to travel, going from group to group of stationary stars. These moving points were called planets, or "wanderers."

The ancient astronomers thought that the positions of celestial bodies revealed what was going to happen on Earth—wars, births, deaths, and good fortune or bad. This system of belief is called astrology. Because the ancient astrologers wanted to predict precisely what would happen on Earth, they studied the

..................................................................................

*This article was contributed by Dr. Gerard P. Kuiper, Late Director of the Lunar and Planetary Laboratory, University of Arizona, and by Dr. Thomas L. Swihart, Professor of Astronomy, University of Arizona.*

motions of the celestial bodies. Most scientists no longer believe in astrology, but they have found that some ancient astrologers were good at observing the motions and positions of stars and planets.

## THE VISIBLE SKY

When you look at the sky without any telescope or binoculars or any other modern instrument, you see basically the same things the ancient astronomers saw. During the day you see the sun and sometimes even a faint moon.

During a clear night you see the stars and usually the moon. If you watch the sky often enough, you can get to recognize groups of stars called constellations. You may even notice a star that seems to be in different positions from night to night: it is really a planet, one of the "wandering stars" of the ancients.

### Day and Night

The day is divided into 24 hours. On average the sun is up 12 hours and down 12 hours. The daily motion of the sun is therefore the source of the time given by our clocks. But the days are not exactly alike. In winter the sun is visible less than 12 hours per day; in summer it is visible longer. This happens because the sun's path through the daytime sky is longer in summer than in winter.

### Earth in Space

The apparent westward motion of the sun, the moon, and the stars is not real. They seem to move around Earth, but it is actually Earth that moves. It is rotating eastward, completing one rotation each day. This

NASA

*Our planet floats freely in space. In this Apollo 8 photograph, North and South America are hidden by clouds. Asia and part of Africa are on Earth's night side.*

*FACT FINDER FOR ASTRONOMY*

The subject of astronomy is a broad one. Readers will obtain additional information in the related articles listed here. (*See also* related references in the Fact-Index.)

| | |
|---|---|
| Asteroid | Meteor and Meteorite |
| Astrology | Moon |
| Aurora | Observatory |
| Black Hole | Planets |
| Calendar | Pulsar |
| Comet | Radiation |
| Constellation | Quasar |
| Cosmology | Satellite |
| Earth | Solar System |
| Eclipse | Sound |
| Energy | Spectrum and Spectroscope |
| Extraterrestrial Life | Star |
| Gravitation | Sun |
| Latitude and Longitude | Telescope |
| Light | X Rays |

*See also* biographies of the following scientists:

| | |
|---|---|
| Alfvén | Huygens |
| Banneker | Jeans |
| Cannon | Kepler |
| Cassini | Laplace |
| Copernicus | Mitchell, Maria |
| Galileo | Newton |
| Halley | Ptolemy |
| Herschel | Sagan |

is hard to believe at first because when we think of motion we also think of the vibrations of moving cars or trains. But Earth moves freely in space, without rubbing against anything, so it does not vibrate. It is this gentle rotation, uninhibited by significant friction, that makes the sun, the moon, and the stars appear to be rising and setting.

Earth is accompanied by the moon, which moves around the planet at a distance of about 30 Earth diameters. At the same time, Earth is moving around the sun. Every year Earth completes one revolution around the sun. This motion accounts for the changes in the seasons because Earth's axis of rotation is tipped. When the northern half of Earth is tipped toward the sun, then the Northern Hemisphere experiences summer and the Southern Hemisphere, which is tipped away from the sun, experiences winter. When Earth has moved to the other side of the sun, six months later, the seasons are reversed because the Southern Hemisphere is then tipped toward the sun and the Northern Hemisphere is tipped away from the sun.

If you watch the moon for three or four weeks, you will see that it does not always look the same. Sometimes it looks like a big disk, sometimes like a tiny curved sliver. These changes are called the phases of the moon. They occur because the moon shines only when the sun's light bounces off its surface. This means that only the side of the moon that faces the sun is bright. When the moon is between Earth and the sun, the light side of the moon faces away from Earth. This is called the new moon, which is not visible. When the moon is on the other side of Earth from the sun, its entire light side faces Earth. This is called the full moon. Halfway between the new and full moons, in locations on either side of Earth, are the first quarter and the last quarter.

## The Night Sky

What else can you see on a clear night with just your eyes? Naturally you can see stars. After a few nights you might even recognize a planet by its motion. Although stars and planets look alike to the unaided eye, they are very different things. The planets all circle the sun, just as Earth does. They are visible to Earth because sunlight bounces off them.

The stars are much farther away. Most stars are like the sun—large, hot, and bright. The stars shine from their own energy, just as the sun does.

As you watch the stars you may notice a broad strip of dim light across the sky. It is a clustering of faint stars known as the Milky Way. The Milky Way is a

The Bettmann Archive

*A woodcut (left) created by Hans Holbein the Younger in 1534 shows astronomical instruments of the time. The astronomers are observing the phases of the moon. The moon has a complicated 30-day path around the Earth as they both travel around the sun (right). As the moon travels in an almost circular path around the Earth, the Earth moves in a similar path around the sun. Both motions combine to give the moon a wavy orbit.*

galaxy—an enormous cluster of stars, of which the sun is only one member. The Milky Way galaxy contains on the order of 1 trillion stars. Other galaxies exist far beyond the Milky Way.

**Eclipses**

In ancient times people were often terrified when the sun or the moon would seem to disappear completely during the day or night when normally it would be visible. They did not understand what caused these eclipses, and they were afraid that the sun or moon might be gone forever, leaving the world in darkness.

Eclipses occur irregularly because the plane of the moon's orbit around Earth is slightly different from the plane of Earth's orbit around the sun. The two planes intersect at an angle of 5° 8'. This means that the moon is usually slightly above or below the line between Earth and the sun, so neither Earth nor the moon throws a shadow on the other. Eclipses can occur only when the moon lies at one of the two points where the planes intersect. If this were not so, we would have total lunar eclipses with every full moon and total solar eclipses with every new moon.

Sometimes the moon crosses a point of intersection of the two planes at the same time that it passes directly behind Earth. The shadow of Earth blocks off the light to the moon, and the moon seems to disappear. Some two hours later, the edge of the moon appears on the other side of Earth's shadow and the whole moon gradually emerges.

### The Moon's Path Around the Sun

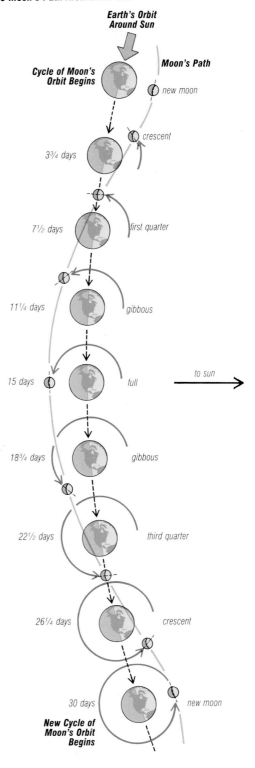

Earth's Orbit Around Sun

Moon's Path

Cycle of Moon's Orbit Begins

new moon

3¾ days — crescent

7½ days — first quarter

11¼ days — gibbous

15 days — full    to sun →

18¾ days — gibbous

22½ days — third quarter

26¼ days — crescent

30 days — new moon

**New Cycle of Moon's Orbit Begins**

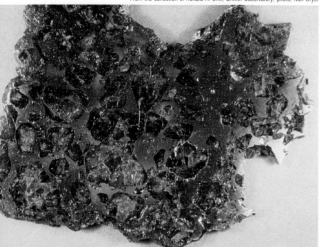

From the collection of Ronald A. Oriti, Griffith Observatory; photo, Ivan Dryer

*A slice from a meteorite has been polished. It contains both stony material and iron. Such meteorites contain large amounts of nickel-iron metal and silicates.*

Robert C. Dickinson

*Auroras are streaks of light that occur high in the sky. They are usually seen far to the north or south, near Earth's poles, but this one was photographed near Pittsburgh, Pa.*

The opposite happens, too. Sometimes the moon crosses the point of intersection of the two planes at the same time that it passes between Earth and the sun. It casts a shadow on Earth, causing an eclipse of the sun. Because the moon is much smaller than Earth, only a small shadow patch on Earth's surface results. To people in the darkest part of the shadow, the umbra, the moon completely blocks out the sun. This is a total eclipse of the sun: the entire bright disk is covered up and only the outer atmosphere of the sun, the corona, is visible. Because the sun is so bright, it is very dangerous to look directly at it, even during an eclipse.

Normally light from the sun's bright disk blots out the faint corona. During total solar eclipses astronomers can study the sun's atmosphere. Unfortunately, such eclipses are always brief; the longest possible total eclipse is about seven minutes.

A larger area of Earth is covered by the shadowy area around the true shadow (this blurry area is the penumbra). To people in the penumbra, the moon blocks off part of the sun, but a light silver or yellow crescent shows along the edge of the moon. This is a partial eclipse of the sun.

When the moon is farthest from Earth during an eclipse, its disk appears a bit smaller than the sun's disk, so that a ring of the sun's disk is seen around the black mass of the moon. This is what astronomers call an annular eclipse.

### Rocks from Outer Space

Sometimes when observing the night sky, a flash of light may streak through the atmosphere and disappear. Although this is commonly called a shooting star, real stars do not shoot through the sky any more than the sun does. But small, solid chunks of stone or metal are in orbit around the sun. Sometimes these pieces of stone or metal enter Earth's atmosphere, and the friction generated by their great speed causes them to burn up. The fragments may either disappear before traveling far or actually hit the ground.

Shooting stars have different names depending on where they are. According to the International Astronomical Union, a rock or metal fragment existing beyond Earth's atmosphere is called a meteoroid. A meteoroid that enters Earth's atmosphere is called a meteor. And a meteor that actually lands on Earth's surface is called a meteorite.

Meteorites, which are sturdy enough to reach the ground, apparently are pieces of asteroids. (Asteroids are huge rocks, up to 500 miles [800 kilometers] across, that orbit the sun.) Most meteors that burn up in the atmosphere are tiny dustlike particles, the remains of disintegrated comets. (Comets are flimsy objects made up primarily of frozen water and frozen gases and some gritty material. They also orbit the sun.)

Sometimes a swarm of meteoroids will enter Earth's atmosphere at one time, causing a meteor shower, with tens or hundreds of shooting stars flashing across the sky at once. But all these meteors burn up in the upper atmosphere.

They are too small and fragile to reach Earth's surface, though a significant amount of dust and ash from meteors settles on Earth each day. The Leonid meteors caused the greatest meteor shower on record on the night spanning Nov. 16 to 17, 1966. These meteors occur only every 33¼ years.

### The Northern and Southern Lights

People who are relatively near the North or South Pole can see one of nature's most lavish and glorious displays—the aurora borealis (northern lights) or the aurora australis (southern lights). High in the skies over Earth's magnetic poles, electrically charged particles from the sun swarm down into Earth's atmosphere. As these particles collide with air molecules,

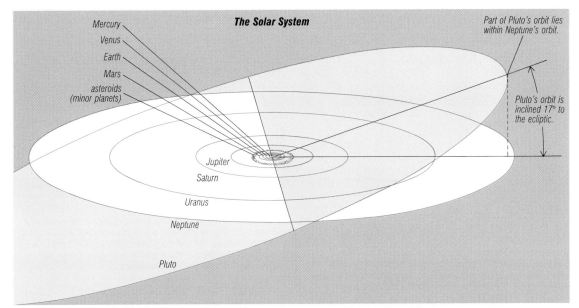

**The Solar System**

Mercury
Venus
Earth
Mars
asteroids (minor planets)

Jupiter
Saturn
Uranus
Neptune
Pluto

Part of Pluto's orbit lies within Neptune's orbit.

Pluto's orbit is inclined 17° to the ecliptic.

*Many pieces of matter are held in the sun's enormous gravitational field. Together with the sun, they make up the solar system. The paths of the planets are huge ellipses with the sun at one focus. All the planets travel in the same direction around the sun. The elliptical paths of the minor bodies are distorted by the gravitational attraction of nearby planets.*

brilliant sheets, streamers, or beams of colored lights are given off at heights ranging from about 50 to 200 miles (80 to 320 kilometers) up in Earth's atmosphere.

The streams of charged particles are known as the solar wind. The sun continually sends a flow of these particles out into space. During periods when the sun is unusually active—that is, when it has large sunspots on its surface—the solar wind is particularly heavy, and huge swarms of the particles reach Earth's atmosphere, causing large and brilliant auroras.

## THE SOLAR SYSTEM

Earth is not the only body to circle the sun. Many chunks of matter, some much larger than Earth and some so small you would need a microscope to see them, are caught in the sun's gravitational field. The nine largest of these chunks are called planets. Earth is the third planet from the sun. The smaller chunks of matter are natural satellites, asteroids, comets, meteors, and the molecules of interplanetary gases.

### Kepler's Laws of Planetary Motion

In the early 1600s, astronomers were beginning to accept the idea that Earth and the planets revolve around the sun, rather than that the sun and the planets revolve around Earth. Astronomers were still unable, however, to describe the motions of the planets with any accuracy. The German astronomer Johannes Kepler was finally able to describe planetary motions using three mathematical expressions, which came to be known as Kepler's laws of planetary motion (*see* Kepler).

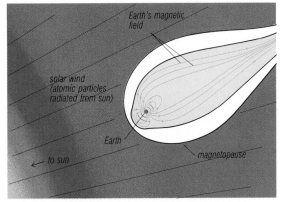

Earth's magnetic field

solar wind (atomic particles radiated from sun)

Earth

to sun

magnetopause

*The sun gives off a continuous stream of charged particles. When this stream, called the solar wind, reaches Earth, it deforms Earth's magnetic field. Some of the particles spiral down near the magnetic poles, where they cause auroras.*

If the average distance from Earth to the sun is arbitrarily called one astronomical unit (A.U.), then Kepler's third law, which describes the mathematical relation between a planet's period of revolution and its distance from the sun, can be used to find the relative distances of the other planets to the sun merely by measuring how long it takes those planets to orbit the sun. Before the actual distance from Earth to the sun was known in miles or kilometers many distances within the solar system were known in astronomical units. The unit is still a useful one. Parallax measurements and, more recently and accurately, radar observations have allowed astronomers to determine that one astronomical unit is equal to 149,597,870 kilometers (92,958,350 miles). Another method of measurement called laser ranging—bouncing laser signals off a mirror placed on the moon's surface—has been used to verify the astronomical unit.

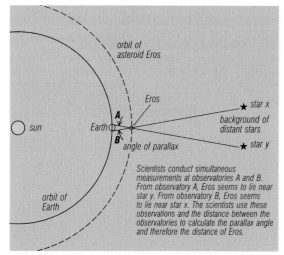

When the asteroid Eros approaches Earth, it frequently comes within 20 million miles, and sometimes it comes within 14 million miles of Earth. At such near approaches its distance is easy to measure by the parallax method.

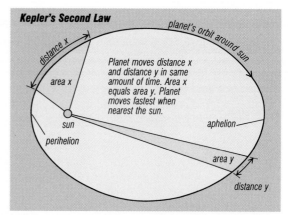

Kepler's second law of planetary motion describes the speed of a planet traveling in an elliptical orbit around the sun. It states that a line between the sun and the planet sweeps equal areas in equal times. Thus, the speed of the planet increases as it nears the sun and decreases as it recedes from the sun.

### Newton's Law of Universal Gravitation

Kepler's laws described the positions and motions of the planets with great accuracy, but they did not explain what caused the planets to follow those paths. If the planets were not acted on by some force, scientists reasoned, then they would simply continue to move in a straight line past the sun and out toward the stars. Some force must be attracting them to the sun.

The English scientist Isaac Newton calculated the acceleration of the moon toward Earth. It was much less than the acceleration of an apple falling from a tree to the ground. Newton concluded that the same force that caused the apple to fall to the ground also caused the moon to fall toward Earth. But the force grew weaker at points farther away from the planet. Following this train of thought, Newton worked out an equation that described this force as it occurred anywhere in the universe (see Gravitation).

### The Planets

Up to the 18th century people knew of seven bodies, besides Earth, that moved against the background of the fixed stars. These were the sun, the moon, and the five planets that are visible to the unaided eye: Mercury, Venus, Mars, Jupiter, and Saturn. Then, in 1781, William Herschel, a German-born English organist and amateur astronomer, discovered a new planet, which became known as Uranus.

Uranus' motion did not follow the exact path predicted by Newton's theory of gravitation. This problem was happily resolved by the discovery of yet another planet, which was named Neptune. Two mathematicians, John Couch Adams and Urbain Leverrier, had calculated Neptune's probable location, but it was the German astronomer Johann Gottfried Galle who located the planet.

Even then some small deviations seemed to remain in the orbits of both planets. This led to the search for yet another planet, based on calculations made by the American astronomer Percival Lowell. In 1930 Clyde W. Tombaugh discovered the new planet, which became known as Pluto.

The mass of Pluto has proved so small—about 1/500 of Earth's mass—that it could not have been responsible for the deviations in the observed paths of Uranus and Neptune. For this reason, some astronomers believe that there may be still other planets in the solar system that would explain the deviations, though none has yet been discovered.

All the planets travel about the sun in elliptical orbits that are close to being circles. Mercury and Pluto have the most eccentric orbits. All the planets travel in one direction around the sun, the same direction in which the sun rotates. Furthermore, all the planetary orbits lie in very nearly the same plane. Again, Mercury and Pluto have the most tilted orbits: Mercury's is tilted 7° to the plane of Earth's orbit (the ecliptic plane); Pluto's is tilted about 17°.

Most of the planets rotate on their axes in the same west-to-east motion (the exceptions are Venus, Uranus, and Pluto). Most of the axes are nearly at right angles to the plane of the planets' orbits. Uranus, however, is tilted so that its axis lies almost in the plane of its orbit.

The planets can be divided into two groups. The inner planets—Mercury, Venus, Earth, and Mars—lie within the asteroid belt, near the sun. They are dense, rocky, and small. Since Earth is a typical inner planet, this group is sometimes called the terrestrial planets.

The outer planets lie beyond the asteroid belt. With the exception of Pluto, they are much larger and more massive than the inner planets, and they are much less dense. Since Jupiter is the main representative of the outer planets, they are sometimes called the Jovian, or giant, planets. Pluto is an outer planet, but it is not usually regarded as a Jovian planet.

*Halley's comet appeared in 1066, when the Normans invaded England. The Bayeux tapestry shows the comet as an evil omen for Harold II, the English king who was defeated.*

*The sun belongs to a group of stars called a galaxy, which has a spiral shape, much like M51, the Whirlpool galaxy, shown above. The smaller companion is a typical irregular galaxy.*

## Natural Satellites of the Planets

Seven of the planets—Earth, Mars, Jupiter, Saturn, Uranus, Pluto, and Neptune—are known to have satellites. Since the moon is large in comparison with Earth, the Earth-moon system is sometimes called a double planet. The same applies to Pluto and its satellite, Charon, since Charon is estimated to be about half the size of Pluto. Although other satellites are much larger than either the moon or Charon, they are much tinier, by comparison, than the planets they circle. No other double planets are known to occur in our solar system.

## Asteroids

On Jan. 1, 1801, the Italian astronomer Giuseppi Piazzi found a small planet in the large gap between Mars and Jupiter. This planet, later named Ceres, was the first and largest of thousands of asteroids, or minor planets, that have been discovered.

## Comets

Comets are the most unusual and unpredictable objects in the solar system. They vary in appearance from small stellar images, like small asteroids, to huge tailed objects so bright that they can be seen in daytime near the sun. The comets are small bodies composed mostly of ices of various substances—principally water and gases—with some silicate grit mixed in. This composition and the nature of the comets' orbits suggest that comets were formed before or about the same time as was the rest of the solar system.

Hundreds of millions of comets may exist in a large cloud, called the Oort cloud, that is believed to surround the solar system. Occasionally comets may leave the Oort cloud when the cloud is perturbed—perhaps by the gravitational force of a passing star. These comets enter the inner solar system and orbit the sun in long elliptical paths. Occasionally one of these intruders may be gravitationally influenced by the larger planets and pulled into a closer, shorter orbit, with a period of about seven years. Most comets, however, have much longer periods. Halley's comet takes about 76 years to complete an orbit, and many comets may take thousands or even millions of years.

As a comet approaches the sun, some of its ices evaporate. The solar wind pushes these evaporated gases away from the head of the comet and away from the sun. This gives the comet a long glowing tail that always points away from the sun.

## The Sun

The spectrum, brightness, mass, dimension, and age of the sun and of nearby stars indicate that the sun is a normal, typical star. Like most stars, the sun produces energy by thermonuclear processes that take place at its core. These processes maintain the conditions needed for life on Earth.

## Origin and Future of the Solar System

The most widely accepted model for the origin of the solar system combines theories elaborated by Gerard P. Kuiper and Thomas Chrowder Chamberlin. Astronomers believe that about 4.5 billion years ago, one of the many dense globules of gas and dust clouds that exist in the galaxy contracted into a disk. The hot, dense center of the disk became our sun. The remaining outer material formed a spinning disk, called the solar nebula, which cooled into small particles of rock and metal that collided and stuck together, gradually growing into larger bodies to become the planets and their satellites.

The future of the solar system cannot be known, because accidents can happen. A star might pass right through and destroy the system, though such events are rare. If no accident occurs, the future depends on the behavior of the sun. The sun is slowly getting brighter as it consumes its reservoir of hydrogen and turns this into helium. If current computations of

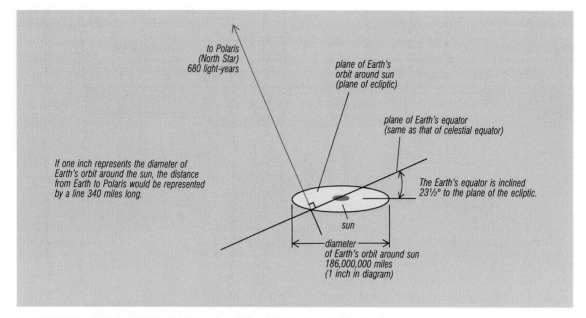

*A vast emptiness of space surrounds the solar system. If the orbit of Earth were 1 inch in diameter, Polaris would be 340 miles away from Earth. When scientists measure the parallax angle of Polaris, they find an angle equal to the smallest angle of a triangle with two sides 340 miles long and one side that is 1 inch long.*

stellar evolution are correct, the sun will grow much brighter and larger in about 5 billion years. In turn, the planets will get too hot for life to endure on Earth.

Much later the sun will have exhausted its nuclear energy source and will begin to cool. In the end it will become a white-dwarf star, with all its matter packed densely into a space not much bigger than Earth. Around it will orbit frozen wastelands, the planets that survived the solar upheavals.

### Does Life Exist Elsewhere in the Solar System?

Life as we know it, and most particularly in its higher forms, can exist only under certain chemical and physical conditions. The major requirements of life are believed to be the availability of a stable liquid or very dense gas, an atmosphere, and some protection from solar radiation. A number of environments within the solar system may meet these criteria. For example, organisms may exist in the clouds of Venus or Jupiter or beneath the surface of the moon. Comets and asteroids may contain organic matter. So far there is no strong evidence either for or against life in such environments.

Exploratory spacecraft have photographed surface features on Mars that suggest that liquid water once existed on the planet's surface. This opens up the possibility that life existed there in a much earlier epoch. However, it seems unlikely that there is any life on Mars now. Thorough analysis of samples of Martian soil obtained by the Viking 1 and 2 space probes in 1976 found no traces of living organisms. In any case, animal life as we know it appears excluded because there is no liquid water on the Martian surface, practi-

cally no free oxygen in the atmosphere, and no ozone to shield against the harmful ultraviolet sunlight.

Earth is a paradise for life as we know it. There is no other place in the solar system that would easily support human colonization. Astronauts will have to take their environment with them to any planets they visit, just as they have taken their environment with them to the moon.

### THE STARS

If you have a chance to look through a telescope at the night sky, you will see a complex display indeed. You must explore this yourself to really appreciate its magnitude. The only comparable experience is to examine a drop of water from a greenish pond under a good microscope and see the drop teeming with unexpected small living creatures.

### Constellations

The stars seem to form groups, or constellations. The Big Dipper is actually part of a larger constellation called the Big Bear (Ursa Major). Orion is another easy-to-recognize constellation. The first step in finding your way among the stars is to learn these constellations. If you begin with a few familiar ones and keep star charts handy, you will quickly learn to recognize others.

The stars in constellations are not necessarily close to each other in space. For example, though the middle five stars of the Big Dipper are relatively close together, the first and last stars only seem to be in the same group. They are actually much farther from Earth than the other five, and they are even

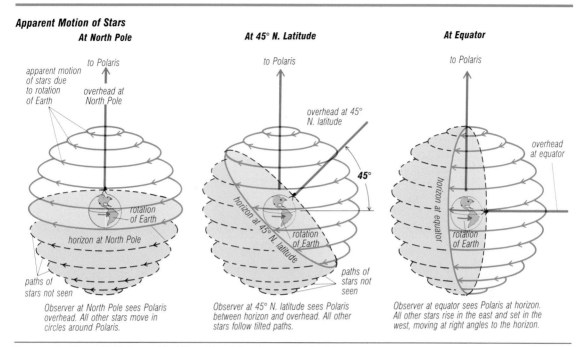

**Apparent Motion of Stars**

**At North Pole**

to Polaris

apparent motion of stars due to rotation of Earth

overhead at North Pole

rotation of Earth

horizon at North Pole

paths of stars not seen

Observer at North Pole sees Polaris overhead. All other stars move in circles around Polaris.

**At 45° N. Latitude**

to Polaris

overhead at 45° N. latitude

45°

horizon at 45° N. latitude

rotation of Earth

paths of stars not seen

Observer at 45° N. latitude sees Polaris between horizon and overhead. All other stars follow tilted paths.

**At Equator**

to Polaris

overhead at equator

horizon at equator

rotation of Earth

Observer at equator sees Polaris at horizon. All other stars rise in the east and set in the west, moving at right angles to the horizon.

*A person standing on Earth does not feel the motion of the planet as it spins. The sun and the stars appear to follow paths that lead from east to west across the sky.*

slowly moving in different directions. Some parts of Orion are relatively close together, but Betelgeuse (pronounced "beetle juice"), the bright red star at the top, is much nearer to Earth.

### Coordinate Systems

Astronomers need to record the exact locations of stars. Within limits, it is useful to locate objects within constellations. An ancient method of recording the motions of planets was to say that a planet was entering, in, or leaving the "house" of a zodiacal constellation. But this method is not really precise.

People who need to record the exact locations of celestial objects use numerical coordinate systems. These systems are like the coordinate system of latitude and longitude used on Earth.

Different celestial coordinate systems have been devised. To be useful they must take into account that Earth has two regular motions in relation to the stars. Its rotation causes the sphere of stars to appear to make a complete circle around the planet once a day. And Earth's revolution around the sun causes the star positions at a particular hour to shift from day to day, returning to the original position after an entire year.

**The horizon, or azimuth, system** is based on Earth's north-south line and the observer's horizon. It uses two angles called the azimuth and the altitude. The azimuth locates the star from the north line, and the altitude locates it from the horizon plane. For this system to be useful, the time of the observation and location from which the observation was made must be accurately known.

**The equator system** is based on the concept of the celestial sphere. All the stars and other heavenly bodies can be imagined to be located on a huge sphere that surrounds Earth. The sphere has several imaginary lines and points. One such line is the celestial equator, which is the projection of Earth's equator onto the celestial sphere. Another is the line of the ecliptic, which is the sun's apparent yearly path along this sphere. The celestial equator and the ecliptic intersect at two points, called the vernal equinox and the autumnal equinox. (When the sun is at either point, day and night on Earth are equally long.) The north and south celestial poles are extensions of the North and South poles of Earth along Earth's axis of rotation.

In the equator system, the position of a star is given by the declination and the right ascension. The declination locates the star from the celestial equator, and the right ascension locates the star from the vernal equinox. Since this system is attached to the celestial sphere, all points on Earth (except the poles) are continually changing their positions under the coordinate system.

### Actual Locations of Stars

Fixing stars on an imaginary sphere is useful for finding them from Earth, but it does not reveal their actual locations. One way to measure the distances of nearby stars from Earth is the parallax method.

For parallax measurements of stars, scientists make use of Earth's yearly motion around the sun. This motion causes us to view the stars from different

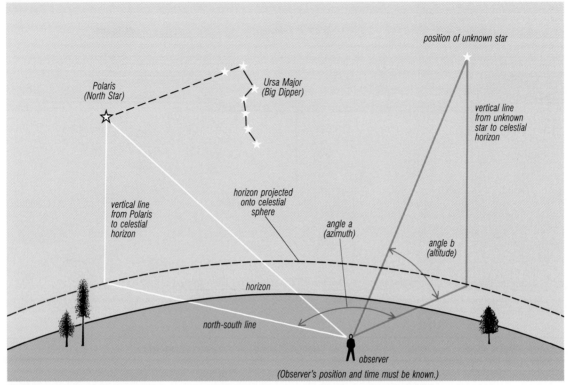

Labels in figure:
- position of unknown star
- Polaris (North Star)
- Ursa Major (Big Dipper)
- vertical line from unknown star to celestial horizon
- vertical line from Polaris to celestial horizon
- horizon projected onto celestial sphere
- angle a (azimuth)
- angle b (altitude)
- horizon
- north-south line
- observer
- (Observer's position and time must be known.)

*The horizon coordinate system provides a way to record the position of a star. The time and location of the observation must also be recorded because the star's altitude and azimuth change from place to place on Earth and with Earth's spin.*

positions at different times of the year. In summer, Earth is on one side of the sun. In winter, Earth is 186 million miles (300 million kilometers) away on the opposite side of the sun. And photographs of a near star, taken through a large telescope and six months apart, will show that the star appears to shift against the background of more distant stars. If this shift is large enough to be measured, astronomers can calculate the distance to the star.

More than four centuries ago the phenomenon of parallax was used to counter Copernicus' suggestion that Earth travels around the sun. Scientists of the time pointed out that if it did, stars should show an annual change in direction due to parallax. Because they were unable to measure any parallax, they concluded that Copernicus was wrong. We know now that the stars are all at such tremendous distances from Earth that their parallax angles are extremely difficult to measure. Even modern instruments cannot measure the parallax of most stars.

Astronomers measure parallaxes of stars in seconds of arc. This is a tiny unit of measure; for example, a penny must be 2½ miles (4 kilometers) away before it appears as small as one second of arc. Yet no star except the sun is close enough to have a parallax that large. Alpha Centauri, a member of the group of three stars nearest to the sun, has a parallax of about three quarters of a second of arc.

Astronomers have devised a unit of distance called the parsec—the distance at which the angle opposite the base of a triangle measures one second of arc when the base of the triangle is the radius of the Earth's orbit around the sun. One parsec is equal to 19.2 trillion ($19.2 \times 10^{12}$) miles (30.9 trillion kilometers). Alpha Centauri is about 1.3 parsecs distant.

Another unit used to record large astronomical distances is the light-year. This is the distance that light travels within a vacuum in one year—about 5.88 trillion ($5.88 \times 10^{12}$) miles (9.46 trillion kilometers). Alpha Centauri is the name of the star that is closest to the Earth (apart from the sun). Yet it is about 4.3 light-years distant from Earth. Light takes more than four years to reach Earth from that distance.

### Demonstrating Parallax

You can demonstrate how parallax happens. You need a wall with a design to represent the background of distant stars. A wallpaper pattern, or even a single vertical stripe, will do. You also need something you can prop in the middle of the room to represent the nearby star whose parallax is being measured. A tall vase on a table, or even a broom leaning against a chair, will do. Put the table with the vase on it (or the broom and the chair) in the middle of the room. Stand at the opposite side of the room with the vase between you and the wallpaper.

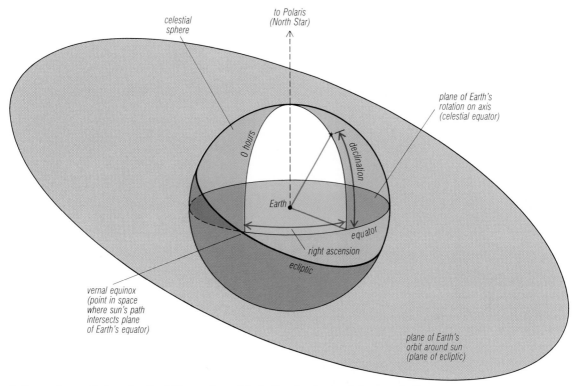

*In the equator coordinate system the right ascension and declination of a star do not change as Earth spins. A star's position is given relative to the vernal equinox, the point where the sun crosses the celestial equator in March.*

To begin with, you are at the position of the sun. Notice where the vase is seen against the wallpaper background. Take a sideways step to your right. This is the position of Earth in summer. Notice that the vase seems to move to the left along the wallpaper background. Take a step back to the sun's position and then take another sideways step to your left. This is the position of Earth in winter. Notice that the vase seems to move to the right along the wallpaper background. The apparent motion of the vase is caused by parallax.

## Estimating Distances of Stars

Each star, including the sun, has its own motion in space. This motion of the sun and the other stars causes the position of any star relative to the sun (its direction) to change evenly with time: the longer the time interval, the greater the change in direction of the star. The yearly change in direction of a star due to the space motions of sun and star is known as the proper motion of the star. Other things being equal, the nearer stars have larger proper motions than the more distant ones. This provides astronomers with a way of estimating distances of stars.

It is not possible to find the distance of an individual star in this way because there is no way to tell whether a certain measured proper motion is caused by a rapidly moving star that is far away or by a slowly moving star that is near. The average individual proper motion of a group of stars, however, can tell astronomers what the average distance of the group is. In this way, approximate distances can be found for many stars that are too far away for their annual parallaxes to be measured.

## What Starlight Tells Astronomers

How can astronomers learn what the stars are made of? Since stars cannot be analyzed in the laboratory, astronomers study the feeble starlight that actually does reach Earth. Fortunately, electromagnetic radiation, including light, can provide much information about the object that emits it.

Visible light is only one form of electromagnetic radiation. There are many more kinds. Gamma rays, X rays, and ultraviolet rays are more energetic than visible light; infrared rays and radio waves are less energetic than visible light.

The forms of electromagnetic radiation differ in their frequencies—that is, in how many times per second their waves crest. Waves with high frequencies have greater energy than waves with low frequencies. Gamma rays have extremely high frequencies and radio waves have low frequencies.

Stars are found to give off a whole range of electromagnetic radiation. The kind of radiation a star gives off is related to the temperature of the star: the

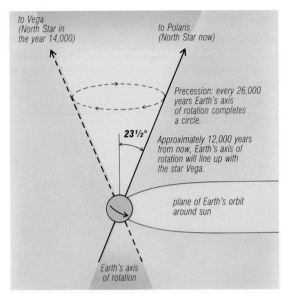

Precession is so slow that a person would not notice it in an entire lifetime. Earth's axis of rotation travels in a complete circle every 26,000 years. This means that the North Pole points toward different stars—and sometimes at no star in particular—as it travels in this circle.

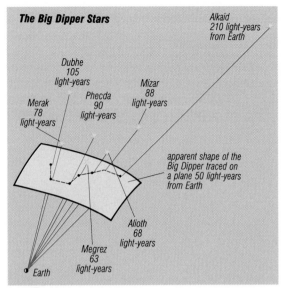

Although the stars of the Big Dipper seem to belong together, they are actually widely separated. A person looking at the Big Dipper stars from a position in space different from that of Earth would see them in a different shape, or they might seem completely unrelated to each other in the sky.

higher the temperature of the star, the more energy it gives off and the more this energy is concentrated in high-frequency radiation. Spectrographs can separate radiation into the different frequencies. The array of frequencies makes up the spectrum of the star.

The color of a star is also an indication of its temperature. Red light has less energy than blue light. A reddish star must have a large amount of its energy in red light. A white or bluish star has a larger amount of higher-energy blue light, so it must be hotter than the reddish star.

Stars have bright or dark lines in their spectra. These bright or dark lines are narrow regions of extra-high emission or absorption of electromagnetic radiation. The presence of a certain chemical, such as hydrogen or calcium, in the star causes a particular set of lines in the star's spectrum. Since most of the lines found in stellar spectra have been identified with specific chemicals, astronomers can learn from a star's spectrum what chemicals it contains.

Spectrum lines are useful in another way, too. When an observer sees radiation coming from a source, such as a star, the frequency of the radiation is affected by the observer's motion toward or away from the source. This is called the Doppler effect. If the observer and the star are moving away from each other, the observer detects a shift to lower frequencies. If the star and the observer are approaching each other, the shift is to higher frequencies.

Astronomers know the normal spectrum-line frequencies for many chemicals. By comparing these known frequencies with those of the same set of lines in a star's spectrum, astronomers can tell how fast the star is moving toward or away from Earth.

## Size and Brightness of Stars

Both the size and the temperature of a star determine how much radiation energy it gives off each second: this is the actual brightness of a star. It is also true, however, that the closer a star is to Earth, the more of its radiation energy will actually reach Earth and the brighter it will appear.

Astronomers express the brightness of a star in terms of its magnitude. Two values of magnitude describe a star. The apparent magnitude refers to how bright the star looks from Earth. The absolute magnitude of a star is the value its apparent magnitude would have if the star were 10 parsecs from Earth. The apparent magnitude of a star depends on its size, temperature, and distance. The temperature is found from its spectrum; if the distance is known, then astronomers can calculate the size of the star and also assign a value for its absolute magnitude. The actual brightness of stars may be compared using their absolute magnitudes.

Astronomers have discovered all kinds of stars—from huge, brilliant supergiants to dense, cool neutron stars. The sun lies in about the middle range of size and brightness of stars and is considered to be a typical star. The largest stars are the cool supergiants: they have low surface temperatures, but they are so bright that they must be extremely large to give off that much energy. In the white-dwarf stars a solar mass is squeezed into a sphere about the size of Earth. A teaspoonful might weigh 10 tons.

Neutron stars are even more strongly compressed than the white dwarfs: they probably have a solar mass compressed to a radius of a few miles. The

The California Institute of Technology

The California Institute of Technology

*Dark nebulas, like the Horsehead nebula in Orion, are made of clouds of interstellar dust, which scatter starlight.*

*The Crab nebula, a cloud of glowing gas in Taurus, is thought to be the remains of a star that exploded in 1054.*

strange objects called pulsars are thought to be neutron stars. While working at the Mullard Radio Astronomy Observatory, Dr. Jocelyn Bell Burnell observed the first pulsar in 1968.

Physicists also speculate about the existence of black holes, which would be the remains of stars after they had undergone complete gravitational collapse. Such an object would be so dense that even light would be unable to escape its gravitational field.

### INTERSTELLAR MATTER

The space between the stars contains gas and dust at extremely low densities. This matter tends to clump into clouds. These clouds are called nebulas when they block more distant starlight, reflect starlight, or get heated by stars so that they glow.

Interstellar dust is made of fine particles or grains. Although only a few of these grains are spread through a cubic mile of space, the distances between the stars are so great that the dust can block the light from distant stars.

Many small, dark regions are known where few or no stars can be seen. These are dark nebulas, dust clouds of higher than average density that are thick enough to obscure the light beyond them.

The dust grains block blue light more than red light, so the color of a star can be changed if it is seen through much dust. To find the temperature of such a star, astronomers must estimate its color to be bluer than it appears because so much of its blue light is lost in the dust. When clouds of dust occur near bright stars they often reflect the starlight in all directions. Such clouds are known as reflection nebulas.

Interstellar gas is about 100 times denser than the dust but still has an extremely low density. The gas does not interfere with starlight passing through it, so it is usually difficult to detect. When a gas cloud occurs close to a hot star, however, the star's radiation causes the gas to glow. This forms a type of bright nebula known as an H II region. Away from hot stars the gas is quite cool. These cooler regions are called H I regions.

The interstellar gas, like most stars, consists mainly of the lightest element, hydrogen, with small amounts of helium and only traces of the other elements. The hydrogen readily glows in the hot H II regions. In the cool H I regions the hydrogen gives off radio-frequency radiation. Most interstellar gas can be located only by detecting these radio waves.

The hydrogen occurs partly as single atoms and partly as molecules (two hydrogen atoms joined together). Molecular hydrogen is even more difficult to detect than atomic hydrogen, but it must exist in abundance. Other molecules have been found in the interstellar gas because they give off low-frequency radiation. These molecules contain other atoms besides hydrogen: oxygen or carbon occurs in hydroxyl radicals ($OH^-$) and in carbon monoxide (CO), formaldehyde ($H_2CO$), and many others, including many organic molecules.

Wherever there are large numbers of young stars, there are also large quantities of interstellar gas and dust. New stars are constantly being formed out of the gas and dust in regions where the clouds have high densities. Although many stars blow off part of their material back into the interstellar regions, the gas and dust are slowly being used up. Astronomers theorize that eventually a time will be reached when no new stars can be formed, and the star system will slowly fade as the stars burn out one by one.

### THE GALAXIES

Stars are found in huge groups called galaxies. Scientists estimate that the larger galaxies may contain

**Kinds of Galaxies**

**Normal Spiral Galaxies**

Sc

Sb

Sa

**Elliptical Galaxies**

E0    E3    E7

**Irregular Galaxies**

SBa

SBb

**Barred Spiral Galaxies**

SBc

In the 1920s Edwin Hubble separated galaxies (top) into four general types according to their appearance and then classified each into subtypes. His method is still used. These four galaxies (left) illustrate Hubble's classification. The irregular galaxy at center left is M82, found in Ursa Major. At center right is an elliptical galaxy, one of the two elliptical galaxies that are companions of the Andromeda galaxy. At bottom left is a spiral galaxy from the constellation Pegasus. A barred spiral galaxy in Eridanus is at bottom right.

Photos, The Observatories of the Carnegie Institution of Washington

as many as a trillion stars, while the smallest may have fewer than a million. Galaxies can be up to 100,000 light-years in diameter.

Galaxies may have any of four general shapes. Elliptical galaxies show little or no structure and vary from moderately flat to spherical in general shape. Spiral galaxies have a small, bright central region, or nucleus, and arms that come out of the nucleus and wind around, trailing off like a giant pinwheel. In barred spiral galaxies, the arms extend sideways

in a short straight line before turning off into the spiral shape. Both kinds of spiral systems are flat. Irregular galaxies are usually rather small and have no particular shape or form.

Galaxies were long thought to be more or less passive objects, containing stars and interstellar gas and dust and shining by the radiation that their stars give off. When astronomers became able to make accurate observations of radio frequencies coming from space, they were surprised to find that a number of galaxies

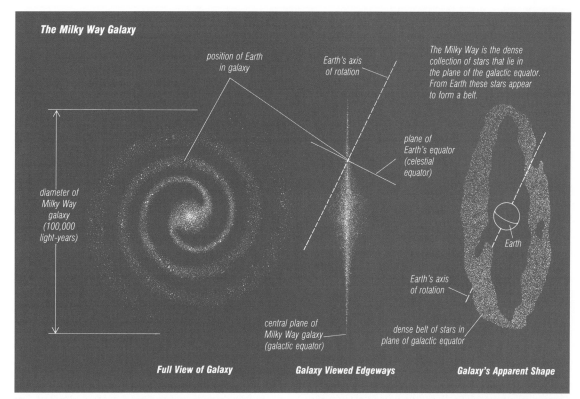

**The Milky Way Galaxy**

position of Earth in galaxy

Earth's axis of rotation

The Milky Way is the dense collection of stars that lie in the plane of the galactic equator. From Earth these stars appear to form a belt.

plane of Earth's equator (celestial equator)

diameter of Milky Way galaxy (100,000 light-years)

Earth

Earth's axis of rotation

central plane of Milky Way galaxy (galactic equator)

dense belt of stars in plane of galactic equator

**Full View of Galaxy**　　　　**Galaxy Viewed Edgeways**　　　　**Galaxy's Apparent Shape**

*The name of our galaxy comes from the visual phenomenon of the Milky Way, a band of stars seen in Earth's night sky. This band is actually the major portion of the galaxy. Since Earth lies in the midst of the galaxy, the spiral structure is hidden by the nearest stars that lie in the plane of the galactic equator and form the Milky Way.*

emit large amounts of energy in the radio region. Ordinary stars are so hot that most of their energy is emitted in visible light, with little energy emitted at radio frequencies. Furthermore, astronomers were able to deduce that this radiation had been given off by charged particles of extremely high energy moving in magnetic fields.

The radio galaxies that have such strong radio emission are usually rather peculiar in appearance. How do they manage to give so much energy to the charged particles and magnetic fields? Many galaxies, and the radio galaxies in particular, show evidence of interstellar matter expanding away from their centers, as though gigantic explosions had taken place in their nuclei. The giant elliptical galaxy known as M 87 has a jet of material nearby that it apparently ejected in the past. The jet itself is the size of an ordinary galaxy.

Another problem has bothered astronomers for years. Most if not all galaxies occur in clusters, presumably held together by the gravity of the cluster members. When the motions of the cluster members are measured, however, it is found in almost every case that the clusters appear to be unstable. The galaxies are moving too fast to be held together by the gravity of the matter that is visible. Then why did the clusters not disintegrate long ago? There is no doubt

Max-Planck-Institut für Radioastronomie, Germany

*The radio telescope at the Max Planck Institute for Radio Astronomy in Effelsberg, Germany, is 328 feet in diameter and is the largest steerable telescope in operation.*

that galaxies contain large amounts of dark matter, matter that has little or no luminosity so that it is not directly visible. However, this matter has enough mass to exert a strong force of gravity that makes the clusters stable. Dark matter constitutes perhaps 90 percent of all matter in the universe. It could be in the form of very-low-luminosity stars, of dead stars, or possibly of other forms of matter. It may be in the form of massive black holes.

## The Doppler Shift

Absorption lines from an approaching object shift toward the violet (shorter wavelength).

The amount of shift depends on the velocity of the object in relationship to the observer: the greater the velocity, the greater the shift.

Absorption lines from the sun are used for comparison.

shift

Absorption lines from a receding object shift toward the red (longer wavelength).

shift

The colored bands are standard spectra. The black lines are absorption lines.

*According to Austrian physicist Christian Doppler, the absorption lines from a star or galaxy shift to longer wavelengths (red shift) when the object is receding from an observer. They shift to shorter wavelengths (blue shift) when the object is approaching an observer. When the absorption lines of an approaching star, a receding star, and the relatively stationary sun are shown against the background of a laboratory spectrum, it is clear that the lines occupy different positions on the spectrum.*

### The Milky Way Galaxy

Like most stars, the sun belongs to a galaxy. Since the sun and Earth are embedded in the galaxy, it is difficult for us to obtain an overall view of the galaxy. In fact, what you can see of its structure is a faint band of stars called the Milky Way (the word galaxy comes from the Greek word for "milk"), so our galaxy has been named the Milky Way galaxy.

The visible band of the Milky Way seems to form a great circle around Earth. This indicates that the galaxy is flat rather than spherical. (If it were spherical, the stars would not be especially concentrated in a single band.) The sun is located on the inner edge of a spiral arm. The center, or nucleus, of the galaxy is about 30,000 light-years distant, in the direction of the constellation Sagittarius. All the stars visible without a telescope belong to the Milky Way galaxy.

Not all the galaxy's stars are confined to the galactic plane. There are a few stars that occur far above or below the disk. They are usually very old stars, and they form what is called the halo of the galaxy. Evidently the galaxy was originally a roughly spherical mass of gas. Its gravity and rotation caused it to collapse into the disklike shape it has today. The stars that had been formed before the collapse remained in their old positions, but after the collapse further star formation could occur only in the flat disk.

All the stars in the galaxy move in orbits around its center. The sun takes about 200 million years to complete an orbit. The orbits of most of these stars are nearly circles and are nearly in the same direction. This gives a sense of rotation to the galaxy as a whole, even as the entire galaxy moves through space. It is possible to calculate how much matter the galaxy must have in order to hold a star in its orbit by the force of gravity. In this way the approximate number of stars in the galaxy can be estimated.

### Velocities of Galaxies

According to the Doppler effect, a general relationship seems to exist throughout the universe: the greater the speed of a galaxy, the greater its distance. This relationship suggests that the system of galaxies is expanding. Suppose the galaxies were at one time in a rather small volume of space. After a time, the fast galaxies would have sped far from the original position, while the slow galaxies would still be nearby. The result would be a velocity-distance relationship exactly like the one observed.

In the early 1960s the new and puzzling quasi-stellar radio source, or quasar, was discovered. In photographs quasars usually look like ordinary stars, but they have Doppler shifts much greater than those of galaxies. This implies that the quasars have enormously large velocities away from us.

If the same relationship between velocity and distance holds for the quasars as for the galaxies, then the quasars are at tremendously large distances from us. But if they are actually so far away, they must be far more luminous than even giant galaxies. And yet, because their energy output varies irregularly over periods of months or less, astronomers have concluded that quasars are actually smaller than ordinary galaxies. The brightest quasar lies at a distance of 2 billion light-years from the Earth.

### THE UNIVERSE

Cosmology is the scientific inquiry into what the universe is like. By making assumptions that are not contradicted by the behavior of the observable universe, scientists build models, or theories, that attempt to describe the universe as a whole, including its origin and its future. They use each model until something is found that contradicts it. Then the model must be modified or discarded.

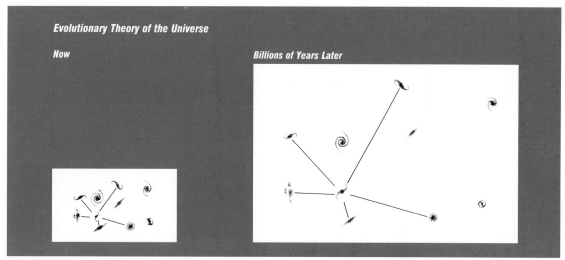

*Evolutionary Theory of the Universe*

*Now*

*Billions of Years Later*

*According to the evolutionary, or big bang, theory of the universe, the universe is expanding while the total energy and matter it contains remain constant. Therefore, as the universe expands, the density of its energy and matter must grow progressively thinner. At left is a representation of the universe as it appears now, with galaxies occupying a typical section of space. At right, billions of years later the same amount of matter will fill a relatively larger volume of space.*

Cosmologists usually assume that the universe, except for small irregularities, has an identical appearance to all observers (and the laws of physics are identical), no matter where in the universe the observers are located. This unproven concept is called the cosmological principle. One consequence of the cosmological principle is that the universe cannot have an edge, for an observer near the edge would have a different view from that of someone near the center. Thus space must be infinite and evenly filled with matter, or, alternatively, the geometry of space must be such that all observers see themselves as at the center. Also, astronomers believe that the only motion that can occur, except for small irregularities, is a uniform expansion or contraction of the universe.

Since the universe appears to be expanding, it seems that it must have been smaller in the past. This is the basis for evolutionary theories of the universe. If one could trace the galaxies back in time, one would find a time at which they were all close together. Observations of the expansion rate indicate that this was between 10 and 20 billion years ago. Thus we have a picture of an evolving universe that started in some kind of explosion—the big bang. Some models of the universe predict that the expansion will continue forever. Others say that it will stop and be followed by a contraction back to a small volume again. Another model suggests that the universe oscillates, with alternate expansions and contractions.

The steady state theory of cosmology was once popular. It is now, however, discredited. The basic assumption of steady state is a perfect cosmological principle, applying to time as well as position. The steady state theory states that the universe must have the same large-scale properties at all times; it cannot evolve, but must remain uniform. But since the

universe is seen to be expanding, which would spread the matter out thinner as time goes on, steady state suggests that new matter must be created to maintain the constant density. In the steady state theory, galaxies are formed, they live and die, and new ones come along to take their places at a rate that keeps the average density of matter constant.

When astronomers observe an object at a great distance, they are seeing it as it looked long ago, because it takes time for light to travel. A galaxy viewed at a distance of a billion light-years is seen as it was a billion years ago. Distant galaxies do seem to be different from nearby galaxies. They seem closer together than nearby ones, contrary to steady state contentions but consistent with the view that the universe had a greater density in the past. Also, a faint glow of radiation has been discovered coming uniformly from all directions. Calculations show that this could be radiation left over from the big bang.

Astronomers supporting the open universe theory believe that the universe will expand forever because they believe it is infinite. Supporters of the closed universe theory believe that at some time in the future the universe will stop expanding and will begin to contract until eventually a situation termed the "big crunch" would occur.

## THE HISTORY OF ASTRONOMY

In many early civilizations, astronomy was sufficiently advanced that reliable calendars had been developed. In ancient Egypt astronomer-priests were responsible for anticipating the season of the annual flooding of the Nile River. The Mayas of the Yucatán peninsula developed a complicated calendar for keeping track of days both in the past and in the future. They could use their calendar to predict astronomical events.

*Between about 1800 and 1400 BC, people in prehistoric Britain constructed Stonehenge, a circle of huge stones that marked various astronomical occurrences. On Midsummer Day a person standing in the center of the circle can see the sun rise directly above the 35-ton heel stone, center.*

In China, a calendar had been developed by the 14th century BC. A Chinese astronomer, Shih Shen, drew up what may be the earliest star catalog, listing about 800 stars. Chinese records mention comets, meteors, large sunspots, and novas.

The early Greek astronomers knew many of the geometrical relationships of the heavenly bodies. Some, including Aristotle, thought Earth was a sphere. Eratosthenes, born in about 276 BC, demonstrated its circumference. Hipparchus, who lived around 140 BC, was a prolific and talented astronomer. Among many other accomplishments, he classified stars according to apparent brightness, estimated the size and distance of the moon, found a way to predict eclipses, and calculated the length of the year to within 6½ minutes.

The most influential ancient astronomer historically was Ptolemy (Claudius Ptolemaeus) of Alexandria, who lived in about 140 AD. His geometric scheme predicted the motions of the planets. In his view, Earth occupied the center of the universe. His theory approximating the true motions of the celestial bodies was held steadfastly through the fall of Rome to the end of the Middle Ages.

In medieval times Western astronomy did not progress. During those centuries Hindu and Arabian astronomers kept the science alive. The records of the Arabian astronomers and their translations of Greek astronomical treatises were the foundation of the later upsurge in Western astronomy.

In 1543, the year of his death, came the publication of Copernicus' theory that Earth and the other planets revolved around the sun. His suggestion contradicted all the authorities of the time and caused great controversy. Galileo supported Copernicus' theory with his observations that other celestial bodies, the satellites of Jupiter, clearly did not circle Earth.

The great Danish astronomer Tycho Brahe rejected Copernicus' theory. Yet his data on planetary positions were later used to support that theory. When Tycho died, his assistant, Johannes Kepler, analyzed Tycho's data and developed the laws of planetary motion. In 1687, Newton's law of gravitation and laws of motion reinforced Kepler's laws.

Meanwhile, the instruments available to astronomers were growing more sophisticated. Beginning with Galileo, the telescope was used to reveal many hitherto invisible phenomena, such as the revolution of satellites about other planets.

The development of the spectroscope in the early 1800s was a major step forward in the development of astronomical instruments. Later, photography became an invaluable aid to astronomers. They could study photographs at leisure and make microscopic measurements on them. Even more recent instrumental developments—radar, the radio telescope, and space probes and manned spaceflights—have helped answer old questions and have opened our eyes to new problems.

## Archaeoastronomy

Archaeoastronomy is an interdisciplinary field that relates archaeology, anthropology, and mythology with astronomy. It is sometimes called historical astronomy. The best-known evidence that early humankind used the sky is Stonehenge, near Salisbury, England. Built between 3100 and 1550 BC, Stonehenge consists of an impressive array of megaliths and lintels arranged as stone portals that are precisely aligned in relationship to the sun on an ancient summer solstice, which occured on June 24. Today the summer solstice falls on June 20 or 21. Over the millenia, solstices shift slightly forward in the calendar. Astronomers have accounted for this shift by observing that the Earth precesses slowly as it rotates on its axis, like a top that wobbles as it spins. This precession makes one complete cycle every 26,000 years. This phenomenon causes the time of the solstices and equinoxes to change and also causes, over time, changes in the apparent location of a polestar, or North Star.

There are at least 900 other structures of a similar nature that exist in the British Isles alone. At Carnac on the western coast of France are more than 3,000 stone monuments for which astronomical alignments have been claimed.

Newgrange, northwest of Dublin, Ireland, is a Neolithic tomb, part of which was built as early as 3100 BC. It also indicates probable early knowledge of astronomy. The tomb has a long, narrow passage with a slitlike opening that appears to have been designed and engineered to permit the sunlight to enter the burial chamber at the far end momentarily on the morning of the winter solstice.

From architectural studies of ancient Egypt, there is considerable evidence of early, though not prehistoric, astronomical knowledge. The base of the Great Pyramid at Giza is aligned closely with the four points of the compass, and its hidden north passage is aligned with the lower culmination of the North Star at the time the pyramids were built (between 2686 and 2345 BC). The great temple of Amon, or Amen (Ra), at El Karnak was aligned with the midwinter sunrise during the epoch of Thutmose III (1479–26 BC). A nearby temple of Khons, the Egyptian moon god, was built to align with the distant hills of Thebes, the northernmost extreme of the setting of the new moon crescent at the time of the summer solstice.

The Dresden Codex, written by the Maya during the 1st millennium of the Christian era, contains astronomical calculations—eclipse-prediction tables, the synodic period of Venus—of exceptional accuracy. Temples and pyramids in what are now Mexico and Guatemala were often constructed and aligned with attention to astronomical phenomena.

The Plains Indians left stone patterns called medicine (magic) wheels, found along the eastern boundary of the Rocky Mountains from Colorado to Alberta and Saskatchewan. One of the best known is on top of Medicine Mountain, in the Bighorn Mountains west of Sheridan, Wyo. It is accessible only in the summer, and calculations have been made relating the arrangements of crude sandstone to the sunrise and sunset about the time of the summer solstice and to bright stars that would have been visible at the time archaeologists estimate its construction, about 200 to 400 years ago. Another medicine wheel, at Moose Mountain in southeastern Saskatchewan, has demonstrably similar relationships but has been estimated as dating from about 2,600 years ago.

A number of stone alignments have also been found in the South Pacific. Such stones on land would, of course, be useless at sea, but it has been suggested that the sites were used for observation and to train voyagers to identify the correct navigational stars before their departure. For example, the Micronesians and Polynesians used as navigational tools strings of bright stars that rose or set near the same point on the horizon. The Caroline Islanders had a 32-point star compass for defining this point, using Vega, the Pleiades, and other stars.

**BIBLIOGRAPHY FOR ASTRONOMY**

**Books for Children**
**Alley, David.** Sky: All About Planets, Stars, Galaxies, Eclipses and More (Firefly Books, 1993).
**Bendick, Jeanne.** Artificial Satellites: Helpers in Space (Millbrook Press, 1991).
**Branley, Franklyn.** The Planets in Our Solar System (Crowell, 1987).
**Couper, Heather, and Henbest, Nigel.** The Moon (Watts, 1987).
**Darling, D.J.** The Planets (Dillon Press, 1984).
**Gallant, R.A.** National Geographic Picture Atlas of Our Universe (National Geographic, 1986).
**Henbest, Nigel.** The Night Sky (EDC, 1993).
**Lampton, Christopher.** Astronomy (Watts, 1987).

**Books for Young Adults**
**Asimov, Isaac.** Our Solar System (Gareth Stevens, 1988).
**Asimov, Isaac, and Giraud, Robert.** The Future in Space (Gareth Stevens, 1993).
**Comins, N.F.** What if the Moon Didn't Exist: Voyages to Earths that Might Have Been (HarperCollins, 1993).
**Fjermedal, Grant.** New Horizons in Amateur Astronomy (Putnam, 1989).
**Friedlander, M.W.** Astronomy: From Stonehenge to Quasars (Prentice, 1985).
**Goldsmith, Donald.** The Astronomers (St. Martin's, 1993).
**Hamburg, Michael.** Astronomy Made Simple (Bantam, 1993).
**Hartmann, William.** Cycles of Fire: Stars, Galaxies and the Wonder of Deep Space (Workman, 1987).
**Hubble, Edwin.** Realm of the Nebulae (Dover, 1991).
**Illingworth, Valerie, ed.** Facts on File Dictionary of Astronomy (Facts on File, 1986).
**Jespersen, James, and Fitz-Randolph, Jane.** From Quarks to Quasars (Atheneum, 1987).
**Kaler, James.** Stars (Scientific American Library, 1993).
**Kelsey, Larry, and Hoff, Darrel.** Recent Revolutions in Astronomy (Watts, 1987).
**Lederman, Leon, and Schramm, David.** From Quarks to the Cosmos (Scientific American Library, 1993).
**Moore, Patrick.** Guinness Book of Astronomy (Sterling, 1988).
**Morris, M.R., ed.** The Center of the Galaxy (Kluwer, 1989).
**Morris, Richard.** Cosmic Questions: Galactic Halos, Cold Dark Matter and the End of Time (Wiley, 1993).
**Ridpath, Ian.** Atlas of Stars and Planets (Facts on File, 1993).
**Riordan, Michael, and Schramm, David.** Shadows of Creation (Scientific American Library, 1993).
**Robinson, M.R.** Our Universe (Scientific American Library, 1993).
**Wilson, D.A.** Star Track (Lorien House, 1994).

**ASTRONOMY, AMATEUR.** Amateur astronomy has become a popular pastime around the world. Astronomy enthusiasts usually subscribe to popular astronomical periodicals and often own moderately priced telescopes. Almost every large city has some kind of astronomy club, and many countries have national organizations of amateur astronomers interested in promoting their hobby. Some of these organizations have grouped together to observe particular types of celestial objects or events.

As amateurs far outnumber professional astronomers, it is often an amateur astronomer who discovers a new comet or an exploding star. Professional astronomers usually concentrate their research efforts on one type of object or may not observe the sky at all. A beginning backyard stargazer, scanning the nighttime sky for pure enjoyment, may see such an object before anyone else.

A dedicated amateur astronomer will observe the sky on a regular basis and take advantage of the vast store of information recorded by others. There are numerous star charts, catalogs, and handbooks that give the positions of objects and predictions for celestial events. Other books describe equipment to use and observational techniques. Many advanced amateurs use home computers, light-sensitive electronic equipment, and special photographic emulsions to record data just like those of professionals.

### Using the Unaided Eye

Some important observations can best be done with very little equipment. Observations of auroral displays and meteor showers, for example, require only the unaided eye (*see* Aurora). All one needs is a good clear horizon and dark skies away from city lights and pollution. A good pair of binoculars, or field glasses, may be helpful but is not essential. It is also quite simple to photograph auroral displays and, with some luck, to photograph a meteor trail with high-speed film in a stationary camera on a tripod.

Much knowledge of meteor showers results from groups of amateur astronomers such as the American Meteor Society or the Federation of European Meteor Astronomers, whose members spend thousands of hours recording the times and locations of individual meteors. From this an average hourly rate is calculated, as well as the radiant, or origin, of the meteor stream. Most annual meteor showers are associated with old comets that have left a trail of dust in space. Normally an observer will see 20 to 50 meteors an hour during a meteor shower, but occasionally a spectacular shower of many thousands of "shooting stars" will reward the meteor watcher.

### Small Telescopes

The two most important aspects of a telescope are light-gathering power and magnification. With binoculars (two telescopes on a single frame) or a small telescope, a person can easily observe many celestial objects not visible to the unaided eye. The sun, moon, planets, and the so-called deep-sky objects—nebulae, star clusters, and galaxies—can all be seen with rather simple instruments.

Observers with such instruments can count the numbers and measure the sizes and locations of sunspots. Since the sun is so bright, the main lens or the telescope mirror can be quite small. To avoid severe eye damage, one must never look directly at the sun with a telescope without a proper sun filter. The sun is even too bright for the unaided eye. During eclipses people are tempted to look at the sun when it is partly blocked, but even a very small part of the sun's surface remaining visible can damage the retina and cause a permanent blind spot in the eye.

A good way to view a solar eclipse or dark sunspots is by projecting the bright image of the sun through a telescope eyepiece onto a screen or white cardboard. An even better way is to use a sun filter, which covers the entrance of the telescope entirely with thin layers of shiny aluminum. This material reflects most sunlight and reduces the brightness to less than a one hundred thousandth of normal intensity, thereby making it safe to view.

The moon is a fascinating object to study with a telescope. With an instrument of less than 50 power one can see craters, mountains, and dark lunar "seas." With an instrument of 200 to 300 power the rugged features are visible in better detail. The best place to observe is along the line created by the border between the dark and light portions of the moon, where sunlight highlights higher elevations. Lunar eclipses are always safe to view because moonlight is much less intense than sunlight. During lunar eclipses amateur astronomers can observe the times at which certain craters slip into the Earth's shadow.

### High-Powered Telescopes

Planets are best viewed with a high-powered telescope of 100 to 300 power. This magnification is needed to make the image sufficiently large for adequate viewing. At a higher power the Earth's atmosphere usually causes the image to deteriorate. A refracting, or lens-type, telescope is recommended. A high-powered reflecting telescope has a small second mirror and several struts in the light path, which scatter some light causing a loss of detail. Lenses, on the other hand, may give some bad color to the image because of certain effects of the lens itself. Color filters are used to increase the contrast of planetary features by subtracting some colors of light from the image. A yellow or blue filter, for example, might highlight patterns in Jupiter's clouds, while a red filter might enhance the dark areas on the surface of Mars. Such details are important to serious amateur astronomers. More than 700 members of the Association of Lunar and Planetary Observers, for example, make careful sketches of planet features and track the motions of faint objects orbiting the sun.

Much research is done by amateur groups studying the thousands of known variable stars in the Milky Way galaxy. These stars vary in brightness over a period of several days or weeks as they swell and contract. Members of the American Association of Variable Star Observers (AAVSO) have made millions of observations of variable-star fluctuations. This organization prepares charts of variable-star fields and light curves of major variable stars and is a source of much information that is nearly impossible to obtain elsewhere. Most European countries and many other nations also have well-organized variable-star observation groups.

Another type of event that can be recorded by amateur astronomers with a good telescope is called an occultation. As the moon, a planet, or even an asteroid moves through space, it will sometimes pass in front of a star. For a short time the star will "blink out" at a particular geographic location on the Earth. If the time of this event is noted accurately and the observer's position is known, it is possible to determine very accurately the speed and position of the moving object. The time it takes for the star to reappear is also noted, and, if information can be gathered from several observers, it may be possible to determine the diameter of the body passing in front of the star. A group called the International Occultation Timing Association (IOTA) was formed to gather such data.

With light meters and high-speed electronic equipment, it is even possible to measure the dimming of a faraway star as it disappears. This information can be used to calculate the star's diameter.

**Larger Telescopes**

A telescope with a larger lens or mirror gathers more light and is best suited for viewing faint comets, asteroids, and deep-sky objects at a low magnification. Binoculars with 3-inch (76-millimeter) lenses or larger are sometimes called "comet hunters" because many comets have been found by amateurs using such binoculars to scan the zodiac near the rising or setting sun. Many amateurs grind their own telescope mirrors and mount them in inexpensive wooden telescope tubes. One type is known as a Dobsonian telescope, named after John Dobson of the San Francisco Sidewalk Astronomers. With telescopes of up to 20 inches (508 millimeters) or more in diameter, some amateurs trek into the mountains to search the skies for distant star clusters and galaxies that can be seen only with large instruments. All of the groups mentioned, as well as local planetariums, are interested in helping the beginning amateur learn more about their specialty. Two periodicals published in the United States are also useful to both beginning and advanced amateur astronomers: *Sky and Telescope* and *Astronomy*. (*See also* Telescope.)    James A. Seevers

**BIBLIOGRAPHY FOR AMATEUR ASTRONOMY**

**Berger, Melvin.** Star Gazing, Comet Tracking and Sky Mapping (Putnam, 1985).
**Muirden, James.** The Amateur Astronomer's Handbook, 3rd ed. (Harper, 1987).
**Muirden, James.** Astronomy Handbook (Arco, 1984).
**Sidgwick, J.B.** Amateur Astronomer's Handbook (Dover, 1981).
**Sidgwick, J.B.** Observational Astronomy for Amateurs (Dover, 1981).

**ASUNCIÓN, Paraguay.** The capital of Paraguay and the nation's largest city is Asunción. It is situated on the east bank of the Paraguay River where it widens to form a broad bay. The Pilcomayo River joins the Paraguay on the opposite shore. The Atlantic Ocean is more than 1,000 miles (1,600 kilometers) distant via the Paraguay, the Paraná, and the Río de la Plata. A shorter, overland route to the port of Paranaguá, Brazil, was completed in 1965.

The city's broad avenues are lined with orange and other flowering trees and interrupted with many plazas and gardens. Most of the older houses are built of plastered brick painted in soft colors and decorated with iron balconies and with iron grillwork. Newer houses are built in a variety of styles that are suitable for the subtropical climate.

Near the riverbank is the Congressional Palace. Across from it are the cathedral and the Archbishop's Palace. The Government Palace, which houses the administrative offices, is also near the river. On Plaza Independencia, the busiest section of the city, is the Pantheon of Heroes, modeled after Les Invalides in Paris. Paraguay's national heroes are buried here. The Hotel Guaraní was designed by Brazilian architect Oscar Niemeyer. Caballero Park, the estate of a former general, houses the National Historical Museum. Carlos Antonio López Park, the estate of Paraguay's first president, is 4 miles (6 kilometers) from the center of the city. Among the city's institutions of higher learning are the Universidad Nacional de Asunción, which was founded in 1890, and the Universidad Católica "Nuestra Señora de la Asunción," which was founded in 1960.

The Presidente General Stroessner Airport is 8 miles (13 kilometers) from the city. Asunción is also the terminus of the Ferrocarril (railway) Presidente Carlos Antonio López, which connects with the Argentine rail systems via a train ferry across the Paraná River at Encarnación, a major port city. Another ferry connection across the Paraguay River provides a road link with Buenos Aires.

Asunción is a busy river port with modern docks and cargo-handling equipment. It is the principal distributing and export center of the most densely populated region of Paraguay. Cotton, sugarcane, corn (maize), tobacco, fruit, and cattle products are processed here. Industrial plants produce textiles, vegetable oils, footwear, flour, small river craft, and tobacco products. There is also a large local transportation system that carries manufactured products to communities throughout the country and brings raw materials into the capital for processing.

The city of Asunción was founded on August 15, the date on which the Feast of the Assumption (*Asunción* in Spanish) of the Virgin Mary is celebrated, in 1537. Until the 17th century, when Buenos Aires assumed the role, it was the most important Spanish colonial city in the eastern part of South America. Paraguay declared its independence from Spain in 1811, and Asunción became the capital of the new republic. (*See also* Paraguay.) Population (1985 census), 567,678.

**ASWAN HIGH DAM.** One of the greatest engineering projects ever executed is the Aswan High Dam, across the Nile River in southern Egypt. The reservoir that it created, Lake Nasser, is one of the world's largest— 1,930 square miles (5,000 square kilometers) in area, with a capacity of 137 million acre-feet (169 billion cubic meters).

The dam, built in the steep granite cliffs, is located about 500 miles (800 kilometers) south of Cairo, the capital of Egypt. The damsite lies within the reservoir of the Aswan Dam that was built by the British in 1902. (*See also* Egypt.) On Jan. 9, 1960, the initial dynamite blast was set off at the damsite. The first of the dam's 12 hydroelectric generators was activated in 1967. When the construction of the dam was completed in 1970, its waters had reclaimed more than 100,000 acres (40,000 hectares) of desert land for cultivation and made one or two extra crops possible on some 800,000 acres (323,700 hectares).

The Aswan High Dam is 364 feet (111 meters) tall and 12,565 feet (3,830 meters) long. To form the earth-and-rock fill dam, some 57.2 million cubic yards (43.7 million cubic meters) of silt, sand, clay, and rock were used. The dam's bulk is 16 times that of the Great Pyramid of King Khufu at Giza.

As the dam was built, Lake Nasser flooded many settlements along the Nile's riverbank, including farmland in Sudan to the south. Egypt agreed to pay the Sudanese for their losses and to let them tap the reservoir for their own irrigation needs.

In 1963, engineers began working to save the great temples and statues of Abu Simbel from being submerged in the lake. They cut them into huge chunks and hoisted them to the top of a cliff, in the face of which they were originally carved, for reassembly.

*The Aswan High Dam was built to control annual flooding in the Nile River valley and to provide irrigation for farming.*

Donald Smetzer

The cost, which was estimated at 36 million dollars, was largely met by contributions from the United States, Kuwait, and the United Nations Educational, Scientific, and Cultural Organization (UNESCO).

Egypt borrowed from other countries to finance the billion-dollar dam. In 1956 the United States withdrew its support when it was learned that Egypt was buying arms from the Soviet Union. The Soviets subsequently underwrote one third of the project's cost. They also trained Egyptian workers and provided engineers, technicians, and equipment. In January 1971 the dam was formally dedicated by President Anwar el-Sadat of Egypt and President Nikolai V. Podgorny of the Soviet Union. (*See also* Nile River.)

**ATATÜRK** (1881–1938). As a founder of Turkey and the country's first president, Mustafa Kemal Atatürk presided over the end of the Ottoman Empire. He inaugurated numerous programs of reform to help modernize his country.

Mustafa was born in Salonika, Greece, in 1881. Early in life he decided on a military career. He attended a military secondary school, and for his excellent work in mathematics he took the name Kemal, an Arabic word meaning "perfection." He entered the military academy in Constantinople (now Istanbul) in 1899 and in 1902 the General Staff College. He served in the Italo-Turkish War in 1911–12 and in the Balkan Wars in 1912–13. These wars undermined the 400-year-old Ottoman Empire.

During World War I Kemal opposed Turkey's alliance with Germany. He nevertheless fought for Turkey. His outstanding military abilities and widely circulated political opinions, calling for an independent Turkish state, won him a popular following. He opposed the presence of foreign powers in Turkey and desired an end to the Ottoman Empire.

In 1920, as leader of a national resistance movement, he set up a rival government in Ankara. He expelled Greek forces from Asia Minor in 1921–22, and in 1922 he proclaimed the end of the Ottoman Empire. He became president of Turkey in 1923 and held the office until his death.

During his presidency Kemal made several changes that affected Turkish life. He proclaimed a secular republic and closed all Islamic religious institutions, including the traditional system of religious education. He abolished the Arabic alphabet and introduced the Latin one. In his effort to align Turkey with the customs of Western nations, he urged the use of Western dress and adopted the use of surnames. He took for himself the name Atatürk, meaning "Father of the Turks." The whole legal system was modernized and a new civil and penal code adopted. Popular forms of entertainment and the use of alcohol were allowed, both normally forbidden in Islamic societies. His attempts to modernize the economy were less successful than his other reforms. The country remained essentially agricultural.

Health problems plagued the last few years of his life. Atatürk died on Nov. 10, 1938, in Istanbul.

**ATGET, Eugène** (1856–1927). In more than 10,000 picturesque scenes of Paris, Eugène Atget—a failed painter who became an influential photographer—recorded moody black-and-white images of the city for others to put in color on canvas. The sign on the door of his studio read "Documents for Artists." Among those who bought Atget's work for inspiration were set designers and the painters Maurice Utrillo and Georges Braque.

Jean-Eugène-Auguste Atget was born in Libourne, France, near Bordeaux, on Feb. 12, 1856. Little is known of his early life. An orphan, he lived with an uncle until he was old enough to be a ship's cabin boy. He eventually abandoned a life at sea for the stage. In about 1898, when he was no longer able to get even minor acting roles, he decided to become a photographer. Atget's main clients were museums and historical societies, who bought his prints of historic buildings and monuments. He also photographed shop fronts, store windows, and poor tradespeople. He made several photographic series of iron grillwork, fountains, statues, and trees.

In 1921 he received a commission to document the brothels of Paris. In 1926 Man Ray, an American artist and photographer living in Paris, saw some of Atget's more unusual prints. Astonished by the bizarre use of reflections to achieve mixtures of images, Ray published four of Atget's photographs in *La Révolution Surréaliste*. This publication was the only recognition that Atget's work received during his lifetime. Because he neglected his health and ate sparingly, Atget was unable to produce much work during his final years. He died on Aug. 4, 1927, in Paris.

*The photograph entitled 'Shop Window: Tailor Dummies' was taken by Eugène Atget in about 1910.*
George Eastman House Collection

**ATHENA.** The war goddess of the ancient Greeks was Athena—often called Pallas Athena, or simply Pallas. The Romans identified her as Minerva and ranked her third among their gods, after Jupiter and Juno. Athena was also worshiped as the goddess of wisdom and of crafts, especially spinning and weaving.

According to mythology, Athena was the favorite daughter of Zeus (Jupiter). She was said to have sprung from his head full grown and clothed in armor. The goddess was usually shown wearing a helmet and carrying a spear and shield. Like her father, she also wore the magic *aegis*—a goatskin breastplate, fringed with snakes, that produced thunderbolts when shaken. Athena was very different from the war god Ares (Mars). She represented the intellectual and civilized side of war—she was not so much a fighter as a wise and prudent adviser.

Athena was regarded as the protector of all cities and states. She was wise not only in war but also in

*The goddess Athena mourns the death of Achilles at Troy in a relief that dates from about 470 BC.*
Alinari/Art Resource

the arts of peace. She supposedly invented the plow and taught men how to yoke oxen.

Athens became the most important seat of the worship of Athena. Zeus had decreed that the city should be given to the god who offered the most useful gift to the people. Poseidon gave them the horse. Athena struck the bare soil with her spear and caused an olive tree to spring up. The people were so delighted with the olive that Zeus gave the city to Athena and named it after her. Athena is often shown with an olive branch, a symbol of peace and plenty.

On the hill of the Acropolis the Athenians built a beautiful temple to Athena called the Parthenon (from *parthenos*, meaning "virgin"). In the temple stood the ivory and gold statue called the Athena Parthenos, by Phidias, the greatest Greek sculptor. (*See also* Acropolis; Phidias.)

The Athenians held their most important festival, the Panathenaea, on the day considered to be the goddess' birthday. It was celebrated by a procession, sacrifices, and games. (*See also* Mythology.)

*The Theseum, one of the best preserved masterpieces of ancient architecture, was mistakenly identified during the Middle Ages as the burial site of the legendary king Theseus. It was actually built as a temple of Hephaestus, god of fire, in about 449 BC.*

The J. Allan Cash Photolibrary

## ATHENS, Greece.

The city of Athens was the birthplace of Western civilization and is still one of Europe's great cities. In ancient times it was the most important Greek city-state. Today it is the capital and chief center of commerce and industry of Greece. The city attracts a large number of tourists each year to visit its historic sites that date to ancient times.

### Location and Climate

Athens is located on a peninsula that stretches southeastward into the Aegean Sea. The city is surrounded by the Plain of Attica, which in turn is surrounded on three sides by mountains. The city proper covers an area of 15 square miles (39 square kilometers), the metropolitan area, 167 square miles (433 square kilometers). Athens' seaport, Piraeus, is 5 miles (8 kilometers) away on the coastal plain. The core of the ancient city consists of a flat-topped mass of rock known as the Acropolis. Close to the Acropolis is a lower rock, the Areopagus. Northeast of the Acropolis, the pointed summit of Mount Lycabettus (Likavittós) rises to a height of more than 1,100 feet (330 meters). There are several other smaller hills.

The location of Athens was favorable for its early growth. The Plain of Attica provided good conditions for farming, while the surrounding mountains gave protection against enemies. There were good natural harbors, yet it was distant enough from the coast to prevent surprise attack from the sea.

The climate of Athens is Mediterranean. The summers are hot and dry, at times oppressive. Winters are mild and wet. Wells, aqueducts, and pipelines were built to hold water to supplement the scanty rainfall.

### Modern City

When Athens became the capital of the new kingdom of Greece in 1833, it was a small town of Turkish-style houses clustered at the foot of the Acropolis. This district, known as Pláka, is popular with tourists because of the picturesque streets, restaurants, and cafés. The modern city developed around this older core. Much of it was constructed in the 19th century around squares and parks that formed part of a planned street pattern. Royal palaces, a university and national library, a parliament house, and a reconstructed stadium for the Olympic Games of 1896 were all built. Most of these public buildings are made of white marble in the classical style.

The center of modern Athens is Síntagma (Constitution) Square. On one side stand the Old Royal Palace and its gardens, the city's largest public park. In front of the Old Palace, now the home of the Greek parliament, is the Monument of the Unknown Soldier, guarded by colorful evzones—members of the select Greek infantry unit who wear the traditional white skirt. Two long avenues lead northwest to Omónia (Concord) Square. The University of Athens, the Greek Academy, and the National Library are on Venizelou Avenue, while Stadiou Avenue has many shops.

Beginning in the 1950s, much of old Athens was demolished to make room for modern buildings. The movement of large numbers of people into the capital from rural areas has led to congestion. The many automobiles, especially taxis, cause air pollution that threatens the ancient monuments. Pollution controls have been introduced to limit the damage caused by the automobiles and by industrial pollution. Other industries and businesses have been developed on the fringes of the city and in adjacent suburbs without adequate planning or control.

Most of the people of Athens are ethnic Greeks, though numerous foreigners also live and work in the city. In particular, people from the Middle East, especially Lebanon, have settled in Athens in recent years. The Athenians have a typical Mediterranean way of life. Because of the predominantly warm and sunny weather they spend a large part of their free time on the streets, sitting in sidewalk cafés.

Apart from the cafés and restaurants and night spots offering traditional Greek music, there are symphony concerts, ballets, operas, and classical dramas. Many of these performances take place in the open-air Theater of Herodes Atticus.

Athens is the commercial and transportation center of Greece. With Piraeus it produces most of

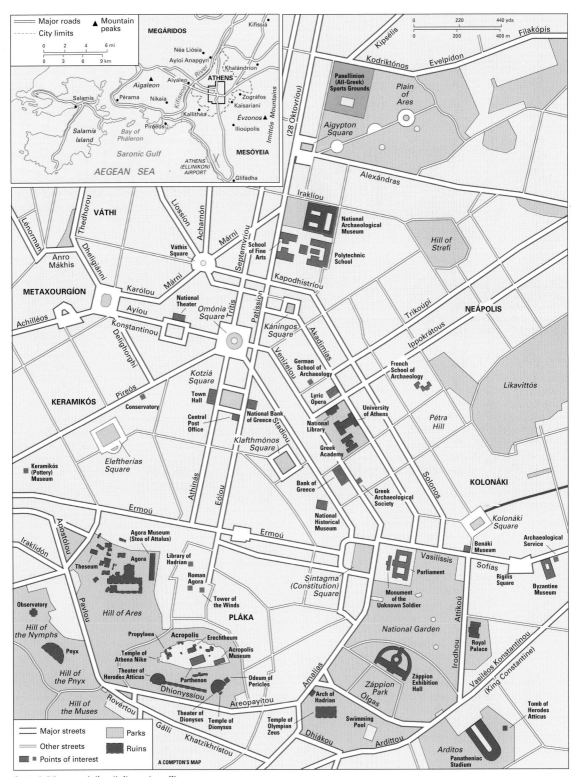

**Central Athens and (inset) its metropolitan area**

The J. Allan Cash Photolibrary

*The arch of Hadrian was erected by the Roman emperor in about AD 132 to mark the boundary of Athens.*

the country's manufactured products. Industries include textiles, shipbuilding, food processing, metallurgy, engineering, oil refining, and chemicals. Publishing and tourism are also major industries. Athens forms the center of the Greek railroad network and is linked by major highways with the northern and southwestern parts of the country. Piraeus accounts for about half the country's seaborne trade. Athens' Ellinikon Airport, south of the city, handles considerable international traffic, especially during the tourist season.

### Ancient City

The site of Athens has been inhabited since before 3000 BC. The earliest buildings date from the late Bronze Age, about 1200 BC, when part of the town spread to the south of the citadel on the Acropolis. During this period a wall was built along the edge of the rock. The 6th century BC was a period of great growth. The old, primitive shrines began to be replaced with large stone temples, thus changing the Acropolis from a citadel to a sanctuary.

In 480 BC the city was captured and destroyed by the Persians. The Acropolis buildings were burned and the houses in the lower town mostly destroyed. When the Athenians returned the next year they immediately began to rebuild. Over the next 30 years they built only fortifications and some secular buildings. The Acropolis and its destroyed temples were left as a reminder of Persian atrocities until a peace with Persia was reached in 449 BC.

Over the next 40 years the city developed its classical form. The Agora, the center of civic life, was located near the Areopagus, where the high court sat, and the Pnyx, where the Athenian assembly met. The Agora was both marketplace and public meeting place. It contained two stoas, or long colonnaded halls. The Agora also contained the Theseum, one of the best preserved temples in Athens. This building is older than the similar but larger Parthenon, which dominates the Acropolis.

The Acropolis was rebuilt in gleaming white marble beginning in 449 BC. Construction on the Parthenon began in 447 BC and was completed nine years later. The large, richly decorated temple was dedicated to Athena and contained a huge statue of the goddess. The Erechtheum, with its caryatids—or marble female figures—supporting the roof, and the Temple of Athena Nike were also built on the Acropolis during the same period. This collection of temples was approached through the Propylaea, a large entrance building. The Theater of Dionysus, built in the 5th century BC at the southern base of the Acropolis, was the city's drama center. The city was connected with the port of Piraeus by the parallel Long Walls, which formed a corridor 550 feet (170 meters) wide. (*See also* Acropolis.)

After Athens lost the Peloponnesian War in 404 BC its place as the premier city-state in Greece was also lost, and the city went into a decline that lasted until the period of Roman control three centuries later. Although the Romans sacked Athens and pulled down the Long Walls in 88 BC, they later built many magnificent buildings. The emperor Hadrian, in particular, completed a huge Temple of Olympian Zeus, built a library and a gymnasium, erected a large arch, and constructed an aqueduct that still serves the city. Herodes Atticus built the Odeum, a theater that has been restored and is still in use. The Romans had their own Agora, which contained the Tower of the Winds, one of the earliest weather observatories. (*See also* Greece, Ancient; Greek and Roman Art; Peloponnesian War.)

At the end of the Roman period, the city began to decay. Several temples were turned into Christian churches during the Byzantine period and after the city fell to the Crusaders in 1204. When the Turks occupied Athens in 1456 and began an almost 400-year rule they turned the Parthenon into a mosque and occupied other classical buildings.

In the 17th century the Propylaea and the Parthenon were severely damaged when explosive powder stored in them exploded. Further damage was done during fighting between the Turks and the Venetians. The latter tried to remove some of the Parthenon sculptures and broke them, while the Turks destroyed several ancient monuments to build defensive walls. In 1801 the British ambassador to Turkey, Thomas Bruce, the seventh earl of Elgin, was given permission by the Turks to remove many remaining sculptures. Known as the Elgin Marbles, they are now in the British Museum in London. Fighting during an uprising in 1821 did further damage.

Population (1981 census), city, 885,737; metropolitan area, 3,027,331. (*See also* Greece.)          Ian Matley

**ATHLETICS** *see* **TRACK AND FIELD.**

**ATLANTA, Ga.** Perhaps the most vivid vision of Atlanta is the torching of the Confederate city during the American Civil War as it was re-created in the film 'Gone With the Wind'. Today Atlanta is the crossroads of the southeastern United States. The commerce of the region revolves around this city, which is the capital of Georgia and the seat of Fulton County. When the city was made the state capital in 1868 it became the symbol of the New South, but it still preserves the aura and traditions of the Old South.

Atlanta lies among the rolling hills of northwestern Georgia, at 1,050 feet (320 meters) above sea level. A southern city, it enjoys mild winters. Its altitude protects it from extreme heat. The average temperature is 61° F (16° C), and temperatures rarely rise above 90° F (32° C) for more than three days in a row.

Peachtree Street, Atlanta's central thoroughfare, follows the route of an old Indian trail. The dome of the Capitol is topped with native gold; it houses the State Museum of Science and Industry. Among the old homes on the 22-acre (9-hectare) grounds of the Atlanta Historical Society are the restored Tullie Smith farmhouse and slave cabin dating from about 1840. On nearby Stone Mountain are carved the gigantic faces of Confederate war heroes Robert E. Lee, Stonewall Jackson, and Jefferson Davis.

The Atlanta Symphony Orchestra and the Alliance Theater Company perform in the Robert W. Woodruff Arts Center, a memorial to the 122 Atlanta art patrons who were killed in an airplane crash in France in 1962. The ten-story, concrete Atlanta Public Library (1980) covers a downtown block. Atlanta–Fulton County Stadium features football's Falcons and baseball's Braves, winners of the National League pennant in 1991. Other professional sports teams are basketball's Hawks and soccer's Attack. New sports facilities were under construction in the early 1990s, in preparation for hosting the Summer Olympics in 1996. These included an Olympic Stadium, the Georgia Dome, and new buildings on the campus of Georgia Tech.

Some 29 degree-granting colleges and universities serve the area. Emory University is especially known for its schools of medicine and law. The Georgia Institute of Technology is known for engineering. The Atlanta University Center is a cluster of schools that focus on black education. Georgia State University is in downtown Atlanta. Research is conducted at the headquarters of the National Centers for Disease Control and at the Fernbank Science Center, the third largest planetarium in the United States.

**Economy.** Atlanta's economic leadership stems from its position as a railway hub for the southeast. Transportation equipment heads the city's list of products manufactured, and 42 of the 50 largest transportation companies in the United States have offices there. Hartsfield–Atlanta International Airport, with worldwide connections, is one of the world's busiest.

© Carl Purcell
*A sculpture called 'Early Mace' stands in Peachtree Center, which is on Atlanta's main thoroughfare.*

Atlanta is a commercial center; wholesale and retail trade employ more people than either the manufacturing or the service sector. The Atlanta Apparel Mart (opened 1979) has more than a thousand permanent showrooms for the clothing and accessory industries.

Atlanta has also become a major convention site. The Georgia World Congress Center features the largest single-level exhibition hall in the United States. Other convention facilities include the Atlanta Civic Center and the Atlanta Merchandise Mart.

**History and Government**

Atlanta was founded in 1837 at the end of the Western and Atlantic Railroad line, a site reflected in its first name, Terminus. The name was briefly changed to Marthasville, after the daughter of the governor of Georgia. In 1847 the city was incorporated as Atlanta, a reference to the Western and Atlantic.

During the war, Confederate weapons were made and stored in Atlanta. In 1864 Gen. William Tecumseh Sherman laid siege to the city for 117 days. After it surrendered, he ordered the city evacuated and burned. Of the 4,500 buildings in Atlanta at the beginning of the siege, only 400 survived the fire. Key events in the city's late-19th-century economic growth were the International Cotton Expositions of 1881 and 1895 and the invention of Coca-Cola, first sold in a drugstore on Peachtree Street in 1886.

The city of Atlanta is governed by a mayor (the chief executive) and an 18-member council. Since the 1970s Atlanta has been served by two black mayors of national reputation: Maynard Jackson and Andrew Young. The latter also served in President Jimmy Carter's administration as ambassador to the United

Nations (*see* Young, Andrew). Each of the 15 counties of the metropolitan area is administered by an elected commission. (*See also* Georgia.) Population (1990 census), 394,017.

Sarah Gibbard Cook

**ATLANTIC CHARTER.** In August 1941 President Franklin D. Roosevelt of the United States and Prime Minister Winston Churchill of Great Britain held secret meetings aboard warships in the North Atlantic off the Newfoundland coast. World War II had begun in Europe nearly two years earlier, and Churchill sought assistance from the United States to combat German aggression. At the conclusion of their conference the two leaders issued the Atlantic Charter, a joint declaration, drafted by Churchill, that stated British-American goals for the postwar world.

The charter stated that (1) neither nation sought any aggrandizement; (2) they desired no territorial changes without the free assent of the peoples concerned; (3) they respected every people's right to choose their own form of government and wanted sovereign rights and self-government restored to those forcibly deprived of them; (4) they would try to promote equal access for all states to trade and raw materials; (5) they hoped for worldwide collaboration to promote improved living standards; (6) they would seek a postwar peace in which all nations could live with security within their boundaries; (7) peace should enable all people to traverse the oceans and seas without hindrance; and (8) all nations should abandon the use of force to settle disputes. The Atlantic Charter was subsequently incorporated into the Declaration of the United Nations on Jan. 1, 1942 (*see* United Nations, "Origin of the United Nations").

**ATLANTIC CITY, N.J.** The city on which the board game Monopoly was based is Atlantic City. It has been a popular oceanside resort since the first wooden walkway was built along the beach in 1870. The novelty of rolling chairs for guests to be wheeled over the famous Boardwalk was introduced in 1884. Today's other attractions include blockbuster entertainment, gambling casinos, and a huge convention center with a 40,000-seat auditorium. The city has been the home of the Miss America Pageant since it was established in 1921.

Located on the southeast coast of New Jersey, Atlantic City is about 60 miles (100 kilometers) southeast of Philadelphia. It is situated on Absecon Island, a sandbar that is 10 miles (16 kilometers) long. A narrow waterway and marshes separate the island from the mainland. Amusement piers jut into the ocean from the Boardwalk, which is 60 feet (18 meters) wide and 5 miles (8 kilometers) long. The first legal casino to be operated in the United States outside of Nevada was opened in Atlantic City in 1978. Beyond the glitter of new hotels financed by gambling proceeds, however, the cityscape is bleak and somewhat shabby.

Atlantic City is a trade and shipping center for agricultural products and seafood as well as a tourism center. The city, incorporated in 1854, has a mayor-council form of government. (*See also* New Jersey.) Population (1990 census), 37,986.

**ATLANTIC OCEAN.** The vast body of water that separates Europe and Africa from North and South America is the Atlantic Ocean. Its name, which comes from the Greek, may refer to Atlantis, the legendary island continent said to have been the site of a great, lost civilization before the island sank.

Extending from the Arctic Ocean in the north to Antarctica in the south, the Atlantic Ocean is divided by the equator into two parts, the North Atlantic and the South Atlantic. Its area is about 31,831,000 square miles (82,442,000 square kilometers), which is about one sixth of the Earth's total area.

Although the South Atlantic is bigger than the North Atlantic, the North Atlantic has a much longer coastline, and large marginal seas and bays adjoin it. On the American side the largest bodies of water are the Gulf of Mexico, the Caribbean Sea, and Hudson Bay. On the European side the largest are the Mediterranean, North, and Baltic seas. More than half of the total land area of the world is drained by rivers that flow into the Atlantic Ocean and its adjoining seas. The large quantities of dissolved minerals carried from this huge area make the Atlantic the saltiest of the world's oceans.

The Atlantic is also the youngest ocean. Its origin and development can be accounted for by the theory of continental drift (*see* Continent, section on "Continental Drift"). This theory supposes that about 200 million years ago a mammoth ancient continent, called Pangaea by today's geologists, broke up into large pieces, which slowly separated to form the present landmasses of the Eastern and Western hemispheres and Antarctica. The coastline of North and South America as observed on a map appears to "fit into" the coastline of Europe and Africa, and there are similarities in rock structures on both sides of the Atlantic. Seafloor spreading, which also supports the theory, continues today in the Mid-Atlantic Ridge, which has been estimated to move at the rate of about ½ to 4 inches (1 to 10 centimeters) each year. (*See also* Earth.)

The outstanding feature of the Atlantic's floor, the Mid-Atlantic Ridge is an immense, volcanic mountain range that stretches its entire length. It covers the central third of the ocean bed and is up to 1,000 miles (1,600 kilometers) wide. On either side of the Mid-Atlantic Ridge are broad mud- and clay-covered abyssal plains and basins. An underwater extension of a continental landmass is called a continental shelf.

In some places the Mid-Atlantic Ridge protrudes to create islands such as the Azores and Iceland. Most islands, however, are isolated portions of the continental shelf, such as Great Britain, Newfoundland, and the Falkland Islands. The deepest point on the Atlantic's ocean floor—27,498 feet (8,381 meters)—

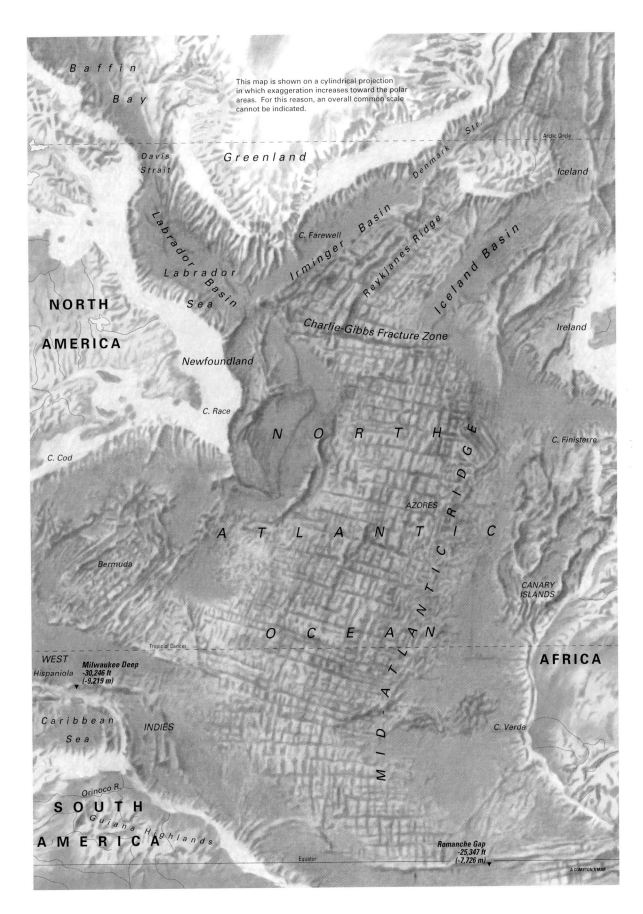

This map is shown on a cylindrical projection in which exaggeration increases toward the polar areas. For this reason, an overall common scale cannot be indicated.

*Baffin*

*Bay*

Arctic Circle

Davis
Strait

*Greenland*

Denmark Str.

Iceland

**NORTH**

**AMERICA**

Labrador

Labrador
Basin
Sea

C. Farewell

*Irminger Basin*

*Reykjanes Ridge*

*Iceland Basin*

Charlie-Gibbs Fracture Zone

Ireland

Newfoundland

C. Race

N  O  R  T  H

C. Finisterre

C. Cod

A  T  L  A  N  T  I  C

AZORES

MID-ATLANTIC RIDGE

Bermuda

CANARY
ISLANDS

O  C  E  A  N

Tropic of Cancer

WEST

**AFRICA**

Hispaniola

Milwaukee Deep
-30,246 ft
(-9,219 m)
▼

*Caribbean*

INDIES

C. Verde

*Sea*

Orinoco R.

**SOUTH**

*Guiana Highlands*

**AMERICA**

Romanche Gap
-25,347 ft
(-7,726 m) ▼

Equator

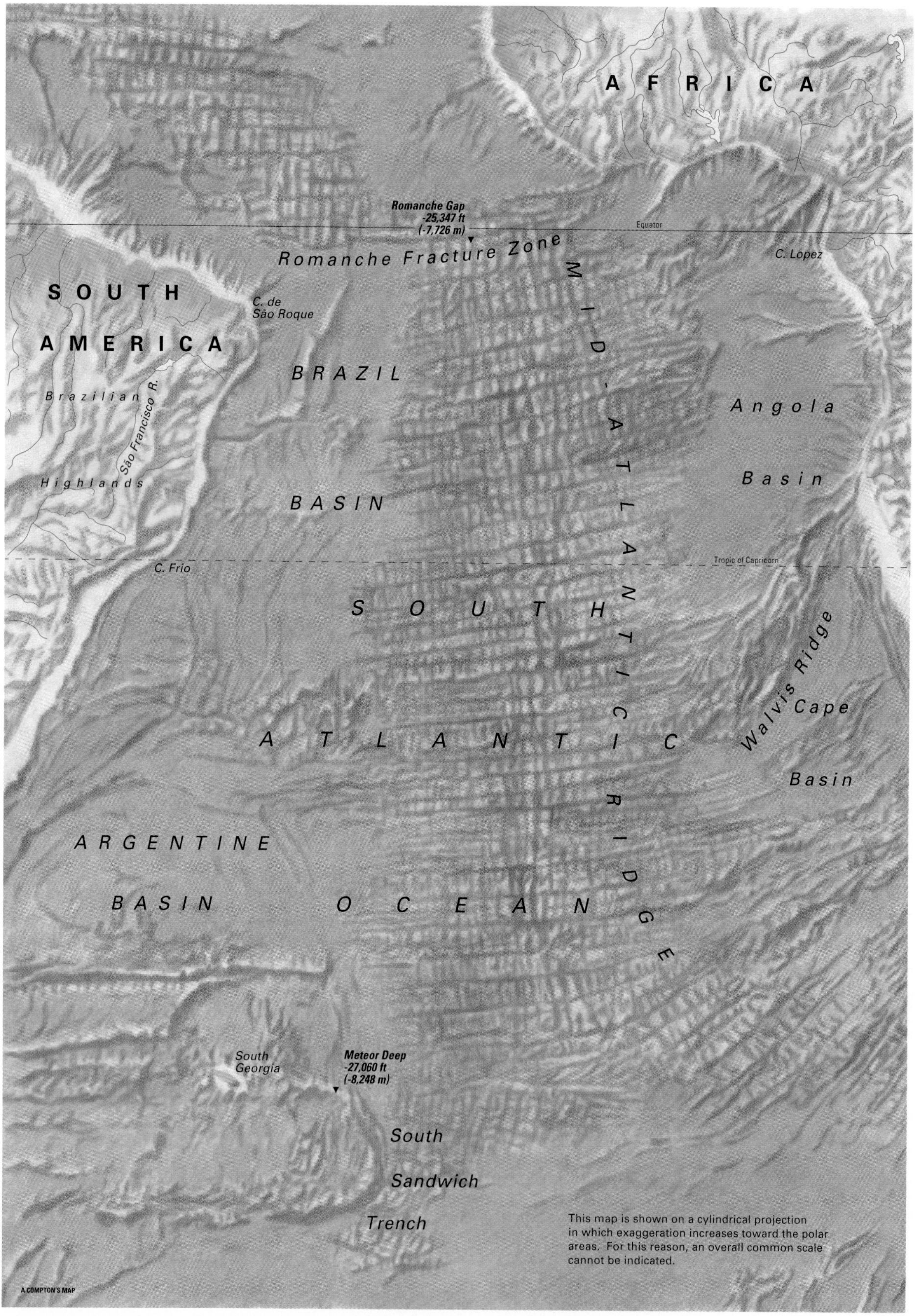

AFRICA

SOUTH
AMERICA

**Romanche Gap**
**-25,347 ft**
**(-7,726 m)** ▼
Equator

C. Lopez

Romanche Fracture Zone

C. de
São Roque

BRAZIL

*Brazilian*

*Angola*

M
I
D
-
A
T
L
A
N
T
I
C

BASIN

*Basin*

*São Francisco R.*

*Highlands*

C. Frio

Tropic of Capricorn

SOUTH

ATLANTIC

R
I
D
G
E

*Walvis Ridge*

*Cape*

*Basin*

ARGENTINE

BASIN

OCEAN

South
Georgia

**Meteor Deep**
**-27,060 ft**
**(-8,248 m)** ▼

*South*

*Sandwich*

*Trench*

This map is shown on a cylindrical projection
in which exaggeration increases toward the polar
areas. For this reason, an overall common scale
cannot be indicated.

A COMPTON'S MAP

is in the Puerto Rico Trench located about 90 miles (145 kilometers) northwest of Puerto Rico.

**Climate and Currents**

Weather over the ocean is largely determined by the prevailing winds and ocean currents. In the North Atlantic, especially during winter, frequent storms occur along fronts, or zones of great temperature contrast. The prevailing westerly winds of the middle latitudes carry cold air masses from Canada over the ocean, where they are met by warm air masses originating over the Gulf of Mexico or associated with a current known as the Gulf Stream. An area of low atmospheric pressure develops where the warm air is forced to rise over the cold air. Storms quickly develop around such a frontal zone. (*See also* Storm; Weather.)

Hurricanes originate in the tropical latitudes of the North Atlantic. During the hottest part of the year large amounts of water vapor enter the atmosphere from the ocean. When the vapor condenses as rain, heat energy is released. Massive hurricanes can develop around large concentrations of such heat.

In the South Atlantic the weather patterns are more regular than in the North Atlantic because there are no adjacent, large land areas in the middle latitudes over which cold or hot air masses can form. However, the prevailing westerly winds frequently carry storms across the South Atlantic creating dangerous gales and heavy winds that are a notorious shipping hazard.

Circulation of the main water currents of the Atlantic Ocean is clockwise in the Northern Hemisphere and counterclockwise in the Southern Hemisphere. In the tropical latitudes the currents of both hemispheres flow generally from east to west, and their temperature becomes relatively warm.

In the North Atlantic the warm current known as the Gulf Stream flows northward along the coast of North America. It continues northward and eastward across the ocean as the somewhat cooler North Atlantic Current and warms the climate of northwestern Europe. After turning southward along the coast of Europe and northwestern Africa, it becomes the relatively cold Canary Current. In the South Atlantic the southward flowing warm current along the east coast of South America is called the Brazil Current, and the northward flowing cold current along the west coast of southern Africa is the Benguela Current. (*See also* Oceanography, "Ocean Surface Currents.")

**Marine Life**

The Atlantic Ocean can be divided into five water layers, or zones, each of which supports a different type of marine life. From top to bottom these zones are the littoral, euphotic, mesopelagic, bathypelagic, and benthic.

The littoral, or tidal, zone is the area along the shore between the high-tide and low-tide levels. It is the habitat for such sea life as clams, oysters, mussels, seaweed, sea moss, and brown algae.

The euphotic zone is the ocean's surface layer into which sunlight can penetrate in sufficient amounts to support photosynthesis. It extends to a depth of about 600 feet (180 meters) and contains most of the sea's organisms. These range from microscopic sea animals (zooplankton) and plants (phytoplankton) to the largest fishes and whales.

The mesopelagic, or midocean, zone extends from about 600 feet to 3,000 feet (180 meters to 900 meters). It contains organic debris from the euphotic zone above and supports such animals as the sperm whale and giant squid.

The bathypelagic, or deep-ocean, zone extends from 3,000 feet (900 meters) to the bottom. About two thirds of the fishes that inhabit this zone are bioluminescent, or capable of producing their own light.

The benthic zone occurs at the bottom of the ocean—from shallow waters to deep-sea trenches—and supports the greatest range of animal and plant life. At depths of 12,000 feet (3,700 meters) or more, fishes are not common on the bottom, but less developed life forms such as tube worms, crinoids (sea lilies), and glass sponges can exist. They feed on the organic matter that settles from the upper zones and, in very specialized deep-sea communities, on minerals that well up with hot water from midocean vents in the seafloor. (*See also* Deep-Sea Life.)

**Economic Resources—Future Prospects**

Approximately 40 percent of the world's fish catch comes from the Atlantic Ocean. In the northwestern Atlantic off Newfoundland is the Grand Banks, where herring, cod, and menhaden are plentiful. Traditional fishing areas in the northeastern Atlantic and the North Sea yield flounder, ocean perch, cod, hake, and herring, but they have been overfished. The warm waters of the Caribbean and Gulf of Mexico abound with shrimp and sponges. Since the 1950s fishing has greatly increased in the South Atlantic, where large quantities of tuna, hake, and herring are caught. Clams, oysters, crabs, and octopuses can be harvested along the coast of much of the Atlantic. The Sargasso Sea, in the center of the North Atlantic, is the breeding ground for the American and European species of migratory eels.

The most important mineral resources derived from the Atlantic are petroleum and natural gas. Offshore fields lie in the North Sea, the Gulf of Mexico, the Caribbean, and along the coasts of Nigeria, Brazil, Canada, Argentina, and the United States. Other minerals being exploited include tin and coal from mines under the ocean floor off Great Britain. Large diamond deposits are found along the southwestern coast of Africa. Salt and bromine are extracted from sea water. Manganese nodules have been found on the deep ocean floor, but technology still needs to be developed to make them economically retrievable.

**History and Trade**

Though human beings have sailed on the waters of the Atlantic from ancient times, the Vikings were the first Europeans to document these voyages. During the 11th century they explored and charted the waters around Iceland, Greenland, and northeastern North America.

In the 15th century the Portuguese discovered the Azores and Madeira and sailed along the entire western coast of Africa. Under the Spanish flag, in 1492, Christopher Columbus made the first of his trans-Atlantic crossings. Europeans explored and settled most of the Atlantic coast of the Americas during the 16th and 17th centuries.

In the mid-1800s Lieut. Matthew Maury of the United States Navy made the first oceanographic study of the Atlantic. He compiled charts on winds and currents that established the first sea lanes, prepared a treatise on the Gulf Stream, and collected other data. The British *Challenger* expedition, made between 1872 and 1876, discovered the Mid-Atlantic Ridge. In more recent times, Jacques Piccard, the Swiss scientist, explored Atlantic waters in *Trieste I*, a deep-sea bathyscaphe. A wide range of other submarine devices have also been used to record new information about the depths of the Atlantic and other oceans. The submersible *Alvin* explored the wreck of the *Titanic* in 1986.

Deep-sea drilling ships, such as the *Glomar Challenger*, have surveyed the bed of the Atlantic and discovered oil fields. The United States Navy established Sealab, an underwater habitat that was set up near Bermuda where aquanauts lived beneath the ocean and studied marine life for extended periods of time. (*See also* Oceanography.)

The North Atlantic, with its hazardous icebergs and winter storms, is the most heavily used and congested ocean trade route in the world. Shipping lanes were established and regulated to ensure the safety of all who sailed the Atlantic. Ice patrols maintain surveillance of icebergs and report on their locations to all ships and oil drilling platforms that could be in danger. Satellites are used to observe iceberg movements throughout the entire Atlantic.

Among the Atlantic's many deep, natural harbors are those at New York City and Rio de Janeiro, Brazil. Other busy ports, such as Amsterdam, The Netherlands, are accessible to oceangoing vessels through dredged channels. Punta Arenas, Chile, is the southernmost port in the South Atlantic, and the northernmost port in the North Atlantic is in Russia, at Archangel. (*See also* Ocean.)

**ATLAS MOUNTAINS.** The vast highlands of North Africa, the Atlas Mountains span three countries and separate the southern rim of the Mediterranean basin from the Sahara Desert. They extend for more than 1,200 miles (1,900 kilometers) across Morocco, Algeria, and Tunisia.

The northern, forested section of the range is called the Tell Atlas. This area receives the most rainfall, and it has moist forests of cork oak trees with an undergrowth of arbutus, heather shrubs, rockroses, and lavender. Where there is less rainfall, light dry forests of green oak trees and arbor vitae (a species of pine tree) cover the soil. In the southern, desertlike

area of the mountain range, called the Saharan Atlas, there are only scattered green oak and juniper trees.

Animal life in the Atlas Mountains is decreasing. Only a few bands of jackals, some monkey tribes, and herds of wild boar remain in the woods.

In spite of severe winters, people still live in the mountains. Here the Berber peoples have survived in fortified villages perched high up on mountain crests. Families live in separate dwellings that form a square around a closed interior courtyard. Berber villages also usually include a mosque, a threshing floor, and an assembly place for the village elders.

The thick rim of the Atlas Mountain range rises to form a high sill, which creates a barrier hindering communication. However, the mountain people have their own internal communication system. Villages are linked by paths that follow the crest lines of the hills. Travel is still on foot or by mule, though the use of local buses is increasing. (*See also* Algeria; Morocco.)

The governments of each of the three countries spanned by the Atlas Mountains are planning for future economic development and are encouraging tourism and the establishment of industry in mountain regions. In Morocco and Algeria dams have been constructed. In all three countries rich mineral deposits are mined, including lead, zinc, copper, and iron ore from Morocco; iron ore and phosphate from Algeria; and phosphate, iron ore, and lead from Tunisia.

**ATMOSPHERE.** The Earth and other planets of the solar system are each enclosed in a thin shell of gas called an atmosphere. Only the Earth's atmosphere will be dealt with in this article. (For information about the atmospheres of the other planets, *see* Planets.)

The atmosphere clings tightly to the Earth by the attraction of gravity. If the Earth is compared to an orange, the atmosphere can be considered the skin of the orange. The air composing the atmosphere moves freely—sometimes violently. The Earth's atmosphere consists mainly of nitrogen, oxygen, argon, water vapor, carbon dioxide, and small amounts of other gases and solid and liquid particles.

---

**FACT FINDER FOR ATMOSPHERE**

The subject of the atmosphere is a broad one. Readers will obtain additional information in the related articles listed here. (*See also* related references in the Fact-Index.)

| | |
|---|---|
| Acid Rain | Meteor and Meteorite |
| Aerosol | Oceanography |
| Aurora | Ocean Waves and Tides |
| Climate | Radiation |
| Cloud | Rainbow |
| Fluorocarbon | Rainfall |
| Fog | Snow |
| Greenhouse Effect | Storm |
| Light | Weather |
| Lightning | Wind |

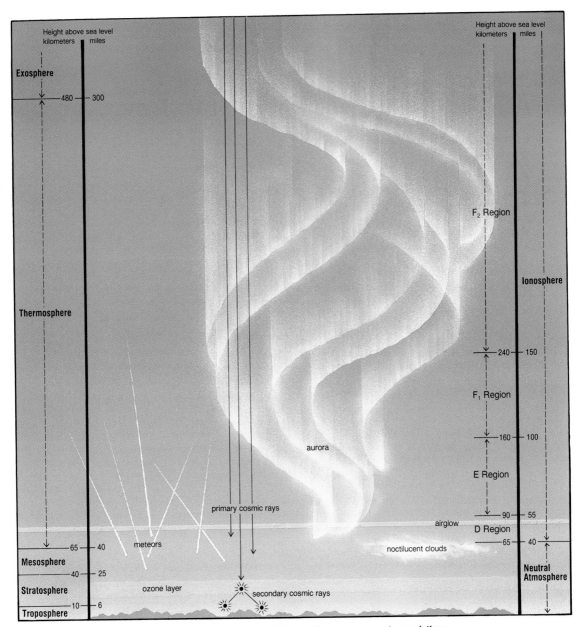

Height above sea level
kilometers ▮ miles ▮

Exosphere
480 — 300

Thermosphere

Mesosphere
65 — 40
40 — 25

Stratosphere
10 — 6

Troposphere

Height above sea level
kilometers ▮ miles ▮

$F_2$ Region

Ionosphere

240 — 150

$F_1$ Region

160 — 100

E Region

90 — 55

D Region
65 — 40

Neutral
Atmosphere

aurora

primary cosmic rays

meteors

ozone layer

secondary cosmic rays

airglow

noctilucent clouds

*Scientists divide the atmosphere into layers, or regions. The divisions are based on temperature variations, indicated by the labels on left side of the drawing, and on electrical properties, indicated by the labels on the right. Each region is characterized by certain atmospheric phenomena.*

The atmosphere serves to moderate the extremes of heat and cold on the Earth. During the day as the heat of the sun penetrates the air and warms the Earth, the atmosphere traps this heat so that it escapes more slowly into space, making the night warmer than it would be without this effect. The atmosphere also protects the Earth's inhabitants to some extent from meteor particles, cosmic rays, radiation from the sun and stars, atmospheric dust, and other hazards.

The atmosphere is in constant motion due to the Earth's rotation and changes in temperature and pressure. The sometimes violent changes that take place in the atmosphere are experienced on Earth as weather, wind, ocean currents, lightning, and rainbows. Large masses of air moving above the Earth's surface can cause changes in weather and produce winds with speeds of over 100 miles per hour (160 kilometers per hour). Vital exchanges of matter and energy occur between the atmosphere and the oceans, which are vast reservoirs of the heat, moisture, and carbon dioxide needed by the atmosphere. The atmosphere, in turn, supplies ocean surfaces with the energy of motion that produces ocean currents. (*See also* Earth, "The Atmosphere.")

## Layers of the Atmosphere

Scientists have developed three different classification systems for the atmosphere. They divide it into layers on the basis of varying temperature, varying electrical characteristics, and varying composition.

**Temperature.** On the basis of temperature, scientists distinguish five layers. The troposphere extends up to 6 miles (10 kilometers) above the Earth's surface. It is the region closest to the Earth's surface and where weather occurs, and it is characterized by a decrease in temperature with increasing altitude. Winds in this layer move mostly in a vertical motion. The stratosphere extends up to 25 miles (40 kilometers) above the Earth and is characterized by an increase in temperature with increasing altitude and by jet streams that move mostly in a horizontal motion. A significant feature of the stratosphere is the ozone layer, which is located between 10 and 20 miles (16 and 32 kilometers) above the Earth. This layer protects the Earth by absorbing harmful ultraviolet radiation from the sun. In the late 1980s there was some concern that the ozone layer was being destroyed by pollution, and an effort was begun to prevent its destruction (*see* Pollution, Environmental).

The mesosphere—up to 40 miles (65 kilometers) above the Earth—is characterized by a rapid decrease in temperature with increasing altitude. Noctilucent clouds, clouds of water vapor or meteor dust that shine at night, are a distinguishable feature of this layer. The thermosphere extends up to 300 miles (480 kilometers) and is characterized by a rapid rise in temperature with increasing altitude. The phenomenon of airglow, luminescence due to reradiation of sunlight by heated atmospheric particles, originates in this layer. Auroras are a spectacular feature of this layer. The highest layer of the atmosphere, the exosphere, extends beyond the thermosphere. The density of the air is so low in this layer that the concept of temperature loses its customary meaning. Ultraviolet rays fill the exosphere, and faint glows called zodiacal light that are due to sunlight reflected from particles of meteoric dust originate in this layer.

**Electrical properties.** Scientists also divide the atmosphere into layers on the basis of electrical properties. Overall they recognize a neutral atmosphere, which lies below about 40 miles, and the ionosphere above it. The ionosphere—a region of electrically charged particles, or ions—may be divided into regions according to the degree of ionization.

The D region extends up to 55 miles (90 kilometers) above the Earth's surface. The E region, also called the Kennelly-Heaviside layer, is a moderately ionized layer extending from 55 to 100 miles (90 to 160 kilometers) high. This region is caused by solar X rays and consists mainly of nitrogen and oxygen atoms. It reflects relatively long radio waves. The F region, also called the Appleton layer, is subdivided into $F_1$ and $F_2$ layers. The $F_1$ layer lies between 100 and 150 miles (160 and 240 kilometers) above the Earth, consists mainly of oxygen atoms, and reflects shorter radio waves. Its ionization varies greatly, and the layer disappears at night. The $F_2$ layer, above 150 miles and the densest of the ionospheric regions, consists mainly of strong nitrogen ions and reflects extremely short radio waves. Beyond its outer boundary is the magnetosphere, a magnetic envelope that shelters the Earth from the ionized blast of the solar wind.

**Composition.** In the lower regions of the atmosphere, up to about 65 miles (100 kilometers) above the Earth, turbulence causes a continuous mixing of the constituent elements of the atmosphere so that the composition is relatively uniform. These regions make up the homosphere. Above this is the heterosphere, where various constituents tend to separate out. The concentrations of heavier elements, such as nitrogen and oxygen, decrease with increasing altitude, so that eventually the atmosphere is dominated by the lighter elements, such as helium and hydrogen. At the outermost part of the ionosphere helium becomes dominant at about 600 miles (960 kilometers), and hydrogen above about 1,500 miles (2,500 kilometers).

## Weight and Pressure of the Atmosphere

The total mass of the atmosphere is estimated to be some 5.5 quadrillion (55 followed by 14 zeros) tons (4.99 quadrillion metric tons). This mass is equal to about one millionth of the mass of the Earth. Air is heaviest at sea level because the air molecules are compressed by the weight of overlying air. As height increases, the air molecules become separated by more space, and the weight decreases. As the weight of the air decreases, so does the air pressure. At sea level, air exerts a pressure of 14.7 pounds per square inch (101.36 kilopascals). At 100,000 feet (30,480 meters), air density is so low that air exerts a pressure of only 0.18 pound per square inch (1.24 kilopascals).

## Why the Sky Is Blue

The sun's rays that stream down to the Earth appear as white light. However, white light is composed of light waves of all the colors of the spectrum, each color having a different wavelength. As it passes through the atmosphere, sunlight is reflected and refracted by the air molecules and by dust particles and molecules of water vapor. This scattering process is called diffusion. The short blue light waves are more widely scattered and rescattered than are the long red waves. Because of this, the sky appears blue. Outer space is black because there is no atmosphere to scatter the light waves.

**BIBLIOGRAPHY FOR ATMOSPHERE**

**Allen, O.E.** Atmosphere (Time-Life, 1983).
**Asimov, Isaac.** How Did We Find Out About the Atmosphere? (Walker, 1985).
**Gedzelman, S.D.** The Science and Wonders of the Atmosphere (Wiley, 1980).
**Maury, Jean-Pierre.** The Atmosphere (Barron, 1989).
**Schaefer, V.J. and Day, J.A.** A Field Guide to the Atmosphere (Houghton, 1983).

Fermilab

*The Fermi National Accelerator Laboratory is one of several large accelerator laboratories in the United States where many of the particle physics experiments are carried out. It is about 40 miles west of Chicago. The large ring has a diameter of more than half a mile. Protons accelerated in the ring are extracted and made to travel down straight or slightly curved paths to where they hit a target. The products of the collision are studied to learn more about the particle interactions, to test theories, and to search for any new kinds of behavior. The 16-story building on the lower left is the main area where people work.*

# ATOMIC PARTICLES

Throughout recorded history human beings have marveled at the universe and have tried to describe and to understand it and their place within it. Furthermore, every culture has tried to explain the universe and to give a unified picture of natural phenomena.

Though the fundamental unified picture was still a goal, great progress was made in around 1600 by concentrating effort on small, manageable questions. Since then many diverse phenomena have been carefully examined and seen as different parts of the same structure. Before the 1970s there were thought to be four main forces in nature, and there was no theory that could mathematically define two of them. A theory now exists for each force. In the late 1980s scientists devised a hypothesis about the existence of a fifth fundamental force in nature. A series of experiments in the early 1990s, however, concluded that there was no strong evidence for a fifth force.

In addition, scientists have increasingly developed techniques to probe ever more deeply into the structure of matter and to break down matter into its most basic elements. The concept of the atom has existed since the 5th century BC, but it was not until the beginning of the 19th century that this concept was developed into a scientific theory. Almost as soon as the modern atomic theory was established, it was discovered that atoms were not the basic pointlike building blocks that were being sought. Instead, atoms consist of electrons that are somehow bound to a tiny nucleus. The nucleus is made of neutrons and protons. For some time it seemed

. . . . . . . . . . . . . . . . . . . . . . . . . . . . . . . . . . . . . . . . . . . . . . . .

*This article was contributed by Gordon Kane, Ph.D., Professor of Physics, University of Michigan; Guggenheim Fellow.*

possible that these objects could be the fundamental building blocks, but in the 1960s it was found that the neutron and proton have structure as well.

Today all the matter in the universe is viewed as being composed of three kinds of elementary objects: (1) particles called quarks, which make up neutrons and protons; (2) particles called leptons, which include electrons and some similar particles; and (3) particles called bosons, or vector mesons, which include the photons seen as light and which carry the electromagnetic force. Other bosons are similar particles that carry the other forces. The forces in nature and the view of how they work cannot be separated from the constituents of matter. Some scientists suggest that leptons and quarks may actually be the same object but in different states. Bosons, too, may be this same object but in still another state.

**Constituents of Matter**

As illustrated in Fig. 1, t he fundamental constituents of matter can be separated into five levels. These levels were discovered in distinct stages. Considered at one level, the everyday world is made of molecules. Because molecules are so small (about one millionth of a centimeter in length), their existence was not easy to establish. Indirect evidence for molecules was strong during the second half of the 19th century, and the first explicit evidence was found when Brownian motion was correctly understood and studied in about 1906 by physicists Albert Einstein and Jean-Baptiste Perrin. (Brownian motion is the random movement of microscopic particles suspended in liquids or gases. This movement is caused by the impact on these particles by the molecules in the surrounding fluid.)

The next stage was already foreseen. There are many kinds of molecules, and it was clear that simplifying ideas were needed. The Russian chemist Dmitri Mendeleev argued that there was a set of more basic entities of which all molecules are constructed, the chemical elements, which consist of atoms of only one kind. In about 1869 he published his periodic table, which exhibited many regularities and sets of recurring properties among these elements.

There are 92 known basic elements, and more can be constructed in the laboratory. The existence of the atoms that make up these elements was confirmed beyond a doubt by the early 1900s. By the 1920s, the behavior and properties of atoms were understood. (*See also* Matter; Molecule; Periodic Table.)

**Structure of the atom.** Even while the existence of atoms was being established, new experimental evidence showed that there would be another stage of matter because atoms were not pointlike objects. One clue was the discovery of the electron in 1897. Then in 1911 the British physicist Ernest Rutherford aimed alpha particles (a form of electrically charged radiation emitted by some elements) at gold foil. He found that most of the radiation went through the foil, sometimes being deflected a little, but occasionally some of the radiation bounced back. This indicated that the atoms constituting the foil were not uniform in structure but instead behaved like an extended object with a hard core at the center. Rutherford had discovered the atomic nucleus.

The atoms of each chemical element have a different nucleus. These nuclei are surrounded by enough electrons to make the atoms electrically neutral. It took some time to determine that the nucleus is made of protons and neutrons (the neutron was discovered in 1932). The protons are electrically charged, and the neutrons are electrically neutral. It became clear that a new force, the nuclear force, was required to hold the nucleus together since the protons repelled one another electrically. The Japanese physicist Hideki Yukawa proposed that a particle named the pion transmitted a strong nuclear force much as the photon transmitted the electromagnetic force. Pions were found shortly after World War II by the British physicist Cecil F. Powell.

Four stages of matter have been discussed: molecules, atoms, the atomic nucleus, and the strong nuclear force. Molecules are combinations of atoms. Atoms consist of electrons bound to a tiny nucleus by the electro-

*Fig. 1. A schematic representation of the present understanding of the constituents of matter shows that there are five levels. Also shown is the force that binds together objects at one level to make the next level. As far as is known today, quarks and leptons are fundamental pointlike particles. Starting at bottom, quarks bind together with the strong force, transmitted by gluons (not shown), to make protons, neutrons, pions, and other hadrons, which are particles with size and structure. Some residual pieces of the strong force bind protons and neutrons to make the nuclei. Then nuclei and electrons bind by the electromagnetic force, transmitted by photons (not shown), to make atoms. Finally, atoms combine by the residual electromagnetic force to make many molecules. See text for further discussion.*

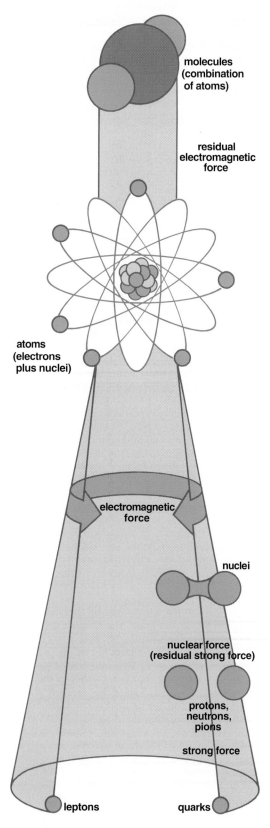

molecules
(combination
of atoms)

residual
electromagnetic
force

atoms
(electrons
plus nuclei)

electromagnetic
force

nuclei

nuclear force
(residual strong force)

protons,
neutrons,
pions

strong force

leptons

quarks

magnetic force. If one atom is put near another, the electromagnetic fields of the nucleus and electrons in one are felt slightly by the electrons of the other atom, giving the residual force that binds atoms into molecules. The nucleus consists of neutrons and protons bound together by a nuclear force strong enough to overcome the electrical repulsion of the protons. The particles so far encountered can be divided into two categories: the electron, which does not experience nuclear or strong interactions, and protons and neutrons, which do feel the nuclear force.

**Quarks, leptons, and bosons.** In the 1960s intensive research revealed that these basic particles were made up of even more basic units called quarks. It was concluded by the mid-1980s that the fundamental constituents of matter were the quarks, which are responsive to the strong force that holds the nucleus together, and the leptons, particles that are unresponsive to the strong force. Quarks are massive particles that have a spin of ½ and carry a fractional electric charge. (Spin is the intrinsic angular momentum that all known particles possess.) Quarks are always found in combination with each other.

There are six types of quarks, called flavors (because once the various types of quarks were named after the ice cream flavors chocolate, strawberry, and vanilla). The flavors are now called up, down, top, bottom, strange, and charm. Only two of these—the up and down flavors—occur in the protons and neutrons of ordinary matter. The other four—top, bottom, strange, and charm flavors—exist only in unstable particles that spontaneously decay in a fraction of a second. The flavors up, charm, and top have an electric charge of ⅔; the down, strange, and bottom flavors have an electric charge of -⅓. All particles made up of quarks are known as hadrons. In turn, protons, neutrons, and other hadrons that consist of three quarks are called baryons. Hadrons formed from a single quark and its antiquark are called mesons. All particles with an odd half-integral spin, such as ½ or ⅔, are known as fermions. Included in this group are leptons and baryons. (*See also* Quark.)

Leptons are always found outside the nucleus because, unlike quarks, they are unresponsive to the strong force that holds the nucleus together. There are six types of leptons, which are always found singly. Leptons have a negative charge and a spin of ½. Electrons, muons, and taus are in this category. Each lepton has an associated neutrino that has no electric charge and either no or very negligible mass. Leptons respond only to the electromagnetic, weak nuclear, and gravitational forces. (The weak nuclear force operates during nuclear fission, when a nucleus spontaneously emits nuclear material.)

While quarks and leptons are the fundamental particles of matter, there is another set of particles called bosons. It is believed that all forces are the result of interactions between particles and that all interactions among quarks or leptons are transmitted by bosons. The most familiar boson is the photon, which transmits the electromagnetic force. The strong force that binds quarks to make protons and other hadrons is transmitted by a set of eight bosons called gluons. The weak force that makes radioactivity occur and that is necessary for the sun to create energy is transmitted by three bosons named the vector mesons. For historical reasons, they are also sometimes called the W+, W-, and Z⁰ bosons. While the photon and gluon are massless, the vector mesons are quite heavy. Presumably, there is also a graviton, which carries the gravitational force. In 1983 researchers at the laboratory of the European Organization for Nuclear Research (CERN) in Geneva, Switzerland, detected particles that formed and decayed as W and Z particles were predicted to do.

In 1997 a group of German physicists claimed to have possibly discovered a new subatomic particle that could, if its existence is proved, revolutionize our understanding of atomic structures. According to the scientists at the Deutsches Elektronen-Synchrotron (DESY), one of the world's most advanced physics

## Some Atomic Particles

**baryons.** Hadrons that consist of three quarks.

**bosons.** Particles that carry the basic physical forces.

**electrons.** The lightest leptons. They have a charge of –1. Electrons play important roles in electrical and chemical reactions.

**fermions.** All particles with an odd half-integral spin, such as ½ or ⅔. Examples include leptons and baryons.

**gluons.** Bosons that carry the strong force between quarks.

**gravitons.** Bosons that presumably carry the gravitational force. Gravitons have not actually been observed yet.

**hadrons.** All particles that are made up of quarks.

**leptons.** Particles that are found outside the nucleus. There are six types of leptons: electrons, muons, taus, and their respective neutrinos.

**mesons.** Hadrons formed from one quark and its antiquark.

**muons.** Leptons that are slightly heavier than the electron. Although these particles existed during the early moments of the beginning of the universe, they now exist only in particle accelerators and cosmic rays.

**neutrinos.** Particles with no electric charge and either no or very little mass.

**neutrons.** Uncharged elementary particles that, along with protons, are constituents of atomic nuclei.

**photons.** Bosons that carry the electromagnetic force. Photons are the particles that make up light.

**protons.** Positively charged elementary particles that, along with neutrons, are constituents of atomic nuclei.

**quarks.** Particles that make up neutrons and protons. Quarks come in six types, called flavors: up, down, charm, strange, top, and bottom.

**taus.** The heaviest leptons. Today these particles can only be found in particle accelerators and cosmic rays, though they were once abundant during the early moments of the universe's creation.

**vector mesons** (also called **W+, W-, and Z⁰ bosons**). Bosons that carry the weak force, which is responsible for some types of radioactive decay.

### The Fundamental Particles of Matter

| Particle | Spin | Electric Charge | Approximate Mass | Color | Flavor |
|---|---|---|---|---|---|
| Leptons | | | | | |
| e | 1/2 | −1 | 1/2,000 | no | yes |
| $\nu_e$ | 1/2 | 0 | 0 | no | yes |
| μ | 1/2 | −1 | 1/10 | no | yes |
| $\nu_\mu$ | 1/2 | 0 | 0 | no | yes |
| τ | 1/2 | −1 | 2 | no | yes |
| $\nu_\tau$ | 1/2 | 0 | 0 | no | yes |
| Quarks | | | | | |
| u | 1/2 | 2/3 | 1/50 | yes | yes |
| d | 1/2 | −1/3 | 1/100 | yes | yes |
| c | 1/2 | 2/3 | 2 | yes | yes |
| s | 1/2 | −1/3 | 1/5 | yes | yes |
| t | 1/2 | 2/3 | >18 | yes | yes |
| b | 1/2 | −1/3 | 5 | yes | yes |

Table A: The attributes color and flavor have precise technical meanings in particle physics (see text). The masses of the particles vary over a wide range and are expressed relative to the mass of a proton as a convenient unit. The electric charge is relative to that of the proton. Spin is the angular momentum resulting from the rotation of a particle on its axis. For each particle there is an antiparticle with opposite electric charge, color, and flavor; the antiparticles are not listed separately.

institutes, the particle, known as a leptoquark, appeared to be a hybrid of two elemental subatomic particles—the quark and the lepton. According to what is known as the standard model of atomic formation, quarks are the building blocks of protons and neutrons, which form the nuclei of atoms. Leptons are particles, such as electrons, which, among other things, occupy shells surrounding the nuclei of atoms. These two types of subatomic particles—quarks and leptons—are unique types of particles that are themselves the basis of all of the mass in the universe. The standard model of atomic formation does not account for particles (other than the quark, the lepton, and the gauge boson) such as the leptoquark.

Most physicists had long speculated that the standard model did not present a complete understanding of atomic formation. For more than two decades, a handful of radical theoretical physicists had hypothesized the existence of the leptoquark, hoping that the discovery of the theoretical particle would allow them to construct a new standard model of atomic structure. Until the observations at the DESY institute, however, no evidence of any other subatomic particle existed to challenge the standard model. The DESY scientists had been conducting research involving the collision of protons and particles that are known as positrons, which are essentially electrons that display a positive charge. In the experiments conducted by the scientists, the two types of particles were accelerated in opposite directions to near light speed and forced to collide.

According to the standard model, the collision of the two types of particles should force the proton to break apart into smaller quark particles, while the positron should bounce off the proton. The scientists observed, however, that in several collisions, the positron

bounced off the proton in patterns not predicted by the standard model, producing high levels of energy and forcing the positron to move away at a sharp angle. The scientists believed that the irregular path of the positron might indicate that a new particle, the leptoquark, was produced in the collision process.

The possibility of the existence of a leptoquark might lead to the creation of a revised standard model of the structure of matter, because it could prove to be a simpler structure that might unify theories of quark and lepton formation. Many physicists, however, questioned whether the German team had indeed discovered a new subatomic particle, pointing to the fact that of the millions of observed collisions, the type of extreme reaction noted by the scientists occurred in only a handful of cases and could possibly be explained simply as random fluctuations in the collision process. The German team cautiously agreed with the suggestion and stated that they would need at least another year of research on the unusual collisions.

**Antiparticles.** In the early 1930s, the British physicist P.A.M. Dirac predicted the existence of antiparticles. For every fundamental particle there must exist another particle with the same mass but with an electrical charge (and any other charges) that is opposite. That this is true is now well understood and verified experimentally.

For example, the antiparticle of an electron is a positron, the antiparticle of a proton is an antiproton, and the antiparticle of a quark is an antiquark. (In the remainder of this article, antiparticles will sometimes appear as the particle name with a bar over it; for example, q̄.)

### Properties of Atomic Particles

Certain distinct properties characterize every atomic particle. Such properties include mass, electric charge, symmetry, color, and flavor.

**Mass and electric charge.** Each elementary particle has a specific mass. Masses can vary greatly from particle to particle, but physicists do not know what accounts for these masses. The next most familiar property is electric charge. Bosons and leptons can have an electric charge that is the same as the electron (called ⁻1 by convention), or they can have the opposite electrical charge (⁺1) as the proton does. They also can

Fig. 2. Illustrating a symmetry, all three objects go into themselves under a rotation by 120 degrees around an axis perpendicular to the paper and through the center of the figures. Objects (b) and (c) are made by combining two of (a), keeping the same center. Obviously, many more complex combinations could be made with the same symmetry. Object (c) is less symmetrical but still has the basic symmetry described for the other two.

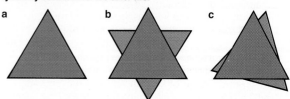

a        b        c

be electrically neutral, as is the neutron or the neutrino. Quarks have an electrical charge of -⅔.

**Symmetry.** Something has a symmetry if there is an operation that can be performed on it that leaves it unchanged. For example, one cannot tell if a circle has been rotated around a line that extends through its center and perpendicular to it. Also the rotation of an equilateral triangle by 120 degrees around a perpendicular line through its center leaves it unchanged (*see* Fig. 2). Mathematicians have generalized and classified ways to leave various systems unchanged in work that is called group theory. If there is a set of operations that acts on a group of objects while leaving the objects and relations among them unchanged, that set is called a symmetry group. It is said that the objects "go into one another" under the operations of the symmetry. Symmetry groups have various names; some of the particular ones that have great relevance in describing how particles and the forces of nature are organized are called the SU(N) groups. The N in this name refers to the basic number of objects on which the operations act.

Physicists discovered that the laws governing particles and their interactions do not change under several sets of operation. In particular, the particles that were discovered in the post–World War II period were found to come in sets that went into one another under the operations of the symmetry group SU(3). But surprisingly the observed particles corresponded to sets of objects that did not include the simplest possible set of objects. This is illustrated by an analogy in Fig. 2. It is as if the observed particles were at the corners in parts (b) and (c) of the figure and the laws of nature did not change when 120-degree rotations were made, so that several sets of particles could be viewed very simply. But the simplest set, at the corners of part (a), was not observed.

In 1964 American physicists Murray Gell-Mann and George Zweig suggested, independently, that all hadrons were made of another level of matter, analogous to part (a) of the figure. Gell-Mann called this matter quarks. (In the language of the next section, they proposed the u, d, and s quarks.) The term quark is adopted from a passage in James Joyce's novel 'Finnegans Wake'—"Three quarks for Muster Mark. . . ." (*See also* Gell-Mann.)

Throughout the 1960s many theoretical physicists tried to account for the ever-growing number of subatomic particles that they observed in experiments. They came to the same conclusion as Gell-Mann and Zweig—that quarks are the most fundamental strongly interacting particles. The most direct reason for concluding that protons and neutrons are made of quarks is the result of an experiment carried out at the Stanford Linear Accelerator Center (SLAC) in Stanford, Calif., in the late 1960s. The researchers essentially repeated Ernest Rutherford's technique for discovering the nucleus of the atom. In this case very energetic electrons were scattered off protons, and a surprisingly large number bounced off at large angles rather than going almost straight through. Careful

study revealed that one should think of a proton as mainly composed of three pointlike objects, the quarks. (Evidence was also found for gluons, the particles that bind the quarks together to make a proton.)

There are additional reasons why scientists are confident that matter is composed of quarks. One is that when protons, neutrons, and other hadrons are constructed from quarks, only certain combinations of quarks are allowed. Protons and neutrons are made of three quarks, and mesons, like pions, are made of quark-antiquark pairs (*see* Fig. 3). Certain hadron states must exist if the theory is valid, and others must not exist. Both conditions are satisfied. Another proof of the existence of quarks is that the theories describing how quarks interact, both strongly and weakly, explain a number of important experiments.

Previously, theoretical physicists had uncovered various clues showing that each stage of matter has structure. The proton did not interact with a magnetic field as a pointlike particle should and was revealed to have structure when electrons were scattered off it. But quarks and leptons have been probed to very small distances and so far reveal no structure; they seem to be pointlike objects.

Quarks have another property that could be very important in this regard. Although they can be observed in a number of ways, it is generally believed that they cannot be separated. The force that binds them together is thought to remain constant as the distance between them is increased, and so more and more work is required to separate a pair of quarks. But

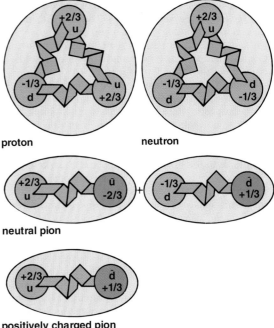

**Fig. 3. Very simplified illustrations of protons, neutrons, pions, and other hadrons show that they are made of quarks (yellow spheres) and antiquarks (green spheres) that are bound together by gluons (bent ribbons). See text for further description.**

proton          neutron

neutral pion

positively charged pion

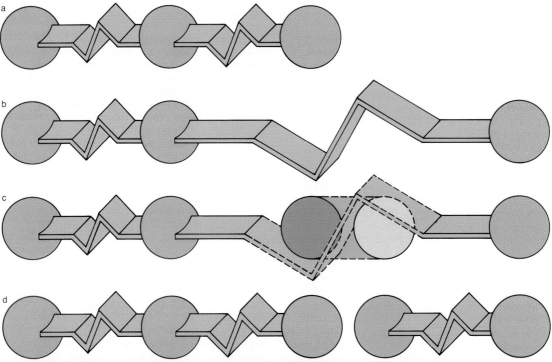

**Fig. 4.** *Individual quarks (circles) cannot be separated from the particles they make up. Imagine a proton as three quarks, laid out in a line for simplicity (a). Now try to pull one quark off (b). We have to supply some energy to do that, and we stretch the gluon (bent ribbon) line. As soon as enough energy is available to create a quark-antiquark pair, that will occur (c). Then the quark of the new pair will go with the other two quarks to make a proton, and the antiquark plus the quark will bind to make a pion. So only ordinary hadrons, such as protons and pions, are produced (d).*

when the energy put into the system reaches a certain level, the system makes a quark-antiquark ($q\bar{q}$) pair. After this occurs, only combinations of qqq or of $q\bar{q}$ can emerge from the system (*see* Figs. 3 and 4). The idea that quarks cannot be separated and that only combinations of them can be seen is called confinement. Confinement may be a new solution to the age-old question of the divisibility of matter.

**Color and flavor.** Particles have two other kinds of properties. Although they have no counterparts in the everyday world, these properties are given familiar names somewhat analogous to their behavior—color and flavor. The names have a precise technical meaning quite unrelated to the everyday definition.

Color is to the strong force that binds quarks as electric charge is to the electromagnetic force. Electrically charged particles make electric and magnetic fields and exchange photons. Quarks carry color charge (as well as electrical charge) and exchange gluons; each quark can have three colors, and the color symmetry is an SU(3) one. Gluons also carry color charge, while photons do not carry electric charge; thus, the color force is different from (and more complicated than) the electrical force. The colored gluons transmit the strong force and interact with anything that carries color charge. All familiar hadrons are made either of three quarks that can combine their three possible

colors so as to make a colorless particle (proton, neutron) or of quark plus antiquark that can again make a colorless object (pion). The rules for combining colors do not allow other ways of making a colorless object.

Flavor seems to be quite a different property from color, though there could be deeper similarities. At present six kinds of leptons (that is, six lepton flavors) and six kinds of quarks (six quark flavors) are known. Three of the lepton flavors have the electric charge ‾1. The lightest is the familiar electron. The next heaviest is the muon (written with a Greek letter $\mu$), and the heaviest is the tau (Greek $\tau$). Apart from the mass and obvious effects associated with mass, the $\mu$ and the $\tau$ behave like electrons with just one difference—they have a hidden attribute that does not allow them to turn into electrons by emitting energy (as might be expected if they were just heavy electrons). Thus they are a different flavor. The e, $\mu$, and $\tau$ each have a neutrino of their own—three flavors of neutrino. Experiments have determined so far that the three kinds of neutrino do not differ, though an electron neutrino always produces an electron when it interacts, never a muon or tau, and a muon neutrino always produces a muon when it interacts, never an electron or a tau. (The tau neutrino has not yet been explicitly detected experimentally, but there is indirect evidence for its existence.)

**Properties of Bosons**

| Boson | Spin | Electric Charge | Mass | Interact with Color? | Interact with Electric Charge? | Change Flavor? | Role |
|---|---|---|---|---|---|---|---|
| $\gamma$ | 1 | 0 | 0 | no | yes | no | Transmits electro-magnetic force |
| 8 gluons | 1 | 0 | 0 | yes | no | no | Transmits strong force |
| W+ | 1 | 1 | about 80 | no | yes | yes | Transmits weak force |
| W− | 1 | −1 | about 80 | no | yes | yes | Transmits weak force |
| Z⁰ | 1 | 0 | about 90 | no | yes | no | Transmits weak force |
| X | 1 | $4/3$ | about $10^{15}$ | yes | yes | yes | Arises in Grand Unified Theories and is expected to mediate the decay of the proton |
| Y | 1 | $-1/3$ | about $10^{15}$ | yes | yes | yes | |

*Table B: Bosons transmit the forces known in nature and also bind quarks and leptons together to make the stages of matter. The photon and gluon have been observed; the effects of the vector mesons ($W^+$, $W^-$, and $Z^0$) have been seen. The X and Y are predicted by the Grand Unified Theories. The attributes color and flavor are properties that particles have, described by familiar words that are given precise technical meanings in particle physics (see text). The masses of the particles vary over a wide range and are expressed relative to the mass of a proton, which serves as a convenient unit. The electric charges are also expressed relative to that of the proton.*

There is one simplification. The six flavors can be grouped into three pairs, called doublets:

$$\binom{\nu_e}{e}, \quad \binom{\nu_\mu}{\mu}, \quad \binom{\nu_\tau}{\tau},$$

where $\nu$ is the Greek letter for neutrino and the subscript identifies the electron neutrino ($\nu_e$), and so on. The three doublets, as described above, seem to have essentially identical properties. The weak interactions connect the top and bottom members of each doublet, but no known interaction connects one doublet to another.

The situation is the same for quarks. There are three quark flavors of electric charge $2/3$ and three of electric charge $-1/3$. The lightest ones are called u and d quarks, for up and down—the up–and–down states of a doublet. The next one found was called s for strange; its discovery was associated with some new particles that behaved in strange ways. The s-quark is in a doublet with the charmed quark (c-quark). It was the discovery in 1974 of the charmed quark, with the properties expected by theorists, that overwhelmingly convinced most particle physicists that the current theories about particles and their interactions were basically correct. The discovery of the charmed baryon was achieved with the help of the bubble chamber and special photographic methods. The third doublet consists of the t- and b-quarks for top and bottom. The b-quark was found in 1977; the t-quark was finally discovered in 1995, but even before that there was strong indirect evidence for its existence (in the theory of weak interactions, the b-quark would behave

differently if there were no t-quark). The discovery of the massive t-quark had to wait on the development of sufficiently powerful accelerators.

Thus, the quarks also come in three doublets:

$$\binom{u}{d}, \quad \binom{c}{s}, \quad \binom{t}{b}.$$

Again the weak interactions connect the two members of each doublet, but there are no known interactions that connect one doublet to another among states of the same electric charge. The properties of bosons are summarized in Table B.

One of the major problems to be solved in particle physics is why the quarks and leptons both seem to come in three families with identical behavior. The universe seems to be constructed from only u, d, e, and $\nu_e$. All other states are unstable particles that decay in a tiny fraction of a second into some combination of u, d, e, and $\nu_e$. The members of the second and third doublets are produced at accelerators and occasionally in a cosmic-ray collision, live for a short time, and decay back to u, d, e, and $\nu_e$. At present no one understands why heavy quarks and leptons exist or whether still heavier ones will be found.

**Evidence of a New Particle**

In 1997 physicists reported the discovery of a rare particle, the exotic meson. The discovery was the result of a collaboration by 51 physicists from laboratories around the world. Part of the reason for the excitement over the new discovery was that the exotic meson might contain a previously unencountered combination of quarks and gluons.

In 1994 an international team of physicists head-quartered at Brookhaven National Laboratory in New York State began a series of experiments in an attempt to create the theorized exotic particle. The physicists created the particle by colliding a beam of high-energy pions into a target of protons in liquid hydrogen. The protons remain unchanged, but the pions were elevated to a higher energy state, forming a new type of particle. Out of approximately 1 billion collisions, roughly 47,000 showed signs of the creation of the short-lived exotic particle, which was called an eta meson.

The discovery of the new particle created a new puzzle to solve. When scientists predicted the existence of this meson, they proposed that the collision producing the particle would cause the gluons to vibrate at a unique frequency though the particle would still contain only a quark and antiquark. After a careful review of the data generated by the study, however, the physicists suspect that the new particle might contain an extra quark-antiquark pair, for a total of four quarks. This would make the eta meson the only known particle to contain more than three quarks.

### Unifying the Forces of Nature

If fundamental particles are to be understood clearly, the forces and interactions that the particles experience must also be understood. Through patient experimentation and observation, scientists slowly began to understand these forces and interactions. In the 18th century, three basic phenomena were known: gravity (G), electricity (E), and magnetism (M). In the first half of the 19th century, the British physicists Michael Faraday and James Clerk Maxwell unified the theories of electricity and magnetism into one basic theory, electromagnetism (EM). At the end of the 19th century, weak interactions (WI) were discovered, and a little later the nuclear force (N) was detected. In about 1970 it was shown that the electromagnetic and weak interactions could be unified into one basic interaction, the electroweak (EW) force. Two American physicists, Sheldon Glashow and Steven Weinberg, and the Pakistani physicist Abdus Salam received the 1979 Nobel prize in physics for their work on the electroweak theory.

The electroweak theory is based on the symmetry group, SU(2) (*see* the discussion of symmetries above). The two objects on which the symmetry acts are the two members of each quark or lepton doublet. Thus the u- and d-quarks, or the electron and the neutrino, are not to be thought of as separate states but as related objects, connected by interactions (which are like rotations in the imaginary space of this symmetry). Since the states that are related have different electric charges, the electromagnetic interactions must be involved, and the weak interactions that cause the transitions u↔d, e$\nu_e$ become unified with the electromagnetic interactions.

At the same time, it became understood that the strongest force is the one between quarks and gluons (S); that force was actually discovered and is actively being studied by physicists and other scientists in an effort to better understand how it works. Scientists have so far discovered that the nuclear force is residual (the nuclear force between protons and neutrons is related to the basic strong force between quarks and gluons in much the same way as the force that makes molecules from atoms is related to the basic electromagnetic force that binds electrons and nuclei into atoms). The full relativistic quantum theory of electromagnetism has come to be known as quantum electrodynamics, and the full relativistic quantum theory of the strong (color) interaction has come to be known as quantum chromodynamics.

The hope of scientists over the ages has been that all basic forces might be understood in terms of one unifying principle. Similarly, it is hoped that the basic kinds of particles are related. In 1974 Salam and, independently, Glashow suggested theories in which the strong, the weak, and the electromagnetic forces were all unified. In addition, quarks and leptons can be grouped together as the basic objects of another symmetry—in the version of Glashow, the three colors of a d-quark plus the electron and the electron neutrino form the five basic objects that are acted on by an SU(5) symmetry. These summations have been dubbed the Unified Field Theory, or the Grand Unified Theory. It is not yet clear whether the Unified Field Theory will be proved true.

In the 1980s and 1990s another unified theory, called the superstring theory (or theory of everything), gained popularity among physicists. It attempted to unify the theory of gravity with the theories of other fundamental forces. The theory regards subatomic particles, such as quarks, leptons, and bosons, as long strings instead of as points in space. These strings are so small that if one billion trillion trillion of them were laid end to end they would be only 0.4 inch (1 centimeter) long. Because of these extremely small measurements and other factors, however, the theory has been criticized as unverifiable by ordinary testing methods. (*See also* Matter.)

The problem of incorporating all known natural forces into a single unified physical theory is being pursued. Although some progress has been made, the ultimate success may require a fundamental revision of the prevailing view of space, time, and even quantum theory. (*See also* Chemistry; Light; Nuclear Energy; Nuclear Physics; Physics; Unified Field Theory.)

---

**FURTHER RESOURCES FOR ATOMIC PARTICLES**

**Atkins, P.W.** Atoms, Electrons and Change (Scientific American Library, 1993).

**Berger, Melvin.** Our Atomic World (Watts, 1989).

**Dandel, Raymond.** The Realm of Molecules (McGraw, 1992).

**Haken, C., and Wolf, H.C.** The Physics of Atoms and Quanta: Introduction to Experiments and Theory, 3rd. ed (Springer-Verlag, 1993).

**Kullander, Sven, and Larsson, Borje.** Out of Sight! From Quarks to Living Cells (Cambridge Univ. Press, 1993).

**Weinberg, Steven.** The Discovery of Subatomic Particles (Scientific American Library, 1993).

**ATTILA** (406?–453). Of all the barbarian leaders who attacked the Roman Empire, none is more famous than Attila the Hun. In western Europe his ferocity earned him the nickname Scourge of God. He was king of the Huns from 434 until his death in 453. He shared power temporarily with his elder brother, Bleda, whom he murdered in about 445.

By the 5th century the Huns ruled a large empire. The Western Roman Empire had almost totally disintegrated. The Eastern, or Byzantine, Empire, which had its capital at Constantinople (now Istanbul, Turkey), was much stronger than its counterpart to the west. But it had extended its boundaries over too wide an area to stop an invasion at any one point. To keep from being attacked, the Eastern emperor paid an annual tribute to the Huns. The emperor's failure to keep up payments led Attila to invade the Byzantine Empire in two campaigns, in 441–443 and in 447–449. Much of what is now the Balkan region was devastated. The empire lost territory and had to pay a larger tribute.

In 450 Attila claimed Honoria, sister of the Western emperor, Valentinian III, as his wife. As a dowry he expected half of the Western Empire. To enforce this claim, Attila invaded Gaul (France) in 451. He was defeated and forced to withdraw. In 452 he overran much of northern Italy but turned back before attacking Rome. His next plan was to lead another invasion of the Byzantine Empire, but he died suddenly after celebrating the last of his marriages. He was succeeded by his sons, who divided his empire. (*See also* Byzantine Empire; Huns.)

**ATTLEE, Clement** (1883–1967). As British prime minister in the first six years after World War II, Clement Attlee presided over the transformation of the British Empire into the Commonwealth of Nations. He also helped organize Britain's postwar austerity program, the nationalization of British industry, and the beginning of the welfare state.

Clement Richard Attlee was born in London on Jan. 3, 1883. After graduating from Oxford he practiced law for a short time. His interest in social welfare led him to enter politics. He joined the socialist Fabian Society in 1907 and a year later became a member of the Labour party. After service in World War I he became mayor of the borough of Stepney in the East End of London. In 1922 he was elected to Parliament. After serving in the first two Labour governments, in 1924 and 1929–31, Attlee rose to the leadership of the party in 1935.

During World War II Attlee served in Winston Churchill's War Cabinet. In the 1945 elections Attlee's Labour party defeated Churchill's Conservatives. As prime minister, Attlee had to deal with the serious postwar problems that plagued Europe. His domestic policies brought about the socialization of Britain's economy and the creation of the National Health Service. He also led his country in granting independence to India, Ceylon (now Sri Lanka), and other portions of the British Empire.

The Conservative party won the elections of 1951, and Attlee resigned his office. In late 1955, after he gave up his Labour party membership, he was made an earl. His memoirs, 'As It Happened', were published in 1954. Attlee died on Oct. 8, 1967, in London.

**AUCKLAND, New Zealand.** The largest city and the major industrial and commercial port of New Zealand, Auckland is situated on an isthmus of the North Island that separates Waitemata and Manukau harbors. The port serves overseas and intercoastal shipping. The largest concentration of Maori (native New Zealand Polynesians) live in Auckland.

Major institutions of interest within the urban area include the War Memorial Museum, the Museum of Transport and Technology, the City Art Gallery, and Auckland University, which was founded in 1883. There are swimming and surfing beaches and several extinct volcanic cones. Among the many parks and reserves is One Tree Hill, which has an obelisk erected in tribute to the Maori by Sir John Logan Campbell, known as the Father of Auckland. The Waitakere Ranges, a native forest preserve, are near the city.

Auckland is a center of road and rail transportation and the site of New Zealand's leading international airport. The Harbour Bridge, opened in 1959, links the city with Devonport, the country's chief naval base and dockyard, and with the rapidly growing North Shore suburbs.

Principal exports include iron, steel, dairy products, and meat and hides. Petroleum, iron and steel products, sugar, wheat, and phosphates are imported.

*Queen Street is a major thoroughfare in the central business district of Auckland, New Zealand.*

© Robert Frerck—Odyssey Productions

There are numerous industries in the Auckland area, including engineering and metal trades, fishing, food processing, brewing, sugar refining, and boatbuilding. The city manufactures a variety of other products that include paint, glass, footwear, plastic, chemicals, cement, and fertilizer.

Auckland was established in 1840 by Gov. William Hobson as the capital of the British colonial government. It was named for George Eden, earl of Auckland, first lord of the admiralty, and, later, governor-general of India. Incorporated as a borough in 1851, Auckland remained the capital until it was replaced in that role by Wellington in 1865. Auckland was officially made a city in 1871. (*See also* New Zealand.) Population (1988 estimate), city, 149,500; metropolitan area, 911,700.

**AUDEN, W.H.** (1907–73). The eminent poet and man of letters W.H. Auden was regarded as a hero of the left in the 1930s. His poems, plays, and essays explored the realms of psychology, politics, and religion.

Wystan Hugh Auden was born in York, England, on Feb. 21, 1907. He studied to be a mining engineer, but by 1922 was determined to make poetry his career. From 1925 to 1928 he attended Oxford University, where he established a reputation as an outstanding young poet. After studying in Germany for a year, he worked as a schoolmaster in England and Scotland for five years.

Auden established his reputation with the poetry in 'Poems' (1930). His psychological insight was matched by his attacks on capitalism and totalitarianism in 'Look, Stranger!' (1936) and other works. He collaborated with Christopher Isherwood on plays including 'The Ascent of F6' (1936). In the mid-1930s Auden married Erika Mann, daughter of the German novelist Thomas Mann, in order to secure a British passport for her, but they never lived together. Auden moved to New York City in 1939 and became a United States citizen in 1946. In these years his commitment to Christianity deepened. He wrote the Christmas oratorio 'For the Time Being' (1944) and won a Pulitzer prize for the poem 'The Age of Anxiety' (1947). He spent much of his time in Italy and Austria and was a professor of poetry at Oxford from 1956 to 1961. In his later years Auden worked on opera libretti for several works, including Igor Stravinsky's 'Rake's Progress' (1951), while he was active as a poet, teacher, lecturer, and essayist. He died in Vienna, Austria, on Sept. 28, 1973.

**AUDIO RECORDING.** The storage of sound for duplication, audio recording is produced through mechanical, electromechanical, or electronic technology. The industry was pioneered in the United States, which is also the largest consumer of long-playing (LP) records, audiotapes, and compact discs (CDs). With steady advances in the recording equipment, disc and tape sales top 3 billion dollars annually.

The first phonographs, invented by Thomas Alva Edison in 1877, played tinfoil-wrapped cylinders.

Later inventors substituted wax. Emile Berliner's gramophone disc records, invented in 1887, made many improvements in Edison's invention possible—for example, easier mass production and enhanced fidelity. Lee De Forest invented the amplifying, three-element electron tube, called the audion, in 1907, and phonographs using amplifiers with one or more tubes appeared in the 1920s. De Forest also demonstrated sound-on-film talking movies as early as 1923. (*See also* De Forest; Edison; Motion Pictures.)

**Audio Recording Equipment**

Audio recordings, and the equipment used to make them and to play them, come in many forms. In the late 1940s manufacturers introduced phonograph discs that revolve at either 45 or 33⅓ revolutions per minute (rpm). Just as they made collections of 78-rpm (the old standard) discs nearly obsolete, CDs in turn replaced LPs in popularity in the late 1980s. In addition to the improved sound of CDs, they can store up to 80 minutes of recorded music on a side, while LPs offer only 60 or 70 minutes on two sides. (*See also* Compact Disc; Phonograph.)

Analog magnetic tape recorders are available in open-reel or cassette formats. Open-reel recorders feature greater fidelity and are easily edited. Cassettes, which were designed for more convenient storage and use, became a high-fidelity medium in about 1970. (*See also* Tape Recorder.)

Digital audiotape (DAT) is a refinement of videotape technology (*see* Video Recording). DAT recorders play cassettes that resemble, but are smaller than, analog audiocassettes. Because DAT technology is digital, it can provide fidelity of sound that is superior to recordings made for analog cassette recorders. Rerecordings of DAT tapes closely resemble the originals in quality, while analog duplicates suffer substantially degraded quality. Recording companies perceive the duplication advantage of DAT as a disadvantage. They believe the availability of excellent amateur-produced recordings would encourage piracy and drastically reduce sales of commercial recordings. (*See also* Electronics.)

**THE RECORDING INDUSTRY**

The recording industry plays an integral part in the music and motion picture branches of the entertainment industry. The techniques used to record sound in each medium are vastly different. Motion picture sound, for example, must be synchronized with the visual performances so it is transferred to film, rather than to discs or cassettes.

**Music Recording**

The two basic approaches to recording music today are the documentary-style and the studio-type recording. On-site equipment is most often used to record

....................................................................................

*This article was contributed by James T. Hawes, senior technical writer for Sentinel Computer Services, Inc.*

classical music and live concerts of popular music. Most rock musicians prefer to record their music in studios, where they can experiment freely, and other pop performers may rely upon electronic gimmicks to alter their sound.

**Documentary-style recording.** In this method, recording engineers set up portable equipment at the recording site. They may employ one or more microphones with or without a microphone mixer. Often they use simple two-, four-, or eight-track recording machines. With only two microphones positioned at 90- to 120-degree angles to the performers, engineers can record an entire orchestra.

Sometimes recording engineers separate the microphones with a screen made of special acoustical insulation in order to approximate the binaural (two-eared) experience of human hearing. Sound personnel may mount a microphone on a tall stand to pick up the airborne waves and the wall-conducted waves. The opposite effect is obtained by placing a microphone on a low tripod. The objective is to permit only one sound path to the microphone, otherwise echoes tend to cloud the original signal.

**Studio recording.** The central components in this kind of recording are tracks—narrow, parallel strips that run the length of the surface of audiotape. A multitrack recorder can tape each track separately. That way, a singer might record on one track one night, the guitarist on another the next night, and the percussionist on still another the third night. The recording engineer can play back the individual tracks at whatever volume is desired for each. The volume of one track does not affect that of any other track. The engineer can also re-equalize (change the ratio of high sounds to low and middle sounds) one track at a time or create a wholly new track by mixing two of the original tracks. In fact, multitrack recording and mixing are routine procedures that allow all kinds of enhancement after the original recording dates.

Studio recording involves the use of several pieces of equipment: a special, acoustically enhanced recording environment (the studio itself); a microphone for each recording voice and acoustic musical instrument; line preamplifiers for electronic instruments; a multitrack mixing console that permits the engineer to adjust the volume of each input separately and a multitrack recorder to store the output signal from the console. This recorder might be digital or analog. For music recording it usually has eight or more tracks; however, many studios are equipped with 24- and 48-track machines.

## Recording for Motion Pictures

Documentary films may be shot with "single-system" or sound-on-film (SOF) cameras that record a magnetic or optical track running parallel to the picture area. Editing such film is difficult, however, and the film's sound quality is inferior. Inventors solved these problems with a technique called double-system sound. Although the sound tape recorder and film camera are separate pieces of equipment, an electronic synchronization signal assures correspondence between the two during filming. Laboratory personnel copy the tape to magnetic film with the same proportions as the picture film. They may also add sound effects in the studio.

During editing picture and sound films are locked side-by-side into an editing console. When one film is cut by an editor, the others must be cut at the same place. If synchronization is lost, it can be regained by advancing one film or another. Back at the laboratory, the picture and sound are married to create a single film with a synchronous soundtrack. This film, called the release print, is what viewers see and hear on television or in the theater. It is equipped with either an optical or a magnetic soundtrack.

Optical soundtracks consist of one or more narrow stripes at the edge of the film. Viewers cannot see these tracks on the screen because they are outside the projected area of the film. There are two basic types of optical soundtracks—variable density and variable area. Many versions of each type are used.

A variable-density sound stripe can vary in color from opaque black to almost clear. An exciter lamp projects through this stripe onto a photoelectric pickup. Depending on the hue of the film, the light falling on the pickup changes in intensity. These changes cause the pickup to send a proportionate, varying current to a sound amplifier. The amplifier fortifies the signal and feeds it to speakers.

Variable-area stripes are composed of a clear center of variable area edged with opaque black. Width differences in the clear center determine the final differences in sound. An exciter lamp shines through the track onto a photoelectric pickup. Like the variable-density stripe, the variable-area stripe constantly alters the amount of light falling on the pickup. From this point on, the two techniques are identical.

A magnetic soundtrack is an iron oxide coating on the edge of the film. A tape head in the projector reads the track. While optical soundtracks are permanent, the magnetic track can be erased for rerecording.

**AUDUBON, John James** (1785–1851). The first lifelike drawings of birds were done by John James Audubon, who used crayons and watercolors to capture all the North American species known in the early 19th century. Audubon's sketches were so realistic because his models were live or freshly killed birds, rather than museum specimens, and he depicted them in natural positions—often in motion—and added authentic details of their habitats.

Some of Audubon's descendants claimed that he was the Lost Dauphin. (Born in the same year as Audubon, the young son of Louis XVI and Marie Antoinette of France reportedly was found dead in prison during the French Revolution, but many royalists believed that the real prince had been spirited away.) Audubon's own claim for a time was that he was born in New Orleans in 1780. Documents later uncovered have shown, however, that he was born with the last name Rabin on his French father's plantation at Les

Howard Jensen—SCALA/Art Resource

*Audubon's 'The Snowy Heron or White Egret' shows the bird now known as the American egret against a background of South Carolina rice fields.*

Cayes, St. Domingue (now Haiti), on April 26, 1785. His Creole mother died soon after his birth, and the child was sent to live near Nantes, France. Adopted by his own father, a naval officer, and his French wife, he was given the name Jean-Jacques Audubon when he was about 9 years old.

Obsessed with nature, young Audubon neglected his schoolwork to roam the French countryside—watching animals in the woods, sketching birds, and collecting specimens. In 1803 his father sent him to Mill Grove, his estate near Philadelphia, with the hope that he would become an American businessman. For Audubon it was a "blessed spot, where hunting, fishing, and drawing occupied my every moment." He made the first American bird-banding experiments there. The girl next door was Lucy Bakewell, whom he married in 1808. The couple moved to Kentucky, and for a decade Audubon tried a variety of occupations—clerk, merchant, miller, and French teacher. His businesses always failed because he deserted them for long periods to follow trails in the woods. Finally, in 1819, he was sent to jail for debt.

### 'Birds of America'

After his bankruptcy Audubon turned to drawing sidewalk portraits. By 1820 he was traveling by flatboat to New Orleans in pursuit of his dream of making life-size pictures of all the birds of America. On the trip down the Mississippi River he earned some of his traveling expenses by painting a portrait of the boat's captain and his wife. From the Kentucky ventures he had salvaged only his crayons, his gun, and his

drawings. Once rats attacked a box containing several hundred of his paintings and completely ruined them, but Audubon redid them all in three years.

In New Orleans, in order to spend even more time on his bird studies, Audubon abandoned all traditional means of earning a living. He supported himself by giving lessons in dancing, fencing, and the violin, and for a time he taught in the private school his wife established to provide for their two sons. By 1826 he had an enormous collection of life-size portraits of birds. Unable to find a publisher for his 'Birds of America' in the United States, he went to England. There he sold enough subscriptions to publish the work over the next dozen years. Although critics pointed out that his drawings were not quite accurate scientifically, subscribers in Great Britain and France were enthusiastic about them.

The original 'Birds of America', which appeared serially, is often called the elephant folio because each page was more than 3 feet (1 meter) long and 2 feet (0.6 meter) wide. The complete edition contained 435 hand-colored plates with 1,065 life-size figures of American birds in characteristic poses and surroundings. At the time the four volumes cost about a thousand dollars. The accompanying text, with descriptions of these birds, was prepared later in collaboration with William MacGillivray, who supplied the more scientific data. 'Ornithological Biography', published from 1831 to 1839 in a five-volume set, included some of Audubon's stories of life on the American frontier.

Audubon's last years were spent on his Hudson River estate (now known as Audubon Park), in what is now New York City. He worked at home on a smaller edition of his masterpiece and, in collaboration with the naturalist John Bachman, began 'The Viviparous Quadrupeds of North America'. He died on Jan. 27, 1851, and the drawings for the work (published 1842–54) were completed by his sons, Victor Gifford and John Woodhouse Audubon.

### The National Audubon Society

One of the oldest conservation organizations in the world, the National Audubon Society was formed in 1905. The society works in cooperation with the United States Fish and Wildlife Service, and it promotes the protection of wildlife, wildlife habitats, plants, soil, water, and forests. Its educational program includes summer ecology camps for teachers and youth leaders, school clubs for children, and the Audubon Expedition Institute for teenagers and adults. The society conducts research programs to aid such endangered species as the bald eagle, whooping crane, eastern timber wolf, and bog turtle.

The society supports a force of wardens for its vast wildlife sanctuaries. Publications include an annual *Wildlife Report* and the bimonthlies *American Birds*, *Audubon*, and *Audubon Activist*. *Audubon Adventures* is a bimonthly children's newspaper.

**AUGUST** *see* **CALENDAR; FESTIVALS AND HOLIDAYS.**

**AUGUSTA, Ga.** The river port of Augusta is one of Georgia's oldest and largest cities. It is located on the south bank of the Savannah River and serves the South as an agricultural and manufacturing center. A bridge connects the city to South Carolina, directly across the Savannah River. Savannah lies 110 miles (177 kilometers) southeast.

Augusta has wide, pleasant streets lined with magnolia trees. It is often called the Garden City of the South. From the center of Broad Street, in the downtown area, rises the tall Confederate monument. The city has many fine old mansions that were built in the early 19th century. Of interest are the First Presbyterian Church and its manse, where President Woodrow Wilson lived as a boy. Augusta is also the site of Augusta State College, the University of Georgia School of Medicine, chartered in 1828 as the Medical College of Georgia, and Paine College. Every April the Masters Invitational Golf Tournament is held at the Augusta National Golf Course.

Projects to control floods, improve navigation, and build power dams on the Savannah River promoted the city's industrial growth. The major industries include the manufacture of cotton textiles, food items, brick, paper products, and chemicals.

Augusta was founded in 1735 by James Oglethorpe (see Oglethorpe). It was named for the princess of Wales, the mother of King George III. This river city served as an Indian fur-trading post, then as a military outpost for Savannah. During the American Revolution the city was captured by the British.

Between 1786 and 1795 Augusta was the state capital. After cotton became the chief crop of the area, bales were shipped to Savannah by raft and steamboat. A railroad to Savannah began operating in 1854. The United States arsenal in Augusta was taken by the Confederates during the American Civil War, and the city became the South's principal supplier of munitions. Augusta College now occupies this property. The city has a mayor-council form of government. (See also Georgia.) Population (1990 census), 44,639.

**AUGUSTA, Me.** Maine's capital is Augusta. It occupies terraced banks on both sides of the Kennebec River in west-central Maine, about 40 miles (64 kilometers) from the Atlantic Ocean. Adjoining the larger, west-bank section is its sister city, Hallowell.

Near the Capitol is the executive mansion. It was once the home of James G. Blaine, an unsuccessful presidential candidate in 1884. A 2,100-foot (640-meter) bridge, built in 1950, spans the Kennebec River in the heart of the city. In 1965 a branch of the University of Maine was established in Augusta. The city is also the site of the Fort Western Museum.

The processing of farm and forest products and state government operations have become the economic mainstays of both Augusta and Hallowell. Manufactures include paper, textiles, food products, and shoes. With the Belgrade chain of lakes 15 miles (24 kilometers) to the north and the Kennebec River flowing south to the Atlantic, Augusta is also one of Maine's vacation centers.

In 1628 the Plymouth Colony established a fur-trading post on the Augusta site. This post was abandoned in the 1660s. The first permanent settlement was made in 1754 with the building of Fort Western on the east bank. By 1762 some 30 settlers had built seven log huts outside the walls of the fort. A new settlement was also started on the west bank, about 2½ miles (4 kilometers) to the south. In 1771 the two villages asked that they be jointly incorporated under the name of the Town of Hallowell.

Lumber and shingles were early products. These, along with fish and furs, were shipped in Hallowell sloops as far as the West Indies. By the end of the American Revolution, the upper village had extended to the river's west bank and had established a ferry. In 1790 the two villages had five sawmills, two gristmills, a bakehouse, and two slaughterhouses.

Rivalry between the two sections of Hallowell flared in 1796 when Massachusetts gave the upper village aid in bridging the Kennebec. The villages separated, and the lower kept the name of Hallowell. The upper village, incorporated as Harrington in 1797, changed its name to Augusta soon after.

In 1827 Augusta was selected as Maine's capital. The granite State House, completed in 1832, was designed by Charles Bulfinch. It was remodeled and enlarged in 1909 and 1910. In 1837 a dam was built across the Kennebec, and a little later a cotton textile plant was added to the city's industries. Augusta was incorporated as a city in 1849 and has a council-manager form of government. (See also Maine.) Population (1990 census), 21,325.

**AUGUSTINE OF CANTERBURY** (died 604?). The founder of the Christian church in England and the first archbishop of Canterbury was a monk named Augustine. Known as the Apostle of the English, he was responsible for the conversion of millions of people to Christianity.

Of his early life nothing is known. He was prior of the Benedictine monastery of St. Andrew in Rome when Pope Gregory I chose him to lead a missionary group of 40 monks going to England. The entourage arrived in the spring of 597 and was well received by King Ethelbert I, whose wife was already a Christian. Ethelbert was soon baptized, which encouraged many of his subjects to be converted. Reportedly thousands were baptized on Christmas Day 597. Augustine sent a report of his remarkable progress to the pope, and Gregory responded by dispatching more missionaries to help with the work.

Augustine was consecrated bishop of the English church in the fall of 597 and made his headquarters at Canterbury in a church provided by the king. He founded Christ Church as his cathedral and started the monastery of Sts. Peter and Paul (later changed to St. Augustine's). Canterbury became the primary see, or seat of authority, for the church in England, a position it has maintained to the present time (*see* Anglican Communion).

Augustine consecrated 12 more bishops and sent them to other districts to carry on the work of preaching and conversion. During the next 90 years most of England was converted by his followers. His only failure to win converts was in Wales, where Christianity antedated his arrival. These churches refused to accept the authority of the pope in Rome and would not cooperate with Augustine in unification with the churches he was founding.

Augustine died in about 604, a few years after he was made archbishop. His feast day is celebrated on May 26 in England.

**AUGUSTINE OF HIPPO** (354–430). The bishop of Hippo in Roman Africa for 35 years, St. Augustine lived during the decline of Roman civilization on that continent. Considered the greatest of the Fathers of the Church in the West, he helped form Christian theology (*see* Fathers of the Church).

Augustine was born Aurelius Augustinus on Nov. 13, 354, at Tagaste in the Roman province of Numidia (now Souk-Ahras in Algeria). Although his mother, St. Monica, was a devout Christian, he was not baptized in infancy. His father, Patricius, a wealthy landowner, was a pagan.

In his 'Confessions' Augustine wrote seven chapters about an incident in his early life—stealing pears from a neighbor's tree. This sin troubled him for the rest of his life. He also confessed to immoral behavior at the University of Carthage, where he was sent at the age of 16.

Augustine remained in Carthage, teaching rhetoric, until he was 29. Then he went to Rome, taking with him his mistress and his son, Adeodatus. His religion at this time was Manichaeism, which combined Christianity with Zoroastrian elements.

By 386 Augustine was teaching in Milan, where his mother joined him. He came under the influence of the city's great bishop, St. Ambrose, who baptized Augustine and Adeodatus on the following Easter.

From this time Augustine lived as an ascetic. He returned to Africa and spent three years with friends on his family's estate. He was ordained a priest and five years later, in 396, was consecrated a bishop. He spent the remainder of his life in Hippo (now Annaba, Algeria) with his clergy, encouraging the formation of religious communities. Augustine, who was ill when the Vandals besieged Hippo, died on Aug. 28, 430, before the town was taken.

Augustine's most widely read book is 'Confessions', a vivid account of his early life and religious development. 'The City of God' was written after 410, when

Alinari—Art Resource

*St. Augustine of Hippo, painted by Botticelli in 1480*

Rome fell to the barbarians. The aim of this book was to restore confidence in the Christian church, which Augustine said would take the place of the earthly city of Rome. During the Middle Ages the book gave strong support to the theory that the church was above the state. Augustine's writings on communal life form the 'Rule of St. Augustine', the basis of many religious orders.

**AUGUSTUS** (63 BC–AD 14). The first emperor of Rome was Augustus. During his long reign, which began in 27 BC during the Golden Age of Latin literature, the Roman world also entered a splendid era of civil peace and prosperity.

Augustus was born Gaius Octavius near Rome on Sept. 23, 63 BC. After Julius Caesar, his great-uncle, adopted him and made him his heir, he was known as Gaius Julius Caesar Octavianus, or Octavian. When Caesar was assassinated in 44 BC, Octavian, then 18, was living in Illyria, across the Adriatic. A letter from his mother warned him to flee eastward. Instead, he hurried to Rome. In the power struggle that followed Caesar's death, his old soldiers rallied to Octavian. The youth also won the support of the Roman senate. Mark Antony and Lepidus, his chief rivals, were forced to come to terms with him. Together they formed a triumvirate (government by three). At Philippi, in 42 BC, they defeated the republican army, headed by Brutus and Cassius. Lepidus was later stripped of his power. Antony and Octavian then divided the Roman world between them, with Octavian supreme in Italy and the West.

Antony took over the eastern provinces but neglected them to spend time at the court of the Egyptian queen, Cleopatra, in Alexandria. Octavian got the Roman senate to declare war on Egypt and won a decisive victory in the naval battle of Actium in 31 BC. Antony and Cleopatra escaped to Alexandria. The next year Octavian defeated Antony again in Egypt. Antony and Cleopatra committed suicide. Egypt was annexed to Rome, and Octavian returned to Rome in triumph. (*See also* Antony; Cleopatra.)

The battle of Actium made Octavian master of Rome and its provinces. He kept up a show of republican government, with himself as first citizen (*princeps civitatis*). However, historians consider the date 31 BC to mark the end of the Roman Republic and the beginning of the Roman Empire. In 27 BC the senate conferred on Octavian the title Augustus (the exalted or sacred one), implying he was more than a man but not quite a god. Later he was acclaimed *Pater Patriae* (father of his country).

After a series of victories, the expansion of Augustus' empire was stopped at the Rhine River by the Germans' defeat of the Roman general Varus in AD 9. From this time Augustus concentrated on domestic problems and the reform of the army. The political system he established endured essentially without change for three centuries. He did so much to beautify Rome that it was said he found a city of brick and left a city of marble. He also founded cities in the provinces, encouraged agriculture, promoted learning, and patronized the arts. The great writers Virgil, Horace, Livy, and Ovid flourished in this Augustan age—a term since used to describe periods of great literary achievement in modern nations (*see* Latin Literature). Although he was never in good health, Augustus' will helped him to survive. After his death, on Aug. 19, AD 14, he was deified. He was succeeded by his adopted son, Tiberius. (*See also* Caesar; Roman Empire; Tiberius.)

**AUK, MURRE, AND PUFFIN.** The seabirds of the family Alcidae nest on the barren islands of the Arctic Sea and on the islands off the far northern coasts of North America, Europe, and Asia. In North America a few kinds nest as far south as northern California and Maine. In the winter they move southward to central California and Long Island.

All members of the family live on fish and other marine life. They are expert swimmers and divers and use their short wings to help propel them underwater. Because of their life in icy waters their plumage is thick, and it is used to make clothing.

The birds are clumsy on land. Their legs are set far back on the body, giving them an awkward waddle. They perch on the flat of the foot instead of on the toes, as most birds do. This gives them the odd appearance of being seated in an upright position. All have black and white plumage, odd bills, quaint crests, and other unusual characteristics.

The birds breed in large colonies on rocky cliffs. They do not build nests. The female lays a single egg in a depression or crevice of the rock. Both parents take turns sitting on the egg until it is hatched.

### Species of Auks and Murres

The razor-billed auk breeds in the North Atlantic and winters from Canada to Long Island. It is about 16½ inches (42 centimeters) long. The large, hooked bill, with a razor-sharp tip, is flattened sideways. Auklets are birds of the Pacific coast. They are about 9 inches (23 centimeters) long. The crested auklet has a beautiful crest of 12 to 20 slender black plumes that curve forward over the bill and a line of white feathers that curve downward and backward from each eye. The rhinoceros auklet has a horn at the base of the bill during the breeding season.

*The crested auklet, or sea sparrow (left), breeds mainly on islands in the Bering Sea but winters as far south as Mexico. The tufted puffin (center) has straw-colored plumes behind the eyes. The habitat of the pigeon guillemot (top right) ranges from the North Pacific to California, and the common murre (bottom right) from the Arctic to Portugal and Korea.*

Murres look like ducks, but murres may be distinguished by the short, thick neck and the pointed bill. Different species are found on both coasts. There are large rookeries of murres on the Farallon Islands of California. The murrelets are Pacific coast birds.

### Puffins, Guillemots, and Dovekies

The puffin, also called the sea parrot or bottlenose, is one of the world's oddest looking birds. The great triangular hooked beak, which is nearly as large as the head, is colored dull yellow at the base, grayish blue in the middle, and vermilion at the end. At each corner of the mouth is an orange circle. The face is white, with grayish blue markings around the eye that make it look like the face of a circus clown. The Atlantic puffin and the large-billed puffin are found on the East coast of North America. The tufted puffin of the West coast has a long crest of yellow feathers over each eye.

Another member of the Alcidae family is the guillemot. The bird is all black except for a large white wing patch. The legs and inside of the mouth are bright red in color. Unlike most of the Alcidae, it lays two or three eggs. In England murres are known as guillemots. The little dovekie, or sea dove, is about 8 inches (20 centimeters) long.

### The Extinct Great Auk

Two centuries ago the great auk was found by the millions on the shores and islands of Northern Europe and North America. Today it is extinct. The last one was seen in 1844. The great auk could neither fly nor run and was easily killed with a club. Its eggs and flesh and its feathered skin were sought by humans. When the birds came to shore to nest, hunters killed them by the thousands.

The great auk had a thick gooselike body about 2 feet (0.6 meter) long. The short black wings, folded against the white vest, looked like small arms.

The scientific name of the razor-billed auk is *Alca torda;* of the great auk, *Pinguinus impennis;* of the murre, *Uria aalge;* of the dovekie (or sea dove), *Alle alle;* of the black guillemot, *Cepphus grylle;* of the Atlantic puffin, *Fratercula arctica;* of the tufted puffin, *Lunda cirrhata;* of the rhinoceros auklet, *Cerorhinea monocerata;* and of the marbled murrelet, *Brachyramphus marmoratus.*

**AURANGZEB** (1618–1707). In the 200-year history of India's Mughal Empire, which was founded in 1530, Aurangzeb was the last great ruler. A warrior-states-man, he was also a zealous follower of the religion of Islam. His fanatic intolerance of other religions gave rise to tensions that eventually led to the dissolution of the empire after his death.

Born on Nov. 3, 1618, Aurangzeb was the son of the emperor Shah Jahan (*see* Shah Jahan). His given name was Muhi-ud-Din Muhammad. Early in life he showed military and administrative abilities and was given a number of troop commands by his father. When Shah Jahan became ill in 1657, Aurangzeb defeated his brothers in the war of succession that followed. His father, meanwhile, was confined to the palace from 1658 until his death in 1666.

Aurangzeb crowned himself emperor in 1658, with the title *Alamgir* (world holder). His reign fell into two parts. Until 1680 he consolidated his power in northern India by war and shrewd politics. He patterned himself after his great-grandfather, Akbar, by reconciling his enemies and placing them in his service (*see* Akbar). Much of the second half of his reign was spent trying to subdue rebellions in the south of India. His wars exhausted the imperial treasury, and he began to lose control of northern India.

The most unfortunate aspect of his reign was his severe persecution of the majority Hindu population. His attempt to force Islam on the people weakened his whole kingdom. Aurangzeb died on March 3, 1707. The failure of his successors to cope with the problems he had created led to the downfall of the Mughal Empire. (*See also* Mughal Empire.)

**AURORA.** An aurora is a display of colored light in the night sky that occurs primarily in high latitudes of both hemispheres. Auroras in the Northern Hemisphere are called the northern lights, or aurora borealis. In the United States they are most frequent and spectacular in Alaska and other Northern states. They are seen approximately 25 times a year. In the Southern Hemisphere auroras are called the southern lights, or aurora australis.

The aurora is usually white with a greenish tinge but may take on a yellowish or reddish cast. Vertical rays, like searchlight beams, are common. In the beautiful corona form of aurora, rays seem to meet overhead in a starlike shape. In the spectacular flame type, tonguelike rays ripple upward. Vertical rays rising from curving bands are called draperies.

Auroras appear when highly charged particles from sunspots and solar flares excite the thin gases of the upper atmosphere and make them glow. Displays are most frequent in spring and fall because the Earth is then most nearly in line with zones of the sun where sunspots are large and frequent. However, auroras may be most frequent during winter in certain areas.

The particles from the sun are deflected by the Earth's magnetic field toward the geomagnetic poles. (These poles mark the axis of the Earth's magnetic field and are not the same as the magnetic poles, which mark points at which lines of magnetic force are vertical.) The particles then collide with oxygen and nitrogen atoms, knocking away electrons to leave ions in excited states. These ions emit radiation at various wavelengths, creating the colors of the aurora.

In the spring of 1989, astronomers across the Northern Hemisphere as far south as southern California, Florida, and Arizona observed a series of spectacular auroras. Especially prominent were the auroras observed in the months of March (auroras which appeared unusually red) and May (auroras which consisted of arcs, rays, and sheets of greenish light). (*See also* Astronomy; Atmosphere; Sun.)

**AUSTEN, Jane** (1775–1817). Through her portrayals of ordinary people in everyday life Jane Austen gave the genre of the novel its modern character. She began writing at an early age. At 15 she was writing plays and sketches for the amusement of her family, and by the time she was 21 she had begun to write novels that are among the finest in English literature.

Jane Austen was born on Dec. 16, 1775, in the parsonage of Steventon, a village in Hampshire, England. She had six brothers and one sister. Her father, the Reverend George Austen, was a rector of the village. Although she and her sister briefly attended several different schools, Jane was educated mainly by her father, who taught his own children and several pupils who boarded with the family.

Her father retired when Jane was 25. By that time her brothers, two of whom later became admirals, had careers and families of their own. Jane, her sister Cassandra, and their parents went to live in Bath. After the father's death in 1805, the family lived temporarily in Southampton before finally settling in Chawton.

All of Jane Austen's novels are love stories. However, neither Jane nor her sister ever married. There are hints of two or three romances in Jane's life, but little is known about them, for Cassandra destroyed all letters of a personal nature after Jane's death. The brothers had large families, and Jane was a favorite with her nephews and nieces.

Jane Austen wrote two novels before she was 22. These she later revised and published as 'Sense and Sensibility' (1811) and 'Pride and Prejudice' (1813). She completed her third novel, 'Northanger Abbey', when she was 27 or 28, but it did not appear in print until after her death. She wrote three more novels in her late 30s: 'Mansfield Park' (1814), 'Emma' (1816), and 'Persuasion' (published together with 'Northanger Abbey' in 1818).

She wrote of the world she knew. Her novels portray the lives of the gentry and clergy of rural England, and they take place in the country villages and neighborhoods, with an occasional visit to Bath and London. Her world was small, but she saw it clearly and portrayed it with wit and detachment. She described her writing as "the little bit (two inches wide) of ivory on which I work with so fine a brush, as produces little effect after much labor."

She died on July 18, 1817, after a long illness. She spent the last weeks of her life in Winchester, near her physician, and is buried in the cathedral there.

**AUSTIN, Stephen Fuller** (1793–1836). Often called the father of Texas, Stephen F. Austin was responsible for settling thousands of American colonists in what was still part of Mexico. He also played a large role in the diplomatic activities that preceded Texan independence.

Stephen Fuller Austin was born on Nov. 3, 1793, in Austinville, Va. When Stephen was 5 years old, the Austin family moved to Missouri. He later attended an academy in Connecticut and Transylvania University in Kentucky.

After losing his wealth in the panic of 1819 Austin's father decided to reestablish himself by bringing American families into Texas. He died soon afterward, and Stephen Austin took over the task. In 1821 Stephen picked a site on the Brazos River for the first settlement. During the next ten years he brought more than 5,000 settlers into Texas.

In 1833 Austin journeyed to Mexico City with the colonists' petition for a separate state government. Various difficulties led him to write the Texans not to wait for approval but to go ahead with their plans for a separate government. This letter was intercepted, and Austin was imprisoned until 1835.

Later that year, when Texas started to fight for independence, Austin was made the commander of the volunteer army. He left the army to win recruits and financial support in the United States. After independence had been won in 1836, he was defeated for the presidency of the new republic by Gen. Sam Houston. Houston appointed him secretary of state. Austin's health was broken, however, and he died on Dec. 27, 1836. The Texas republic's capital (now the state capital) was named in his honor. (*See also* Texas; Austin, Tex.)

**AUSTIN, Tex.** The capital of Texas, Austin was named for Stephen F. Austin, one of the founders of the state (*see* Austin, Stephen F.). The city is located along a bend of the Colorado River, in the south-central part of the state.

In Austin, at the University of Texas, is the Lyndon Baines Johnson Library. Other schools are St. Edward's University, Huston-Tillotson College, Concordia Lutheran College, and Austin Community College. Museums are housed in the former residences of sculptor Elisabet Ney and writer O. Henry.

Caverns, springs, and unusual rock outcrops are features of recreational areas around a series of lakes formed by dams built by the Lower Colorado River Authority for flood control and hydroelectric power.

Austin is a research and development center for defense and consumer industries, including electronic and business equipment. Other industries include food processing, printing, and the manufacture of brick, tile and concrete, furniture, bus bodies, boats, and chemicals. Bergstrom Air Force Base is nearby.

The city originated as the village of Waterloo, which was chosen in 1839 as the site for the capital of the Republic of Texas and renamed in honor of Austin. The government was moved from Austin in 1842 because of the threat of a Mexican invasion, but it returned when Texas became a state in 1845. The city flourished after the arrival of the Houston and Texas Central Railroad in 1871.

Austin has a council-manager form of government. (*See also* Texas.) Population (1990 census), city, 465,622; metropolitan area, 781,572.

Craig Lamotte—Australian Picture Library

***Ayers Rock, known to the aborigines as Uluru, is in the southwestern part of Australia's Northern Territory. It rises to 1,143 feet (348 meters) and is 2.2 miles (3.5 kilometers) long by 1.5 miles (2.4 kilomters) wide and is thought to be the world's largest monolith.***

# AUSTRALIA

Wedged between the Indian and Pacific oceans, Australia lies south of the Eurasian landmass. It is an island continent and, like the island continent of Antarctica, it is located entirely in the Southern Hemisphere. Australia is also the only continent occupied entirely by a single nation. Tasmania, a much smaller island off the southeast coast, is also considered to be a part of the continent of Australia.

Australia is the smallest, flattest, most arid, and least populated of the inhabited continents. Its southern coasts are washed by the cold Antarctic Ocean—those portions of the Pacific, Atlantic, and Indian oceans encircling Antarctica—while Australia's northern coasts are separated from the archipelagoes of Southeast Asia by warm, shallow, tropical seas. Although Australia is a small continent, it is a large country: only Russia, Canada, the United States, China, and Brazil have larger areas. Of Australia's 17.7 million inhabitants, about 23 percent were born elsewhere, and 1.5 percent are of aboriginal descent. Over 86 percent of Australia's people live in cities, yet only 10 percent of its area is cultivated. Two thirds of the continent is desert or semidesert.

Australia has a diverse, technologically advanced industrial economy, very productive primary industries, and abundant mineral and other resources. It leads the world in wool production and coal exports, and its iron ore and bauxite mines also make significant contributions to world production. With a gross national product per capita of 17,070 dollars in 1992, Australia enjoys one of the world's highest standards of living, ranking sixteenth among the industrialized nations.

## PREVIEW

*The article Australia is divided into the following sections:*

*This article was contributed by Dr. Bruce Ryan, Professor of Geography at the University of Cincinnati.*

Australia began its political independence in 1901 as a remote European country near Asia. Since 1945, it has become increasingly an Asian country with European origins and culture. Politically, Australia may be variously described as an independent Western democracy, a liberal welfare state, a federal parliamentary democracy, or a constitutional monarchy. England's reigning monarch remains the head of state. Australia contains six states (New South Wales, Victoria, Queensland, South Australia, Western Australia, and Tasmania) and two internal territories (the Northern Territory and the Australian Capital Territory). Australia also administers seven external territories: Norfolk Island, the Coral Sea Islands Territory, the Cocos (Keeling) Islands, Christmas Island, Ashmore and Cartier Islands Territory, Heard and McDonald Islands, and the Australian Antarctic Territory—the latter covering 42 percent of that landmass (see Australian External Territories).

Australia claims sovereignty over three maritime zones around its coasts. Its territorial seas extend 3 nautical miles beyond the line of lowest tide. The Australian Fishing Zone extends 200 nautical miles beyond the coastal base line. Australia also claims its entire continental margin—approximating the shallow continental shelf—extending farther than 200 nautical miles in some northwestern coastal sections. Maritime delimitation agreements have been formalized with Indonesia, Papua New Guinea, the Solomon Islands, and France (regarding New Caledonia). Australia was one of the twelve original signatories to the Antarctic Treaty in 1959. This reserved the area south of 60° S. latitude for peaceful purposes and placed it under international management, while preserving the status quo with regard to territorial rights and claims.

Australia was a founding member of the United Nations and served four terms on its Security Council. It was also one of four founding members of the (formerly British) Commonwealth. It has been a partner in the ANZUS (Australia, New Zealand, and United States) Treaty since its inception in 1952, in the Organisation for Economic Cooperation and Development (OECD) since 1971, and in the Colombo Plan, the South Pacific Commission, and the South Pacific Forum. Australia ratified the Nuclear Non-Proliferation Treaty in 1973, and the Convention on the Law of the Sea in 1982. The Australian flag incorporates the Union Jack in the top left quarter, representing British colonial origins; the large seven-pointed Commonwealth Star below it, representing the federation of six states and other territories; and the Southern Cross constellation of five stars in the fly. The Blue Ensign places these symbols on a dark blue background, whereas the Red Ensign is reserved for merchant ships registered in Australia. The Australian coat of arms consists of a shield containing the badges of all six states. The coat of arms is supported on either side by a kangaroo and emu, the national fauna; swathed in golden wattle, the national flower; and surmounted by the Commonwealth Star. The national colors are green and gold. 'Advance Australia Fair' was adopted as the National Anthem in 1984, replacing 'God Save the Queen', which was designated as the Royal Anthem and played only during the monarch's presence. 'Waltzing Matilda', Australia's best-known song, was written in about 1895 by A.B. Paterson.

Australia Day is celebrated on January 26, commemorating the arrival of the First Fleet at Sydney Cove in 1788. Other public holidays observed throughout Australia include Anzac Day, April 25, to honor war veterans; Good Friday; Easter Monday; Queen's Birthday; Christmas Day; and Boxing Day (December 26). Different States observe Labour Day, or Eight-Hour Day; Bank Holiday; Proclamation Day, in South Australia; Foundation Day, in Western Australia; Remembrance Day (November 11); and Melbourne Cup Day, in Victoria, to permit attendance at Australia's richest and most popular horse race.

The school year extends from late January or early February into mid-December. Students attend class for about 120 days per year. Literacy stands at 99.5 percent of the population. The summer months are December through February. Australia has three standard time zones. The eastern states are ten hours ahead of Greenwich (15 hours ahead of New York). South Australia, the Northern Territory, and the city of Broken Hill are 30 minutes behind the eastern states, which are two hours ahead of Western Australia. Conversion to the metric system was completed by 1981, and decimal currency—dollars and cents—replaced pounds, shillings, and pence in 1966.

The language of Australia is English, by common usage rather than law. There are an Australian accent and a vivid Australian slang. Western Australians are 'sand gropers', cattle duffers are 'poddy-dodgers', and a home run in cricket is a 'bewdy bottler.' There is no national costume, except the slouch hat, and no national motto, though "Advance Australia" is widely used.

## LAND

Australia is sometimes called "the land down under," because it lies in the Southern Hemisphere. It is almost halfway around the world from England, its mother country. The continent extends between 113° 9' and 153° 39' E. longitude and between 10° 41' and 43° 39' S. latitude. It is crossed by the Tropic of Capricorn, and a little more than one third of the continent is in the tropics.

### Geology and Landforms

Australia is the least mountainous and most level of the world's continents. Two thirds of its surface forms a plateau only 1,000 to 2,000 feet (300 to 600 meters) in elevation. The few peaks that exceed 6,500 feet (2,000 meters) would be considered foothills in any other continent. One may drive to the summit of Mount Kosciusko, at 7,310 feet (2,228 meters) the continent's highest point. Unlike North America and Europe, where spectacular tectonic and glacial activity created most landforms within the last 20,000 years, Australia's geological history dates back to the Precambrian, the

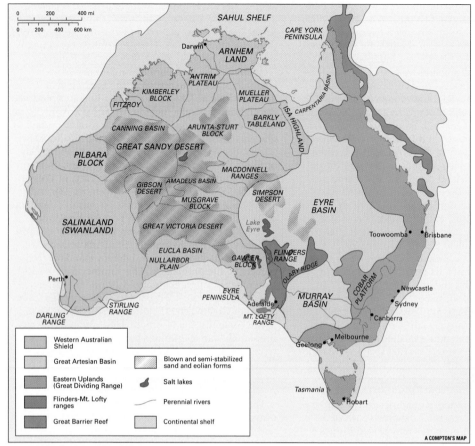

**Physiographic regions of Australia**

oldest era of all, over 600 million years ago. The dominant geological processes have been sedimentation in shallow seas that once inundated parts of the present continent, interspersed with long periods of erosion.

Australian fossils are among the oldest on Earth, revealing some algae and soft-bodied invertebrates dating from 3 billion years ago. These indicate that Australia was once joined to South America, Africa, India, and Antarctica to form the southern part of a supercontinent called Gondwanaland. This great landmass began to split and drift apart some 85 to 100 million years ago. The plate carrying Australia is still drifting northward by about 2¾ inches (7 centimeters) per year, having shifted the continent from subpolar latitudes where rain forest was almost universal to tropical and arid latitudes where dry eucalyptus forests and Asian vegetation, better adapted to the changing climate, could invade and displace much of the rain forest.

The Australian continent has remained separate for the past 40 million years, during which its distinctive flora and fauna evolved in isolation. Fossils of mammals are scarce but reveal giant wombats; goannas, a type of lizard; kangaroos; and mihirungs, flightless birds standing 10 feet (3 meters) high, the largest that ever lived on Earth. Rich sources of Australian fossils include the Gogo formation of Western Australia, where the internal anatomy of ancient fish can be studied; and the Riversleigh deposit in North Queensland, where giant pythons, carniverous kangaroos, and horned turtles have been discovered.

Australia has three major physiographic, or landform, areas: the Western Plateau, containing two thirds of the continent; the Eastern Highlands, extending from Cape York Peninsula (Queensland) to Victoria and Tasmania; and, between them, the Central Lowlands from the Gulf of Carpentaria to the Murray-Darling drainage basin. The first consists mainly of Precambrian rocks, with such uplifted blocks as the central Macdonnell Ranges. Desert dunefields cover its parched surface. The wetter, usually forest-covered highlands are a succession of separate tablelands, or plateaus, escarpments, and low ranges. Some were glaciated during the Pleistocene period—the Snowy Mountains and central Tasmania, for instance. Others are of volcanic origin—for example, the border ranges between Queensland and New South Wales.

Parts of the Central Lowlands drain sluggishly into the ocean along the Murray River and its tributaries. Most of the water dissipates and evaporates in such

*The dry riverbeds (top) in the Northern Territory's Macdonnell Ranges are among Australia's varied features. Salt lakes (bottom left) lie near Ravensthor, wheatlands, in Western Australia. Hardy Reef (bottom right) is a popular tourist destination in the central section of the Great Barrier Reef.*

*Twelve Apostles Rocks (top) are one of the striking features along the shore in Port Campbell National Park in southern Victoria. The Pinnacles Desert (bottom left) in Nambung National Park, north of Perth, Western Australia, has its own unusual formations made of limestone. Some of the pillars are 15 feet (4.5 meters) high. The Murchison River (bottom right) can be viewed through the Natural Bridge near the small town of Kalbarri in Western Australia.*

dry saline depressions as Lakes Eyre, Torrens, and Gairdner. Underlying these lowlands are the largest artesian basins in the world, from which bore water is pumped to sustain grazing animals in the arid zone. Representative caves include the intricate dripstone at Jenolan, New South Wales; the fossil bones at Mammoth Cave, Western Australia; and the flint

quarrying and aboriginal rock paintings, 20,000 years old, at Koonalda Cave, 250 feet (75 meters) below the Nullarbor Plain. The highest waterfall in Australia is Wollomombi, at 1,100 feet (335 meters), in northern New South Wales.

The Australian coastline extends for 22,826 miles (36,734 kilometers), including Tasmania, which has

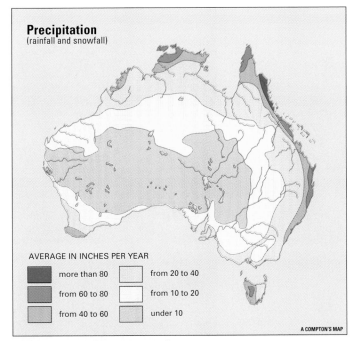

**Precipitation**
(rainfall and snowfall)

AVERAGE IN INCHES PER YEAR

more than 80

from 60 to 80

from 40 to 60

from 20 to 40

from 10 to 20

under 10

A COMPTON'S MAP

*Average annual precipitation in Australia*

1,990 miles (3,200 kilometers) of coastline. Warm, shallow tropical seas connect the northern coasts with Indonesia. More typical of the southern coasts are drowned river valleys (where rising sea levels followed the melting of polar ice) and alternations of cliffed headlands and sandy beaches. Huge sea stacks—jagged rocks—called the Twelve Apostles line the Victoria coast near Port Campbell.

The Great Barrier Reef is a spectacular ribbon of reefs and islands extending for 1,240 miles (2,000 kilometers) along the Queensland coast. Its pools, lagoons, and grottoes display the most complex diversity of marine life in the world. It teems with 10,000 species of sponge, 350 species of coral, 4,000 species of mollusk, and 1,200 species of fish. The reef originated about 18 million years ago when coral polyps began to colonize the subsiding continental shelf. As the lowermost polyps die, their skeletons fuse into a massive limestone foundation on which new coral grows. Coral survives only in shallow, moving water where sunlight can reach the algae on which it feeds, in seas never colder than 64°F (18° C). As the sea level rose, so did the coral reefs, until there were 2,100 reefs forming the outer barrier. Another 540 continental islands (fragments of the coast) have their own fringing reefs. Only four shipping passages connect the mainland to the Coral Sea. The Hydrographers Passage alone is navigable by large vessels. Near Cairns, the reef has been degenerating since the 1960s, when the voracious crown of thorns starfish destroyed as much as 80 percent of the living coral. Since 1976, the Great Barrier Reef Marine Park Authority has had responsibility for reef management. (*See also* Great Barrier Reef.)

## Climate

For so large an area, Australia experiences a relatively small variation in climate. The landmass extends over only 33° of latitude, one third of which lies within the tropics. Its generally low, flat topography lacks the mountain ranges that diversify climatic regimes elsewhere. Summer temperatures hover around 84° F (29° C) in the north and 64° F (18° C) in the south, compared with winter temperatures of 75° F (24° C) and 50° F (10° C). Cloncurry, Queensland, claims the highest temperature ever recorded, 127° F (52.7° C) in 1889, but Marble Bar, Western Australia, set the heat wave record by surpassing 100° F (37.8° C) on 170 consecutive days in 1923–24. The lowest temperature, –3° F (–23° C) was recorded at Charlotte Pass near Mount Kosciusko.

As an island continent, Australia displays major contrasts between its interior continental climates (with large temperature ranges and erratic rainfall) and its coastal maritime climates (with small temperature ranges and more reliable rainfall). Of all the continents, only Antarctica receives less precipitation than Australia—an annual average of 16½ inches (42 centimeters). Periodic droughts, flooding, heat, and aridity are constant threats. Dry conditions create the potential for disastrous fires, such as those that charred thousands of acres and destroyed many homes in the vicinity of Sydney early in 1994. Almost all of northern Australia endures heat discomfort for over 150 days a year. The tropical seas along the coast offer little relief from the heat.

Very different wind belts cross northern, central, and southern Australia. Humid easterlies blow off the Pacific Ocean across the tropical north, making the coastal rain forests of Tully, Queensland, the wettest place in Australia; they receive an average of 159 inches (405 centimeters) per year. These summer winds are augmented by monsoonal westerlies which blow out of Indonesia into Arnhem Land, Northern Territory, and the Kimberleys, Western Australia, and by destructive tropical cyclones (or hurricanes) off the Coral Sea and Gulf of Carpentaria. Northern Australians refer to summer as "the wet" and to winter as "the dry."

Across the center of Australia move the subtropical anticyclones, from west to east. These cells of high pressure bring clear skies, summer heat, and almost no rain to the desert core of the continent. Southern Australia extends into the belt of westerlies that encircle the Earth around 40° S. latitude: the "roaring forties." These bring cloudy cold fronts (cyclones) twice weekly to Tasmania and Victoria during the winter, when rainfall is concentrated. Perth enjoys a classic mild Mediterranean-like climate, with its cool,

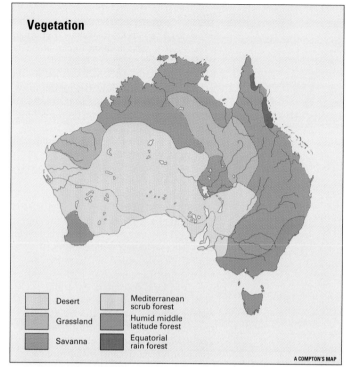

**Vegetation**

Desert

Grassland

Savanna

Mediterranean scrub forest

Humid middle latitude forest

Equatorial rain forest

A COMPTON'S MAP

*Vegetation zones of Australia*

*The golden wattle, floral symbol of Australia, is the most common of the acacias, or wattles, in Australia. Some early English settlers built dwellings out of wattle branches and mud.*

moist winter and warm, rainless summer. Australia's erratic weather has been attributed to the El Niño Southern Oscillation effect. Because of this effect, when unusually warm water gathers off the Pacific coast of South America, it disrupts the usual climatic rhythms of atmospheric pressure on the opposite side of the Pacific. Thus, every five years or so, rainfall due in Australia falls instead in the central Pacific, to be followed a few years later by an equally perturbing inundation of usually dry areas.

Climate does change. The last Ice Age ended only 10,000 years ago. Today, despite scientific skepticism, many Australians are concerned that rapid global warming caused by the 'greenhouse effect' may ruin agriculture and flood coastal cities (*see* Greenhouse Effect).

A recurrent summer hazard is the bushfire—a forest fire, or wildfire—especially after seasons of intense heat which dry out plant litter. Fanned by hot winds, the leaves of oil-bearing eucalyptus trees burn explosively. Careless campers and arsonists are often responsible. Killer fires that damaged many towns occurred in 1851, in 1983, and during the January 1994 conflagration.

Conservationists advocate the reintroduction of trees and deep-rooted perennials, the preservation of bushland, the use of more native predators instead of pesticides (and biological control by fungi and insects rather than herbicides), the diversification and scaling

down of the farming-forestry system, and a more self-sufficient, less urban population.

**Plant Life**

Although only a dozen plant families are unique to Australia, there are 530 unique genera and many unique species within these genera. As the Australian fragment of prehistoric Gondwanaland drifted north, its ancient flora became the basis for the present plant systems. Increasing aridity modified this vegetation, giving much of it hardened, pointed leaves of reduced size—a condition called scleromorphy.

Australia's native vegetation is divisible into seven types. The first type of vegetation consists of remnants of Gondwanan rain forests, with primitive flowering plants, palms, and laurels. These occur where high rainfall and high temperatures coincide with fertile, often volcanic soils, mainly in coastal north Queensland. In climax rain forests, three layers of trees appear, entangled with shrubs, lianas, and epiphytes. Closest to original Gondwanan conditions are the temperate rain forests of Tasmania, dominated by the myrtle beech and swathed in tree-ferns and mosses—called moss forests.

The second type of vegetation, communities dominated by the tall, straggly eucalyptus trees, is the most ubiquitous, forming a wide, concentric band around the desert core. Of the 500 species, two or three typically form a mosaic in one locality and

*The red box and white brittle gum (or eucalyptus) trees (top) grow on the lower slopes of Black Mountain near Canberra. Eucalyptus communities ring Australia's desert core. Primitive pandanus (bottom left) flourish in the high rainfall of Cradle Valley, Tasmania. After recent rains flowers bloom in the desert (bottom right) near Alice Springs, Northern Territory.*

intermingle with other plant associations. Eucalyptus trees are classified according to their bark types—hence the names stringybark, ironbark, bloodwood, and smoothbark (the gums that shed their outer bark annually). The most widespread is the river red gum. Mallee eucalypts survive in semiarid regions by growing multiple stems (lignotubers) from a common rootstock. The world's tallest flowering plant is a southern eucalyptus, the mountain ash. Its height can exceed 325 feet (100 meters). Building timbers are obtained in Victoria from alpine ash and mountain ash, in New South Wales and Queensland from blackbutt, spotted gum, bluegum, and ironbark, and in Western Australia from jarrah and karri, another type of eucalypt.

A third type of plant community is dominated by wattles (the genus *Acacia* of the Mimosa family) and advances beyond the last eucalyptus trees into the desert. Although more than 900 species are known, vast regions are dominated by just a few, including brigalow, mulga, and gidgee. Their tannin-rich bark is used in tanning leather. One of the less attractive of the varieties of acacia is the mulga. This small tree grows on thousands of square miles of arid inland Australia. The slang term "out in the mulga" refers to the distant outback areas. Aborigines had a number of uses for this tree. Its wood provided a slow-burning fuel for cooking fires, and it was also used to make spear blades.

The golden wattle is the acacia most familiar to natives. It is the floral symbol of Australia. There is even a Wattle Day, which may be celebrated on August 1 or September 1. Eucalyptus or acacia trees are dominant over 75 percent of the continent.

Three other types of vegetation are found over smaller areas. Communities dominated by casuarinas (and Allocasuarina species, including she-oaks) occupy semiarid niches between eucalyptus and acacia woodlands. Native conifers command no large areas as they do in the Northern Hemisphere, although white cypress pine grows widely on infertile soils. Pioneer builders were gratified to discover that it withstands drought, fire, and termites. Salt-tolerant shrublands devoid of trees are found mainly along the southern edges of the arid core. Mallee, saltbush, and bluebush are common, and Banksia and Grevillea are of local

*Perth's skyline can be seen from nearby Kings Park and its 42-acre (17-hectare) Botanic Garden. The park displays more than 2,000 different plant species from Western Australia, including natural bushland.*

importance. Finally, grasslands occur where rainfall is insufficient for larger plants. Summer-growing species tend to be more northerly and winter-growing species more southerly. Hummock grasslands (including spinifex) spread across the dunes, sandy plains, and rocky ranges of the Western Plateau.

Minor coastal plant communities include salt marsh, seagrass, and mangroves. Alpine herb fields, often flattened by the wind, are dotted with sphagnum moss bogs. Weeds introduced from outside Australia, such as wild turnip and hoary cress, compete with crops. Lantana, blackberries, bracken fern, and Paterson's curse overrun pastures. Cape tulip and Saint-John's-wort can poison livestock or taint food. Algae block drainage and smother plants. Only 5.3 percent of Australia's 2,966,200 square miles (7,682,300 square kilometers) is covered in forest. Of that, 75 percent is in public domain. Forest plantations account for another 3,759 square miles (9,737 square kilometers), 69 percent of them under California radiata pine. Fine specimens of Australian flora can be seen in the National Botanic Gardens in Canberra, the Royal Botanic Gardens of Sydney and Melbourne, and Kings Park in Perth.

### Animal Life

Native to Australia are 250 species of mammals (half of them pouched marsupials); 750 species of birds; more than 500 species of reptiles and amphibians, including 150 species of snakes; 22,000 species of fish, but only 150 of them freshwater; 65,000 known insect species; and 1,500 species of spiders. The continent is world-famous for these zoological curiosities. It became a veritable Noah's ark for monotremes, which include the platypus, and marsupials, saved from competition with carnivores and herbivores and free to evolve uniquely, when Australia split from Gondwanaland

between 45 and 70 million years ago. By contrast, other animals drifted free with South America and Africa but became extinct when those continents encountered Northern Hemisphere landmasses that were home to predators.

When Australia drifted closer to Asia 20 million years ago, Asian animal immigrants reached northern Australia across shallow continental shelves. Bats and rodents island-hopped. The dingo, a type of wild dog, came with migrating aborigines or Asian fishermen 5,000 years ago. Other creatures used the broad land bridges which surfaced when the expansion of the ice caps resulted in lowered sea levels, linking the Australian mainland with New Guinea and Tasmania. Marine animals dispersed easily across the entire tropical and subtropical Indian and Pacific oceans. Wallace's line, drawn in 1868 between the Indonesian islands of Bali and Lombok, marked the proximal separation of Australasian and Oriental faunas.

The present Australian fauna thus contains three main elements—those uniquely Australian (like the monotremes and lyrebirds), those of Gondwanan origin with affinities to other continents (some marsupials, the emu and cassawary, geckos, side-necked tortoises, most frogs, lungfish, and barramundis), and those which flew or floated on drifting vegetation from Asia within the last 30 million years (rodents, lizards, insects, birds, bats, and snakes), still comfortably acclimatized in tropical northern Australia.

The monotremes, an egg-laying order of mammals, include only the platypus and two species of echidnas, or spiny anteaters. Platypuses are found nowhere else in the world, not even in fossil form. Echidnas are found also in New Guinea. The platypus uses its webbed feet and broad, sensitive bill to nuzzle food from the bottoms of coastal creeks from northern Queensland to South Australia. The bill has a unique sensing device that detects changes in electrical fields. The platypus is a skilled swimmer and can remain underwater for up to five minutes at a time. It spends only a few hours of each day in the water. The males have a poisonous spur on each hind leg. Although the poison is not fatal to humans, it can cause agonizing pain.

The shy echidna uses its snout to probe for termites and insects, which adhere to the saliva on its tongue. It settles into the ground, spikes erect, when disturbed. The heavily armored echidna has small spines on the back of its head and long spines on the upper surface and sides of its body. Its clawed limbs are short and powerful. The male has a retractable spur on each hind limb that releases a weak poison. It is from this that the animal gets its name—echidna is derived from a Greek word for viper. The echidna is toothless but has a tongue up to 12 inches (30 centimeters) long, the sticky surface of which is used for catching ants.

For a study in sheer animal cunning it would be difficult to surpass the dingo, also known by the aboriginal name *warrigal*. It is an animal very similar in appearance to the domestic dog. It probably arrived from mainland Asia about 5,000 years ago, along with

*A koala perched in a eucalyptus tree carries its baby on its back. These animals will spend most of their lives in eucalyptus trees, devouring the leaves which make up the koala's diet.*

*A platypus (top), which is quite at home in the water, catches a crustacean for its meal. Like the platypus, the echidna (bottom) is an egg-laying mammal. At home on land, its claws are long and sharp for digging.*

an immigration of aborigines. The dingo is a fairly large canine, growing to about 4 feet (1.2 meters) long, including its 12-inch tail. The dingo has long been the killer of the outback. It hunts kangaroos, wallabies, rabbits, and ground birds—with a special fondness for the echidna. It also runs down and kills sheep and cattle. Like wolves, these animals hunt alone or in packs. Its ferocity resulted in the elimination of the Tasmanian devil and the Tasmanian wolf from mainland Australia. The dingo carries a bounty on its head, and Queensland once erected a 3,000-mile (4,800-kilometer) fence to keep the animal out.

**Marsupials.** Of the world's 19 marsupial families, 16 are native to Australia. They include opossums, koalas, wombats, kangaroos, and wallabies. Whereas placental mammals connect the unborn baby to the mother's uterus, the marsupials give birth to their young at a very early stage of development, retaining, carrying, and suckling them in an abdominal pouch. A vivid example is the joey, or baby kangaroo, scrambling into the mother kangaroo's pouch.

There are 50 species of kangaroos in Australia. These macropods have large hind legs for hopping. Their heavy tails serve as a counterbalance during locomotion and as a prop when standing upright.

Kangaroo sizes and characteristics vary widely. There are burrowing rat kangaroos, tree kangaroos with shortened hind legs and exceedingly long tails, rock wallabies with granulated footpads for gripping, pademelons, and quokkas. The largest species are the grey (or forester) kangaroo and the red kangaroo. Males of both species may exceed 8 feet (2.4 meters) from nose to tail.

Many ranchers regard kangaroos as vermin, especially during plagues. Conservationists deplore their slaughter for skins, for pet food, or simply to cut down the size of a herd. (*See also* Kangaroo.)

Koala is an aboriginal word meaning "it does not drink," though these animals do drink when ill. Koalas are tree-dwelling marsupials with a home range of 14 to 15 eucalyptus trees. One tree will be an animal's favorite. They feed exclusively on specific eucalyptus leaves which provide sufficient moisture. An exceptionally long intestine and special liver mechanism cope with the harsh oils and tannin in the leaves. Lacking the tails typical of most arboreal animals, and with pouches that open inconveniently backwards (like their closest relative, the wombat), koalas may have originated as ground-dwelling, burrowing animals.

Koalas were abundant in coastal forests from northern Queensland to southeastern South Australia.

(Top left and bottom left) John Carnemolla—Australian Picture Library; (right) Fritz Prenzel—Australian Picture Library

*The kangaroo is recognized around the world as symbolic of Australia. A gray kangaroo (top left) plays in the surf at Pebbly Beach on the coast of New South Wales. Bennett's tree kangaroo (right) is one of seven species of these medium-sized marsupials. Like other kangaroos, the yellow-footed rock wallaby (bottom left) uses its long tail to maintain balance.*

Hunters exported their pelts in large numbers (two million in 1924 alone) until public revulsion and an American ban on imports led to total protection by law. Continuing problems include habitat fragmentation—especially in their southern Queensland stronghold—serious fires, and a virulent form of the disease trachoma.

Australian opossums, or phalangers, are also arboreal marsupials. They include the cuscus, a monkeylike marsupial; the ringtail opossum, which has a prehensile tail; and the gliders, which are also called flying phalangers.

Another tree-dwelling marsupial is the tiny pygmy gliding opossum, an acrobatic, mouselike animal and the smallest marsupial adapted for gliding. One of the numerous kinds of Australian possums, it is found in eastern regions of the country. However, it is rarely seen because it is active at night and extremely furtive. It glides from tree to tree in flights that are really prolonged leaps. Membranes between its limbs have a parachute effect, and its fringed tail provides an additional airplanelike surface.

The doglike Tasmanian devil is also a marsupial. It is a slow-moving, clumsy animal that lives in open forest areas. It takes shelter in any available cover by day and scavenges for food by night. Although widely regarded as a fierce killer of animals, the Tasmanian devil is actually a poor hunter and usually feeds on carrion, much like a vulture. The animal is usually about 28 inches (71 centimeters) long with a 10-inch (25-centimeter) tail. It is mostly black, with white bands across its chest and rump. The forefeet have five toes and the rear feet have four. All of its toes are strongly clawed. (*See also* Marsupials.)

**Reptiles.** All three orders of reptiles—crocodiles, lizards and snakes, turtles and tortoises—are well represented in Australia. The seagoing estuarine crocodile ranges from India to China and the western Pacific. It is found along the northern coasts of Australia between Broome and Maryborough, in saltwater estuaries and river mouths. Males average 16 feet (5 meters) in length but do reach 23 feet (7 meters). Crocodiles feed on fish, crabs, water rats, and occasionally on larger prey—including horses,

cattle, and humans—which they first drown and then dismember. The smaller freshwater crocodile, found in the billabongs (streambeds) and lagoons of monsoonal rivers, is harmless to humans.

Besides estuarine crocodiles, the only Australian animals that will feed on humans are sharks and, of course, mosquitos and fleas. Crocodile-skin handbags and shoes were once highly prized luxury items, but crocodile hunting has been completely banned in Western Australia and the Northern Territory since 1971 and in Queensland since 1974. Crocodile farms, several of them run by aborigines, now market meat.

Australia's 450 species of lizard probably originated in tropical Asia. Today they are the dominant predators in desert ecosystems. The largest of them is the desert perenty, averaging 5.2 feet (1.6 meters) but known to reach 8.2 feet (2.5 meters). Fossil monitor lizards, called goannas, at 20 feet (6 meters) and 1,300 pounds (600 kilograms), were twice as big as today's record-holder, the Komodo dragon. Curiosities include the gecko, whose padded, adhesive digits enable it to move and rest on ceilings. Geckoes are able to snap off their still-wriggling tails to distract predators while making their escape. Among the dragon lizards are the thorny devil, the water dragon, and the spectacular frill-necked lizard, which unfolds its ruff like an umbrella when alarmed. Skinks with smooth, silky scales are common sights in suburban gardens.

Of Australia's marine turtles, the largest is the leathey, or luth, turtle, up to 10 feet (3 meters) in length and 1,100 pounds (500 kilograms) in weight. Among reptiles, only the estuarine crocodile exceeds it in size. Marine turtles thrive in the warm tropical seas, coming ashore—vulnerable to human predators—to lay scores of eggs in chambers dug into beach sand. An extraordinary navigational sense permits turtles to return to the very beach where they were hatched.

Australia is the only continent where venomous snakes outnumber the nonvenomous, though only 20 or so of the 160 species (including 32 of sea snakes) are fatal to humans. Among the nonvenomous are blind or worm snakes, tree snakes, file snakes, and 13 species of pythons that suffocate their prey by constriction. The longest is the amethystine, or rock, python, which averages 11½ feet (3.5 meters), and

whose maximum length is 28 feet (8.5 meters). The most widespread is the common carpet snake.

All 65 species of venomous snakes are front-fanged elapids. Venom is secreted from modified saliva glands at the base of grooved, hollow fangs. It kills either by destroying the linings of blood vessels, causing blood to clot, destroying the red blood cells, or, in the case of neurotoxins, paralyzing nerves that control the heart and lungs. Australia's most dangerous snakes are the tiger snake, the Eastern brown snake, the mulga or king brown snake, death adders, the red-bellied black snake, the taipan, and its look-alike, the fierce or giant brown snake. The latter's neurotoxic venom can kill 100,000 mice, making it the most deadly of all the world's land snakes. Antivenins developed in the Commonwealth Serum Laboratories, if administered promptly, can now counteract most of these venoms.

**Insects.** Other poisonous animals include the Sydney funnelweb spider, which spins a silken tube at the entrance to its burrow and has killed unsuspecting gardeners; the trapdoor spider, which seals its burrow with a plug of earth; and the red-back spider, which lurks in outhouses under toilet lids. Many of Australia's 80,000 known insect species also sting.

The largest insect nests are the towering termites' nests, or termitaria, some of which surpass 23 feet (7 meters) in height, connected to food sources by 110 yards (100 meters) of tunnels and galleries. Those built in the Northern Territory by the compass, or magnetic, termite are aligned north–south to minimize exposure to the tropical sun.

*The kookaburra (left) is a member of the kingfisher family. Its call is famous for its resemblance to human laughter. The flightless emu (right) is the world's second largest bird after the ostrich.*

**Birds.** Of the world's more than 8,000 species of birds, about 750 are found in Australia. Of these, 368 are peculiar to Australia, 125 are nonbreeding visitors, and 20 or so were introduced, usually by human migrants longing for the birdsongs of their homelands. Acclimatized birds include the house sparrow, starling, song thrush, blackbird, pigeon, and, from India, the mynah and red-whiskered bulbul. Although Australia has 19 of the 25 orders of living birds, it lacks woodpeckers, vultures, true finches, and flamingos. Many of the indigenous birds originated in Asia or Gondwanaland. Many still live in New Guinea, among them the birds of paradise, bowerbirds, and spangled drongo.

The flightless, nomadic emu is the largest native bird and the second largest in the world. It accelerates in short bursts to 30 miles (48 kilometers) per hour and may surpass 6½ feet (2 meters) in height. It is found almost anywhere in inland Australia. Having laid from 7 to 20 green eggs on the ground, the larger female emu wanders off, leaving the male with nest duties of hatching and tending the chicks.

The lyrebird is unique to Australia and is one of the largest songbirds in the world. It can reproduce the sounds of more than 20 other songbirds. Similar in appearance to the peacock, the lyrebid can grow to more than 3 feet (0.9 meter) in length. Rarely seen by humans, it is native to eastern Australia. It is famous for its tail-twirling courtship display, as well as for its incomparable mimicry.

Other native species are mound-building birds, nesting in hot anthills, and the black swan, the symbol of Western Australia. Also peculiar to the continent are honeyeaters, bowerbirds, nocturnal frogmouths, and kingfishers. Singularly Australian birdcalls come from the kookaburra, or laughing jackass—a raucous, throaty, mocking peal of laughter—and the bellbird, which has ringing, tinkling tones. A survey by the Royal Australasian Ornithologists Union, founded in 1901, reported that the ten most commonly sighted Australian birds were the Australian magpie, willie wagtail, Australian magpie-lark, welcome swallow, black-faced cuckoo-shrike, galah, white-faced heron, laughing kookaburra, Australian kestrel, and common starling.

The drab, brown plains of inland Australia are brightened by the brilliant plumage of 55 species of parrots, one sixth of the world total. The gaudily colored rosellas take their name from Rose Hill, the Sydney locality where they were first observed. There are small grass-eating parakeets, tree-dwelling lorikeets, and budgerigars, but the aristocracy must be the cockatoos—among them the galahs (sometimes in flocks of a thousand), the screeching sulphur-crested white cockatoos, gang-gangs, and the glossy black cockatoo. The illegal smuggling of parrots out of Australia remains a problem.

Many seabirds and waders are migratory, even reaching Asia and New Zealand. The muttonbird, or short-tailed shearwater, follows a 19,000-mile (31,000-kilometer) figure-eight loop between Japan and Bass Strait, managing to summer in both the northern and southern hemispheres.

**Sea animals.** Australia's tropical coral reefs teem with fish, but the scarcity of rivers in an arid continent limits its freshwater fishes to only 150 species, including the carnivorous barramundi (giant perch). Commercial trawlers fish for barricuda, gemfish, or hake, tuna, and Australian salmon in the deeper, colder waters off the southern coasts, nominally inside the 200-nautical-mile Australian Fishing Zone adopted in 1979. Australia's last whaling station, at Albany, Western Australia, was closed in 1978. The Whale Protection Act of 1980 outlawed whaling in all Australian waters.

Whales still migrate along the Australian coast, where they are sometimes stranded, between Antarctica and their tropical breeding grounds. Two suborders are seen in these waters—the baleen whales, which filter water and plankton through a whalebone screen, and toothed whales, which chew their food. The baleen species are the southern right whale, formerly the prime target of whalers; the blue whale, largest of known mammals, averaging 95 feet (29 meters) but reaching 130 feet (40 meters); and the humpback whale. Toothed species include killer whales, which hunt in packs of 40 or more, preying on dolphins, seals, penguins, and other whales; and sperm whales, which in the 19th century were hunted almost to extinction for their oil and spermaceti.

Thirteen species of dolphins frolic off the Australian coast. The spinner dolphin leaps almost vertically above the waves while rotating at high speed. From 1790 to 1850, an industry that hunted fur seals for their oil and skins operated from the islands of Bass Strait.

The major scavengers in Australian waters today are sharks. They shred and swallow marine carrion indiscriminately and voraciously, but they also attack living creatures. Sharks differ from most other marine species in that their skeletons are cartilage, not bone. Lacking a swim bladder, they must swim ceaselessly to circulate water through the gills and maintain their height above the bottom. That is why sharks quickly drown if snared in nets strung across swimming beaches, just below the surface. Since the installation of such nets in Sydney Harbour in 1937, there has not been a single fatality from shark attacks. An average of less than one shark fatality per year has been reported in all Australian waters over the past 150 years. Attacks occur almost only in summer where water temperatures exceed 72° F (22° C).

Of Australia's 90 species of shark, the only dangerous man-eaters are the bronze whaler and grey whaler—with which the grey nurse shark is often confused—the tiger shark, the blue pointer (which prefers surfboards and small craft to swimmers), and the most dangerous of them all, variously known as the white pointer, great white shark, or white death. It may be 40 feet (12 meters) long and displays up to 200 replaceable teeth. Other common sharks are the thresher, hammerhead, checkerboard, and paisley-patterned wobbegong. The Australian coast is also plagued by the blue-ringed octopus, which delivers a fatal bite, the box jellyfish, whose trailing tentacles carry venomous cells, the poisonous geographer cone, the well-camouflaged stonefish, and assorted stingrays.

**Nature parks.** Representative slices of Australia's natural environment can be seen in more 2,000 national parks and other conservation reserves. These protected areas contain over 154,400 square miles (399,000 square kilometers) and cover 5 percent of the total land area, compared with 8.6 percent of total land area in the United States going to parks, and about 4 percent worldwide. Except in federal territories, they were established and remain controlled by state governments. Australia was one of the first countries to create national parks and nature reserves. Kings Park in Perth dates from 1872 and Sydney's Royal National Park from 1879. Yet most of the significant natural and cultural sites have been identified, inventoried, and protected systematically only since 1970. National parks are intended primarily for public recreation.

Other reserves are dedicated to protecting such significant or endangered features as prehistoric rock art, sacred or ceremonial aboriginal sites, wilderness areas, marine and terrestrial habitats, and sites of historic or scientific interest. Australia has five major zoos: Taronga Park, Sydney; Royal Melbourne Zoological Gardens; Adelaide Zoo; Perth Zoo; and the Western Plains Zoo, an open-range park at Dubbo, New South Wales. Native fauna parks include the Cleland National Park, South Australia; Sir Colin Mackenzie Zoological Park, Victoria; and the Currumbin Sanctuary, Queensland, where friendly perching parrots almost envelop visitors.

**Environmental Concerns**

Australian aborigines lived for millennia in respectful harmony with the land. Only during the time of European settlement have mechanized farming, deforestation, and the dispersal of exotic species of flora and fauna created environmental degradation. Extinction has been the fate of 18 species of native birds and mammals. Among them are the Tasmanian tiger, certain bandicoots and wallabies, and the hopping mouse.

At least 97 vascular plant species have disappeared. Another 3,300 species (17 percent of the total) are considered rare or threatened, and another 1,000 are considered endangered or vulnerable.

Sixty percent of all soils now require treatment for erosion, compaction, acidification, or salinity. The Australian Conservation Foundation, created in 1966, became a powerful lobby by bringing nature conservation into the public arena. During the 1970s, called the decade of the environment, the federal government began requiring environmental effects statements before resource exploitation could be approved. The government passed the Australian Heritage Commission Act in 1975. This created a register of the National Estate for the protection of both the natural and cultural heritage.

Previously conservation in Australia was a matter left mostly to the states. Belated federal involvement had to fall back on constitutional prerogatives in external affairs, mainly by nominating crucial environments for World heritage designation by UNESCO.

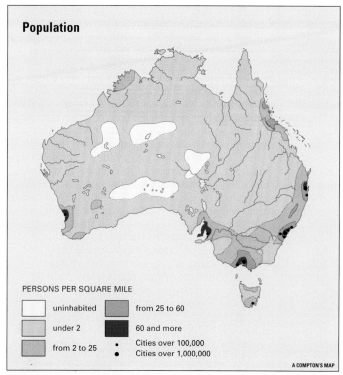

**Population**

PERSONS PER SQUARE MILE

| | |
|---|---|
| uninhabited | from 25 to 60 |
| under 2 | 60 and more |
| from 2 to 25 | • Cities over 100,000 |
| | ● Cities over 1,000,000 |

A COMPTON'S MAP

*Population density of Australia*

## PEOPLE

In 1788, when the first permanent European settlers arrived in Australia, the population of the continent consisted of these 1,030 Europeans and an estimated 750,000 aborigines. Two hundred years later, by the census of 1991, that population had grown to 17.3 million, of whom only 250,000 (1.5 percent) were indigenous, either aboriginals or Torres Strait Islanders of Melanesian origin.

With 63.6 percent of the total population concentrated in just eight capital cities, and 86 percent in all cities, Australia now lays claim to being the most urbanized nation on Earth. This population is largely concentrated within 220 miles (350 kilometers) of the eastern and southeastern coasts, including Tasmania. The only other center of dense population is in the southwestern corner of Western Australia. Another entire third of the continent is sparsely settled semiarid rangeland. The remaining third is virtually empty desert.

### Migrants and Population

Throughout the 19th century, North America was the main destination for migrants from Europe. Luring them to Australia required strong incentives and financial assistance.

Immigration policy was aimed at occupying—and then defending—a seemingly empty continent and developing its resources, preferably through family migration. Edward Gibbon Wakefield, a British official

who spearheaded colonization of the continent, realized that sole reliance on the transportation of convicts could not produce a stable, civil society. He tried using the proceeds of land sales to finance the migration of free settlers, notably in the founding of South Australia in 1836. The Australian colonies eventually paid the fares of some 700,000 British migrants between 1831 and 1900. Since then, federal programs have controlled the types, numbers, and skills of subsidized migrants, as economic conditions permitted.

The continuous influx of largely male immigrants during the past two centuries has distorted the Australian population. The ratio of males to females stood at 121 to 100 in 1881 and remained at 102 to 100 during the 1950s and 1960s, while postwar immigration policies were in full force. Before 1870, the majority of residents were British-born; since 1870, the majority have been Australian-born. Average life expectancy now stands at 80 years for females and 74 years for males. For aborigines, it is 64 for females and 56 years for males.

Seventy-two percent of all Australian householders now own or are purchasing their own dwellings, compared with 40 percent in 1947. Three fourths of all homes are separate houses. Entrenched government policies favoring home ownership have kept welfare, or public, housing at 5 percent of the total. During the 1980s, new policies to encourage urban consolidation saw many inner-city single-family residences replaced by townhouses and row houses.

To exclude cheap Asian labor and to avert racial conflict, the "white Australia" policy was embodied officially in the Immigration Restriction Act of 1901. It applied until 1973. Immigration in Australia today is no longer restricted by race or nationality, but only by employability and skills. The only refugees who have received financial assistance since 1947 have been Jews fleeing from Nazi Germany, Eastern Europeans and Asians fleeing from Communist regimes, and persons displaced by war. During the 1950s and 1960s, migration from Britain was eclipsed by migration from Southern Europe, especially from Italy, Greece, Croatia, and Malta. During the 1970s and 1980s, migrants from Asia, notably Chinese and Vietnamese, accounted for up to 35 percent of the total. The restriction of government assistance to only British migrants ended in the 1950s. Australians abandoned the old ideal of perpetuating an exclusively British heritage by establishing a federal Office of Multicultural Affairs in 1987. Social cohesion was to be attained, not through the previous policy of assimilation, but by tolerating ethnic differences within an accepted legal code. Now only New Zealanders are granted unrestricted entry.

*Aboriginal handprints and paintings (top left) can be found in Carnarvon National Park in Queensland. Aborigines have created a rock art gallery (top right) at Nourlangie Rock, an isolated outlier of the Arnhem Land escarpment. Samuel Thomas Gill painted an aboriginal ceremony (bottom), as viewed by Europeans, in 1855.*

(Top left and top right) R. Smith—SUPERSTOCK; (bottom) National Library of Australia

Of the 17.5 million Australians, four million identify themselves in some way with an ethnic group, though the other 75 percent of the population do not. Two million were born in a non-English-speaking country and speak its language. Official sources no longer categorize people by race or ethnicity, but refer simply to NESB, or non-English-speaking background, Australians. These form 100 distinctive groups with 4,000 ethnic organizations.

Despite the background diversity of five million postwar immigrants, surprisingly few social conflicts have erupted on the continent. Only the Jewish and Greek Orthodox communities have established their own school systems. Such government initiatives as a telephone interpreting service (operating since 1973) and the multilingual Special Broadcasting Service (since 1977) made migrants welcome in Australia. Public debate continues on the issues of Asian migration, sustainable levels of development, and zero population growth.

## Aborigines

Of the 250,000 indigenous people, only a fourth are pure aborigines still pursuing the traditional seminomadic life of hunter-gatherers and following a seasonal, cyclical calendar. Another fourth live in big cities. The remainder live in rural areas. Many are still devoted to notions of kinship and walkabout—the desire to revisit the sacred sites.

Aborigines hold inalienable freehold title to 34 percent of the Northern Territory, including the great Arnhem Land Reserve created in 1931. They comprise 22 percent of the Northern Territory population. Other aboriginal concentrations are found in the Kimberleys in Western Australia and Cape York Peninsula in Queensland. Since 1988, when the European bicentenary of Australia was celebrated, many aborigines have rejected the anthropological term aborigine. Instead, they refer to themselves in their own languages: Koorie (Our People) in the southern and

*An aboriginal artist creates a bark painting depicting a large bird surrounded by fish. The bark is actually cloth made of fibers from a tree's inner bark. Animal motifs are common subjects.*

*Aboriginal hunters (top) hunt with spears covered with mud or clay. Women (bottom) dig for honey ants, a source of food when game is scarce during droughts.*

eastern states, Yolngu in Northern Territory, Arangu in central Australia, Nyunga in Western Australia, and Nungga in South Australia.

Aboriginal oral history traces their origins to ancestral beings such as the Rainbow Serpent. These spirits moved across the land before the Pleistocene ice ages, two million years ago, leaving "dreaming tracks" along which nomads still travel to distant ceremonial gatherings. By contrast, scientists using radiocarbon and thermoluminescence dating techniques believe that the aborigines canoed to Australia in successive waves from Southeast Asia some 30,000 to 50,000 years before the present, when sea levels were lower and when *Homo sapiens* was replacing the Neanderthals in Europe. A female skull, 30,000 years old, was found in Lake Mungo, New South Wales.

Aboriginal religion is deeply involved with the land, the mother of all living things to which the spirit returns for rebirth following death. Aborigines do not own the land: it owns them. They are its custodians, believing that the ancestral beings of the Dreamtime, or Dreaming, created plants, animals, people, and places. Some of these are sacred to men, others sacred to women—who have religious autonomy in aboriginal society—still others sacred to both. The exact place of birth determines a person's position within a clan or kinship group and provides a secret personal name.

Traditionally, aboriginal education required separate ceremonies, or rites of passage, at each stage of the life cycle for males and females. A group's history was passed on through song cycles recounting the creation myths and the cautionary tales. At the physically painful initiation into adulthood, sacred secrets were passed down. Only initiates could inherit land, sing certain songs, or paint certain images. Group territorial boundaries were known and respected without recourse to fences or permanent housing. Wars over property were therefore unnecessary. There were 230 distinct aboriginal languages and 500 dialects, half of them now extinct.

Nomads had few material possessions and built temporary shelters from bark and brush (*gunyahs* or *mia mias*). They wore little clothing in hot areas but used marsupial-skin cloaks in colder areas. In thick forests, their hunting weapons were killer sticks and specialized spears. On the open plains, they hunted with woomeras (hooked spear-throwers) and boomerangs, firing the grasslands to drive game animals in their direction. Fishing required string nets, stone traps, and tined spears. When game was scarce during droughts, tribal aborigines depended on the women's work with digging sticks to supply yams, witchetty grubs, and honey ants. Edible native plants included epacrids (a family of small trees and shrubs), geebungs, and lillypilly. Traditional aborigines may have had a sparse material culture, but they gloried in a richly imaginative spiritual life. Their art, their dances—including the festive corroboree—and their music were intimately linked with this spiritual life and the land which embodied it. "Songlines" of communication carried ideas and images across the continent. Their art was both symbolic and educational, from tree-bark paintings of animals and fish—with depictions of the placement of vital organs to illustrate spear targets—to rock engravings, hard sand sculptures, and petroglyphs (rock paintings) of Mimi, a clan of spirit beings. The oldest petroglyphs in the world were created 43,000 years ago in the Olary region of South Australia.

The forms and content of this art persisted for thousands of years. Its ceremonial association with the ancestral past is seen in the Pukimani burial poles, mortuary figures, and hollow log coffins. The earth tones of clays and ochres conveyed specific meanings: white for mourning and grief; yellow for anger and belligerence; red for love and joy; black (from charcoal) for death and revenge. Some convergence of aboriginal and Western art was achieved by Albert Namatjira, whose embrace of watercolors enchanted many Euro-Australians; and Geoffrey Bardon of Papunya, whose acrylic, mosaic-like, abstract dot paintings incorporated layers of aboriginal symbolism. (*See also* Namatjira, Albert.)

European contact with the aborigines, until quite recently, has been a painful and tragic tale of incomprehension and rapacity. The earliest British settlers did not recognize aboriginal rights to the land, but regarded it as a *terra nullius*—a land unoccupied and unclaimed by prior inhabitants. They saw aborigines as uncivilized relics of the Stone Age, lacking agriculture, permanent habitations, written languages, or the use of metal. Many groups were physically or culturally exterminated, uprooted from land which held for them sacred, ceremonial, or hunting significance. Massacres, food poisoning, rape, and punitive expeditions were employed.

By 1930, only 67,000 aborigines remained in Australia, and there was fear of complete genocide. Christian missions were largely unsuccessful except in furthering segregation. Protection acts were passed in all states between 1860 and 1911, and many reserves were set aside for the "use and benefit" of aborigines, typically in remote, isolated, arid areas. Aborigines were eventually granted Australian citizenship by the government in 1967, and they were granted the right to vote in 1984.

In 1976, the Aboriginal Land Rights Act of the Northern Territory gave ownership of its reserves to the aborigines, and permitted them, as traditional owners, to claim other vacant public land—up to 30 percent of the entire territory. Aboriginal groups or communities now own 11 percent of Australia's land, despite fierce opposition from the governments of Queensland and Western Australia, and from the mining companies.

## Women

Australian society was long characterized by the concerns of dominant patriarchy, and the rights of women were often subject to discrimination. Feminist reforms have almost as long a history as this discrimination. In 1902, Australia granted women the right to vote in national elections and the right to stand for Parliament—just a decade after New Zealand passed similar legislation and 18 years before women in the United States could vote. Women could vote in all state elections by 1909. One setback was depression-era legislation that resulted in the dismissal of 220 married female teachers in New South Wales in 1932. The law was repealed in 1947.

The Country Women's Association, founded in 1922 as a nonsectarian, nonpolitical organization to alleviate the hardships of rural life for women and children, brought rest rooms, rest homes, and baby health centers to hundreds of country towns. Equal-opportunity legislation was promoted by two parliamentary watchdog groups, the Australian Federation of Women Voters, from 1921, and the Women's Electoral Lobby, from 1972. Equal pay for women was legislated in 1974, but immigrant women who spoke no English remained an exploited group. The 1975 Family Law Act resulted in raising the divorce rate to one in every three marriages.

## Welfare

Australia has 40,000 welfare organizations which complement the government's formal provision of social services. They include the Red Cross Society, the Smith Family (established in Sydney in 1922 for the needy), the Salvation Army (1881), the St. Vincent de Paul Society (Roman Catholic), and the Brotherhood of St. Lawrence (Anglican). Underprivileged children have enjoyed free seaside holidays with Barnardo Australia since 1921. St. John Ambulance teaches first aid and provides voluntary paramedic services at sporting and other public events. LifeLine is a telephone emergency service, founded in Sydney in 1963. It is now international in scope. Another 3,000 organizations provide social, recreational, and spiritual programs for the youth of Australia. In 1908, just one year after Robert Baden-Powell founded the Boy Scouts in England, they were established in Australia. Of the international networks, the largest are the YMCA, the YWCA, and the Youth Hostels Association, with some 100 hostels throughout the nation and no age limit on membership.

## CULTURE

The social and cultural life of Australia is rooted first of all in the land itself—a vast island continent cut off from the rest of the world. It is a continent with distinctive features found nowhere else. Secondly, the culture grew out of what gradually became a truly multicultural population. To an already rich aboriginal culture was added a European heritage that became more ethnically diverse as the decades passed.

The Sydney Opera House (top), one of the world's most striking pieces of modern architecture, has become a well-recognized symbol of the city. A concert is taking place in the foreground interior area. The Queen Victoria Building in Sydney (bottom), built in 1898, was designed to resemble a Byzantine palace.

(Left) Robin Smith—Australian Picture Library; (bottom) R. Fretwell—Australian Picture Library

## Architecture and Urban Design

Apart from some striking late 20th-century structures, Australian architecture is largely derivative. It makes use of diverse styles, copied mainly from Europe and North America. Since there have been no powerful patrons and few specifically designed city plans, large-scale civic precincts and housing projects are the exception. Most building has been small-scale and private. Canberra, the exhaustively planned national capital, is the only monumental garden city in Australia. Its designer, the Chicago architect Walter Burley Griffin, introduced Frank Lloyd Wright's design precepts to Australia.

A colonial Georgian style was imported from Britain before 1840. It produced simple buildings of fine proportions to which shady eaves, shutters, and verandas were added in deference to the dry Australian heat. Georgian was superseded by about 1850 by ornate, exuberant Victorian styles. These monuments to the British Empire and the ostentatious new wealth from gold and sheep ranching included Gothic churches, extravaganzas like the Queen Victoria Building in Sydney, and dignified public buildings.

A more picturesque, domestically comfortable Federation style, from the 1890s, incorporated elements of the English Arts and Crafts Movement and the California bungalow, which set the sprawling suburban fashion of large lots and single-story cottages. Perhaps the most distinctively Australian structure to emerge was the Queensland high-set house (or Queensland elevated), a bungalow homestead raised on stilts or stumps for tropical ventilation. By 1950, Australian architecture was afflicted with what Robin Boyd dubbed Austerica, meaning a shoddy amalgam of "Australia, America, austerity, and hysteria."

After 1970, a more humane architecture emerged, more conservative of energy and the cultural heritage. The Builders' Labourers Federation, led by Jack Mundy, staged "green bans" to stop the demolition of important structures or encroachment on unique environments. Office, industrial, apartment, and institutional buildings followed international trends, usually a few years behind the wave. One Australian building did capture the world's imagination—Jørn

Utzon's soaring Sydney Opera House, designed and built from 1957 to 1973.

Military surveyors laid out Australia's first town plans in conventional grid patterns. Melbourne, Perth, and Adelaide are the chief examples. William Light's parkland towns in South Australia, designed in 1836–38, were early experiments with an encircling greenbelt. Urban development thrived in an unregulated environment until the coordination of land uses and public works was eventually attempted by state governments after World War II. These statutory land-use plans imitated British precedents but borrowed zoning procedures from the United States. Federal government involvement was limited by the constitution until 1945, when an agreement between the Commonwealth and the states on funding public housing projects required metropolis-wide planning schemes. Sydney's was the first, in 1947, and Brisbane's the last, in 1964. Since 1980, urban planning has stressed community participation, with planning appeals and negotiated incentives directed to a state minister.

## Literature

In the beginning, Australia's colonial writers simply recorded their impressions of a strange continent for the benefit of a curious British public. Watkin Tench published his journal of the First Fleet and the first European settlement at Sydney. James Hardy Vaux recorded convict slang in his memoirs of the penal days. The first Australian ballads were convict songs and stories, often based on Irish originals. They have survived in the folksong repertories played by bush bands. Stylish travel accounts were also published by such inland explorers as Charles Sturt, who sailed down the Murray River; Edward John Eyre, who crossed the Nullarbor Plain; and Ernest Giles, the first nonnative to behold Ayers Rock.

The first works of fiction were guidebook novels, some romantic, others realistic, mainly intended to lure immigrants to Australia. The lyrics of Charles Harpur, praising the landscape in the manner of William Wordsworth, were the first important Australian poems, soon followed by those of Henry Kendall. The first major work of fiction was Henry Kingsley's 'The Recollections of Geoffrey Hamlyn' (1859), one of many tales of pioneering life. Another was Rolf Boldrewood's 'Robbery Under Arms' (1888), extolling the bushranger (highwayman) and the gold miner. Marcus Clarke's 'His Natural Life' (1874) best conveyed the convict life. Outback comedy was Steele Rudd's speciality in 'On Our Selection' (1899). Much of this writing was antiauthoritarian or expressed a stoic acceptance of fate.

During the last decades of the 19th century, Australian writers began to shed the British heritage. They espoused a nationalism that led to political independence and federation in 1901. Their catalyst was *The Bulletin*, a radical, racist, influential, widely read Sydney journal of politics and literature. It was founded in 1880 by John Haynes. J.F. Archibald, its

editor, encouraged his authors to seek their inspiration in the bush, unsettled or only sparsely settled country districts. Such authors included Henry Lawson, the leading bush balladist and the first writer depicted on an Australian banknote; A.B. (Banjo) Paterson, author of 'The Man from Snowy River' (1895) and the words for "Waltzing Matilda" (about 1895); Joseph Furphy, who wrote 'Such is Life' (1903); Miles Franklin, author of 'My Brilliant Career' (1901), a very popular film version of which was made in 1978; Christopher Brennan; Shaw Neilson; Bernard O'Dowd; and Mary Gilmore. Poems memorized by generations of Australian schoolchildren date from this period, including Dorothea Mackellar's patriotic 'My Country' (1908).

Between the two world wars, Australian writing saw an increasing output of novels. Some were historical sagas of pioneering, but others tackled more contemporary concerns—the 1930s Depression, urban life, and black-white sexual relations. A hedonistic Sydney circle around Norman Lindsay produced many exotic works, including Lindsay's 'The Magic Pudding' (1918), Australia's outstanding children's classic. Individualists who enlarged Lindsay's scope included the poets Kenneth Slessor, James McAuley, and Robert FitzGerald. Some writers left Australia for Europe and Great Britain. Among them were Christina Stead, Martin Boyd, and Henry Handel Richardson (the pen name of Ethel Florence Robertson).

After World War II there was an upsurge of modernism, exemplified in the poetry of A.D. Hope, Judith Wright, and Les Murray. Patrick White returned from exile in Britain to become the first Australian to win the Nobel prize for Literature, in 1973. His novels include 'The Tree of Man' (1955), 'Voss' (1957), and 'The Eye of the Storm' (1973).

The 1950s and 1960s so hastened the emigration of creative artists and scientists that A.A. Phillips called Australia's deference to foreign achievement its "cultural cringe." Yet a less self-righteously parochial writing emerged from the quest for national identity. Aboriginal authors, including the poet Oodgeroo Noonuccal and the novelist Mudrooroo Narogin, began contributing to a less prejudiced, less guilt-laden literature of race relations.

The British Booker Prize was won by novelists Thomas Keneally (1982) and Peter Cary (1988). Distinguished histories of Australia were written by Manning Clark and Robert Hughes. Very Australian autobiographies came from Hal Porter, Bernard Smith, Jack Lindsay, Patrick White, Clive James, and Jill Ker Conway.

Foreign authors came to envy the government's support for writers, through the Commonwealth Literary Fund from 1908, and by its successor, the Literature Board of the Arts Council, from 1973. A public lending-rights scheme was introduced in 1975, whereby libraries paid 80 cents to the author and 20 cents to the publisher for the use of their books. The main literary journals are *Southerly,* founded in 1939, *Meanjin* (1940), *Overland* (1954), *Quadrant* (1956), and *Scripsi* (1981).

Many public buildings in Australia are graced with sculpture. 'Two Figure Group' (top left), a bronze sculpture by Lyndon Dadswell, is in the Newcastle city building. The Art Gallery of New South Wales has many noted works. 'The Sleeping Greek' (top right), 1936, oil on canvas on hard board, 38 by 32.7 centimeters, is a painting by William Dobell. 'Departure of the Orient—Circular Quay' (bottom), 1888, oil on canvas, 45.1 by 50.1 centimeters, is by Charles Conder.

(Top left) The Newcastle City Council; (top right) Art Gallery of New South Wales, Sydney; gift of the NSW Society of Artists in Memory of its President, Sydney Ure Smith, 1950; (bottom) Art Gallery of New South Wales, Sydney; purchased 1888

## Graphic Arts

Initially, taste and style in the graphic arts were largely imported from Europe, then from the United States after World War II. Australia's unique environment and cultural experience found their artistic expression only gradually, as green, nostalgic, pseudo-English landscapes were replaced with the harsh, brown reality of deserts and eucalyptus forests. S.T. Gill's watercolors of the gold rushes of the 1850s opened the eyes of settlers to the authentic Australian landscape, and made Melbourne the leading art center. There the Heidelberg School of impressionists was founded in the 1880s by Tom Roberts, Frederick McCubbin, Arthur Streeton, and Charles Condor. This was the first truly Australian school of painting. Its masterpieces make the Victorian National Gallery Australia's finest.

Twentieth-century Australian painting has contributed to every avant-garde movement. Distinctively Australian idioms have been created by Sidney Nolan, Arthur Boyd, Albert Tucker, John Olsen, and Brett Whitely. Outside the mainstream were William Dobell; Russell Drysdale, of the empty red landscapes and lonely, surreal figures; and Fred Williams. Important stimuli for the art world were several well-endowed prizes—the Archibald Prize for portraiture, the Wynne Prize for landscape painting, the Blake Prize for religious art, the Sulman Prize, and the Moet Chandon Art Fellowship. The Australian National Gallery opened in Canberra in 1982, and Sydney's Museum of Contemporary Art in 1991.

Australia's finest sculpture adorns its war memorials, most notably Melbourne's Shrine of Remembrance and Sydney's Anzac Memorial. One sculptor, Clement Meadmore, gained his reputation as an expatriate. Making his headquarters in New York City in 1963, he readily found world markets for his enormous steel fabrications.

Early works in Australian sculpture date from the 1830s and include some very fine work on a famous bridge in Tasmania. Most of the early artists expressed themselves in statues of notables from early local history. Thomas Woolner's statue of Capt. James Cook, still standing in Sydney's Hyde Park, is an example. William Stanford received a pardon from a jail sentence in 1870 and carved the bluestone fountain in Melbourne.

During the period from the 1890s to 1930, Sir Bertram MacKennal became the first major name in sculpture. The Cenotaph and the Shakespeare Memorial in Sydney are his best-known pieces. MacKennal brought sculpture to the public's attention and helped pave the way for Rayner Hoff, who won the international Prix de Rome in 1922. Hoff designed and carved the figures, some of them 16 feet (5 meters) high, on the Anzac War Memorial in Sydney and the South Australian War Memorial in Adelaide.

Among the moderns, Lyndon Dadswell and Thomas Bass probably have more public sculptures than any other native artists. Women have been among Australia's leading sculptors, including Norma Redpath, Margel Hinder, and Margaret Priest. Gerald Lewis, Robert Klippel, and Lenton Parr are also notable.

*An eternal flame burns before the Shrine of Remembrance, a World War I memorial located in King's Domain Park in Melbourne. The massive structure was built during the 1930s and 1940s to honor citizens from Victoria who died in the war.*
Cameramann International

Australia has also produced a host of inimitable, irreverent, sardonic political cartoonists. Phil May, Norman Lindsay, and David Low worked for *The Bulletin* and Stan Cross and George Finey for *Smith's Weekly*. The newspaper editorial pages employed the idiosyncratic George Molnar, Bruce Petty, Michael Leunig, and Pat Oliphant, a Pulitzer prizewinning American cartoonist who emigrated from Australia in 1964.

## Music

In colonial times, the customary domestic musical entertainments were choral singing, instrumental ensembles, and harmonizing with the drawing-room piano. Outings took people to amateur concerts in public halls and to hear military bands in the parks. University courses for professional musicians were first offered in Adelaide in 1885 and in Melbourne in 1891. Music societies lasted until recorded music universalized passive listening.

The Victoria Orchestra was Australia's first, performing during 1888–91. An amateur Melbourne Symphony Orchestra was assembled in 1906 and the Sydney Symphony Orchestra in 1915. Also in 1915, a Belgian immigrant named Henri Verbrugghen arrived in Sydney to become founding director of the New South Wales State Conservatorium of Music. This was a significant step by a state government in providing official help to the arts. State orchestras were established in the 1920s, with the Australian Broadcasting Commission as impresario, a role only relinquished in the last years of the 20th century. In 1946, Musica Viva began sponsoring chamber-music concerts. Like Percy Grainger and Peggy Glanville-Hicks, many Australian composers became expatriates, leaving their homeland for Europe and North America.

Contemporary classical composers who express Australian themes while experimenting with Asian imagery are Peter Sculthorpe and Richard Meale. The Australian Opera was established in 1970, with the government providing 25 percent of its budget. Australia has produced a surprising number of world-class operatic and concert-hall performers, among them Nellie Melba, Florence Austral, and Joan Sutherland, as well as the operatic conductors Charles Mackerras and Richard Bonynge.

Traditional folk music is favored in cities, whereas rural areas prefer American-style country music. Rock and pop music, introduced in the 1950s, monopolize the local scene. Australian exports have included Men at Work, Air Supply, Midnight Oil, and Olivia Newton-John. Classical ballet, with 2,500 schools, is the most widely appreciated dance form in Australia. The Australian Ballet was formed in 1962.

## Theater

The first play performed in Australia, with a convict cast in 1789, was George Farquhar's 'The Recruiting Officer'. Six years after this performance, a convict named Robert Sidaway opened Australia's first licensed theater. He had been transported to the colony from England for stealing, but in 1794 he was granted an absolute pardon. In 1796 he built a playhouse in Bell Row, now Bligh Street, in the heart of Sydney's business district. After about two years he was ordered to close it because Sydney's underclass routinely robbed the homes of those in the audience while they were at the theater. A second attempt at operating a theater was tried in 1800, but it soon met the same fate as the first.

Gold miners, pastoralists, and city workers found simple pleasure and relief from drudgery in vaudeville, burlesque, pantomime, domestic farce, and melodrama. Stock actors played bushrangers, diggers, sensible heroines, and credulous English "new chums," or recent immigrants.

By the late 1820s theater was in the air again. Onto the scene came the prodigious Barnett Levey. He built a commercial complex including a large warehouse, a mill, the Royal Hotel, and eventually Sydney's first true commercial theater. Named the Theatre Royal, it opened on Oct. 5, 1833. Through this effort, theater became permanently established and respected in Australia.

Within a decade, full-time professional theaters were built in the main population centers. By 1840 actors and actresses were freely playing roles and doing management chores on the Sydney-Hobart-Adelaide circuit. The number of plays presented in a single season was remarkable. Sydney's Theatre Royal staged 50 works during 1835. London hits made their appearance on Australian stages as soon as they had played a hundred nights at the Surrey or Drury Lane theaters in London.

Local performers of more than adequate talent never seemed to be lacking in number. Eliza Winstanley O'Flaherty became the first native Australian actress to make a world reputation for herself and play in London and New York. Another major figure in the life of the theater was George Seth Coppin, an English actor who arrived in Sydney in 1843. There he acted in the Victoria Theatre's productions. This was a very attractive theater building that seated 1,900 people. It had a stage 100 feet (30 meters) deep and 47 feet (14 meters) wide. Coppin lived in Australia for 47 years. He made and lost several fortunes, built six theaters, and was the first local producer to import some of the world's great talents from overseas.

The nationwide expansion of theater came with the discovery of gold. The Australian gold-rush days began in 1851–52, bringing a massive increase in population and a great explosion of wealth, especially in the growing young cities. Of all the arts, theater shared most in the new wealth and in the excitement of the times. In Victorian towns such as Geelong, fine theaters were built to cater to the miners going to and from the goldfields. Miners showered popular players with gold nuggets. Serious drama seemed to take the fancy of the gold-seekers as much as circuses and other light entertainments did.

Visiting entrepreneurs and theatrical stars quickly became aware that there was money to be made in Australia. Good theater buildings were constructed in the major population centers, and productions of world standing became the rule rather than the exception. Many entrepreneurs, actors, and producers arrived for extended tours. Some settled permanently. This collection of new talent raised the standards of local theater considerably.

The already-famous Coppin backed the visit, in 1874, of the American actor James Cassius Williamson and his wife, actress Maggie Moore. With a comedy-drama of their own called 'Struck Oil', the couple made a fortune in Australia and took the play on tour to other countries. Williamson's future became tied to Australia. In 1879, after seeing the special genius of Gilbert and Sullivan musicals, he negotiated the rights to perform these works in Australia. (*See also* Gilbert and Sullivan.)

The immediate and enormous success of Gilbert and Sullivan convinced Williamson of a fact so far unnoticed about the Australian population: a vast appetite for opera. He toured such world-class artists as Nellie Melba, Ada Crossley, Madame Albani, and Sarah Bernhardt in opera and drama. Grand opera, light opera, and comic opera became a regular staple right up to World War II. The Australian theater became very much a part of the world stage circuits.

In addition to Coppin and Williamson, other management talents came to the fore in the late 19th and early 20th centuries. Among them were Bland Holt, Harry Rikards (with his great chain of Tivoli vaudeville), and the Tait brothers, John and Nevin. After the death of Williamson in 1913, the Taits became the leading theatrical producers in Australia. They maintained a dominant position until the 1950s.

Ireland's nationalist Abbey Theatre in the early 20th century inspired the hope that an equally national Australian drama might emerge not long after federation. Louis Essen's Pioneer Players in Melbourne (1922–26) pursued that dream. So did Doris Fitton's Independent Theatre in Sydney (1930–77), where Sumner Locke Elliott's allegedly blasphemous 'Rusty Bugles' premiered in 1948. Ray Lawler's 'Summer of the Seventeenth Doll' (1955), a vernacular portrayal of aging cane-cutters shedding their illusions, brought local drama to maturity. It was staged by the Australian Elizabethan Theatre Trust, established in 1954 during the euphoria that followed the first visit to Australia by a reigning British monarch.

By the 1970s, a self-confident national drama had diversified into a score of radical, groundbreaking little theaters, well represented by women dramatists and black theater, including 'The First Born' by aboriginal playwright Jack Davis of Perth. The most celebrated and popular contemporary Australian dramatist is David Williamson. His plays include 'Don's Party' (1973), 'Travelling North' (1980), and 'Emerald City' (1987). His defection from Melbourne to Sydney unsettled many admirers, since Melbourne had long and legitimately claimed to be Australia's cultural trendsetter. Music-hall satirical comedy survived brilliantly in Roy Rene (as Mo McCackie) and Barry Humphries (as Dame Edna Everidge, the housewife megastar from Moonee Ponds). Humphries, as Dame Edna, played on stage in London, England, and appeared on television in the United States.

## Motion Pictures

Australian filmmaking dates back to 1896, when two Frenchmen filmed the running of the Melbourne Cup, Australia's most prestigious horse race. Between 1903 and 1914, about 50 feature films had been made in Australia, and the film industry was firmly established.

In the 1920s overseas interests, mainly from the United States, gained control of the distribution of movies in Australia. The distributors of American films became the most potent force in the industry. Without access to a world market, the Australian film producer needed protection for survival. Until 1970, overseas groups controlled film distribution and cinema management. They screened American and British productions almost exclusively. A golden age dawned in 1970 to break this stranglehold: the federal government established the Australian Film Development Corporation—reconstituted in 1975 as the Australian Film Commission, championed and later chaired by Phillip Adams—to make its own documentaries and fund local features.

In 1973, the Australian Film and Television School was founded in Sydney. Its graduates include such directors as Peter Weir ('Picnic at Hanging Rock', 1975; 'Gallipoli', 1981); Fred Schepisi ('The Chant of Jimmie Blacksmith', 1978); Gillian Armstrong ('My Brilliant Career', 1978, with Judy Davis); and Bruce Beresford ('Breaker Morant', 1980). Worldwide box-office successes were scored by George Miller's 'Mad Max' series (beginning with 'Road Warrior', 1981, with Mel Gibson) and by Peter Faiman's 'Crocodile Dundee' (1986, with Paul Hogan).

## Sports

Recreation has been central to Australian culture ever since European migrants found no harsh winters to curtail year-long outdoor games. They had good reason to build their cities alongside coastal beaches. Water temperatures suitable for swimming last about seven months a year. Learn to Swim organizations are widespread, and most children can swim by the time they are 7 or 8. Australians introduced the crawl and the butterfly stroke in competitive swimming, and the continent has produced many world-class swimmers.

The surf, stretching 5,000 miles (8,000 kilometers) from just north of Brisbane on the east coast around the south to Perth on the west coast, broken only by the cliffs of the Nullarbor plateau. This has spawned a huge number of surfers. But sailing, boating, skin diving, and water skiing are nearly as popular. The Sydney-Hobart Yacht Race, held on Boxing Day—December 26—has become a blue-water classic attracting many international entries.

During the 19th century, intercolonial cricket and football matches helped evoke the sense of becoming a nation. Sporting successes put Australia on the world map, most notably during the 1950s, when the 1956 Olympics were held in Melbourne and Australia began scoring victories in Davis Cup tennis. To redress dismal failures in the 1976 Olympics, the Australian Institute of Sport was established in Canberra in 1981. Its goal is to nurture sporting excellence and promote fitness for everyone. (The Summer Olympics were again scheduled for Australia in the year 2000.)

Milestones in recreational development include the inauguration of Australian Rules Football in Melbourne in 1858, codified to exclude the violence of Rugby football; the popularization of the Australian crawl stroke in swimming (in about 1900); the 1983 capture of the America's Cup for yachting, beating an American crew for the first time since the race

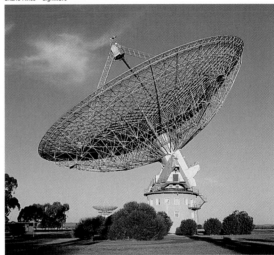

Charle Avice—Lightwave

*The radio telescope at Parkes, New South Wales, is operated by the Commonwealth Scientific and Industrial Research Organisation. The telescope identified the first known quasars in 1960.*

series began in 1851; and the introduction of surf life-saving at Sydney's Bondi and Manly beaches. World-champion Australian athletes, arguably the best ever in their sports, include cricketer Don Bradman, runner Herb Elliott, swimmer Dawn Fraser, and tennis player Rod Laver.

## Sciences

Australian science began with amateur naturalists collecting, describing, and classifying the unique flora and fauna that so amazed the earliest European explorers. Capt. James Cook's first landfall in 1770 was named Botany Bay to celebrate the large number of new plants discovered there. Initial efforts to acclimatize useful plants and animals, including the familiar flowers and birds of Britain, were followed by efforts to eradicate pests and weeds from pioneer farmlands.

Key figures in agricultural research were William Farrer, whose development of rust-resistant strains of wheat helped launch a major export industry, and Hugh McKay, who designed a harvester that stripped, threshed, and winnowed grain. The focused research thrust of World War II saw major advances in biotechnology, information technology, radio astronomy, pharmacology, and medical research. Since then, commercial applications of scientific discoveries have lagged in the private sector, where overseas suppliers win contracts because local markets and investment are too small. To encourage scientific literacy for a postindustrial age, the Australian Research Council was established in 1988. Nobel prizewinners include Howard Florey, Macfarlane Burnet, and John Eccles, all in physiology or medicine.

Most scientific research is conducted by the universities, specialized agencies such as Telecom Australia, multinational corporations, and government departments. New technology parks have been established jointly by state governments and

Photo Index

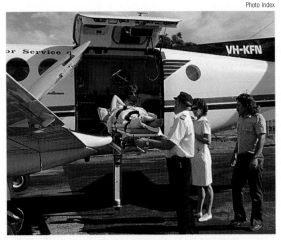

*Health workers in Australia's outback board a patient onto an airplane of the Radio Flying Doctor Service.*

was carried in a hammock slung between horses to Oodnadatta, 400 miles (640 kilometers) away. There he waited two weeks for a train to take him 600 miles (970 kilometers) to a hospital in Adelaide.

In 1928 Alfred Traeger invented the pedal-driven radio transmitter and receiver, which most homesteads could afford. He and Flynn traveled the country installing the two-way radios and showing settlers how to use them to call mission headquarters. In the same year the Australian Inland Mission established its first flying-doctor base at Cloncurry, Queensland. The first flying doctor was K. St. Vincent Welch.

### Religion

Between the censuses of 1976 and 1986, the proportion of the Australian population professing Christianity fell from 79 percent to 73 percent. One fourth of the population had no religion or did not state a religion. The largest non-Christian groups, comprising another two percent of the total population, adhere to Islam (100,000), Buddhism (80,400), and Judaism (69,000). For the first 50 years of European settlement, the Church of England (Anglicans) had the hallmarks of an established church for the richer, ruling class. This included a monopoly of education.

The Roman Catholic church served poorer, often Irish communities. It supported the working class and later its political wing, the Australian Labor party. Both denominations now minister to all classes, but the Anglicans are in decline, claiming 24 percent of the Australian population. The Catholics, with 26 percent, are now more Italian than Irish. The international trend toward ecumenism has ended some feuds. The Australian Council of Churches was established in 1946, and many of the Presbyterians, Methodists, and Congregationalists coalesced into the Uniting Church in Australia in 1977.

Christian religious practice began in Australia on the first Sunday of February 1788, when the Reverend Richard Johnson, chaplain to the colony of New South Wales, conducted a service at what is now the intersection of Bligh and Hunter streets. Johnson also built the first church in the colony. The first service was held there on Aug. 25, 1793. The little building was destroyed by fire five years later.

### Education

Australian children are required to attend school between the ages of 6 and 15 or 16. Ninety percent of them attend government-operated primary schools, but 30 percent attend nongovernment secondary schools. Government schools are usually coeducational, whereas the custom in private school has been single-sex. About 60 percent of all pupils complete high school. But this figure is somewhat misleading since it includes a range from 50 percent for boys in government schools to 80 percent for girls in nongovernment schools.

The states have had primary responsibility for schooling since the mid-19th century, when the School Acts created centralized education authorities. This

universities. The Commonwealth Scientific and Industrial Research Organisation (CSIRO), begun in 1926 as the federal government's research agency, gradually enlarged its scope from the primary to the secondary industries. Its discovery of processes that made woolen textiles shrink-proof, mothproof, and permanently pressed saved the wool industry from the onslaught of artificial fibers after 1950. Its aeronautical, chemical, and standards laboratories underwrote Australian industry. CSIRO pioneered land-systems research in Northern Australia. Australia is one of the world's key astronomical centers, thanks to its political stability, clear dry air, and clear wide view of the southern skies. The ingenious Mills Cross radio telescopes originated in Australia. The CSIRO's radiophysics laboratory pioneered the use of the interferometer in 1946, while the 210-foot (64-meter) dish at Parkes, New South Wales, identified the first known quasars in 1960. One of the world's largest ensembles of mobile radio telescopes, the Australia Telescope, opened at Culgoora, New South Wales, in 1988. Optical astronomy is pursued at Mount Stromlo, near Canberra.

### The Flying-Doctor Service

Australia's vast distances have always presented a problem to settlers. In the early years, one of the biggest worries of people in the outback was becoming ill. It was not until the appearance of a clergyman named John Flynn—Flynn of the Inland, as he was called—that some form of medical service became available to people in remote areas of the country.

In 1912 the Presbyterian church set up the Australian Inland Mission, of which Flynn spent most of his adult life as superintendent. He gave spiritual solace to inland settlers, but he soon realized that medical aid was also desperately needed. Settlers often died because they were too far from a doctor or medical assistance.

This was made clear to Flynn most forcefully when a ranch hand with a spear embedded in his chest legislation still mandates predetermined curricula in primary schools as well as teacher assignments. However, a common national curriculum was adopted for tenth grade in 1989 to simplify transfers among school systems. The earlier dual system of government and denominational schools caused such bickering that an attempt to unite them through a "common Christianity" was attempted, but it failed. As a result, the public schools have been free, compulsory, and secular since the 1870s. Remote areas of the country are reached by correspondence education or the School of the Air.

Since the seasons in Australia are the opposite of those in the Northern Hemisphere, the school year begins at the end of January or early in February, and it ends in mid-December. A vacation of about six weeks is taken over the summer months, December to February. There are two shorter vacations that divide the school year into three terms.

Matriculation in secondary education depends on continuous school-based assessments of a student's aptitude and competence or by a combination of school-based assessment and public examinations. Since the 1970s, Australian authorities have expressed concern about the small number of students taking science and mathematics courses, the high school dropout rate, broadening the curriculum for girls, and integrating children with physical and mental disabilities into local schools. The federal government was long reluctant to take on responsibilities delegated to the states, but it has taken upon itself responsibility for schooling in the Capital Territory (the area around Canberra) and for the education of immigrants and aborigines. Since one fifth of the population in the early 1990s had a non-English-speaking background, federal funds were provided for teaching English as a second language. Aborigines can pursue a bilingual education at mission stations, with bridging courses to ease access to further schooling. Relatively few actually seize these opportunities.

Federal contributions to school libraries, science facilities, and teacher training were increased after 1974 by direct per capita grants to religious and independent schools, ranging from 20 to 75 percent of the fees charged. These grants carried no obligation on the part of the recipient schools to offer free access to qualified students, as is the case in the United Kingdom and other countries.

Post–high school education is available in over 1,000 TAFE (technical-and-further-education) colleges, operated as part of state-wide systems since 1974. There are also about two dozen self-governing universities. About 1.5 million students were enrolled in TAFE colleges in the early 1990s. Another 485,000 students attend universities, 62 percent of them full-time, 27 percent part-time, and 11 percent as correspondence students. Women comprise 52 percent of university students.

The first Australian university was founded in Sydney in 1850. In later years universities were built in Melbourne (1853), Adelaide (1874), Tasmania (1890),

*A primary school at Kuranda in northern Queensland has pupils of various ethnic backgrounds, including aborigines. The schools in Australia have long been integrated.*

Queensland (1909), and Western Australia (1911). Except in Western Australia, tuition fees were charged until 1974, when a Labour government abolished them to encourage lifelong learning. Tuition was reinstated in 1988, but at only 20 percent of actual cost. Australia's first private university was established in 1989.

Libraries and museums augment Australia's formal educational institutions. Sydney was the first city to get a private library, in 1821, and it had the first public library and reading room by 1827. With the opening of the State Library of Victoria in 1853, state libraries remained the main source of books until community libraries became widespread in the mid-20th century.

The Mitchell Library and the Dixson Galleries in Sydney retain the nation's preeminent collections of Australiana. The National Library of Australia, founded in 1901 as the Commonwealth Parliamentary Library, launched the computerized Australian Information Network—called Ausinet—in 1977 and the Australian Bibliographic Network in 1981. Its holdings are now the largest of any Australian library. Sydney University's Fisher Library ranks second.

The Australian Museum was established in Sydney in 1827. It contains a fine collection of aboriginal artifacts. The structure itself epitomizes the imposing architectural styles that so fascinated people during the Victorian era. The Australian War Memorial, in Canberra, and the National Gallery of Victoria contain other notable national collections. Portraits of prominent Australians are displayed at the Australian National Gallery in Canberra. There are a number of open-air museums, including Sovereign Hill, a reconstructed gold mining town in Ballarat, Victoria; and Old Sydney Town, where the days of convict immigrants are recalled.

During the 20th century there has been a proliferation of regional, local, and natural history museums. Official Commonwealth records are now held by the Australian National Archives, established in 1961. Major museums started during the national bicentennial celebration of 1988 include the Australian National Maritime Museum and the Sydney Aquarium.

## ECONOMY

The penal colony that was established at Sydney by the first British settlers in 1788 was initially unable to feed itself and offered only the most dismal prospects for economic development. For the first 30 years, its tiny population of convicts and their military guards occupied an economic backwater as remote from the markets, finance, and technology of Europe as any place on Earth. Only when pastoralists managed to cross the encircling knot of sandstone canyons after 1813, and discovered the far more fertile inland plains, was an agricultural export trade feasible.

After 1830, wool emerged as the most profitable staple commodity. Its labor requirements were low, and its value was high in relation to its weight. It would not perish during a long voyage back to Europe, and the Industrial Revolution in Britain had created textile mills eagerly seeking business. By 1850, half of these mills were using Australian wool. Wheat became a competitive export only after 1860, with the boom in railroad construction. Meats and perishable dairy products became exportable only after 1880, with the development of refrigerated shipping. Meanwhile, in the 1850s, gold rushes had boosted the Australian population and diversified its industries, laying essential foundations for economic development.

By 1900, when Australia's population was still barely three million, its export economy remained specialized in just a few agricultural and mineral products. Wool still earned half the export income. Producers often felt helplessly dependent on the fluctuations of commodity prices and sales in foreign markets. This is one of the perils associated with being an exporter mainly of raw materials instead of finished products. Efficient pastoral production and high wages for farmworkers had dampened the development of manufacturing industry while making Australia seem like a working man's paradise to prospective migrants.

That optimistic view was dashed by a series of unfortunate circumstances: the depression of the 1890s, a massive foreign debt incurred from World War I, costly land settlement schemes, the road building and utilities needed to create an urban infrastructure for what was already a highly urbanized nation, and the depression of the 1930s. Governments felt unable to affect the course of events, and they dreaded the possibility of defaulting on foreign loans. Although plants for iron and steel and for motor-vehicle bodies were established after 1915, Australia's industrial maturation was drawn out. Labor costs were too high, technology was largely imported, and tariff barriers protected inefficient manufacturers from foreign competition.

The outbreak of World War II in 1939 brought such a demand for industrial products that resources were no longer underutilized. In addition, government direction of the economy was increased, for the purpose of combating inflation. The six states surrendered their roles as tax collectors when uniform taxation was introduced in 1942, and the federal government became, and has remained, the sole levier of income tax. Its Commonwealth Bank became a central bank, and its Treasury Department usurped national macroeconomic policy. Postwar social welfare reforms and the reconstruction of the economy further enhanced the federal role, a development by no means unique to Australia.

Until the oil crisis engineered by the Organization of Petroleum Exporting Countries (OPEC) in 1973, the Australian economy boomed. Unemployment remained below a negligible 2 percent of the workforce, and a materialistic modern consumer society emerged. Home ownership rose from 50 percent in 1945 to 70 percent by the 1960s.

Since 1973, the nation's traditional exports have suffered because of serious fluctuations in the prices of basic commodities, such as wool, minerals, and foodstuffs. National trends toward economic self-sufficiency, often by developing synthetic substitutes for wool and other raw materials, also proved detrimental. In Australia there were serious consequences. Industrial militancy rose, wage rates and inflation accelerated, local markets were invaded by the newly industrialized nations of Eastern and Southern Asia, growth faltered, and the public sector was downsized through privatization. This situation was somewhat alleviated by the extraordinary discoveries of mineral wealth after 1960. Mineral exports surpassed those of agricultural and pastoral products by 1980.

### Primary Industries

Australian prosperity has long depended on the agricultural industries, which still attract 35 to 40 percent of the nation's export earnings. Nevertheless, their 30 percent of the Gross National Product in 1950 shrank to less than 5 percent by the 1990s. Many European farming methods initially proved ill adapted to the dry and unfamiliar Australian environment. Scientific research and the insights gained by pioneer settlers helped overcome water deficiencies, salinity, infertile soils, and natural hazards. Advances included the stripper-harvester in 1843, the stump-jump plow in 1876, applications of superphosphate fertilizer to pastures beginning in the 1890s, the selective breeding of animals and crops, and the extension of irrigation, from 1914.

Securing government support for rural Australia became the political mission of the Country Party—formed in 1920, then reorganized as the National Party in 1975—and the National Farmers' Federation. Agricultural exports were hurt when Britain joined the European Economic Community (EEC; now the European Union, or EU) in 1973. There was also, for a time, more restricted access to Japanese and American markets. The decline in exports to Europe has now been offset by a reorientation of sales to Japan, the Middle East, the United States, the former Soviet Union, China, and Southeast Asia.

**Livestock.** With about 12 percent of the world's sheep—170 million, with an annual fluctuation of nine million or so—Australia produces one fourth

J. Cowan—SUPERSTOCK

*Sheep have been herded into pens in Western Australia in preparation for a sheep auction. One quarter of the world's wool is produced in Australia.*

Cameramann International

*Instead of a horse, this Australian cowboy rides a motorcycle. Carrying his dog in a basket on the back of his motorcycle, he is checking on cattle grazing in the outback.*

of the world's wool clip. Of that, 95 percent is sold for export, mostly in its greasy natural state, through public auctions. The main purchasers are Japan, the EU (especially France and Italy), the remnants of the former Soviet Union, Eastern Europe, and, increasingly, China and Taiwan. Marketing and promotion are controlled by the Australian Wool Corporation, a federal statutory authority, which manages a reserve price scheme, hoping to maintain price stability in a wildly fluctuating market.

Australia is also a major exporter of lamb, mutton, and live sheep. About seven million of these are sent each year to the Muslim populations of the Middle East, many for ceremonial slaughter, over the protests of animal-welfare groups. During the 1980s, sheep products accounted for 20 to 25 percent of the value of all rural production.

Cape fat-tailed sheep from South Africa arrived in Australia with the First Fleet in 1788, but only when John Macarthur imported fine-wooled Spanish merinos in 1797 was a breed found that flourished under Australian conditions and supplied the export staple necessary for economic growth. Merinos now comprise 85 percent of all flocks. Other breeds include Corriedales; Polwarths; and Tukidales, a New Zealand breed from which carpet wool is produced; and the crossbred merino–Border Leicester, the ewes of which are mated with Poll Dorset rams to supply table lamb. Since sheep are afflicted by blowflies, internal parasites (including liver fluke), and foot rot, southern pastoral regions are more suitable than the tropical north.

Cattle numbers peaked at 33.4 million in 1976 and declined to 23.2 million by 1990. Most of the decline occurred in southern Australia where grazing is more intensive and other crop-combinations more profitable. Most cattle grazing is now in northern Australia. Of those that remain, 2.7 million are dairy cattle, half of them Holstein-Friesians, with enclaves where Jerseys and Australian Illawarra Shorthorns also feed on improved pastures and fodder crops. Half the beef

herds graze, mainly on natural pastures, in the tropical interior of Queensland. dairying is concentrated in temperate, coastal, southeastern Australia.

In 1933, to produce a strain more resistant to heat and ticks, Brahman cattle were crossed with British breeds. To the same end, the King Ranch of Texas introduced the Santa Gertrudis; and the Braford, Brangus, and Droughtmaster were bred in Australia. Water buffalo were introduced into the Northern Territory in the 1820s and 1830s. Abandoned, they formed feral herds which have since damaged wetlands and waterways with their wallowing, and have been slaughtered (often by game hunters) to control buffalo fly infestations.

After cattle production first surpassed demand in 1843, slaughtered beasts were boiled down for their tallow and hides, which were exported. Canned meat was exported from Newcastle, New South Wales, after 1847, and frozen meat after 1880. Exports of chilled meat, the present mode, began in 1932. The principal markets during the 1980s were North America and Japan.

Dairy output is divided about equally between butter, cheese (production having doubled between 1970 and 1986), and liquid milk. Total output has been decreasing in the face of a world butter glut, growing consumer preference for margarine, competition from imported cheeses, and pollution from the disposal of cheese factory wastes. National dairy policy dates from the 1950s, through price-fixing and production quotas. Poultry meats have also made inroads into the Australian diet at the expense of beef and lamb, 85 percent of it sold fresh. There were 11,000 egg farms (mainly backyard operations) in the late 1960s, but only 691 large, automated hatcheries in 1989.

*Wheat is Australia's primary crop. Although it produces less than 2 percent of the world total, the country ranks second only to Canada as a chief exporter of wheat.*

*Sugar cane fields near Bundaberg, Queensland, are set afire to burn off the dried leaves. Australia is the world's third largest producer of sugar. Cultivation of the crop started in the 1860s.*

**Crops.** Wheat is Australia's primary crop, for both domestic consumption and export. Although Australia harvests less than 2 percent of the world's production, it vies with Canada for second place in the volume exported. Grain purchases by China, Egypt, the successors to the Soviet Union, and Japan account for much of the 80 percent shipped overseas. Wheat is planted in all six states, with New South Wales the greatest producer but Western Australia having the largest area. All Australian wheat is white-grained, planted in winter, harvested in late spring through summer, and bred for resistance to drought, disease, and extreme summer temperatures. The Australian Wheat Board was set up in 1930 to control domestic prices, guarantee minimum prices, and oversee 19 export shipping terminals and a thousand clusters of silos.

After Cuba and Brazil, Australia is the world's third largest exporter of sugar, and is arguably the most efficient producer. Commercial cultivation dates from the 1860s, near Brisbane, and has spread along the Queensland coast as far north as Cairns. The Colonial

Sugar Refining Company, founded in 1853 and still operating sugar mills and refineries as CSR, organized the industry in the 19th century.

Falling world demand and European Union subsidies of beet sugar have created a chronic over-supply of sugar, obliging the Queensland government to impose cane quotas on growers. By-products include molasses and bagasse, fibrous plant residue used as fuel. Cane toads were introduced from South America in 1935 to control beetle pests but are now invading southeastern Australia.

The gold rushes of the 1850s brought Chinese market gardeners into Australia. They dominated vegetable growing for the ensuing 50 years, at first around the suburban fringes of cities but later, with improvements in irrigation, food processing, and storage, around remoter country towns.

The cultivated area reached its peak at 490,000 acres (200,000 hectares) in 1945 but, with higher-yielding varieties and technology, has stabilized around 270,000 acres (110,000 hectares) since 1975. Potatoes occupy about one third of the cultivated area. Less than 10 percent of all vegetable production is sold abroad, mainly as out-of-season curiosities in the Northern Hemisphere.

An even lower proportion of Australian wine production—2 to 3 percent—enters a foreign market, but what is exported is judged to be on a par with South African and California vineyards. Australians no longer consume record-setting volumes of tea and beer, but they lead the English-speaking nations in wine consumption per capita. Viticulturists established wineries near Sydney in 1817, in the Hunter Valley of central New South Wales in 1830, and in the Germanic Barossa Valley of South Australia in 1847–51. Some of the areas achieved notoriety after 1880 when the insect pest phylloxera devastated the vineyards of Victoria and New South Wales. The industry became economically significant only in the 1950s.

**Fishing industries.** With their wines, gourmets enjoy lobsters and prawns, abalone and scallops, and the delicate Sydney rock oyster, for which ready export markets exist, especially in Asia. Otherwise, the Australian fishing industry is surprisingly small and distinctly local, apart from canned tuna, barracuda, and Australian salmon. The smallness of the industry seems odd, since the continent has a coastal circumference of 23,000 miles (37,000 kilometers) and 3,000 varieties of neighboring fish. But Australia's continental shelf is generally too narrow for extensive trawling, and the relatively warm surrounding oceans lack the vast shoals of fish found in colder, shallower waters.

After a 200-mile (320-kilometer) Australian Fishing Zone was adopted in 1979, partly to curtail over-fishing, foreign fishing boats were required to hold licenses and pay access fees. The main fishing grounds are along the northeastern, southeastern, and southwestern coasts of the continent. Barramundi are taken in estuaries but, given Australia's aridity, the freshwater industry is negligible.

Oysters were a traditional food of the aborigines, whose shell middens, or refuse dumps, dot the coast. The larger Pacific oyster was introduced from Japan in 1947 and is cultivated mainly in Tasmania. From about 1860, pearl divers sought natural pearls from the mother-of-pearl shell. They operated mainly from Broome in Western Australia, where 350 luggers berthed until the 1930s. Then depletion of the pearl beds ruined the industry. It was revived in the 1950s along the tropical coasts, but is based today on the artificial culture of pearls. Japanese companies have a joint interest in these pearl farms.

## Water Resources

Crucial to the modern agricultural economy are the available water resources and their impoundment be-hind dams and reservoirs. On this driest of the settled continents, two thirds of the area depends on surface-water conservation and irrigation, the other third on subterranean water. Following the drought of 1877–81, large irrigation projects were constructed along the Murray River and its tributaries, where evaporation and transpiration already reduce the effective rainfall by 50 percent. Even high rainfall regions present problems. Half of Australia's total surface runoff enters the sea in northeastern Queensland. There, low-lying terrain confounded plans to construct big storages for monsoonal rains until the Burdekin Falls dam was built in the late 1980s.

Groundwater is brought to the surface either from shallow, uncompacted sediments or, in greater volume, from deeper-lying sedimentary aquifers. The Great Artesian Basin of Queensland is the largest concentration of subterranean water in the world, but its extraction for stock watering has so greatly exceeded natural replenishment that many bores have run dry or require pumping. Australia has more than 320 large dams, the largest of them at Dartmouth in Victoria. In western Tasmania, dam construction for hydroelectric power dates from the 1930s but from the 1970s was opposed by environmental activists, who succeeded in stopping the controversial Franklin gorge project in a scenic wilderness later awarded World Heritage status.

Water quality is impaired by pollution, notably from the use of farm fertilizers. Runoff from fertilizers finds its way into the waterways. Overgrazing hastens soil erosion, and the remains of salt deposits also deplete usefulness of the soil.

Compared with its effects in the Northern Hemisphere, acid rain has caused only minor damage. Severe and almost universal water deficits encourage Australians to establish tree plantations in strategic parts of watersheds, to install drip or trickle appliances in their gardens, and to replace suburban lawns with native shrubberies.

## Mining and Mineral Industries

Between the primary, or farming, industries and the secondary, or manufacturing, industries lies the mining industry, now the prime source of Australia's export income and a recurring catalyst to economic development. Now practically self-sufficient in minerals, Australia is a leading world exporter of coal, bauxite, alumina, copper, gold, iron ore, silver, lead, zinc, nickel, mineral sands (rutile, ilmenite, zircon, and monazite), diamonds, and uranium. A prodigious array of lesser minerals is also present, from sapphires and manganese to the world's largest concentration of opals. By 1980, mineral exports surpassed those from agriculture and pastoralism.

Sandstone quarrying began by using convict labor, but the 19th century could ultimately rejoice in the gold rushes of the 1850s—concentrated in Victoria—and the 1890s—around Kalgoorlie in Western Australia; the first production of pig iron (1848); and, in 1885, the founding of Broken Hill, the "Silver City" built on the world's richest lode of lead and zinc. Its labor unionists created the militant Barrier Industrial Council. Its members walked out on strike for 18 months in 1919–20, an industrial trauma that resulted in more conciliatory employee relations nationally.

The steel industry at Lithgow ushered in the 20th century but took deeper root at Newcastle in 1915, when Broken Hill Propriety Ltd. diversified its activities. BHP is now Australia's largest production company—the outgrowth of mining enterprises at Broken Hill. It operates in 40 countries and accounts for 10 percent of Australia's export receipts. BHP has branched into engineering and transportation, joined with Esso in developing the Bass Strait oil and gas field, and is now exploiting the same fuels in the Timor Sea. Queensland's Mount Isa began its rivalry with Broken Hill when the mining of silver, lead, zinc, and copper began in 1923. Heavy sand mining commenced in 1934 and the processing of uranium in 1947.

Mineral exploration peaked in the 1970s, but it has resumed using such new tools as satellite scanning and geochemical searches. Exports no longer go

Australia is rich in mineral resources. Alumina is refined at a refinery in Gladstone, Queensland, (top left). Australia is the world's largest producer of aluminum ore bauxite and its derivative, alumina. Uranium is extracted from the Ranger mine (bottom left), in Kakadu National Park in Northern Territory. The Ulan coal mine (center right) near Sydney is a source of much of the country's coal exports. An opal mine (bottom right) near Coober Pedy, South Australia, is one of hundreds of small mines in the area.

(Top left and bottom left) Leo Meier—Australian Picture Library; (center right and bottom right) Paul Steel—Lightwave

primarily to Europe and the United Kingdom, but to Asia. Japan remains the primary destination, with South Korea, China, and India increasingly significant. Prospects for the mining industry are encouraging, even if the exploitation of Aboriginal lands is restricted. There are, however, concerns over environmental degradation and the incidence of such diseases as silicosis and mesothelioma among miners.

Coal was discovered at Newcastle in 1793 and has been exported since 1800, though production barely met domestic consumption until 1965. While not the world's biggest producer, Australia has exported more coal than any other nation since 1985, at times almost half of those shipments going to Japan. Steaming and coking coal are also exported. The richest deposits of black, or bituminous, coal are found in the Sydney Basin, where both underground and open-pit mines operate, and in the Bowen Basin of Queensland, where open-pit mines predominate. Both locations are efficiently close to coastal ports. Less volatile brown coal, or lignite, is cut only in Victoria, where the State Electricity Commission operates on-site generating stations which supply 80 percent of the state's power. BHP burns 15 percent of Australia's black coal in its own iron and steel plants.

Before 1965, isolated Australia was strategically vulnerable in the matter of energy resources, depending almost entirely on imports of crude oil and petroleum products. Estimates now suggest that it is 70 to 90 percent self-sufficient in petroleum and completely self-sufficient in natural gas. Its first commercial oil field at Moonie in Queensland began operating only in 1961. Drilling began as late as 1964 in the offshore Bass Strait field, which now pumps 78 percent of the nation's production. More recent commercial prospects are being exploited off the coast of Western Australia at Barrow Island, and at Jabiru in the Timor Sea, where direct exports began in 1986.

Natural gas flows by long pipelines to all mainland capital cities. The first to benefit were Adelaide and Melbourne in 1969, with supplies from remote inland or offshore wells.

The systematic search for uranium began only in 1944, but reserves are now estimated at 28 percent of the western world's. Four fifths of the known deposits are in the Alligator Rivers area of the Northern Territory, with earlier finds at Rum Jungle, Mary Kathleen, and Radium Hill. Uranium oxide, sometimes called yellow cake, is exported only to countries with which Australia has concluded a nuclear safeguards agreement, since uranium is used in nuclear weapons.

Australia is the world's largest producer of bauxite and its derivative, alumina. Primary aluminum output ranks fourth. Following ore discoveries in 1952, Alcoa began mining in 1963 at Jarrahdale, just east of Perth. Richer mines were soon established at Gove and Weipa on the Gulf of Carpentaria, on or alongside aboriginal lands. Built near the electric generating station which meets 60 percent of Queensland's demand, the alumina refinery at Gladstone is the world's largest. Two thirds of production is exported.

## Forests and Lumbering

Forests suitable for timber amount to only 50,000 square miles (129,500 square kilometers), a fairly small area considering the size of the continent. The forests are found in areas of high and regular rainfall in the Eastern Highlands, in Tasmania, and in the southwest. Dense tropical forests grow on the moist Queensland slopes. Elsewhere trees are too scattered for logging to make economic sense, and much of the desert is treeless. The country produces only about 80 percent of its timber requirements. About four fifths of the timber is hardwood—mainly from the various kinds of eucalyptus. The trees that are softwoods grow in parts of Queensland and Tasmania. Pine plantations have been established in New South Wales, South Australia, Victoria, and Western Australia.

## Manufacturing

In the 19th century, Australia's manufacturing industries were initially restrained by the British mercantilist policy of regarding its colonies as exclusively markets for British goods. Later, nurturing industrial growth relied on high tariff barriers aimed at excluding foreign manufactures. The tariffs were set after 1921 by the federal Tariff Board and its successors, the Industries Assistance Commission from 1974 and the Industry Commission from 1990.

By World War II, major Australian industries included iron and steel, building products, engineering, electrical goods, clothing, printing, and motor assembly. A twenty-year post-war boom saw 28 percent of the workforce in manufacturing by 1960-61, contributing 29 percent of the gross domestic product (GDP). Those proportions have now shrunk to 17 percent of both GDP and labor force participation. Mining, which employs only one percent of the workforce, accounts for 5 percent of GDP.

The older industries were also beset by competition from the newly industrializing nations of nearby Asia. During the 1980s, Australia followed the international trend toward lower tariffs.

After tentative beginnings in the 19th century, Australia's iron and steel industry took firm root in 1913, when BHP inaugurated its steelworks at Newcastle. In 1935, BHP absorbed the rival Australian Iron & Steel plant at Port Kembla. This plant now supplies more than half the nation's output. BHP then rode a wartime boom and confirmed its monopoly by establishing its own blast furnace at Whyalla in 1940. Between 1915 and 1970, all three coastal locations shipped in most of their iron ore from the Middleback Ranges of South Australia. A Western Australian steel facility operated at Kwinana from 1957 to 1983, and the most recent facility to be built was erected in Geelong in 1976.

When Lang Hancock and Stan Hilditch discovered the Pilbara deposits of hematite (iron-ore crystals) in the 1950s, they triggered the minerals boom of the 1970s which recast the resources map and transformed the entire Australian economy. Initially financed by

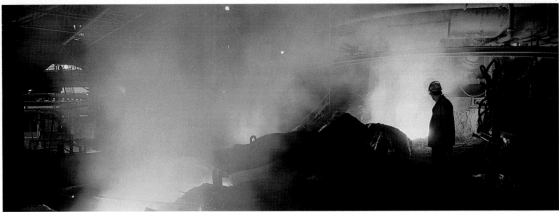

*The Broken Hill Propriety, Ltd., steel plant in Newcastle, New South Wales, was established in 1913 on the south bank of the Hunter River. Founded in 1885, Broken Hill is the largest Australian company.*

American and British interests, development of the hitherto desolate Pilbara region demanded an assured Japanese market for pelletized ore as well as new ports, railroads, and infrastructures. Australia became the world's second largest exporter of iron ore, and the huge Pilbara mines at Mount Tom Price, Newman, and Paraburdoo became household words.

Before 1917, only fully imported motor vehicles were available in Australia. After 1917, motor bodies and certain components were manufactured domestically, and assembled on imported chassis. The first completely Australian-made vehicle was the General Motors Holden, which began rolling off the Fisherman's Bend production line in 1948 and racked up its millionth sale in 1962.

Five foreign-controlled companies now dominate the automobile industry: General Motors, Ford, Nissan, Toyota, and Mitsubishi. Only in the last two corporations is even minority ownership held by Australian investors. Over the years too many companies sought a place in too small a domestic market, and Chrysler, Volkswagen, and the British Motor Corporation have ceased production. Though protected historically by high tariffs and considered essential for a healthy balance of trade, the motor-vehicle industry has been urged to rationalize production. The 1984 Button Plan recommended more interindustry cooperation, fewer car models, less duplication of facilities, higher local content, and increased exports of engines and components.

Many other manufacturing industries dot Australia's economic landscape in an attempt to enhance self-sufficiency through import replacement. Nevertheless, 30 percent of all manufacturing is foreign-owned. Initially providing sulfuric and nitric acids for farm fertilizers, the chemical industry was forced into producing more complex chemicals by World War II. After the war it continued growing at twice the overall rate of industry into the 1960s. Petrochemicals and plastic by-products became significant only after Australia's first oil refinery began operating in 1954. The printing industry caters to a population that is among the most voracious per capita purchasers of books, newspapers, and periodicals in the world, although high local labor costs have now shifted much book printing into Asia. The related papermaking industry now meets 70 percent of Australia's needs.

Eucalyptus pulp was first used in papermaking in 1929, when the dominant firms were emerging. Australian Paper Manufacturers now specializes in heavy industrial paper and packaging, while Associated Pulp & Paper Manufacturers controls the fine-paper market. The clothing and footwear industry remains concentrated in Victoria, where protectionist policies during the 19th century provided an early impetus. Its workers are largely women (84 percent) and immigrants (52 percent), and its factories share inner suburban locations where alternative employment is often lacking.

A nationwide market for brewery products has now eclipsed the statewide dominance of capital-city brewers with tied houses—hotels that sold only one brand of beer—just as these superseded the local rural breweries where the industry began almost 200 years ago. Mergers and takeovers within the brewing industry have left Elders-IXL and the Bond Corporation in shaky control.

There are some 90 biotechnology companies in Australia, half of them engaged in veterinary or medical healthcare. Notable achievements of this small but promising research industry include the isolation of jumping genes, the breeding of a "superpig," and the development of a vaccine for malaria.

**Energy Resource**

Australia is richly endowed with the energy resources on which manufacturers rely. It claims an estimated 6 percent of the world's black-coal reserves and can afford to export two thirds of what is cut each year. Crude oil and condensate compose less than 1 percent of Australia's energy resources but meet 39 percent of total energy demand, two thirds of it from transport. The 1973 OPEC oil crisis sharpened concerns about obtaining more reliable foreign suppliers. Alternative fuels include clean-burning liquid petroleum gas (LPG), which supplies one fifth of the transport demand, and synthetic liquid fuels, such as the Japanese-financed experimental liquefaction of brown coal in the Latrobe Valley.

Remote areas unconnected to state electricity grids increasingly depend on such renewable energy sources as wind turbines, geothermal systems, and ocean energy, or tidal, conversion systems. Five percent of Australian households already use solar water heaters, but that figure has reached 25 percent in Western Australia and 75 percent in the Northern Territory.

Public authorities supply 92 percent of Australia's electricity, of which 60 percent is consumed in the two states of New South Wales and Victoria. Their grids were interconnected in 1960, and then connected with South Australia's in 1990. Australia has no national power grid, and no nuclear power. Steam-powered generating stations, fueled by coal, natural gas, or fuel oil, produce 86.5 percent of this electricity, and hydroelectric power another 2.3 percent. Hydroelectric power peaked at 22 percent of the total in the mid-1970s, when the Snowy Mountains Scheme came into full operation, diverting coastal streams to irrigate inland farms and building seven power stations. Since then, environmentalists have effectively opposed more dam-building in Tasmania and high-voltage power lines through cities.

### Service Industries

Nonmanufacturing businesses now comprise the fastest-growing sector of the Australian economy. The tourist industry is typical. It now employs as many as the clothing, footwear, textiles, and motor vehicle industries combined. Yet only in 1988, boosted by the Australian Bicentennial celebrations and Brisbane's World Expo 88, did Australia first become a net importer of tourists. New Zealanders accounted for 18 percent of those visitors, and the Japanese 14 percent, surpassing Americans for the first time.

The Australian Tourist Commission (now Tourism Australia) was established by the federal government only in 1967. It advertises Australia as uncongested, unpolluted, friendly, climatically superb, and politically quiescent. It does not advertise its remoteness from the populous Northern Hemisphere, its lack of cultural and natural diversity, and its expensive domestic travel. Nor does it mention that Venice attracts more tourists in one summer month than Australia does in a year.

The development of retail trade has imitated the Anglo-American pattern of department stores, discount chains, supermarkets, and suburban malls. As car ownership increased, malls were built farther out from the cities. Attempts to avert central business district decline, usually by pedestrian-oriented planning, have been more successful than similar projects in the United States. In 1974, the Trade Practices Act prohibited retail price maintenance by denying manufacturers the right to set and stamp mandatory

retail prices on their products. Longer trading hours became universal during the 1980s, after decades of union-enforced early closing. Credit-card purchases are blamed for the rise in consumer indebtedness to $1,300 per capita by 1989.

### Finance and Banking

Australian business cycles, with alternating prosperity and recession, have typically lagged behind international trends. Depressions in the 1840s, 1890s, and 1930s were deepened by the unavoidable and continuing reliance on foreign finance, though regionally localized booms reflected pastoral expansion and mineral discoveries. Such was the Poseidon Boom of 1968–70, which fueled an unprecedented bull market in stocks before collapsing in 1974.

Few family-owned dynastic enterprises survived the 19th century. New firms sprang up in the 20th century, scattering old family fortunes, and attracting more American than British capital after 1920, especially from multinational corporations. They diversified their products and markets after 1945 under the twin stimuli of a national immigration program and the closing of traditional European markets as the European Communities became a trading bloc.

The decade of 1975–85 brought major economic uncertainties, with rising oil prices, erratic commodities markets, two recessions, and the heyday of corporate raiders. When the traditionally socialist Labor government won federal office in 1983, it startled the business community by deregulating the financial system, exposing it to world market forces, and allowing a 10 percent devaluation of the Australian dollar to offset reverses in the terms of trade. Sixteen foreign banks were authorized to operate in Australia. In return, the more enterprising Australian banks were permitted to launch overseas offices. Previously, the Banking Act of 1959 had tightened control of private banks while legalizing unregulated competition from savings-and-loan and similar financial institutions for the next 20 years. State banks trading in their own states were exempted.

By establishing the Reserve Bank in 1960, the federal government stripped from its earlier creation, the Commonwealth Bank of Australia, the central banking role it had gradually appropriated after its establishment in 1911.

Before the Australian colonies formed a federal union in 1901, central bank functions had been performed by the Bank of England. An attempt by Joseph B. Chifley's Labor government to nationalize all private banks in 1947 was declared unconstitutional.

Australian banking dates from 1817, when the Bank of New South Wales was chartered. Its amalgamation with the Commercial Bank of Australia in 1982–83 created Westpac, the nation's largest private banking corporation. Three banks are now among Australia's top ten companies, ranked by 1992 revenues. First and second on this list are the Australian Mutual Provident Society, an insurance company, and Coles Meyer, in retail.

The Indian Pacific Railroad (top) has the longest straight stretch of track in the world—300 miles (480 kilometers). The track runs through the Nullarbor Plain in the southern part of Western Australia. Fremantle Harbor (bottom), in Perth, is the chief port of Western Australia.

Photos, Photo Index

Trading in stocks and shares began in the 1840s, and is now controlled by the Australian Stock Exchange. Formed in 1986 from six preexisting exchanges, it now operates trading floors in all state capitals, lists more than 1,000 companies, and has 115 registered, self-regulating brokers.

## Transportation

The immense area and sparse population of Australia still combine to impede development. Long distances between small settlements inevitably inflate the costs of transportation, so that the main roads are often inferior to those in other developed nations.

The earliest road network beyond Sydney reached the inland provincial city of Bathurst by 1815. The Hume Highway from Sydney to Melbourne, following a route discovered in 1824 between what are now the nation's preeminent cities, remains the busiest link. Since World War I, most roads have been controlled and financed by the state governments. The road from Adelaide to Darwin was paved during World War II at the insistence of Gen. Douglas MacArthur, the United States Army officer in charge of Allied operations in the Pacific theater. The highway from Adelaide to Perth across the Nullarbor Plain was paved only in 1976. Federal highway initiatives in 1974 and 1989 effectively upgraded the national road, Highway 1, linking all mainland state capitals. Several highway segments have been named after the explorers who first blazed the trails: Stuart, Eyre, Hume, Sturt, Landsborough, Oxley, and Mitchell.

Of the coaching companies which braved floods, fires, bushrangers (outlaws), and deplorable roads to carry passengers and mail to inland destinations, the most famous was Cobb and Company, founded in 1853 by four Americans. They replaced lighter English coaches with sturdier, leather-sprung, American-built models. Their teams served the outback margins of settlement until 1924, when the expanding railway network finally drove them out of business.

Railways were constructed in all colonies between 1854, when a line was built between Melbourne and Port Melbourne, and 1871, when the inland wheat belts were being developed. Trivial disagreements among the self-protecting colonies blocked the creation of any master plan and saddled Australia with three different rail gauges: the standard gauge of 4 feet 8½ inches (144 centimeters) in New South Wales; the broad gauge of 5 feet 3 inches (160 centimeters) in Victoria and South Australia; and the narrow gauge of 3 feet 6 inches (107 centimeters) in Queensland, Tasmania, Western Australia, and the northern extremities of South Australia. It took until 1970 to standardize one continuous line between Perth and Brisbane, along which the India–Pacific train now travels. It crosses the Nullarbor Plain on the longest straight stretch of rail track in the world—300 miles (480 kilometers).

State governments control most of the railways, including the profitable electrified commuter lines in the cities. These help offset the losses on run-down rural services. The Commonwealth government controls the railways of Tasmania, the Northern Territory, and parts of the transcontinental line. Private freight lines convey iron ore, sugar, coal, and other goods to the nearest ports. Trams, or streetcars, served the larger cities until buses replaced them by the 1960s—except in Melbourne, where trains still run along broad streets laid out in a grid pattern.

Australia's busiest ports are Sydney, Melbourne, Newcastle, Hay Point, Dampier, and Port Hedland. The last three of these are occupied primarily with carrying mineral exports.

Australia originally depended on shipping for all contact with England, Europe, and other trading partners. In 1787–88, the fleet bringing the original convict settlers arrived after being eight months at sea. The travel time from England to Australia was cut to 60 days—a time set in 1871 by the *Thermopylae,* after clipper ships, including the famous *Cutty Sark,* had entered the Australian run. They mainly carried wool to Europe.

The airplane made connections with other countries much more swift. Qantas and Imperial Airways flew their first passengers to Britain in 1935. By the 1960s, shipping lines to Southampton, Genoa, and San Francisco had carried their last passengers, though fleets of cruise ships still ply the Australian waters.

Mercantile shipping is now dominated by the Australian National Line, established by the federal government in 1956. River transport is negligible in a land beset by droughts, sand-clogged channels, and the scarcity of navigable streams.

Aviation solved the problem of Australia's vast internal distances and remoteness from overseas centers. In 1919, Keith and Ross Smith flew from England to Darwin in 28 days. The first flight across the Pacific, from California to Brisbane, was completed in 1928 by Charles Kingsford-Smith, after whom Sydney's airport is named. Such exploits made Australians air-conscious and promoted the domestic market. Queensland and Northern Territory Aerial Services (Qantas) was founded in 1920. It became the nation's flagship carrier after being nationalized by the federal government in 1947. Its safety record is unmatched.

Thirty overseas carriers now serve Australia, mostly under bilateral agreements which give Qantas reciprocal landing rights. Domestic airline services were controlled between 1952 and 1987 by a two-airline policy. This maintained a regulated monopoly on interstate routes, with the government airline (Australian Airlines) in sole direct competition with one private airline (Ansett). Remote outposts have been served by the Royal Flying Doctor Service since 1928, using aerial ambulances, radio and landline networks, and mobile clinics. The School of the Air for outback children began in 1951 by using the same two-way radio transmitters.

## Communication

There were post offices in most Australian towns by the 1850s. Telegraphy became widespread in the 1860s. The triumphant completion of the Overland Telegraph Line in 1870–72 was a remarkable feat: a line 1,860 miles (3,000 kilometers) long ran across the deserts from Adelaide to Darwin, and thence underwater as cable to Java, to link Australia with Europe. This finally supplanted the tedious reliance on slow steamship mail. Telephone exchanges were established in the major cities during the 1870s.

After the federation of 1901, the new postmaster–general integrated the services previously provided by the independent colonies. In time the postmaster–general also took over radio broadcasting, started motorizing mail delivery in 1910, began airmail service in 1930, and started overseas airmail in 1934. The postmaster–general's department was split in 1975 into Australia Post and the highly profitable Telecom Australia. These are two government monopolies, which private entrepreneurs continue to challenge. Telecom's coaxial cables now link all major cities. Fiber optic undersea cables link Australia with North America; and Aussat receives and transmits radio signals via an Earth satellite.

Regular radio broadcasts started in 1923 using a "sealed-set" system: listeners could tune in only to pre-programmed stations by subscribing to Amalgamated Wireless (Australasia) Ltd. and paying a license fee to the federal government. A rival, advertising-based service began in 1925. Network radio was introduced in 1930, and the first frequency modulation (FM) stations were licensed in 1980. The Australian Broadcasting Commission (ABC) was established in 1932 and was reconstituted as the Australian Broadcasting Corporation in 1983. Controlling 384 radio stations and 393 television stations, the ABC is now the world's largest English-language broadcaster.

Television transmission began in Sydney in 1956, in all other state capitals by 1960, and in Canberra and the major provincial centers by 1964. Australia has 343 commercial television channels and 393 national, or government, channels. Foreign ownership of broadcasting licenses is forbidden, and no single operator may command more than 60 percent of the national audience.

Australia's first newspaper, the *Sydney Gazette & New South Wales Advertiser,* began publication in 1803. There are now two national dailies, 15 metropolitan dailies, and more than 450 other newspapers. Australians remain among the most avid newspaper readers in the world. A few labor-oriented papers survived until World War II, but current media views tend to be conservative. Rupert Murdoch's News Ltd. now controls 62 percent of all newspaper circulation, and the Fairfax group—publishers of the venerable *Sydney Morning Herald* since 1841—a dwindling 18 percent.

## Government Regulation

Government intervention in the Australian economy deepened during World War II with the introduction of uniform taxation in 1942. Tax-sharing arrangements with the states were revised in 1971 and 1976, but the federal government still collects 80 percent of all taxes, compared with 16 percent by state governments and four percent by local authorities. A national tax summit in 1985 vainly tried to replace progressive direct taxation with a broad-based consumption tax—the Value Added Tax (VAT).

Maintaining full employment has been another government objective. This goal was achieved briefly, without government stimulus, during the golden decade of the 1850s, the building boom of the 1880s, and the postwar reconstruction era from 1950 through the mid-1970s. Unemployment peaked at 20 percent of the workforce during the depression in 1932 but remained around 3 percent from 1942 until 1975. It peaked again in 1983 at 10 percent, as women and casual or part-time employees entered the workforce in greater proportions, and wage increases and the oil crisis of 1973 led to retrenchments. Matters improved with the devaluation of the currency and improved industrial competitiveness. By 1989, unemployment had fallen to six percent. In 1983, a Prices and Incomes Accord was hammered out between the Australian Council of Trade Unions and the federal government. It provided for wage indexation—tying wage increases to the consumer price index. Trade union membership comprised 54 percent of the total workforce in 1989.

Since 1905, as the Australian constitution provided, wage determinations have been made by the Commonwealth Court of Conciliation and Arbitration, and after 1956 by its successor, the Australian Conciliation and Arbitration Commission. The concept of a basic wage was introduced in 1907 through the celebrated Harvester judgment, whereby a minimum wage for unskilled male workers was established. Its provision for automatic quarterly cost-of-living adjustments was abandoned in 1953, and the concept of a basic wage was replaced in 1967 by a total (variable) wage, which included skill margins for different occupations. Equal pay for women was effected between 1966 and 1972.

### International Trade

The exchange of raw materials for finished products sums up Australian trade until World War II. Between 1850 and 1900, exports and imports accounted for about half of Australia's Gross National Product. Foreign trade simply dominated an economy where a tiny, globally isolated population depended on European products, both industrial and cultural, and could pay for them only with the continent's immense natural resources. Imports routinely exceeded exports until 1940–55.

The orientation of trade shifted after Britain joined the European Community (now European Union) in 1973. Britain alone had taken 40 to 50 percent of Australia's exports before 1950 and had supplied a comparable proportion of its imports. By 1989–90, Japan was buying 26 percent of Australia's exports and the entire EC only 14 percent. Japan was supplying 19 percent of the imports and the United States 24 percent, mainly machinery, chemicals, and transport equipment. Australia was undeniably a partner in the booming Pacific Rim. Australia is also an active member of the General Agreement on Trade and Tariffs (GATT), the Organization for Economic Cooperation and Development (OECD), and the United Nations Conference on Trade and Development (UNCTAD).

The regulation of foreign trade remains a constant national concern. Since 1986, Australia has played a leading role among the world's 14 nonsubsidizing, agricultural fair traders. Within Australia, restrictive trade practices which hinder competition, either by collusion or monopoly, have been regulated stringently since 1974, when the Trade Practices Act offered consumer protection. But it exempted mergers and takeovers unless they created monopolies.

## GOVERNMENT

Australia is a parliamentary democracy, generally modeled on the British system—but with a few differences. In Australia the primacy of parliament is limited by a written constitution. Australia's three-tiered system of federal, state, and local governments also differs from the unitary British model, because it took over some aspects of the American federal system.

Each of the six states has a bicameral parliament, except Queensland, where the upper house was abolished in 1922. Local government now embraces 835 urban municipalities and rural shires, making Australia possibly the most overgoverned nation on Earth for the size of its population. Australia is also to some extent a constitutional monarchy, since the British monarch serves as titular head of the government through her nominated representatives, the governor-general in Canberra and the six state governors. A sentimental but widespread attachment to the British Crown is increasingly under challenge by would-be republicans, whom pollsters in 1993 believed comprise 70 percent of the electorate.

In all seven parliaments, the right to govern is held by the political party, or coalition of parties, with the most representatives in the lower house. The leader of the majority party automatically becomes prime minister, in the federal parliament, or premier in state parliaments. In Canberra's federal parliament, the legislature consists of the House of Representatives, with 148 members, elected every three years or less; and the Senate, with 76 members, 12 from each state and two each from the Northern Territory and the Australian Capital Territory. The constitution states that the number of members of the lower house of Parliament must be approximately twice the number in the Senate. The Representation Act of 1983 provided for election of 12 senators from each state, while allotting two each to the territories.

Executive power is technically vested in the British monarch, but it is exercised in reality by a cabinet of ministers, drawn from the leading members of the ruling party or coalition. These ministers serve as heads of specific government agencies. Unlike the heads of American government agencies, they must also be elected as members of Parliament. They are thus answerable to both Parliament and the public. (*See also* Cabinet Government.)

### Historical Background

The Australian Constitution was drafted at conventions in 1891 and from 1897 to 1898, approved by referendum, and ratified by the British parliament on July 9, 1900. It came into force on the first day of the 20th century, Jan. 1, 1901, the founding date of the Commonwealth of Australia. State constitutions,

*Parliament House in Canberra, the Australian capital, faces Lake Burley Griffin, opposite the Anzac Parade in the foreground. Designed by architect Romaldo Giurgola, the building took eight years to construct and was opened in 1988.*

J.P. & E.S. Baker—Australian Picture Library

legislatures, and laws continued to operate as before, though federal laws were to prevail over any contradictory state laws. The Commonwealth was given specific powers to regulate commerce, communications, industrial disputes, defense, external affairs, and immigration, as well as marriage and divorce, where uniform laws were desirable.

Since its creation in 1903, the High Court of Australia has been responsible for interpreting the constitution. Its decisions have expanded and centralized Commonwealth power in such areas as education, health, housing, transport, environment, aviation, urban development, trade practices, and international treaty obligations. The constitution permits either house of Parliament to introduce legislation and requires both to approve it, though only the House of Representatives may introduce most appropriation and taxation bills. The constitution may be altered by referendum if approved by a majority of electors nationally and by majorities in four out of the six states. Only eight of 42 referenda have succeeded.

For the entire 20th century, Australian nationalism remained feeble. National identity crises were recurrent, as loyalties were torn between the emergent Australian Commonwealth, Britain and the Empire (especially during World War I), and older allegiances to home states. No civil war or foreign invasion

unified Australia, and a recent multiculturalism— with aboriginal rights resurgent—has again diluted any emotional or cultural attachment to the continent. Controversy still surrounds the national song and the national flag, from which Asia-oriented republicans would like to see the Union Jack discarded forever.

### Elections and Political Parties

Australia has led the world in many phases of electoral reform, though voting rights were granted to aborigines only in 1967. The secret ballot, universally known as the Australian ballot, was first used in Victoria in 1856. The South Australian government was the first in the world to adopt adult male suffrage (1856), and the second—after New Zealand—to enfranchise women (1894).

Since 1915, voting has been compulsory. Those who fail to vote in an election may be fined up to 50 dollars. Voter turnout exceeds 90 percent, though 10 percent of these may cast informal—intentionally invalid—votes. The government adopted a preferential voting system in 1919: voters number the candidates in order of preference on the ballot. Proportional representation is retained in multimember electorates such as those for the senate. This assures that the parties will divide the seats in the legislative houses according to the number of votes they receive.

The Australian public service, or bureaucracy, has been built on a departmental framework begun in New South Wales by Gov. Ralph Darling in the 1820s. Appointments to the public service by political patronage were ended in Victoria in 1883 and in all other states shortly thereafter. Senior public servants are appointed as nonpolitical permanent heads of government departments, to ensure continuity of technical and professional expertise during political transitions. After public servants took unprecedented industrial action in the 1970s, the federal Labor government legislated reforms in 1984 and 1987 to improve accountability and efficiency.

Australia enjoys a strong but polarized political party system. During the 19th century, conservative coalitions were splintered among rural, urban, Whig, and Tory factions. These were forced to present a more unified front after 1891, when forerunners of the Australian Labor party (ALP) emerged. From 1910 to 1990, over 90 percent of the federal vote was split between the ALP and the Liberal (conservative) party, the latter usually in coalition with the National, or Country, party. Smaller parties—including Communist, "green," Democratic Labor, and Australian Democrat—seldom captured more than 10 percent of the total vote collectively.

The Country party was formed in 1920 to promote the interests of farmers and isolated rural communities, but it broadened its base and changed its name to the National party in 1982. In uneasy coalition with the Liberals, it has regularly held the balance of parliamentary power. All three major parties have extensive networks of local branches, but only the state branches of the ALP preselect candidates, set policy, and cement trade-union affiliations. The ALP has been the left-wing party of reform as well as the workers' party. It arose as Australia's first political party in 1891 when strikes failed to secure better working conditions and direct political action seemed more promising. Its early platform advocated electoral reforms, improved working conditions, government aid to agriculture and education, and the "white Australia" policy, which was officially abandoned in 1973.

### The Legal System

British authority to pass statutes affecting the Australian Commonwealth and States ended with the passage of the Australia Acts in 1986, but the traditions of British statutes and case law remain firmly embedded in the Australian legal system. State courts are structured hierarchically. Magistrate's courts (called local courts in some States) have jurisdiction over less serious offenses. District courts are presided over by judges who hear indictable felonies—except those formerly punishable by death—and civil claims of less than 100,000 dollars.

The State supreme courts, with a full bench of three judges, have general appellate jurisdiction, hearing the most serious indictable offenses, including admiralty and probate cases. The more recently established federal court system includes the Family Court,

dating from 1976, and responsible for settling disputes over marriage and offspring; and the Federal Court, dedicated since 1977 to labor law, bankruptcy, and restrictive trade practices.

The final arbiter is the High Court of Australia, which seats a Chief Justice and six Justices, now appointed to the age of 70. Appeals beyond it to the Judicial Committee of the Privy Council in London have not been permitted since 1968 in federal matters, nor since 1985 in state matters. Since 1987, cases involving locations in several jurisdictions need no longer be litigated in several courts, possibly in different states, but can be presented in any federal or State court. Lawyers may practice as both solicitors and barristers, except in New South Wales and Queensland. (Barristers represent clients in court proceedings, while solicitors perform most other legal tasks.)

Criminal offenses are codified entirely in statutes in Queensland, Western Australia, and Tasmania. The other states and territories have common-law jurisdictions that also recognize court decisions in their criminal law. Although the constitutional powers of the Commonwealth do not include criminal jurisdiction, the importation of prohibited drugs is regulated by its Customs Act.

Each state and the Northern Territory has its own police force. Local communities have none but rely on district offices of state patrols. Until 1833, soldiers supervising convicts performed police duties. For the remainder of the 19th century, urban police units were supplemented by native police, known as blacktrackers, and mounted troopers who patrolled remote areas where bushrangers, escaped convicts, and violent miners provoked disorder. Allegations of corruption and links to organized crime continue to dog the police.

The Australian Federal Police was consolidated in 1979 from the older Commonwealth Police to enforce federal laws. It deals mainly with drug trafficking, organized crime, and large-scale fraud. The Australian Security Intelligence Organisation (ASIO) was established in 1949 and formalized by legislation in 1956. It handles internal counterespionage, leaving external (foreign) operations to the Australian Secret Intelligence Service (ASIS) and the electronic interception of intelligence run by the Defence Signals Directorate (DSD).

### Foreign and Military Affairs

The attainment of nationhood in 1901 occasioned no immediate break with the colonial past. Australia remained so dependent on Britain economically, culturally, and politically that its own department of foreign affairs was not established until 1935. Until 1941, the Royal Navy was Australia's reliable first line of defense. When the Japanese captured Singapore from the British in 1942 and bombed Darwin in the same month, Australia's vulnerability and isolation were fearfully exposed. Its precarious location on the edge of an Asia that was rapidly throwing off colonial status was further emphasized by Mao's Communist victory in China (1949), the Korean War (1950–53), and the implications of the "domino theory" as Communist insurgents rampaged southward through Indochina into neighboring Indonesia. The domino theory, enunciated by United States President Dwight D. Eisenhower, suggested that if one country fell to Communism, neighboring countries would soon follow suit.

After World War II, like most other countries stranded in a world of antagonistic superpowers, Australia sought security through defense alliances, mainly with the United States. Since 1980 Australia has taken a more independent stance internationally, focusing on economic and diplomatic issues affecting the Pacific Rim rather than the old militaristic, ideological, and white-supremacist attitudes.

An Australian, Sir Percy Spender, initiated the Colombo Plan in 1950, to channel economic and technical assistance to British Commonwealth countries in Asia and their dependent territories. Australia eagerly signed the ANZUS Treaty with New Zealand and the United States in 1951, under which an ultimately worthless policy of forward defense sent troops to Korea, Malaysia (1963–65), and Vietnam. Australia joined the Southeast Asia Treaty Organisation (SEATO) in 1954, after French Indochina disintegrated (see Vietnam War).

Over one fourth of Australia's foreign aid was directed to Papua New Guinea (PNG), which became self-governing in 1973. It had been an Australian responsibility since 1883, as an annexation, a protectorate, a League of Nations mandated territory, and a United Nations Trust Territory. This aid (335 million dollars) accounted for 25 percent of PNG's operating budget (1991–92). Another 116.3 million dollars of aid went to Indonesia. Guiding Papua New Guinea to independence was a major commitment in Australian foreign policy after World War II, as was the reorientation of immigration and trade from Europe towards Asia. More stable conditions now permit the Royal Australian Navy to concentrate on antisubmarine surveillance and coastal patrol.

The defense of the continent is managed by the Australian Defence Force (ADF) and the Department of Defence. The ADF consists of the military branches—the army, navy, and air force. The Department of Defence is the civilian control over military affairs. It sets policy, deals with military procurement, and handles financial, budgetary, logistic, and scientific support for the military branches.

The Australian army now trains primarily for tropical jungle warfare, not for the desert battles it fought with distinction in both World Wars. For its flexible role in Australia's defense, the Royal Australian Air Force is equipped with F-111 fighter-bombers and FA-18 Hornet multirole fighters. Orion P-3Cs are used for maritime surveillance around Australia's long, largely uninhabited northern coastline.

Since 1963, Australia and the United States have established joint strategic facilities within Australia to monitor international arms movements and to anticipate surprise attacks. They provide satellite ground control and sea navigation information, and plot submarine movements in the Indian and western Pacific oceans. Critics argued that their presence makes Australia a nuclear target, but this threat was lessened by the end of the Cold War in 1991.

## HISTORY

The Australian past can be divided into four broad eras. There is a geologic history of Australia, an anthropological prehistory before 1788, a European colonial history after 1788, and now, since World War II, a contemporary Asian-Pacific history.

### Precolonial Era

The continent and its natural environment were created when the Australian fragment of Gondwanaland drifted into its present, partly tropical location. The current, more arid climatic regime succeeded the ice ages. Aborigines occupied the continent over 40,000 years ago and established a sensitive living relationship with the land. But they knew nothing of the wider world.

Incorporating Australia into a worldview was left to the Europeans who systematically explored the oceans and colonized their coasts, beginning by about AD 700. Medieval geographers conjectured a perfectly round globe with frigid polar regions, temperate midlatitudes, and a torrid equatorial zone. To counterbalance the landmasses of the northern hemisphere, they postulated the existence of a Terra Australis Incognita (unknown southern continent) and sent navigators to find it. Asians and Pacific Islanders probably sighted the uninviting northern coast of Australia before the Europeans did, but left neither maps, records, nor settlements.

### The European Discovery

Overland trade routes between Asia and Europe through the Middle East were interrupted by Muslim control of much of this area in the late Middle Ages. In addition, many of the waterways to the East were under Muslim control. Muslim taxation and harassment persuaded Europeans to seek other ways to reach the Far East. Portuguese and Spanish navigators sought an alternative oceanic route around Africa to India and the Spice Islands (the Moluccas). They had found a route by 1509. As is well known, Columbus sailed west in 1492 to reach East Asia, discovering the Americas in the process. The archipelagoes north of Australia were soon discovered—New Guinea by 1526, the New Hebrides (now Vanuatu) by 1606.

The Dutch vessel, Duyfken, under master Willem Jansz, made the first indisputable sighting of Australia in 1606, in the Gulf of Carpentaria. From Batavia (now Jakarta), the Dutch spread their mercantile interests throughout the East Indies (now Indonesia), seeking new lands. Sailing ships bound for Batavia soon found that hugging the coasts of Africa and India made for a slow passage. Running due east from the Cape of

*'Captain Cook Taking Possession of the Australian Continent on Behalf of the British Crown, AD 1700' is a colored wood engraving by Samuel Calvert.*

Good Hope with the brisk westerlies, then cutting north at the last possible moment, some 2,000 miles (3,200 kilometers) across the Indian Ocean, was much faster. Not all turned north in time. Dirck Hartog, Frederik de Houtman, and other Dutch navigators thus discovered the wreck-littered western coast of Australia between 1616 and 1628.

In 1642–43, Abel Tasman was sent by the Dutch East India Company to seek new lands south and east of Batavia. He sailed eastward across the Indian Ocean at 50° S. latitude, shifted course to avoid bad weather, and ran against the stormy west coast of Tasmania, which he named Van Diemen's Land after the governor-general in Batavia. He sailed on eastward and discovered New Zealand.

All of these coastal discoveries revealed only desolate deserts and hostile natives. The better-endowed east coast was long avoided by navigators, fearful that prevailing winds would trap them against its dead lee shore. It was discovered and charted in 1770 by James Cook, arguably the greatest navigator of them all. Six years later, Britain lost its American Colonies and the dumping ground for convicts that they had provided.

### A New British Penal Colony

A recommendation that Botany Bay—Cook's first landfall, now part of Sydney—might be suitable for a British penal settlement was accepted, and the First Fleet sailed for Australia from Portsmouth, England, in 1787. It was under the command of Arthur Phillip, the first governor-designate of New South Wales. The 11 ships set out with a complement of 443 seamen, 586 male and 192 female convicts, 211 marines, and officials, wives, and children. They arrived 250 days later.

Finding Botany Bay too exposed and lacking drinking water, Phillip investigated the next inlet north. He "had the satisfaction of finding the finest Harbour in the World, in which a thousand Sail of the line may ride in the most perfect security." It was Sydney Harbour. He selected a deepwater cove with a freshwater stream, named it Sydney Cove, and inaugurated

the settlement on Jan. 26, 1788, now celebrated as Australia Day. The first circumnavigation of Australia was achieved in 1801–03 by Matthew Flinders. He proposed the name Australia for the entire continent. The continent had been divided into New South Wales and New Holland at 135° E. longitude.

A surrounding canyonland of precipitous sandstone confined Phillip's settlement to the immediate vicinity of Sydney Harbour for 25 years. The Blue Mountains were finally crossed in 1813 by explorers who kept to the level ridges and avoided the blind valleys. Pastoralists seized this unauthorized opportunity to drive their sheep and cattle inland, following reports of suitable pastures. They left behind a brutalized penal colony, often living on starvation rations, 15,000 miles (24,000 kilometers) from a home country to which they could never hope to return.

Exile to overseas prison settlements—the so-called transportation system—was devised by the British in the early 18th century as a punitive measure for more than 200 crimes. Conditions below decks on convict ships were appalling until surgeon-superintendants were assigned to all voyages after 1815. The mortality rate during passages fell to below 1 percent—lower than on emigrant ships to North America.

There were altogether 825 passages by convict ships, with only five wrecks and 550 convicts lost. Of all the convicts transported, 137,000 were males. They were mostly young and poor from the industrial cities, and often thieves. Some 25,000 exiles were females. Not more than 1,000 were political offenders or exiles, 600 of them from Ireland. Another 4,000 Irish were transported for rebellious land agitation. By 1800, free settlers already outnumbered the convicts in New South Wales and were twice as numerous by 1839. Satellite penal stations were also established, among them Norfolk Island and Moreton Bay (now Brisbane).

Abolitionist sentiment began in Britain, with clergy questioning both the deterrent and reforming capabilities of transportation. In Australia, the growing proportion of free settlers resented the social stigma of the "convict stain," which was recklessly attached to all colonists. The free colonists also feared competition from cheap labor. Only the squatters, wealthier rural landholders, wanted to prolong transportation. They benefited from the assignment system which placed convicts in private service, where good conduct could obtain for them a "ticket of leave" entitling them to work for wages, or even a conditional pardon—the condition being that they never return to Britain. Only 15 percent of the convicts were sentenced to chain gangs or actual incarceration.

Hard labor did leave a colonial legacy of simple but dignified stone buildings. In Sydney, there were the Hyde Park Barracks, the Mint Building, St. James' Anglican Church—the convict architect Francis Greenway's masterpiece—and Elizabeth Farm House, the oldest extant building in Australia. In Tasmania there remain the ruins of Port Arthur, grimmest of the penitentiaries. Parts of Fremantle in Perth were also convict-built. Transportation to New South Wales

ceased in 1840, to Tasmania in 1852, and to Western Australia in 1868.

Many escaped convicts, called bolters, became bushrangers, the Australian counterparts of Europe's 19th-century highwaymen or the outlaws of the frontier in the United States. Bushranging originally meant familiarity with the bush, but it came to imply rural crime, such as stock thefts, robbery of banks and mail coaches, and the murder of policemen. Since Tasmania's Port Arthur and Macquarie Harbour received the most hardened criminals, that was where the bushranging Vandemonians of Van Diemen's Land were legion. Many in New South Wales and Victoria roamed in well-organized gangs, often with the connivance of local residents, themselves contemptuous of the law.

Bushrangers personified the antiauthoritarian aspects of the Australian character, the comradeship of the bush, the conflict between squatter and free selector, the transplanted hatred of Irish Catholics for English Protestants, the rivalry between immigrants and the native-born, and the disorderliness of settlement itself, for all its rules and regulations. Bushrangers thus became an enduring part of Australian folklore. Among the most notorious were Jack Donahoe (the original wild colonial boy), Captain Thunderbolt, Mad Dog Morgan, and the armor-clad Ned Kelly. Kelly's exploits were portrayed in a dramatic series of paintings by the modern Australian artist Sidney Nolan (*see* Kelly, Ned).

## Inland Exploration

The map of inland Australia was gradually and arduously compiled by the explorers who traversed its length and breadth between 1815 and 1939. Settlers who followed them pushed the pioneering frontier as far as they could into the arid center and the tropical north, first from the southeast and then from the southwest. Fanning out from the more fertile coastal fringes into the least productive and last explored regions, they established the present pattern of sparse rural settlement. It has remained tethered and

subordinate to the handful of coastal ports where the British once held power, and where the lifelines from Europe terminated. Having crossed the Blue Mountains in 1813, explorers looked for potential croplands and pastures. John Oxley found only marshes but wishfully hoped they were the edges of a vast inland sea. That vision of a well-watered interior led other explorers astray. For example, Charles Sturt unraveled the mystery of the west-flowing rivers by tracing the Murray-Darling to its outlet, but he later went half-blind in the blazing heat of the Simpson Desert.

Others forged overland links between the coastal ports. In 1824, Hamilton Hume and William Hovell were the first to traverse the 540 miles (870 kilometers) between what are now the cities of Sydney and Melbourne. Edward John Eyre was commissioned in 1841 to find a land route between South Australia and Western Australia, but in crossing the Nullarbor Plain on foot he found no running water for 1,240 miles (2,000 kilometers). Ludwig Leichhardt discovered a route across reliable rivers from Brisbane to Darwin in 1844–45 but vanished without trace on a second expedition. His epic journeys are the subject of Patrick White's novel 'Voss' (*see* Australian Literature).

The race to cross the continent from south to north pitted the Victorian party of Robert O'Hara Burke and William Wills against the South Australian expeditions of John McDouall Stuart. Burke and Wills reached the Gulf of Carpentaria first, but they died of starvation on the tragic return journey (*see* Burke and Wills Expedition). Stuart crossed the very center of the continent to reach Darwin. He blazed the trail followed later, in 1870–72, by the Overland Telegraph Line from Adelaide to Darwin, from which the underwater cable to Java finally linked Australia with the rest of the world.

Most colonies appointed a surveyor-general to systematize mapping and land subdivision. One of them was the explorer Thomas Mitchell, a British soldier who had come to New South Wales in 1827, a veteran of fighting in Spain. He discovered the fertile Western Districts of Victoria. His unfulfilled obsession

*'Alluvial Gold Washing', a steel engraving by J.S. Prout and S. Bradshaw, celebrates the Australian gold rush of 1851. Today, most of the nation's gold is mined in Western Australia.*

National Library of Australia, Rex Nan Kivell Collection

was to find a great river that flowed northwesterly, an "Australian Ganges" that would channel trade towards Asia. The National Mapping Council was established in 1945 to coordinate these state and federal cartographic agencies. Since 1921, the mapping of coastal waters has been the responsibility of the Royal Australian Navy Hydrographic Service.

## Land Settlement

Autocratic governors, acting under royal instructions from London, ruled the Australian colonies until advisory councils and representative governments were formed between 1823 and 1890. From the moment Captain Cook took possession of all eastern Australia in 1770, it became British Crown land. Governors were generous in granting this land to free settlers, marines, military officers, and emancipated convicts.

Actual sales of land began in 1825. So uncontrolled was the spread of settlement inland that an artificial cordon was drawn around the Nineteen Counties surrounding Sydney, outside which settlers were forbidden to trespass. By 1836, this unworkable arrangement had to be abandoned, and grazing rights were permitted in these remote squatting districts for an annual fee of ten pounds sterling.

These leases did not guarantee security of tenure, as squatters discovered when the "free selection" acts were passed in every colony between 1858 and 1872. They permitted anyone to purchase Crown land, whether already leased by a squatter or not. Squatters retaliated through recourse to bribery at land auctions; "peacocking," preemptively purchasing the choicest sites, and leaving only the waterless intervening wastes for rivals to bid on; and "dummying," acquiring property in the names of others.

Free selection failed to create a yeoman class of small farmers. Nor did the land settlement schemes of the 1890s and the "soldier settlements" for veterans following both world wars. Agricultural land remained firmly under the control of the "squattocracy," as the self-styled landed gentry were called. The Torrens system of transferring land titles originated in South Australia in 1858, when Sir Robert Torrens sponsored the Real Property Act. His simplified land registration system was subsequently adopted in New Zealand

## Gold Rushes

Complicating this grab for land were the gold rushes of the 1850s and 1890s. These had profound and far-reaching impacts on Australian development. Reports of early gold discoveries between 1823 and 1844 were suppressed by the colonial governors, for fear of rampant disorder. This policy was reversed when the great California Gold Rush of 1848 lured away many Australians.

The first officially acknowledged gold discovery was that by Edward Hargraves in 1851, at Ophir. Other finds attracted such an influx of miners into New South Wales that Victorians, already suffering from a labor shortage, were galvanized into offering a reward for the first discovery of payable gold in that state. It was won by James Esmond at Clunes, but much richer finds were made later in 1851 at Castlemaine, Bendigo, and Ballarat—which boasts the richest alluvial goldfield ever discovered anywhere.

Victoria's richer fields were also more compact and accessible than those of the other eastern states. During the decade of the 1850s, Victoria produced 25 million ounces (709 million grams) of gold, representing 87 percent of the total Australian production and 35 percent of world production. Its population boomed from 97,000 to 539,000, an increase larger than the entire previous population of Australia. Victoria became the most populous colony, and "marvelous Melbourne" the continent's largest city.

The Welcome Stranger, recovered at Moliagul in 1869, was Victoria's largest pure gold nugget. Its gross weight was 176 pounds (80 kilograms). Larger still, but containing impurities, was Holtermann's Nugget, at 205 pounds (93 kilograms of gold) from Hill End, New South Wales. Other gold rushes helped populate north Queensland, at Rockhampton (1858), Gympie (1867), Charters Towers (1872), and Mount Morgan, the "mountain of gold" (1882).

As surface diggings in quartz rocks and old river courses were exhausted, deeper leads in buried alluvium required more capital and rock-crushing machinery, and more advanced metallurgical technology. These the independent diggers could not afford. They looked for other work, leaving behind scores of ghost towns and mine tailings.

Victorian production was slumping in the 1890s when Paddy Hannan picked up what he thought was a stone to throw at a crow, only to discover that it was a gold nugget. Thus began the 1893 rush to Coolgardie in Western Australia, and the genesis of the fabled Golden Mile at nearby Kalgoorlie. It became another dusty tent city in a parched lunar landscape for victims of the 1890s depression, but its revival in the 1980s has made Australia the world's third-ranking gold producer.

The gold rushes of the 1850s tripled Australia's population, created a demand for suffrage that quickened constitutional development, and empowered the cities to challenge what had previously been a rural monopoly in capital and government. Gold cast aside forever the "convict stain," and pumped wealth into a diversifying economy that entered its long boom from 1860 to 1890.

Discipline and honesty among miners were exemplary, until grievances over the licensing of mining claims gave rise to violence at Ballarat. There the Eureka Stockade was erected in 1854 and deadly shots were exchanged between police and intransigent miners, who were led by Peter Lalor. These rebels are sentimentally credited with the first call for an Australian democracy. Chinese miners began to arrive in Australia in 1853. By 1858, they constituted one fifth of the mining population of Victoria, and 11 percent of its total population. Riots broke out and restrictions were placed on Chinese immigration in Victoria (1855), South Australia (1857), and New South Wales (1861). These were the ripening seeds of the "white Australia" policy.

### Federation and Independence

The latter half of the 19th century saw a network of railroads constructed to serve and extend the wheat belts of the inland plains, and incidentally to foster national integration. As Australia's isolation from Europe shrank, with the opening of the Suez Canal in 1869 and the replacement of sailing vessels by steamships, that period saw an export-oriented economy emerge with nonperishable wool, wheat, refrigerated meat, and other rural commodities in the vanguard. It saw the pastoral frontiers pushed into northern and western Australia to the very margins of the desert, despite the warnings of soothsayers like George Goyder, who identified the line of rainfall that

officially separated the drought-prone region of South Australia from the potentially arable areas.

There were pandemics of measles, smallpox, Asian flu, and bubonic plague, and the beginning of quarantine regulations to protect both agriculture and human health. Constitutional conventions and parliaments appeared in every colony, exploring the prospects for federation as a nation. These assemblies were urged on by Henry Parkes, premier of New South Wales and Father of Federation. When national independence from Britain was granted on the first day of the 20th century, Jan. 1, 1901, six colonies became six states; interstate customs barriers and tariffs fell; the development of a national capital at Canberra was planned; and an increasingly independent phase of integration and growth began.

### World War I and Gallipoli

The newly created Commonwealth of Australia remained a staunchly loyal dominion of the British Empire. When a state of war against Germany was declared in London on Aug. 4, 1914, Australia immediately, automatically, and wholeheartedly formed an expeditionary army of 20,000 men—the Australian Imperial Force (AIF). Australian and New Zealand troops, soon known as the Anzacs (Australian and New Zealand Army Corps), embarked for desert training in Egypt on Nov. 1, 1914. They were sent in April 1915 to the Dardanelles, the narrow strait between the Mediterranean and Black seas, to help capture the Gallipoli peninsula from the Turkish allies of Germany.

They landed at dawn on April 25, still celebrated as Anzac Day, the most solemn occasion of the Australian year. Few other countries celebrate a defeat in war. The Turks were prepared, entrenched, and determined. During the eight futile months before the British allies withdrew, Turks killed 33,532 soldiers, including 8,587 Australians. The Gallipoli campaign, devised by Winston Churchill, was an ill-contrived attempt to gain access to the Russian breadbasket and to split Turkish power, but it blooded Australians as Australians for the first time. The survivors came home as heroes, and recruitment boomed.

Other army divisions were sent to France and Belgium, where they fought as shock troops on the Somme, at Bullecourt, Bapaume, Messines, Ypres, and the appalling disaster of Passchendaele. Just east of Amiens, the AIF suffered 23,000 casualties. It is said that no other part of the Earth is as soaked with the blood of Australians. Their commanders were John Monash and Thomas Blamey. From Egypt, the 1st Light Horse Brigade under Maj. Gen. Henry George Chauvel made spectacular captures of Beersheba and Damascus. Altogether, 331,000 Australians served in World War I. Those killed in battle numbered 59,993—the highest ratio of deaths to total national population of any country in the Empire. Another 6,291 died from other causes.

Australia's second Labor government was then in office. Under Prime Minister W.M. Hughes, an ardent advocate of conscription, two very divisive referenda failed to endorse it. Newly urgent policies geared towards industrial self-sufficiency saw Broken Hill Propriety Ltd. enter the iron and steel industry, previously dominated by German suppliers. Government-guaranteed purchases of foodstuffs boosted the land industries. World War I put Australia on the world map, baptized its nationalism by fire, and began a martial tradition of fighting foreign wars in the expectation that grateful allies would in turn defend Australia under different contingencies.

**Between the Wars**

The 20th century has seen a continuous erosion of the "tyranny of distance" which impeded trade and communications for so long, stranding Australia on the far side of the Earth. Aviation led the way.

The first direct flight from England reached Australia in 1919, the first solo flight, by Bert Hinkler in 1928, and the first solo flight by a woman, Amy Johnson, in 1930. By then, Charles Kingsford-Smith and an intrepid crew had flown across the Pacific Ocean for the first time, in the *Southern Cross,* a Fokker monoplane, taking 83 hours and 11 minutes in 1928. Kingsford-Smith also piloted the first flights across Australia (from Melbourne to Perth), and across the Tasman Sea to New Zealand.

Qantas (Queensland and Northern Territory Aerial Services) was founded in 1920. Passengers on internal airline services rose from 3,663 in 1925 to 18,014,600 in 199192. Flying times between Adelaide and Sydney fell from five hours (in a Douglas DC3, in about 1946) to 1 hour and 55 minutes (in a Boeing 727, in about 1965), though the corresponding fare increased from $20.85 to $45.40. The Royal Flying Doctor Service made its inaugural flight out of Cloncurry, Queensland, in 1928. It was the humane creation of the Rev. John Flynn and the Australian Inland Mission of the Presbyterian Church.

Railway construction steadily carried the agricultural frontier inland, peaking in 1941 with 27,233 miles (43,826 kilometers) of open track, since declining to 22,222 miles (35,762 kilometers) by 1989. Australia's first air-conditioned train, the *Spirit of Progress,* linked Melbourne in 1937 with the border town of Albury, where the infuriating change of rail gauges (and change of trains) between states occurred. The completion of one standardized rail gauge between Brisbane and Perth was accomplished only in 1970. The Eyre Highway crossing the Nullarbor Plain from Adelaide to Perth was fully paved as recently as 1976. Sprawling port cities were consolidated when the Sydney Harbour Bridge opened in 1932 and Brisbane's Story Bridge in 1940. Large construction projects induced the Ready Mix Concrete Company to begin trucking the world's first premade concrete in 1936.

The nationwide calamity between World Wars I and II was the Great Depression of 1930–33, following the Wall Street stock-market crash of October 1929. The economic downturn spread around the world. Unemployment rose to as much as 29 percent in 1932

by some estimates. When the New South Wales government could not meet interest payments on its London borrowings, the Commonwealth government footed the bill, under pressure from the Bank of England. Export income fell to half what it had been in 1928. In New South Wales, the state treasury exhausted its reserves and could not pay public servants for two months. The State Savings Bank also closed its doors following a run by panicking depositors, and had to be taken over by the Commonwealth Bank. The Australian pound was devalued, and prices for wool and wheat fell. Unemployment relief work was found in water supply and sewerage schemes, road construction, and rural development. Happier economic times returned for the Australian Sesquicentenary in 1938, though aborigines observed a day of mourning.

**World War II**

Australia entered the war on Sept. 3, 1939, the moment that Britain declared war on Germany and its allies for persisting in their invasion of Poland. Once again, Australian public sentiment and the Labor Party opposition were fervently behind Britain. A second Australian Imperial Force was formed, fighting a losing rearguard action in Greece and Crete, helping to overthrow the Vichy regime in Syria, and opposing German Field Marshal Erwin Rommel in North Africa. In Egypt, the Australian "Rats of Tobruk" withstood a siege for 242 days until relief arrived. The Royal Australian Air Force sustained its heaviest losses in bombing raids against Germany.

The Pacific phase of the Second World War opened badly for Australia, when Japan crippled the American naval base at Pearl Harbor on Dec. 7, 1941. The Japanese offensive of 1941 brought war into Australia's northern backyard. Australians were petrified by the ignominious fall of Singapore, that supposedly impregnable British bastion, in Feb. 1942. Of 130,000 prisoners taken, 15,384 were Australians. Perth was closer to Singapore than it was to the Royal Australian Navy in Sydney Harbour.

On Feb. 19, 1942, 54 Japanese planes bombed Darwin in the first assault on Australian soil since Governor Phillip had arrived in 1788. They sank or damaged 16 ships, destroyed 20 aircraft, and killed 243 people. They also bombed the northern coastal towns of Broome, Wyndham, Derby, Katherine, Port Hedland, and Townsville. On May 30, 1942, two miniature submarines briefly eluded pursuers inside Sydney Harbour, causing minor material damage but traumatic psychological shock.

The Japanese, now in control of virtually all Southeast Asia and most of the critical Pacific islands, set their sights on Port Moresby, the principal town of Papua New Guinea. They also planned to seize the United States base in the Midway Islands. It was at this point, during the first half of 1942, that the tide of combat began to turn against Japan. In the battle of the Coral Sea, American and Australian warships defeated Japanese invaders. In New Guinea—at Milne Bay, Rabaul, and along the Kokoda Trail—Australians helped repulse the Japanese, hounding their retreat into the Solomon Islands and Borneo.

Australia became the base for Pacific operations. By 1943, there were 120,000 American troops stationed in Australia, under the command of Gen. Douglas MacArthur. He insisted on the construction of a supply road across the Northern Territory.

Victory in Europe came in May 1945. Japan surrendered on Aug. 15, 1945, after the first atomic bombs were dropped on Hiroshima and Nagasaki. Australian enlistment in World War II totaled 990,900 men and women. There were 37,000 war-related deaths, including 27,291 in battle. Of the 22,376 taken prisoner by the Japanese, 8,031 died in captivity, many from starvation in such camps as Singapore's Changi, or from forced labor on the Burma railroad.

When Singapore fell, Prime Minister John Curtin turned to the United States for help, beginning an alliance that has hardly faltered since. Curtin instituted the rationing of food, gasoline, and some clothing, curtailed travel and investment, and extended conscription. The volunteer Women's Land Army boosted food production, and 9,000 women became nurses. The regulated war economy stimulated and decentralized industry inland, away from coastal targets. Commonwealth encroachment on states' powers proceeded apace. It monopolized income tax collection and foreign borrowing.

### Reorientation Toward Asia

After World War II, with 766,000 migrant settlers arriving between 1947 and 1955, Australians became more proudly and self-consciously Australian. They searched for a common purpose in a newly Asian and multicultural context. The debate over a collective national identity raged on during the 1970s and 1980s. Universities which had never offered courses in Australian literature and regarded Australian history as a primitive subspecies of British history found themselves enthralled by Australian Studies programs. Soprano Joan Sutherland, writer Patrick White, publisher Rupert Murdoch, and the sporting heroes and heroines made the world their stage, and Australia its spotlight. Radio Australia began broadcasting in 1940, as Australia Calls. Sir Isaac Isaacs became the first Australian-born (and first Jewish) governor-general in 1931.

Lovers of the Australian landscape, long mute and scattered, found their focus and voice in 1975 with the creation of the Australian Heritage Commission. Its Register of the National Estate listed 1,698 natural places and 7,850 historic places as of the early 1990s. Increasing numbers of women were elected to local government councils, from 6.2 percent of their membership in 1980 to 19.4 percent in 1990. Such ethnic soccer teams as West Adelaide Hellas, Marconi Fairfield, and Melbourne Croatia changed the nature of sporting rivalries. Japanese surpassed French, Italian, and German as the most commonly studied foreign language in higher education.

During the Cold War, Australia remained a firm ally of the United States, even to the point of participating in the Korean and Vietnam wars. But gradually, as the postwar modernization of the economy took place, Australians began to view themselves within the context of Asia. The sudden end of the Cold war accelerated this trend. The economies of East Asia, from Japan and South Korea in the north to Hong Kong, Taiwan, and Singapore in the south, became dynamos of productivity. They also became vital trading partners for Australia.

Prime Minister Robert Menzies also strove to attract investment and technology transfers from the United States, Japan, and Europe as guarantees, or in the hope, that these allies would protect their stake in Australian development, if necessary, against foreign aggressors. New resource frontiers were opened in the iron-rich Pilbara region of Western Australia, the oil and gas fields of Bass Strait and the desert interior, the Snowy Mountains hydroelectric scheme, and the tourist islands of the Great Barrier Reef.

Australia also shifted somewhat away from its 200-year connection with Great Britain. Britain turned toward Europe, both politically and economically, especially through its involvement in the North Atlantic Treaty Organization and the European Union. To symbolize the break, Australia changed its monetary unit from the British pound to the dollar in 1966.

Between 1983 and 1989, even while the Prime Minister Robert Hawke's Labor Party controlled federal parliament, foreign investment in Australia grew from 81,873 million Australian dollars to 229,314 million Australian dollars, of which 55 percent came from British, American, or Japanese sources. Import tariffs on industrial goods were phased out, and such government enterprises as Qantas, the Commonwealth Bank, Telecom, and Australian Airlines seemed ripe for privatization. Overseas visitors, possibly reflecting world interest in Australia, arrived in swelling numbers, from 23,236 in 1925 to 2.4 million in 1991.

Hawke was called the most popular prime minister in Australian history, winning reelection in 1984, 1987, and 1991. He was the first Labor party leader to serve more than two consecutive terms. In the 1990 election, however, his party's majority was narrowed. In December 1991 he was undone by a steep recession. The unemployment rate rose to more than ten percent, and several major banks failed. His party voted him out of the leadership post, and he was succeeded by Paul Keating—his former treasurer. The recession would later be seen as part of a worldwide economic downturn. Keating cemented relationships with Japan, Indonesia, and Papua New Guinea. But he played on nationalist sentiment by alienating the British on several issues, including the monarchy, a demand for a new Australian flag, and accusations that Britain had failed to defend Commonwealth countries adequately during World War II. (*See also* Hawke, Bob; Keating, Paul. For table of prime ministers, *see* Australia in the Fact-Index.)

In March 1996 a coalition of Liberal and National parties led by John Howard won a solid victory in national elections and ended 13 years of rule by the

Labor party. The conservative Liberal-National coalition captured 94 of the 148 seats in the House of Representatives, while the Labor party managed to hold only 47 of the 79 seats it controlled before the election. Howard replaced Keating as head of the government.

### A New Australia

Toward the end of the 20th century, Australian society had matured to a level that would be almost incomprehensible to the early colonizers. A welfare state had emerged, with old age pensions available since 1900, a 40-hour working week since 1939, a pharmaceutical benefits plan since 1950, and a national health plan since 1975.

At the same time, Australia was attracting international attention. Brisbane was the site of Expo 88, which drew more than 18 million visitors. That same year the country celebrated its 200th anniversary. In September 2000 Australia staged its second Olympic Games (Melbourne hosted in 1956) in Sydney.

Australia celebrated the Centenary of Federation in 2001. Amid a year of festivities, a meeting of elected members of the state and commonwealth parliaments took place. The event was held in the Royal Exhibition Building in Melbourne, where 100 years earlier the Australian states had formally convened the first federal Parliament. Also in 2001, the Right Rev. Peter Hollingworth, the Anglican archbishop of Brisbane, replaced Sir William Deane as governor-general.

The 1990s saw the aboriginal issue intensify and many large events were marked with demonstrations by aborigines, who claimed they were victims of discrimination. A federal policy of assimilation lasted from 1939 until the 1970s, when it was replaced by a policy of integration. Crucial in the advancement of aborigine claims of native lands were decisions of the nation's High Court which recognized the validity of native title to traditionally-occupied lands. Meanwhile, despite recent advances, the aboriginal experience often remained stark and disturbing, with illness, alcoholism, and violence all having their part.

On Feb. 13, 1998, Australia's Parliament voted to turn the country into a fully independent republic by severing Australia's longstanding ties to the British Crown. When the matter came to referendum vote in 1999, however, republicans divided over how radical their intended change should be. With many other Australians still attached to traditional and even monarchical modes, the referendum failed decisively.

### Growing International Participation

Before 1940 Australia had only a tiny diplomatic service, but thereafter this arm of government expanded. The nation's new ethnic diversity increased the need for professional diplomats. Activity continued within the United Nations and the British Commonwealth, but increasing emphasis lay on Australia's role in Southeast Asia and the South Pacific. While this stance was appropriate to Australia's geopolitical reality, it entailed problems. Prime Minister Mahatir of Malaysia long scorned Australia's claims to Asian empathy. Relations with Indonesia fluctuated and were never so tense as in 1999 and 2000, when Australia abandoned its earlier acceptance of the absorption of East Timor within Indonesia and led the United Nations forces which oversaw its independence. Troubles in Fiji, New Guinea, and the Solomons, all provoking violence in 2000, also presented difficulties.

The government faced an international crisis when the Norwegian freighter *Tampa* picked up a boatload of over 430 refugees on Aug. 26, 2001, and sailed with them to Christmas Island, an Australian dependency. Prime Minister John Howard took a hard line and declared that none of the refugees could enter Australia. Despite international protests, Australian troops boarded the ship and transferred the refugees to the troopship HMAS *Manoora* for transport to Nauru and New Zealand, which had agreed to hold them. Despite an Australian court ruling that the refugees were being illegally detained, the government remained adamant and pushed through legislation that tightened laws on refugees.

### FURTHER RESOURCES FOR AUSTRALIA

**Brewster, B.M.** Down Under All Over (Four Winds, 1991).
**Cobb, Vicki.** This Place is Lonely (Walker, 1991).
**Cowan, James.** The Elements of the Aborigine Tradition (Element, 1992).
**Crump, D.J., ed.** Surprising Lands Down Under (National Geographic, 1989).
**Dolce, Laura.** Australia (Chelsea House, 1990).
**Hughes, Robert.** The Fatal Shore: The Epic of Australia's Founding (Random, 1988).
**Jackomos, Alick, and Fowell, Derk.** Aboriginal Living Histories: Stories in the Oral Tradition (Cambridge Univ. Press, 1992).
**Kurian, G.T.** Australia and New Zealand (Facts on File, 1990).

### States and Territories of Australia

| States and Internal Territories | Area (sq mi) | Area (sq km) | Rank in Area | Population | Rank in Population | Capital |
|---|---|---|---|---|---|---|
| Australian Capital Territory | 900 | 2,300 | 8 | 308,400 | 7 | Canberra |
| New South Wales | 309,500 | 801,600 | 5 | 6,341,600 | 1 | Sydney |
| Northern Territory | 519,800 | 1,346,300 | 3 | 190,000 | 8 | Darwin |
| Queensland | 666,900 | 1,727,300 | 2 | 3,456,300 | 3 | Brisbane |
| South Australia | 379,900 | 984,000 | 4 | 1,487,300 | 5 | Adelaide |
| Tasmania | 26,200 | 67,900 | 7 | 471,900 | 6 | Hobart |
| Victoria | 87,900 | 227,700 | 6 | 4,660,900 | 2 | Melbourne |
| Western Australia | 975,100 | 2,525,500 | 1 | 1,831,400 | 4 | Perth |

# Australia Fact Summary

## THE LAND

Area*
2,966,200 sq mi
(7,682,300 sq km)

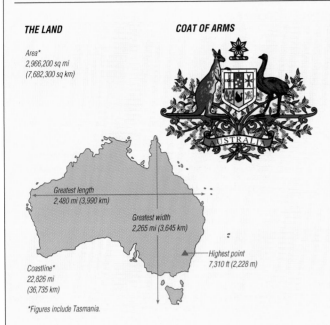

Greatest length
2,480 mi (3,990 km)

Greatest width
2,265 mi (3,645 km)

Highest point
7,310 ft (2,228 m)

Coastline*
22,826 mi
(36,735 km)

*Figures include Tasmania.

## COAT OF ARMS

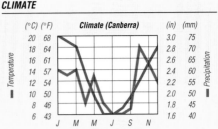

## CLIMATE

Climate (Canberra)

## POPULATION GROWTH

| Year | Population |
|------|-----------|
| 1900 | 3,765,300 |
| 1931 | 6,526,500 |
| 1951 | 8,421,800 |
| 1961 | 10,508,200 |
| 1971 | 13,067,300 |
| 1981 | 14,923,300 |
| 1992 | 17,529,000 |

**Official Name.** Commonwealth of Australia.

**Capital.** Canberra.

**Coat of Arms.** A shield, bearing the coats of arms of the 6 states of Australia, flanked by a kangaroo on the left and an emu on the right. The background is filled in with golden wattle blossoms. A 7-pointed star above the shield represents the states and territories. Granted in 1912.

**National Emblems.** Kangaroo, emu, and golden wattle.

**Flag.** The British Union Jack in the upper left corner of a blue field; large, white 7-pointed star directly underneath the Union Jack; to the right, 5 smaller white stars representing the Southern Cross ( *see* Flags of the World).

**Motto.** Advance Australia.

**Anthem.** 'Advance Australia Fair'.

### NATURAL FEATURES

**Border.** *Coast*—17,365 miles (27,945 kilometers).

**Natural Regions.** Great Western Plateau, Central-Eastern Lowlands, Eastern Highlands (Great Dividing Range), Australian Alps.

**Major Ranges.** Australian Alps, Flinders Ranges, Great Western Tiers, Blue Mountains.

**Notable Peaks.** Mount Kosciusko, 7,310 feet (2,228 meters); Mount Wellington, 4,167 feet (1,270 meters).

**Major Rivers.** Murray, Darling, Murrumbidgee.

**Major Lakes.** Lake Eyre, Lake Torrens, Lake Gairdner.

**Major Islands.** Tasmania, Melville.

**Climate.** Central and southern Queensland are subtropical; north and central New South Wales, Victoria, Western Australia, and Tasmania are warm temperate; Northern Australia has a wet season from November to March. Most rain falls during winter.

### PEOPLE

**Population** (1996 estimate). 18,287,000; 6.2 persons per square mile (2.4 persons per square kilometer); 85 percent urban, 15 percent rural (1995 estimate).

**Vital Statistics** (rate per 1,000 population). *Births*—14.1; *deaths*—6.9; *marriages*—6.0.

**Life Expectancy** (at birth). *Males*—75.4 years; *females*—81.1 years.

**Official Language.** English.

**Ethnic Groups.** European, aboriginal, Asian.

**Major Religions.** Roman Catholicism, Protestantism, Orthodox Christianity.

### MAJOR CITIES (1995 estimate)

**Sydney** (3,772,700). Capital of New South Wales; oil refining; mercantile port; transport equipment; foods and beverages; fabricated metals; printing; chemicals; Opera House; Anzac Memorial; St. Mary's Roman Catholic Cathedral ( *see* Sydney, Australia ).

**Melbourne** (3,218,100). Capital of Victoria; metal processing; engineering; textile and clothing manufacture; food processing; papermaking; building materials; chemicals; Royal Melbourne Institute of Technology; Flinders Street Railway Station; Treasury Gardens ( *see* Melbourne, Australia ).

**Brisbane** (1,489,100). Capital and port of Queensland; engineering; food processing; shipbuilding; lumber; rubber goods; automobiles; cement; fertilizer; petroleum refining; University of Queensland; Parliament House ( *see* Brisbane, Australia ).

**Perth** (1,262,600). Capital of Western Australia; banking and insurance center; paint; furniture; sheet metal; cement; rubber; tractors; fertilizer; paper; automobiles; nickel and petroleum refining; Kings Park; Perry Lakes Stadium; Coolgardie-Kalgoorlie gold mines ( *see* Perth, Australia ).

**Adelaide** (1,081,000). Capital of South Australia; automobile parts; machinery; textiles; chemicals; transportation hub; Adelaide Festival of Arts; St. Peter's Anglican Cathedral; State War Memorial ( *see* Adelaide, Australia ).

**Newcastle** (466,000). Industrial and shipping center; coal; iron and steel; textiles; wood fiber; electrical equipment; zircon mining; fertilizers; University of Newcastle; College of Advanced Education; War Memorial Cultural Centre.

**Canberra-Queanbeyan** (331,800). Capital of Australia; light industry; tourist trade; National Library of Australia; Australian National Gallery; Mount Stromlo Observatory; Church of St. John the Baptist; Australian War Memorial ( *see* Canberra, Australia ).

**Gold Coast-Tweed** (326,900). Resort area includes such famous resorts as Surfers Paradise, Currumbin, Mermaid Beach, and Broadbeach; surfing; swimming; fishing; wildlife reserves.

**Wollongong** (2563,600). Commercial, railway, and educational center; fishing; coal processing; steel manufacturing; copper refining; brick making; food processing; St. Michael's Cathedral.

**Hobart** (194,700). Capital of Tasmania; industrial, trade, and communications hub; textiles; chemicals; cement; confectionery; paper pulp; metal products; fruit and jam processing; Wrest Point Casino; St. George's Church; Theatre Royal; Anglesea Barracks ( *see* Hobart, Australia ).

## Australia Fact Summary

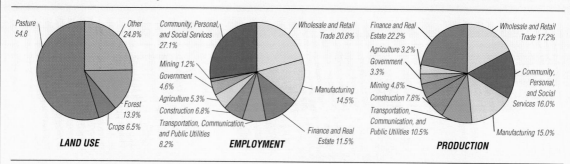

LAND USE
- Pasture 54.8
- Other 24.8%
- Forest 13.9%
- Crops 6.5%

EMPLOYMENT
- Community, Personal, and Social Services 27.1%
- Mining 1.2%
- Government 4.6%
- Agriculture 5.3%
- Construction 6.8%
- Transportation, Communication, and Public Utilities 8.2%
- Wholesale and Retail Trade 20.8%
- Manufacturing 14.5%
- Finance and Real Estate 11.5%

PRODUCTION
- Finance and Real Estate 22.2%
- Agriculture 3.2%
- Government 3.3%
- Mining 4.8%
- Construction 7.8%
- Transportation, Communication, and Public Utilities 10.5%
- Wholesale and Retail Trade 17.2%
- Community, Personal, and Social Services 16.0%
- Manufacturing 15.0%

### ECONOMY

**Chief Agricultural Products.** *Crops*—wheat, sugarcane, cotton, barley, grapes, potatoes, apples, bananas, oats, tomatoes, oranges, rice, sorghum. *Livestock*—sheep, cattle, pigs, poultry.

**Chief Mined Products.** Iron ore, bauxite, zinc, lead, copper, tin, gold, diamonds, coal, petroleum, natural gas.

**Chief Manufactured Products.** Cement, pig iron, textile floor coverings, woven cotton and woolen cloth, beer, electrical motors, refrigerators, motor vehicles.

**Foreign Trade.** Imports, 52%; exports, 48%.

**Chief Imports.** Machinery, basic manufactures, paper and paper products, nonferrous metals, transport equipment, chemicals, mineral fuels and lubricants, food and live animals.

**Chief Exports.** Metal ores and metal scrap, textile fibers, cereals, meat, mineral fuels and lubricants, petroleum, natural gas, machinery and transport equipment, chemicals.

**Chief Trading Partners.** United States, Japan, Germany, New Zealand.

**Monetary Unit.** 1 Australian dollar = 100 cents.

### EDUCATION

**Public Schools.** The governments of the Australian states and the Northern Territory administer and fund the majority of primary, secondary, and technical education. They also have special responsibilities for educational and assistance programs for aboriginal people.

**Compulsory School Age.** Attendance is compulsory from ages 6 to 15 (16 years in Tasmania).

**Literacy.** 99.5 percent of population.

**Leading Universities.** Australian National University; University of Melbourne; University of Adelaide; University of Tasmania; Murdoch University, Perth; Griffith University, Brisbane; University of New South Wales; Macquarie University, Sydney; Latrobe University, Melbourne.

**Notable Libraries.** National Library of Australia; Parliamentary Library; State Library of New South Wales; State Library of Victoria.

**Notable Museums and Art Galleries.** National Gallery of Australia, Canberra; Northern Territory Museum and Art Gallery, Darwin; Royal Botanic Gardens and Australian Museum, Sydney; National Maritime Museum, Sydney; Museum of Applied Arts and Sciences, Sydney; Tasmanian Museum and Art Gallery; Ballarat Art Gallery; National Gallery of Victoria; Art Gallery of New South Wales.

### GOVERNMENT

**Form of Government.** Federal parliamentary state.

**Constitution.** Took effect Jan. 1, 1901.

**Sovereign.** British monarch represented by governor-general.

**Governor-General.** Appointed by British monarch on advice of local government ministers; acts on advice of Federal Executive Council.

**Prime Minister.** Leader of majority party in Parliament; term, as long as party retains majority.

**Cabinet.** Selected by prime minister from House of Representatives.

**Parliament.** Senate and House of Representatives; annual sessions. *Senate*—76 members, elected by universal suffrage; term, 6 years. *House of Representatives*—148 elected members; term, 3 years.

**Judiciary.** *High Court of Australia*—chief justice and 6 other justices; term, life, with retirement at age 70. Federal Court, Family Court, state courts, industrial tribunals.

**Political Divisions.** 6 states—New South Wales, Queensland, South Australia, Tasmania, Victoria, Western Australia; 2 territories—Australian Capital Territory, Northern Territory.

**Voting Qualification.** Age 18.

### PLACES OF INTEREST

**Ayers Rock and Mount Olga National Park.** In Northern Territory; Ayers Rock is world's largest monolith; area is important to mythological beliefs and ritual life of aborigines; cave paintings within rock.

**Beaconsfield.** In Tasmania; ruins of Tasmania Gold Mine; replica of miner's school and home; Auld Kirk; Batman Bridge; fishing; boating in Tamar Valley; surfing at Greens Beach; Fern Gorge Reserve; hiking; camping.

**Braidwood.** In New South Wales; early pastoral settlement; grasslands; rolling granite plateau; preserved convict barracks; abandoned Bellevue Station gold mine; alluvial Bombay diggings; Ballalaba homestead; preserved flour mill; World War I Memorial.

**Bunbury.** In Perth; major historical port district; used by whalers in colonial days; old steam trains displayed at railway station; Collie River cruises; Australind, Australia's smallest church.

**Burleigh Heads National Park and Fauna Reserve.** In Gold Coast; vintage aircraft museum with life-size displays; beach resort.

**The Grampians.** In Victoria; range of large hills; walking tracks; lakes; waterfalls; painted aboriginal rock shelters; beekeeping; champagne production.

**Great Barrier Reef.** In Queensland; largest coral structure in the world; includes some 700 islands; 350 species of coral; diving; snorkeling.

**Hunter Valley.** In New South Wales; old agricultural and timber area; rain forest; cedar stands; wineries and distilleries; archaeological sites; Grossman House; Morpeth; pottery works; Newcastle iron- and steelworks; Gostwick.

**Kapunda-Burra.** In South Australia; old copper mining district; preserved mine structures; ruins of chimneys; dugouts; Kooringa settlement; miners' cottages; Baptist church; railway station; ruins of St. John's Roman Catholic church.

**Noosa Heads.** In Queensland; booming resort area; famous surfing beach; other aquatic sports; display of life-size tall ships; colored sand cliffs nearby; Cooloola National Park; picnicking; hiking.

**Norfolk Island.** In New South Wales; volcanic island; Mount Pitt rain forest reserve; famous pine forests; penal colony ruins; Beach Store Museum; Arthurs Vale watermill; Longridge Barracks; Slaughter Bay; St. Barnabas's Chapel.

**Swan River Valley.** In Western Australia; early agricultural settlement; Walyunga National Park; hiking trails; ancient aboriginal campsite; rock formations; St. George's Anglican Cathedral; Woodbridge House; Round House; Fremantle Town Hall.

**Sydney Opera House.** Contains a concert hall, opera theater, drama theater, cinema, recording hall, and reception hall; daily tours.

**Warwick and the Southern Darling Downs.** In Queensland; pastoral countryside; sheep stations; eucalyptus forests; wool processing center; Warwick Courthouse; Masonic Hall; Glengallan homestead; Allora railway; Yangan Masonic Temple.

# Australia

### ASHMORE AND CARTIER ISLANDS, TERRITORY OF

#### PHYSICAL FEATURES

Ashmore (isls.) C 2
Cartier (isl.) C 2

### AUSTRALIAN CAPITAL TERRITORY

#### CITIES AND TOWNS

Canberra (cap.), 276,162 H 7
Canberra (met. area), 278,894 H 7

### CORAL SEA ISLANDS TERRITORY

#### PHYSICAL FEATURES

Bougainville (reef) H 3
Coringa (isls.) H 3
Coral (sea) H 2
Flinders (reef) H 3
Holmes (reefs) H 3
Lihou (cays) J 3
Magdelaine (cays) H 3
Saumarez (reef) J 4
Willis (isls.) J 3

### NEW SOUTH WALES

#### CITY AND TOWNS

Albury, 39,975 H 7
Armidale, 21,605 J 6
Ashfield, 40,558 K 4
Auburn, 48,566 K 4
Balranald, 1,327 G 6
Bankstown, 153,904 K 4
Bathurst, 24,682 H 6
Baulkham Hills, 114,059 K 4
Bega, 4,202 J 7
Blacktown, 211,710 K 4
Blue Mountains, 69,420 J 6
Bonnyrigg K 4
Boomi H 5
Botany, 34,435 L 4
Bourke, 2,976 H 6
Brewarrina, 1,168 H 5
Brisbane Water J 6
Broken Hill, 23,263 G 6
Burwood, 28,362 K 4
Canterbury, 129,232 K 4
Carrathool, 3,239 G 6
Casino, 10,164 J 5
Cessnock-Bellbird, 17,932 J 6
Cobar, 4,138 H 6
Coffs Harbour, 20,326 J 6
Concord, 23,150 K 4
Condobolin, 3,163 H 6
Cooma, 7,385 H 7
Coonamble, 2,886 H 6
Cootamundra, 6,386 H 6
Cowra, 8,422 H 6
Cronulla L 5
Dee Why L 4
Deniliquin, 7,895 G 7
Drummoyne, 30,192 K 4
Dubbo, 28,064 H 6
Eastwood K 4
Fairfield, 175,099 K 4
Finley, 2,220 H 7
Forbes, 7,552 H 6
Gilgandra, 5,056 H 6
Glen Innes, 6,140 J 5
Goulburn, 21,451 J 6
Grafton, 16,642 J 5
Griffith, 13,296 H 6
Gunnedah, 8,874 H 6
Hay, 2,817 H 6
Hilston, 1,030 G 6
Holroyd, 79,132 K 4
Hornsby, 127,672 K 3
Hunters Hill, 11,977 K 4
Hurtsville, 63,757 K 4
Inverell, 9,736 J 5
Ivanhoe, 355 G 6
Kempsey, 9,049 J 6
Kogarah, 46,518 K 4
Ku-ring-gai, 99,193 K 4
Lane Cove, 28,954 L 4
La Perouse L 4
Leeton, 6,245 H 6
Leichhardt, 58,484 L 4
Lismore, 27,246 J 5
Lithgow, 11,968 J 6
Liverpool, 98,203 K 4
Maitland, 45,209 J 6
Manly, 34,895 L 4
Marrickville, 78,023 L 4
Mona Vale L 3
Moree, 10,062 H 5
Mosman, 25,353 L 4
Mudgee, 7,447 J 6
Murwillumbah, 8,003 J 5
Muswellbrook, 10,140 J 6
Narrabeen L 3
Narrabri, 6,694 J 6
Narrandera, 4,649 H 6
Narromine, 3,378 H 6
Newcastle, 262,331 J 6
Newcastle (met. area), 427,703 J 6
North Sydney, 50,446 L 4
Nowra-Bomaderry, 21,942 J 6
Nyngan, 2,311 J 6
Orange, 29,635 H 6
Parkes, 8,784 H 6
Parramatta, 132,798 K 4
Penrith, 149,630 J 6
Port Macquarie, 26,798 J 6
Queanbeyan, 23,714 H 7
Randwick, 115,349 L 4
Rockdale, 84,074 K 4
Ryde, 90,197 K 4
South Sydney, 77,818 L 4
Strathfield, 25,833 K 4
Sutherland, 184,399 K 5
Sydney (cap.), 3,097,956 L 4
Sydney (met. area), 3,538,970 L 4
Tamworth, 31,716 J 6
Taree, 16,303 J 6
Temora, 4,279 H 6
Tenterfield, 3,310 J 5
Terrey Hills L 3
The Entrance–Terrigal J 6
Tibooburra G 5
Tumut, 5,955 H 7
Villawood K 4
Wagga Wagga, 40,875 H 7
Walgett, 2,091 H 6
Warren, 2,036 H 6
Waverly, 59,095 L 4
West Wyalong, 3,458 H 6
Wilcannia, 942 G 6
Willoughby, 51,503 K 3
Wollongong, 211,417 J 6
Wollongong (met. area), 236,010 J 6
Woollahra, 49,904 L 4
Young, 6,666 H 6

#### OTHER FEATURES

Banks (cape) L 4
Barwon (riv.) H 5
Birrie (riv.) H 5
Blue (mts.) H 6
Bogan (riv.) H 6
Botany (bay) L 4
Byron (cape) J 5
Clarence (riv.) J 5
Darling (riv.) G 6
Georges (riv.) K 4
Great Dividing (range) J 6
Howe (cape) J 7
Kingsford Smith Airport L 4
Kosciusko (mt.) H 7
Lachlan (riv.) G 6
Lane Cove (riv.) K 4
Macintyre (riv.) J 5
Macquarie (riv.) H 6
Main Barrier (range) G 6
Middle Harbour (creek) K 3
Murray (riv.) G 6
Murrumbidgee (riv.) H 6
Paroo (riv.) G 5
Parramatta (riv.) K 4
Port Jackson (inlet) L 4
Prospect (res.) K 4
Riverina (reg.) H 7
Sugarloaf (pt.) J 6
Warrumbungle (range) H 6
Woronora (riv.) K 5

### NORTHERN TERRITORY

#### CITIES AND TOWNS

Adelaide River E 2
Alice Springs, 20,448 E 4
Alyangula, 1,113 F 2
Anthony Lagoon E 3
Areyonga E 4
Avon Downs F 4
Beswick E 2
Borrolloola, 594 F 3
Croker Island Mission E 2
Daly River E 2
Daly Waters, 298 E 3
Darwin (cap.), 67,946 E 2
Darwin (met. area), 70,071 E 2
Elliott, 423 E 3
Haasts Bluff E 4
Harts Range F 4
Hatches Creek F 4
Hermannsburg, 422 E 4
Hooker Creek E 3
Jay Creek E 4
Jervois Range F 4
Katherine, 7,064 E 2
Kulgera E 5
Lake Nash F 4
Larrimah E 3
McArthur River F 3
Nhulunbuy, 3,934 F 2
Numbulwar, 440 F 2
Pine Creek, 437 E 2
Port Keats Mission, 1,363 D 2
Roper River Mission E 2
Rum Jungle E 2
Tennant Creek, 3,480 E 3
Timber Creek E 3
Victoria River Downs E 3
Wave Hill E 3
Wollogorang F 3

#### OTHER FEATURES

Amadeus (lake) E 4
Anson (bay) D 2
Arafura (sea) E 2
Arnhem (cape) F 2
Arnhem Land (reg.) E 2
Arnhem Land Aboriginal Reserve E 2
Ayers Rock (mt.) E 5
Ayers Rock, Mount Olga Nat'l Park E 5
Barkly Tableland F 3
Bathurst (isl.) D 2
Bathurst Island Mission E 2
Beatrice (cape) F 2
Beswick Aboriginal Reserve E 2
Blaze (pt.) D 2
Carpentaria (gulf) F 2
Clarence (str.) E 2
Cobourg (pen.) E 2
Croker (cape) E 2
Daly (riv.) E 2
Daly River Aboriginal Reserve D 2
Dry (riv.) E 3
Dundas (str.) E 2
Finke (riv.) E 5
Ford (cape) D 2
Goulburn (isls.) E 2
Grey (cape) F 2
Groote (isl.) F 2
Haasts Bluff Aboriginal Reserve E 5
Hay (dry riv.) E 4
Hooker Creek Aboriginal Reserve E 3
Lake Mackay Aboriginal Reserve D 4
Lander (dry riv.) E 4
Limmen (bight) F 2
Limmen Bight (riv.) F 3
Macdonnell (ranges) E 4
Mackay (lake) D 4
Marshall (riv.) F 4
Melville (bay) F 2
Melville (isl.) E 2
Neale (lake) D 4
Nicholson (riv.) F 3
Peron (isls.) D 2
Petermann Ranges Aboriginal Reserve D 4
Roper (riv.) E 3
Simpson (des.) F 4
Sir Edward Pellew Group (isls.) F 3
South Alligator (riv.) E 2
Stirling (creek) D 3
Tanami (des.) E 3
Timor (sea) D 2
Vanderlin (isl.) F 3
Van Diemen (cape) D 2
Van Diemen (gulf) E 2
Victoria (riv.) E 3
Warrabri Aboriginal Reserve E 4
Wessel (cape) F 2
Wessel (isls.) F 2
White (lake) D 4
Woods (lake) E 3
Ziel (mt.) E 4

### QUEENSLAND

#### CITIES AND TOWNS

Adavale G 5
Albany Creek J 2
Alpha H 4
Archerfield K 3
Ascot K 2
Ashgrove K 2
Aspley K 2
Atherton, 9,518 G 3
Augathella, 431 H 5
Ayr, 8,637 H 3
Bald Hills, 4,228 K 2
Balmoral, 2,915 K 2
Banyo, 4,892 K 2
Barcaldine, 1,530 G 4
Bedourie F 4
Beenleigh, 16,388 J 5
Biloela, 5,051 J 4
Birdsville F 5
Blackall, 1,578 H 4
Blackwater, 6,760 H 4
Bollon H 5
Boondall K 2
Boulia, 281 F 4
Bowen, 8,312 H 3
Brisbane (cap.), 1,145,537 K 3
Brisbane (met. area), 1,334,746 K 3
Bulgroo G 5
Bulloo Downs G 5
Bundaberg, 38,074 J 4
Burketown F 3
Cairns, 64,463 H 3
Caloundra, 22,094 J 5
Camooweal, 234 F 3
Camp Hill K 3
Carina K 3
Carleville H 5
Charters Towers, 9,016 H 4
Chermside K 2
Childers J 5
Chinchilla, 3,152 J 5
Clermont 2,727 H 4
Cloncurry, 2,309 G 4
Coen G 2
Collinsville, 2,552 H 4
Cooktown, 1,342 H 3
Cooladdi H 5
Coopers Plains K 3
Corfield G 4
Corinda K 3
Croydon, 281 G 3
Cunnamulla, 1,683 H 5
Dajarra F 4
Dalby, 9,385 J 5
Darra K 3
Dirranbandi, 460 H 5
Duchess F 4
East Brisbane K 3
Ekibin K 3
Emerald, 6,557 H 4
Emmet G 4
Enoggera K 2
Eromanga G 5
Fernberg K 3
Forsayth G 3
Fruitgrove K 3
Gatton, 5,098 J 5
Gayndah, 1,750 J 5
Geebung K 2
Georgetown, 310 G 3
Gladstone, 23,462 J 4
Gold Coast, 225,773 J 5
Goondiwindi, 4,331 H 5
Gordonvale, 2,658 H 3
Graceville K 3
Greenslopes K 3
Gunpowder F 3
Gympie, 10,791 J 5
Hendra K 2
Hervey Bay, 22,205 J 5
Holland Park K 3
Home Hill, 3,197 H 3
Hughenden, 1,592 G 4
Inala K 3
Indooroopilly K 3
Ingham, 5,075 H 3
Injune, 394 H 5
Innisfail, 8,520 H 3
Ipswich, 73,299 J 3
Isisford, 440 G 4
Ithaca K 2
Julia Creek, 572 G 4
Jundah G 4
Kajabbi G 3
Kalinga K 2
Karumba, 708 G 3
Kenmore J 3
Kingaroy, 6,672 J 5
Laura G 3
Longreach, 3,607 G 4
Mackay, 40,250 H 4
McKinlay, 1,306 G 4
Manly L 2
Mapoon Mission Station G 2
Mareeba, 6,795 G 3
Marian, 587 H 4
Maroochydore-Moolooba, 28,509 J 5
Maryborough, 20,790 J 5
Mary Kathleen G 4
Maryvale H 3
Maxwelton G 4
Meeandah K 2
Miles H 5
Mitchell, 1,101 H 5
Mitchelton J 2
Monto, 1,339 J 4
Moorooka K 3
Morella G 4
Morningside K 2
Mossman, 1,771 G 3
Mount Gravatt K 3
Mount Isa, 23,667 F 4
Mount Morgan, 2,782 J 4
Moura, 2,367 J 4
Munbura G 2
Mundubbera J 5
Murarrie K 2
Murgon, 2,210 J 5
Nambour, 10,355 J 5
Newmarket K 2
Normanby K 2
Normanton, 1,189 G 3
Nudgee K 2
Nundah K 2
Ogmore J 4
Proserpine, 3,034 H 4
Quilpie, 624 G 5
Ravenshoe, 875 H 3
Redcliffe, 47,799 J 5
Richmond, 1,108 G 4
Rockhampton, 59,394 H 4
Roma, 6,220 H 5
St. George, 2,512 H 5
St. Lucia K 3
Sandgate K 2
Sarina, 3,094 H 4
Springfield G 5
Stafford K 2
Stamford G 4
Stanthorpe, 4,187 J 5
Stonehenge G 4
Surat, 468 H 5
Tambo, 351 H 4
Tara, 876 J 5
Thargomindah, 267 G 5
The Gap J 2
Thursday Island, 2,652 G 2
Toowoomba, 75,990 J 5
Townsville, 101,398 H 3
Tully, 2,715 H 3
Walkerston, 1,351 H 4
Warwick, 10,393 J 5
Weipa, 2,510 G 2
Windorah G 5
Windsor K 2
Winton, 1,156 G 4
Wynnum L 2
Yeppoon, 7,542 J 4
Yeronga K 3

#### OTHER FEATURES

Albatross (bay) G 2
Balonne (riv.) H 5
Banks (isl.) G 2
Barcoo (creek) G 4
Bartle Frere (mt.) H 3
Barwon (riv.) H 5
Belyando (riv.) H 4
Bentinck (isl.) F 3
Bowling Green (cape) H 3
Brisbane (riv.) J 3
Brisbane International Airport K 2
Broad (sound) H 4
Bulloo (riv.) G 5
Burdekin (riv.) H 3
Cape York (pen.) G 2
Capricorn Group (isls.) J 4
Carpentaria (gulf) F 2
Comet (riv.) H 4
Condamine (riv.) H 5
Cumberland (isls.) H 4
Curtis (isl.) J 4
Dawson (riv.) H 4
Diamantina (riv.) G 4
Direction (cape) G 2
Drummond (range) H 4
Duifken (pt.) G 2
Endeavor (str.) G 2
Eyre (riv.) F 5
Fitzroy (riv.) J 4
Flattery (cape) H 2
Flinders (riv.) G 3
Fraser (Great Sandy) (isl.) J 4
Georgina (riv.) F 4
Gilbert (riv.) G 3
Great Barrier (reef) H 2
Great Dividing (range) H 4
Great Sandy (Fraser) (isl.) J 5
Gregory (riv.) F 3
Grenville (cape) G 2
Grey (range) G 5
Halifax (bay) H 3
Herbert (riv). H 3
Hervey (bay) J 4
Hinchinbrook (isl.) H 3
Hook (isl.) H 4
Isaacs (riv.) H 4
Keerweer (cape) G 2
Leichhardt (riv.) F 3
Machattie (lake) G 5
Manifold (cape) J 4
Marion (reef) J 3
Melville (cape) G 2
Mitchell (riv. ) G 3
Moreton (bay) K 2
Moreton (isl.) J 5
Mornington (isl.) F 3
Nogoa (riv.) H 4
Norman (riv.) G 3
Northern Peninsula Aboriginal Reserve G 2
Osprey (reef) H 2
Pera (head) G 2
Prince of Wales (isl.) G 2
Princess Charlotte (bay) G 2
Repulse (bay) H 4
Sandy (cape) J 4
Shoalwater (bay) J 4
Staaten (riv.) G 3
Sturt (des.) G 5
Suttor (riv.) H 4
Swain (reefs) J 4
Thomson (riv.) G 4
Torres (str.) G 2
Trinity (bay) H 3
Warrego (range) H 5
Warrego (riv.) H 5
Wellesley (isls) F 3
Wenlock (riv.) G 2
Whitsunday (isl.) H 4
Yamma Yamma (lake) G 5
York (cape) G 2

### SOUTH AUSTRALIA

#### CITIES AND TOWNS

Adelaide (cap.), 957,480 D 8
Adelaide (met. area), 1,023,617 D 8
Berri, 3,733 G 6
Blinman F 6
Bordertown, 2,235 F 7
Brighton, 18,423 D 8
Burnside, 20,243 E 8
Campbelltown, 43,516 E 8

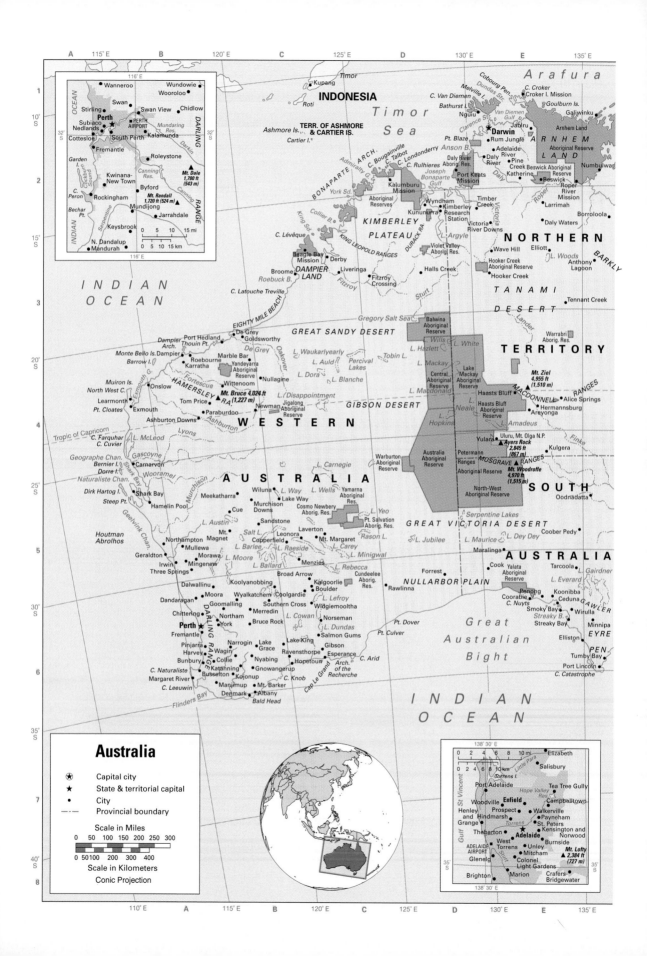

# Australia

Ceduna, 2,735 E 6
Cleve, 738 F 6
Colonel Light Gardens D 8
Coober Pedy, 2,491 E 5
Cook E 6
Coorabie E 6
Cowell, 695 F 6
Crafers-Bridgewater, 11,887 E 8
Elizabeth, 28,954 E 7
Elliston, 1,314 E 6
Enfield, 61,502 D 7
Gawler, 15,068 F 6
Hawker, 345 F 6
Henley and Grange, 14,207 D 8
Hindmarsh, 8,097 D 8
Iron Knob, 293 F 6
Jamestown, 1,359 F 6
Kadina, 3,536 F 6
Kensington and Norwood, 8,803 E 8
Kimba, 683 F 6
Kingoonya E 6
Kingscote, 1,443 F 7
Koonibba E 6
Leigh Creek, 1,378 F 6
Lyndhurst F 6
Maralinga E 6
Marion, 73,942 D 8
Marree F 5
Millicent, 5,118 F 7
Minnipa F 5
Mitcham, 60,939 D 8
Mount Gambier, 21,153 G 7
Murray Bridge, 12,725 F 7
Naracoorte, 4,711 F 7
Oodnadatta E 5
Parachilna F 6
Payneham, 15,327 E 8
Penola, 1,147 G 7
Penong E 6
Peterborough, 2,138 F 6
Pinnaroo, 645 G 7
Port Adelaide, 38,205 D 7
Port Augusta, 14,965 F 6
Port Lincoln, 11,809 E 6
Port Pirie, 14,398 F 6
Prospect, 18,601 D 8
Quorn, 1,056 F 6
Radium Hill G 6
Renmark, 4,256 G 6
St. Peters, 8,142 E 8
Salisbury, 106,007 E 7
Smoky Bay E 6
Streaky Bay, 957 E 6
Tailem Bend, 1,502 F 7
Tarcoola E 6
Tea Tree Gully, 83,969 E 7
Thebarton, 7,701 D 8
Tumby Bay, 1,147 F 6
Unley, 35,692 D 8
Victor Harbor, 5,930 F 7
Walkerville E 8
West Torrens 42,863 D 8
Whyalla, 25,739 F 6
Wirulla E 6
Woodville, 78,824 D 7
Wooltana F 6
Woomera, 1,600 F 6
Wudinna, 573 E 6
Yorketown, 738 F 6

#### OTHER FEATURES

Adelaide Airport D 8
Alberga, The (riv.) E 5
Barcoo (Coopers) (creek) F 5
Blanche (lake) F 5
Callabonna (lake) G 5
Catastrophe (cape) F 7
Coopers (Barcoo) (creek) G 5
Dey Dey (lake) E 5
Encounter (bay) F 7
Everard (lake) E 6
Eyre (lake) F 5
Eyre (pen.) F 6
Flinders (range) F 6
Frome (lake) G 6
Gairdner (lake) F 6
Gawler (ranges) F 6
Great Australian (bight) D 6
Great Victoria (des.) D 5
Gregory (lake) F 5
Hamilton, The (riv.) E 5
Hope Valley (res.) E 7
Investigator (str.) F 7
Investigator Group (isls) E 6
Kangaroo (isl.) F 7
Lacepede (bay) F 7
Lagoon (lake) F 6
Little Para (riv.) D 7
Lofty (mt.) E 8
Macfarlane (lake) F 6
Macumba (riv.) F 5
Maurice (lake) E 5
Mount Lofty (range) F 6
Murray (riv.) G 6
Musgrave (ranges) E 5
Namoi (riv.) H 6
Neals, The (riv.) F 5
North-West Aboriginal Reserve E 5
Nullarbor (plain) D 6
Nuyts (cape) E 6
Onkaparinga (riv.) D 8
St. Vincent (gulf) D 8
Serpentine (lakes) D 5
Siccus (riv.) F 6
Spencer (cape) F 7
Spencer (gulf) F 6
Streaky (bay) E 6
Strzelecki (creek) G 5
Sturt (riv.) D 8
Torrens (isl.) D 7
Torrens (lake) F 6
Torrens (riv.) E 7
Warburton, The (riv.) F 5
Woodroffe (mt.) E 5
Yalata Aboriginal Reserve E 6
Yorke (pen.) F 7

### TASMANIA

#### CITIES AND TOWNS

Burnie-Somerset, 20,505 H 8
Devonport, 22,600 H 8
George Town, 5,026 H 8
Glenorchy, 42,172 H 8
Hobart (cap.), 127,134 H 8
Hobart (met. area), 181,838 H 8
Launceston, 66,747 H 8
New Norfolk, 5,822 H 8
Queenstown, 3,368 H 8
Smithton, 3,495 H 8
Wynyard, 4,679 H 8

#### OTHER FEATURES

Banks (str.) H 8
Bass (str.) H 7
Cape Barren (isl.) H 8
Eddystone (pt.) H 8
Flinders (isl.) H 7
Furneaux Group (isls.) H 8
Hunter (isls.) G 8
King (isl.) G 7
Macquarie (harb.) G 8
Ossa (mt.) H 8
Oyster (bay) H 8
Pillar (cape) H 8
Port Davey (inlet) G 8
South East (cape) H 8
South West (cape) G 7
Tasman (pen.) H 8
Tasman (sea) J 7

### VICTORIA

#### CITIES AND TOWNS

Altona, 35,900 K 7
Ararat, 8,050 G 7
Bairnsdale, 11,740 H 7
Ballarat, 19,320 G 7
Bendigo, 31,880 G 7
Box Hill, 47,500 L 7
Brighton, 34,200 L 7
Broadmeadows, 107,000 L 6
Brunswick, 41,500 K 7
Camberwell, 88,000 L 7
Caulfield, 71,100 L 7
Chelsea, 27,100 L 8
Coburg, 52,800 K 7
Colac, 9,690 G 7
Collingwood, 14,000 L 7
Cranbourne, 73,600 M 8
Croydon, 47,700 M 7
Dandenong, 59,400 M 7
Doncaster and Templestowe, 107,600 L 7
Echuca, 9,780 G 7
Eltham, 44,600 L 6
Essendon, 55,100 K 7
Fitzroy, 18,400 L 7
Footscray, 48,600 K 7
Geelong, 13,310 G 7
Geelong (met. area), 145,323 G 7
Geelong West, 14,440 G 7
Hamilton, 10,200 G 7
Hampton Park M 8
Hawthorn, 31,700 L 7
Heidelberg, 62,800 L 7
Horsham, 13,110 G 7
Keilor, 110,000 K 7
Kew, 28,600 L 7
Knox, 126,900 M 7
Malvern, 43,700 L 7
Maryborough, 7,800 G 7
Melbourne (cap.), 3,145,600 H 7
Melbourne (met. area), 3,022,150 H 7
Mildura, 20,640 G 6
Moe, 17,500 H 7
Moorabbin, 98,500 L 7
Mordialloc, 27,500 L 7
Morwell, 27,950 H 7
Nhill G 7
Northcote, 48,500 L 7
Nunawading, 95,700 L 7
Oakleigh, 57,300 L 7
Orbost, 6,740 H 7
Ouyen G 7
Portland, 10,670 G 7
Port Melbourne, 7,800 K 7
Prahran, 44,300 L 7
Preston, 79,700 L 7
Richmond, 23,500 L 7
Ringwood, 41,900 M 7
St. Kilda, 47,700 L 7
Sale, 14,120 H 7
Sandringham, 32,200 L 7
Seymour, 12,240 H 7
Shepparton, 26,290 G 7
South Melbourne, 18,300 K 7
Springvale, 92,700 L 7
Sunshine, 97,900 K 7
Swan Hill, 9,710 G 7
Traralgon, 20,521 H 7
Wangaratta, 16,190 H 7
Warracknabeal, 3,870 G 7
Warrnambool, 24,900 G 7
Waverly, 123,900 L 7
Werribee, 74,800 G 7
Williamstown, 23,100 K 7
Wodonga, 27,290 H 7
Wonthaggi, 6,800 G 7

#### OTHER FEATURES

Altona (bay) K 7
Australian Alps (mts.) H 7
Bass (str.) H 7
Beaumaris (bay) L 8
Cook (pt.) K 7
Dandenong (creek) M 7
Discovery (bay) E 7
Hobsons (bay) L 7
Kororoit (creek) K 7
Loddon (riv.) G 7
Maribyrnong (riv.) K 7
Melbourne Airport K 7
Merri (riv.) L 7
Murray (riv.) G 6
Otway (cape) G 7
Plenty (riv.) L 6
Portland (bay) G 7
Port Philip (bay) K 7
Ricketts (pt.) L 8
Snowy (riv.) H 7
Wilsons (prom.) H 7
Yarra (riv.) L 6

### WESTERN AUSTRALIA

#### CITIES AND TOWNS

Albany, 18,826 B 6
Ashburton Downs B 4
Bay Mission C 3
Beagle C 3
Boulder C 6
Broad Arrow C 6
Bridgetown, 2,017 B 6
Broome, 8,906 C 3
Bruce Rock, 562 B 6
Bunbury, 24,003 B 6
Busselton, 8,936 A 6
Byford, 1,308 B 2
Carnarvon, 6,901 A 4
Chidlow, 630 B 2
Chittering, 1,920 B 6
Collie, 7,684 B 6
Coolgardie, 1,063 C 6
Copperfield C 5
Cottesloe B 2
Cue, 394 B 5
Dalwallinu, 602 B 6
Dampier, 1,810 B 4
Dandaragan, 2,371 B 6
De Grey B 4
Denmark, 1,586 B 7
Derby, 3,022 C 3
Esperance, 7,066 C 6
Exmouth, 3,128 A 4
Fitzroy Crossing D 3
Forrest D 6
Fremantle, 23,834 B 6
Geraldton, 20,587 A 5
Gibson C 6
Gnowangerup, 762 B 6
Goldsworthy, 379 C 4
Goomalling, 534 B 6
Halls Creek, 1,305 D 3
Hamelin Pool A 5
Harvey, 2,597 B 6
Hopetoun C 6
Irwin A 5
Jarrahdale, 393 B 3
Kalamunda, 45,898 B 2
Kalgoorlie, 25,016 C 6
Kalumburu Mission D 2
Kambalda, 4,259 C 6
Karratha, 11,325 B 4
Katanning, 4,139 B 6
Kellerberrin, 920 B 6
Keysbrook B 3
Kojonup, 1,023 B 6
Koolyanobbing B 6
Kununurra, 4,061 D 3
Kwinana–New Town, 13,517 B 2
Lake Grace, 596 B 6
Lake King C 6
Lake Way C 5
Laverton, 1,197 C 5
Learmonth A 4
Leonora, 1,196 C 5
Liberinga C 3
Mandurah, 23,343 B 3
Manjimup, 4,353 B 6
Marble Bar, 383 B 4
Margaret River, 1,725 A 6
Meekatharra, 1,414 B 5
Menzies, 303 C 5
Merredin, 3,068 B 6
Mingenew, 357 B 5
Moora, 1,687 B 6
Morawa, 624 B 5
Mount Barker, 1,520 B 6
Mount Magnet, 1,076 B 5
Mount Margaret C 5
Mullewa, 739 B 5
Mundijong, 725 B 3
Murchison Downs B 5
Narrogin, 4,638 B 6
Nedlands, 20,409 B 2
Newman, 5,627 C 4
Norseman, 1,398 C 6
Northam, 6,560 B 6
Northampton, 786 A 5
North Dandalup B 3
Nullagine C 4
Nyabing B 6
Onslow, 881 B 4
Paraburdoo, 2,218 B 4
Perth (cap.), 1,018,782 B 2
Perth (met. area), 1,143,265 B 2
Pingelly, 763 B 6
Pinjarra, 1,779 B 6
Port Hedland, 11,344 B 3
Ravensthorpe, 392 C 6
Rawlinna C 6
Rockingham, 36,675 B 2
Roebourne, 1,213 B 4
Roleystone, B 2
Salmon Gums C 6
Sandstone, 347 B 5
Shark Bay A 5
Southern Cross, 982 B 6
South Perth, 34,279 B 2
Stirling, 172,731 B 2
Subiaco B 2
Swan B 2
Swan View B 2
Three Springs, 473 B 5
Tom Price, 3,634 B 4
Wagin, 1,293 B 6
Wanneroo, 167,873 B 2
Widgiemooltha C 6
Wiluna, 236 C 5
Wittenoom B 4
Wooroloo B 2
Wundowie, 711 C 2
Wyalkatchem, 411 B 6
Wydham, 860 D 3
Yampi Sound C 3
York, 1,562 B 6

#### OTHER FEATURES

Adele (isl.) C 3
Admiralty (gulf) D 2
Argyle (lake) D 3
Arid (cape) C 6
Ashburton (riv.) B 4
Auld (lake) C 4
Austin (lake) B 5
Australia Aboriginal Reserve D 5
Avon (riv.) B 6
Bald (head) B 7
Ballard (lake) B 5
Balwina Aboriginal Reserve D 4
Barlee (lake) B 5
Barrow (isl.) A 4
Bechar (pt.) A 3
Bernier (isl.) A 4
Blanche (lake) C 4
Bonaparte (arch.) C 2
Bougainville (cape) D 2
Browse (isl.) C 2
Bruce (mt.) B 4
Brunswick (bay) C 3
Buccaneer (arch.) C 3
Canning (res.) B 2
Canning (riv.) B 3
Carey (lake) C 5
Carnegie (lake) C 5
Central Aboriginal Reserve D 4
Christmas (riv.) D 3
Cockburn (sound) B 2
Collier (bay) C 3
Cosmo Newbery Aboriginal Reserve C 5
Cowan (lake) C 6
Culver (pt.) D 6
Cundeelee Aboriginal Reserve C 6
Cuvier (cape) A 4
Dale (mt.) B 2
Dampier (arch.) B 4
Dampier Land (reg.) C 3
Darkin (riv.) B 2
Darling (range) B 6
De Grey (riv.) C 4
D'Entrecasteaux (pt.) B 7
Dirk Hartogs (isl.) A 5
Disappointment (lake) C 4
Dora (lake) C 4
Dorre (isl.) A 5
Dover (pt.) D 6
Drysdale (riv.) D 3
Dundas (lake) C 6
Durack (range) D 3
Eighty Mile (beach) C 3
Exmouth (gulf) A 4
Farquhar (cape) A 4
Fitzroy (riv.) C 3
Flinders (bay) A 6
Fortescue (riv.) B 4
Garden (isl.) A 2
Gascoyne (riv.) A 4
Geelvink (chan.) A 5
Geographe (chan.) A 4
Gibson (des.) C 4
Great Australian (bight) D 6
Great Sandy (des.) C 4
Great Victoria (des.) D 5
Hamersley (range) B 4
Hazlett (lake) D 4
Hopkins (lake) D 4
Houtman Abrolhos (isls.) A 5
Jigalong Aboriginal Reserve C 4
Johnston, The (lakes) C 6
Joseph Bonaparte (gulf) D 2
Jubilee (lake) D 5
Kimberley (plat.) D 3
Kimberley Research Station D 3
King (sound) C 3
King Leopold (range) D 3
Koolan (isl.) C 3
Lacepede (isls.) C 3
Latouche Treville (cape) C 3
Leeuwin (cape) A 6
Lefroy (lake) C 6
Le Grand (cape) C 6
Lévêque (cape) C 3
Londonderry (cape) D 2
Lort (riv.) C 6
Lyons (riv.) B 4
Macdonald (lake) D 4
McLeod (lake) A 4
Margaret (riv.) D 3
Minigwal (lake) C 5
Montague (sound) C 2
Monte Bello (isls.) A 4
Moore (lake) B 5
Muiron (isls.) A 4
Mundaring (res.) B 2
Murchison (riv.) B 5
Naturaliste (cape) A 6
Naturaliste (chan.) A 5
North West (cape) A 4
Nullarbor (plain) D 6
Oakover (riv.) C 4
Ord (riv.) D 3
Percival (lakes) C 4
Peron (cape) A 2
Perth Airport B 2
Point Salvation Aboriginal Reserve C 5
Raeside (lake) C 5
Randal (mt.) B 3
Rason (lake) C 5
Rebecca (lake) C 6
Recherche (arch.) C 6
Roebuck (bay) C 3
Rulhieres (cape) D 2
Salt (lake) B 5
Serpentine (riv.) B 3
Shark (bay) A 5
Steep (pt.) A 5
Sturt (creek) D 3
Talbot (cape) D 2
Tay (lake) C 6
Thouin (pt.) B 4
Timor (sea) D 2
Tobin (lake) D 4
Violet Valley Aboriginal Reserve D 3
Warburton Aboriginal Reserve D 5
Waukarlyearly (lake) C 4
Way (lake) C 5
Wells (lake) C 5
Wills (lake) D 4
Wooramel (riv.) A 5
Yamarna Aboriginal Reserve C 5
Yandeyarra Aboriginal Reserve B 4
Yeo (lake) D 5
York (sound) C 2

### NORFOLK ISLAND

#### CITIES AND TOWNS

Cascade L 5
Kingston (cap.) L 6
Middlegate L 6

#### OTHER FEATURES

Anson (bay) K 5
Anson (pt.) K 5
Ball (bay) L 6
Bates (mt.) L 5
Blackbourne (pt.) L 6
Cascade (bay) L 5
Collins (head) L 6
Duncombe (bay) L 5
Nepean (isl.) L 6
Rocky (pt.) K 6
Ross (pt.) L 6
Steels (pt.) L 5
Sydney (bay) L 6
Vincent (pt.) K 5

**AUSTRALIAN CAPITAL TERRITORY** *see* CANBERRA.

**AUSTRALIAN EXTERNAL TERRITORIES.** Except for the Antarctic Territory, which is on the continent of Antarctica, the Australian External Territories are all islands in the Indian, Pacific, and Southern oceans. They span one third of the Southern Hemisphere and include virtually every type of climate and physical environment. There are few inhabitants, however. The Territories comprise the Territory of Ashmore and Cartier Islands, the Australian Antarctic Territory, Christmas Island, the Cocos (Keeling) Islands, the Coral Sea Islands Territory, Heard Island and the McDonald Islands, and Norfolk Island.

**The Territory of Ashmore and Cartier Islands** is composed of two groups of islands and reefs in the Indian Ocean off the northwest Australian coast. The territory, within an area of 2 square miles (5 square kilometers), is uninhabited and was transferred from British control in 1931. Ashmore Reef was declared a national nature reserve in 1983.

**The Australian Antarctic Territory,** with an area of some 2,400,000 square miles (6,200,000 square kilometers), covers about one third of Antarctica. It was transferred to Australia from Great Britain in 1933. The area is permanently frozen, and strong winds and blizzards dominate the climate. Plant life is limited to mosses and lichens. The coastal region contains migratory seabirds, penguins, and seals. There is no permanent population, but the territory is regularly visited by scientists based at Mawson, Davis, and Casey stations. With other countries, Australia has taken part in international research projects in Antarctica such as the BIOMASS program, which studies the marine life of Antarctic waters. Members of the Antarctic Treaty, including Australia, adopted the Convention for the Conservation of Antarctic Marine Living Resources in 1980. (*See also* Antarctica.)

**Christmas Island,** northeast of the Cocos and about 1,630 miles (2,623 kilometers) from Perth, covers some 52 square miles (135 square kilometers) in the Indian Ocean. The islanders depend almost entirely on the mining of phosphate rock for their livelihood. Yearly rainfall averages 81 inches (205 centimeters), with a summer wet season. Temperatures range from 64° to 85° F (18° to 30° C). Christmas Island supports a dense rain forest and various animals.

The population (1989 estimate) is about 1,200, of whom some 60 percent are of Chinese descent and 20 percent are of Malay descent. The supply of phosphate rock, mined since 1891 for use in fertilizer manufacturing in Australia, is becoming depleted, though in 1990 a joint venture took over the operation of the phosphate mine.

**The Cocos (Keeling) Islands,** some 1,720 miles (2,768 kilometers) northwest of Perth, comprise 27 small coral islands forming two atolls in the Indian Ocean. Their total area is five square miles (14 square kilometers). Temperatures on the islands range from 75° to 85° F (24° to 29° C), and rainfall averages 79 inches (200 centimeters) annually.

The Cocos has some 555 residents, about 300 of whom are Cocos Malays—descendants of workers, mostly of Malay origin, brought there beginning in 1827. Copra is the sole cash crop. Other activities are subsistence farming, fishing, and boatbuilding.

The first European to visit the islands was Capt. William Keeling in 1609. In 1857 the islands were claimed by Britain and in 1955 transferred to Australia. The copra plantation was owned by the Clunies-Ross family from 1827 to 1978, when Australia purchased it. The Cocos Malay population controls local affairs.

**The Territory of Coral Sea Islands** is made up of scattered reefs and islands off the northeast Australian coast. The islands are mainly coral and sand, though some have grassy or low shrub vegetation. They are the home of 49 seabird species and also turtles that nest in the sand. Abundant marine life inhabits the clear waters, and the island has stopover facilities for visitors to the Great Barrier Reef Marine Park. There is no population apart from a manned weather station on Willis Island. Australia claimed the territory in 1969.

**Heard Island** lies off the Antarctic ice shelf in the south Indian Ocean, about 2,500 miles (4,000 kilometers) southwest of Perth, Australia. Glaciers cover much of it.

**The McDonald Islands,** small and rocky, are 27 miles (43 kilometers) to the west of Heard Island. Together Heard and McDonald islands cover an area of about 159 square miles (412 square kilometers). The islands have no permanent human population. Plant cover is sparse, but Heard and McDonald support many seabird breeding colonies, including penguins and albatross. Elephant seals and leopard seals frequent the shores. During the 19th century, the seals and penguins were exploited for oil. Australia gained control of the islands from Great Britain in 1947. Beginning in 1985, several major research programs were undertaken to study the islands' wildlife.

**Norfolk Island,** with an area of 14 square miles (36 square kilometers), lies 1,041 miles (1,675 kilometers) northeast of Sydney, Australia. It is noted for its rugged coastline, graceful stone buildings, and the native Norfolk Island pine. Temperatures range from 50° to 82° F (10° to 28° C). The presence of pine timber and flax encouraged British settlement of the island, but both have been extensively cleared. Attention is now being given to reforestation.

The resident population is about 2,000 (1986 estimate), one third of whom are descendants of crew members of the British ship *Bounty* who mutinied in 1789. They moved to Norfolk Island from Pitcairn Island in 1856. Tourism is the island's main industry. Farming and fishing are carried on, but most items that support the tourist trade are imported. Postage stamps account for one third of government revenue.

The island was discovered in 1774 by Capt. James Cook and became a penal settlement in 1788. It became an Australian Commonwealth Territory in 1914. In 1979 the Norfolk Island Act established a framework for self-government. (*See also* Australia.)

Kevin J. Frawley

## AUSTRALIAN LITERATURE.

Before European settlers arrived in Australia late in the 18th century, the sole human inhabitants of the continent were the aborigines. These people had no written language. Their songs, myths, legends, and stories were part of an oral tradition handed down over centuries. Much of this tradition served to explain the origin of the land and of the people in the dreamtime, or the dreaming, a mythological period in which the natural world, its laws, and the human race were created. The land itself was the focal point of aboriginal narratives, because it was the source of the people's livelihood. The stories also told of journeys across the land, of specific events tied to special places. The stories traced the origins of each tribal organization back to a revered ancestor.

Not until well after Australia had become an extension of European civilization were some of the aboriginal stories collected and translated. One collection was published in 1896 by Catherine Langloh Parker under the title 'Australian Legendary Tales'. In 1952 Alan Marshall published 'People of the Dreamtime'. By the 1960s aboriginal writers were publishing their own works in English.

Oodgeroo Noonuccal (or Kath Walker) published the first volume of her poems, 'We Are Going', in 1964. The novel 'Wild Cat Falling' by Mudrooroo Narogin (or Colin Johnson) came out in 1965. His later novels included 'Long Live Sandawara' (1979), 'Doctor Wooreddy's Prescription for Enduring the End of the World' (1983), and 'Doin' Wildcat' (1988). Sally Morgan's autobiography, 'My Place', was published in 1987. It deals with her search for identity.

**The first century.** The first English immigrants arrived in 1788. For several decades the bulk of the settlers were convicts shipped to Australia by British authorities. The writings that emerged from these early immigrants and their descendants had two main emphases: the distinctive qualities of the land itself and the lives the former convicts made in their new home. One of the first reports sent back to Europe was 'A Narrative of the Expedition to Botany Bay' (1789), by sea captain Watkin Tench. He followed with 'A Complete Account of the Settlement at Port Jackson' in 1793. Physician John White published 'Journal of a Voyage to New South Wales' in 1789.

The transition from factual—if sometimes exaggerated—narratives to more literary forms happened in 1819, the year the first volume of poetry appeared. It was Barron Field's 'First Fruits of Australian Poetry'. Another work of 1819 was 'The Memoirs of James Hardy Vaux'. Vaux was a convict writer. His autobiography, while not fictionalized, was an attempt to justify himself and to portray himself more a victim than as felon. An other convict writer, Henry Savery, took the next step by publishing a thinly veiled autobiography as a novel. 'Quintus Servinton' (1831) was the author's attempt to justify the events of his life and to defend his character to a reading audience. Memoirs similar to those of Savery's included Charles Rowcroft's 'Tales of the Colonies' (1843) and Alexander Harris' 'Settlers and Convicts' (1847).

*WHITE*

*McCULLOUGH*

Rowcroft and Harris also wrote novels. Rowcroft published 'The Bushranger of Van Diemen's Land' in 1846 and Harris 'The Emigrant Family' in 1849. These were novels of the land as well as convict stories. They were about life in a more settled Australia, including the violence and uncertainty that faced the inhabitants. Other novels in a similar vein included James Tucker's 'Ralph Rashleigh' (1844), 'The Recollections of Geoffry Hamlyn' (1859) by Henry Kingsley, Catherine Helen Spence's 'Clara Morison' (1854), Caroline Leakey's 'The Broad Arrow' (1859), John Lang's 'The Forger's Wife' (1855), Marcus Clarke's 'His Natural Life' (1874), and Rosa Praed's 'Policy and Passion' (1881).

The most successful writer of the late colonial era was Thomas Alexander Browne, who wrote under the pen name Rolf Boldrewood. His 'Robbery Under Arms' was a classic adventure story about life in the bush and the goldfields. Serialized in a magazine in 1883, it came out as a book in 1888. Among his 17 other fiction works were 'A Colonial Reformer' (1890) and 'The Miner's Right (1890).

In addition to the fiction and poetry of the first century were numerous journals by explorers of the outback, Australia's inland frontier. Those written by such intrepid adventurers as Charles Stuart, Edward John Eyre, and Thomas Livingstone Mitchell had a good deal of literary merit.

**From 1888 to 1945.** The year 1888 was the centennial of the first settlement. The anniversary was a literary watershed. Novels of convicts and exploration gave way to a spirit of nationalism that would lead, in 1901, to the end of colonial status. A "Young Australia" attitude was growing among Australians—a conviction that theirs was a new country with a bright future. This notion was reflected in the literature of the time. The focal point of the new trend was *The Bulletin,* a weekly publication with the slogan "Australia for the Australians." The fiction medium of the time was as often the short story as the novel.

Among the best-known writers before World War I were Henry Lawson, Barbara Baynton, William Astley, Joseph Furphy, Henry Handel Richardson (the pen name of Ethel Florence Lindesay Robertson), William Gosse Hay, Louis Stone, Miles Franklin, and Norman Lindsay. Their writings often centered on life in the bush, with all of its difficulties—not unlike frontier

Photos, Jerry Bauer

*KENEALLY*  *MOORHOUSE*

tales in the United States. Lawson, for instance, published 'Short Stories in Prose and Verse' (1894), with such tales as "The Drover's Wife" and "The Bush Undertaker." Baynton's 'Bush Studies' (1902) is a collection of stories on the difficulties of rural living. Astley drew on the convict system for his 'Tales of the Early Days' (1894), 'Tales of the Isle of Death' (1898), and other works. His 'Half-Crown Bob and Tales of the Riverine' were bush narratives. Furphy celebrated rural life in his sprawling novel 'Such is Life' (1903), in which he explored the unspoken code of behavior of the bush dwellers.

Richardson was an expatriate writer. She spent much of her life in Europe. Yet she was perhaps the best Australian novelist of the era. Her 'Maurice Guest' (1908) was set in Leipzig, Germany, but her three-volume 'The Fortunes of Richard Mahony' (1917–29) is a saga of an immigrant family's fortunes in Australia. W.G. Hay's main work was 'The Escape of the Notorious Sir William Heans', a peculiar combination of romantic melodrama with historical events.

Louis Stone was both dramatist and novelist, although there was little demand for theater in Australia then. His literary reputation rests mostly on the novel 'Jonah' (1911), a story set in Sydney instead of the rural setting preferred by most writers. Miles Franklin, a woman, is best remembered for 'My Brilliant Career' (1901). She was an early feminist whose works spanned several decades. Among her good later books was 'All That Swagger' (1936). Norman Lindsay's career also covered many decades. His short story 'Lone Hand' came out in 1907 and his last novel, 'Rooms and Houses', in 1968.

The two leading writers of the period between the world wars were Vance Palmer and Katherine Susannah Pritchard. Palmer was a very influential writer whose first collection of stories, 'The World of Men' came out in 1915. His first novel, 'Cronulla' (1924) was set in the outback of Queensland. His last work was a trilogy published from 1948 to 1959— 'Golconda', 'Seedtime', and 'The Big Fellow', about the mining industry and the men who developed it.

Pritchard was born in Fiji, but she settled in Western Australia after her marriage. She was a feminist and a Marxist. Her novel 'Coondaroo' (1929), on white mistreatment of the aborigines, aroused a great deal of opposition. Like Palmer, she wrote a trilogy about

the mining industry: 'The Roaring Nineties' (1946), 'Golden Miles' (1948), and 'Winged Seeds' (1950). Her least political novel was 'Intimate Strangers' (1937).

**Since 1945.** Three writers who made a worldwide reputation after World War II were Patrick White, Morris West, and Colleen McCullough. White won the Nobel prize for literature in 1973. He is considered the major Australian writer of the late 20th century. His first novel was 'Happy Valley' (1939), a story of rural New South Wales. Altogether he published 12 large novels. His best-known work was 'Voss' (1957), about an expedition to inland Australia.

Morris West is known outside Australia mainly for his religious novels: 'The Shoes of the Fisherman' (1963), 'The Clowns of God' (1981), and 'Lazarus' (1990), which form a trilogy. Colleen McCullough was born in New Zealand but settled in Australia. Her novel 'The Thorn Birds' (1977) became a worldwide bestseller and was made into a television miniseries. It is the story of one family over three generations and its relationship to a priest, Father de Bricassart. Her later novels included 'A Creed for the Third Millennium' (1985), 'The First Man in Rome' (1990), and 'The Grass Crown' (1990).

Significant writers of the immediate postwar decades included Martin Boyd, Christina Stead, and Randolph Stow. Boyd's novels were primarily family histories: 'Lucinda Brayford' (1946) and the tetralogy consisting of 'The Cardboard Crown' (1952), 'A Difficult Young Man' (1955), 'Outbreak of Love' (1957), and 'When Blackbirds Sing' (1962). Stead first won recognition with 'The Man Who Loved Children' in 1940. Her later books included 'For Love Alone' (1945) and 'The People with the Dogs' (1952). Stow's first success was 'To the Islands' (1958), followed by 'The Merry-Go-Round in the Sea' (1965), 'Visitants' (1979), 'The Suburbs of Hell' (1984), and others.

By the 1960s Australian fiction was as far-ranging in its subject matter as any literature in the world. Thomas Keneally was one of the era's most productive authors. His most highly regarded book is probably 'Schindler's Ark' (1982), based on a true story of the Holocaust that was made into the Academy awardwinning film 'Schindler's List' in 1993. His other novels included 'The Chant of Jimmie Blacksmith' (1972), which was also made into a film, 'Passenger' (1979), and 'A Family Madness' (1985). Some of the other major novelists of the 1980s and after were Jon Cleary, Frank Hardy, Thea Astley, David Malouf, David Ireland, Christopher J. Koch, Frank Moorhouse, Gerald Murnane, Glenda Adams, Nicholas Hasluck, and Amanda Lohrey.

**BIBLIOGRAPHY FOR AUSTRALIAN LITERATURE**

**Bennett, Brice, and others, eds.** The Penguin New Literary History of Australia (Penguin, 1988).

**Clancy, Laurie.** A Reader's Guide to Australian Fiction (Oxford, 1992).

**Goodwin, K.L.** A History of Australian Literature (St. Martin's, 1986).

**Kramer, Leonie, ed.** The Oxford History of Australian Literature (Oxford, 1981).

Bavaria—Viesti Associates, Inc.

*The Dachstein Mountains of the northern Alps loom over Hallstatt, Austria. Hallstatt has given its name to the earliest European Iron Age because of the many archaeological excavations done in the surrounding area.*

**AUSTRIA.** A small, mountainous country in Central Europe, Austria was once at the center of a great empire and one of the great powers of Europe. Its position at the middle of Europe made it a center of trade, transportation, and culture.

### Land and Climate

The Republic of Austria occupies the eastern end of the great mountain ranges of the Alps. The highest peaks are in the western and central parts of Austria. A number of ranges extend west to east with several major river valleys between them. The highest peak is the Grossglockner (12,457 feet; 3,797 meters), located in the Hohe Tauern range. The high ranges of the Austrian Alps are glaciated.

The major lowland areas lie in the northern and eastern parts of the country. The northern lowland is the wide valley of the Danube River, which flows across northern Austria. At the eastern end of this lowland, where the Danube emerges from the mountains into the drier plains, lies the capital city of Vienna. South of Vienna a second area of plains extends to the Slovenian border. These lowlands occupy about 20 percent of the country's total area. North of the Danube is an area of hills that is an extension of a mountain area in the southern part of the Czech Republic.

A number of rivers, such as the Enns, Inn, Drava, Ill, Salzach, and Mur, flow through the interior valleys of the Alps. These valleys provide conditions suitable for farming as well as for the development of cities and towns. Among a number of Alpine passes, the most important is the Brenner Pass, which connects Austria with Italy. The city of Innsbruck, located in the valley of the Inn, owes its importance to its location at the approaches to the Brenner Pass. The Semmering Pass south of Vienna leads to the northern end of the Adriatic Sea. The largest lake is Neusiedler Lake, south of Vienna. The western tip of Austria lies on the shores of Lake Constance (Bodensee), which borders Austria, Switzerland, and Germany.

The climate of Austria is not uniform throughout its whole territory. The western mountainous region receives considerable moisture from the Atlantic Ocean and thus tends to have higher rainfall and snowfall totals than the east. The difference between summer and winter temperatures is greater in the east than in the west. The interior valleys and the eastern lowlands have the warmest summer temperatures. In the latter area summers have average temperatures of about 68° F (20° C) and winter temperatures of about 29° F (–2° C). In the mountains temperatures decrease with altitude, and the permanent snow line averages between 8,000 and 9,000 feet (2,400 and 2,700 meters).

Most of the western and central parts of landlocked Austria are covered by mountains of the Alps. To the east the mountains become lower and less rugged. The Danube River, the country's only important water route, and Vienna, the capital city, are located in the northeast, which consists mostly of plains.

Alpine weather is affected by winds. The most important is the foehn, a warm, dry wind that occurs on the leeward slopes of the mountain ranges. (See also Alps.)

### Plant and Animal Life

The original vegetation of the Austrian Alps consisted of deciduous trees, such as beech, birch, and oak, on the lower slopes, and coniferous trees, such as spruce, pine, fir, and larch, on the upper slopes. Much of the forest on the lower slopes and on the lowlands has been removed to allow crop farming. A large number of the native species—bears, wolves, and wild swine—have vanished, but there are still marmots, deer, foxes, martens, badgers, squirrels, hares, partridges, pheasants, and a number of other birds. In the high parts of the Alps chamois and a few ibex are found. Above the timberline grow numerous species of berries and flowers, including the rare edelweiss.

### The People

About 96 percent of the inhabitants of Austria are German-speaking. The small minority groups include Czechs, Croats, Slovenes, and Hungarians. Dominant in Austrian society, along with German language and culture, is the Roman Catholic religion. The few Protestants and Jews reside mainly in Vienna.

Austrian culture has made many contributions to the world. In particular, several great composers— such as Wolfgang Amadeus Mozart, Ludwig van Beethoven, Franz Schubert, Johannes Brahms, Johann Strauss, and Gustav Mahler—have lived or worked in Austria. Austrian writers such as Hugo von Hofmannsthal and Arthur Schnitzler have made important contributions to German literature. Austrian folk culture is rich in music, dance, arts, and crafts.

Since the 1970s the growth rate of the population has decreased to near zero, due to a balancing out of the birthrate and the death rate. About 65 percent of the population lives in cities. The largest city by far is the capital, Vienna, with a little more than 1.5 million

inhabitants. The second city, Graz, is much smaller, with only about 237,000 inhabitants. Other important cities include Linz, Salzburg, and Innsbruck. (See also Vienna, Austria.)

### The Economy

Because of its large region of mountains only about half of Austria's total area is suitable for farming or pasture. More than one third of its area is forest and woodland, and more than 15 percent is unproductive. More than half of the farmland consists of natural meadows and pastures where cattle, goats, and sheep are grazed. Of the country's agricultural output more than two thirds consists of animal products, especially milk, butter, and cheese. The major grain crops are corn (maize), barley, wheat, and rye. Other important crops include potatoes and sugar beets. Orchards and vineyards are found mainly in the eastern part of the country. The main tree orchard fruits are apples, pears, plums, apricots, and peaches. Wine is produced both for home consumption and for export. A typical farm is small and is usually owned by the family that lives and works on it.

The forest-products industry is important, and about one eighth of Austria's exports consists of timber, timber products, and paper. The country is one of the world's leading producers of coniferous sawn timber. Much of the forest land has been severely overcut, but extensive reforestation and other forest management techniques such as controlled thinning are being encouraged by the government. About one third of the forest land is in small, private holdings, and many of the owners have formed efficient forest-utilization cooperatives.

The lack of energy resources is the weakest aspect of Austria's economy. Austria must import more than 70 percent of its bituminous coal and lignite. It also imports more than 80 percent of its oil and natural gas. Some petroleum and natural gas come from wells east of Vienna. There is a refinery at Schwechat, a suburb of Vienna. Oil from the Middle East is brought by pipeline from Trieste in Italy. Natural gas is imported from Russia by pipeline. Lignite is mined locally in small quantities and is burned to generate electricity. About half of the electricity produced comes from hydroelectric power stations on Alpine rivers and on the Danube. A nuclear power station built near Vienna was protested, and, after a national referendum in 1978, it was not used.

Production of metallic minerals is significant, and Austria mines iron ore, lead, zinc, copper, and magnesite. Iron ore is mined in the southern area of the country. Magnesite is an important export.

Austrian industry is in general characterized by a number of small specialized enterprises, many of them state-owned. The iron and steel industry is important and produces enough for the country's needs and for export. The major plants are at Linz and in the south near the iron ore deposits. The Austrian iron and steel industry expanded rapidly after World War II. There is also a sizable aluminum industry that processes primarily imported aluminum, which is economically feasible because of the abundance of inexpensive hydroelectric power. One of the largest plants in Western Europe is located near Braunau. The chemical industry produces fertilizer, plastics, and synthetic fibers, mainly for use in Austria. The paper industry is important, and cellulose, paper, and cardboard are exported. Other industries include construction, machinery, transportation equipment, electrical equipment, and cotton and wool textiles.

The development of the tourist trade also contributes much to the Austrian economy. The main attractions are the alpine scenery and the skiing resorts in the mountains. Many art and music enthusiasts and historians are attracted to the galleries, concert halls, and museums of Vienna. Salzburg, with its annual music festival, also brings many visitors.

## Transportation, Communication, and Education

Austria is located at the meeting place of several important transportation routes. In the west is the Brenner Pass to Italy, and in the east is the Danube River, which flows through southeastern Europe. Austria also lies on the land route between the head of the Adriatic Sea and the Danube Plain.

Austria has a good railroad network, half of which is electrified. There are several mountain railroads and many cableways and chair lifts that provide access to the high slopes for skiers and hikers. Austria also has several four-lane highways that are connected to the German and Italian road networks and permit easy access to the country for tourists. The two most important river ports are Vienna and Linz. The national airline links Vienna with many cities of the world.

Austria has a well-organized postal and telegraph network, as well as a state radio and television service. All of these services are controlled and operated by the Post and Telegraph Administration.

The Austrian educational system is based on compulsory, free education for all children between the ages of 6 and 15 in a variety of primary and secondary schools. There are six universities, located at Vienna, Graz, Innsbruck, Salzburg, and Krems. They are particularly noted for their technical and medical schools and clinics. Austria has produced Nobel prizewinners in the fields of medicine, physics, chemistry, peace, and economics. Sigmund Freud, the founder of psychoanalysis, was an Austrian.

## Government

Austria is a federal republic, consisting of nine democratic states, known as *Bundesländer*. The states of Lower Austria, Upper Austria, Styria, Tirol (Tyrol), Carinthia, Salzburg, Vorarlberg, and Burgenland have their own capitals and legislative assemblies. The federal capital, Vienna, is also a state.

The country is governed under the constitution of 1920, as amended in 1929, which gives the federal government considerable political and economic power. The residual powers are left to the provincial governments. The federal president is elected by popular vote for a term of six years. He is the head of state, but his power is largely limited to appointing the chancellor (head of government) and the Cabinet ministers. The legislature consists of a lower house, the National Council (*Nationalrat*), and an upper house, the Federal Council (*Bundesrat*). There are two major political parties, the People's party and the Social Democratic party. The former is, in general, a conservative party representing businessmen and farmers, and it has the unofficial support of the Roman Catholic church. The Social Democrats count on the support of industrial workers.

## History

The present nation of Austria is the remnant of a once-powerful empire that controlled a large area of central and eastern Europe. With the breakdown of the empire of Austria-Hungary after World War I, Austria found itself only one eighth of its former size. (*See also* Austria-Hungary).

This sudden reduction from world power to a small and relatively weak country was a major blow to the Austrian people. In 1918 the German members of the imperial parliament declared the formation of an Austrian nation consisting of the German-speaking areas of former Austria-Hungary. This new republic, however, was threatened by Communist attempts at a takeover along with the attempts by several of the provinces to break away and form independent states.

The republic in its early days wished to be united with Germany, but this was expressly forbidden in the World War I peace treaty signed with the Allies in 1919. The main task of the government was the restoration of the economy, which was in chaos. Although economic conditions improved considerably in the 1920s, the internal political situation did not, due to a continuous confrontation between the Socialists and right-wing groups. Many people turned to the Nazi party after a financial crisis in 1931 discredited the major parties. The Christian Socialist party under Chancellor Engelbert Dollfuss was attacked by both the left and right, and in 1934 the conflict led to a brief civil war. In the same year the Nazis attempted to take over the government by force and murdered Dollfuss. The leaders of this attempt were arrested, and the new chancellor tried to resist Nazi Germany. In 1938 the Germans marched into Austria and declared a union, or *Anschluss.* Renamed Ostmark by the Nazis, Austria fought World War II as part of the Axis powers.

In 1945 Austria was divided into zones of occupation by the United States, the Soviet Union, the United Kingdom, and France. Economic problems retarded the recovery of the country, but by the early 1950s considerable prosperity had been restored. In 1955 the four countries signed a treaty with the Austrian government and removed their troops. Austria was prohibited from union with Germany and undertook to maintain a democratic political system. The constitution was amended to make the nation neutral. Austria was admitted to the United Nations in 1955.

Controversy erupted during Austria's 1986 presidential election when candidate Kurt Waldheim, former secretary-general of the United Nations (UN), was accused of participating in war crimes while serving in the German army during World War II. Despite this, Waldheim won the election.

Austria's neutrality had prevented it from joining the European Communities (EU; formerly the European Communities) or any major European military organization. With the end of the Cold War, this situation changed (*see* Cold War). Austria was a member of the European Free Trade Association (EFTA). In 1991 the EFTA signed a free-trade agreement with the EU, and in June 1994 Austrians voted overwhelmingly to join the EU in 1995. Elections held in Austria in October 1996 yielded results that raised concern throughout Europe. The Freedom party, led by Jorg Haider, won over its largely working-class constituency by campaigning against immigration, government corruption, and a United Europe. Haider raised eyebrows when he spoke, in terms reminiscent of Third Reich rhetoric, of a need to create a "Europe of Fatherlands." Haider spoke of the dangers of immigration and blamed Turkish immigrants for the increase of criminal activity in Austria, and warned that a unified Europe would lead to the loss of jobs for Austrian workers.

Ian Matley

## Austria Fact Summary

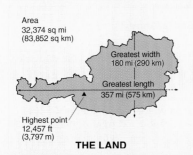

Area
32,374 sq mi
(83,852 sq km)

Greatest width
180 mi (290 km)

Greatest length
357 mi (575 km)

Highest point
12,457 ft
(3,797 m)

**THE LAND**

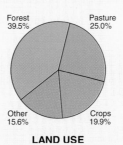

Forest 39.5%
Pasture 25.0%
Other 15.6%
Crops 19.9%

**LAND USE**

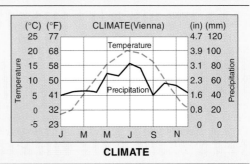

CLIMATE(Vienna)

**CLIMATE**

**Official Name.** Republic of Austria.
**Capital.** Vienna.

### NATURAL FEATURES

**Mountain Ranges.** Alps (Hohe Tauern, Niedere Tauern, Ötztaler Alps, Zillertaler Alps).
**Highest Peaks.** Grossglockner, 12,457 feet (3,797 meters); Wildspitze, 12,383 feet (3,774 meters); Grossvenediger, 12,054 feet (3,674 meters); Hochfeiler 11,516 feet (3,510 meters).
**Largest Lakes.** Lake Constance (Bodensee), Neusiedler Lake.
**Major Rivers.** Danube, Drava, Enns, Ill, Inn, Mur, Rhine, Salzach, Traun.

### PEOPLE

**Population** (1996 estimate). 8,102,000; 250.2 persons per square mile (96.6 persons per square kilometer); 64.5 percent urban, 35.5 percent rural (1991 estimate).
**Major Cities** (1991 census). Vienna (1,539,848), Graz (237,810), Linz (203,044), Salzburg (143,978), Innsbruck (118,112).
**Chief Religion.** Roman Catholicism.
**Official Language.** German.
**Literacy.** 100 percent.
**Leading Universities and Colleges.** University of Vienna, University of Graz, University of Innsbruck, University of Technology (Vienna), University of Salzburg, Danube University of Krems.

### GOVERNMENT

**Form of Government.** Federal Republic.
**Chief of State.** President.

**Head of Government.** Chancellor, leader of the Council of Ministers (cabinet) of the National Council (*Nationalrat*).
**Legislature.** Parliament of two houses: the National Council (*Nationalrat*), elected by the people; the Federal Council (*Bundesrat*), elected by the state assemblies.
**Voting Qualification.** Age 20.
**Political Divisions.** 9 states (*Bundesländer*): Burgenland, Carinthia, Lower Austria, Salzburg, Styria, Tirol (Tyrol), Upper Austria, Vienna, Vorarlberg.
**Flag.** Three horizontal stripes of equal width: red, white, and red (*see* Flags of the World).

### ECONOMY

**Chief Agricultural Products.** *Crops*—sugar beets, corn (maize), barley, wheat, potatoes, rye. *Livestock*—pigs, cattle, chickens.
**Chief Mined Products.** Iron ore, magnesite, high-grade graphite, coal, petroleum, natural gas.
**Chief Manufactured Products.** Electrical and nonelectrical machinery and equipment, base metals and fabricated metals, beverages and tobacco products, chemicals and chemical products, transport equipment.
**Chief Exports.** Machinery and transport equipment, chemicals and related products, paper and paper products, iron and steel.
**Chief Imports.** Machinery and transport equipment, chemicals and related products, clothing, food products.
**Monetary Unit.** 1 Austrian Schilling = 100 Groschen.

*Schönbrunn Palace in Vienna was built as an official residence for Leopold I. It was designed by Johann B. Fischer von Erlach as an imitation of Versailles in France, but his plans were modified before construction began in 1695.*
SUPERSTOCK

**AUSTRIA-HUNGARY.** After centuries as one of the most powerful nations of Europe, proud Austria was forced to divide its empire with Hungary in 1867. The two nations formed a dual monarchy—Austria-Hungary.

In Europe, only Russia surpassed Austria-Hungary in size, population, and variety of nationalities. The empire lay in the Danube Basin, inhabited by German-speaking Austrians in the west and by Magyars in the broad Hungarian plain to the east. Slavs lived on the fringes of the empire, and Italians on the Adriatic coast. Language divided these groups; however, the Danube and the roads and railways radiating from Vienna held them together as an economic unit.

Austria began as a frontier land of Charlemagne's empire and rose to be the chief German state, ruling many neighboring peoples. Austria-Hungary ceased to exist when the empire split apart at the end of World War I. (*See also* Austria; Bosnia and Herzegovina; Croatia; Czechoslovakia; Czech Republic; Hungary; Poland; Romania; Serbia; Slovakia; Slovenia; Ukraine; Yugoslavia.)

### The Eastern Outpost of Europe

In the 1st century AD the Romans conquered the Celts south of the Danube and set up a frontier colony. As Rome's power declined, Germanic tribes from the north overcame the Celts. Christianity took hold in the area in the 7th century, and Salzburg began its rise as a great ecclesiastical center. In the 9th century Charlemagne added the region to his empire as the Ostmark (East March), hoping to stem the invasions from the east. In the next century, however, Magyar invaders ravaged the land. Otto the Great crushed them in the battle of Lechfeld (955) and pushed them back into Hungary. (*See also* Charlemagne; Otto I.)

Austria's rise to power began with the Babenberg dynasty, which began when Leopold I became Margrave of Austria in 976. Elevated to a duchy, the Ostmark became the Österreich (Eastern Realm). Its fortunes improved when Leopold V joined the Third Crusade. Leopold quarreled with Richard I (the Lion-Hearted) of England and imprisoned him as he tried to slip through Austria on his way home. With the ransom money England was forced to pay for

Richard, Leopold improved the roads and towns of the realm. The Babenberg dynasty came to an end in 1246 when Frederick II, the last of the line, was killed in battle against the Magyars.

After Frederick's death his lands were divided; they eventually came under the control of the Hapsburg king of Germany, Rudolph I. The Hapsburgs' power mounted when Albert V was crowned Holy Roman emperor as Albert II in 1438. The title then became virtually hereditary. (*See also* Hapsburg, House of; Holy Roman Empire.)

### "Thou, Happy Austria, Marry!"

"Let others make wars," so the saying went, "thou, happy Austria, marry!" Albert II married the daughter of the king of Hungary and Bohemia. His successor, Frederick III, came into possession of both these crowns. Frederick's son Maximilian I, crowned emperor in 1493, married Mary, daughter of Charles the Bold, duke of Burgundy and ruler of the Netherlands. Maximilian's son Philip married Joan, daughter of Ferdinand and Isabella of Spain. Charles V, Maximilian's grandson, thus inherited Germany, Austria, the Netherlands, Naples and Sicily, Spain, and the Spanish New World domain.

Austria, however, did fight as well as marry. For centuries it struggled with France; and with the help of the Magyars, it fought against the Turks, who besieged Vienna itself. Charles V tried to crush the Protestant revolt in Germany (*see* Reformation). He was made to sign the Peace of Augsburg (1555), however, which allowed each prince to determine whether his people should be Roman Catholic or Lutheran.

Before his death Charles divided his empire, creating two branches of the Hapsburg line. He transferred his German possessions to his brother, Ferdinand I. To his son, Philip II, he gave Milan, Sicily, the Netherlands, and Spain with its American colonies.

Encouraged by the Peace of Augsburg, Protestantism spread. In 1608 Protestant rulers banded together into the Protestant Union. The Roman Catholics countered with the Catholic League. In 1619 the Hapsburg emperor Ferdinand II appealed to the League for help in putting down a Protestant uprising

*Before the outbreak of World War I, Austria-Hungary was a vast and powerful empire. After its defeat in the war it was divided into a number of smaller nations.*

**Austria-Hungary**
From One Empire
to Many Nations
— Austria-Hungary in 1914
— Current political boundaries

A COMPTON'S MAP

in Bohemia. Soon Austria was involved with all of Europe in a religious conflict (*see* Thirty Years' War).

## Effects of the Peace of Augsburg

The Peace of Augsburg had weakened the authority of the Holy Roman emperors. At the end of the Thirty Years' War the empire received its final blow from the Treaty of Westphalia (1648), which further strengthened the local princes by allowing them to make treaties with foreign powers. The way was thus opened for the rise of Prussia, which was eventually to humble the Hapsburgs and assume the leadership in a new German empire (*see* Prussia).

The Hapsburgs' influence in European affairs diminished. The remains of their power lay in their rule over those territories from which the empire of Austria-Hungary was beginning to evolve. Successful at last in their long struggle with the Turks, the Hapsburgs forced them out of Hungary by the end of the 17th century.

## The War of the Spanish Succession

The Spanish line of the Hapsburgs ended in 1700 when Charles II of Spain died childless and brotherless. One of his sisters had married Louis XIV of France; another married Emperor Leopold I. These rulers had each planned how the rich Spanish possessions should be divided. Charles left a will, however, that made Louis's younger grandson, Philip, heir to all his possessions.

England became alarmed at this growth in French power and joined with France's enemies, Austria and Holland, in a Grand Alliance (1701). This led to the War of the Spanish Succession, which spread through Europe and even to America, where it was called Queen Anne's War (*see* Queen Anne's War).

In Europe the Austrian commander, Prince Eugene of Savoy, and the English general, the duke of

Marlborough, won the major battles against France but won no decisive victory over the country. Finally Louis XIV agreed to a compromise.

The Treaty of Utrecht (1713) gave each of the foes a share in the Spanish booty. Philip V retained Spain. Some of the colonies went to England, along with Gibraltar. The Spanish Netherlands became the Austrian Netherlands, and Austria also received Naples and Milan, obtaining a hold on Italy that it would greatly enlarge later.

## The War of the Austrian Succession

With the death of Charles VI in 1740, the male line of the Austrian Hapsburgs ended. In order to secure all the Austrian possessions to his daughter Maria Theresa, Charles had drawn up a code of succession (the Pragmatic Sanction) and worked tirelessly to have it accepted by the European powers. It seemed at first that they would. However, a new enemy arose to confront Austria. In the same year that Maria Theresa received her inheritance, the ambitious Frederick came to the throne of Prussia. (See also Maria Theresa; Frederick the Great.)

Without bothering to declare war, Frederick marched his armies into Austrian Silesia less than two months after the death of Charles VI. France came to his aid. England and Spain were already at war—the War of Jenkins' Ear. The two wars merged, with Britain as Austria's ally. Frederick the Great, having secured Silesia, sat back and quoted, "Happy are they who, having secured their own advantage, can look tranquilly upon the embarrassment of others."

The peace treaties restored the position of the Austrian crown to what it had been before the war. As far as Austria was concerned, the powers accepted the Pragmatic Sanction; and Frederick the Great ratified the election of Maria Theresa's consort, Francis I of Lorraine, as Holy Roman emperor. Thus the empire

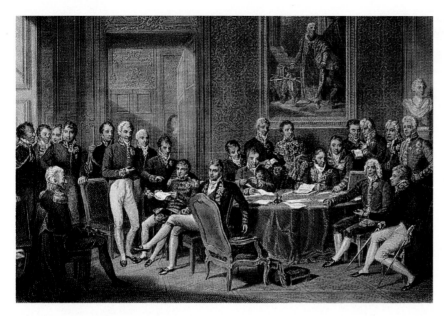

*The great powers of Europe meet for the Congress of Vienna (left). The duke of Wellington is at the far left. Prince Metternich is shown standing at the left and in a portrait (right).*

(Left) The Granger Collection; (right) Brown Brothers

was returned to the new ruling house of Austria—the house of Hapsburg-Lorraine.

### The Seven Years' War

The peace proved to be merely a truce. Maria Theresa would not accept the loss of Silesia. When Russia offered to help her regain it, she gladly accepted. Louis XV of France also had a score to settle with the Prussian king for withdrawing from the earlier conflict. Frederick, aware that an alliance was being built up against him, sought the help of England, Austria's former friend. Without waiting to be attacked, he marched into Saxony. Thus began the Seven Years' War (1756–63). It was to be fought not only in Europe but also in India and America. Again the peace left Silesia in Prussia's hands. (*See also* Seven Years' War; French and Indian War.)

Frederick the Great then decided to seize Poland and invited Catherine of Russia and Maria Theresa to divide it with him. Austria thus added to its territory the large province of Galicia (1772).

### The Holy Roman Empire Comes to an End

Before her death Maria Theresa saw her ill-fated daughter Marie Antoinette crowned queen of France as the wife of Louis XVI (*see* Marie Antoinette). Her son Joseph II, who had become coruler with his mother on the death of his father, succeeded her in 1780. An "enlightened despot," he freed the serfs and tried to put through many other reforms. His brother Leopold II, who followed him, repealed most of his decrees. Leopold died after a reign of two years. His son Francis II succeeded him.

When the French revolutionists executed Louis XVI and Marie Antoinette, Austria found itself ranged with most of Europe's powers against the new French Republic (*see* French Revolution). Forced to surrender in 1797 after a short campaign, Austria again went to

war against France after Napoleon I's rise and suffered a terrible defeat at Austerlitz in 1805 (*see* Napoleon I). By now the disintegration of the German states was complete. To preserve his imperial title, Francis II decided to call himself simply emperor of Austria and king of Hungary. In 1806 he formally renounced the title of emperor of Germany. The Holy Roman Empire, which had lasted a thousand years, thus came to an end.

### The Age of Metternich

Austria's foreign minister, Prince Metternich, tried to heal the breach with France. He arranged a marriage between Napoleon and Marie Louise, daughter of Francis II. After Napoleon's failure in Russia, however, Austria again joined the allies against him. At the great Congress of Vienna (1814–15), the astute Metternich regained for Austria its former position as a dominant power in Europe.

Vienna soon was the gayest capital in Europe. The masses lived in poverty, however, and the Magyars, Slavs, and Italians clamored for equality with the Germans. In 1848 revolts against Metternich's reactionary rule broke out in Hungary, Italy, the Tyrol, and Vienna. Metternich fled to England, and Emperor Ferdinand yielded the crown to his nephew, Francis Joseph I (*see* Francis Joseph I).

### Birth of the Dual Monarchy

In the Congress of Vienna, Austria had won a dominating place among the German states that replaced the Holy Roman Empire. Prussia was now a strong military state. William I and his statesman Bismarck plotted to lay Austria low (*see* Bismarck, Otto von). In the Seven Weeks' War (1866), Prussia defeated Austria and enforced a peace which weakened the Hapsburg rule. Austria lost its possessions in Italy and the German Confederation was dissolved.

Austria then turned to the east and decided to strengthen its precarious hold over the Danube Valley. Above all, the demands of Hungary had to be met. In 1867 Francis Joseph agreed to divide his empire into halves, giving it the name of the Austro-Hungarian Monarchy. As king of Hungary and emperor of Austria he was still sovereign over both states, but each was allowed to manage its own internal affairs.

This arrangement satisfied the Magyars for a time. But discontent grew among the Slavic peoples, who formed a majority of the population. They saw the Slavs of the Balkans freeing themselves from Turkish rule with the help of Russia; and they too began to look to Russia for assistance. The government made some concessions, but it was interested chiefly in spreading its rule to new Slav provinces. In 1878 the Congress of Berlin permitted Austria-Hungary to occupy the Turkish provinces of Bosnia and Herzegovina. In 1908 the government announced their annexation. This intensified the rivalry with Russia. It also inflamed the Serbs, who had hoped to gain the territory. The issue came to a head when Archduke Francis Ferdinand was assassinated in Bosnia, leading to World War I (see World War I).

After the war Austria-Hungary was no more. The Poles and the Czechs had proclaimed their independence before the armistice was signed. Hungary broke away, and the South Slavs joined together in the new state of Yugoslavia. Austria proclaimed itself a republic. Charles I, successor to Francis Joseph, died in exile.

**AUTOBIOGRAPHY.** The life story of an individual, as written by himself, is called autobiography. It differs from biography in that the person presents himself to his readers as he views himself and as he wants to be understood by others (see Biography). The autobiographer's most useful source of information is his own memory, aided by diaries, notes, letters, and papers to help him recall information, impressions, and events chronologically.

A similar kind of writing is the memoir. It is usually written by someone who has played a significant role in public life, such as a prime minister or a president. It differs from autobiography in that it emphasizes events and other persons rather than concentrating on unfolding the life of the writer. Most United States presidents since Harry Truman, for instance, have written memoirs to explain and justify their actions while in office.

While the word autobiography did not come into general English usage until about 1800, the first such work was written in about AD 399 by St. Augustine, bishop of the Christian church at Hippo, in North Africa (see Augustine of Hippo). His 'Confessions' traces the story of his childhood and education, his search for philosophical truth, and his conversion to Christianity.

Probably one of the most candid, objective, and well-written autobiographies ever composed, it has remained a model for succeeding writers. Shortly before his death in 430, Augustine published a book called 'Retractions', a survey of his later life; but it never gained the fame of his earlier work.

For a thousand years after Augustine no major autobiographical writing was done. The tradition of modern autobiographies began with the Renaissance in Italy during the 16th century in the works of Benvenuto Cellini and Girolamo Cardano. Cellini, who was an outstanding sculptor and goldsmith, wrote his life story between 1558 and 1562, although it was not published until 1728. In it Cellini told the story of his eventful life in the papal court at Rome, in the royal court of France, and in Florence during the rule of Cosimo de' Medici. Cardano, who was an outstanding astrologer and physician of the time, wrote 'De propria vita' (Book of My Life) in 1574 and 1575 as a study in human nature. It is an objective observation on his own life. Cardano's work exemplified two characteristics of the Renaissance that were to be a continuing influence on the writing of autobiography: freedom of scientific inquiry and interest in the human personality for its own sake.

Several autobiographies of the 18th century became classic works that helped to establish autobiography as a significant and influential literary genre. In 'Memoirs of My Life and Writings', the English historian Edward Gibbon gave an account of how he came to write his great work, 'The Decline and Fall of the Roman Empire'. Benjamin Franklin toward the end of his life wrote his 'Autobiography'. He intended the recounting of his life and thoughts to serve as a model for those who came after him (see Franklin, Benjamin). The major autobiography of the century was the 'Confessions' of Jean-Jacques Rousseau, the French writer of works on social and political theory (see Rousseau, Jean-Jacques). In this masterpiece, the author delves deeply into the workings of his mind, his emotions, and his motives to discern how his own attitudes shaped the way in which he perceived events. Indeed, Rousseau's work exemplified a revolution in expression of self-awareness and private aspirations.

In the 19th and 20th centuries, the popularity of autobiographies as reading matter increased enormously, as did the writing of them. Individuals in nearly every field of endeavor wrote their life stories: poets, novelists, painters, politicians, educators, and members of the clergy, to name a few. This trend has continued into the second half of the 20th century with the writing of autobiographies by celebrities of every type—rock stars, prizefighters, movie stars, country-western singers, politicians, military men, and convicted criminals.

Since the middle of the 19th century, few autobiographies have established themselves as classics. Among those likely to endure are 'Autobiography' by John Stuart Mill, the English philosopher and economist; 'The Education of Henry Adams' by the American historian Henry Adams; and 'Apologia pro Vita Sua' (Apology for His Life) by John Henry Newman, the English religious leader.

**AUTOGRAPH.** Derived from Greek terminology that means "self-writing," an autograph is commonly understood to be the signature of an individual. People who collect famous signatures as a hobby are said to be autograph hunters. The origin of this use of the word autograph dates back to the 16th century when university students in Germany and the Low Countries collected each others' signatures in small albums. This practice has continued to the present in Europe and in a modified form in the United States, when each year, graduating students ask their classmates to sign their yearbooks.

In its original usage, autograph has a broader meaning than just a signature. It is any manuscript written in the author's own handwriting. Such a manuscript may be a letter, diary, notebook, novel, poem, essay, or musical composition. In the late 20th century the manuscript would probably be typed rather than handwritten, then signed by the writer.

Autographs in the sense of original manuscripts are valuable sources of historical information. Literary or musical autographs can reveal to scholars how an author or composer brought a work from first draft to final form. The sketchbooks of the composer Ludwig van Beethoven throw much light on his original intentions and methods of revision. Musical autographs have been used to correct errors that were introduced by copyists or editors and to confirm authenticity when authorship was in dispute. Because literary and musical autographs are so significant and useful, they are often preserved and collected in libraries. Sometimes they are photographically reproduced and bound in books. The unique collection of literary autographs on permanent exhibit at the British Museum contains famous specimens from the 16th century onward.

The most valuable autographs in the world, if they existed, would be those belonging to ancient Roman, Greek, and early Christian writers. Unfortunately no original manuscripts by such eminent authors as Plato, Aristotle, Virgil, or Plutarch have survived. Nor have any of the original writings of the authors of the Old and New Testaments of the Bible. The writings of ancient authors that do exist are copies, often with variant readings and errors.

From the late Middle Ages and the Renaissance some autographs have survived. The most famous original manuscript from the Renaissance is the collection of notebooks by Leonardo da Vinci, the Italian artist and inventor. The greatest of the English writers, William Shakespeare, has left several signatures but only one manuscript; and there is controversy over its authenticity.

From the 18th century to the present the amount of autograph material has become abundant. Writers in virtually every field have left original copies of their works. The popularity or notoriety of some individuals has made their autographs, whether as manuscript or as signature, very valuable as collector's items. This has frequently led to the manufacture of forgeries of famous autographs.

**Autographs of Famous People**

**Authors**

Oliver Wendell Holmes

John Greenleaf Whittier

Victor Hugo

William Makepeace Thackeray

Jane Austen

Henry Wadsworth Longfellow

**Historical**

Daniel Boone

Queen Elizabeth I

Benjamin Franklin

Oliver Cromwell

**Composers**

Edward Elgar

Richard Strauss

Richard Wagner

E. A. MacDowell — Edward A. MacDowell

**Others**

Thomas Gainsborough

# AUTOMATION.

A clock radio goes on automatically, awakening a student from his nap with the sound of music. Meanwhile his sister turns on the video recorder to play back television shows that it had been programmed to record several nights earlier. The house has become chilly, but the furnace fires up to provide heat. These familiar occurrences are only a few examples of the ways in which automation has come to pervade daily life. The term automation, coined from the words automatic and operation, describes all such processes in which mechanical or electronic devices are employed to carry out tasks without human intervention.

Automation is sometimes confused with mechanization, but the two are quite distinct. Mechanization simply involves the use of machines instead of human physical effort—that is, muscle power—to accomplish a given task. True automation, by contrast, is the performance of an operation by automatically controlled equipment capable of self-regulation.

Machines or systems of machines achieve automatic control and self-regulation through feedback. In a typical automated system, what is actually done by the system (the output) depends on what is desired of the system (the input). Accordingly, such a system is frequently called a closed loop system. A feedback control loop is formed when the output is measured and compared with the input and the difference between the two values is used to adjust the input. A thermostatically controlled home heating system is an example of a simple feedback loop. If the temperature of the house drops below some desired level, a mechanism in the thermostat opens an electric switch that turns on the furnace. When the room temperature rises to the desired level, the mechanism closes the switch and shuts off the furnace.

## DEVELOPMENT OF AUTOMATION

Although fully automated systems were not developed until the 20th century, many simple, semi-automated devices were invented hundreds of years before. Among the many notebooks of the Italian Renaissance painter and inventor Leonardo da Vinci were designs for various devices of this sort. For example, one of his sketches, prepared during the early 1500s, is a drawing of a partially automated spit for roasting meat. During the 1700s there appeared in England and Scotland a number of inventions that helped to bring about the first Industrial Revolution. These inventions included feedback systems for controlling the temperature of industrial furnaces and the action of water mills. One of the most notable of the early feedback control mechanisms was the flyball governor, developed in 1788 by the Scottish inventor James Watt to regulate automatically the output of the steam engines he had

This article was contributed by Thomas T. Liao, Ed.D., Professor and Chairman, Department of Technology and Society, State University of New York, Stony Brook; Coeditor, Journal of Educational Technology Systems.

invented. The governor consisted of an upright shaft (belt-driven to spin with the speed of the engine), which had two arms connected to it near the top. A small, heavy ball was attached to the end of each arm. When the engine was started, the governor spun. As the engine speed increased, the governor spun faster and the weighted arms flew outward. The rising arms steadily closed the steam valve, lowering the pressure of the steam supplied to the piston cylinder. When the speed decreased, the arms fell so that the governor eased the valve open again. By means of such feedback action, the engine was made to regulate itself.

As the Industrial Revolution progressed, other inventors applied the principle of negative feedback, designing variable brakes and moderators that could regulate the operations of machines by adjusting input on the basis of output. The principle, however, received little attention until the 20th century.

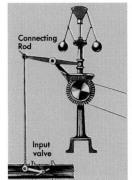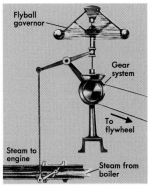

Automation Magazine

*The flyball governor is an early automatic control system for a steam engine. At rest, the weight of the balls keeps the input valve open. Spinning, their outward motion closes the valve to a degree that is determined by their speed.*

By the late 1930s, electronic amplifiers and circuits had reached a stage of development where they could be employed to perform control tasks. But perhaps more important to the advancement of automation was the work of the United States mathematician Norbert Wiener. In his book *Cybernetics: On Control and Communication in the Animal and the Machine* (1948), Wiener unified the findings of the research on control and information transmission of the first half of the century and thereby provided a theoretical base for the creative use of automatic control that has revolutionized technological systems.

## COMPONENTS OF AUTOMATED SYSTEMS

Many modern automated systems, such as those used in automobile factories, petrochemical plants, and supermarkets, are extremely complex and require numerous feedback loops. Each of these subsystems consists of only five basic components: (1) action element, (2) sensing mechanism, (3) control element, (4) decision element, and (5) program.

Action elements are those parts of an automated system that provide energy to achieve the desired task or goal. Energy can be applied in several different forms, such as heat to change the temperature of a room or electricity to run motors, which in turn drive conveyors for moving materials.

Sensing mechanisms measure either the performance of an automated system or a particular property of an object processed by the system. The measurements obtained make it possible to determine whether the operation or process is proceeding as desired. The sensors are often connected to indicators such as dials and gauges. A thermocouple inserted in a pipe, for example, measures the temperature of a liquid flowing through the pipe; the temperature reading is then indicated on a thermometer.

Control elements use information provided by the sensing mechanisms to regulate the action elements of a system. For instance, a control device in a fluid-flow system causes a valve to open, allowing a liquid to flow into a tank. In response to measurements from a sensor, the control may automatically close the valve.

Decision elements differentiate automated systems from ordinary mechanized systems. In the latter, a human operator has to monitor sensor gauges and decide whether or not to activate the control elements. In an automated system, this decision-making is performed either by a comparer such as a thermostat or by a program stored in the memory of a computer.

Programs of complex automated systems include both process and command information. The process information contains data that indicate how the various components of the system have to function in order to achieve a desired result. The command information consists of a series of instructions that tell the system's control elements how to perform certain specific operations. In most computer-controlled automated systems, these complex programs are stored in magnetic tape, magnetic disk, or ferrite core auxiliary memory units.

### Supermarket Automation as an Example

The interaction of the five principal components of an automated system can be illustrated by the automated checkout and inventory system employed by many supermarkets. This system makes use of an optical laser scanner and high-speed digital computer (*see* Computer). The laser scanner is designed to sense a special code, called the Universal Product Code (UPC), that is printed on nearly all prepackaged grocery items. The code, consisting of a series of dark and light vertical bars, identifies both the product type (*e.g.,* chicken noodle soup) and the brand name. Each individual bar corresponds to a number, which is printed alongside or under the bar. Such numbers are provided so that a checkout clerk can readily identify the code in the event that the scanner malfunctions.

As the checkout clerk moves a grocery item across a small opening in the counter, a helium-neon laser sends a light beam up to the label bearing the code. The dark areas absorb the light, whereas the lighter colored regions reflect the light down toward a detector (sensing component) that reads the pattern of bars by measuring the reflections. This input data is converted into electrical signals, which are relayed to a central computer where the specific product is identified from the coded information (program element). The computer (functioning as both control and decision-making components) then performs two different operations. First, it orders the cash register (action component) to ring up the price of the item, display the price on an indicator visible to the customer, and print it on the sales slip, along with a description of the product and other pertinent information. Second, the computer updates the supermarket inventory stored in its memory by subtracting one item from the total number of items of the same kind and brand available in the store.

*A supermarket checkout clerk passes a coded cereal box over a scanner on the counter. A special laser reacts to the code, signaling the computer simultaneously to order the cash register to ring up the item and to update the market's inventory, which is stored in the computer's memory.*

IBM Corporation

The principal benefit of supermarket automation is inventory control. The computer has a complete record of each item sold as well as a record of the quantity still in stock. Once this information is in the computer's memory, it is a simple matter to have the computer print out daily a list of those items that have gone below a predetermined number and, so, need to be reordered. In effect, the responsibility of having to decide whether to reorder each of perhaps 8,000 products is taken from the store manager, who cannot accurately analyze every one of the 8,000 situations continuously, and is given to a system ideally suited for such routine decision-making.

## ADVANTAGES AND DISADVANTAGES

Should a system be automated? Before this question can be answered, the various positive and negative effects of introducing automation must be considered. Two primary types of effects are technical and economic. There are others, but they are more complex. One reason for the complexity is that the benefits and problems of automating a system vary considerably not only with each area of application but also with the people who work with the system or who are affected by it.

Because automated systems are able to perform routine decision-making tasks, they enable a company or organization to increase productivity. In other words, more goods are manufactured or more services rendered. Often quality can be improved as well. Such has been the case with the automation of the supermarket. The number of grocery items that can be checked out per minute has been greatly increased—in some cases nearly doubled—and the extensive delays occasionally experienced when a checkout clerk does not know the price of an item have been eliminated. More important, the automated reordering of goods has helped to even out the workload at warehouses and distributors, which is of particular importance to large supermarket chains. In addition, studies show that the computerized checkout system reduces errors in charging customers by as much as 75 percent.

Automation also makes possible the performance of tasks that are well beyond the limits of human capabilities, as for example the launching, tracking, and control of the United States space shuttle. A project of this kind requires so many complex computations and such rapid control responses that it can only be accomplished through the employment of high-speed computerized systems.

Automated systems, however, do have certain limitations and drawbacks. Although usually very reliable, they can malfunction. Moreover, an entire system may fail to operate properly if there is a single error in setting it up. A backup system has to be provided or a human "override" capability built into the system so that operations can be handled manually. Automated systems also lack the flexibility of humans. Any significant change in their function may thus require extensive redesigning of the equipment. This problem has been mitigated by the use of computer

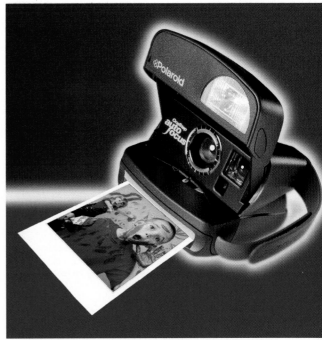

Polaroid Corporation

*A modern camera combines advanced electronics, optics, film, and battery technology for those who want all functional photographic decisions made automatically.*

programs that can be modified with relative ease, but action, sensing, and control components still have to be tailored to specific applications. This is one reason that large amounts of money are required as a company or industry becomes increasingly more automated. In the long term, automation generally yields economic benefits. An exception would be a situation where an operation has to be automated for technical or safety reasons only.

## APPLICATIONS OF AUTOMATION

The development of sophisticated sensing equipment and low-cost microprocessors (miniature multicircuited devices capable of performing all of the logic functions of a computer) has made it possible to automate a vast array of machines and systems. In industrially developed nations, nearly every aspect of daily life is affected by automation. This section gives a small sampling of its manifold applications.

### Consumer Products

Consumer products of all kinds, from automobiles to household appliances and home entertainment systems, are becoming increasingly automated. Most recent-model cars are equipped with computerized ignition and fuel systems designed to increase fuel economy and performance. Japanese engineers also have developed a car with an on-board computer that the driver can use to plan his route. The driver simply enters his intended destination into the computer, which transmits the information to special roadside

MLS/A-Kurzweil Computer Products

*A reading machine for the blind automatically scans the lines of a printed page, converts the information into digital form, and then translates this into audible words.*

computer-sensor units. These units measure and analyze the traffic flow on all possible routes to the desired destination and recommend the one with the least amount of traffic.

Even smaller consumer products such as cameras feature automatic capabilities. One type of camera makes use of sonar to provide automatic focusing. It transmits an ultrasonic wave, which is reflected when it strikes the subject to be photographed. As the reflected sound signal is picked up by a receiver in the camera, a microprocessor determines the distance from the camera to the subject by measuring the time it took the signal to reach the subject and return. The microprocessor then activates a motor that properly adjusts the lens.

An automated reading machine has been developed for the blind and the visually handicapped. Known as the Kurzweil Reading Machine (KRM), the device consists of an optical scanner, microcomputer, and speech synthesizer. The KRM automatically scans the lines of a printed page and converts the information into digital form, which in turn is translated into spoken words. The system reads hundreds of different styles and sizes of type.

### Manufacturing Industries

The manufacturing industries rely heavily on automation. Some of the most advanced automated systems are employed by those industries that process petroleum and iron and steel. The automobile industry operates elaborate systems that include computer-controlled robot devices. Other assembly industries have also begun to use such industrial robots. Aircraft manufacturers employ single-arm robots for drilling and riveting body sections, while some electronics firms utilize high-performance robot mechanisms together with computerized instruments to test finished products.

Another development that has greatly affected the manufacturing industries is the integration of engineering design and manufacturing into one continuous automated activity through the use of computers. The introduction of CAD/CAM, which stand for Computer-Aided Design and Computer-Aided Manufacturing, has significantly increased productivity and reduced the time required to develop new products. When using a CAD/CAM system, an engineer sketches the design of some mechanical part, such as an automobile part or aircraft component, directly on the display screen of a computer terminal with a special pen. The computer programs that are provided by the system can be used to manipulate this first draft to improve it.

After the design has been revised as needed, the system prepares instructions for numerically controlled machine tools and places orders for materials and auxiliary equipment. In essence, a CAD/CAM system enables an engineer to sit down at a computer terminal, perform all the activities of engineering design while interacting with the computer, and then walk over to the computer-controlled machine tool and pick up the finished part.

**The petroleum industry,** one of the first industrial users of automation, leads in the employment of automatic control apparatus. The petroleum refining process is particularly suited to automation application. It exemplifies a manufacturing operation known as continuous process, which is characterized by the handling of a continuous flow of materials from basic components or raw materials to finished products. Crude oil is fed through a maze of pipes, towers, and vessels after which it appears in the form of usable products such as gasoline, jet fuel, and lubricating oil.

*An operator sits at a console in the central control room of an oil refinery complex and monitors controls that regulate the flow of crude oil through the refinery.*

Honeywell, Inc./American Petroleum Institute

*A control center at a hot strip rolling mill contains the monitoring equipment and controls for the mill. Automatic instruments measure the dimensions and temperature of the steel pieces as they pass through the rollers.*
American Iron and Steel Institute

Another reason for emphasis on automation in an oil refinery is the complexity of its operation. Processes occur under varied temperatures and pressures and involve numerous chemical and physical changes that make human control impractical. Moreover, the extensive use of automatic mechanisms results in increased productivity when the refinery is running and it also reduces shutdown time.

The heart of a modern refinery is the control room with its computerized control panels. The thousands of individual functions carried out in the distillation units, catalytic cracking plants, and purification facilities of the refinery are monitored from this center. Each of its control panels has a set of indicators for measurements, valve positions, controller settings, alarms, and safety devices. It shows clearly the relationships between all these units. If any of them is not performing as it should, corrective actions are initiated automatically. Because of this, only a handful of human operators are needed to watch the panels, and rarely is it necessary for them to make manual adjustments. In addition to the computer-controlled equipment that is at the refinery itself, automatic control devices are used at the pumping stations situated along pipelines.

**The iron and steel industry** uses automation for a large number of its operations. Automatic control has been applied to blast furnaces in which iron ore is reduced to pig iron. Automatic instruments measure the pressure and composition of the gases released by the furnaces. This data is analyzed by computer and the results are used to regulate blast air volume, temperature, humidity, and other variables that affect the efficiency of the production process and the quality of the resulting iron.

Automation also plays an important role in certain steelmaking operations, as for example the shaping of steel ingots into sheets, coils, and strips in rolling mills. In this process steel ingots are passed between large, cylindrical rollers that squeeze them into the desired shape. Automatic instruments measure the

dimensions and temperature of the steel pieces each time they pass through the rollers. This information is transmitted to a computer that adjusts the distance between the rollers for the next pass.

**The automobile industry** initially applied automation to isolated areas of production, primarily continuous process operations such as the forging of crankshafts. This resulted in a pattern of integrated manufacturing steps, with functions performed by automated equipment followed by manual operations requiring human dexterity and flexibility.

During the 1970s Japanese car manufacturers triggered a revolution in automaking. They introduced improved, computer-controlled robot mechanisms to highly automate their assembly lines. These one-arm robotic devices, capable of simulating the articulation and movement of the human arm and hand, are used for varied functions, such as welding and painting auto bodies. The mechanical arms are programmed by physically moving them through the desired motions. The different movements are recorded in the computer's memory so that they can be repeated precisely. Some advanced high-performance robots have built-in sensors that enable them to correct their movements if they deviate from the programmed patterns.

In the 1980s United States automakers also began employing similar kinds of industrial robots. In some plants robots equipped with optical lasers are even used to scan auto bodies to make certain that their dimensions meet specified standards.

### Service Industries

Most of the service industries, which include banking, communications, transportation, and government, have been relatively slow to embrace automation technology. The United States telephone system was one of the few notable exceptions until the 1970s when banks and certain other businesses began introducing innovative systems. The computerized grocery checkout and inventory system is a highly visible example of automation in the service industries.

**Banking.** Automated systems are very useful in areas of service that require the analysis of data. In nearly all United States banks, computers handle the sorting of checks and verification of balances in accounts. A growing number of banks throughout the country have gone a step further, establishing a system of electronic banking that includes the use of automated teller machines. These automated tellers, often located in shopping centers and business buildings, permit patrons to complete basic transactions without standing in long bank lines. By simply inserting a special plastic card into a slot in the machine and typing a personal code number on its keyboard, a patron can transact bank business instantly.

A more sophisticated form of electronic banking that may eventually become the standard means of conducting financial transactions is electronic funds transfer (EFT). This system permits the movement of money by means of electronic signals relayed between computers via such means as telephone lines and radio waves. Designed primarily to reduce banking costs by decreasing paperwork, EFT virtually eliminates the use of cash, checks, and conventional credit cards. In such a system, salaries, social security payments, and other income are credited directly to a user's account. Payment of utility bills, rent, or home mortgage loans are likewise made directly, with the amount of the outlays deducted from the balance of the account.

Another EFT feature is the extensive use of remote point-of-sale terminals linking stores and banks, which allows purchases to be charged against bank accounts. An EFT transaction of this kind requires the use of a debit card similar to the one employed with automated tellers. The card is coded with information that identifies the bank and account number of the cardholder. The store clerk inserts the customer's card into an EFT terminal and enters the price of the item. The terminal, equipped with either a magnetic tape reader or laser scanner, reads the encoded information and contacts the customer's bank whose computer checks the appropriate account, compares the balance and the amount of the funds requested, and then sends back approval to the store. The funds are transferred electronically to the merchant's bank and credited to his account. The entire transaction is accomplished within minutes regardless of the geographical distances between the point of sale and the banks involved.

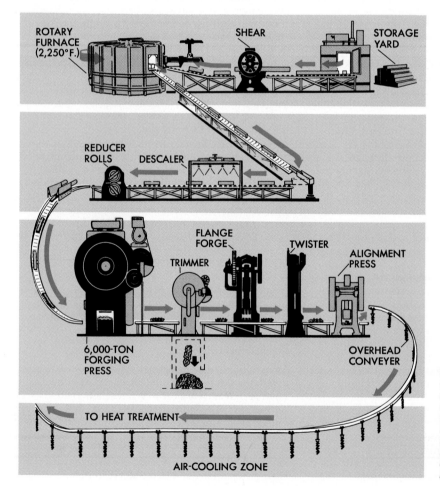

*The manufacture of crankshafts is not completely automated but the forging operation is continuous. It takes 8 hours to complete the forging of a shaft, but the operation is designed so that pieces move through in a continuous flow at 30-second intervals.*

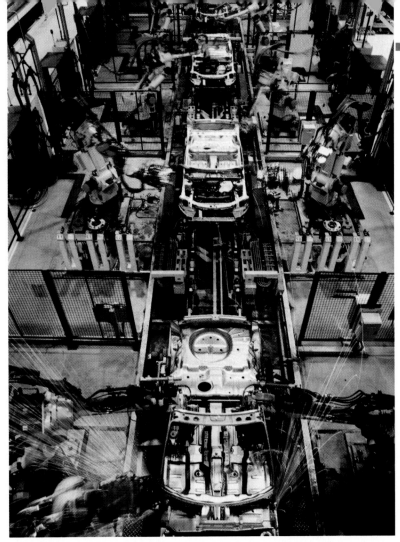

**Robots work on chassis assembly at the Opel Division of the Eisenach Plant in Germany.**
2001 GM Corp. Used with permission of GM Media Archives

**Communications.** One of the earliest practical applications of automation was in telephone switching. The first generation of truly automatic switching equipment consisted of relays and other electromechanical switches. Systems of such devices, which appeared during the 1920s and 1930s, monitored thousands of telephone lines, determined which were demanding service, provided dial tone, checked calls that were in progress, and disconnected the phones when calls were completed. They thus performed most of the functions of a human operator.

Modern telephone switching systems, which use integrated circuits and related miniature electronic devices, are more reliable, faster, and less expensive than their electromechanical predecessors. They not only perform the functions mentioned above but also automatically transfer calls to alternate numbers and provide other customer services in response to simple dialed codes, usually without human intervention. The handling of today's huge volume of phone calls and computer data transmissions would be impossible without the use of electronically automated systems. Even the human operators who handle services that machines cannot provide, such as directory assistance, depend on automated machines for help.

Automation is employed in many other areas of communications. Satellite communications has been made possible through the utilization of automated guidance systems that place and hold satellites in predetermined orbits around the Earth. Many national postal systems have partially automated their operations. The sorting of mail is carried out by automatic machines, as is the grading of letters and parcels. Fully automated systems to aid in the collection and redistribution of mail have been proposed but have not yet been implemented. A key technical problem that prevents the total automation of postal systems is the extreme difficulty of designing machines that can reliably read the countless types of human handwriting.

**Transportation.** The most sophisticated applications of automation in transportation have been made in the guidance and control of aircraft and spacecraft. Other applications include railroad operations and automotive traffic control.

**Aviation.** Automated systems combining radar, computers, and auxiliary electronic equipment have been developed to accommodate the ever-increasing volume of air traffic. Air traffic controllers at large airports depend on such systems to direct the

Passengers (left) await a special train service on the fully automated Bay Area Rapid Transit (BART) system in the San Francisco–Oakland area of California. A young girl (right) gets her ticket from BART's automatic vendor, which accepts and discerns between not only nickels, dimes, quarters, and half dollars, but also one- and five-dollar bills.

(Photos) Bay Area Rapid Transit District

continuous flow of incoming and outgoing airplanes. They can pinpoint the position of every plane within 50 miles (80 kilometers) of the airfield on a special display screen of the radar unit. This information allows the controllers to select the safest route for pilots to follow as they approach and leave the airport.

Many of the systems of the aircraft itself are automated. Oxygen masks, for instance, automatically drop down from overhead compartments when the cabin pressure becomes too low. Most modern planes have an automatic pilot that can take over for the human pilot. Commercial passenger planes are usually equipped with an automatic landing system that can be used when runway visibility is poor. The system employs radio beams from the ground to operate an instrument on board the plane. By watching this

An air traffic controller depends on automated systems combining radar, computers, and other electronic equipment to direct the continuous flow of airport traffic.

© Jim West

instrument, a pilot can determine the exact position of his craft in relation to the landing strip.

*Space missions.* Automated control and guidance systems are vital to the success of space missions. The launching of the United States space shuttle and the subsequent guidance and staging of its various modules require a coordination of measurement and control well beyond human capability. From the moment of ignition to the powered phases of the launch, the vehicle is continuously tracked by radar. Any deviation from the predetermined trajectory produces automatic control signals that correct the vehicle's flight path. The flight and reentry of the shuttle are also automatically controlled. The crew monitors the performance of the automated systems and takes corrective action in case of problems.

*Railroads.* Automation has become an important factor in railroad operations. The management of rail yards has been facilitated by computerized systems that integrate the signaling and switching functions of classification yards, where freight trains are sorted and assembled. Electronic scanners read color-coded identification labels on all freight cars entering a classification yard and relay the information to yard computers that assign the cars to the proper track.

Automation has also been adopted by many passenger rail lines. In a number of systems, automatic equipment is used so extensively that the function of the train operator has been reduced to simple on and off operations during station stops. Since commands from automatic controls are continuously fed to other automatic mechanisms in response to information collected by sensors strategically positioned on the engine and track, human control of the engine is only required in an emergency.

An impressive example of automated rail transportation is the Bay Area Rapid Transit (BART) system serving the San Francisco–Oakland area of California. BART consists of more than 75 miles (121 kilometers) of track and about 100 trains operating between 33 stations at peak hours. Both the operation of trains and ticketing of passengers are fully automated. As a train enters a station, it automatically transmits its identification and destination to the control center and to a display board for passengers to see. The control center, in turn, sends signals to the train that regulate its time in the station and its running time to the next destination.

An ideal schedule is established every morning and, as the day progresses, the performance of each train is compared with that schedule. The performances of individual trains are then adjusted as required. The entire BART system is controlled by essentially one computer. There is an identical backup computer that can assume control if necessary.

*Automatic traffic control.* The principles of automation have been applied to traffic signal control for decades. Automatic control systems range from signal controllers that respond to vehicles passing over sensing elements on the roadway to a series of traffic lights whose interrelated timing is regulated by computers at a remote traffic control center. In the future, microcomputers may be installed in vehicles to interact with roadside sensors to provide traffic flow and density data, allowing rapid signal adjustment and preventing congestion.

## AUTOMATION AND SOCIETY

By the mid-1990s, automation had made great headway in manufacturing, in the service industries, and in government. Manufacturing led the way, because business leaders desired to cut costs while remaining competitive. The progress of automation brought both benefits and challenges to the larger society.

Automation often reduces cost and improves output both in terms of quantity and quality. If properly applied, it also can free workers from unpleasant, tedious, and hazardous jobs. In a growing number of factories, robots are programmed to perform dull, repetitive tasks on the assembly line and to load and unload heavy objects. Various cities have provided professional firefighters with robot devices that can be used to carry hoses into burning buildings in danger of collapse, and thereby reduce risk.

In spite of its beneficial effects, however, increased automation can cause serious problems for workers in manufacturing plants. In many plants, such as pulp mills and steel mills, production levels have been greatly increased, while the number of workers has been cut sharply. Large steel mills once required thousands of employees; today's automated mills need only a few hundred at most. The new mills, however, can outproduce the older ones.

Such a restructuring of industry obviously upsets workers who have toiled for decades in semiskilled jobs. They find jobs disappearing, and they have little hope that new ones will replace them. Even if they are retained in their employment, working conditions are drastically altered by automated processes. The worker's expertise, gained over years of experience, is undermined by the new procedures. Overtime pay is a thing of the past for many. Workers wonder what kind of opportunities will be available for their children, as the high-paying jobs of an earlier industrial era gradually disappear. For older workers, too, the idea of

retraining for a new career is difficult to accept. The complexity of the new kinds of knowledge required is daunting for those who have not been in a classroom for many years.

Even in nonindustrial work automation tends to displace unskilled and semiskilled workers whose abilities no longer meet the job requirements of automated facilities. The automation of supermarkets is a case in point. It has reduced the number of checkout clerks needed to serve customers and virtually eliminated the use of support personnel to stamp prices on grocery items. On the other hand, supermarket automation has increased the need for specialists in electronics and computer engineering, not only to design, manufacture, and install equipment but also to maintain and repair it.

The proliferation of automated consumer products, including cars equipped with computerized components, necessitates a large number of highly skilled service technicians. This situation has raised several far-reaching questions: Who will provide the necessary training? Can today's service personnel be adequately retrained? If not, will there be enough new people with the necessary talents? Or will the advanced technological environment break down because of a lack of qualified individuals? In Germany this dilemma has been solved by an elaborate apprenticeship program for all graduates of secondary schools who do not go to college. Close cooperation between the private sector and the government has created a program that assures all major segments of the economy have a well-trained labor force. This training is often highly technical and would be considered college-level work in the United States.

In contrast to Germany, the United States does not have an official apprenticeship program. High school graduates who do not go to college are left to fend for themselves in an economy that is continually demanding a more skilled workforce. The number of unskilled and semiskilled jobs is shrinking while the number of people available to fill such jobs has been growing. A huge increase in immigration, both legal and illegal, has only served to worsen the problem. Many of the new immigrants arrive in the United States with little or no schooling and are surprised to find a job market that is almost closed.

The economic and social benefits of technological change have proved enormous. As the pace of change continues, society will have to find a way to assist poorly schooled and underemployed individuals whose abilities and attitudes reflect an earlier industrial era.

**FURTHER RESOURCES FOR AUTOMATION**

**Giordano, Lorraine.** Beyond Taylorism (St. Martin, 1992).
**Groover, M.P.** Automation, Production Systems, and Computer Integrated Manufacturing (Prentice, 1987).
**Mody, Ashoka, and Wheeler, David.** Automation and World Competition (St. Martin, 1990).
**Stone, Rod.** The Push-Button Manager: A Guide to Office Automation (McGraw, 1985).
**Zuboff, Shoshana.** In the Age of the Smart Machine (Basic Books, 1988).

Pete Saloutos—Tony Stone Worldwide

*Traffic on the Los Angeles freeways is frequently bumper-to-bumper. California has more cars than any other state, which leads to highway congestion and air pollution problems.*

# AUTOMOBILE

Soon after automobiles were mass-produced early in the 20th century, they began to change styles of living. The automobile is still causing changes. Easy access by passenger car or by truck helps to determine where people build homes, buy food, seek recreation, and locate businesses. The term automotive means "self-propelling." It generally refers to passenger cars, trucks, buses, and tractors. The words automobile, motorcar, and car may include any conveyance in the general range of automotive vehicles, but they usually refer specifically to passenger vehicles that seat from two to six people. (*See also* Bus; Truck and Trucking.)

Cars and trucks are unique. Unlike other types of transportation, they enable the driver to get in and go at a moment's notice. They move near the source or destination of farm or manufactured products, unrestricted by the need for rails, runways, or waterways. Roads are needed, of course, and these cover the industrial countries of the world in a vast network.

Many automotive vehicles have been developed for travel over primitive roads and open terrain (*see* Roads and Streets).

The automobile is a mixed blessing. Millions of people driving passenger cars create huge traffic jams around major cities. The exhaust from automobiles pollutes the air. Each year thousands of people are killed and injured in automobile accidents.

Most of the world's automobiles run on gasoline, which is made from petroleum, a resource in limited supply. The Arab oil embargo of 1973, in which major oil-producing nations stopped making shipments, revealed how dependent many countries had become upon petroleum imports. The rapid gasoline price increases that followed the embargo disrupted every national economy in the world.

The automobile underwent many changes in the 1970s, 1980s, and early 1990s. Concern with safety and pollution led to design changes and the introduction of new technology. Automobile bodies and engines were made smaller and lighter to save gasoline. Researchers worked on alternatives to the gasoline engine and on fuel-efficient transportation.

### Industry's Vast Influence

By the early 1990s more than 50 million automobiles were being manufactured worldwide annually. Leading manufacturing areas were Japan, the United States, and Western Europe. There was also significant production in Eastern Europe and Latin America. The automotive industry is so vast that it influences, directly or indirectly, most of the people on Earth. In industrial nations the level of automobile production

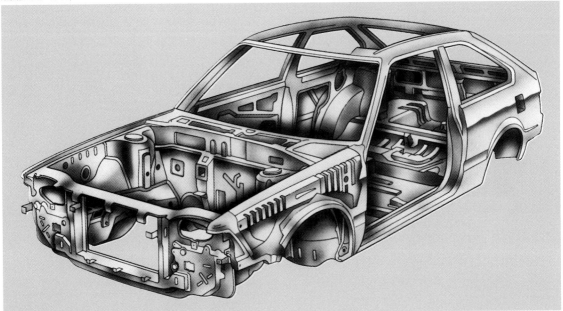

*An integrated body frame used for compact cars for strength is shaped and punched to take parts.*

has become a barometer of the economy and is closely watched by political leaders and business analysts. Changes in auto production directly affect the large steel, aluminum, petroleum, and rubber industries and their suppliers and employees. A long strike in the automobile industry or a sharp drop in sales can result in a general business decline (*see* Automobile Industry).

## Uses

Although the size of the automobile industry is impressive, it is the use of automotive vehicles that has had the greatest effect on people's lives. Foods arrive fresh at processing plants or at local markets because of the automotive vehicle. Many other products in common use are also distributed quickly and inexpensively by motor trucks.

Many services other than transportation depend on the automobile. Public utilities are built and maintained by crews using automotive equipment. Ambulance, fire, and police services depend on the automobile. The construction industry uses a variety of special vehicles to prepare building sites and to haul materials and to put them in place. Farmers use automobiles, trucks, tractors, and motorized harvest and planting equipment.

The armies of the world rely on motor vehicles to move soldiers and supplies and to assault the enemy. Modern military strategy involves highly mobile armies supported by tanks, armored personnel carriers, and supply trucks.

### Way of Life

Before the automobile was developed, people lived near their places of work. Many now commute between suburban residential areas and industrial or office areas in the city. Shopping centers, banks, restaurants, and even churches have been arranged to serve people in automobiles. Because so much vacation and other pleasure touring is done in automobiles, motels and parks have accommodations for large numbers of passenger cars, vehicles towing trailers, and light trucks (often called recreational vehicles, or RV's) that contain kitchen facilities and beds. An entire industry supports automotive hobbyists who collect and restore antique or classic cars, collect and drive sports cars, or modify their vehicles in many ways. Both children and adults make miniature car models.

## BODY

The body of an automobile encloses or partly encloses the vehicle's mechanical parts and the driver and passengers. The term body does not include the car's motor, transmission, chassis, or frame. Sometimes, however, the body is integrated with the frame as a solid unit. The body of a truck includes the structure that carries the cargo.

Passenger car bodies usually are stamped out of sheets of metal. They are shaped and punched to accommodate the elements that make up the car.

The first automobiles were called horseless carriages because they resembled horse-drawn vehicles. Gradually cars were styled for greater comfort and convenience. In order to provide a more pleasing appearance and to reduce wind resistance, streamlining was introduced.

### Types and Styles

A closed automobile that seats from four to six people is called a sedan. It may be a four-door or a two-door

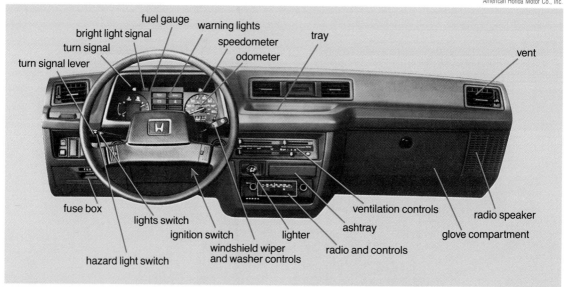

American Honda Motor Co., Inc.

fuel gauge
bright light signal
turn signal
turn signal lever
warning lights
speedometer
odometer
tray
vent
fuse box
lights switch
ignition switch
hazard light switch
windshield wiper
and washer controls
lighter
radio and controls
ventilation controls
ashtray
radio speaker
glove compartment

*The dashboard of a modern automobile includes a wide variety of switches, gauges, indicator lights, and conveniences for the driver and passengers.*

### SOME PASSENGER-CAR BODY STYLES

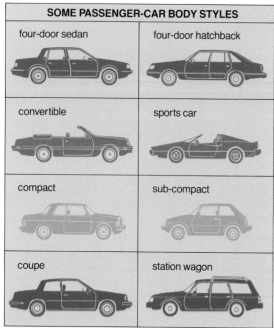

four-door sedan  
four-door hatchback  
convertible  
sports car  
compact  
sub-compact  
coupe  
station wagon

*Passenger cars come in a variety of body styles. Compact and subcompact refer also to body size.*

between front and back windows but has a permanent rigid top. A station wagon usually accommodates more people and cargo than a standard passenger car, and the backseats can be removed or turned down to provide still more cargo space. There is also a rear-end door, often a lift-up type as in a hatchback.

The long, heavy, and extravagantly designed full-size cars of the 1950s and 1960s were largely supplanted in the 1970s and 1980s by smaller, lighter, compact and subcompact cars. This happened as gasoline prices rose, making fuel-efficient cars economically desirable, and as manufacturers complied in some countries with government gas consumption mandates. The shrinking automobile was most evident in the United States, where fuel prices had been low, and large, powerful cars had long been popular. Some United States manufacturers produced models that lost as much as 1,000 pounds (450 kilograms) of weight and a foot (30 centimeters) in length from one year to the next.

A sports car is one of a variety of automobiles ordinarily used for pleasure driving. The typical sports car has low, sleek lines, high top speeds, and rapid acceleration. A limousine is a long luxury car usually driven by a chauffeur.

Two hybrid-type automotive vehicles are the van, a boxy truck that may be decorated elaborately and used to carry passengers, and the recreational vehicle (RV), a long van that is often equipped with beds and a kitchen.

### Interior

The passenger car interior is designed to keep the driver safely in control. Gauges and switches, grouped and recessed into the dashboard, are surrounded with stiff padding.

model. Two-door sedans sometimes have a rear lift-up door and a backseat that can be turned down to produce a flat storage, or hauling, space. This sedan is called a hatchback.

A coupe, or coupé, originally was a two-door automobile with a single wide seat. The modern coupe, or club coupe, usually has a backseat, enclosed in a somewhat smaller area than the rear seat of a sedan. A convertible is a car with a soft top that may be folded back and down. A hardtop is styled to resemble a convertible in the omission of a center post

General Electric Co.

## ANTIGLARE HEADLIGHT

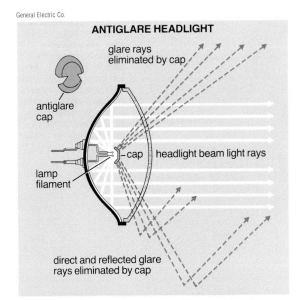

glare rays eliminated by cap

antiglare cap

cap — headlight beam light rays

lamp filament

direct and reflected glare rays eliminated by cap

*Antiglare headlights provide good general illumination and eliminate glare problems for drivers of oncoming vehicles.*

Contemporary electronic instrumentation is reliable and informative. Much of the instrumentation has been computerized. Lights and alarms may indicate low fuel, outside light malfunction, improperly closed doors, or unfastened seat belts.

Some automobiles have microcomputer instrumentation, including a bar chart fuel gauge, digital speedometer, and message center. The center can provide information about numerous mechanical conditions and can tell how many miles remain to a particular destination. Some vehicles use a computer chip to determine fuel consumption on both an overall average and an instantaneous basis.

Many cars have bucket seats in front. These are individual rounded seats, set close to the floor. Other automobile interior features include heaters and air conditioners, power-operated windows and seats, and radios and audio tape players.

### Bumpers, Lights, and Accessories

Bumpers that absorb impact from minor collisions at low speeds, therefore protecting a car's body from damage, are standard on many automobiles. These bumpers are of two types: the mechanical telescoping model and the one made of material that yields on impact and springs back into shape.

An automobile's lighting system includes dim and bright headlights, parking lights, turn signals, tail lights, backup lights, stoplights, ceiling lights, and dashboard lights. Some cars have map lights, floor lights, and cornering lights, or sidelights, that switch on automatically when the car is turned.

Other accessories, which can be both standard and optional, include safety glass, defrosters, rearview and side view mirrors, windshield wipers and washers, clocks, and cigarette lighters. Safety belts are now standard equipment.

## ENGINES IN COMMON USE

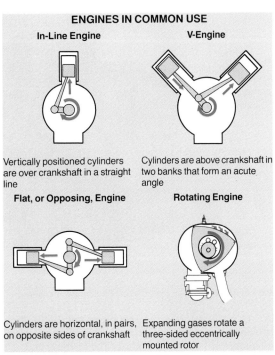

**In-Line Engine**

**V-Engine**

Vertically positioned cylinders are over crankshaft in a straight line

Cylinders are above crankshaft in two banks that form an acute angle

**Flat, or Opposing, Engine**

**Rotating Engine**

Cylinders are horizontal, in pairs, on opposite sides of crankshaft

Expanding gases rotate a three-sided eccentrically mounted rotor

*Most passenger-car power plants are internal-combustion engines that employ the expansion of gases to move a number of pistons or a single rotor.*

### POWER PLANT

An internal-combustion engine, which obtains its power from the expansion of gases, is used to propel most modern automobiles. A fuel, usually gasoline, is burned with air to create the expanding gas.

Through the use of pistons or a rotor, the energy that is produced is converted into torque, or rotating force, for transmission to the vehicle's wheels. The internal-combustion engine may be mounted in either the front or the rear.

### Classification

There are many types of automotive power plants. They may be classified in a number of ways—by the number and arrangement of pistons and cylinders, by the means of ignition, or by the type of cooling system. When vertical pistons are arranged in a single row, the engine is called in-line. When the cylinders are in two rows, sloping inward at the bottom, the engine is called a V-type. Designations such as V-8 or V-6 indicate the number of cylinders.

Some compact cars have flat, or opposing, cylinder arrangements in their power plants. The pistons lie horizontally in pairs and oppose each other, with a crankshaft between them. Gas turbine engines have been used in trucks and military vehicles. The turbine is rotated by the force of expanding gas. Some of the heat given off by the gas is in turn reused, or regenerated, by the engine.

The free-piston engine, an experimental type, operates by internal combustion, though the pistons

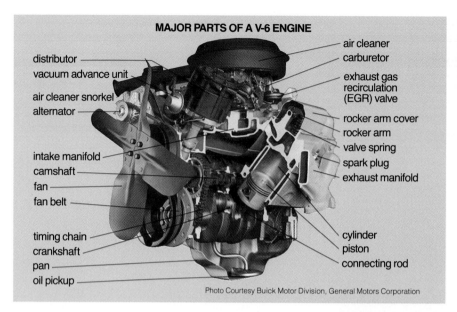

## MAJOR PARTS OF A V-6 ENGINE

distributor
vacuum advance unit
air cleaner snorkel
alternator
intake manifold
camshaft
fan
fan belt
timing chain
crankshaft
pan
oil pickup

air cleaner
carburetor
exhaust gas recirculation (EGR) valve
rocker arm cover
rocker arm
valve spring
spark plug
exhaust manifold
cylinder
piston
connecting rod

*Photo Courtesy Buick Motor Division, General Motors Corporation*

*An automobile engine (top) consists of many working parts. The carburetor (bottom) regulates the amounts of both air and fuel and mixes them. The choke valve reduces the amount of air to provide a fuel-rich mixture for easier starting on cold days. The throttle valve is controlled through the gas pedal.*

do not produce torque, or rotating power. Riding free in a chamber, they are bounced back by trapped air to compress the air-fuel mixture. The burning and expanding gas is ignited and then expelled into a turbine to provide torque.

There is an engine without pistons or a turbine. This is the rotating engine. Sometimes it is called a rotary engine, though this term is also used to describe a piston engine with cylinders that rotate around a crankshaft. The Wankel rotating engine, which was developed by Felix Wankel of West Germany, has three moving parts.

A three-sided rotor in the engine is mounted eccentrically (off-center) on a drive shaft. Compartments are formed between each side of the rotor and the chamber walls. As the rotor turns, the sealed compartments alternately become larger and smaller in rapid succession, serving much like the varying chambers of a piston engine—drawing in fuel and air, compressing the mixture and igniting it, and expelling the burned gas. The expansion of the gas forces the rotor to spin in a circular motion and turn the shaft. The Wankel engine is used by one automobile manufacturer. It is much smaller and lighter than the conventional piston engine.

### Fuel System

The fuel system of an automobile includes the fuel tank, fuel pump, one or more carburetors, and connecting fuel lines. An air cleaner is mounted on top of the carburetor to remove dust and dirt from incoming air that is to be mixed with fuel and used for combustion. The throttle valve is controlled by the accelerator pedal. A choke valve is used to shut off some of the air during the starting of the car. This produces an air-fuel mixture rich in fuel. The choke valve is controlled either manually from the car's dashboard or, more often, automatically.

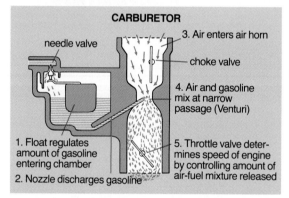

## CARBURETOR

needle valve

3. Air enters air horn
choke valve
4. Air and gasoline mix at narrow passage (Venturi)
1. Float regulates amount of gasoline entering chamber
2. Nozzle discharges gasoline
5. Throttle valve determines speed of engine by controlling amount of air-fuel mixture released

Most carburetors have at least two fuel passages, called jets, from the float chamber to the mixing chamber. The first jet provides fuel for idling and low speeds; the second provides fuel for higher speeds. Passages called intake manifolds transmit the air-fuel mixture to the cylinders. Some engines, and all diesel engines, use fuel injection, a system whereby a carefully measured amount of fuel is forced into the combustion chamber at high pressure.

### Valves and Camshaft

The air-fuel mixture enters a combustion chamber, or cylinder, of the engine whenever the corresponding valve is opened. The opening and closing of the valves are accomplished by the camshaft, which turns with the engine. In most engines projections on the camshaft raise a pushrod that is connected with a valve. In the overhead valve engine the pushrod moves the rocker arm, which in turn opens the intake valve. As the cam continues to turn, the pushrod moves down again, and the intake valve closes. The exhaust valve operates on the same principle. The camshaft is geared to the crankshaft, or central power

## WORKING PARTS OF AN ENGINE

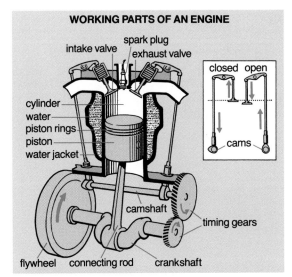

*The spark plug ignites fuel. The fuel expands, forcing the piston to move. Through the connecting rod, this motion is passed on to a series of devices that provide vehicle power.*

## ELECTRONIC IGNITION

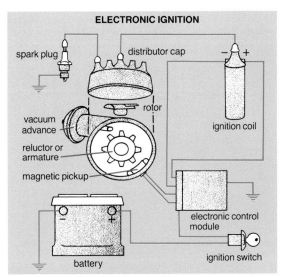

*The electronic ignition system, combined with spark plugs of extended life, eliminated the need for points and a condenser and is more reliable than earlier systems.*

shaft. Gearing of the two shafts so that the valves will open and close at the correct moment is called timing the valves.

### Electrical System

Instantaneous ignition of the explosive air-fuel mixture in each cylinder of the engine requires a strong, hot electric spark. This spark is caused by a momentary surge of high voltage, which may reach 20,000 to 25,000 volts. The voltage is supplied by a small induction coil. The surge occurs when the flow of electricity in the primary winding of the induction coil is interrupted by the opening of a breaker arm. A rotor permits the high-voltage surge to pass to each spark plug and trigger combustion in the cylinders in precisely timed sequence.

In the 1970s transistorized circuitry replaced the points and condenser in automotive ignitions. The resulting electronic ignition, combined with spark plugs of extended life, improved automotive reliability and lengthened the normal interval between tune-ups from 4,000 to 12,000 miles (6,000 to 18,000 kilometers).

The ignition system, as well as lights and other electrical devices in the car, is supplied with current from a 6- or 12-volt storage battery (*see* Battery and Fuel Cell). The battery is charged during operation of the vehicle by a direct-current (DC) generator powered by the engine. A variation of the generator, called an alternator, or alternating-current (AC) generator, has been developed. The AC is changed, or rectified, to DC by means of a diode, or type of electron tube. Unlike the ordinary car generator, the alternator continues to charge the battery while the engine is at its lowest, or idling, speed. The storage battery also powers the starter. This is an electric motor that cranks, or turns, the engine until the spark plugs ignite the air-fuel mixture.

### Four-Stroke Cycle Engine

Most automotive engines are four-stroke cycle engines. Each up and each down movement of the piston is a stroke. Four strokes are needed to complete one cycle. The strokes of the cycle are the intake, compression, power, and exhaust strokes.

An important characteristic of engine operation is the compression ratio. This is the relation of the size of the piston chamber when the piston is at its lowest position to its size when the piston is in the top position. If the total volume of a cylinder is, for example, 35 cubic inches (574 cubic centimeters) and the piston at the top of the stroke leaves a space of 5 cubic inches (82 cubic centimeters), the air-fuel mixture has been compacted to one seventh of its original volume, and the compression ratio is seven to one.

The ability of gasoline to operate at a specified compression ratio is measured in octane ratings (*see* Gasoline). Gasoline rated too low for a specified engine may ignite prematurely and produce a pinging sound, called knock.

Another cause of engine knock is accumulation of soot (carbon) as a hard deposit inside the cylinder. Pieces of carbon become red-hot and act like a spark to cause premature ignition. Occasionally running the engine at high speed or driving the car at maximum highway speeds does much to avoid or clean out this accumulation of carbon. Missing is a term used to describe failure of the air-fuel mixture to ignite. It may be caused by a cold engine. The compression ratio is a good indication of engine performance. The greater the ratio of an engine, the more power it delivers per unit of fuel. An automobile's horsepower rating is also usually given. One horsepower is the force needed to move 33,000 pounds (15,000 kilograms) one foot (30 centimeters) in one minute.

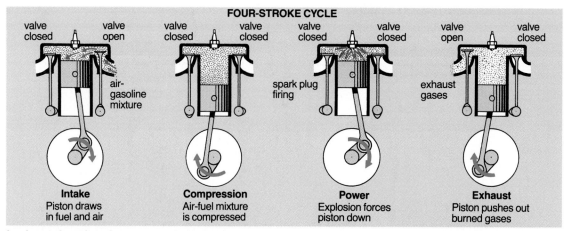

**FOUR-STROKE CYCLE**

| valve closed | valve open | valve closed | valve closed | valve closed | valve closed | valve open | valve closed |

air-gasoline mixture

spark plug firing

exhaust gases

**Intake**
Piston draws in fuel and air

**Compression**
Air-fuel mixture is compressed

**Power**
Explosion forces piston down

**Exhaust**
Piston pushes out burned gases

*In a four-stroke cycle engine, only one of the four strokes delivers power. The strokes are the intake, compression, power, and exhaust strokes. The firing of other cylinders and the momentum of a flywheel keep the piston moving during the other three strokes.*

The cylinders of the engine are molded into a cylinder block, a heavy block of metal. The cylinder head is a separate casting that is bolted to the block. Most cylinder blocks and heads are made of cast iron, though some are made of aluminum. The pistons turn the crankshaft by means of connecting rods. Attached to the crankshaft is a heavy flywheel, which helps keep engine speed steady.

**Exhaust System**

The exhaust system includes the exhaust manifold, muffler, exhaust pipe, and tail pipe. Through the manifold the burned gases are carried off to the muffler, which reduces the pressure of the gases and discharges them quietly through the tail pipe.

Since about 1975 most automotive exhaust systems have been equipped with catalytic converters—flat and rectangular devices placed along the tail pipe in much the same fashion as a muffler. They contain pellets that are coated with tiny amounts of platinum and palladium. These metals act as catalysts in a chemical reaction within the converter that transforms the exhaust pollutants into carbon dioxide and water.

Until the mid-1970s most automobiles used gasoline to which compounds of lead had been added. These substances improve engine performance but enter the atmosphere in automotive exhausts, causing pollution. Most cars now use lead-free gasoline. Leaded fuel contaminates catalytic converters, reducing their effectiveness.

Afterburners have also been devloped to reduce pollution. They burn compounds in exhaust gases so they do not reach the atmosphere. The blow-by, a variation, recirculates smog-producing gases into the combustion chamber to be burned.

**Cooling System**

Water from the radiator is circulated through the water jacket, or passages around the cylinders, to cool

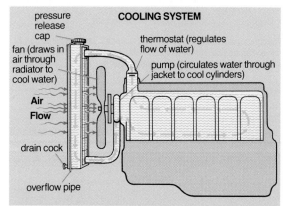

**COOLING SYSTEM**

pressure release cap

fan (draws in air through radiator to cool water)

thermostat (regulates flow of water)

pump (circulates water through jacket to cool cylinders)

**Air Flow**

drain cock

overflow pipe

*In the cooling system, air is drawn through the radiator grill by the fan. This cools the water, which is circulated through the jacket around the engine's cylinders.*

the engine. A centrifugal water pump generally is used in automobiles. The water, entering at the center, is caught by the vanes of the pump and is thrown to the outside by centrifugal force. The pressure imparted to the water carries it to the pipe leading to the water jacket. A thermostatic valve prevents water from circulating through the radiator until the temperature has reached a degree suitable for efficient engine operation. Some engines depend on a flow of air over the engine and have no liquid coolant.

**Lubrication System**

The presence of an oil film between two metal surfaces working together reduces friction and prevents parts from overheating and wearing. Several different systems are used to keep the engine parts of a car lubricated. The one most in use is a pressure system called force feed. A pump supplies oil through lines to wherever it is needed.

A simpler arrangement is the splash system. Troughs of oil are located inside the crankcase under the connecting rods. The rods are fitted with dippers at the lower ends. As the engine runs, these throw and splash oil inside the engine.

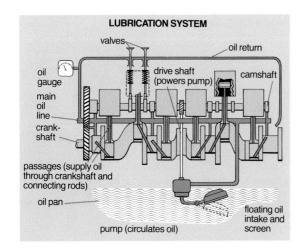

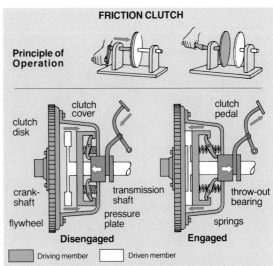

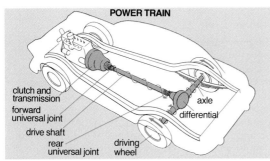

*In a force-feed lubrication system (top), oil is pumped to the moving parts of the engine. The force-feed system is used by most manufacturers of automotive vehicles. The power train (bottom) includes those parts that transmit power from the engine through the transmission, drive shaft, and axles to the driving wheels. In most cars, the power is transmitted to the rear wheels.*

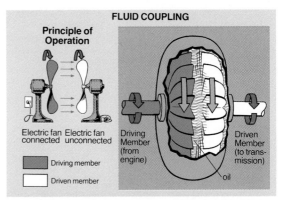

*When a friction clutch (top) is engaged, the disk is held against the flywheel. Pressure on the clutch pedal disengages the disk. Oil permits the fluid coupling (bottom) to slip at low speeds. At high speeds the coupling functions like a solid connection.*

Few cars now depend on the splash system alone. Oil is usually pumped to the main bearings of the crankshaft, the connecting rod bearings, and the camshaft bearings. In most systems it reaches the main bearings through passages in the crankshaft.

Screens are provided at the intake opening of the oil pump to prevent the entrance of dirt. To permit a change of the engine oil supply, a drain plug is provided. Some parts of the car that formerly needed lubrication are now greased permanently. The lubricant is sealed in before the car leaves the factory.

## POWER TRAIN

The parts of the automobile that transmit power from the engine to the driving wheels make up the power train. These are the clutch, transmission, drive shaft, and differential. In most cars power is delivered to the rear wheels (rear-wheel drive). Increasing numbers of car engines, however, transmit power to the front wheels (front-wheel drive). This improves traction because the engine's weight is centered over the wheels that power the car. It also eliminates the drive shaft and the hump in the car's floor to accommodate it. This, in turn, increases interior legroom. An

alternative with similar advantages is the rear-engine, rear-wheel drive car. Four-wheel drive cars have even better traction and are generally used to travel rough country or to drive through snow. Some have a part-time feature in which a flick of a lever transmits power to a set of wheels to provide four-wheel drive.

### Clutch

It is not practical to connect the wheels of an automobile directly to the engine. A device is needed to uncouple the wheels from the running engine so that the driver can warm the engine and keep it running while the vehicle is not moving. The engine must also be separated from the gearbox when the driver is shifting gears. Most automobiles provide for this uncoupling either with a friction (disk) clutch or with a fluid coupling.

**Friction clutch.** In the operation of a friction clutch, the driver slowly releases the clutch pedal, and the disk slips against the flywheel. As the clutch is further let in, or engaged, springs hold the disk more

## HOW A PLANETARY TRANSMISSION WORKS

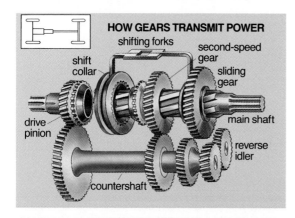

pinions, or planet gears
ring gear
sun gear
planet carrier
**Parts Unassembled**
**Low Speed**
**Second Speed**
**High Speed and Overdrive**
**Reverse**

Driving member
Driven member
Stationary member

*In a planetary transmission, the torque, or rotating power, is varied by a change in the role each gear plays. A gear may be driving (providing power), driven (receiving power), or stationary, as shown in the color key.*

## HOW GEARS TRANSMIT POWER

shifting forks
second-speed gear
shift collar
sliding gear
drive pinion
main shaft
reverse idler
countershaft

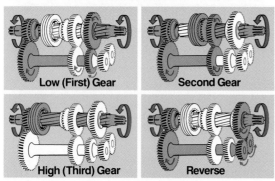

**Low (First) Gear**
**Second Gear**
**High (Third) Gear**
**Reverse**

*The gearshift lever (center) moves the shifting forks, which changes the relative positions of the gears. This results in different power ratios for varying speeds and a different direction for reversing the vehicle. Most modern cars feature an automatic transmission, which alters the gears without a hand-operated lever. The arrangement of gears (bottom) for low, or first, gear provides maximum power. The arrangement for second gear serves for intermediate power. In high, or third, gear the main shaft turns at engine speed. In reverse the idler reverses the direction in which the main shaft turns.*

firmly. Friction on the disk gradually increases until finally the disk and flywheel move together as a unit without slipping.

**Fluid coupling.** The fluid coupling is also called a fluid flywheel or hydraulic coupling. In it there is no solid connection between the driving and driven members. Oil permits the fluid coupling to slip easily at low engine speeds. At high speeds the slippage is almost eliminated, and the fluid coupling functions

like a solid connection. Sometimes both a fluid coupling and a friction clutch are used.

### Transmission

The transmission is a device installed at some point between the engine and the driving wheels of a vehicle to change speed and power. Power from the engine is provided in the form of torque, or twisting force. The amount of this force varies a great deal, depending on the individual characteristics of the engine and the speed at which the engine is running. At high speeds the torque is greater. The amount of torque needed to move a car is not always directly related to speed. When a car is traveling at moderate speed on a level road, the engine does not need to supply much torque to keep it going. When the car is starting from a dead stop or moving up a hill, however, the engine must deliver enough torque to get or keep the car moving. Turning speed (revolutions per minute) from the engine may be reduced or increased by gears and thus converted to provide greater torque or greater speed.

The gearshift lever of a car moves shifting forks, which engage or disengage various combinations of gears. These combinations provide more or less torque and speed, and they determine the direction in which the vehicle will move. Most modern cars are equipped with an automatic transmission, which alters the combinations of gears or of torque converters without the movement of a lever by hand.

**Standard gear transmission.** The conversion of engine speed and the resulting torque may be accomplished by engaging various combinations of large and small gears. The so-called standard transmission for many years has been a gearbox with a combination of gears. The standard gearbox usually provides three forward speeds and one reverse speed. Four and five forward speeds are not uncommon, especially on sports cars, and some trucks have even more.

Most standard transmissions manufactured after 1965 were equipped with synchromesh, a system in which all forward gears have a similar mesh design. This makes it easier for slow-moving gears to engage smoothly with fast-moving ones and eliminates clashing and grinding when the driver shifts.

# HYDRAULIC TORQUE CONVERTER

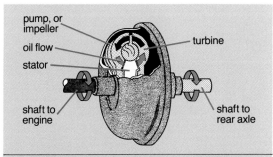

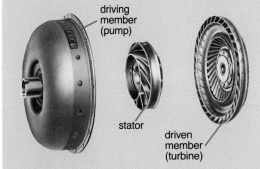

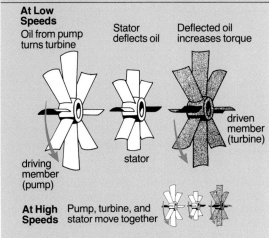

*In a hydraulic torque converter oil circulates between the pump, stator, and turbine. The stator is stationary at low speeds but moves with the pump and turbine at higher speeds.*

**Planetary gear transmission.** Another means of changing speed and torque is through the use of planetary transmission. Just as the planets in space move about the sun, so planetary gears move around a sun gear. Both of these types of gears move within a ring gear, which has its teeth on the inside. The same principles of torque conversion that govern the standard gear transmission apply to the planetary system. Small and large gears follow the same mechanical laws of speed and power. In the planetary transmission system the parts may be either driving or driven (that is, providing power or receiving power) depending on the torque conversion needed.

**Automatic transmission.** Although all automatic transmissions essentially eliminate the driver's need to shift gears and use a clutch, the design and construction of automatic transmissions may vary with each manufacturer. All modern systems, however, incorporate one or more fluid couplings or a torque converter, one or more sets of planetary gears, and valves (with suitable controls) that direct the flow of automatic transmission fluid.

One form of automatic transmission is a hydraulic torque converter, which achieves the same shifting effect as a gear transmission. This method somewhat resembles the fluid coupling. Oil transmits power in both. At lower speeds the blades of the pump, or impeller, force oil against the blades of a stator. These blades deflect the oil against a turbine, therefore increasing torque. At higher speeds, as in the case of the fluid coupling, the oil, pump, and turbine turn together as a unit.

The oil moves in different directions in different parts of a hydraulic torque converter. The pump spins and throws the oil outward. The doughnut-shaped housing that encloses the pump and turbine forces the oil toward the turbine. There it strikes the turbine blades and slides inward toward the turbine hub and then returns back through the stator.

The stator is equipped with an overrunning, or one-way, clutch. This device permits the stator to be used for deflection of oil at low speeds and to move with the pump and turbine at high speeds.

There are many variations of the hydraulic torque converter. They involve complexities not described here. The number of elements to deflect and direct the oil vary with the type of unit. Some torque converters have as many as five elements. Others are combined with gear transmissions.

Systems with hydraulic torque converters provide excellent smoothness in shifting gears. The torque ratio changes automatically to produce changes in car speed or to meet the need of extra torque, as in climbing hills.

**Other systems.** Hydraulic transmissions may not be fully automatic. Some of them are semiautomatic. In the most common type of semiautomatic transmission, the driver moves a lever but does not use a clutch pedal. In this case the clutch operates automatically in response to a control such as engine oil pressure or intake manifold vacuum. The initial movement of the automobile's shift lever releases the clutch, and, when the shifting is completed, the clutch automatically reengages.

A European development is the magnetic powder coupling. This has some of the characteristics of a fluid coupling. The system is electromechanical; no hydraulics or pneumatics are involved. The unit provides three automatically changing forward speeds and reverse gears. One magnetic powder coupling gives direct drive from the engine. A second powder coupling gives an indirect drive. The transmission for this system performs automatically in response to road speed and accelerator pedal position.

## HOW REAR WHEELS CAN TURN AT DIFFERENT SPEEDS

Straight Ahead     Turning Left     Turning Right     Left Wheel Stopped

Driving

Driven

Faster than ring-gear speed

Slower than ring-gear speed

Stationary

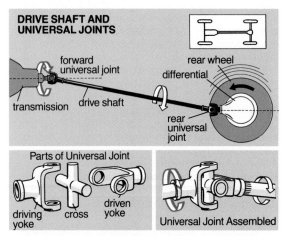

### DRIVE SHAFT AND UNIVERSAL JOINTS

forward universal joint

rear wheel

differential

transmission     drive shaft

rear universal joint

Parts of Universal Joint

driving yoke     cross     driven yoke

Universal Joint Assembled

*The drive shaft is equipped with universal joints to enable it to move up and down and from side to side. The driving yoke permits the shaft to move from side to side. The driven yoke allows it to move up and down.*

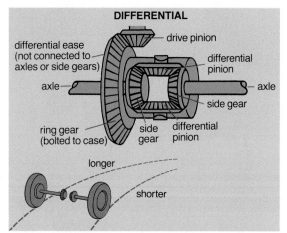

### DIFFERENTIAL

differential ease (not connected to axles or side gears)

drive pinion

differential pinion

axle

axle

side gear

ring gear (bolted to case)     side gear     differential pinion

longer

shorter

*The drive pinion (top) turns steadily while either of the side gears may move at varying speeds, or even stop, during turning maneuvers or when one axle and wheel is stopped. The gears in a differential (bottom) so mesh that different axles and wheels can turn at different speeds. This is necessary in turns, where different distances must be covered in the same amount of time by the wheels in a pair.*

### Drive Shaft

The drive shaft carries the torque from the transmission to the axle. The shaft must be equipped with several universal joints. These permit the axle to move freely up and down or from side to side as the wheels roll over road irregularities.

A sliding, or telescoping, joint also is used on drive shafts. This joint permits the shaft to change its length slightly with the up-and-down movement of the rear axle.

A flexible drive shaft with a minimum number of joints has been used on some cars. This small-diameter shaft is of alloy steel. Vibration and whip of the shaft as it turns are limited by two center bearings mounted around the shaft. A plastic-type coating prevents corrosion.

### Differential

The rear end of the drive shaft leads into a bulge in the rear-axle housing where the differential is located. The differential applies power as needed to the wheels while they turn at different speeds on curves.

The difference in speeds is necessary because the outer wheels must travel both farther and faster than the inner wheels when the vehicle is going around a turn. This could not occur if the two wheels were rigidly attached to a solid axle. The two front wheels of an automobile with rear-wheel drive present no problem, as each is mounted on its own spindle and turns independently. The rear wheels, however, drive the car, and they must be attached to a strong axle supplying torque from the engine. The rear axle, therefore, is in two pieces connected through the differential.

In some ways the differential works like planetary gears, for, depending on need, some gears will move slower or faster than others or even remain stationary. The system turns the wheel that is easiest to turn. This aids in turning corners but has other disadvantages.

One of these disadvantages, for example, if one wheel of an automobile is on dry pavement and the other is in slippery mud, the wheel in the mud will spin and the other will remain stationary. To eliminate this problem, a complex controlled slip differential has been developed. It prevents one wheel from slipping while the other is standing still.

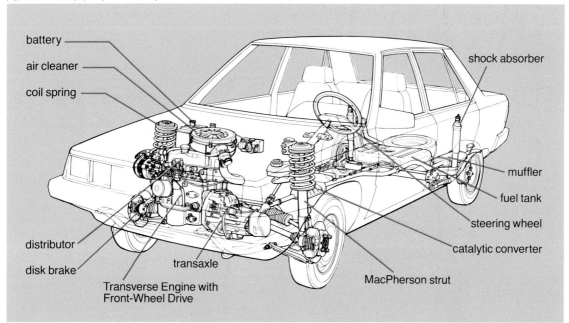

battery

air cleaner

coil spring

shock absorber

muffler

fuel tank

steering wheel

catalytic converter

distributor

disk brake

transaxle

Transverse Engine with
Front-Wheel Drive

MacPherson strut

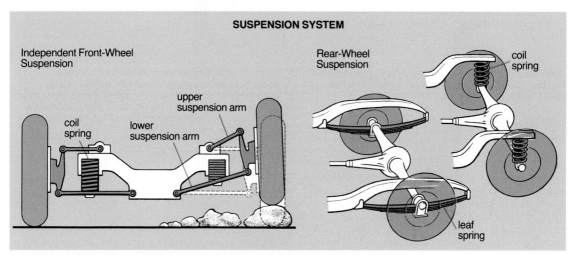

**SUSPENSION SYSTEM**

Independent Front-Wheel
Suspension

Rear-Wheel
Suspension

coil
spring

upper
suspension arm

coil
spring

lower
suspension arm

leaf
spring

*A chassis (top) with an integrated body frame and MacPherson strut front suspension supports a
transverse-mounted engine. The vehicle has front-wheel drive and disk brakes. Various types of suspension
systems (bottom) are used to absorb up-and-down movement and tilting from side to side as the wheels
move over road irregularities.*

Some front-wheel drive and rear-engine cars use
a transmission-axle combination called a transaxle.
In this arrangement a gearbox or torque converter
is positioned so that it will drive the axle directly,
eliminating a drive shaft connection. Few cars of this
type are currently manufactured.

### CHASSIS

The under portion of an automobile, generally
excluding those parts that develop and transmit
power, is called the chassis. The chassis consists of the
frame, springs, shock absorbers, axles, brakes, wheels,
tires, and steering mechanism.

The frame supports the power plant. The frame is
supported by the suspension system, and that in turn
is supported by the axles and wheels. The frame must
be sufficiently stiff and strong to resist severe twisting
and bending. Large cars have separate bodies and
frames, but compact cars are usually built with the
frame and body integrated.

### Suspension System

The suspension assembly is designed to absorb much
of the up-and-down movement and tilting from side
to side as the wheels move over irregularities in the
road. The system keeps the body of the car more or

## DISK BRAKE

piston

friction pad

rotating disk

## DRUM BRAKE

hydraulic cylinder

brake shoe
brake lining
rotating wheel drum

*In the disk brake, pistons squeeze friction pads against the brake disk from both sides. In the drum brake the brake shoes are pushed outward against the inside of the drum.*

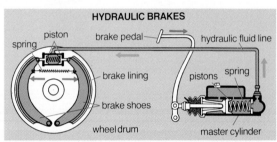

General Motors Corp.

### POWER BRAKES

3. Atmospheric pressure moves large piston

2. Pressure of fluid opens valve to admit atmospheric pressure (air)

1. Pressure on pedal causes brake fluid to flow from master cylinder to slave cylinder

diaphragm

slave cylinder

master cylinder

5. Small piston, pushed by rod from large piston, transmits pressure through tubing to brake shoes

4. Tubing from manifold of engine creates vacuum, aiding atmospheric pressure to move large piston

Hydraulic fluid | Atmospheric pressure | Vacuum

### HYDRAULIC BRAKES

spring
piston
brake pedal
hydraulic fluid line

brake lining
pistons
spring

brake shoes

wheel drum

master cylinder

*The power brake (top), or slave, cylinder and associated mechanisms function between the master cylinder and the hydraulic-fluid line that leads to the pistons in each wheel. When the brake pedal is engaged (bottom), the master cylinder forces fluid through the line to pistons at each wheel. The pistons press the brake shoes against the wheel drum.*

less at an even level as well as relatively free from road shock.

Most cars made in North America use coil springs to provide what is called independent front suspension. This permits each front wheel to move up and down independently. Another system uses a torsion bar— a round, heat-treated steel bar that is sufficiently elastic to twist slightly and act as a spring. Leaf springs usually consist of several layers. A durable single-leaf spring has also been developed. Air or air-oil springs are used on some European cars.

Shock absorbers slow the reaction during compression and rebound of the springs. They are filled with a fluid or use Freon gas in a plastic bag.

### Axles and Wheels

A rear axle called a swing axle is free to move or swing as either wheel goes up or down. There are variations of this axle. Rear axles are equipped with differentials as described earlier. Trucks usually have rigid front axles.

Most wheels are disks of steel or aluminum. An early type had spokes; spoked wheels are still used on some sports cars.

### Tires

Automobiles use pneumatic (air-filled) tires. In the past they had separate inner tubes to hold air. Today's tires

are tubeless, sealed airtight to the wheel rim at the bead (edge of their inner circumference).

Tires may be bias type, belted bias, or belted radial. Bias tires, which were standard through the late 1960s, are made of two, four, or more layers of rayon, nylon, polyester, or other synthetic cords laid at an angle from one bead to another. Successive layers, or plies, alternate in direction to strengthen the tire's body. Belted bias tires are made the same way but have belts of synthetic or fine steel wire just beneath the tread (the part of the tire that touches the road). The belts add strength and stability. A belted radial tire has layers of rubber-coated synthetic cords that are laid straight across the tire from bead to bead and covered along the tread with belts. The radial tire's tread is very stable, therefore making the car easier to control. It also reduces rolling resistance and improves fuel economy.

### Braking System

Every car has a service brake system, operated by foot pressure on a pedal while the car is in motion, and a hand-operated emergency brake system employed for parking and as a backup to the service brake system. The service brake system uses fluid forced by pistons through small flexible pipes (brake lines) to

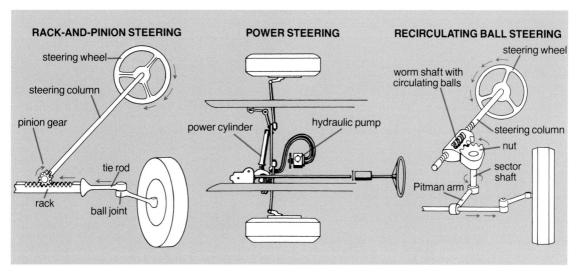

## RACK-AND-PINION STEERING

steering wheel

steering column

pinion gear

tie rod

rack

ball joint

## POWER STEERING

power cylinder

hydraulic pump

## RECIRCULATING BALL STEERING

steering wheel

worm shaft with circulating balls

steering column

nut

sector shaft

Pitman arm

*In rack-and-pinion steering (left), a pinion gear at the base of the steering column moves a rack, which transmits the turning motion to the wheels. In the recirculating ball type (right), a worm shaft gear turns a Pitman arm that causes a drag link to turn the wheels. In power steering (center), a hydraulic pump and cylinder add power to the manual turning by the driver.*

transmit the pressure of the driver's foot to the brake mechanisms within each wheel and is, therefore, a hydraulic system. Emergency brakes make use of purely mechanical techniques (cables attached to the brake lever) to stop the car. They are intended to be effective if the hydraulic system fades (loses its braking ability).

**Drum brakes.** A drum brake operates by pressing two crescent-shaped brake shoes outward against the interior of a brake drum. One end of each shoe is linked to a pivot while the other end is attached to the piston. The shoes are faced with a brake lining, which is a replaceable friction surface of asbestos or some other material.

**Disk brakes.** Disk brakes use fluid to transmit pressure from the driver's foot but have a piston that presses against a rotating disk attached to the car's axle. Unlike the more common drum brake, disk brakes run cool and thus have little tendency to fade. Cars equipped with disk brakes normally have them on the front axle only.

**Power brakes.** Power brakes have a mechanical assist that reduces the physical effort required to stop a car. (*See also* Brake.)

### Steering System

The recirculating ball steering system involves a worm shaft steering gear at the base of the steering column that turns a Pitman arm, causing a device called the drag link to turn the wheels. A simpler system is rack-and-pinion steering. A pinion gear at the base of the steering column moves a rack, transmitting turning motion to the wheels. Rack-and-pinion steering improves control but is not suitable for larger cars because it requires too much strength. Power steering systems make steering virtually effortless. They employ a hydraulic pump and a power cylinder.

### HISTORY

In the 15th century the Renaissance genius Leonardo da Vinci considered the concept of a self-propelled vehicle, and Robert Valturio planned for a cart powered by windmills geared to its wheels. As early as the 16th century, steam propulsion was proposed, and in 1678 a Belgian missionary to China, Ferdinand Verbiest, made a model steam carriage based on a principle that suggests the modern turbine. Another early proponent of steam power, however, was certified to be insane. In the 17th century the great Dutch physicist Christiaan Huygens built an engine that worked by air pressure developed by exploding a powder charge. A carriage propelled by a large clockwork engine was demonstrated in about 1750 by the French inventor Jacques de Vaucanson.

#### Forerunners of the Automobile

Nicolas Cugnot of France built a three-wheeled steam-powered artillery carriage in 1769. This was probably the first automotive vehicle.

Steam carriages were produced in England during the late 18th and early 19th centuries. In 1786 William Murdock built a three-wheeled steam-driven wagon. Richard Trevithick produced several steam carriages in the early 1800s. Steam-driven carriages, built and operated by Goldsworthy Gurney and by Walter Hancock, transported passengers in the London area during this same period. Hancock's "steam bus," built in 1832, was in regular service between London and Paddington.

Oliver Evans built the first steam-powered motor vehicle in the United States in 1805. A combination dredge and flatboat, it operated on land and water. Richard Dudgeon's road engine of 1867 could carry ten passengers. It resembled a farm tractor.

## Some Leading Figures in the Development of the Automobile

*Some prominent persons are not included below because they are covered in the main text of this article or in other articles in Compton's Encyclopedia (see Fact-Index).*

**Agnelli, Giovanni** (1866–1945). Italian industrialist and founder (in 1899) of Fabbrica Italiana Automobili Torino (Fiat), the first automobile factory in Italy. He also founded companies that manufactured roll and ball bearings and airplane engines. In 1923 he was made a senator by the Italian dictator, Benito Mussolini.

**Benz, Carl** (1844–1929). German engineer who in 1885 designed and built the first practical automobile powered by an internal-combustion engine. His company, founded in 1883 to build engines, merged in 1926 with Daimler to form Daimler-Benz, maker of Mercedes-Benz cars. Benz had left his firm in about 1906 to organize another company with his sons.

**Buick, David Dunbar** (1854–1929). Scottish-born United States auto manufacturer who founded Buick in 1902. Originally a plumber, he lost control of his company before selling a single car and at his death was a clerk in a Detroit trade school.

**Chevrolet, Louis** (1878–1941). Swiss-born United States automobile racer, designer, and manufacturer who in his first race in 1905 set a speed record of 68 mph (109 kilometers per hour). With William C. Durant he built the first Chevrolet car in 1911. He sold his interest to Durant in 1915. The next year Durant brought the Chevrolet Motor Company into the General Motors organization.

**Chrysler, Walter P.** (1875–1940). United States auto manufacturer who was with Buick from 1912 (president and general manager, 1916–19), Willys-Overland until 1921, and Maxwell from 1923, which he turned into the Chrysler Corporation in 1925. He purchased Dodge Brothers, Inc., in 1928 and introduced the Plymouth the same year.

**Cugnot, Nicolas-Joseph** (1725–1804). French military engineer who built a steam-powered, three-wheeled vehicle in 1769 that is recognized by the British Royal Automobile Club and Automobile Club de France as the first true automobile.

**Daimler, Gottlieb** (1834–1900). German mechanical engineer who patented a high-speed internal-combustion engine in 1885 and developed a carburetor that made possible the use of gasoline as fuel. In 1890 he founded Daimler-Motoren-Gesellschaft, which built the first Mercedes car in 1899.

**Dodge, John F.** (1864–1920), and **Horace E.** (1868–1920). United States machinist brothers who manufactured auto parts, founding their own automobile firm in 1914 largely with capital earned from their 1903 investment in Ford. The firm was purchased in 1928 by Chrysler.

**Durant, William C.** (1861–1947). Founder of General Motors Corporation. He began with a horse-drawn carriage company in 1886 and took over Buick in 1904, forming the General Motors (GM) Company in 1908. He lost control in 1910, cofounded Chevrolet in 1911, and acquired control of GM again in 1915. He was forced out finally in 1920 and founded Durant Motors, Inc., in 1921.

**Duryea, Charles E.** (1861–1938), and **J. Frank** (1869–1967). Brothers who in 1893 built the first successful gasoline-powered automobile in the United States. An improved version, driven by Frank Duryea, won in 1895 the first auto race in Chicago.

**Fisher, Frederic J.** (1878–1941). United States manufacturer of auto bodies who, with his uncle and five brothers, founded the Fisher Body Company in 1908. The company was acquired by General Motors (60 percent in 1918 and completely in 1926).

**Iacocca, Lee** (born 1924). Engineer who became president of the failing Chrysler Corporation in 1979 and negotiated the largest federal loan ever made to a private firm, reversing the corporate slump. He began his career at Ford in 1945 and was its president from 1970 to 1978. He retired from Chrysler in December 1992.

**Kettering, Charles F.** (1876–1958). United States engineer who cofounded Delco (Dayton Engineering Laboratories Company) in 1909 and developed improved lighting and ignition systems and the first electric starter, which were introduced on Cadillacs in 1912. Delco became a subsidiary of United Motors (later part of General Motors) in 1916. Kettering served as vice-president and director of research for General Motors from 1920 to 1947. He also helped develop quick-drying finishes and antiknock fuels.

**Leland, Henry M.** (1843–1932). United States engineer whose rigorous standards aided development of the automobile. He built the first Cadillac in 1903 and founded the Lincoln Motor Company in 1917. His innovations include the V-8 engine.

**Lenoir, Étienne** (1822–1900). French inventor who in 1860 made the first practical internal-combustion engine. In 1862 he built the first vehicle to be powered by such an engine.

**Nash, Charles W.** (1864–1948). United States automobile manufacturer who was president of Buick from 1910 to 1916 and of General Motors from 1912 to 1916, and who founded the Nash Motorcar Company in 1916.

**Olds, Ransom E.** (1864–1950). United States inventor who founded the Olds Motor Works in 1899, marketing the first Oldsmobile in 1901. He left his company in 1904 and formed the Reo (from his initials) Motor Car Company. His Oldsmobile was the first commercially successful American-made auto.

**Sloan, Alfred P.** (1875–1966). United States automotive engineer and industrialist who was president of General Motors from 1923 to 1937 and chairman of the board from 1937 to 1956.

**Stanley, Francis E.** (1849–1918), and **Freelan O.** (1849–1940). Twin brothers who invented the first United States steam car in 1897. They manufactured Stanley Steamers until they retired during World War I, but their steam cars continued being built until 1927.

**Tucker, Preston T.** (1903–57). United States automobile maker who founded the Tucker Corporation in 1946. His innovative designs for the "first new car in 50 years" garnered much interest and many advance orders. After building 51 cars his corporation went bankrupt in the wake of his indictment for fraud by the federal government. He was acquitted in 1950.

## Steam Automobiles

Steam-driven automobiles were turned out by some 100 manufacturers during the late 1890s and early 1900s. The most famous of these steam-car makers were Francis E. and Freelan O. Stanley of the United States—twin brothers who developed an automobile called the "Stanley Steamer" in 1897. Steam cars burned kerosene to heat water in a tank that was part of the car. The pressure of escaping steam activated the car's driving mechanism. Perhaps the chief asset of the steam car was its simple power mechanism. It did not have an ignition system or a clutch. No transmission was needed because its engine was connected directly to the wheel axle.

The steam car had some disadvantages, however. Most of these centered in the water tank, also called the "boiler." It took too long for the water to heat up. In addition there was a constant fear of explosion, though this proved groundless. The popularity of the steam car declined at about the time of World War I. Steam car production came to an end in 1929.

## Electric Automobiles

Several experimental, electrically powered automobiles were built in Europe during the 1880s. One of the first "electrics" in the United States was produced by William Morrison in 1891. About 54 United States manufacturers turned out almost 35,000 electric cars between 1896 and 1915—the period of their greatest

*The world's first automobile show was held in New York City in 1900. More than half of the vehicles exhibited were steam cars and electric cars.*
Automobile Manufacturers Association

popularity. The Columbia, the Baker, and the Riker were among the more famous makes.

The electric car ran smoothly and was simple to operate. However, it did not run efficiently at speeds of more than 20 miles per hour and could not travel more than 50 miles without having its batteries recharged. Thus it was limited to city use.

### Early Gasoline Automobiles

Gasoline-driven automobiles were developed in Europe. A practical gas engine was designed and built by Étienne Lenoir of France in 1860. It ran on illuminating gas. In 1862 he built a vehicle powered by one of his engines. Siegfried Marcus of Austria built several four-wheeled gasoline-powered vehicles. By 1876 Nikolaus Otto, a German, was perfecting his four-stroke cycle engine (*see* Internal-Combustion Engine). Two other Germans, Karl Benz and Gottlieb Daimler, built gasoline cars in 1885.

### Beginning of the Automobile Industry

By the early 1900s many inventors in the United States were developing new models. In 1893 J. Frank and Charles E. Duryea produced the first successful gasoline-powered automobile in the United States. They began commercial production of the Duryea car in 1896—the same year in which Henry Ford operated his first successful automobile in Detroit.

The first automobile salesroom was opened in New York City in 1899 by Percy Owen. In 1900 the first automobile show was held—also in New York City.

Mass production in the automobile industry was introduced in 1901 by Ransom E. Olds, a pioneer experimenter since 1886. His company manufactured more than 400 of the now historic curved-dash Oldsmobiles in that first year. Each car sold for only $650. Henry M. Leland and Henry Ford further developed mass production methods during the early 1900s. (*See also* Automobile Industry.)

### The Selden Patent

In 1879 George B. Selden, an American attorney, applied for a patent which covered the general features of a gasoline-powered automobile. He received his patent in 1895. In 1903 the Association of

Licensed Vehicle Manufacturers was formed by companies who recognized the Selden patent. They agreed to pay Selden a royalty on each car built.

Henry Ford refused to join this association. He sued to break Selden's hold on the industry. After extensive litigation, Ford won. In 1911 a District Court of Appeals held that Selden's patent applied only to a two-stroke cycle engine—not to the Otto engine. This decision permitted all manufacturers to use the Otto engine. It also led to a cross-licensing agreement among most of the American manufacturers. This is administered by the Automobile Manufacturers Association. The association can license any signer of the agreement to use a patent held by another signer. Usually the patent holder has a year of exclusive use first.

### Developments of the Early 1900s

The Ford Motor Company was organized in 1903, the General Motors Corporation in 1908, and the Chrysler Corporation in 1925. The first Model T Ford was made in 1908. More than 15 million were to be sold in the next 20 years. The Model T, nicknamed the "flivver" and the "tin lizzie," was probably more responsible for the development of large-scale motoring than was any other car in automotive history. It also spurred the building of roads and streets in the United States (*see* Automobile Driving).

Many men contributed to the development of the automobile industry in the United States. These included Elmer and Edgar Apperson, who built a car conceived by Elwood G. Haynes in 1894; the Studebaker brothers, manufacturers of horse-drawn vehicles, who began making motorcars in 1902; David Dunbar Buick, who built his first car in 1903; Frederic J. Fisher, founder of the Fisher Body Company (1908), which became a part of General Motors in 1926; Louis Chevrolet, the Swiss-American who founded the Chevrolet Motor Company in 1911; Charles F. Kettering, who invented the self-starter in 1911; John and Horace Dodge, the bicycle parts producers who founded the Dodge Motor Company in 1914; and Charles W. Nash, an executive with other automobile manufacturers until he founded the Nash Motors Company in 1916.

## *A Gallery of Historic Automobiles*

**1875 MARCUS**   **1888 BENZ**   **1893 DURYEA**

**1904 OLDSMOBILE**   **1908 MODEL T FORD**   **1912 CADILLAC**

**1929 CORD**   **1931 DUESENBERG**   **1936 CHRYSLER**

### World War I and After

By 1916 annual passenger-car sales in the United States had reached more than 1½ million. During World War I the manufacture of automobiles for civilian uses was virtually halted as the industry was mobilized to produce vehicles, motors, and other war matériel for the armed forces.

The automobile assumed a significant new role in the American way of life immediately after World War I. No longer an extravagant novelty, the motorcar was rapidly becoming a necessity rather than a luxury for many American families. By the early 1920s most of the basic mechanical problems of automotive engineering had been solved. Manufacturers then concentrated their efforts on making motorcars safer, more stylish, and more comfortable.

Four-wheel brakes were used in production models in 1920. By the late 1920s safety glass and balloon tires were standard equipment. Steel bodies, hydraulic brakes, and hot-water heaters were also common. In 1919, 90 percent of the passenger cars made were open touring cars and roadsters. In 1929 about 90 percent were closed models.

By the mid-1920s Henry Ford had decided to abandon the three-pedaled Model T and replace it with the Model A, which was to be equipped with a conventional gearshift. The last Model T was produced in May 1927. A slowdown in Model T production had been in effect for several months. The first Model A rolled off the assembly line in October 1927, and several were in the showrooms by Dec. 1, 1927. An enthusiastic public was soon buying thousands. In 1928 the Chrysler Corporation announced the production of its answer to the Model A—a new low-cost automobile called the Plymouth.

Despite the Great Depression, the United States automotive industry continued to make engineering progress. The Chrysler Corporation introduced its airflow streamlined models in 1934. Window defrosters became available in 1936, automatic transmissions in 1937, and sealed-beam headlights were introduced in

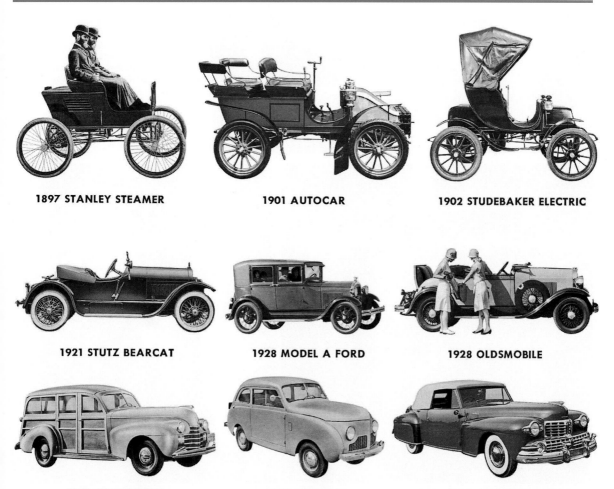

1897 STANLEY STEAMER      1901 AUTOCAR      1902 STUDEBAKER ELECTRIC

1921 STUTZ BEARCAT      1928 MODEL A FORD      1928 OLDSMOBILE

1940 OLDSMOBILE      1946 CROSLEY      1948 LINCOLN CONTINENTAL

1940 before the industry once more went into full-time war production for World War II.

### Innovations After World War II

Power steering, power brakes, wraparound windshields, tubeless tires, and automatic window and seat controls were among the innovations developed after World War II. Engines became more powerful—horsepower ratings of 200 or 300 were commonplace. Streamlined contours gave way to the boxier shapes of the 1950s. The 1960s models featured longer silhouettes and more window area.

Small European and Japanese compact cars began to capture a larger share of the American market in the mid-1950s. United States manufacturers introduced their own compacts, but it was not until the fuel crisis of the 1970s that they became significant.

### Alternatives to Gasoline

In the 1970s came a renewed interest in automobiles propelled by electric motors powered by storage

batteries. Enormous expense and two technological problems prevented widespread adoption. However, General Motors announced in 1990 that it would begin work on a new experimental electric car, called the Impact, that would perform as well as internal-combustion engine vehicles. Electric cars are made and used in limited numbers for light passenger use and for mail delivery.

Some passenger cars have diesel engines, which function differently from gas-burning engines. Diesels use less-expensive fuel and can get 20 to 30 percent more miles or kilometers per gallon. They are high polluters and are noisy, however, so research has gone into solving these problems. Also promising is the stratified-charge engine, which supplies lean and rich fuel mixtures simultaneously to each cylinder.

Ethyl alcohol, or ethanol, has been used in cars for many years, either alone or in combination with gasoline to make gasohol. Ethanol is easy to manufacture from renewable plant sources such as corn and sugarcane. It is neither difficult nor expensive to

adjust most automobile engines to burn ethanol. This fuel is used widely in Brazil, which depends heavily on imported oil but produces a large sugar crop. In the Philippines there are cars that burn ethanol distilled from coconut husks.

Ethanol's major disadvantage is its high cost in most countries. It can also cause some damage to metal engine parts in high concentrations and should be used only as a supplement rather than a complete substitute for gasoline. If research and development can reduce the drawbacks of ethanol while gasoline prices continue to rise, it may be used on a broader scale.

Other substitutes for gasoline include methyl alcohol, or methanol, which is distilled from wood products or natural gas, and synthetic fuels that can be made from coal, oil, shale, or tar sands. Electric cars would eliminate the need for gasoline entirely, but they face technological obstacles before they can be used widely.

### Reducing Pollution

Government regulations have reduced automotive air pollution by forcing the adoption of lead-free gasoline and catalytic converters. Newer engines that burn fuel more efficiently can reduce the volume of emissions while they economize on gasoline.

In the United States, Congress passed the Clean Air Act of 1990, calling for reductions of some auto emissions by as much as 70 percent. California introduced the strictest auto emission standards in the world. The goal was to decrease output of hydrocarbons by 70 percent in new cars by the year 2003.

### Increased Safety

In response to legislative requirements, automakers have made many improvements. Disk brakes, for example, are safer than most others because they are less prone to fading, or loss of braking ability. Anti-lock braking systems (ABS), which control skidding on roads during hard braking, are often available. Impact-absorbing bumpers are now standard on many cars. Makers have investigated the crashworthiness of their vehicles and have developed models that have a rigid central box to protect passengers.

All cars are equipped with seat belts, and many have an alarm that warns the driver to fasten them before

*The Precept is a 2000 concept car created by the ATV (Advanced Technology Vehicles) department at GM. Targeted to achieve 80 mpg it contains a hybrid electric propulsion with a 35kw electric motor and a 1.31, 3 cylinder, 12 valve engine and a 3 camera rear vision display that replaces outside and rear-view mirrors.*

2001 GM Corp. Used with permission of GM Media Archives.

starting the vehicle. One alternative to seat belts is the air bag. This has a sensor that in a crash activates a gas cylinder in one tenth of a second. The cylinder inflates a nylon bag positioned so that it will prevent a passenger from pitching forward.

Other safety research has centered on improvements in exterior body design to reduce injuries to pedestrians. Electronic instrumentation has been improved so that drivers are warned of unsafe conditions such as an unfastened door.

### Fuel Efficiency

Much work goes into transmission improvements. Manual transmissions with four or five speeds are roughly 10 percent more efficient than automatic transmissions. Makers also try to improve automatic transmission performance. A possible substitute for current transmissions is the continuously variable transmission (CVT), which has an infinitely variable set of gears for close matching between engine speed and engine load. Laboratory models indicate a possible savings of as much as 20 percent.

Turbochargers, which force the air-fuel mixture into the cylinder with the pressure of exhaust gases, have been modified from racing cars in which they were first used. Turbochargers improve mileage from 5 to 10 percent. Other possible means to improve economy include styling to reduce wind resistance, improvements in tires, more efficient accessories, and better ignition control. Almost anything that reduces the overall weight of a car will allow it to travel farther on a gallon of fuel.

### Better Manufacturing

Research and development in automobile manufacturing are centered on substituting machines for labor and the employment of better materials. One recent manufacturing technique is the use of robotic arms for welding, painting, and assembling

automobiles and parts. Plastics have been used as substitutes for metal in many parts of automobiles. As technology has advanced, early durability problems with plastics have been overcome. Because plastic weighs less than metal, its use also saves fuel. Ceramic materials were of interest as possible replacements for engines or engine parts.

### Styling for Efficiency

An average-size car traveling at 55 miles (85 kilometers) per hour uses more than 60 percent of its fuel and power to overcome wind resistance. Aerodynamically efficient design greatly reduces the car's drag, improving gas mileage. This information comes from wind tunnel tests on auto bodies.

Better designs are usually considered to be better looking as well. With windshields raked back and a lower hood, a car takes on a dashing, sporty look. Some of the most sensible designs are incidentally attractive. (*See also* Automobile Industry.)

---

**FURTHER RESOURCES FOR AUTOMOBILE**

**Brown, Lester and others.** Running on Empty (Norton, 1979).
**Chilton's Auto Repair Manual 1982–89** (Chilton, 1988).
**Consumer Guide to Used Cars** (New American, 1988).
**Dark, Harris.** The Wankel Rotary Engine (Ind. Univ. Press, 1974).
**Doty, Dennis.** Model Car Building: Advanced Techniques (TAB, 1988).
**Drane, Keat.** Convert Your Car to Alcohol (Love Street, 1980).
**Engen, Gavin.** Kit Cars (Lerner, 1977).
**Gillis, Jack.** The Car Book (Harper, 1988).
**Hirsch, Jay.** Great American Dream Machines (Random, 1988).
**Marsh, Peter and Collet, Peter.** Driving Passion: The Psychology of the Car (Faber, 1989).
**Silk, Gerald and others.** Automobile and Culture (Abrams, 1984).
**Slater, Teddy.** The Big Book of Real Race Cars and Race Car Driving (Putnam, 1989).
**Weissler, Paul.** Weekend Mechanic's Handbook: Complete Auto Repairs You Can Make, rev. ed. (Prentice, 1987).
**Whole Car Catalog by the Editors of Consumer Guide** (Simon & Schuster, 1978).

Courtesy of the American Automobile Association

*Students learn the functions and interrelationships of driving controls with the aid of a device that simulates such operations as shifting gears, steering, and braking.*

## What To Do in Case of an Automobile Accident

1. Prevent further accidents—clear the road, in most cases; warn traffic; help the victims; turn off vehicle ignition.

2. Get help—call local or state police; summon medical aid, including ambulance, if needed.

3. Obtain all necessary information, such as name of driver, license number.

4. Obtain names and addresses of all available witnesses.

5. Report accident to state authorities.

6. Report accident to your insurance company representative.

**AUTOMOBILE DRIVING.** There are approximately 165 million registered automotive vehicles in the United States. In Canada there are more than 13 million; in Italy, 19 million; France, 21 million; and Japan, 37 million. Most of these automobiles, trucks, buses, and other motor vehicles travel along busy thoroughfares each day.

About 65 percent of all the people in the United States and some 45 percent of all Canadians are licensed motor vehicle drivers. Unfortunately, not all of these drivers have the necessary physical or emotional makeup to operate such a complicated machine as the modern motorcar.

In the United States alone, more than 1.8 million persons have died in traffic accidents since 1900. More than 5,900 persons are killed each year in automobile accidents in Canada. In France more than 12,000 people per year lose their lives in traffic accidents. The same is true in Italy and Japan. In Mexico the toll is almost 9,000 deaths related to motor vehicles per year. Based on numbers per population, Kuwait has the highest death rate in the world, followed by Portugal and Venezuela.

### The Most Common Causes of Accidents

Almost 18 million traffic accidents are reported in the United States annually, and more than 450,000 are reported in Canada each year. Human error is responsible for about 90 percent of these accidents.

The most frequent traffic violations committed by poor drivers are: (1) speeding—the principal contributing factor in fatal and nonfatal traffic accidents; (2) failing to yield the right-of-way—ranks second in nonfatal and third in fatal accidents; and (3) driving under the influence of alcohol—a factor in at least half of the fatal accidents.

### Safe Drivers Must Be Trained

The final responsibility for preventing traffic accidents rests with the driver. The best way to be sure that every motorist is capable of operating an automobile is to offer formal training in the techniques and mechanics of driving. Friends or relatives do not make ideal instructors. Frequently such persons did not have formal instruction and, although they mean well, often pass their own bad habits on to the pupil.

The driver education programs offered by many high schools in the United States, Canada, and other countries provide the best means of training

*Arm Signals To Use When Turn Signals Don't Work*
*Left Turn*                          *Right Turn*                          *Slow or Stop*

*The arm is held straight out to signal a left turn. For a right turn, the arm is bent at the elbow so that the forearm points upward. To signal slow or stop, the arm is bent at the elbow so that the forearm points downward.*

prospective drivers. These programs are conducted by teachers who have been trained to instruct new drivers. Some schools also include driver training in their adult education programs.

Standards for a unified program to be presented by all high schools in the United States have been established by the National Conference of Safety Education. The standards call for 90 hours of classroom instruction and practical driving experience.

### What a Driver-Trainee Learns

A typical course for training prospective drivers consists of three phases. One phase is classroom instruction. The second phase is a laboratory phase, which includes either driver simulation techniques or practice on a driver's range or both. The third phase is actual driving experience on the street.

In the classroom the trainee learns the basic mechanical principles of how and why an automobile runs. A student also masters the rules of the road and learns to identify and know the meanings of various traffic signs and warning signals. Sound safety practices are also taught.

No amount of classroom instruction, however, can teach a person how to drive. This skill must be acquired by practical experience. For this reason the trainee learns how to perform basic operations—starting the motor, guiding a car through traffic, stopping, and parking—by actually driving an automobile. This is done in a special training car equipped with dual controls. The extra controls are for the instructor who supervises the student's practical driving training.

### The Human Element in Driving

Throughout the driver education program, both in the classroom and in the training car, one major fact is emphasized over and over again. This fact is that the habits a student acquires during the training period will be reflected in future behavior behind the wheel—and these habits will largely determine whether one becomes a safe, competent driver or a dangerous driver.

Every motorist must understand that an automobile is a large, powerful machine. It can move at very high speeds. Even at speeds of 55 miles an hour or more it can be operated so smoothly and easily that its driver

*Rules Governing the Right-of-Way*

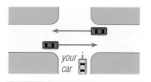

The red cars reach the intersection before your car does; thus they have the right-of-way, regardless of direction.

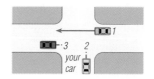

The car to your right has the right-of-way. It crosses first, you follow, and the third car goes next.

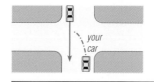

Wait for the approaching car to cross the intersection before you turn left.

Wait for the signaling car to make its left turn.

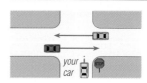

Wait until the traffic is clear before you cross a stop street.

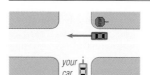

If your car is traveling on a through street, watch for crossing cars.

may be lulled into a feeling of false security. It is therefore imperative that every driver remain alert.

The motorist who is not alert cannot cope with a sudden emergency as quickly as is necessary. An overly relaxed driver requires more time to react to an emergency than does an alert one. For example, it takes longer for a daydreaming driver to react and

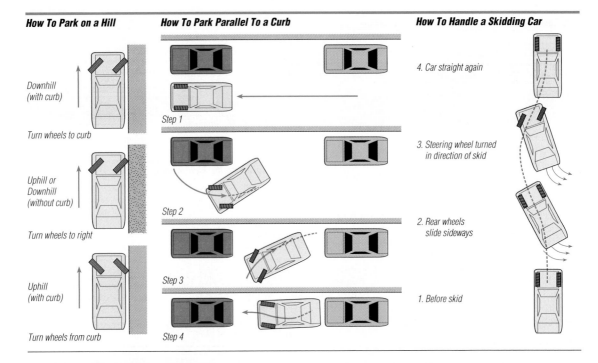

*How To Park on a Hill*

Downhill (with curb)

Turn wheels to curb

Uphill or Downhill (without curb)

Turn wheels to right

Uphill (with curb)

Turn wheels from curb

*How To Park Parallel To a Curb*

Step 1

Step 2

Step 3

Step 4

*How To Handle a Skidding Car*

4. Car straight again

3. Steering wheel turned in direction of skid

2. Rear wheels slide sideways

1. Before skid

apply the brakes when a child darts into the car's path than it takes for an alert driver to do so.

The time interval between a driver's first recognition of danger and the response to it is called reaction time. The average reaction time for most drivers is three fourths of a second. The alert driver in the situation cited above would apply the brakes within three quarters of a second after detecting the child.

A driver's reaction time may be affected by many different factors. Some of these are permanent handicaps; others are only temporary. Certain cases of arthritis and paralysis, for example, are permanent handicaps that may prevent some persons from reacting fast enough in an emergency. The normal slowing down that occurs as a person grows older may also lengthen reaction time. Temporary, correctable factors include faulty eyesight, defective hearing, and such illnesses as the common cold.

An emotionally immature person is almost always a dangerous driver. Examples of emotionally immature persons are: those who show off; those who resent authority; those who act impulsively and take chances; those who are aggressive and intolerant of the shortcomings of others; those who exaggerate their own importance and abilities; and those who do not respect the rights of others.

Reaction time is also severely slowed by alcohol consumption. Alcohol is involved in almost half of all annual road traffic fatalities in the United States. Laws equating specified blood alcohol concentrations with evidence of being drunk have been passed in most countries. Attempts to curb drunk driving have taken the form of heavy fines, jail sentences, and loss of driving licenses.

### Safety Devices and Safety Legislation

Since its beginnings the automobile industry has developed many safety devices and features, such as four-wheel brakes, brake lights, turn signals, and safety glass. One of the most significant safety devices is the seat belt. This helps prevent a person's being thrown from a car or tossed about in it when an accident occurs. An estimated 12,000 lives could be saved each year if all passengers and drivers used seat belts. (*See also* Safety.)

In 1966 the National Traffic Safety Agency was established to set federal safety standards for cars, buses, trucks, and motorcycles. In 1967 the agency issued its first list of standards for most motor vehicles. It included such features as seat belts for all occupants, shatter-resistant windshields, and energy-absorbing steering mechanisms. Most of the features listed were required on all new motor vehicles sold in the United States after Jan. 1, 1968. Also created in 1966 was the National Highway Safety Agency. Its function was to set standards for state highway safety programs. In 1967 the two agencies were merged into the National Highway Traffic Safety Bureau. The bureau was named the National Highway Traffic Safety Administration in 1970.

In 1978 Tennessee became the first state to adopt child passenger protection legislation, requiring some sort of child restraint apparatus for children under four years of age. This resulted in a reduction of the fatality and serious injury rates in that state by 50 percent in 1978 and 71 percent in 1979. Since that time, almost all states have passed similar child passenger protection laws.

Motor Vehicle Manufacturers Association of the U.S.

*Ford's Rouge industrial complex in River Rouge, Mich., uses one million tons of iron ore and more than two million tons of coal each year. Construction of the complex began in 1919.*

**AUTOMOBILE INDUSTRY.** Although once considered to be little but status items, motor vehicles are now regarded as necessities in most developed nations. The number of cars, vans, trucks, and buses in the world now averages at least one for every 12 human beings. The automobile industry, one of the world's major manufacturing industries, encompasses all companies and activities involved in the production of these vehicles and special-purpose vehicles such as fire engines, hearses, and ambulances. This production includes the manufacture of components such as engines and bodies as well as the design and assembly of the final product.

The principal product of the industry is the passenger automobile. The word automobile comes from the Greek word *auto,* meaning "self," and the French word *mobile,* meaning "moving."

Although the automobile was first produced in Europe, the United States completely dominated world production for the first half of the 20th century. This domination was possible because of the extensive use of mass production techniques. In the second half of the century, the situation changed considerably, and Western European and Japanese companies became major producers and exporters. It was the Japanese who ultimately emerged as the world leader in automobile manufacturing. Led by Toyota and Nissan (Datsun), Japanese production figures surged past those of the United States in 1980.

Today most of the world's major automobile companies are international in technology and organization. Companies that produce only at home but sell products internationally are called multinational trading companies. Companies that own or control production facilities in more than one country are called multinational corporations.

## MODEL DESIGN

As part of an effort to persuade drivers to buy new cars, manufacturers regularly implement engineering advances and major styling changes. Engineering changes may stem from the desire or need to increase safety or energy efficiency or decrease exhaust emissions that pollute the air. The annual model change, along with a yearly price increase, was established in the 1930s by General Motors. The company had created an art and color department in 1927, which was later called the styling division.

For decades the consumer has had a variety of automobile models from which to choose. Today there is a choice from hundreds of named or numbered models and thousands of variations based on body type, engine capacity, and price class.

The design process is lengthy and complicated. Although the process has become largely standardized, the time gap between the first display of a model on a drawing board and its debut in a dealer's showroom can be as long as five years.

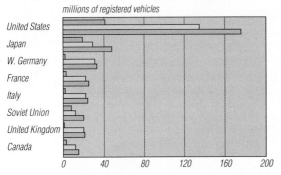

**Leading Countries in Motor-Vehicle Registrations for 1986**

millions of registered vehicles

United States
Japan
W. Germany
France
Italy
Soviet Union
United Kingdom
Canada

0    40    80    120    160    200

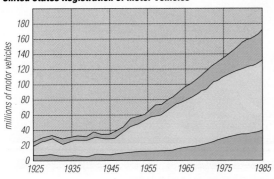

**United States Registration of Motor Vehicles**

millions of motor vehicles

180
160
140
120
100
80
60
40
20
0

1925    1935    1945    1955    1965    1975    1985

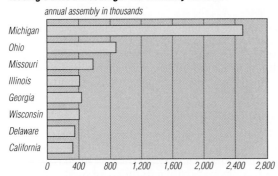

**Leading States in Passenger-Car Assembly for 1988**

annual assembly in thousands

Michigan
Ohio
Missouri
Illinois
Georgia
Wisconsin
Delaware
California

0    400    800    1,200    1,600    2,000    2,400    2,800

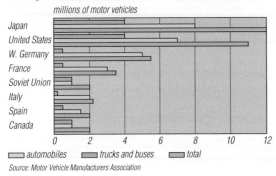

**Leading Countries in Motor-Vehicle Production for 1987**

millions of motor vehicles

Japan
United States
W. Germany
France
Soviet Union
Italy
Spain
Canada

0    2    4    6    8    10    12

automobiles    trucks and buses    total

Source: Motor Vehicle Manufacturers Association

Usually even before initial planning begins, experts called market-research analysts collect information that indicates what kind of automobile the general public seems to prefer. Occasionally, however, style innovations can be traced to the whims of particular individuals. The tail fins of the 1950s, for example, originated with General Motors' chief stylist at the time, Harley J. Earl. After seeing them on World War II fighter planes, he decided to add fins to the 1948 Cadillac. The design spread to other cars and retained its popularity for more than ten years.

Before a new model design can be approved for mass manufacturing, there are several important steps. These are prototype building, testing, evaluation, correction, design of production machinery, and the manufacture of that machinery. The prototype process begins with clay models that are covered with colored plastic and other materials to simulate the surface of a real car. This mock-up provides the basis for engineering drawings and blueprints. The model changeover finally occurs when a plant's machinery is altered to meet the requirements of the new parts for the new design. Certain parts, however, can be produced more economically and efficiently by outside manufacturers. The decision to make or buy a part is made by the management team and the industrial engineering staff.

Cars have traditionally been designed for two markets—North America, which preferred larger and heavier cars as long as fuel prices were low, and Europe and Japan, which because of different economic conditions preferred smaller, more fuel-efficient vehicles. Economic situations, particularly the rising cost of gasoline in the 1970s and '80s, however, prompted the development of a "world class car." Fuel-efficient, lightweight, boxy in profile, suited for most climates, and able to be produced with components manufactured around the world, this type of car has been produced by many manufacturers, including Ford, Honda, Volkswagen, Chrysler, and Fiat.

### Safety

From its beginnings, the automobile posed serious safety problems because of its weight and its speed. Over the 20th century the rates of death and injury have declined in terms of passenger miles, yet the numbers have risen because of the increased numbers of vehicles on the road.

Early attempts to improve auto safety statistics focused on driver training, vehicle maintenance, highway improvement, and law enforcement. The automobile industry in the United States became heavily involved during the 1960s, when the basic design of the vehicle and the need to add special safety features began to undergo increasing scrutiny. Government regulations on auto design had been imposed as early as 1903 in Great Britain, when the Motor Car Act regulated details of the width, tires, and brakes of the London taxicab. But it was in the United States that some of the strictest safety regulations affecting automobile design were established. The bulk of these regulations stemmed from the creation of the National Traffic and Motor Vehicle Safety Act of 1966. That same year the publication of consumer advocate Ralph Nader's book, 'Unsafe at Any Speed', increased public concern with automobile safety.

Government regulations issued worldwide in the 1960s and '70s were concerned with making cars that were less likely to get into accidents and in which, once in them, occupants were protected as completely as possible. Several features were introduced or improved. These included safety belts, bumpers, braking systems, and door locks.

The trend toward regulation was reversed in the early 1980s. Some standards were eased, rescinded, or delayed as part of a deregulation movement of the United States government. The effect was worldwide. The United States had become the pacesetter in safety innovations, and manufacturers in other countries adopted United States standards if only to be able to sell their cars in the American market.

### Emissions

Although pollution of the atmosphere has always existed to some extent, the concentration of thousands of motor vehicles in some areas increased the problem dramatically. Auto engine exhausts contribute from half of the atmospheric pollution in most industri- alized cities up to about 80 percent in Los Angeles, Calif. These exhausts include hydrocarbons and oxides of three elements: carbon, nitrogen, and sulfur. Tiny amounts of poisonous trace elements such as lead, cadmium, and nickel are also present.

*A car undergoes a full-scale barrier test at 30.6 mph (49.2 kph) with dummies restrained by lap and shoulder belts.*

General Motors Safety Research & Development Lab, General Motors Corporation

Pollution control devices have been demanded, particularly by the governments of Japan, Canada, and the United States. A major improvement occurred in 1975, when catalytic converters that substantially reduce toxic emissions were introduced by major automobile manufacturers. By the 1980s cars equipped with emission control devices produced 92 percent less carbon monoxide, 95 percent fewer hydrocarbons, and 51 percent fewer oxides of nitrogen than did most uncontrolled cars.

### Energy Efficiency

Rising gasoline costs and worries of dependence on oil-producing nations spurred public demand for fuel- efficient cars in the United States in the 1970s and '80s. The United States had lagged behind Western Europe and Japan in accepting and producing smaller, fuel-efficient vehicles. In 1975, however, the Energy Policy and Conservation Act (EPCA) set minimum standards for gasoline mileage that each domestic and imported automobile in the United States must reach by 1985. Automobile manufacturers complained that the technology required to meet the standards would be too expensive to develop. But the public was strongly behind the change, as indicated by increasing sales of foreign cars. In 1976 General Motors began "downsizing" their models in an attempt to compete with the smaller, more fuel-efficient Japanese and European models.

Some major automakers build cars with diesel engines. Diesel fuel is cheaper and provides increased mileage, but the diesel engine is expensive, raising the cost of a car considerably. Also diesel fuel is not available at all gasoline stations.

Research has begun anew on battery-powered cars. Along with some powered by steam, these were popular in the early days of the automobile, but they could not compete with cars powered by the then inexpensive gasoline. Some electric cars and trucks are in use today, but mass production of such vehicles awaits the discovery of batteries that are far superior to any now available.

### MASS PRODUCTION

The production of an automobile involves the assembly of more than 15,000 individual parts. In a modern manufacturing plant these parts are moved in a variety of ways: through the air suspended from traveling hooks, carried along on conveyor belts, or transported by forklift trucks or electronic "mules." Each part is directed to the exact spot at which it is needed at precisely the proper time.

This method of manufacture is called assembly line production. The system is laid out in a river-like pattern. Similar to tributary streams merging to form a principal river, numerous tributary lines converge at assembly points, or stations. There the parts they carry are put together and then moved on to a further stage of assembly. The windows and windshield and appliances such as the radio, heater, windshield wipers, and cigarette lighter are installed as the car

*Sheet metal pieces are welded (top left) to the floor pan, or basic body component. Body joints are soldered (bottom left) in enclosed booths for cleaner conditions. Bodies are dipped into electrically charged anti-rust solution (bottom right) before painting. Four coats of paint are applied (top right) before baking.*

Photos (both pages), GM Assembly Division, General Motors Corporation

nears the end of the assembly line. All along the line inspectors test the various parts of the car. At a large plant using an assembly line, vehicles can be produced at the rate of 60 to 80 per hour.

The assembly line is, perhaps, the outstanding contribution of the automobile industry to technology. First introduced in the United States on a large scale by Henry Ford in 1913, it consists of two basic elements: a conveyor system and the limitation of each worker to a single, repetitive task. Today the largest companies produce frames and components in regional assembly factories. The final assembly is then completed at a separate plant.

The boredom that often results from performing the same task all day is a major problem for some workers on assembly lines. In Sweden, Saab and Volvo employees have devised various methods by which each worker is responsible for a number of tasks rather than for just one.

## History

The development of the gasoline engine is generally attributed to Karl Benz and Gottlieb Daimler of Germany in about 1885. The firm of Daimler-Benz, along with the Panhard company of France, is one of the oldest automobile firms in the world. By 1888 Benz employed 50 workers to produce his automobile. Today products of the Daimler-Benz company are sold under the name Mercedes-Benz.

The major manufacturing companies of Western Europe dominated the automotive world before World War I. With the development of the assembly line, however, the United States was propelled into the lead by the end of the war. By 1926 Ford, then the leading world manufacturer, was producing half of all motor vehicles. Advanced organizational strategies of General Motors, including its development of manufacturing divisions, carried it into the primary

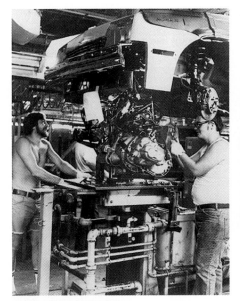

An instrument panel is put together (bottom left) on a sub-assembly line before being installed in an auto body. A transverse engine and front-wheel-drive assembly (top left) is lifted into a body. An assembled car (top right) is given a simulated road test. Completed vehicles (bottom right) are loaded on haulaway transports for shipment to dealers.

position by the late 1920s. The third major United States manufacturer, Chrysler, was founded in 1925.

The close of World War II ended the dominance of the United States. Major companies sprang up in Western Europe and then in Japan. In Britain, Leyland Motors and British Motor Holdings united in 1968 to form the British Leyland Motor Corporation. After three name changes, the company assumed the name BL Public Limited Company in 1982. In a joint venture with Honda Motor Company of Japan, it now produces Triumph Acclaims in the United Kingdom.

German automobile production has centered on the Volkswagen company. Originally state-owned, the company was denationalized in the 1960s. Fiat continued to dominate Italian motor vehicle production, and the French industry was based on Renault, Peugeot, Citroën, and Simca. Swedish-built Volvos and Saabs were also of increasing importance in world automobile production.

Since World War II the world output of motor vehicles has more than tripled, and Japan has become the world leader. From the early 1980s to the early 1990s there was a general decline in the automobile industry. Japan continued to fare quite well, but the industry suffered badly elsewhere.

Motor vehicles and various automotive products are significant commodities in world trade today. About 25 percent of the world output of motor vehicles enters international commerce. The automotive industry is an indicator of a nation's economic health in such industrialized countries as the United States, the United Kingdom, Japan, France, Italy, Sweden, and Germany.

Some national governments have been unhappy about the enormous economic influence of this industry. Prior to 1991, in a few countries, such as the Soviet Union, the government was directly involved in the ownership, planning, and development of motor

*A computer model of an automobile is designed with detailed characteristics recorded. The computer can then predict the interactions of various elements before a prototype is built.*

vehicle firms. Since World War II the industry has been an important consideration in the economic policies of the British and Japanese governments, among others. State support of the nations' automobile industries has been granted in the form of subsidies in Italy, the United Kingdom, and France. In addition many governments impose tariffs and quotas in order to protect domestic automakers against competition from imports.

This concern and activity are the result, in part, to the great number of people employed by the industry in the United States, Western Europe, and Japan. For example, the manufacture of automobiles and other vehicles is the primary industry in the United States. Nearly one-fifth of the population works for the companies that produce, distribute, maintain, or are in some other way connected with motor vehicles. A decline in sales affects not only those directly involved in the industry but those in peripheral businesses as well. These include, among others, the manufacturing of steel and rubber as well as the processing of scrap metal.

The rise in gasoline prices in the 1970s and '80s had a major impact on the automobile industry and illustrates the industry's significance to national economies. As fuel prices increased, so did the demand for smaller, fuel-efficient cars. In the United States consumers turned to imports, particularly the Japanese models, which they perceived to be not only fuel-efficient but also of better quality. In fact, in 1980 only auto manufacturing companies in Japan made significant economic gains. This was attributed not only to the increased number of cars they sold but also to lower labor costs in Japan as well as to Japanese

companies' increased use of robotics, a trend predicted to increase worldwide in the 1980s and '90s. (*See also* Automobile.)

## CAREERS IN THE INDUSTRY

Automobiles are important worldwide. Although Western Europe, North America, and Japan are manufacturing centers, every nation has a highway system, numerous vehicles, and many automobile-related jobs. Cars are probably most important to the economy of the United States, where one out of six wage earners makes a living in or related to the industry.

There are so many types of jobs related to automobiles that the average person can barely imagine them. Industry workers include such diverse types as the mechanic who uses sophisticated electronic equipment to diagnose an automatic transmission problem; the chemical engineer whose objective is to improve the durability of auto paint; the specialist who hand-sews the upholstery for a restored classic car; and the clerk in an auto parts store who serves weekend home mechanics.

Many automotive jobs require a high degree of education, intelligence, and talent. Cars have miniature computers and electronic ignitions that must be designed, installed, and maintained. Manufacturers use automated techniques for maximum productivity, and great skill and much training are needed to operate these machines. Repair shops have complex testing devices in order to save time and improve automotive performance.

### Research

The first steps in the production of an automotive vehicle are in a research laboratory. Here chemists, physicists, and computer scientists work with metallurgists and engineers. Together they plan, evaluate, and test all promising ideas.

*A designer sits in a "seating buck" in order to study the interior and its basic structural aesthetics.*

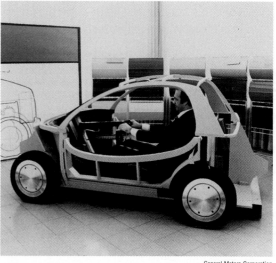

*A sculptor creates a precise clay model of a proposed design.*
General Motors Corporation

**Chemist.** Seeks to improve existing forms of fuel and to develop new ones; looks for ways to improve existing products such as rubber, plastics, and paints; tries to discover new materials that are better than the ones in use.

**Computer scientist.** Helps to improve automotive design and many of the manufacturing operations by use of the computer.

**Electronics engineer.** Develops transistorized systems for improving safety, performance, and reliability of the vehicle.

**Instrumentation engineer.** Develops new methods for measuring automotive characteristics, from fuel consumption to the best angles for seating comfort.

**Librarian.** Catalogs, files, and maintains data pertaining to all phases of automotive research, engineering, and production.

**Mechanical engineer.** Develops new engines, bearings, transmission and gear mechanisms, and other products; studies stress and vibration analysis and the means of reducing injuries in accidents.

**Metallurgist.** Develops new metal materials and products and the processes for making them.

**Physicist.** Investigates fundamental problems of matter and energy as they relate to automotive design and performance.

### Engineering Laboratories

The next steps in the production or improvement of an automobile take place in engineering laboratories. Here the findings of research scientists and engineers are put to practical use. It is here also that the new ideas that are produced by research are converted into products that have practical application in automotive vehicles.

**Acoustical engineer.** Works on sound-deadening problems, traces car noises to their sources, and specifies means of reducing noise.

**Body engineer.** Works with stylists and design engineers to lay out durable automobile bodies that can be manufactured efficiently.

**Drafter.** Makes drawings of engineering ideas.

**Electrical engineer.** Works on wiring circuitry, storage battery problems, and related projects.

**Executive engineer.** Acts as engineering branch business manager.

**Hydraulic engineer.** Works with specific problems concerning automobile transmissions, brakes, and other parts that are wholly or partly driven hydraulically.

**Mechanical engineer.** Makes layouts for engines, transmissions, and chassis and for their components such as carburetors and differential gears.

**Safety engineer.** Develops systems for improving motoring safety and makes recommendations for changes that improve driving safety.

### Styling

While the current year's automobile models are being manufactured and sold, designers are working on models to be marketed four or five years hence.

**Clay modeler.** Translates the designer's sketches into clay models, first in miniature, then in full size.

**Color engineer.** Specifies the color schemes to be used on upcoming models.

**Designer.** Originates the general body style of the new motorcar.

**Interior stylist.** Designs items for interiors, including upholstery, dashboard, and hardware.

**Styling engineer.** Serves as a liaison between stylists and engineers and sees that the work of both departments is coordinated.

### Testing

Proposed new automobile models are given exhaustive tests on proving grounds and test racks.

It is here that engineers learn how the vehicle will react to actual driving conditions. Most occupations in this category are for engineers.

**Instrumentation layout person.** Devises the special equipment that enables test drivers to measure the performance of an automobile.

**Test analyst.** Studies test data and compiles reports.

**Test driver.** Drives the car over varying terrains at high speeds and under severe conditions. The driver makes full reports on how the cars handle and must be able to offer suggestions for improvement.

## Preparation for Production

After a new model has been designed, built, tested, and approved, its blueprints, working models, and test results are given to the manufacturing department. Here skilled production workers begin the task of mass-producing the automobile. A wide variety of specialists in the production area contribute their skills.

The tool-and-die maker is largely responsible for making the new machinery that is needed to form and build the automobile. First the tool-and-die maker fabricates parts by hand. Then models are duplicated on computerized, robotic machines. There are about 75 classifications for tool-and-die makers. Each requires a four-year apprenticeship.

**Drop-forge repairer.** Restores to original condition a special die that has become worn after normal use.

**Keller operator.** Runs a kind of duplicating machine that shapes metal to the contours and dimensions of a model handmade from mahogany or metal.

**Pattern maker.** Reads blueprints of patterns and coreboxes (the forms for molds and cores) for foundries and builds them by hand machining.

**Toolmaker.** Reads blueprints describing a new cutting tool and then runs machines that fabricate the tool to precise dimensions.

## Manufacturing

The first step in manufacturing an automobile is the stamping, forging, casting, and machining of such materials as steel, aluminum, zinc, and plastics.

**Coremaker.** Forms sand into a solid and places it in a mold to create space for hollow castings.

---

### *Some Notable Automobiles and Their Manufacturers*

*Some famous automobiles are not included below because they are covered in the main text of this article or in other articles in Compton's Encyclopedia (see Fact-Index).*

**Alfa Romeo** (1910– ). Italy. Most recently made by Alfa Romeo SpA in Milan.

**Alpine** (1955– ). France. Most recently by Régie Nationale des Usines Renault.

**AMC Cars** (1954–87). United States. American Motors Corporation, Kenosha, Wis. (now a division of Chrysler).

**Aston Martin** (1922– ). Great Britain. Most recently made by Aston Martin Lagonda Ltd., Newport Pagnell (a division of Ford).

**Audi** (1910–39; 1965– ). Germany. Most recently made by Auto Union GmbH, Ingolstadt, Germany.

**Austin** (1902–18) and **Austin-Healey** (1946–71). Great Britain. Austin Motor Company Ltd., Longbridge, Birmingham.

**Avanti II** (1965– ). United States. Avanti Motor Company, South Bend, Ind.

**Bentley** (1920– ). Great Britain. Most recently by Bentley Motors Ltd., Crewe, Cheshire (owned by Rolls-Royce).

**Benz** (1885–1926). Germany. Benz & Cie, Rheinische Automobil und Motorenfabrik AG, Mannheim.

**BMW** (1928– ). Germany. Most recently by Bayerische Motoren-Werke AG, Munich.

**Bugatti** (1909–15; 1919–56). France. Automobiles Ettore Bugatti, Molsheim.

**Buick** (1903– ). United States. Buick Motor Car Company, Flint, Mich. (a division of General Motors).

**Cadillac** (1903– ). United States. Cadillac Motor Car Company, Detroit, Mich. (a division of General Motors).

**Checker** (1923–82). United States. Checker Motors Corporation, Kalamazoo, Mich.

**Chevrolet** (1911– ). United States. Chevrolet Motor Company, Detroit, Mich. (a division of General Motors).

**Chrysler** (1923– ). United States. Chrysler Corporation, Detroit, Mich.

**Citroën** (1919– ). France. Most recently by Peugeot SA, Paris.

**Cooper** (1948–71). Great Britain. Cooper Car Company Ltd., Byfleet, Surrey.

**Cord** (1929–37). United States. Last made by Elfman Motors, Inc., Philadelphia, Pa.

**Crossley** (1904–37). Great Britain. Crossley Motors Ltd., Gorton, Manchester.

**Daimler** (1896– ). Great Britain. Most recently by BL Public, Ltd., Company.

**Datsun** (intermittently, 1912– ). Japan. Most recently by Nissan Motor Company Ltd., Tokyo.

**De Soto** (1928–60). United States. Chrysler Motors Corporation.

**Dodge** (1914– ). United States. Most recently by Chrysler Motors Corporation, Detroit, Mich.

**Duesenberg** (1920–37; 1966– ). United States. Duesenberg Motor Company, Gardena, Calif.

**Edsel** (1957–59). United States. Ford Motor Company, Detroit, Mich.

**Essex** (1918–32). United States. Hudson Motor Car Company, Detroit, Mich.

**Excalibur SS** (1964– ). Excalibur Automobile Corporation, Milwaukee, Wis.

**Ferrari** (1940– ). Italy. Most recently by Società Esercizio Fabbriche Automobili e Corse Ferrari Maranello, Modena.

**Fiat** (1899– ). Italy. Fabbrica Italiana Automobili Torino (now Fiat SpA).

**Ford** (1903– ). United States. Ford Motor Company, Detroit, Mich.

**Frazer** (1946–51). United States. Kaiser-Frazer Corporation, Willow Run, Mich.

**Hillman** (1907–78). Great Britain. Last made by Hillman Motor Car Company Ltd., Coventry, Warwickshire.

**Hispano-Suiza** (1904–44). Spain. SA Hispano-Suiza, Barcelona.

**Honda** (1962– ). Japan. Honda Motor Company Ltd., Tokyo.

**Hudson** (1909–57). United States. Last made by American Motors Corporation, Kenosha, Wis.

**Humber** (1901–76). Great Britain. Last made by Humber Ltd., Ryton-on-Dunamore, Warwickshire.

**Hyundai** (1968– ). South Korea. Hyundai Motor Company, Ulsan.

**Jaguar** (1936– ). Great Britain. Most recently by BL Public, Ltd., Company.

**Jeep** (intermittently, 1903– ). United States. Originally Willys-Overland. Most recently by Chrysler Corporation.

**Die-casting machine operator.** Supervises pouring of materials into machines that automatically produce cast parts at high speeds.

**Forge operator.** Runs a hammer or press that forges hot metal blanks to desired dimensions.

**Foundry melter.** Operates a furnace in which various combinations of metals are liquefied by extreme heat so they can be poured into shaping molds.

**Machine operator.** Runs a machine, such as a lathe, drill, mill, or plane, that fabricates a material to specification standards.

**Maintenance person.** Repairs and renovates factory equipment.

**Materials handler.** Loads and unloads supplies that are carried by trucks, cars, and other vehicles.

**Metal finisher.** Files and polishes the body to prepare its surfaces for painting.

### Sales and Service

Once the automobile has been manufactured, it must be sold and maintained. There are numerous jobs in new and used auto sales and in all the related service areas. As automobiles have become more complex, the number of auto shops performing specialized work has increased.

**Mechanic.** Performs a broad range of light and heavy repair work that can include changing tires, diagnosing engine problems, estimating repair costs for insurance purposes, and performing a complete engine overhaul.

**Salesperson.** Works on the showroom floor or lot of a new or used car dealership. A salesperson needs excellent mechanical knowledge to answer the many questions of prospective buyers.

**Service manager.** Supervises the entire automotive service operation, dealing with customers, directing mechanics, and handling billings. The service manager has responsibility for shop efficiency.

**Specialty mechanic.** Acquires and uses expert knowledge of one aspect of automotive service. Special fields include transmissions and electrical equipment.

A useful book for career guidance is 'Opportunities in Automotive Service Careers' by Robert Weber (1988). (*See also* bibliography for Automobile.)

---

**Kaiser** (1946–55). United States. Last made by Willys Motors Inc., Willow Run, Mich.

**Lancia** (1906– ). Italy. Most recently by Fabbrica Automobili Lancia e Cia, Bolzano (a division of Fiat).

**La Salle** (1927–40). United States. Cadillac Motor Car Company, Detroit, Mich. (a division of General Motors).

**Lincoln** (1920– ). United States. Lincoln Motor Company, Detroit, Mich. (a division of Ford Motor Company).

**Lotus** (1952– ). Great Britain. Most recently by Lotus Cars Ltd. (a division of General Motors).

**Maserati** (1926– ). Italy. Officine Alfieri Maserati SpA, Modena.

**Mazda** (1960– ). Japan. Mazda Motor Corporation, Hiroshima.

**Mercedes-Benz** (1926– ). Germany. Daimler-Benz AG, Stuttgart-Untertürkheim. Preceded by the **Mercedes** (1901–26).

**Mercury** (1938– ). United States. Ford Motor Company, Detroit, Mich.

**M.G.** (1924–80). Great Britain. Morris Garages Ltd., Oxford. Most recently by BL Public, Ltd., Company.

**Mitsubishi** (1917–21; 1959– ). Japan. Mitsubishi Heavy Industries Ltd., Tokyo.

**Morgan** (1910– ). Great Britain. Morgan Motor Company Ltd., Malvern Link.

**Morris** (1913– ). Great Britain. Most recently by BL Public, Ltd., Company.

**Nash** (1917–57). United States. Last made by American Motors Corporation, Kenosha, Wis.

**Nissan** (1937–43; 1960– ). Japan. Nissan Motor Company Ltd., Tokyo.

**Oldsmobile** (1896– ). United States. Oldsmobile Division of General Motors Corporation, Lansing, Mich.

**Opel** (1898– ). Germany. Adam Opel AG, Rüsselsheim, Germany, (a subsidiary of General Motors).

**Packard** (1899–1958). United States. Last made by Studebaker-Packard Corporation, Detroit, Mich.

**Peugeot** (1889– ). France. Most recently by Peugeot SA, Paris.

**Pierce** and **Pierce-Arrow** (1901–38). United States. Last made by Pierce-Arrow Motor Car Company, Buffalo, N.Y.

**Plymouth** (1928– ). United States. Chrysler Corporation.

**Pontiac** (1926– ). United States. Pontiac Motor Company, Pontiac, Mich. (a division of General Motors).

**Porsche** (1948– ). Germany. Most recently by Dr Ing.h.c. F. Porsche KG, Stuttgart-Zuffenhausen, Germany.

**Rambler** (1902–13; 1950–69). United States. Last made by American Motors Corporation, Kenosha, Wis.

**Renault** (1898– ). France. Most recently by Renault-Volvo RVA, Boulogne-Billancourt.

**Riley** (1898–1969). Great Britain. Last made by Riley Motors Ltd., Abingdon.

**Rolls-Royce** (1904– ). Great Britain. Most recently by Rolls-Royce PLC, London.

**Rover** (1904– ). Great Britain. The Rover Company Ltd., Solihull, Warwickshire (a division of BMW AG, Munich).

**Saab** (1950– ). Sweden. Saab-Scania AB, Linköping.

**Simca** (1935–81). France. Sté Industrielle de Mécanique et Carrosserie Automobile, Poissy.

**Singer** (1905–70). Great Britain. Last made by Singer Motors Ltd., Ryton-on-Dunsmore, Warwickshire.

**Stanley** (1897–1927). United States. Last made by Steam Vehicle Corporation of America, Newton, Mass.

**Studebaker** (1902–66). United States–Canada. Last made by Studebaker Corporation of Canada Ltd., Hamilton, Ontario.

**Stutz** (1911–35). United States. Last made by Stutz Motor Car Company of America, Indianapolis, Ind.

**Subaru** (1958– ). Japan. Fuji Heavy Industries Ltd., Tokyo.

**Sunbeam** (1899–1937; 1953–68). Great Britain. Last made by Sunbeam-Talbot Ltd., Ryton-on-Dunsmore, Warwickshire.

**Toyota** (1936– ). Japan. Most recently by Toyota Motor Corporation, Toyota City.

**Trabant** (1945–91). East Germany. Industrie-Vereinigung Volkseigner Fahrzeugwerke, Zwickau.

**Triumph** (1923– ). Great Britain. Most recently by Triumph Motor Company Ltd. (a division of BL Public, Ltd., Company).

**Tucker** (1946–48). United States. Tucker Corporation, Chicago.

**Vauxhall** (1903– ). Great Britain. Most recently by Vauxhall Motors Ltd., Luton.

**Volkswagen** (1936– ). Germany. Most recently by Volkswagenwerk AG, Wolfsburg, Germany.

**Volvo** (1927– ). Sweden. Most recently by Renault-Volvo RVA.

**Wolseley-Siddeley** (1904– ). Great Britain. Most recently by BL Public, Ltd., Company.

*The annual Memorial Day Indianapolis 500-mile race is about to start (left). The Borg-Warner trophy (right) is presented to the winner.*

**AUTOMOBILE RACING AND RALLIES.** For millions of people automobile racing and rallies are among the most exciting and colorful of all spectator sports. Rallies are not speed contests but tests of driving skill on the part of sports-car owners. A major automobile race probably attracts more spectators than does any other single sporting event. In the United States, for example, the particularly popular annual Memorial Day 500-mile (805-kilometer) race at Indianapolis, Ind., is attended by more than 300,000 persons. Crowds greater than 500,000 have attended the grueling contest that is run over the mountain roads of the Nürburgring, in the rugged Eifel region of western Germany.

The first official automobile race was held in France in 1894. The 19 competing cars traveled from Paris to Rouen. A similar race took place near Chicago, Ill., on Thanksgiving Day in 1895. It required 8 hours and 23 minutes for the winner, J. Frank Duryea, to travel the 54-mile (87-kilometer) course. In 1904 a world governing body of automobile racing was founded. It has had its present name, International Automobile Federation, since 1947.

The first Indianapolis 500-mile race was in 1911. The winning car averaged about 75 miles (121 kilometers) per hour. In 1990 the winner's average speed was a record 185.981 miles (299 kilometers) per hour. Cars were covering the required 200 laps in about 3 hours. Each lap is 2½ miles (4 kilometers). (For Indianapolis 500 winners, *see* table in Fact-Index.)

### The Grand Prix and Other Competitions

Grand Prix cars are built according to a variety of formulas. The contest is for open-wheeled, single-seater racing cars and is run on a closed road circuit. Some are run on regular roads, others on specially built tracklike circuits. Major Grand Prix races are run throughout Europe and North America. Probably the world's best known is the Le Mans 24-hour Grand Prix d'Endurance, which has been run annually, with few exceptions, since 1923 at the Sarthe road-racing circuit near Le Mans, France.

Rebuilt stock cars—standard mass-produced automobiles—compete in stock-car races. They may run in measured-mile trials and in circular- or oval-track races. Stock cars also compete in long-distance road races and in so-called "economy runs" that demonstrate which model can travel a given highway distance with the lowest gasoline consumption. Lap speeds of about 200 miles (322 kilometers) per hour are not uncommon for these cars.

The sole purpose of a drag race is to measure acceleration. From a standing start, the driver tries to cover a given distance in the shortest possible time. The course is usually ¼ mile (0.4 kilometer). The cars used are generally of the hot-rod variety, with rebuilt (souped-up) light stock-car engines.

Other types of automobile competition include off-road racing, hill climbs, hill trials, gymkhanas, and even historic (classic or antique) meets. Off-road racing allows for different vehicle categories, including two- and four-wheel drive, motorcycles, and "Baja Bugs," which are modified Volkswagen sedans. One major off-road race is the Mexican 1,000, with a course that includes long, straight stretches of open desert, sudden detours, rock-strewn washes, boulder-covered rock beds, sandy beaches, and tufted dunes.

Hill climbs are short-distance races against the clock, on mountain roads. Only one car races at a time, from a standing start to a flying finish. Hill trials refer to a particular British event consisting of an off-road hill climb for two-wheel-drive sports cars. The typical vehicle usually consists of a small, lightweight chassis

On a twisting 2½-mile (4-kilometer) course, cars compete at the Daytona International Speedway. Except for the streamlined bodies, the cars are made of regular Volkswagen automobile components.
Daytona International Speedway

powered by a mass-produced engine, with thin front tires and fat rear ones. This type of competition is especially rough on the low gears of a car's transmission and on its tires. In Europe, hill climbs for motorcycles are also held.

The gymkhana is a driving skill and maneuverability test with obstacles, usually including a selection of slalom S-bends, short straights, a reversing test, U-turns, and other similar elements. Each car goes through alone and is timed. Drivers in a sports-car rally must maintain—within tenths of a second— a carefully set average speed over public roads. The driver does not know what course to follow or the constantly varying speeds at which he is to travel until formal instructions are given at the starting line. A navigator spots landmarks and figures speeds. Secret speed checks and control points along the way record the drivers' progress. The rally winner is the driver who adheres most closely to the average speed established by the rally organizers.

**AUTOPSY.** The dissection, or cutting apart, and examination of a dead body is called autopsy. Also called postmortem (from the Latin for "after death"), or necropsy, it is usually used to determine the cause of death or to observe the effects of disease.

An autopsy is performed by a pathologist, a medical doctor with special training in analyzing body tissues and substances. The pathologist examines the body both externally and by removing organs and tissue samples. The modern autopsy often includes highly specialized scientific instruments and procedures. These can extend the examination to body structures too small to be seen except with an electron microscope and to chemical analyses that reveal concentrations of only a few parts per billion.

Although often associated only with forensic, or legal, medicine in the determination of the cause or details of death from foul play, the autopsy serves a number of other purposes as well. It provides opportunities for the salvage of organs and hormones for use in medical treatment of living persons. It is invaluable in the anatomical education of physicians. It is also very important in studying how and why certain illnesses cause death and what happens to the various body systems in illness.

The first dissections for the study of disease were done by the Alexandrian physicians Herophilus and Erasistratus in about 300 BC. The Greeks and Indians cremated their dead without examination. The Romans, Chinese, and Muslims all had taboos about opening the body. Human dissections were not permitted in the West during the Middle Ages. Not until the rebirth of anatomy in the Renaissance was it possible to distinguish the abnormal from the normal. Leonardo da Vinci dissected 30 corpses, noting abnormal anatomy. His anatomical drawings are well-known. The autopsy came of age with Giovanni Morgagni, the Italian father of modern pathology, who in 1761 described what could be seen in the body with the naked eye. The gross (naked-eye) autopsy reached its culmination with the Viennese Karl von Rokitansky in the 19th century. It was the German pathologist Rudolf Virchow who in 1858 promoted the cellular doctrine—that changes in cells are the basis of the understanding of disease—in both pathology and autopsy. He established that all cells come from preexisting cells and that disease is altered cell function or altered relations or both. Ann Giudici Fettner

**AVERROËS** (1126–98). One of the major Islamic scholars of the Middle Ages, Averroës wrote commentaries on the Greek philosophers Plato and Aristotle. These works contributed significantly to the development of both Jewish and Christian thought in subsequent centuries.

Averroës was born in Córdoba, Spain, in 1126. He was thoroughly educated in Muslim science, medicine, philosophy, and law. He became chief judge at Córdoba and personal physician to the city rulers.

Between 1169 and 1195 Averroës wrote a series of commentaries on most of Aristotle's works and on Plato's 'Republic'. His penetrating mind enabled him to present the thought of these philosophers competently and to add considerably to its understanding. (See also Aristotle; Plato.)

Averroës wrote several original works. His first book, 'General Medicine', was written from 1162 to 1169. Three religious-philosophical treatises written in 1179 to 1180 have survived, but most of his legal works and all his theological books have been lost. He died at Marrakesh in North Africa in 1198.

*The Boeing 717-200 twinjet is the first airplane to come of the combined heritage of Boeing and McDonnell Douglas. It is also the first airplane to be cooperatively certified by both the United States Federal Aviation Administration (FAA) and Europe's Joint Airworthiness Authority (JAA).*

# AVIATION

The development of the boat for transportation on water and of the wheel for travel on land took centuries. In contrast, the development of the airplane for carrying passengers and goods through the air has occurred in only about half a century (*see* Airplane, "Airplane History").

Today, record distances set while traveling in the air are measured in hours rather than in miles. Jet airliners, for example, have made a continent only a few hours wide (*see* Transportation). Aviation has shrunk the globe and enlarged people's horizons by bringing nations closer. In war and in peace, aviation had a far-reaching influence on the economic, social, and political climate of the 20th century.

## ECONOMIC IMPACT OF AVIATION

The airplane is a vital machine in the transportation system. It facilitates the production and distribution of a nation's goods and services. It also furnishes employment for a large number of people.

The airplane has brought into being a whole new industry—the aviation industry. Each of its three segments is a great industry in itself. These segments are aircraft, missile, and spacecraft manufacturing; air transport; and general aviation. The airplane has also brought changes in trade routes, national economies, and municipal development. (*See also* Aerospace Industry; Guided Missile; Rocket; Space Travel.)

From its simple beginning in the Dayton, Ohio, bicycle shop of the Wright brothers, aircraft manufacturing has grown rapidly into an industrial giant (*see*

. . . . . . . . . . . . . . . . . . . . . . . . . . . . . . . . . . . . . . . . . . .

*This article was critically reviewed by Robert van der Linden, Associate Curator of Aeronautics, National Air and Space Museum, Smithsonian Institution, and Richard D. Gless, aviator and flight engineer and former basic flight instructor, U.S. Navy.*

Wright, Wilbur and Orville). Today, the buildings of one large aircraft manufacturer alone sprawl over an area that is equal to that of a dozen football fields.

In 1940, a year before the United States entered World War II, President Franklin D. Roosevelt called on the aviation industry to produce 50,000 airplanes a year. This was more than it had produced in its entire history. In 1944, when United States aircraft production reached an all-time high, almost double that number had been manufactured.

### Air Transport

The airplane has increased in importance from a means of emergency or luxury travel to one of the basic forms of transportation. Today the world's airlines fly some 1.1 billion passengers yearly (*see* Airline). The air carriers handle more intercity passenger-miles of traffic than the railroads. Many times more people cross the oceans by air than cross by ship. The possibilities of air transportation have reached even greater proportions with the high-speed and large-capacity jets. (*See also* Airplane; Jet Propulsion.)

The rise of the airplane has affected other industries as well. Airways crisscrossing a country or girdling the globe make it possible for people to enjoy fresh fruit and vegetables from faraway places. Letters sent from across an ocean may reach their destination on the same day. Besides maintaining a steady increase in air express and airmail, the airlines have moved into the field of heavy freight. While cost of air transportation is high compared with costs per mile of water, rail, and truck transport, manufacturers can save money by shipping by air if total distribution costs are computed. They can, for example, reduce inventories, warehouse space, and crating costs and make faster deliveries. (*See also* Postal Service.)

## THE USERS OF AIRSPACE

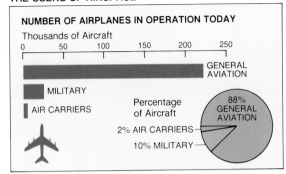

**NUMBER OF AIRPLANES IN OPERATION TODAY**

Thousands of Aircraft

GENERAL AVIATION

MILITARY

AIR CARRIERS

Percentage of Aircraft

88% GENERAL AVIATION

2% AIR CARRIERS

10% MILITARY

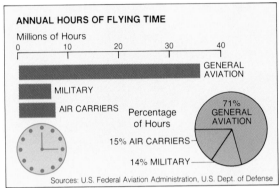

**ANNUAL HOURS OF FLYING TIME**

Millions of Hours

GENERAL AVIATION

MILITARY

AIR CARRIERS

Percentage of Hours

71% GENERAL AVIATION

15% AIR CARRIERS

14% MILITARY

Sources: U.S. Federal Aviation Administration, U.S. Dept. of Defense

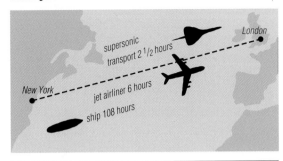

*Crossing the Atlantic*

supersonic transport 2 1/2 hours

London

New York

jet airliner 6 hours

ship 108 hours

*Supersonic transport allows a traveler to eat breakfast in New York City and arrive in London before lunchtime.*

### General Aviation

The greatest part of civil flying consists of general, or utility, aviation. The more than 100 purposes served by general aviation are classified into four major types. These are business, commercial, instructional, and pleasure. General aviation underwent phenomenal growth after World War II. Although the airlines have achieved a leading place in transportation, general aviation exceeds them in the number of aircraft and the hours and miles flown annually.

In 1990 there were about 5,800 airliners in the United States, utility aircraft totaled more than 220,000, or about 38 times as many. Moreover, aircraft in general aviation flew more than 43 million hours annually—5.7 times as many hours as were flown by the airliners, for four times as many miles.

Business corporation executives, sales people, engineers, and others who save money by saving time have made the most use of the fast transportation offered by the airplane. Small jet planes such as the Learjet and the French-built Dassault Falcon are produced specifically for use by corporations. Business people running their own small businesses often pilot their own planes.

Commercial flying consists of aviation services performed for hire. Conventional airplanes and helicopters, for example, dust and spray crops, orchards, and forests with insecticides and fertilizers, and they can also sow seeds. They also deposit chemicals for controlling weeds or defoliating (taking the leaves off) cotton and other crops, which makes

mechanical picking easier. Airplanes are used for patrolling pipelines and power and telephone lines. Planes are excellent observation posts for forest fire patrol, mapping, aerial photography, weather study, exploration, and mineral prospecting. Airplanes are also chartered for skywriting. Air taxi operators haul passengers and cargo.

Instructional flying by civilians, which boomed after World War II, is again increasing. Pleasure flying includes local and cross-country hops for sight-seeing, vacationing, and hunting, fishing, and other sports.

### New Routes for Trade and Travel

Another important effect of aviation has been to change the pattern of world trade. The airplane made the need for trade routes over oceans, through mountain passes, and around deserts obsolete. The airplane not only flies over these obstacles but also reduces the total miles of travel because its route is more direct.

The airplane can fly the great circle routes, which are the shortest distances around the globe when wind and other factors are taken into consideration. For example, a traveler going from Los Angeles, Calif., to the Scandinavian countries does not go across the United States from west to east and then across the Atlantic Ocean and up the English Channel, as land- and sea-based transportation modes would dictate. Instead the air passenger flies northeast from Los Angeles over Canada, Greenland, and Iceland, along the great circle route, to Copenhagen, Denmark.

Another economic benefit of aviation is the development of isolated and sparsely populated areas. Alaska, for example, has many sections that are rich in natural resources yet are inaccessible except by air. The mountain backbone of South America is a barrier to land transportation from coast to coast, but airplanes fly across it daily. Countries with scattered populations, such as Australia, are unified by the airplane.

However, the airplane both benefits cities and creates problems for them. It improves transportation, but airports are costly (*see* Airport). The jet transports need longer runways than do piston-engine aircraft because jet transports carry greater fuel and passenger loads.

**Air Distances from United States Gateway Cities to Foreign Places**

Air Distance $\dfrac{1,000}{\text{Statute Miles}}$

1 statute mile = 1.6 kilometers

*Most of the mileages are airport-to-airport distances along great circle routes. However, they may not agree with perfect great circle mileages because they follow airline routes, which may not be direct.*

A COMPTON'S MAP

If the airport is too close to a city or is surrounded by homes, industries, or unfavorable terrain, it may not be possible to lengthen the runways for the jetliners that need extended distances to land and take off. This, combined with similar problems associated with the early jet airplanes, created difficulties at Washington National Airport, which for many years was the only airport to serve the Washington, D.C. area. Washington-Dulles International Airport was built in Virginia to solve these problems because the area had more land space. In Chicago jet traffic was shifted from Midway Airport to O'Hare International Airport after World War II for similar reasons. In the New York City area jet traffic was shifted from the La Guardia and Newark, N.J., terminals to the John F. Kennedy International Airport in the 1970s.

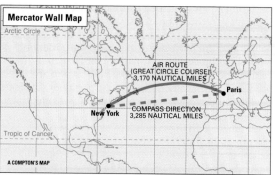

**Mercator Wall Map**

AIR ROUTE (GREAT CIRCLE COURSE) 3,170 NAUTICAL MILES

COMPASS DIRECTION 3,285 NAUTICAL MILES

New York

Paris

A COMPTON'S MAP

*Mercator maps are designed for use by ships. On this type of map projection, the shortest distance plotted for aircraft would be a curve rather than a straight line.*

Chris Sorensen

*Aircraft have varied recreational uses. Hunters and fishers can fly to remote lake areas, often for just a weekend, on seaplanes.*

The entire traffic pattern of cities has been changed because of jets. Air travel is of little advantage if it takes an hour to drive to the airport just to fly to another city that is only an hour away. Highways have therefore been built for the specific purpose of connecting airports to cities.

There are more than 16,000 civil airports in the United States, including military airports with joint civil and military use. To meet the continuing demands of general aviation, federal funds are granted to city and state governments for improving existing airports and building new ones.

## SOCIAL EFFECTS OF AVIATION

Besides affecting economic life, aviation has had an important impact on the individual's relationship with society. It has shaped many aspects of daily life, including communication, education, culture, and recreation.

The airplane has speeded up communication by making person-to-person contact easier and by accelerating the movement of mail and printed matter, such as books, newspapers, and periodicals. A letter mailed by a writer from Paris can be read in New York City the following day. This advantage, however, has disappeared somewhat with the everyday use of even faster means of communication, such as the computer and the fax machine.

Even the educational system has felt the influence of aviation. At the elementary, secondary, and college levels, schools can equip young people with the skills needed for careers in aviation (*see* Aerospace Industry, "Careers in Aerospace"). The students also learn about the significant role that aviation plays in their daily lives.

### Influence on Culture and Recreation

Aviation has also molded the culture of many nations. A whole new vocabulary has come into being to describe aviation practices, policies, and social impacts. Aviation themes, for example, are found in stories, poems, paintings, movies, and songs.

The airplane has altered recreational habits as well. A person on vacation can see historic and scenic sites thousands of miles away within a short time. A visit to distant relatives, furthermore, can be made in a few hours.

Hunters and fishers can fly to remote lake areas, often for just a weekend. Fishes are stocked in lakes and mountain streams by airplane. Many resort areas have landing strips for private planes. Amateur and professional sports teams and players can maintain their playing schedules by traveling by air.

## POLITICAL IMPACT OF AVIATION

In the field of political life—in a citizen's relation to government—aviation has had a great influence. It has brought about sweeping changes in military, governmental, and international affairs.

The airplane revolutionized modern warfare. Aerial duels were fought in World War I, but in World War II the airplane played a vital part in the total war. A strong air force is a balanced combination of aircraft and missiles. Jet bombers and push-button missiles can deliver deadly bombs. No nation in the world is invincible to air attack. (*See also* Air Force; Guided Missile; Warfare.)

### Campaigning and Diplomacy

The airplane has brought a change in political campaigning. For example, presidential candidates can fly from one corner of the United States to the other, giving a speech in Los Angeles in the morning and one in New York City in the evening. By doing this they can reach many more voters than they could with any other form of campaigning, except for messages broadcast by radio or television.

Air travel by government officials is commonplace. The president of the United States has airplanes and helicopters for his own use. An important function of the federal government is the regulation of aviation for its safe and orderly operation (*see* section on Aviation Regulation).

It can be said that the airplane has reduced the world to neighborhood size. As people are brought closer together, it is hoped that their understanding of each other would grow accordingly. India is now no farther away from the United States than Europe was only a few decades ago.

Diplomats can fly quickly to trouble spots in any part of the globe. For many decades many countries' presidents never went far abroad while in office because of the time it took to travel to distant countries. Today, however, there are summit conferences attended by many government officials all over the world, thanks to speedy air travel.

# Aviation Regulation

Commercial aviation is a worldwide business. Governments of almost all nations have some control over it, and some countries have nationalized the industry. Private flying is also subject to regulation by government agencies.

The rules for commercial aviation are extensive. Those for private flying are similar to those for driving an automobile. The private pilot, for example, must pass an examination to get a license to fly.

Until 1978, in the United States the federal government regulated aviation. This was done to promote safety and to make sure the country had a sound national and international airline system. Because the airplane is one of the major means of transportation, rates, schedules, routes, and certain financial aspects of the airline industry were regulated in the public interest (see Airline).

While today the United States government no longer controls fares, schedules, routes, or the financial aspects of the domestic airline industry, it still regulates safety, controls the airways, and supervises the certification of aircraft and flight crews. Various cities, counties, and states within the United States also have aviation laws. (See also Airline, "Regulation and Deregulation"; Airport.)

The first major legislation to regulate aviation in the United States was the Air Commerce Act of 1926. It established an Aeronautics Branch in the Department of Commerce. Later this agency became the Bureau of Air Commerce. The department was authorized to license pilots, develop air navigation facilities, promote aviation safety, map airways, and furnish flight information. As civil aviation became big business, Congress wrote the Civil Aeronautics Act of 1938. Under the act the Civil Aeronautics Administration (CAA) and the Civil Aeronautics Board (CAB) came into existence in 1940. Until 1959 the CAA, under the Department of Commerce, was responsible for air safety, air-traffic control, operation of airways, aviation communications, and airport improvements. The CAB controlled fares, routes, and certain financial aspects of the industry.

The Federal Aviation Act of 1958 established the independent Federal Aviation Agency (FAA), which absorbed the CAA. The FAA also took over the CAB's authority to make and enforce safety rules. In 1966 the FAA was renamed the Federal Aviation Administration and became part of the Department of Transportation (DOT). The CAB investigated all airline accidents until 1967, when its safety functions were transferred to DOT. The FAA controls civil and military use of airspace. Its responsibilities include modernizing airways, installing radar, and training air-traffic controllers.

In an effort to phase out some federal control of airlines and to promote competition in the industry, Congress passed the Airline Deregulation Act of 1978. Gradually the CAB gave up control over fares, schedules, and routes until it went out of business altogether in 1985.

Today the National Transportation Safety Board (NTSB) and the DOT handle the CAB's other functions, including safety and the administration of the Small Communities Air Service Program, which subsidizes air service to smaller areas.

Deregulation has generally reduced fares by increasing competition among air carriers, and it has thus allowed the airlines to operate more efficiently. It has also, however, greatly increased airport congestion. Also, because of high operating costs, many airlines have either consolidated through mergers and acquisitions, or have gone out of business because they could not compete.

## Other Agencies Important to Aviation

Other United States agencies are also closely tied to the aviation industry. For example, the National Weather Service reports and forecasts weather for aviation. The Federal Communications Commission (FCC) controls radio facilities. The National Ocean Service publishes aeronautical charts. The National Aeronautics and Space Administration (NASA) conducts research in aviation and manages the nation's space program.

Connecticut became the first state to regulate aviation, in 1911. Now almost all states in the United States have aeronautics departments or commissions for licensing pilots and aircraft, zoning airports, and enforcing air safety.

Counties and municipalities are concerned chiefly with airport regulation. The states have granted local governments condemnation and zoning powers. The counties or cities may administer the airports. Sometimes neighboring cities establish an airport district. For example, the Port Authority of New York and New Jersey has jurisdiction over terminals in New York City and Newark, N.J.

## Control in Other Countries

While most nations regulate commercial aviation to some degree, recent economic and political trends have greatly changed aviation regulation policy throughout the world. Until 1984, Canadian civil aviation was heavily regulated. Following the United States's example, the Canadian government began its "freedom to move" policy, which increased competition among air carriers and also resulted in mergers and acquisitions. Now there are only two large airlines in Canada: Air Canada, which was privatized in 1989, and Canadian Airlines International.

As a result of Australia's economic upsurge in 1987, the Australian government also deregulated its airlines. Before 1987 only Qantas, Ansett, and Trans Australia were allowed to fly within Australia. Today other airlines are allowed to compete for passenger and freight dollars within the country.

In the early 1990s members of the European Union (formerly the European Communities) greatly liberalized the decades-old restrictions on commercial aviation within Europe. The privatization of several formerly state-run airlines, particularly British Airways, led the way towards greater competition within an economically "borderless" Europe. Great Britain was the first to promote a gradual, less traumatic liberalization for its home market under the administration of the Civil Aviation Authority. The impact of the new rules on the European Union is expected to be great.

The turmoil in the former Soviet Union also greatly altered the face of civil aviation. Once Aeroflot operated as the sole airline in the Soviet Union. Today in the Commonwealth of Independent States, Aeroflot survives as the airline of Russia and the international carrier of the Commonwealth of Independent States. In addition, Aeroflot's domestic operations in the other former Soviet republics served as the foundation for the emergence of new national airlines, such as Air Ukraine and Uzbek Air.

## International Regulation

Air policy agreements on an international level began after World War I. The Paris Convention of 1919 assigned sovereignty to each country over the airspace above it. The Pan American Convention on Commercial Aviation, held in Havana, Cuba, in 1928, defined the principles of air transport. The Warsaw Convention in 1929 established the rules that govern the liability of airlines for passengers, luggage, and cargo in international air travel. In 1944, representatives from about 50 nations met in Chicago, Ill., and founded the International Civil Aviation Organization (ICAO). The ICAO was made a specialized agency of the United Nations in 1947 (see United Nations). Headquartered in Montreal, Que., the organization had more than 160 members by the early 1990s. The work of the ICAO covers civil navigation, safety and regulation of international flights, economic aspects of transportation, and international law.

Another organization is the International Air Transport Association. This nongovernmental organization of world airlines was established in 1945. Its major purpose is to assure that international airline traffic moves with speed, efficiency, and economy.

## AVIATION SAFETY

Air transportation is safer, in terms of passenger-miles, than travel by automobile, and it compares favorably with travel by railroad and bus. Airlines have made it a priority to improve safety for passengers over the years. In 1930 there were 28 passenger fatalities for each 100 million passenger-miles (160 million kilometers). Today the figure is far less than one fatality for the same number of passenger-miles. More people die in automobile accidents each year than have been killed in the entire history of peacetime aviation in the United States.

In addition to the governmental organizations concerned with air safety, there are many private organizations. They include the Air Transport Association of America, composed of various airlines;

### Aircraft Nationality Marks*

| Country | Mark | Country | Mark |
|---|---|---|---|
| Afghanistan | YA | Lebanon | OD |
| Algeria | 7T | Lesotho | 7P |
| Angola | D2 | Liberia | EL |
| Argentina | LV, LQ | Libya | 5A |
| Australia | VH | Liechtenstein | HB |
| Austria | OE | Luxembourg | LX |
| Bahamas, The | C6 | Madagascar | 5R |
| Bangladesh | S2 | Malawi | 7QY |
| Barbados | 8P | Malaysia | 9M |
| Belgium | OO | Maldives | 8Q |
| Belize | V3 | Mali | TZ |
| Benin | TY | Malta | 9H |
| Bolivia | CP | Mauritania | 5T |
| Botswana | A2 | Mauritius | 3B |
| Brazil | PP, PT | Mexico | XA, XB, XC |
| Bulgaria | LZ | Monaco | 3A |
| Burkina Faso | XT | Morocco | CN |
| Burundi | 9U | Mozambique | C9 |
| Cambodia | XU | Myanmar | XY, XZ |
| Cameroon | TJ | Nepal | 9N |
| Canada | C, CF | Netherlands, The | PH |
| Central African Republic | TL | New Zealand | ZK, ZL, ZM |
| Chad | TT | Nicaragua | YN |
| Chile | CC | Niger | 5U |
| China | B | Nigeria | 5N |
| Colombia | HK | Norway | LN |
| Congo | TN | Oman | A40 |
| Costa Rica | TI | Pakistan | AP |
| Côte d'Ivoire | TU | Panama | HP |
| Cuba | CU | Paraguay | ZP |
| Cyprus | 5B | Peru | OB |
| Czech Republic | OK | Philippines | RP |
| Denmark | OY | Poland | SP |
| Djibouti | J2 | Portugal | CS, CR |
| Dominica | J7 | Qatar | A7 |
| Dominican Republic | HI | Romania | YR |
| Ecuador | HC | Rwanda | 9XR |
| Egypt | SU | Saudi Arabia | HZ |
| El Salvador | YS | Senegal | 6V, 6W |
| Equatorial Guinea | 3C | Sierra Leone | 9L |
| Ethiopia | ET | Singapore | 9V |
| Fiji | DQ | Somalia | 60 |
| Finland | OH | South Africa | ZS, ZT, ZU |
| France | F | Spain | EC |
| Gabon | TR | Sri Lanka | 4R |
| Germany | D | Sudan | ST |
| Ghana | 9G | Suriname | PZ |
| Greece | SX | Swaziland | 3D |
| Guatemala | TG | Sweden | SE |
| Guinea | 3X | Switzerland | HB |
| Guyana | 8R | Syria | YK |
| Haiti | HH | Tanzania | 5H |
| Honduras | HR | Thailand | HS |
| Hong Kong | VRH | Togo | 5V |
| Hungary | HA | Trinidad and Tobago | 9Y |
| Iceland | TF | Tunisia | TS |
| India | VT | Turkey | TC |
| Indonesia | PK | Uganda | 5X |
| Iran | EP | United Arab Emirates | A6 |
| Iraq | YI | United Kingdom | G |
| Ireland | EI, EJ | Colonies and | |
| Israel | 4X | Protectorates | VP, VQ, VR |
| Italy | I | United States | N |
| Jamaica | 6Y | Uruguay | CX |
| Japan | JA | Venezuela | YV |
| Jordan | JY | Vietnam | XV |
| Kenya | 5Y | Western Samoa | 5W |
| Korea, South | HL | Yemen | 70, 4W |
| Kuwait | 9K | Zaire | 9Q |
| Laos | RDPL | Zambia | 9J |

*May appear anywhere on aircraft, but usually appear on tail.

the International Air Line Pilots Association; the International Council of Aircraft Owner and Pilot Associations; and the International Society of Air Safety Investigators.

Human error is the cause of about one half of all air-carrier accidents, with about a third of the total attributed to the pilot. Other causes are equipment failure, weather, and airport terrain. The National Transportation Safety Board, an independent agency of the federal government, investigates all United States civil-aviation accidents. (*See also* Airline.)

### Safety Equipment and Practices

Equipment has been developed for the aircraft, crew, and passengers to make civil and military aviation safer. Fireproof fabrics, fire extinguishers, and fire and smoke detectors aid in fire protection. Safety belts protect passengers during takeoffs, landings, rough weather, or turbulence.

Sophisticated anti-icing and deicing equipment keeps ice from forming on wings, tail assemblies, propellers, windshields, and carburetors. Radio and radar equipment in the aircraft and on the ground assists in air-traffic control.

Parachutes are not carried on most civilian aircraft, including small private planes such as those owned by corporations. They are, however, used by all military personnel on military aircraft (*see* Parachute). Airliners do not carry parachutes because it is impractical to instruct passengers in their use, and studies indicate it would be almost impossible to deal with hundreds of passengers handling parachutes in an emergency situation. Ejection seats on military aircraft hurl pilots from disabled high-speed planes, usually without injury. Military pilots wear special suits and other equipment that prevent blackouts during sharp turns and dives.

*The remains of Pan American flight 103 lie on the ground at Lockerbie, Scotland, on Dec. 21, 1988. The Boeing 747 crashed after a bomb explosion, killing 270 people.*

A. Nogues—Sygma

For protection in ditching (abandoning) aircraft at sea, aircraft carry automatically inflating life rafts, life jackets, emergency rations and drinking water, dyes that can be seen by rescuers for marking the water, fishing and hunting equipment, maps, and signaling devices, such as mirrors, flares, and radio sets. Much of this equipment, notably the rafts and life jackets, is provided on commercial planes because passengers can easily be instructed to use these even in emergency situations.

## Aviation Navigation

A pilot flies an airplane from one place to another by using aerial navigation. With it the pilot plots the course, follows it while in flight, and determines the plane's position if it gets off course.

Aerial navigation is similar to nautical navigation (*see* Navigation). An airplane, however, is faster than a ship and travels in three dimensions. It is also affected more by winds than a ship is by sea currents. Finally, winds are more variable than sea currents.

### Forms of Navigation

Five basic forms of aerial navigation have been developed. They are pilotage, dead reckoning, radio navigation, celestial navigation, and inertial navigation.

In the early days of flying, pilots took their planes up only for short hops and kept them close to the ground. They found their way by using road maps, following roads and rivers, and looking for landmarks, such as water towers and bridges. Navigation solely by reference to landmarks is called pilotage. Improved weather reporting made it possible for the pilot to plan the flight (*see* "Aviation Meteorology" in this article). The pilot considered wind direction and wind velocity in calculating the heading and arrival time.

When the plane was airborne, the pilot turned to the predetermined heading, checked the time, and flew until the estimated flying time had elapsed. If the calculations were correct, the plane arrived at the proper destination. At any time the pilot could determine any position by computing direction and distance from the last known position. Navigation of this type is called dead reckoning. First known as deduced reckoning, it was abbreviated "ded. reckoning" and finally became "dead reckoning."

In the early days, pilots, however, were handicapped if they flew in bad weather. When they installed a radio receiver in the plane, they could communicate with the ground. Later, a network of ground-based radio stations made it possible for planes to navigate by radio, essentially laying down "highways" in the sky.

Another method for guiding an airplane through the air is celestial navigation. With this method the pilot determines the plane's geographic position by observing heavenly bodies.

A United States Air Force navigator on a Boeing KC-135 Stratotanker uses specially designed charts to plot the airplane's course while he communicates with ground operations by radio.
DOD—Kulik Photographic

Celestial navigation has, to a large degree, been replaced by inertial navigation. The onboard inertial navigation system (INS) tracks the aircraft's position with sensitive accelerometers. INS, in turn, may be entirely replaced by a satellite-based global positioning system, also known as GPS.

When flying over familiar terrain, the pilot uses pilotage. On cross-country flights the pilot may rely on pilotage, dead reckoning, and radio signals. The celestial and inertial navigation systems are used primarily for transoceanic flights. The pilot generally does his or her own navigating on small aircraft. Airliners on international flights and military aircraft, however, usually employ a specially trained navigator.

### Navigation Equipment

Because air navigation is concerned with direction and distance, the pilot must have equipment for measuring these factors. On the instrument panel are the magnetic compass, heading indicator, airspeed indicator, altimeter, and chronometer (or clock) (see Airplane, "Airplane Instruments"). The pilot's navigational aids also include charts, a plotter, and a computer. Many aircraft are equipped with loran (long-range navigation) receivers or inertial navigation systems.

The National Ocean Service publishes many types of maps and charts. These charts are specially designed maps for use in navigation. The United States (excluding Alaska and Hawaii) is divided into 54 sectional charts. The scale of these charts is 1 to 500,000, or about one inch (2.5 centimeters) to every eight statute miles (13 kilometers). In the 18 World Aeronautical Charts covering the United States the scale is one inch to 16 miles (26 kilometers). The charts are made from the Lambert conformal conic projection. They show elevations, landmarks, radio aids, and other data. The

Three Commonly Used Types of Navigation for Aircraft

Pilotage
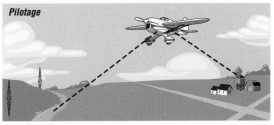

Dead Reckoning
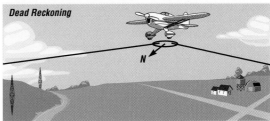

Radio Navigation
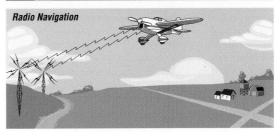

Pilotage (top) was used when planes were small and pilots could fly low enough to see identifiable landmarks to be used for guidance. The next step was dead reckoning (center), which depended on computing the distance to be traveled. Radio navigation (bottom) greatly improved plane safety.

*Plotting a Course*

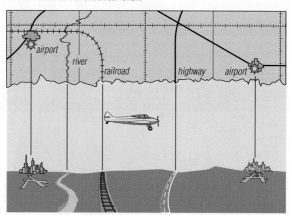

*Check Points on Aeronautical Chart*

*In pilotage the flier plots the course on a chart, marks checkpoints along the course, and while in flight looks for them on the ground to check position.*

agency also publishes changes in navigational facilities in the Airport Facility Directory. The FAA updates information on navigation aids for pilots in periodicals called "Notices to Airmen." The plotter is a combination plastic straightedge and protractor used to draw and measure a course. The computer is a circular slide rule for solving problems of time, speed, distance, and fuel consumption. Electronic computers that perform these same functions are also frequently used.

### Pilotage

Before takeoff on a flight navigated by pilotage, the pilot draws a course line on a chart from the point of departure to the destination. To avoid mountains, forests, or other hazards a new route may be selected. The distance is usually marked off in 10-mile (16-kilometer) intervals. Then the terrain must be studied for checkpoints, such as railroads, quarries, or lakes. The pilot locates brackets, or conspicuous features, on either side of the line of flight to avoid getting lost. End brackets prevent overflying the destination.

With a protractor, the pilot measures the angle of direction between the course line and the North Pole. This angle is called the true course. It is always measured in degrees clockwise from true north.

Because the compass does not point to the geographic North Pole but to the magnetic pole, the pilot compensates by adding or subtracting the magnetic variation from the true course as shown on the prepared chart (*see* Compass, Magnetic). This is the magnetic course. Electric currents and the great amount of electronic equipment in the plane exert additional magnetic influences. The compass deviation card tells the pilot how much error must be allowed for. After all this computation is complete, the pilot has the compass course.

After the course has been plotted, the pilot usually files a flight plan with air-traffic control and enters the data in the flight log. When the craft is airborne

Dave Bartruff—FPG

*A flight crew in Hong Kong—pilot, copilot, and flight engineer—study charts in preparation for a flight across the Pacific to North America. The flight takes more than 12 hours.*

and passes from one checkpoint to another, the pilot reports by radio on the arrival time. This information is also recorded in the pilot's log.

### Dead Reckoning

If the plane is flying over terrain that is lacking in prominent landmarks, pilotage cannot be used. If the plane has no radio equipment, the pilot navigates by dead reckoning.

The pilot first plots the true course, which is measured in degrees from true north. Since the wind may blow the plane off course, a pilot must compensate for drift by drawing a wind triangle or by using a computer. A wind triangle is a vector diagram that shows the effect of the wind's force and direction. The

## Flight Log

| | | PREFLIGHT | | | | | | | | | | ENROUTE | | | | | |
|---|---|---|---|---|---|---|---|---|---|---|---|---|---|---|---|---|---|
| From | To | True Course | Wind Corr. | True Head. | Var. | Mag. Head. | Dist. Leg / Total | Est. GS | Time Leg / Total | Est. Fuel | Act'l. Time | Act'l. GS | Dist. Next Pt. | Est. Arrv'l. | Fuel Used | Fuel Remain |
| | | | | | | | | | | | | | | | | |

| Weather Reports | Winds Aloft |
|---|---|
| | |
| **Terminal Forecasts** | **NOTAMS** |
| | |

U.S. DEPARTMENT OF TRANSPORTATION FEDERAL AVIATION ADMINISTRATION — FLIGHT PLAN (FAA USE ONLY) □ PILOT BRIEFING □ VNR □ STOPOVER TIME STARTED SPECIALIST INITIALS

1. TYPE — VFR / IFR / DVFR  2. AIRCRAFT IDENTIFICATION  3. AIRCRAFT TYPE/SPECIAL EQUIPMENT  4. TRUE AIRSPEED KTS  5. DEPARTURE POINT  6. DEPARTURE TIME PROPOSED (Z) ACTUAL (Z)  7. CRUISING ALTITUDE  8. ROUTE OF FLIGHT  9. DESTINATION (Name of airport and city)  10. EST. TIME ENROUTE HOURS MINUTES  11. REMARKS  12. FUEL ON BOARD HOURS MINUTES  13. ALTERNATE AIRPORT(S)  14. PILOT'S NAME, ADDRESS & TELEPHONE NUMBER & AIRCRAFT HOME BASE  15. NUMBER ABOARD  17. DESTINATION CONTACT/TELEPHONE (OPTIONAL)  16. COLOR OF AIRCRAFT  CIVIL AIRCRAFT PILOTS, FAR Part 91 requires you to file an IFR flight plan to operate under instrument flight rules in controlled airspace. Failure to file could result in a civil penalty not to exceed $1,000 for each violation (Section 901 of the Federal Aviation act of 1958, as amended). Filing of a VFR flight plan is recommended as a good operating practice. See also Part 99 for requirements concerning DVFR flight plans.

FAA Form 7233-1 (8-82)     CLOSE VFR FLIGHT PLAN WITH_____ FSS ON ARRIVAL

Source: Aircraft Owners and Pilots Association

direction in which an airplane is pointed is its heading, while the actual path of a plane over the ground is its track. The pilot finds the true heading by adding or subtracting the wind correction angle. The pilot then adjusts the true heading for magnetic variation and compass deviation.

The distance to be flown is found by measuring the course line. The time for the flight is calculated by dividing the distance by ground speed, which is obtained from the wind triangle. The pilot can compute fuel consumption by multiplying the fuel rate by the total flight time.

### Radio Navigation

Only radio navigation can be used for all-weather flying. The first radio aid to navigation was two-way communication with a transmitter and a receiver in the airplane and on the ground.

Today there are many radio navigation aids and instruments on board almost every plane. These complicated devices are designed to help pilots find their way accurately. The very high frequency omnidirectional range (VOR) transmits radio signals, or radials, in all directions like spokes of a wheel. The automatic direction finder (ADF) has a loop antenna that swings toward the ground-based radio station. The instrument landing system (ILS) guides an airplane toward a runway by using radio transmitters.

Other electronic navigational aids are radar and loran (see Radar). Airborne radar can send out signals that gauge the terrain in order to provide a maplike picture of the terrain. This radar also serves as a means of avoiding collisions with mountains and of locating storms. Distance-measuring equipment (DME) is a radarlike device that tells the pilot how far the plane is from a station. The course line computer is an airborne electronic "brain" that continually fixes an airplane's position. The Doppler navigation system utilizes radar and the Doppler effect for long-range navigation (see Sound).

Ground-based radar is used for surveillance, air traffic control, and precision approach guidance of airplanes. Precision approach radar (PAR) is the most frequently used guidance system. Loran (long-range navigation) is a ground-based radio system that gives the aircraft's position both over land and on transoceanic flights.

The global positioning system (GPS) is a satellite-based direction-finding system. The inertial navigation system (INS) is a self-contained system carried onboard an airplane to provide essentially the same service, but in a much more scaled-down version.

### Celestial Navigation

For centuries sailors have steered their ships by the stars (see Astronomy). Celestial navigation once used for long flights was based on the same principle.

The equipment needed to perform celestial navigation includes a sextant for measuring the altitude of the stars, a watch, an air almanac for locating the position of the celestial bodies, and navigation tables for making rapid calculations.

## Wind Drift

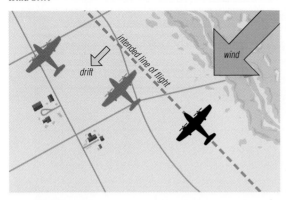
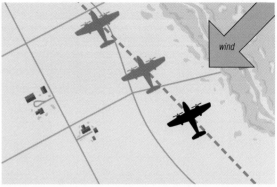

## Wind Triangle

*A crosswind (top) can blow an aircraft off its line of flight. This is called wind drift. To counteract the effect of wind drift the pilot heads the airplane at an angle into the wind. Pilots use the wind triangle (bottom) to find ground speed, heading, and flying time. These factors can be found graphically or by computer.*

Chris Sorensen

*Inertial navigation systems use precision instruments to track position without the use of external references. These systems are computerized and highly efficient.*

The navigator determines the plane's position by observing the angles formed above the horizon by two or more stars, meanwhile noting the time. Each star at any instant is directly above some point on the Earth. This is called the subpoint.

To the observer at the subpoint, the angle formed by a line drawn between the star and the horizon must measure 90 degrees. Any movement from the subpoint decreases the angle.

The navigator measures this angle and draws a circle with the subpoint as its center. At any place on this circle of position the star's altitude is the same. The observer verifies this calculation using at least two stars and draws a circle for each. The position, or fix, is where the circles intersect. Doing this for only two stars will provide a fix, but a three-star fix is more accurate and was common practice among professional navigators. (*See also* Navigation.)

## Aviation Meteorology

Weather is as important to an aircrew in the skies as it is to sailors on the seas. Atmospheric conditions can either add to the danger of flying or aid in overcoming the danger of flying. Thunderstorms, turbulent air, fog, snow, hail, and icy conditions are all hazards to the pilot. On the other hand, tailwinds and the jet stream may assist a pilot by adding as much as 250 miles (400 kilometers) per hour to the airplane's speed.

### Celestial Navigation by Circles of Altitude

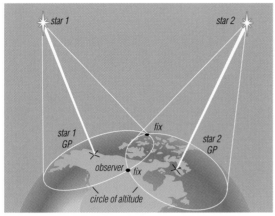

*When an observer is at the star's geographic position (GP), the altitude is 90° (top). An observer at a distance from the star's GP records an altitude of less than 90° (bottom).*

### Typical Aviation Weather Symbols

Aircraft Owners and Pilots Association Air Safety Foundation

*A pilot must be able to interpret weather reports that carry a large number of special symbols. In the United States more than 500 weather stations provide this kind of information.*

A knowledge of aviation meteorology helps the pilot avoid hazardous weather and take advantage of good weather. Meteorology, the science of weather, includes the study of the Earth's atmosphere and its phenomena. Weather is the condition of the atmosphere at a particular time and place (*see* Weather). Aviation meteorology is the study of the atmosphere as it affects flying. A pilot must understand the properties of air temperature, pressure, moisture content, and motion. (*See also* Atmosphere; Barometer; Cloud; Rainfall; Weather; Wind.)

#### Planning the Flight

Pilots rely on four aids to help them plan a flight through different weather conditions—weather reports, weather forecasts, their knowledge of meteorology, and their own experience. Some 500 weather stations in the United States report local conditions each hour to each other and to subscribers. Pilots inform these stations if they encounter unusual weather conditions. Every six hours the stations report their local findings to a central bureau. The information they submit is charted on maps that show the weather conditions throughout the country. The maps are transmitted by various means to pilots as they require them.

#### Ceiling and Visibility

Before a flight, a pilot checks the ceiling and visibility at the departure point, along the route, and at the destination. The ceiling is the distance between the ground and the lowest cloud layer that covers more than half the sky. The phrase unlimited ceiling means that there are no clouds to interfere with flying. A limited ceiling is low enough to affect flight. Zero ceiling means that there is no vertical space between the Earth and the clouds. A pilot must also know the visibility, or range of clear vision. This is measured in the number of miles that can be seen horizontally by the pilot in the air. Restricted visibility is caused by rain, snow, haze, and fog (*see* Fog). Conditions such as smog, a mixture of fog and smoke, reduce visibility over cities and industrial areas.

#### Turbulence, Icing, and Thunderstorms

Once pilots are airborne, they may encounter weather conditions that they did not expect, because certain conditions often come on without warning. These conditions include turbulence, icing, and thunderstorms. Turbulence results from irregular movements of the air. It makes the flight of the airplane bumpy and may even cause the plane to lose or gain altitude quickly.

Icing affects all airplanes, even those with anti-icing and deicing equipment. Ice formation slightly changes the shape of the wings and propellers. By doing this, it increases drag and weight and decreases thrust and lift. Icing can usually be avoided by changing altitude.

Thunderstorms may combine severe icing, violent turbulence, heavy rain, lightning, and hail (*see* Storm). All pilots avoid thunderstorms if at all possible—even by delaying the flight if necessary. Pilots fly around or over thunderstorms if they cannot delay the flight. If weather conditions prevent pilots from seeing the ground, they may navigate by using instruments (*see* Airplane, "Airplane Instruments"). (*See also* Helicopter.)

888 ■ AVIATION

## How Radar is Used to Avoid Storms

*Pilot Flies Around Storm*

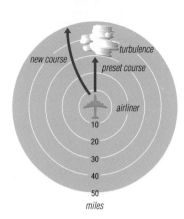

*Pilot May Also Fly Under Storm*

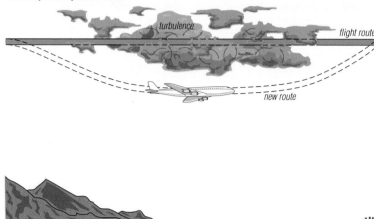

A radar scope reading (left) in the cockpit warns of turbulence ahead and shows how the pilot can change course to avoid it. Aircraft can also fly under the storm.

## BIBLIOGRAPHY FOR AVIATION

Baxter, Leon. Famous Flying Machines (Ideals, 1992).
Barrett, N.S. Airliners (Watts, 1989).
Berliner, Don. Before the Wright Brothers (Lerner, 1990).
Biddle, Wayne. Barons of the Sky from Early Flight to Strategic Warfare (Holt, 1993).
Brenlove, M.S. Vectors to Spare: The Life of an Air Traffic Controller (Iowa State Univ. Press, 1993).
Calderone, Robert. The Complete Aviation-Aerospace Career Guide (TAB Books, 1989).
Carter, Sharon. Careers in Aviation (Rosen Group, 1989).
Cohn, R.L. They Called It Pilot Error: True Stories Behind General Aviation Accidents (TAB Books, 1993).
Cushing, Steven. Fatal Words: Communication Clashes and Airplane Crashes (Univ. of Christchurch Press, 1994).
Fitzpatrick, Julie. In the Air (Silver Burdett, 1989).
Gonzales, Laurence. One-Zero-Charley: Adventures in Grassroots Aviation (Simon & Schuster, 1993).
Hawkes, Nigel. Safety in the Sky (Watts, 1990).
Hook, Jason. Twenty Names in Aviation (Marshall Cavendish, 1990).
Maher, E.R. Pilot's Avionics Survival Guide (TAB Books, 1993).
Maynard, Chris. Planes Have Wings and Other Questions About Transport (Kingfisher, 1993).
Millspaugh, Ben. Aviation and Space Science Projects (TAB Books, 1991).
Nader, Ralph, and Smith, W.J. Collision Course: The Truth About Airline Safety (TAB Books, 1993).
National Aeronautic Association. World and U.S.A. National Aviation Space Records (NAA, 1987).
Pearl, Lizzy. The Story of Flight (Troll, 1993).
Recknagel, Carl. Just Off The Ground: Memoirs of an Aviator (Fithian Press, 1993).
Seller, Mick. Air, Wind, and Flight (Watts, 1992).
Seymour, Peter. Pilots (Dutton Child Books, 1992).
Smith, H.L. Airways: The History of Commercial Aviation in the United States (Smithsonian, 1991).
Taneja, N.K. Introduction to Civil Aviation (Lexington Books, 1989).
Teitelbaum, Michael. First Facts About Flying Machines (Kidbooks, 1991).
Tessendorf, K.C. Wings Around the World (Macmillan, 1991).
Williams, Neil. Aerobatics (Specialty Press, 1991).

(See also bibliography for **Navigation**.)

## How Ice Forms on a Wing

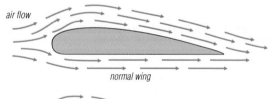

Photo, Chris Sorensen

*(Top) Efficient flight requires smooth airflow over a wing. (Bottom) Chemical deicers are used to remove ice from an airplane wing. Ice disturbs airflow, increases drag and weight, and decreases lift.*

**AVICENNA** (980–1037). During the Middle Ages, few scholars contributed more to science and philosophy than the Muslim scholar Avicenna. By his writings he helped convey the thought of the Greek philosopher Aristotle to the thinkers of western Europe, and his 'Canon of Medicine' became the definitive work in its field for centuries.

Born in Bukhara, Persia (now in Iran), in 980, he spent his childhood and youth studying Islamic law, literature, and medicine. By age 21 he was considered a great scholar and an outstanding physician.

After his father's death, Avicenna left Bukhara and for about twenty years lived in different Persian cities, working as a physician and completing two of his major works. 'The Book of Healing' was a large encyclopedia covering the natural sciences, logic, mathematics, psychology, astronomy, music, and philosophy. It is probably the largest work of its kind ever written by one man. 'The Canon of Medicine' was a systematic exposition of the achievements of Greek and Roman physicians.

For the last 14 years of his life, Avicenna lived in the city of Isfahan and continued his prodigious writing career. He died in 1037.

In the next century much of Avicenna's work was translated into Latin and thereby became available to the philosophers and theologians of Europe. In Islam his contributions in medicine, theology, and philosophy are still recognized as valuable.

**AVOCADO.** A fruit of high nutritional value popular in salads, soups, and sandwiches, the avocado has been grown for centuries in Central America and southern Mexico. The name avocado is a variation of the Spanish *aguacate,* which is derived from the Aztec name for the fruit, *ahuacatl.*

The avocado tree is a member of the laurel family. Its scientific name is *Persea americana.* It is distinguished by egg-shaped leaves, which can be 4 to 12 inches (10 to 30 centimeters) long, and by greenish flowers that lack petals. The oval or round fruit can have thick or thin green, purple, or black skin and can grow up to 9 inches (23 centimeters) in diameter and 4 pounds (2 kilograms) in weight. The butter-smooth flesh is yellow or pale green and surrounds a single large seed. There are three distinct varieties of avocados, each differing in fat content, appearance, and season of maturity.

In addition to containing as much as 25 percent oil (the highest percentage of oil in any fruit except the olive), the flesh provides thiamine, riboflavin, vitamin A, and up to 2 percent protein.

In their native habitats the trees originally grew from scattered seedlings. In about 1900 horticulturists discovered that avocados of good quality could be efficiently grown in orchards from grafted trees. Avocados for commercial use are now grown in Mexico and Central America, Chile, Brazil, Florida, some Caribbean islands, California, Hawaii, South Africa, Australia, and several Mediterranean countries, including Israel and Turkey.

**AYUB KHAN, Mohammad** (1907–74). As president of Pakistan from 1958 to 1969, Mohammad Ayub Khan played a critical role in the modern development of his nation.

Born in Hazara, India (now in Pakistan), on May 14, 1907, Ayub Khan studied at Aligarh Muslim University in Uttar Pradesh, India, and at the British Royal Military College in Sandhurst, England. In 1928 he was commissioned an officer in the Indian Army. After British India was partitioned into the countries of India and Pakistan in 1947, he rose in rank to become commander in chief of the army.

After several years of political turmoil in Pakistan, the president, Iskander Mirza, did away with the constitution in 1958 and appointed Ayub to administer martial law. A few months later Ayub had himself declared president and Mirza exiled.

Ayub set out to reorganize the administration and revitalize the economy. He enacted agrarian reforms and attempted to stimulate industry by means of foreign investment. In 1960 he introduced a system of "basic democracies," a network of local, self-governing bodies linking the government and the people. He was re-elected president in 1965.

In 1965 a dispute with India over the states of Jammu and Kashmir led to war. A boundary settlement was reached, but Pakistan's failure to win Kashmir led to such political turmoil that Ayub did not run again. He resigned in March 1969. He died near Islamabad, Pakistan, on April 19, 1974.

**AZERBAIJAN.** On the Caspian Sea at the eastern end of the Caucasus mountains is Azerbaijan, one of the 15 republics that made up the Soviet Union until that country was dissolved and the republics gained their independence in December 1991. Azerbaijan is bordered by Russia and Georgia to the north, the Caspian Sea to the east, Armenia to the west, and Iran to the south.

**The Land and Climate**

The republic has an area of 33,400 square miles (86,600 square kilometers), about the size of Portugal. Much of the north and south is mountainous, the highest peak being Bazardyuze (14,698 feet; 4,480 meters). The central area consists of a large lowland through which flows the Kura River.

The climate is dry and subtropical, with hot summers and mild winters. Much of the plains has a dry and even semidesert type of climate, while more rain falls in the mountains and on the narrow Lenkoran coastal plain in the southeast. Cactus, scrub growth, and steppe grass grow in the lowlands and foothills, and there are hardwood forests and alpine grazing meadows at higher elevations.

## People

The Azerbaijanis are traditionally farmers and herders, though more than half of the people now live in urban areas. The largest city and the republic's capital is Baku (*see* Baku, Azerbaijan). The petroleum industry in particular has attracted many people to Baku. Some three quarters of the republic's more than 7 million people are Turkic Azerbaijanis. They speak Azeri-Turkish, which differs somewhat from the language of Turkey. They are Muslims of the Shi'ah sect, the predominant sect of Iran. There are some 9 million Azerbaijanis living across the border in Iran. Azerbaijan administers Nakhichevan, an ethnically Azerbaijani territory located within Armenia.

Armenians make up more than 80 percent of the population living in the Nagorno-Karabakh Autonomous Oblast, a district in the south of the republic. There have been violent ethnic riots since 1988 between Azerbaijanis and Armenians after Armenian demands that Nagorno-Karabakh be united with the Armenian republic. The Soviet government intervened to stop the violence, but the fighting escalated when the Soviet troops were withdrawn after the dissolution of the Soviet Union. (*See also* Armenia.)

## Economy

Raw cotton and tobacco are the leading crops. Wheat, barley, and corn are the major grain crops. Rice is grown through irrigation. Potatoes, fruits, grapes, and vegetables are other crops. Tea and citrus fruits are specialties of the humid Lenkoran lowland. Cattle, sheep, and goats graze the lowlands and the mountains and are the basis of wool and meat production. Silk is a major product.

The Baku area is the site of extensive petroleum and natural gas fields. Most of the republic's industry is in the Baku-Sumgait area, where petroleum refining and the manufacture of steel, oil equipment, and chemicals are significant. A petroleum pipeline extends from Baku to Batumi in Georgia, and gas pipelines also extend to the nearby republics.

## Government and History

Before the 19th century the territory of the present republic consisted of a number of khanates, which were conquered by the Russians by the 1820s. At the time of the Russian Revolution in 1918, an independent Azerbaijan republic was declared with the help of the Turks and, later, the British. In 1920 the Soviets invaded the republic, and in 1936 it was declared a republic of the Soviet Union. Azerbaijan declared its independence in August 1991. When the Soviet Union was dissolved in December, Azerbaijan tentatively joined ten other republics in forming the Commonwealth of Independent States. It did not become a member, however, because its parliament failed to ratify the agreement. (*See also* Independent States, Commonwealth of; Union of Soviet Socialist Republics.) Population (1992 estimate), 7,237,000.

Ian Matley

**AZORES.** The Portuguese islands called the Azores lie almost midway between North America and Europe. This makes them a key link to air travel and cable communication. Cables from the Americas, Europe, and Africa meet at Faial Island. A major refueling station for transatlantic aircraft is on Santa Maria Island.

The nine islands and several islets of the Azores are broken into three administrative districts and form a group that stretches for about 400 miles (640 kilometers). Flores, the westernmost island, is only about 1,200 miles (1,930 kilometers) from Cape Race, Newfoundland. São Miguel, one of the easternmost islands, is some 800 miles (1,300 kilometers) from Portugal. The Azores have a land area of 868 square miles (2,248 square kilometers). The highest point is Pico Alto, at 7,713 feet (2,351 meters), on Pico Island. The chief cities are Ponta Delgada, Angra do Heroísmo, and Horta.

The Azores are of volcanic origin. In 1522 the town of Vila Franca was buried under volcanic debris. The mild climate and fertile volcanic soil support fine vineyards, orchards, pastures, and gardens. Exports include embroideries, pineapples, wine, and canned fish. Imports include textiles, coal, and automobiles.

The Azores remained virtually unknown until they were reputedly discovered by a Portuguese navigator in 1427. Faial Island was given to Flanders in 1466, but then ceded to Portugal in 1480. Settlement began in 1432. Population (1991 census), 236,700.

**AZTECS.** When Hernando Cortez and his Spanish soldiers reached the Valley of Mexico in 1519, they found a splendid city standing on an island in a lake. Three wide causeways led to huge white palaces and ornate temples on pyramids.

This proud city was Tenochtitlán, capital of the Aztecs. Its grandeur showed their power and wealth. From the city their armies went out to conquer. To the city came tribute from subject peoples—foodstuffs, pottery, gold, jade, turquoise, and ornaments. Beside porters marched captive soldiers who were to be sacrificed on the altars of Aztec gods.

When the Spanish arrived, the Aztecs ruled the area from the Gulf of Mexico to the Cordilleras and southward into present-day Guatemala. However, their emperor, Montezuma II, did not have a firmly organized empire. When vassal tribes or cities revolted, he had no governors or standing armies to control them. He had to reconquer them. This weakness in government helped the Spaniards conquer the warlike Aztecs in about two years. Cortez was aided throughout his campaign by rebellious tribes. (*See also* Montezuma II; Cortez, Hernando.)

The Aztecs had the most advanced civilization in North America at the time of Cortez, but they did not originate it. When they invaded the region, they took over the culture of earlier, advanced peoples—

*The central plaza of an Aztec castle (top) included a pyramid temple to the war god, left, temples to other gods, and palaces. This reconstruction was created by Ignacio Marquina. The relic of an Aztec calendar stone (bottom) weighs some 20 tons. The sun god is shown in the center. Other symbols tell of the world's creation and foretell its destruction.*

(Top) Field Museum of Natural History (Neg#A111653c), Chicago; (bottom) Robert Frerck—Odyssey Productions

the Toltecs, Mayas, Zapotecs, and others. The barbarian Aztecs came to Mexico in about AD 1200.

Religion was the great controlling force in Aztec life. In architecture and sculpture they gave their best efforts to building and decorating huge temples. They had picture writing, hieroglyphics, and number symbols with which they recorded religious events and historic annals. They had learned from the Mayas how to determine the solar year accurately (*see* Calendar). With this knowledge their priests kept an exact solar calendar. An almanac gave dates for fixed and movable festivals and listed the various deities who held sway over each day and hour.

A trade system linked the far parts of the empire with Tenochtitlán. Soldiers guarded the traders, and troops of porters carried the heavy loads, for the Aztecs had no pack animals. Canoes brought the crops from nearby farms through the canals to markets in Tenochtitlán. Their chief produce included corn, beans, peppers, squash, alligator pears, tomatoes, tobacco, cotton, and turkeys. Trade was carried on by barter, since the Aztecs had not invented money. Change could be made in cacao beans.

### Life in the Capital

The Aztecs used their wealth and power to provide a brilliant life in their capital. Montezuma lived in a splendid palace. He was surrounded by his nobles and served by thousands of slaves. In the palace grounds were beautiful gardens and menageries.

The city streets and palace walls were scrubbed dazzlingly white by sweating slaves. Bridges carried the streets over the network of canals which laced the city. An aqueduct brought drinking water from Chapultepec, a rocky height nearby.

Strange floating islands fringed the oval main island. They were made of mud dredged up from the lake bottom, supported on a network of branches and water grass. At first, the farmers could tow them with canoes. Then, as trees sent down roots, they became permanent island farms, called *chinampas.*

Farmers lived in wattle-and-daub huts on these islands. In the older sections of the city officials lived in houses of stone and adobe. Each house was built around a patio and raised on a platform for protection against lake floods. Most Aztecs were farmers. There were also traders and craftsmen.

### Training of Children

Custom governed many details of child rearing— even the number of tortillas to be fed at various ages. Children were taught courtesy, respect for their elders, truthfulness, and self-control.

Aztec boys learned practical tasks from their fathers at home, then went to the house of youth (called *telpuchcalli*) at the age of 15. Here older men of each clan taught the boys the duties of citizenship, religious observances, the history and traditions of their people, and arts and crafts. Training for war included learning to use the javelin thrower (called the *atlatl*), bows and arrows, and wooden war clubs with sharp blades of obsidian. In another school, the *calmecac,* boys studied for the priesthood. Girls could learn to be priestesses in temple schools.

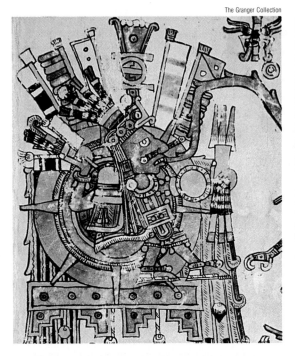

The Granger Collection

The Granger Collection

*The Aztec sun deity, Tonatiuh (left), was depicted in a drawing from the Codex Borgia. An event from the 1530 Nuno de Guzman expedition during the Spanish conquest was portrayed by an Aztec artist on the now-destroyed 'Lienzo de Tlascala Canvas'.*

### Tribal Organization

Aztec tribes were divided into families and clans. Each clan had its own elected officials and sent representatives to the council of the tribe. The council appointed officials to govern the four quarters (*phratries*) in which the city was organized. The council also elected and advised the supreme chief, who led the tribe in wars and alliances. A second chief supervised internal affairs. Although the system was theoretically democratic, actually the chiefs were selected from powerful families. The priesthood had a strong influence in tribal affairs but probably took no active part in government.

Land was held in common by the tribes. The council apportioned shares to heads of families. They controlled the land, however, only as long as it was cultivated. Sections were also farmed to provide food for chiefs and priests.

Strict laws and courts protected common citizens and even slaves from many forms of injustice. Crimes and disorder were severely suppressed. Theft of growing corn was punished by slavery or execution.

The Aztecs worshiped a host of gods who personified the forces of nature. To obtain the gods' aid, the worshipers performed penances and took part in innumerable elaborate rituals and ceremonies. Human sacrifice played an important part in the rites. Since life was man's most precious possession, the Aztecs reasoned, it was the most acceptable gift for the gods. As the Aztec nation grew powerful, more and more sacrifices were needed to keep the favor of the gods. At the dedication of the great pyramid temple in Tenochtitlán, 20,000 captives were killed. They were led up the steps of the high pyramid to the altar,

where chiefs and priests took turns at slitting open their bodies and tearing out their hearts.

The Aztecs sometimes practiced cannibalism; that is, they ate the flesh of their victims, believing that they would then absorb the virtues of the slain. The sacrificed victims were thought to win a high place in paradise. The need for collecting captives led Aztec warriors to seek prisoners instead of killing their enemies in battle. (*See also* Cannibalism.)

The Spaniards were horrified by these Aztec rites, and after the conquest they ruthlessly destroyed the temples in order to blot out the old faith. The friars who came to convert the Indians to Christianity and to educate them added to the destruction by burning records and shattering idols. They frequently built a Christian church on the rubble left when the old temple was torn down.

### History of the Aztec Nation

The Aztecs are believed to have come from the north. They spoke the Nahuan, or Nahuatl, language. This tongue belongs to the Uto-Aztecan linguistic stock. It is related to the languages of the Piman and Shoshonean tribes of the western United States.

Their legends reveal the early Aztecs as a nomadic farming people, wandering about in search of fertile land. In the Valley of Mexico, they fought with the settled tribes and at times were forced to serve them. Finally they took refuge on islands in the shallow lakes and founded Tenochtitlán on the site of modern Mexico City in about 1325.

Here they prospered and reached out to win new lands. They allied themselves with other Nahua tribes. Soon the Tenocha Aztecs dominated the Aztec Confederacy. They were at the height of their power when the Spaniards attacked them. The Indians living in the Mexico City region today are largely descendants of those whom Cortez conquered.